Anatomy & Physiology

Part 2 of 2
Chapters 15-28

Download for free at http://cnx.org/content/col11496/latest/

© 2016 Rice University

Rice University
6100 Main Street MS-375
Houston, Texas 77005

Textbook content produced by OpenStax is licensed under a Creative Commons Attribution 4.0 International License.
https://creativecommons.org/licenses/by/4.0/
https://creativecommons.org/licenses/by/4.0/legalcode

Changes to original document:
Non-numbered pages 1, 2, 3 and 4 were removed. The previous title page, this page, non-numbered pages 5 and 6, and the final blank page have been added. Chapters 1 through 14 (pages 9-656) were removed. The pages for chapters 15 through 28 were re-numbered. The Table of Contents pages, the References pages, the Solutions pages and the Index pages were modified, re-formatted and re-numbered to reflect the removal of Chapters 1 through 14 and any related pages. Color images and text were converted to grayscale.

Download the original document for free at:
http://cnx.org/content/col11496/latest/

Table of Contents

Preface 1
Chapter 15: The Autonomic Nervous System 9
   15.1 Divisions of the Autonomic Nervous System 10
   15.2 Autonomic Reflexes and Homeostasis 19
   15.3 Central Control 27
   15.4 Drugs that Affect the Autonomic System 31
Chapter 16: The Neurological Exam 45
   16.1 Overview of the Neurological Exam 46
   16.2 The Mental Status Exam 50
   16.3 The Cranial Nerve Exam 57
   16.4 The Sensory and Motor Exams 66
   16.5 The Coordination and Gait Exams 71
Chapter 17: The Endocrine System 85
   17.1 An Overview of the Endocrine System 86
   17.2 Hormones 89
   17.3 The Pituitary Gland and Hypothalamus 97
   17.4 The Thyroid Gland 105
   17.5 The Parathyroid Glands 110
   17.6 The Adrenal Glands 113
   17.7 The Pineal Gland 116
   17.8 Gonadal and Placental Hormones 117
   17.9 The Endocrine Pancreas 118
   17.10 Organs with Secondary Endocrine Functions 124
   17.11 Development and Aging of the Endocrine System 126
Unit 4: Fluids and Transport
Chapter 18: The Cardiovascular System: Blood 137
   18.1 An Overview of Blood 138
   18.2 Production of the Formed Elements 142
   18.3 Erythrocytes 145
   18.4 Leukocytes and Platelets 153
   18.5 Hemostasis 159
   18.6 Blood Typing 165
Chapter 19: The Cardiovascular System: The Heart 179
   19.1 Heart Anatomy 180
   19.2 Cardiac Muscle and Electrical Activity 202
   19.3 Cardiac Cycle 216
   19.4 Cardiac Physiology 221
   19.5 Development of the Heart 232
Chapter 20: The Cardiovascular System: Blood Vessels and Circulation 243
   20.1 Structure and Function of Blood Vessels 244
   20.2 Blood Flow, Blood Pressure, and Resistance 256
   20.3 Capillary Exchange 266
   20.4 Homeostatic Regulation of the Vascular System 268
   20.5 Circulatory Pathways 278
   20.6 Development of Blood Vessels and Fetal Circulation 314
Chapter 21: The Lymphatic and Immune System 331
   21.1 Anatomy of the Lymphatic and Immune Systems 332
   21.2 Barrier Defenses and the Innate Immune Response 346
   21.3 The Adaptive Immune Response: T lymphocytes and Their Functional Types 352
   21.4 The Adaptive Immune Response: B-lymphocytes and Antibodies 361
   21.5 The Immune Response against Pathogens 367
   21.6 Diseases Associated with Depressed or Overactive Immune Responses 370
   21.7 Transplantation and Cancer Immunology 374
Unit 5: Energy, Maintenance, and Environmental Exchange
Chapter 22: The Respiratory System 389
   22.1 Organs and Structures of the Respiratory System 390
   22.2 The Lungs 401
   22.3 The Process of Breathing 404

    22.4 Gas Exchange 413
    22.5 Transport of Gases 419
    22.6 Modifications in Respiratory Functions 425
    22.7 Embryonic Development of the Respiratory System 427
Chapter 23: The Digestive System 441
    23.1 Overview of the Digestive System 442
    23.2 Digestive System Processes and Regulation 448
    23.3 The Mouth, Pharynx, and Esophagus 453
    23.4 The Stomach 463
    23.5 The Small and Large Intestines 469
    23.6 Accessory Organs in Digestion: The Liver, Pancreas, and Gallbladder 480
    23.7 Chemical Digestion and Absorption: A Closer Look 486
Chapter 24: Metabolism and Nutrition 507
    24.1 Overview of Metabolic Reactions 508
    24.2 Carbohydrate Metabolism 513
    24.3 Lipid Metabolism 526
    24.4 Protein Metabolism 532
    24.5 Metabolic States of the Body 538
    24.6 Energy and Heat Balance 543
    24.7 Nutrition and Diet 545
Chapter 25: The Urinary System 559
    25.1 Physical Characteristics of Urine 560
    25.2 Gross Anatomy of Urine Transport 563
    25.3 Gross Anatomy of the Kidney 567
    25.4 Microscopic Anatomy of the Kidney 572
    25.5 Physiology of Urine Formation 576
    25.6 Tubular Reabsorption 579
    25.7 Regulation of Renal Blood Flow 589
    25.8 Endocrine Regulation of Kidney Function 590
    25.9 Regulation of Fluid Volume and Composition 592
    25.10 The Urinary System and Homeostasis 595
Chapter 26: Fluid, Electrolyte, and Acid-Base Balance 607
    26.1 Body Fluids and Fluid Compartments 608
    26.2 Water Balance 616
    26.3 Electrolyte Balance 619
    26.4 Acid-Base Balance 624
    26.5 Disorders of Acid-Base Balance 629
Unit 6: Human Development and the Continuity of Life
Chapter 27: The Reproductive System 637
    27.1 Anatomy and Physiology of the Male Reproductive System 638
    27.2 Anatomy and Physiology of the Female Reproductive System 649
    27.3 Development of the Male and Female Reproductive Systems 667
Chapter 28: Development and Inheritance 677
    28.1 Fertilization 678
    28.2 Embryonic Development 683
    28.3 Fetal Development 695
    28.4 Maternal Changes During Pregnancy, Labor, and Birth 700
    28.5 Adjustments of the Infant at Birth and Postnatal Stages 706
    28.6 Lactation 709
    28.7 Patterns of Inheritance 713
Index 741

PREFACE

Welcome to *Anatomy and Physiology*, an OpenStax resource. We created this textbook with several goals in mind: accessibility, customization, and student engagement—helping students reach high levels of academic scholarship. Instructors and students alike will find that this textbook offers a thorough introduction to the content in an accessible format.

About OpenStax

OpenStax is a nonprofit organization committed to improving student access to quality learning materials. Our free textbooks are developed and peer-reviewed by educators to ensure that they are readable, accurate, and organized in accordance with the scope and sequence requirements of today's college courses. Unlike traditional textbooks, OpenStax resources live online and are owned by the community of educators using them. Through partnerships with companies and foundations committed to reducing costs for students, we are working to improve access to higher education for all. OpenStax is an initiative of Rice University and is made possible through the generous support of several philanthropic foundations.

About OpenStax's Resources

OpenStax resources provide quality academic instruction. Three key features set our materials apart from others: 1) They can be easily customized by instructors for each class, 2) they are "living" resources that grow online through contributions from science educators, and 3) they are available for free or for a minimal cost.

Customization

OpenStax learning resources are conceived and written with flexibility in mind so that they can be customized for each course. Our textbooks provide a solid foundation on which instructors can build their own texts. Instructors can select the sections that are most relevant to their curricula and create a textbook that speaks directly to the needs of their students. Instructors are encouraged to expand on existing examples in the text by adding unique context via geographically localized applications and topical connections.

Anatomy and Physiology can be easily customized using our online platform (https://openstaxcollege.org/textbooks/anatomy-and-physiology/adapt). The text is arranged in a modular chapter format. Simply select the content most relevant to your syllabus and create a textbook that addresses the needs of your class. This customization feature will ensure that your textbook reflects the goals of your course.

Curation

To broaden access and encourage community curation, *Anatomy and Physiology* is "open source" under a Creative Commons Attribution (CC BY) license. Members of the scientific community are invited to submit examples, emerging research, and other feedback to enhance and strengthen the material, keeping it current and relevant for today's students. You can submit your suggestions to info@openstaxcollege.org.

Cost

Our textbooks are available for free online, and in low-cost print and tablet editions.

About *Anatomy and Physiology*

Anatomy and Physiology is designed for the two-semester anatomy and physiology course taken by life science and allied health students. It supports effective teaching and learning, and prepares students for further learning and future careers. The text focuses on the most important concepts and aims to minimize distracting students with more minor details.

The development choices for this textbook were made with the guidance of hundreds of faculty who are deeply involved in teaching this course. These choices led to innovations in art, terminology, career orientation, practical applications, and multimedia-based learning, all with a goal of increasing relevance to students. We strove to make the discipline meaningful and memorable to students, so that they can draw from it a working knowledge that will enrich their future studies.

Coverage and Scope

The units of our *Anatomy and Physiology* textbook adhere to the scope and sequence followed by most two-semester courses nationwide.

Unit 1: Levels of Organization

Chapters 1–4 provide students with a basic understanding of human anatomy and physiology, including its language, the levels of organization, and the basics of chemistry and cell biology. These chapters provide a foundation for the further study of the body. They also focus particularly on how the body's regions, important chemicals, and cells maintain homeostasis.

Chapter 1 An Introduction to the Human Body
Chapter 2 The Chemical Level of Organization
Chapter 3 The Cellular Level of Organization
Chapter 4 The Tissue Level of Organization

Unit 2: Support and Movement

In Chapters 5–11, students explore the skin, the largest organ of the body, and examine the body's skeletal and muscular systems, following a traditional sequence of topics. This unit is the first to walk students through specific systems of the body, and as it does so, it maintains a focus on homeostasis as well as those diseases and conditions that can disrupt it.

Chapter 5 The Integumentary System
Chapter 6 Bone and Skeletal Tissue
Chapter 7 The Axial Skeleton
Chapter 8 The Appendicular Skeleton
Chapter 9 Joints
Chapter 10 Muscle Tissue
Chapter 11 The Muscular System

Unit 3: Regulation, Integration, and Control

Chapters 12–17 help students answer questions about nervous and endocrine system control and regulation. In a break with the traditional sequence of topics, the special senses are integrated into the chapter on the somatic nervous system. The chapter on the neurological examination offers students a unique approach to understanding nervous system function using five simple but powerful diagnostic tests.

Chapter 12 Introduction to the Nervous System
Chapter 13 The Anatomy of the Nervous System
Chapter 14 The Somatic Nervous System
Chapter 15 The Autonomic Nervous System
Chapter 16 The Neurological Exam
Chapter 17 The Endocrine System

Unit 4: Fluids and Transport

In Chapters 18–21, students examine the principal means of transport for materials needed to support the human body, regulate its internal environment, and provide protection.

Chapter 18 Blood
Chapter 19 The Cardiovascular System: The Heart
Chapter 20 The Cardiovascular System: Blood Vessels and Circulation
Chapter 21 The Lymphatic System and Immunity

Unit 5: Energy, Maintenance, and Environmental Exchange

In Chapters 22–26, students discover the interaction between body systems and the outside environment for the exchange of materials, the capture of energy, the release of waste, and the overall maintenance of the internal systems that regulate the exchange. The explanations and illustrations are particularly focused on how structure relates to function.

Chapter 22 The Respiratory System
Chapter 23 The Digestive System
Chapter 24 Nutrition and Metabolism
Chapter 25 The Urinary System
Chapter 26 Fluid, Electrolyte, and Acid–Base Balance

Unit 6: Human Development and the Continuity of Life

The closing chapters examine the male and female reproductive systems, describe the process of human development and the different stages of pregnancy, and end with a review of the mechanisms of inheritance.

Chapter 27 The Reproductive System
Chapter 28 Development and Genetic Inheritance

Pedagogical Foundation and Features

Anatomy and Physiology is designed to promote scientific literacy. Throughout the text, you will find features that engage the students by taking selected topics a step further.

Homeostatic Imbalances discusses the effects and results of imbalances in the body.

Disorders showcases a disorder that is relevant to the body system at hand. This feature may focus on a specific disorder, or a set of related disorders.

Diseases showcases a disease that is relevant to the body system at hand.

Aging explores the effect aging has on a body's system and specific disorders that manifest over time.

Career Connections presents information on the various careers often pursued by allied health students, such as medical technician, medical examiner, and neurophysiologist. Students are introduced to the educational requirements for and day-to-day responsibilities in these careers.

Everyday Connections tie anatomical and physiological concepts to emerging issues and discuss these in terms of everyday life. Topics include "Anabolic Steroids" and "The Effect of Second-Hand Tobacco Smoke."

Interactive Links direct students to online exercises, simulations, animations, and videos to add a fuller context to core content and help improve understanding of the material. Many features include links to the University of Michigan's interactive WebScopes, which allow students to zoom in on micrographs in the collection. These resources were vetted by reviewers and other subject matter experts to ensure that they are effective and accurate. We strongly urge students to explore these links, whether viewing a video or inputting data into a simulation, to gain the fullest experience and to learn how to search for information independently.

Dynamic, Learner-Centered Art

Our unique approach to visuals is designed to emphasize only the components most important in any given illustration. The art style is particularly aimed at focusing student learning through a powerful blend of traditional depictions and instructional innovations.

Much of the art in this book consists of black line illustrations. The strongest line is used to highlight the most important structures, and shading is used to show dimension and shape. Color is used sparingly to highlight and clarify the primary anatomical or functional point of the illustration. This technique is intended to draw students' attention to the critical learning point in the illustration, without distraction from excessive gradients, shadows, and highlights. Full color is used when the structure or process requires it (for example, muscle diagrams and cardiovascular system illustrations).

Download for free at http://cnx.org/content/col11496/latest/

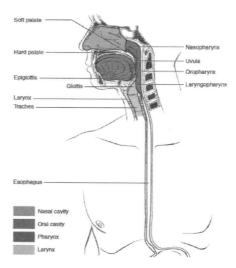

By highlighting the most important portions of the illustration, the artwork helps students focus on the most important points, without overwhelming them.

Micrographs

Micrograph magnifications have been calculated based on the objective provided with the image. If a micrograph was recorded at 40×, and the image was magnified an additional 2×, we calculated the final magnification of the micrograph to be 80×.

Please note that, when viewing the textbook electronically, the micrograph magnification provided in the text does not take into account the size and magnification of the screen on your electronic device. There may be some variation.

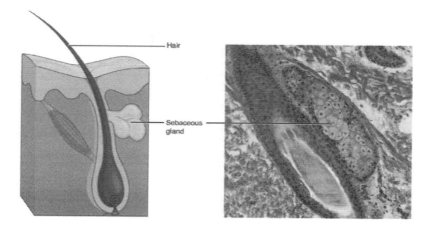

These glands secrete oils that lubricate and protect the skin. LM × 400. (Micrograph provided by the Regents of University of Michigan Medical School © 2012)

Learning Resources

The following resources are (or will be) available in addition to main text:

PowerPoint slides: For each chapter, the illustrations are presented, one per slide, with their respective captions.

Pronunciation guide: A subset of the text's key terms are presented with easy-to-follow phonetic transcriptions. For example, blastocyst is rendered as "blas'to-sist"

About Our Team

Senior Contributing Authors

J. Gordon Betts	Tyler Junior College
Peter Desaix	University of North Carolina at Chapel Hill
Eddie Johnson	Central Oregon Community College
Jody E. Johnson	Arapahoe Community College
Oksana Korol	Aims Community College
Dean Kruse	Portland Community College
Brandon Poe	Springfield Technical Community College
James A. Wise	Hampton University
Mark Womble	Youngstown State University
Kelly A. Young	California State University, Long Beach

Advisor

Robin J. Heyden

Contributing Authors

Kim Aaronson	Aquarius Institute; Triton College
Lopamudra Agarwal	Augusta Technical College
Gary Allen	Dalhousie University
Robert Allison	McLennan Community College
Heather Armbruster	Southern Union State Community College
Timothy Ballard	University of North Carolina Wilmington
Matthew Barlow	Eastern New Mexico University
William Blaker	Furman University
Julie Bowers	East Tennessee State University
Emily Bradshaw	Florida Southern College
Nishi Bryska	University of North Carolina, Charlotte
Susan Caley Opsal	Illinois Valley Community College
Boyd Campbell	Southwest College of Naturopathic Medicine and Health Sciences
Ann Caplea	Walsh University
Marnie Chapman	University of Alaska, Sitka
Barbara Christie-Pope	Cornell College
Kenneth Crane	Texarkana College
Maurice Culver	Florida State College at Jacksonville
Heather Cushman	Tacoma Community College

Noelle Cutter	Molloy College
Lynnette Danzl-Tauer	Rock Valley College
Jane Davis	Aurora University
AnnMarie DelliPizzi	Dominican College
Susan Dentel	Washtenaw Community College
Pamela Dobbins	Shelton State Community College
Patty Dolan	Pacific Lutheran University
Sondra Dubowsky	McLennan Community College
Peter Dukehart	Three Rivers Community College
Ellen DuPré	Central College
Elizabeth DuPriest	Warner Pacific College
Pam Elf	University of Minnesota
Sharon Ellerton	Queensborough Community College
Carla Endres	Utah State University - College of Eastern Utah: San Juan Campus
Myriam Feldman	Lake Washington Institute of Technology; Cascadia Community College
Greg Fitch	Avila University
Lynn Gargan	Tarant County College
Michael Giangrande	Oakland Community College
Chaya Gopalan	St. Louis College of Pharmacy
Victor Greco	Chattahoochee Technical College
Susanna Heinze	Skagit Valley College
Ann Henninger	Wartburg College
Dale Horeth	Tidewater Community College
Michael Hortsch	University of Michigan
Rosemary Hubbard	Marymount University
Mark Hubley	Prince George's Community College
Branko Jablanovic	College of Lake County
Norman Johnson	University of Massachusetts Amherst
Mark Jonasson	North Arkansas College
Jeff Keyte	College of Saint Mary
William Kleinelp	Middlesex County College
Leigh Kleinert	Grand Rapids Community College
Brenda Leady	University of Toledo
John Lepri	University of North Carolina, Greensboro
Sarah Leupen	University of Maryland, Baltimore County
Lihua Liang	Johns Hopkins University
Robert Mallet	University of North Texas Health Science Center
Bruce Maring	Daytona State College
Elisabeth Martin	College of Lake County
Natalie Maxwell	Carl Albert State College, Sallisaw
Julie May	William Carey University

Debra McLaughlin	University of Maryland University College
Nicholas Mitchell	St. Bonaventure University
Shobhana Natarajan	Brookhaven College
Phillip Nicotera	St. Petersburg College
Mary Jane Niles	University of San Francisco
Ikemefuna Nwosu	Parkland College; Lake Land College
Betsy Ott	Tyler Junior College
Ivan Paul	John Wood Community College
Aaron Payette	College of Southern Nevada
Scott Payne	Kentucky Wesleyan College
Cameron Perkins	South Georgia College
David Pfeiffer	University of Alaska, Anchorage
Thomas Pilat	Illinois Central College
Eileen Preston	Tarrant County College
Mike Pyle	Olivet Nazarene University
Robert Rawding	Gannon University
Jason Schreer	State University of New York at Potsdam
Laird Sheldahl	Mt. Hood Community College
Brian Shmaefsky	Lone Star College System
Douglas Sizemore	Bevill State Community College
Susan Spencer	Mount Hood Community College
Cynthia Standley	University of Arizona
Robert Sullivan	Marist College
Eric Sun	Middle Georgia State College
Tom Swenson	Ithaca College
Kathleen Tallman	Azusa Pacific University
Rohinton Tarapore	University of Pennsylvania
Elizabeth Tattersall	Western Nevada College
Mark Thomas	University of Northern Colorado
Janis Thompson	Lorain County Community College
Rita Thrasher	Pensacola State College
David Van Wylen	St. Olaf College
Lynn Wandrey	Mott Community College
Margaret Weck	St. Louis College of Pharmacy
Kathleen Weiss	George Fox University
Neil Westergaard	Williston State College
David Wortham	West Georgia Technical College
Umesh Yadav	University of Texas Medical Branch
Tony Yates	Oklahoma Baptist University
Justin York	Glendale Community College
Cheri Zao	North Idaho College

| Elena Zoubina | Bridgewater State University; Massasoit Community College |
| Shobhana Natarajan | Alcon Laboratories, Inc. |

Special Thanks

OpenStax wishes to thank the Regents of University of Michigan Medical School for the use of their extensive micrograph collection. Many of the UM micrographs that appear in *Anatomy and Physiology* are interactive WebScopes, which students can explore by zooming in and out.

We also wish to thank the Open Learning Initiative at Carnegie Mellon University, with whom we shared and exchanged resources during the development of *Anatomy and Physiology*.

15 | THE AUTONOMIC NERVOUS SYSTEM

Figure 15.1 Fight or Flight? Though the threats that modern humans face are not large predators, the autonomic nervous system is adapted to this type of stimulus. The modern world presents stimuli that trigger the same response. (credit: Vernon Swanepoel)

Introduction

Chapter Objectives

After studying this chapter, you will be able to:

- Describe the components of the autonomic nervous system
- Differentiate between the structures of the sympathetic and parasympathetic divisions in the autonomic nervous system
- Name the components of a visceral reflex specific to the autonomic division to which it belongs
- Predict the response of a target effector to autonomic input on the basis of the released signaling molecule
- Describe how the central nervous system coordinates and contributes to autonomic functions

The autonomic nervous system is often associated with the "fight-or-flight response," which refers to the preparation of the body to either run away from a threat or to stand and fight in the face of that threat. To suggest what this means, consider the (very unlikely) situation of seeing a lioness hunting out on the savannah. Though this is not a common threat that humans deal with in the modern world, it represents the type of environment in which the human species thrived and adapted. The spread of humans around the world to the present state of the modern age occurred much more quickly than any species would adapt to environmental pressures such as predators. However, the reactions modern humans have in the modern world are based on these prehistoric situations. If your boss is walking down the hallway on Friday afternoon looking for "volunteers" to come in on the weekend, your response is the same as the prehistoric human seeing the lioness running across the savannah: fight or flight.

Most likely, your response to your boss—not to mention the lioness—would be flight. Run away! The autonomic system is responsible for the physiological response to make that possible, and hopefully successful. Adrenaline starts to flood your circulatory system. Your heart rate increases. Sweat glands become active. The bronchi of the lungs dilate to allow more air exchange. Pupils dilate to increase visual information. Blood pressure increases in general, and blood vessels dilate in skeletal muscles. Time to run. Similar physiological responses would occur in preparation for fighting off the threat.

This response should sound a bit familiar. The autonomic nervous system is tied into emotional responses as well, and the fight-or-flight response probably sounds like a panic attack. In the modern world, these sorts of reactions are associated with anxiety as much as with response to a threat. It is engrained in the nervous system to respond like this. In fact, the adaptations of the autonomic nervous system probably predate the human species and are likely to be common to all mammals, and perhaps shared by many animals. That lioness might herself be threatened in some other situation.

However, the autonomic nervous system is not just about responding to threats. Besides the fight-or-flight response, there are the responses referred to as "rest and digest." If that lioness is successful in her hunting, then she is going to rest from the exertion. Her heart rate will slow. Breathing will return to normal. The digestive system has a big job to do. Much of the function of the autonomic system is based on the connections within an autonomic, or visceral, reflex.

15.1 | Divisions of the Autonomic Nervous System

By the end of this section, you will be able to:

- Name the components that generate the sympathetic and parasympathetic responses of the autonomic nervous system
- Explain the differences in output connections within the two divisions of the autonomic nervous system
- Describe the signaling molecules and receptor proteins involved in communication within the two divisions of the autonomic nervous system

The nervous system can be divided into two functional parts: the somatic nervous system and the autonomic nervous system. The major differences between the two systems are evident in the responses that each produces. The somatic nervous system causes contraction of skeletal muscles. The autonomic nervous system controls cardiac and smooth muscle, as well as glandular tissue. The somatic nervous system is associated with voluntary responses (though many can happen without conscious awareness, like breathing), and the autonomic nervous system is associated with involuntary responses, such as those related to homeostasis.

The autonomic nervous system regulates many of the internal organs through a balance of two aspects, or divisions. In addition to the endocrine system, the autonomic nervous system is instrumental in homeostatic mechanisms in the body. The two divisions of the autonomic nervous system are the **sympathetic division** and **parasympathetic division**. The sympathetic system is associated with the **fight-or-flight response**, and parasympathetic activity is referred to by the epithet of **rest and digest**. Homeostasis is the balance between the two systems. At each target effector, dual innervation determines activity. For example, the heart receives connections from both the sympathetic and parasympathetic divisions. One causes heart rate to increase, whereas the other causes heart rate to decrease.

Interactive LINK

Watch this video (http://openstaxcollege.org/l/fightflight) to learn more about adrenaline and the fight-or-flight response. When someone is said to have a rush of adrenaline, the image of bungee jumpers or skydivers usually comes to mind. But adrenaline, also known as epinephrine, is an important chemical in coordinating the body's fight-or-flight response. In this video, you look inside the physiology of the fight-or-flight response, as envisioned for a firefighter. His body's reaction is the result of the sympathetic division of the autonomic nervous system causing system-wide changes as it prepares for extreme responses. What two changes does adrenaline bring about to help the skeletal muscle response?

Sympathetic Division of the Autonomic Nervous System

To respond to a threat—to fight or to run away—the sympathetic system causes divergent effects as many different effector organs are activated together for a common purpose. More oxygen needs to be inhaled and delivered to skeletal muscle. The respiratory, cardiovascular, and musculoskeletal systems are all activated together. Additionally, sweating keeps the excess heat that comes from muscle contraction from causing the body to overheat. The digestive system shuts down so that blood is not absorbing nutrients when it should be delivering oxygen to skeletal muscles. To coordinate all these responses, the connections in the sympathetic system diverge from a limited region of the central nervous system (CNS) to a wide array of ganglia that project to the many effector organs simultaneously. The complex set of structures that compose the output of the sympathetic system make it possible for these disparate effectors to come together in a coordinated, systemic change.

The sympathetic division of the autonomic nervous system influences the various organ systems of the body through connections emerging from the thoracic and upper lumbar spinal cord. It is referred to as the **thoracolumbar system** to reflect this anatomical basis. A **central neuron** in the lateral horn of any of these spinal regions projects to ganglia adjacent to the vertebral column through the ventral spinal roots. The majority of ganglia of the sympathetic system belong to a network of **sympathetic chain ganglia** that runs alongside the vertebral column. The ganglia appear as a series of clusters of neurons linked by axonal bridges. There are typically 23 ganglia in the chain on either side of the spinal column. Three correspond to the cervical region, 12 are in the thoracic region, four are in the lumbar region, and four correspond to the sacral region. The cervical and sacral levels are not connected to the spinal cord directly through the spinal roots, but through ascending or descending connections through the bridges within the chain.

A diagram that shows the connections of the sympathetic system is somewhat like a circuit diagram that shows the electrical connections between different receptacles and devices. In Figure 15.2, the "circuits" of the sympathetic system are intentionally simplified.

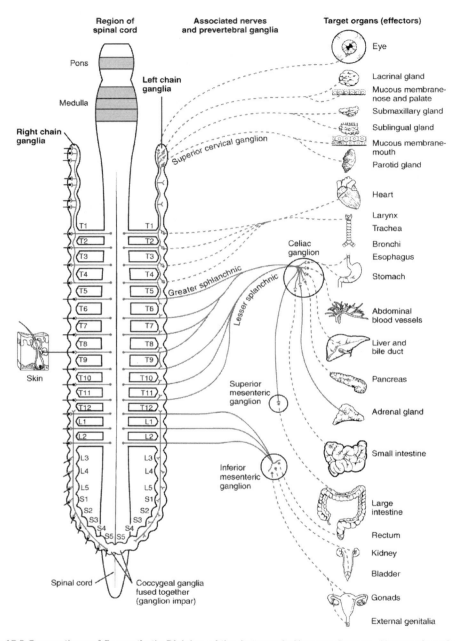

Figure 15.2 Connections of Sympathetic Division of the Autonomic Nervous System Neurons from the lateral horn of the spinal cord (preganglionic nerve fibers - solid lines)) project to the chain ganglia on either side of the vertebral column or to collateral (prevertebral) ganglia that are anterior to the vertebral column in the abdominal cavity. Axons from these ganglionic neurons (postganglionic nerve fibers - dotted lines) then project to target effectors throughout the body.

To continue with the analogy of the circuit diagram, there are three different types of "junctions" that operate within the sympathetic system (Figure 15.3). The first type is most direct: the sympathetic nerve projects to the chain ganglion at the same level as the **target effector** (the organ, tissue, or gland to be innervated). An example of this type is spinal nerve T1 that synapses with the T1 chain ganglion to innervate the trachea. The fibers of this branch are called **white rami communicantes** (singular = ramus communicans); they are myelinated and therefore referred to as white (see Figure 15.3a). The axon from the central neuron (the preganglionic fiber shown as a solid line) synapses with the **ganglionic neuron** (with the postganglionic fiber shown as a dashed line). This neuron then projects to a target effector—in this case, the trachea—via **gray rami communicantes**, which are unmyelinated axons.

In some cases, the target effectors are located superior or inferior to the spinal segment at which the preganglionic fiber emerges. With respect to the "wiring" involved, the synapse with the ganglionic neuron occurs at chain ganglia superior or inferior to the location of the central neuron. An example of this is spinal nerve T1 that innervates the eye. The spinal nerve tracks up through the chain until it reaches the **superior cervical ganglion**, where it synapses with the postganglionic neuron (see Figure 15.3b). The cervical ganglia are referred to as **paravertebral ganglia**, given their location adjacent to prevertebral ganglia in the sympathetic chain.

Not all axons from the central neurons terminate in the chain ganglia. Additional branches from the ventral nerve root continue through the chain and on to one of the collateral ganglia as the **greater splanchnic nerve** or **lesser splanchnic nerve**. For example, the greater splanchnic nerve at the level of T5 synapses with a collateral ganglion outside the chain before making the connection to the postganglionic nerves that innervate the stomach (see Figure 15.3c).

Collateral ganglia, also called **prevertebral ganglia**, are situated anterior to the vertebral column and receive inputs from splanchnic nerves as well as central sympathetic neurons. They are associated with controlling organs in the abdominal cavity, and are also considered part of the enteric nervous system. The three collateral ganglia are the **celiac ganglion**, the **superior mesenteric ganglion**, and the **inferior mesenteric ganglion** (see Figure 15.2). The word celiac is derived from the Latin word "coelom," which refers to a body cavity (in this case, the abdominal cavity), and the word mesenteric refers to the digestive system.

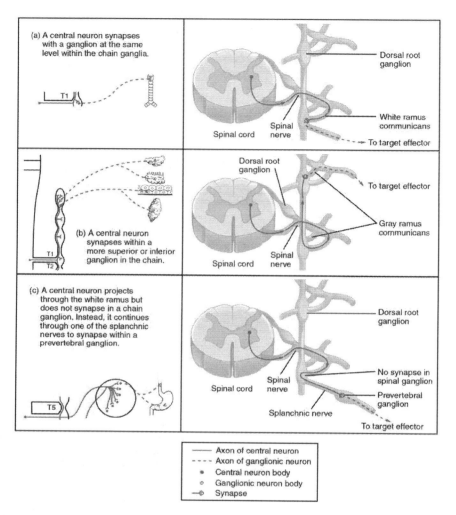

Figure 15.3 Sympathetic Connections and Chain Ganglia The axon from a central sympathetic neuron in the spinal cord can project to the periphery in a number of different ways. (a) The fiber can project out to the ganglion at the same level and synapse on a ganglionic neuron. (b) A branch can project to more superior or inferior ganglion in the chain. (c) A branch can project through the white ramus communicans, but not terminate on a ganglionic neuron in the chain. Instead, it projects through one of the splanchnic nerves to a collateral ganglion or the adrenal medulla (not pictured).

An axon from the central neuron that projects to a sympathetic ganglion is referred to as a **preganglionic fiber** or neuron, and represents the output from the CNS to the ganglion. Because the sympathetic ganglia are adjacent to the vertebral column, preganglionic sympathetic fibers are relatively short, and they are myelinated. A **postganglionic fiber**—the axon from a ganglionic neuron that projects to the target effector—represents the output of a ganglion that directly influences the organ. Compared with the preganglionic fibers, postganglionic sympathetic fibers are long because of the relatively greater distance from the ganglion to the target effector. These fibers are unmyelinated. (Note that the term "postganglionic neuron" may be used to describe the projection from a ganglion to the target. The problem with that usage is that the cell body is in the ganglion, and only the fiber is postganglionic. Typically, the term neuron applies to the entire cell.)

One type of preganglionic sympathetic fiber does not terminate in a ganglion. These are the axons from central sympathetic neurons that project to the **adrenal medulla**, the interior portion of the adrenal gland. These axons are still referred to as preganglionic fibers, but the target is not a ganglion. The adrenal medulla releases signaling molecules into the bloodstream, rather than using axons to communicate with target structures. The cells in the adrenal medulla that are contacted by the preganglionic fibers are called **chromaffin cells**. These cells are neurosecretory cells that develop from the neural crest along with the sympathetic ganglia, reinforcing the idea that the gland is, functionally, a sympathetic ganglion.

The projections of the sympathetic division of the autonomic nervous system diverge widely, resulting in a broad influence of the system throughout the body. As a response to a threat, the sympathetic system would increase heart rate and breathing rate and cause blood flow to the skeletal muscle to increase and blood flow to the digestive system to decrease. Sweat gland secretion should also increase as part of an integrated response. All of those physiological changes are going to be required to occur together to run away from the hunting lioness, or the modern equivalent. This divergence is seen in the branching patterns of preganglionic sympathetic neurons—a single preganglionic sympathetic neuron may have 10–20 targets. An axon that leaves a central neuron of the lateral horn in the thoracolumbar spinal cord will pass through the white ramus communicans and enter the sympathetic chain, where it will branch toward a variety of targets. At the level of the spinal cord at which the preganglionic sympathetic fiber exits the spinal cord, a branch will synapse on a neuron in the adjacent chain ganglion. Some branches will extend up or down to a different level of the chain ganglia. Other branches will pass through the chain ganglia and project through one of the splanchnic nerves to a collateral ganglion. Finally, some branches may project through the splanchnic nerves to the adrenal medulla. All of these branches mean that one preganglionic neuron can influence different regions of the sympathetic system very broadly, by acting on widely distributed organs.

Parasympathetic Division of the Autonomic Nervous System

The parasympathetic division of the autonomic nervous system is named because its central neurons are located on either side of the thoracolumbar region of the spinal cord (para- = "beside" or "near"). The parasympathetic system can also be referred to as the **craniosacral system** (or outflow) because the preganglionic neurons are located in nuclei of the brain stem and the lateral horn of the sacral spinal cord.

The connections, or "circuits," of the parasympathetic division are similar to the general layout of the sympathetic division with a few specific differences (Figure 15.4). The preganglionic fibers from the cranial region travel in cranial nerves, whereas preganglionic fibers from the sacral region travel in spinal nerves. The targets of these fibers are **terminal ganglia**, which are located near—or even within—the target effector. These ganglia are often referred to as **intramural ganglia** when they are found within the walls of the target organ. The postganglionic fiber projects from the terminal ganglia a short distance to the target effector, or to the specific target tissue within the organ. Comparing the relative lengths of axons in the parasympathetic system, the preganglionic fibers are long and the postganglionic fibers are short because the ganglia are close to—and sometimes within—the target effectors.

The cranial component of the parasympathetic system is based in particular nuclei of the brain stem. In the midbrain, the **Edinger–Westphal nucleus** is part of the oculomotor complex, and axons from those neurons travel with the fibers in the oculomotor nerve (cranial nerve III) that innervate the extraocular muscles. The preganglionic parasympathetic fibers within cranial nerve III terminate in the **ciliary ganglion**, which is located in the posterior orbit. The postganglionic parasympathetic fibers then project to the smooth muscle of the iris to control pupillary size. In the upper medulla, the salivatory nuclei contain neurons with axons that project through the facial and glossopharyngeal nerves to ganglia that control salivary glands. Tear production is influenced by parasympathetic fibers in the facial nerve, which activate a ganglion, and ultimately the lacrimal (tear) gland. Neurons in the **dorsal nucleus of the vagus nerve** and the **nucleus ambiguus** project through the vagus nerve (cranial nerve X) to the terminal ganglia of the thoracic and abdominal cavities. Parasympathetic preganglionic fibers primarily influence the heart, bronchi, and esophagus in the thoracic cavity and the stomach, liver, pancreas, gall bladder, and small intestine of the abdominal cavity. The postganglionic fibers from the ganglia activated by the vagus nerve are often incorporated into the structure of the organ, such as the **mesenteric plexus** of the digestive tract organs and the intramural ganglia.

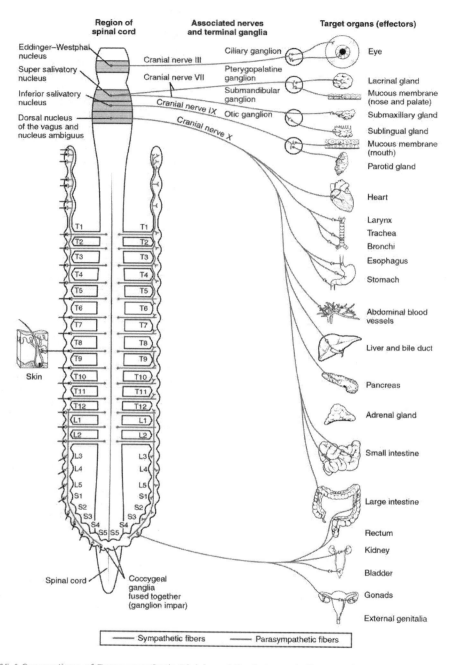

Figure 15.4 Connections of Parasympathetic Division of the Autonomic Nervous System   Neurons from brainstem nuclei, or from the lateral horn of the sacral spinal cord, project to terminal ganglia near or within the various organs of the body. Axons from these ganglionic neurons then project the short distance to those target effectors.

Chemical Signaling in the Autonomic Nervous System

Where an autonomic neuron connects with a target, there is a synapse. The electrical signal of the action potential causes the release of a signaling molecule, which will bind to receptor proteins on the target cell. Synapses of the autonomic system are classified as either **cholinergic**, meaning that **acetylcholine (ACh)** is released, or **adrenergic**, meaning that **norepinephrine** is released. The terms cholinergic and adrenergic refer not only to the signaling molecule that is released but also to the class of receptors that each binds.

The cholinergic system includes two classes of receptor: the **nicotinic receptor** and the **muscarinic receptor**. Both receptor types bind to ACh and cause changes in the target cell. The nicotinic receptor is a **ligand-gated cation channel** and the muscarinic receptor is a **G protein–coupled receptor**. The receptors are named for, and differentiated by, other molecules that bind to them. Whereas nicotine will bind to the nicotinic receptor, and muscarine will bind to the muscarinic receptor, there is no cross-reactivity between the receptors. The situation is similar to locks and keys. Imagine two locks—one for a classroom and the other for an office—that are opened by two separate keys. The classroom key will not open the office door and the office key will not open the classroom door. This is similar to the specificity of nicotine and muscarine for their receptors. However, a master key can open multiple locks, such as a master key for the Biology Department that opens both the classroom and the office doors. This is similar to ACh that binds to both types of receptors. The molecules that define these receptors are not crucial—they are simply tools for researchers to use in the laboratory. These molecules are **exogenous**, meaning that they are made outside of the human body, so a researcher can use them without any confounding **endogenous** results (results caused by the molecules produced in the body).

The adrenergic system also has two types of receptors, named the **alpha (α)-adrenergic receptor** and **beta (β)-adrenergic receptor**. Unlike cholinergic receptors, these receptor types are not classified by which drugs can bind to them. All of them are G protein–coupled receptors. There are three types of α-adrenergic receptors, termed $α_1$, $α_2$, and $α_3$, and there are two types of β-adrenergic receptors, termed $β_1$ and $β_2$. An additional aspect of the adrenergic system is that there is a second signaling molecule called **epinephrine**. The chemical difference between norepinephrine and epinephrine is the addition of a methyl group (CH_3) in epinephrine. The prefix "nor-" actually refers to this chemical difference, in which a methyl group is missing.

The term adrenergic should remind you of the word adrenaline, which is associated with the fight-or-flight response described at the beginning of the chapter. Adrenaline and epinephrine are two names for the same molecule. The adrenal gland (in Latin, ad- = "on top of"; renal = "kidney") secretes adrenaline. The ending "-ine" refers to the chemical being derived, or extracted, from the adrenal gland. A similar construction from Greek instead of Latin results in the word epinephrine (epi- = "above"; nephr- = "kidney"). In scientific usage, epinephrine is preferred in the United States, whereas adrenaline is preferred in Great Britain, because "adrenalin" was once a registered, proprietary drug name in the United States. Though the drug is no longer sold, the convention of referring to this molecule by the two different names persists. Similarly, norepinephrine and noradrenaline are two names for the same molecule.

Having understood the cholinergic and adrenergic systems, their role in the autonomic system is relatively simple to understand. All preganglionic fibers, both sympathetic and parasympathetic, release ACh. All ganglionic neurons—the targets of these preganglionic fibers—have nicotinic receptors in their cell membranes. The nicotinic receptor is a ligand-gated cation channel that results in depolarization of the postsynaptic membrane. The postganglionic parasympathetic fibers also release ACh, but the receptors on their targets are muscarinic receptors, which are G protein–coupled receptors and do not exclusively cause depolarization of the postsynaptic membrane. Postganglionic sympathetic fibers release norepinephrine, except for fibers that project to sweat glands and to blood vessels associated with skeletal muscles, which release ACh (Table 15.1).

Autonomic System Signaling Molecules

	Sympathetic	Parasympathetic
Preganglionic	Acetylcholine → nicotinic receptor	Acetylcholine → nicotinic receptor
Postganglionic	Norepinephrine → α- or β-adrenergic receptors Acetylcholine → muscarinic receptor (associated with sweat glands and the blood vessels associated with skeletal muscles only)	Acetylcholine → muscarinic receptor

Table 15.1

Signaling molecules can belong to two broad groups. Neurotransmitters are released at synapses, whereas hormones are released into the bloodstream. These are simplistic definitions, but they can help to clarify this point. Acetylcholine can be considered a neurotransmitter because it is released by axons at synapses. The adrenergic system, however, presents a challenge. Postganglionic sympathetic fibers release norepinephrine, which can be considered a neurotransmitter. But the adrenal medulla releases epinephrine and norepinephrine into circulation, so they should be considered hormones.

What are referred to here as synapses may not fit the strictest definition of synapse. Some sources will refer to the connection between a postganglionic fiber and a target effector as neuroeffector junctions; neurotransmitters, as defined above, would be called neuromodulators. The structure of postganglionic connections are not the typical synaptic end bulb that is found at the neuromuscular junction, but rather are chains of swellings along the length of a postganglionic fiber called a **varicosity** (Figure 15.5).

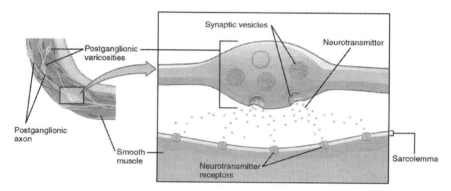

Figure 15.5 Autonomic Varicosities The connection between autonomic fibers and target effectors is not the same as the typical synapse, such as the neuromuscular junction. Instead of a synaptic end bulb, a neurotransmitter is released from swellings along the length of a fiber that makes an extended network of connections in the target effector.

Everyday CONNECTION

Fight or Flight? What About Fright and Freeze?

The original usage of the epithet "fight or flight" comes from a scientist named Walter Cannon who worked at Harvard in 1915. The concept of homeostasis and the functioning of the sympathetic system had been introduced in France in the previous century. Cannon expanded the idea, and introduced the idea that an animal responds to a threat by preparing to stand and fight or run away. The nature of this response was thoroughly explained in a book on the physiology of pain, hunger, fear, and rage.

When students learn about the sympathetic system and the fight-or-flight response, they often stop and wonder about other responses. If you were faced with a lioness running toward you as pictured at the beginning of this chapter, would you run or would you stand your ground? Some people would say that they would freeze and not know what to do. So isn't there really more to what the autonomic system does than fight, flight, rest, or digest. What about fear and paralysis in the face of a threat?

The common epithet of "fight or flight" is being enlarged to be "fight, flight, or fright" or even "fight, flight, fright, or freeze." Cannon's original contribution was a catchy phrase to express some of what the nervous system does in response to a threat, but it is incomplete. The sympathetic system is responsible for the physiological responses to emotional states. The name "sympathetic" can be said to mean that (sym- = "together"; -pathos = "pain," "suffering," or "emotion").

Watch this video (http://openstaxcollege.org/l/nervsystem1) to learn more about the nervous system. As described in this video, the nervous system has a way to deal with threats and stress that is separate from the conscious control of the somatic nervous system. The system comes from a time when threats were about survival, but in the modern age, these responses become part of stress and anxiety. This video describes how the autonomic system is only part of the response to threats, or stressors. What other organ system gets involved, and what part of the brain coordinates the two systems for the entire response, including epinephrine (adrenaline) and cortisol?

15.2 | Autonomic Reflexes and Homeostasis

By the end of this section, you will be able to:
- Compare the structure of somatic and autonomic reflex arcs
- Explain the differences in sympathetic and parasympathetic reflexes
- Differentiate between short and long reflexes
- Determine the effect of the autonomic nervous system on the regulation of the various organ systems on the basis of the signaling molecules involved
- Describe the effects of drugs that affect autonomic function

The autonomic nervous system regulates organ systems through circuits that resemble the reflexes described in the somatic nervous system. The main difference between the somatic and autonomic systems is in what target tissues are effectors. Somatic responses are solely based on skeletal muscle contraction. The autonomic system, however, targets cardiac and smooth muscle, as well as glandular tissue. Whereas the basic circuit is a **reflex arc**, there are differences in the structure of those reflexes for the somatic and autonomic systems.

The Structure of Reflexes

One difference between a **somatic reflex**, such as the withdrawal reflex, and a **visceral reflex**, which is an autonomic reflex, is in the **efferent branch**. The output of a somatic reflex is the lower motor neuron in the ventral horn of the spinal cord that projects directly to a skeletal muscle to cause its contraction. The output of a visceral reflex is a two-step pathway starting with the preganglionic fiber emerging from a lateral horn neuron in the spinal cord, or a cranial nucleus neuron in the brain stem, to a ganglion—followed by the postganglionic fiber projecting to a target effector. The other part of a reflex, the **afferent branch**, is often the same between the two systems. Sensory neurons receiving input from the periphery—with cell bodies in the sensory ganglia, either of a cranial nerve or a dorsal root ganglion adjacent to the spinal cord—project into the CNS to initiate the reflex (Figure 15.6). The Latin root "effere" means "to carry." Adding the prefix "ef-" suggests the meaning "to carry away," whereas adding the prefix "af-" suggests "to carry toward or inward."

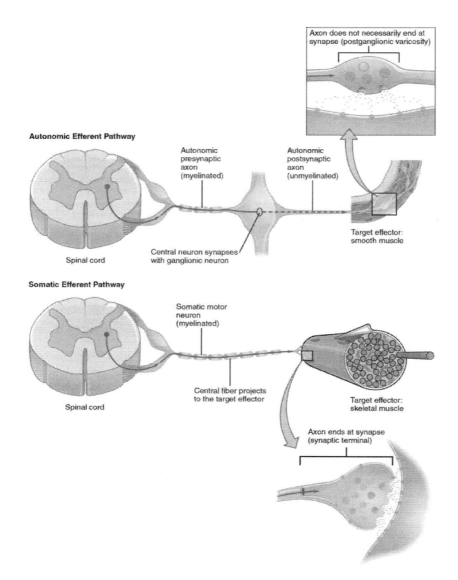

Figure 15.6 Comparison of Somatic and Visceral Reflexes The afferent inputs to somatic and visceral reflexes are essentially the same, whereas the efferent branches are different. Somatic reflexes, for instance, involve a direct connection from the ventral horn of the spinal cord to the skeletal muscle. Visceral reflexes involve a projection from the central neuron to a ganglion, followed by a second projection from the ganglion to the target effector.

Afferent Branch

The afferent branch of a reflex arc does differ between somatic and visceral reflexes in some instances. Many of the inputs to visceral reflexes are from special or somatic senses, but particular senses are associated with the viscera that are not part of the conscious perception of the environment through the somatic nervous system. For example, there is a specific type of mechanoreceptor, called a **baroreceptor**, in the walls of the aorta and carotid sinuses that senses the stretch of those organs when blood volume or pressure increases. You do not have a conscious perception of having high blood pressure, but that is an important afferent branch of the cardiovascular and, particularly, vasomotor reflexes. The sensory neuron is essentially the same as any other general sensory neuron. The baroreceptor apparatus is part of the ending of a unipolar neuron that has a cell body in a sensory ganglion. The baroreceptors from the carotid arteries have axons in the glossopharyngeal nerve, and those from the aorta have axons in the vagus nerve.

Though visceral senses are not primarily a part of conscious perception, those sensations sometimes make it to conscious awareness. If a visceral sense is strong enough, it will be perceived. The sensory homunculus—the representation of the body in the primary somatosensory cortex—only has a small region allotted for the perception of internal stimuli. If you swallow a large bolus of food, for instance, you will probably feel the lump of that food as it pushes through your esophagus, or even if your stomach is distended after a large meal. If you inhale especially cold air, you can feel it as it enters your larynx and trachea. These sensations are not the same as feeling high blood pressure or blood sugar levels.

When particularly strong visceral sensations rise to the level of conscious perception, the sensations are often felt in unexpected places. For example, strong visceral sensations of the heart will be felt as pain in the left shoulder and left arm. This irregular pattern of projection of conscious perception of visceral sensations is called **referred pain**. Depending on the organ system affected, the referred pain will project to different areas of the body (Figure 15.7). The location of referred pain is not random, but a definitive explanation of the mechanism has not been established. The most broadly accepted theory for this phenomenon is that the visceral sensory fibers enter into the same level of the spinal cord as the somatosensory fibers of the referred pain location. By this explanation, the visceral sensory fibers from the mediastinal region, where the heart is located, would enter the spinal cord at the same level as the spinal nerves from the shoulder and arm, so the brain misinterprets the sensations from the mediastinal region as being from the axillary and brachial regions. Projections from the medial and inferior divisions of the cervical ganglia do enter the spinal cord at the middle to lower cervical levels, which is where the somatosensory fibers enter.

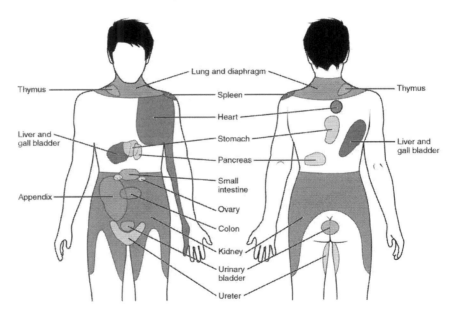

Figure 15.7 Referred Pain Chart Conscious perception of visceral sensations map to specific regions of the body, as shown in this chart. Some sensations are felt locally, whereas others are perceived as affecting areas that are quite distant from the involved organ.

Nervous System: Kehr's Sign

Kehr's sign is the presentation of pain in the left shoulder, chest, and neck regions following rupture of the spleen. The spleen is in the upper-left abdominopelvic quadrant, but the pain is more in the shoulder and neck. How can this be? The sympathetic fibers connected to the spleen are from the celiac ganglion, which would be from the mid-thoracic to lower thoracic region whereas parasympathetic fibers are found in the vagus nerve, which connects in the medulla of the brain stem. However, the neck and shoulder would connect to the spinal cord at the mid-cervical level of the spinal cord. These connections do not fit with the expected correspondence of visceral and somatosensory fibers entering at the same level of the spinal cord.

The incorrect assumption would be that the visceral sensations are coming from the spleen directly. In fact, the visceral fibers are coming from the diaphragm. The nerve connecting to the diaphragm takes a special route. The phrenic nerve is connected to the spinal cord at cervical levels 3 to 5. The motor fibers that make up this nerve are responsible for the muscle contractions that drive ventilation. These fibers have left the spinal cord to enter the phrenic nerve, meaning that spinal cord damage below the mid-cervical level is not fatal by making ventilation impossible. Therefore, the visceral fibers from the diaphragm enter the spinal cord at the same level as the somatosensory fibers from the neck and shoulder.

The diaphragm plays a role in Kehr's sign because the spleen is just inferior to the diaphragm in the upper-left quadrant of the abdominopelvic cavity. When the spleen ruptures, blood spills into this region. The accumulating hemorrhage then puts pressure on the diaphragm. The visceral sensation is actually in the diaphragm, so the referred pain is in a region of the body that corresponds to the diaphragm, not the spleen.

Efferent Branch

The efferent branch of the visceral reflex arc begins with the projection from the central neuron along the preganglionic fiber. This fiber then makes a synapse on the ganglionic neuron that projects to the target effector.

The effector organs that are the targets of the autonomic system range from the iris and ciliary body of the eye to the urinary bladder and reproductive organs. The thoracolumbar output, through the various sympathetic ganglia, reaches all of these organs. The cranial component of the parasympathetic system projects from the eye to part of the intestines. The sacral component picks up with the majority of the large intestine and the pelvic organs of the urinary and reproductive systems.

Short and Long Reflexes

Somatic reflexes involve sensory neurons that connect sensory receptors to the CNS and motor neurons that project back out to the skeletal muscles. Visceral reflexes that involve the thoracolumbar or craniosacral systems share similar connections. However, there are reflexes that do not need to involve any CNS components. A **long reflex** has afferent branches that enter the spinal cord or brain and involve the efferent branches, as previously explained. A **short reflex** is completely peripheral and only involves the local integration of sensory input with motor output (Figure 15.8).

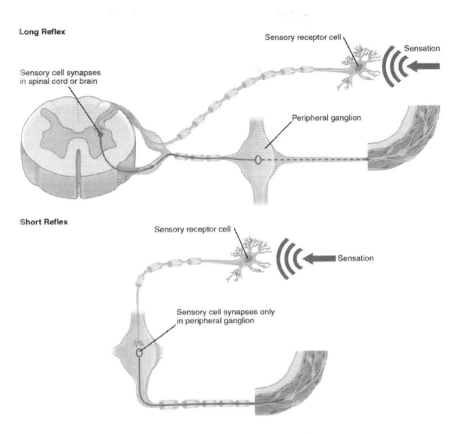

Figure 15.8 Short and Long Reflexes Sensory input can stimulate either a short or a long reflex. A sensory neuron can project to the CNS or to an autonomic ganglion. The short reflex involves the direct stimulation of a postganglionic fiber by the sensory neuron, whereas the long reflex involves integration in the spinal cord or brain.

The difference between short and long reflexes is in the involvement of the CNS. Somatic reflexes always involve the CNS, even in a monosynaptic reflex in which the sensory neuron directly activates the motor neuron. That synapse is in the spinal cord or brain stem, so it has to involve the CNS. However, in the autonomic system there is the possibility that the CNS is not involved. Because the efferent branch of a visceral reflex involves two neurons—the central neuron and the ganglionic neuron—a "short circuit" can be possible. If a sensory neuron projects directly to the ganglionic neuron and causes it to activate the effector target, then the CNS is not involved.

A division of the nervous system that is related to the autonomic nervous system is the enteric nervous system. The word enteric refers to the digestive organs, so this represents the nervous tissue that is part of the digestive system. There are a few myenteric plexuses in which the nervous tissue in the wall of the digestive tract organs can directly influence digestive function. If stretch receptors in the stomach are activated by the filling and distension of the stomach, a short reflex will directly activate the smooth muscle fibers of the stomach wall to increase motility to digest the excessive food in the stomach. No CNS involvement is needed because the stretch receptor is directly activating a neuron in the wall of the stomach that causes the smooth muscle to contract. That neuron, connected to the smooth muscle, is a postganglionic parasympathetic neuron that can be controlled by a fiber found in the vagus nerve.

Interactive LINK

Read this article (http://openstaxcollege.org/l/strokespell) to learn about a teenager who experiences a series of spells that suggest a stroke. He undergoes endless tests and seeks input from multiple doctors. In the end, one expert, one question, and a simple blood pressure cuff answers the question. Why would the heart have to beat faster when the teenager changes his body position from lying down to sitting, and then to standing?

Balance in Competing Autonomic Reflex Arcs

The autonomic nervous system is important for homeostasis because its two divisions compete at the target effector. The balance of homeostasis is attributable to the competing inputs from the sympathetic and parasympathetic divisions (dual innervation). At the level of the target effector, the signal of which system is sending the message is strictly chemical. A signaling molecule binds to a receptor that causes changes in the target cell, which in turn causes the tissue or organ to respond to the changing conditions of the body.

Competing Neurotransmitters

The postganglionic fibers of the sympathetic and parasympathetic divisions both release neurotransmitters that bind to receptors on their targets. Postganglionic sympathetic fibers release norepinephrine, with a minor exception, whereas postganglionic parasympathetic fibers release ACh. For any given target, the difference in which division of the autonomic nervous system is exerting control is just in what chemical binds to its receptors. The target cells will have adrenergic and muscarinic receptors. If norepinephrine is released, it will bind to the adrenergic receptors present on the target cell, and if ACh is released, it will bind to the muscarinic receptors on the target cell.

In the sympathetic system, there are exceptions to this pattern of dual innervation. The postganglionic sympathetic fibers that contact the blood vessels within skeletal muscle and that contact sweat glands do not release norepinephrine, they release ACh. This does not create any problem because there is no parasympathetic input to the sweat glands. Sweat glands have muscarinic receptors and produce and secrete sweat in response to the presence of ACh.

At most of the other targets of the autonomic system, the effector response is based on which neurotransmitter is released and what receptor is present. For example, regions of the heart that establish heart rate are contacted by postganglionic fibers from both systems. If norepinephrine is released onto those cells, it binds to an adrenergic receptor that causes the cells to depolarize faster, and the heart rate increases. If ACh is released onto those cells, it binds to a muscarinic receptor that causes the cells to hyperpolarize so that they cannot reach threshold as easily, and the heart rate slows. Without this parasympathetic input, the heart would work at a rate of approximately 100 beats per minute (bpm). The sympathetic system speeds that up, as it would during exercise, to 120–140 bpm, for example. The parasympathetic system slows it down to the resting heart rate of 60–80 bpm.

Another example is in the control of pupillary size (Figure 15.9). The afferent branch responds to light hitting the retina. Photoreceptors are activated, and the signal is transferred to the retinal ganglion cells that send an action potential along the optic nerve into the diencephalon. If light levels are low, the sympathetic system sends a signal out through the upper thoracic spinal cord to the superior cervical ganglion of the sympathetic chain. The postganglionic fiber then projects to the iris, where it releases norepinephrine onto the radial fibers of the iris (a smooth muscle). When those fibers contract, the pupil dilates—increasing the amount of light hitting the retina. If light levels are too high, the parasympathetic system sends a signal out from the Eddinger–Westphal nucleus through the oculomotor nerve. This fiber synapses in the ciliary ganglion in the posterior orbit. The postganglionic fiber then projects to the iris, where it releases ACh onto the circular fibers of the iris—another smooth muscle. When those fibers contract, the pupil constricts to limit the amount of light hitting the retina.

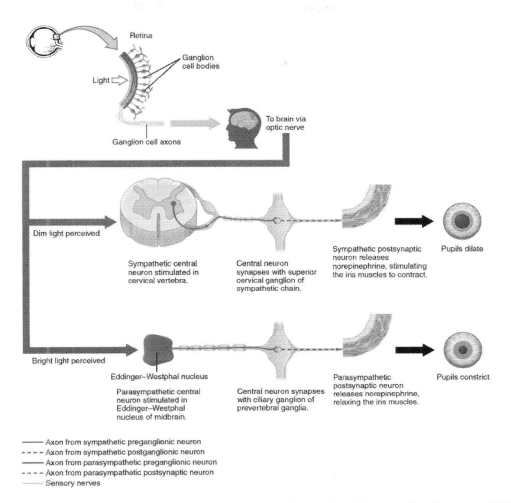

Figure 15.9 Autonomic Control of Pupillary Size Activation of the pupillary reflex comes from the amount of light activating the retinal ganglion cells, as sent along the optic nerve. The output of the sympathetic system projects through the superior cervical ganglion, whereas the parasympathetic system originates out of the midbrain and projects through the oculomotor nerve to the ciliary ganglion, which then projects to the iris. The postganglionic fibers of either division release neurotransmitters onto the smooth muscles of the iris to cause changes in the pupillary size. Norepinephrine results in dilation and ACh results in constriction.

In this example, the autonomic system is controlling how much light hits the retina. It is a homeostatic reflex mechanism that keeps the activation of photoreceptors within certain limits. In the context of avoiding a threat like the lioness on the savannah, the sympathetic response for fight or flight will increase pupillary diameter so that more light hits the retina and more visual information is available for running away. Likewise, the parasympathetic response of rest reduces the amount of light reaching the retina, allowing the photoreceptors to cycle through bleaching and be regenerated for further visual perception; this is what the homeostatic process is attempting to maintain.

Interactive LINK

Watch this video (http://openstaxcollege.org/l/pupillary) to learn about the pupillary reflexes. The pupillary light reflex involves sensory input through the optic nerve and motor response through the oculomotor nerve to the ciliary ganglion, which projects to the circular fibers of the iris. As shown in this short animation, pupils will constrict to limit the amount of light falling on the retina under bright lighting conditions. What constitutes the afferent and efferent branches of the competing reflex (dilation)?

Autonomic Tone

Organ systems are balanced between the input from the sympathetic and parasympathetic divisions. When something upsets that balance, the homeostatic mechanisms strive to return it to its regular state. For each organ system, there may be more of a sympathetic or parasympathetic tendency to the resting state, which is known as the **autonomic tone** of the system. For example, the heart rate was described above. Because the resting heart rate is the result of the parasympathetic system slowing the heart down from its intrinsic rate of 100 bpm, the heart can be said to be in parasympathetic tone.

In a similar fashion, another aspect of the cardiovascular system is primarily under sympathetic control. Blood pressure is partially determined by the contraction of smooth muscle in the walls of blood vessels. These tissues have adrenergic receptors that respond to the release of norepinephrine from postganglionic sympathetic fibers by constricting and increasing blood pressure. The hormones released from the adrenal medulla—epinephrine and norepinephrine—will also bind to these receptors. Those hormones travel through the bloodstream where they can easily interact with the receptors in the vessel walls. The parasympathetic system has no significant input to the systemic blood vessels, so the sympathetic system determines their tone.

There are a limited number of blood vessels that respond to sympathetic input in a different fashion. Blood vessels in skeletal muscle, particularly those in the lower limbs, are more likely to dilate. It does not have an overall effect on blood pressure to alter the tone of the vessels, but rather allows for blood flow to increase for those skeletal muscles that will be active in the fight-or-flight response. The blood vessels that have a parasympathetic projection are limited to those in the erectile tissue of the reproductive organs. Acetylcholine released by these postganglionic parasympathetic fibers cause the vessels to dilate, leading to the engorgement of the erectile tissue.

Orthostatic Hypotension

Have you ever stood up quickly and felt dizzy for a moment? This is because, for one reason or another, blood is not getting to your brain so it is briefly deprived of oxygen. When you change position from sitting or lying down to standing, your cardiovascular system has to adjust for a new challenge, keeping blood pumping up into the head while gravity is pulling more and more blood down into the legs.

The reason for this is a sympathetic reflex that maintains the output of the heart in response to postural change. When a person stands up, proprioceptors indicate that the body is changing position. A signal goes to the CNS, which then sends a signal to the upper thoracic spinal cord neurons of the sympathetic division. The sympathetic system then causes the heart to beat faster and the blood vessels to constrict. Both changes will make it possible for the cardiovascular system to maintain the rate of blood delivery to the brain. Blood is being pumped superiorly through the internal branch of the carotid arteries into the brain, against the force of gravity. Gravity is not increasing while standing, but blood is more likely to flow down into the legs as they are extended for standing. This sympathetic reflex keeps the brain well oxygenated so that cognitive and other neural processes are not interrupted.

Sometimes this does not work properly. If the sympathetic system cannot increase cardiac output, then blood pressure into the brain will decrease, and a brief neurological loss can be felt. This can be brief, as a slight "wooziness" when standing up too quickly, or a loss of balance and neurological impairment for a period of time. The name for this is orthostatic hypotension, which means that blood pressure goes below the homeostatic set point when standing. It can be the result of standing up faster than the reflex can occur, which may be referred to as a benign "head rush," or it may be the result of an underlying cause.

There are two basic reasons that orthostatic hypotension can occur. First, blood volume is too low and the sympathetic reflex is not effective. This hypovolemia may be the result of dehydration or medications that affect fluid balance, such as diuretics or vasodilators. Both of these medications are meant to lower blood pressure, which may be necessary in the case of systemic hypertension, and regulation of the medications may alleviate the problem. Sometimes increasing fluid intake or water retention through salt intake can improve the situation.

The second underlying cause of orthostatic hypotension is autonomic failure. There are several disorders that result in compromised sympathetic functions. The disorders range from diabetes to multiple system atrophy (a loss of control over many systems in the body), and addressing the underlying condition can improve the hypotension. For example, with diabetes, peripheral nerve damage can occur, which would affect the postganglionic sympathetic fibers. Getting blood glucose levels under control can improve neurological deficits associated with diabetes.

15.3 | Central Control

By the end of this section, you will be able to:

- Describe the role of higher centers of the brain in autonomic regulation
- Explain the connection of the hypothalamus to homeostasis
- Describe the regions of the CNS that link the autonomic system with emotion
- Describe the pathways important to descending control of the autonomic system

The pupillary light reflex (Figure 15.10) begins when light hits the retina and causes a signal to travel along the optic nerve. This is visual sensation, because the afferent branch of this reflex is simply sharing the special sense pathway. Bright light hitting the retina leads to the parasympathetic response, through the oculomotor nerve, followed by the postganglionic fiber from the ciliary ganglion, which stimulates the circular fibers of the iris to contract and constrict the pupil. When light hits the retina in one eye, both pupils contract. When that light is removed, both pupils dilate again back to the resting position. When the stimulus is unilateral (presented to only one eye), the response is bilateral (both eyes). The same is not true for somatic reflexes. If you touch a hot radiator, you only pull that arm back, not both. Central control of autonomic reflexes is different than for somatic reflexes. The hypothalamus, along with other CNS locations, controls the autonomic system.

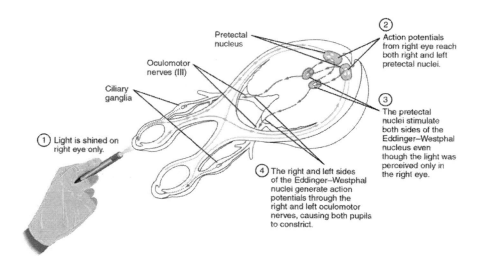

Figure 15.10 Pupillary Reflex Pathways The pupil is under competing autonomic control in response to light levels hitting the retina. The sympathetic system will dilate the pupil when the retina is not receiving enough light, and the parasympathetic system will constrict the pupil when too much light hits the retina.

Forebrain Structures

Autonomic control is based on the visceral reflexes, composed of the afferent and efferent branches. These homeostatic mechanisms are based on the balance between the two divisions of the autonomic system, which results in tone for various organs that is based on the predominant input from the sympathetic or parasympathetic systems. Coordinating that balance requires integration that begins with forebrain structures like the hypothalamus and continues into the brain stem and spinal cord.

The Hypothalamus

The hypothalamus is the control center for many homeostatic mechanisms. It regulates both autonomic function and endocrine function. The roles it plays in the pupillary reflexes demonstrates the importance of this control center. The optic nerve projects primarily to the thalamus, which is the necessary relay to the occipital cortex for conscious visual perception. Another projection of the optic nerve, however, goes to the hypothalamus.

The hypothalamus then uses this visual system input to drive the pupillary reflexes. If the retina is activated by high levels of light, the hypothalamus stimulates the parasympathetic response. If the optic nerve message shows that low levels of light are falling on the retina, the hypothalamus activates the sympathetic response. Output from the hypothalamus follows two main tracts, the **dorsal longitudinal fasciculus** and the **medial forebrain bundle** (Figure 15.11). Along these two tracts, the hypothalamus can influence the Eddinger–Westphal nucleus of the oculomotor complex or the lateral horns of the thoracic spinal cord.

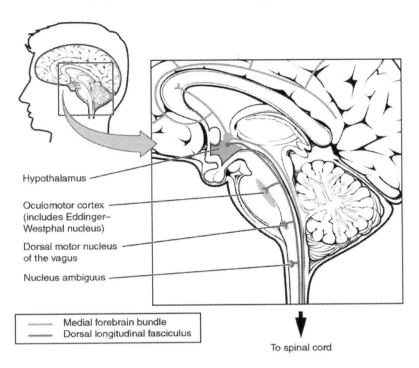

Figure 15.11 Fiber Tracts of the Central Autonomic System The hypothalamus is the source of most of the central control of autonomic function. It receives input from cerebral structures and projects to brain stem and spinal cord structures to regulate the balance of sympathetic and parasympathetic input to the organ systems of the body. The main pathways for this are the medial forebrain bundle and the dorsal longitudinal fasciculus.

These two tracts connect the hypothalamus with the major parasympathetic nuclei in the brain stem and the preganglionic (central) neurons of the thoracolumbar spinal cord. The hypothalamus also receives input from other areas of the forebrain through the medial forebrain bundle. The olfactory cortex, the septal nuclei of the basal forebrain, and the amygdala project into the hypothalamus through the medial forebrain bundle. These forebrain structures inform the hypothalamus about the state of the nervous system and can influence the regulatory processes of homeostasis. A good example of this is found in the amygdala, which is found beneath the cerebral cortex of the temporal lobe and plays a role in our ability to remember and feel emotions.

The Amygdala

The amygdala is a group of nuclei in the medial region of the temporal lobe that is part of the **limbic lobe** (Figure 15.12). The limbic lobe includes structures that are involved in emotional responses, as well as structures that contribute to memory function. The limbic lobe has strong connections with the hypothalamus and influences the state of its activity on the basis of emotional state. For example, when you are anxious or scared, the amygdala will send signals to the hypothalamus along the medial forebrain bundle that will stimulate the sympathetic fight-or-flight response. The hypothalamus will also stimulate the release of stress hormones through its control of the endocrine system in response to amygdala input.

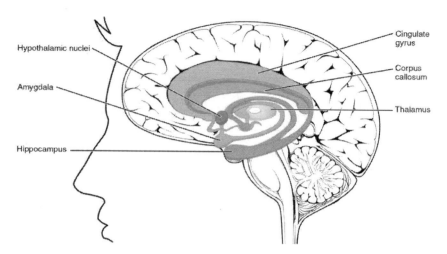

Figure 15.12 The Limbic Lobe Structures arranged around the edge of the cerebrum constitute the limbic lobe, which includes the amygdala, hippocampus, and cingulate gyrus, and connects to the hypothalamus.

The Medulla

The medulla contains nuclei referred to as the **cardiovascular center**, which controls the smooth and cardiac muscle of the cardiovascular system through autonomic connections. When the homeostasis of the cardiovascular system shifts, such as when blood pressure changes, the coordination of the autonomic system can be accomplished within this region. Furthermore, when descending inputs from the hypothalamus stimulate this area, the sympathetic system can increase activity in the cardiovascular system, such as in response to anxiety or stress. The preganglionic sympathetic fibers that are responsible for increasing heart rate are referred to as the **cardiac accelerator nerves**, whereas the preganglionic sympathetic fibers responsible for constricting blood vessels compose the **vasomotor nerves**.

Several brain stem nuclei are important for the visceral control of major organ systems. One brain stem nucleus involved in cardiovascular function is the solitary nucleus. It receives sensory input about blood pressure and cardiac function from the glossopharyngeal and vagus nerves, and its output will activate sympathetic stimulation of the heart or blood vessels through the upper thoracic lateral horn. Another brain stem nucleus important for visceral control is the dorsal motor nucleus of the vagus nerve, which is the motor nucleus for the parasympathetic functions ascribed to the vagus nerve, including decreasing the heart rate, relaxing bronchial tubes in the lungs, and activating digestive function through the enteric nervous system. The nucleus ambiguus, which is named for its ambiguous histology, also contributes to the parasympathetic output of the vagus nerve and targets muscles in the pharynx and larynx for swallowing and speech, as well as contributing to the parasympathetic tone of the heart along with the dorsal motor nucleus of the vagus.

Everyday CONNECTION

Exercise and the Autonomic System

In addition to its association with the fight-or-flight response and rest-and-digest functions, the autonomic system is responsible for certain everyday functions. For example, it comes into play when homeostatic mechanisms dynamically change, such as the physiological changes that accompany exercise. Getting on the treadmill and putting in a good workout will cause the heart rate to increase, breathing to be stronger and deeper, sweat glands to activate, and the digestive system to suspend activity. These are the same physiological changes associated with the fight-or-flight response, but there is nothing chasing you on that treadmill.

This is not a simple homeostatic mechanism at work because "maintaining the internal environment" would mean getting all those changes back to their set points. Instead, the sympathetic system has become active during exercise so that your body can cope with what is happening. A homeostatic mechanism is dealing with the conscious decision to push the body away from a resting state. The heart, actually, is moving away from its homeostatic set point. Without any input from the autonomic system, the heart would beat at approximately 100 bpm, and the parasympathetic system slows that down to the resting rate of approximately 70 bpm. But in the middle of a good workout, you should see your heart rate at 120–140 bpm. You could say that the body is stressed because of what you are doing to it. Homeostatic mechanisms are trying to keep blood pH in the normal range, or to keep body temperature under control, but those are in response to the choice to exercise.

Interactive LINK

Watch this video (http://openstaxcollege.org/l/emotions) to learn about physical responses to emotion. The autonomic system, which is important for regulating the homeostasis of the organ systems, is also responsible for our physiological responses to emotions such as fear. The video summarizes the extent of the body's reactions and describes several effects of the autonomic system in response to fear. On the basis of what you have already studied about autonomic function, which effect would you expect to be associated with parasympathetic, rather than sympathetic, activity?

15.4 | Drugs that Affect the Autonomic System

By the end of this section, you will be able to:
- List the classes of pharmaceuticals that interact with the autonomic nervous system
- Differentiate between cholinergic and adrenergic compounds
- Differentiate between sympathomimetic and sympatholytic drugs
- Relate the consequences of nicotine abuse with respect to autonomic control of the cardiovascular system

An important way to understand the effects of native neurochemicals in the autonomic system is in considering the effects of pharmaceutical drugs. This can be considered in terms of how drugs change autonomic function. These effects will primarily be based on how drugs act at the receptors of the autonomic system neurochemistry. The signaling molecules of the nervous system interact with proteins in the cell membranes of various target cells. In fact, no effect can be attributed to just the signaling molecules themselves without considering the receptors. A chemical that the body produces to interact with those receptors is called an **endogenous chemical**, whereas a chemical introduced to the system from outside is an **exogenous chemical**. Exogenous chemicals may be of a natural origin, such as a plant extract, or they may be synthetically produced in a pharmaceutical laboratory.

Broad Autonomic Effects

One important drug that affects the autonomic system broadly is not a pharmaceutical therapeutic agent associated with the system. This drug is nicotine. The effects of nicotine on the autonomic nervous system are important in considering the role smoking can play in health.

All ganglionic neurons of the autonomic system, in both sympathetic and parasympathetic ganglia, are activated by ACh released from preganglionic fibers. The ACh receptors on these neurons are of the nicotinic type, meaning that they are ligand-gated ion channels. When the neurotransmitter released from the preganglionic fiber binds to the receptor protein, a channel opens to allow positive ions to cross the cell membrane. The result is depolarization of the ganglia. Nicotine acts as an ACh analog at these synapses, so when someone takes in the drug, it binds to these ACh receptors and activates the ganglionic neurons, causing them to depolarize.

Ganglia of both divisions are activated equally by the drug. For many target organs in the body, this results in no net change. The competing inputs to the system cancel each other out and nothing significant happens. For example, the sympathetic system will cause sphincters in the digestive tract to contract, limiting digestive propulsion, but the parasympathetic system will cause the contraction of other muscles in the digestive tract, which will try to push the contents of the digestive system along. The end result is that the food does not really move along and the digestive system has not appreciably changed.

The system in which this can be problematic is in the cardiovascular system, which is why smoking is a risk factor for cardiovascular disease. First, there is no significant parasympathetic regulation of blood pressure. Only a limited number of blood vessels are affected by parasympathetic input, so nicotine will preferentially cause the vascular tone to become more sympathetic, which means blood pressure will be increased. Second, the autonomic control of the heart is special. Unlike skeletal or smooth muscles, cardiac muscle is intrinsically active, meaning that it generates its own action potentials. The autonomic system does not cause the heart to beat, it just speeds it up (sympathetic) or slows it down (parasympathetic). The mechanisms for this are not mutually exclusive, so the heart receives conflicting signals, and the rhythm of the heart can be affected (Figure 15.13).

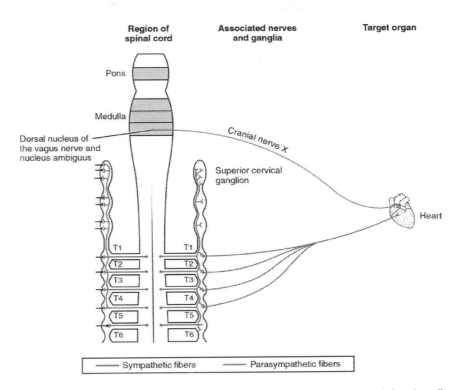

Figure 15.13 Autonomic Connections to Heart and Blood Vessels The nicotinic receptor is found on all autonomic ganglia, but the cardiovascular connections are particular, and do not conform to the usual competitive projections that would just cancel each other out when stimulated by nicotine. The opposing signals to the heart would both depolarize and hyperpolarize the heart cells that establish the rhythm of the heartbeat, likely causing arrhythmia. Only the sympathetic system governs systemic blood pressure so nicotine would cause an increase.

Sympathetic Effect

The neurochemistry of the sympathetic system is based on the adrenergic system. Norepinephrine and epinephrine influence target effectors by binding to the α-adrenergic or β-adrenergic receptors. Drugs that affect the sympathetic system affect these chemical systems. The drugs can be classified by whether they enhance the functions of the sympathetic system or interrupt those functions. A drug that enhances adrenergic function is known as a **sympathomimetic drug**, whereas a drug that interrupts adrenergic function is a **sympatholytic drug**.

Sympathomimetic Drugs

When the sympathetic system is not functioning correctly or the body is in a state of homeostatic imbalance, these drugs act at postganglionic terminals and synapses in the sympathetic efferent pathway. These drugs either bind to particular adrenergic receptors and mimic norepinephrine at the synapses between sympathetic postganglionic fibers and their targets, or they increase the production and release of norepinephrine from postganglionic fibers. Also, to increase the effectiveness of adrenergic chemicals released from the fibers, some of these drugs may block the removal or reuptake of the neurotransmitter from the synapse.

A common sympathomimetic drug is phenylephrine, which is a common component of decongestants. It can also be used to dilate the pupil and to raise blood pressure. Phenylephrine is known as an α_1-adrenergic **agonist**, meaning that it binds to a specific adrenergic receptor, stimulating a response. In this role, phenylephrine will bind to the adrenergic receptors in bronchioles of the lungs and cause them to dilate. By opening these structures, accumulated mucus can be cleared out of the lower respiratory tract. Phenylephrine is often paired with other pharmaceuticals, such as analgesics, as in the "sinus" version of many over-the-counter drugs, such as Tylenol Sinus® or Excedrin Sinus®, or in expectorants for chest congestion such as in Robitussin CF®.

A related molecule, called pseudoephedrine, was much more commonly used in these applications than was phenylephrine, until the molecule became useful in the illicit production of amphetamines. Phenylephrine is not as effective as a drug because it can be partially broken down in the digestive tract before it is ever absorbed. Like the adrenergic agents, phenylephrine is effective in dilating the pupil, known as **mydriasis** (Figure 15.14). Phenylephrine is used during an eye exam in an ophthalmologist's or optometrist's office for this purpose. It can also be used to increase blood pressure in situations in which cardiac function is compromised, such as under anesthesia or during septic shock.

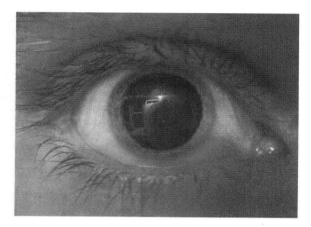

Figure 15.14 Mydriasis The sympathetic system causes pupillary dilation when norepinephrine binds to an adrenergic receptor in the radial fibers of the iris smooth muscle. Phenylephrine mimics this action by binding to the same receptor when drops are applied onto the surface of the eye in a doctor's office. (credit: Corey Theiss)

Other drugs that enhance adrenergic function are not associated with therapeutic uses, but affect the functions of the sympathetic system in a similar fashion. Cocaine primarily interferes with the uptake of dopamine at the synapse and can also increase adrenergic function. Caffeine is an antagonist to a different neurotransmitter receptor, called the adenosine receptor. Adenosine will suppress adrenergic activity, specifically the release of norepinephrine at synapses, so caffeine indirectly increases adrenergic activity. There is some evidence that caffeine can aid in the therapeutic use of drugs, perhaps by potentiating (increasing) sympathetic function, as is suggested by the inclusion of caffeine in over-the-counter analgesics such as Excedrin®.

Sympatholytic Drugs

Drugs that interfere with sympathetic function are referred to as sympatholytic, or sympathoplegic, drugs. They primarily work as an **antagonist** to the adrenergic receptors. They block the ability of norepinephrine or epinephrine to bind to the receptors so that the effect is "cut" or "takes a blow," to refer to the endings "-lytic" and "-plegic," respectively. The various drugs of this class will be specific to α-adrenergic or β-adrenergic receptors, or to their receptor subtypes.

Possibly the most familiar type of sympatholytic drug are the β-blockers. These drugs are often used to treat cardiovascular disease because they block the β-receptors associated with vasoconstriction and cardioacceleration. By allowing blood vessels to dilate, or keeping heart rate from increasing, these drugs can improve cardiac function in a compromised system, such as for a person with congestive heart failure or who has previously suffered a heart attack. A couple of common versions of β-blockers are metoprolol, which specifically blocks the $β_2$-receptor, and propanolol, which nonspecifically blocks β-receptors. There are other drugs that are α-blockers and can affect the sympathetic system in a similar way.

Other uses for sympatholytic drugs are as antianxiety medications. A common example of this is clonidine, which is an α-agonist. The sympathetic system is tied to anxiety to the point that the sympathetic response can be referred to as "fight, flight, or fright." Clonidine is used for other treatments aside from hypertension and anxiety, including pain conditions and attention deficit hyperactivity disorder.

Parasympathetic Effects

Drugs affecting parasympathetic functions can be classified into those that increase or decrease activity at postganglionic terminals. Parasympathetic postganglionic fibers release ACh, and the receptors on the targets are muscarinic receptors. There are several types of muscarinic receptors, M1–M5, but the drugs are not usually specific to the specific types. Parasympathetic drugs can be either muscarinic agonists or antagonists, or have indirect effects on the cholinergic system. Drugs that enhance cholinergic effects are called **parasympathomimetic drugs**, whereas those that inhibit cholinergic effects are referred to as **anticholinergic drugs**.

Pilocarpine is a nonspecific muscarinic agonist commonly used to treat disorders of the eye. It reverses mydriasis, such as is caused by phenylephrine, and can be administered after an eye exam. Along with constricting the pupil through the smooth muscle of the iris, pilocarpine will also cause the ciliary muscle to contract. This will open perforations at the base of the cornea, allowing for the drainage of aqueous humor from the anterior compartment of the eye and, therefore, reducing intraocular pressure related to glaucoma.

Atropine and scopolamine are part of a class of muscarinic antagonists that come from the *Atropa* genus of plants that include belladonna or deadly nightshade (Figure 15.15). The name of one of these plants, belladonna, refers to the fact that extracts from this plant were used cosmetically for dilating the pupil. The active chemicals from this plant block the muscarinic receptors in the iris and allow the pupil to dilate, which is considered attractive because it makes the eyes appear larger. Humans are instinctively attracted to anything with larger eyes, which comes from the fact that the ratio of eye-to-head size is different in infants (or baby animals) and can elicit an emotional response. The cosmetic use of belladonna extract was essentially acting on this response. Atropine is no longer used in this cosmetic capacity for reasons related to the other name for the plant, which is deadly nightshade. Suppression of parasympathetic function, especially when it becomes systemic, can be fatal. Autonomic regulation is disrupted and anticholinergic symptoms develop. The berries of this plant are highly toxic, but can be mistaken for other berries. The antidote for atropine or scopolamine poisoning is pilocarpine.

Figure 15.15 Belladonna Plant The plant from the genus *Atropa*, which is known as belladonna or deadly nightshade, was used cosmetically to dilate pupils, but can be fatal when ingested. The berries on the plant may seem attractive as a fruit, but they contain the same anticholinergic compounds as the rest of the plant.

Sympathetic and Parasympathetic Effects of Different Drug Types

Drug type	Example(s)	Sympathetic effect	Parasympathetic effect	Overall result
Nicotinic agonists	Nicotine	Mimic ACh at preganglionic synapses, causing activation of postganglionic fibers and the release of norepinephrine onto the target organ	Mimic ACh at preganglionic synapses, causing activation of postganglionic fibers and the release of ACh onto the target organ	Most conflicting signals cancel each other out, but cardiovascular system is susceptible to hypertension and arrhythmias
Sympathomimetic drugs	Phenylephrine	Bind to adrenergic receptors or mimics sympathetic action in some other way	No effect	Increase sympathetic tone
Sympatholytic drugs	β-blockers such as propanolol or metoprolol; α-agonists such as clonidine	Block binding to adrenergic drug or decrease adrenergic signals	No effect	Increase parasympathetic tone
Parasympatho-mimetics/ muscarinic agonists	Pilocarpine	No effect, except on sweat glands	Bind to muscarinic receptor, similar to ACh	Increase parasympathetic tone
Anticholinergics/ muscarinic antagonists	Atropine, scopolamine, dimenhydrinate	No effect	Block muscarinic receptors and parasympathetic function	Increase sympathetic tone

Table 15.2

Disorders OF THE...

Autonomic Nervous System

Approximately 33 percent of people experience a mild problem with motion sickness, whereas up to 66 percent experience motion sickness under extreme conditions, such as being on a tossing boat with no view of the horizon. Connections between regions in the brain stem and the autonomic system result in the symptoms of nausea, cold sweats, and vomiting.

The part of the brain responsible for vomiting, or emesis, is known as the area postrema. It is located next to the fourth ventricle and is not restricted by the blood–brain barrier, which allows it to respond to chemicals in the bloodstream—namely, toxins that will stimulate emesis. There are significant connections between this area, the solitary nucleus, and the dorsal motor nucleus of the vagus nerve. These autonomic system and nuclei connections are associated with the symptoms of motion sickness.

Motion sickness is the result of conflicting information from the visual and vestibular systems. If motion is perceived by the visual system without the complementary vestibular stimuli, or through vestibular stimuli without visual confirmation, the brain stimulates emesis and the associated symptoms. The area postrema, by itself, appears to be able to stimulate emesis in response to toxins in the blood, but it is also connected to the autonomic system and can trigger a similar response to motion.

Autonomic drugs are used to combat motion sickness. Though it is often described as a dangerous and deadly drug, scopolamine is used to treat motion sickness. A popular treatment for motion sickness is the transdermal scopolamine patch. Scopolamine is one of the substances derived from the *Atropa* genus along with atropine. At higher doses, those substances are thought to be poisonous and can lead to an extreme sympathetic syndrome. However, the transdermal patch regulates the release of the drug, and the concentration is kept very low so that the dangers are avoided. For those who are concerned about using "The Most Dangerous Drug," as some websites will call it, antihistamines such as dimenhydrinate (Dramamine®) can be used.

Watch this video (http://openstaxcollege.org/l/3Dmovies) to learn about the side effects of 3-D movies. As discussed in this video, movies that are shot in 3-D can cause motion sickness, which elicits the autonomic symptoms of nausea and sweating. The disconnection between the perceived motion on the screen and the lack of any change in equilibrium stimulates these symptoms. Why do you think sitting close to the screen or right in the middle of the theater makes motion sickness during a 3-D movie worse?

KEY TERMS

acetylcholine (ACh) neurotransmitter that binds at a motor end-plate to trigger depolarization

adrenal medulla interior portion of the adrenal (or suprarenal) gland that releases epinephrine and norepinephrine into the bloodstream as hormones

adrenergic synapse where norepinephrine is released, which binds to α- or β-adrenergic receptors

afferent branch component of a reflex arc that represents the input from a sensory neuron, for either a special or general sense

agonist any exogenous substance that binds to a receptor and produces a similar effect to the endogenous ligand

alpha (α)-adrenergic receptor one of the receptors to which epinephrine and norepinephrine bind, which comes in three subtypes: $α_1$, $α_2$, and $α_3$

antagonist any exogenous substance that binds to a receptor and produces an opposing effect to the endogenous ligand

anticholinergic drugs drugs that interrupt or reduce the function of the parasympathetic system

autonomic tone tendency of an organ system to be governed by one division of the autonomic nervous system over the other, such as heart rate being lowered by parasympathetic input at rest

baroreceptor mechanoreceptor that senses the stretch of blood vessels to indicate changes in blood pressure

beta (β)-adrenergic receptor one of the receptors to which epinephrine and norepinephrine bind, which comes in two subtypes: $β_1$ and $β_2$

cardiac accelerator nerves preganglionic sympathetic fibers that cause the heart rate to increase when the cardiovascular center in the medulla initiates a signal

cardiovascular center region in the medulla that controls the cardiovascular system through cardiac accelerator nerves and vasomotor nerves, which are components of the sympathetic division of the autonomic nervous system

celiac ganglion one of the collateral ganglia of the sympathetic system that projects to the digestive system

central neuron specifically referring to the cell body of a neuron in the autonomic system that is located in the central nervous system, specifically the lateral horn of the spinal cord or a brain stem nucleus

cholinergic synapse at which acetylcholine is released and binds to the nicotinic or muscarinic receptor

chromaffin cells neuroendocrine cells of the adrenal medulla that release epinephrine and norepinephrine into the bloodstream as part of sympathetic system activity

ciliary ganglion one of the terminal ganglia of the parasympathetic system, located in the posterior orbit, axons from which project to the iris

collateral ganglia ganglia outside of the sympathetic chain that are targets of sympathetic preganglionic fibers, which are the celiac, inferior mesenteric, and superior mesenteric ganglia

craniosacral system alternate name for the parasympathetic division of the autonomic nervous system that is based on the anatomical location of central neurons in brain-stem nuclei and the lateral horn of the sacral spinal cord; also referred to as craniosacral outflow

dorsal longitudinal fasciculus major output pathway of the hypothalamus that descends through the gray matter of the brain stem and into the spinal cord

dorsal nucleus of the vagus nerve location of parasympathetic neurons that project through the vagus nerve to terminal ganglia in the thoracic and abdominal cavities

Eddinger–Westphal nucleus location of parasympathetic neurons that project to the ciliary ganglion

efferent branch component of a reflex arc that represents the output, with the target being an effector, such as muscle or glandular tissue

endogenous describes substance made in the human body

endogenous chemical substance produced and released within the body to interact with a receptor protein

epinephrine signaling molecule released from the adrenal medulla into the bloodstream as part of the sympathetic response

exogenous describes substance made outside of the human body

exogenous chemical substance from a source outside the body, whether it be another organism such as a plant or from the synthetic processes of a laboratory, that binds to a transmembrane receptor protein

fight-or-flight response set of responses induced by sympathetic activity that lead to either fleeing a threat or standing up to it, which in the modern world is often associated with anxious feelings

G protein–coupled receptor membrane protein complex that consists of a receptor protein that binds to a signaling molecule—a G protein—that is activated by that binding and in turn activates an effector protein (enzyme) that creates a second-messenger molecule in the cytoplasm of the target cell

ganglionic neuron specifically refers to the cell body of a neuron in the autonomic system that is located in a ganglion

gray rami communicantes (singular = ramus communicans) unmyelinated structures that provide a short connection from a sympathetic chain ganglion to the spinal nerve that contains the postganglionic sympathetic fiber

greater splanchnic nerve nerve that contains fibers of the central sympathetic neurons that do not synapse in the chain ganglia but project onto the celiac ganglion

inferior mesenteric ganglion one of the collateral ganglia of the sympathetic system that projects to the digestive system

intramural ganglia terminal ganglia of the parasympathetic system that are found within the walls of the target effector

lesser splanchnic nerve nerve that contains fibers of the central sympathetic neurons that do not synapse in the chain ganglia but project onto the inferior mesenteric ganglion

ligand-gated cation channel ion channel, such as the nicotinic receptor, that is specific to positively charged ions and opens when a molecule such as a neurotransmitter binds to it

limbic lobe structures arranged around the edges of the cerebrum that are involved in memory and emotion

long reflex reflex arc that includes the central nervous system

medial forebrain bundle fiber pathway that extends anteriorly into the basal forebrain, passes through the hypothalamus, and extends into the brain stem and spinal cord

mesenteric plexus nervous tissue within the wall of the digestive tract that contains neurons that are the targets of autonomic preganglionic fibers and that project to the smooth muscle and glandular tissues in the digestive organ

muscarinic receptor type of acetylcholine receptor protein that is characterized by also binding to muscarine and is a metabotropic receptor

mydriasis dilation of the pupil; typically the result of disease, trauma, or drugs

nicotinic receptor type of acetylcholine receptor protein that is characterized by also binding to nicotine and is an ionotropic receptor

norepinephrine signaling molecule released as a neurotransmitter by most postganglionic sympathetic fibers as part of the sympathetic response, or as a hormone into the bloodstream from the adrenal medulla

nucleus ambiguus brain-stem nucleus that contains neurons that project through the vagus nerve to terminal ganglia in the thoracic cavity; specifically associated with the heart

parasympathetic division division of the autonomic nervous system responsible for restful and digestive functions

parasympathomimetic drugs drugs that enhance or mimic the function of the parasympathetic system

paravertebral ganglia autonomic ganglia superior to the sympathetic chain ganglia

postganglionic fiber axon from a ganglionic neuron in the autonomic nervous system that projects to and synapses with the target effector; sometimes referred to as a postganglionic neuron

preganglionic fiber axon from a central neuron in the autonomic nervous system that projects to and synapses with a ganglionic neuron; sometimes referred to as a preganglionic neuron

prevertebral ganglia autonomic ganglia that are anterior to the vertebral column and functionally related to the sympathetic chain ganglia

referred pain the conscious perception of visceral sensation projected to a different region of the body, such as the left shoulder and arm pain as a sign for a heart attack

reflex arc circuit of a reflex that involves a sensory input and motor output, or an afferent branch and an efferent branch, and an integrating center to connect the two branches

rest and digest set of functions associated with the parasympathetic system that lead to restful actions and digestion

short reflex reflex arc that does not include any components of the central nervous system

somatic reflex reflex involving skeletal muscle as the effector, under the control of the somatic nervous system

superior cervical ganglion one of the paravertebral ganglia of the sympathetic system that projects to the head

superior mesenteric ganglion one of the collateral ganglia of the sympathetic system that projects to the digestive system

sympathetic chain ganglia series of ganglia adjacent to the vertebral column that receive input from central sympathetic neurons

sympathetic division division of the autonomic nervous system associated with the fight-or-flight response

sympatholytic drug drug that interrupts, or "lyses," the function of the sympathetic system

sympathomimetic drug drug that enhances or mimics the function of the sympathetic system

target effector organ, tissue, or gland that will respond to the control of an autonomic or somatic or endocrine signal

terminal ganglia ganglia of the parasympathetic division of the autonomic system, which are located near or within the target effector, the latter also known as intramural ganglia

thoracolumbar system alternate name for the sympathetic division of the autonomic nervous system that is based on the anatomical location of central neurons in the lateral horn of the thoracic and upper lumbar spinal cord

varicosity structure of some autonomic connections that is not a typical synaptic end bulb, but a string of swellings along the length of a fiber that makes a network of connections with the target effector

vasomotor nerves preganglionic sympathetic fibers that cause the constriction of blood vessels in response to signals from the cardiovascular center

visceral reflex reflex involving an internal organ as the effector, under the control of the autonomic nervous system

white rami communicantes (singular = ramus communicans) myelinated structures that provide a short connection from a sympathetic chain ganglion to the spinal nerve that contains the preganglionic sympathetic fiber

CHAPTER REVIEW

15.1 Divisions of the Autonomic Nervous System

The primary responsibilities of the autonomic nervous system are to regulate homeostatic mechanisms in the body, which is also part of what the endocrine system does. The key to understanding the autonomic system is to explore the response pathways—the output of the nervous system. The way we respond to the world around us, to manage the internal environment on the basis of the external environment, is divided between two parts of the autonomic nervous system. The sympathetic division responds to threats and produces a readiness to confront the threat or to run away: the fight-or-flight response. The parasympathetic division plays the opposite role. When the external environment does not present any immediate danger, a restful mode descends on the body, and the digestive system is more active.

The sympathetic output of the nervous system originates out of the lateral horn of the thoracolumbar spinal cord. An axon from one of these central neurons projects by way of the ventral spinal nerve root and spinal nerve to a sympathetic ganglion, either in the sympathetic chain ganglia or one of the collateral locations, where it synapses on a ganglionic neuron. These preganglionic fibers release ACh, which excites the ganglionic neuron through the nicotinic receptor. The axon from the ganglionic neuron—the postganglionic fiber—then projects to a target effector where it will release norepinephrine to bind to an adrenergic receptor, causing a change in the physiology of that organ in keeping with the broad, divergent sympathetic response. The postganglionic connections to sweat glands in the skin and blood vessels supplying skeletal muscle are, however, exceptions; those fibers release ACh onto muscarinic receptors. The sympathetic system has a specialized preganglionic connection to the adrenal medulla that causes epinephrine and norepinephrine to be released into the bloodstream rather than exciting a neuron that contacts an organ directly. This hormonal component means that the sympathetic chemical signal can spread throughout the body very quickly and affect many organ systems at once.

The parasympathetic output is based in the brain stem and sacral spinal cord. Neurons from particular nuclei in the brain stem or from the lateral horn of the sacral spinal cord (preganglionic neurons) project to terminal (intramural) ganglia located close to or within the wall of target effectors. These preganglionic fibers also release ACh onto nicotinic receptors to excite the ganglionic neurons. The postganglionic fibers then contact the target tissues within the organ to release ACh, which binds to muscarinic receptors to induce rest-and-digest responses.

Signaling molecules utilized by the autonomic nervous system are released from axons and can be considered as either neurotransmitters (when they directly interact with the effector) or as hormones (when they are released into the bloodstream). The same molecule, such as norepinephrine, could be considered either a neurotransmitter or a hormone on the basis of whether it is released from a postganglionic sympathetic axon or from the adrenal gland. The synapses in the autonomic system are not always the typical type of connection first described in the neuromuscular junction. Instead of having synaptic end bulbs at the very end of an axonal fiber, they may have swellings—called varicosities—along the length of a fiber so that it makes a network of connections within the target tissue.

15.2 Autonomic Reflexes and Homeostasis

Autonomic nervous system function is based on the visceral reflex. This reflex is similar to the somatic reflex, but the efferent branch is composed of two neurons. The central neuron projects from the spinal cord or brain stem to synapse on the ganglionic neuron that projects to the effector. The afferent branch of the somatic and visceral reflexes is very similar, as many somatic and special senses activate autonomic responses. However, there are visceral senses that do not form part of conscious perception. If a visceral sensation, such as cardiac pain, is strong enough, it will rise to the level of consciousness. However, the sensory homunculus does not provide a representation of the internal structures to the same degree as the surface of the body, so visceral sensations are often experienced as referred pain, such as feelings of pain in the left shoulder and arm in connection with a heart attack.

The role of visceral reflexes is to maintain a balance of function in the organ systems of the body. The two divisions of the autonomic system each play a role in effecting change, usually in competing directions. The sympathetic system increases heart rate, whereas the parasympathetic system decreases heart rate. The sympathetic system dilates the pupil of the eye, whereas the parasympathetic system constricts the pupil. The competing inputs can contribute to the resting tone of the organ system. Heart rate is normally under parasympathetic tone, whereas blood pressure is normally under sympathetic tone. The heart rate is slowed by the autonomic system at rest, whereas blood vessels retain a slight constriction at rest.

In a few systems of the body, the competing input from the two divisions is not the norm. The sympathetic tone of blood vessels is caused by the lack of parasympathetic input to the systemic circulatory system. Only certain regions receive parasympathetic input that relaxes the smooth muscle wall of the blood vessels. Sweat glands are another example, which only receive input from the sympathetic system.

15.3 Central Control

The autonomic system integrates sensory information and higher cognitive processes to generate output, which balances homeostatic mechanisms. The central autonomic structure is the hypothalamus, which coordinates sympathetic and parasympathetic efferent pathways to regulate activities of the organ systems of the body. The majority of hypothalamic output travels through the medial forebrain bundle and the dorsal longitudinal fasciculus to influence brain stem and spinal components of the autonomic nervous system. The medial forebrain bundle also connects the hypothalamus with higher centers of the limbic system where emotion can influence visceral responses. The amygdala is a structure within the limbic system that influences the hypothalamus in the regulation of the autonomic system, as well as the endocrine system.

These higher centers have descending control of the autonomic system through brain stem centers, primarily in the medulla, such as the cardiovascular center. This collection of medullary nuclei regulates cardiac function, as well as blood pressure. Sensory input from the heart, aorta, and carotid sinuses project to these regions of the medulla. The solitary nucleus increases sympathetic tone of the cardiovascular system through the cardiac accelerator and vasomotor nerves. The nucleus ambiguus and the dorsal motor nucleus both contribute fibers to the vagus nerve, which exerts parasympathetic control of the heart by decreasing heart rate.

15.4 Drugs that Affect the Autonomic System

The autonomic system is affected by a number of exogenous agents, including some that are therapeutic and some that are illicit. These drugs affect the autonomic system by mimicking or interfering with the endogenous agents or their receptors. A survey of how different drugs affect autonomic function illustrates the role that the neurotransmitters and hormones play in autonomic function. Drugs can be thought of as chemical tools to effect changes in the system with some precision, based on where those drugs are effective.

Nicotine is not a drug that is used therapeutically, except for smoking cessation. When it is introduced into the body via products, it has broad effects on the autonomic system. Nicotine carries a risk for cardiovascular disease because of these broad effects. The drug stimulates both sympathetic and parasympathetic ganglia at the preganglionic fiber synapse. For most organ systems in the body, the competing input from the two postganglionic fibers will essentially cancel each other out. However, for the cardiovascular system, the results are different. Because there is essentially no parasympathetic influence on blood pressure for the entire body, the sympathetic input is increased by nicotine, causing an increase in blood pressure. Also, the influence that the autonomic system has on the heart is not the same as for other organs. Other organs have smooth muscle or glandular tissue that is activated or inhibited by the autonomic system. Cardiac muscle is intrinsically active and is modulated by the autonomic system. The contradictory signals do not just cancel each other out, they alter the regularity of the heart rate and can cause arrhythmias. Both hypertension and arrhythmias are risk factors for heart disease.

Other drugs affect one division of the autonomic system or the other. The sympathetic system is affected by drugs that mimic the actions of adrenergic molecules (norepinephrine and epinephrine) and are called sympathomimetic drugs. Drugs such as phenylephrine bind to the adrenergic receptors and stimulate target organs just as sympathetic activity would. Other drugs are sympatholytic because they block adrenergic activity and cancel the sympathetic influence on the target organ. Drugs that act on the parasympathetic system also work by either enhancing the postganglionic signal or blocking it. A muscarinic agonist (or parasympathomimetic drug) acts just like ACh released by the parasympathetic postganglionic fiber. Anticholinergic drugs block muscarinic receptors, suppressing parasympathetic interaction with the organ.

INTERACTIVE LINK QUESTIONS

1. Watch this video (http://openstaxcollege.org/l/fightflight) to learn more about adrenaline and the fight-or-flight response. When someone is said to have a rush of adrenaline, the image of bungee jumpers or skydivers usually comes to mind. But adrenaline, also known as epinephrine, is an important chemical in coordinating the body's fight-or-flight response. In this video, you look inside the physiology of the fight-or-flight response, as envisioned for a firefighter. His body's reaction is the result of the sympathetic division of the autonomic nervous system causing system-wide changes as it prepares for extreme responses. What two changes does adrenaline bring about to help the skeletal muscle response?

2. Watch this video (http://openstaxcollege.org/l/nervsystem1) to learn more about the nervous system. As described in this video, the nervous system has a way to deal with threats and stress that is separate from the conscious control of the somatic nervous system. The system comes from a time when threats were about survival, but in the modern age, these responses become part of stress and anxiety. This video describes how the autonomic system is only part of the response to threats, or stressors. What other organ system gets involved, and what part of the brain coordinates the two systems for the entire response, including epinephrine (adrenaline) and cortisol?

3. Read this article (http://openstaxcollege.org/l/strokespell) to learn about a teenager who experiences a series of spells that suggest a stroke. He undergoes endless tests and seeks input from multiple doctors. In the end, one expert, one question, and a simple blood pressure cuff answers the question. Why would the heart have to beat faster when the teenager changes his body position from lying down to sitting, and then to standing?

4. Watch this video (http://openstaxcollege.org/l/pupillary) to learn about the pupillary reflexes. The pupillary light reflex involves sensory input through the optic nerve and motor response through the oculomotor nerve to the ciliary ganglion, which projects to the circular fibers of the iris. As shown in this short animation, pupils will constrict to limit the amount of light falling on the retina under bright lighting conditions. What constitutes the afferent and efferent branches of the competing reflex (dilation)?

5. Watch this video (http://openstaxcollege.org/l/emotions) to learn about physical responses to emotion. The autonomic system, which is important for regulating the homeostasis of the organ systems, is also responsible for our physiological responses to emotions such as fear. The video summarizes the extent of the body's reactions and describes several effects of the autonomic system in response to fear. On the basis of what you have already studied about autonomic function, which effect would you expect to be associated with parasympathetic, rather than sympathetic, activity?

6. Watch this video (http://openstaxcollege.org/l/3Dmovies) to learn about the side effects of 3-D movies. As discussed in this video, movies that are shot in 3-D can cause motion sickness, which elicits the autonomic symptoms of nausea and sweating. The disconnection between the perceived motion on the screen and the lack of any change in equilibrium stimulates these symptoms. Why do you think sitting close to the screen or right in the middle of the theater makes motion sickness during a 3-D movie worse?

REVIEW QUESTIONS

7. Which of these physiological changes would *not* be considered part of the sympathetic fight-or-flight response?

   a. increased heart rate
   b. increased sweating
   c. dilated pupils
   d. increased stomach motility

8. Which type of fiber could be considered the longest?

   a. preganglionic parasympathetic
   b. preganglionic sympathetic
   c. postganglionic parasympathetic
   d. postganglionic sympathetic

9. Which signaling molecule is *most likely* responsible for an increase in digestive activity?
   a. epinephrine
   b. norepinephrine
   c. acetylcholine
   d. adrenaline

10. Which of these cranial nerves contains preganglionic parasympathetic fibers?
   a. optic, CN II
   b. facial, CN VII
   c. trigeminal, CN V
   d. hypoglossal, CN XII

11. Which of the following is *not* a target of a sympathetic preganglionic fiber?
   a. intermural ganglion
   b. collateral ganglion
   c. adrenal gland
   d. chain ganglion

12. Which of the following represents a sensory input that is *not* part of both the somatic and autonomic systems?

   a. vision
   b. taste
   c. baroreception
   d. proprioception

13. What is the term for a reflex that does *not* include a CNS component?
   a. long reflex
   b. visceral reflex
   c. somatic reflex
   d. short reflex

14. What neurotransmitter will result in constriction of the pupil?
   a. norepinephrine
   b. acetylcholine
   c. epinephrine
   d. serotonin

15. What gland produces a secretion that causes fight-or-flight responses in effectors?
   a. adrenal medulla
   b. salivatory gland
   c. reproductive gland
   d. thymus

16. Which of the following is an incorrect pairing?

   a. norepinephrine dilates the pupil
   b. epinephrine increases blood pressure
   c. acetylcholine decreases digestion
   d. norepinephrine increases heart rate

17. Which of these locations in the forebrain is the master control center for homeostasis through the autonomic and endocrine systems?
   a. hypothalamus
   b. thalamus
   c. amygdala

d. cerebral cortex

18. Which nerve projects to the hypothalamus to indicate the level of light stimuli in the retina?
  a. glossopharyngeal
  b. oculomotor
  c. optic
  d. vagus

19. What region of the limbic lobe is responsible for generating stress responses via the hypothalamus?
  a. hippocampus
  b. amygdala
  c. mammillary bodies
  d. prefrontal cortex

20. What is another name for the preganglionic sympathetic fibers that project to the heart?
  a. solitary tract
  b. vasomotor nerve
  c. vagus nerve
  d. cardiac accelerator nerve

21. What central fiber tract connects forebrain and brain stem structures with the hypothalamus?
  a. cardiac accelerator nerve
  b. medial forebrain bundle
  c. dorsal longitudinal fasciculus
  d. corticospinal tract

22. A drug that affects both divisions of the autonomic system is going to bind to, or block, which type of neurotransmitter receptor?
  a. nicotinic
  b. muscarinic
  c. α-adrenergic
  d. β-adrenergic

23. A drug is called an agonist if it _____.
  a. blocks a receptor
  b. interferes with neurotransmitter reuptake
  c. acts like the endogenous neurotransmitter by binding to its receptor
  d. blocks the voltage-gated calcium ion channel

24. Which type of drug would be an antidote to atropine poisoning?
  a. nicotinic agonist
  b. anticholinergic
  c. muscarinic agonist
  d. α-blocker

25. Which kind of drug would have anti-anxiety effects?
  a. nicotinic agonist
  b. anticholinergic
  c. muscarinic agonist
  d. α-blocker

26. Which type of drug could be used to treat asthma by opening airways wider?
  a. sympatholytic drug
  b. sympathomimetic drug
  c. anticholinergic drug
  d. parasympathomimetic drug

CRITICAL THINKING QUESTIONS

27. In the context of a lioness hunting on the savannah, why would the sympathetic system *not* activate the digestive system?

28. A target effector, such as the heart, receives input from the sympathetic and parasympathetic systems. What is the actual difference between the sympathetic and parasympathetic divisions at the level of those connections (i.e., at the synapse)?

29. Damage to internal organs will present as pain associated with a particular surface area of the body. Why would something like irritation to the diaphragm, which is between the thoracic and abdominal cavities, feel like pain in the shoulder or neck?

30. Medical practice is paying more attention to the autonomic system in considering disease states. Why would autonomic tone be important in considering cardiovascular disease?

31. Horner's syndrome is a condition that presents with changes in one eye, such as pupillary constriction and dropping of eyelids, as well as decreased sweating in the face. Why could a tumor in the thoracic cavity have an effect on these autonomic functions?

32. The cardiovascular center is responsible for regulating the heart and blood vessels through homeostatic mechanisms. What tone does each component of the cardiovascular system have? What connections does the cardiovascular center invoke to keep these two systems in their resting tone?

33. Why does smoking increase the risk of heart disease? Provide two reasons based on autonomic function.

34. Why might topical, cosmetic application of atropine or scopolamine from the belladonna plant not cause fatal poisoning, as would occur with ingestion of the plant?

16 | THE NEUROLOGICAL EXAM

Figure 16.1 Neurological Exam Health care professionals, such as this air force nurse, can rapidly assess the neurological functions of a patient using the neurological exam. One part of the exam is the inspection of the oral cavity and pharynx, which enables the doctor to not only inspect the tissues for signs of infection, but also provides a means to test the functions of the cranial nerves associated with the oral cavity. (credit: U.S. Department of Defense)

Introduction

Chapter Objectives

After studying this chapter, you will be able to:

- Describe the major sections of the neurological exam
- Outline the benefits of rapidly assessing neurological function
- Relate anatomical structures of the nervous system to specific functions
- Diagram the connections of the nervous system to the musculature and integument involved in primary sensorimotor responses
- Compare and contrast the somatic and visceral reflexes with respect to how they are assessed through the neurological exam

A man arrives at the hospital after feeling faint and complaining of a "pins-and-needles" feeling all along one side of his body. The most likely explanation is that he has suffered a stroke, which has caused a loss of oxygen to a particular part of the central nervous system (CNS). The problem is finding where in the entire nervous system the stroke has occurred. By checking reflexes, sensory responses, and motor control, a health care provider can focus on what abilities the patient may have lost as a result of the stroke and can use this information to determine where the injury occurred. In the emergency department of the hospital, this kind of rapid assessment of neurological function is key to treating trauma to the nervous system. In the classroom, the neurological exam is a valuable tool for learning the anatomy and physiology of the nervous system because it allows you to relate the functions of the system to particular locations in the nervous system.

As a student of anatomy and physiology, you may be planning to go into an allied health field, perhaps nursing or physical therapy. You could be in the emergency department treating a patient such as the one just described. An important part of this course is to understand the nervous system. This can be especially challenging because you need to learn about the nervous system using your own nervous system. The first chapter in this unit about the nervous system began with a quote: "If the human brain were simple enough for us to understand, we would be too simple to understand it." However, you are being asked to understand aspects of it. A healthcare provider can pinpoint problems with the nervous system in minutes by running through the series of tasks to test neurological function that are described in this chapter. You can use the same approach, though not as quickly, to learn about neurological function and its relationship to the structures of the nervous system.

Nervous tissue is different from other tissues in that it is not classified into separate tissue types. It does contain two types of cells, neurons and glia, but it is all just nervous tissue. White matter and gray matter are not types of nervous tissue, but indications of different specializations within the nervous tissue. However, not all nervous tissue performs the same function. Furthermore, specific functions are not wholly localized to individual brain structures in the way that other bodily functions occur strictly within specific organs. In the CNS, we must consider the connections between cells over broad areas, not just the function of cells in one particular nucleus or region. In a broad sense, the nervous system is responsible for the majority of electrochemical signaling in the body, but the use of those signals is different in various regions.

The nervous system is made up of the brain and spinal cord as the central organs, and the ganglia and nerves as organs in the periphery. The brain and spinal cord can be thought of as a collection of smaller organs, most of which would be the nuclei (such as the oculomotor nuclei), but white matter structures play an important role (such as the corpus callosum). Studying the nervous system requires an understanding of the varied physiology of the nervous system. For example, the hypothalamus plays a very different role than the visual cortex. The neurological exam provides a way to elicit behavior that represents those varied functions.

16.1 | Overview of the Neurological Exam

By the end of this section, you will be able to:
- List the major sections of the neurological exam
- Explain the connection between location and function in the nervous system
- Explain the benefit of a rapid assessment for neurological function in a clinical setting
- List the causes of neurological deficits
- Describe the different ischemic events in the nervous system

The **neurological exam** is a clinical assessment tool used to determine what specific parts of the CNS are affected by damage or disease. It can be performed in a short time—sometimes as quickly as 5 minutes—to establish neurological function. In the emergency department, this rapid assessment can make the difference with respect to proper treatment and the extent of recovery that is possible.

The exam is a series of subtests separated into five major sections. The first of these is the **mental status exam**, which assesses the higher cognitive functions such as memory, orientation, and language. Then there is the **cranial nerve exam**, which tests the function of the 12 cranial nerves and, therefore, the central and peripheral structures associated with them. The cranial nerve exam tests the sensory and motor functions of each of the nerves, as applicable. Two major sections, the **sensory exam** and the **motor exam**, test the sensory and motor functions associated with spinal nerves. Finally, the **coordination exam** tests the ability to perform complex and coordinated movements. The **gait exam**, which is often considered a sixth major exam, specifically assesses the motor function of walking and can be considered part of the coordination exam because walking is a coordinated movement.

Neuroanatomy and the Neurological Exam

Localization of function is the concept that circumscribed locations are responsible for specific functions. The neurological exam highlights this relationship. For example, the cognitive functions that are assessed in the mental status exam are based on functions in the cerebrum, mostly in the cerebral cortex. Several of the subtests examine language function. Deficits in neurological function uncovered by these examinations usually point to damage to the left cerebral cortex. In the majority of individuals, language function is localized to the left hemisphere between the superior temporal lobe and the posterior frontal lobe, including the intervening connections through the inferior parietal lobe.

The five major sections of the neurological exam are related to the major regions of the CNS (Figure 16.2). The mental status exam assesses functions related to the cerebrum. The cranial nerve exam is for the nerves that connect to the diencephalon and brain stem (as well as the olfactory connections to the forebrain). The coordination exam and the related gait exam primarily assess the functions of the cerebellum. The motor and sensory exams are associated with the spinal cord and its connections through the spinal nerves.

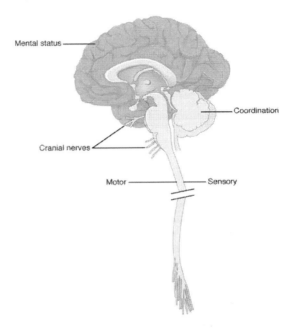

Figure 16.2 Anatomical Underpinnings of the Neurological Exam The different regions of the CNS relate to the major sections of the neurological exam: the mental status exam, cranial nerve exam, sensory exam, motor exam, and coordination exam (including the gait exam).

Part of the power of the neurological exam is this link between structure and function. Testing the various functions represented in the exam allows an accurate estimation of where the nervous system may be damaged. Consider the patient described in the chapter introduction. In the emergency department, he is given a quick exam to find where the deficit may be localized. Knowledge of where the damage occurred will lead to the most effective therapy.

In rapid succession, he is asked to smile, raise his eyebrows, stick out his tongue, and shrug his shoulders. The doctor tests muscular strength by providing resistance against his arms and legs while he tries to lift them. With his eyes closed, he has to indicate when he feels the tip of a pen touch his legs, arms, fingers, and face. He follows the tip of a pen as the doctor moves it through the visual field and finally toward his face. A formal mental status exam is not needed at this point; the patient will demonstrate any possible deficits in that area during normal interactions with the interviewer. If cognitive or language deficits are apparent, the interviewer can pursue mental status in more depth. All of this takes place in less than 5 minutes. The patient reports that he feels pins and needles in his left arm and leg, and has trouble feeling the tip of the pen when he is touched on those limbs. This suggests a problem with the sensory systems between the spinal cord and the brain. The emergency department has a lead to follow before a CT scan is performed. He is put on aspirin therapy to limit the possibility of blood clots forming, in case the cause is an **embolus**—an obstruction such as a blood clot that blocks the flow of blood in an artery or vein.

Watch this video (http://openstaxcollege.org/l/neuroexam) to see a demonstration of the neurological exam—a series of tests that can be performed rapidly when a patient is initially brought into an emergency department. The exam can be repeated on a regular basis to keep a record of how and if neurological function changes over time. In what order were the sections of the neurological exam tested in this video, and which section seemed to be left out?

Causes of Neurological Deficits

Damage to the nervous system can be limited to individual structures or can be distributed across broad areas of the brain and spinal cord. Localized, limited injury to the nervous system is most often the result of circulatory problems. Neurons are very sensitive to oxygen deprivation and will start to deteriorate within 1 or 2 minutes, and permanent damage (cell death) could result within a few hours. The loss of blood flow to part of the brain is known as a **stroke**, or a cerebrovascular accident (CVA).

There are two main types of stroke, depending on how the blood supply is compromised: ischemic and hemorrhagic. An **ischemic stroke** is the loss of blood flow to an area because vessels are blocked or narrowed. This is often caused by an embolus, which may be a blood clot or fat deposit. Ischemia may also be the result of thickening of the blood vessel wall, or a drop in blood volume in the brain known as **hypovolemia**.

A related type of CVA is known as a **transient ischemic attack (TIA)**, which is similar to a stroke although it does not last as long. The diagnostic definition of a stroke includes effects that last at least 24 hours. Any stroke symptoms that are resolved within a 24-hour period because of restoration of adequate blood flow are classified as a TIA.

A **hemorrhagic stroke** is bleeding into the brain because of a damaged blood vessel. Accumulated blood fills a region of the cranial vault and presses against the tissue in the brain (Figure 16.3). Physical pressure on the brain can cause the loss of function, as well as the squeezing of local arteries resulting in compromised blood flow beyond the site of the hemorrhage. As blood pools in the nervous tissue and the vasculature is damaged, the blood-brain barrier can break down and allow additional fluid to accumulate in the region, which is known as **edema**.

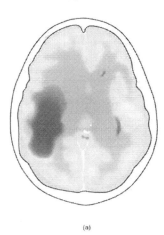 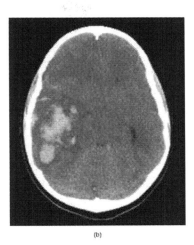

Figure 16.3 Hemorrhagic Stroke (a) A hemorrhage into the tissue of the cerebrum results in a large accumulation of blood with an additional edema in the adjacent tissue. The hemorrhagic area causes the entire brain to be disfigured as suggested here by the lateral ventricles being squeezed into the opposite hemisphere. (b) A CT scan shows an intraparenchymal hemorrhage within the parietal lobe. (credit b: James Heilman)

Whereas hemorrhagic stroke may involve bleeding into a large region of the CNS, such as into the deep white matter of a cerebral hemisphere, other events can cause widespread damage and loss of neurological functions. Infectious diseases can lead to loss of function throughout the CNS as components of nervous tissue, specifically astrocytes and microglia, react to the disease. Blunt force trauma, such as from a motor vehicle accident, can physically damage the CNS.

A class of disorders that affect the nervous system are the neurodegenerative diseases: Alzheimer's disease, Parkinson's disease, Huntington's disease, amyotrophic lateral sclerosis (ALS), Creutzfeld–Jacob disease, multiple sclerosis (MS), and other disorders that are the result of nervous tissue degeneration. In diseases like Alzheimer's, Parkinson's, or ALS, neurons die; in diseases like MS, myelin is affected. Some of these disorders affect motor function, and others present with dementia. How patients with these disorders perform in the neurological exam varies, but is often broad in its effects, such as memory deficits that compromise many aspects of the mental status exam, or movement deficits that compromise aspects of the cranial nerve exam, the motor exam, or the coordination exam. The causes of these disorders are also varied. Some are the result of genetics, such as Huntington's disease, or the result of autoimmunity, such as MS; others are not entirely understood, such as Alzheimer's and Parkinson's diseases. Current research suggests that many of these diseases are related in how the degeneration takes place and may be treated by common therapies.

Finally, a common cause of neurological changes is observed in developmental disorders. Whether the result of genetic factors or the environment during development, there are certain situations that result in neurological functions being different from the expected norms. Developmental disorders are difficult to define because they are caused by defects that existed in the past and disrupted the normal development of the CNS. These defects probably involve multiple environmental and genetic factors—most of the time, we don't know what the cause is other than that it is more complex than just one factor. Furthermore, each defect on its own may not be a problem, but when several are added together, they can disrupt growth processes that are not well understand in the first place. For instance, it is possible for a stroke to damage a specific region of the brain and lead to the loss of the ability to recognize faces (prosopagnosia). The link between cell death in the fusiform gyrus and the symptom is relatively easy to understand. In contrast, similar deficits can be seen in children with the developmental disorder, autism spectrum disorder (ASD). However, these children do not lack a fusiform gyrus, nor is there any damage or defect visible to this brain region. We conclude, rather poorly, that this brain region is not connected properly to other brain regions.

Infection, trauma, and congenital disorders can all lead to significant signs, as identified through the neurological exam. It is important to differentiate between an acute event, such as stroke, and a chronic or global condition such as blunt force trauma. Responses seen in the neurological exam can help. A loss of language function observed in all its aspects is more likely a global event as opposed to a discrete loss of one function, such as not being able to say certain types of words. A concern, however, is that a specific function—such as controlling the muscles of speech—may mask other language functions. The various subtests within the mental status exam can address these finer points and help clarify the underlying cause of the neurological loss.

Watch this video (http://openstaxcollege.org/l/neuroexam2) for an introduction to the neurological exam. Studying the neurological exam can give insight into how structure and function in the nervous system are interdependent. This is a tool both in the clinic and in the classroom, but for different reasons. In the clinic, this is a powerful but simple tool to assess a patient's neurological function. In the classroom, it is a different way to think about the nervous system. Though medical technology provides noninvasive imaging and real-time functional data, the presenter says these cannot replace the history at the core of the medical examination. What does history mean in the context of medical practice?

16.2 | The Mental Status Exam

By the end of this section, you will be able to:
- Describe the relationship of mental status exam results to cerebral functions
- Explain the categorization of regions of the cortex based on anatomy and physiology
- Differentiate between primary, association, and integration areas of the cerebral cortex
- Provide examples of localization of function related to the cerebral cortex

In the clinical setting, the set of subtests known as the mental status exam helps us understand the relationship of the brain to the body. Ultimately, this is accomplished by assessing behavior. Tremors related to intentional movements, incoordination, or the neglect of one side of the body can be indicative of failures of the connections of the cerebrum either within the hemispheres, or from the cerebrum to other portions of the nervous system. There is no strict test for what the cerebrum does alone, but rather in what it does through its control of the rest of the CNS, the peripheral nervous system (PNS), and the musculature.

Sometimes eliciting a behavior is as simple as asking a question. Asking a patient to state his or her name is not only to verify that the file folder in a health care provider's hands is the correct one, but also to be sure that the patient is aware, oriented, and capable of interacting with another person. If the answer to "What is your name?" is "Santa Claus," the person may have a problem understanding reality. If the person just stares at the examiner with a confused look on their face, the person may have a problem understanding or producing speech.

Functions of the Cerebral Cortex

The cerebrum is the seat of many of the higher mental functions, such as memory and learning, language, and conscious perception, which are the subjects of subtests of the mental status exam. The cerebral cortex is the thin layer of gray matter on the outside of the cerebrum. It is approximately a millimeter thick in most regions and highly folded to fit within the limited space of the cranial vault. These higher functions are distributed across various regions of the cortex, and specific locations can be said to be responsible for particular functions. There is a limited set of regions, for example, that are involved in language function, and they can be subdivided on the basis of the particular part of language function that each governs.

The basis for parceling out areas of the cortex and attributing them to various functions has its root in pure anatomical underpinnings. The German neurologist and histologist Korbinian Brodmann, who made a careful study of the **cytoarchitecture** of the cerebrum around the turn of the nineteenth century, described approximately 50 regions of the cortex that differed enough from each other to be considered separate areas (Figure 16.4). Brodmann made preparations of many different regions of the cerebral cortex to view with a microscope. He compared the size, shape, and number of neurons to find anatomical differences in the various parts of the cerebral cortex. Continued investigation into these anatomical areas over the subsequent 100 or more years has demonstrated a strong correlation between the structures and the functions attributed to those structures. For example, the first three areas in Brodmann's list—which are in the postcentral gyrus—compose the primary somatosensory cortex. Within this area, finer separation can be made on the basis of the concept of the sensory homunculus, as well as the different submodalities of somatosensation such as touch, vibration, pain, temperature, or proprioception. Today, we more frequently refer to these regions by their function (i.e., primary sensory cortex) than by the number Brodmann assigned to them, but in some situations the use of Brodmann numbers persists.

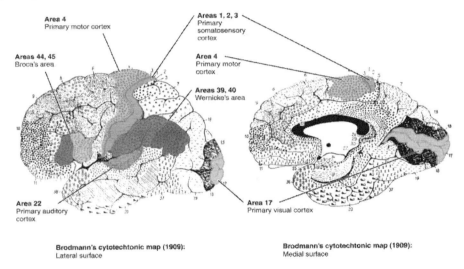

Figure 16.4 Brodmann's Areas of the Cerebral Cortex On the basis of cytoarchitecture, the anatomist Korbinian Brodmann described the extensive array of cortical regions, as illustrated in his figure. Subsequent investigations found that these areas corresponded very well to functional differences in the cerebral cortex. (credit: modification of work by "Looie496"/Wikimedia Commons, based on original work by Korvinian Brodmann)

Area 17, as Brodmann described it, is also known as the primary visual cortex. Adjacent to that are areas 18 and 19, which constitute subsequent regions of visual processing. Area 22 is the primary auditory cortex, and it is followed by area 23, which further processes auditory information. Area 4 is the primary motor cortex in the precentral gyrus, whereas area 6 is the premotor cortex. These areas suggest some specialization within the cortex for functional processing, both in sensory and motor regions. The fact that Brodmann's areas correlate so closely to functional localization in the cerebral cortex demonstrates the strong link between structure and function in these regions.

Areas 1, 2, 3, 4, 17, and 22 are each described as primary cortical areas. The adjoining regions are each referred to as association areas. Primary areas are where sensory information is initially received from the thalamus for conscious perception, or—in the case of the primary motor cortex—where descending commands are sent down to the brain stem or spinal cord to execute movements (Figure 16.5).

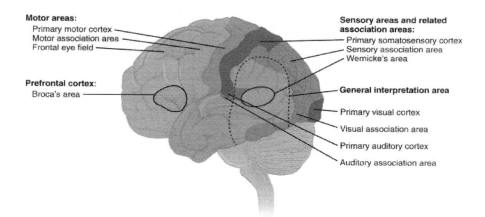

Figure 16.5 Types of Cortical Areas The cerebral cortex can be described as containing three types of processing regions: primary, association, and integration areas. The primary cortical areas are where sensory information is initially processed, or where motor commands emerge to go to the brain stem or spinal cord. Association areas are adjacent to primary areas and further process the modality-specific input. Multimodal integration areas are found where the modality-specific regions meet; they can process multiple modalities together or different modalities on the basis of similar functions, such as spatial processing in vision or somatosensation.

A number of other regions, which extend beyond these primary or association areas of the cortex, are referred to as integrative areas. These areas are found in the spaces between the domains for particular sensory or motor functions, and they integrate multisensory information, or process sensory or motor information in more complex ways. Consider, for example, the posterior parietal cortex that lies between the somatosensory cortex and visual cortex regions. This has been ascribed to the coordination of visual and motor functions, such as reaching to pick up a glass. The somatosensory function that would be part of this is the proprioceptive feedback from moving the arm and hand. The weight of the glass, based on what it contains, will influence how those movements are executed.

Cognitive Abilities

Assessment of cerebral functions is directed at cognitive abilities. The abilities assessed through the mental status exam can be separated into four groups: orientation and memory, language and speech, sensorium, and judgment and abstract reasoning.

Orientation and Memory

Orientation is the patient's awareness of his or her immediate circumstances. It is awareness of time, not in terms of the clock, but of the date and what is occurring around the patient. It is awareness of place, such that a patient should know where he or she is and why. It is also awareness of who the patient is—recognizing personal identity and being able to relate that to the examiner. The initial tests of orientation are based on the questions, "Do you know what the date is?" or "Do you know where you are?" or "What is your name?" Further understanding of a patient's awareness of orientation can come from questions that address remote memory, such as "Who is the President of the United States?", or asking what happened on a specific date.

There are also specific tasks to address memory. One is the three-word recall test. The patient is given three words to recall, such as book, clock, and shovel. After a short interval, during which other parts of the interview continue, the patient is asked to recall the three words. Other tasks that assess memory—aside from those related to orientation—have the patient recite the months of the year in reverse order to avoid the overlearned sequence and focus on the memory of the months in an order, or to spell common words backwards, or to recite a list of numbers back.

Memory is largely a function of the temporal lobe, along with structures beneath the cerebral cortex such as the hippocampus and the amygdala. The storage of memory requires these structures of the medial temporal lobe. A famous case of a man who had both medial temporal lobes removed to treat intractable epilepsy provided insight into the relationship between the structures of the brain and the function of memory.

Henry Molaison, who was referred to as patient HM when he was alive, had epilepsy localized to both of his medial temporal lobes. In 1953, a bilateral lobectomy was performed that alleviated the epilepsy but resulted in the inability for HM to form new memories—a condition called **anterograde amnesia**. HM was able to recall most events from before his surgery, although there was a partial loss of earlier memories, which is referred to as **retrograde amnesia**. HM became the subject of extensive studies into how memory works. What he was unable to do was form new memories of what happened to him, what are now called **episodic memory**. Episodic memory is autobiographical in nature, such as remembering riding a bicycle as a child around the neighborhood, as opposed to the **procedural memory** of how to ride a bike. HM also retained his **short-term memory**, such as what is tested by the three-word task described above. After a brief period, those memories would dissipate or decay and not be stored in the long-term because the medial temporal lobe structures were removed.

The difference in short-term, procedural, and episodic memory, as evidenced by patient HM, suggests that there are different parts of the brain responsible for those functions. The long-term storage of episodic memory requires the hippocampus and related medial temporal structures, and the location of those memories is in the multimodal integration areas of the cerebral cortex. However, short-term memory—also called working or active memory—is localized to the prefrontal lobe. Because patient HM had only lost his medial temporal lobe—and lost very little of his previous memories, and did not lose the ability to form new short-term memories—it was concluded that the function of the hippocampus, and adjacent structures in the medial temporal lobe, is to move (or consolidate) short-term memories (in the pre-frontal lobe) to long-term memory (in the temporal lobe).

The prefrontal cortex can also be tested for the ability to organize information. In one subtest of the mental status exam called set generation, the patient is asked to generate a list of words that all start with the same letter, but not to include proper nouns or names. The expectation is that a person can generate such a list of at least 10 words within 1 minute. Many people can likely do this much more quickly, but the standard separates the accepted normal from those with compromised prefrontal cortices.

Read this article (http://openstaxcollege.org/l/3word) to learn about a young man who texts his fiancée in a panic as he finds that he is having trouble remembering things. At the hospital, a neurologist administers the mental status exam, which is mostly normal except for the three-word recall test. The young man could not recall them even 30 seconds after hearing them and repeating them back to the doctor. An undiscovered mass in the mediastinum region was found to be Hodgkin's lymphoma, a type of cancer that affects the immune system and likely caused antibodies to attack the nervous system. The patient eventually regained his ability to remember, though the events in the hospital were always elusive. Considering that the effects on memory were temporary, but resulted in the loss of the specific events of the hospital stay, what regions of the brain were likely to have been affected by the antibodies and what type of memory does that represent?

Language and Speech

Language is, arguably, a very human aspect of neurological function. There are certainly strides being made in understanding communication in other species, but much of what makes the human experience seemingly unique is its basis in language. Any understanding of our species is necessarily reflective, as suggested by the question "What am I?" And the fundamental answer to this question is suggested by the famous quote by René Descartes: "Cogito Ergo Sum" (translated from Latin as "I think, therefore I am"). Formulating an understanding of yourself is largely describing who you are to yourself. It is a confusing topic to delve into, but language is certainly at the core of what it means to be self-aware.

The neurological exam has two specific subtests that address language. One measures the ability of the patient to understand language by asking them to follow a set of instructions to perform an action, such as "touch your right finger to your left elbow and then to your right knee." Another subtest assesses the fluency and coherency of language by having the patient generate descriptions of objects or scenes depicted in drawings, and by reciting sentences or explaining a written passage.

Language, however, is important in so many ways in the neurological exam. The patient needs to know what to do, whether it is as simple as explaining how the knee-jerk reflex is going to be performed, or asking a question such as "What is your name?" Often, language deficits can be determined without specific subtests; if a person cannot reply to a question properly, there may be a problem with the reception of language.

An important example of multimodal integrative areas is associated with language function (Figure 16.6). Adjacent to the auditory association cortex, at the end of the lateral sulcus just anterior to the visual cortex, is **Wernicke's area**. In the lateral aspect of the frontal lobe, just anterior to the region of the motor cortex associated with the head and neck, is Broca's area. Both regions were originally described on the basis of losses of speech and language, which is called **aphasia**. The aphasia associated with Broca's area is known as an **expressive aphasia**, which means that speech production is compromised. This type of aphasia is often described as non-fluency because the ability to say some words leads to broken or halting speech. Grammar can also appear to be lost. The aphasia associated with Wernicke's area is known as a **receptive aphasia**, which is not a loss of speech production, but a loss of understanding of content. Patients, after recovering from acute forms of this aphasia, report not being able to understand what is said to them or what they are saying themselves, but they often cannot keep from talking.

The two regions are connected by white matter tracts that run between the posterior temporal lobe and the lateral aspect of the frontal lobe. **Conduction aphasia** associated with damage to this connection refers to the problem of connecting the understanding of language to the production of speech. This is a very rare condition, but is likely to present as an inability to faithfully repeat spoken language.

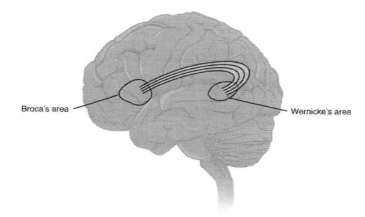

Figure 16.6 Broca's and Wernicke's Areas Two important integration areas of the cerebral cortex associated with language function are Broca's and Wernicke's areas. The two areas are connected through the deep white matter running from the posterior temporal lobe to the frontal lobe.

Sensorium

Those parts of the brain involved in the reception and interpretation of sensory stimuli are referred to collectively as the sensorium. The cerebral cortex has several regions that are necessary for sensory perception. From the primary cortical areas of the somatosensory, visual, auditory, and gustatory senses to the association areas that process information in these modalities, the cerebral cortex is the seat of conscious sensory perception. In contrast, sensory information can also be processed by deeper brain regions, which we may vaguely describe as subconscious—for instance, we are not constantly aware of the proprioceptive information that the cerebellum uses to maintain balance. Several of the subtests can reveal activity associated with these sensory modalities, such as being able to hear a question or see a picture. Two subtests assess specific functions of these cortical areas.

The first is **praxis**, a practical exercise in which the patient performs a task completely on the basis of verbal description without any demonstration from the examiner. For example, the patient can be told to take their left hand and place it palm down on their left thigh, then flip it over so the palm is facing up, and then repeat this four times. The examiner describes the activity without any movements on their part to suggest how the movements are to be performed. The patient needs to understand the instructions, transform them into movements, and use sensory feedback, both visual and proprioceptive, to perform the movements correctly.

The second subtest for sensory perception is **gnosis**, which involves two tasks. The first task, known as **stereognosis**, involves the naming of objects strictly on the basis of the somatosensory information that comes from manipulating them. The patient keeps their eyes closed and is given a common object, such as a coin, that they have to identify. The patient should be able to indicate the particular type of coin, such as a dime versus a penny, or a nickel versus a quarter, on the basis of the sensory cues involved. For example, the size, thickness, or weight of the coin may be an indication, or to differentiate the pairs of coins suggested here, the smooth or corrugated edge of the coin will correspond to the particular denomination. The second task, **graphesthesia**, is to recognize numbers or letters written on the palm of the hand with a dull pointer, such as a pen cap.

Praxis and gnosis are related to the conscious perception and cortical processing of sensory information. Being able to transform verbal commands into a sequence of motor responses, or to manipulate and recognize a common object and associate it with a name for that object. Both subtests have language components because language function is integral to these functions. The relationship between the words that describe actions, or the nouns that represent objects, and the cerebral location of these concepts is suggested to be localized to particular cortical areas. Certain aphasias can be characterized by a deficit of verbs or nouns, known as V impairment or N impairment, or may be classified as V–N dissociation. Patients have difficulty using one type of word over the other. To describe what is happening in a photograph as part of the expressive language subtest, a patient will use active- or image-based language. The lack of one or the other of these components of language can relate to the ability to use verbs or nouns. Damage to the region at which the frontal and temporal lobes meet, including the region known as the insula, is associated with V impairment; damage to the middle and inferior temporal lobe is associated with N impairment.

Judgment and Abstract Reasoning

Planning and producing responses requires an ability to make sense of the world around us. Making judgments and reasoning in the abstract are necessary to produce movements as part of larger responses. For example, when your alarm goes off, do you hit the snooze button or jump out of bed? Is 10 extra minutes in bed worth the extra rush to get ready for your day? Will hitting the snooze button multiple times lead to feeling more rested or result in a panic as you run late? How you mentally process these questions can affect your whole day.

The prefrontal cortex is responsible for the functions responsible for planning and making decisions. In the mental status exam, the subtest that assesses judgment and reasoning is directed at three aspects of frontal lobe function. First, the examiner asks questions about problem solving, such as "If you see a house on fire, what would you do?" The patient is also asked to interpret common proverbs, such as "Don't look a gift horse in the mouth." Additionally, pairs of words are compared for similarities, such as apple and orange, or lamp and cabinet.

The prefrontal cortex is composed of the regions of the frontal lobe that are not directly related to specific motor functions. The most posterior region of the frontal lobe, the precentral gyrus, is the primary motor cortex. Anterior to that are the premotor cortex, Broca's area, and the frontal eye fields, which are all related to planning certain types of movements. Anterior to what could be described as motor association areas are the regions of the prefrontal cortex. They are the regions in which judgment, abstract reasoning, and working memory are localized. The antecedents to planning certain movements are judging whether those movements should be made, as in the example of deciding whether to hit the snooze button.

To an extent, the prefrontal cortex may be related to personality. The neurological exam does not necessarily assess personality, but it can be within the realm of neurology or psychiatry. A clinical situation that suggests this link between the prefrontal cortex and personality comes from the story of Phineas Gage, the railroad worker from the mid-1800s who had a metal spike impale his prefrontal cortex. There are suggestions that the steel rod led to changes in his personality. A man who was a quiet, dependable railroad worker became a raucous, irritable drunkard. Later anecdotal evidence from his life suggests that he was able to support himself, although he had to relocate and take on a different career as a stagecoach driver.

A psychiatric practice to deal with various disorders was the prefrontal lobotomy. This procedure was common in the 1940s and early 1950s, until antipsychotic drugs became available. The connections between the prefrontal cortex and other regions of the brain were severed. The disorders associated with this procedure included some aspects of what are now referred to as personality disorders, but also included mood disorders and psychoses. Depictions of lobotomies in popular media suggest a link between cutting the white matter of the prefrontal cortex and changes in a patient's mood and personality, though this correlation is not well understood.

Left Brain, Right Brain

Popular media often refer to right-brained and left-brained people, as if the brain were two independent halves that work differently for different people. This is a popular misinterpretation of an important neurological phenomenon. As an extreme measure to deal with a debilitating condition, the corpus callosum may be sectioned to overcome intractable epilepsy. When the connections between the two cerebral hemispheres are cut, interesting effects can be observed.

If a person with an intact corpus callosum is asked to put their hands in their pockets and describe what is there on the basis of what their hands feel, they might say that they have keys in their right pocket and loose change in the left. They may even be able to count the coins in their pocket and say if they can afford to buy a candy bar from the vending machine. If a person with a sectioned corpus callosum is given the same instructions, they will do something quite peculiar. They will only put their right hand in their pocket and say they have keys there. They will not even move their left hand, much less report that there is loose change in the left pocket.

The reason for this is that the language functions of the cerebral cortex are localized to the left hemisphere in 95 percent of the population. Additionally, the left hemisphere is connected to the right side of the body through the corticospinal tract and the ascending tracts of the spinal cord. Motor commands from the precentral gyrus control the opposite side of the body, whereas sensory information processed by the postcentral gyrus is received from the opposite side of the body. For a verbal command to initiate movement of the right arm and hand, the left side of the brain needs to be connected by the corpus callosum. Language is processed in the left side of the brain and directly influences the left brain and right arm motor functions, but is sent to influence the right brain and left arm motor functions through the corpus callosum. Likewise, the left-handed sensory perception of what is in the left pocket travels across the corpus callosum from the right brain, so no verbal report on those contents would be possible if the hand happened to be in the pocket.

Watch the video (http://openstaxcollege.org/l/2brains) titled "The Man With Two Brains" to see the neuroscientist Michael Gazzaniga introduce a patient he has worked with for years who has had his corpus callosum cut, separating his two cerebral hemispheres. A few tests are run to demonstrate how this manifests in tests of cerebral function. Unlike normal people, this patient can perform two independent tasks at the same time because the lines of communication between the right and left sides of his brain have been removed. Whereas a person with an intact corpus callosum cannot overcome the dominance of one hemisphere over the other, this patient can. If the left cerebral hemisphere is dominant in the majority of people, why would right-handedness be most common?

The Mental Status Exam

The cerebrum, particularly the cerebral cortex, is the location of important cognitive functions that are the focus of the mental status exam. The regionalization of the cortex, initially described on the basis of anatomical evidence of cytoarchitecture, reveals the distribution of functionally distinct areas. Cortical regions can be described as primary sensory or motor areas, association areas, or multimodal integration areas. The functions attributed to these regions include attention, memory, language, speech, sensation, judgment, and abstract reasoning.

The mental status exam addresses these cognitive abilities through a series of subtests designed to elicit particular behaviors ascribed to these functions. The loss of neurological function can illustrate the location of damage to the cerebrum. Memory functions are attributed to the temporal lobe, particularly the medial temporal lobe structures known as the hippocampus and amygdala, along with the adjacent cortex. Evidence of the importance of these structures comes from the side effects of a bilateral temporal lobectomy that were studied in detail in patient HM.

Losses of language and speech functions, known as aphasias, are associated with damage to the important integration areas in the left hemisphere known as Broca's or Wernicke's areas, as well as the connections in the white matter between them. Different types of aphasia are named for the particular structures that are damaged. Assessment of the functions of the sensorium includes praxis and gnosis. The subtests related to these functions depend on multimodal integration, as well as language-dependent processing.

The prefrontal cortex contains structures important for planning, judgment, reasoning, and working memory. Damage to these areas can result in changes to personality, mood, and behavior. The famous case of Phineas Gage suggests a role for this cortex in personality, as does the outdated practice of prefrontal lobectomy.

16.3 | The Cranial Nerve Exam

By the end of this section, you will be able to:
- Describe the functional grouping of cranial nerves
- Match the regions of the forebrain and brain stem that are connected to each cranial nerve
- Suggest diagnoses that would explain certain losses of function in the cranial nerves
- Relate cranial nerve deficits to damage of adjacent, unrelated structures

The twelve cranial nerves are typically covered in introductory anatomy courses, and memorizing their names is facilitated by numerous mnemonics developed by students over the years of this practice. But knowing the names of the nerves in order often leaves much to be desired in understanding what the nerves do. The nerves can be categorized by functions, and subtests of the cranial nerve exam can clarify these functional groupings.

Three of the nerves are strictly responsible for special senses whereas four others contain fibers for special and general senses. Three nerves are connected to the extraocular muscles resulting in the control of gaze. Four nerves connect to muscles of the face, oral cavity, and pharynx, controlling facial expressions, mastication, swallowing, and speech. Four nerves make up the cranial component of the parasympathetic nervous system responsible for pupillary constriction, salivation, and the regulation of the organs of the thoracic and upper abdominal cavities. Finally, one nerve controls the muscles of the neck, assisting with spinal control of the movement of the head and neck.

The cranial nerve exam allows directed tests of forebrain and brain stem structures. The twelve cranial nerves serve the head and neck. The vagus nerve (cranial nerve X) has autonomic functions in the thoracic and superior abdominal cavities. The special senses are served through the cranial nerves, as well as the general senses of the head and neck. The movement of the eyes, face, tongue, throat, and neck are all under the control of cranial nerves. Preganglionic parasympathetic nerve fibers that control pupillary size, salivary glands, and the thoracic and upper abdominal viscera are found in four of the nerves. Tests of these functions can provide insight into damage to specific regions of the brain stem and may uncover deficits in adjacent regions.

Sensory Nerves

The olfactory, optic, and vestibulocochlear nerves (cranial nerves I, II, and VIII) are dedicated to four of the special senses: smell, vision, equilibrium, and hearing, respectively. Taste sensation is relayed to the brain stem through fibers of the facial and glossopharyngeal nerves. The trigeminal nerve is a mixed nerve that carries the general somatic senses from the head, similar to those coming through spinal nerves from the rest of the body.

Testing smell is straightforward, as common smells are presented to one nostril at a time. The patient should be able to recognize the smell of coffee or mint, indicating the proper functioning of the olfactory system. Loss of the sense of smell is called anosmia and can be lost following blunt trauma to the head or through aging. The short axons of the first cranial nerve regenerate on a regular basis. The neurons in the olfactory epithelium have a limited life span, and new cells grow to replace the ones that die off. The axons from these neurons grow back into the CNS by following the existing axons—representing one of the few examples of such growth in the mature nervous system. If all of the fibers are sheared when the brain moves within the cranium, such as in a motor vehicle accident, then no axons can find their way back to the olfactory bulb to re-establish connections. If the nerve is not completely severed, the anosmia may be temporary as new neurons can eventually reconnect.

Olfaction is not the pre-eminent sense, but its loss can be quite detrimental. The enjoyment of food is largely based on our sense of smell. Anosmia means that food will not seem to have the same taste, though the gustatory sense is intact, and food will often be described as being bland. However, the taste of food can be improved by adding ingredients (e.g., salt) that stimulate the gustatory sense.

Testing vision relies on the tests that are common in an optometry office. The **Snellen chart** (Figure 16.7) demonstrates visual acuity by presenting standard Roman letters in a variety of sizes. The result of this test is a rough generalization of the acuity of a person based on the normal accepted acuity, such that a letter that subtends a visual angle of 5 minutes of an arc at 20 feet can be seen. To have 20/60 vision, for example, means that the smallest letters that a person can see at a 20-foot distance could be seen by a person with normal acuity from 60 feet away. Testing the extent of the visual field means that the examiner can establish the boundaries of peripheral vision as simply as holding their hands out to either side and asking the patient when the fingers are no longer visible without moving the eyes to track them. If it is necessary, further tests can establish the perceptions in the visual fields. Physical inspection of the optic disk, or where the optic nerve emerges from the eye, can be accomplished by looking through the pupil with an ophthalmoscope.

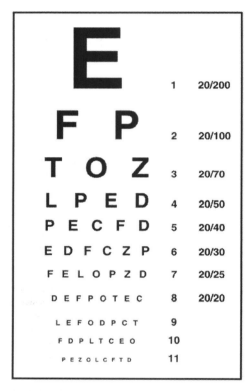

Figure 16.7 The Snellen Chart The Snellen chart for visual acuity presents a limited number of Roman letters in lines of decreasing size. The line with letters that subtend 5 minutes of an arc from 20 feet represents the smallest letters that a person with normal acuity should be able to read at that distance. The different sizes of letters in the other lines represent rough approximations of what a person of normal acuity can read at different distances. For example, the line that represents 20/200 vision would have larger letters so that they are legible to the person with normal acuity at 200 feet.

The optic nerves from both sides enter the cranium through the respective optic canals and meet at the optic chiasm at which fibers sort such that the two halves of the visual field are processed by the opposite sides of the brain. Deficits in visual field perception often suggest damage along the length of the optic pathway between the orbit and the diencephalon. For example, loss of peripheral vision may be the result of a pituitary tumor pressing on the optic chiasm (Figure 16.8). The pituitary, seated in the sella turcica of the sphenoid bone, is directly inferior to the optic chiasm. The axons that decussate in the chiasm are from the medial retinae of either eye, and therefore carry information from the peripheral visual field.

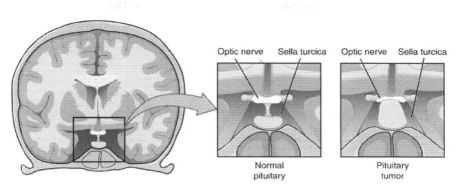

Figure 16.8 Pituitary Tumor The pituitary gland is located in the sella turcica of the sphenoid bone within the cranial floor, placing it immediately inferior to the optic chiasm. If the pituitary gland develops a tumor, it can press against the fibers crossing in the chiasm. Those fibers are conveying peripheral visual information to the opposite side of the brain, so the patient will experience "tunnel vision"—meaning that only the central visual field will be perceived.

The vestibulocochlear nerve (CN VIII) carries both equilibrium and auditory sensations from the inner ear to the medulla. Though the two senses are not directly related, anatomy is mirrored in the two systems. Problems with balance, such as vertigo, and deficits in hearing may both point to problems with the inner ear. Within the petrous region of the temporal bone is the bony labyrinth of the inner ear. The vestibule is the portion for equilibrium, composed of the utricle, saccule, and the three semicircular canals. The cochlea is responsible for transducing sound waves into a neural signal. The sensory nerves from these two structures travel side-by-side as the vestibulocochlear nerve, though they are really separate divisions. They both emerge from the inner ear, pass through the internal auditory meatus, and synapse in nuclei of the superior medulla. Though they are part of distinct sensory systems, the vestibular nuclei and the cochlear nuclei are close neighbors with adjacent inputs. Deficits in one or both systems could occur from damage that encompasses structures close to both. Damage to structures near the two nuclei can result in deficits to one or both systems.

Balance or hearing deficits may be the result of damage to the middle or inner ear structures. Ménière's disease is a disorder that can affect both equilibrium and audition in a variety of ways. The patient can suffer from vertigo, a low-frequency ringing in the ears, or a loss of hearing. From patient to patient, the exact presentation of the disease can be different. Additionally, within a single patient, the symptoms and signs may change as the disease progresses. Use of the neurological exam subtests for the vestibulocochlear nerve illuminates the changes a patient may go through. The disease appears to be the result of accumulation, or over-production, of fluid in the inner ear, in either the vestibule or cochlea.

Tests of equilibrium are important for coordination and gait and are related to other aspects of the neurological exam. The vestibulo-ocular reflex involves the cranial nerves for gaze control. Balance and equilibrium, as tested by the Romberg test, are part of spinal and cerebellar processes and involved in those components of the neurological exam, as discussed later.

Hearing is tested by using a tuning fork in a couple of different ways. The **Rinne test** involves using a tuning fork to distinguish between **conductive hearing** and **sensorineural hearing**. Conductive hearing relies on vibrations being conducted through the ossicles of the middle ear. Sensorineural hearing is the transmission of sound stimuli through the neural components of the inner ear and cranial nerve. A vibrating tuning fork is placed on the mastoid process and the patient indicates when the sound produced from this is no longer present. Then the fork is immediately moved to just next to the ear canal so the sound travels through the air. If the sound is not heard through the ear, meaning the sound is conducted better through the temporal bone than through the ossicles, a conductive hearing deficit is present. The **Weber test** also uses a tuning fork to differentiate between conductive versus sensorineural hearing loss. In this test, the tuning fork is placed at the top of the skull, and the sound of the tuning fork reaches both inner ears by travelling through bone. In a healthy patient, the sound would appear equally loud in both ears. With unilateral conductive hearing loss, however, the tuning fork sounds louder in the ear with hearing loss. This is because the sound of the tuning fork has to compete with background noise coming from the outer ear, but in conductive hearing loss, the background noise is blocked in the damaged ear, allowing the tuning fork to sound relatively louder in that ear. With unilateral sensorineural hearing loss, however, damage to the cochlea or associated nervous tissue means that the tuning fork sounds quieter in that ear.

The trigeminal system of the head and neck is the equivalent of the ascending spinal cord systems of the dorsal column and the spinothalamic pathways. Somatosensation of the face is conveyed along the nerve to enter the brain stem at the level of the pons. Synapses of those axons, however, are distributed across nuclei found throughout the brain stem. The mesencephalic nucleus processes proprioceptive information of the face, which is the movement and position of facial muscles. It is the sensory component of the **jaw-jerk reflex**, a stretch reflex of the masseter muscle. The chief nucleus, located in the pons, receives information about light touch as well as proprioceptive information about the mandible, which are both relayed to the thalamus and, ultimately, to the postcentral gyrus of the parietal lobe. The spinal trigeminal nucleus, located in the medulla, receives information about crude touch, pain, and temperature to be relayed to the thalamus and cortex. Essentially, the projection through the chief nucleus is analogous to the dorsal column pathway for the body, and the projection through the spinal trigeminal nucleus is analogous to the spinothalamic pathway.

Subtests for the sensory component of the trigeminal system are the same as those for the sensory exam targeting the spinal nerves. The primary sensory subtest for the trigeminal system is sensory discrimination. A cotton-tipped applicator, which is cotton attached to the end of a thin wooden stick, can be used easily for this. The wood of the applicator can be snapped so that a pointed end is opposite the soft cotton-tipped end. The cotton end provides a touch stimulus, while the pointed end provides a painful, or sharp, stimulus. While the patient's eyes are closed, the examiner touches the two ends of the applicator to the patient's face, alternating randomly between them. The patient must identify whether the stimulus is sharp or dull. These stimuli are processed by the trigeminal system separately. Contact with the cotton tip of the applicator is a light touch, relayed by the chief nucleus, but contact with the pointed end of the applicator is a painful stimulus relayed by the spinal trigeminal nucleus. Failure to discriminate these stimuli can localize problems within the brain stem. If a patient cannot recognize a painful stimulus, that might indicate damage to the spinal trigeminal nucleus in the medulla. The medulla also contains important regions that regulate the cardiovascular, respiratory, and digestive systems, as well as being the pathway for ascending and descending tracts between the brain and spinal cord. Damage, such as a stroke, that results in changes in sensory discrimination may indicate these unrelated regions are affected as well.

Gaze Control

The three nerves that control the extraocular muscles are the oculomotor, trochlear, and abducens nerves, which are the third, fourth, and sixth cranial nerves. As the name suggests, the abducens nerve is responsible for abducting the eye, which it controls through contraction of the lateral rectus muscle. The trochlear nerve controls the superior oblique muscle to rotate the eye along its axis in the orbit medially, which is called **intorsion**, and is a component of focusing the eyes on an object close to the face. The oculomotor nerve controls all the other extraocular muscles, as well as a muscle of the upper eyelid. Movements of the two eyes need to be coordinated to locate and track visual stimuli accurately. When moving the eyes to locate an object in the horizontal plane, or to track movement horizontally in the visual field, the lateral rectus muscle of one eye and medial rectus muscle of the other eye are both active. The lateral rectus is controlled by neurons of the abducens nucleus in the superior medulla, whereas the medial rectus is controlled by neurons in the oculomotor nucleus of the midbrain.

Coordinated movement of both eyes through different nuclei requires integrated processing through the brain stem. In the midbrain, the superior colliculus integrates visual stimuli with motor responses to initiate eye movements. The **paramedian pontine reticular formation (PPRF)** will initiate a rapid eye movement, or **saccade**, to bring the eyes to bear on a visual stimulus quickly. These areas are connected to the oculomotor, trochlear, and abducens nuclei by the **medial longitudinal fasciculus (MLF)** that runs through the majority of the brain stem. The MLF allows for **conjugate gaze**, or the movement of the eyes in the same direction, during horizontal movements that require the lateral and medial rectus muscles. Control of conjugate gaze strictly in the vertical direction is contained within the oculomotor complex. To elevate the eyes, the oculomotor nerve on either side stimulates the contraction of both superior rectus muscles; to depress the eyes, the oculomotor nerve on either side stimulates the contraction of both inferior rectus muscles.

Purely vertical movements of the eyes are not very common. Movements are often at an angle, so some horizontal components are necessary, adding the medial and lateral rectus muscles to the movement. The rapid movement of the eyes used to locate and direct the fovea onto visual stimuli is called a saccade. Notice that the paths that are traced in Figure 16.9 are not strictly vertical. The movements between the nose and the mouth are closest, but still have a slant to them. Also, the superior and inferior rectus muscles are not perfectly oriented with the line of sight. The origin for both muscles is medial to their insertions, so elevation and depression may require the lateral rectus muscles to compensate for the slight adduction inherent in the contraction of those muscles, requiring MLF activity as well.

Figure 16.9 Saccadic Eye Movements Saccades are rapid, conjugate movements of the eyes to survey a complicated visual stimulus, or to follow a moving visual stimulus. This image represents the shifts in gaze typical of a person studying a face. Notice the concentration of gaze on the major features of the face and the large number of paths traced between the eyes or around the mouth.

Testing eye movement is simply a matter of having the patient track the tip of a pen as it is passed through the visual field. This may appear similar to testing visual field deficits related to the optic nerve, but the difference is that the patient is asked to not move the eyes while the examiner moves a stimulus into the peripheral visual field. Here, the extent of movement is the point of the test. The examiner is watching for conjugate movements representing proper function of the related nuclei and the MLF. Failure of one eye to abduct while the other adducts in a horizontal movement is referred to as **internuclear ophthalmoplegia**. When this occurs, the patient will experience **diplopia**, or double vision, as the two eyes are temporarily pointed at different stimuli. Diplopia is not restricted to failure of the lateral rectus, because any of the extraocular muscles may fail to move one eye in perfect conjugation with the other.

The final aspect of testing eye movements is to move the tip of the pen in toward the patient's face. As visual stimuli move closer to the face, the two medial recti muscles cause the eyes to move in the one nonconjugate movement that is part of gaze control. When the two eyes move to look at something closer to the face, they both adduct, which is referred to as **convergence**. To keep the stimulus in focus, the eye also needs to change the shape of the lens, which is controlled through the parasympathetic fibers of the oculomotor nerve. The change in focal power of the eye is referred to as **accommodation**. Accommodation ability changes with age; focusing on nearer objects, such as the written text of a book or on a computer screen, may require corrective lenses later in life. Coordination of the skeletal muscles for convergence and coordination of the smooth muscles of the ciliary body for accommodation are referred to as the **accommodation–convergence reflex**.

A crucial function of the cranial nerves is to keep visual stimuli centered on the fovea of the retina. The **vestibulo-ocular reflex (VOR)** coordinates all of the components (Figure 16.10), both sensory and motor, that make this possible. If the head rotates in one direction—for example, to the right—the horizontal pair of semicircular canals in the inner ear indicate the movement by increased activity on the right and decreased activity on the left. The information is sent to the abducens nuclei and oculomotor nuclei on either side to coordinate the lateral and medial rectus muscles. The left lateral rectus and right medial rectus muscles will contract, rotating the eyes in the opposite direction of the head, while nuclei controlling the right lateral rectus and left medial rectus muscles will be inhibited to reduce antagonism of the contracting muscles.

These actions stabilize the visual field by compensating for the head rotation with opposite rotation of the eyes in the orbits. Deficits in the VOR may be related to vestibular damage, such as in Ménière's disease, or from dorsal brain stem damage that would affect the eye movement nuclei or their connections through the MLF.

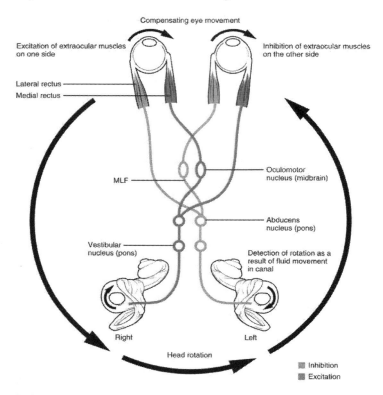

Figure 16.10 Vestibulo-ocular Reflex If the head is turned in one direction, the coordination of that movement with the fixation of the eyes on a visual stimulus involves a circuit that ties the vestibular sense with the eye movement nuclei through the MLF.

Nerves of the Face and Oral Cavity

An iconic part of a doctor's visit is the inspection of the oral cavity and pharynx, suggested by the directive to "open your mouth and say 'ah.'" This is followed by inspection, with the aid of a tongue depressor, of the back of the mouth, or the opening of the oral cavity into the pharynx known as the **fauces**. Whereas this portion of a medical exam inspects for signs of infection, such as in tonsillitis, it is also the means to test the functions of the cranial nerves that are associated with the oral cavity.

The facial and glossopharyngeal nerves convey gustatory stimulation to the brain. Testing this is as simple as introducing salty, sour, bitter, or sweet stimuli to either side of the tongue. The patient should respond to the taste stimulus before retracting the tongue into the mouth. Stimuli applied to specific locations on the tongue will dissolve into the saliva and may stimulate taste buds connected to either the left or right of the nerves, masking any lateral deficits. Along with taste, the glossopharyngeal nerve relays general sensations from the pharyngeal walls. These sensations, along with certain taste stimuli, can stimulate the gag reflex. If the examiner moves the tongue depressor to contact the lateral wall of the fauces, this should elicit the gag reflex. Stimulation of either side of the fauces should elicit an equivalent response. The motor response, through contraction of the muscles of the pharynx, is mediated through the vagus nerve. Normally, the vagus nerve is considered autonomic in nature. The vagus nerve directly stimulates the contraction of skeletal muscles in the pharynx and larynx to contribute to the swallowing and speech functions. Further testing of vagus motor function has the patient repeating consonant sounds that require movement of the muscles around the fauces. The patient is asked to say "lah-kah-pah" or a similar set of alternating sounds while the examiner observes the movements of the soft palate and arches between the palate and tongue.

The facial and glossopharyngeal nerves are also responsible for the initiation of salivation. Neurons in the salivary nuclei of the medulla project through these two nerves as preganglionic fibers, and synapse in ganglia located in the head. The parasympathetic fibers of the facial nerve synapse in the pterygopalatine ganglion, which projects to the submandibular gland and sublingual gland. The parasympathetic fibers of the glossopharyngeal nerve synapse in the otic ganglion, which projects to the parotid gland. Salivation in response to food in the oral cavity is based on a visceral reflex arc within the facial or glossopharyngeal nerves. Other stimuli that stimulate salivation are coordinated through the hypothalamus, such as the smell and sight of food.

The hypoglossal nerve is the motor nerve that controls the muscles of the tongue, except for the palatoglossus muscle, which is controlled by the vagus nerve. There are two sets of muscles of the tongue. The **extrinsic muscles of the tongue** are connected to other structures, whereas the **intrinsic muscles of the tongue** are completely contained within the lingual tissues. While examining the oral cavity, movement of the tongue will indicate whether hypoglossal function is impaired. The test for hypoglossal function is the "stick out your tongue" part of the exam. The genioglossus muscle is responsible for protrusion of the tongue. If the hypoglossal nerves on both sides are working properly, then the tongue will stick straight out. If the nerve on one side has a deficit, the tongue will stick out to that side—pointing to the side with damage. Loss of function of the tongue can interfere with speech and swallowing. Additionally, because the location of the hypoglossal nerve and nucleus is near the cardiovascular center, inspiratory and expiratory areas for respiration, and the vagus nuclei that regulate digestive functions, a tongue that protrudes incorrectly can suggest damage in adjacent structures that have nothing to do with controlling the tongue.

Watch this short video (http://openstaxcollege.org/l/facialnerve) to see an examination of the facial nerve using some simple tests. The facial nerve controls the muscles of facial expression. Severe deficits will be obvious in watching someone use those muscles for normal control. One side of the face might not move like the other side. But directed tests, especially for contraction against resistance, require a formal testing of the muscles. The muscles of the upper and lower face need to be tested. The strength test in this video involves the patient squeezing her eyes shut and the examiner trying to pry her eyes open. Why does the examiner ask her to try a second time?

Motor Nerves of the Neck

The accessory nerve, also referred to as the spinal accessory nerve, innervates the sternocleidomastoid and trapezius muscles (Figure 16.11). When both the sternocleidomastoids contract, the head flexes forward; individually, they cause rotation to the opposite side. The trapezius can act as an antagonist, causing extension and hyperextension of the neck. These two superficial muscles are important for changing the position of the head. Both muscles also receive input from cervical spinal nerves. Along with the spinal accessory nerve, these nerves contribute to elevating the scapula and clavicle through the trapezius, which is tested by asking the patient to shrug both shoulders, and watching for asymmetry. For the sternocleidomastoid, those spinal nerves are primarily sensory projections, whereas the trapezius also has lateral insertions to the clavicle and scapula, and receives motor input from the spinal cord. Calling the nerve the spinal accessory nerve suggests that it is aiding the spinal nerves. Though that is not precisely how the name originated, it does help make the association between the function of this nerve in controlling these muscles and the role these muscles play in movements of the trunk or shoulders.

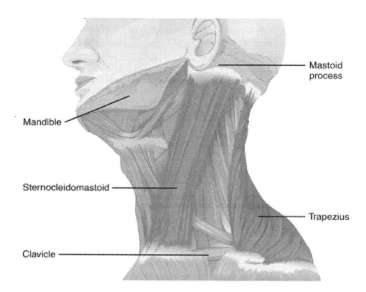

Figure 16.11 Muscles Controlled by the Accessory Nerve The accessory nerve innervates the sternocleidomastoid and trapezius muscles, both of which attach to the head and to the trunk and shoulders. They can act as antagonists in head flexion and extension, and as synergists in lateral flexion toward the shoulder.

To test these muscles, the patient is asked to flex and extend the neck or shrug the shoulders against resistance, testing the strength of the muscles. Lateral flexion of the neck toward the shoulder tests both at the same time. Any difference on one side versus the other would suggest damage on the weaker side. These strength tests are common for the skeletal muscles controlled by spinal nerves and are a significant component of the motor exam. Deficits associated with the accessory nerve may have an effect on orienting the head, as described with the VOR.

The Pupillary Light Response

The autonomic control of pupillary size in response to a bright light involves the sensory input of the optic nerve and the parasympathetic motor output of the oculomotor nerve. When light hits the retina, specialized photosensitive ganglion cells send a signal along the optic nerve to the pretectal nucleus in the superior midbrain. A neuron from this nucleus projects to the Eddinger–Westphal nuclei in the oculomotor complex in both sides of the midbrain. Neurons in this nucleus give rise to the preganglionic parasympathetic fibers that project through the oculomotor nerve to the ciliary ganglion in the posterior orbit. The postganglionic parasympathetic fibers from the ganglion project to the iris, where they release acetylcholine onto circular fibers that constrict the pupil to reduce the amount of light hitting the retina. The sympathetic nervous system is responsible for dilating the pupil when light levels are low.

Shining light in one eye will elicit constriction of both pupils. The efferent limb of the pupillary light reflex is bilateral. Light shined in one eye causes a constriction of that pupil, as well as constriction of the contralateral pupil. Shining a penlight in the eye of a patient is a very artificial situation, as both eyes are normally exposed to the same light sources. Testing this reflex can illustrate whether the optic nerve or the oculomotor nerve is damaged. If shining the light in one eye results in no changes in pupillary size but shining light in the opposite eye elicits a normal, bilateral response, the damage is associated with the optic nerve on the nonresponsive side. If light in either eye elicits a response in only one eye, the problem is with the oculomotor system.

If light in the right eye only causes the left pupil to constrict, the direct reflex is lost and the consensual reflex is intact, which means that the right oculomotor nerve (or Eddinger–Westphal nucleus) is damaged. Damage to the right oculomotor connections will be evident when light is shined in the left eye. In that case, the direct reflex is intact but the consensual reflex is lost, meaning that the left pupil will constrict while the right does not.

The Cranial Nerve Exam

The cranial nerves can be separated into four major groups associated with the subtests of the cranial nerve exam. First are the sensory nerves, then the nerves that control eye movement, the nerves of the oral cavity and superior pharynx, and the nerve that controls movements of the neck.

The olfactory, optic, and vestibulocochlear nerves are strictly sensory nerves for smell, sight, and balance and hearing, whereas the trigeminal, facial, and glossopharyngeal nerves carry somatosensation of the face, and taste—separated between the anterior two-thirds of the tongue and the posterior one-third. Special senses are tested by presenting the particular stimuli to each receptive organ. General senses can be tested through sensory discrimination of touch versus painful stimuli.

The oculomotor, trochlear, and abducens nerves control the extraocular muscles and are connected by the medial longitudinal fasciculus to coordinate gaze. Testing conjugate gaze is as simple as having the patient follow a visual target, like a pen tip, through the visual field ending with an approach toward the face to test convergence and accommodation. Along with the vestibular functions of the eighth nerve, the vestibulo-ocular reflex stabilizes gaze during head movements by coordinating equilibrium sensations with the eye movement systems.

The trigeminal nerve controls the muscles of chewing, which are tested for stretch reflexes. Motor functions of the facial nerve are usually obvious if facial expressions are compromised, but can be tested by having the patient raise their eyebrows, smile, and frown. Movements of the tongue, soft palate, or superior pharynx can be observed directly while the patient swallows, while the gag reflex is elicited, or while the patient says repetitive consonant sounds. The motor control of the gag reflex is largely controlled by fibers in the vagus nerve and constitutes a test of that nerve because the parasympathetic functions of that nerve are involved in visceral regulation, such as regulating the heartbeat and digestion.

Movement of the head and neck using the sternocleidomastoid and trapezius muscles is controlled by the accessory nerve. Flexing of the neck and strength testing of those muscles reviews the function of that nerve.

16.4 | The Sensory and Motor Exams

By the end of this section, you will be able to:
- Describe the arrangement of sensory and motor regions in the spinal cord
- Relate damage in the spinal cord to sensory or motor deficits
- Differentiate between upper motor neuron and lower motor neuron diseases
- Describe the clinical indications of common reflexes

Connections between the body and the CNS occur through the spinal cord. The cranial nerves connect the head and neck directly to the brain, but the spinal cord receives sensory input and sends motor commands out to the body through the spinal nerves. Whereas the brain develops into a complex series of nuclei and fiber tracts, the spinal cord remains relatively simple in its configuration (Figure 16.12). From the initial neural tube early in embryonic development, the spinal cord retains a tube-like structure with gray matter surrounding the small central canal and white matter on the surface in three columns. The dorsal, or posterior, horns of the gray matter are mainly devoted to sensory functions whereas the ventral, or anterior, and lateral horns are associated with motor functions. In the white matter, the dorsal column relays sensory information to the brain, and the anterior column is almost exclusively relaying motor commands to the ventral horn motor neurons. The lateral column, however, conveys both sensory and motor information between the spinal cord and brain.

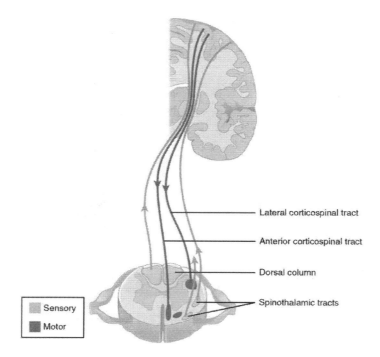

Figure 16.12 Locations of Spinal Fiber Tracts

Sensory Modalities and Location

The general senses are distributed throughout the body, relying on nervous tissue incorporated into various organs. Somatic senses are incorporated mostly into the skin, muscles, or tendons, whereas the visceral senses come from nervous tissue incorporated into the majority of organs such as the heart or stomach. The somatic senses are those that usually make up the conscious perception of the how the body interacts with the environment. The visceral senses are most often below the limit of conscious perception because they are involved in homeostatic regulation through the autonomic nervous system.

The sensory exam tests the somatic senses, meaning those that are consciously perceived. Testing of the senses begins with examining the regions known as dermatomes that connect to the cortical region where somatosensation is perceived in the postcentral gyrus. To test the sensory fields, a simple stimulus of the light touch of the soft end of a cotton-tipped applicator is applied at various locations on the skin. The spinal nerves, which contain sensory fibers with dendritic endings in the skin, connect with the skin in a topographically organized manner, illustrated as dermatomes (Figure 16.13). For example, the fibers of eighth cervical nerve innervate the medial surface of the forearm and extend out to the fingers. In addition to testing perception at different positions on the skin, it is necessary to test sensory perception within the dermatome from distal to proximal locations in the appendages, or lateral to medial locations in the trunk. In testing the eighth cervical nerve, the patient would be asked if the touch of the cotton to the fingers or the medial forearm was perceptible, and whether there were any differences in the sensations.

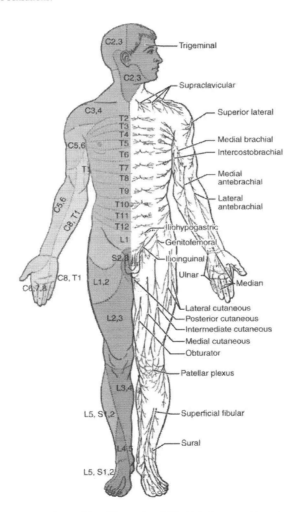

Figure 16.13 Dermatomes The surface of the skin can be divided into topographic regions that relate to the location of sensory endings in the skin based on the spinal nerve that contains those fibers. (credit: modification of work by Mikael Häggström)

Other modalities of somatosensation can be tested using a few simple tools. The perception of pain can be tested using the broken end of the cotton-tipped applicator. The perception of vibratory stimuli can be testing using an oscillating tuning fork placed against prominent bone features such as the distal head of the ulna on the medial aspect of the elbow. When the tuning fork is still, the metal against the skin can be perceived as a cold stimulus. Using the cotton tip of the applicator, or even just a fingertip, the perception of tactile movement can be assessed as the stimulus is drawn across the skin for approximately 2–3 cm. The patient would be asked in what direction the stimulus is moving. All of these tests are repeated in distal and proximal locations and for different dermatomes to assess the spatial specificity of perception. The sense of position and motion, proprioception, is tested by moving the fingers or toes and asking the patient if they sense the movement. If the distal locations are not perceived, the test is repeated at increasingly proximal joints.

The various stimuli used to test sensory input assess the function of the major ascending tracts of the spinal cord. The dorsal column pathway conveys fine touch, vibration, and proprioceptive information, whereas the spinothalamic pathway primarily conveys pain and temperature. Testing these stimuli provides information about whether these two major ascending pathways are functioning properly. Within the spinal cord, the two systems are segregated. The dorsal column information ascends ipsilateral to the source of the stimulus and decussates in the medulla, whereas the spinothalamic pathway decussates at the level of entry and ascends contralaterally. The differing sensory stimuli are segregated in the spinal cord so that the various subtests for these stimuli can distinguish which ascending pathway may be damaged in certain situations.

Whereas the basic sensory stimuli are assessed in the subtests directed at each submodality of somatosensation, testing the ability to discriminate sensations is important. Pairing the light touch and pain subtests together makes it possible to compare the two submodalities at the same time, and therefore the two major ascending tracts at the same time. Mistaking painful stimuli for light touch, or vice versa, may point to errors in ascending projections, such as in a **hemisection** of the spinal cord that might come from a motor vehicle accident.

Another issue of sensory discrimination is not distinguishing between different submodalities, but rather location. The two-point discrimination subtest highlights the density of sensory endings, and therefore receptive fields in the skin. The sensitivity to fine touch, which can give indications of the texture and detailed shape of objects, is highest in the fingertips. To assess the limit of this sensitivity, two-point discrimination is measured by simultaneously touching the skin in two locations, such as could be accomplished with a pair of forceps. Specialized calipers for precisely measuring the distance between points are also available. The patient is asked to indicate whether one or two stimuli are present while keeping their eyes closed. The examiner will switch between using the two points and a single point as the stimulus. Failure to recognize two points may be an indication of a dorsal column pathway deficit.

Similar to two-point discrimination, but assessing laterality of perception, is double simultaneous stimulation. Two stimuli, such as the cotton tips of two applicators, are touched to the same position on both sides of the body. If one side is not perceived, this may indicate damage to the contralateral posterior parietal lobe. Because there is one of each pathway on either side of the spinal cord, they are not likely to interact. If none of the other subtests suggest particular deficits with the pathways, the deficit is likely to be in the cortex where conscious perception is based. The mental status exam contains subtests that assess other functions that are primarily localized to the parietal cortex, such as stereognosis and graphesthesia.

A final subtest of sensory perception that concentrates on the sense of proprioception is known as the **Romberg test**. The patient is asked to stand straight with feet together. Once the patient has achieved their balance in that position, they are asked to close their eyes. Without visual feedback that the body is in a vertical orientation relative to the surrounding environment, the patient must rely on the proprioceptive stimuli of joint and muscle position, as well as information from the inner ear, to maintain balance. This test can indicate deficits in dorsal column pathway proprioception, as well as problems with proprioceptive projections to the cerebellum through the **spinocerebellar tract**.

Interactive LINK

Watch this video (http://openstaxcollege.org/l/2point) to see a quick demonstration of two-point discrimination. Touching a specialized caliper to the surface of the skin will measure the distance between two points that are perceived as distinct stimuli versus a single stimulus. The patient keeps their eyes closed while the examiner switches between using both points of the caliper or just one. The patient then must indicate whether one or two stimuli are in contact with the skin. Why is the distance between the caliper points closer on the fingertips as opposed to the palm of the hand? And what do you think the distance would be on the arm, or the shoulder?

Muscle Strength and Voluntary Movement

The skeletomotor system is largely based on the simple, two-cell projection from the precentral gyrus of the frontal lobe to the skeletal muscles. The corticospinal tract represents the neurons that send output from the primary motor cortex. These fibers travel through the deep white matter of the cerebrum, then through the midbrain and pons, into the medulla where most of them decussate, and finally through the spinal cord white matter in the lateral (crossed fibers) or anterior (uncrossed fibers) columns. These fibers synapse on motor neurons in the ventral horn. The ventral horn motor neurons then project to skeletal muscle and cause contraction. These two cells are termed the upper motor neuron (UMN) and the lower motor neuron (LMN). Voluntary movements require these two cells to be active.

The motor exam tests the function of these neurons and the muscles they control. First, the muscles are inspected and palpated for signs of structural irregularities. Movement disorders may be the result of changes to the muscle tissue, such as scarring, and these possibilities need to be ruled out before testing function. Along with this inspection, muscle tone is assessed by moving the muscles through a passive range of motion. The arm is moved at the elbow and wrist, and the leg is moved at the knee and ankle. Skeletal muscle should have a resting tension representing a slight contraction of the fibers. The lack of muscle tone, known as **hypotonicity** or **flaccidity**, may indicate that the LMN is not conducting action potentials that will keep a basal level of acetylcholine in the neuromuscular junction.

If muscle tone is present, muscle strength is tested by having the patient contract muscles against resistance. The examiner will ask the patient to lift the arm, for example, while the examiner is pushing down on it. This is done for both limbs, including shrugging the shoulders. Lateral differences in strength—being able to push against resistance with the right arm but not the left—would indicate a deficit in one corticospinal tract versus the other. An overall loss of strength, without laterality, could indicate a global problem with the motor system. Diseases that result in UMN lesions include cerebral palsy or MS, or it may be the result of a stroke. A sign of UMN lesion is a negative result in the subtest for **pronator drift**. The patient is asked to extend both arms in front of the body with the palms facing up. While keeping the eyes closed, if the patient unconsciously allows one or the other arm to slowly relax, toward the pronated position, this could indicate a failure of the motor system to maintain the supinated position.

Reflexes

Reflexes combine the spinal sensory and motor components with a sensory input that directly generates a motor response. The reflexes that are tested in the neurological exam are classified into two groups. A **deep tendon reflex** is commonly known as a stretch reflex, and is elicited by a strong tap to a tendon, such as in the knee-jerk reflex. A **superficial reflex** is elicited through gentle stimulation of the skin and causes contraction of the associated muscles.

For the arm, the common reflexes to test are of the biceps, brachioradialis, triceps, and flexors for the digits. For the leg, the knee-jerk reflex of the quadriceps is common, as is the ankle reflex for the gastrocnemius and soleus. The tendon at the insertion for each of these muscles is struck with a rubber mallet. The muscle is quickly stretched, resulting in activation of the muscle spindle that sends a signal into the spinal cord through the dorsal root. The fiber synapses directly on the ventral horn motor neuron that activates the muscle, causing contraction. The reflexes are physiologically useful for stability. If a muscle is stretched, it reflexively contracts to return the muscle to compensate for the change in length. In the context of the neurological exam, reflexes indicate that the LMN is functioning properly.

The most common superficial reflex in the neurological exam is the **plantar reflex** that tests for the **Babinski sign** on the basis of the extension or flexion of the toes at the plantar surface of the foot. The plantar reflex is commonly tested in newborn infants to establish the presence of neuromuscular function. To elicit this reflex, an examiner brushes a stimulus, usually the examiner's fingertip, along the plantar surface of the infant's foot. An infant would present a positive Babinski sign, meaning the foot dorsiflexes and the toes extend and splay out. As a person learns to walk, the plantar reflex changes to cause curling of the toes and a moderate plantar flexion. If superficial stimulation of the sole of the foot caused extension of the foot, keeping one's balance would be harder. The descending input of the corticospinal tract modifies the response of the plantar reflex, meaning that a negative Babinski sign is the expected response in testing the reflex. Other superficial reflexes are not commonly tested, though a series of abdominal reflexes can target function in the lower thoracic spinal segments.

Watch this video (http://openstaxcollege.org/l/reflextest) to see how to test reflexes in the abdomen. Testing reflexes of the trunk is not commonly performed in the neurological exam, but if findings suggest a problem with the thoracic segments of the spinal cord, a series of superficial reflexes of the abdomen can localize function to those segments. If contraction is not observed when the skin lateral to the umbilicus (belly button) is stimulated, what level of the spinal cord may be damaged?

Comparison of Upper and Lower Motor Neuron Damage

Many of the tests of motor function can indicate differences that will address whether damage to the motor system is in the upper or lower motor neurons. Signs that suggest a UMN lesion include muscle weakness, strong deep tendon reflexes, decreased control of movement or slowness, pronator drift, a positive Babinski sign, **spasticity**, and the **clasp-knife response**. Spasticity is an excess contraction in resistance to stretch. It can result in **hyperflexia**, which is when joints are overly flexed. The clasp-knife response occurs when the patient initially resists movement, but then releases, and the joint will quickly flex like a pocket knife closing.

A lesion on the LMN would result in paralysis, or at least partial loss of voluntary muscle control, which is known as **paresis**. The paralysis observed in LMN diseases is referred to as **flaccid paralysis**, referring to a complete or partial loss of muscle tone, in contrast to the loss of control in UMN lesions in which tone is retained and spasticity is exhibited. Other signs of an LMN lesion are **fibrillation**, **fasciculation**, and compromised or lost reflexes resulting from the denervation of the muscle fibers.

Disorders OF THE...

Spinal Cord

In certain situations, such as a motorcycle accident, only half of the spinal cord may be damaged in what is known as a hemisection. Forceful trauma to the trunk may cause ribs or vertebrae to fracture, and debris can crush or section through part of the spinal cord. The full section of a spinal cord would result in paraplegia, or loss of voluntary motor control of the lower body, as well as loss of sensations from that point down. A hemisection, however, will leave spinal cord tracts intact on one side. The resulting condition would be hemiplegia on the side of the trauma—one leg would be paralyzed. The sensory results are more complicated.

The ascending tracts in the spinal cord are segregated between the dorsal column and spinothalamic pathways. This means that the sensory deficits will be based on the particular sensory information each pathway conveys. Sensory discrimination between touch and painful stimuli will illustrate the difference in how these pathways divide these functions.

On the paralyzed leg, a patient will acknowledge painful stimuli, but not fine touch or proprioceptive sensations. On the functional leg, the opposite is true. The reason for this is that the dorsal column pathway ascends ipsilateral to the sensation, so it would be damaged the same way as the lateral corticospinal tract. The spinothalamic pathway decussates immediately upon entering the spinal cord and ascends contralateral to the source; it would therefore bypass the hemisection.

The motor system can indicate the loss of input to the ventral horn in the lumbar enlargement where motor neurons to the leg are found, but motor function in the trunk is less clear. The left and right anterior corticospinal tracts are directly adjacent to each other. The likelihood of trauma to the spinal cord resulting in a hemisection that affects one anterior column, but not the other, is very unlikely. Either the axial musculature will not be affected at all, or there will be bilateral losses in the trunk.

Sensory discrimination can pinpoint the level of damage in the spinal cord. Below the hemisection, pain stimuli will be perceived in the damaged side, but not fine touch. The opposite is true on the other side. The pain fibers on the side with motor function cross the midline in the spinal cord and ascend in the contralateral lateral column as far as the hemisection. The dorsal column will be intact ipsilateral to the source on the intact side and reach the brain for conscious perception. The trauma would be at the level just before sensory discrimination returns to normal, helping to pinpoint the trauma. Whereas imaging technology, like magnetic resonance imaging (MRI) or computed tomography (CT) scanning, could localize the injury as well, nothing more complicated than a cotton-tipped applicator can localize the damage. That may be all that is available on the scene when moving the victim requires crucial decisions be made.

16.5 | The Coordination and Gait Exams

By the end of this section, you will be able to:
- Explain the relationship between the location of the cerebellum and its function in movement
- Chart the major divisions of the cerebellum
- List the major connections of the cerebellum
- Describe the relationship of the cerebellum to axial and appendicular musculature
- Explain the prevalent causes of cerebellar ataxia

The role of the cerebellum is a subject of debate. There is an obvious connection to motor function based on the clinical implications of cerebellar damage. There is also strong evidence of the cerebellar role in procedural memory. The two are not incompatible; in fact, procedural memory is motor memory, such as learning to ride a bicycle. Significant work has been performed to describe the connections within the cerebellum that result in learning. A model for this learning is classical conditioning, as shown by the famous dogs from the physiologist Ivan Pavlov's work. This classical conditioning, which can be related to motor learning, fits with the neural connections of the cerebellum. The cerebellum is 10 percent of the mass of the brain and has varied functions that all point to a role in the motor system.

Location and Connections of the Cerebellum

The cerebellum is located in apposition to the dorsal surface of the brain stem, centered on the pons. The name of the pons is derived from its connection to the cerebellum. The word means "bridge" and refers to the thick bundle of myelinated axons that form a bulge on its ventral surface. Those fibers are axons that project from the gray matter of the pons into the contralateral cerebellar cortex. These fibers make up the **middle cerebellar peduncle (MCP)** and are the major physical connection of the cerebellum to the brain stem (Figure 16.14). Two other white matter bundles connect the cerebellum to the other regions of the brain stem. The **superior cerebellar peduncle (SCP)** is the connection of the cerebellum to the midbrain and forebrain. The **inferior cerebellar peduncle (ICP)** is the connection to the medulla.

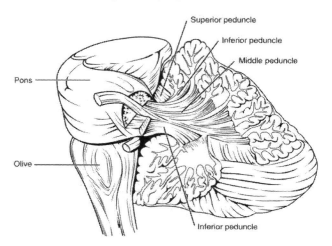

Figure 16.14 Cerebellar Peduncles The connections to the cerebellum are the three cerebellar peduncles, which are close to each other. The ICP arises from the medulla—specifically from the inferior olive, which is visible as a bulge on the ventral surface of the brain stem. The MCP is the ventral surface of the pons. The SCP projects into the midbrain.

These connections can also be broadly described by their functions. The ICP conveys sensory input to the cerebellum, partially from the spinocerebellar tract, but also through fibers of the **inferior olive**. The MCP is part of the **cortico-ponto-cerebellar pathway** that connects the cerebral cortex with the cerebellum and preferentially targets the lateral regions of the cerebellum. It includes a copy of the motor commands sent from the precentral gyrus through the corticospinal tract, arising from collateral branches that synapse in the gray matter of the pons, along with input from other regions such as the visual cortex. The SCP is the major output of the cerebellum, divided between the **red nucleus** in the midbrain and the thalamus, which will return cerebellar processing to the motor cortex. These connections describe a circuit that compares motor commands and sensory feedback to generate a new output. These comparisons make it possible to coordinate movements. If the cerebral cortex sends a motor command to initiate walking, that command is copied by the pons and sent into the cerebellum through the MCP. Sensory feedback in the form of proprioception from the spinal cord, as well as vestibular sensations from the inner ear, enters through the ICP. If you take a step and begin to slip on the floor because it is wet, the output from the cerebellum—through the SCP—can correct for that and keep you balanced and moving. The red nucleus sends new motor commands to the spinal cord through the **rubrospinal tract**.

The cerebellum is divided into regions that are based on the particular functions and connections involved. The midline regions of the cerebellum, the **vermis** and **flocculonodular lobe**, are involved in comparing visual information, equilibrium, and proprioceptive feedback to maintain balance and coordinate movements such as walking, or **gait**, through the descending output of the red nucleus (Figure 16.15). The lateral hemispheres are primarily concerned with planning motor functions through frontal lobe inputs that are returned through the thalamic projections back to the premotor and motor cortices. Processing in the midline regions targets movements of the axial musculature, whereas the lateral regions target movements of the appendicular musculature. The vermis is referred to as the **spinocerebellum** because it primarily receives input from the dorsal columns and spinocerebellar pathways. The flocculonodular lobe is referred to as the **vestibulocerebellum** because of the vestibular projection into that region. Finally, the lateral cerebellum is referred to as the **cerebrocerebellum**, reflecting the significant input from the cerebral cortex through the cortico-ponto-cerebellar pathway.

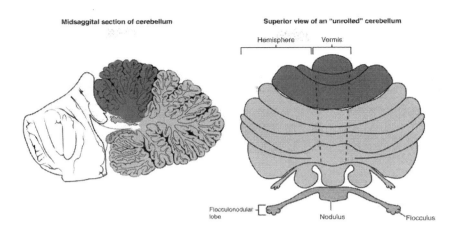

Figure 16.15 Major Regions of the Cerebellum The cerebellum can be divided into two basic regions: the midline and the hemispheres. The midline is composed of the vermis and the flocculonodular lobe, and the hemispheres are the lateral regions.

Coordination and Alternating Movement

Testing for cerebellar function is the basis of the coordination exam. The subtests target appendicular musculature, controlling the limbs, and axial musculature for posture and gait. The assessment of cerebellar function will depend on the normal functioning of other systems addressed in previous sections of the neurological exam. Motor control from the cerebrum, as well as sensory input from somatic, visual, and vestibular senses, are important to cerebellar function.

The subtests that address appendicular musculature, and therefore the lateral regions of the cerebellum, begin with a check for tremor. The patient extends their arms in front of them and holds the position. The examiner watches for the presence of tremors that would not be present if the muscles are relaxed. By pushing down on the arms in this position, the examiner can check for the rebound response, which is when the arms are automatically brought back to the extended position. The extension of the arms is an ongoing motor process, and the tap or push on the arms presents a change in the proprioceptive feedback. The cerebellum compares the cerebral motor command with the proprioceptive feedback and adjusts the descending input to correct. The red nucleus would send an additional signal to the LMN for the arm to increase contraction momentarily to overcome the change and regain the original position.

The **check reflex** depends on cerebellar input to keep increased contraction from continuing after the removal of resistance. The patient flexes the elbow against resistance from the examiner to extend the elbow. When the examiner releases the arm, the patient should be able to stop the increased contraction and keep the arm from moving. A similar response would be seen if you try to pick up a coffee mug that you believe to be full but turns out to be empty. Without checking the contraction, the mug would be thrown from the overexertion of the muscles expecting to lift a heavier object.

Several subtests of the cerebellum assess the ability to alternate movements, or switch between muscle groups that may be antagonistic to each other. In the finger-to-nose test, the patient touches their finger to the examiner's finger and then to their nose, and then back to the examiner's finger, and back to the nose. The examiner moves the target finger to assess a range of movements. A similar test for the lower extremities has the patient touch their toe to a moving target, such as the examiner's finger. Both of these tests involve flexion and extension around a joint—the elbow or the knee and the shoulder or hip—as well as movements of the wrist and ankle. The patient must switch between the opposing muscles, like the biceps and triceps brachii, to move their finger from the target to their nose. Coordinating these movements involves the motor cortex communicating with the cerebellum through the pons and feedback through the thalamus to plan the movements. Visual cortex information is also part of the processing that occurs in the cerebrocerebellum while it is involved in guiding movements of the finger or toe.

Rapid, alternating movements are tested for the upper and lower extremities. The patient is asked to touch each finger to their thumb, or to pat the palm of one hand on the back of the other, and then flip that hand over and alternate back-and-forth. To test similar function in the lower extremities, the patient touches their heel to their shin near the knee and slides it down toward the ankle, and then back again, repetitively. Rapid, alternating movements are part of speech as well. A patient is asked to repeat the nonsense consonants "lah-kah-pah" to alternate movements of the tongue, lips, and palate. All of these rapid alternations require planning from the cerebrocerebellum to coordinate movement commands that control the coordination.

Posture and Gait

Gait can either be considered a separate part of the neurological exam or a subtest of the coordination exam that addresses walking and balance. Testing posture and gait addresses functions of the spinocerebellum and the vestibulocerebellum because both are part of these activities. A subtest called station begins with the patient standing in a normal position to check for the placement of the feet and balance. The patient is asked to hop on one foot to assess the ability to maintain balance and posture during movement. Though the station subtest appears to be similar to the Romberg test, the difference is that the patient's eyes are open during station. The Romberg test has the patient stand still with the eyes closed. Any changes in posture would be the result of proprioceptive deficits, and the patient is able to recover when they open their eyes.

Subtests of walking begin with having the patient walk normally for a distance away from the examiner, and then turn and return to the starting position. The examiner watches for abnormal placement of the feet and the movement of the arms relative to the movement. The patient is then asked to walk with a few different variations. Tandem gait is when the patient places the heel of one foot against the toe of the other foot and walks in a straight line in that manner. Walking only on the heels or only on the toes will test additional aspects of balance.

Ataxia

A movement disorder of the cerebellum is referred to as **ataxia**. It presents as a loss of coordination in voluntary movements. Ataxia can also refer to sensory deficits that cause balance problems, primarily in proprioception and equilibrium. When the problem is observed in movement, it is ascribed to cerebellar damage. Sensory and vestibular ataxia would likely also present with problems in gait and station.

Ataxia is often the result of exposure to exogenous substances, focal lesions, or a genetic disorder. Focal lesions include strokes affecting the cerebellar arteries, tumors that may impinge on the cerebellum, trauma to the back of the head and neck, or MS. Alcohol intoxication or drugs such as ketamine cause ataxia, but it is often reversible. Mercury in fish can cause ataxia as well. Hereditary conditions can lead to degeneration of the cerebellum or spinal cord, as well as malformation of the brain, or the abnormal accumulation of copper seen in Wilson's disease.

Watch this short video (http://openstaxcollege.org/l/stationtest) to see a test for station. Station refers to the position a person adopts when they are standing still. The examiner would look for issues with balance, which coordinates proprioceptive, vestibular, and visual information in the cerebellum. To test the ability of a subject to maintain balance, asking them to stand or hop on one foot can be more demanding. The examiner may also push the subject to see if they can maintain balance. An abnormal finding in the test of station is if the feet are placed far apart. Why would a wide stance suggest problems with cerebellar function?

Everyday CONNECTION

The Field Sobriety Test

The neurological exam has been described as a clinical tool throughout this chapter. It is also useful in other ways. A variation of the coordination exam is the Field Sobriety Test (FST) used to assess whether drivers are under the influence of alcohol. The cerebellum is crucial for coordinated movements such as keeping balance while walking, or moving appendicular musculature on the basis of proprioceptive feedback. The cerebellum is also very sensitive to ethanol, the particular type of alcohol found in beer, wine, and liquor.

Walking in a straight line involves comparing the motor command from the primary motor cortex to the proprioceptive and vestibular sensory feedback, as well as following the visual guide of the white line on the side of the road. When the cerebellum is compromised by alcohol, the cerebellum cannot coordinate these movements effectively, and maintaining balance becomes difficult.

Another common aspect of the FST is to have the driver extend their arms out wide and touch their fingertip to their nose, usually with their eyes closed. The point of this is to remove the visual feedback for the movement and force the driver to rely just on proprioceptive information about the movement and position of their fingertip relative to their nose. With eyes open, the corrections to the movement of the arm might be so small as to be hard to see, but proprioceptive feedback is not as immediate and broader movements of the arm will probably be needed, particularly if the cerebellum is affected by alcohol.

Reciting the alphabet backwards is not always a component of the FST, but its relationship to neurological function is interesting. There is a cognitive aspect to remembering how the alphabet goes and how to recite it backwards. That is actually a variation of the mental status subtest of repeating the months backwards. However, the cerebellum is important because speech production is a coordinated activity. The speech rapid alternating movement subtest is specifically using the consonant changes of "lah-kah-pah" to assess coordinated movements of the lips, tongue, pharynx, and palate. But the entire alphabet, especially in the nonrehearsed backwards order, pushes this type of coordinated movement quite far. It is related to the reason that speech becomes slurred when a person is intoxicated.

KEY TERMS

accommodation in vision, a change in the ability of the eye to focus on objects at different distances

accommodation–convergence reflex coordination of somatic control of the medial rectus muscles of either eye with the parasympathetic control of the ciliary bodies to maintain focus while the eyes converge on visual stimuli near to the face

anterograde amnesia inability to form new memories from a particular time forward

aphasia loss of language function

ataxia movement disorder related to damage of the cerebellum characterized by loss of coordination in voluntary movements

Babinski sign dorsiflexion of the foot with extension and splaying of the toes in response to the plantar reflex, normally suppressed by corticospinal input

cerebrocerebellum lateral regions of the cerebellum; named for the significant input from the cerebral cortex

check reflex response to a release in resistance so that the contractions stop, or check, movement

clasp-knife response sign of UMN disease when a patient initially resists passive movement of a muscle but will quickly release to a lower state of resistance

conduction aphasia loss of language function related to connecting the understanding of speech with the production of speech, without either specific function being lost

conductive hearing hearing dependent on the conduction of vibrations of the tympanic membrane through the ossicles of the middle ear

conjugate gaze coordinated movement of the two eyes simultaneously in the same direction

convergence in vision, the movement of the eyes so that they are both pointed at the same point in space, which increases for stimuli that are closer to the subject

coordination exam major section of the neurological exam that assesses complex, coordinated motor functions of the cerebellum and associated motor pathways

cortico-ponto-cerebellar pathway projection from the cerebral cortex to the cerebellum by way of the gray matter of the pons

cranial nerve exam major section of the neurological exam that assesses sensory and motor functions of the cranial nerves and their associated central and peripheral structures

cytoarchitecture study of a tissue based on the structure and organization of its cellular components; related to the broader term, histology

deep tendon reflex another term for stretch reflex, based on the elicitation through deep stimulation of the tendon at the insertion

diplopia double vision resulting from a failure in conjugate gaze

edema fluid accumulation in tissue; often associated with circulatory deficits

embolus obstruction in a blood vessel such as a blood clot, fatty mass, air bubble, or other foreign matter that interrupts the flow of blood to an organ or some part of the body

episodic memory memory of specific events in an autobiographical sense

expressive aphasia loss of the ability to produce language; usually associated with damage to Broca's area in the frontal lobe

extrinsic muscles of the tongue muscles that are connected to other structures, such as the hyoid bone or the mandible, and control the position of the tongue

fasciculation small muscle twitch as a result of spontaneous activity from an LMN

fauces opening from the oral cavity into the pharynx

fibrillation in motor responses, a spontaneous muscle action potential that occurs in the absence of neuromuscular input, resulting from LMN lesions

flaccid paralysis loss of voluntary muscle control and muscle tone, as the result of LMN disease

flaccidity presentation of a loss of muscle tone, observed as floppy limbs or a lack of resistance to passive movement

flocculonodular lobe lobe of the cerebellum that receives input from the vestibular system to help with balance and posture

gait rhythmic pattern of alternating movements of the lower limbs during locomotion

gait exam major section of the neurological exam that assesses the cerebellum and descending pathways in the spinal cord through the coordinated motor functions of walking; a portion of the coordination exam

gnosis in a neurological exam, intuitive experiential knowledge tested by interacting with common objects or symbols

graphesthesia perception of symbols, such as letters or numbers, traced in the palm of the hand

hemisection cut through half of a structure, such as the spinal cord

hemorrhagic stroke disruption of blood flow to the brain caused by bleeding within the cranial vault

hyperflexia overly flexed joints

hypotonicity low muscle tone, a sign of LMN disease

hypovolemia decrease in blood volume

inferior cerebellar peduncle (ICP) input to the cerebellum, largely from the inferior olive, that represents sensory feedback from the periphery

inferior olive large nucleus in the medulla that receives input from sensory systems and projects into the cerebellar cortex

internuclear ophthalmoplegia deficit of conjugate lateral gaze because the lateral rectus muscle of one eye does not contract resulting from damage to the abducens nerve or the MLF

intorsion medial rotation of the eye around its axis

intrinsic muscles of the tongue muscles that originate out of, and insert into, other tissues within the tongue and control the shape of the tongue

ischemic stroke disruption of blood flow to the brain because blood cannot flow through blood vessels as a result of a blockage or narrowing of the vessel

jaw-jerk reflex stretch reflex of the masseter muscle

localization of function principle that circumscribed anatomical locations are responsible for specific functions in an organ system

medial longitudinal fasciculus (MLF) fiber pathway that connects structures involved in the control of eye and head position, from the superior colliculus to the vestibular nuclei and cerebellum

mental status exam major section of the neurological exam that assesses cognitive functions of the cerebrum

middle cerebellar peduncle (MCP) large, white-matter bridge from the pons that constitutes the major input to the cerebellar cortex

motor exam major section of the neurological exam that assesses motor functions of the spinal cord and spinal nerves

neurological exam clinical assessment tool that can be used to quickly evaluate neurological function and determine if specific parts of the nervous system have been affected by damage or disease

paramedian pontine reticular formation (PPRF) region of the brain stem adjacent to the motor nuclei for gaze control that coordinates rapid, conjugate eye movements

paresis partial loss of, or impaired, voluntary muscle control

plantar reflex superficial reflex initiated by gentle stimulation of the sole of the foot

praxis in a neurological exam, the act of doing something using ready knowledge or skills in response to verbal instruction

procedural memory memory of how to perform a specific task

pronator drift sign of contralateral corticospinal lesion when the one arm will drift into a pronated position when held straight out with the palms facing upward

receptive aphasia loss of the ability to understand received language, such as what is spoken to the subject or given in written form

red nucleus nucleus in the midbrain that receives output from the cerebellum and projects onto the spinal cord in the rubrospinal tract

retrograde amnesia loss of memories before a particular event

Rinne test use of a tuning fork to test conductive hearing loss versus sensorineural hearing loss

Romberg test test of equilibrium that requires the patient to maintain a straight, upright posture without visual feedback of position

rubrospinal tract descending tract from the red nucleus of the midbrain that results in modification of ongoing motor programs

saccade small, rapid movement of the eyes used to locate and direct the fovea onto visual stimuli

sensorineural hearing hearing dependent on the transduction and propagation of auditory information through the neural components of the peripheral auditory structures

sensory exam major section of the neurological exam that assesses sensory functions of the spinal cord and spinal nerves

short-term memory capacity to retain information actively in the brain for a brief period of time

Snellen chart standardized arrangement of letters in decreasing size presented to a subject at a distance of 20 feet to test visual acuity

spasticity increased contraction of a muscle in response to resistance, often resulting in hyperflexia

spinocerebellar tract ascending fibers that carry proprioceptive input to the cerebellum used in maintaining balance and coordinated movement

spinocerebellum midline region of the cerebellum known as the vermis that receives proprioceptive input from the spinal cord

stereognosis perception of common objects placed in the hand solely on the basis of manipulation of that object in the hand

stroke (also, cerebrovascular accident (CVA)) loss of neurological function caused by an interruption of blood flow to a region of the central nervous system

superficial reflex reflexive contraction initiated by gentle stimulation of the skin

superior cerebellar peduncle (SCP) white-matter tract representing output of the cerebellum to the red nucleus of the midbrain

transient ischemic attack (TIA) temporary disruption of blood flow to the brain in which symptoms occur rapidly but last only a short time

vermis prominent ridge along the midline of the cerebellum that is referred to as the spinocerebellum

vestibulo-ocular reflex (VOR) reflex based on connections between the vestibular system and the cranial nerves of eye movements that ensures that images are stabilized on the retina as the head and body move

vestibulocerebellum flocculonodular lobe of the cerebellum named for the vestibular input from the eighth cranial nerve

Weber test use of a tuning fork to test the laterality of hearing loss by placing it at several locations on the midline of the skull

Wernicke's area region at the posterior end of the lateral sulcus in which speech comprehension is localized

CHAPTER REVIEW

16.1 Overview of the Neurological Exam

The neurological exam is a clinical assessment tool to determine the extent of function from the nervous system. It is divided into five major sections that each deal with a specific region of the CNS. The mental status exam is concerned with the cerebrum and assesses higher functions such as memory, language, and emotion. The cranial nerve exam tests the functions of all of the cranial nerves and, therefore, their connections to the CNS through the forebrain and brain stem. The sensory and motor exams assess those functions as they relate to the spinal cord, as well as the combination of the functions in spinal reflexes. The coordination exam targets cerebellar function in coordinated movements, including those functions associated with gait.

Damage to and disease of the nervous system lead to loss of function. The location of the injury will correspond to the functional loss, as suggested by the principle of localization of function. The neurological exam provides the opportunity for a clinician to determine where damage has occurred on the basis of the function that is lost. Damage from acute injuries such as strokes may result in specific functions being lost, whereas broader effects in infection or developmental disorders may result in general losses across an entire section of the neurological exam.

16.4 The Sensory and Motor Exams

The sensory and motor exams assess function related to the spinal cord and the nerves connected to it. Sensory functions are associated with the dorsal regions of the spinal cord, whereas motor function is associated with the ventral side. Localizing damage to the spinal cord is related to assessments of the peripheral projections mapped to dermatomes.

Sensory tests address the various submodalities of the somatic senses: touch, temperature, vibration, pain, and proprioception. Results of the subtests can point to trauma in the spinal cord gray matter, white matter, or even in connections to the cerebral cortex.

Motor tests focus on the function of the muscles and the connections of the descending motor pathway. Muscle tone and strength are tested for upper and lower extremities. Input to the muscles comes from the descending cortical input of upper motor neurons and the direct innervation of lower motor neurons.

Reflexes can either be based on deep stimulation of tendons or superficial stimulation of the skin. The presence of reflexive contractions helps to differentiate motor disorders between the upper and lower motor neurons. The specific signs associated with motor disorders can establish the difference further, based on the type of paralysis, the state of muscle tone, and specific indicators such as pronator drift or the Babinski sign.

16.5 The Coordination and Gait Exams

The cerebellum is an important part of motor function in the nervous system. It apparently plays a role in procedural learning, which would include motor skills such as riding a bike or throwing a football. The basis for these roles is likely to be tied into the role the cerebellum plays as a comparator for voluntary movement.

The motor commands from the cerebral hemispheres travel along the corticospinal pathway, which passes through the pons. Collateral branches of these fibers synapse on neurons in the pons, which then project into the cerebellar cortex through the middle cerebellar peduncles. Ascending sensory feedback, entering through the inferior cerebellar peduncles, provides information about motor performance. The cerebellar cortex compares the command to the actual performance and can adjust the descending input to compensate for any mismatch. The output from deep cerebellar nuclei projects through the superior cerebellar peduncles to initiate descending signals from the red nucleus to the spinal cord.

The primary role of the cerebellum in relation to the spinal cord is through the spinocerebellum; it controls posture and gait with significant input from the vestibular system. Deficits in cerebellar function result in ataxias, or a specific kind of movement disorder. The root cause of the ataxia may be the sensory input—either the proprioceptive input from the spinal cord or the equilibrium input from the vestibular system, or direct damage to the cerebellum by stroke, trauma, hereditary factors, or toxins.

INTERACTIVE LINK QUESTIONS

1. Watch this video (http://openstaxcollege.org/l/neuroexam) that provides a demonstration of the neurological exam—a series of tests that can be performed rapidly when a patient is initially brought into an emergency department. The exam can be repeated on a regular basis to keep a record of how and if neurological function changes over time. In what order were the sections of the neurological exam tested in this video, and which section seemed to be left out?

2. Watch this video (http://openstaxcollege.org/l/neuroexam2) for an introduction to the neurological exam. Studying the neurological exam can give insight into how structure and function in the nervous system are interdependent. This is a tool both in the clinic and in the classroom, but for different reasons. In the clinic, this is a powerful but simple tool to assess a patient's neurological function. In the classroom, it is a different way to think about the nervous system. Though medical technology provides noninvasive imaging and real-time functional data, the presenter says these cannot replace the history at the core of the medical examination. What does history mean in the context of medical practice?

3. Read this article (http://openstaxcollege.org/l/3word) to learn about a young man who texts his fiancée in a panic as he finds that he is having trouble remembering things. At the hospital, a neurologist administers the mental status exam, which is mostly normal except for the three-word recall test. The young man could not recall them even 30 seconds after hearing them and repeating them back to the doctor. An undiscovered mass in the mediastinum region was found to be Hodgkin's lymphoma, a type of cancer that affects the immune system and likely caused antibodies to attack the nervous system. The patient eventually regained his ability to remember, though the events in the hospital were always elusive. Considering that the effects on memory were temporary, but resulted in the loss of the specific events of the hospital stay, what regions of the brain were likely to have been affected by the antibodies and what type of memory does that represent?

4. Watch the video (http://openstaxcollege.org/l/2brains) titled "The Man With Two Brains" to see the neuroscientist Michael Gazzaniga introduce a patient he has worked with for years who has had his corpus callosum cut, separating his two cerebral hemispheres. A few tests are run to demonstrate how this manifests in tests of cerebral function. Unlike normal people, this patient can perform two independent tasks at the same time because the lines of communication between the right and left sides of his brain have been removed. Whereas a person with an intact corpus callosum cannot overcome the dominance of one hemisphere over the other, this patient can. If the left cerebral hemisphere is dominant in the majority of people, why would right-handedness be most common?

5. Watch this short video (http://openstaxcollege.org/l/facialnerve) to see an examination of the facial nerve using some simple tests. The facial nerve controls the muscles of facial expression. Severe deficits will be obvious in watching someone use those muscles for normal control. One side of the face might not move like the other side. But directed tests, especially for contraction against resistance, require a formal testing of the muscles. The muscles of the upper and lower face need to be tested. The strength test in this video involves the patient squeezing her eyes shut and the examiner trying to pry her eyes open. Why does the examiner ask her to try a second time?

6. Watch this video (http://openstaxcollege.org/l/2point) to see a quick demonstration of two-point discrimination. Touching a specialized caliper to the surface of the skin will measure the distance between two points that are perceived as distinct stimuli versus a single stimulus. The patient keeps their eyes closed while the examiner switches between using both points of the caliper or just one. The patient then must indicate whether one or two stimuli are in contact with the skin. Why is the distance between the caliper points closer on the fingertips as opposed to the palm of the hand? And what do you think the distance would be on the arm, or the shoulder?

7. Watch this video (http://openstaxcollege.org/l/reflextest) to see how to test reflexes in the abdomen. Testing reflexes of the trunk is not commonly performed in the neurological exam, but if findings suggest a problem with the thoracic segments of the spinal cord, a series of superficial reflexes of the abdomen can localize function to those segments. If contraction is not observed when the skin lateral to the umbilicus (belly button) is stimulated, what level of the spinal cord may be damaged?

8. Watch this short video (http://openstaxcollege.org/l/stationtest) to see a test for station. Station refers to the position a person adopts when they are standing still. The examiner would look for issues with balance, which coordinates proprioceptive, vestibular, and visual information in the cerebellum. To test the ability of a subject to maintain balance, asking them to stand or hop on one foot can be more demanding. The examiner may also push the subject to see if they can maintain balance. An abnormal finding in the test of station is if the feet are placed far apart. Why would a wide stance suggest problems with cerebellar function?

REVIEW QUESTIONS

9. Which major section of the neurological exam is *most likely* to reveal damage to the cerebellum?
   a. cranial nerve exam
   b. mental status exam
   c. sensory exam
   d. coordination exam

10. What function would *most likely* be affected by a restriction of a blood vessel in the cerebral cortex?
   a. language
   b. gait
   c. facial expressions
   d. knee-jerk reflex

11. Which major section of the neurological exam includes subtests that are sometimes considered a separate set of tests concerned with walking?
   a. mental status exam
   b. cranial nerve exam
   c. coordination exam
   d. sensory exam

12. Memory, emotional, language, and sensorimotor deficits together are *most likely* the result of what kind of damage?
   a. stroke
   b. developmental disorder
   c. whiplash
   d. gunshot wound

13. Where is language function localized in the majority of people?
   a. cerebellum
   b. right cerebral hemisphere
   c. hippocampus
   d. left cerebral hemisphere

14. Which of the following could be elements of cytoarchitecture, as related to Brodmann's microscopic studies of the cerebral cortex?
   a. connections to the cerebellum
   b. activation by visual stimuli
   c. number of neurons per square millimeter
   d. number of gyri or sulci

15. Which of the following could be a multimodal integrative area?
   a. primary visual cortex
   b. premotor cortex
   c. hippocampus
   d. Wernicke's area

16. Which is an example of episodic memory?
   a. how to bake a cake
   b. your last birthday party
   c. how old you are
   d. needing to wear an oven mitt to take a cake out of the oven

17. Which type of aphasia is more like hearing a foreign language spoken?
   a. receptive aphasia
   b. expressive aphasia
   c. conductive aphasia
   d. Broca's aphasia

18. What region of the cerebral cortex is associated with understanding language, both from another person and the language a person generates himself or herself?
   a. medial temporal lobe
   b. ventromedial prefrontal cortex
   c. superior temporal gyrus
   d. postcentral gyrus

19. Without olfactory sensation to complement gustatory stimuli, food will taste bland unless it is seasoned with which substance?
   a. salt
   b. thyme
   c. garlic
   d. olive oil

20. Which of the following cranial nerves is *not* part of the VOR?
   a. optic
   b. oculomotor
   c. abducens
   d. vestibulocochlear

21. Which nerve is responsible for controlling the muscles that result in the gag reflex?
   a. trigeminal

b. facial
c. glossopharyngeal
d. vagus

22. Which nerve is responsible for taste, as well as salivation, in the anterior oral cavity?
   a. facial
   b. glossopharyngeal
   c. vagus
   d. hypoglossal

23. Which of the following nerves controls movements of the neck?
   a. oculomotor
   b. vestibulocochlear
   c. spinal accessory
   d. hypoglossal

24. Which of the following is *not* part of the corticospinal pathway?
   a. cerebellar deep white matter
   b. midbrain
   c. medulla
   d. lateral column

25. Which subtest is directed at proprioceptive sensation?
   a. two-point discrimination
   b. tactile movement
   c. vibration
   d. Romberg test

26. What term describes the inability to lift the arm above the level of the shoulder?
   a. paralysis
   b. paresis
   c. fasciculation
   d. fibrillation

27. Which type of reflex is the jaw-jerk reflex that is part of the cranial nerve exam for the vestibulocochlear nerve?
   a. visceral reflex
   b. withdrawal reflex
   c. stretch reflex
   d. superficial reflex

28. Which of the following is a feature of both somatic and visceral senses?
   a. requires cerebral input
   b. causes skeletal muscle contraction
   c. projects to a ganglion near the target effector
   d. involves an axon in the ventral nerve root

29. Which white matter structure carries information from the cerebral cortex to the cerebellum?
   a. cerebral peduncle
   b. superior cerebellar peduncle
   c. middle cerebellar peduncle
   d. inferior cerebellar peduncle

30. Which region of the cerebellum receives proprioceptive input from the spinal cord?
   a. vermis
   b. left hemisphere
   c. flocculonodular lobe
   d. right hemisphere

31. Which of the following tests cerebellar function related to gait?
   a. toe-to-finger
   b. station
   c. lah-kah-pah
   d. finger-to-nose

32. Which of the following is *not* a cause of cerebellar ataxia?
   a. mercury from fish
   b. drinking alcohol
   c. antibiotics
   d. hereditary degeneration of the cerebellum

33. Which of the following functions *cannot* be attributed to the cerebellum?
   a. comparing motor commands and sensory feedback
   b. associating sensory stimuli with learned behavior
   c. coordinating complex movements
   d. processing visual information

CRITICAL THINKING QUESTIONS

34. Why is a rapid assessment of neurological function important in an emergency situation?

35. How is the diagnostic category of TIA different from a stroke?

36. A patient's performance of the majority of the mental status exam subtests is in line with the expected norms, but the patient cannot repeat a string of numbers given by the examiner. What is a likely explanation?

37. A patient responds to the question "What is your name?" with a look of incomprehension. Which of the two major language areas is most likely affected and what is the name for that type of aphasia?

38. As a person ages, their ability to focus on near objects (accommodation) changes. If a person is already myopic (near-sighted), why would corrective lenses not be necessary to read a book or computer screen?

39. When a patient flexes their neck, the head tips to the right side. Also, their tongue sticks out slightly to the left when they try to stick it straight out. Where is the damage to the brain stem most likely located?

40. The location of somatosensation is based on the topographical map of sensory innervation. What does this mean?

41. Why are upper motor neuron lesions characterized by "spastic paralysis"?

42. Learning to ride a bike is a motor function dependent on the cerebellum. Why are the different regions of the cerebellum involved in this complex motor learning?

43. Alcohol intoxication can produce slurred speech. How is this related to cerebellar function?

17 | THE ENDOCRINE SYSTEM

Figure 17.1 A Child Catches a Falling Leaf Hormones of the endocrine system coordinate and control growth, metabolism, temperature regulation, the stress response, reproduction, and many other functions. (credit: "seenthroughmylense"/flickr.com)

Introduction

Chapter Objectives

After studying this chapter, you will be able to:

- Identify the contributions of the endocrine system to homeostasis
- Discuss the chemical composition of hormones and the mechanisms of hormone action

- Summarize the site of production, regulation, and effects of the hormones of the pituitary, thyroid, parathyroid, adrenal, and pineal glands
- Discuss the hormonal regulation of the reproductive system
- Explain the role of the pancreatic endocrine cells in the regulation of blood glucose
- Identify the hormones released by the heart, kidneys, and other organs with secondary endocrine functions
- Discuss several common diseases associated with endocrine system dysfunction
- Discuss the embryonic development of, and the effects of aging on, the endocrine system

You may never have thought of it this way, but when you send a text message to two friends to meet you at the dining hall at six, you're sending digital signals that (you hope) will affect their behavior—even though they are some distance away. Similarly, certain cells send chemical signals to other cells in the body that influence their behavior. This long-distance intercellular communication, coordination, and control is critical for homeostasis, and it is the fundamental function of the endocrine system.

17.1 | An Overview of the Endocrine System

By the end of this section, you will be able to:
- Distinguish the types of intercellular communication, their importance, mechanisms, and effects
- Identify the major organs and tissues of the endocrine system and their location in the body

Communication is a process in which a sender transmits signals to one or more receivers to control and coordinate actions. In the human body, two major organ systems participate in relatively "long distance" communication: the nervous system and the endocrine system. Together, these two systems are primarily responsible for maintaining homeostasis in the body.

Neural and Endocrine Signaling

The nervous system uses two types of intercellular communication—electrical and chemical signaling—either by the direct action of an electrical potential, or in the latter case, through the action of chemical neurotransmitters such as serotonin or norepinephrine. Neurotransmitters act locally and rapidly. When an electrical signal in the form of an action potential arrives at the synaptic terminal, they diffuse across the synaptic cleft (the gap between a sending neuron and a receiving neuron or muscle cell). Once the neurotransmitters interact (bind) with receptors on the receiving (post-synaptic) cell, the receptor stimulation is transduced into a response such as continued electrical signaling or modification of cellular response. The target cell responds within milliseconds of receiving the chemical "message"; this response then ceases very quickly once the neural signaling ends. In this way, neural communication enables body functions that involve quick, brief actions, such as movement, sensation, and cognition.In contrast, the **endocrine system** uses just one method of communication: chemical signaling. These signals are sent by the endocrine organs, which secrete chemicals—the **hormone**—into the extracellular fluid. Hormones are transported primarily via the bloodstream throughout the body, where they bind to receptors on target cells, inducing a characteristic response. As a result, endocrine signaling requires more time than neural signaling to prompt a response in target cells, though the precise amount of time varies with different hormones. For example, the hormones released when you are confronted with a dangerous or frightening situation, called the fight-or-flight response, occur by the release of adrenal hormones—epinephrine and norepinephrine—within seconds. In contrast, it may take up to 48 hours for target cells to respond to certain reproductive hormones.

Visit this link (http://openstaxcollege.org/l/hormonebind) to watch an animation of the events that occur when a hormone binds to a cell membrane receptor. What is the secondary messenger made by adenylyl cyclase during the activation of liver cells by epinephrine?

In addition, endocrine signaling is typically less specific than neural signaling. The same hormone may play a role in a variety of different physiological processes depending on the target cells involved. For example, the hormone oxytocin promotes uterine contractions in women in labor. It is also important in breastfeeding, and may be involved in the sexual response and in feelings of emotional attachment in both males and females.

In general, the nervous system involves quick responses to rapid changes in the external environment, and the endocrine system is usually slower acting—taking care of the internal environment of the body, maintaining homeostasis, and controlling reproduction (Table 17.1). So how does the fight-or-flight response that was mentioned earlier happen so quickly if hormones are usually slower acting? It is because the two systems are connected. It is the fast action of the nervous system in response to the danger in the environment that stimulates the adrenal glands to secrete their hormones. As a result, the nervous system can cause rapid endocrine responses to keep up with sudden changes in both the external and internal environments when necessary.

Endocrine and Nervous Systems

	Endocrine system	Nervous system
Signaling mechanism(s)	Chemical	Chemical/electrical
Primary chemical signal	Hormones	Neurotransmitters
Distance traveled	Long or short	Always short
Response time	Fast or slow	Always fast
Environment targeted	Internal	Internal and external

Table 17.1

Structures of the Endocrine System

The endocrine system consists of cells, tissues, and organs that secrete hormones as a primary or secondary function. The **endocrine gland** is the major player in this system. The primary function of these ductless glands is to secrete their hormones directly into the surrounding fluid. The interstitial fluid and the blood vessels then transport the hormones throughout the body. The endocrine system includes the pituitary, thyroid, parathyroid, adrenal, and pineal glands (Figure 17.2). Some of these glands have both endocrine and non-endocrine functions. For example, the pancreas contains cells that function in digestion as well as cells that secrete the hormones insulin and glucagon, which regulate blood glucose levels. The hypothalamus, thymus, heart, kidneys, stomach, small intestine, liver, skin, female ovaries, and male testes are other organs that contain cells with endocrine function. Moreover, adipose tissue has long been known to produce hormones, and recent research has revealed that even bone tissue has endocrine functions.

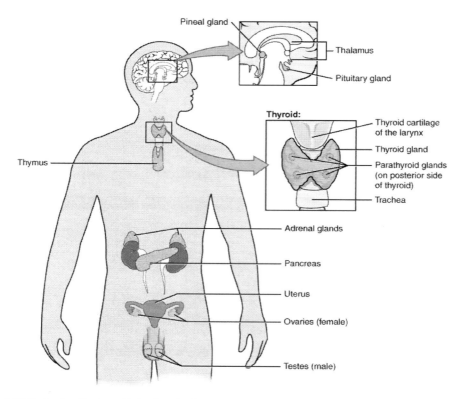

Figure 17.2 Endocrine System Endocrine glands and cells are located throughout the body and play an important role in homeostasis.

The ductless endocrine glands are not to be confused with the body's **exocrine system**, whose glands release their secretions through ducts. Examples of exocrine glands include the sebaceous and sweat glands of the skin. As just noted, the pancreas also has an exocrine function: most of its cells secrete pancreatic juice through the pancreatic and accessory ducts to the lumen of the small intestine.

Other Types of Chemical Signaling

In endocrine signaling, hormones secreted into the extracellular fluid diffuse into the blood or lymph, and can then travel great distances throughout the body. In contrast, autocrine signaling takes place within the same cell. An **autocrine** (auto- = "self") is a chemical that elicits a response in the same cell that secreted it. Interleukin-1, or IL-1, is a signaling molecule that plays an important role in inflammatory response. The cells that secrete IL-1 have receptors on their cell surface that bind these molecules, resulting in autocrine signaling.

Local intercellular communication is the province of the **paracrine**, also called a paracrine factor, which is a chemical that induces a response in neighboring cells. Although paracrines may enter the bloodstream, their concentration is generally too low to elicit a response from distant tissues. A familiar example to those with asthma is histamine, a paracrine that is released by immune cells in the bronchial tree. Histamine causes the smooth muscle cells of the bronchi to constrict, narrowing the airways. Another example is the neurotransmitters of the nervous system, which act only locally within the synaptic cleft.

Endocrinologist

Endocrinology is a specialty in the field of medicine that focuses on the treatment of endocrine system disorders. Endocrinologists—medical doctors who specialize in this field—are experts in treating diseases associated with hormonal systems, ranging from thyroid disease to diabetes mellitus. Endocrine surgeons treat endocrine disease through the removal, or resection, of the affected endocrine gland.

Patients who are referred to endocrinologists may have signs and symptoms or blood test results that suggest excessive or impaired functioning of an endocrine gland or endocrine cells. The endocrinologist may order additional blood tests to determine whether the patient's hormonal levels are abnormal, or they may stimulate or suppress the function of the suspect endocrine gland and then have blood taken for analysis. Treatment varies according to the diagnosis. Some endocrine disorders, such as type 2 diabetes, may respond to lifestyle changes such as modest weight loss, adoption of a healthy diet, and regular physical activity. Other disorders may require medication, such as hormone replacement, and routine monitoring by the endocrinologist. These include disorders of the pituitary gland that can affect growth and disorders of the thyroid gland that can result in a variety of metabolic problems.

Some patients experience health problems as a result of the normal decline in hormones that can accompany aging. These patients can consult with an endocrinologist to weigh the risks and benefits of hormone replacement therapy intended to boost their natural levels of reproductive hormones.

In addition to treating patients, endocrinologists may be involved in research to improve the understanding of endocrine system disorders and develop new treatments for these diseases.

17.2 | Hormones

By the end of this section, you will be able to:
- Identify the three major classes of hormones on the basis of chemical structure
- Compare and contrast intracellular and cell membrane hormone receptors
- Describe signaling pathways that involve cAMP and IP3
- Identify several factors that influence a target cell's response
- Discuss the role of feedback loops and humoral, hormonal, and neural stimuli in hormone control

Although a given hormone may travel throughout the body in the bloodstream, it will affect the activity only of its target cells; that is, cells with receptors for that particular hormone. Once the hormone binds to the receptor, a chain of events is initiated that leads to the target cell's response. Hormones play a critical role in the regulation of physiological processes because of the target cell responses they regulate. These responses contribute to human reproduction, growth and development of body tissues, metabolism, fluid, and electrolyte balance, sleep, and many other body functions. The major hormones of the human body and their effects are identified in Table 17.2.

Endocrine Glands and Their Major Hormones

Endocrine gland	Associated hormones	Chemical class	Effect
Pituitary (anterior)	Growth hormone (GH)	Protein	Promotes growth of body tissues
Pituitary (anterior)	Prolactin (PRL)	Peptide	Promotes milk production

Table 17.2

Endocrine Glands and Their Major Hormones

Endocrine gland	Associated hormones	Chemical class	Effect
Pituitary (anterior)	Thyroid-stimulating hormone (TSH)	Glycoprotein	Stimulates thyroid hormone release
Pituitary (anterior)	Adrenocorticotropic hormone (ACTH)	Peptide	Stimulates hormone release by adrenal cortex
Pituitary (anterior)	Follicle-stimulating hormone (FSH)	Glycoprotein	Stimulates gamete production
Pituitary (anterior)	Luteinizing hormone (LH)	Glycoprotein	Stimulates androgen production by gonads
Pituitary (posterior)	Antidiuretic hormone (ADH)	Peptide	Stimulates water reabsorption by kidneys
Pituitary (posterior)	Oxytocin	Peptide	Stimulates uterine contractions during childbirth
Thyroid	Thyroxine (T_4), triiodothyronine (T_3)	Amine	Stimulate basal metabolic rate
Thyroid	Calcitonin	Peptide	Reduces blood Ca^{2+} levels
Parathyroid	Parathyroid hormone (PTH)	Peptide	Increases blood Ca^{2+} levels
Adrenal (cortex)	Aldosterone	Steroid	Increases blood Na^+ levels
Adrenal (cortex)	Cortisol, corticosterone, cortisone	Steroid	Increase blood glucose levels
Adrenal (medulla)	Epinephrine, norepinephrine	Amine	Stimulate fight-or-flight response
Pineal	Melatonin	Amine	Regulates sleep cycles
Pancreas	Insulin	Protein	Reduces blood glucose levels
Pancreas	Glucagon	Protein	Increases blood glucose levels
Testes	Testosterone	Steroid	Stimulates development of male secondary sex characteristics and sperm production
Ovaries	Estrogens and progesterone	Steroid	Stimulate development of female secondary sex characteristics and prepare the body for childbirth

Table 17.2

Types of Hormones

The hormones of the human body can be divided into two major groups on the basis of their chemical structure. Hormones derived from amino acids include amines, peptides, and proteins. Those derived from lipids include steroids (Figure 17.3). These chemical groups affect a hormone's distribution, the type of receptors it binds to, and other aspects of its function.

Hormone Class	Components	Example(s)
Amine Hormone	Amino acids with modified groups (e.g. norepinephrine's carboxyl group is replaced with a benzene ring)	Norepinephrine 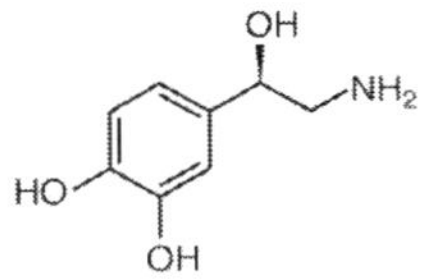
Peptide Hormone	Short chains of linked amino acids	Oxytocin 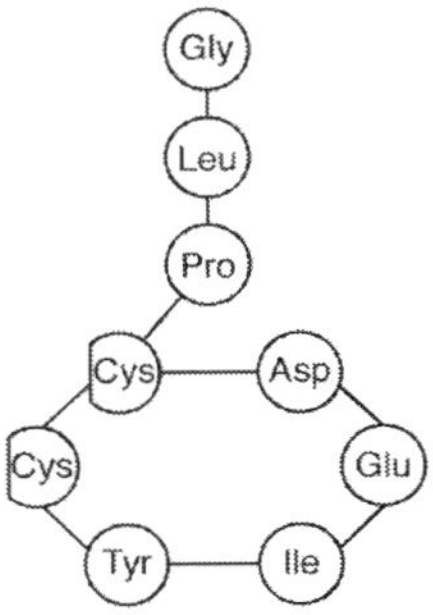
Protein Hormone	Long chains of linked amino acids	Human Growth Hormone 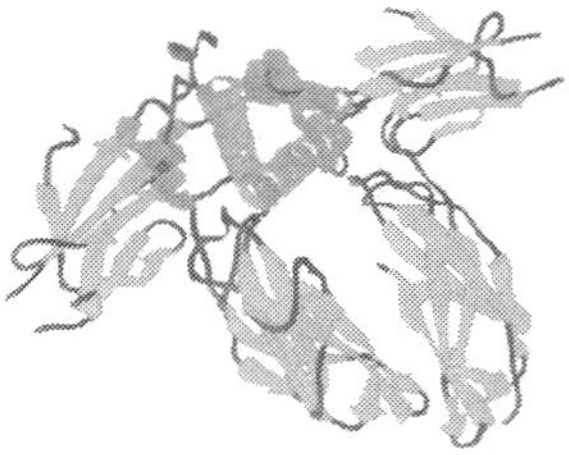
Steroid Hormones	Derived from the lipid cholesterol	Testosterone, 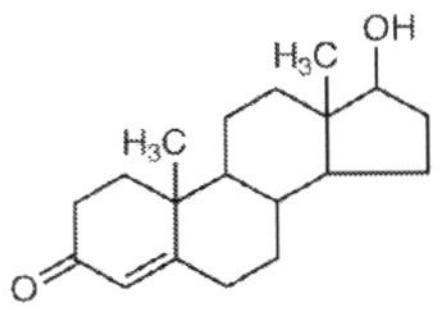 Progesterone 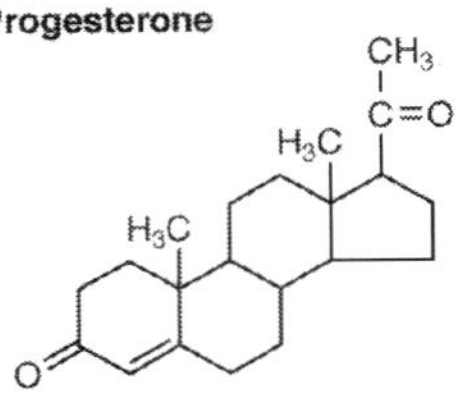

Figure 17.3 Amine, Peptide, Protein, and Steroid Hormone Structure

Amine Hormones

Hormones derived from the modification of amino acids are referred to as amine hormones. Typically, the original structure of the amino acid is modified such that a –COOH, or carboxyl, group is removed, whereas the $-\text{NH}_3^+$, or amine, group remains.

Amine hormones are synthesized from the amino acids tryptophan or tyrosine. An example of a hormone derived from tryptophan is melatonin, which is secreted by the pineal gland and helps regulate circadian rhythm. Tyrosine derivatives include the metabolism-regulating thyroid hormones, as well as the catecholamines, such as epinephrine, norepinephrine, and dopamine. Epinephrine and norepinephrine are secreted by the adrenal medulla and play a role in the fight-or-flight response, whereas dopamine is secreted by the hypothalamus and inhibits the release of certain anterior pituitary hormones.

Peptide and Protein Hormones

Whereas the amine hormones are derived from a single amino acid, peptide and protein hormones consist of multiple amino acids that link to form an amino acid chain. Peptide hormones consist of short chains of amino acids, whereas protein hormones are longer polypeptides. Both types are synthesized like other body proteins: DNA is transcribed into mRNA, which is translated into an amino acid chain.

Examples of peptide hormones include antidiuretic hormone (ADH), a pituitary hormone important in fluid balance, and atrial-natriuretic peptide, which is produced by the heart and helps to decrease blood pressure. Some examples of protein hormones include growth hormone, which is produced by the pituitary gland, and follicle-stimulating hormone (FSH), which has an attached carbohydrate group and is thus classified as a glycoprotein. FSH helps stimulate the maturation of eggs in the ovaries and sperm in the testes.

Steroid Hormones

The primary hormones derived from lipids are steroids. Steroid hormones are derived from the lipid cholesterol. For example, the reproductive hormones testosterone and the estrogens—which are produced by the gonads (testes and ovaries)—are steroid hormones. The adrenal glands produce the steroid hormone aldosterone, which is involved in osmoregulation, and cortisol, which plays a role in metabolism.

Like cholesterol, steroid hormones are not soluble in water (they are hydrophobic). Because blood is water-based, lipid-derived hormones must travel to their target cell bound to a transport protein. This more complex structure extends the half-life of steroid hormones much longer than that of hormones derived from amino acids. A hormone's half-life is the time required for half the concentration of the hormone to be degraded. For example, the lipid-derived hormone cortisol has a half-life of approximately 60 to 90 minutes. In contrast, the amino acid–derived hormone epinephrine has a half-life of approximately one minute.

Pathways of Hormone Action

The message a hormone sends is received by a **hormone receptor**, a protein located either inside the cell or within the cell membrane. The receptor will process the message by initiating other signaling events or cellular mechanisms that result in the target cell's response. Hormone receptors recognize molecules with specific shapes and side groups, and respond only to those hormones that are recognized. The same type of receptor may be located on cells in different body tissues, and trigger somewhat different responses. Thus, the response triggered by a hormone depends not only on the hormone, but also on the target cell.

Once the target cell receives the hormone signal, it can respond in a variety of ways. The response may include the stimulation of protein synthesis, activation or deactivation of enzymes, alteration in the permeability of the cell membrane, altered rates of mitosis and cell growth, and stimulation of the secretion of products. Moreover, a single hormone may be capable of inducing different responses in a given cell.

Pathways Involving Intracellular Hormone Receptors

Intracellular hormone receptors are located inside the cell. Hormones that bind to this type of receptor must be able to cross the cell membrane. Steroid hormones are derived from cholesterol and therefore can readily diffuse through the lipid bilayer of the cell membrane to reach the intracellular receptor (Figure 17.4). Thyroid hormones, which contain benzene rings studded with iodine, are also lipid-soluble and can enter the cell.

The location of steroid and thyroid hormone binding differs slightly: a steroid hormone may bind to its receptor within the cytosol or within the nucleus. In either case, this binding generates a hormone-receptor complex that moves toward the chromatin in the cell nucleus and binds to a particular segment of the cell's DNA. In contrast, thyroid hormones bind to receptors already bound to DNA. For both steroid and thyroid hormones, binding of the hormone-receptor complex with DNA triggers transcription of a target gene to mRNA, which moves to the cytosol and directs protein synthesis by ribosomes.

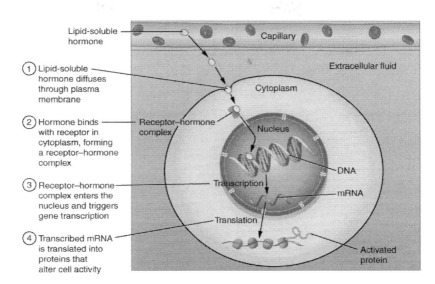

Figure 17.4 Binding of Lipid-Soluble Hormones A steroid hormone directly initiates the production of proteins within a target cell. Steroid hormones easily diffuse through the cell membrane. The hormone binds to its receptor in the cytosol, forming a receptor–hormone complex. The receptor–hormone complex then enters the nucleus and binds to the target gene on the DNA. Transcription of the gene creates a messenger RNA that is translated into the desired protein within the cytoplasm.

Pathways Involving Cell Membrane Hormone Receptors

Hydrophilic, or water-soluble, hormones are unable to diffuse through the lipid bilayer of the cell membrane and must therefore pass on their message to a receptor located at the surface of the cell. Except for thyroid hormones, which are lipid-soluble, all amino acid–derived hormones bind to cell membrane receptors that are located, at least in part, on the extracellular surface of the cell membrane. Therefore, they do not directly affect the transcription of target genes, but instead initiate a signaling cascade that is carried out by a molecule called a **second messenger**. In this case, the hormone is called a **first messenger**.

The second messenger used by most hormones is **cyclic adenosine monophosphate (cAMP)**. In the cAMP second messenger system, a water-soluble hormone binds to its receptor in the cell membrane (Step 1 in Figure 17.5). This receptor is associated with an intracellular component called a **G protein**, and binding of the hormone activates the G-protein component (Step 2). The activated G protein in turn activates an enzyme called **adenylyl cyclase**, also known as adenylate cyclase (Step 3), which converts adenosine triphosphate (ATP) to cAMP (Step 4). As the second messenger, cAMP activates a type of enzyme called a **protein kinase** that is present in the cytosol (Step 5). Activated protein kinases initiate a **phosphorylation cascade**, in which multiple protein kinases phosphorylate (add a phosphate group to) numerous and various cellular proteins, including other enzymes (Step 6).

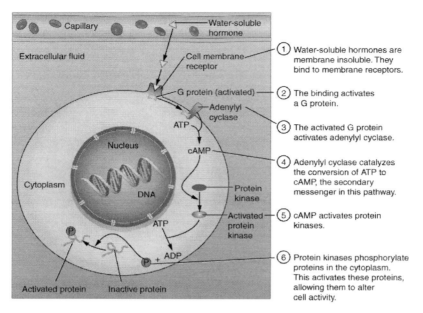

Figure 17.5 Binding of Water-Soluble Hormones Water-soluble hormones cannot diffuse through the cell membrane. These hormones must bind to a surface cell-membrane receptor. The receptor then initiates a cell-signaling pathway within the cell involving G proteins, adenylyl cyclase, the secondary messenger cyclic AMP (cAMP), and protein kinases. In the final step, these protein kinases phosphorylate proteins in the cytoplasm. This activates proteins in the cell that carry out the changes specified by the hormone.

The phosphorylation of cellular proteins can trigger a wide variety of effects, from nutrient metabolism to the synthesis of different hormones and other products. The effects vary according to the type of target cell, the G proteins and kinases involved, and the phosphorylation of proteins. Examples of hormones that use cAMP as a second messenger include calcitonin, which is important for bone construction and regulating blood calcium levels; glucagon, which plays a role in blood glucose levels; and thyroid-stimulating hormone, which causes the release of T_3 and T_4 from the thyroid gland.

Overall, the phosphorylation cascade significantly increases the efficiency, speed, and specificity of the hormonal response, as thousands of signaling events can be initiated simultaneously in response to a very low concentration of hormone in the bloodstream. However, the duration of the hormone signal is short, as cAMP is quickly deactivated by the enzyme **phosphodiesterase (PDE)**, which is located in the cytosol. The action of PDE helps to ensure that a target cell's response ceases quickly unless new hormones arrive at the cell membrane.

Importantly, there are also G proteins that decrease the levels of cAMP in the cell in response to hormone binding. For example, when growth hormone–inhibiting hormone (GHIH), also known as somatostatin, binds to its receptors in the pituitary gland, the level of cAMP decreases, thereby inhibiting the secretion of human growth hormone.

Not all water-soluble hormones initiate the cAMP second messenger system. One common alternative system uses calcium ions as a second messenger. In this system, G proteins activate the enzyme phospholipase C (PLC), which functions similarly to adenylyl cyclase. Once activated, PLC cleaves a membrane-bound phospholipid into two molecules: **diacylglycerol (DAG)** and **inositol triphosphate (IP$_3$)**. Like cAMP, DAG activates protein kinases that initiate a phosphorylation cascade. At the same time, IP$_3$ causes calcium ions to be released from storage sites within the cytosol, such as from within the smooth endoplasmic reticulum. The calcium ions then act as second messengers in two ways: they can influence enzymatic and other cellular activities directly, or they can bind to calcium-binding proteins, the most common of which is calmodulin. Upon binding calcium, calmodulin is able to modulate protein kinase within the cell. Examples of hormones that use calcium ions as a second messenger system include angiotensin II, which helps regulate blood pressure through vasoconstriction, and growth hormone–releasing hormone (GHRH), which causes the pituitary gland to release growth hormones.

Factors Affecting Target Cell Response

You will recall that target cells must have receptors specific to a given hormone if that hormone is to trigger a response. But several other factors influence the target cell response. For example, the presence of a significant level of a hormone circulating in the bloodstream can cause its target cells to decrease their number of receptors for that hormone. This process is called **downregulation**, and it allows cells to become less reactive to the excessive hormone levels. When the level of a hormone is chronically reduced, target cells engage in **upregulation** to increase their number of receptors. This process allows cells to be more sensitive to the hormone that is present. Cells can also alter the sensitivity of the receptors themselves to various hormones.

Two or more hormones can interact to affect the response of cells in a variety of ways. The three most common types of interaction are as follows:

- The permissive effect, in which the presence of one hormone enables another hormone to act. For example, thyroid hormones have complex permissive relationships with certain reproductive hormones. A dietary deficiency of iodine, a component of thyroid hormones, can therefore affect reproductive system development and functioning.
- The synergistic effect, in which two hormones with similar effects produce an amplified response. In some cases, two hormones are required for an adequate response. For example, two different reproductive hormones—FSH from the pituitary gland and estrogens from the ovaries—are required for the maturation of female ova (egg cells).
- The antagonistic effect, in which two hormones have opposing effects. A familiar example is the effect of two pancreatic hormones, insulin and glucagon. Insulin increases the liver's storage of glucose as glycogen, decreasing blood glucose, whereas glucagon stimulates the breakdown of glycogen stores, increasing blood glucose.

Regulation of Hormone Secretion

To prevent abnormal hormone levels and a potential disease state, hormone levels must be tightly controlled. The body maintains this control by balancing hormone production and degradation. Feedback loops govern the initiation and maintenance of most hormone secretion in response to various stimuli.

Role of Feedback Loops

The contribution of feedback loops to homeostasis will only be briefly reviewed here. Positive feedback loops are characterized by the release of additional hormone in response to an original hormone release. The release of oxytocin during childbirth is a positive feedback loop. The initial release of oxytocin begins to signal the uterine muscles to contract, which pushes the fetus toward the cervix, causing it to stretch. This, in turn, signals the pituitary gland to release more oxytocin, causing labor contractions to intensify. The release of oxytocin decreases after the birth of the child.

The more common method of hormone regulation is the negative feedback loop. Negative feedback is characterized by the inhibition of further secretion of a hormone in response to adequate levels of that hormone. This allows blood levels of the hormone to be regulated within a narrow range. An example of a negative feedback loop is the release of glucocorticoid hormones from the adrenal glands, as directed by the hypothalamus and pituitary gland. As glucocorticoid concentrations in the blood rise, the hypothalamus and pituitary gland reduce their signaling to the adrenal glands to prevent additional glucocorticoid secretion (Figure 17.6).

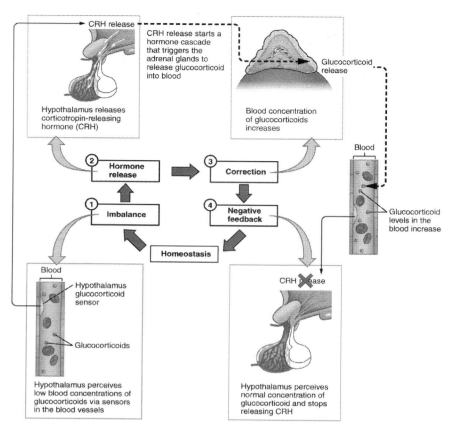

Figure 17.6 Negative Feedback Loop   The release of adrenal glucocorticoids is stimulated by the release of hormones from the hypothalamus and pituitary gland. This signaling is inhibited when glucocorticoid levels become elevated by causing negative signals to the pituitary gland and hypothalamus.

Role of Endocrine Gland Stimuli

Reflexes triggered by both chemical and neural stimuli control endocrine activity. These reflexes may be simple, involving only one hormone response, or they may be more complex and involve many hormones, as is the case with the hypothalamic control of various anterior pituitary–controlled hormones.

Humoral stimuli are changes in blood levels of non-hormone chemicals, such as nutrients or ions, which cause the release or inhibition of a hormone to, in turn, maintain homeostasis. For example, osmoreceptors in the hypothalamus detect changes in blood osmolarity (the concentration of solutes in the blood plasma). If blood osmolarity is too high, meaning that the blood is not dilute enough, osmoreceptors signal the hypothalamus to release ADH. The hormone causes the kidneys to reabsorb more water and reduce the volume of urine produced. This reabsorption causes a reduction of the osmolarity of the blood, diluting the blood to the appropriate level. The regulation of blood glucose is another example. High blood glucose levels cause the release of insulin from the pancreas, which increases glucose uptake by cells and liver storage of glucose as glycogen.

An endocrine gland may also secrete a hormone in response to the presence of another hormone produced by a different endocrine gland. Such hormonal stimuli often involve the hypothalamus, which produces releasing and inhibiting hormones that control the secretion of a variety of pituitary hormones.

In addition to these chemical signals, hormones can also be released in response to neural stimuli. A common example of neural stimuli is the activation of the fight-or-flight response by the sympathetic nervous system. When an individual perceives danger, sympathetic neurons signal the adrenal glands to secrete norepinephrine and epinephrine. The two hormones dilate blood vessels, increase the heart and respiratory rate, and suppress the digestive and immune systems. These responses boost the body's transport of oxygen to the brain and muscles, thereby improving the body's ability to fight or flee.

Everyday CONNECTION

Bisphenol A and Endocrine Disruption

You may have heard news reports about the effects of a chemical called bisphenol A (BPA) in various types of food packaging. BPA is used in the manufacturing of hard plastics and epoxy resins. Common food-related items that may contain BPA include the lining of aluminum cans, plastic food-storage containers, drinking cups, as well as baby bottles and "sippy" cups. Other uses of BPA include medical equipment, dental fillings, and the lining of water pipes.

Research suggests that BPA is an endocrine disruptor, meaning that it negatively interferes with the endocrine system, particularly during the prenatal and postnatal development period. In particular, BPA mimics the hormonal effects of estrogens and has the opposite effect—that of androgens. The U.S. Food and Drug Administration (FDA) notes in their statement about BPA safety that although traditional toxicology studies have supported the safety of low levels of exposure to BPA, recent studies using novel approaches to test for subtle effects have led to some concern about the potential effects of BPA on the brain, behavior, and prostate gland in fetuses, infants, and young children. The FDA is currently facilitating decreased use of BPA in food-related materials. Many US companies have voluntarily removed BPA from baby bottles, "sippy" cups, and the linings of infant formula cans, and most plastic reusable water bottles sold today boast that they are "BPA free." In contrast, both Canada and the European Union have completely banned the use of BPA in baby products.

The potential harmful effects of BPA have been studied in both animal models and humans and include a large variety of health effects, such as developmental delay and disease. For example, prenatal exposure to BPA during the first trimester of human pregnancy may be associated with wheezing and aggressive behavior during childhood. Adults exposed to high levels of BPA may experience altered thyroid signaling and male sexual dysfunction. BPA exposure during the prenatal or postnatal period of development in animal models has been observed to cause neurological delays, changes in brain structure and function, sexual dysfunction, asthma, and increased risk for multiple cancers. In vitro studies have also shown that BPA exposure causes molecular changes that initiate the development of cancers of the breast, prostate, and brain. Although these studies have implicated BPA in numerous ill health effects, some experts caution that some of these studies may be flawed and that more research needs to be done. In the meantime, the FDA recommends that consumers take precautions to limit their exposure to BPA. In addition to purchasing foods in packaging free of BPA, consumers should avoid carrying or storing foods or liquids in bottles with the recycling code 3 or 7. Foods and liquids should not be microwave-heated in any form of plastic: use paper, glass, or ceramics instead.

17.3 | The Pituitary Gland and Hypothalamus

By the end of this section, you will be able to:
- Explain the interrelationships of the anatomy and functions of the hypothalamus and the posterior and anterior lobes of the pituitary gland
- Identify the two hormones released from the posterior pituitary, their target cells, and their principal actions
- Identify the six hormones produced by the anterior lobe of the pituitary gland, their target cells, their principal actions, and their regulation by the hypothalamus

The hypothalamus–pituitary complex can be thought of as the "command center" of the endocrine system. This complex secretes several hormones that directly produce responses in target tissues, as well as hormones that regulate the synthesis and secretion of hormones of other glands. In addition, the hypothalamus–pituitary complex coordinates the messages of the endocrine and nervous systems. In many cases, a stimulus received by the nervous system must pass through the hypothalamus–pituitary complex to be translated into hormones that can initiate a response.

The **hypothalamus** is a structure of the diencephalon of the brain located anterior and inferior to the thalamus (Figure 17.7). It has both neural and endocrine functions, producing and secreting many hormones. In addition, the hypothalamus is anatomically and functionally related to the **pituitary gland** (or hypophysis), a bean-sized organ suspended from it by a stem called the **infundibulum** (or pituitary stalk). The pituitary gland is cradled within the sellaturcica of the sphenoid bone of the skull. It consists of two lobes that arise from distinct parts of embryonic tissue: the posterior pituitary (neurohypophysis) is neural tissue, whereas the anterior pituitary (also known as the adenohypophysis) is glandular tissue that develops from the primitive digestive tract. The hormones secreted by the posterior and anterior pituitary, and the intermediate zone between the lobes are summarized in Table 17.3.

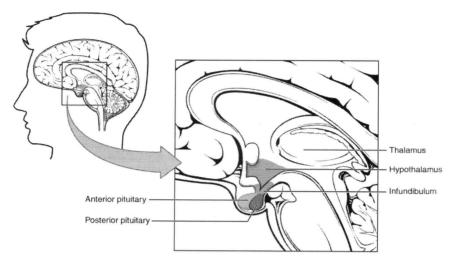

Figure 17.7 Hypothalamus–Pituitary Complex The hypothalamus region lies inferior and anterior to the thalamus. It connects to the pituitary gland by the stalk-like infundibulum. The pituitary gland consists of an anterior and posterior lobe, with each lobe secreting different hormones in response to signals from the hypothalamus.

Pituitary Hormones

Pituitary lobe	Associated hormones	Chemical class	Effect
Anterior	Growth hormone (GH)	Protein	Promotes growth of body tissues
Anterior	Prolactin (PRL)	Peptide	Promotes milk production from mammary glands
Anterior	Thyroid-stimulating hormone (TSH)	Glycoprotein	Stimulates thyroid hormone release from thyroid
Anterior	Adrenocorticotropic hormone (ACTH)	Peptide	Stimulates hormone release by adrenal cortex
Anterior	Follicle-stimulating hormone (FSH)	Glycoprotein	Stimulates gamete production in gonads
Anterior	Luteinizing hormone (LH)	Glycoprotein	Stimulates androgen production by gonads
Posterior	Antidiuretic hormone (ADH)	Peptide	Stimulates water reabsorption by kidneys
Posterior	Oxytocin	Peptide	Stimulates uterine contractions during childbirth

Table 17.3

Pituitary Hormones

Pituitary lobe	Associated hormones	Chemical class	Effect
Intermediate zone	Melanocyte-stimulating hormone	Peptide	Stimulates melanin formation in melanocytes

Table 17.3

Posterior Pituitary

The posterior pituitary is actually an extension of the neurons of the paraventricular and supraoptic nuclei of the hypothalamus. The cell bodies of these regions rest in the hypothalamus, but their axons descend as the hypothalamic–hypophyseal tract within the infundibulum, and end in axon terminals that comprise the posterior pituitary (Figure 17.8).

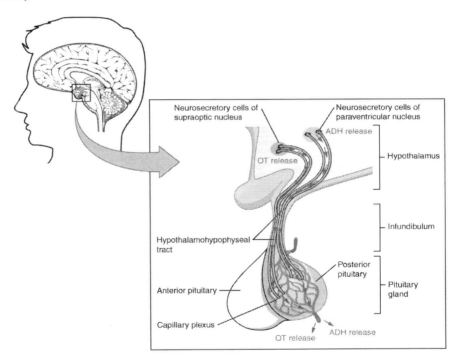

Figure 17.8 Posterior Pituitary. Neurosecretory cells in the hypothalamus release oxytocin (OT) or ADH into the posterior lobe of the pituitary gland. These hormones are stored or released into the blood via the capillary plexus.

The posterior pituitary gland does not produce hormones, but rather stores and secretes hormones produced by the hypothalamus. The paraventricular nuclei produce the hormone oxytocin, whereas the supraoptic nuclei produce ADH. These hormones travel along the axons into storage sites in the axon terminals of the posterior pituitary. In response to signals from the same hypothalamic neurons, the hormones are released from the axon terminals into the bloodstream.

Oxytocin

When fetal development is complete, the peptide-derived hormone **oxytocin** (tocia- = "childbirth") stimulates uterine contractions and dilation of the cervix. Throughout most of pregnancy, oxytocin hormone receptors are not expressed at high levels in the uterus. Toward the end of pregnancy, the synthesis of oxytocin receptors in the uterus increases, and the smooth muscle cells of the uterus become more sensitive to its effects. Oxytocin is continually released throughout childbirth through a positive feedback mechanism. As noted earlier, oxytocin prompts uterine contractions that push the fetal head toward the cervix. In response, cervical stretching stimulates additional oxytocin to be synthesized by the hypothalamus and released from the pituitary. This increases the intensity and effectiveness of uterine contractions and prompts additional dilation of the cervix. The feedback loop continues until birth.

Although the mother's high blood levels of oxytocin begin to decrease immediately following birth, oxytocin continues to play a role in maternal and newborn health. First, oxytocin is necessary for the milk ejection reflex (commonly referred to as "let-down") in breastfeeding women. As the newborn begins suckling, sensory receptors in the nipples transmit signals to the hypothalamus. In response, oxytocin is secreted and released into the bloodstream. Within seconds, cells in the mother's milk ducts contract, ejecting milk into the infant's mouth. Secondly, in both males and females, oxytocin is thought to contribute to parent–newborn bonding, known as attachment. Oxytocin is also thought to be involved in feelings of love and closeness, as well as in the sexual response.

Antidiuretic Hormone (ADH)

The solute concentration of the blood, or blood osmolarity, may change in response to the consumption of certain foods and fluids, as well as in response to disease, injury, medications, or other factors. Blood osmolarity is constantly monitored by **osmoreceptors**—specialized cells within the hypothalamus that are particularly sensitive to the concentration of sodium ions and other solutes.

In response to high blood osmolarity, which can occur during dehydration or following a very salty meal, the osmoreceptors signal the posterior pituitary to release **antidiuretic hormone (ADH)**. The target cells of ADH are located in the tubular cells of the kidneys. Its effect is to increase epithelial permeability to water, allowing increased water reabsorption. The more water reabsorbed from the filtrate, the greater the amount of water that is returned to the blood and the less that is excreted in the urine. A greater concentration of water results in a reduced concentration of solutes. ADH is also known as vasopressin because, in very high concentrations, it causes constriction of blood vessels, which increases blood pressure by increasing peripheral resistance. The release of ADH is controlled by a negative feedback loop. As blood osmolarity decreases, the hypothalamic osmoreceptors sense the change and prompt a corresponding decrease in the secretion of ADH. As a result, less water is reabsorbed from the urine filtrate.

Interestingly, drugs can affect the secretion of ADH. For example, alcohol consumption inhibits the release of ADH, resulting in increased urine production that can eventually lead to dehydration and a hangover. A disease called diabetes insipidus is characterized by chronic underproduction of ADH that causes chronic dehydration. Because little ADH is produced and secreted, not enough water is reabsorbed by the kidneys. Although patients feel thirsty, and increase their fluid consumption, this doesn't effectively decrease the solute concentration in their blood because ADH levels are not high enough to trigger water reabsorption in the kidneys. Electrolyte imbalances can occur in severe cases of diabetes insipidus.

Anterior Pituitary

The anterior pituitary originates from the digestive tract in the embryo and migrates toward the brain during fetal development. There are three regions: the pars distalis is the most anterior, the pars intermedia is adjacent to the posterior pituitary, and the pars tuberalis is a slender "tube" that wraps the infundibulum.

Recall that the posterior pituitary does not synthesize hormones, but merely stores them. In contrast, the anterior pituitary does manufacture hormones. However, the secretion of hormones from the anterior pituitary is regulated by two classes of hormones. These hormones—secreted by the hypothalamus—are the releasing hormones that stimulate the secretion of hormones from the anterior pituitary and the inhibiting hormones that inhibit secretion.

Hypothalamic hormones are secreted by neurons, but enter the anterior pituitary through blood vessels (Figure 17.9). Within the infundibulum is a bridge of capillaries that connects the hypothalamus to the anterior pituitary. This network, called the **hypophyseal portal system**, allows hypothalamic hormones to be transported to the anterior pituitary without first entering the systemic circulation. The system originates from the superior hypophyseal artery, which branches off the carotid arteries and transports blood to the hypothalamus. The branches of the superior hypophyseal artery form the hypophyseal portal system (see Figure 17.9). Hypothalamic releasing and inhibiting hormones travel through a primary capillary plexus to the portal veins, which carry them into the anterior pituitary. Hormones produced by the anterior pituitary (in response to releasing hormones) enter a secondary capillary plexus, and from there drain into the circulation.

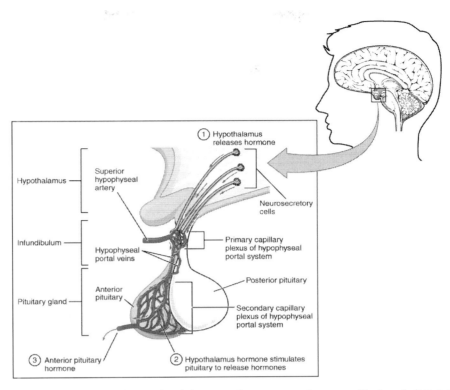

Figure 17.9 Anterior Pituitary The anterior pituitary manufactures seven hormones. The hypothalamus produces separate hormones that stimulate or inhibit hormone production in the anterior pituitary. Hormones from the hypothalamus reach the anterior pituitary via the hypophyseal portal system.

The anterior pituitary produces seven hormones. These are the growth hormone (GH), thyroid-stimulating hormone (TSH), adrenocorticotropic hormone (ACTH), follicle-stimulating hormone (FSH), luteinizing hormone (LH), beta endorphin, and prolactin. Of the hormones of the anterior pituitary, TSH, ACTH, FSH, and LH are collectively referred to as tropic hormones (trope- = "turning") because they turn on or off the function of other endocrine glands.

Growth Hormone

The endocrine system regulates the growth of the human body, protein synthesis, and cellular replication. A major hormone involved in this process is **growth hormone (GH)**, also called somatotropin—a protein hormone produced and secreted by the anterior pituitary gland. Its primary function is anabolic; it promotes protein synthesis and tissue building through direct and indirect mechanisms (Figure 17.10). GH levels are controlled by the release of GHRH and GHIH (also known as somatostatin) from the hypothalamus.

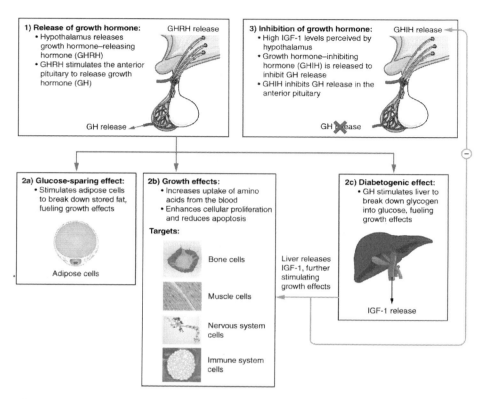

Figure 17.10 Hormonal Regulation of Growth Growth hormone (GH) directly accelerates the rate of protein synthesis in skeletal muscle and bones. Insulin-like growth factor 1 (IGF-1) is activated by growth hormone and indirectly supports the formation of new proteins in muscle cells and bone.

A glucose-sparing effect occurs when GH stimulates lipolysis, or the breakdown of adipose tissue, releasing fatty acids into the blood. As a result, many tissues switch from glucose to fatty acids as their main energy source, which means that less glucose is taken up from the bloodstream.

GH also initiates the diabetogenic effect in which GH stimulates the liver to break down glycogen to glucose, which is then deposited into the blood. The name "diabetogenic" is derived from the similarity in elevated blood glucose levels observed between individuals with untreated diabetes mellitus and individuals experiencing GH excess. Blood glucose levels rise as the result of a combination of glucose-sparing and diabetogenic effects.

GH indirectly mediates growth and protein synthesis by triggering the liver and other tissues to produce a group of proteins called **insulin-like growth factors (IGFs)**. These proteins enhance cellular proliferation and inhibit apoptosis, or programmed cell death. IGFs stimulate cells to increase their uptake of amino acids from the blood for protein synthesis. Skeletal muscle and cartilage cells are particularly sensitive to stimulation from IGFs.

Dysfunction of the endocrine system's control of growth can result in several disorders. For example, **gigantism** is a disorder in children that is caused by the secretion of abnormally large amounts of GH, resulting in excessive growth. A similar condition in adults is **acromegaly**, a disorder that results in the growth of bones in the face, hands, and feet in response to excessive levels of GH in individuals who have stopped growing. Abnormally low levels of GH in children can cause growth impairment—a disorder called **pituitary dwarfism** (also known as growth hormone deficiency).

Thyroid-Stimulating Hormone

The activity of the thyroid gland is regulated by **thyroid-stimulating hormone (TSH)**, also called thyrotropin. TSH is released from the anterior pituitary in response to thyrotropin-releasing hormone (TRH) from the hypothalamus. As discussed shortly, it triggers the secretion of thyroid hormones by the thyroid gland. In a classic negative feedback loop, elevated levels of thyroid hormones in the bloodstream then trigger a drop in production of TRH and subsequently TSH.

Adrenocorticotropic Hormone

The **adrenocorticotropic hormone (ACTH)**, also called corticotropin, stimulates the adrenal cortex (the more superficial "bark" of the adrenal glands) to secrete corticosteroid hormones such as cortisol. ACTH come from a precursor molecule known as pro-opiomelanotropin (POMC) which produces several biologically active molecules when cleaved, including ACTH, melanocyte-stimulating hormone, and the brain opioid peptides known as endorphins.

The release of ACTH is regulated by the corticotropin-releasing hormone (CRH) from the hypothalamus in response to normal physiologic rhythms. A variety of stressors can also influence its release, and the role of ACTH in the stress response is discussed later in this chapter.

Follicle-Stimulating Hormone and Luteinizing Hormone

The endocrine glands secrete a variety of hormones that control the development and regulation of the reproductive system (these glands include the anterior pituitary, the adrenal cortex, and the gonads—the testes in males and the ovaries in females). Much of the development of the reproductive system occurs during puberty and is marked by the development of sex-specific characteristics in both male and female adolescents. Puberty is initiated by gonadotropin-releasing hormone (GnRH), a hormone produced and secreted by the hypothalamus. GnRH stimulates the anterior pituitary to secrete **gonadotropins**—hormones that regulate the function of the gonads. The levels of GnRH are regulated through a negative feedback loop; high levels of reproductive hormones inhibit the release of GnRH. Throughout life, gonadotropins regulate reproductive function and, in the case of women, the onset and cessation of reproductive capacity.

The gonadotropins include two glycoprotein hormones: **follicle-stimulating hormone (FSH)** stimulates the production and maturation of sex cells, or gametes, including ova in women and sperm in men. FSH also promotes follicular growth; these follicles then release estrogens in the female ovaries. **Luteinizing hormone (LH)** triggers ovulation in women, as well as the production of estrogens and progesterone by the ovaries. LH stimulates production of testosterone by the male testes.

Prolactin

As its name implies, **prolactin (PRL)** promotes lactation (milk production) in women. During pregnancy, it contributes to development of the mammary glands, and after birth, it stimulates the mammary glands to produce breast milk. However, the effects of prolactin depend heavily upon the permissive effects of estrogens, progesterone, and other hormones. And as noted earlier, the let-down of milk occurs in response to stimulation from oxytocin.

In a non-pregnant woman, prolactin secretion is inhibited by prolactin-inhibiting hormone (PIH), which is actually the neurotransmitter dopamine, and is released from neurons in the hypothalamus. Only during pregnancy do prolactin levels rise in response to prolactin-releasing hormone (PRH) from the hypothalamus.

Intermediate Pituitary: Melanocyte-Stimulating Hormone

The cells in the zone between the pituitary lobes secrete a hormone known as melanocyte-stimulating hormone (MSH) that is formed by cleavage of the pro-opiomelanocortin (POMC) precursor protein. Local production of MSH in the skin is responsible for melanin production in response to UV light exposure. The role of MSH made by the pituitary is more complicated. For instance, people with lighter skin generally have the same amount of MSH as people with darker skin. Nevertheless, this hormone is capable of darkening of the skin by inducing melanin production in the skin's melanocytes. Women also show increased MSH production during pregnancy; in combination with estrogens, it can lead to darker skin pigmentation, especially the skin of the areolas and labia minora. Figure 17.11 is a summary of the pituitary hormones and their principal effects.

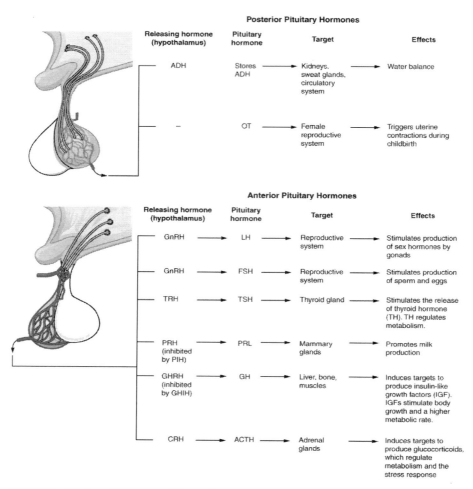

Figure 17.11 Major Pituitary Hormones Major pituitary hormones and their target organs.

Visit this link (http://openstaxcollege.org/l/roleofhypo) to watch an animation showing the role of the hypothalamus and the pituitary gland. Which hormone is released by the pituitary to stimulate the thyroid gland?

17.4 | The Thyroid Gland

By the end of this section, you will be able to:
- Describe the location and anatomy of the thyroid gland
- Discuss the synthesis of triiodothyronine and thyroxine
- Explain the role of thyroid hormones in the regulation of basal metabolism
- Identify the hormone produced by the parafollicular cells of the thyroid

A butterfly-shaped organ, the **thyroid gland** is located anterior to the trachea, just inferior to the larynx (Figure 17.12). The medial region, called the isthmus, is flanked by wing-shaped left and right lobes. Each of the thyroid lobes are embedded with parathyroid glands, primarily on their posterior surfaces. The tissue of the thyroid gland is composed mostly of thyroid follicles. The follicles are made up of a central cavity filled with a sticky fluid called **colloid**. Surrounded by a wall of epithelial follicle cells, the colloid is the center of thyroid hormone production, and that production is dependent on the hormones' essential and unique component: iodine.

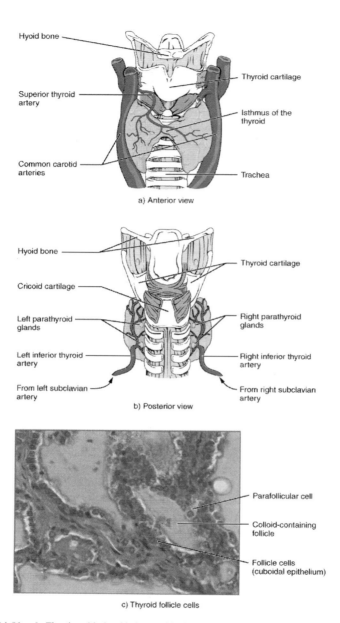

Figure 17.12 Thyroid Gland The thyroid gland is located in the neck where it wraps around the trachea. (a) Anterior view of the thyroid gland. (b) Posterior view of the thyroid gland. (c) The glandular tissue is composed primarily of thyroid follicles. The larger parafollicular cells often appear within the matrix of follicle cells. LM × 1332. (Micrograph provided by the Regents of University of Michigan Medical School © 2012)

Synthesis and Release of Thyroid Hormones

Hormones are produced in the colloid when atoms of the mineral iodine attach to a glycoprotein, called thyroglobulin, that is secreted into the colloid by the follicle cells. The following steps outline the hormones' assembly:

1. Binding of TSH to its receptors in the follicle cells of the thyroid gland causes the cells to actively transport iodide ions (I^-) across their cell membrane, from the bloodstream into the cytosol. As a result, the concentration of iodide ions "trapped" in the follicular cells is many times higher than the concentration in the bloodstream.
2. Iodide ions then move to the lumen of the follicle cells that border the colloid. There, the ions undergo oxidation (their negatively charged electrons are removed). The oxidation of two iodide ions ($2\ I^-$) results in iodine (I_2), which passes through the follicle cell membrane into the colloid.
3. In the colloid, peroxidase enzymes link the iodine to the tyrosine amino acids in thyroglobulin to produce two intermediaries: a tyrosine attached to one iodine and a tyrosine attached to two iodines. When one of each of these intermediaries is linked by covalent bonds, the resulting compound is **triiodothyronine** (T_3), a thyroid hormone with three iodines. Much more commonly, two copies of the second intermediary bond, forming tetraiodothyronine, also known as **thyroxine** (T_4), a thyroid hormone with four iodines.

These hormones remain in the colloid center of the thyroid follicles until TSH stimulates endocytosis of colloid back into the follicle cells. There, lysosomal enzymes break apart the thyroglobulin colloid, releasing free T_3 and T_4, which diffuse across the follicle cell membrane and enter the bloodstream.

In the bloodstream, less than one percent of the circulating T_3 and T_4 remains unbound. This free T_3 and T_4 can cross the lipid bilayer of cell membranes and be taken up by cells. The remaining 99 percent of circulating T_3 and T_4 is bound to specialized transport proteins called thyroxine-binding globulins (TBGs), to albumin, or to other plasma proteins. This "packaging" prevents their free diffusion into body cells. When blood levels of T_3 and T_4 begin to decline, bound T_3 and T_4 are released from these plasma proteins and readily cross the membrane of target cells. T_3 is more potent than T_4, and many cells convert T_4 to T_3 through the removal of an iodine atom.

Regulation of TH Synthesis

The release of T_3 and T_4 from the thyroid gland is regulated by thyroid-stimulating hormone (TSH). As shown in Figure 17.13, low blood levels of T_3 and T_4 stimulate the release of thyrotropin-releasing hormone (TRH) from the hypothalamus, which triggers secretion of TSH from the anterior pituitary. In turn, TSH stimulates the thyroid gland to secrete T_3 and T_4. The levels of TRH, TSH, T_3, and T_4 are regulated by a negative feedback system in which increasing levels of T_3 and T_4 decrease the production and secretion of TSH.

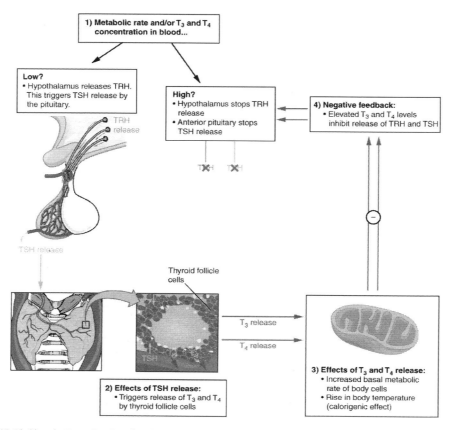

Figure 17.13 Classic Negative Feedback Loop A classic negative feedback loop controls the regulation of thyroid hormone levels.

Functions of Thyroid Hormones

The thyroid hormones, T_3 and T_4, are often referred to as metabolic hormones because their levels influence the body's basal metabolic rate, the amount of energy used by the body at rest. When T_3 and T_4 bind to intracellular receptors located on the mitochondria, they cause an increase in nutrient breakdown and the use of oxygen to produce ATP. In addition, T_3 and T_4 initiate the transcription of genes involved in glucose oxidation. Although these mechanisms prompt cells to produce more ATP, the process is inefficient, and an abnormally increased level of heat is released as a byproduct of these reactions. This so-called calorigenic effect (calor- = "heat") raises body temperature.

Adequate levels of thyroid hormones are also required for protein synthesis and for fetal and childhood tissue development and growth. They are especially critical for normal development of the nervous system both in utero and in early childhood, and they continue to support neurological function in adults. As noted earlier, these thyroid hormones have a complex interrelationship with reproductive hormones, and deficiencies can influence libido, fertility, and other aspects of reproductive function. Finally, thyroid hormones increase the body's sensitivity to catecholamines (epinephrine and norepinephrine) from the adrenal medulla by upregulation of receptors in the blood vessels. When levels of T_3 and T_4 hormones are excessive, this effect accelerates the heart rate, strengthens the heartbeat, and increases blood pressure. Because thyroid hormones regulate metabolism, heat production, protein synthesis, and many other body functions, thyroid disorders can have severe and widespread consequences.

Endocrine System: Iodine Deficiency, Hypothyroidism, and Hyperthyroidism

As discussed above, dietary iodine is required for the synthesis of T_3 and T_4. But for much of the world's population, foods do not provide adequate levels of this mineral, because the amount varies according to the level in the soil in which the food was grown, as well as the irrigation and fertilizers used. Marine fish and shrimp tend to have high levels because they concentrate iodine from seawater, but many people in landlocked regions lack access to seafood. Thus, the primary source of dietary iodine in many countries is iodized salt. Fortification of salt with iodine began in the United States in 1924, and international efforts to iodize salt in the world's poorest nations continue today.

Dietary iodine deficiency can result in the impaired ability to synthesize T_3 and T_4, leading to a variety of severe disorders. When T_3 and T_4 cannot be produced, TSH is secreted in increasing amounts. As a result of this hyperstimulation, thyroglobulin accumulates in the thyroid gland follicles, increasing their deposits of colloid. The accumulation of colloid increases the overall size of the thyroid gland, a condition called a **goiter** (Figure 17.14). A goiter is only a visible indication of the deficiency. Other iodine deficiency disorders include impaired growth and development, decreased fertility, and prenatal and infant death. Moreover, iodine deficiency is the primary cause of preventable mental retardation worldwide. **Neonatal hypothyroidism** (cretinism) is characterized by cognitive deficits, short stature, and sometimes deafness and muteness in children and adults born to mothers who were iodine-deficient during pregnancy.

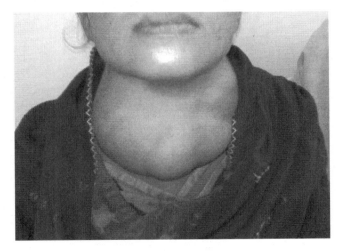

Figure 17.14 Goiter (credit: "Almazi"/Wikimedia Commons)

In areas of the world with access to iodized salt, dietary deficiency is rare. Instead, inflammation of the thyroid gland is the more common cause of low blood levels of thyroid hormones. Called **hypothyroidism**, the condition is characterized by a low metabolic rate, weight gain, cold extremities, constipation, reduced libido, menstrual irregularities, and reduced mental activity. In contrast, **hyperthyroidism**—an abnormally elevated blood level of thyroid hormones—is often caused by a pituitary or thyroid tumor. In Graves' disease, the hyperthyroid state results from an autoimmune reaction in which antibodies overstimulate the follicle cells of the thyroid gland. Hyperthyroidism can lead to an increased metabolic rate, excessive body heat and sweating, diarrhea, weight loss, tremors, and increased heart rate. The person's eyes may bulge (called exophthalmos) as antibodies produce inflammation in the soft tissues of the orbits. The person may also develop a goiter.

Calcitonin

The thyroid gland also secretes a hormone called **calcitonin** that is produced by the parafollicular cells (also called C cells) that stud the tissue between distinct follicles. Calcitonin is released in response to a rise in blood calcium levels. It appears to have a function in decreasing blood calcium concentrations by:

- Inhibiting the activity of osteoclasts, bone cells that release calcium into the circulation by degrading bone matrix
- Increasing osteoblastic activity
- Decreasing calcium absorption in the intestines
- Increasing calcium loss in the urine

However, these functions are usually not significant in maintaining calcium homeostasis, so the importance of calcitonin is not entirely understood. Pharmaceutical preparations of calcitonin are sometimes prescribed to reduce osteoclast activity in people with osteoporosis and to reduce the degradation of cartilage in people with osteoarthritis. The hormones secreted by thyroid are summarized in Table 17.4.

Thyroid Hormones

Associated hormones	Chemical class	Effect
Thyroxine (T$_4$), triiodothyronine (T$_3$)	Amine	Stimulate basal metabolic rate
Calcitonin	Peptide	Reduces blood Ca^{2+} levels

Table 17.4

Of course, calcium is critical for many other biological processes. It is a second messenger in many signaling pathways, and is essential for muscle contraction, nerve impulse transmission, and blood clotting. Given these roles, it is not surprising that blood calcium levels are tightly regulated by the endocrine system. The organs involved in the regulation are the parathyroid glands.

17.5 | The Parathyroid Glands

By the end of this section, you will be able to:

- Describe the location and structure of the parathyroid glands
- Describe the hormonal control of blood calcium levels
- Discuss the physiological response of parathyroid dysfunction

The **parathyroid glands** are tiny, round structures usually found embedded in the posterior surface of the thyroid gland (Figure 17.15). A thick connective tissue capsule separates the glands from the thyroid tissue. Most people have four parathyroid glands, but occasionally there are more in tissues of the neck or chest. The function of one type of parathyroid cells, the oxyphil cells, is not clear. The primary functional cells of the parathyroid glands are the chief cells. These epithelial cells produce and secrete the **parathyroid hormone (PTH)**, the major hormone involved in the regulation of blood calcium levels.

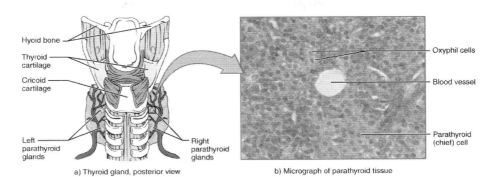

Figure 17.15 Parathyroid Glands The small parathyroid glands are embedded in the posterior surface of the thyroid gland. LM × 760. (Micrograph provided by the Regents of University of Michigan Medical School © 2012)

View the University of Michigan WebScope at http://141.214.65.171/Histology/Endocrine%20System/217_HISTO_40X.svs/view.apml (http://openstaxcollege.org/l/parathyroid) to explore the tissue sample in greater detail.

The parathyroid glands produce and secrete PTH, a peptide hormone, in response to low blood calcium levels (Figure 17.16). PTH secretion causes the release of calcium from the bones by stimulating osteoclasts, which secrete enzymes that degrade bone and release calcium into the interstitial fluid. PTH also inhibits osteoblasts, the cells involved in bone deposition, thereby sparing blood calcium. PTH causes increased reabsorption of calcium (and magnesium) in the kidney tubules from the urine filtrate. In addition, PTH initiates the production of the steroid hormone calcitriol (also known as 1,25-dihydroxyvitamin D), which is the active form of vitamin D_3, in the kidneys. Calcitriol then stimulates increased absorption of dietary calcium by the intestines. A negative feedback loop regulates the levels of PTH, with rising blood calcium levels inhibiting further release of PTH.

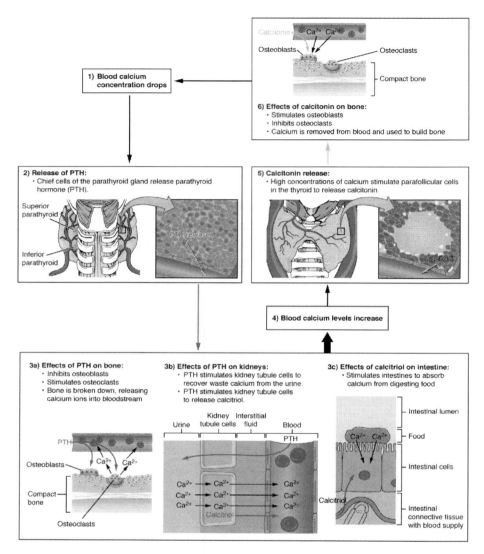

Figure 17.16 Parathyroid Hormone in Maintaining Blood Calcium Homeostasis Parathyroid hormone increases blood calcium levels when they drop too low. Conversely, calcitonin, which is released from the thyroid gland, decreases blood calcium levels when they become too high. These two mechanisms constantly maintain blood calcium concentration at homeostasis.

Abnormally high activity of the parathyroid gland can cause **hyperparathyroidism**, a disorder caused by an overproduction of PTH that results in excessive calcium reabsorption from bone. Hyperparathyroidism can significantly decrease bone density, leading to spontaneous fractures or deformities. As blood calcium levels rise, cell membrane permeability to sodium is decreased, and the responsiveness of the nervous system is reduced. At the same time, calcium deposits may collect in the body's tissues and organs, impairing their functioning.

In contrast, abnormally low blood calcium levels may be caused by parathyroid hormone deficiency, called **hypoparathyroidism**, which may develop following injury or surgery involving the thyroid gland. Low blood calcium increases membrane permeability to sodium, resulting in muscle twitching, cramping, spasms, or convulsions. Severe deficits can paralyze muscles, including those involved in breathing, and can be fatal.

When blood calcium levels are high, calcitonin is produced and secreted by the parafollicular cells of the thyroid gland. As discussed earlier, calcitonin inhibits the activity of osteoclasts, reduces the absorption of dietary calcium in the intestine, and signals the kidneys to reabsorb less calcium, resulting in larger amounts of calcium excreted in the urine.

17.6 | The Adrenal Glands

By the end of this section, you will be able to:
- Describe the location and structure of the adrenal glands
- Identify the hormones produced by the adrenal cortex and adrenal medulla, and summarize their target cells and effects

The **adrenal glands** are wedges of glandular and neuroendocrine tissue adhering to the top of the kidneys by a fibrous capsule (Figure 17.17). The adrenal glands have a rich blood supply and experience one of the highest rates of blood flow in the body. They are served by several arteries branching off the aorta, including the suprarenal and renal arteries. Blood flows to each adrenal gland at the adrenal cortex and then drains into the adrenal medulla. Adrenal hormones are released into the circulation via the left and right suprarenal veins.

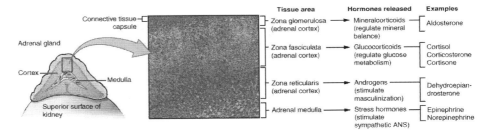

Figure 17.17 Adrenal Glands Both adrenal glands sit atop the kidneys and are composed of an outer cortex and an inner medulla, all surrounded by a connective tissue capsule. The cortex can be subdivided into additional zones, all of which produce different types of hormones. LM × 204. (Micrograph provided by the Regents of University of Michigan Medical School © 2012)

View the University of Michigan WebScope at http://141.214.65.171/Histology/Endocrine%20System/New%20Scans/230_HISTO_40x.svs/view.apml (http://openstaxcollege.org/l/adrenal) to explore the tissue sample in greater detail.

The adrenal gland consists of an outer cortex of glandular tissue and an inner medulla of nervous tissue. The cortex itself is divided into three zones: the **zona glomerulosa**, the **zona fasciculata**, and the **zona reticularis**. Each region secretes its own set of hormones.

The **adrenal cortex**, as a component of the hypothalamic-pituitary-adrenal (HPA) axis, secretes steroid hormones important for the regulation of the long-term stress response, blood pressure and blood volume, nutrient uptake and storage, fluid and electrolyte balance, and inflammation. The HPA axis involves the stimulation of hormone release of adrenocorticotropic hormone (ACTH) from the pituitary by the hypothalamus. ACTH then stimulates the adrenal cortex to produce the hormone cortisol. This pathway will be discussed in more detail below.

The **adrenal medulla** is neuroendocrine tissue composed of postganglionic sympathetic nervous system (SNS) neurons. It is really an extension of the autonomic nervous system, which regulates homeostasis in the body. The sympathomedullary (SAM) pathway involves the stimulation of the medulla by impulses from the hypothalamus via neurons from the thoracic spinal cord. The medulla is stimulated to secrete the amine hormones epinephrine and norepinephrine.

One of the major functions of the adrenal gland is to respond to stress. Stress can be either physical or psychological or both. Physical stresses include exposing the body to injury, walking outside in cold and wet conditions without a coat on, or malnutrition. Psychological stresses include the perception of a physical threat, a fight with a loved one, or just a bad day at school.

The body responds in different ways to short-term stress and long-term stress following a pattern known as the **general adaptation syndrome (GAS)**. Stage one of GAS is called the **alarm reaction**. This is short-term stress, the fight-or-flight response, mediated by the hormones epinephrine and norepinephrine from the adrenal medulla via the SAM pathway. Their function is to prepare the body for extreme physical exertion. Once this stress is relieved, the body quickly returns to normal. The section on the adrenal medulla covers this response in more detail.

If the stress is not soon relieved, the body adapts to the stress in the second stage called the **stage of resistance**. If a person is starving for example, the body may send signals to the gastrointestinal tract to maximize the absorption of nutrients from food.

If the stress continues for a longer term however, the body responds with symptoms quite different than the fight-or-flight response. During the **stage of exhaustion**, individuals may begin to suffer depression, the suppression of their immune response, severe fatigue, or even a fatal heart attack. These symptoms are mediated by the hormones of the adrenal cortex, especially cortisol, released as a result of signals from the HPA axis.

Adrenal hormones also have several non–stress-related functions, including the increase of blood sodium and glucose levels, which will be described in detail below.

Adrenal Cortex

The adrenal cortex consists of multiple layers of lipid-storing cells that occur in three structurally distinct regions. Each of these regions produces different hormones.

Visit this link (http://openstaxcollege.org/l/adrenalglands) to view an animation describing the location and function of the adrenal glands. Which hormone produced by the adrenal glands is responsible for the mobilization of energy stores?

Chapter 17 | The Endocrine System

Hormones of the Zona Glomerulosa

The most superficial region of the adrenal cortex is the zona glomerulosa, which produces a group of hormones collectively referred to as **mineralocorticoids** because of their effect on body minerals, especially sodium and potassium. These hormones are essential for fluid and electrolyte balance.

Aldosterone is the major mineralocorticoid. It is important in the regulation of the concentration of sodium and potassium ions in urine, sweat, and saliva. For example, it is released in response to elevated blood K^+, low blood Na^+, low blood pressure, or low blood volume. In response, aldosterone increases the excretion of K^+ and the retention of Na^+, which in turn increases blood volume and blood pressure. Its secretion is prompted when CRH from the hypothalamus triggers ACTH release from the anterior pituitary.

Aldosterone is also a key component of the renin-angiotensin-aldosterone system (RAAS) in which specialized cells of the kidneys secrete the enzyme renin in response to low blood volume or low blood pressure. Renin then catalyzes the conversion of the blood protein angiotensinogen, produced by the liver, to the hormone angiotensin I. Angiotensin I is converted in the lungs to angiotensin II by **angiotensin-converting enzyme** (ACE). Angiotensin II has three major functions:

1. Initiating vasoconstriction of the arterioles, decreasing blood flow
2. Stimulating kidney tubules to reabsorb NaCl and water, increasing blood volume
3. Signaling the adrenal cortex to secrete aldosterone, the effects of which further contribute to fluid retention, restoring blood pressure and blood volume

For individuals with hypertension, or high blood pressure, drugs are available that block the production of angiotensin II. These drugs, known as ACE inhibitors, block the ACE enzyme from converting angiotensin I to angiotensin II, thus mitigating the latter's ability to increase blood pressure.

Hormones of the Zona Fasciculata

The intermediate region of the adrenal cortex is the zona fasciculata, named as such because the cells form small fascicles (bundles) separated by tiny blood vessels. The cells of the zona fasciculata produce hormones called **glucocorticoids** because of their role in glucose metabolism. The most important of these is **cortisol**, some of which the liver converts to cortisone. A glucocorticoid produced in much smaller amounts is corticosterone. In response to long-term stressors, the hypothalamus secretes CRH, which in turn triggers the release of ACTH by the anterior pituitary. ACTH triggers the release of the glucocorticoids. Their overall effect is to inhibit tissue building while stimulating the breakdown of stored nutrients to maintain adequate fuel supplies. In conditions of long-term stress, for example, cortisol promotes the catabolism of glycogen to glucose, the catabolism of stored triglycerides into fatty acids and glycerol, and the catabolism of muscle proteins into amino acids. These raw materials can then be used to synthesize additional glucose and ketones for use as body fuels. The hippocampus, which is part of the temporal lobe of the cerebral cortices and important in memory formation, is highly sensitive to stress levels because of its many glucocorticoid receptors.

You are probably familiar with prescription and over-the-counter medications containing glucocorticoids, such as cortisone injections into inflamed joints, prednisone tablets and steroid-based inhalers used to manage severe asthma, and hydrocortisone creams applied to relieve itchy skin rashes. These drugs reflect another role of cortisol—the downregulation of the immune system, which inhibits the inflammatory response.

Hormones of the Zona Reticularis

The deepest region of the adrenal cortex is the zona reticularis, which produces small amounts of a class of steroid sex hormones called androgens. During puberty and most of adulthood, androgens are produced in the gonads. The androgens produced in the zona reticularis supplement the gonadal androgens. They are produced in response to ACTH from the anterior pituitary and are converted in the tissues to testosterone or estrogens. In adult women, they may contribute to the sex drive, but their function in adult men is not well understood. In post-menopausal women, as the functions of the ovaries decline, the main source of estrogens becomes the androgens produced by the zona reticularis.

Adrenal Medulla

As noted earlier, the adrenal cortex releases glucocorticoids in response to long-term stress such as severe illness. In contrast, the adrenal medulla releases its hormones in response to acute, short-term stress mediated by the sympathetic nervous system (SNS).

The medullary tissue is composed of unique postganglionic SNS neurons called **chromaffin** cells, which are large and irregularly shaped, and produce the neurotransmitters **epinephrine** (also called adrenaline) and **norepinephrine** (or noradrenaline). Epinephrine is produced in greater quantities—approximately a 4 to 1 ratio with norepinephrine—and is the more powerful hormone. Because the chromaffin cells release epinephrine and norepinephrine into the systemic circulation, where they travel widely and exert effects on distant cells, they are considered hormones. Derived from the amino acid tyrosine, they are chemically classified as catecholamines.

The secretion of medullary epinephrine and norepinephrine is controlled by a neural pathway that originates from the hypothalamus in response to danger or stress (the SAM pathway). Both epinephrine and norepinephrine signal the liver and skeletal muscle cells to convert glycogen into glucose, resulting in increased blood glucose levels. These hormones increase the heart rate, pulse, and blood pressure to prepare the body to fight the perceived threat or flee from it. In addition, the pathway dilates the airways, raising blood oxygen levels. It also prompts vasodilation, further increasing the oxygenation of important organs such as the lungs, brain, heart, and skeletal muscle. At the same time, it triggers vasoconstriction to blood vessels serving less essential organs such as the gastrointestinal tract, kidneys, and skin, and downregulates some components of the immune system. Other effects include a dry mouth, loss of appetite, pupil dilation, and a loss of peripheral vision. The major hormones of the adrenal glands are summarized in Table 17.5.

Hormones of the Adrenal Glands

Adrenal gland	Associated hormones	Chemical class	Effect
Adrenal cortex	Aldosterone	Steroid	Increases blood Na^+ levels
Adrenal cortex	Cortisol, corticosterone, cortisone	Steroid	Increase blood glucose levels
Adrenal medulla	Epinephrine, norepinephrine	Amine	Stimulate fight-or-flight response

Table 17.5

Disorders Involving the Adrenal Glands

Several disorders are caused by the dysregulation of the hormones produced by the adrenal glands. For example, Cushing's disease is a disorder characterized by high blood glucose levels and the accumulation of lipid deposits on the face and neck. It is caused by hypersecretion of cortisol. The most common source of Cushing's disease is a pituitary tumor that secretes cortisol or ACTH in abnormally high amounts. Other common signs of Cushing's disease include the development of a moon-shaped face, a buffalo hump on the back of the neck, rapid weight gain, and hair loss. Chronically elevated glucose levels are also associated with an elevated risk of developing type 2 diabetes. In addition to hyperglycemia, chronically elevated glucocorticoids compromise immunity, resistance to infection, and memory, and can result in rapid weight gain and hair loss.

In contrast, the hyposecretion of corticosteroids can result in Addison's disease, a rare disorder that causes low blood glucose levels and low blood sodium levels. The signs and symptoms of Addison's disease are vague and are typical of other disorders as well, making diagnosis difficult. They may include general weakness, abdominal pain, weight loss, nausea, vomiting, sweating, and cravings for salty food.

17.7 | The Pineal Gland

By the end of this section, you will be able to:
- Describe the location and structure of the pineal gland
- Discuss the function of melatonin

Recall that the hypothalamus, part of the diencephalon of the brain, sits inferior and somewhat anterior to the thalamus. Inferior but somewhat posterior to the thalamus is the **pineal gland**, a tiny endocrine gland whose functions are not entirely clear. The **pinealocyte** cells that make up the pineal gland are known to produce and secrete the amine hormone **melatonin**, which is derived from serotonin.

The secretion of melatonin varies according to the level of light received from the environment. When photons of light stimulate the retinas of the eyes, a nerve impulse is sent to a region of the hypothalamus called the suprachiasmatic nucleus (SCN), which is important in regulating biological rhythms. From the SCN, the nerve signal is carried to the spinal cord and eventually to the pineal gland, where the production of melatonin is inhibited. As a result, blood levels of melatonin fall, promoting wakefulness. In contrast, as light levels decline—such as during the evening—melatonin production increases, boosting blood levels and causing drowsiness.

Visit this link (http://openstaxcollege.org/l/melatonin) to view an animation describing the function of the hormone melatonin. What should you avoid doing in the middle of your sleep cycle that would lower melatonin?

The secretion of melatonin may influence the body's circadian rhythms, the dark-light fluctuations that affect not only sleepiness and wakefulness, but also appetite and body temperature. Interestingly, children have higher melatonin levels than adults, which may prevent the release of gonadotropins from the anterior pituitary, thereby inhibiting the onset of puberty. Finally, an antioxidant role of melatonin is the subject of current research.

Jet lag occurs when a person travels across several time zones and feels sleepy during the day or wakeful at night. Traveling across multiple time zones significantly disturbs the light-dark cycle regulated by melatonin. It can take up to several days for melatonin synthesis to adjust to the light-dark patterns in the new environment, resulting in jet lag. Some air travelers take melatonin supplements to induce sleep.

17.8 | Gonadal and Placental Hormones

By the end of this section, you will be able to:
- Identify the most important hormones produced by the testes and ovaries
- Name the hormones produced by the placenta and state their functions

This section briefly discusses the hormonal role of the gonads—the male testes and female ovaries—which produce the sex cells (sperm and ova) and secrete the gonadal hormones. The roles of the gonadotropins released from the anterior pituitary (FSH and LH) were discussed earlier.

The primary hormone produced by the male testes is **testosterone**, a steroid hormone important in the development of the male reproductive system, the maturation of sperm cells, and the development of male secondary sex characteristics such as a deepened voice, body hair, and increased muscle mass. Interestingly, testosterone is also produced in the female ovaries, but at a much reduced level. In addition, the testes produce the peptide hormone **inhibin**, which inhibits the secretion of FSH from the anterior pituitary gland. FSH stimulates spermatogenesis.

The primary hormones produced by the ovaries are **estrogens**, which include estradiol, estriol, and estrone. Estrogens play an important role in a larger number of physiological processes, including the development of the female reproductive system, regulation of the menstrual cycle, the development of female secondary sex characteristics such as increased adipose tissue and the development of breast tissue, and the maintenance of pregnancy. Another significant ovarian hormone is **progesterone**, which contributes to regulation of the menstrual cycle and is important in preparing the body for pregnancy as well as maintaining pregnancy. In addition, the granulosa cells of the ovarian follicles produce inhibin, which—as in males—inhibits the secretion of FSH.During the initial stages of pregnancy, an organ called the placenta develops within the uterus. The placenta supplies oxygen and nutrients to the fetus, excretes waste products, and produces and secretes estrogens and progesterone. The placenta produces human chorionic gonadotropin (hCG) as well. The hCG hormone promotes progesterone synthesis and reduces the mother's immune function to protect the fetus from immune rejection. It also secretes human placental lactogen (hPL), which plays a role in preparing the breasts for lactation, and relaxin, which is thought to help soften and widen the pubic symphysis in preparation for childbirth. The hormones controlling reproduction are summarized in Table 17.6.

Reproductive Hormones

Gonad	Associated hormones	Chemical class	Effect
Testes	Testosterone	Steroid	Stimulates development of male secondary sex characteristics and sperm production
Testes	Inhibin	Protein	Inhibits FSH release from pituitary
Ovaries	Estrogens and progesterone	Steroid	Stimulate development of female secondary sex characteristics and prepare the body for childbirth
Placenta	Human chorionic gonadotropin	Protein	Promotes progesterone synthesis during pregnancy and inhibits immune response against fetus

Table 17.6

Everyday CONNECTION

Anabolic Steroids

The endocrine system can be exploited for illegal or unethical purposes. A prominent example of this is the use of steroid drugs by professional athletes.

Commonly used for performance enhancement, anabolic steroids are synthetic versions of the male sex hormone, testosterone. By boosting natural levels of this hormone, athletes experience increased muscle mass. Synthetic versions of human growth hormone are also used to build muscle mass.

The use of performance-enhancing drugs is banned by all major collegiate and professional sports organizations in the United States because they impart an unfair advantage to athletes who take them. In addition, the drugs can cause significant and dangerous side effects. For example, anabolic steroid use can increase cholesterol levels, raise blood pressure, and damage the liver. Altered testosterone levels (both too low or too high) have been implicated in causing structural damage to the heart, and increasing the risk for cardiac arrhythmias, heart attacks, congestive heart failure, and sudden death. Paradoxically, steroids can have a feminizing effect in males, including shriveled testicles and enlarged breast tissue. In females, their use can cause masculinizing effects such as an enlarged clitoris and growth of facial hair. In both sexes, their use can promote increased aggression (commonly known as "roid-rage"), depression, sleep disturbances, severe acne, and infertility.

17.9 | The Endocrine Pancreas

By the end of this section, you will be able to:
- Describe the location and structure of the pancreas, and the morphology and function of the pancreatic islets
- Compare and contrast the functions of insulin and glucagon

The **pancreas** is a long, slender organ, most of which is located posterior to the bottom half of the stomach (Figure 17.18). Although it is primarily an exocrine gland, secreting a variety of digestive enzymes, the pancreas has an endocrine function. Its **pancreatic islets**—clusters of cells formerly known as the islets of Langerhans—secrete the hormones glucagon, insulin, somatostatin, and pancreatic polypeptide (PP).

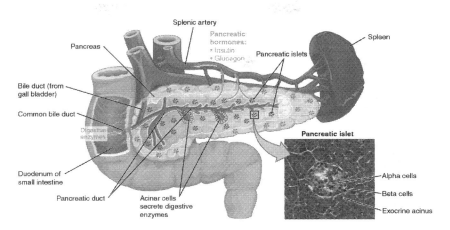

Figure 17.18 Pancreas The pancreatic exocrine function involves the acinar cells secreting digestive enzymes that are transported into the small intestine by the pancreatic duct. Its endocrine function involves the secretion of insulin (produced by beta cells) and glucagon (produced by alpha cells) within the pancreatic islets. These two hormones regulate the rate of glucose metabolism in the body. The micrograph reveals pancreatic islets. LM × 760. (Micrograph provided by the Regents of University of Michigan Medical School © 2012)

View the University of Michigan WebScope at http://141.214.65.171/Histology/Digestive%20System/Liver%20and%20Pancreas/188B_HISTO_40X.svs/view.apml (http://openstaxcollege.org/l/pancreaticislet) to explore the tissue sample in greater detail.

Cells and Secretions of the Pancreatic Islets

The pancreatic islets each contain four varieties of cells:

- The **alpha cell** produces the hormone glucagon and makes up approximately 20 percent of each islet. Glucagon plays an important role in blood glucose regulation; low blood glucose levels stimulate its release.
- The **beta cell** produces the hormone insulin and makes up approximately 75 percent of each islet. Elevated blood glucose levels stimulate the release of insulin.
- The **delta cell** accounts for four percent of the islet cells and secretes the peptide hormone somatostatin. Recall that somatostatin is also released by the hypothalamus (as GHIH), and the stomach and intestines also secrete it. An inhibiting hormone, pancreatic somatostatin inhibits the release of both glucagon and insulin.
- The **PP cell** accounts for about one percent of islet cells and secretes the pancreatic polypeptide hormone. It is thought to play a role in appetite, as well as in the regulation of pancreatic exocrine and endocrine secretions. Pancreatic polypeptide released following a meal may reduce further food consumption; however, it is also released in response to fasting.

Regulation of Blood Glucose Levels by Insulin and Glucagon

Glucose is required for cellular respiration and is the preferred fuel for all body cells. The body derives glucose from the breakdown of the carbohydrate-containing foods and drinks we consume. Glucose not immediately taken up by cells for fuel can be stored by the liver and muscles as glycogen, or converted to triglycerides and stored in the adipose tissue. Hormones regulate both the storage and the utilization of glucose as required. Receptors located in the pancreas sense blood glucose levels, and subsequently the pancreatic cells secrete glucagon or insulin to maintain normal levels.

Glucagon

Receptors in the pancreas can sense the decline in blood glucose levels, such as during periods of fasting or during prolonged labor or exercise (Figure 17.19). In response, the alpha cells of the pancreas secrete the hormone **glucagon**, which has several effects:

- It stimulates the liver to convert its stores of glycogen back into glucose. This response is known as glycogenolysis. The glucose is then released into the circulation for use by body cells.
- It stimulates the liver to take up amino acids from the blood and convert them into glucose. This response is known as gluconeogenesis.
- It stimulates lipolysis, the breakdown of stored triglycerides into free fatty acids and glycerol. Some of the free glycerol released into the bloodstream travels to the liver, which converts it into glucose. This is also a form of gluconeogenesis.

Taken together, these actions increase blood glucose levels. The activity of glucagon is regulated through a negative feedback mechanism; rising blood glucose levels inhibit further glucagon production and secretion.

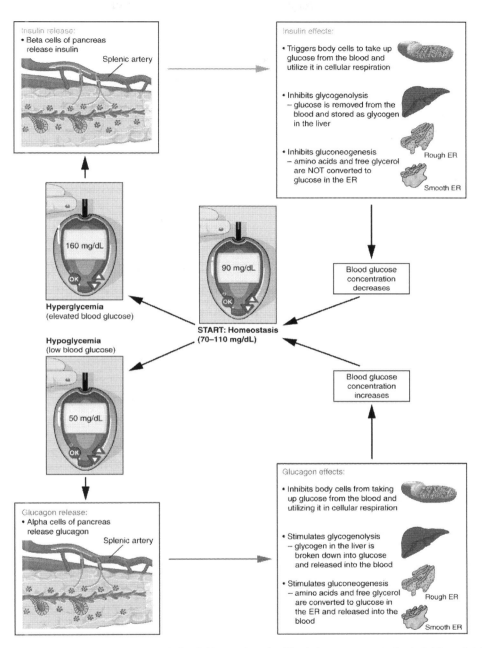

Figure 17.19 Homeostatic Regulation of Blood Glucose Levels Blood glucose concentration is tightly maintained between 70 mg/dL and 110 mg/dL. If blood glucose concentration rises above this range, insulin is released, which stimulates body cells to remove glucose from the blood. If blood glucose concentration drops below this range, glucagon is released, which stimulates body cells to release glucose into the blood.

Insulin

The primary function of **insulin** is to facilitate the uptake of glucose into body cells. Red blood cells, as well as cells of the brain, liver, kidneys, and the lining of the small intestine, do not have insulin receptors on their cell membranes and do not require insulin for glucose uptake. Although all other body cells do require insulin if they are to take glucose from the bloodstream, skeletal muscle cells and adipose cells are the primary targets of insulin.

The presence of food in the intestine triggers the release of gastrointestinal tract hormones such as glucose-dependent insulinotropic peptide (previously known as gastric inhibitory peptide). This is in turn the initial trigger for insulin production and secretion by the beta cells of the pancreas. Once nutrient absorption occurs, the resulting surge in blood glucose levels further stimulates insulin secretion.

Precisely how insulin facilitates glucose uptake is not entirely clear. However, insulin appears to activate a tyrosine kinase receptor, triggering the phosphorylation of many substrates within the cell. These multiple biochemical reactions converge to support the movement of intracellular vesicles containing facilitative glucose transporters to the cell membrane. In the absence of insulin, these transport proteins are normally recycled slowly between the cell membrane and cell interior. Insulin triggers the rapid movement of a pool of glucose transporter vesicles to the cell membrane, where they fuse and expose the glucose transporters to the extracellular fluid. The transporters then move glucose by facilitated diffusion into the cell interior.

Visit this link (http://openstaxcollege.org/l/pancreas1) to view an animation describing the location and function of the pancreas. What goes wrong in the function of insulin in type 2 diabetes?

Insulin also reduces blood glucose levels by stimulating glycolysis, the metabolism of glucose for generation of ATP. Moreover, it stimulates the liver to convert excess glucose into glycogen for storage, and it inhibits enzymes involved in glycogenolysis and gluconeogenesis. Finally, insulin promotes triglyceride and protein synthesis. The secretion of insulin is regulated through a negative feedback mechanism. As blood glucose levels decrease, further insulin release is inhibited. The pancreatic hormones are summarized in Table 17.7.

Hormones of the Pancreas

Associated hormones	Chemical class	Effect
Insulin (beta cells)	Protein	Reduces blood glucose levels
Glucagon (alpha cells)	Protein	Increases blood glucose levels
Somatostatin (delta cells)	Protein	Inhibits insulin and glucagon release
Pancreatic polypeptide (PP cells)	Protein	Role in appetite

Table 17.7

Disorders OF THE...
Endocrine System: Diabetes Mellitus

Dysfunction of insulin production and secretion, as well as the target cells' responsiveness to insulin, can lead to a condition called **diabetes mellitus**. An increasingly common disease, diabetes mellitus has been diagnosed in more than 18 million adults in the United States, and more than 200,000 children. It is estimated that up to 7 million more adults have the condition but have not been diagnosed. In addition, approximately 79 million people in the US are estimated to have pre-diabetes, a condition in which blood glucose levels are abnormally high, but not yet high enough to be classified as diabetes.

There are two main forms of diabetes mellitus. Type 1 diabetes is an autoimmune disease affecting the beta cells of the pancreas. Certain genes are recognized to increase susceptibility. The beta cells of people with type 1 diabetes do not produce insulin; thus, synthetic insulin must be administered by injection or infusion. This form of diabetes accounts for less than five percent of all diabetes cases.

Type 2 diabetes accounts for approximately 95 percent of all cases. It is acquired, and lifestyle factors such as poor diet, inactivity, and the presence of pre-diabetes greatly increase a person's risk. About 80 to 90 percent of people with type 2 diabetes are overweight or obese. In type 2 diabetes, cells become resistant to the effects of insulin. In response, the pancreas increases its insulin secretion, but over time, the beta cells become exhausted. In many cases, type 2 diabetes can be reversed by moderate weight loss, regular physical activity, and consumption of a healthy diet; however, if blood glucose levels cannot be controlled, the diabetic will eventually require insulin.

Two of the early manifestations of diabetes are excessive urination and excessive thirst. They demonstrate how the out-of-control levels of glucose in the blood affect kidney function. The kidneys are responsible for filtering glucose from the blood. Excessive blood glucose draws water into the urine, and as a result the person eliminates an abnormally large quantity of sweet urine. The use of body water to dilute the urine leaves the body dehydrated, and so the person is unusually and continually thirsty. The person may also experience persistent hunger because the body cells are unable to access the glucose in the bloodstream.

Over time, persistently high levels of glucose in the blood injure tissues throughout the body, especially those of the blood vessels and nerves. Inflammation and injury of the lining of arteries lead to atherosclerosis and an increased risk of heart attack and stroke. Damage to the microscopic blood vessels of the kidney impairs kidney function and can lead to kidney failure. Damage to blood vessels that serve the eyes can lead to blindness. Blood vessel damage also reduces circulation to the limbs, whereas nerve damage leads to a loss of sensation, called neuropathy, particularly in the hands and feet. Together, these changes increase the risk of injury, infection, and tissue death (necrosis), contributing to a high rate of toe, foot, and lower leg amputations in people with diabetes. Uncontrolled diabetes can also lead to a dangerous form of metabolic acidosis called ketoacidosis. Deprived of glucose, cells increasingly rely on fat stores for fuel. However, in a glucose-deficient state, the liver is forced to use an alternative lipid metabolism pathway that results in the increased production of ketone bodies (or ketones), which are acidic. The build-up of ketones in the blood causes ketoacidosis, which—if left untreated—may lead to a life-threatening "diabetic coma." Together, these complications make diabetes the seventh leading cause of death in the United States.

Diabetes is diagnosed when lab tests reveal that blood glucose levels are higher than normal, a condition called **hyperglycemia**. The treatment of diabetes depends on the type, the severity of the condition, and the ability of the patient to make lifestyle changes. As noted earlier, moderate weight loss, regular physical activity, and consumption of a healthful diet can reduce blood glucose levels. Some patients with type 2 diabetes may be unable to control their disease with these lifestyle changes, and will require medication. Historically, the first-line treatment of type 2 diabetes was insulin. Research advances have resulted in alternative options, including medications that enhance pancreatic function.

Interactive Link

Visit this link (http://openstaxcollege.org/l/insulin) to view an animation describing the role of insulin and the pancreas in diabetes.

17.10 | Organs with Secondary Endocrine Functions

By the end of this section, you will be able to:
- Identify the organs with a secondary endocrine function, the hormone they produce, and its effects

In your study of anatomy and physiology, you have already encountered a few of the many organs of the body that have secondary endocrine functions. Here, you will learn about the hormone-producing activities of the heart, gastrointestinal tract, kidneys, skeleton, adipose tissue, skin, and thymus.

Heart

When the body experiences an increase in blood volume or pressure, the cells of the heart's atrial wall stretch. In response, specialized cells in the wall of the atria produce and secrete the peptide hormone **atrial natriuretic peptide (ANP)**. ANP signals the kidneys to reduce sodium reabsorption, thereby decreasing the amount of water reabsorbed from the urine filtrate and reducing blood volume. Other actions of ANP include the inhibition of renin secretion and the initiation of the renin-angiotensin-aldosterone system (RAAS) and vasodilation. Therefore, ANP aids in decreasing blood pressure, blood volume, and blood sodium levels.

Gastrointestinal Tract

The endocrine cells of the GI tract are located in the mucosa of the stomach and small intestine. Some of these hormones are secreted in response to eating a meal and aid in digestion. An example of a hormone secreted by the stomach cells is gastrin, a peptide hormone secreted in response to stomach distention that stimulates the release of hydrochloric acid. Secretin is a peptide hormone secreted by the small intestine as acidic chyme (partially digested food and fluid) moves from the stomach. It stimulates the release of bicarbonate from the pancreas, which buffers the acidic chyme, and inhibits the further secretion of hydrochloric acid by the stomach. Cholecystokinin (CCK) is another peptide hormone released from the small intestine. It promotes the secretion of pancreatic enzymes and the release of bile from the gallbladder, both of which facilitate digestion. Other hormones produced by the intestinal cells aid in glucose metabolism, such as by stimulating the pancreatic beta cells to secrete insulin, reducing glucagon secretion from the alpha cells, or enhancing cellular sensitivity to insulin.

Kidneys

The kidneys participate in several complex endocrine pathways and produce certain hormones. A decline in blood flow to the kidneys stimulates them to release the enzyme renin, triggering the renin-angiotensin-aldosterone (RAAS) system, and stimulating the reabsorption of sodium and water. The reabsorption increases blood flow and blood pressure. The kidneys also play a role in regulating blood calcium levels through the production of calcitriol from vitamin D_3, which is released in response to the secretion of parathyroid hormone (PTH). In addition, the kidneys produce the hormone **erythropoietin (EPO)** in response to low oxygen levels. EPO stimulates the production of red blood cells (erythrocytes) in the bone marrow, thereby increasing oxygen delivery to tissues. You may have heard of EPO as a performance-enhancing drug (in a synthetic form).

Skeleton

Although bone has long been recognized as a target for hormones, only recently have researchers recognized that the skeleton itself produces at least two hormones. Fibroblast growth factor 23 (FGF23) is produced by bone cells in response to increased blood levels of vitamin D_3 or phosphate. It triggers the kidneys to inhibit the formation of calcitriol from vitamin D_3 and to increase phosphorus excretion. Osteocalcin, produced by osteoblasts, stimulates the pancreatic beta cells to increase insulin production. It also acts on peripheral tissues to increase their sensitivity to insulin and their utilization of glucose.

Adipose Tissue

Adipose tissue produces and secretes several hormones involved in lipid metabolism and storage. One important example is **leptin**, a protein manufactured by adipose cells that circulates in amounts directly proportional to levels of body fat. Leptin is released in response to food consumption and acts by binding to brain neurons involved in energy intake and expenditure. Binding of leptin produces a feeling of satiety after a meal, thereby reducing appetite. It also appears that the binding of leptin to brain receptors triggers the sympathetic nervous system to regulate bone metabolism, increasing deposition of cortical bone. Adiponectin—another hormone synthesized by adipose cells—appears to reduce cellular insulin resistance and to protect blood vessels from inflammation and atherosclerosis. Its levels are lower in people who are obese, and rise following weight loss.

Skin

The skin functions as an endocrine organ in the production of the inactive form of vitamin D_3, cholecalciferol. When cholesterol present in the epidermis is exposed to ultraviolet radiation, it is converted to cholecalciferol, which then enters the blood. In the liver, cholecalciferol is converted to an intermediate that travels to the kidneys and is further converted to calcitriol, the active form of vitamin D_3. Vitamin D is important in a variety of physiological processes, including intestinal calcium absorption and immune system function. In some studies, low levels of vitamin D have been associated with increased risks of cancer, severe asthma, and multiple sclerosis. Vitamin D deficiency in children causes rickets, and in adults, osteomalacia—both of which are characterized by bone deterioration.

Thymus

The **thymus** is an organ of the immune system that is larger and more active during infancy and early childhood, and begins to atrophy as we age. Its endocrine function is the production of a group of hormones called **thymosins** that contribute to the development and differentiation of T lymphocytes, which are immune cells. Although the role of thymosins is not yet well understood, it is clear that they contribute to the immune response. Thymosins have been found in tissues other than the thymus and have a wide variety of functions, so the thymosins cannot be strictly categorized as thymic hormones.

Liver

The liver is responsible for secreting at least four important hormones or hormone precursors: insulin-like growth factor (somatomedin), angiotensinogen, thrombopoetin, and hepcidin. Insulin-like growth factor-1 is the immediate stimulus for growth in the body, especially of the bones. Angiotensinogen is the precursor to angiotensin, mentioned earlier, which increases blood pressure. Thrombopoetin stimulates the production of the blood's platelets. Hepcidins block the release of iron from cells in the body, helping to regulate iron homeostasis in our body fluids. The major hormones of these other organs are summarized in Table 17.8.

Organs with Secondary Endocrine Functions and Their Major Hormones

Organ	Major hormones	Effects
Heart	Atrial natriuretic peptide (ANP)	Reduces blood volume, blood pressure, and Na^+ concentration
Gastrointestinal tract	Gastrin, secretin, and cholecystokinin	Aid digestion of food and buffering of stomach acids
Gastrointestinal tract	Glucose-dependent insulinotropic peptide (GIP) and glucagon-like peptide 1 (GLP-1)	Stimulate beta cells of the pancreas to release insulin

Table 17.8

Organs with Secondary Endocrine Functions and Their Major Hormones

Organ	Major hormones	Effects
Kidneys	Renin	Stimulates release of aldosterone
Kidneys	Calcitriol	Aids in the absorption of Ca^{2+}
Kidneys	Erythropoietin	Triggers the formation of red blood cells in the bone marrow
Skeleton	FGF23	Inhibits production of calcitriol and increases phosphate excretion
Skeleton	Osteocalcin	Increases insulin production
Adipose tissue	Leptin	Promotes satiety signals in the brain
Adipose tissue	Adiponectin	Reduces insulin resistance
Skin	Cholecalciferol	Modified to form vitamin D
Thymus (and other organs)	Thymosins	Among other things, aids in the development of T lymphocytes of the immune system
Liver	Insulin-like growth factor-1	Stimulates bodily growth
Liver	Angiotensinogen	Raises blood pressure
Liver	Thrombopoetin	Causes increase in platelets
Liver	Hepcidin	Blocks release of iron into body fluids

Table 17.8

17.11 | Development and Aging of the Endocrine System

By the end of this section, you will be able to:
- Describe the embryonic origins of the endocrine system
- Discuss the effects of aging on the endocrine system

The endocrine system arises from all three embryonic germ layers. The endocrine glands that produce the steroid hormones, such as the gonads and adrenal cortex, arise from the mesoderm. In contrast, endocrine glands that arise from the endoderm and ectoderm produce the amine, peptide, and protein hormones. The pituitary gland arises from two distinct areas of the ectoderm: the anterior pituitary gland arises from the oral ectoderm, whereas the posterior pituitary gland arises from the neural ectoderm at the base of the hypothalamus. The pineal gland also arises from the ectoderm. The two structures of the adrenal glands arise from two different germ layers: the adrenal cortex from the mesoderm and the adrenal medulla from ectoderm neural cells. The endoderm gives rise to the thyroid and parathyroid glands, as well as the pancreas and the thymus.

As the body ages, changes occur that affect the endocrine system, sometimes altering the production, secretion, and catabolism of hormones. For example, the structure of the anterior pituitary gland changes as vascularization decreases and the connective tissue content increases with increasing age. This restructuring affects the gland's hormone production. For example, the amount of human growth hormone that is produced declines with age, resulting in the reduced muscle mass commonly observed in the elderly.

The adrenal glands also undergo changes as the body ages; as fibrous tissue increases, the production of cortisol and aldosterone decreases. Interestingly, the production and secretion of epinephrine and norepinephrine remain normal throughout the aging process.

A well-known example of the aging process affecting an endocrine gland is menopause and the decline of ovarian function. With increasing age, the ovaries decrease in both size and weight and become progressively less sensitive to gonadotropins. This gradually causes a decrease in estrogen and progesterone levels, leading to menopause and the inability to reproduce.

Low levels of estrogens and progesterone are also associated with some disease states, such as osteoporosis, atherosclerosis, and hyperlipidemia, or abnormal blood lipid levels.

Testosterone levels also decline with age, a condition called andropause (or viropause); however, this decline is much less dramatic than the decline of estrogens in women, and much more gradual, rarely affecting sperm production until very old age. Although this means that males maintain their ability to father children for decades longer than females, the quantity, quality, and motility of their sperm is often reduced.

As the body ages, the thyroid gland produces less of the thyroid hormones, causing a gradual decrease in the basal metabolic rate. The lower metabolic rate reduces the production of body heat and increases levels of body fat. Parathyroid hormones, on the other hand, increase with age. This may be because of reduced dietary calcium levels, causing a compensatory increase in parathyroid hormone. However, increased parathyroid hormone levels combined with decreased levels of calcitonin (and estrogens in women) can lead to osteoporosis as PTH stimulates demineralization of bones to increase blood calcium levels. Notice that osteoporosis is common in both elderly males and females.

Increasing age also affects glucose metabolism, as blood glucose levels spike more rapidly and take longer to return to normal in the elderly. In addition, increasing glucose intolerance may occur because of a gradual decline in cellular insulin sensitivity. Almost 27 percent of Americans aged 65 and older have diabetes.

KEY TERMS

acromegaly disorder in adults caused when abnormally high levels of GH trigger growth of bones in the face, hands, and feet

adenylyl cyclase membrane-bound enzyme that converts ATP to cyclic AMP, creating cAMP, as a result of G-protein activation

adrenal cortex outer region of the adrenal glands consisting of multiple layers of epithelial cells and capillary networks that produces mineralocorticoids and glucocorticoids

adrenal glands endocrine glands located at the top of each kidney that are important for the regulation of the stress response, blood pressure and blood volume, water homeostasis, and electrolyte levels

adrenal medulla inner layer of the adrenal glands that plays an important role in the stress response by producing epinephrine and norepinephrine

adrenocorticotropic hormone (ACTH) anterior pituitary hormone that stimulates the adrenal cortex to secrete corticosteroid hormones (also called corticotropin)

alarm reaction the short-term stress, or the fight-or-flight response, of stage one of the general adaptation syndrome mediated by the hormones epinephrine and norepinephrine

aldosterone hormone produced and secreted by the adrenal cortex that stimulates sodium and fluid retention and increases blood volume and blood pressure

alpha cell pancreatic islet cell type that produces the hormone glucagon

angiotensin-converting enzyme the enzyme that converts angiotensin I to angiotensin II

antidiuretic hormone (ADH) hypothalamic hormone that is stored by the posterior pituitary and that signals the kidneys to reabsorb water

atrial natriuretic peptide (ANP) peptide hormone produced by the walls of the atria in response to high blood pressure, blood volume, or blood sodium that reduces the reabsorption of sodium and water in the kidneys and promotes vasodilation

autocrine chemical signal that elicits a response in the same cell that secreted it

beta cell pancreatic islet cell type that produces the hormone insulin

calcitonin peptide hormone produced and secreted by the parafollicular cells (C cells) of the thyroid gland that functions to decrease blood calcium levels

chromaffin neuroendocrine cells of the adrenal medulla

colloid viscous fluid in the central cavity of thyroid follicles, containing the glycoprotein thyroglobulin

cortisol glucocorticoid important in gluconeogenesis, the catabolism of glycogen, and downregulation of the immune system

cyclic adenosine monophosphate (cAMP) second messenger that, in response to adenylyl cyclase activation, triggers a phosphorylation cascade

delta cell minor cell type in the pancreas that secretes the hormone somatostatin

diabetes mellitus condition caused by destruction or dysfunction of the beta cells of the pancreas or cellular resistance to insulin that results in abnormally high blood glucose levels

diacylglycerol (DAG) molecule that, like cAMP, activates protein kinases, thereby initiating a phosphorylation cascade

downregulation decrease in the number of hormone receptors, typically in response to chronically excessive levels of a hormone

endocrine gland tissue or organ that secretes hormones into the blood and lymph without ducts such that they may be transported to organs distant from the site of secretion

endocrine system cells, tissues, and organs that secrete hormones as a primary or secondary function and play an integral role in normal bodily processes

epinephrine primary and most potent catecholamine hormone secreted by the adrenal medulla in response to short-term stress; also called adrenaline

erythropoietin (EPO) protein hormone secreted in response to low oxygen levels that triggers the bone marrow to produce red blood cells

estrogens class of predominantly female sex hormones important for the development and growth of the female reproductive tract, secondary sex characteristics, the female reproductive cycle, and the maintenance of pregnancy

exocrine system cells, tissues, and organs that secrete substances directly to target tissues via glandular ducts

first messenger hormone that binds to a cell membrane hormone receptor and triggers activation of a second messenger system

follicle-stimulating hormone (FSH) anterior pituitary hormone that stimulates the production and maturation of sex cells

G protein protein associated with a cell membrane hormone receptor that initiates the next step in a second messenger system upon activation by hormone–receptor binding

general adaptation syndrome (GAS) the human body's three-stage response pattern to short- and long-term stress

gigantism disorder in children caused when abnormally high levels of GH prompt excessive growth

glucagon pancreatic hormone that stimulates the catabolism of glycogen to glucose, thereby increasing blood glucose levels

glucocorticoids hormones produced by the zona fasciculata of the adrenal cortex that influence glucose metabolism

goiter enlargement of the thyroid gland either as a result of iodine deficiency or hyperthyroidism

gonadotropins hormones that regulate the function of the gonads

growth hormone (GH) anterior pituitary hormone that promotes tissue building and influences nutrient metabolism (also called somatotropin)

hormone secretion of an endocrine organ that travels via the bloodstream or lymphatics to induce a response in target cells or tissues in another part of the body

hormone receptor protein within a cell or on the cell membrane that binds a hormone, initiating the target cell response

hyperglycemia abnormally high blood glucose levels

hyperparathyroidism disorder caused by overproduction of PTH that results in abnormally elevated blood calcium

hyperthyroidism clinically abnormal, elevated level of thyroid hormone in the blood; characterized by an increased metabolic rate, excess body heat, sweating, diarrhea, weight loss, and increased heart rate

hypoparathyroidism disorder caused by underproduction of PTH that results in abnormally low blood calcium

hypophyseal portal system network of blood vessels that enables hypothalamic hormones to travel into the anterior lobe of the pituitary without entering the systemic circulation

hypothalamus region of the diencephalon inferior to the thalamus that functions in neural and endocrine signaling

hypothyroidism clinically abnormal, low level of thyroid hormone in the blood; characterized by low metabolic rate, weight gain, cold extremities, constipation, and reduced mental activity

infundibulum stalk containing vasculature and neural tissue that connects the pituitary gland to the hypothalamus (also called the pituitary stalk)

inhibin hormone secreted by the male and female gonads that inhibits FSH production by the anterior pituitary

inositol triphosphate (IP$_3$) molecule that initiates the release of calcium ions from intracellular stores

insulin pancreatic hormone that enhances the cellular uptake and utilization of glucose, thereby decreasing blood glucose levels

insulin-like growth factors (IGF) protein that enhances cellular proliferation, inhibits apoptosis, and stimulates the cellular uptake of amino acids for protein synthesis

leptin protein hormone secreted by adipose tissues in response to food consumption that promotes satiety

luteinizing hormone (LH) anterior pituitary hormone that triggers ovulation and the production of ovarian hormones in females, and the production of testosterone in males

melatonin amino acid–derived hormone that is secreted in response to low light and causes drowsiness

mineralocorticoids hormones produced by the zona glomerulosa cells of the adrenal cortex that influence fluid and electrolyte balance

neonatal hypothyroidism condition characterized by cognitive deficits, short stature, and other signs and symptoms in people born to women who were iodine-deficient during pregnancy

norepinephrine secondary catecholamine hormone secreted by the adrenal medulla in response to short-term stress; also called noradrenaline

osmoreceptor hypothalamic sensory receptor that is stimulated by changes in solute concentration (osmotic pressure) in the blood

oxytocin hypothalamic hormone stored in the posterior pituitary gland and important in stimulating uterine contractions in labor, milk ejection during breastfeeding, and feelings of attachment (also produced in males)

pancreas organ with both exocrine and endocrine functions located posterior to the stomach that is important for digestion and the regulation of blood glucose

pancreatic islets specialized clusters of pancreatic cells that have endocrine functions; also called islets of Langerhans

paracrine chemical signal that elicits a response in neighboring cells; also called paracrine factor

parathyroid glands small, round glands embedded in the posterior thyroid gland that produce parathyroid hormone (PTH)

parathyroid hormone (PTH) peptide hormone produced and secreted by the parathyroid glands in response to low blood calcium levels

phosphodiesterase (PDE) cytosolic enzyme that deactivates and degrades cAMP

phosphorylation cascade signaling event in which multiple protein kinases phosphorylate the next protein substrate by transferring a phosphate group from ATP to the protein

pineal gland endocrine gland that secretes melatonin, which is important in regulating the sleep-wake cycle

pinealocyte cell of the pineal gland that produces and secretes the hormone melatonin

pituitary dwarfism disorder in children caused when abnormally low levels of GH result in growth retardation

pituitary gland bean-sized organ suspended from the hypothalamus that produces, stores, and secretes hormones in response to hypothalamic stimulation (also called hypophysis)

PP cell minor cell type in the pancreas that secretes the hormone pancreatic polypeptide

progesterone predominantly female sex hormone important in regulating the female reproductive cycle and the maintenance of pregnancy

prolactin (PRL) anterior pituitary hormone that promotes development of the mammary glands and the production of breast milk

protein kinase enzyme that initiates a phosphorylation cascade upon activation

second messenger molecule that initiates a signaling cascade in response to hormone binding on a cell membrane receptor and activation of a G protein

stage of exhaustion stage three of the general adaptation syndrome; the body's long-term response to stress mediated by the hormones of the adrenal cortex

stage of resistance stage two of the general adaptation syndrome; the body's continued response to stress after stage one diminishes

testosterone steroid hormone secreted by the male testes and important in the maturation of sperm cells, growth and development of the male reproductive system, and the development of male secondary sex characteristics

thymosins hormones produced and secreted by the thymus that play an important role in the development and differentiation of T cells

thymus organ that is involved in the development and maturation of T-cells and is particularly active during infancy and childhood

thyroid gland large endocrine gland responsible for the synthesis of thyroid hormones

thyroid-stimulating hormone (TSH) anterior pituitary hormone that triggers secretion of thyroid hormones by the thyroid gland (also called thyrotropin)

thyroxine (also, tetraiodothyronine, T_4) amino acid–derived thyroid hormone that is more abundant but less potent than T_3 and often converted to T_3 by target cells

triiodothyronine (also, T_3) amino acid–derived thyroid hormone that is less abundant but more potent than T_4

upregulation increase in the number of hormone receptors, typically in response to chronically reduced levels of a hormone

zona fasciculata intermediate region of the adrenal cortex that produce hormones called glucocorticoids

zona glomerulosa most superficial region of the adrenal cortex, which produces the hormones collectively referred to as mineralocorticoids

zona reticularis deepest region of the adrenal cortex, which produces the steroid sex hormones called androgens

CHAPTER REVIEW

17.1 An Overview of the Endocrine System

The endocrine system consists of cells, tissues, and organs that secrete hormones critical to homeostasis. The body coordinates its functions through two major types of communication: neural and endocrine. Neural communication includes both electrical and chemical signaling between neurons and target cells. Endocrine communication involves chemical signaling via the release of hormones into the extracellular fluid. From there, hormones diffuse into the bloodstream and may travel to distant body regions, where they elicit a response in target cells. Endocrine glands are ductless glands that secrete hormones. Many organs of the body with other primary functions—such as the heart, stomach, and kidneys—also have hormone-secreting cells.

Download for free at http://cnx.org/content/col11496/latest/

17.2 Hormones

Hormones are derived from amino acids or lipids. Amine hormones originate from the amino acids tryptophan or tyrosine. Larger amino acid hormones include peptides and protein hormones. Steroid hormones are derived from cholesterol.

Steroid hormones and thyroid hormone are lipid soluble. All other amino acid–derived hormones are water soluble. Hydrophobic hormones are able to diffuse through the membrane and interact with an intracellular receptor. In contrast, hydrophilic hormones must interact with cell membrane receptors. These are typically associated with a G protein, which becomes activated when the hormone binds the receptor. This initiates a signaling cascade that involves a second messenger, such as cyclic adenosine monophosphate (cAMP). Second messenger systems greatly amplify the hormone signal, creating a broader, more efficient, and faster response.

Hormones are released upon stimulation that is of either chemical or neural origin. Regulation of hormone release is primarily achieved through negative feedback. Various stimuli may cause the release of hormones, but there are three major types. Humoral stimuli are changes in ion or nutrient levels in the blood. Hormonal stimuli are changes in hormone levels that initiate or inhibit the secretion of another hormone. Finally, a neural stimulus occurs when a nerve impulse prompts the secretion or inhibition of a hormone.

17.3 The Pituitary Gland and Hypothalamus

The hypothalamus–pituitary complex is located in the diencephalon of the brain. The hypothalamus and the pituitary gland are connected by a structure called the infundibulum, which contains vasculature and nerve axons. The pituitary gland is divided into two distinct structures with different embryonic origins. The posterior lobe houses the axon terminals of hypothalamic neurons. It stores and releases into the bloodstream two hypothalamic hormones: oxytocin and antidiuretic hormone (ADH). The anterior lobe is connected to the hypothalamus by vasculature in the infundibulum and produces and secretes six hormones. Their secretion is regulated, however, by releasing and inhibiting hormones from the hypothalamus. The six anterior pituitary hormones are: growth hormone (GH), thyroid-stimulating hormone (TSH), adrenocorticotropic hormone (ACTH), follicle-stimulating hormone (FSH), luteinizing hormone (LH), and prolactin (PRL).

17.4 The Thyroid Gland

The thyroid gland is a butterfly-shaped organ located in the neck anterior to the trachea. Its hormones regulate basal metabolism, oxygen use, nutrient metabolism, the production of ATP, and calcium homeostasis. They also contribute to protein synthesis and the normal growth and development of body tissues, including maturation of the nervous system, and they increase the body's sensitivity to catecholamines. The thyroid hormones triiodothyronine (T_3) and thyroxine (T_4) are produced and secreted by the thyroid gland in response to thyroid-stimulating hormone (TSH) from the anterior pituitary. Synthesis of the amino acid–derived T_3 and T_4 hormones requires iodine. Insufficient amounts of iodine in the diet can lead to goiter, cretinism, and many other disorders.

17.5 The Parathyroid Glands

Calcium is required for a variety of important physiologic processes, including neuromuscular functioning; thus, blood calcium levels are closely regulated. The parathyroid glands are small structures located on the posterior thyroid gland that produce parathyroid hormone (PTH), which regulates blood calcium levels. Low blood calcium levels cause the production and secretion of PTH. In contrast, elevated blood calcium levels inhibit secretion of PTH and trigger secretion of the thyroid hormone calcitonin. Underproduction of PTH can result in hypoparathyroidism. In contrast, overproduction of PTH can result in hyperparathyroidism.

17.6 The Adrenal Glands

The adrenal glands, located superior to each kidney, consist of two regions: the adrenal cortex and adrenal medulla. The adrenal cortex—the outer layer of the gland—produces mineralocorticoids, glucocorticoids, and androgens. The adrenal medulla at the core of the gland produces epinephrine and norepinephrine.

The adrenal glands mediate a short-term stress response and a long-term stress response. A perceived threat results in the secretion of epinephrine and norepinephrine from the adrenal medulla, which mediate the fight-or-flight response. The long-term stress response is mediated by the secretion of CRH from the hypothalamus, which triggers ACTH, which in turn stimulates the secretion of corticosteroids from the adrenal cortex. The mineralocorticoids, chiefly aldosterone, cause sodium and fluid retention, which increases blood volume and blood pressure.

17.7 The Pineal Gland

The pineal gland is an endocrine structure of the diencephalon of the brain, and is located inferior and posterior to the thalamus. It is made up of pinealocytes. These cells produce and secrete the hormone melatonin in response to low light levels. High blood levels of melatonin induce drowsiness. Jet lag, caused by traveling across several time zones, occurs because melatonin synthesis takes several days to readjust to the light-dark patterns in the new environment.

17.8 Gonadal and Placental Hormones

The male and female reproductive system is regulated by follicle-stimulating hormone (FSH) and luteinizing hormone (LH) produced by the anterior lobe of the pituitary gland in response to gonadotropin-releasing hormone (GnRH) from the hypothalamus. In males, FSH stimulates sperm maturation, which is inhibited by the hormone inhibin. The steroid hormone testosterone, a type of androgen, is released in response to LH and is responsible for the maturation and maintenance of the male reproductive system, as well as the development of male secondary sex characteristics. In females, FSH promotes egg maturation and LH signals the secretion of the female sex hormones, the estrogens and progesterone. Both of these hormones are important in the development and maintenance of the female reproductive system, as well as maintaining pregnancy. The placenta develops during early pregnancy, and secretes several hormones important for maintaining the pregnancy.

17.9 The Endocrine Pancreas

The pancreas has both exocrine and endocrine functions. The pancreatic islet cell types include alpha cells, which produce glucagon; beta cells, which produce insulin; delta cells, which produce somatostatin; and PP cells, which produce pancreatic polypeptide. Insulin and glucagon are involved in the regulation of glucose metabolism. Insulin is produced by the beta cells in response to high blood glucose levels. It enhances glucose uptake and utilization by target cells, as well as the storage of excess glucose for later use. Dysfunction of the production of insulin or target cell resistance to the effects of insulin causes diabetes mellitus, a disorder characterized by high blood glucose levels. The hormone glucagon is produced and secreted by the alpha cells of the pancreas in response to low blood glucose levels. Glucagon stimulates mechanisms that increase blood glucose levels, such as the catabolism of glycogen into glucose.

17.10 Organs with Secondary Endocrine Functions

Some organs have a secondary endocrine function. For example, the walls of the atria of the heart produce the hormone atrial natriuretic peptide (ANP), the gastrointestinal tract produces the hormones gastrin, secretin, and cholecystokinin, which aid in digestion, and the kidneys produce erythropoietin (EPO), which stimulates the formation of red blood cells. Even bone, adipose tissue, and the skin have secondary endocrine functions.

17.11 Development and Aging of the Endocrine System

The endocrine system originates from all three germ layers of the embryo, including the endoderm, ectoderm, and mesoderm. In general, different hormone classes arise from distinct germ layers. Aging affects the endocrine glands, potentially affecting hormone production and secretion, and can cause disease. The production of hormones, such as human growth hormone, cortisol, aldosterone, sex hormones, and the thyroid hormones, decreases with age.

INTERACTIVE LINK QUESTIONS

1. Visit this link (http://openstaxcollege.org/l/hormonebind) to watch an animation of the events that occur when a hormone binds to a cell membrane receptor. What is the secondary messenger made by adenylyl cyclase during the activation of liver cells by epinephrine?

2. Visit this link (http://openstaxcollege.org/l/roleofhypo) to watch an animation showing the role of the hypothalamus and the pituitary gland. Which hormone is released by the pituitary to stimulate the thyroid gland?

3. Visit this link (http://openstaxcollege.org/l/adrenalglands) to view an animation describing the location and function of the adrenal glands. Which hormone produced by the adrenal glands is responsible for mobilization of energy stores?

4. Visit this link (http://openstaxcollege.org/l/melatonin) to view an animation describing the function of the hormone melatonin. What should you avoid doing in the middle of your sleep cycle that would lower melatonin?

5. Visit this link (http://openstaxcollege.org/l/pancreas1) to view an animation describing the location and function of the pancreas. What goes wrong in the function of insulin in type 2 diabetes?

REVIEW QUESTIONS

6. Endocrine glands _____.
   a. secrete hormones that travel through a duct to the target organs
   b. release neurotransmitters into the synaptic cleft
   c. secrete chemical messengers that travel in the bloodstream
   d. include sebaceous glands and sweat glands

7. Chemical signaling that affects neighboring cells is called _____.
   a. autocrine
   b. paracrine
   c. endocrine
   d. neuron

8. A newly developed pesticide has been observed to bind to an intracellular hormone receptor. If ingested, residue from this pesticide could disrupt levels of _____.
   a. melatonin
   b. thyroid hormone
   c. growth hormone
   d. insulin

9. A small molecule binds to a G protein, preventing its activation. What direct effect will this have on signaling that involves cAMP?
   a. The hormone will not be able to bind to the hormone receptor.
   b. Adenylyl cyclase will not be activated.
   c. Excessive quantities of cAMP will be produced.
   d. The phosphorylation cascade will be initiated.

10. A student is in a car accident, and although not hurt, immediately experiences pupil dilation, increased heart rate, and rapid breathing. What type of endocrine system stimulus did the student receive?
   a. humoral
   b. hormonal
   c. neural
   d. positive feedback

11. The hypothalamus is functionally and anatomically connected to the posterior pituitary lobe by a bridge of _____.
   a. blood vessels
   b. nerve axons
   c. cartilage
   d. bone

12. Which of the following is an anterior pituitary hormone?
   a. ADH
   b. oxytocin
   c. TSH
   d. cortisol

13. How many hormones are produced by the posterior pituitary?
   a. 0
   b. 1
   c. 2
   d. 6

14. Which of the following hormones contributes to the regulation of the body's fluid and electrolyte balance?
   a. adrenocorticotropic hormone
   b. antidiuretic hormone
   c. luteinizing hormone
   d. all of the above

15. Which of the following statements about the thyroid gland is true?
   a. It is located anterior to the trachea and inferior to the larynx.
   b. The parathyroid glands are embedded within it.
   c. It manufactures three hormones.
   d. all of the above

16. The secretion of thyroid hormones is controlled by _____.
   a. TSH from the hypothalamus
   b. TSH from the anterior pituitary
   c. thyroxine from the anterior pituitary
   d. thyroglobulin from the thyroid's parafollicular cells

17. The development of a goiter indicates that _____.
   a. the anterior pituitary is abnormally enlarged
   b. there is hypertrophy of the thyroid's follicle cells
   c. there is an excessive accumulation of colloid in the thyroid follicles
   d. the anterior pituitary is secreting excessive growth hormone

18. Iodide ions cross from the bloodstream into follicle cells via _____.
   a. simple diffusion
   b. facilitated diffusion
   c. active transport
   d. osmosis

19. When blood calcium levels are low, PTH stimulates _____.
   a. urinary excretion of calcium by the kidneys
   b. a reduction in calcium absorption from the intestines
   c. the activity of osteoblasts
   d. the activity of osteoclasts

20. Which of the following can result from hyperparathyroidism?
   a. increased bone deposition
   b. fractures
   c. convulsions
   d. all of the above

21. The adrenal glands are attached superiorly to which organ?

a. thyroid
b. liver
c. kidneys
d. hypothalamus

22. What secretory cell type is found in the adrenal medulla?

a. chromaffin cells
b. neuroglial cells
c. follicle cells
d. oxyphil cells

23. Cushing's disease is a disorder caused by _____.

a. abnormally low levels of cortisol
b. abnormally high levels of cortisol
c. abnormally low levels of aldosterone
d. abnormally high levels of aldosterone

24. Which of the following responses s not part of the fight-or-flight response?

a. pupil dilation
b. increased oxygen supply to the lungs
c. suppressed digestion
d. reduced mental activity

25. What cells secrete melatonin?

a. melanocytes
b. pinealocytes
c. suprachiasmatic nucleus cells
d. retinal cells

26. The production of melatonin is inhibited by _____.

a. declining levels of light
b. exposure to bright light
c. the secretion of serotonin
d. the activity of pinealocytes

27. The gonads produce what class of hormones?

a. amine hormones
b. peptide hormones
c. steroid hormones
d. catecholamines

28. The production of FSH by the anterior pituitary is reduced by which hormone?

a. estrogens
b. progesterone
c. relaxin
d. inhibin

29. The function of the placental hormone human placental lactogen (hPL) is to _____.

a. prepare the breasts for lactation
b. nourish the placenta
c. regulate the menstrual cycle
d. all of the above

30. If an autoimmune disorder targets the alpha cells, production of which hormone would be directly affected?

a. somatostatin
b. pancreatic polypeptide
c. insulin
d. glucagon

31. Which of the following statements about insulin is true?

a. Insulin acts as a transport protein, carrying glucose across the cell membrane.
b. Insulin facilitates the movement of intracellular glucose transporters to the cell membrane.
c. Insulin stimulates the breakdown of stored glycogen into glucose.
d. Insulin stimulates the kidneys to reabsorb glucose into the bloodstream.

32. The walls of the atria produce which hormone?

a. cholecystokinin
b. atrial natriuretic peptide
c. renin
d. calcitriol

33. The end result of the RAAS is to _____.

a. reduce blood volume
b. increase blood glucose
c. reduce blood pressure
d. increase blood pressure

34. Athletes may take synthetic EPO to boost their _____.

a. blood calcium levels
b. secretion of growth hormone
c. blood oxygen levels
d. muscle mass

35. Hormones produced by the thymus play a role in the _____.

a. development of T cells
b. preparation of the body for childbirth
c. regulation of appetite
d. release of hydrochloric acid in the stomach

36. The anterior pituitary gland develops from which embryonic germ layer?

a. oral ectoderm
b. neural ectoderm
c. mesoderm
d. endoderm

37. In the elderly, decreased thyroid function causes _____.

a. increased tolerance for cold
b. decreased basal metabolic rate
c. decreased body fat
d. osteoporosis

CRITICAL THINKING QUESTIONS

38. Describe several main differences in the communication methods used by the endocrine system and the nervous system.

39. Compare and contrast endocrine and exocrine glands.

40. True or false: Neurotransmitters are a special class of paracrines. Explain your answer.

41. Compare and contrast the signaling events involved with the second messengers cAMP and IP_3.

42. Describe the mechanism of hormone response resulting from the binding of a hormone with an intracellular receptor.

43. Compare and contrast the anatomical relationship of the anterior and posterior lobes of the pituitary gland to the hypothalamus.

44. Name the target tissues for prolactin.

45. Explain why maternal iodine deficiency might lead to neurological impairment in the fetus.

46. Define hyperthyroidism and explain why one of its symptoms is weight loss.

47. Describe the role of negative feedback in the function of the parathyroid gland.

48. Explain why someone with a parathyroid gland tumor might develop kidney stones.

49. What are the three regions of the adrenal cortex and what hormones do they produce?

50. If innervation to the adrenal medulla were disrupted, what would be the physiological outcome?

51. Compare and contrast the short-term and long-term stress response.

52. Seasonal affective disorder (SAD) is a mood disorder characterized by, among other symptoms, increased appetite, sluggishness, and increased sleepiness. It occurs most commonly during the winter months, especially in regions with long winter nights. Propose a role for melatonin in SAD and a possible non-drug therapy.

53. Retinitis pigmentosa (RP) is a disease that causes deterioration of the retinas of the eyes. Describe the impact RP would have on melatonin levels.

54. Compare and contrast the role of estrogens and progesterone.

55. Describe the role of placental secretion of relaxin in preparation for childbirth.

56. What would be the physiological consequence of a disease that destroyed the beta cells of the pancreas?

57. Why is foot care extremely important for people with diabetes mellitus?

58. Summarize the role of GI tract hormones following a meal.

59. Compare and contrast the thymus gland in infancy and adulthood.

60. Distinguish between the effects of menopause and andropause on fertility.

18 | THE CARDIOVASCULAR SYSTEM: BLOOD

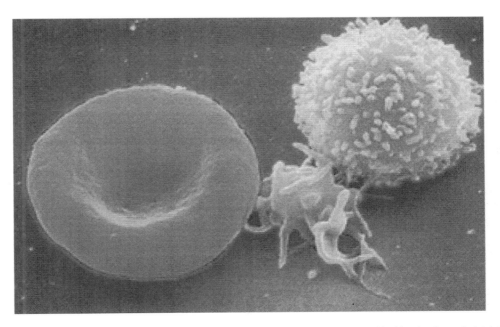

Figure 18.1 Blood Cells A single drop of blood contains millions of red blood cells, white blood cells, and platelets. One of each type is shown here, isolated from a scanning electron micrograph.

Introduction

Chapter Objectives

After studying this chapter, you will be able to:

- Identify the primary functions of blood, its fluid and cellular components, and its physical characteristics
- Identify the most important proteins and other solutes present in blood plasma
- Describe the formation of the formed element components of blood
- Discuss the structure and function of red blood cells and hemoglobin
- Classify and characterize white blood cells
- Describe the structure of platelets and explain the process of hemostasis
- Explain the significance of AB and Rh blood groups in blood transfusions
- Discuss a variety of blood disorders

Single-celled organisms do not need blood. They obtain nutrients directly from and excrete wastes directly into their environment. The human organism cannot do that. Our large, complex bodies need blood to deliver nutrients to and remove wastes from our trillions of cells. The heart pumps blood throughout the body in a network of blood vessels. Together, these three components—blood, heart, and vessels—makes up the cardiovascular system. This chapter focuses on the medium of transport: blood.

18.1 | An Overview of Blood

By the end of this section, you will be able to:
- Identify the primary functions of blood in transportation, defense, and maintenance of homeostasis
- Name the fluid component of blood and the three major types of formed elements, and identify their relative proportions in a blood sample
- Discuss the unique physical characteristics of blood
- Identify the composition of blood plasma, including its most important solutes and plasma proteins

Recall that **blood** is a connective tissue. Like all connective tissues, it is made up of cellular elements and an extracellular matrix. The cellular elements—referred to as the **formed elements**—include **red blood cells (RBCs)**, **white blood cells (WBCs)**, and cell fragments called **platelets**. The extracellular matrix, called **plasma**, makes blood unique among connective tissues because it is fluid. This fluid, which is mostly water, perpetually suspends the formed elements and enables them to circulate throughout the body within the cardiovascular system.

Functions of Blood

The primary function of blood is to deliver oxygen and nutrients to and remove wastes from body cells, but that is only the beginning of the story. The specific functions of blood also include defense, distribution of heat, and maintenance of homeostasis.

Transportation

Nutrients from the foods you eat are absorbed in the digestive tract. Most of these travel in the bloodstream directly to the liver, where they are processed and released back into the bloodstream for delivery to body cells. Oxygen from the air you breathe diffuses into the blood, which moves from the lungs to the heart, which then pumps it out to the rest of the body. Moreover, endocrine glands scattered throughout the body release their products, called hormones, into the bloodstream, which carries them to distant target cells. Blood also picks up cellular wastes and byproducts, and transports them to various organs for removal. For instance, blood moves carbon dioxide to the lungs for exhalation from the body, and various waste products are transported to the kidneys and liver for excretion from the body in the form of urine or bile.

Defense

Many types of WBCs protect the body from external threats, such as disease-causing bacteria that have entered the bloodstream in a wound. Other WBCs seek out and destroy internal threats, such as cells with mutated DNA that could multiply to become cancerous, or body cells infected with viruses.

When damage to the vessels results in bleeding, blood platelets and certain proteins dissolved in the plasma, the fluid portion of the blood, interact to block the ruptured areas of the blood vessels involved. This protects the body from further blood loss.

Maintenance of Homeostasis

Recall that body temperature is regulated via a classic negative-feedback loop. If you were exercising on a warm day, your rising core body temperature would trigger several homeostatic mechanisms, including increased transport of blood from your core to your body periphery, which is typically cooler. As blood passes through the vessels of the skin, heat would be dissipated to the environment, and the blood returning to your body core would be cooler. In contrast, on a cold day, blood is diverted away from the skin to maintain a warmer body core. In extreme cases, this may result in frostbite.

Blood also helps to maintain the chemical balance of the body. Proteins and other compounds in blood act as buffers, which thereby help to regulate the pH of body tissues. Blood also helps to regulate the water content of body cells.

Composition of Blood

You have probably had blood drawn from a superficial vein in your arm, which was then sent to a lab for analysis. Some of the most common blood tests—for instance, those measuring lipid or glucose levels in plasma—determine which substances are present within blood and in what quantities. Other blood tests check for the composition of the blood itself, including the quantities and types of formed elements.

One such test, called a **hematocrit**, measures the percentage of RBCs, clinically known as erythrocytes, in a blood sample. It is performed by spinning the blood sample in a specialized centrifuge, a process that causes the heavier elements suspended within the blood sample to separate from the lightweight, liquid plasma (Figure 18.2). Because the heaviest elements in blood are the erythrocytes, these settle at the very bottom of the hematocrit tube. Located above the erythrocytes is a pale, thin layer composed of the remaining formed elements of blood. These are the WBCs, clinically known as leukocytes, and the platelets, cell fragments also called thrombocytes. This layer is referred to as the **buffy coat** because of its color; it normally constitutes less than 1 percent of a blood sample. Above the buffy coat is the blood plasma, normally a pale, straw-colored fluid, which constitutes the remainder of the sample.

The volume of erythrocytes after centrifugation is also commonly referred to as **packed cell volume (PCV)**. In normal blood, about 45 percent of a sample is erythrocytes. The hematocrit of any one sample can vary significantly, however, about 36–50 percent, according to gender and other factors. Normal hematocrit values for females range from 37 to 47, with a mean value of 41; for males, hematocrit ranges from 42 to 52, with a mean of 47. The percentage of other formed elements, the WBCs and platelets, is extremely small so it is not normally considered with the hematocrit. So the mean plasma percentage is the percent of blood that is not erythrocytes: for females, it is approximately 59 (or 100 minus 41), and for males, it is approximately 53 (or 100 minus 47).

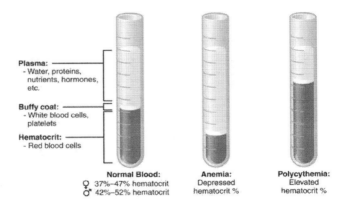

Figure 18.2 Composition of Blood The cellular elements of blood include a vast number of erythrocytes and comparatively fewer leukocytes and platelets. Plasma is the fluid in which the formed elements are suspended. A sample of blood spun in a centrifuge reveals that plasma is the lightest component. It floats at the top of the tube separated from the heaviest elements, the erythrocytes, by a buffy coat of leukocytes and platelets. Hematocrit is the percentage of the total sample that is comprised of erythrocytes. Depressed and elevated hematocrit levels are shown for comparison.

Characteristics of Blood

When you think about blood, the first characteristic that probably comes to mind is its color. Blood that has just taken up oxygen in the lungs is bright red, and blood that has released oxygen in the tissues is a more dusky red. This is because hemoglobin is a pigment that changes color, depending upon the degree of oxygen saturation.

Blood is viscous and somewhat sticky to the touch. It has a viscosity approximately five times greater than water. Viscosity is a measure of a fluid's thickness or resistance to flow, and is influenced by the presence of the plasma proteins and formed elements within the blood. The viscosity of blood has a dramatic impact on blood pressure and flow. Consider the difference in flow between water and honey. The more viscous honey would demonstrate a greater resistance to flow than the less viscous water. The same principle applies to blood.

The normal temperature of blood is slightly higher than normal body temperature—about 38 °C (or 100.4 °F), compared to 37 °C (or 98.6 °F) for an internal body temperature reading, although daily variations of 0.5 °C are normal. Although the surface of blood vessels is relatively smooth, as blood flows through them, it experiences some friction and resistance, especially as vessels age and lose their elasticity, thereby producing heat. This accounts for its slightly higher temperature.

The pH of blood averages about 7.4; however, it can range from 7.35 to 7.45 in a healthy person. Blood is therefore somewhat more basic (alkaline) on a chemical scale than pure water, which has a pH of 7.0. Blood contains numerous buffers that actually help to regulate pH.

Blood constitutes approximately 8 percent of adult body weight. Adult males typically average about 5 to 6 liters of blood. Females average 4–5 liters.

Blood Plasma

Like other fluids in the body, plasma is composed primarily of water: In fact, it is about 92 percent water. Dissolved or suspended within this water is a mixture of substances, most of which are proteins. There are literally hundreds of substances dissolved or suspended in the plasma, although many of them are found only in very small quantities.

Visit this site (http://openstaxcollege.org/l/normallevels) for a list of normal levels established for many of the substances found in a sample of blood. Serum, one of the specimen types included, refers to a sample of plasma after clotting factors have been removed. What types of measurements are given for levels of glucose in the blood?

Plasma Proteins

About 7 percent of the volume of plasma—nearly all that is not water—is made of proteins. These include several plasma proteins (proteins that are unique to the plasma), plus a much smaller number of regulatory proteins, including enzymes and some hormones. The major components of plasma are summarized in Figure 18.3.

The three major groups of plasma proteins are as follows:

- **Albumin** is the most abundant of the plasma proteins. Manufactured by the liver, albumin molecules serve as binding proteins—transport vehicles for fatty acids and steroid hormones. Recall that lipids are hydrophobic; however, their binding to albumin enables their transport in the watery plasma. Albumin is also the most significant contributor to the osmotic pressure of blood; that is, its presence holds water inside the blood vessels and draws water from the tissues, across blood vessel walls, and into the bloodstream. This in turn helps to maintain both blood volume and blood pressure. Albumin normally accounts for approximately 54 percent of the total plasma protein content, in clinical levels of 3.5–5.0 g/dL blood.
- The second most common plasma proteins are the **globulins**. A heterogeneous group, there are three main subgroups known as alpha, beta, and gamma globulins. The alpha and beta globulins transport iron, lipids, and the fat-soluble vitamins A, D, E, and K to the cells; like albumin, they also contribute to osmotic pressure. The gamma globulins are proteins involved in immunity and are better known as an **antibodies** or **immunoglobulins**. Although other plasma proteins are produced by the liver, immunoglobulins are produced by specialized leukocytes known as plasma cells. (Seek additional content for more information about immunoglobulins.) Globulins make up approximately 38 percent of the total plasma protein volume, in clinical levels of 1.0–1.5 g/dL blood.
- The least abundant plasma protein is **fibrinogen**. Like albumin and the alpha and beta globulins, fibrinogen is produced by the liver. It is essential for blood clotting, a process described later in this chapter. Fibrinogen accounts for about 7 percent of the total plasma protein volume, in clinical levels of 0.2–0.45 g/dL blood.

Other Plasma Solutes

In addition to proteins, plasma contains a wide variety of other substances. These include various electrolytes, such as sodium, potassium, and calcium ions; dissolved gases, such as oxygen, carbon dioxide, and nitrogen; various organic nutrients, such as vitamins, lipids, glucose, and amino acids; and metabolic wastes. All of these nonprotein solutes combined contribute approximately 1 percent to the total volume of plasma.

Component and % of blood	Subcomponent and % of component	Type and % (where appropriate)	Site of production	Major function(s)
Plasma 46–63 percent	Water 92 percent	Fluid	Absorbed by intestinal tract or produced by metabolism	Transport medium
	Plasma proteins 7 percent	Albumin 54–60 percent	Liver	Maintain osmotic concentration, transport lipid molecules
		Globulins 35–38 percent	Alpha globulins— liver	Transport, maintain osmotic concentration
			Beta globulins— liver	Transport, maintain osmotic concentration
			Gamma globulins (immunoglobulins) —plasma cells	Immune responses
		Fibrinogen 4–7 percent	Liver	Blood clotting in hemostasis
	Regulatory proteins <1 percent	Hormones and enzymes	Various sources	Regulate various body functions
	Other solutes 1 percent	Nutrients, gases, and wastes	Absorbed by intestinal tract, exchanged in respiratory system, or produced by cells	Numerous and varied
Formed elements 37–54 percent	Erythrocytes 99 percent	Erythrocytes	Red bone marrow	Transport gases, primarily oxygen and some carbon dioxide
	Leukocytes <1 percent Platelets <1 percent	Granular leukocytes: neutrophils eosinophils basophils	Red bone marrow	Nonspecific immunity
		Agranular leukocytes: lymphocytes monocytes	Lymphocytes: bone marrow and lymphatic tissue	Lymphocytes: specific immunity
			Monocytes: red bone marrow	Monocytes: nonspecific immunity
	Platelets <1 percent		Megakaryocytes: red bone marrow	Hemostasis

Figure 18.3 Major Blood Components

Phlebotomy and Medical Lab Technology

Phlebotomists are professionals trained to draw blood (phleb- = "a blood vessel"; -tomy = "to cut"). When more than a few drops of blood are required, phlebotomists perform a venipuncture, typically of a surface vein in the arm. They perform a capillary stick on a finger, an earlobe, or the heel of an infant when only a small quantity of blood is required. An arterial stick is collected from an artery and used to analyze blood gases. After collection, the blood may be analyzed by medical laboratories or perhaps used for transfusions, donations, or research. While many allied health professionals practice phlebotomy, the American Society of Phlebotomy Technicians issues certificates to individuals passing a national examination, and some large labs and hospitals hire individuals expressly for their skill in phlebotomy.

Medical or clinical laboratories employ a variety of individuals in technical positions:

- Medical technologists (MT), also known as clinical laboratory technologists (CLT), typically hold a bachelor's degree and certification from an accredited training program. They perform a wide variety of tests on various body fluids, including blood. The information they provide is essential to the primary care providers in determining a diagnosis and in monitoring the course of a disease and response to treatment.
- Medical laboratory technicians (MLT) typically have an associate's degree but may perform duties similar to those of an MT.
- Medical laboratory assistants (MLA) spend the majority of their time processing samples and carrying out routine assignments within the lab. Clinical training is required, but a degree may not be essential to obtaining a position.

18.2 | Production of the Formed Elements

By the end of this section, you will be able to:

- Trace the generation of the formed elements of blood from bone marrow stem cells
- Discuss the role of hemopoietic growth factors in promoting the production of the formed elements

The lifespan of the formed elements is very brief. Although one type of leukocyte called memory cells can survive for years, most erythrocytes, leukocytes, and platelets normally live only a few hours to a few weeks. Thus, the body must form new blood cells and platelets quickly and continuously. When you donate a unit of blood during a blood drive (approximately 475 mL, or about 1 pint), your body typically replaces the donated plasma within 24 hours, but it takes about 4 to 6 weeks to replace the blood cells. This restricts the frequency with which donors can contribute their blood. The process by which this replacement occurs is called **hemopoiesis**, or hematopoiesis (from the Greek root haima- = "blood"; -poiesis = "production").

Sites of Hemopoiesis

Prior to birth, hemopoiesis occurs in a number of tissues, beginning with the yolk sac of the developing embryo, and continuing in the fetal liver, spleen, lymphatic tissue, and eventually the red bone marrow. Following birth, most hemopoiesis occurs in the red marrow, a connective tissue within the spaces of spongy (cancellous) bone tissue. In children, hemopoiesis can occur in the medullary cavity of long bones; in adults, the process is largely restricted to the cranial and pelvic bones, the vertebrae, the sternum, and the proximal epiphyses of the femur and humerus.

Throughout adulthood, the liver and spleen maintain their ability to generate the formed elements. This process is referred to as extramedullary hemopoiesis (meaning hemopoiesis outside the medullary cavity of adult bones). When a disease such as bone cancer destroys the bone marrow, causing hemopoiesis to fail, extramedullary hemopoiesis may be initiated.

Differentiation of Formed Elements from Stem Cells

All formed elements arise from stem cells of the red bone marrow. Recall that stem cells undergo mitosis plus cytokinesis (cellular division) to give rise to new daughter cells: One of these remains a stem cell and the other differentiates into one of any number of diverse cell types. Stem cells may be viewed as occupying a hierarchal system, with some loss of the ability to diversify at each step. The **totipotent stem cell** is the zygote, or fertilized egg. The totipotent (toti- = "all") stem cell gives rise to all cells of the human body. The next level is the **pluripotent stem cell**, which gives rise to multiple types of cells of the body and some of the supporting fetal membranes. Beneath this level, the mesenchymal cell is a stem cell that develops only into types of connective tissue, including fibrous connective tissue, bone, cartilage, and blood, but not epithelium, muscle, and nervous tissue. One step lower on the hierarchy of stem cells is the **hemopoietic stem cell**, or **hemocytoblast**. All of the formed elements of blood originate from this specific type of cell.

Hemopoiesis begins when the hemopoietic stem cell is exposed to appropriate chemical stimuli collectively called **hemopoietic growth factors**, which prompt it to divide and differentiate. One daughter cell remains a hemopoietic stem cell, allowing hemopoiesis to continue. The other daughter cell becomes either of two types of more specialized stem cells (Figure 18.4):

- **Lymphoid stem cells** give rise to a class of leukocytes known as lymphocytes, which include the various T cells, B cells, and natural killer (NK) cells, all of which function in immunity. However, hemopoiesis of lymphocytes progresses somewhat differently from the process for the other formed elements. In brief, lymphoid stem cells quickly migrate from the bone marrow to lymphatic tissues, including the lymph nodes, spleen, and thymus, where their production and differentiation continues. B cells are so named since they mature in the bone marrow, while T cells mature in the thymus.
- **Myeloid stem cells** give rise to all the other formed elements, including the erythrocytes; megakaryocytes that produce platelets; and a myeloblast lineage that gives rise to monocytes and three forms of granular leukocytes: neutrophils, eosinophils, and basophils.

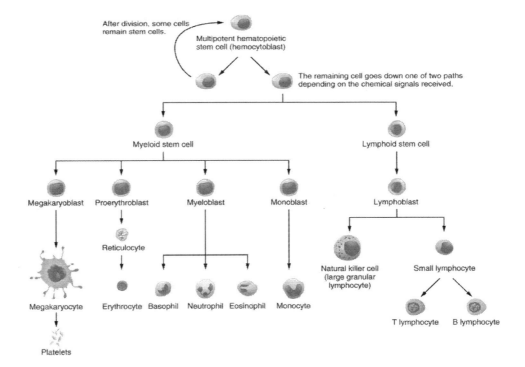

Figure 18.4 Hematopoietic System of Bone Marrow Hemopoiesis is the proliferation and differentiation of the formed elements of blood.

Lymphoid and myeloid stem cells do not immediately divide and differentiate into mature formed elements. As you can see in Figure 18.4, there are several intermediate stages of precursor cells (literally, forerunner cells), many of which can be recognized by their names, which have the suffix -blast. For instance, megakaryoblasts are the precursors of megakaryocytes, and proerythroblasts become reticulocytes, which eject their nucleus and most other organelles before maturing into erythrocytes.

Hemopoietic Growth Factors

Development from stem cells to precursor cells to mature cells is again initiated by hemopoietic growth factors. These include the following:

- **Erythropoietin (EPO)** is a glycoprotein hormone secreted by the interstitial fibroblast cells of the kidneys in response to low oxygen levels. It prompts the production of erythrocytes. Some athletes use synthetic EPO as a performance-enhancing drug (called blood doping) to increase RBC counts and subsequently increase oxygen delivery to tissues throughout the body. EPO is a banned substance in most organized sports, but it is also used medically in the treatment of certain anemia, specifically those triggered by certain types of cancer, and other disorders in which increased erythrocyte counts and oxygen levels are desirable.
- **Thrombopoietin**, another glycoprotein hormone, is produced by the liver and kidneys. It triggers the development of megakaryocytes into platelets.
- **Cytokines** are glycoproteins secreted by a wide variety of cells, including red bone marrow, leukocytes, macrophages, fibroblasts, and endothelial cells. They act locally as autocrine or paracrine factors, stimulating the proliferation of progenitor cells and helping to stimulate both nonspecific and specific resistance to disease. There are two major subtypes of cytokines known as colony-stimulating factors and interleukins.
  - **Colony-stimulating factors (CSFs)** are glycoproteins that act locally, as autocrine or paracrine factors. Some trigger the differentiation of myeloblasts into granular leukocytes, namely, neutrophils, eosinophils, and basophils. These are referred to as granulocyte CSFs. A different CSF induces the production of monocytes, called monocyte CSFs. Both granulocytes and monocytes are stimulated by GM-CSF; granulocytes, monocytes, platelets, and erythrocytes are stimulated by multi-CSF. Synthetic forms of these hormones are often administered to patients with various forms of cancer who are receiving chemotherapy to revive their WBC counts.
  - **Interleukins** are another class of cytokine signaling molecules important in hemopoiesis. They were initially thought to be secreted uniquely by leukocytes and to communicate only with other leukocytes, and were named accordingly, but are now known to be produced by a variety of cells including bone marrow and endothelium. Researchers now suspect that interleukins may play other roles in body functioning, including differentiation and maturation of cells, producing immunity and inflammation. To date, more than a dozen interleukins have been identified, with others likely to follow. They are generally numbered IL-1, IL-2, IL-3, etc.

Everyday CONNECTION

Blood Doping

In its original intent, the term blood doping was used to describe the practice of injecting by transfusion supplemental RBCs into an individual, typically to enhance performance in a sport. Additional RBCs would deliver more oxygen to the tissues, providing extra aerobic capacity, clinically referred to as VO_2 max. The source of the cells was either from the recipient (autologous) or from a donor with compatible blood (homologous). This practice was aided by the well-developed techniques of harvesting, concentrating, and freezing of the RBCs that could be later thawed and injected, yet still retain their functionality. These practices are considered illegal in virtually all sports and run the risk of infection, significantly increasing the viscosity of the blood and the potential for transmission of blood-borne pathogens if the blood was collected from another individual.

With the development of synthetic EPO in the 1980s, it became possible to provide additional RBCs by artificially stimulating RBC production in the bone marrow. Originally developed to treat patients suffering from anemia, renal failure, or cancer treatment, large quantities of EPO can be generated by recombinant DNA technology. Synthetic EPO is injected under the skin and can increase hematocrit for many weeks. It may also induce polycythemia and raise hematocrit to 70 or greater. This increased viscosity raises the resistance of the blood and forces the heart to pump more powerfully; in extreme cases, it has resulted in death. Other drugs such as cobalt II chloride have been shown to increase natural EPO gene expression. Blood doping has become problematic in many sports, especially cycling. Lance Armstrong, winner of seven Tour de France and many other cycling titles, was stripped of his victories and admitted to blood doping in 2013.

Interactive LINK

Watch this video (http://openstaxcollege.org/l/doping) to see doctors discuss the dangers of blood doping in sports. What are the some potential side effects of blood doping?

Bone Marrow Sampling and Transplants

Sometimes, a healthcare provider will order a **bone marrow biopsy**, a diagnostic test of a sample of red bone marrow, or a **bone marrow transplant**, a treatment in which a donor's healthy bone marrow—and its stem cells—replaces the faulty bone marrow of a patient. These tests and procedures are often used to assist in the diagnosis and treatment of various severe forms of anemia, such as thalassemia major and sickle cell anemia, as well as some types of cancer, specifically leukemia.

In the past, when a bone marrow sample or transplant was necessary, the procedure would have required inserting a large-bore needle into the region near the iliac crest of the pelvic bones (os coxae). This location was preferred, since its location close to the body surface makes it more accessible, and it is relatively isolated from most vital organs. Unfortunately, the procedure is quite painful.

Now, direct sampling of bone marrow can often be avoided. In many cases, stem cells can be isolated in just a few hours from a sample of a patient's blood. The isolated stem cells are then grown in culture using the appropriate hemopoietic growth factors, and analyzed or sometimes frozen for later use.

For an individual requiring a transplant, a matching donor is essential to prevent the immune system from destroying the donor cells—a phenomenon known as tissue rejection. To treat patients with bone marrow transplants, it is first necessary to destroy the patient's own diseased marrow through radiation and/or chemotherapy. Donor bone marrow stem cells are then intravenously infused. From the bloodstream, they establish themselves in the recipient's bone marrow.

18.3 | Erythrocytes

By the end of this section, you will be able to:
- Describe the anatomy of erythrocytes
- Discuss the various steps in the lifecycle of an erythrocyte
- Explain the composition and function of hemoglobin

The **erythrocyte**, commonly known as a red blood cell (or RBC), is by far the most common formed element: A single drop of blood contains millions of erythrocytes and just thousands of leukocytes. Specifically, males have about 5.4 million erythrocytes per microliter (μL) of blood, and females have approximately 4.8 million per μL. In fact, erythrocytes are estimated to make up about 25 percent of the total cells in the body. As you can imagine, they are quite small cells, with a mean diameter of only about 7–8 micrometers (μm) (Figure 18.5). The primary functions of erythrocytes are to pick up inhaled oxygen from the lungs and transport it to the body's tissues, and to pick up some (about 24 percent) carbon dioxide waste at the tissues and transport it to the lungs for exhalation. Erythrocytes remain within the vascular network. Although leukocytes typically leave the blood vessels to perform their defensive functions, movement of erythrocytes from the blood vessels is abnormal.

Formed element	Major subtypes	Numbers present per microliter (µL) and mean (range)	Appearance in a standard blood smear	Summary of functions	Comments
Erythrocytes (red blood cells)		5.2 million (4.4–6.0 million)	Flattened biconcave disk; no nucleus; pale red color	Transport oxygen and some carbon dioxide between tissues and lungs	Lifespan of approximately 120 days
Leukocytes (white blood cells)		7000 (5000–10,000)	Obvious dark-staining nucleus	All function in body defenses	Exit capillaries and move into tissues; lifespan of usually a few hours or days
	Granulocytes including neutrophils, eosinophils, and basophils	4360 (1800–9950)	Abundant granules in cytoplasm; nucleus normally lobed	Nonspecific (innate) resistance to disease	Classified according to membrane-bound granules in cytoplasm
	Neutrophils	4150 (1800–7300)	Nuclear lobes increase with age; pale lilac granules	Phagocytic; particularly effective against bacteria. Release cytotoxic chemicals from granules	Most common leukocyte; lifespan of minutes to days
	Eosinophils	165 (0–700)	Nucleus generally two-lobed; bright red-orange granules	Phagocytic cells; particularly effective with antigen-antibody complexes. Release antihistamines. Increase in allergies and parasitic infections	Lifespan of minutes to days
	Basophils	44 (0–150)	Nucleus generally two-lobed but difficult to see due to presence of heavy, dense, dark purple granules	Promotes inflammation	Least common leukocyte; lifespan unknown
	Agranulocytes including lymphocytes and monocytes	2640 (1700–4950)	Lack abundant granules in cytoplasm; have a simple-shaped nucleus that may be indented	Body defenses	Group consists of two major cell types from different lineages
	Lymphocytes	2185 (1500–4000)	Spherical cells with a single often large nucleus occupying much of the cell's volume; stains purple; seen in large (natural killer cells) and small (B and T cells) variants	Primarily specific (adaptive) immunity: T cells directly attack other cells (cellular immunity); B cells release antibodies (humoral immunity); natural killer cells are similar to T cells but nonspecific	Initial cells originate in bone marrow, but secondary production occurs in lymphatic tissue; several distinct subtypes; memory cells form after exposure to a pathogen and rapidly increase responses to subsequent exposure; lifespan of many years
	Monocytes	455 (200–950)	Largest leukocyte with an indented or horseshoe-shaped nucleus	Very effective phagocytic cells engulfing pathogens or worn out cells; also serve as antigen-presenting cells (APCs) for other components of the immune system	Produced in red bone marrow; referred to as macrophages after leaving circulation
Platelets		350,000 (150,000–500,000)	Cellular fragments surrounded by a plasma membrane and containing granules; purple stain	Hemostasis plus release growth factors for repair and healing of tissue	Formed from megakaryocytes that remain in the red bone marrow and shed platelets into circulation

Figure 18.5 Summary of Formed Elements in Blood

Shape and Structure of Erythrocytes

As an erythrocyte matures in the red bone marrow, it extrudes its nucleus and most of its other organelles. During the first day or two that it is in the circulation, an immature erythrocyte, known as a **reticulocyte**, will still typically contain remnants of organelles. Reticulocytes should comprise approximately 1–2 percent of the erythrocyte count and provide a rough estimate of the rate of RBC production, with abnormally low or high rates indicating deviations in the production of these cells. These remnants, primarily of networks (reticulum) of ribosomes, are quickly shed, however, and mature, circulating erythrocytes have few internal cellular structural components. Lacking mitochondria, for example, they rely on anaerobic respiration. This means that they do not utilize any of the oxygen they are transporting, so they can deliver it all to the tissues. They also lack endoplasmic reticula and do not synthesize proteins. Erythrocytes do, however, contain some structural proteins that help the blood cells maintain their unique structure and enable them to change their shape to squeeze through capillaries. This includes the protein spectrin, a cytoskeletal protein element.

Erythrocytes are biconcave disks; that is, they are plump at their periphery and very thin in the center (Figure 18.6). Since they lack most organelles, there is more interior space for the presence of the hemoglobin molecules that, as you will see shortly, transport gases. The biconcave shape also provides a greater surface area across which gas exchange can occur, relative to its volume; a sphere of a similar diameter would have a lower surface area-to-volume ratio. In the capillaries, the oxygen carried by the erythrocytes can diffuse into the plasma and then through the capillary walls to reach the cells, whereas some of the carbon dioxide produced by the cells as a waste product diffuses into the capillaries to be picked up by the erythrocytes. Capillary beds are extremely narrow, slowing the passage of the erythrocytes and providing an extended opportunity for gas exchange to occur. However, the space within capillaries can be so minute that, despite their own small size, erythrocytes may have to fold in on themselves if they are to make their way through. Fortunately, their structural proteins like spectrin are flexible, allowing them to bend over themselves to a surprising degree, then spring back again when they enter a wider vessel. In wider vessels, erythrocytes may stack up much like a roll of coins, forming a rouleaux, from the French word for "roll."

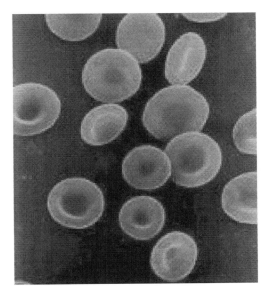

Figure 18.6 Shape of Red Blood Cells Erythrocytes are biconcave discs with very shallow centers. This shape optimizes the ratio of surface area to volume, facilitating gas exchange. It also enables them to fold up as they move through narrow blood vessels.

Hemoglobin

Hemoglobin is a large molecule made up of proteins and iron. It consists of four folded chains of a protein called **globin**, designated alpha 1 and 2, and beta 1 and 2 (Figure 18.7**a**). Each of these globin molecules is bound to a red pigment molecule called **heme**, which contains an ion of iron (Fe^{2+}) (Figure 18.7**b**).

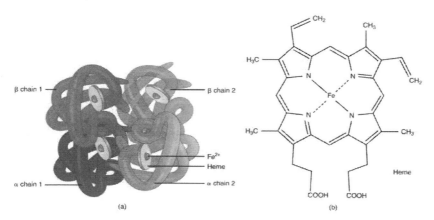

Figure 18.7 Hemoglobin (a) A molecule of hemoglobin contains four globin proteins, each of which is bound to one molecule of the iron-containing pigment heme. (b) A single erythrocyte can contain 300 million hemoglobin molecules, and thus more than 1 billion oxygen molecules.

Each iron ion in the heme can bind to one oxygen molecule; therefore, each hemoglobin molecule can transport four oxygen molecules. An individual erythrocyte may contain about 300 million hemoglobin molecules, and therefore can bind to and transport up to 1.2 billion oxygen molecules (see Figure 18.7**b**).

In the lungs, hemoglobin picks up oxygen, which binds to the iron ions, forming **oxyhemoglobin**. The bright red, oxygenated hemoglobin travels to the body tissues, where it releases some of the oxygen molecules, becoming darker red **deoxyhemoglobin**, sometimes referred to as reduced hemoglobin. Oxygen release depends on the need for oxygen in the surrounding tissues, so hemoglobin rarely if ever leaves all of its oxygen behind. In the capillaries, carbon dioxide enters the bloodstream. About 76 percent dissolves in the plasma, some of it remaining as dissolved CO_2, and the remainder forming bicarbonate ion. About 23–24 percent of it binds to the amino acids in hemoglobin, forming a molecule known as **carbaminohemoglobin**. From the capillaries, the hemoglobin carries carbon dioxide back to the lungs, where it releases it for exchange of oxygen.

Changes in the levels of RBCs can have significant effects on the body's ability to effectively deliver oxygen to the tissues. Ineffective hematopoiesis results in insufficient numbers of RBCs and results in one of several forms of anemia. An overproduction of RBCs produces a condition called polycythemia. The primary drawback with polycythemia is not a failure to directly deliver enough oxygen to the tissues, but rather the increased viscosity of the blood, which makes it more difficult for the heart to circulate the blood.

In patients with insufficient hemoglobin, the tissues may not receive sufficient oxygen, resulting in another form of anemia. In determining oxygenation of tissues, the value of greatest interest in healthcare is the percent saturation; that is, the percentage of hemoglobin sites occupied by oxygen in a patient's blood. Clinically this value is commonly referred to simply as "percent sat."

Percent saturation is normally monitored using a device known as a pulse oximeter, which is applied to a thin part of the body, typically the tip of the patient's finger. The device works by sending two different wavelengths of light (one red, the other infrared) through the finger and measuring the light with a photodetector as it exits. Hemoglobin absorbs light differentially depending upon its saturation with oxygen. The machine calibrates the amount of light received by the photodetector against the amount absorbed by the partially oxygenated hemoglobin and presents the data as percent saturation. Normal pulse oximeter readings range from 95–100 percent. Lower percentages reflect **hypoxemia**, or low blood oxygen. The term hypoxia is more generic and simply refers to low oxygen levels. Oxygen levels are also directly monitored from free oxygen in the plasma typically following an arterial stick. When this method is applied, the amount of oxygen present is expressed in terms of partial pressure of oxygen or simply pO₂ and is typically recorded in units of millimeters of mercury, mm Hg.

The kidneys filter about 180 liters (~380 pints) of blood in an average adult each day, or about 20 percent of the total resting volume, and thus serve as ideal sites for receptors that determine oxygen saturation. In response to hypoxemia, less oxygen will exit the vessels supplying the kidney, resulting in hypoxia (low oxygen concentration) in the tissue fluid of the kidney where oxygen concentration is actually monitored. Interstitial fibroblasts within the kidney secrete EPO, thereby increasing erythrocyte production and restoring oxygen levels. In a classic negative-feedback loop, as oxygen saturation rises, EPO secretion falls, and vice versa, thereby maintaining homeostasis. Populations dwelling at high elevations, with inherently lower levels of oxygen in the atmosphere, naturally maintain a hematocrit higher than people living at sea level. Consequently, people traveling to high elevations may experience symptoms of hypoxemia, such as fatigue, headache, and shortness of breath, for a few days after their arrival. In response to the hypoxemia, the kidneys secrete EPO to step up the production of erythrocytes until homeostasis is achieved once again. To avoid the symptoms of hypoxemia, or altitude sickness, mountain climbers typically rest for several days to a week or more at a series of camps situated at increasing elevations to allow EPO levels and, consequently, erythrocyte counts to rise. When climbing the tallest peaks, such as Mt. Everest and K2 in the Himalayas, many mountain climbers rely upon bottled oxygen as they near the summit.

Lifecycle of Erythrocytes

Production of erythrocytes in the marrow occurs at the staggering rate of more than 2 million cells per second. For this production to occur, a number of raw materials must be present in adequate amounts. These include the same nutrients that are essential to the production and maintenance of any cell, such as glucose, lipids, and amino acids. However, erythrocyte production also requires several trace elements:

- Iron. We have said that each heme group in a hemoglobin molecule contains an ion of the trace mineral iron. On average, less than 20 percent of the iron we consume is absorbed. Heme iron, from animal foods such as meat, poultry, and fish, is absorbed more efficiently than non-heme iron from plant foods. Upon absorption, iron becomes part of the body's total iron pool. The bone marrow, liver, and spleen can store iron in the protein compounds **ferritin** and **hemosiderin**. Ferroportin transports the iron across the intestinal cell plasma membranes and from its storage sites into tissue fluid where it enters the blood. When EPO stimulates the production of erythrocytes, iron is released from storage, bound to transferrin, and carried to the red marrow where it attaches to erythrocyte precursors.
- Copper. A trace mineral, copper is a component of two plasma proteins, hephaestin and ceruloplasmin. Without these, hemoglobin could not be adequately produced. Located in intestinal villi, hephaestin enables iron to be absorbed by intestinal cells. Ceruloplasmin transports copper. Both enable the oxidation of iron from Fe^{2+} to Fe^{3+}, a form in which it can be bound to its transport protein, **transferrin**, for transport to body cells. In a state of copper deficiency, the transport of iron for heme synthesis decreases, and iron can accumulate in tissues, where it can eventually lead to organ damage.
- Zinc. The trace mineral zinc functions as a co-enzyme that facilitates the synthesis of the heme portion of hemoglobin.
- B vitamins. The B vitamins folate and vitamin B_{12} function as co-enzymes that facilitate DNA synthesis. Thus, both are critical for the synthesis of new cells, including erythrocytes.

Erythrocytes live up to 120 days in the circulation, after which the worn-out cells are removed by a type of myeloid phagocytic cell called a **macrophage**, located primarily within the bone marrow, liver, and spleen. The components of the degraded erythrocytes' hemoglobin are further processed as follows:

- Globin, the protein portion of hemoglobin, is broken down into amino acids, which can be sent back to the bone marrow to be used in the production of new erythrocytes. Hemoglobin that is not phagocytized is broken down in the circulation, releasing alpha and beta chains that are removed from circulation by the kidneys.
- The iron contained in the heme portion of hemoglobin may be stored in the liver or spleen, primarily in the form of ferritin or hemosiderin, or carried through the bloodstream by transferrin to the red bone marrow for recycling into new erythrocytes.
- The non-iron portion of heme is degraded into the waste product **biliverdin**, a green pigment, and then into another waste product, **bilirubin**, a yellow pigment. Bilirubin binds to albumin and travels in the blood to the liver, which uses it in the manufacture of bile, a compound released into the intestines to help emulsify dietary fats. In the large intestine, bacteria breaks the bilirubin apart from the bile and converts it to urobilinogen and then into stercobilin. It is then eliminated from the body in the feces. Broad-spectrum antibiotics typically eliminate these bacteria as well and may alter the color of feces. The kidneys also remove any circulating bilirubin and other related metabolic byproducts such as urobilins and secrete them into the urine.

The breakdown pigments formed from the destruction of hemoglobin can be seen in a variety of situations. At the site of an injury, biliverdin from damaged RBCs produces some of the dramatic colors associated with bruising. With a failing liver, bilirubin cannot be removed effectively from circulation and causes the body to assume a yellowish tinge associated with jaundice. Stercobilins within the feces produce the typical brown color associated with this waste. And the yellow of urine is associated with the urobilins.

The erythrocyte lifecycle is summarized in Figure 18.8.

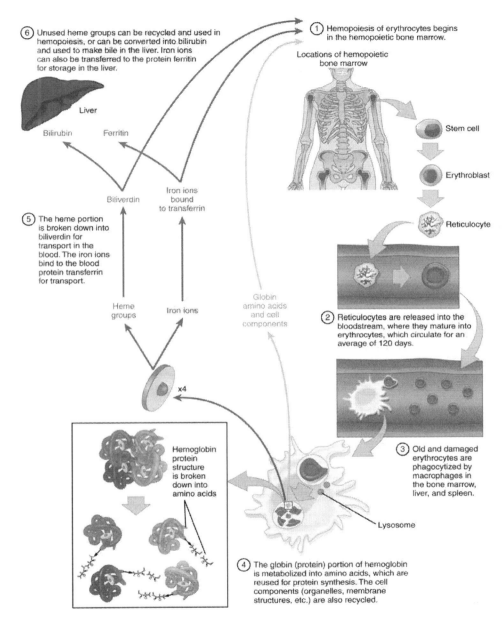

Figure 18.8 Erythrocyte Lifecycle Erythrocytes are produced in the bone marrow and sent into the circulation. At the end of their lifecycle, they are destroyed by macrophages, and their components are recycled.

Disorders of Erythrocytes

The size, shape, and number of erythrocytes, and the number of hemoglobin molecules can have a major impact on a person's health. When the number of RBCs or hemoglobin is deficient, the general condition is called **anemia**. There are more than 400 types of anemia and more than 3.5 million Americans suffer from this condition. Anemia can be broken down into three major groups: those caused by blood loss, those caused by faulty or decreased RBC production, and those caused by excessive destruction of RBCs. Clinicians often use two groupings in diagnosis: The kinetic approach focuses on evaluating the production, destruction, and removal of RBCs, whereas the morphological approach examines the RBCs themselves, paying particular emphasis to their size. A common test is the mean corpuscle volume (MCV), which measures size. Normal-sized cells are referred to as normocytic, smaller-than-normal cells are referred to as microcytic, and larger-than-normal cells are referred to as macrocytic. Reticulocyte counts are also important and may reveal inadequate production of RBCs. The effects of the various anemias are widespread, because reduced numbers of RBCs or hemoglobin will result in lower levels of oxygen being delivered to body tissues. Since oxygen is required for tissue functioning, anemia produces fatigue, lethargy, and an increased risk for infection. An oxygen deficit in the brain impairs the ability to think clearly, and may prompt headaches and irritability. Lack of oxygen leaves the patient short of breath, even as the heart and lungs work harder in response to the deficit.

Blood loss anemias are fairly straightforward. In addition to bleeding from wounds or other lesions, these forms of anemia may be due to ulcers, hemorrhoids, inflammation of the stomach (gastritis), and some cancers of the gastrointestinal tract. The excessive use of aspirin or other nonsteroidal anti-inflammatory drugs such as ibuprofen can trigger ulceration and gastritis. Excessive menstruation and loss of blood during childbirth are also potential causes.

Anemias caused by faulty or decreased RBC production include sickle cell anemia, iron deficiency anemia, vitamin deficiency anemia, and diseases of the bone marrow and stem cells.

- A characteristic change in the shape of erythrocytes is seen in **sickle cell disease** (also referred to as sickle cell anemia). A genetic disorder, it is caused by production of an abnormal type of hemoglobin, called hemoglobin S, which delivers less oxygen to tissues and causes erythrocytes to assume a sickle (or crescent) shape, especially at low oxygen concentrations (Figure 18.9). These abnormally shaped cells can then become lodged in narrow capillaries because they are unable to fold in on themselves to squeeze through, blocking blood flow to tissues and causing a variety of serious problems from painful joints to delayed growth and even blindness and cerebrovascular accidents (strokes). Sickle cell anemia is a genetic condition particularly found in individuals of African descent.

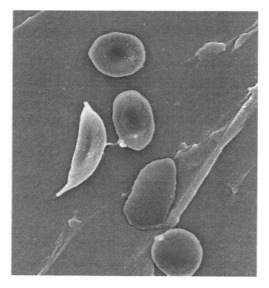

Figure 18.9 Sickle Cells Sickle cell anemia is caused by a mutation in one of the hemoglobin genes. Erythrocytes produce an abnormal type of hemoglobin, which causes the cell to take on a sickle or crescent shape. (credit: Janice Haney Carr)

- Iron deficiency anemia is the most common type and results when the amount of available iron is insufficient to allow production of sufficient heme. This condition can occur in individuals with a deficiency of iron in the diet and is especially common in teens and children as well as in vegans and vegetarians. Additionally, iron deficiency anemia may be caused by either an inability to absorb and transport iron or slow, chronic bleeding.
- Vitamin-deficient anemias generally involve insufficient vitamin B12 and folate.

- Megaloblastic anemia involves a deficiency of vitamin B12 and/or folate, and often involves diets deficient in these essential nutrients. Lack of meat or a viable alternate source, and overcooking or eating insufficient amounts of vegetables may lead to a lack of folate.
- Pernicious anemia is caused by poor absorption of vitamin B12 and is often seen in patients with Crohn's disease (a severe intestinal disorder often treated by surgery), surgical removal of the intestines or stomach (common in some weight loss surgeries), intestinal parasites, and AIDS.
- Pregnancies, some medications, excessive alcohol consumption, and some diseases such as celiac disease are also associated with vitamin deficiencies. It is essential to provide sufficient folic acid during the early stages of pregnancy to reduce the risk of neurological defects, including spina bifida, a failure of the neural tube to close.

• Assorted disease processes can also interfere with the production and formation of RBCs and hemoglobin. If myeloid stem cells are defective or replaced by cancer cells, there will be insufficient quantities of RBCs produced.
- Aplastic anemia is the condition in which there are deficient numbers of RBC stem cells. Aplastic anemia is often inherited, or it may be triggered by radiation, medication, chemotherapy, or infection.
- **Thalassemia** is an inherited condition typically occurring in individuals from the Middle East, the Mediterranean, African, and Southeast Asia, in which maturation of the RBCs does not proceed normally. The most severe form is called Cooley's anemia.
- Lead exposure from industrial sources or even dust from paint chips of iron-containing paints or pottery that has not been properly glazed may also lead to destruction of the red marrow.

• Various disease processes also can lead to anemias. These include chronic kidney diseases often associated with a decreased production of EPO, hypothyroidism, some forms of cancer, lupus, and rheumatoid arthritis.

In contrast to anemia, an elevated RBC count is called **polycythemia** and is detected in a patient's elevated hematocrit. It can occur transiently in a person who is dehydrated; when water intake is inadequate or water losses are excessive, the plasma volume falls. As a result, the hematocrit rises. For reasons mentioned earlier, a mild form of polycythemia is chronic but normal in people living at high altitudes. Some elite athletes train at high elevations specifically to induce this phenomenon. Finally, a type of bone marrow disease called polycythemia vera (from the Greek vera = "true") causes an excessive production of immature erythrocytes. Polycythemia vera can dangerously elevate the viscosity of blood, raising blood pressure and making it more difficult for the heart to pump blood throughout the body. It is a relatively rare disease that occurs more often in men than women, and is more likely to be present in elderly patients those over 60 years of age.

18.4 | Leukocytes and Platelets

By the end of this section, you will be able to:
- Describe the general characteristics of leukocytes
- Classify leukocytes according to their lineage, their main structural features, and their primary functions
- Discuss the most common malignancies involving leukocytes
- Identify the lineage, basic structure, and function of platelets

The **leukocyte**, commonly known as a white blood cell (or WBC), is a major component of the body's defenses against disease. Leukocytes protect the body against invading microorganisms and body cells with mutated DNA, and they clean up debris. Platelets are essential for the repair of blood vessels when damage to them has occurred; they also provide growth factors for healing and repair. See Figure 18.5 for a summary of leukocytes and platelets.

Characteristics of Leukocytes

Although leukocytes and erythrocytes both originate from hematopoietic stem cells in the bone marrow, they are very different from each other in many significant ways. For instance, leukocytes are far less numerous than erythrocytes: Typically there are only 5000 to 10,000 per μL. They are also larger than erythrocytes and are the only formed elements that are complete cells, possessing a nucleus and organelles. And although there is just one type of erythrocyte, there are many types of leukocytes. Most of these types have a much shorter lifespan than that of erythrocytes, some as short as a few hours or even a few minutes in the case of acute infection.

One of the most distinctive characteristics of leukocytes is their movement. Whereas erythrocytes spend their days circulating within the blood vessels, leukocytes routinely leave the bloodstream to perform their defensive functions in the body's tissues. For leukocytes, the vascular network is simply a highway they travel and soon exit to reach their true destination. When they arrive, they are often given distinct names, such as macrophage or microglia, depending on their function. As shown in Figure 18.10, they leave the capillaries—the smallest blood vessels—or other small vessels through a process known as **emigration** (from the Latin for "removal") or **diapedesis** (dia- = "through"; -pedan = "to leap") in which they squeeze through adjacent cells in a blood vessel wall.

Once they have exited the capillaries, some leukocytes will take up fixed positions in lymphatic tissue, bone marrow, the spleen, the thymus, or other organs. Others will move about through the tissue spaces very much like amoebas, continuously extending their plasma membranes, sometimes wandering freely, and sometimes moving toward the direction in which they are drawn by chemical signals. This attracting of leukocytes occurs because of **positive chemotaxis** (literally "movement in response to chemicals"), a phenomenon in which injured or infected cells and nearby leukocytes emit the equivalent of a chemical "911" call, attracting more leukocytes to the site. In clinical medicine, the differential counts of the types and percentages of leukocytes present are often key indicators in making a diagnosis and selecting a treatment.

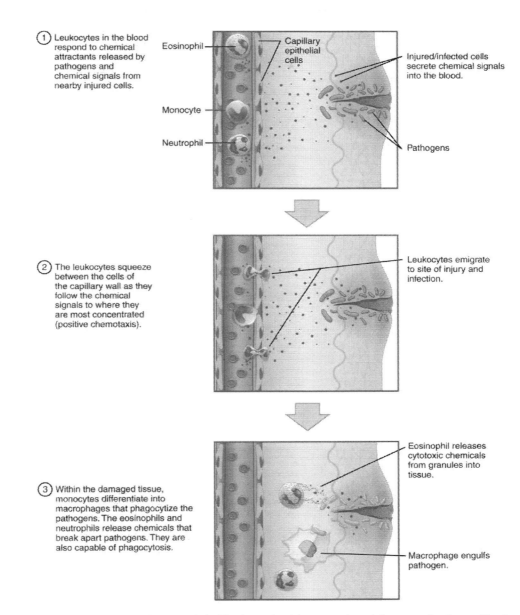

Figure 18.10 Emigration Leukocytes exit the blood vessel and then move through the connective tissue of the dermis toward the site of a wound. Some leukocytes, such as the eosinophil and neutrophil, are characterized as granular leukocytes. They release chemicals from their granules that destroy pathogens; they are also capable of phagocytosis. The monocyte, an agranular leukocyte, differentiates into a macrophage that then phagocytizes the pathogens.

Classification of Leukocytes

When scientists first began to observe stained blood slides, it quickly became evident that leukocytes could be divided into two groups, according to whether their cytoplasm contained highly visible granules:

- **Granular leukocytes** contain abundant granules within the cytoplasm. They include neutrophils, eosinophils, and basophils (you can view their lineage from myeloid stem cells in Figure 18.4).
- While granules are not totally lacking in **agranular leukocytes**, they are far fewer and less obvious. Agranular leukocytes include monocytes, which mature into macrophages that are phagocytic, and lymphocytes, which arise from the lymphoid stem cell line.

Granular Leukocytes

We will consider the granular leukocytes in order from most common to least common. All of these are produced in the red bone marrow and have a short lifespan of hours to days. They typically have a lobed nucleus and are classified according to which type of stain best highlights their granules (Figure 18.11).

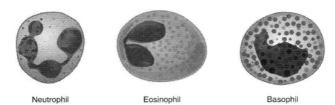

Figure 18.11 Granular Leukocytes A neutrophil has small granules that stain light lilac and a nucleus with two to five lobes. An eosinophil's granules are slightly larger and stain reddish-orange, and its nucleus has two to three lobes. A basophil has large granules that stain dark blue to purple and a two-lobed nucleus.

The most common of all the leukocytes, **neutrophils** will normally comprise 50–70 percent of total leukocyte count. They are 10–12 μm in diameter, significantly larger than erythrocytes. They are called neutrophils because their granules show up most clearly with stains that are chemically neutral (neither acidic nor basic). The granules are numerous but quite fine and normally appear light lilac. The nucleus has a distinct lobed appearance and may have two to five lobes, the number increasing with the age of the cell. Older neutrophils have increasing numbers of lobes and are often referred to as **polymorphonuclear** (a nucleus with many forms), or simply "polys." Younger and immature neutrophils begin to develop lobes and are known as "bands."

Neutrophils are rapid responders to the site of infection and are efficient phagocytes with a preference for bacteria. Their granules include **lysozyme**, an enzyme capable of lysing, or breaking down, bacterial cell walls; oxidants such as hydrogen peroxide; and **defensins**, proteins that bind to and puncture bacterial and fungal plasma membranes, so that the cell contents leak out. Abnormally high counts of neutrophils indicate infection and/or inflammation, particularly triggered by bacteria, but are also found in burn patients and others experiencing unusual stress. A burn injury increases the proliferation of neutrophils in order to fight off infection that can result from the destruction of the barrier of the skin. Low counts may be caused by drug toxicity and other disorders, and may increase an individual's susceptibility to infection.

Eosinophils typically represent 2–4 percent of total leukocyte count. They are also 10–12 μm in diameter. The granules of eosinophils stain best with an acidic stain known as eosin. The nucleus of the eosinophil will typically have two to three lobes and, if stained properly, the granules will have a distinct red to orange color.

The granules of eosinophils include antihistamine molecules, which counteract the activities of histamines, inflammatory chemicals produced by basophils and mast cells. Some eosinophil granules contain molecules toxic to parasitic worms, which can enter the body through the integument, or when an individual consumes raw or undercooked fish or meat. Eosinophils are also capable of phagocytosis and are particularly effective when antibodies bind to the target and form an antigen-antibody complex. High counts of eosinophils are typical of patients experiencing allergies, parasitic worm infestations, and some autoimmune diseases. Low counts may be due to drug toxicity and stress.

Basophils are the least common leukocytes, typically comprising less than one percent of the total leukocyte count. They are slightly smaller than neutrophils and eosinophils at 8–10 μm in diameter. The granules of basophils stain best with basic (alkaline) stains. Basophils contain large granules that pick up a dark blue stain and are so common they may make it difficult to see the two-lobed nucleus.

In general, basophils intensify the inflammatory response. They share this trait with mast cells. In the past, mast cells were considered to be basophils that left the circulation. However, this appears not to be the case, as the two cell types develop from different lineages.

The granules of basophils release histamines, which contribute to inflammation, and heparin, which opposes blood clotting. High counts of basophils are associated with allergies, parasitic infections, and hypothyroidism. Low counts are associated with pregnancy, stress, and hyperthyroidism.

Agranular Leukocytes

Agranular leukocytes contain smaller, less-visible granules in their cytoplasm than do granular leukocytes. The nucleus is simple in shape, sometimes with an indentation but without distinct lobes. There are two major types of agranulocytes: lymphocytes and monocytes (see Figure 18.4).

Lymphocytes are the only formed element of blood that arises from lymphoid stem cells. Although they form initially in the bone marrow, much of their subsequent development and reproduction occurs in the lymphatic tissues. Lymphocytes are the second most common type of leukocyte, accounting for about 20–30 percent of all leukocytes, and are essential for the immune response. The size range of lymphocytes is quite extensive, with some authorities recognizing two size classes and others three. Typically, the large cells are 10–14 μm and have a smaller nucleus-to-cytoplasm ratio and more granules. The smaller cells are typically 6–9 μm with a larger volume of nucleus to cytoplasm, creating a "halo" effect. A few cells may fall outside these ranges, at 14–17 μm. This finding has led to the three size range classification.

The three major groups of lymphocytes include natural killer cells, B cells, and T cells. **Natural killer (NK) cells** are capable of recognizing cells that do not express "self" proteins on their plasma membrane or that contain foreign or abnormal markers. These "nonself" cells include cancer cells, cells infected with a virus, and other cells with atypical surface proteins. Thus, they provide generalized, nonspecific immunity. The larger lymphocytes are typically NK cells.

B cells and T cells, also called **B lymphocytes** and **T lymphocytes**, play prominent roles in defending the body against specific pathogens (disease-causing microorganisms) and are involved in specific immunity. One form of B cells (plasma cells) produces the antibodies or immunoglobulins that bind to specific foreign or abnormal components of plasma membranes. This is also referred to as humoral (body fluid) immunity. T cells provide cellular-level immunity by physically attacking foreign or diseased cells. A **memory cell** is a variety of both B and T cells that forms after exposure to a pathogen and mounts rapid responses upon subsequent exposures. Unlike other leukocytes, memory cells live for many years. B cells undergo a maturation process in the bone marrow, whereas T cells undergo maturation in the thymus. This site of the maturation process gives rise to the name B and T cells. The functions of lymphocytes are complex and will be covered in detail in the chapter covering the lymphatic system and immunity. Smaller lymphocytes are either B or T cells, although they cannot be differentiated in a normal blood smear.

Abnormally high lymphocyte counts are characteristic of viral infections as well as some types of cancer. Abnormally low lymphocyte counts are characteristic of prolonged (chronic) illness or immunosuppression, including that caused by HIV infection and drug therapies that often involve steroids.

Monocytes originate from myeloid stem cells. They normally represent 2–8 percent of the total leukocyte count. They are typically easily recognized by their large size of 12–20 μm and indented or horseshoe-shaped nuclei. Macrophages are monocytes that have left the circulation and phagocytize debris, foreign pathogens, worn-out erythrocytes, and many other dead, worn out, or damaged cells. Macrophages also release antimicrobial defensins and chemotactic chemicals that attract other leukocytes to the site of an infection. Some macrophages occupy fixed locations, whereas others wander through the tissue fluid.

Abnormally high counts of monocytes are associated with viral or fungal infections, tuberculosis, and some forms of leukemia and other chronic diseases. Abnormally low counts are typically caused by suppression of the bone marrow.

Lifecycle of Leukocytes

Most leukocytes have a relatively short lifespan, typically measured in hours or days. Production of all leukocytes begins in the bone marrow under the influence of CSFs and interleukins. Secondary production and maturation of lymphocytes occurs in specific regions of lymphatic tissue known as germinal centers. Lymphocytes are fully capable of mitosis and may produce clones of cells with identical properties. This capacity enables an individual to maintain immunity throughout life to many threats that have been encountered in the past.

Disorders of Leukocytes

Leukopenia is a condition in which too few leukocytes are produced. If this condition is pronounced, the individual may be unable to ward off disease. Excessive leukocyte proliferation is known as **leukocytosis**. Although leukocyte counts are high, the cells themselves are often nonfunctional, leaving the individual at increased risk for disease.

Leukemia is a cancer involving an abundance of leukocytes. It may involve only one specific type of leukocyte from either the myeloid line (myelocytic leukemia) or the lymphoid line (lymphocytic leukemia). In chronic leukemia, mature leukocytes accumulate and fail to die. In acute leukemia, there is an overproduction of young, immature leukocytes. In both conditions the cells do not function properly.

Lymphoma is a form of cancer in which masses of malignant T and/or B lymphocytes collect in lymph nodes, the spleen, the liver, and other tissues. As in leukemia, the malignant leukocytes do not function properly, and the patient is vulnerable to infection. Some forms of lymphoma tend to progress slowly and respond well to treatment. Others tend to progress quickly and require aggressive treatment, without which they are rapidly fatal.

Platelets

You may occasionally see platelets referred to as **thrombocytes**, but because this name suggests they are a type of cell, it is not accurate. A platelet is not a cell but rather a fragment of the cytoplasm of a cell called a **megakaryocyte** that is surrounded by a plasma membrane. Megakaryocytes are descended from myeloid stem cells (see Figure 18.4) and are large, typically 50–100 μm in diameter, and contain an enlarged, lobed nucleus. As noted earlier, thrombopoietin, a glycoprotein secreted by the kidneys and liver, stimulates the proliferation of megakaryoblasts, which mature into megakaryocytes. These remain within bone marrow tissue (Figure 18.12) and ultimately form platelet-precursor extensions that extend through the walls of bone marrow capillaries to release into the circulation thousands of cytoplasmic fragments, each enclosed by a bit of plasma membrane. These enclosed fragments are platelets. Each megakarocyte releases 2000–3000 platelets during its lifespan. Following platelet release, megakaryocyte remnants, which are little more than a cell nucleus, are consumed by macrophages.

Platelets are relatively small, 2–4 μm in diameter, but numerous, with typically 150,000–160,000 per μL of blood. After entering the circulation, approximately one-third migrate to the spleen for storage for later release in response to any rupture in a blood vessel. They then become activated to perform their primary function, which is to limit blood loss. Platelets remain only about 10 days, then are phagocytized by macrophages.

Platelets are critical to hemostasis, the stoppage of blood flow following damage to a vessel. They also secrete a variety of growth factors essential for growth and repair of tissue, particularly connective tissue. Infusions of concentrated platelets are now being used in some therapies to stimulate healing.

Disorders of Platelets

Thrombocytosis is a condition in which there are too many platelets. This may trigger formation of unwanted blood clots (thrombosis), a potentially fatal disorder. If there is an insufficient number of platelets, called **thrombocytopenia**, blood may not clot properly, and excessive bleeding may result.

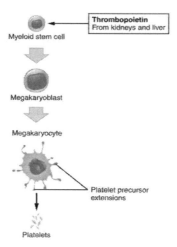

Figure 18.12 Platelets Platelets are derived from cells called megakaryocytes.

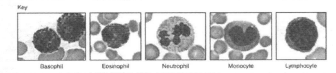

Figure 18.13 Leukocytes (Micrographs provided by the Regents of University of Michigan Medical School © 2012)

View University of Michigan Webscopes at http://virtualslides.med.umich.edu/Histology/Cardiovascular%20System/081-2_HISTO_40X.svs/view.apml?cwidth=860&cheight=733&chost=virtualslides.med.umich.edu&listview=1&title=&csis=1 and explore the blood slides in greater detail. The Webscope feature allows you to move the slides as you would with a mechanical stage. You can increase and decrease the magnification. There is a chance to review each of the leukocytes individually after you have attempted to identify them from the first two blood smears. In addition, there are a few multiple choice questions.

Are you able to recognize and identify the various formed elements? You will need to do this is a systematic manner, scanning along the image. The standard method is to use a grid, but this is not possible with this resource. Try constructing a simple table with each leukocyte type and then making a mark for each cell type you identify. Attempt to classify at least 50 and perhaps as many as 100 different cells. Based on the percentage of cells that you count, do the numbers represent a normal blood smear or does something appear to be abnormal?

18.5 | Hemostasis

By the end of this section, you will be able to:
- Describe the three mechanisms involved in hemostasis
- Explain how the extrinsic and intrinsic coagulation pathways lead to the common pathway, and the coagulation factors involved in each
- Discuss disorders affecting hemostasis

Platelets are key players in **hemostasis**, the process by which the body seals a ruptured blood vessel and prevents further loss of blood. Although rupture of larger vessels usually requires medical intervention, hemostasis is quite effective in dealing with small, simple wounds. There are three steps to the process: vascular spasm, the formation of a platelet plug, and coagulation (blood clotting). Failure of any of these steps will result in **hemorrhage**—excessive bleeding.

Vascular Spasm

When a vessel is severed or punctured, or when the wall of a vessel is damaged, vascular spasm occurs. In **vascular spasm**, the smooth muscle in the walls of the vessel contracts dramatically. This smooth muscle has both circular layers; larger vessels also have longitudinal layers. The circular layers tend to constrict the flow of blood, whereas the longitudinal layers, when present, draw the vessel back into the surrounding tissue, often making it more difficult for a surgeon to locate, clamp, and tie off a severed vessel. The vascular spasm response is believed to be triggered by several chemicals called endothelins that are released by vessel-lining cells and by pain receptors in response to vessel injury. This phenomenon typically lasts for up to 30 minutes, although it can last for hours.

Formation of the Platelet Plug

In the second step, platelets, which normally float free in the plasma, encounter the area of vessel rupture with the exposed underlying connective tissue and collagenous fibers. The platelets begin to clump together, become spiked and sticky, and bind to the exposed collagen and endothelial lining. This process is assisted by a glycoprotein in the blood plasma called von Willebrand factor, which helps stabilize the growing **platelet plug**. As platelets collect, they simultaneously release chemicals from their granules into the plasma that further contribute to hemostasis. Among the substances released by the platelets are:

- adenosine diphosphate (ADP), which helps additional platelets to adhere to the injury site, reinforcing and expanding the platelet plug
- serotonin, which maintains vasoconstriction
- prostaglandins and phospholipids, which also maintain vasoconstriction and help to activate further clotting chemicals, as discussed next

A platelet plug can temporarily seal a small opening in a blood vessel. Plug formation, in essence, buys the body time while more sophisticated and durable repairs are being made. In a similar manner, even modern naval warships still carry an assortment of wooden plugs to temporarily repair small breaches in their hulls until permanent repairs can be made.

Coagulation

Those more sophisticated and more durable repairs are collectively called **coagulation**, the formation of a blood clot. The process is sometimes characterized as a cascade, because one event prompts the next as in a multi-level waterfall. The result is the production of a gelatinous but robust clot made up of a mesh of **fibrin**—an insoluble filamentous protein derived from fibrinogen, the plasma protein introduced earlier—in which platelets and blood cells are trapped. Figure 18.14 summarizes the three steps of hemostasis.

Chapter 18 | The Cardiovascular System: Blood

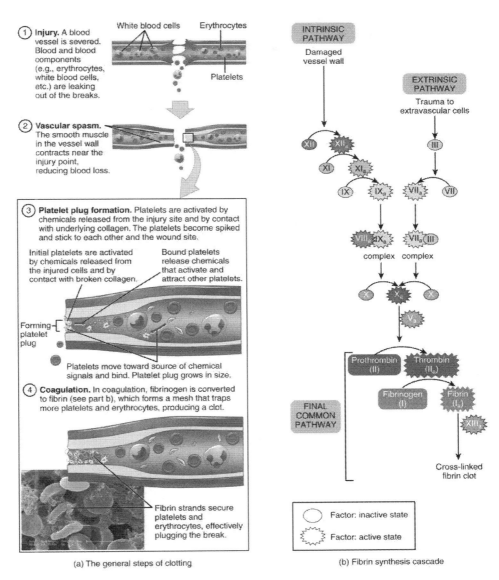

(a) The general steps of clotting (b) Fibrin synthesis cascade

Figure 18.14 Hemostasis (a) An injury to a blood vessel initiates the process of hemostasis. Blood clotting involves three steps. First, vascular spasm constricts the flow of blood. Next, a platelet plug forms to temporarily seal small openings in the vessel. Coagulation then enables the repair of the vessel wall once the leakage of blood has stopped. (b) The synthesis of fibrin in blood clots involves either an intrinsic pathway or an extrinsic pathway, both of which lead to a common pathway. (credit a: Kevin MacKenzie)

Clotting Factors Involved in Coagulation

In the coagulation cascade, chemicals called **clotting factors** (or coagulation factors) prompt reactions that activate still more coagulation factors. The process is complex, but is initiated along two basic pathways:

- The extrinsic pathway, which normally is triggered by trauma.

- The intrinsic pathway, which begins in the bloodstream and is triggered by internal damage to the wall of the vessel.

Both of these merge into a third pathway, referred to as the common pathway (see Figure 18.14b). All three pathways are dependent upon the 12 known clotting factors, including Ca^{2+} and vitamin K (Table 18.1). Clotting factors are secreted primarily by the liver and the platelets. The liver requires the fat-soluble vitamin K to produce many of them. Vitamin K (along with biotin and folate) is somewhat unusual among vitamins in that it is not only consumed in the diet but is also synthesized by bacteria residing in the large intestine. The calcium ion, considered factor IV, is derived from the diet and from the breakdown of bone. Some recent evidence indicates that activation of various clotting factors occurs on specific receptor sites on the surfaces of platelets.

The 12 clotting factors are numbered I through XIII according to the order of their discovery. Factor VI was once believed to be a distinct clotting factor, but is now thought to be identical to factor V. Rather than renumber the other factors, factor VI was allowed to remain as a placeholder and also a reminder that knowledge changes over time.

Clotting Factors

Factor number	Name	Type of molecule	Source	Pathway(s)
I	Fibrinogen	Plasma protein	Liver	Common; converted into fibrin
II	Prothrombin	Plasma protein	Liver*	Common; converted into thrombin
III	Tissue thromboplastin or tissue factor	Lipoprotein mixture	Damaged cells and platelets	Extrinsic
IV	Calcium ions	Inorganic ions in plasma	Diet, platelets, bone matrix	Entire process
V	Proaccelerin	Plasma protein	Liver, platelets	Extrinsic and intrinsic
VI	Not used	Not used	Not used	Not used
VII	Proconvertin	Plasma protein	Liver *	Extrinsic
VIII	Antihemolytic factor A	Plasma protein factor	Platelets and endothelial cells	Intrinsic; deficiency results in hemophilia A
IX	Antihemolytic factor B (plasma thromboplastin component)	Plasma protein	Liver*	Intrinsic; deficiency results in hemophilia B
X	Stuart–Prower factor (thrombokinase)	Protein	Liver*	Extrinsic and intrinsic
XI	Antihemolytic factor C (plasma thromboplastin antecedent)	Plasma protein	Liver	Intrinsic; deficiency results in hemophilia C
XII	Hageman factor	Plasma protein	Liver	Intrinsic; initiates clotting in vitro also activates plasmin
XIII	Fibrin-stabilizing factor	Plasma protein	Liver, platelets	Stabilizes fibrin; slows fibrinolysis

Table 18.1 *Vitamin K required.

Extrinsic Pathway

The quicker responding and more direct **extrinsic pathway** (also known as the **tissue factor** pathway) begins when damage occurs to the surrounding tissues, such as in a traumatic injury. Upon contact with blood plasma, the damaged extravascular cells, which are extrinsic to the bloodstream, release factor III (thromboplastin). Sequentially, Ca^{2+} then factor

VII (proconvertin), which is activated by factor III, are added, forming an enzyme complex. This enzyme complex leads to activation of factor X (Stuart–Prower factor), which activates the common pathway discussed below. The events in the extrinsic pathway are completed in a matter of seconds.

Intrinsic Pathway

The **intrinsic pathway** (also known as the contact activation pathway) is longer and more complex. In this case, the factors involved are intrinsic to (present within) the bloodstream. The pathway can be prompted by damage to the tissues, resulting from internal factors such as arterial disease; however, it is most often initiated when factor XII (Hageman factor) comes into contact with foreign materials, such as when a blood sample is put into a glass test tube. Within the body, factor XII is typically activated when it encounters negatively charged molecules, such as inorganic polymers and phosphate produced earlier in the series of intrinsic pathway reactions. Factor XII sets off a series of reactions that in turn activates factor XI (antihemolytic factor C or plasma thromboplastin antecedent) then factor IX (antihemolytic factor B or plasma thromboplasmin). In the meantime, chemicals released by the platelets increase the rate of these activation reactions. Finally, factor VIII (antihemolytic factor A) from the platelets and endothelial cells combines with factor IX (antihemolytic factor B or plasma thromboplasmin) to form an enzyme complex that activates factor X (Stuart–Prower factor or thrombokinase), leading to the common pathway. The events in the intrinsic pathway are completed in a few minutes.

Common Pathway

Both the intrinsic and extrinsic pathways lead to the **common pathway**, in which fibrin is produced to seal off the vessel. Once factor X has been activated by either the intrinsic or extrinsic pathway, the enzyme prothrombinase converts factor II, the inactive enzyme prothrombin, into the active enzyme **thrombin**. (Note that if the enzyme thrombin were not normally in an inactive form, clots would form spontaneously, a condition not consistent with life.) Then, thrombin converts factor I, the insoluble fibrinogen, into the soluble fibrin protein strands. Factor XIII then stabilizes the fibrin clot.

Fibrinolysis

The stabilized clot is acted upon by contractile proteins within the platelets. As these proteins contract, they pull on the fibrin threads, bringing the edges of the clot more tightly together, somewhat as we do when tightening loose shoelaces (see Figure 18.14a). This process also wrings out of the clot a small amount of fluid called **serum**, which is blood plasma without its clotting factors.

To restore normal blood flow as the vessel heals, the clot must eventually be removed. **Fibrinolysis** is the gradual degradation of the clot. Again, there is a fairly complicated series of reactions that involves factor XII and protein-catabolizing enzymes. During this process, the inactive protein plasminogen is converted into the active **plasmin**, which gradually breaks down the fibrin of the clot. Additionally, bradykinin, a vasodilator, is released, reversing the effects of the serotonin and prostaglandins from the platelets. This allows the smooth muscle in the walls of the vessels to relax and helps to restore the circulation.

Plasma Anticoagulants

An **anticoagulant** is any substance that opposes coagulation. Several circulating plasma anticoagulants play a role in limiting the coagulation process to the region of injury and restoring a normal, clot-free condition of blood. For instance, a cluster of proteins collectively referred to as the protein C system inactivates clotting factors involved in the intrinsic pathway. TFPI (tissue factor pathway inhibitor) inhibits the conversion of the inactive factor VII to the active form in the extrinsic pathway. **Antithrombin** inactivates factor X and opposes the conversion of prothrombin (factor II) to thrombin in the common pathway. And as noted earlier, basophils release **heparin**, a short-acting anticoagulant that also opposes prothrombin. Heparin is also found on the surfaces of cells lining the blood vessels. A pharmaceutical form of heparin is often administered therapeutically, for example, in surgical patients at risk for blood clots.

View these animations (http://openstaxcollege.org/l/coagulation) to explore the intrinsic, extrinsic, and common pathways that are involved the process of coagulation. The coagulation cascade restores hemostasis by activating coagulation factors in the presence of an injury. How does the endothelium of the blood vessel walls prevent the blood from coagulating as it flows through the blood vessels?

Disorders of Clotting

Either an insufficient or an excessive production of platelets can lead to severe disease or death. As discussed earlier, an insufficient number of platelets, called thrombocytopenia, typically results in the inability of blood to form clots. This can lead to excessive bleeding, even from minor wounds.

Another reason for failure of the blood to clot is the inadequate production of functional amounts of one or more clotting factors. This is the case in the genetic disorder **hemophilia**, which is actually a group of related disorders, the most common of which is hemophilia A, accounting for approximately 80 percent of cases. This disorder results in the inability to synthesize sufficient quantities of factor VIII. Hemophilia B is the second most common form, accounting for approximately 20 percent of cases. In this case, there is a deficiency of factor IX. Both of these defects are linked to the X chromosome and are typically passed from a healthy (carrier) mother to her male offspring, since males are XY. Females would need to inherit a defective gene from each parent to manifest the disease, since they are XX. Patients with hemophilia bleed from even minor internal and external wounds, and leak blood into joint spaces after exercise and into urine and stool. Hemophilia C is a rare condition that is triggered by an autosomal (not sex) chromosome that renders factor XI nonfunctional. It is not a true recessive condition, since even individuals with a single copy of the mutant gene show a tendency to bleed. Regular infusions of clotting factors isolated from healthy donors can help prevent bleeding in hemophiliac patients. At some point, genetic therapy will become a viable option.

In contrast to the disorders characterized by coagulation failure is thrombocytosis, also mentioned earlier, a condition characterized by excessive numbers of platelets that increases the risk for excessive clot formation, a condition known as **thrombosis**. A **thrombus** (plural = thrombi) is an aggregation of platelets, erythrocytes, and even WBCs typically trapped within a mass of fibrin strands. While the formation of a clot is normal following the hemostatic mechanism just described, thrombi can form within an intact or only slightly damaged blood vessel. In a large vessel, a thrombus will adhere to the vessel wall and decrease the flow of blood, and is referred to as a mural thrombus. In a small vessel, it may actually totally block the flow of blood and is termed an occlusive thrombus. Thrombi are most commonly caused by vessel damage to the endothelial lining, which activates the clotting mechanism. These may include venous stasis, when blood in the veins, particularly in the legs, remains stationary for long periods. This is one of the dangers of long airplane flights in crowded conditions and may lead to deep vein thrombosis or atherosclerosis, an accumulation of debris in arteries. Thrombophilia, also called hypercoagulation, is a condition in which there is a tendency to form thrombosis. This may be familial (genetic) or acquired. Acquired forms include the autoimmune disease lupus, immune reactions to heparin, polycythemia vera, thrombocytosis, sickle cell disease, pregnancy, and even obesity. A thrombus can seriously impede blood flow to or from a region and will cause a local increase in blood pressure. If flow is to be maintained, the heart will need to generate a greater pressure to overcome the resistance.

When a portion of a thrombus breaks free from the vessel wall and enters the circulation, it is referred to as an **embolus**. An embolus that is carried through the bloodstream can be large enough to block a vessel critical to a major organ. When it becomes trapped, an embolus is called an embolism. In the heart, brain, or lungs, an embolism may accordingly cause a heart attack, a stroke, or a pulmonary embolism. These are medical emergencies.

Among the many known biochemical activities of aspirin is its role as an anticoagulant. Aspirin (acetylsalicylic acid) is very effective at inhibiting the aggregation of platelets. It is routinely administered during a heart attack or stroke to reduce the adverse effects. Physicians sometimes recommend that patients at risk for cardiovascular disease take a low dose of aspirin on a daily basis as a preventive measure. However, aspirin can also lead to serious side effects, including increasing the risk of ulcers. A patient is well advised to consult a physician before beginning any aspirin regimen.

A class of drugs collectively known as thrombolytic agents can help speed up the degradation of an abnormal clot. If a thrombolytic agent is administered to a patient within 3 hours following a thrombotic stroke, the patient's prognosis improves significantly. However, some strokes are not caused by thrombi, but by hemorrhage. Thus, the cause must be determined before treatment begins. Tissue plasminogen activator is an enzyme that catalyzes the conversion of plasminogen to plasmin, the primary enzyme that breaks down clots. It is released naturally by endothelial cells but is also used in clinical medicine. New research is progressing using compounds isolated from the venom of some species of snakes, particularly vipers and cobras, which may eventually have therapeutic value as thrombolytic agents.

18.6 | Blood Typing

By the end of this section, you will be able to:
- Describe the two basic physiological consequences of transfusion of incompatible blood
- Compare and contrast ABO and Rh blood groups
- Identify which blood groups may be safely transfused into patients with different ABO types
- Discuss the pathophysiology of hemolytic disease of the newborn

Blood transfusions in humans were risky procedures until the discovery of the major human blood groups by Karl Landsteiner, an Austrian biologist and physician, in 1900. Until that point, physicians did not understand that death sometimes followed blood transfusions, when the type of donor blood infused into the patient was incompatible with the patient's own blood. Blood groups are determined by the presence or absence of specific marker molecules on the plasma membranes of erythrocytes. With their discovery, it became possible for the first time to match patient-donor blood types and prevent transfusion reactions and deaths.

Antigens, Antibodies, and Transfusion Reactions

Antigens are substances that the body does not recognize as belonging to the "self" and that therefore trigger a defensive response from the leukocytes of the immune system. (Seek more content for additional information on immunity.) Here, we will focus on the role of immunity in blood transfusion reactions. With RBCs in particular, you may see the antigens referred to as isoantigens or agglutinogens (surface antigens) and the antibodies referred to as isoantibodies or agglutinins. In this chapter, we will use the more common terms antigens and antibodies.

Antigens are generally large proteins, but may include other classes of organic molecules, including carbohydrates, lipids, and nucleic acids. Following an infusion of incompatible blood, erythrocytes with foreign antigens appear in the bloodstream and trigger an immune response. Proteins called antibodies (immunoglobulins), which are produced by certain B lymphocytes called plasma cells, attach to the antigens on the plasma membranes of the infused erythrocytes and cause them to adhere to one another.

- Because the arms of the Y-shaped antibodies attach randomly to more than one nonself erythrocyte surface, they form clumps of erythrocytes. This process is called **agglutination**.
- The clumps of erythrocytes block small blood vessels throughout the body, depriving tissues of oxygen and nutrients.
- As the erythrocyte clumps are degraded, in a process called **hemolysis**, their hemoglobin is released into the bloodstream. This hemoglobin travels to the kidneys, which are responsible for filtration of the blood. However, the load of hemoglobin released can easily overwhelm the kidney's capacity to clear it, and the patient can quickly develop kidney failure.

More than 50 antigens have been identified on erythrocyte membranes, but the most significant in terms of their potential harm to patients are classified in two groups: the ABO blood group and the Rh blood group.

The ABO Blood Group

Although the **ABO blood group** name consists of three letters, ABO blood typing designates the presence or absence of just two antigens, A and B. Both are glycoproteins. People whose erythrocytes have A antigens on their erythrocyte membrane surfaces are designated blood type A, and those whose erythrocytes have B antigens are blood type B. People can also have both A and B antigens on their erythrocytes, in which case they are blood type AB. People with neither A nor B antigens are designated blood type O. ABO blood types are genetically determined.

Normally the body must be exposed to a foreign antigen before an antibody can be produced. This is not the case for the ABO blood group. Individuals with type A blood—without any prior exposure to incompatible blood—have preformed antibodies to the B antigen circulating in their blood plasma. These antibodies, referred to as anti-B antibodies, will cause agglutination and hemolysis if they ever encounter erythrocytes with B antigens. Similarly, an individual with type B blood has pre-formed anti-A antibodies. Individuals with type AB blood, which has both antigens, do not have preformed antibodies to either of these. People with type O blood lack antigens A and B on their erythrocytes, but both anti-A and anti-B antibodies circulate in their blood plasma.

Rh Blood Groups

The **Rh blood group** is classified according to the presence or absence of a second erythrocyte antigen identified as Rh. (It was first discovered in a type of primate known as a rhesus macaque, which is often used in research, because its blood is similar to that of humans.) Although dozens of Rh antigens have been identified, only one, designated D, is clinically important. Those who have the Rh D antigen present on their erythrocytes—about 85 percent of Americans—are described as Rh positive (Rh^+) and those who lack it are Rh negative (Rh^-). Note that the Rh group is distinct from the ABO group, so any individual, no matter their ABO blood type, may have or lack this Rh antigen. When identifying a patient's blood type, the Rh group is designated by adding the word positive or negative to the ABO type. For example, A positive (A^+) means ABO group A blood with the Rh antigen present, and AB negative (AB^-) means ABO group AB blood without the Rh antigen.

Table 18.2 summarizes the distribution of the ABO and Rh blood types within the United States.

Summary of ABO and Rh Blood Types within the United States

Blood Type	African-Americans	Asian-Americans	Caucasian-Americans	Latino/Latina-Americans
A^+	24	27	33	29
A^-	2	0.5	7	2
B^+	18	25	9	9
B^-	1	0.4	2	1
AB^+	4	7	3	2
AB^-	0.3	0.1	1	0.2
O^+	47	39	37	53
O^-	4	1	8	4

Table 18.2

In contrast to the ABO group antibodies, which are preformed, antibodies to the Rh antigen are produced only in Rh^- individuals after exposure to the antigen. This process, called sensitization, occurs following a transfusion with Rh-incompatible blood or, more commonly, with the birth of an Rh^+ baby to an Rh^- mother. Problems are rare in a first pregnancy, since the baby's Rh^+ cells rarely cross the placenta (the organ of gas and nutrient exchange between the baby and the mother). However, during or immediately after birth, the Rh^- mother can be exposed to the baby's Rh^+ cells (Figure 18.15). Research has shown that this occurs in about 13–14 percent of such pregnancies. After exposure, the mother's immune system begins to generate anti-Rh antibodies. If the mother should then conceive another Rh^+ baby, the Rh antibodies she has produced can cross the placenta into the fetal bloodstream and destroy the fetal RBCs. This condition, known as **hemolytic disease of the newborn (HDN)** or erythroblastosis fetalis, may cause anemia in mild cases, but the agglutination and hemolysis can be so severe that without treatment the fetus may die in the womb or shortly after birth.

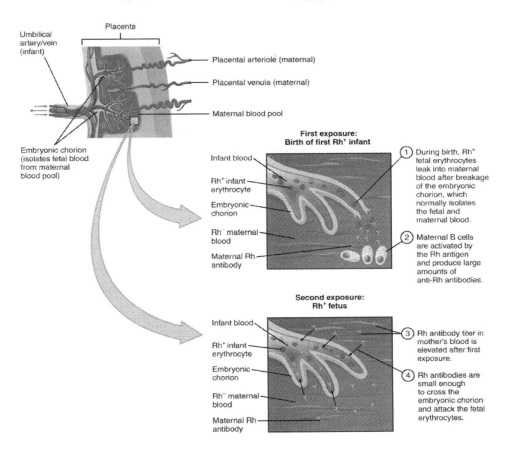

Figure 18.15 Erythroblastosis Fetalis The first exposure of an Rh⁻ mother to Rh⁺ erythrocytes during pregnancy induces sensitization. Anti-Rh antibodies begin to circulate in the mother's bloodstream. A second exposure occurs with a subsequent pregnancy with an Rh⁺ fetus in the uterus. Maternal anti-Rh antibodies may cross the placenta and enter the fetal bloodstream, causing agglutination and hemolysis of fetal erythrocytes.

A drug known as RhoGAM, short for Rh immune globulin, can temporarily prevent the development of Rh antibodies in the Rh⁻ mother, thereby averting this potentially serious disease for the fetus. RhoGAM antibodies destroy any fetal Rh⁺ erythrocytes that may cross the placental barrier. RhoGAM is normally administered to Rh⁻ mothers during weeks 26–28 of pregnancy and within 72 hours following birth. It has proven remarkably effective in decreasing the incidence of HDN. Earlier we noted that the incidence of HDN in an Rh⁺ subsequent pregnancy to an Rh⁻ mother is about 13–14 percent without preventive treatment. Since the introduction of RhoGAM in 1968, the incidence has dropped to about 0.1 percent in the United States.

Determining ABO Blood Types

Clinicians are able to determine a patient's blood type quickly and easily using commercially prepared antibodies. An unknown blood sample is allocated into separate wells. Into one well a small amount of anti-A antibody is added, and to another a small amount of anti-B antibody. If the antigen is present, the antibodies will cause visible agglutination of the cells (Figure 18.16). The blood should also be tested for Rh antibodies.

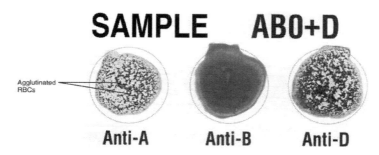

Figure 18.16 Cross Matching Blood Types This sample of a commercially produced "bedside" card enables quick typing of both a recipient's and donor's blood before transfusion. The card contains three reaction sites or wells. One is coated with an anti-A antibody, one with an anti-B antibody, and one with an anti-D antibody (tests for the presence of Rh factor D). Mixing a drop of blood and saline into each well enables the blood to interact with a preparation of type-specific antibodies, also called anti-seras. Agglutination of RBCs in a given site indicates a positive identification of the blood antigens, in this case A and Rh antigens for blood type A^+. For the purpose of transfusion, the donor's and recipient's blood types must match.

ABO Transfusion Protocols

To avoid transfusion reactions, it is best to transfuse only matching blood types; that is, a type B^+ recipient should ideally receive blood only from a type B^+ donor and so on. That said, in emergency situations, when acute hemorrhage threatens the patient's life, there may not be time for cross matching to identify blood type. In these cases, blood from a **universal donor**—an individual with type O^- blood—may be transfused. Recall that type O erythrocytes do not display A or B antigens. Thus, anti-A or anti-B antibodies that might be circulating in the patient's blood plasma will not encounter any erythrocyte surface antigens on the donated blood and therefore will not be provoked into a response. One problem with this designation of universal donor is if the O^- individual had prior exposure to Rh antigen, Rh antibodies may be present in the donated blood. Also, introducing type O blood into an individual with type A, B, or AB blood will nevertheless introduce antibodies against both A and B antigens, as these are always circulating in the type O blood plasma. This may cause problems for the recipient, but because the volume of blood transfused is much lower than the volume of the patient's own blood, the adverse effects of the relatively few infused plasma antibodies are typically limited. Rh factor also plays a role. If Rh^- individuals receiving blood have had prior exposure to Rh antigen, antibodies for this antigen may be present in the blood and trigger agglutination to some degree. Although it is always preferable to cross match a patient's blood before transfusing, in a true life-threatening emergency situation, this is not always possible, and these procedures may be implemented.

A patient with blood type AB^+ is known as the **universal recipient**. This patient can theoretically receive any type of blood, because the patient's own blood—having both A and B antigens on the erythrocyte surface—does not produce anti-A or anti-B antibodies. In addition, an Rh^+ patient can receive both Rh^+ and Rh^- blood. However, keep in mind that the donor's blood will contain circulating antibodies, again with possible negative implications. Figure 18.17 summarizes the blood types and compatibilities.

At the scene of multiple-vehicle accidents, military engagements, and natural or human-caused disasters, many victims may suffer simultaneously from acute hemorrhage, yet type O blood may not be immediately available. In these circumstances, medics may at least try to replace some of the volume of blood that has been lost. This is done by intravenous administration of a saline solution that provides fluids and electrolytes in proportions equivalent to those of normal blood plasma. Research is ongoing to develop a safe and effective artificial blood that would carry out the oxygen-carrying function of blood without the RBCs, enabling transfusions in the field without concern for incompatibility. These blood substitutes normally contain hemoglobin- as well as perfluorocarbon-based oxygen carriers.

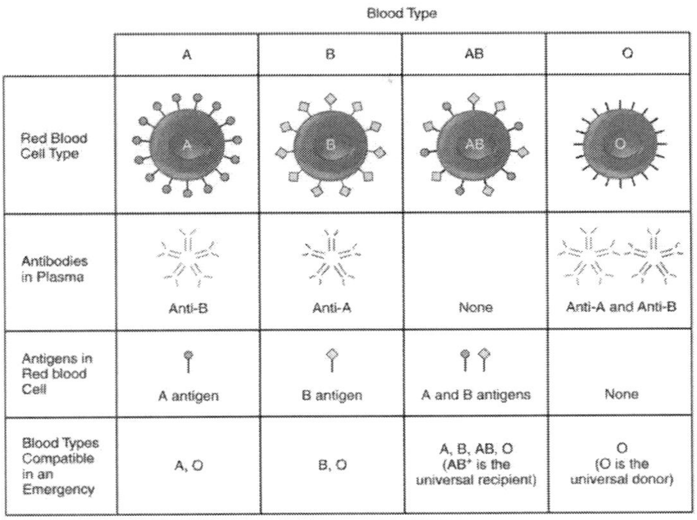

Chapter 18 | The Cardiovascular System: Blood

	Blood Type			
	A	B	AB	O
Red Blood Cell Type				
Antibodies in Plasma	Anti-B	Anti-A	None	Anti-A and Anti-B
Antigens in Red blood Cell	A antigen	B antigen	A and B antigens	None
Blood Types Compatible in an Emergency	A, O	B, O	A, B, AB, O (AB⁺ is the universal recipient)	O (O is the universal donor)

Figure 18.17 ABO Blood Group This chart summarizes the characteristics of the blood types in the ABO blood group. See the text for more on the concept of a universal donor or recipient.

KEY TERMS

ABO blood group blood-type classification based on the presence or absence of A and B glycoproteins on the erythrocyte membrane surface

agglutination clustering of cells into masses linked by antibodies

agranular leukocytes leukocytes with few granules in their cytoplasm; specifically, monocytes, lymphocytes, and NK cells

albumin most abundant plasma protein, accounting for most of the osmotic pressure of plasma

anemia deficiency of red blood cells or hemoglobin

antibodies (also, immunoglobulins or gamma globulins) antigen-specific proteins produced by specialized B lymphocytes that protect the body by binding to foreign objects such as bacteria and viruses

anticoagulant substance such as heparin that opposes coagulation

antithrombin anticoagulant that inactivates factor X and opposes the conversion of prothrombin (factor II) into thrombin in the common pathway

B lymphocytes (also, B cells) lymphocytes that defend the body against specific pathogens and thereby provide specific immunity

basophils granulocytes that stain with a basic (alkaline) stain and store histamine and heparin

bilirubin yellowish bile pigment produced when iron is removed from heme and is further broken down into waste products

biliverdin green bile pigment produced when the non-iron portion of heme is degraded into a waste product; converted to bilirubin in the liver

blood liquid connective tissue composed of formed elements—erythrocytes, leukocytes, and platelets—and a fluid extracellular matrix called plasma; component of the cardiovascular system

bone marrow biopsy diagnostic test of a sample of red bone marrow

bone marrow transplant treatment in which a donor's healthy bone marrow with its stem cells replaces diseased or damaged bone marrow of a patient

buffy coat thin, pale layer of leukocytes and platelets that separates the erythrocytes from the plasma in a sample of centrifuged blood

carbaminohemoglobin compound of carbon dioxide and hemoglobin, and one of the ways in which carbon dioxide is carried in the blood

clotting factors group of 12 identified substances active in coagulation

coagulation formation of a blood clot; part of the process of hemostasis

colony-stimulating factors (CSFs) glycoproteins that trigger the proliferation and differentiation of myeloblasts into granular leukocytes (basophils, neutrophils, and eosinophils)

common pathway final coagulation pathway activated either by the intrinsic or the extrinsic pathway, and ending in the formation of a blood clot

cross matching blood test for identification of blood type using antibodies and small samples of blood

cytokines class of proteins that act as autocrine or paracrine signaling molecules; in the cardiovascular system, they stimulate the proliferation of progenitor cells and help to stimulate both nonspecific and specific resistance to disease

defensins antimicrobial proteins released from neutrophils and macrophages that create openings in the plasma membranes to kill cells

deoxyhemoglobin molecule of hemoglobin without an oxygen molecule bound to it

diapedesis (also, emigration) process by which leukocytes squeeze through adjacent cells in a blood vessel wall to enter tissues

embolus thrombus that has broken free from the blood vessel wall and entered the circulation

emigration (also, diapedesis) process by which leukocytes squeeze through adjacent cells in a blood vessel wall to enter tissues

eosinophils granulocytes that stain with eosin; they release antihistamines and are especially active against parasitic worms

erythrocyte (also, red blood cell) mature myeloid blood cell that is composed mostly of hemoglobin and functions primarily in the transportation of oxygen and carbon dioxide

erythropoietin (EPO) glycoprotein that triggers the bone marrow to produce RBCs; secreted by the kidney in response to low oxygen levels

extrinsic pathway initial coagulation pathway that begins with tissue damage and results in the activation of the common pathway

ferritin protein-containing storage form of iron found in the bone marrow, liver, and spleen

fibrin insoluble, filamentous protein that forms the structure of a blood clot

fibrinogen plasma protein produced in the liver and involved in blood clotting

fibrinolysis gradual degradation of a blood clot

formed elements cellular components of blood; that is, erythrocytes, leukocytes, and platelets

globin heme-containing globular protein that is a constituent of hemoglobin

globulins heterogeneous group of plasma proteins that includes transport proteins, clotting factors, immune proteins, and others

granular leukocytes leukocytes with abundant granules in their cytoplasm; specifically, neutrophils, eosinophils, and basophils

hematocrit (also, packed cell volume) volume percentage of erythrocytes in a sample of centrifuged blood

heme red, iron-containing pigment to which oxygen binds in hemoglobin

hemocytoblast hemopoietic stem cell that gives rise to the formed elements of blood

hemoglobin oxygen-carrying compound in erythrocytes

hemolysis destruction (lysis) of erythrocytes and the release of their hemoglobin into circulation

hemolytic disease of the newborn (HDN) (also, erythroblastosis fetalis) disorder causing agglutination and hemolysis in an Rh^+ fetus or newborn of an Rh^- mother

hemophilia genetic disorder characterized by inadequate synthesis of clotting factors

hemopoiesis production of the formed elements of blood

hemopoietic growth factors chemical signals including erythropoietin, thrombopoietin, colony-stimulating factors, and interleukins that regulate the differentiation and proliferation of particular blood progenitor cells

hemopoietic stem cell type of pluripotent stem cell that gives rise to the formed elements of blood (hemocytoblast)

hemorrhage excessive bleeding

hemosiderin protein-containing storage form of iron found in the bone marrow, liver, and spleen

hemostasis physiological process by which bleeding ceases

heparin short-acting anticoagulant stored in mast cells and released when tissues are injured, opposes prothrombin

hypoxemia below-normal level of oxygen saturation of blood (typically <95 percent)

immunoglobulins (also, antibodies or gamma globulins) antigen-specific proteins produced by specialized B lymphocytes that protect the body by binding to foreign objects such as bacteria and viruses

interleukins signaling molecules that may function in hemopoiesis, inflammation, and specific immune responses

intrinsic pathway initial coagulation pathway that begins with vascular damage or contact with foreign substances, and results in the activation of the common pathway

leukemia cancer involving leukocytes

leukocyte (also, white blood cell) colorless, nucleated blood cell, the chief function of which is to protect the body from disease

leukocytosis excessive leukocyte proliferation

leukopenia below-normal production of leukocytes

lymphocytes agranular leukocytes of the lymphoid stem cell line, many of which function in specific immunity

lymphoid stem cells type of hemopoietic stem cells that gives rise to lymphocytes, including various T cells, B cells, and NK cells, all of which function in immunity

lymphoma form of cancer in which masses of malignant T and/or B lymphocytes collect in lymph nodes, the spleen, the liver, and other tissues

lysozyme digestive enzyme with bactericidal properties

macrophage phagocytic cell of the myeloid lineage; a matured monocyte

megakaryocyte bone marrow cell that produces platelets

memory cell type of B or T lymphocyte that forms after exposure to a pathogen

monocytes agranular leukocytes of the myeloid stem cell line that circulate in the bloodstream; tissue monocytes are macrophages

myeloid stem cells type of hemopoietic stem cell that gives rise to some formed elements, including erythrocytes, megakaryocytes that produce platelets, and a myeloblast lineage that gives rise to monocytes and three forms of granular leukocytes (neutrophils, eosinophils, and basophils)

natural killer (NK) cells cytotoxic lymphocytes capable of recognizing cells that do not express "self" proteins on their plasma membrane or that contain foreign or abnormal markers; provide generalized, nonspecific immunity

neutrophils granulocytes that stain with a neutral dye and are the most numerous of the leukocytes; especially active against bacteria

oxyhemoglobin molecule of hemoglobin to which oxygen is bound

packed cell volume (PCV) (also, hematocrit) volume percentage of erythrocytes present in a sample of centrifuged blood

plasma in blood, the liquid extracellular matrix composed mostly of water that circulates the formed elements and dissolved materials throughout the cardiovascular system

plasmin blood protein active in fibrinolysis

platelet plug accumulation and adhesion of platelets at the site of blood vessel injury

platelets (also, thrombocytes) one of the formed elements of blood that consists of cell fragments broken off from megakaryocytes

pluripotent stem cell stem cell that derives from totipotent stem cells and is capable of differentiating into many, but not all, cell types

polycythemia elevated level of hemoglobin, whether adaptive or pathological

polymorphonuclear having a lobed nucleus, as seen in some leukocytes

positive chemotaxis process in which a cell is attracted to move in the direction of chemical stimuli

red blood cells (RBCs) (also, erythrocytes) one of the formed elements of blood that transports oxygen

reticulocyte immature erythrocyte that may still contain fragments of organelles

Rh blood group blood-type classification based on the presence or absence of the antigen Rh on the erythrocyte membrane surface

serum blood plasma that does not contain clotting factors

sickle cell disease (also, sickle cell anemia) inherited blood disorder in which hemoglobin molecules are malformed, leading to the breakdown of RBCs that take on a characteristic sickle shape

T lymphocytes (also, T cells) lymphocytes that provide cellular-level immunity by physically attacking foreign or diseased cells

thalassemia inherited blood disorder in which maturation of RBCs does not proceed normally, leading to abnormal formation of hemoglobin and the destruction of RBCs

thrombin enzyme essential for the final steps in formation of a fibrin clot

thrombocytes platelets, one of the formed elements of blood that consists of cell fragments broken off from megakaryocytes

thrombocytopenia condition in which there are too few platelets, resulting in abnormal bleeding (hemophilia)

thrombocytosis condition in which there are too many platelets, resulting in abnormal clotting (thrombosis)

thrombopoietin hormone secreted by the liver and kidneys that prompts the development of megakaryocytes into thrombocytes (platelets)

thrombosis excessive clot formation

thrombus aggregation of fibrin, platelets, and erythrocytes in an intact artery or vein

tissue factor protein thromboplastin, which initiates the extrinsic pathway when released in response to tissue damage

totipotent stem cell embryonic stem cell that is capable of differentiating into any and all cells of the body; enabling the full development of an organism

transferrin plasma protein that binds reversibly to iron and distributes it throughout the body

universal donor individual with type O^- blood

universal recipient individual with type AB^+ blood

vascular spasm initial step in hemostasis, in which the smooth muscle in the walls of the ruptured or damaged blood vessel contracts

white blood cells (WBCs) (also, leukocytes) one of the formed elements of blood that provides defense against disease agents and foreign materials

CHAPTER REVIEW

18.1 An Overview of Blood

Blood is a fluid connective tissue critical to the transportation of nutrients, gases, and wastes throughout the body; to defend the body against infection and other threats; and to the homeostatic regulation of pH, temperature, and other internal conditions. Blood is composed of formed elements—erythrocytes, leukocytes, and cell fragments called platelets—and a fluid extracellular matrix called plasma. More than 90 percent of plasma is water. The remainder is mostly plasma proteins—mainly albumin, globulins, and fibrinogen—and other dissolved solutes such as glucose, lipids, electrolytes, and dissolved gases. Because of the formed elements and the plasma proteins and other solutes, blood is sticky and more viscous than water. It is also slightly alkaline, and its temperature is slightly higher than normal body temperature.

18.2 Production of the Formed Elements

Through the process of hemopoiesis, the formed elements of blood are continually produced, replacing the relatively short-lived erythrocytes, leukocytes, and platelets. Hemopoiesis begins in the red bone marrow, with hemopoietic stem cells that differentiate into myeloid and lymphoid lineages. Myeloid stem cells give rise to most of the formed elements. Lymphoid stem cells give rise only to the various lymphocytes designated as B and T cells, and NK cells. Hemopoietic growth factors, including erythropoietin, thrombopoietin, colony-stimulating factors, and interleukins, promote the proliferation and differentiation of formed elements.

18.3 Erythrocytes

The most abundant formed elements in blood, erythrocytes are red, biconcave disks packed with an oxygen-carrying compound called hemoglobin. The hemoglobin molecule contains four globin proteins bound to a pigment molecule called heme, which contains an ion of iron. In the bloodstream, iron picks up oxygen in the lungs and drops it off in the tissues; the amino acids in hemoglobin then transport carbon dioxide from the tissues back to the lungs. Erythrocytes live only 120 days on average, and thus must be continually replaced. Worn-out erythrocytes are phagocytized by macrophages and their hemoglobin is broken down. The breakdown products are recycled or removed as wastes: Globin is broken down into amino acids for synthesis of new proteins; iron is stored in the liver or spleen or used by the bone marrow for production of new erythrocytes; and the remnants of heme are converted into bilirubin, or other waste products that are taken up by the liver and excreted in the bile or removed by the kidneys. Anemia is a deficiency of RBCs or hemoglobin, whereas polycythemia is an excess of RBCs.

18.4 Leukocytes and Platelets

Leukocytes function in body defenses. They squeeze out of the walls of blood vessels through emigration or diapedesis, then may move through tissue fluid or become attached to various organs where they fight against pathogenic organisms, diseased cells, or other threats to health. Granular leukocytes, which include neutrophils, eosinophils, and basophils, originate with myeloid stem cells, as do the agranular monocytes. The other agranular leukocytes, NK cells, B cells, and T cells, arise from the lymphoid stem cell line. The most abundant leukocytes are the neutrophils, which are first responders to infections, especially with bacteria. About 20–30 percent of all leukocytes are lymphocytes, which are critical to the body's defense against specific threats. Leukemia and lymphoma are malignancies involving leukocytes. Platelets are fragments of cells known as megakaryocytes that dwell within the bone marrow. While many platelets are stored in the spleen, others enter the circulation and are essential for hemostasis; they also produce several growth factors important for repair and healing.

18.5 Hemostasis

Hemostasis is the physiological process by which bleeding ceases. Hemostasis involves three basic steps: vascular spasm, the formation of a platelet plug, and coagulation, in which clotting factors promote the formation of a fibrin clot. Fibrinolysis is the process in which a clot is degraded in a healing vessel. Anticoagulants are substances that oppose coagulation. They are important in limiting the extent and duration of clotting. Inadequate clotting can result from too few platelets, or inadequate production of clotting factors, for instance, in the genetic disorder hemophilia. Excessive clotting, called thrombosis, can be caused by excessive numbers of platelets. A thrombus is a collection of fibrin, platelets, and erythrocytes that has accumulated along the lining of a blood vessel, whereas an embolus is a thrombus that has broken free from the vessel wall and is circulating in the bloodstream.

18.6 Blood Typing

Antigens are nonself molecules, usually large proteins, which provoke an immune response. In transfusion reactions, antibodies attach to antigens on the surfaces of erythrocytes and cause agglutination and hemolysis. ABO blood group antigens are designated A and B. People with type A blood have A antigens on their erythrocytes, whereas those with type B blood have B antigens. Those with AB blood have both A and B antigens, and those with type O blood have neither A nor B antigens. The blood plasma contains preformed antibodies against the antigens not present on a person's erythrocytes.

A second group of blood antigens is the Rh group, the most important of which is Rh D. People with Rh^- blood do not have this antigen on their erythrocytes, whereas those who are Rh^+ do. About 85 percent of Americans are Rh^+. When a woman who is Rh^- becomes pregnant with an Rh^+ fetus, her body may begin to produce anti-Rh antibodies. If she subsequently becomes pregnant with a second Rh^+ fetus and is not treated preventively with RhoGAM, the fetus will be at risk for an antigen-antibody reaction, including agglutination and hemolysis. This is known as hemolytic disease of the newborn.

Cross matching to determine blood type is necessary before transfusing blood, unless the patient is experiencing hemorrhage that is an immediate threat to life, in which case type O^- blood may be transfused.

INTERACTIVE LINK QUESTIONS

1. Visit this site (http://openstaxcollege.org/l/normallevels) for a list of normal levels established for many of the substances found in a sample of blood. Serum, one of the specimen types included, refers to a sample of plasma after clotting factors have been removed. What types of measurements are given for levels of glucose in the blood?

2. Watch this video (http://openstaxcollege.org/l/doping) to see doctors discuss the dangers of blood doping in sports. What are the some potential side effects of blood doping?

3. Figure 18.13 Are you able to recognize and identify the various formed elements? You will need to do this is a systematic manner, scanning along the image. The standard method is to use a grid, but this is not possible with this resource. Try constructing a simple table with each leukocyte type and then making a mark for each cell type you identify. Attempt to classify at least 50 and perhaps as many as 100 different cells. Based on the percentage of cells that you count, do the numbers represent a normal blood smear or does something appear to be abnormal?

4. View these animations (http://openstaxcollege.org/l/coagulation) to explore the intrinsic, extrinsic, and common pathways that are involved the process of coagulation. The coagulation cascade restores hemostasis by activating coagulation factors in the presence of an injury. How does the endothelium of the blood vessel walls prevent the blood from coagulating as it flows through the blood vessels?

REVIEW QUESTIONS

5. Which of the following statements about blood is true?

   a. Blood is about 92 percent water.
   b. Blood is slightly more acidic than water.
   c. Blood is slightly more viscous than water.
   d. Blood is slightly more salty than seawater.

6. Which of the following statements about albumin is true?

   a. It draws water out of the blood vessels and into the body's tissues.
   b. It is the most abundant plasma protein.
   c. It is produced by specialized leukocytes called plasma cells.
   d. All of the above are true.

7. Which of the following plasma proteins is *not* produced by the liver?

   a. fibrinogen
   b. alpha globulin
   c. beta globulin
   d. immunoglobulin

8. Which of the formed elements arise from myeloid stem cells?

   a. B cells
   b. natural killer cells
   c. platelets
   d. all of the above

9. Which of the following statements about erythropoietin is true?

   a. It facilitates the proliferation and differentiation of the erythrocyte lineage.
   b. It is a hormone produced by the thyroid gland.

c. It is a hemopoietic growth factor that prompts lymphoid stem cells to leave the bone marrow.
  d. Both a and b are true.

10. Interleukins are associated primarily with which of the following?
  a. production of various lymphocytes
  b. immune responses
  c. inflammation
  d. all of the above

11. Which of the following statements about mature, circulating erythrocytes is true?
  a. They have no nucleus.
  b. They are packed with mitochondria.
  c. They survive for an average of 4 days.
  d. All of the above

12. A molecule of hemoglobin _____.
  a. is shaped like a biconcave disk packed almost entirely with iron
  b. contains four glycoprotein units studded with oxygen
  c. consists of four globin proteins, each bound to a molecule of heme
  d. can carry up to 120 molecules of oxygen

13. The production of healthy erythrocytes depends upon the availability of _____.
  a. copper
  b. zinc
  c. vitamin B_{12}
  d. copper, zinc, and vitamin B_{12}

14. Aging and damaged erythrocytes are removed from the circulation by _____.
  a. myeoblasts
  b. monocytes
  c. macrophages
  d. mast cells

15. A patient has been suffering for 2 months with a chronic, watery diarrhea. A blood test is likely to reveal _____.
  a. a hematocrit below 30 percent
  b. hypoxemia
  c. anemia
  d. polycythemia

16. The process by which leukocytes squeeze through adjacent cells in a blood vessel wall is called _____.
  a. leukocytosis
  b. positive chemotaxis
  c. emigration
  d. cytoplasmic extending

17. Which of the following describes a neutrophil?
  a. abundant, agranular, especially effective against cancer cells
  b. abundant, granular, especially effective against bacteria
  c. rare, agranular, releases antimicrobial defensins
  d. rare, granular, contains multiple granules packed with histamine

18. T and B lymphocytes _____.
  a. are polymorphonuclear
  b. are involved with specific immune function
  c. proliferate excessively in leukopenia
  d. are most active against parasitic worms

19. A patient has been experiencing severe, persistent allergy symptoms that are reduced when she takes an antihistamine. Before the treatment, this patient was likely to have had increased activity of which leukocyte?
  a. basophils
  b. neutrophils
  c. monocytes
  d. natural killer cells

20. Thrombocytes are more accurately called _____.
  a. clotting factors
  b. megakaryoblasts
  c. megakaryocytes
  d. platelets

21. The first step in hemostasis is _____.
  a. vascular spasm
  b. conversion of fibrinogen to fibrin
  c. activation of the intrinsic pathway
  d. activation of the common pathway

22. Prothrombin is converted to thrombin during the _____.
  a. intrinsic pathway
  b. extrinsic pathway
  c. common pathway
  d. formation of the platelet plug

23. Hemophilia is characterized by _____.
  a. inadequate production of heparin
  b. inadequate production of clotting factors
  c. excessive production of fibrinogen
  d. excessive production of platelets

24. The process in which antibodies attach to antigens, causing the formation of masses of linked cells, is called _____.
  a. sensitization
  b. coagulation
  c. agglutination
  d. hemolysis

25. People with ABO blood type O _____.
  a. have both antigens A and B on their erythrocytes
  b. lack both antigens A and B on their erythrocytes
  c. have neither anti-A nor anti-B antibodies circulating in their blood plasma
  d. are considered universal recipients

26. Hemolytic disease of the newborn is a risk during a subsequent pregnancy in which _____.
  a. a type AB mother is carrying a type O fetus

b. a type O mother is carrying a type AB fetus
c. an Rh$^+$ mother is carrying an Rh$^-$ fetus
d. an Rh$^-$ mother is carrying a second Rh$^+$ fetus

CRITICAL THINKING QUESTIONS

27. A patient's hematocrit is 42 percent. Approximately what percentage of the patient's blood is plasma?

28. Why would it be incorrect to refer to the formed elements as cells?

29. True or false: The buffy coat is the portion of a blood sample that is made up of its proteins.

30. Myelofibrosis is a disorder in which inflammation and scar tissue formation in the bone marrow impair hemopoiesis. One sign is an enlarged spleen. Why?

31. Would you expect a patient with a form of cancer called acute myelogenous leukemia to experience impaired production of erythrocytes, or impaired production of lymphocytes? Explain your choice.

32. A young woman has been experiencing unusually heavy menstrual bleeding for several years. She follows a strict vegan diet (no animal foods). She is at risk for what disorder, and why?

33. A patient has thalassemia, a genetic disorder characterized by abnormal synthesis of globin proteins and excessive destruction of erythrocytes. This patient is jaundiced and is found to have an excessive level of bilirubin in his blood. Explain the connection.

34. One of the more common adverse effects of cancer chemotherapy is the destruction of leukocytes. Before his next scheduled chemotherapy treatment, a patient undergoes a blood test called an absolute neutrophil count (ANC), which reveals that his neutrophil count is 1900 cells per microliter. Would his healthcare team be likely to proceed with his chemotherapy treatment? Why?

35. A patient was admitted to the burn unit the previous evening suffering from a severe burn involving his left upper extremity and shoulder. A blood test reveals that he is experiencing leukocytosis. Why is this an expected finding?

36. A lab technician collects a blood sample in a glass tube. After about an hour, she harvests serum to continue her blood analysis. Explain what has happened during the hour that the sample was in the glass tube.

37. Explain why administration of a thrombolytic agent is a first intervention for someone who has suffered a thrombotic stroke.

38. Following a motor vehicle accident, a patient is rushed to the emergency department with multiple traumatic injuries, causing severe bleeding. The patient's condition is critical, and there is no time for determining his blood type. What type of blood is transfused, and why?

39. In preparation for a scheduled surgery, a patient visits the hospital lab for a blood draw. The technician collects a blood sample and performs a test to determine its type. She places a sample of the patient's blood in two wells. To the first well she adds anti-A antibody. To the second she adds anti-B antibody. Both samples visibly agglutinate. Has the technician made an error, or is this a normal response? If normal, what blood type does this indicate?

19 | THE CARDIOVASCULAR SYSTEM: THE HEART

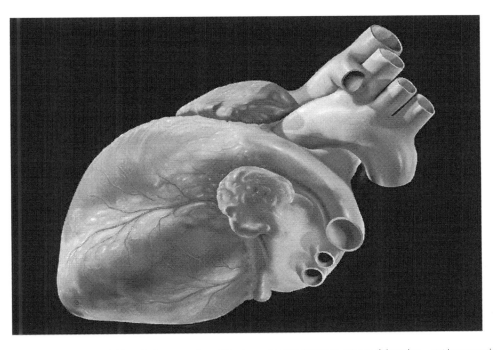

Figure 19.1 Human Heart This artist's conception of the human heart suggests a powerful engine—not inappropriate for a muscular pump that keeps the body continually supplied with blood. (credit: Patrick J. Lynch)

Introduction

Chapter Objectives

After studying this chapter, you will be able to:

- Identify and describe the interior and exterior parts of the human heart
- Describe the path of blood through the cardiac circuits
- Describe the size, shape, and location of the heart
- Compare cardiac muscle to skeletal and smooth muscle
- Explain the cardiac conduction system
- Describe the process and purpose of an electrocardiogram
- Explain the cardiac cycle

- Calculate cardiac output
- Describe the effects of exercise on cardiac output and heart rate
- Name the centers of the brain that control heart rate and describe their function
- Identify other factors affecting heart rate
- Describe fetal heart development

In this chapter, you will explore the remarkable pump that propels the blood into the vessels. There is no single better word to describe the function of the heart other than "pump," since its contraction develops the pressure that ejects blood into the major vessels: the aorta and pulmonary trunk. From these vessels, the blood is distributed to the remainder of the body. Although the connotation of the term "pump" suggests a mechanical device made of steel and plastic, the anatomical structure is a living, sophisticated muscle. As you read this chapter, try to keep these twin concepts in mind: pump and muscle.

Although the term "heart" is an English word, cardiac (heart-related) terminology can be traced back to the Latin term, "kardia." Cardiology is the study of the heart, and cardiologists are the physicians who deal primarily with the heart.

19.1 | Heart Anatomy

By the end of this section, you will be able to:

- Describe the location and position of the heart within the body cavity
- Describe the internal and external anatomy of the heart
- Identify the tissue layers of the heart
- Relate the structure of the heart to its function as a pump
- Compare systemic circulation to pulmonary circulation
- Identify the veins and arteries of the coronary circulation system
- Trace the pathway of oxygenated and deoxygenated blood thorough the chambers of the heart

The vital importance of the heart is obvious. If one assumes an average rate of contraction of 75 contractions per minute, a human heart would contract approximately 108,000 times in one day, more than 39 million times in one year, and nearly 3 billion times during a 75-year lifespan. Each of the major pumping chambers of the heart ejects approximately 70 mL blood per contraction in a resting adult. This would be equal to 5.25 liters of fluid per minute and approximately 14,000 liters per day. Over one year, that would equal 10,000,000 liters or 2.6 million gallons of blood sent through roughly 60,000 miles of vessels. In order to understand how that happens, it is necessary to understand the anatomy and physiology of the heart.

Location of the Heart

The human heart is located within the thoracic cavity, medially between the lungs in the space known as the mediastinum. Figure 19.2 shows the position of the heart within the thoracic cavity. Within the mediastinum, the heart is separated from the other mediastinal structures by a tough membrane known as the pericardium, or pericardial sac, and sits in its own space called the **pericardial cavity**. The dorsal surface of the heart lies near the bodies of the vertebrae, and its anterior surface sits deep to the sternum and costal cartilages. The great veins, the superior and inferior venae cavae, and the great arteries, the aorta and pulmonary trunk, are attached to the superior surface of the heart, called the base. The base of the heart is located at the level of the third costal cartilage, as seen in Figure 19.2. The inferior tip of the heart, the apex, lies just to the left of the sternum between the junction of the fourth and fifth ribs near their articulation with the costal cartilages. The right side of the heart is deflected anteriorly, and the left side is deflected posteriorly. It is important to remember the position and orientation of the heart when placing a stethoscope on the chest of a patient and listening for heart sounds, and also when looking at images taken from a midsagittal perspective. The slight deviation of the apex to the left is reflected in a depression in the medial surface of the inferior lobe of the left lung, called the **cardiac notch**.

Chapter 19 | The Cardiovascular System: The Heart

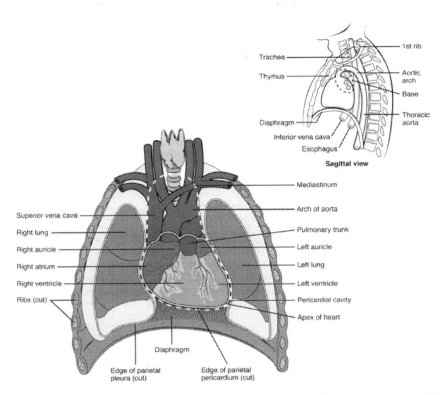

Figure 19.2 Position of the Heart in the Thorax The heart is located within the thoracic cavity, medially between the lungs in the mediastinum. It is about the size of a fist, is broad at the top, and tapers toward the base.

Everyday CONNECTION

CPR

The position of the heart in the torso between the vertebrae and sternum (see Figure 19.2 for the position of the heart within the thorax) allows for individuals to apply an emergency technique known as cardiopulmonary resuscitation (CPR) if the heart of a patient should stop. By applying pressure with the flat portion of one hand on the sternum in the area between the line at T4 and T9 (Figure 19.3), it is possible to manually compress the blood within the heart enough to push some of the blood within it into the pulmonary and systemic circuits. This is particularly critical for the brain, as irreversible damage and death of neurons occur within minutes of loss of blood flow. Current standards call for compression of the chest at least 5 cm deep and at a rate of 100 compressions per minute, a rate equal to the beat in "Staying Alive," recorded in 1977 by the Bee Gees. If you are unfamiliar with this song, a version is available on www.youtube.com. At this stage, the emphasis is on performing high-quality chest compressions, rather than providing artificial respiration. CPR is generally performed until the patient regains spontaneous contraction or is declared dead by an experienced healthcare professional.

When performed by untrained or overzealous individuals, CPR can result in broken ribs or a broken sternum, and can inflict additional severe damage on the patient. It is also possible, if the hands are placed too low on the sternum, to manually drive the xiphoid process into the liver, a consequence that may prove fatal for the patient. Proper training is essential. This proven life-sustaining technique is so valuable that virtually all medical personnel as well as concerned members of the public should be certified and routinely recertified in its application. CPR courses are offered at a variety of locations, including colleges, hospitals, the American Red Cross, and some commercial companies. They normally include practice of the compression technique on a mannequin.

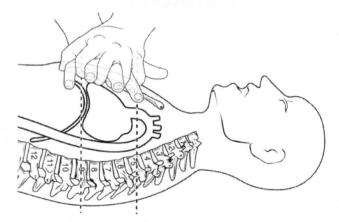

Figure 19.3 CPR Technique If the heart should stop, CPR can maintain the flow of blood until the heart resumes beating. By applying pressure to the sternum, the blood within the heart will be squeezed out of the heart and into the circulation. Proper positioning of the hands on the sternum to perform CPR would be between the lines at T4 and T9.

Interactive Link

Visit the American Heart Association website (http://openstaxcollege.org/l/AHA) to help locate a course near your home in the United States. There are also many other national and regional heart associations that offer the same service, depending upon the location.

Shape and Size of the Heart

The shape of the heart is similar to a pinecone, rather broad at the superior surface and tapering to the apex (see Figure 19.2). A typical heart is approximately the size of your fist: 12 cm (5 in) in length, 8 cm (3.5 in) wide, and 6 cm (2.5 in) in thickness. Given the size difference between most members of the sexes, the weight of a female heart is approximately 250–300 grams (9 to 11 ounces), and the weight of a male heart is approximately 300–350 grams (11 to 12 ounces). The heart of a well-trained athlete, especially one specializing in aerobic sports, can be considerably larger than this. Cardiac muscle responds to exercise in a manner similar to that of skeletal muscle. That is, exercise results in the addition of protein myofilaments that increase the size of the individual cells without increasing their numbers, a concept called hypertrophy. Hearts of athletes can pump blood more effectively at lower rates than those of nonathletes. Enlarged hearts are not always a result of exercise; they can result from pathologies, such as **hypertrophic cardiomyopathy**. The cause of an abnormally enlarged heart muscle is unknown, but the condition is often undiagnosed and can cause sudden death in apparently otherwise healthy young people.

Chambers and Circulation through the Heart

The human heart consists of four chambers: The left side and the right side each have one **atrium** and one **ventricle**. Each of the upper chambers, the right atrium (plural = atria) and the left atrium, acts as a receiving chamber and contracts to push blood into the lower chambers, the right ventricle and the left ventricle. The ventricles serve as the primary pumping chambers of the heart, propelling blood to the lungs or to the rest of the body.

There are two distinct but linked circuits in the human circulation called the pulmonary and systemic circuits. Although both circuits transport blood and everything it carries, we can initially view the circuits from the point of view of gases. The **pulmonary circuit** transports blood to and from the lungs, where it picks up oxygen and delivers carbon dioxide for exhalation. The **systemic circuit** transports oxygenated blood to virtually all of the tissues of the body and returns relatively deoxygenated blood and carbon dioxide to the heart to be sent back to the pulmonary circulation.

The right ventricle pumps deoxygenated blood into the **pulmonary trunk**, which leads toward the lungs and bifurcates into the left and right **pulmonary arteries**. These vessels in turn branch many times before reaching the **pulmonary capillaries**, where gas exchange occurs: Carbon dioxide exits the blood and oxygen enters. The pulmonary arteries and their branches are the only arteries in the post-natal body that carry relatively deoxygenated blood. Highly oxygenated blood returning from the pulmonary capillaries in the lungs passes through a series of vessels that join together to form the **pulmonary veins**—the only post-natal veins in the body that carry highly oxygenated blood. The pulmonary veins conduct blood into the left atrium, which pumps the blood into the left ventricle, which in turn pumps oxygenated blood into the aorta and on to the many branches of the systemic circuit. Eventually, these vessels will lead to the systemic capillaries, where exchange with the tissue fluid and cells of the body occurs. In this case, oxygen and nutrients exit the systemic capillaries to be used by the cells in their metabolic processes, and carbon dioxide and waste products will enter the blood.

The blood exiting the systemic capillaries is lower in oxygen concentration than when it entered. The capillaries will ultimately unite to form venules, joining to form ever-larger veins, eventually flowing into the two major systemic veins, the **superior vena cava** and the **inferior vena cava**, which return blood to the right atrium. The blood in the superior and inferior venae cavae flows into the right atrium, which pumps blood into the right ventricle. This process of blood circulation continues as long as the individual remains alive. Understanding the flow of blood through the pulmonary and systemic circuits is critical to all health professions (Figure 19.4).

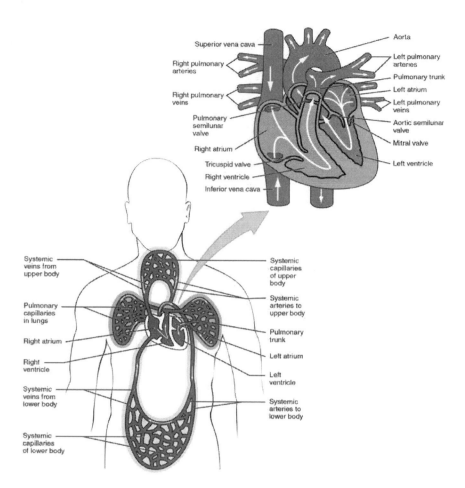

Figure 19.4 Dual System of the Human Blood Circulation Blood flows from the right atrium to the right ventricle, where it is pumped into the pulmonary circuit. The blood in the pulmonary artery branches is low in oxygen but relatively high in carbon dioxide. Gas exchange occurs in the pulmonary capillaries (oxygen into the blood, carbon dioxide out), and blood high in oxygen and low in carbon dioxide is returned to the left atrium. From here, blood enters the left ventricle, which pumps it into the systemic circuit. Following exchange in the systemic capillaries (oxygen and nutrients out of the capillaries and carbon dioxide and wastes in), blood returns to the right atrium and the cycle is repeated.

Membranes, Surface Features, and Layers

Our exploration of more in-depth heart structures begins by examining the membrane that surrounds the heart, the prominent surface features of the heart, and the layers that form the wall of the heart. Each of these components plays its own unique role in terms of function.

Membranes

The membrane that directly surrounds the heart and defines the pericardial cavity is called the **pericardium** or **pericardial sac**. It also surrounds the "roots" of the major vessels, or the areas of closest proximity to the heart. The pericardium, which literally translates as "around the heart," consists of two distinct sublayers: the sturdy outer fibrous pericardium and the inner serous pericardium. The fibrous pericardium is made of tough, dense connective tissue that protects the heart and maintains its position in the thorax. The more delicate serous pericardium consists of two layers: the parietal pericardium, which is fused to the fibrous pericardium, and an inner visceral pericardium, or **epicardium**, which is fused to the heart and is part of the heart wall. The pericardial cavity, filled with lubricating serous fluid, lies between the epicardium and the pericardium.

In most organs within the body, visceral serous membranes such as the epicardium are microscopic. However, in the case of the heart, it is not a microscopic layer but rather a macroscopic layer, consisting of a simple squamous epithelium called a **mesothelium**, reinforced with loose, irregular, or areolar connective tissue that attaches to the pericardium. This mesothelium secretes the lubricating serous fluid that fills the pericardial cavity and reduces friction as the heart contracts. Figure 19.5 illustrates the pericardial membrane and the layers of the heart.

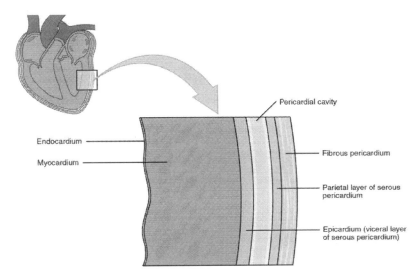

Figure 19.5 Pericardial Membranes and Layers of the Heart Wall   The pericardial membrane that surrounds the heart consists of three layers and the pericardial cavity. The heart wall also consists of three layers. The pericardial membrane and the heart wall share the epicardium.

Heart: Cardiac Tamponade

If excess fluid builds within the pericardial space, it can lead to a condition called cardiac tamponade, or pericardial tamponade. With each contraction of the heart, more fluid—in most instances, blood—accumulates within the pericardial cavity. In order to fill with blood for the next contraction, the heart must relax. However, the excess fluid in the pericardial cavity puts pressure on the heart and prevents full relaxation, so the chambers within the heart contain slightly less blood as they begin each heart cycle. Over time, less and less blood is ejected from the heart. If the fluid builds up slowly, as in hypothyroidism, the pericardial cavity may be able to expand gradually to accommodate this extra volume. Some cases of fluid in excess of one liter within the pericardial cavity have been reported. Rapid accumulation of as little as 100 mL of fluid following trauma may trigger cardiac tamponade. Other common causes include myocardial rupture, pericarditis, cancer, or even cardiac surgery. Removal of this excess fluid requires insertion of drainage tubes into the pericardial cavity. Premature removal of these drainage tubes, for example, following cardiac surgery, or clot formation within these tubes are causes of this condition. Untreated, cardiac tamponade can lead to death.

Surface Features of the Heart

Inside the pericardium, the surface features of the heart are visible, including the four chambers. There is a superficial leaf-like extension of the atria near the superior surface of the heart, one on each side, called an **auricle**—a name that means "ear like"—because its shape resembles the external ear of a human (Figure 19.6). Auricles are relatively thin-walled structures that can fill with blood and empty into the atria or upper chambers of the heart. You may also hear them referred to as atrial appendages. Also prominent is a series of fat-filled grooves, each of which is known as a **sulcus** (plural = sulci), along the superior surfaces of the heart. Major coronary blood vessels are located in these sulci. The deep **coronary sulcus** is located between the atria and ventricles. Located between the left and right ventricles are two additional sulci that are not as deep as the coronary sulcus. The **anterior interventricular sulcus** is visible on the anterior surface of the heart, whereas the **posterior interventricular sulcus** is visible on the posterior surface of the heart. Figure 19.6 illustrates anterior and posterior views of the surface of the heart.

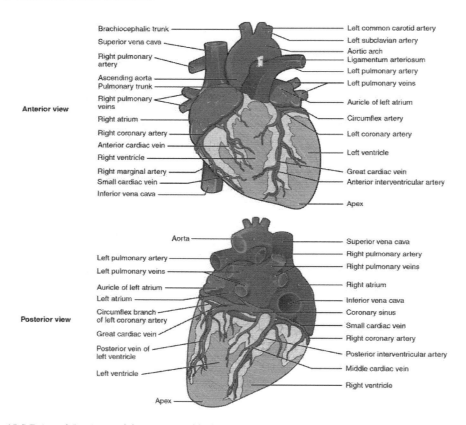

Figure 19.6 External Anatomy of the Heart Inside the pericardium, the surface features of the heart are visible.

Layers

The wall of the heart is composed of three layers of unequal thickness. From superficial to deep, these are the epicardium, the myocardium, and the endocardium (see Figure 19.5). The outermost layer of the wall of the heart is also the innermost layer of the pericardium, the epicardium, or the visceral pericardium discussed earlier.

The middle and thickest layer is the **myocardium**, made largely of cardiac muscle cells. It is built upon a framework of collagenous fibers, plus the blood vessels that supply the myocardium and the nerve fibers that help regulate the heart. It is the contraction of the myocardium that pumps blood through the heart and into the major arteries. The muscle pattern is elegant and complex, as the muscle cells swirl and spiral around the chambers of the heart. They form a figure 8 pattern around the atria and around the bases of the great vessels. Deeper ventricular muscles also form a figure 8 around the two ventricles and proceed toward the apex. More superficial layers of ventricular muscle wrap around both ventricles. This complex swirling pattern allows the heart to pump blood more effectively than a simple linear pattern would. Figure 19.7 illustrates the arrangement of muscle cells.

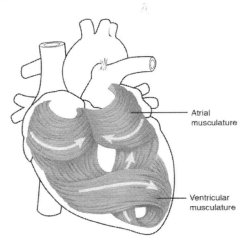

Figure 19.7 Heart Musculature   The swirling pattern of cardiac muscle tissue contributes significantly to the heart's ability to pump blood effectively.

Although the ventricles on the right and left sides pump the same amount of blood per contraction, the muscle of the left ventricle is much thicker and better developed than that of the right ventricle. In order to overcome the high resistance required to pump blood into the long systemic circuit, the left ventricle must generate a great amount of pressure. The right ventricle does not need to generate as much pressure, since the pulmonary circuit is shorter and provides less resistance. Figure 19.8 illustrates the differences in muscular thickness needed for each of the ventricles.

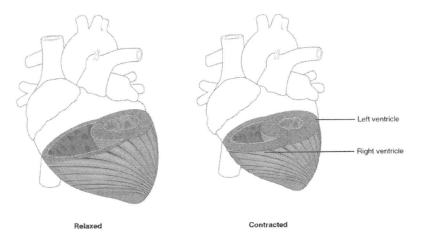

Figure 19.8 Differences in Ventricular Muscle Thickness   The myocardium in the left ventricle is significantly thicker than that of the right ventricle. Both ventricles pump the same amount of blood, but the left ventricle must generate a much greater pressure to overcome greater resistance in the systemic circuit. The ventricles are shown in both relaxed and contracting states. Note the differences in the relative size of the lumens, the region inside each ventricle where the blood is contained.

The innermost layer of the heart wall, the **endocardium**, is joined to the myocardium with a thin layer of connective tissue. The endocardium lines the chambers where the blood circulates and covers the heart valves. It is made of simple squamous epithelium called **endothelium**, which is continuous with the endothelial lining of the blood vessels (see Figure 19.5).

Once regarded as a simple lining layer, recent evidence indicates that the endothelium of the endocardium and the coronary capillaries may play active roles in regulating the contraction of the muscle within the myocardium. The endothelium may also regulate the growth patterns of the cardiac muscle cells throughout life, and the endothelins it secretes create an environment in the surrounding tissue fluids that regulates ionic concentrations and states of contractility. Endothelins are potent vasoconstrictors and, in a normal individual, establish a homeostatic balance with other vasoconstrictors and vasodilators.

Internal Structure of the Heart

Recall that the heart's contraction cycle follows a dual pattern of circulation—the pulmonary and systemic circuits—because of the pairs of chambers that pump blood into the circulation. In order to develop a more precise understanding of cardiac function, it is first necessary to explore the internal anatomical structures in more detail.

Septa of the Heart

The word septum is derived from the Latin for "something that encloses;" in this case, a **septum** (plural = septa) refers to a wall or partition that divides the heart into chambers. The septa are physical extensions of the myocardium lined with endocardium. Located between the two atria is the **interatrial septum**. Normally in an adult heart, the interatrial septum bears an oval-shaped depression known as the **fossa ovalis**, a remnant of an opening in the fetal heart known as the **foramen ovale**. The foramen ovale allowed blood in the fetal heart to pass directly from the right atrium to the left atrium, allowing some blood to bypass the pulmonary circuit. Within seconds after birth, a flap of tissue known as the **septum primum** that previously acted as a valve closes the foramen ovale and establishes the typical cardiac circulation pattern.

Between the two ventricles is a second septum known as the **interventricular septum**. Unlike the interatrial septum, the interventricular septum is normally intact after its formation during fetal development. It is substantially thicker than the interatrial septum, since the ventricles generate far greater pressure when they contract.

The septum between the atria and ventricles is known as the **atrioventricular septum**. It is marked by the presence of four openings that allow blood to move from the atria into the ventricles and from the ventricles into the pulmonary trunk and aorta. Located in each of these openings between the atria and ventricles is a **valve**, a specialized structure that ensures one-way flow of blood. The valves between the atria and ventricles are known generically as **atrioventricular valves**. The valves at the openings that lead to the pulmonary trunk and aorta are known generically as **semilunar valves**. The interventricular septum is visible in Figure 19.9. In this figure, the atrioventricular septum has been removed to better show the bicupid and tricuspid valves; the interatrial septum is not visible, since its location is covered by the aorta and pulmonary trunk. Since these openings and valves structurally weaken the atrioventricular septum, the remaining tissue is heavily reinforced with dense connective tissue called the **cardiac skeleton**, or skeleton of the heart. It includes four rings that surround the openings between the atria and ventricles, and the openings to the pulmonary trunk and aorta, and serve as the point of attachment for the heart valves. The cardiac skeleton also provides an important boundary in the heart electrical conduction system.

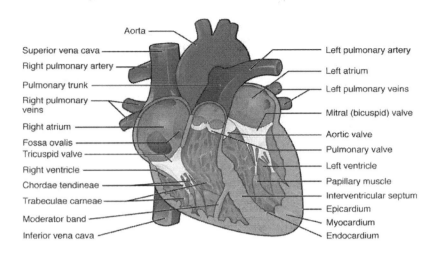

Anterior view

Figure 19.9 Internal Structures of the Heart This anterior view of the heart shows the four chambers, the major vessels and their early branches, as well as the valves. The presence of the pulmonary trunk and aorta covers the interatrial septum, and the atrioventricular septum is cut away to show the atrioventricular valves.

Heart: Heart Defects

One very common form of interatrial septum pathology is patent foramen ovale, which occurs when the septum primum does not close at birth, and the fossa ovalis is unable to fuse. The word patent is from the Latin root patens for "open." It may be benign or asymptomatic, perhaps never being diagnosed, or in extreme cases, it may require surgical repair to close the opening permanently. As much as 20–25 percent of the general population may have a patent foramen ovale, but fortunately, most have the benign, asymptomatic version. Patent foramen ovale is normally detected by auscultation of a heart murmur (an abnormal heart sound) and confirmed by imaging with an echocardiogram. Despite its prevalence in the general population, the causes of patent ovale are unknown, and there are no known risk factors. In nonlife-threatening cases, it is better to monitor the condition than to risk heart surgery to repair and seal the opening.

Coarctation of the aorta is a congenital abnormal narrowing of the aorta that is normally located at the insertion of the ligamentum arteriosum, the remnant of the fetal shunt called the ductus arteriosus. If severe, this condition drastically restricts blood flow through the primary systemic artery, which is life threatening. In some individuals, the condition may be fairly benign and not detected until later in life. Detectable symptoms in an infant include difficulty breathing, poor appetite, trouble feeding, or failure to thrive. In older individuals, symptoms include dizziness, fainting, shortness of breath, chest pain, fatigue, headache, and nosebleeds. Treatment involves surgery to resect (remove) the affected region or angioplasty to open the abnormally narrow passageway. Studies have shown that the earlier the surgery is performed, the better the chance of survival.

A patent ductus arteriosus is a congenital condition in which the ductus arteriosus fails to close. The condition may range from severe to benign. Failure of the ductus arteriosus to close results in blood flowing from the higher pressure aorta into the lower pressure pulmonary trunk. This additional fluid moving toward the lungs increases pulmonary pressure and makes respiration difficult. Symptoms include shortness of breath (dyspnea), tachycardia, enlarged heart, a widened pulse pressure, and poor weight gain in infants. Treatments include surgical closure (ligation), manual closure using platinum coils or specialized mesh inserted via the femoral artery or vein, or nonsteroidal anti-inflammatory drugs to block the synthesis of prostaglandin E2, which maintains the vessel in an open position. If untreated, the condition can result in congestive heart failure.

Septal defects are not uncommon in individuals and may be congenital or caused by various disease processes. Tetralogy of Fallot is a congenital condition that may also occur from exposure to unknown environmental factors; it occurs when there is an opening in the interventricular septum caused by blockage of the pulmonary trunk, normally at the pulmonary semilunar valve. This allows blood that is relatively low in oxygen from the right ventricle to flow into the left ventricle and mix with the blood that is relatively high in oxygen. Symptoms include a distinct heart murmur, low blood oxygen percent saturation, dyspnea or difficulty in breathing, polycythemia, broadening (clubbing) of the fingers and toes, and in children, difficulty in feeding or failure to grow and develop. It is the most common cause of cyanosis following birth. The term "tetralogy" is derived from the four components of the condition, although only three may be present in an individual patient: pulmonary infundibular stenosis (rigidity of the pulmonary valve), overriding aorta (the aorta is shifted above both ventricles), ventricular septal defect (opening), and right ventricular hypertrophy (enlargement of the right ventricle). Other heart defects may also accompany this condition, which is typically confirmed by echocardiography imaging. Tetralogy of Fallot occurs in approximately 400 out of one million live births. Normal treatment involves extensive surgical repair, including the use of stents to redirect blood flow and replacement of valves and patches to repair the septal defect, but the condition has a relatively high mortality. Survival rates are currently 75 percent during the first year of life; 60 percent by 4 years of age; 30 percent by 10 years; and 5 percent by 40 years.

In the case of severe septal defects, including both tetralogy of Fallot and patent foramen ovale, failure of the heart to develop properly can lead to a condition commonly known as a "blue baby." Regardless of normal skin pigmentation, individuals with this condition have an insufficient supply of oxygenated blood, which leads to cyanosis, a blue or purple coloration of the skin, especially when active.

Septal defects are commonly first detected through auscultation, listening to the chest using a stethoscope. In this case, instead of hearing normal heart sounds attributed to the flow of blood and closing of heart valves, unusual heart sounds may be detected. This is often followed by medical imaging to confirm or rule out a diagnosis. In many cases, treatment may not be needed. Some common congenital heart defects are illustrated in Figure 19.10.

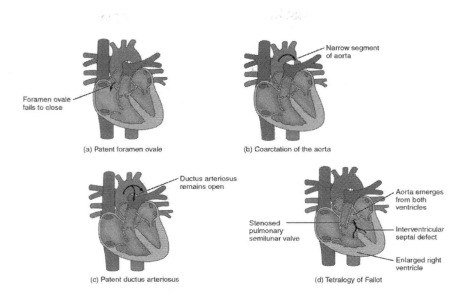

Figure 19.10 Congenital Heart Defects (a) A patent foramen ovale defect is an abnormal opening in the interatrial septum, or more commonly, a failure of the foramen ovale to close. (b) Coarctation of the aorta is an abnormal narrowing of the aorta. (c) A patent ductus arteriosus is the failure of the ductus arteriosus to close. (d) Tetralogy of Fallot includes an abnormal opening in the interventricular septum.

Right Atrium

The right atrium serves as the receiving chamber for blood returning to the heart from the systemic circulation. The two major systemic veins, the superior and inferior venae cavae, and the large coronary vein called the **coronary sinus** that drains the heart myocardium empty into the right atrium. The superior vena cava drains blood from regions superior to the diaphragm: the head, neck, upper limbs, and the thoracic region. It empties into the superior and posterior portions of the right atrium. The inferior vena cava drains blood from areas inferior to the diaphragm: the lower limbs and abdominopelvic region of the body. It, too, empties into the posterior portion of the atria, but inferior to the opening of the superior vena cava. Immediately superior and slightly medial to the opening of the inferior vena cava on the posterior surface of the atrium is the opening of the coronary sinus. This thin-walled vessel drains most of the coronary veins that return systemic blood from the heart. The majority of the internal heart structures discussed in this and subsequent sections are illustrated in Figure 19.9.

While the bulk of the internal surface of the right atrium is smooth, the depression of the fossa ovalis is medial, and the anterior surface demonstrates prominent ridges of muscle called the **pectinate muscles**. The right auricle also has pectinate muscles. The left atrium does not have pectinate muscles except in the auricle.

The atria receive venous blood on a nearly continuous basis, preventing venous flow from stopping while the ventricles are contracting. While most ventricular filling occurs while the atria are relaxed, they do demonstrate a contractile phase and actively pump blood into the ventricles just prior to ventricular contraction. The opening between the atrium and ventricle is guarded by the tricuspid valve.

Right Ventricle

The right ventricle receives blood from the right atrium through the tricuspid valve. Each flap of the valve is attached to strong strands of connective tissue, the **chordae tendineae**, literally "tendinous cords," or sometimes more poetically referred to as "heart strings." There are several chordae tendineae associated with each of the flaps. They are composed of approximately 80 percent collagenous fibers with the remainder consisting of elastic fibers and endothelium. They connect each of the flaps to a **papillary muscle** that extends from the inferior ventricular surface. There are three papillary muscles in the right ventricle, called the anterior, posterior, and septal muscles, which correspond to the three sections of the valves.

When the myocardium of the ventricle contracts, pressure within the ventricular chamber rises. Blood, like any fluid, flows from higher pressure to lower pressure areas, in this case, toward the pulmonary trunk and the atrium. To prevent any potential backflow, the papillary muscles also contract, generating tension on the chordae tendineae. This prevents the flaps of the valves from being forced into the atria and regurgitation of the blood back into the atria during ventricular contraction. Figure 19.11 shows papillary muscles and chordae tendineae attached to the tricuspid valve.

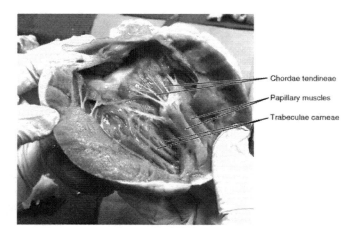

Figure 19.11 Chordae Tendineae and Papillary Muscles In this frontal section, you can see papillary muscles attached to the tricuspid valve on the right as well as the mitral valve on the left via chordae tendineae. (credit: modification of work by "PV KS"/flickr.com)

The walls of the ventricle are lined with **trabeculae carneae**, ridges of cardiac muscle covered by endocardium. In addition to these muscular ridges, a band of cardiac muscle, also covered by endocardium, known as the **moderator band** (see Figure 19.9) reinforces the thin walls of the right ventricle and plays a crucial role in cardiac conduction. It arises from the inferior portion of the interventricular septum and crosses the interior space of the right ventricle to connect with the inferior papillary muscle.

When the right ventricle contracts, it ejects blood into the pulmonary trunk, which branches into the left and right pulmonary arteries that carry it to each lung. The superior surface of the right ventricle begins to taper as it approaches the pulmonary trunk. At the base of the pulmonary trunk is the pulmonary semilunar valve that prevents backflow from the pulmonary trunk.

Left Atrium

After exchange of gases in the pulmonary capillaries, blood returns to the left atrium high in oxygen via one of the four pulmonary veins. While the left atrium does not contain pectinate muscles, it does have an auricle that includes these pectinate ridges. Blood flows nearly continuously from the pulmonary veins back into the atrium, which acts as the receiving chamber, and from here through an opening into the left ventricle. Most blood flows passively into the heart while both the atria and ventricles are relaxed, but toward the end of the ventricular relaxation period, the left atrium will contract, pumping blood into the ventricle. This atrial contraction accounts for approximately 20 percent of ventricular filling. The opening between the left atrium and ventricle is guarded by the mitral valve.

Left Ventricle

Recall that, although both sides of the heart will pump the same amount of blood, the muscular layer is much thicker in the left ventricle compared to the right (see Figure 19.8). Like the right ventricle, the left also has trabeculae carneae, but there is no moderator band. The mitral valve is connected to papillary muscles via chordae tendineae. There are two papillary muscles on the left—the anterior and posterior—as opposed to three on the right.

The left ventricle is the major pumping chamber for the systemic circuit; it ejects blood into the aorta through the aortic semilunar valve.

Heart Valve Structure and Function

A transverse section through the heart slightly above the level of the atrioventricular septum reveals all four heart valves along the same plane (Figure 19.12). The valves ensure unidirectional blood flow through the heart. Between the right atrium and the right ventricle is the **right atrioventricular valve**, or **tricuspid valve**. It typically consists of three flaps, or leaflets, made of endocardium reinforced with additional connective tissue. The flaps are connected by chordae tendineae to the papillary muscles, which control the opening and closing of the valves.

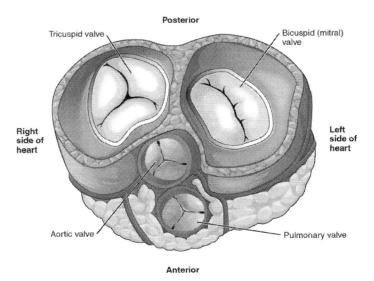

Figure 19.12 Heart Valves With the atria and major vessels removed, all four valves are clearly visible, although it is difficult to distinguish the three separate cusps of the tricuspid valve.

Emerging from the right ventricle at the base of the pulmonary trunk is the pulmonary semilunar valve, or the **pulmonary valve**; it is also known as the pulmonic valve or the right semilunar valve. The pulmonary valve is comprised of three small flaps of endothelium reinforced with connective tissue. When the ventricle relaxes, the pressure differential causes blood to flow back into the ventricle from the pulmonary trunk. This flow of blood fills the pocket-like flaps of the pulmonary valve, causing the valve to close and producing an audible sound. Unlike the atrioventricular valves, there are no papillary muscles or chordae tendineae associated with the pulmonary valve.

Located at the opening between the left atrium and left ventricle is the **mitral valve**, also called the **bicuspid valve** or the **left atrioventricular valve**. Structurally, this valve consists of two cusps, known as the anterior medial cusp and the posterior medial cusp, compared to the three cusps of the tricuspid valve. In a clinical setting, the valve is referred to as the mitral valve, rather than the bicuspid valve. The two cusps of the mitral valve are attached by chordae tendineae to two papillary muscles that project from the wall of the ventricle.

At the base of the aorta is the aortic semilunar valve, or the **aortic valve**, which prevents backflow from the aorta. It normally is composed of three flaps. When the ventricle relaxes and blood attempts to flow back into the ventricle from the aorta, blood will fill the cusps of the valve, causing it to close and producing an audible sound.

In Figure 19.13a, the two atrioventricular valves are open and the two semilunar valves are closed. This occurs when both atria and ventricles are relaxed and when the atria contract to pump blood into the ventricles. Figure 19.13b shows a frontal view. Although only the left side of the heart is illustrated, the process is virtually identical on the right.

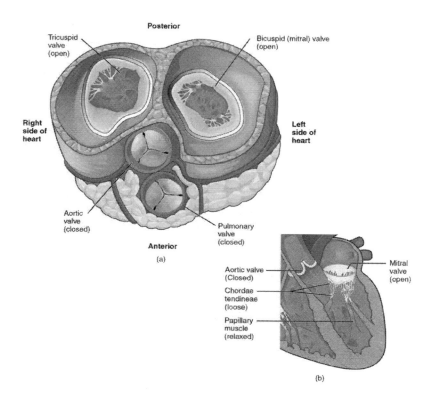

Figure 19.13 Blood Flow from the Left Atrium to the Left Ventricle (a) A transverse section through the heart illustrates the four heart valves. The two atrioventricular valves are open; the two semilunar valves are closed. The atria and vessels have been removed. (b) A frontal section through the heart illustrates blood flow through the mitral valve. When the mitral valve is open, it allows blood to move from the left atrium to the left ventricle. The aortic semilunar valve is closed to prevent backflow of blood from the aorta to the left ventricle.

Figure 19.14a shows the atrioventricular valves closed while the two semilunar valves are open. This occurs when the ventricles contract to eject blood into the pulmonary trunk and aorta. Closure of the two atrioventricular valves prevents blood from being forced back into the atria. This stage can be seen from a frontal view in Figure 19.14b.

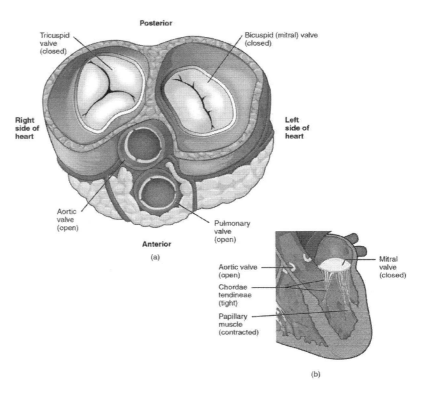

Figure 19.14 Blood Flow from the Left Ventricle into the Great Vessels (a) A transverse section through the heart illustrates the four heart valves during ventricular contraction. The two atrioventricular valves are closed, but the two semilunar valves are open. The atria and vessels have been removed. (b) A frontal view shows the closed mitral (bicuspid) valve that prevents backflow of blood into the left atrium. The aortic semilunar valve is open to allow blood to be ejected into the aorta.

When the ventricles begin to contract, pressure within the ventricles rises and blood flows toward the area of lowest pressure, which is initially in the atria. This backflow causes the cusps of the tricuspid and mitral (bicuspid) valves to close. These valves are tied down to the papillary muscles by chordae tendineae. During the relaxation phase of the cardiac cycle, the papillary muscles are also relaxed and the tension on the chordae tendineae is slight (see Figure 19.13**b**). However, as the myocardium of the ventricle contracts, so do the papillary muscles. This creates tension on the chordae tendineae (see Figure 19.14**b**), helping to hold the cusps of the atrioventricular valves in place and preventing them from being blown back into the atria.

The aortic and pulmonary semilunar valves lack the chordae tendineae and papillary muscles associated with the atrioventricular valves. Instead, they consist of pocket-like folds of endocardium reinforced with additional connective tissue. When the ventricles relax and the change in pressure forces the blood toward the ventricles, the blood presses against these cusps and seals the openings.

Interactive LINK

Visit this site (http://openstaxcollege.org/l/heartvalve) to observe an echocardiogram of actual heart valves opening and closing. Although much of the heart has been "removed" from this gif loop so the chordae tendineae are not visible, why is their presence more critical for the atrioventricular valves (tricuspid and mitral) than the semilunar (aortic and pulmonary) valves?

Disorders OF THE...

Heart Valves

When heart valves do not function properly, they are often described as incompetent and result in valvular heart disease, which can range from benign to lethal. Some of these conditions are congenital, that is, the individual was born with the defect, whereas others may be attributed to disease processes or trauma. Some malfunctions are treated with medications, others require surgery, and still others may be mild enough that the condition is merely monitored since treatment might trigger more serious consequences.

Valvular disorders are often caused by carditis, or inflammation of the heart. One common trigger for this inflammation is rheumatic fever, or scarlet fever, an autoimmune response to the presence of a bacterium, *Streptococcus pyogenes*, normally a disease of childhood.

While any of the heart valves may be involved in valve disorders, mitral regurgitation is the most common, detected in approximately 2 percent of the population, and the pulmonary semilunar valve is the least frequently involved. When a valve malfunctions, the flow of blood to a region will often be disrupted. The resulting inadequate flow of blood to this region will be described in general terms as an insufficiency. The specific type of insufficiency is named for the valve involved: aortic insufficiency, mitral insufficiency, tricuspid insufficiency, or pulmonary insufficiency.

If one of the cusps of the valve is forced backward by the force of the blood, the condition is referred to as a prolapsed valve. Prolapse may occur if the chordae tendineae are damaged or broken, causing the closure mechanism to fail. The failure of the valve to close properly disrupts the normal one-way flow of blood and results in regurgitation, when the blood flows backward from its normal path. Using a stethoscope, the disruption to the normal flow of blood produces a heart murmur.

Stenosis is a condition in which the heart valves become rigid and may calcify over time. The loss of flexibility of the valve interferes with normal function and may cause the heart to work harder to propel blood through the valve, which eventually weakens the heart. Aortic stenosis affects approximately 2 percent of the population over 65 years of age, and the percentage increases to approximately 4 percent in individuals over 85 years. Occasionally, one or more of the chordae tendineae will tear or the papillary muscle itself may die as a component of a myocardial infarction (heart attack). In this case, the patient's condition will deteriorate dramatically and rapidly, and immediate surgical intervention may be required.

Auscultation, or listening to a patient's heart sounds, is one of the most useful diagnostic tools, since it is proven, safe, and inexpensive. The term auscultation is derived from the Latin for "to listen," and the technique has been used for diagnostic purposes as far back as the ancient Egyptians. Valve and septal disorders will trigger abnormal heart sounds. If a valvular disorder is detected or suspected, a test called an echocardiogram, or simply an "echo," may be ordered. Echocardiograms are sonograms of the heart and can help in the diagnosis of valve disorders as well as a wide variety of heart pathologies.

Visit this site (http://openstaxcollege.org/l/heartsounds) for a free download, including excellent animations and audio of heart sounds.

Cardiologist

Cardiologists are medical doctors that specialize in the diagnosis and treatment of diseases of the heart. After completing 4 years of medical school, cardiologists complete a three-year residency in internal medicine followed by an additional three or more years in cardiology. Following this 10-year period of medical training and clinical experience, they qualify for a rigorous two-day examination administered by the Board of Internal Medicine that tests their academic training and clinical abilities, including diagnostics and treatment. After successful completion of this examination, a physician becomes a board-certified cardiologist. Some board-certified cardiologists may be invited to become a Fellow of the American College of Cardiology (FACC). This professional recognition is awarded to outstanding physicians based upon merit, including outstanding credentials, achievements, and community contributions to cardiovascular medicine.

Visit this site (http://openstaxcollege.org/l/cardiologist) to learn more about cardiologists.

Cardiovascular Technologist/Technician

Cardiovascular technologists/technicians are trained professionals who perform a variety of imaging techniques, such as sonograms or echocardiograms, used by physicians to diagnose and treat diseases of the heart. Nearly all of these positions require an associate degree, and these technicians earn a median salary of $49,410 as of May 2010, according to the U.S. Bureau of Labor Statistics. Growth within the field is fast, projected at 29 percent from 2010 to 2020.

There is a considerable overlap and complementary skills between cardiac technicians and vascular technicians, and so the term cardiovascular technician is often used. Special certifications within the field require documenting appropriate experience and completing additional and often expensive certification examinations. These subspecialties include Certified Rhythm Analysis Technician (CRAT), Certified Cardiographic Technician (CCT), Registered Congenital Cardiac Sonographer (RCCS), Registered Cardiac Electrophysiology Specialist (RCES), Registered Cardiovascular Invasive Specialist (RCIS), Registered Cardiac Sonographer (RCS), Registered Vascular Specialist (RVS), and Registered Phlebology Sonographer (RPhS).

Visit this site (http://openstaxcollege.org/l/cardiotech) for more information on cardiovascular technologists/technicians.

Coronary Circulation

You will recall that the heart is a remarkable pump composed largely of cardiac muscle cells that are incredibly active throughout life. Like all other cells, a **cardiomyocyte** requires a reliable supply of oxygen and nutrients, and a way to remove wastes, so it needs a dedicated, complex, and extensive coronary circulation. And because of the critical and nearly ceaseless activity of the heart throughout life, this need for a blood supply is even greater than for a typical cell. However, coronary circulation is not continuous; rather, it cycles, reaching a peak when the heart muscle is relaxed and nearly ceasing while it is contracting.

Coronary Arteries

Coronary arteries supply blood to the myocardium and other components of the heart. The first portion of the aorta after it arises from the left ventricle gives rise to the coronary arteries. There are three dilations in the wall of the aorta just superior to the aortic semilunar valve. Two of these, the left posterior aortic sinus and anterior aortic sinus, give rise to the left and right coronary arteries, respectively. The third sinus, the right posterior aortic sinus, typically does not give rise to a vessel. Coronary vessel branches that remain on the surface of the artery and follow the sulci are called **epicardial coronary arteries**.

The left coronary artery distributes blood to the left side of the heart, the left atrium and ventricle, and the interventricular septum. The **circumflex artery** arises from the left coronary artery and follows the coronary sulcus to the left. Eventually, it will fuse with the small branches of the right coronary artery. The larger **anterior interventricular artery**, also known as the left anterior descending artery (LAD), is the second major branch arising from the left coronary artery. It follows the anterior interventricular sulcus around the pulmonary trunk. Along the way it gives rise to numerous smaller branches that interconnect with the branches of the posterior interventricular artery, forming anastomoses. An **anastomosis** is an area where vessels unite to form interconnections that normally allow blood to circulate to a region even if there may be partial blockage in another branch. The anastomoses in the heart are very small. Therefore, this ability is somewhat restricted in the heart so a coronary artery blockage often results in death of the cells (myocardial infarction) supplied by the particular vessel.

The right coronary artery proceeds along the coronary sulcus and distributes blood to the right atrium, portions of both ventricles, and the heart conduction system. Normally, one or more marginal arteries arise from the right coronary artery inferior to the right atrium. The **marginal arteries** supply blood to the superficial portions of the right ventricle. On the posterior surface of the heart, the right coronary artery gives rise to the **posterior interventricular artery**, also known as the posterior descending artery. It runs along the posterior portion of the interventricular sulcus toward the apex of the heart, giving rise to branches that supply the interventricular septum and portions of both ventricles. Figure 19.15 presents views of the coronary circulation from both the anterior and posterior views.

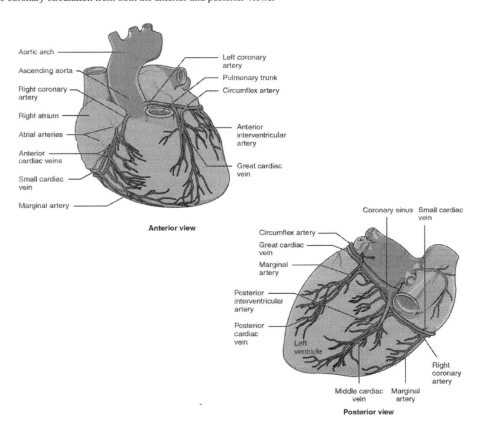

Figure 19.15 Coronary Circulation The anterior view of the heart shows the prominent coronary surface vessels. The posterior view of the heart shows the prominent coronary surface vessels.

Diseases OF THE...

Heart: Myocardial Infarction

Myocardial infarction (MI) is the formal term for what is commonly referred to as a heart attack. It normally results from a lack of blood flow (ischemia) and oxygen (hypoxia) to a region of the heart, resulting in death of the cardiac muscle cells. An MI often occurs when a coronary artery is blocked by the buildup of atherosclerotic plaque consisting of lipids, cholesterol and fatty acids, and white blood cells, primarily macrophages. It can also occur when a portion of an unstable atherosclerotic plaque travels through the coronary arterial system and lodges in one of the smaller vessels. The resulting blockage restricts the flow of blood and oxygen to the myocardium and causes death of the tissue. MIs may be triggered by excessive exercise, in which the partially occluded artery is no longer able to pump sufficient quantities of blood, or severe stress, which may induce spasm of the smooth muscle in the walls of the vessel.

In the case of acute MI, there is often sudden pain beneath the sternum (retrosternal pain) called angina pectoris, often radiating down the left arm in males but not in female patients. Until this anomaly between the sexes was discovered, many female patients suffering MIs were misdiagnosed and sent home. In addition, patients typically present with difficulty breathing and shortness of breath (dyspnea), irregular heartbeat (palpations), nausea and vomiting, sweating (diaphoresis), anxiety, and fainting (syncope), although not all of these symptoms may be present. Many of the symptoms are shared with other medical conditions, including anxiety attacks and simple indigestion, so differential diagnosis is critical. It is estimated that between 22 and 64 percent of MIs present without any symptoms.

An MI can be confirmed by examining the patient's ECG, which frequently reveals alterations in the ST and Q components. Some classification schemes of MI are referred to as ST-elevated MI (STEMI) and non-elevated MI (non-STEMI). In addition, echocardiography or cardiac magnetic resonance imaging may be employed. Common blood tests indicating an MI include elevated levels of creatine kinase MB (an enzyme that catalyzes the conversion of creatine to phosphocreatine, consuming ATP) and cardiac troponin (the regulatory protein for muscle contraction), both of which are released by damaged cardiac muscle cells.

Immediate treatments for MI are essential and include administering supplemental oxygen, aspirin that helps to break up clots, and nitroglycerine administered sublingually (under the tongue) to facilitate its absorption. Despite its unquestioned success in treatments and use since the 1880s, the mechanism of nitroglycerine is still incompletely understood but is believed to involve the release of nitric oxide, a known vasodilator, and endothelium-derived releasing factor, which also relaxes the smooth muscle in the tunica media of coronary vessels. Longer-term treatments include injections of thrombolytic agents such as streptokinase that dissolve the clot, the anticoagulant heparin, balloon angioplasty and stents to open blocked vessels, and bypass surgery to allow blood to pass around the site of blockage. If the damage is extensive, coronary replacement with a donor heart or coronary assist device, a sophisticated mechanical device that supplements the pumping activity of the heart, may be employed. Despite the attention, development of artificial hearts to augment the severely limited supply of heart donors has proven less than satisfactory but will likely improve in the future.

MIs may trigger cardiac arrest, but the two are not synonymous. Important risk factors for MI include cardiovascular disease, age, smoking, high blood levels of the low-density lipoprotein (LDL, often referred to as "bad" cholesterol), low levels of high-density lipoprotein (HDL, or "good" cholesterol), hypertension, diabetes mellitus, obesity, lack of physical exercise, chronic kidney disease, excessive alcohol consumption, and use of illegal drugs.

Coronary Veins

Coronary veins drain the heart and generally parallel the large surface arteries (see Figure 19.15). The **great cardiac vein** can be seen initially on the surface of the heart following the interventricular sulcus, but it eventually flows along the coronary sulcus into the coronary sinus on the posterior surface. The great cardiac vein initially parallels the anterior interventricular artery and drains the areas supplied by this vessel. It receives several major branches, including the posterior cardiac vein, the middle cardiac vein, and the small cardiac vein. The **posterior cardiac vein** parallels and drains the areas supplied by the marginal artery branch of the circumflex artery. The **middle cardiac vein** parallels and drains the areas supplied by the posterior interventricular artery. The **small cardiac vein** parallels the right coronary artery and drains the blood from the posterior surfaces of the right atrium and ventricle. The coronary sinus is a large, thin-walled vein on the posterior surface of the heart lying within the atrioventricular sulcus and emptying directly into the right atrium. The **anterior cardiac veins** parallel the small cardiac arteries and drain the anterior surface of the right ventricle. Unlike these other cardiac veins, it bypasses the coronary sinus and drains directly into the right atrium.

Heart: Coronary Artery Disease

Coronary artery disease is the leading cause of death worldwide. It occurs when the buildup of plaque—a fatty material including cholesterol, connective tissue, white blood cells, and some smooth muscle cells—within the walls of the arteries obstructs the flow of blood and decreases the flexibility or compliance of the vessels. This condition is called atherosclerosis, a hardening of the arteries that involves the accumulation of plaque. As the coronary blood vessels become occluded, the flow of blood to the tissues will be restricted, a condition called ischemia that causes the cells to receive insufficient amounts of oxygen, called hypoxia. Figure 19.16 shows the blockage of coronary arteries highlighted by the injection of dye. Some individuals with coronary artery disease report pain radiating from the chest called angina pectoris, but others remain asymptomatic. If untreated, coronary artery disease can lead to MI or a heart attack.

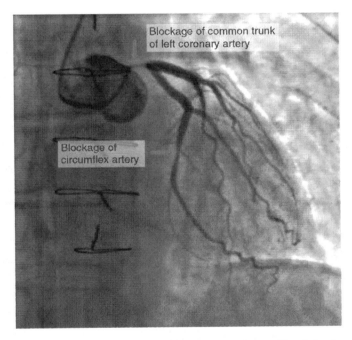

Figure 19.16 Atherosclerotic Coronary Arteries In this coronary angiogram (X-ray), the dye makes visible two occluded coronary arteries. Such blockages can lead to decreased blood flow (ischemia) and insufficient oxygen (hypoxia) delivered to the cardiac tissues. If uncorrected, this can lead to cardiac muscle death (myocardial infarction).

The disease progresses slowly and often begins in children and can be seen as fatty "streaks" in the vessels. It then gradually progresses throughout life. Well-documented risk factors include smoking, family history, hypertension, obesity, diabetes, high alcohol consumption, lack of exercise, stress, and hyperlipidemia or high circulating levels of lipids in the blood. Treatments may include medication, changes to diet and exercise, angioplasty with a balloon catheter, insertion of a stent, or coronary bypass procedure.

Angioplasty is a procedure in which the occlusion is mechanically widened with a balloon. A specialized catheter with an expandable tip is inserted into a superficial vessel, normally in the leg, and then directed to the site of the occlusion. At this point, the balloon is inflated to compress the plaque material and to open the vessel to increase blood flow. Then, the balloon is deflated and retracted. A stent consisting of a specialized mesh is typically inserted at the site of occlusion to reinforce the weakened and damaged walls. Stent insertions have been routine in cardiology for more than 40 years.

Coronary bypass surgery may also be performed. This surgical procedure grafts a replacement vessel obtained from another, less vital portion of the body to bypass the occluded area. This procedure is clearly effective in treating patients experiencing a MI, but overall does not increase longevity. Nor does it seem advisable in patients with stable although diminished cardiac capacity since frequently loss of mental acuity occurs following the procedure. Long-term changes to behavior, emphasizing diet and exercise plus a medicine regime tailored to lower blood pressure, lower cholesterol and lipids, and reduce clotting are equally as effective.

19.2 | Cardiac Muscle and Electrical Activity

By the end of this section, you will be able to:
- Describe the structure of cardiac muscle
- Identify and describe the components of the conducting system that distributes electrical impulses through the heart
- Compare the effect of ion movement on membrane potential of cardiac conductive and contractile cells
- Relate characteristics of an electrocardiogram to events in the cardiac cycle
- Identify blocks that can interrupt the cardiac cycle

Recall that cardiac muscle shares a few characteristics with both skeletal muscle and smooth muscle, but it has some unique properties of its own. Not the least of these exceptional properties is its ability to initiate an electrical potential at a fixed rate that spreads rapidly from cell to cell to trigger the contractile mechanism. This property is known as **autorhythmicity**. Neither smooth nor skeletal muscle can do this. Even though cardiac muscle has autorhythmicity, heart rate is modulated by the endocrine and nervous systems.

There are two major types of cardiac muscle cells: myocardial contractile cells and myocardial conducting cells. The **myocardial contractile cells** constitute the bulk (99 percent) of the cells in the atria and ventricles. Contractile cells conduct impulses and are responsible for contractions that pump blood through the body. The **myocardial conducting cells** (1 percent of the cells) form the conduction system of the heart. Except for Purkinje cells, they are generally much smaller than the contractile cells and have few of the myofibrils or filaments needed for contraction. Their function is similar in many respects to neurons, although they are specialized muscle cells. Myocardial conduction cells initiate and propagate the action potential (the electrical impulse) that travels throughout the heart and triggers the contractions that propel the blood.

Structure of Cardiac Muscle

Compared to the giant cylinders of skeletal muscle, cardiac muscle cells, or cardiomyocytes, are considerably shorter with much smaller diameters. Cardiac muscle also demonstrates striations, the alternating pattern of dark A bands and light I bands attributed to the precise arrangement of the myofilaments and fibrils that are organized in sarcomeres along the length of the cell (Figure 19.17a). These contractile elements are virtually identical to skeletal muscle. T (transverse) tubules penetrate from the surface plasma membrane, the sarcolemma, to the interior of the cell, allowing the electrical impulse to reach the interior. The T tubules are only found at the Z discs, whereas in skeletal muscle, they are found at the junction of the A and I bands. Therefore, there are one-half as many T tubules in cardiac muscle as in skeletal muscle. In addition, the sarcoplasmic reticulum stores few calcium ions, so most of the calcium ions must come from outside the cells. The result is a slower onset of contraction. Mitochondria are plentiful, providing energy for the contractions of the heart. Typically, cardiomyocytes have a single, central nucleus, but two or more nuclei may be found in some cells.

Cardiac muscle cells branch freely. A junction between two adjoining cells is marked by a critical structure called an **intercalated disc**, which helps support the synchronized contraction of the muscle (Figure 19.17b). The sarcolemmas from adjacent cells bind together at the intercalated discs. They consist of desmosomes, specialized linking proteoglycans, tight junctions, and large numbers of gap junctions that allow the passage of ions between the cells and help to synchronize the contraction (Figure 19.17c). Intercellular connective tissue also helps to bind the cells together. The importance of strongly binding these cells together is necessitated by the forces exerted by contraction.

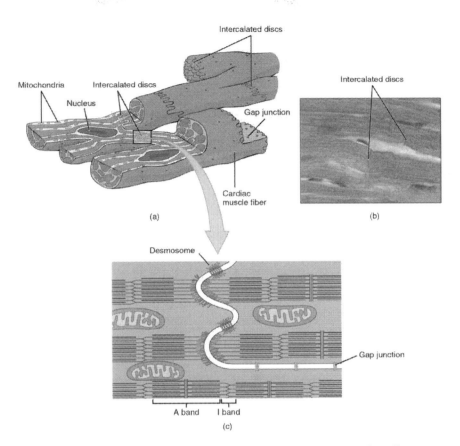

Figure 19.17 Cardiac Muscle (a) Cardiac muscle cells have myofibrils composed of myofilaments arranged in sarcomeres, T tubules to transmit the impulse from the sarcolemma to the interior of the cell, numerous mitochondria for energy, and intercalated discs that are found at the junction of different cardiac muscle cells. (b) A photomicrograph of cardiac muscle cells shows the nuclei and intercalated discs. (c) An intercalated disc connects cardiac muscle cells and consists of desmosomes and gap junctions. LM × 1600. (Micrograph provided by the Regents of the University of Michigan Medical School © 2012)

Cardiac muscle undergoes aerobic respiration patterns, primarily metabolizing lipids and carbohydrates. Myoglobin, lipids, and glycogen are all stored within the cytoplasm. Cardiac muscle cells undergo twitch-type contractions with long refractory periods followed by brief relaxation periods. The relaxation is essential so the heart can fill with blood for the next cycle. The refractory period is very long to prevent the possibility of tetany, a condition in which muscle remains involuntarily contracted. In the heart, tetany is not compatible with life, since it would prevent the heart from pumping blood.

Everyday CONNECTION

Repair and Replacement

Damaged cardiac muscle cells have extremely limited abilities to repair themselves or to replace dead cells via mitosis. Recent evidence indicates that at least some stem cells remain within the heart that continue to divide and at least potentially replace these dead cells. However, newly formed or repaired cells are rarely as functional as the original cells, and cardiac function is reduced. In the event of a heart attack or MI, dead cells are often replaced by patches of scar tissue. Autopsies performed on individuals who had successfully received heart transplants show some proliferation of original cells. If researchers can unlock the mechanism that generates new cells and restore full mitotic capabilities to heart muscle, the prognosis for heart attack survivors will be greatly enhanced. To date, myocardial cells produced within the patient (*in situ*) by cardiac stem cells seem to be nonfunctional, although those grown in Petri dishes (*in vitro*) do beat. Perhaps soon this mystery will be solved, and new advances in treatment will be commonplace.

Conduction System of the Heart

If embryonic heart cells are separated into a Petri dish and kept alive, each is capable of generating its own electrical impulse followed by contraction. When two independently beating embryonic cardiac muscle cells are placed together, the cell with the higher inherent rate sets the pace, and the impulse spreads from the faster to the slower cell to trigger a contraction. As more cells are joined together, the fastest cell continues to assume control of the rate. A fully developed adult heart maintains the capability of generating its own electrical impulse, triggered by the fastest cells, as part of the cardiac conduction system. The components of the cardiac conduction system include the sinoatrial node, the atrioventricular node, the atrioventricular bundle, the atrioventricular bundle branches, and the Purkinje cells (Figure 19.18).

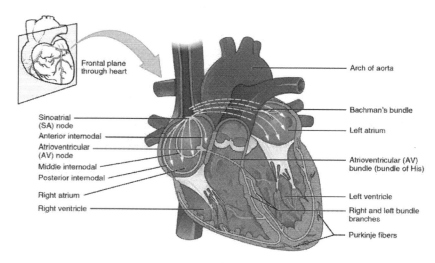

Figure 19.18 Conduction System of the Heart Specialized conducting components of the heart include the sinoatrial node, the internodal pathways, the atrioventricular node, the atrioventricular bundle, the right and left bundle branches, and the Purkinje fibers.

Sinoatrial (SA) Node

Normal cardiac rhythm is established by the **sinoatrial (SA) node**, a specialized clump of myocardial conducting cells located in the superior and posterior walls of the right atrium in close proximity to the orifice of the superior vena cava. The

SA node has the highest inherent rate of depolarization and is known as the **pacemaker** of the heart. It initiates the **sinus rhythm**, or normal electrical pattern followed by contraction of the heart.

This impulse spreads from its initiation in the SA node throughout the atria through specialized **internodal pathways**, to the atrial myocardial contractile cells and the atrioventricular node. The internodal pathways consist of three bands (anterior, middle, and posterior) that lead directly from the SA node to the next node in the conduction system, the atrioventricular node (see Figure 19.18). The impulse takes approximately 50 ms (milliseconds) to travel between these two nodes. The relative importance of this pathway has been debated since the impulse would reach the atrioventricular node simply following the cell-by-cell pathway through the contractile cells of the myocardium in the atria. In addition, there is a specialized pathway called **Bachmann's bundle** or the **interatrial band** that conducts the impulse directly from the right atrium to the left atrium. Regardless of the pathway, as the impulse reaches the atrioventricular septum, the connective tissue of the cardiac skeleton prevents the impulse from spreading into the myocardial cells in the ventricles except at the atrioventricular node. Figure 19.19 illustrates the initiation of the impulse in the SA node that then spreads the impulse throughout the atria to the atrioventricular node.

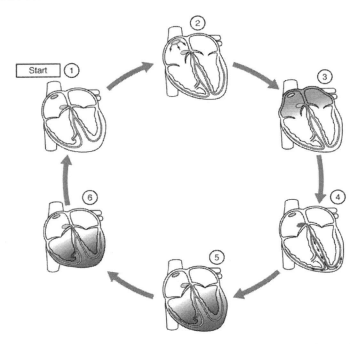

Figure 19.19 Cardiac Conduction (1) The sinoatrial (SA) node and the remainder of the conduction system are at rest. (2) The SA node initiates the action potential, which sweeps across the atria. (3) After reaching the atrioventricular node, there is a delay of approximately 100 ms that allows the atria to complete pumping blood before the impulse is transmitted to the atrioventricular bundle. (4) Following the delay, the impulse travels through the atrioventricular bundle and bundle branches to the Purkinje fibers, and also reaches the right papillary muscle via the moderator band. (5) The impulse spreads to the contractile fibers of the ventricle. (6) Ventricular contraction begins.

The electrical event, the wave of depolarization, is the trigger for muscular contraction. The wave of depolarization begins in the right atrium, and the impulse spreads across the superior portions of both atria and then down through the contractile cells. The contractile cells then begin contraction from the superior to the inferior portions of the atria, efficiently pumping blood into the ventricles.

Atrioventricular (AV) Node

The **atrioventricular (AV) node** is a second clump of specialized myocardial conductive cells, located in the inferior portion of the right atrium within the atrioventricular septum. The septum prevents the impulse from spreading directly to the ventricles without passing through the AV node. There is a critical pause before the AV node depolarizes and transmits the impulse to the atrioventricular bundle (see Figure 19.19, step 3). This delay in transmission is partially attributable to the small diameter of the cells of the node, which slow the impulse. Also, conduction between nodal cells is less efficient than between conducting cells. These factors mean that it takes the impulse approximately 100 ms to pass through the node. This pause is critical to heart function, as it allows the atrial cardiomyocytes to complete their contraction that pumps blood into the ventricles before the impulse is transmitted to the cells of the ventricle itself. With extreme stimulation by the SA node, the AV node can transmit impulses maximally at 220 per minute. This establishes the typical maximum heart rate in a healthy young individual. Damaged hearts or those stimulated by drugs can contract at higher rates, but at these rates, the heart can no longer effectively pump blood.

Atrioventricular Bundle (Bundle of His), Bundle Branches, and Purkinje Fibers

Arising from the AV node, the **atrioventricular bundle**, or **bundle of His**, proceeds through the interventricular septum before dividing into two **atrioventricular bundle branches**, commonly called the left and right bundle branches. The left bundle branch has two fascicles. The left bundle branch supplies the left ventricle, and the right bundle branch the right ventricle. Since the left ventricle is much larger than the right, the left bundle branch is also considerably larger than the right. Portions of the right bundle branch are found in the moderator band and supply the right papillary muscles. Because of this connection, each papillary muscle receives the impulse at approximately the same time, so they begin to contract simultaneously just prior to the remainder of the myocardial contractile cells of the ventricles. This is believed to allow tension to develop on the chordae tendineae prior to right ventricular contraction. There is no corresponding moderator band on the left. Both bundle branches descend and reach the apex of the heart where they connect with the Purkinje fibers (see Figure 19.19, step 4). This passage takes approximately 25 ms.

The **Purkinje fibers** are additional myocardial conductive fibers that spread the impulse to the myocardial contractile cells in the ventricles. They extend throughout the myocardium from the apex of the heart toward the atrioventricular septum and the base of the heart. The Purkinje fibers have a fast inherent conduction rate, and the electrical impulse reaches all of the ventricular muscle cells in about 75 ms (see Figure 19.19, step 5). Since the electrical stimulus begins at the apex, the contraction also begins at the apex and travels toward the base of the heart, similar to squeezing a tube of toothpaste from the bottom. This allows the blood to be pumped out of the ventricles and into the aorta and pulmonary trunk. The total time elapsed from the initiation of the impulse in the SA node until depolarization of the ventricles is approximately 225 ms.

Membrane Potentials and Ion Movement in Cardiac Conductive Cells

Action potentials are considerably different between cardiac conductive cells and cardiac contractive cells. While Na^+ and K^+ play essential roles, Ca^{2+} is also critical for both types of cells. Unlike skeletal muscles and neurons, cardiac conductive cells do not have a stable resting potential. Conductive cells contain a series of sodium ion channels that allow a normal and slow influx of sodium ions that causes the membrane potential to rise slowly from an initial value of −60 mV up to about −40 mV. The resulting movement of sodium ions creates **spontaneous depolarization** (or **prepotential depolarization**). At this point, calcium ion channels open and Ca^{2+} enters the cell, further depolarizing it at a more rapid rate until it reaches a value of approximately +5 mV. At this point, the calcium ion channels close and K^+ channels open, allowing outflux of K^+ and resulting in repolarization. When the membrane potential reaches approximately −60 mV, the K^+ channels close and Na^+ channels open, and the prepotential phase begins again. This phenomenon explains the autorhythmicity properties of cardiac muscle (Figure 19.20).

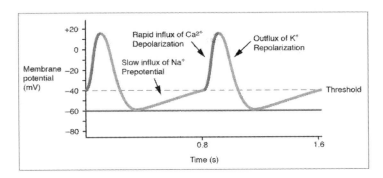

Figure 19.20 Action Potential at the SA Node The prepotential is due to a slow influx of sodium ions until the threshold is reached followed by a rapid depolarization and repolarization. The prepotential accounts for the membrane reaching threshold and initiates the spontaneous depolarization and contraction of the cell. Note the lack of a resting potential.

Membrane Potentials and Ion Movement in Cardiac Contractile Cells

There is a distinctly different electrical pattern involving the contractile cells. In this case, there is a rapid depolarization, followed by a plateau phase and then repolarization. This phenomenon accounts for the long refractory periods required for the cardiac muscle cells to pump blood effectively before they are capable of firing for a second time. These cardiac myocytes normally do not initiate their own electrical potential, although they are capable of doing so, but rather wait for an impulse to reach them.

Contractile cells demonstrate a much more stable resting phase than conductive cells at approximately −80 mV for cells in the atria and −90 mV for cells in the ventricles. Despite this initial difference, the other components of their action potentials are virtually identical. In both cases, when stimulated by an action potential, voltage-gated channels rapidly open, beginning the positive-feedback mechanism of depolarization. This rapid influx of positively charged ions raises the membrane potential to approximately +30 mV, at which point the sodium channels close. The rapid depolarization period typically lasts 3–5 ms. Depolarization is followed by the plateau phase, in which membrane potential declines relatively slowly. This is due in large part to the opening of the slow Ca^{2+} channels, allowing Ca^{2+} to enter the cell while few K^+ channels are open, allowing K^+ to exit the cell. The relatively long plateau phase lasts approximately 175 ms. Once the membrane potential reaches approximately zero, the Ca^{2+} channels close and K^+ channels open, allowing K^+ to exit the cell. The repolarization lasts approximately 75 ms. At this point, membrane potential drops until it reaches resting levels once more and the cycle repeats. The entire event lasts between 250 and 300 ms (Figure 19.21).

The absolute refractory period for cardiac contractile muscle lasts approximately 200 ms, and the relative refractory period lasts approximately 50 ms, for a total of 250 ms. This extended period is critical, since the heart muscle must contract to pump blood effectively and the contraction must follow the electrical events. Without extended refractory periods, premature contractions would occur in the heart and would not be compatible with life.

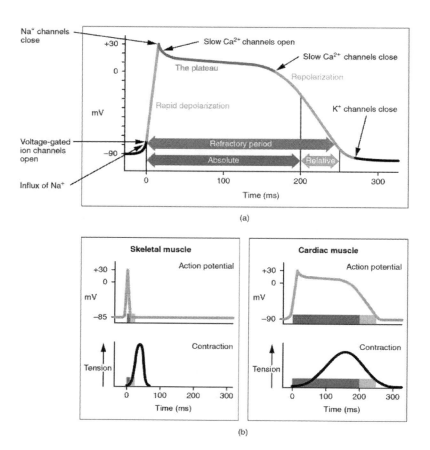

Figure 19.21 Action Potential in Cardiac Contractile Cells (a) Note the long plateau phase due to the influx of calcium ions. The extended refractory period allows the cell to fully contract before another electrical event can occur. (b) The action potential for heart muscle is compared to that of skeletal muscle.

Calcium Ions

Calcium ions play two critical roles in the physiology of cardiac muscle. Their influx through slow calcium channels accounts for the prolonged plateau phase and absolute refractory period that enable cardiac muscle to function properly. Calcium ions also combine with the regulatory protein troponin in the troponin-tropomyosin complex; this complex removes the inhibition that prevents the heads of the myosin molecules from forming cross bridges with the active sites on actin that provide the power stroke of contraction. This mechanism is virtually identical to that of skeletal muscle. Approximately 20 percent of the calcium required for contraction is supplied by the influx of Ca^{2+} during the plateau phase. The remaining Ca^{2+} for contraction is released from storage in the sarcoplasmic reticulum.

Comparative Rates of Conduction System Firing

The pattern of prepotential or spontaneous depolarization, followed by rapid depolarization and repolarization just described, are seen in the SA node and a few other conductive cells in the heart. Since the SA node is the pacemaker, it reaches threshold faster than any other component of the conduction system. It will initiate the impulses spreading to the other conducting cells. The SA node, without nervous or endocrine control, would initiate a heart impulse approximately 80–100 times per minute. Although each component of the conduction system is capable of generating its own impulse, the rate progressively slows as you proceed from the SA node to the Purkinje fibers. Without the SA node, the AV node would generate a heart rate of 40–60 beats per minute. If the AV node were blocked, the atrioventricular bundle would fire at a rate of approximately 30–40 impulses per minute. The bundle branches would have an inherent rate of 20–30 impulses per minute, and the Purkinje fibers would fire at 15–20 impulses per minute. While a few exceptionally trained aerobic athletes demonstrate resting heart rates in the range of 30–40 beats per minute (the lowest recorded figure is 28 beats per minute for Miguel Indurain, a cyclist), for most individuals, rates lower than 50 beats per minute would indicate a condition called bradycardia. Depending upon the specific individual, as rates fall much below this level, the heart would be unable to maintain adequate flow of blood to vital tissues, initially resulting in decreasing loss of function across the systems, unconsciousness, and ultimately death.

Electrocardiogram

By careful placement of surface electrodes on the body, it is possible to record the complex, compound electrical signal of the heart. This tracing of the electrical signal is the **electrocardiogram (ECG)**, also commonly abbreviated EKG (K coming kardiology, from the German term for cardiology). Careful analysis of the ECG reveals a detailed picture of both normal and abnormal heart function, and is an indispensable clinical diagnostic tool. The standard electrocardiograph (the instrument that generates an ECG) uses 3, 5, or 12 leads. The greater the number of leads an electrocardiograph uses, the more information the ECG provides. The term "lead" may be used to refer to the cable from the electrode to the electrical recorder, but it typically describes the voltage difference between two of the electrodes. The 12-lead electrocardiograph uses 10 electrodes placed in standard locations on the patient's skin (Figure 19.22). In continuous ambulatory electrocardiographs, the patient wears a small, portable, battery-operated device known as a Holter monitor, or simply a Holter, that continuously monitors heart electrical activity, typically for a period of 24 hours during the patient's normal routine.

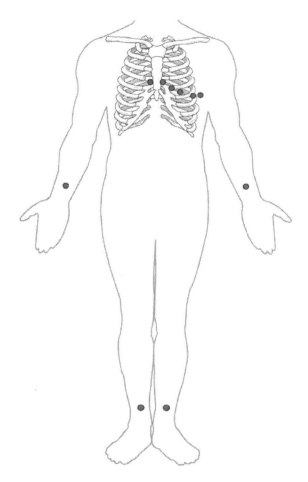

Figure 19.22 Standard Placement of ECG Leads In a 12-lead ECG, six electrodes are placed on the chest, and four electrodes are placed on the limbs.

A normal ECG tracing is presented in Figure 19.23. Each component, segment, and interval is labeled and corresponds to important electrical events, demonstrating the relationship between these events and contraction in the heart.

There are five prominent points on the ECG: the P wave, the QRS complex, and the T wave. The small **P wave** represents the depolarization of the atria. The atria begin contracting approximately 25 ms after the start of the P wave. The large **QRS complex** represents the depolarization of the ventricles, which requires a much stronger electrical signal because of the larger size of the ventricular cardiac muscle. The ventricles begin to contract as the QRS reaches the peak of the R wave. Lastly, the **T wave** represents the repolarization of the ventricles. The repolarization of the atria occurs during the QRS complex, which masks it on an ECG.

The major segments and intervals of an ECG tracing are indicated in Figure 19.23. Segments are defined as the regions between two waves. Intervals include one segment plus one or more waves. For example, the PR segment begins at the end of the P wave and ends at the beginning of the QRS complex. The PR interval starts at the beginning of the P wave and ends with the beginning of the QRS complex. The PR interval is more clinically relevant, as it measures the duration from the beginning of atrial depolarization (the P wave) to the initiation of the QRS complex. Since the Q wave may be difficult to view in some tracings, the measurement is often extended to the R that is more easily visible. Should there be a delay in passage of the impulse from the SA node to the AV node, it would be visible in the PR interval. Figure 19.24 correlates events of heart contraction to the corresponding segments and intervals of an ECG.

Visit this site (http://openstaxcollege.org/l/ECG) for a more detailed analysis of ECGs.

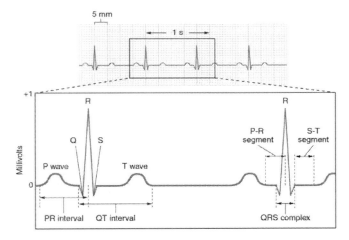

Figure 19.23 Electrocardiogram   A normal tracing shows the P wave, QRS complex, and T wave. Also indicated are the PR, QT, QRS, and ST intervals, plus the P-R and S-T segments.

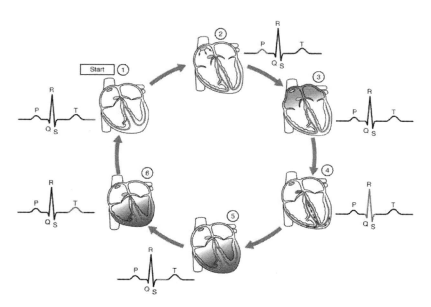

Figure 19.24 ECG Tracing Correlated to the Cardiac Cycle This diagram correlates an ECG tracing with the electrical and mechanical events of a heart contraction. Each segment of an ECG tracing corresponds to one event in the cardiac cycle.

Everyday CONNECTION

ECG Abnormalities

Occassionally, an area of the heart other than the SA node will initiate an impulse that will be followed by a premature contraction. Such an area, which may actually be a component of the conduction system or some other contractile cells, is known as an ectopic focus or ectopic pacemaker. An ectopic focus may be stimulated by localized ischemia; exposure to certain drugs, including caffeine, digitalis, or acetylcholine; elevated stimulation by both sympathetic or parasympathetic divisions of the autonomic nervous system; or a number of disease or pathological conditions. Occasional occurances are generally transitory and nonlife threatening, but if the condition becomes chronic, it may lead to either an arrhythmia, a deviation from the normal pattern of impulse conduction and contraction, or to fibrillation, an uncoordinated beating of the heart.

While interpretation of an ECG is possible and extremely valuable after some training, a full understanding of the complexities and intricacies generally requires several years of experience. In general, the size of the electrical variations, the duration of the events, and detailed vector analysis provide the most comprehensive picture of cardiac function. For example, an amplified P wave may indicate enlargement of the atria, an enlarged Q wave may indicate a MI, and an enlarged suppressed or inverted Q wave often indicates enlarged ventricles. T waves often appear flatter when insufficient oxygen is being delivered to the myocardium. An elevation of the ST segment above baseline is often seen in patients with an acute MI, and may appear depressed below the baseline when hypoxia is occurring.

As useful as analyzing these electrical recordings may be, there are limitations. For example, not all areas suffering a MI may be obvious on the ECG. Additionally, it will not reveal the effectiveness of the pumping, which requires further testing, such as an ultrasound test called an echocardiogram or nuclear medicine imaging. It is also possible for there to be pulseless electrical activity, which will show up on an ECG tracing, although there is no corresponding pumping action. Common abnormalities that may be detected by the ECGs are shown in Figure 19.25.

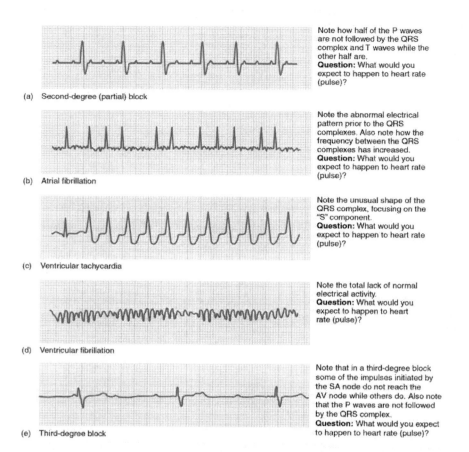

Figure 19.25 Common ECG Abnormalities (a) In a second-degree or partial block, one-half of the P waves are not followed by the QRS complex and T waves while the other half are. (b) In atrial fibrillation, the electrical pattern is abnormal prior to the QRS complex, and the frequency between the QRS complexes has increased. (c) In ventricular tachycardia, the shape of the QRS complex is abnormal. (d) In ventricular fibrillation, there is no normal electrical activity. (e) In a third-degree block, there is no correlation between atrial activity (the P wave) and ventricular activity (the QRS complex).

Interactive Link

Visit this site (http://openstaxcollege.org/l/abnormalECG) for a more complete library of abnormal ECGs.

Everyday Connection

External Automated Defibrillators

In the event that the electrical activity of the heart is severely disrupted, cessation of electrical activity or fibrillation may occur. In fibrillation, the heart beats in a wild, uncontrolled manner, which prevents it from being able to pump effectively. Atrial fibrillation (see Figure 19.25**b**) is a serious condition, but as long as the ventricles continue to pump blood, the patient's life may not be in immediate danger. Ventricular fibrillation (see Figure 19.25**d**) is a medical emergency that requires life support, because the ventricles are not effectively pumping blood. In a hospital setting, it is often described as "code blue." If untreated for as little as a few minutes, ventricular fibrillation may lead to brain death. The most common treatment is defibrillation, which uses special paddles to apply a charge to the heart from an external electrical source in an attempt to establish a normal sinus rhythm (Figure 19.26). A defibrillator effectively stops the heart so that the SA node can trigger a normal conduction cycle. Because of their effectiveness in reestablishing a normal sinus rhythm, external automated defibrillators (EADs) are being placed in areas frequented by large numbers of people, such as schools, restaurants, and airports. These devices contain simple and direct verbal instructions that can be followed by nonmedical personnel in an attempt to save a life.

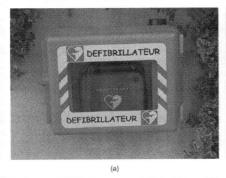

(a) (b)

Figure 19.26 Defibrillators (a) An external automatic defibrillator can be used by nonmedical personnel to reestablish a normal sinus rhythm in a person with fibrillation. (b) Defibrillator paddles are more commonly used in hospital settings. (credit b: "widerider107"/flickr.com)

A **heart block** refers to an interruption in the normal conduction pathway. The nomenclature for these is very straightforward. SA nodal blocks occur within the SA node. AV nodal blocks occur within the AV node. Infra-Hisian blocks involve the bundle of His. Bundle branch blocks occur within either the left or right atrioventricular bundle branches.

Hemiblocks are partial and occur within one or more fascicles of the atrioventricular bundle branch. Clinically, the most common types are the AV nodal and infra-Hisian blocks.

AV blocks are often described by degrees. A first-degree or partial block indicates a delay in conduction between the SA and AV nodes. This can be recognized on the ECG as an abnormally long PR interval. A second-degree or incomplete block occurs when some impulses from the SA node reach the AV node and continue, while others do not. In this instance, the ECG would reveal some P waves not followed by a QRS complex, while others would appear normal. In the third-degree or complete block, there is no correlation between atrial activity (the P wave) and ventricular activity (the QRS complex). Even in the event of a total SA block, the AV node will assume the role of pacemaker and continue initiating contractions at 40–60 contractions per minute, which is adequate to maintain consciousness. Second- and third-degree blocks are demonstrated on the ECG presented in Figure 19.25.

When arrhythmias become a chronic problem, the heart maintains a junctional rhythm, which originates in the AV node. In order to speed up the heart rate and restore full sinus rhythm, a cardiologist can implant an **artificial pacemaker**, which delivers electrical impulses to the heart muscle to ensure that the heart continues to contract and pump blood effectively. These artificial pacemakers are programmable by the cardiologists and can either provide stimulation temporarily upon demand or on a continuous basis. Some devices also contain built-in defibrillators.

Cardiac Muscle Metabolism

Normally, cardiac muscle metabolism is entirely aerobic. Oxygen from the lungs is brought to the heart, and every other organ, attached to the hemoglobin molecules within the erythrocytes. Heart cells also store appreciable amounts of oxygen in myoglobin. Normally, these two mechanisms, circulating oxygen and oxygen attached to myoglobin, can supply sufficient oxygen to the heart, even during peak performance.

Fatty acids and glucose from the circulation are broken down within the mitochondria to release energy in the form of ATP. Both fatty acid droplets and glycogen are stored within the sarcoplasm and provide additional nutrient supply. (Seek additional content for more detail about metabolism.)

19.3 | Cardiac Cycle

By the end of this section, you will be able to:
- Describe the relationship between blood pressure and blood flow
- Summarize the events of the cardiac cycle
- Compare atrial and ventricular systole and diastole
- Relate heart sounds detected by auscultation to action of heart's valves

The period of time that begins with contraction of the atria and ends with ventricular relaxation is known as the **cardiac cycle** (Figure 19.27). The period of contraction that the heart undergoes while it pumps blood into circulation is called **systole**. The period of relaxation that occurs as the chambers fill with blood is called **diastole**. Both the atria and ventricles undergo systole and diastole, and it is essential that these components be carefully regulated and coordinated to ensure blood is pumped efficiently to the body.

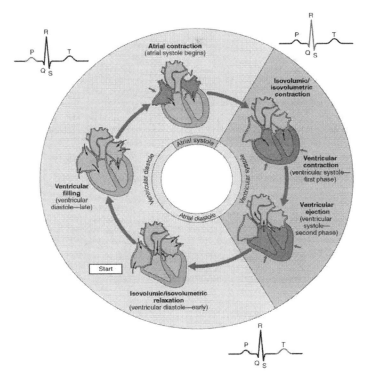

Figure 19.27 Overview of the Cardiac Cycle The cardiac cycle begins with atrial systole and progresses to ventricular systole, atrial diastole, and ventricular diastole, when the cycle begins again. Correlations to the ECG are highlighted.

Pressures and Flow

Fluids, whether gases or liquids, are materials that flow according to pressure gradients—that is, they move from regions that are higher in pressure to regions that are lower in pressure. Accordingly, when the heart chambers are relaxed (diastole), blood will flow into the atria from the veins, which are higher in pressure. As blood flows into the atria, the pressure will rise, so the blood will initially move passively from the atria into the ventricles. When the action potential triggers the muscles in the atria to contract (atrial systole), the pressure within the atria rises further, pumping blood into the ventricles. During ventricular systole, pressure rises in the ventricles, pumping blood into the pulmonary trunk from the right ventricle and into the aorta from the left ventricle. Again, as you consider this flow and relate it to the conduction pathway, the elegance of the system should become apparent.

Phases of the Cardiac Cycle

At the beginning of the cardiac cycle, both the atria and ventricles are relaxed (diastole). Blood is flowing into the right atrium from the superior and inferior venae cavae and the coronary sinus. Blood flows into the left atrium from the four pulmonary veins. The two atrioventricular valves, the tricuspid and mitral valves, are both open, so blood flows unimpeded from the atria and into the ventricles. Approximately 70–80 percent of ventricular filling occurs by this method. The two semilunar valves, the pulmonary and aortic valves, are closed, preventing backflow of blood into the right and left ventricles from the pulmonary trunk on the right and the aorta on the left.

Atrial Systole and Diastole

Contraction of the atria follows depolarization, represented by the P wave of the ECG. As the atrial muscles contract from the superior portion of the atria toward the atrioventricular septum, pressure rises within the atria and blood is pumped into the ventricles through the open atrioventricular (tricuspid, and mitral or bicuspid) valves. At the start of atrial systole, the ventricles are normally filled with approximately 70–80 percent of their capacity due to inflow during diastole. Atrial contraction, also referred to as the "atrial kick," contributes the remaining 20–30 percent of filling (see Figure 19.27). Atrial systole lasts approximately 100 ms and ends prior to ventricular systole, as the atrial muscle returns to diastole.

Ventricular Systole

Ventricular systole (see Figure 19.27) follows the depolarization of the ventricles and is represented by the QRS complex in the ECG. It may be conveniently divided into two phases, lasting a total of 270 ms. At the end of atrial systole and just prior to atrial contraction, the ventricles contain approximately 130 mL blood in a resting adult in a standing position. This volume is known as the **end diastolic volume (EDV)** or **preload**.

Initially, as the muscles in the ventricle contract, the pressure of the blood within the chamber rises, but it is not yet high enough to open the semilunar (pulmonary and aortic) valves and be ejected from the heart. However, blood pressure quickly rises above that of the atria that are now relaxed and in diastole. This increase in pressure causes blood to flow back toward the atria, closing the tricuspid and mitral valves. Since blood is not being ejected from the ventricles at this early stage, the volume of blood within the chamber remains constant. Consequently, this initial phase of ventricular systole is known as **isovolumic contraction**, also called isovolumetric contraction (see Figure 19.27).

In the second phase of ventricular systole, the **ventricular ejection phase**, the contraction of the ventricular muscle has raised the pressure within the ventricle to the point that it is greater than the pressures in the pulmonary trunk and the aorta. Blood is pumped from the heart, pushing open the pulmonary and aortic semilunar valves. Pressure generated by the left ventricle will be appreciably greater than the pressure generated by the right ventricle, since the existing pressure in the aorta will be so much higher. Nevertheless, both ventricles pump the same amount of blood. This quantity is referred to as stroke volume. Stroke volume will normally be in the range of 70–80 mL. Since ventricular systole began with an EDV of approximately 130 mL of blood, this means that there is still 50–60 mL of blood remaining in the ventricle following contraction. This volume of blood is known as the **end systolic volume (ESV)**.

Ventricular Diastole

Ventricular relaxation, or diastole, follows repolarization of the ventricles and is represented by the T wave of the ECG. It too is divided into two distinct phases and lasts approximately 430 ms.

During the early phase of ventricular diastole, as the ventricular muscle relaxes, pressure on the remaining blood within the ventricle begins to fall. When pressure within the ventricles drops below pressure in both the pulmonary trunk and aorta, blood flows back toward the heart, producing the dicrotic notch (small dip) seen in blood pressure tracings. The semilunar valves close to prevent backflow into the heart. Since the atrioventricular valves remain closed at this point, there is no change in the volume of blood in the ventricle, so the early phase of ventricular diastole is called the **isovolumic ventricular relaxation phase**, also called isovolumetric ventricular relaxation phase (see Figure 19.27).

In the second phase of ventricular diastole, called late ventricular diastole, as the ventricular muscle relaxes, pressure on the blood within the ventricles drops even further. Eventually, it drops below the pressure in the atria. When this occurs, blood flows from the atria into the ventricles, pushing open the tricuspid and mitral valves. As pressure drops within the ventricles, blood flows from the major veins into the relaxed atria and from there into the ventricles. Both chambers are in diastole, the atrioventricular valves are open, and the semilunar valves remain closed (see Figure 19.27). The cardiac cycle is complete.

Figure 19.28 illustrates the relationship between the cardiac cycle and the ECG.

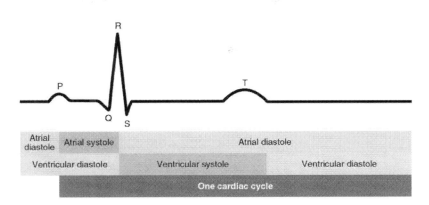

Figure 19.28 Relationship between the Cardiac Cycle and ECG Initially, both the atria and ventricles are relaxed (diastole). The P wave represents depolarization of the atria and is followed by atrial contraction (systole). Atrial systole extends until the QRS complex, at which point, the atria relax. The QRS complex represents depolarization of the ventricles and is followed by ventricular contraction. The T wave represents the repolarization of the ventricles and marks the beginning of ventricular relaxation.

Heart Sounds

One of the simplest, yet effective, diagnostic techniques applied to assess the state of a patient's heart is auscultation using a stethoscope.

In a normal, healthy heart, there are only two audible **heart sounds**: S_1 and S_2. S_1 is the sound created by the closing of the atrioventricular valves during ventricular contraction and is normally described as a "lub," or first heart sound. The second heart sound, S_2, is the sound of the closing of the semilunar valves during ventricular diastole and is described as a "dub" (Figure 19.29). In both cases, as the valves close, the openings within the atrioventricular septum guarded by the valves will become reduced, and blood flow through the opening will become more turbulent until the valves are fully closed. There is a third heart sound, S_3, but it is rarely heard in healthy individuals. It may be the sound of blood flowing into the atria, or blood sloshing back and forth in the ventricle, or even tensing of the chordae tendineae. S_3 may be heard in youth, some athletes, and pregnant women. If the sound is heard later in life, it may indicate congestive heart failure, warranting further tests. Some cardiologists refer to the collective S_1, S_2, and S_3 sounds as the "Kentucky gallop," because they mimic those produced by a galloping horse. The fourth heart sound, S_4, results from the contraction of the atria pushing blood into a stiff or hypertrophic ventricle, indicating failure of the left ventricle. S_4 occurs prior to S_1 and the collective sounds S_4, S_1, and S_2 are referred to by some cardiologists as the "Tennessee gallop," because of their similarity to the sound produced by a galloping horse with a different gait. A few individuals may have both S_3 and S_4, and this combined sound is referred to as S_7.

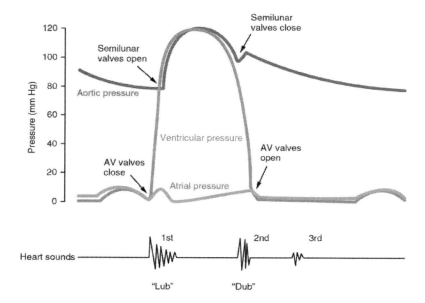

Figure 19.29 Heart Sounds and the Cardiac Cycle In this illustration, the x-axis reflects time with a recording of the heart sounds. The y-axis represents pressure.

The term **murmur** is used to describe an unusual sound coming from the heart that is caused by the turbulent flow of blood. Murmurs are graded on a scale of 1 to 6, with 1 being the most common, the most difficult sound to detect, and the least serious. The most severe is a 6. Phonocardiograms or auscultograms can be used to record both normal and abnormal sounds using specialized electronic stethoscopes.

During auscultation, it is common practice for the clinician to ask the patient to breathe deeply. This procedure not only allows for listening to airflow, but it may also amplify heart murmurs. Inhalation increases blood flow into the right side of the heart and may increase the amplitude of right-sided heart murmurs. Expiration partially restricts blood flow into the left side of the heart and may amplify left-sided heart murmurs. Figure 19.30 indicates proper placement of the bell of the stethoscope to facilitate auscultation.

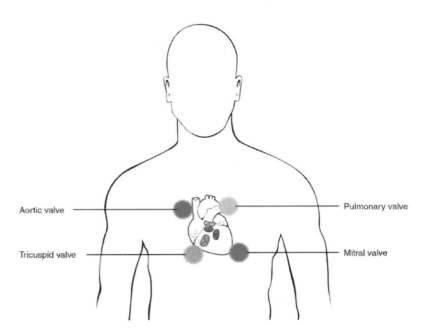

Figure 19.30 Stethoscope Placement for Auscultation   Proper placement of the bell of the stethoscope facilitates auscultation. At each of the four locations on the chest, a different valve can be heard.

19.4 | Cardiac Physiology

By the end of this section, you will be able to:
- Relate heart rate to cardiac output
- Describe the effect of exercise on heart rate
- Identify cardiovascular centers and cardiac reflexes that regulate heart function
- Describe factors affecting heart rate
- Distinguish between positive and negative factors that affect heart contractility
- Summarize factors affecting stroke volume and cardiac output
- Describe the cardiac response to variations in blood flow and pressure

The autorhythmicity inherent in cardiac cells keeps the heart beating at a regular pace; however, the heart is regulated by and responds to outside influences as well. Neural and endocrine controls are vital to the regulation of cardiac function. In addition, the heart is sensitive to several environmental factors, including electrolytes.

Resting Cardiac Output

Cardiac output (CO) is a measurement of the amount of blood pumped by each ventricle in one minute. To calculate this value, multiply **stroke volume (SV)**, the amount of blood pumped by each ventricle, by **heart rate (HR)**, in contractions per minute (or beats per minute, bpm). It can be represented mathematically by the following equation:

$CO = HR \times SV$

SV is normally measured using an echocardiogram to record EDV and ESV, and calculating the difference: $SV = EDV - ESV$. SV can also be measured using a specialized catheter, but this is an invasive procedure and far more dangerous to the patient. A mean SV for a resting 70-kg (150-lb) individual would be approximately 70 mL. There are several important variables, including size of the heart, physical and mental condition of the individual, sex, contractility, duration of contraction, preload or EDV, and afterload or resistance. Normal range for SV would be 55–100 mL. An average resting HR would be approximately 75 bpm but could range from 60–100 in some individuals.

Using these numbers, the mean CO is 5.25 L/min, with a range of 4.0–8.0 L/min. Remember, however, that these numbers refer to CO from each ventricle separately, not the total for the heart. Factors influencing CO are summarized in Figure 19.31.

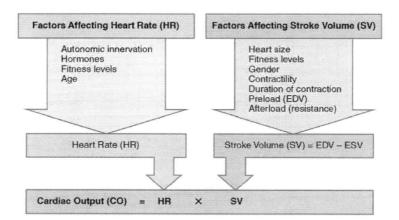

Figure 19.31 Major Factors Influencing Cardiac Output Cardiac output is influenced by heart rate and stroke volume, both of which are also variable.

SVs are also used to calculate **ejection fraction**, which is the portion of the blood that is pumped or ejected from the heart with each contraction. To calculate ejection fraction, SV is divided by EDV. Despite the name, the ejection fraction is normally expressed as a percentage. Ejection fractions range from approximately 55–70 percent, with a mean of 58 percent.

Exercise and Maximum Cardiac Output

In healthy young individuals, HR may increase to 150 bpm during exercise. SV can also increase from 70 to approximately 130 mL due to increased strength of contraction. This would increase CO to approximately 19.5 L/min, 4–5 times the resting rate. Top cardiovascular athletes can achieve even higher levels. At their peak performance, they may increase resting CO by 7–8 times.

Since the heart is a muscle, exercising it increases its efficiency. The difference between maximum and resting CO is known as the **cardiac reserve**. It measures the residual capacity of the heart to pump blood.

Heart Rates

HRs vary considerably, not only with exercise and fitness levels, but also with age. Newborn resting HRs may be 120 bpm. HR gradually decreases until young adulthood and then gradually increases again with age.

Maximum HRs are normally in the range of 200–220 bpm, although there are some extreme cases in which they may reach higher levels. As one ages, the ability to generate maximum rates decreases. This may be estimated by taking the maximal value of 220 bpm and subtracting the individual's age. So a 40-year-old individual would be expected to hit a maximum rate of approximately 180, and a 60-year-old person would achieve a HR of 160.

Heart: Abnormal Heart Rates

For an adult, normal resting HR will be in the range of 60–100 bpm. Bradycardia is the condition in which resting rate drops below 60 bpm, and tachycardia is the condition in which the resting rate is above 100 bpm. Trained athletes typically have very low HRs. If the patient is not exhibiting other symptoms, such as weakness, fatigue, dizziness, fainting, chest discomfort, palpitations, or respiratory distress, bradycardia is not considered clinically significant. However, if any of these symptoms are present, they may indicate that the heart is not providing sufficient oxygenated blood to the tissues. The term relative bradycardia may be used with a patient who has a HR in the normal range but is still suffering from these symptoms. Most patients remain asymptomatic as long as the HR remains above 50 bpm.

Bradycardia may be caused by either inherent factors or causes external to the heart. While the condition may be inherited, typically it is acquired in older individuals. Inherent causes include abnormalities in either the SA or AV node. If the condition is serious, a pacemaker may be required. Other causes include ischemia to the heart muscle or diseases of the heart vessels or valves. External causes include metabolic disorders, pathologies of the endocrine system often involving the thyroid, electrolyte imbalances, neurological disorders including inappropriate autonomic responses, autoimmune pathologies, over-prescription of beta blocker drugs that reduce HR, recreational drug use, or even prolonged bed rest. Treatment relies upon establishing the underlying cause of the disorder and may necessitate supplemental oxygen.

Tachycardia is not normal in a resting patient but may be detected in pregnant women or individuals experiencing extreme stress. In the latter case, it would likely be triggered by stimulation from the limbic system or disorders of the autonomic nervous system. In some cases, tachycardia may involve only the atria. Some individuals may remain asymptomatic, but when present, symptoms may include dizziness, shortness of breath, lightheadedness, rapid pulse, heart palpations, chest pain, or fainting (syncope). While tachycardia is defined as a HR above 100 bpm, there is considerable variation among people. Further, the normal resting HRs of children are often above 100 bpm, but this is not considered to be tachycardia Many causes of tachycardia may be benign, but the condition may also be correlated with fever, anemia, hypoxia, hyperthyroidism, hypersecretion of catecholamines, some cardiomyopathies, some disorders of the valves, and acute exposure to radiation. Elevated rates in an exercising or resting patient are normal and expected. Resting rate should always be taken after recovery from exercise. Treatment depends upon the underlying cause but may include medications, implantable cardioverter defibrillators, ablation, or surgery.

Correlation Between Heart Rates and Cardiac Output

Initially, physiological conditions that cause HR to increase also trigger an increase in SV. During exercise, the rate of blood returning to the heart increases. However as the HR rises, there is less time spent in diastole and consequently less time for the ventricles to fill with blood. Even though there is less filling time, SV will initially remain high. However, as HR continues to increase, SV gradually decreases due to decreased filling time. CO will initially stabilize as the increasing HR compensates for the decreasing SV, but at very high rates, CO will eventually decrease as increasing rates are no longer able to compensate for the decreasing SV. Consider this phenomenon in a healthy young individual. Initially, as HR increases from resting to approximately 120 bpm, CO will rise. As HR increases from 120 to 160 bpm, CO remains stable, since the increase in rate is offset by decreasing ventricular filling time and, consequently, SV. As HR continues to rise above 160 bpm, CO actually decreases as SV falls faster than HR increases. So although aerobic exercises are critical to maintain the health of the heart, individuals are cautioned to monitor their HR to ensure they stay within the **target heart rate** range of between 120 and 160 bpm, so CO is maintained. The target HR is loosely defined as the range in which both the heart and lungs receive the maximum benefit from the aerobic workout and is dependent upon age.

Cardiovascular Centers

Nervous control over HR is centralized within the two paired cardiovascular centers of the medulla oblongata (Figure 19.32). The cardioaccelerator regions stimulate activity via sympathetic stimulation of the cardioaccelerator nerves, and the cardioinhibitory centers decrease heart activity via parasympathetic stimulation as one component of the vagus nerve, cranial nerve X. During rest, both centers provide slight stimulation to the heart, contributing to **autonomic tone**. This is a similar concept to tone in skeletal muscles. Normally, vagal stimulation predominates as, left unregulated, the SA node would initiate a sinus rhythm of approximately 100 bpm.

Both sympathetic and parasympathetic stimulations flow through a paired complex network of nerve fibers known as the **cardiac plexus** near the base of the heart. The cardioaccelerator center also sends additional fibers, forming the cardiac nerves via sympathetic ganglia (the cervical ganglia plus superior thoracic ganglia T1–T4) to both the SA and AV nodes, plus additional fibers to the atria and ventricles. The ventricles are more richly innervated by sympathetic fibers than parasympathetic fibers. Sympathetic stimulation causes the release of the neurotransmitter norepinephrine (NE) at the neuromuscular junction of the cardiac nerves. NE shortens the repolarization period, thus speeding the rate of depolarization and contraction, which results in an increase in HR. It opens chemical- or ligand-gated sodium and calcium ion channels, allowing an influx of positively charged ions.

NE binds to the beta-1 receptor. Some cardiac medications (for example, beta blockers) work by blocking these receptors, thereby slowing HR and are one possible treatment for hypertension. Overprescription of these drugs may lead to bradycardia and even stoppage of the heart.

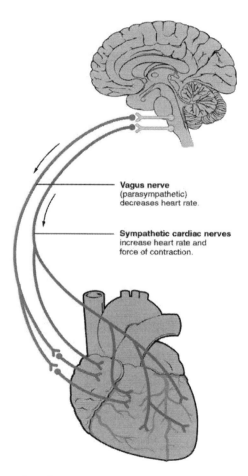

Figure 19.32 Autonomic Innervation of the Heart Cardioaccelerator and cardioinhibitory areas are components of the paired cardiac centers located in the medulla oblongata of the brain. They innervate the heart via sympathetic cardiac nerves that increase cardiac activity and vagus (parasympathetic) nerves that slow cardiac activity.

Parasympathetic stimulation originates from the cardioinhibitory region with impulses traveling via the vagus nerve (cranial nerve X). The vagus nerve sends branches to both the SA and AV nodes, and to portions of both the atria and ventricles. Parasympathetic stimulation releases the neurotransmitter acetylcholine (ACh) at the neuromuscular junction. ACh slows HR by opening chemical- or ligand-gated potassium ion channels to slow the rate of spontaneous depolarization, which extends repolarization and increases the time before the next spontaneous depolarization occurs. Without any nervous stimulation, the SA node would establish a sinus rhythm of approximately 100 bpm. Since resting rates are considerably less than this, it becomes evident that parasympathetic stimulation normally slows HR. This is similar to an individual driving a car with one foot on the brake pedal. To speed up, one need merely remove one's foot from the break and let the engine increase speed. In the case of the heart, decreasing parasympathetic stimulation decreases the release of ACh, which allows HR to increase up to approximately 100 bpm. Any increases beyond this rate would require sympathetic stimulation. Figure 19.33 illustrates the effects of parasympathetic and sympathetic stimulation on the normal sinus rhythm.

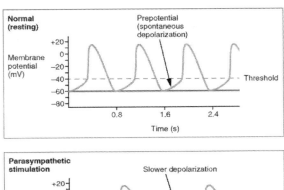
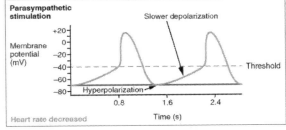
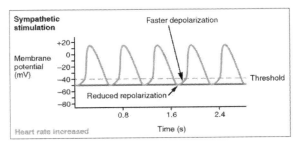

Figure 19.33 Effects of Parasympathetic and Sympathetic Stimulation on Normal Sinus Rhythm The wave of depolarization in a normal sinus rhythm shows a stable resting HR. Following parasympathetic stimulation, HR slows. Following sympathetic stimulation, HR increases.

Input to the Cardiovascular Center

The cardiovascular center receives input from a series of visceral receptors with impulses traveling through visceral sensory fibers within the vagus and sympathetic nerves via the cardiac plexus. Among these receptors are various proprioreceptors, baroreceptors, and chemoreceptors, plus stimuli from the limbic system. Collectively, these inputs normally enable the cardiovascular centers to regulate heart function precisely, a process known as **cardiac reflexes**. Increased physical activity results in increased rates of firing by various proprioreceptors located in muscles, joint capsules, and tendons. Any such increase in physical activity would logically warrant increased blood flow. The cardiac centers monitor these increased rates of firing, and suppress parasympathetic stimulation and increase sympathetic stimulation as needed in order to increase blood flow.

Similarly, baroreceptors are stretch receptors located in the aortic sinus, carotid bodies, the venae cavae, and other locations, including pulmonary vessels and the right side of the heart itself. Rates of firing from the baroreceptors represent blood pressure, level of physical activity, and the relative distribution of blood. The cardiac centers monitor baroreceptor firing to maintain cardiac homeostasis, a mechanism called the **baroreceptor reflex**. With increased pressure and stretch, the rate of baroreceptor firing increases, and the cardiac centers decrease sympathetic stimulation and increase parasympathetic stimulation. As pressure and stretch decrease, the rate of baroreceptor firing decreases, and the cardiac centers increase sympathetic stimulation and decrease parasympathetic stimulation.

There is a similar reflex, called the **atrial reflex** or **Bainbridge reflex**, associated with varying rates of blood flow to the atria. Increased venous return stretches the walls of the atria where specialized baroreceptors are located. However, as the atrial baroreceptors increase their rate of firing and as they stretch due to the increased blood pressure, the cardiac center responds by increasing sympathetic stimulation and inhibiting parasympathetic stimulation to increase HR. The opposite is also true.

Increased metabolic byproducts associated with increased activity, such as carbon dioxide, hydrogen ions, and lactic acid, plus falling oxygen levels, are detected by a suite of chemoreceptors innervated by the glossopharyngeal and vagus nerves. These chemoreceptors provide feedback to the cardiovascular centers about the need for increased or decreased blood flow, based on the relative levels of these substances.

The limbic system can also significantly impact HR related to emotional state. During periods of stress, it is not unusual to identify higher than normal HRs, often accompanied by a surge in the stress hormone cortisol. Individuals experiencing extreme anxiety may manifest panic attacks with symptoms that resemble those of heart attacks. These events are typically transient and treatable. Meditation techniques have been developed to ease anxiety and have been shown to lower HR effectively. Doing simple deep and slow breathing exercises with one's eyes closed can also significantly reduce this anxiety and HR.

Heart: Broken Heart Syndrome

Extreme stress from such life events as the death of a loved one, an emotional break up, loss of income, or foreclosure of a home may lead to a condition commonly referred to as broken heart syndrome. This condition may also be called Takotsubo cardiomyopathy, transient apical ballooning syndrome, apical ballooning cardiomyopathy, stress-induced cardiomyopathy, Gebrochenes-Herz syndrome, and stress cardiomyopathy. The recognized effects on the heart include congestive heart failure due to a profound weakening of the myocardium not related to lack of oxygen. This may lead to acute heart failure, lethal arrhythmias, or even the rupture of a ventricle. The exact etiology is not known, but several factors have been suggested, including transient vasospasm, dysfunction of the cardiac capillaries, or thickening of the myocardium—particularly in the left ventricle—that may lead to the critical circulation of blood to this region. While many patients survive the initial acute event with treatment to restore normal function, there is a strong correlation with death. Careful statistical analysis by the Cass Business School, a prestigious institution located in London, published in 2008, revealed that within one year of the death of a loved one, women are more than twice as likely to die and males are six times as likely to die as would otherwise be expected.

Other Factors Influencing Heart Rate

Using a combination of autorhythmicity and innervation, the cardiovascular center is able to provide relatively precise control over HR. However, there are a number of other factors that have an impact on HR as well, including epinephrine, NE, and thyroid hormones; levels of various ions including calcium, potassium, and sodium; body temperature; hypoxia; and pH balance (Table 19.1 and Table 19.2). After reading this section, the importance of maintaining homeostasis should become even more apparent.

Major Factors Increasing Heart Rate and Force of Contraction

Factor	Effect
Cardioaccelerator nerves	Release of norepinephrine
Proprioreceptors	Increased rates of firing during exercise
Chemoreceptors	Decreased levels of O_2; increased levels of H^+, CO_2, and lactic acid
Baroreceptors	Decreased rates of firing, indicating falling blood volume/pressure
Limbic system	Anticipation of physical exercise or strong emotions
Catecholamines	Increased epinephrine and norepinephrine
Thyroid hormones	Increased T_3 and T_4
Calcium	Increased Ca^{2+}
Potassium	Decreased K^+
Sodium	Decreased Na^+
Body temperature	Increased body temperature
Nicotine and caffeine	Stimulants, increasing heart rate

Table 19.1

Factors Decreasing Heart Rate and Force of Contraction

Factor	Effect
Cardioinhibitor nerves (vagus)	Release of acetylcholine
Proprioreceptors	Decreased rates of firing following exercise
Chemoreceptors	Increased levels of O_2; decreased levels of H^+ and CO_2
Baroreceptors	Increased rates of firing, indicating higher blood volume/pressure
Limbic system	Anticipation of relaxation
Catecholamines	Decreased epinephrine and norepinephrine
Thyroid hormones	Decreased T_3 and T_4
Calcium	Decreased Ca^{2+}
Potassium	Increased K^+
Sodium	Increased Na^+
Body temperature	Decrease in body temperature

Table 19.2

Epinephrine and Norepinephrine

The catecholamines, epinephrine and NE, secreted by the adrenal medulla form one component of the extended fight-or-flight mechanism. The other component is sympathetic stimulation. Epinephrine and NE have similar effects: binding to the beta-1 receptors, and opening sodium and calcium ion chemical- or ligand-gated channels. The rate of depolarization is increased by this additional influx of positively charged ions, so the threshold is reached more quickly and the period of repolarization is shortened. However, massive releases of these hormones coupled with sympathetic stimulation may actually lead to arrhythmias. There is no parasympathetic stimulation to the adrenal medulla.

Thyroid Hormones

In general, increased levels of thyroid hormone, or thyroxin, increase cardiac rate and contractility. The impact of thyroid hormone is typically of a much longer duration than that of the catecholamines. The physiologically active form of thyroid hormone, T_3 or triiodothyronine, has been shown to directly enter cardiomyocytes and alter activity at the level of the genome. It also impacts the beta adrenergic response similar to epinephrine and NE described above. Excessive levels of thyroxin may trigger tachycardia.

Calcium

Calcium ion levels have great impacts upon both HR and contractility; as the levels of calcium ions increase, so do HR and contractility. High levels of calcium ions (hypercalcemia) may be implicated in a short QT interval and a widened T wave in the ECG. The QT interval represents the time from the start of depolarization to repolarization of the ventricles, and includes the period of ventricular systole. Extremely high levels of calcium may induce cardiac arrest. Drugs known as calcium channel blockers slow HR by binding to these channels and blocking or slowing the inward movement of calcium ions.

Caffeine and Nicotine

Caffeine and nicotine are not found naturally within the body. Both of these nonregulated drugs have an excitatory effect on membranes of neurons in general and have a stimulatory effect on the cardiac centers specifically, causing an increase in HR. Caffeine works by increasing the rates of depolarization at the SA node, whereas nicotine stimulates the activity of the sympathetic neurons that deliver impulses to the heart.

Although it is the world's most widely consumed psychoactive drug, caffeine is legal and not regulated. While precise quantities have not been established, "normal" consumption is not considered harmful to most people, although it may cause disruptions to sleep and acts as a diuretic. Its consumption by pregnant women is cautioned against, although no evidence of negative effects has been confirmed. Tolerance and even physical and mental addiction to the drug result in individuals who routinely consume the substance.

Nicotine, too, is a stimulant and produces addiction. While legal and nonregulated, concerns about nicotine's safety and documented links to respiratory and cardiac disease have resulted in warning labels on cigarette packages.

Factors Decreasing Heart Rate

HR can be slowed when a person experiences altered sodium and potassium levels, hypoxia, acidosis, alkalosis, and hypothermia (see Table 19.1). The relationship between electrolytes and HR is complex, but maintaining electrolyte balance is critical to the normal wave of depolarization. Of the two ions, potassium has the greater clinical significance. Initially, both hyponatremia (low sodium levels) and hypernatremia (high sodium levels) may lead to tachycardia. Severely high hypernatremia may lead to fibrillation, which may cause CO to cease. Severe hyponatremia leads to both bradycardia and other arrhythmias. Hypokalemia (low potassium levels) also leads to arrhythmias, whereas hyperkalemia (high potassium levels) causes the heart to become weak and flaccid, and ultimately to fail.

Heart muscle relies exclusively on aerobic metabolism for energy. Hypoxia (an insufficient supply of oxygen) leads to decreasing HRs, since metabolic reactions fueling heart contraction are restricted.

Acidosis is a condition in which excess hydrogen ions are present, and the patient's blood expresses a low pH value. Alkalosis is a condition in which there are too few hydrogen ions, and the patient's blood has an elevated pH. Normal blood pH falls in the range of 7.35–7.45, so a number lower than this range represents acidosis and a higher number represents alkalosis. Recall that enzymes are the regulators or catalysts of virtually all biochemical reactions; they are sensitive to pH and will change shape slightly with values outside their normal range. These variations in pH and accompanying slight physical changes to the active site on the enzyme decrease the rate of formation of the enzyme-substrate complex, subsequently decreasing the rate of many enzymatic reactions, which can have complex effects on HR. Severe changes in pH will lead to denaturation of the enzyme.

The last variable is body temperature. Elevated body temperature is called hyperthermia, and suppressed body temperature is called hypothermia. Slight hyperthermia results in increasing HR and strength of contraction. Hypothermia slows the rate and strength of heart contractions. This distinct slowing of the heart is one component of the larger diving reflex that diverts blood to essential organs while submerged. If sufficiently chilled, the heart will stop beating, a technique that may be employed during open heart surgery. In this case, the patient's blood is normally diverted to an artificial heart-lung machine to maintain the body's blood supply and gas exchange until the surgery is complete, and sinus rhythm can be restored. Excessive hyperthermia and hypothermia will both result in death, as enzymes drive the body systems to cease normal function, beginning with the central nervous system.

Stroke Volume

Many of the same factors that regulate HR also impact cardiac function by altering SV. While a number of variables are involved, SV is ultimately dependent upon the difference between EDV and ESV. The three primary factors to consider are preload, or the stretch on the ventricles prior to contraction; the contractility, or the force or strength of the contraction itself; and afterload, the force the ventricles must generate to pump blood against the resistance in the vessels. These factors are summarized in Table 19.1 and Table 19.2.

Preload

Preload is another way of expressing EDV. Therefore, the greater the EDV is, the greater the preload is. One of the primary factors to consider is **filling time**, or the duration of ventricular diastole during which filling occurs. The more rapidly the heart contracts, the shorter the filling time becomes, and the lower the EDV and preload are. This effect can be partially overcome by increasing the second variable, contractility, and raising SV, but over time, the heart is unable to compensate for decreased filling time, and preload also decreases.

With increasing ventricular filling, both EDV or preload increase, and the cardiac muscle itself is stretched to a greater degree. At rest, there is little stretch of the ventricular muscle, and the sarcomeres remain short. With increased ventricular filling, the ventricular muscle is increasingly stretched and the sarcomere length increases. As the sarcomeres reach their optimal lengths, they will contract more powerfully, because more of the myosin heads can bind to the actin on the thin filaments, forming cross bridges and increasing the strength of contraction and SV. If this process were to continue and the sarcomeres stretched beyond their optimal lengths, the force of contraction would decrease. However, due to the physical constraints of the location of the heart, this excessive stretch is not a concern.

The relationship between ventricular stretch and contraction has been stated in the well-known **Frank-Starling mechanism** or simply Starling's Law of the Heart. This principle states that, within physiological limits, the force of heart contraction is directly proportional to the initial length of the muscle fiber. This means that the greater the stretch of the ventricular muscle (within limits), the more powerful the contraction is, which in turn increases SV. Therefore, by increasing preload, you increase the second variable, contractility.

Otto Frank (1865–1944) was a German physiologist; among his many published works are detailed studies of this important heart relationship. Ernest Starling (1866–1927) was an important English physiologist who also studied the heart. Although they worked largely independently, their combined efforts and similar conclusions have been recognized in the name "Frank-Starling mechanism."

Any sympathetic stimulation to the venous system will increase venous return to the heart, which contributes to ventricular filling, and EDV and preload. While much of the ventricular filling occurs while both atria and ventricles are in diastole, the contraction of the atria, the atrial kick, plays a crucial role by providing the last 20–30 percent of ventricular filling.

Contractility

It is virtually impossible to consider preload or ESV without including an early mention of the concept of contractility. Indeed, the two parameters are intimately linked. Contractility refers to the force of the contraction of the heart muscle, which controls SV, and is the primary parameter for impacting ESV. The more forceful the contraction is, the greater the SV and smaller the ESV are. Less forceful contractions result in smaller SVs and larger ESVs. Factors that increase contractility are described as **positive inotropic factors**, and those that decrease contractility are described as **negative inotropic factors** (ino- = "fiber;" -tropic = "turning toward").

Not surprisingly, sympathetic stimulation is a positive inotrope, whereas parasympathetic stimulation is a negative inotrope. Sympathetic stimulation triggers the release of NE at the neuromuscular junction from the cardiac nerves and also stimulates the adrenal cortex to secrete epinephrine and NE. In addition to their stimulatory effects on HR, they also bind to both alpha and beta receptors on the cardiac muscle cell membrane to increase metabolic rate and the force of contraction. This combination of actions has the net effect of increasing SV and leaving a smaller residual ESV in the ventricles. In comparison, parasympathetic stimulation releases ACh at the neuromuscular junction from the vagus nerve. The membrane hyperpolarizes and inhibits contraction to decrease the strength of contraction and SV, and to raise ESV. Since parasympathetic fibers are more widespread in the atria than in the ventricles, the primary site of action is in the upper chambers. Parasympathetic stimulation in the atria decreases the atrial kick and reduces EDV, which decreases ventricular stretch and preload, thereby further limiting the force of ventricular contraction. Stronger parasympathetic stimulation also directly decreases the force of contraction of the ventricles.

Several synthetic drugs, including dopamine and isoproterenol, have been developed that mimic the effects of epinephrine and NE by stimulating the influx of calcium ions from the extracellular fluid. Higher concentrations of intracellular calcium ions increase the strength of contraction. Excess calcium (hypercalcemia) also acts as a positive inotropic agent. The drug digitalis lowers HR and increases the strength of the contraction, acting as a positive inotropic agent by blocking the sequestering of calcium ions into the sarcoplasmic reticulum. This leads to higher intracellular calcium levels and greater strength of contraction. In addition to the catecholamines from the adrenal medulla, other hormones also demonstrate positive inotropic effects. These include thyroid hormones and glucagon from the pancreas.

Negative inotropic agents include hypoxia, acidosis, hyperkalemia, and a variety of synthetic drugs. These include numerous beta blockers and calcium channel blockers. Early beta blocker drugs include propranolol and pronethalol, and are credited with revolutionizing treatment of cardiac patients experiencing angina pectoris. There is also a large class of dihydropyridine, phenylalkylamine, and benzothiazepine calcium channel blockers that may be administered decreasing the strength of contraction and SV.

Afterload

Afterload refers to the tension that the ventricles must develop to pump blood effectively against the resistance in the vascular system. Any condition that increases resistance requires a greater afterload to force open the semilunar valves and pump the blood. Damage to the valves, such as stenosis, which makes them harder to open will also increase afterload. Any decrease in resistance decreases the afterload. Figure 19.34 summarizes the major factors influencing SV, Figure 19.35 summarizes the major factors influencing CO, and Table 19.3 and Table 19.4 summarize cardiac responses to increased and decreased blood flow and pressure in order to restore homeostasis.

	Factors Affecting Stroke Volume (SV)		
	Preload	**Contractility**	**Afterload**
Raised due to:	• fast filling time • increased venous return	• sympathetic stimulation • epinephrine and norepinephrine • high intracellular calcium ions • high blood calcium level • thyroid hormones • glucagon	• increased vascular resistance • semilunar valve damage
	Increases end diastolic volume, Increases stroke volume	**Decreases end systolic volume, Increases stroke volume**	**Increases end systolic volume Decreases stroke volume**
Lowered due to:	• decreased thyroid hormones • decreased calcium ions • high or low potassium ions • high or low sodium • low body temperature • hypoxia • abnormal pH balance • drugs (i.e., calcium channel blockers)	• parasympathetic stimulation • acetylcholine • hypoxia • hyperkalemia	• decreased vascular resistance
	Decreases end diastolic volume, Decreases stroke volume	**Increases end systolic volume Decreases stroke volume**	**Decreases end systolic volume Increases stroke volume**

Figure 19.34 Major Factors Influencing Stroke Volume Multiple factors impact preload, afterload, and contractility, and are the major considerations influencing SV.

Chapter 19 | The Cardiovascular System: The Heart

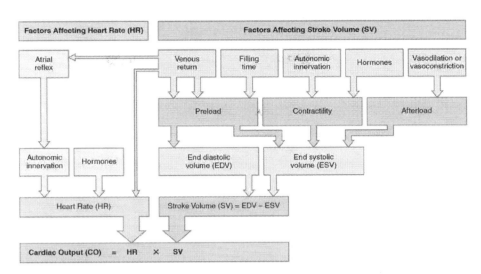

Figure 19.35 Summary of Major Factors Influencing Cardiac Output The primary factors influencing HR include autonomic innervation plus endocrine control. Not shown are environmental factors, such as electrolytes, metabolic products, and temperature. The primary factors controlling SV include preload, contractility, and afterload. Other factors such as electrolytes may be classified as either positive or negative inotropic agents.

Cardiac Response to Decreasing Blood Flow and Pressure Due to Decreasing Cardiac Output

	Baroreceptors (aorta, carotid arteries, venae cavae, and atria)	Chemoreceptors (both central nervous system and in proximity to baroreceptors)
Sensitive to	Decreasing stretch	Decreasing O_2 and increasing CO_2, H^+, and lactic acid
Target	Parasympathetic stimulation suppressed	Sympathetic stimulation increased
Response of heart	Increasing heart rate and increasing stroke volume	Increasing heart rate and increasing stroke volume
Overall effect	Increasing blood flow and pressure due to increasing cardiac output; hemostasis restored	Increasing blood flow and pressure due to increasing cardiac output; hemostasis restored

Table 19.3

Cardiac Response to Increasing Blood Flow and Pressure Due to Increasing Cardiac Output

	Baroreceptors (aorta, carotid arteries, venae cavae, and atria)	Chemoreceptors (both central nervous system and in proximity to baroreceptors)
Sensitive to	Increasing stretch	Increasing O_2 and decreasing CO_2, H^+, and lactic acid
Target	Parasympathetic stimulation increased	Sympathetic stimulation suppressed
Response of heart	Decreasing heart rate and decreasing stroke volume	Decreasing heart rate and decreasing stroke volume
Overall effect	Decreasing blood flow and pressure due to decreasing cardiac output; hemostasis restored	Decreasing blood flow and pressure due to decreasing cardiac output; hemostasis restored

Table 19.4

19.5 | Development of the Heart

By the end of this section, you will be able to:
- Describe the embryological development of heart structures
- Identify five regions of the fetal heart
- Relate fetal heart structures to adult counterparts

The human heart is the first functional organ to develop. It begins beating and pumping blood around day 21 or 22, a mere three weeks after fertilization. This emphasizes the critical nature of the heart in distributing blood through the vessels and the vital exchange of nutrients, oxygen, and wastes both to and from the developing baby. The critical early development of the heart is reflected by the prominent **heart bulge** that appears on the anterior surface of the embryo.

The heart forms from an embryonic tissue called **mesoderm** around 18 to 19 days after fertilization. Mesoderm is one of the three primary germ layers that differentiates early in development that collectively gives rise to all subsequent tissues and organs. The heart begins to develop near the head of the embryo in a region known as the **cardiogenic area**. Following chemical signals called factors from the underlying endoderm (another of the three primary germ layers), the cardiogenic area begins to form two strands called the **cardiogenic cords** (Figure 19.36). As the cardiogenic cords develop, a lumen rapidly develops within them. At this point, they are referred to as **endocardial tubes**. The two tubes migrate together and fuse to form a single **primitive heart tube**. The primitive heart tube quickly forms five distinct regions. From head to tail, these include the truncus arteriosus, bulbus cordis, primitive ventricle, primitive atrium, and the sinus venosus. Initially, all venous blood flows into the sinus venosus, and contractions propel the blood from tail to head, or from the sinus venosus to the truncus arteriosus. This is a very different pattern from that of an adult.

Chapter 19 | The Cardiovascular System: The Heart

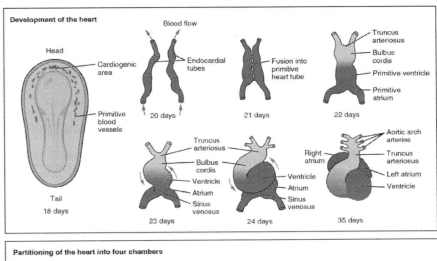

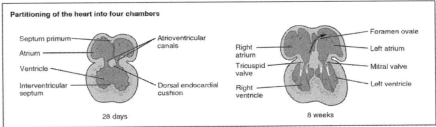

Figure 19.36 Development of the Human Heart This diagram outlines the embryological development of the human heart during the first eight weeks and the subsequent formation of the four heart chambers.

The five regions of the primitive heart tube develop into recognizable structures in a fully developed heart. The **truncus arteriosus** will eventually divide and give rise to the ascending aorta and pulmonary trunk. The **bulbus cordis** develops into the right ventricle. The **primitive ventricle** forms the left ventricle. The **primitive atrium** becomes the anterior portions of both the right and left atria, and the two auricles. The **sinus venosus** develops into the posterior portion of the right atrium, the SA node, and the coronary sinus.

As the primitive heart tube elongates, it begins to fold within the pericardium, eventually forming an S shape, which places the chambers and major vessels into an alignment similar to the adult heart. This process occurs between days 23 and 28. The remainder of the heart development pattern includes development of septa and valves, and remodeling of the actual chambers. Partitioning of the atria and ventricles by the interatrial septum, interventricular septum, and atrioventricular septum is complete by the end of the fifth week, although the fetal blood shunts remain until birth or shortly after. The atrioventricular valves form between weeks five and eight, and the semilunar valves form between weeks five and nine.

KEY TERMS

afterload force the ventricles must develop to effectively pump blood against the resistance in the vessels

anastomosis (plural = anastomoses) area where vessels unite to allow blood to circulate even if there may be partial blockage in another branch

anterior cardiac veins vessels that parallel the small cardiac arteries and drain the anterior surface of the right ventricle; bypass the coronary sinus and drain directly into the right atrium

anterior interventricular artery (also, left anterior descending artery or LAD) major branch of the left coronary artery that follows the anterior interventricular sulcus

anterior interventricular sulcus sulcus located between the left and right ventricles on the anterior surface of the heart

aortic valve (also, aortic semilunar valve) valve located at the base of the aorta

artificial pacemaker medical device that transmits electrical signals to the heart to ensure that it contracts and pumps blood to the body

atrial reflex (also, called Bainbridge reflex) autonomic reflex that responds to stretch receptors in the atria that send impulses to the cardioaccelerator area to increase HR when venous flow into the atria increases

atrioventricular (AV) node clump of myocardial cells located in the inferior portion of the right atrium within the atrioventricular septum; receives the impulse from the SA node, pauses, and then transmits it into specialized conducting cells within the interventricular septum

atrioventricular bundle (also, bundle of His) group of specialized myocardial conductile cells that transmit the impulse from the AV node through the interventricular septum; form the left and right atrioventricular bundle branches

atrioventricular bundle branches (also, left or right bundle branches) specialized myocardial conductile cells that arise from the bifurcation of the atrioventricular bundle and pass through the interventricular septum; lead to the Purkinje fibers and also to the right papillary muscle via the moderator band

atrioventricular septum cardiac septum located between the atria and ventricles; atrioventricular valves are located here

atrioventricular valves one-way valves located between the atria and ventricles; the valve on the right is called the tricuspid valve, and the one on the left is the mitral or bicuspid valve

atrium (plural = atria) upper or receiving chamber of the heart that pumps blood into the lower chambers just prior to their contraction; the right atrium receives blood from the systemic circuit that flows into the right ventricle; the left atrium receives blood from the pulmonary circuit that flows into the left ventricle

auricle extension of an atrium visible on the superior surface of the heart

autonomic tone contractile state during resting cardiac activity produced by mild sympathetic and parasympathetic stimulation

autorhythmicity ability of cardiac muscle to initiate its own electrical impulse that triggers the mechanical contraction that pumps blood at a fixed pace without nervous or endocrine control

Bachmann's bundle (also, interatrial band) group of specialized conducting cells that transmit the impulse directly from the SA node in the right atrium to the left atrium

Bainbridge reflex (also, called atrial reflex) autonomic reflex that responds to stretch receptors in the atria that send impulses to the cardioaccelerator area to increase HR when venous flow into the atria increases

baroreceptor reflex autonomic reflex in which the cardiac centers monitor signals from the baroreceptor stretch receptors and regulate heart function based on blood flow

bicuspid valve (also, mitral valve or left atrioventricular valve) valve located between the left atrium and ventricle; consists of two flaps of tissue

bulbus cordis portion of the primitive heart tube that will eventually develop into the right ventricle

bundle of His (also, atrioventricular bundle) group of specialized myocardial conductile cells that transmit the impulse from the AV node through the interventricular septum; form the left and right atrioventricular bundle branches

cardiac cycle period of time between the onset of atrial contraction (atrial systole) and ventricular relaxation (ventricular diastole)

cardiac notch depression in the medial surface of the inferior lobe of the left lung where the apex of the heart is located

cardiac output (CO) amount of blood pumped by each ventricle during one minute; equals HR multiplied by SV

cardiac plexus paired complex network of nerve fibers near the base of the heart that receive sympathetic and parasympathetic stimulations to regulate HR

cardiac reflexes series of autonomic reflexes that enable the cardiovascular centers to regulate heart function based upon sensory information from a variety of visceral sensors

cardiac reserve difference between maximum and resting CO

cardiac skeleton (also, skeleton of the heart) reinforced connective tissue located within the atrioventricular septum; includes four rings that surround the openings between the atria and ventricles, and the openings to the pulmonary trunk and aorta; the point of attachment for the heart valves

cardiogenic area area near the head of the embryo where the heart begins to develop 18–19 days after fertilization

cardiogenic cords two strands of tissue that form within the cardiogenic area

cardiomyocyte muscle cell of the heart

chordae tendineae string-like extensions of tough connective tissue that extend from the flaps of the atrioventricular valves to the papillary muscles

circumflex artery branch of the left coronary artery that follows coronary sulcus

coronary arteries branches of the ascending aorta that supply blood to the heart; the left coronary artery feeds the left side of the heart, the left atrium and ventricle, and the interventricular septum; the right coronary artery feeds the right atrium, portions of both ventricles, and the heart conduction system

coronary sinus large, thin-walled vein on the posterior surface of the heart that lies within the atrioventricular sulcus and drains the heart myocardium directly into the right atrium

coronary sulcus sulcus that marks the boundary between the atria and ventricles

coronary veins vessels that drain the heart and generally parallel the large surface arteries

diastole period of time when the heart muscle is relaxed and the chambers fill with blood

ejection fraction portion of the blood that is pumped or ejected from the heart with each contraction; mathematically represented by SV divided by EDV

electrocardiogram (ECG) surface recording of the electrical activity of the heart that can be used for diagnosis of irregular heart function; also abbreviated as EKG

end diastolic volume (EDV) (also, preload) the amount of blood in the ventricles at the end of atrial systole just prior to ventricular contraction

end systolic volume (ESV) amount of blood remaining in each ventricle following systole

endocardial tubes stage in which lumens form within the expanding cardiogenic cords, forming hollow structures

endocardium innermost layer of the heart lining the heart chambers and heart valves; composed of endothelium reinforced with a thin layer of connective tissue that binds to the myocardium

endothelium layer of smooth, simple squamous epithelium that lines the endocardium and blood vessels

epicardial coronary arteries surface arteries of the heart that generally follow the sulci

epicardium innermost layer of the serous pericardium and the outermost layer of the heart wall

filling time duration of ventricular diastole during which filling occurs

foramen ovale opening in the fetal heart that allows blood to flow directly from the right atrium to the left atrium, bypassing the fetal pulmonary circuit

fossa ovalis oval-shaped depression in the interatrial septum that marks the former location of the foramen ovale

Frank-Starling mechanism relationship between ventricular stretch and contraction in which the force of heart contraction is directly proportional to the initial length of the muscle fiber

great cardiac vein vessel that follows the interventricular sulcus on the anterior surface of the heart and flows along the coronary sulcus into the coronary sinus on the posterior surface; parallels the anterior interventricular artery and drains the areas supplied by this vessel

heart block interruption in the normal conduction pathway

heart bulge prominent feature on the anterior surface of the heart, reflecting early cardiac development

heart rate (HR) number of times the heart contracts (beats) per minute

heart sounds sounds heard via auscultation with a stethoscope of the closing of the atrioventricular valves ("lub") and semilunar valves ("dub")

hypertrophic cardiomyopathy pathological enlargement of the heart, generally for no known reason

inferior vena cava large systemic vein that returns blood to the heart from the inferior portion of the body

interatrial band (also, Bachmann's bundle) group of specialized conducting cells that transmit the impulse directly from the SA node in the right atrium to the left atrium

interatrial septum cardiac septum located between the two atria; contains the fossa ovalis after birth

intercalated disc physical junction between adjacent cardiac muscle cells; consisting of desmosomes, specialized linking proteoglycans, and gap junctions that allow passage of ions between the two cells

internodal pathways specialized conductile cells within the atria that transmit the impulse from the SA node throughout the myocardial cells of the atrium and to the AV node

interventricular septum cardiac septum located between the two ventricles

isovolumic contraction (also, isovolumetric contraction) initial phase of ventricular contraction in which tension and pressure in the ventricle increase, but no blood is pumped or ejected from the heart

isovolumic ventricular relaxation phase initial phase of the ventricular diastole when pressure in the ventricles drops below pressure in the two major arteries, the pulmonary trunk, and the aorta, and blood attempts to flow back into the ventricles, producing the dicrotic notch of the ECG and closing the two semilunar valves

left atrioventricular valve (also, mitral valve or bicuspid valve) valve located between the left atrium and ventricle; consists of two flaps of tissue

marginal arteries branches of the right coronary artery that supply blood to the superficial portions of the right ventricle

mesoderm one of the three primary germ layers that differentiate early in embryonic development

mesothelium simple squamous epithelial portion of serous membranes, such as the superficial portion of the epicardium (the visceral pericardium) and the deepest portion of the pericardium (the parietal pericardium)

middle cardiac vein vessel that parallels and drains the areas supplied by the posterior interventricular artery; drains into the great cardiac vein

mitral valve (also, left atrioventricular valve or bicuspid valve) valve located between the left atrium and ventricle; consists of two flaps of tissue

moderator band band of myocardium covered by endocardium that arises from the inferior portion of the interventricular septum in the right ventricle and crosses to the anterior papillary muscle; contains conductile fibers that carry electrical signals followed by contraction of the heart

murmur unusual heart sound detected by auscultation; typically related to septal or valve defects

myocardial conducting cells specialized cells that transmit electrical impulses throughout the heart and trigger contraction by the myocardial contractile cells

myocardial contractile cells bulk of the cardiac muscle cells in the atria and ventricles that conduct impulses and contract to propel blood

myocardium thickest layer of the heart composed of cardiac muscle cells built upon a framework of primarily collagenous fibers and blood vessels that supply it and the nervous fibers that help to regulate it

negative inotropic factors factors that negatively impact or lower heart contractility

P wave component of the electrocardiogram that represents the depolarization of the atria

pacemaker cluster of specialized myocardial cells known as the SA node that initiates the sinus rhythm

papillary muscle extension of the myocardium in the ventricles to which the chordae tendineae attach

pectinate muscles muscular ridges seen on the anterior surface of the right atrium

pericardial cavity cavity surrounding the heart filled with a lubricating serous fluid that reduces friction as the heart contracts

pericardial sac (also, pericardium) membrane that separates the heart from other mediastinal structures; consists of two distinct, fused sublayers: the fibrous pericardium and the parietal pericardium

pericardium (also, pericardial sac) membrane that separates the heart from other mediastinal structures; consists of two distinct, fused sublayers: the fibrous pericardium and the parietal pericardium

positive inotropic factors factors that positively impact or increase heart contractility

posterior cardiac vein vessel that parallels and drains the areas supplied by the marginal artery branch of the circumflex artery; drains into the great cardiac vein

posterior interventricular artery (also, posterior descending artery) branch of the right coronary artery that runs along the posterior portion of the interventricular sulcus toward the apex of the heart and gives rise to branches that supply the interventricular septum and portions of both ventricles

posterior interventricular sulcus sulcus located between the left and right ventricles on the anterior surface of the heart

preload (also, end diastolic volume) amount of blood in the ventricles at the end of atrial systole just prior to ventricular contraction

prepotential depolarization (also, spontaneous depolarization) mechanism that accounts for the autorhythmic property of cardiac muscle; the membrane potential increases as sodium ions diffuse through the always-open sodium ion channels and causes the electrical potential to rise

primitive atrium portion of the primitive heart tube that eventually becomes the anterior portions of both the right and left atria, and the two auricles

primitive heart tube singular tubular structure that forms from the fusion of the two endocardial tubes

primitive ventricle portion of the primitive heart tube that eventually forms the left ventricle

pulmonary arteries left and right branches of the pulmonary trunk that carry deoxygenated blood from the heart to each of the lungs

pulmonary capillaries capillaries surrounding the alveoli of the lungs where gas exchange occurs: carbon dioxide exits the blood and oxygen enters

pulmonary circuit blood flow to and from the lungs

pulmonary trunk large arterial vessel that carries blood ejected from the right ventricle; divides into the left and right pulmonary arteries

pulmonary valve (also, pulmonary semilunar valve, the pulmonic valve, or the right semilunar valve) valve at the base of the pulmonary trunk that prevents backflow of blood into the right ventricle; consists of three flaps

pulmonary veins veins that carry highly oxygenated blood into the left atrium, which pumps the blood into the left ventricle, which in turn pumps oxygenated blood into the aorta and to the many branches of the systemic circuit

Purkinje fibers specialized myocardial conduction fibers that arise from the bundle branches and spread the impulse to the myocardial contraction fibers of the ventricles

QRS complex component of the electrocardiogram that represents the depolarization of the ventricles and includes, as a component, the repolarization of the atria

right atrioventricular valve (also, tricuspid valve) valve located between the right atrium and ventricle; consists of three flaps of tissue

semilunar valves valves located at the base of the pulmonary trunk and at the base of the aorta

septum (plural = septa) walls or partitions that divide the heart into chambers

septum primum flap of tissue in the fetus that covers the foramen ovale within a few seconds after birth

sinoatrial (SA) node known as the pacemaker, a specialized clump of myocardial conducting cells located in the superior portion of the right atrium that has the highest inherent rate of depolarization that then spreads throughout the heart

sinus rhythm normal contractile pattern of the heart

sinus venosus develops into the posterior portion of the right atrium, the SA node, and the coronary sinus

small cardiac vein parallels the right coronary artery and drains blood from the posterior surfaces of the right atrium and ventricle; drains into the great cardiac vein

spontaneous depolarization (also, prepotential depolarization) the mechanism that accounts for the autorhythmic property of cardiac muscle; the membrane potential increases as sodium ions diffuse through the always-open sodium ion channels and causes the electrical potential to rise

stroke volume (SV) amount of blood pumped by each ventricle per contraction; also, the difference between EDV and ESV

sulcus (plural = sulci) fat-filled groove visible on the surface of the heart; coronary vessels are also located in these areas

superior vena cava large systemic vein that returns blood to the heart from the superior portion of the body

systemic circuit blood flow to and from virtually all of the tissues of the body

systole period of time when the heart muscle is contracting

T wave component of the electrocardiogram that represents the repolarization of the ventricles

target heart rate range in which both the heart and lungs receive the maximum benefit from an aerobic workout

trabeculae carneae ridges of muscle covered by endocardium located in the ventricles

tricuspid valve term used most often in clinical settings for the right atrioventricular valve

truncus arteriosus portion of the primitive heart that will eventually divide and give rise to the ascending aorta and pulmonary trunk

valve in the cardiovascular system, a specialized structure located within the heart or vessels that ensures one-way flow of blood

ventricle one of the primary pumping chambers of the heart located in the lower portion of the heart; the left ventricle is the major pumping chamber on the lower left side of the heart that ejects blood into the systemic circuit via the aorta and receives blood from the left atrium; the right ventricle is the major pumping chamber on the lower right side of the heart that ejects blood into the pulmonary circuit via the pulmonary trunk and receives blood from the right atrium

ventricular ejection phase second phase of ventricular systole during which blood is pumped from the ventricle

CHAPTER REVIEW

19.1 Heart Anatomy

The heart resides within the pericardial sac and is located in the mediastinal space within the thoracic cavity. The pericardial sac consists of two fused layers: an outer fibrous capsule and an inner parietal pericardium lined with a serous membrane. Between the pericardial sac and the heart is the pericardial cavity, which is filled with lubricating serous fluid. The walls of the heart are composed of an outer epicardium, a thick myocardium, and an inner lining layer of endocardium. The human heart consists of a pair of atria, which receive blood and pump it into a pair of ventricles, which pump blood into the vessels. The right atrium receives systemic blood relatively low in oxygen and pumps it into the right ventricle, which pumps it into the pulmonary circuit. Exchange of oxygen and carbon dioxide occurs in the lungs, and blood high in oxygen returns to the left atrium, which pumps blood into the left ventricle, which in turn pumps blood into the aorta and the remainder of the systemic circuit. The septa are the partitions that separate the chambers of the heart. They include the interatrial septum, the interventricular septum, and the atrioventricular septum. Two of these openings are guarded by the atrioventricular valves, the right tricuspid valve and the left mitral valve, which prevent the backflow of blood. Each is attached to chordae tendineae that extend to the papillary muscles, which are extensions of the myocardium, to prevent the valves from being blown back into the atria. The pulmonary valve is located at the base of the pulmonary trunk, and the left semilunar valve is located at the base of the aorta. The right and left coronary arteries are the first to branch off the aorta and arise from two of the three sinuses located near the base of the aorta and are generally located in the sulci. Cardiac veins parallel the small cardiac arteries and generally drain into the coronary sinus.

19.2 Cardiac Muscle and Electrical Activity

The heart is regulated by both neural and endocrine control, yet it is capable of initiating its own action potential followed by muscular contraction. The conductive cells within the heart establish the heart rate and transmit it through the myocardium. The contractile cells contract and propel the blood. The normal path of transmission for the conductive cells is the sinoatrial (SA) node, internodal pathways, atrioventricular (AV) node, atrioventricular (AV) bundle of His, bundle branches, and Purkinje fibers. The action potential for the conductive cells consists of a prepotential phase with a slow influx of Na^+ followed by a rapid influx of Ca^{2+} and outflux of K^+. Contractile cells have an action potential with an extended plateau phase that results in an extended refractory period to allow complete contraction for the heart to pump blood effectively. Recognizable points on the ECG include the P wave that corresponds to atrial depolarization, the QRS complex that corresponds to ventricular depolarization, and the T wave that corresponds to ventricular repolarization.

19.3 Cardiac Cycle

The cardiac cycle comprises a complete relaxation and contraction of both the atria and ventricles, and lasts approximately 0.8 seconds. Beginning with all chambers in diastole, blood flows passively from the veins into the atria and past the atrioventricular valves into the ventricles. The atria begin to contract (atrial systole), following depolarization of the atria, and pump blood into the ventricles. The ventricles begin to contract (ventricular systole), raising pressure within the ventricles. When ventricular pressure rises above the pressure in the atria, blood flows toward the atria, producing the first heart sound, S_1 or lub. As pressure in the ventricles rises above two major arteries, blood pushes open the two semilunar valves and moves into the pulmonary trunk and aorta in the ventricular ejection phase. Following ventricular repolarization, the ventricles begin to relax (ventricular diastole), and pressure within the ventricles drops. As ventricular pressure drops, there is a tendency for blood to flow back into the atria from the major arteries, producing the dicrotic notch in the ECG and closing the two semilunar valves. The second heart sound, S_2 or dub, occurs when the semilunar valves close. When the pressure falls below that of the atria, blood moves from the atria into the ventricles, opening the atrioventricular valves and marking one complete heart cycle. The valves prevent backflow of blood. Failure of the valves to operate properly produces turbulent blood flow within the heart; the resulting heart murmur can often be heard with a stethoscope.

19.4 Cardiac Physiology

Many factors affect HR and SV, and together, they contribute to cardiac function. HR is largely determined and regulated by autonomic stimulation and hormones. There are several feedback loops that contribute to maintaining homeostasis dependent upon activity levels, such as the atrial reflex, which is determined by venous return.

SV is regulated by autonomic innervation and hormones, but also by filling time and venous return. Venous return is determined by activity of the skeletal muscles, blood volume, and changes in peripheral circulation. Venous return determines preload and the atrial reflex. Filling time directly related to HR also determines preload. Preload then impacts both EDV and ESV. Autonomic innervation and hormones largely regulate contractility. Contractility impacts EDV as does afterload. CO is the product of HR multiplied by SV. SV is the difference between EDV and ESV.

19.5 Development of the Heart

The heart is the first organ to form and become functional, emphasizing the importance of transport of material to and from the developing infant. It originates about day 18 or 19 from the mesoderm and begins beating and pumping blood about day 21 or 22. It forms from the cardiogenic region near the head and is visible as a prominent heart bulge on the surface of the embryo. Originally, it consists of a pair of strands called cardiogenic cords that quickly form a hollow lumen and are referred to as endocardial tubes. These then fuse into a single heart tube and differentiate into the truncus arteriosus, bulbus cordis, primitive ventricle, primitive atrium, and sinus venosus, starting about day 22. The primitive heart begins to form an S shape within the pericardium between days 23 and 28. The internal septa begin to form about day 28, separating the heart into the atria and ventricles, although the foramen ovale persists until shortly after birth. Between weeks five and eight, the atrioventricular valves form. The semilunar valves form between weeks five and nine.

INTERACTIVE LINK QUESTIONS

1. Visit this site (http://openstaxcollege.org/l/heartvalve) to observe an echocardiogram of actual heart valves opening and closing. Although much of the heart has been "removed" from this gif loop so the chordae tendineae are not visible, why is their presence more critical for the atrioventricular valves (tricuspid and mitral) than the semilunar (aortic and pulmonary) valves?

REVIEW QUESTIONS

2. Which of the following is not important in preventing backflow of blood?
   a. chordae tendineae
   b. papillary muscles
   c. AV valves
   d. endocardium

3. Which valve separates the left atrium from the left ventricle?
   a. mitral
   b. tricuspid
   c. pulmonary
   d. aortic

4. Which of the following lists the valves in the order through which the blood flows from the vena cava through the heart?
   a. tricuspid, pulmonary semilunar, bicuspid, aortic semilunar
   b. mitral, pulmonary semilunar, bicuspid, aortic semilunar
   c. aortic semilunar, pulmonary semilunar, tricuspid, bicuspid

d. bicuspid, aortic semilunar, tricuspid, pulmonary semilunar

5. Which chamber initially receives blood from the systemic circuit?
   a. left atrium
   b. left ventricle
   c. right atrium
   d. right ventricle

6. The _____ layer secretes chemicals that help to regulate ionic environments and strength of contraction and serve as powerful vasoconstrictors.
   a. pericardial sac
   b. endocardium
   c. myocardium
   d. epicardium

7. The myocardium would be the thickest in the _____.
   a. left atrium
   b. left ventricle
   c. right atrium
   d. right ventricle

8. In which septum is it normal to find openings in the adult?
   a. interatrial septum
   b. interventricular septum
   c. atrioventricular septum
   d. all of the above

9. Which of the following is unique to cardiac muscle cells?
   a. Only cardiac muscle contains a sarcoplasmic reticulum.
   b. Only cardiac muscle has gap junctions.
   c. Only cardiac muscle is capable of autorhythmicity
   d. Only cardiac muscle has a high concentration of mitochondria.

10. The influx of which ion accounts for the plateau phase?
   a. sodium
   b. potassium
   c. chloride
   d. calcium

11. Which portion of the ECG corresponds to repolarization of the atria?
   a. P wave
   b. QRS complex
   c. T wave
   d. none of the above: atrial repolarization is masked by ventricular depolarization

12. Which component of the heart conduction system would have the slowest rate of firing?
   a. atrioventricular node
   b. atrioventricular bundle
   c. bundle branches
   d. Purkinje fibers

13. The cardiac cycle consists of a distinct relaxation and contraction phase. Which term is typically used to refer ventricular contraction while no blood is being ejected?
   a. systole
   b. diastole
   c. quiescent
   d. isovolumic contraction

14. Most blood enters the ventricle during _____.
   a. atrial systole
   b. atrial diastole
   c. ventricular systole
   d. isovolumic contraction

15. The first heart sound represents which portion of the cardiac cycle?
   a. atrial systole
   b. ventricular systole
   c. closing of the atrioventricular valves
   d. closing of the semilunar valves

16. Ventricular relaxation immediately follows _____.
   a. atrial depolarization
   b. ventricular repolarization
   c. ventricular depolarization
   d. atrial repolarization

17. The force the heart must overcome to pump blood is known as _____.
   a. preload
   b. afterload
   c. cardiac output
   d. stroke volume

18. The cardiovascular centers are located in which area of the brain?
   a. medulla oblongata
   b. pons
   c. mesencephalon (midbrain)
   d. cerebrum

19. In a healthy young adult, what happens to cardiac output when heart rate increases above 160 bpm?
   a. It increases.
   b. It decreases.
   c. It remains constant.
   d. There is no way to predict.

20. What happens to preload when there is venous constriction in the veins?
   a. It increases.
   b. It decreases.
   c. It remains constant.
   d. There is no way to predict.

21. Which of the following is a positive inotrope?
   a. Na^+
   b. K^+

c. Ca^{2+}
d. both Na^+ and K^+

22. The earliest organ to form and begin function within the developing human is the _____.
   a. brain
   b. stomach
   c. lungs
   d. heart

23. Of the three germ layers that give rise to all adult tissues and organs, which gives rise to the heart?
   a. ectoderm
   b. endoderm
   c. mesoderm
   d. placenta

24. The two tubes that eventually fuse to form the heart are referred to as the _____.

   a. primitive heart tubes
   b. endocardial tubes
   c. cardiogenic region
   d. cardiogenic tubes

25. Which primitive area of the heart will give rise to the right ventricle?
   a. bulbus cordis
   b. primitive ventricle
   c. sinus venosus
   d. truncus arteriosus

26. The pulmonary trunk and aorta are derived from which primitive heart structure?
   a. bulbus cordis
   b. primitive ventricle
   c. sinus venosus
   d. truncus arteriosus

CRITICAL THINKING QUESTIONS

27. Describe how the valves keep the blood moving in one direction.

28. Why is the pressure in the pulmonary circulation lower than in the systemic circulation?

29. Why is the plateau phase so critical to cardiac muscle function?

30. How does the delay of the impulse at the atrioventricular node contribute to cardiac function?

31. How do gap junctions and intercalated disks aid contraction of the heart?

32. Why do the cardiac muscles cells demonstrate autorhythmicity?

33. Describe one cardiac cycle, beginning with both atria and ventricles relaxed.

34. Why does increasing EDV increase contractility?

35. Why is afterload important to cardiac function?

36. Why is it so important for the human heart to develop early and begin functioning within the developing embryo?

37. Describe how the major pumping chambers, the ventricles, form within the developing heart.

20 | THE CARDIOVASCULAR SYSTEM: BLOOD VESSELS AND CIRCULATION

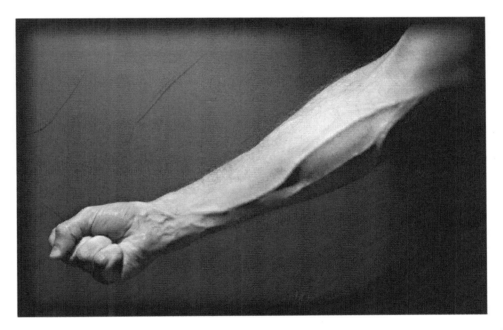

Figure 20.1 Blood Vessels While most blood vessels are located deep from the surface and are not visible, the superficial veins of the upper limb provide an indication of the extent, prominence, and importance of these structures to the body. (credit: Colin Davis)

Introduction

Chapter Objectives

After studying this chapter, you will be able to:

- Compare and contrast the anatomical structure of arteries, arterioles, capillaries, venules, and veins
- Accurately describe the forces that account for capillary exchange
- List the major factors affecting blood flow, blood pressure, and resistance
- Describe how blood flow, blood pressure, and resistance interrelate
- Discuss how the neural and endocrine mechanisms maintain homeostasis within the blood vessels
- Describe the interaction of the cardiovascular system with other body systems
- Label the major blood vessels of the pulmonary and systemic circulations
- Identify and describe the hepatic portal system
- Describe the development of blood vessels and fetal circulation
- Compare fetal circulation to that of an individual after birth

In this chapter, you will learn about the vascular part of the cardiovascular system, that is, the vessels that transport blood throughout the body and provide the physical site where gases, nutrients, and other substances are exchanged with body cells. When vessel functioning is reduced, blood-borne substances do not circulate effectively throughout the body. As a result, tissue injury occurs, metabolism is impaired, and the functions of every bodily system are threatened.

20.1 | Structure and Function of Blood Vessels

By the end of this section, you will be able to:
- Compare and contrast the three tunics that make up the walls of most blood vessels
- Distinguish between elastic arteries, muscular arteries, and arterioles on the basis of structure, location, and function
- Describe the basic structure of a capillary bed, from the supplying metarteriole to the venule into which it drains
- Explain the structure and function of venous valves in the large veins of the extremities

Blood is carried through the body via blood vessels. An artery is a blood vessel that carries blood away from the heart, where it branches into ever-smaller vessels. Eventually, the smallest arteries, vessels called arterioles, further branch into tiny capillaries, where nutrients and wastes are exchanged, and then combine with other vessels that exit capillaries to form venules, small blood vessels that carry blood to a vein, a larger blood vessel that returns blood to the heart.

Arteries and veins transport blood in two distinct circuits: the systemic circuit and the pulmonary circuit (Figure 20.2). Systemic arteries provide blood rich in oxygen to the body's tissues. The blood returned to the heart through systemic veins has less oxygen, since much of the oxygen carried by the arteries has been delivered to the cells. In contrast, in the pulmonary circuit, arteries carry blood low in oxygen exclusively to the lungs for gas exchange. Pulmonary veins then return freshly oxygenated blood from the lungs to the heart to be pumped back out into systemic circulation. Although arteries and veins differ structurally and functionally, they share certain features.

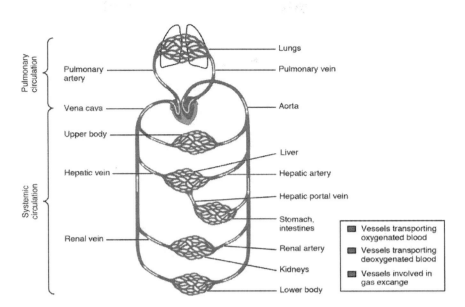

Figure 20.2 Cardiovascular Circulation The pulmonary circuit moves blood from the right side of the heart to the lungs and back to the heart. The systemic circuit moves blood from the left side of the heart to the head and body and returns it to the right side of the heart to repeat the cycle. The arrows indicate the direction of blood flow, and the colors show the relative levels of oxygen concentration.

Shared Structures

Different types of blood vessels vary slightly in their structures, but they share the same general features. Arteries and arterioles have thicker walls than veins and venules because they are closer to the heart and receive blood that is surging at a far greater pressure (Figure 20.3). Each type of vessel has a **lumen**—a hollow passageway through which blood flows. Arteries have smaller lumens than veins, a characteristic that helps to maintain the pressure of blood moving through the system. Together, their thicker walls and smaller diameters give arterial lumens a more rounded appearance in cross section than the lumens of veins.

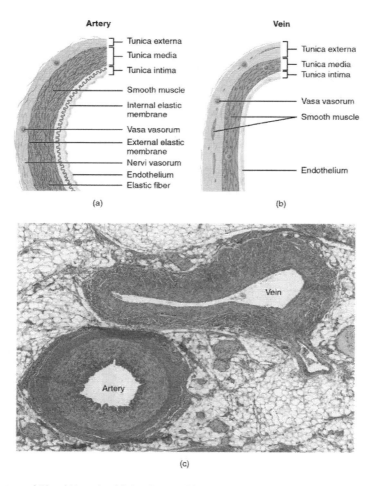

Figure 20.3 Structure of Blood Vessels (a) Arteries and (b) veins share the same general features, but the walls of arteries are much thicker because of the higher pressure of the blood that flows through them. (c) A micrograph shows the relative differences in thickness. LM × 160. (Micrograph provided by the Regents of the University of Michigan Medical School © 2012)

By the time blood has passed through capillaries and entered venules, the pressure initially exerted upon it by heart contractions has diminished. In other words, in comparison to arteries, venules and veins withstand a much lower pressure from the blood that flows through them. Their walls are considerably thinner and their lumens are correspondingly larger in diameter, allowing more blood to flow with less vessel resistance. In addition, many veins of the body, particularly those of the limbs, contain valves that assist the unidirectional flow of blood toward the heart. This is critical because blood flow becomes sluggish in the extremities, as a result of the lower pressure and the effects of gravity.

The walls of arteries and veins are largely composed of living cells and their products (including collagenous and elastic fibers); the cells require nourishment and produce waste. Since blood passes through the larger vessels relatively quickly, there is limited opportunity for blood in the lumen of the vessel to provide nourishment to or remove waste from the vessel's cells. Further, the walls of the larger vessels are too thick for nutrients to diffuse through to all of the cells. Larger arteries and veins contain small blood vessels within their walls known as the **vasa vasorum**—literally "vessels of the vessel"—to provide them with this critical exchange. Since the pressure within arteries is relatively high, the vasa vasorum must function in the outer layers of the vessel (see Figure 20.3) or the pressure exerted by the blood passing through the vessel would collapse it, preventing any exchange from occurring. The lower pressure within veins allows the vasa vasorum to be located closer to the lumen. The restriction of the vasa vasorum to the outer layers of arteries is thought to be one reason that arterial diseases are more common than venous diseases, since its location makes it more difficult to nourish the cells of the arteries and remove waste products. There are also minute nerves within the walls of both types of vessels that control the contraction and dilation of smooth muscle. These minute nerves are known as the nervi vasorum.

Both arteries and veins have the same three distinct tissue layers, called tunics (from the Latin term tunica), for the garments first worn by ancient Romans; the term tunic is also used for some modern garments. From the most interior layer to the outer, these tunics are the tunica intima, the tunica media, and the tunica externa (see Figure 20.3). Table 20.1 compares and contrasts the tunics of the arteries and veins.

Comparison of Tunics in Arteries and Veins

	Arteries	Veins
General appearance	Thick walls with small lumens Generally appear rounded	Thin walls with large lumens Generally appear flattened
Tunica intima	Endothelium usually appears wavy due to constriction of smooth muscle Internal elastic membrane present in larger vessels	Endothelium appears smooth Internal elastic membrane absent
Tunica media	Normally the thickest layer in arteries Smooth muscle cells and elastic fibers predominate (the proportions of these vary with distance from the heart) External elastic membrane present in larger vessels	Normally thinner than the tunica externa Smooth muscle cells and collagenous fibers predominate Nervi vasorum and vasa vasorum present External elastic membrane absent
Tunica externa	Normally thinner than the tunica media in all but the largest arteries Collagenous and elastic fibers Nervi vasorum and vasa vasorum present	Normally the thickest layer in veins Collagenous and smooth fibers predominate Some smooth muscle fibers Nervi vasorum and vasa vasorum present

Table 20.1

Tunica Intima

The **tunica intima** (also called the tunica interna) is composed of epithelial and connective tissue layers. Lining the tunica intima is the specialized simple squamous epithelium called the endothelium, which is continuous throughout the entire vascular system, including the lining of the chambers of the heart. Damage to this endothelial lining and exposure of blood to the collagenous fibers beneath is one of the primary causes of clot formation. Until recently, the endothelium was viewed simply as the boundary between the blood in the lumen and the walls of the vessels. Recent studies, however, have shown that it is physiologically critical to such activities as helping to regulate capillary exchange and altering blood flow. The endothelium releases local chemicals called endothelins that can constrict the smooth muscle within the walls of the vessel to increase blood pressure. Uncompensated overproduction of endothelins may contribute to hypertension (high blood pressure) and cardiovascular disease.

Next to the endothelium is the basement membrane, or basal lamina, that effectively binds the endothelium to the connective tissue. The basement membrane provides strength while maintaining flexibility, and it is permeable, allowing materials to pass through it. The thin outer layer of the tunica intima contains a small amount of areolar connective tissue that consists primarily of elastic fibers to provide the vessel with additional flexibility; it also contains some collagenous fibers to provide additional strength.

In larger arteries, there is also a thick, distinct layer of elastic fibers known as the **internal elastic membrane** (also called the internal elastic lamina) at the boundary with the tunica media. Like the other components of the tunica intima, the internal elastic membrane provides structure while allowing the vessel to stretch. It is permeated with small openings that allow exchange of materials between the tunics. The internal elastic membrane is not apparent in veins. In addition, many veins, particularly in the lower limbs, contain valves formed by sections of thickened endothelium that are reinforced with connective tissue, extending into the lumen.

Under the microscope, the lumen and the entire tunica intima of a vein will appear smooth, whereas those of an artery will normally appear wavy because of the partial constriction of the smooth muscle in the tunica media, the next layer of blood vessel walls.

Tunica Media

The **tunica media** is the substantial middle layer of the vessel wall (see Figure 20.3). It is generally the thickest layer in arteries, and it is much thicker in arteries than it is in veins. The tunica media consists of layers of smooth muscle supported by connective tissue that is primarily made up of elastic fibers, most of which are arranged in circular sheets. Toward the outer portion of the tunic, there are also layers of longitudinal muscle. Contraction and relaxation of the circular muscles decrease and increase the diameter of the vessel lumen, respectively. Specifically in arteries, **vasoconstriction** decreases blood flow as the smooth muscle in the walls of the tunica media contracts, making the lumen narrower and increasing blood pressure. Similarly, **vasodilation** increases blood flow as the smooth muscle relaxes, allowing the lumen to widen and blood pressure to drop. Both vasoconstriction and vasodilation are regulated in part by small vascular nerves, known as **nervi vasorum**, or "nerves of the vessel," that run within the walls of blood vessels. These are generally all sympathetic fibers, although some trigger vasodilation and others induce vasoconstriction, depending upon the nature of the neurotransmitter and receptors located on the target cell. Parasympathetic stimulation does trigger vasodilation as well as erection during sexual arousal in the external genitalia of both sexes. Nervous control over vessels tends to be more generalized than the specific targeting of individual blood vessels. Local controls, discussed later, account for this phenomenon. (Seek additional content for more information on these dynamic aspects of the autonomic nervous system.) Hormones and local chemicals also control blood vessels. Together, these neural and chemical mechanisms reduce or increase blood flow in response to changing body conditions, from exercise to hydration. Regulation of both blood flow and blood pressure is discussed in detail later in this chapter.

The smooth muscle layers of the tunica media are supported by a framework of collagenous fibers that also binds the tunica media to the inner and outer tunics. Along with the collagenous fibers are large numbers of elastic fibers that appear as wavy lines in prepared slides. Separating the tunica media from the outer tunica externa in larger arteries is the **external elastic membrane** (also called the external elastic lamina), which also appears wavy in slides. This structure is not usually seen in smaller arteries, nor is it seen in veins.

Tunica Externa

The outer tunic, the **tunica externa** (also called the tunica adventitia), is a substantial sheath of connective tissue composed primarily of collagenous fibers. Some bands of elastic fibers are found here as well. The tunica externa in veins also contains groups of smooth muscle fibers. This is normally the thickest tunic in veins and may be thicker than the tunica media in some larger arteries. The outer layers of the tunica externa are not distinct but rather blend with the surrounding connective tissue outside the vessel, helping to hold the vessel in relative position. If you are able to palpate some of the superficial veins on your upper limbs and try to move them, you will find that the tunica externa prevents this. If the tunica externa did not hold the vessel in place, any movement would likely result in disruption of blood flow.

Arteries

An **artery** is a blood vessel that conducts blood away from the heart. All arteries have relatively thick walls that can withstand the high pressure of blood ejected from the heart. However, those close to the heart have the thickest walls, containing a high percentage of elastic fibers in all three of their tunics. This type of artery is known as an **elastic artery** (Figure 20.4). Vessels larger than 10 mm in diameter are typically elastic. Their abundant elastic fibers allow them to expand, as blood pumped from the ventricles passes through them, and then to recoil after the surge has passed. If artery walls were rigid and unable to expand and recoil, their resistance to blood flow would greatly increase and blood pressure would rise to even higher levels, which would in turn require the heart to pump harder to increase the volume of blood expelled by each pump (the stroke volume) and maintain adequate pressure and flow. Artery walls would have to become even thicker in response to this increased pressure. The elastic recoil of the vascular wall helps to maintain the pressure gradient that drives the blood through the arterial system. An elastic artery is also known as a conducting artery, because the large diameter of the lumen enables it to accept a large volume of blood from the heart and conduct it to smaller branches.

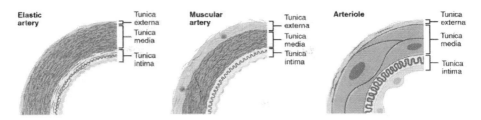

Figure 20.4 Types of Arteries and Arterioles Comparison of the walls of an elastic artery, a muscular artery, and an arteriole is shown. In terms of scale, the diameter of an arteriole is measured in micrometers compared to millimeters for elastic and muscular arteries.

Farther from the heart, where the surge of blood has dampened, the percentage of elastic fibers in an artery's tunica intima decreases and the amount of smooth muscle in its tunica media increases. The artery at this point is described as a **muscular artery**. The diameter of muscular arteries typically ranges from 0.1 mm to 10 mm. Their thick tunica media allows muscular arteries to play a leading role in vasoconstriction. In contrast, their decreased quantity of elastic fibers limits their ability to expand. Fortunately, because the blood pressure has eased by the time it reaches these more distant vessels, elasticity has become less important.

Notice that although the distinctions between elastic and muscular arteries are important, there is no "line of demarcation" where an elastic artery suddenly becomes muscular. Rather, there is a gradual transition as the vascular tree repeatedly branches. In turn, muscular arteries branch to distribute blood to the vast network of arterioles. For this reason, a muscular artery is also known as a distributing artery.

Arterioles

An **arteriole** is a very small artery that leads to a capillary. Arterioles have the same three tunics as the larger vessels, but the thickness of each is greatly diminished. The critical endothelial lining of the tunica intima is intact. The tunica media is restricted to one or two smooth muscle cell layers in thickness. The tunica externa remains but is very thin (see Figure 20.4).

With a lumen averaging 30 micrometers or less in diameter, arterioles are critical in slowing down—or resisting—blood flow and, thus, causing a substantial drop in blood pressure. Because of this, you may see them referred to as resistance vessels. The muscle fibers in arterioles are normally slightly contracted, causing arterioles to maintain a consistent muscle tone—in this case referred to as vascular tone—in a similar manner to the muscular tone of skeletal muscle. In reality, all blood vessels exhibit vascular tone due to the partial contraction of smooth muscle. The importance of the arterioles is that they will be the primary site of both resistance and regulation of blood pressure. The precise diameter of the lumen of an arteriole at any given moment is determined by neural and chemical controls, and vasoconstriction and vasodilation in the arterioles are the primary mechanisms for distribution of blood flow.

Capillaries

A **capillary** is a microscopic channel that supplies blood to the tissues themselves, a process called **perfusion**. Exchange of gases and other substances occurs in the capillaries between the blood and the surrounding cells and their tissue fluid (interstitial fluid). The diameter of a capillary lumen ranges from 5–10 micrometers; the smallest are just barely wide enough for an erythrocyte to squeeze through. Flow through capillaries is often described as **microcirculation**.

The wall of a capillary consists of the endothelial layer surrounded by a basement membrane with occasional smooth muscle fibers. There is some variation in wall structure: In a large capillary, several endothelial cells bordering each other may line the lumen; in a small capillary, there may be only a single cell layer that wraps around to contact itself.

For capillaries to function, their walls must be leaky, allowing substances to pass through. There are three major types of capillaries, which differ according to their degree of "leakiness:" continuous, fenestrated, and sinusoid capillaries (Figure 20.5).

Continuous Capillaries

The most common type of capillary, the **continuous capillary**, is found in almost all vascularized tissues. Continuous capillaries are characterized by a complete endothelial lining with tight junctions between endothelial cells. Although a tight junction is usually impermeable and only allows for the passage of water and ions, they are often incomplete in capillaries, leaving intercellular clefts that allow for exchange of water and other very small molecules between the blood plasma and the interstitial fluid. Substances that can pass between cells include metabolic products, such as glucose, water, and small hydrophobic molecules like gases and hormones, as well as various leukocytes. Continuous capillaries not associated with the brain are rich in transport vesicles, contributing to either endocytosis or exocytosis. Those in the brain are part of the blood-brain barrier. Here, there are tight junctions and no intercellular clefts, plus a thick basement membrane and astrocyte extensions called end feet; these structures combine to prevent the movement of nearly all substances.

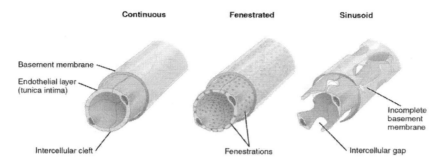

Figure 20.5 Types of Capillaries The three major types of capillaries: continuous, fenestrated, and sinusoid.

Fenestrated Capillaries

A **fenestrated capillary** is one that has pores (or fenestrations) in addition to tight junctions in the endothelial lining. These make the capillary permeable to larger molecules. The number of fenestrations and their degree of permeability vary, however, according to their location. Fenestrated capillaries are common in the small intestine, which is the primary site of nutrient absorption, as well as in the kidneys, which filter the blood. They are also found in the choroid plexus of the brain and many endocrine structures, including the hypothalamus, pituitary, pineal, and thyroid glands.

Sinusoid Capillaries

A **sinusoid capillary** (or sinusoid) is the least common type of capillary. Sinusoid capillaries are flattened, and they have extensive intercellular gaps and incomplete basement membranes, in addition to intercellular clefts and fenestrations. This gives them an appearance not unlike Swiss cheese. These very large openings allow for the passage of the largest molecules, including plasma proteins and even cells. Blood flow through sinusoids is very slow, allowing more time for exchange of gases, nutrients, and wastes. Sinusoids are found in the liver and spleen, bone marrow, lymph nodes (where they carry lymph, not blood), and many endocrine glands including the pituitary and adrenal glands. Without these specialized capillaries, these organs would not be able to provide their myriad of functions. For example, when bone marrow forms new blood cells, the cells must enter the blood supply and can only do so through the large openings of a sinusoid capillary; they cannot pass through the small openings of continuous or fenestrated capillaries. The liver also requires extensive specialized sinusoid capillaries in order to process the materials brought to it by the hepatic portal vein from both the digestive tract and spleen, and to release plasma proteins into circulation.

Metarterioles and Capillary Beds

A **metarteriole** is a type of vessel that has structural characteristics of both an arteriole and a capillary. Slightly larger than the typical capillary, the smooth muscle of the tunica media of the metarteriole is not continuous but forms rings of smooth muscle (sphincters) prior to the entrance to the capillaries. Each metarteriole arises from a terminal arteriole and branches to supply blood to a **capillary bed** that may consist of 10–100 capillaries.

The **precapillary sphincters**, circular smooth muscle cells that surround the capillary at its origin with the metarteriole, tightly regulate the flow of blood from a metarteriole to the capillaries it supplies. Their function is critical: If all of the capillary beds in the body were to open simultaneously, they would collectively hold every drop of blood in the body and there would be none in the arteries, arterioles, venules, veins, or the heart itself. Normally, the precapillary sphincters are closed. When the surrounding tissues need oxygen and have excess waste products, the precapillary sphincters open, allowing blood to flow through and exchange to occur before closing once more (Figure 20.6). If all of the precapillary sphincters in a capillary bed are closed, blood will flow from the metarteriole directly into a **thoroughfare channel** and then into the venous circulation, bypassing the capillary bed entirely. This creates what is known as a **vascular shunt**. In addition, an **arteriovenous anastomosis** may bypass the capillary bed and lead directly to the venous system.

Although you might expect blood flow through a capillary bed to be smooth, in reality, it moves with an irregular, pulsating flow. This pattern is called **vasomotion** and is regulated by chemical signals that are triggered in response to changes in internal conditions, such as oxygen, carbon dioxide, hydrogen ion, and lactic acid levels. For example, during strenuous exercise when oxygen levels decrease and carbon dioxide, hydrogen ion, and lactic acid levels all increase, the capillary beds in skeletal muscle are open, as they would be in the digestive system when nutrients are present in the digestive tract. During sleep or rest periods, vessels in both areas are largely closed; they open only occasionally to allow oxygen and nutrient supplies to travel to the tissues to maintain basic life processes.

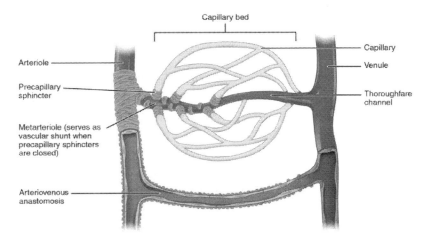

Figure 20.6 Capillary Bed In a capillary bed, arterioles give rise to metarterioles. Precapillary sphincters located at the junction of a metarteriole with a capillary regulate blood flow. A thoroughfare channel connects the metarteriole to a venule. An arteriovenous anastomosis, which directly connects the arteriole with the venule, is shown at the bottom.

Venules

A **venule** is an extremely small vein, generally 8–100 micrometers in diameter. Postcapillary venules join multiple capillaries exiting from a capillary bed. Multiple venules join to form veins. The walls of venules consist of endothelium, a thin middle layer with a few muscle cells and elastic fibers, plus an outer layer of connective tissue fibers that constitute a very thin tunica externa (Figure 20.7). Venules as well as capillaries are the primary sites of emigration or diapedesis, in which the white blood cells adhere to the endothelial lining of the vessels and then squeeze through adjacent cells to enter the tissue fluid.

Veins

Compared to arteries, veins are thin-walled vessels with large pressure vessels, larger veins are commonly equipped with heart and prevent backflow toward the capillaries caused gravity. Table 20.2 compares the features of arteries and

---

Venous valves
- Because they are ↓ pressure vessels, larger veins are given valves.
- Promote unidirectional flow of blood toward the heart & prevent backflow toward capillaries caused by inherent low blood pressure in veins & pull of gravity
- In limbs & veins below heart

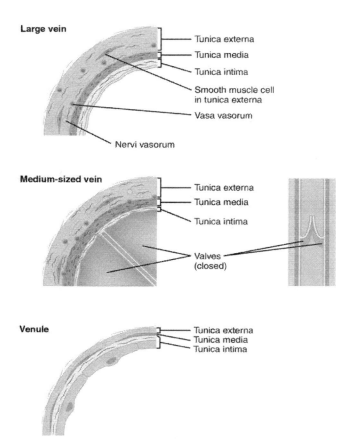

Figure 20.7 Comparison of Veins and Venules Many veins have valves to prevent back flow of blood, whereas venules do not. In terms of scale, the diameter of a venule is measured in micrometers compared to millimeters for veins.

Comparison of Arteries and Veins

	Arteries	Veins
Direction of blood flow	Conducts blood away from the heart	Conducts blood toward the heart
General appearance	Rounded	Irregular, often collapsed
Pressure	High	Low
Wall thickness	Thick	Thin
Relative oxygen concentration	Higher in systemic arteries Lower in pulmonary arteries	Lower in systemic veins Higher in pulmonary veins
Valves	Not present	Present most commonly in limbs and in veins inferior to the heart

Table 20.2

Cardiovascular System: Edema and Varicose Veins

Despite the presence of valves and the contributions of other anatomical and physiological adaptations we will cover shortly, over the course of a day, some blood will inevitably pool, especially in the lower limbs, due to the pull of gravity. Any blood that accumulates in a vein will increase the pressure within it, which can then be reflected back into the smaller veins, venules, and eventually even the capillaries. Increased pressure will promote the flow of fluids out of the capillaries and into the interstitial fluid. The presence of excess tissue fluid around the cells leads to a condition called edema.

Most people experience a daily accumulation of tissue fluid, especially if they spend much of their work life on their feet (like most health professionals). However, clinical edema goes beyond normal swelling and requires medical treatment. Edema has many potential causes, including hypertension and heart failure, severe protein deficiency, renal failure, and many others. In order to treat edema, which is a sign rather than a discrete disorder, the underlying cause must be diagnosed and alleviated.

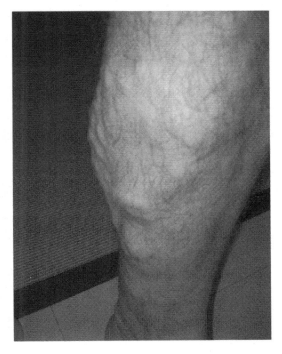

Figure 20.8 Varicose Veins Varicose veins are commonly found in the lower limbs. (credit: Thomas Kriese)

Edema may be accompanied by varicose veins, especially in the superficial veins of the legs (Figure 20.8). This disorder arises when defective valves allow blood to accumulate within the veins, causing them to distend, twist, and become visible on the surface of the integument. Varicose veins may occur in both sexes, but are more common in women and are often related to pregnancy. More than simple cosmetic blemishes, varicose veins are often painful and sometimes itchy or throbbing. Without treatment, they tend to grow worse over time. The use of support hose, as well as elevating the feet and legs whenever possible, may be helpful in alleviating this condition. Laser surgery and interventional radiologic procedures can reduce the size and severity of varicose veins. Severe cases may require conventional surgery to remove the damaged vessels. As there are typically redundant circulation patterns, that is, anastomoses, for the smaller and more superficial veins, removal does not typically impair the circulation. There is evidence that patients with varicose veins suffer a greater risk of developing a thrombus or clot.

Veins as Blood Reservoirs

In addition to their primary function of returning blood to the heart, veins may be considered blood reservoirs, since systemic veins contain approximately 64 percent of the blood volume at any given time (Figure 20.9). Their ability to hold this much blood is due to their high **capacitance**, that is, their capacity to distend (expand) readily to store a high volume of blood, even at a low pressure. The large lumens and relatively thin walls of veins make them far more distensible than arteries; thus, they are said to be **capacitance vessels**.

Systemic circulation 84%	Systemic veins 64%	Large veins 18%
		Large venous networks (liver, bone marrow, and integument) 21%
		Venules and medium-sized veins 25%
	Systemic arteries 13%	Arterioles 2%
		Muscular arteries 5%
		Elastic arteries 4%
		Aorta 2%
	Systemic capillaries 7%	Systemic capillaries 7%
Pulmonary circulation 9%	Pulmonary veins 4%	
	Pulmonary capillaries 2%	
	Pulmonary arteries 3%	
Heart 7%		

Figure 20.9 Distribution of Blood Flow

When blood flow needs to be redistributed to other portions of the body, the vasomotor center located in the medulla oblongata sends sympathetic stimulation to the smooth muscles in the walls of the veins, causing constriction—or in this case, venoconstriction. Less dramatic than the vasoconstriction seen in smaller arteries and arterioles, venoconstriction may be likened to a "stiffening" of the vessel wall. This increases pressure on the blood within the veins, speeding its return to the heart. As you will note in Figure 20.9, approximately 21 percent of the venous blood is located in venous networks within the liver, bone marrow, and integument. This volume of blood is referred to as **venous reserve**. Through venoconstriction, this "reserve" volume of blood can get back to the heart more quickly for redistribution to other parts of the circulation.

Vascular Surgeons and Technicians

Vascular surgery is a specialty in which the physician deals primarily with diseases of the vascular portion of the cardiovascular system. This includes repair and replacement of diseased or damaged vessels, removal of plaque from vessels, minimally invasive procedures including the insertion of venous catheters, and traditional surgery. Following completion of medical school, the physician generally completes a 5-year surgical residency followed by an additional 1 to 2 years of vascular specialty training. In the United States, most vascular surgeons are members of the Society of Vascular Surgery.

Vascular technicians are specialists in imaging technologies that provide information on the health of the vascular system. They may also assist physicians in treating disorders involving the arteries and veins. This profession often overlaps with cardiovascular technology, which would also include treatments involving the heart. Although recognized by the American Medical Association, there are currently no licensing requirements for vascular technicians, and licensing is voluntary. Vascular technicians typically have an Associate's degree or certificate, involving 18 months to 2 years of training. The United States Bureau of Labor projects this profession to grow by 29 percent from 2010 to 2020.

Visit this site (http://openstaxcollege.org/l/vascsurgery) to learn more about vascular surgery.

Visit this site (http://openstaxcollege.org/l/vasctechs) to learn more about vascular technicians.

20.2 | Blood Flow, Blood Pressure, and Resistance

By the end of this section, you will be able to:
- Distinguish between systolic pressure, diastolic pressure, pulse pressure, and mean arterial pressure
- Describe the clinical measurement of pulse and blood pressure
- Identify and discuss five variables affecting arterial blood flow and blood pressure
- Discuss several factors affecting blood flow in the venous system

Blood flow refers to the movement of blood through a vessel, tissue, or organ, and is usually expressed in terms of volume of blood per unit of time. It is initiated by the contraction of the ventricles of the heart. Ventricular contraction ejects blood into the major arteries, resulting in flow from regions of higher pressure to regions of lower pressure, as blood encounters smaller arteries and arterioles, then capillaries, then the venules and veins of the venous system. This section discusses a number of critical variables that contribute to blood flow throughout the body. It also discusses the factors that impede or slow blood flow, a phenomenon known as **resistance**.

As noted earlier, hydrostatic pressure is the force exerted by a fluid due to gravitational pull, usually against the wall of the container in which it is located. One form of hydrostatic pressure is **blood pressure**, the force exerted by blood upon the walls of the blood vessels or the chambers of the heart. Blood pressure may be measured in capillaries and veins, as well as the vessels of the pulmonary circulation; however, the term blood pressure without any specific descriptors typically refers to systemic arterial blood pressure—that is, the pressure of blood flowing in the arteries of the systemic circulation. In clinical practice, this pressure is measured in mm Hg and is usually obtained using the brachial artery of the arm.

Components of Arterial Blood Pressure

Arterial blood pressure in the larger vessels consists of several distinct components (Figure 20.10): systolic and diastolic pressures, pulse pressure, and mean arterial pressure.

Systolic and Diastolic Pressures

When systemic arterial blood pressure is measured, it is recorded as a ratio of two numbers (e.g., 120/80 is a normal adult blood pressure), expressed as systolic pressure over diastolic pressure. The **systolic pressure** is the higher value (typically around 120 mm Hg) and reflects the arterial pressure resulting from the ejection of blood during ventricular contraction, or systole. The **diastolic pressure** is the lower value (usually about 80 mm Hg) and represents the arterial pressure of blood during ventricular relaxation, or diastole.

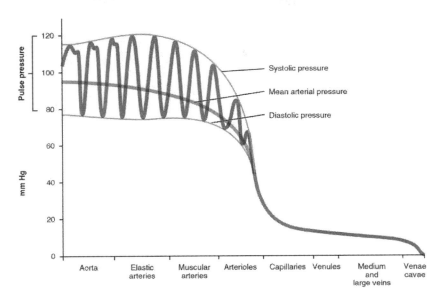

Figure 20.10 Systemic Blood Pressure The graph shows the components of blood pressure throughout the blood vessels, including systolic, diastolic, mean arterial, and pulse pressures.

Pulse Pressure

As shown in Figure 20.10, the difference between the systolic pressure and the diastolic pressure is the **pulse pressure**. For example, an individual with a systolic pressure of 120 mm Hg and a diastolic pressure of 80 mm Hg would have a pulse pressure of 40 mmHg.

Generally, a pulse pressure should be at least 25 percent of the systolic pressure. A pulse pressure below this level is described as low or narrow. This may occur, for example, in patients with a low stroke volume, which may be seen in congestive heart failure, stenosis of the aortic valve, or significant blood loss following trauma. In contrast, a high or wide pulse pressure is common in healthy people following strenuous exercise, when their resting pulse pressure of 30–40 mm Hg may increase temporarily to 100 mm Hg as stroke volume increases. A persistently high pulse pressure at or above 100 mm Hg may indicate excessive resistance in the arteries and can be caused by a variety of disorders. Chronic high resting pulse pressures can degrade the heart, brain, and kidneys, and warrant medical treatment.

Mean Arterial Pressure

Mean arterial pressure (MAP) represents the "average" pressure of blood in the arteries, that is, the average force driving blood into vessels that serve the tissues. Mean is a statistical concept and is calculated by taking the sum of the values divided by the number of values. Although complicated to measure directly and complicated to calculate, MAP can be approximated by adding the diastolic pressure to one-third of the pulse pressure or systolic pressure minus the diastolic pressure:

$$\text{MAP} = \text{diastolic BP} + \frac{(\text{systolic-diastolic BP})}{3}$$

In Figure 20.10, this value is approximately $80 + (120 - 80) / 3$, or 93.33. Normally, the MAP falls within the range of 70–110 mm Hg. If the value falls below 60 mm Hg for an extended time, blood pressure will not be high enough to ensure circulation to and through the tissues, which results in **ischemia**, or insufficient blood flow. A condition called **hypoxia**, inadequate oxygenation of tissues, commonly accompanies ischemia. The term hypoxemia refers to low levels of oxygen in systemic arterial blood. Neurons are especially sensitive to hypoxia and may die or be damaged if blood flow and oxygen supplies are not quickly restored.

Pulse

After blood is ejected from the heart, elastic fibers in the arteries help maintain a high-pressure gradient as they expand to accommodate the blood, then recoil. This expansion and recoiling effect, known as the **pulse**, can be palpated manually or measured electronically. Although the effect diminishes over distance from the heart, elements of the systolic and diastolic components of the pulse are still evident down to the level of the arterioles.

Because pulse indicates heart rate, it is measured clinically to provide clues to a patient's state of health. It is recorded as beats per minute. Both the rate and the strength of the pulse are important clinically. A high or irregular pulse rate can be caused by physical activity or other temporary factors, but it may also indicate a heart condition. The pulse strength indicates the strength of ventricular contraction and cardiac output. If the pulse is strong, then systolic pressure is high. If it is weak, systolic pressure has fallen, and medical intervention may be warranted.

Pulse can be palpated manually by placing the tips of the fingers across an artery that runs close to the body surface and pressing lightly. While this procedure is normally performed using the radial artery in the wrist or the common carotid artery in the neck, any superficial artery that can be palpated may be used (Figure 20.11). Common sites to find a pulse include temporal and facial arteries in the head, brachial arteries in the upper arm, femoral arteries in the thigh, popliteal arteries behind the knees, posterior tibial arteries near the medial tarsal regions, and dorsalis pedis arteries in the feet. A variety of commercial electronic devices are also available to measure pulse.

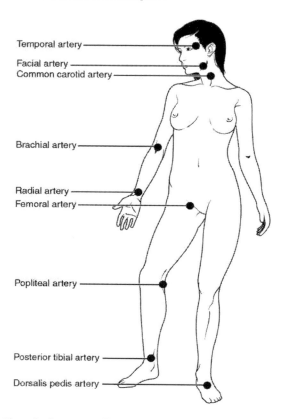

Figure 20.11 Pulse Sites The pulse is most readily measured at the radial artery, but can be measured at any of the pulse points shown.

Measurement of Blood Pressure

Blood pressure is one of the critical parameters measured on virtually every patient in every healthcare setting. The technique used today was developed more than 100 years ago by a pioneering Russian physician, Dr. Nikolai Korotkoff.

Turbulent blood flow through the vessels can be heard as a soft ticking while measuring blood pressure; these sounds are known as **Korotkoff sounds**. The technique of measuring blood pressure requires the use of a **sphygmomanometer** (a blood pressure cuff attached to a measuring device) and a stethoscope. The technique is as follows:

- The clinician wraps an inflatable cuff tightly around the patient's arm at about the level of the heart.
- The clinician squeezes a rubber pump to inject air into the cuff, raising pressure around the artery and temporarily cutting off blood flow into the patient's arm.
- The clinician places the stethoscope on the patient's antecubital region and, while gradually allowing air within the cuff to escape, listens for the Korotkoff sounds.

Although there are five recognized Korotkoff sounds, only two are normally recorded. Initially, no sounds are heard since there is no blood flow through the vessels, but as air pressure drops, the cuff relaxes, and blood flow returns to the arm. As shown in Figure 20.12, the first sound heard through the stethoscope—the first Korotkoff sound—indicates systolic pressure. As more air is released from the cuff, blood is able to flow freely through the brachial artery and all sounds disappear. The point at which the last sound is heard is recorded as the patient's diastolic pressure.

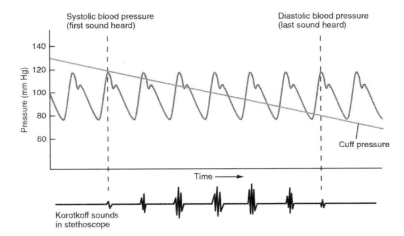

Figure 20.12 Blood Pressure Measurement When pressure in a sphygmomanometer cuff is released, a clinician can hear the Korotkoff sounds. In this graph, a blood pressure tracing is aligned to a measurement of systolic and diastolic pressures.

The majority of hospitals and clinics have automated equipment for measuring blood pressure that work on the same principles. An even more recent innovation is a small instrument that wraps around a patient's wrist. The patient then holds the wrist over the heart while the device measures blood flow and records pressure.

Variables Affecting Blood Flow and Blood Pressure

Five variables influence blood flow and blood pressure:

- Cardiac output
- Compliance
- Volume of the blood
- Viscosity of the blood
- Blood vessel length and diameter

Recall that blood moves from higher pressure to lower pressure. It is pumped from the heart into the arteries at high pressure. If you increase pressure in the arteries (afterload), and cardiac function does not compensate, blood flow will actually decrease. In the venous system, the opposite relationship is true. Increased pressure in the veins does not decrease flow as it does in arteries, but actually increases flow. Since pressure in the veins is normally relatively low, for blood to flow back into the heart, the pressure in the atria during atrial diastole must be even lower. It normally approaches zero, except when the atria contract (see Figure 20.10).

Cardiac Output

Cardiac output is the measurement of blood flow from the heart through the ventricles, and is usually measured in liters per minute. Any factor that causes cardiac output to increase, by elevating heart rate or stroke volume or both, will elevate blood pressure and promote blood flow. These factors include sympathetic stimulation, the catecholamines epinephrine and norepinephrine, thyroid hormones, and increased calcium ion levels. Conversely, any factor that decreases cardiac output, by decreasing heart rate or stroke volume or both, will decrease arterial pressure and blood flow. These factors include parasympathetic stimulation, elevated or decreased potassium ion levels, decreased calcium levels, anoxia, and acidosis.

Compliance

Compliance is the ability of any compartment to expand to accommodate increased content. A metal pipe, for example, is not compliant, whereas a balloon is. The greater the compliance of an artery, the more effectively it is able to expand to accommodate surges in blood flow without increased resistance or blood pressure. Veins are more compliant than arteries and can expand to hold more blood. When vascular disease causes stiffening of arteries, compliance is reduced and resistance to blood flow is increased. The result is more turbulence, higher pressure within the vessel, and reduced blood flow. This increases the work of the heart.

A Mathematical Approach to Factors Affecting Blood Flow

Jean Louis Marie Poiseuille was a French physician and physiologist who devised a mathematical equation describing blood flow and its relationship to known parameters. The same equation also applies to engineering studies of the flow of fluids. Although understanding the math behind the relationships among the factors affecting blood flow is not necessary to understand blood flow, it can help solidify an understanding of their relationships. Please note that even if the equation looks intimidating, breaking it down into its components and following the relationships will make these relationships clearer, even if you are weak in math. Focus on the three critical variables: radius (r), vessel length (λ), and viscosity (η).

Poiseuille's equation:

$$\text{Blood flow} = \frac{\pi \, \Delta P \, r^4}{8 \eta \lambda}$$

- π is the Greek letter pi, used to represent the mathematical constant that is the ratio of a circle's circumference to its diameter. It may commonly be represented as 3.14, although the actual number extends to infinity.
- ΔP represents the difference in pressure.
- r^4 is the radius (one-half of the diameter) of the vessel to the fourth power.
- η is the Greek letter eta and represents the viscosity of the blood.
- λ is the Greek letter lambda and represents the length of a blood vessel.

One of several things this equation allows us to do is calculate the resistance in the vascular system. Normally this value is extremely difficult to measure, but it can be calculated from this known relationship:

$$\text{Blood flow} = \frac{\Delta P}{\text{Resistance}}$$

If we rearrange this slightly,

$$\text{Resistance} = \frac{\Delta P}{\text{Blood flow}}$$

Then by substituting Pouseille's equation for blood flow:

$$\text{Resistance} = \frac{8 \eta \lambda}{\pi r^4}$$

By examining this equation, you can see that there are only three variables: viscosity, vessel length, and radius, since 8 and π are both constants. The important thing to remember is this: Two of these variables, viscosity and vessel length, will change slowly in the body. Only one of these factors, the radius, can be changed rapidly by vasoconstriction and vasodilation, thus dramatically impacting resistance and flow. Further, small changes in the radius will greatly affect flow, since it is raised to the fourth power in the equation.

We have briefly considered how cardiac output and blood volume impact blood flow and pressure; the next step is to see how the other variables (contraction, vessel length, and viscosity) articulate with Pouseille's equation and what they can teach us about the impact on blood flow.

Blood Volume

The relationship between blood volume, blood pressure, and blood flow is intuitively obvious. Water may merely trickle along a creek bed in a dry season, but rush quickly and under great pressure after a heavy rain. Similarly, as blood volume decreases, pressure and flow decrease. As blood volume increases, pressure and flow increase.

Under normal circumstances, blood volume varies little. Low blood volume, called **hypovolemia**, may be caused by bleeding, dehydration, vomiting, severe burns, or some medications used to treat hypertension. It is important to recognize that other regulatory mechanisms in the body are so effective at maintaining blood pressure that an individual may be asymptomatic until 10–20 percent of the blood volume has been lost. Treatment typically includes intravenous fluid replacement.

Hypervolemia, excessive fluid volume, may be caused by retention of water and sodium, as seen in patients with heart failure, liver cirrhosis, some forms of kidney disease, hyperaldosteronism, and some glucocorticoid steroid treatments. Restoring homeostasis in these patients depends upon reversing the condition that triggered the hypervolemia.

Blood Viscosity

Viscosity is the thickness of fluids that affects their ability to flow. Clean water, for example, is less viscous than mud. The viscosity of blood is directly proportional to resistance and inversely proportional to flow; therefore, any condition that causes viscosity to increase will also increase resistance and decrease flow. For example, imagine sipping milk, then a milkshake, through the same size straw. You experience more resistance and therefore less flow from the milkshake. Conversely, any condition that causes viscosity to decrease (such as when the milkshake melts) will decrease resistance and increase flow.

Normally the viscosity of blood does not change over short periods of time. The two primary determinants of blood viscosity are the formed elements and plasma proteins. Since the vast majority of formed elements are erythrocytes, any condition affecting erythropoiesis, such as polycythemia or anemia, can alter viscosity. Since most plasma proteins are produced by the liver, any condition affecting liver function can also change the viscosity slightly and therefore decrease blood flow. Liver abnormalities include hepatitis, cirrhosis, alcohol damage, and drug toxicities. While leukocytes and platelets are normally a small component of the formed elements, there are some rare conditions in which severe overproduction can impact viscosity as well.

Vessel Length and Diameter

The length of a vessel is directly proportional to its resistance: the longer the vessel, the greater the resistance and the lower the flow. As with blood volume, this makes intuitive sense, since the increased surface area of the vessel will impede the flow of blood. Likewise, if the vessel is shortened, the resistance will decrease and flow will increase.

The length of our blood vessels increases throughout childhood as we grow, of course, but is unchanging in adults under normal physiological circumstances. Further, the distribution of vessels is not the same in all tissues. Adipose tissue does not have an extensive vascular supply. One pound of adipose tissue contains approximately 200 miles of vessels, whereas skeletal muscle contains more than twice that. Overall, vessels decrease in length only during loss of mass or amputation. An individual weighing 150 pounds has approximately 60,000 miles of vessels in the body. Gaining about 10 pounds adds from 2000 to 4000 miles of vessels, depending upon the nature of the gained tissue. One of the great benefits of weight reduction is the reduced stress to the heart, which does not have to overcome the resistance of as many miles of vessels.

In contrast to length, the diameter of blood vessels changes throughout the body, according to the type of vessel, as we discussed earlier. The diameter of any given vessel may also change frequently throughout the day in response to neural and chemical signals that trigger vasodilation and vasoconstriction. The **vascular tone** of the vessel is the contractile state of the smooth muscle and the primary determinant of diameter, and thus of resistance and flow. The effect of vessel diameter on resistance is inverse: Given the same volume of blood, an increased diameter means there is less blood contacting the vessel wall, thus lower friction and lower resistance, subsequently increasing flow. A decreased diameter means more of the blood contacts the vessel wall, and resistance increases, subsequently decreasing flow.

The influence of lumen diameter on resistance is dramatic: A slight increase or decrease in diameter causes a huge decrease or increase in resistance. This is because resistance is inversely proportional to the radius of the blood vessel (one-half of the vessel's diameter) raised to the fourth power ($R = 1/r^4$). This means, for example, that if an artery or arteriole constricts to one-half of its original radius, the resistance to flow will increase 16 times. And if an artery or arteriole dilates to twice its initial radius, then resistance in the vessel will decrease to 1/16 of its original value and flow will increase 16 times.

The Roles of Vessel Diameter and Total Area in Blood Flow and Blood Pressure

Recall that we classified arterioles as resistance vessels, because given their small lumen, they dramatically slow the flow of blood from arteries. In fact, arterioles are the site of greatest resistance in the entire vascular network. This may seem surprising, given that capillaries have a smaller size. How can this phenomenon be explained?

Figure 20.13 compares vessel diameter, total cross-sectional area, average blood pressure, and blood velocity through the systemic vessels. Notice in parts (a) and (b) that the total cross-sectional area of the body's capillary beds is far greater than any other type of vessel. Although the diameter of an individual capillary is significantly smaller than the diameter of an arteriole, there are vastly more capillaries in the body than there are other types of blood vessels. Part (c) shows that blood pressure drops unevenly as blood travels from arteries to arterioles, capillaries, venules, and veins, and encounters greater resistance. However, the site of the most precipitous drop, and the site of greatest resistance, is the arterioles. This explains why vasodilation and vasoconstriction of arterioles play more significant roles in regulating blood pressure than do the vasodilation and vasoconstriction of other vessels.

Part (d) shows that the velocity (speed) of blood flow decreases dramatically as the blood moves from arteries to arterioles to capillaries. This slow flow rate allows more time for exchange processes to occur. As blood flows through the veins, the rate of velocity increases, as blood is returned to the heart.

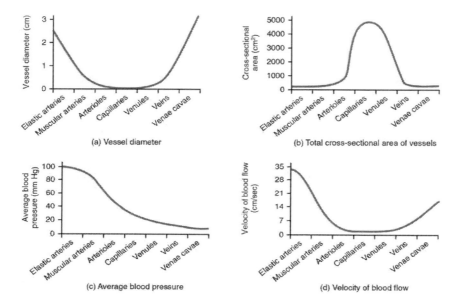

Figure 20.13 Relationships among Vessels in the Systemic Circuit The relationships among blood vessels that can be compared include (a) vessel diameter, (b) total cross-sectional area, (c) average blood pressure, and (d) velocity of blood flow.

Cardiovascular System: Arteriosclerosis

Compliance allows an artery to expand when blood is pumped through it from the heart, and then to recoil after the surge has passed. This helps promote blood flow. In arteriosclerosis, compliance is reduced, and pressure and resistance within the vessel increase. This is a leading cause of hypertension and coronary heart disease, as it causes the heart to work harder to generate a pressure great enough to overcome the resistance.

Arteriosclerosis begins with injury to the endothelium of an artery, which may be caused by irritation from high blood glucose, infection, tobacco use, excessive blood lipids, and other factors. Artery walls that are constantly stressed by blood flowing at high pressure are also more likely to be injured—which means that hypertension can promote arteriosclerosis, as well as result from it.

Recall that tissue injury causes inflammation. As inflammation spreads into the artery wall, it weakens and scars it, leaving it stiff (sclerotic). As a result, compliance is reduced. Moreover, circulating triglycerides and cholesterol can seep between the damaged lining cells and become trapped within the artery wall, where they are frequently joined by leukocytes, calcium, and cellular debris. Eventually, this buildup, called plaque, can narrow arteries enough to impair blood flow. The term for this condition, atherosclerosis (athero- = "porridge") describes the mealy deposits (Figure 20.14).

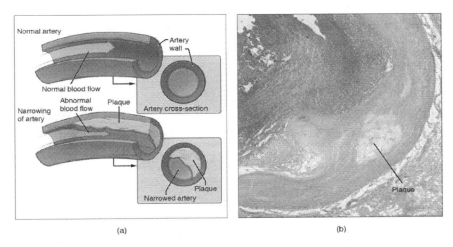

Figure 20.14 Atherosclerosis (a) Atherosclerosis can result from plaques formed by the buildup of fatty, calcified deposits in an artery. (b) Plaques can also take other forms, as shown in this micrograph of a coronary artery that has a buildup of connective tissue within the artery wall. LM × 40. (Micrograph provided by the Regents of University of Michigan Medical School © 2012)

Sometimes a plaque can rupture, causing microscopic tears in the artery wall that allow blood to leak into the tissue on the other side. When this happens, platelets rush to the site to clot the blood. This clot can further obstruct the artery and—if it occurs in a coronary or cerebral artery—cause a sudden heart attack or stroke. Alternatively, plaque can break off and travel through the bloodstream as an embolus until it blocks a more distant, smaller artery.

Even without total blockage, vessel narrowing leads to ischemia—reduced blood flow—to the tissue region "downstream" of the narrowed vessel. Ischemia in turn leads to hypoxia—decreased supply of oxygen to the tissues. Hypoxia involving cardiac muscle or brain tissue can lead to cell death and severe impairment of brain or heart function.

A major risk factor for both arteriosclerosis and atherosclerosis is advanced age, as the conditions tend to progress over time. Arteriosclerosis is normally defined as the more generalized loss of compliance, "hardening of the arteries," whereas atherosclerosis is a more specific term for the build-up of plaque in the walls of the vessel and is a specific type of arteriosclerosis. There is also a distinct genetic component, and pre-existing hypertension and/or diabetes also greatly increase the risk. However, obesity, poor nutrition, lack of physical activity, and tobacco use all are major risk factors.

Treatment includes lifestyle changes, such as weight loss, smoking cessation, regular exercise, and adoption of a diet low in sodium and saturated fats. Medications to reduce cholesterol and blood pressure may be prescribed. For blocked coronary arteries, surgery is warranted. In angioplasty, a catheter is inserted into the vessel at the point of narrowing, and a second catheter with a balloon-like tip is inflated to widen the opening. To prevent subsequent collapse of the vessel, a small mesh tube called a stent is often inserted. In an endarterectomy, plaque is surgically removed from the walls of a vessel. This operation is typically performed on the carotid arteries of the neck, which are a prime source of oxygenated blood for the brain. In a coronary bypass procedure, a non-vital superficial vessel from another part of the body (often the great saphenous vein) or a synthetic vessel is inserted to create a path around the blocked area of a coronary artery.

Venous System

The pumping action of the heart propels the blood into the arteries, from an area of higher pressure toward an area of lower pressure. If blood is to flow from the veins back into the heart, the pressure in the veins must be greater than the pressure in the atria of the heart. Two factors help maintain this pressure gradient between the veins and the heart. First, the pressure in the atria during diastole is very low, often approaching zero when the atria are relaxed (atrial diastole). Second, two physiologic "pumps" increase pressure in the venous system. The use of the term "pump" implies a physical device that speeds flow. These physiological pumps are less obvious.

Skeletal Muscle Pump

In many body regions, the pressure within the veins can be increased by the contraction of the surrounding skeletal muscle. This mechanism, known as the **skeletal muscle pump** (Figure 20.15), helps the lower-pressure veins counteract the force of gravity, increasing pressure to move blood back to the heart. As leg muscles contract, for example during walking or running, they exert pressure on nearby veins with their numerous one-way valves. This increased pressure causes blood to flow upward, opening valves superior to the contracting muscles so blood flows through. Simultaneously, valves inferior to the contracting muscles close; thus, blood should not seep back downward toward the feet. Military recruits are trained to flex their legs slightly while standing at attention for prolonged periods. Failure to do so may allow blood to pool in the lower limbs rather than returning to the heart. Consequently, the brain will not receive enough oxygenated blood, and the individual may lose consciousness.

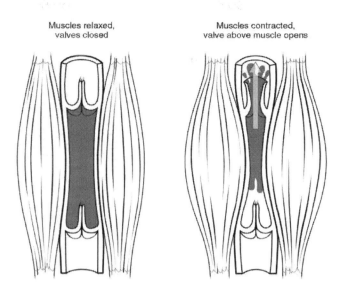

Figure 20.15 Skeletal Muscle Pump The contraction of skeletal muscles surrounding a vein compresses the blood and increases the pressure in that area. This action forces blood closer to the heart where venous pressure is lower. Note the importance of the one-way valves to assure that blood flows only in the proper direction.

Respiratory Pump

The **respiratory pump** aids blood flow through the veins of the thorax and abdomen. During inhalation, the volume of the thorax increases, largely through the contraction of the diaphragm, which moves downward and compresses the abdominal cavity. The elevation of the chest caused by the contraction of the external intercostal muscles also contributes to the increased volume of the thorax. The volume increase causes air pressure within the thorax to decrease, allowing us to inhale. Additionally, as air pressure within the thorax drops, blood pressure in the thoracic veins also decreases, falling below the pressure in the abdominal veins. This causes blood to flow along its pressure gradient from veins outside the thorax, where pressure is higher, into the thoracic region, where pressure is now lower. This in turn promotes the return of blood from the thoracic veins to the atria. During exhalation, when air pressure increases within the thoracic cavity, pressure in the thoracic veins increases, speeding blood flow into the heart while valves in the veins prevent blood from flowing backward from the thoracic and abdominal veins.

Pressure Relationships in the Venous System

Although vessel diameter increases from the smaller venules to the larger veins and eventually to the venae cavae (singular = vena cava), the total cross-sectional area actually decreases (see Figure 20.15a and b). The individual veins are larger in diameter than the venules, but their total number is much lower, so their total cross-sectional area is also lower.

Also notice that, as blood moves from venules to veins, the average blood pressure drops (see Figure 20.15c), but the blood velocity actually increases (see Figure 20.15). This pressure gradient drives blood back toward the heart. Again, the presence of one-way valves and the skeletal muscle and respiratory pumps contribute to this increased flow. Since approximately 64 percent of the total blood volume resides in systemic veins, any action that increases the flow of blood through the veins will increase venous return to the heart. Maintaining vascular tone within the veins prevents the veins from merely distending, dampening the flow of blood, and as you will see, vasoconstriction actually enhances the flow.

The Role of Venoconstriction in Resistance, Blood Pressure, and Flow

As previously discussed, vasoconstriction of an artery or arteriole decreases the radius, increasing resistance and pressure, but decreasing flow. Venoconstriction, on the other hand, has a very different outcome. The walls of veins are thin but irregular; thus, when the smooth muscle in those walls constricts, the lumen becomes more rounded. The more rounded the lumen, the less surface area the blood encounters, and the less resistance the vessel offers. Vasoconstriction increases pressure within a vein as it does in an artery, but in veins, the increased pressure increases flow. Recall that the pressure in the atria, into which the venous blood will flow, is very low, approaching zero for at least part of the relaxation phase of the cardiac cycle. Thus, venoconstriction increases the return of blood to the heart. Another way of stating this is that venoconstriction increases the preload or stretch of the cardiac muscle and increases contraction.

20.3 | Capillary Exchange

By the end of this section, you will be able to:
- Identify the primary mechanisms of capillary exchange
- Distinguish between capillary hydrostatic pressure and blood colloid osmotic pressure, explaining the contribution of each to net filtration pressure
- Compare filtration and reabsorption
- Explain the fate of fluid that is not reabsorbed from the tissues into the vascular capillaries

The primary purpose of the cardiovascular system is to circulate gases, nutrients, wastes, and other substances to and from the cells of the body. Small molecules, such as gases, lipids, and lipid-soluble molecules, can diffuse directly through the membranes of the endothelial cells of the capillary wall. Glucose, amino acids, and ions—including sodium, potassium, calcium, and chloride—use transporters to move through specific channels in the membrane by facilitated diffusion. Glucose, ions, and larger molecules may also leave the blood through intercellular clefts. Larger molecules can pass through the pores of fenestrated capillaries, and even large plasma proteins can pass through the great gaps in the sinusoids. Some large proteins in blood plasma can move into and out of the endothelial cells packaged within vesicles by endocytosis and exocytosis. Water moves by osmosis.

Bulk Flow

The mass movement of fluids into and out of capillary beds requires a transport mechanism far more efficient than mere diffusion. This movement, often referred to as bulk flow, involves two pressure-driven mechanisms: Volumes of fluid move from an area of higher pressure in a capillary bed to an area of lower pressure in the tissues via **filtration**. In contrast, the movement of fluid from an area of higher pressure in the tissues into an area of lower pressure in the capillaries is **reabsorption**. Two types of pressure interact to drive each of these movements: hydrostatic pressure and osmotic pressure.

Hydrostatic Pressure

The primary force driving fluid transport between the capillaries and tissues is hydrostatic pressure, which can be defined as the pressure of any fluid enclosed in a space. **Blood hydrostatic pressure** is the force exerted by the blood confined within blood vessels or heart chambers. Even more specifically, the pressure exerted by blood against the wall of a capillary is called **capillary hydrostatic pressure (CHP)**, and is the same as capillary blood pressure. CHP is the force that drives fluid out of capillaries and into the tissues.

As fluid exits a capillary and moves into tissues, the hydrostatic pressure in the interstitial fluid correspondingly rises. This opposing hydrostatic pressure is called the **interstitial fluid hydrostatic pressure (IFHP)**. Generally, the CHP originating from the arterial pathways is considerably higher than the IFHP, because lymphatic vessels are continually absorbing excess fluid from the tissues. Thus, fluid generally moves out of the capillary and into the interstitial fluid. This process is called filtration.

Osmotic Pressure

The net pressure that drives reabsorption—the movement of fluid from the interstitial fluid back into the capillaries—is called osmotic pressure (sometimes referred to as oncotic pressure). Whereas hydrostatic pressure forces fluid out of the capillary, osmotic pressure draws fluid back in. Osmotic pressure is determined by osmotic concentration gradients, that is, the difference in the solute-to-water concentrations in the blood and tissue fluid. A region higher in solute concentration (and lower in water concentration) draws water across a semipermeable membrane from a region higher in water concentration (and lower in solute concentration).

As we discuss osmotic pressure in blood and tissue fluid, it is important to recognize that the formed elements of blood do not contribute to osmotic concentration gradients. Rather, it is the plasma proteins that play the key role. Solutes also move across the capillary wall according to their concentration gradient, but overall, the concentrations should be similar and not have a significant impact on osmosis. Because of their large size and chemical structure, plasma proteins are not truly solutes, that is, they do not dissolve but are dispersed or suspended in their fluid medium, forming a colloid rather than a solution.

The pressure created by the concentration of colloidal proteins in the blood is called the **blood colloidal osmotic pressure (BCOP)**. Its effect on capillary exchange accounts for the reabsorption of water. The plasma proteins suspended in blood cannot move across the semipermeable capillary cell membrane, and so they remain in the plasma. As a result, blood has a higher colloidal concentration and lower water concentration than tissue fluid. It therefore attracts water. We can also say that the BCOP is higher than the **interstitial fluid colloidal osmotic pressure (IFCOP)**, which is always very low because interstitial fluid contains few proteins. Thus, water is drawn from the tissue fluid back into the capillary, carrying dissolved molecules with it. This difference in colloidal osmotic pressure accounts for reabsorption.

Interaction of Hydrostatic and Osmotic Pressures

The normal unit used to express pressures within the cardiovascular system is millimeters of mercury (mm Hg). When blood leaving an arteriole first enters a capillary bed, the CHP is quite high—about 35 mm Hg. Gradually, this initial CHP declines as the blood moves through the capillary so that by the time the blood has reached the venous end, the CHP has dropped to approximately 18 mm Hg. In comparison, the plasma proteins remain suspended in the blood, so the BCOP remains fairly constant at about 25 mm Hg throughout the length of the capillary and considerably below the osmotic pressure in the interstitial fluid.

The **net filtration pressure (NFP)** represents the interaction of the hydrostatic and osmotic pressures, driving fluid out of the capillary. It is equal to the difference between the CHP and the BCOP. Since filtration is, by definition, the movement of fluid out of the capillary, when reabsorption is occurring, the NFP is a negative number.

NFP changes at different points in a capillary bed (Figure 20.16). Close to the arterial end of the capillary, it is approximately 10 mm Hg, because the CHP of 35 mm Hg minus the BCOP of 25 mm Hg equals 10 mm Hg. Recall that the hydrostatic and osmotic pressures of the interstitial fluid are essentially negligible. Thus, the NFP of 10 mm Hg drives a net movement of fluid out of the capillary at the arterial end. At approximately the middle of the capillary, the CHP is about the same as the BCOP of 25 mm Hg, so the NFP drops to zero. At this point, there is no net change of volume: Fluid moves out of the capillary at the same rate as it moves into the capillary. Near the venous end of the capillary, the CHP has dwindled to about 18 mm Hg due to loss of fluid. Because the BCOP remains steady at 25 mm Hg, water is drawn into the capillary, that is, reabsorption occurs. Another way of expressing this is to say that at the venous end of the capillary, there is an NFP of −7 mm Hg.

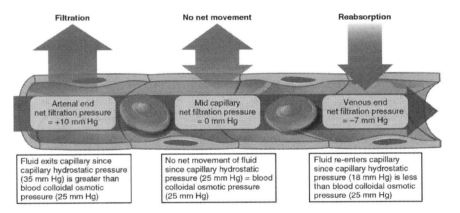

Figure 20.16 Capillary Exchange Net filtration occurs near the arterial end of the capillary since capillary hydrostatic pressure (CHP) is greater than blood colloidal osmotic pressure (BCOP). There is no net movement of fluid near the midpoint since CHP = BCOP. Net reabsorption occurs near the venous end since BCOP is greater than CHP.

The Role of Lymphatic Capillaries

Since overall CHP is higher than BCOP, it is inevitable that more net fluid will exit the capillary through filtration at the arterial end than enters through reabsorption at the venous end. Considering all capillaries over the course of a day, this can be quite a substantial amount of fluid: Approximately 24 liters per day are filtered, whereas 20.4 liters are reabsorbed. This excess fluid is picked up by capillaries of the lymphatic system. These extremely thin-walled vessels have copious numbers of valves that ensure unidirectional flow through ever-larger lymphatic vessels that eventually drain into the subclavian veins in the neck. An important function of the lymphatic system is to return the fluid (lymph) to the blood. Lymph may be thought of as recycled blood plasma. (Seek additional content for more detail on the lymphatic system.)

Watch this video (http://openstaxcollege.org/l/capillaryfunct) to explore capillaries and how they function in the body. Capillaries are never more than 100 micrometers away. What is the main component of interstitial fluid?

20.4 | Homeostatic Regulation of the Vascular System

By the end of this section, you will be able to:
- Discuss the mechanisms involved in the neural regulation of vascular homeostasis
- Describe the contribution of a variety of hormones to the renal regulation of blood pressure
- Identify the effects of exercise on vascular homeostasis
- Discuss how hypertension, hemorrhage, and circulatory shock affect vascular health

In order to maintain homeostasis in the cardiovascular system and provide adequate blood to the tissues, blood flow must be redirected continually to the tissues as they become more active. In a very real sense, the cardiovascular system engages in resource allocation, because there is not enough blood flow to distribute blood equally to all tissues simultaneously. For example, when an individual is exercising, more blood will be directed to skeletal muscles, the heart, and the lungs. Following a meal, more blood is directed to the digestive system. Only the brain receives a more or less constant supply of blood whether you are active, resting, thinking, or engaged in any other activity.

Table 20.3 provides the distribution of systemic blood at rest and during exercise. Although most of the data appears logical, the values for the distribution of blood to the integument may seem surprising. During exercise, the body distributes more blood to the body surface where it can dissipate the excess heat generated by increased activity into the environment.

Systemic Blood Flow During Rest, Mild Exercise, and Maximal Exercise in a Healthy Young Individual

Organ	Resting (mL/min)	Mild exercise (mL/min)	Maximal exercise (mL/min)
Skeletal muscle	1200	4500	12,500
Heart	250	350	750
Brain	750	750	750
Integument	500	1500	1900
Kidney	1100	900	600
Gastrointestinal	1400	1100	600
Others (i.e., liver, spleen)	600	400	400

Table 20.3

Systemic Blood Flow During Rest, Mild Exercise, and Maximal Exercise in a Healthy Young Individual

Organ	Resting (mL/min)	Mild exercise (mL/min)	Maximal exercise (mL/min)
Total	5800	9500	17,500

Table 20.3

Three homeostatic mechanisms ensure adequate blood flow, blood pressure, distribution, and ultimately perfusion: neural, endocrine, and autoregulatory mechanisms. They are summarized in Figure 20.17.

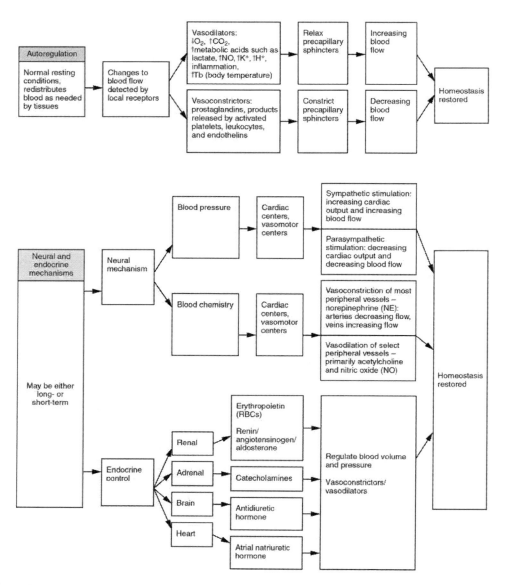

Figure 20.17 Summary of Factors Maintaining Vascular Homeostasis Adequate blood flow, blood pressure, distribution, and perfusion involve autoregulatory, neural, and endocrine mechanisms.

Neural Regulation

The nervous system plays a critical role in the regulation of vascular homeostasis. The primary regulatory sites include the cardiovascular centers in the brain that control both cardiac and vascular functions. In addition, more generalized neural responses from the limbic system and the autonomic nervous system are factors.

The Cardiovascular Centers in the Brain

Neurological regulation of blood pressure and flow depends on the cardiovascular centers located in the medulla oblongata. This cluster of neurons responds to changes in blood pressure as well as blood concentrations of oxygen, carbon dioxide, and hydrogen ions. The cardiovascular center contains three distinct paired components:

- The cardioaccelerator centers stimulate cardiac function by regulating heart rate and stroke volume via sympathetic stimulation from the cardiac accelerator nerve.
- The cardioinhibitor centers slow cardiac function by decreasing heart rate and stroke volume via parasympathetic stimulation from the vagus nerve.
- The vasomotor centers control vessel tone or contraction of the smooth muscle in the tunica media. Changes in diameter affect peripheral resistance, pressure, and flow, which affect cardiac output. The majority of these neurons act via the release of the neurotransmitter norepinephrine from sympathetic neurons.

Although each center functions independently, they are not anatomically distinct.

There is also a small population of neurons that control vasodilation in the vessels of the brain and skeletal muscles by relaxing the smooth muscle fibers in the vessel tunics. Many of these are cholinergic neurons, that is, they release acetylcholine, which in turn stimulates the vessels' endothelial cells to release nitric oxide (NO), which causes vasodilation. Others release norepinephrine that binds to β_2 receptors. A few neurons release NO directly as a neurotransmitter.

Recall that mild stimulation of the skeletal muscles maintains muscle tone. A similar phenomenon occurs with vascular tone in vessels. As noted earlier, arterioles are normally partially constricted: With maximal stimulation, their radius may be reduced to one-half of the resting state. Full dilation of most arterioles requires that this sympathetic stimulation be suppressed. When it is, an arteriole can expand by as much as 150 percent. Such a significant increase can dramatically affect resistance, pressure, and flow.

Baroreceptor Reflexes

Baroreceptors are specialized stretch receptors located within thin areas of blood vessels and heart chambers that respond to the degree of stretch caused by the presence of blood. They send impulses to the cardiovascular center to regulate blood pressure. Vascular baroreceptors are found primarily in sinuses (small cavities) within the aorta and carotid arteries: The **aortic sinuses** are found in the walls of the ascending aorta just superior to the aortic valve, whereas the **carotid sinuses** are in the base of the internal carotid arteries. There are also low-pressure baroreceptors located in the walls of the venae cavae and right atrium.

When blood pressure increases, the baroreceptors are stretched more tightly and initiate action potentials at a higher rate. At lower blood pressures, the degree of stretch is lower and the rate of firing is slower. When the cardiovascular center in the medulla oblongata receives this input, it triggers a reflex that maintains homeostasis (Figure 20.18):

- When blood pressure rises too high, the baroreceptors fire at a higher rate and trigger parasympathetic stimulation of the heart. As a result, cardiac output falls. Sympathetic stimulation of the peripheral arterioles will also decrease, resulting in vasodilation. Combined, these activities cause blood pressure to fall.
- When blood pressure drops too low, the rate of baroreceptor firing decreases. This will trigger an increase in sympathetic stimulation of the heart, causing cardiac output to increase. It will also trigger sympathetic stimulation of the peripheral vessels, resulting in vasoconstriction. Combined, these activities cause blood pressure to rise.

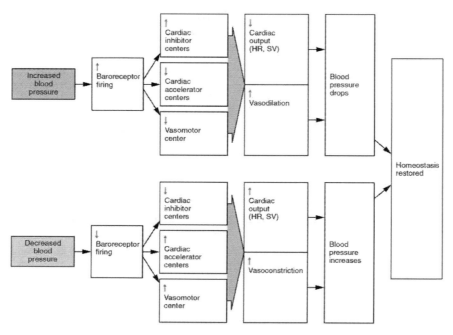

Figure 20.18 Baroreceptor Reflexes for Maintaining Vascular Homeostasis   Increased blood pressure results in increased rates of baroreceptor firing, whereas decreased blood pressure results in slower rates of fire, both initiating the homeostatic mechanism to restore blood pressure.

The baroreceptors in the venae cavae and right atrium monitor blood pressure as the blood returns to the heart from the systemic circulation. Normally, blood flow into the aorta is the same as blood flow back into the right atrium. If blood is returning to the right atrium more rapidly than it is being ejected from the left ventricle, the atrial receptors will stimulate the cardiovascular centers to increase sympathetic firing and increase cardiac output until homeostasis is achieved. The opposite is also true. This mechanism is referred to as the **atrial reflex**.

Chemoreceptor Reflexes

In addition to the baroreceptors are chemoreceptors that monitor levels of oxygen, carbon dioxide, and hydrogen ions (pH), and thereby contribute to vascular homeostasis. Chemoreceptors monitoring the blood are located in close proximity to the baroreceptors in the aortic and carotid sinuses. They signal the cardiovascular center as well as the respiratory centers in the medulla oblongata.

Since tissues consume oxygen and produce carbon dioxide and acids as waste products, when the body is more active, oxygen levels fall and carbon dioxide levels rise as cells undergo cellular respiration to meet the energy needs of activities. This causes more hydrogen ions to be produced, causing the blood pH to drop. When the body is resting, oxygen levels are higher, carbon dioxide levels are lower, more hydrogen is bound, and pH rises. (Seek additional content for more detail about pH.)

The chemoreceptors respond to increasing carbon dioxide and hydrogen ion levels (falling pH) by stimulating the cardioaccelerator and vasomotor centers, increasing cardiac output and constricting peripheral vessels. The cardioinhibitor centers are suppressed. With falling carbon dioxide and hydrogen ion levels (increasing pH), the cardioinhibitor centers are stimulated, and the cardioaccelerator and vasomotor centers are suppressed, decreasing cardiac output and causing peripheral vasodilation. In order to maintain adequate supplies of oxygen to the cells and remove waste products such as carbon dioxide, it is essential that the respiratory system respond to changing metabolic demands. In turn, the cardiovascular system will transport these gases to the lungs for exchange, again in accordance with metabolic demands. This interrelationship of cardiovascular and respiratory control cannot be overemphasized.

Other neural mechanisms can also have a significant impact on cardiovascular function. These include the limbic system that links physiological responses to psychological stimuli, as well as generalized sympathetic and parasympathetic stimulation.

Endocrine Regulation

Endocrine control over the cardiovascular system involves the catecholamines, epinephrine and norepinephrine, as well as several hormones that interact with the kidneys in the regulation of blood volume.

Epinephrine and Norepinephrine

The catecholamines epinephrine and norepinephrine are released by the adrenal medulla, and enhance and extend the body's sympathetic or "fight-or-flight" response (see Figure 20.17). They increase heart rate and force of contraction, while temporarily constricting blood vessels to organs not essential for flight-or-fight responses and redirecting blood flow to the liver, muscles, and heart.

Antidiuretic Hormone

Antidiuretic hormone (ADH), also known as vasopressin, is secreted by the cells in the hypothalamus and transported via the hypothalamic-hypophyseal tracts to the posterior pituitary where it is stored until released upon nervous stimulation. The primary trigger prompting the hypothalamus to release ADH is increasing osmolarity of tissue fluid, usually in response to significant loss of blood volume. ADH signals its target cells in the kidneys to reabsorb more water, thus preventing the loss of additional fluid in the urine. This will increase overall fluid levels and help restore blood volume and pressure. In addition, ADH constricts peripheral vessels.

Renin-Angiotensin-Aldosterone Mechanism

The renin-angiotensin-aldosterone mechanism has a major effect upon the cardiovascular system (Figure 20.19). Renin is an enzyme, although because of its importance in the renin-angiotensin-aldosterone pathway, some sources identify it as a hormone. Specialized cells in the kidneys found in the juxtaglomerular apparatus respond to decreased blood flow by secreting renin into the blood. Renin converts the plasma protein angiotensinogen, which is produced by the liver, into its active form—angiotensin I. Angiotensin I circulates in the blood and is then converted into angiotensin II in the lungs. This reaction is catalyzed by the enzyme angiotensin-converting enzyme (ACE).

Angiotensin II is a powerful vasoconstrictor, greatly increasing blood pressure. It also stimulates the release of ADH and aldosterone, a hormone produced by the adrenal cortex. Aldosterone increases the reabsorption of sodium into the blood by the kidneys. Since water follows sodium, this increases the reabsorption of water. This in turn increases blood volume, raising blood pressure. Angiotensin II also stimulates the thirst center in the hypothalamus, so an individual will likely consume more fluids, again increasing blood volume and pressure.

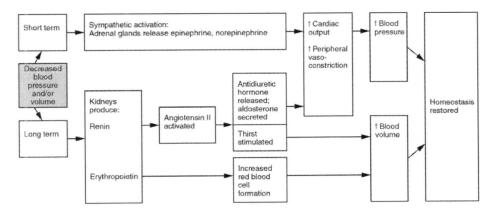

Figure 20.19 Hormones Involved in Renal Control of Blood Pressure In the renin-angiotensin-aldosterone mechanism, increasing angiotensin II will stimulate the production of antidiuretic hormone and aldosterone. In addition to renin, the kidneys produce erythropoietin, which stimulates the production of red blood cells, further increasing blood volume.

Erythropoietin

Erythropoietin (EPO) is released by the kidneys when blood flow and/or oxygen levels decrease. EPO stimulates the production of erythrocytes within the bone marrow. Erythrocytes are the major formed element of the blood and may contribute 40 percent or more to blood volume, a significant factor of viscosity, resistance, pressure, and flow. In addition, EPO is a vasoconstrictor. Overproduction of EPO or excessive intake of synthetic EPO, often to enhance athletic performance, will increase viscosity, resistance, and pressure, and decrease flow in addition to its contribution as a vasoconstrictor.

Atrial Natriuretic Hormone

Secreted by cells in the atria of the heart, atrial natriuretic hormone (ANH) (also known as atrial natriuretic peptide) is secreted when blood volume is high enough to cause extreme stretching of the cardiac cells. Cells in the ventricle produce a hormone with similar effects, called B-type natriuretic hormone. Natriuretic hormones are antagonists to angiotensin II. They promote loss of sodium and water from the kidneys, and suppress renin, aldosterone, and ADH production and release. All of these actions promote loss of fluid from the body, so blood volume and blood pressure drop.

Autoregulation of Perfusion

As the name would suggest, autoregulation mechanisms require neither specialized nervous stimulation nor endocrine control. Rather, these are local, self-regulatory mechanisms that allow each region of tissue to adjust its blood flow—and thus its perfusion. These local mechanisms include chemical signals and myogenic controls.

Chemical Signals Involved in Autoregulation

Chemical signals work at the level of the precapillary sphincters to trigger either constriction or relaxation. As you know, opening a precapillary sphincter allows blood to flow into that particular capillary, whereas constricting a precapillary sphincter temporarily shuts off blood flow to that region. The factors involved in regulating the precapillary sphincters include the following:

- Opening of the sphincter is triggered in response to decreased oxygen concentrations; increased carbon dioxide concentrations; increasing levels of lactic acid or other byproducts of cellular metabolism; increasing concentrations of potassium ions or hydrogen ions (falling pH); inflammatory chemicals such as histamines; and increased body temperature. These conditions in turn stimulate the release of NO, a powerful vasodilator, from endothelial cells (see Figure 20.17).

- Contraction of the precapillary sphincter is triggered by the opposite levels of the regulators, which prompt the release of endothelins, powerful vasoconstricting peptides secreted by endothelial cells. Platelet secretions and certain prostaglandins may also trigger constriction.

Again, these factors alter tissue perfusion via their effects on the precapillary sphincter mechanism, which regulates blood flow to capillaries. Since the amount of blood is limited, not all capillaries can fill at once, so blood flow is allocated based upon the needs and metabolic state of the tissues as reflected in these parameters. Bear in mind, however, that dilation and constriction of the arterioles feeding the capillary beds is the primary control mechanism.

The Myogenic Response

The **myogenic response** is a reaction to the stretching of the smooth muscle in the walls of arterioles as changes in blood flow occur through the vessel. This may be viewed as a largely protective function against dramatic fluctuations in blood pressure and blood flow to maintain homeostasis. If perfusion of an organ is too low (ischemia), the tissue will experience low levels of oxygen (hypoxia). In contrast, excessive perfusion could damage the organ's smaller and more fragile vessels. The myogenic response is a localized process that serves to stabilize blood flow in the capillary network that follows that arteriole.

When blood flow is low, the vessel's smooth muscle will be only minimally stretched. In response, it relaxes, allowing the vessel to dilate and thereby increase the movement of blood into the tissue. When blood flow is too high, the smooth muscle will contract in response to the increased stretch, prompting vasoconstriction that reduces blood flow.

Figure 20.20 summarizes the effects of nervous, endocrine, and local controls on arterioles.

Control	Factor	Vasoconstriction	Vasodilation
Neural	Sympathetic stimulation	Arterioles within integument, abdominal viscera, and mucosa membrane; skeletal muscle (at high levels); varied in veins and venules	Arterioles within heart; skeletal muscles at low to moderate levels
	Parasympathetic	No known innervation for most	Arterioles in external genitalia, no known innervation for most other arterioles or veins
Endocrine	Epinephrine	Similar to sympathetic stimulation for extended flight-or-fight responses; at high levels, binds to specialized alpha (α) receptors	Similar to sympathetic stimulation for extended flight-or-fight responses; at low to moderate levels, binds to specialized beta (β) receptors
	Norepinephrine	Similar to epinephrine	Similar to epinephrine
	Angiotensin II	Powerful generalized vasoconstrictor; also stimulates release of aldosterone and ADH	n/a
	ANH (peptide)	n/a	Powerful generalized vasodilator; also promotes loss of fluid volume from kidneys, hence reducing blood volume, pressure, and flow
	ADH	Moderately strong generalized vasoconstrictor; also causes body to retain more fluid via kidneys, increasing blood volume and pressure	n/a
Other factors	Decreasing levels of oxygen	n/a	Vasodilation, also opens precapillary sphincters
	Decreasing pH	n/a	Vasodilation, also opens precapillary sphincters
	Increasing levels of carbon dioxide	n/a	Vasodilation, also opens precapillary sphincters
	Increasing levels of potassium ion	n/a	Vasodilation, also opens precapillary sphincters
	Increasing levels of prostaglandins	Vasoconstriction, closes precapillary sphincters for many	Vasodilation, opens precapillary sphincters for many
	Increasing levels of adenosine	n/a	Vasodilation
	Increasing levels of NO	n/a	Vasodilation, also opens precapillary sphincters
	Increasing levels of lactic acid and other metabolites	n/a	Vasodilation, also opens precapillary sphincters
	Increasing levels of endothelins	Vasoconstriction	n/a
	Increasing levels of platelet secretions	Vasoconstriction	n/a
	Increasing hyperthermia	n/a	Vasodilation
	Stretching of vascular wall (myogenic)	Vasoconstriction	n/a
	Increasing levels of histamines from basophils and mast cells	n/a	Vasodilation

Figure 20.20 Summary of Mechanisms Regulating Arteriole Smooth Muscle and Veins

Effect of Exercise on Vascular Homeostasis

The heart is a muscle and, like any muscle, it responds dramatically to exercise. For a healthy young adult, cardiac output (heart rate × stroke volume) increases in the nonathlete from approximately 5.0 liters (5.25 quarts) per minute to a maximum of about 20 liters (21 quarts) per minute. Accompanying this will be an increase in blood pressure from about 120/80 to 185/75. However, well-trained aerobic athletes can increase these values substantially. For these individuals, cardiac output soars from approximately 5.3 liters (5.57 quarts) per minute resting to more than 30 liters (31.5 quarts) per minute during maximal exercise. Along with this increase in cardiac output, blood pressure increases from 120/80 at rest to 200/90 at maximum values.

In addition to improved cardiac function, exercise increases the size and mass of the heart. The average weight of the heart for the nonathlete is about 300 g, whereas in an athlete it will increase to 500 g. This increase in size generally makes the heart stronger and more efficient at pumping blood, increasing both stroke volume and cardiac output.

Tissue perfusion also increases as the body transitions from a resting state to light exercise and eventually to heavy exercise (see Figure 20.20). These changes result in selective vasodilation in the skeletal muscles, heart, lungs, liver, and integument. Simultaneously, vasoconstriction occurs in the vessels leading to the kidneys and most of the digestive and reproductive organs. The flow of blood to the brain remains largely unchanged whether at rest or exercising, since the vessels in the brain largely do not respond to regulatory stimuli, in most cases, because they lack the appropriate receptors.

As vasodilation occurs in selected vessels, resistance drops and more blood rushes into the organs they supply. This blood eventually returns to the venous system. Venous return is further enhanced by both the skeletal muscle and respiratory pumps. As blood returns to the heart more quickly, preload rises and the Frank-Starling principle tells us that contraction of the cardiac muscle in the atria and ventricles will be more forceful. Eventually, even the best-trained athletes will fatigue and must undergo a period of rest following exercise. Cardiac output and distribution of blood then return to normal.

Regular exercise promotes cardiovascular health in a variety of ways. Because an athlete's heart is larger than a nonathlete's, stroke volume increases, so the athletic heart can deliver the same amount of blood as the nonathletic heart but with a lower heart rate. This increased efficiency allows the athlete to exercise for longer periods of time before muscles fatigue and places less stress on the heart. Exercise also lowers overall cholesterol levels by removing from the circulation a complex form of cholesterol, triglycerides, and proteins known as low-density lipoproteins (LDLs), which are widely associated with increased risk of cardiovascular disease. Although there is no way to remove deposits of plaque from the walls of arteries other than specialized surgery, exercise does promote the health of vessels by decreasing the rate of plaque formation and reducing blood pressure, so the heart does not have to generate as much force to overcome resistance.

Generally as little as 30 minutes of noncontinuous exercise over the course of each day has beneficial effects and has been shown to lower the rate of heart attack by nearly 50 percent. While it is always advisable to follow a healthy diet, stop smoking, and lose weight, studies have clearly shown that fit, overweight people may actually be healthier overall than sedentary slender people. Thus, the benefits of moderate exercise are undeniable.

Clinical Considerations in Vascular Homeostasis

Any disorder that affects blood volume, vascular tone, or any other aspect of vascular functioning is likely to affect vascular homeostasis as well. That includes hypertension, hemorrhage, and shock.

Hypertension and Hypotension

Chronically elevated blood pressure is known clinically as **hypertension**. It is defined as chronic and persistent blood pressure measurements of 140/90 mm Hg or above. Pressures between 120/80 and 140/90 mm Hg are defined as prehypertension. About 68 million Americans currently suffer from hypertension. Unfortunately, hypertension is typically a silent disorder; therefore, hypertensive patients may fail to recognize the seriousness of their condition and fail to follow their treatment plan. The result is often a heart attack or stroke. Hypertension may also lead to an aneurism (ballooning of a blood vessel caused by a weakening of the wall), peripheral arterial disease (obstruction of vessels in peripheral regions of the body), chronic kidney disease, or heart failure.

Listen to this CDC podcast (http://openstaxcollege.org/l/CDCpodcast) to learn about hypertension, often described as a "silent killer." What steps can you take to reduce your risk of a heart attack or stroke?

Hemorrhage

Minor blood loss is managed by hemostasis and repair. Hemorrhage is a loss of blood that cannot be controlled by hemostatic mechanisms. Initially, the body responds to hemorrhage by initiating mechanisms aimed at increasing blood pressure and maintaining blood flow. Ultimately, however, blood volume will need to be restored, either through physiological processes or through medical intervention.

In response to blood loss, stimuli from the baroreceptors trigger the cardiovascular centers to stimulate sympathetic responses to increase cardiac output and vasoconstriction. This typically prompts the heart rate to increase to about 180–200 contractions per minute, restoring cardiac output to normal levels. Vasoconstriction of the arterioles increases vascular resistance, whereas constriction of the veins increases venous return to the heart. Both of these steps will help increase blood pressure. Sympathetic stimulation also triggers the release of epinephrine and norepinephrine, which enhance both cardiac output and vasoconstriction. If blood loss were less than 20 percent of total blood volume, these responses together would usually return blood pressure to normal and redirect the remaining blood to the tissues.

Additional endocrine involvement is necessary, however, to restore the lost blood volume. The angiotensin-renin-aldosterone mechanism stimulates the thirst center in the hypothalamus, which increases fluid consumption to help restore the lost blood. More importantly, it increases renal reabsorption of sodium and water, reducing water loss in urine output. The kidneys also increase the production of EPO, stimulating the formation of erythrocytes that not only deliver oxygen to the tissues but also increase overall blood volume. Figure 20.21 summarizes the responses to loss of blood volume.

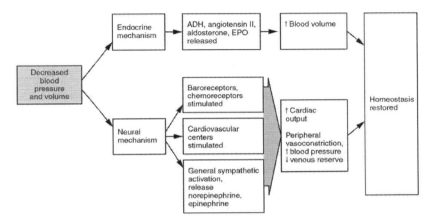

Figure 20.21 Homeostatic Responses to Loss of Blood Volume

Circulatory Shock

The loss of too much blood may lead to **circulatory shock**, a life-threatening condition in which the circulatory system is unable to maintain blood flow to adequately supply sufficient oxygen and other nutrients to the tissues to maintain cellular metabolism. It should not be confused with emotional or psychological shock. Typically, the patient in circulatory shock will demonstrate an increased heart rate but decreased blood pressure, but there are cases in which blood pressure will remain normal. Urine output will fall dramatically, and the patient may appear confused or lose consciousness. Urine output less than 1 mL/kg body weight/hour is cause for concern. Unfortunately, shock is an example of a positive-feedback loop that, if uncorrected, may lead to the death of the patient.

There are several recognized forms of shock:

- **Hypovolemic shock** in adults is typically caused by hemorrhage, although in children it may be caused by fluid losses related to severe vomiting or diarrhea. Other causes for hypovolemic shock include extensive burns, exposure to some toxins, and excessive urine loss related to diabetes insipidus or ketoacidosis. Typically, patients present with a rapid, almost tachycardic heart rate; a weak pulse often described as "thread;" cool, clammy skin, particularly in the extremities, due to restricted peripheral blood flow; rapid, shallow breathing; hypothermia; thirst; and dry mouth. Treatments generally involve providing intravenous fluids to restore the patient to normal function and various drugs such as dopamine, epinephrine, and norepinephrine to raise blood pressure.
- **Cardiogenic shock** results from the inability of the heart to maintain cardiac output. Most often, it results from a myocardial infarction (heart attack), but it may also be caused by arrhythmias, valve disorders, cardiomyopathies, cardiac failure, or simply insufficient flow of blood through the cardiac vessels. Treatment involves repairing the damage to the heart or its vessels to resolve the underlying cause, rather than treating cardiogenic shock directly.

- **Vascular shock** occurs when arterioles lose their normal muscular tone and dilate dramatically. It may arise from a variety of causes, and treatments almost always involve fluid replacement and medications, called inotropic or pressor agents, which restore tone to the muscles of the vessels. In addition, eliminating or at least alleviating the underlying cause of the condition is required. This might include antibiotics and antihistamines, or select steroids, which may aid in the repair of nerve damage. A common cause is **sepsis** (or septicemia), also called "blood poisoning," which is a widespread bacterial infection that results in an organismal-level inflammatory response known as **septic shock**. **Neurogenic shock** is a form of vascular shock that occurs with cranial or spinal injuries that damage the cardiovascular centers in the medulla oblongata or the nervous fibers originating from this region. **Anaphylactic shock** is a severe allergic response that causes the widespread release of histamines, triggering vasodilation throughout the body.

- **Obstructive shock**, as the name would suggest, occurs when a significant portion of the vascular system is blocked. It is not always recognized as a distinct condition and may be grouped with cardiogenic shock, including pulmonary embolism and cardiac tamponade. Treatments depend upon the underlying cause and, in addition to administering fluids intravenously, often include the administration of anticoagulants, removal of fluid from the pericardial cavity, or air from the thoracic cavity, and surgery as required. The most common cause is a pulmonary embolism, a clot that lodges in the pulmonary vessels and interrupts blood flow. Other causes include stenosis of the aortic valve; cardiac tamponade, in which excess fluid in the pericardial cavity interferes with the ability of the heart to fully relax and fill with blood (resulting in decreased preload); and a pneumothorax, in which an excessive amount of air is present in the thoracic cavity, outside of the lungs, which interferes with venous return, pulmonary function, and delivery of oxygen to the tissues.

20.5 | Circulatory Pathways

By the end of this section, you will be able to:

- Identify the vessels through which blood travels within the pulmonary circuit, beginning from the right ventricle of the heart and ending at the left atrium
- Create a flow chart showing the major systemic arteries through which blood travels from the aorta and its major branches, to the most significant arteries feeding into the right and left upper and lower limbs
- Create a flow chart showing the major systemic veins through which blood travels from the feet to the right atrium of the heart

Virtually every cell, tissue, organ, and system in the body is impacted by the circulatory system. This includes the generalized and more specialized functions of transport of materials, capillary exchange, maintaining health by transporting white blood cells and various immunoglobulins (antibodies), hemostasis, regulation of body temperature, and helping to maintain acid-base balance. In addition to these shared functions, many systems enjoy a unique relationship with the circulatory system. Figure 20.22 summarizes these relationships.

System	Role of Circulatory System
Digestive 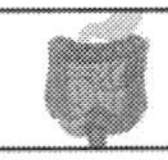	Absorbs nutrients and water; delivers nutrients (except most lipids) to liver for processing by hepatic portal vein; provides nutrients essential for hematopoiesis and building hemoglobin
Endocrine 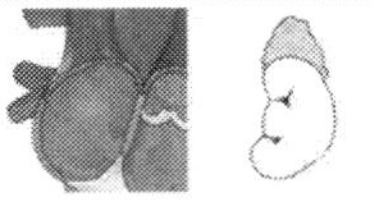	Delivers hormones: atrial natriuretic hormone (peptide) secreted by the heart atrial cells to help regulate blood volumes and pressures; epinephrine, ANH, angiotensin II, ADH, and thyroxine to help regulate blood pressure; estrogen to promote vascular health in women and men
Integumentary 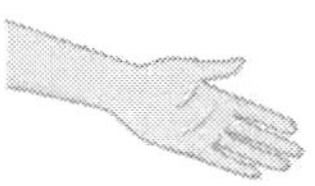	Carries clotting factors, platelets, and white blood cells for hemostasis, fighting infection, and repairing damage; regulates temperature by controlling blood flow to the surface, where heat can be dissipated; provides some coloration of integument; acts as a blood reservoir
Lymphatic 	Transports various white blood cells, including those produced by lymphatic tissue, and immunoglobulins (antibodies) throughout the body to maintain health; carries excess tissue fluid not able to be reabsorbed by the vascular capillaries back to the lymphatic system for processing
Muscular 	Provides nutrients and oxygen for contraction; removes lactic acid and distributes heat generated by contraction; muscular pumps aid in venous return; exercise contributes to cardiovascular health and helps to prevent atherosclerosis
Nervous 	Produces cerebrospinal fluid (CSF) within choroid plexuses; contributes to blood–brain barrier; cardiac and vasomotor centers regulate cardiac output and blood flow through vessels via autonomic system
Reproductive 	Aids in erection of genitalia in both sexes during sexual arousal; transports gonadotropic hormones that regulate reproductive functions
Respiratory 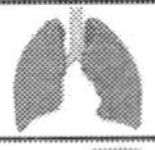	Provides blood for critical exchange of gases to carry oxygen needed for metabolic reactions and carbon dioxide generated as byproducts of these processes
Skeletal 	Provides calcium, phosphate, and other minerals critical for bone matrix; transports hormones regulating buildup and absorption of matrix including growth hormone (somatotropin), thyroid hormone, calcitonins, and parathyroid hormone; erythropoietin stimulates myeloid cell hematopoiesis; some level of protection for select vessels by bony structures
Urinary 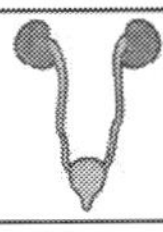	Delivers 20% of resting circulation to kidneys for filtering, reabsorption of useful products, and secretion of excesses; regulates blood volume and pressure by regulating fluid loss in the form of urine and by releasing the enzyme renin that is essential in the renin-angiotensin-aldosterone mechanism

Figure 20.22 Interaction of the Circulatory System with Other Body Systems

As you learn about the vessels of the systemic and pulmonary circuits, notice that many arteries and veins share the same names, parallel one another throughout the body, and are very similar on the right and left sides of the body. These pairs of vessels will be traced through only one side of the body. Where differences occur in branching patterns or when vessels are singular, this will be indicated. For example, you will find a pair of femoral arteries and a pair of femoral veins, with one vessel on each side of the body. In contrast, some vessels closer to the midline of the body, such as the aorta, are unique. Moreover, some superficial veins, such as the great saphenous vein in the femoral region, have no arterial counterpart. Another phenomenon that can make the study of vessels challenging is that names of vessels can change with location. Like a street that changes name as it passes through an intersection, an artery or vein can change names as it passes an anatomical landmark. For example, the left subclavian artery becomes the axillary artery as it passes through the body wall and into the axillary region, and then becomes the brachial artery as it flows from the axillary region into the upper arm (or brachium). You will also find examples of anastomoses where two blood vessels that previously branched reconnect. Anastomoses are especially common in veins, where they help maintain blood flow even when one vessel is blocked or narrowed, although there are some important ones in the arteries supplying the brain.

As you read about circular pathways, notice that there is an occasional, very large artery referred to as a **trunk**, a term indicating that the vessel gives rise to several smaller arteries. For example, the celiac trunk gives rise to the left gastric, common hepatic, and splenic arteries.

As you study this section, imagine you are on a "Voyage of Discovery" similar to Lewis and Clark's expedition in 1804–1806, which followed rivers and streams through unfamiliar territory, seeking a water route from the Atlantic to the Pacific Ocean. You might envision being inside a miniature boat, exploring the various branches of the circulatory system. This simple approach has proven effective for many students in mastering these major circulatory patterns. Another approach that works well for many students is to create simple line drawings similar to the ones provided, labeling each of the major vessels. It is beyond the scope of this text to name every vessel in the body. However, we will attempt to discuss the major pathways for blood and acquaint you with the major named arteries and veins in the body. Also, please keep in mind that individual variations in circulation patterns are not uncommon.

Visit this site (http://openstaxcollege.org/l/arts1) for a brief summary of the arteries.

Pulmonary Circulation

Recall that blood returning from the systemic circuit enters the right atrium (Figure 20.23) via the superior and inferior venae cavae and the coronary sinus, which drains the blood supply of the heart muscle. These vessels will be described more fully later in this section. This blood is relatively low in oxygen and relatively high in carbon dioxide, since much of the oxygen has been extracted for use by the tissues and the waste gas carbon dioxide was picked up to be transported to the lungs for elimination. From the right atrium, blood moves into the right ventricle, which pumps it to the lungs for gas exchange. This system of vessels is referred to as the **pulmonary circuit**.

The single vessel exiting the right ventricle is the **pulmonary trunk**. At the base of the pulmonary trunk is the pulmonary semilunar valve, which prevents backflow of blood into the right ventricle during ventricular diastole. As the pulmonary trunk reaches the superior surface of the heart, it curves posteriorly and rapidly bifurcates (divides) into two branches, a left and a right **pulmonary artery**. To prevent confusion between these vessels, it is important to refer to the vessel exiting the heart as the pulmonary trunk, rather than also calling it a pulmonary artery. The pulmonary arteries in turn branch many times within the lung, forming a series of smaller arteries and arterioles that eventually lead to the pulmonary capillaries. The pulmonary capillaries surround lung structures known as alveoli that are the sites of oxygen and carbon dioxide exchange.

Once gas exchange is completed, oxygenated blood flows from the pulmonary capillaries into a series of pulmonary venules that eventually lead to a series of larger **pulmonary veins**. Four pulmonary veins, two on the left and two on the right, return blood to the left atrium. At this point, the pulmonary circuit is complete. Table 20.4 defines the major arteries and veins of the pulmonary circuit discussed in the text.

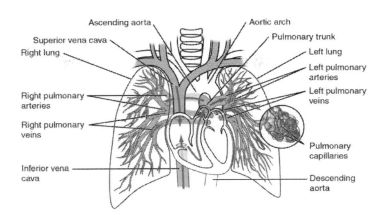

Figure 20.23 Pulmonary Circuit Blood exiting from the right ventricle flows into the pulmonary trunk, which bifurcates into the two pulmonary arteries. These vessels branch to supply blood to the pulmonary capillaries, where gas exchange occurs within the lung alveoli. Blood returns via the pulmonary veins to the left atrium.

Pulmonary Arteries and Veins

Vessel	Description
Pulmonary trunk	Single large vessel exiting the right ventricle that divides to form the right and left pulmonary arteries
Pulmonary arteries	Left and right vessels that form from the pulmonary trunk and lead to smaller arterioles and eventually to the pulmonary capillaries
Pulmonary veins	Two sets of paired vessels—one pair on each side—that are formed from the small venules, leading away from the pulmonary capillaries to flow into the left atrium

Table 20.4

Overview of Systemic Arteries

Blood relatively high in oxygen concentration is returned from the pulmonary circuit to the left atrium via the four pulmonary veins. From the left atrium, blood moves into the left ventricle, which pumps blood into the aorta. The aorta and its branches—the systemic arteries—send blood to virtually every organ of the body (Figure 20.24).

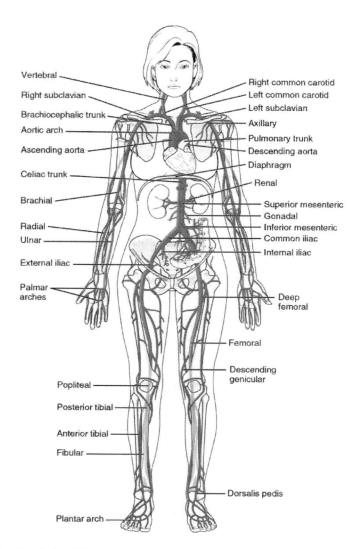

Figure 20.24 Systemic Arteries The major systemic arteries shown here deliver oxygenated blood throughout the body.

The Aorta

The **aorta** is the largest artery in the body (Figure 20.25). It arises from the left ventricle and eventually descends to the abdominal region, where it bifurcates at the level of the fourth lumbar vertebra into the two common iliac arteries. The aorta consists of the ascending aorta, the aortic arch, and the descending aorta, which passes through the diaphragm and a landmark that divides into the superior thoracic and inferior abdominal components. Arteries originating from the aorta ultimately distribute blood to virtually all tissues of the body. At the base of the aorta is the aortic semilunar valve that prevents backflow of blood into the left ventricle while the heart is relaxing. After exiting the heart, the **ascending aorta** moves in a superior direction for approximately 5 cm and ends at the sternal angle. Following this ascent, it reverses direction, forming a graceful arc to the left, called the **aortic arch**. The aortic arch descends toward the inferior portions of the body and ends at the level of the intervertebral disk between the fourth and fifth thoracic vertebrae. Beyond this point, the **descending aorta** continues close to the bodies of the vertebrae and passes through an opening in the diaphragm known as the **aortic hiatus**. Superior to the diaphragm, the aorta is called the **thoracic aorta**, and inferior to the diaphragm, it is called the **abdominal aorta**. The abdominal aorta terminates when it bifurcates into the two common iliac arteries at the level of the fourth lumbar vertebra. See Figure 20.25 for an illustration of the ascending aorta, the aortic arch, and the initial segment of the descending aorta plus major branches; Table 20.5 summarizes the structures of the aorta.

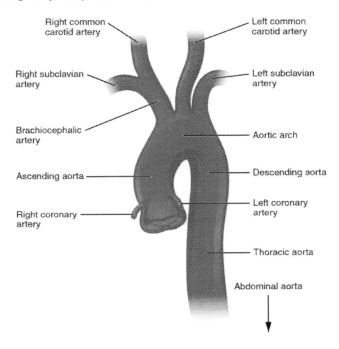

Figure 20.25 Aorta The aorta has distinct regions, including the ascending aorta, aortic arch, and the descending aorta, which includes the thoracic and abdominal regions.

Components of the Aorta

Vessel	Description
Aorta	Largest artery in the body, originating from the left ventricle and descending to the abdominal region, where it bifurcates into the common iliac arteries at the level of the fourth lumbar vertebra; arteries originating from the aorta distribute blood to virtually all tissues of the body
Ascending aorta	Initial portion of the aorta, rising superiorly from the left ventricle for a distance of approximately 5 cm
Aortic arch	Graceful arc to the left that connects the ascending aorta to the descending aorta; ends at the intervertebral disk between the fourth and fifth thoracic vertebrae
Descending aorta	Portion of the aorta that continues inferiorly past the end of the aortic arch; subdivided into the thoracic aorta and the abdominal aorta
Thoracic aorta	Portion of the descending aorta superior to the aortic hiatus
Abdominal aorta	Portion of the aorta inferior to the aortic hiatus and superior to the common iliac arteries

Table 20.5

Coronary Circulation

The first vessels that branch from the ascending aorta are the paired coronary arteries (see Figure 20.25), which arise from two of the three sinuses in the ascending aorta just superior to the aortic semilunar valve. These sinuses contain the aortic baroreceptors and chemoreceptors critical to maintain cardiac function. The left coronary artery arises from the left posterior aortic sinus. The right coronary artery arises from the anterior aortic sinus. Normally, the right posterior aortic sinus does not give rise to a vessel.

The coronary arteries encircle the heart, forming a ring-like structure that divides into the next level of branches that supplies blood to the heart tissues. (Seek additional content for more detail on cardiac circulation.)

Aortic Arch Branches

There are three major branches of the aortic arch: the brachiocephalic artery, the left common carotid artery, and the left subclavian (literally "under the clavicle") artery. As you would expect based upon proximity to the heart, each of these vessels is classified as an elastic artery.

The brachiocephalic artery is located only on the right side of the body; there is no corresponding artery on the left. The brachiocephalic artery branches into the right subclavian artery and the right common carotid artery. The left subclavian and left common carotid arteries arise independently from the aortic arch but otherwise follow a similar pattern and distribution to the corresponding arteries on the right side (see Figure 20.23).

Each **subclavian artery** supplies blood to the arms, chest, shoulders, back, and central nervous system. It then gives rise to three major branches: the internal thoracic artery, the vertebral artery, and the thyrocervical artery. The **internal thoracic artery**, or mammary artery, supplies blood to the thymus, the pericardium of the heart, and the anterior chest wall. The **vertebral artery** passes through the vertebral foramen in the cervical vertebrae and then through the foramen magnum into the cranial cavity to supply blood to the brain and spinal cord. The paired vertebral arteries join together to form the large basilar artery at the base of the medulla oblongata. This is an example of an anastomosis. The subclavian artery also gives rise to the **thyrocervical artery** that provides blood to the thyroid, the cervical region of the neck, and the upper back and shoulder.

The **common carotid artery** divides into internal and external carotid arteries. The right common carotid artery arises from the brachiocephalic artery and the left common carotid artery arises directly from the aortic arch. The **external carotid artery** supplies blood to numerous structures within the face, lower jaw, neck, esophagus, and larynx. These branches include the lingual, facial, occipital, maxillary, and superficial temporal arteries. The **internal carotid artery** initially forms an expansion known as the carotid sinus, containing the carotid baroreceptors and chemoreceptors. Like their counterparts in the aortic sinuses, the information provided by these receptors is critical to maintaining cardiovascular homeostasis (see Figure 20.23).

The internal carotid arteries along with the vertebral arteries are the two primary suppliers of blood to the human brain. Given the central role and vital importance of the brain to life, it is critical that blood supply to this organ remains uninterrupted. Recall that blood flow to the brain is remarkably constant, with approximately 20 percent of blood flow directed to this organ at any given time. When blood flow is interrupted, even for just a few seconds, a **transient ischemic attack (TIA)**, or mini-stroke, may occur, resulting in loss of consciousness or temporary loss of neurological function. In some cases, the damage may be permanent. Loss of blood flow for longer periods, typically between 3 and 4 minutes, will likely produce irreversible brain damage or a stroke, also called a **cerebrovascular accident (CVA)**. The locations of the arteries in the brain not only provide blood flow to the brain tissue but also prevent interruption in the flow of blood. Both the carotid and vertebral arteries branch once they enter the cranial cavity, and some of these branches form a structure known as the **arterial circle** (or **circle of Willis**), an anastomosis that is remarkably like a traffic circle that sends off branches (in this case, arterial branches to the brain). As a rule, branches to the anterior portion of the cerebrum are normally fed by the internal carotid arteries; the remainder of the brain receives blood flow from branches associated with the vertebral arteries.

The internal carotid artery continues through the carotid canal of the temporal bone and enters the base of the brain through the carotid foramen where it gives rise to several branches (Figure 20.26 and Figure 20.27). One of these branches is the **anterior cerebral artery** that supplies blood to the frontal lobe of the cerebrum. Another branch, the **middle cerebral artery**, supplies blood to the temporal and parietal lobes, which are the most common sites of CVAs. The **ophthalmic artery**, the third major branch, provides blood to the eyes.

The right and left anterior cerebral arteries join together to form an anastomosis called the **anterior communicating artery**. The initial segments of the anterior cerebral arteries and the anterior communicating artery form the anterior portion of the arterial circle. The posterior portion of the arterial circle is formed by a left and a right **posterior communicating artery** that branches from the **posterior cerebral artery**, which arises from the basilar artery. It provides blood to the posterior portion of the cerebrum and brain stem. The **basilar artery** is an anastomosis that begins at the junction of the two vertebral arteries and sends branches to the cerebellum and brain stem. It flows into the posterior cerebral arteries. Table 20.6 summarizes the aortic arch branches, including the major branches supplying the brain.

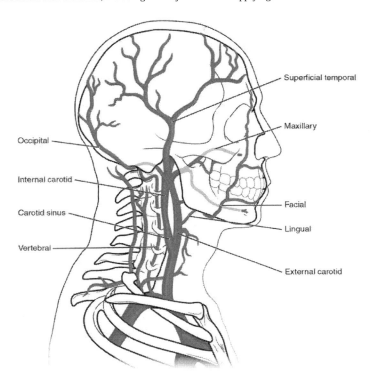

Figure 20.26 Arteries Supplying the Head and Neck The common carotid artery gives rise to the external and internal carotid arteries. The external carotid artery remains superficial and gives rise to many arteries of the head. The internal carotid artery first forms the carotid sinus and then reaches the brain via the carotid canal and carotid foramen, emerging into the cranium via the foramen lacerum. The vertebral artery branches from the subclavian artery and passes through the transverse foramen in the cervical vertebrae, entering the base of the skull at the vertebral foramen. The subclavian artery continues toward the arm as the axillary artery.

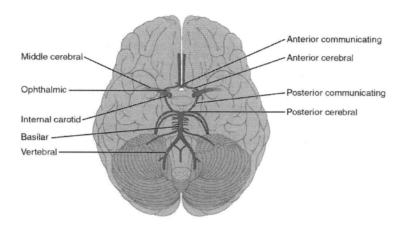

Figure 20.27 Arteries Serving the Brain This inferior view shows the network of arteries serving the brain. The structure is referred to as the arterial circle or circle of Willis.

Aortic Arch Branches and Brain Circulation

Vessel	Description
Brachiocephalic artery	Single vessel located on the right side of the body; the first vessel branching from the aortic arch; gives rise to the right subclavian artery and the right common carotid artery; supplies blood to the head, neck, upper limb, and wall of the thoracic region
Subclavian artery	The right subclavian artery arises from the brachiocephalic artery while the left subclavian artery arises from the aortic arch; gives rise to the internal thoracic, vertebral, and thyrocervical arteries; supplies blood to the arms, chest, shoulders, back, and central nervous system
Internal thoracic artery	Also called the mammary artery; arises from the subclavian artery; supplies blood to the thymus, pericardium of the heart, and anterior chest wall
Vertebral artery	Arises from the subclavian artery and passes through the vertebral foramen through the foramen magnum to the brain; joins with the internal carotid artery to form the arterial circle; supplies blood to the brain and spinal cord
Thyrocervical artery	Arises from the subclavian artery; supplies blood to the thyroid, the cervical region, the upper back, and shoulder
Common carotid artery	The right common carotid artery arises from the brachiocephalic artery and the left common carotid artery arises from the aortic arch; each gives rise to the external and internal carotid arteries; supplies the respective sides of the head and neck
External carotid artery	Arises from the common carotid artery; supplies blood to numerous structures within the face, lower jaw, neck, esophagus, and larynx
Internal carotid artery	Arises from the common carotid artery and begins with the carotid sinus; goes through the carotid canal of the temporal bone to the base of the brain; combines with the branches of the vertebral artery, forming the arterial circle; supplies blood to the brain
Arterial circle or circle of Willis	An anastomosis located at the base of the brain that ensures continual blood supply; formed from the branches of the internal carotid and vertebral arteries; supplies blood to the brain

Table 20.6

Aortic Arch Branches and Brain Circulation

Vessel	Description
Anterior cerebral artery	Arises from the internal carotid artery; supplies blood to the frontal lobe of the cerebrum
Middle cerebral artery	Another branch of the internal carotid artery; supplies blood to the temporal and parietal lobes of the cerebrum
Ophthalmic artery	Branch of the internal carotid artery; supplies blood to the eyes
Anterior communicating artery	An anastomosis of the right and left internal carotid arteries; supplies blood to the brain
Posterior communicating artery	Branches of the posterior cerebral artery that form part of the posterior portion of the arterial circle; supplies blood to the brain
Posterior cerebral artery	Branch of the basilar artery that forms a portion of the posterior segment of the arterial circle of Willis; supplies blood to the posterior portion of the cerebrum and brain stem
Basilar artery	Formed from the fusion of the two vertebral arteries; sends branches to the cerebellum, brain stem, and the posterior cerebral arteries; the main blood supply to the brain stem

Table 20.6

Thoracic Aorta and Major Branches

The thoracic aorta begins at the level of vertebra T5 and continues through to the diaphragm at the level of T12, initially traveling within the mediastinum to the left of the vertebral column. As it passes through the thoracic region, the thoracic aorta gives rise to several branches, which are collectively referred to as visceral branches and parietal branches (Figure 20.28). Those branches that supply blood primarily to visceral organs are known as the **visceral branches** and include the bronchial arteries, pericardial arteries, esophageal arteries, and the mediastinal arteries, each named after the tissues it supplies. Each **bronchial artery** (typically two on the left and one on the right) supplies systemic blood to the lungs and visceral pleura, in addition to the blood pumped to the lungs for oxygenation via the pulmonary circuit. The bronchial arteries follow the same path as the respiratory branches, beginning with the bronchi and ending with the bronchioles. There is considerable, but not total, intermingling of the systemic and pulmonary blood at anastomoses in the smaller branches of the lungs. This may sound incongruous—that is, the mixing of systemic arterial blood high in oxygen with the pulmonary arterial blood lower in oxygen—but the systemic vessels also deliver nutrients to the lung tissue just as they do elsewhere in the body. The mixed blood drains into typical pulmonary veins, whereas the bronchial artery branches remain separate and drain into bronchial veins described later. Each **pericardial artery** supplies blood to the pericardium, the **esophageal artery** provides blood to the esophagus, and the **mediastinal artery** provides blood to the mediastinum. The remaining thoracic aorta branches are collectively referred to as **parietal branches** or somatic branches, and include the intercostal and superior phrenic arteries. Each **intercostal artery** provides blood to the muscles of the thoracic cavity and vertebral column. The **superior phrenic artery** provides blood to the superior surface of the diaphragm. Table 20.7 lists the arteries of the thoracic region.

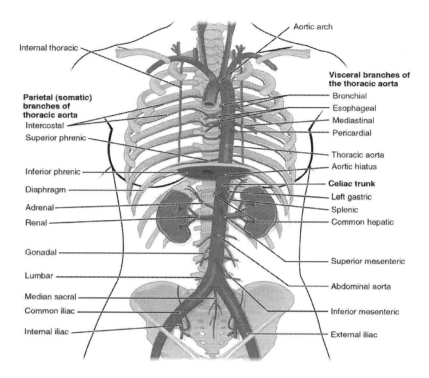

Figure 20.28 Arteries of the Thoracic and Abdominal Regions The thoracic aorta gives rise to the arteries of the visceral and parietal branches.

Arteries of the Thoracic Region

Vessel	Description
Visceral branches	A group of arterial branches of the thoracic aorta; supplies blood to the viscera (i.e., organs) of the thorax
Bronchial artery	Systemic branch from the aorta that provides oxygenated blood to the lungs; this blood supply is in addition to the pulmonary circuit that brings blood for oxygenation
Pericardial artery	Branch of the thoracic aorta; supplies blood to the pericardium
Esophageal artery	Branch of the thoracic aorta; supplies blood to the esophagus
Mediastinal artery	Branch of the thoracic aorta; supplies blood to the mediastinum
Parietal branches	Also called somatic branches, a group of arterial branches of the thoracic aorta; include those that supply blood to the thoracic wall, vertebral column, and the superior surface of the diaphragm

Table 20.7

Arteries of the Thoracic Region

Vessel	Description
Intercostal artery	Branch of the thoracic aorta; supplies blood to the muscles of the thoracic cavity and vertebral column
Superior phrenic artery	Branch of the thoracic aorta; supplies blood to the superior surface of the diaphragm

Table 20.7

Abdominal Aorta and Major Branches

After crossing through the diaphragm at the aortic hiatus, the thoracic aorta is called the abdominal aorta (see Figure 20.28). This vessel remains to the left of the vertebral column and is embedded in adipose tissue behind the peritoneal cavity. It formally ends at approximately the level of vertebra L4, where it bifurcates to form the common iliac arteries. Before this division, the abdominal aorta gives rise to several important branches. A single **celiac trunk** (artery) emerges and divides into the **left gastric artery** to supply blood to the stomach and esophagus, the **splenic artery** to supply blood to the spleen, and the **common hepatic artery**, which in turn gives rise to the **hepatic artery proper** to supply blood to the liver, the **right gastric artery** to supply blood to the stomach, the **cystic artery** to supply blood to the gall bladder, and several branches, one to supply blood to the duodenum and another to supply blood to the pancreas. Two additional single vessels arise from the abdominal aorta. These are the superior and inferior mesenteric arteries. The **superior mesenteric artery** arises approximately 2.5 cm after the celiac trunk and branches into several major vessels that supply blood to the small intestine (duodenum, jejunum, and ileum), the pancreas, and a majority of the large intestine. The **inferior mesenteric artery** supplies blood to the distal segment of the large intestine, including the rectum. It arises approximately 5 cm superior to the common iliac arteries.

In addition to these single branches, the abdominal aorta gives rise to several significant paired arteries along the way. These include the inferior phrenic arteries, the adrenal arteries, the renal arteries, the gonadal arteries, and the lumbar arteries. Each **inferior phrenic artery** is a counterpart of a superior phrenic artery and supplies blood to the inferior surface of the diaphragm. The **adrenal artery** supplies blood to the adrenal (suprarenal) glands and arises near the superior mesenteric artery. Each **renal artery** branches approximately 2.5 cm inferior to the superior mesenteric arteries and supplies a kidney. The right renal artery is longer than the left since the aorta lies to the left of the vertebral column and the vessel must travel a greater distance to reach its target. Renal arteries branch repeatedly to supply blood to the kidneys. Each **gonadal artery** supplies blood to the gonads, or reproductive organs, and is also described as either an ovarian artery or a testicular artery (internal spermatic), depending upon the sex of the individual. An **ovarian artery** supplies blood to an ovary, uterine (Fallopian) tube, and the uterus, and is located within the suspensory ligament of the uterus. It is considerably shorter than a **testicular artery**, which ultimately travels outside the body cavity to the testes, forming one component of the spermatic cord. The gonadal arteries arise inferior to the renal arteries and are generally retroperitoneal. The ovarian artery continues to the uterus where it forms an anastomosis with the uterine artery that supplies blood to the uterus. Both the uterine arteries and vaginal arteries, which distribute blood to the vagina, are branches of the internal iliac artery. The four paired **lumbar arteries** are the counterparts of the intercostal arteries and supply blood to the lumbar region, the abdominal wall, and the spinal cord. In some instances, a fifth pair of lumbar arteries emerges from the median sacral artery.

The aorta divides at approximately the level of vertebra L4 into a left and a right **common iliac artery** but continues as a small vessel, the **median sacral artery**, into the sacrum. The common iliac arteries provide blood to the pelvic region and ultimately to the lower limbs. They split into external and internal iliac arteries approximately at the level of the lumbar-sacral articulation. Each **internal iliac artery** sends branches to the urinary bladder, the walls of the pelvis, the external genitalia, and the medial portion of the femoral region. In females, they also provide blood to the uterus and vagina. The much larger **external iliac artery** supplies blood to each of the lower limbs. Figure 20.29 shows the distribution of the major branches of the aorta into the thoracic and abdominal regions. Figure 20.30 shows the distribution of the major branches of the common iliac arteries. Table 20.8 summarizes the major branches of the abdominal aorta.

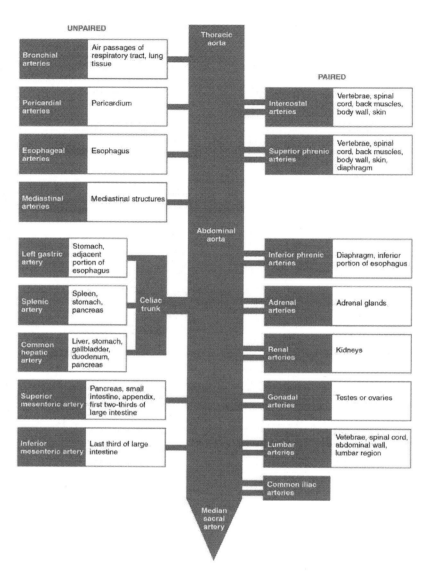

Figure 20.29 Major Branches of the Aorta The flow chart summarizes the distribution of the major branches of the aorta into the thoracic and abdominal regions.

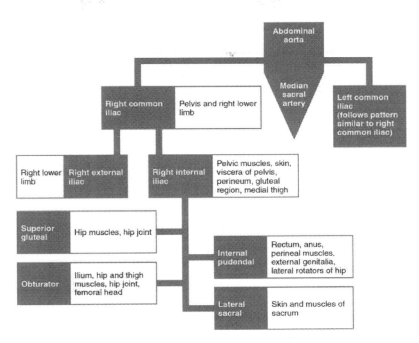

Figure 20.30 Major Branches of the Iliac Arteries The flow chart summarizes the distribution of the major branches of the common iliac arteries into the pelvis and lower limbs. The left side follows a similar pattern to the right.

Vessels of the Abdominal Aorta

Vessel	Description
Celiac trunk	Also called the celiac artery; a major branch of the abdominal aorta; gives rise to the left gastric artery, the splenic artery, and the common hepatic artery that forms the hepatic artery to the liver, the right gastric artery to the stomach, and the cystic artery to the gall bladder
Left gastric artery	Branch of the celiac trunk; supplies blood to the stomach
Splenic artery	Branch of the celiac trunk; supplies blood to the spleen
Common hepatic artery	Branch of the celiac trunk that forms the hepatic artery, the right gastric artery, and the cystic artery
Hepatic artery proper	Branch of the common hepatic artery; supplies systemic blood to the liver
Right gastric artery	Branch of the common hepatic artery; supplies blood to the stomach
Cystic artery	Branch of the common hepatic artery; supplies blood to the gall bladder
Superior mesenteric artery	Branch of the abdominal aorta; supplies blood to the small intestine (duodenum, jejunum, and ileum), the pancreas, and a majority of the large intestine

Table 20.8

Vessels of the Abdominal Aorta

Vessel	Description
Inferior mesenteric artery	Branch of the abdominal aorta; supplies blood to the distal segment of the large intestine and rectum
Inferior phrenic arteries	Branches of the abdominal aorta; supply blood to the inferior surface of the diaphragm
Adrenal artery	Branch of the abdominal aorta; supplies blood to the adrenal (suprarenal) glands
Renal artery	Branch of the abdominal aorta; supplies each kidney
Gonadal artery	Branch of the abdominal aorta; supplies blood to the gonads or reproductive organs; also described as ovarian arteries or testicular arteries, depending upon the sex of the individual
Ovarian artery	Branch of the abdominal aorta; supplies blood to ovary, uterine (Fallopian) tube, and uterus
Testicular artery	Branch of the abdominal aorta; ultimately travels outside the body cavity to the testes and forms one component of the spermatic cord
Lumbar arteries	Branches of the abdominal aorta; supply blood to the lumbar region, the abdominal wall, and spinal cord
Common iliac artery	Branch of the aorta that leads to the internal and external iliac arteries
Median sacral artery	Continuation of the aorta into the sacrum
Internal iliac artery	Branch from the common iliac arteries; supplies blood to the urinary bladder, walls of the pelvis, external genitalia, and the medial portion of the femoral region; in females, also provides blood to the uterus and vagina
External iliac artery	Branch of the common iliac artery that leaves the body cavity and becomes a femoral artery; supplies blood to the lower limbs

Table 20.8

Arteries Serving the Upper Limbs

As the subclavian artery exits the thorax into the axillary region, it is renamed the **axillary artery**. Although it does branch and supply blood to the region near the head of the humerus (via the humeral circumflex arteries), the majority of the vessel continues into the upper arm, or brachium, and becomes the brachial artery (Figure 20.31). The **brachial artery** supplies blood to much of the brachial region and divides at the elbow into several smaller branches, including the deep brachial arteries, which provide blood to the posterior surface of the arm, and the ulnar collateral arteries, which supply blood to the region of the elbow. As the brachial artery approaches the coronoid fossa, it bifurcates into the radial and ulnar arteries, which continue into the forearm, or antebrachium. The **radial artery** and **ulnar artery** parallel their namesake bones, giving off smaller branches until they reach the wrist, or carpal region. At this level, they fuse to form the superficial and deep **palmar arches** that supply blood to the hand, as well as the **digital arteries** that supply blood to the digits. Figure 20.32 shows the distribution of systemic arteries from the heart into the upper limb. Table 20.9 summarizes the arteries serving the upper limbs.

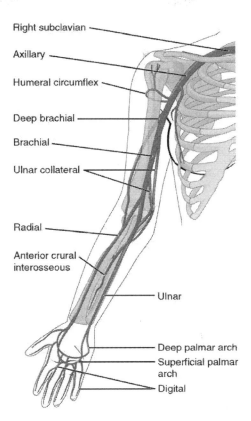

Figure 20.31 Major Arteries Serving the Thorax and Upper Limb The arteries that supply blood to the arms and hands are extensions of the subclavian arteries.

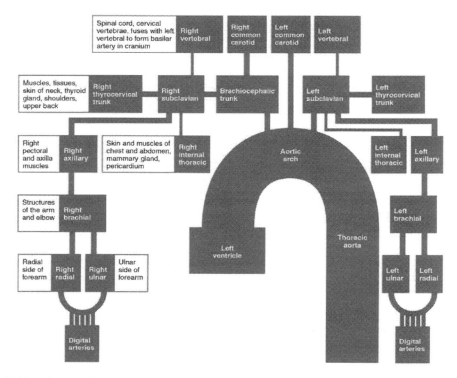

Figure 20.32 Major Arteries of the Upper Limb The flow chart summarizes the distribution of the major arteries from the heart into the upper limb.

Arteries Serving the Upper Limbs

Vessel	Description
Axillary artery	Continuation of the subclavian artery as it penetrates the body wall and enters the axillary region; supplies blood to the region near the head of the humerus (humeral circumflex arteries); the majority of the vessel continues into the brachium and becomes the brachial artery
Brachial artery	Continuation of the axillary artery in the brachium; supplies blood to much of the brachial region; gives off several smaller branches that provide blood to the posterior surface of the arm in the region of the elbow; bifurcates into the radial and ulnar arteries at the coronoid fossa
Radial artery	Formed at the bifurcation of the brachial artery; parallels the radius; gives off smaller branches until it reaches the carpal region where it fuses with the ulnar artery to form the superficial and deep palmar arches; supplies blood to the lower arm and carpal region
Ulnar artery	Formed at the bifurcation of the brachial artery; parallels the ulna; gives off smaller branches until it reaches the carpal region where it fuses with the radial artery to form the superficial and deep palmar arches; supplies blood to the lower arm and carpal region

Table 20.9

Arteries Serving the Upper Limbs

Vessel	Description
Palmar arches (superficial and deep)	Formed from anastomosis of the radial and ulnar arteries; supply blood to the hand and digital arteries
Digital arteries	Formed from the superficial and deep palmar arches; supply blood to the digits

Table 20.9

Arteries Serving the Lower Limbs

The external iliac artery exits the body cavity and enters the femoral region of the lower leg (Figure 20.33). As it passes through the body wall, it is renamed the **femoral artery**. It gives off several smaller branches as well as the lateral **deep femoral artery** that in turn gives rise to a **lateral circumflex artery**. These arteries supply blood to the deep muscles of the thigh as well as ventral and lateral regions of the integument. The femoral artery also gives rise to the **genicular artery**, which provides blood to the region of the knee. As the femoral artery passes posterior to the knee near the popliteal fossa, it is called the popliteal artery. The **popliteal artery** branches into the anterior and posterior tibial arteries.

The **anterior tibial artery** is located between the tibia and fibula, and supplies blood to the muscles and integument of the anterior tibial region. Upon reaching the tarsal region, it becomes the **dorsalis pedis artery**, which branches repeatedly and provides blood to the tarsal and dorsal regions of the foot. The **posterior tibial artery** provides blood to the muscles and integument on the posterior surface of the tibial region. The fibular or peroneal artery branches from the posterior tibial artery. It bifurcates and becomes the **medial plantar artery** and **lateral plantar artery**, providing blood to the plantar surfaces. There is an anastomosis with the dorsalis pedis artery, and the medial and lateral plantar arteries form two arches called the **dorsal arch** (also called the arcuate arch) and the **plantar arch**, which provide blood to the remainder of the foot and toes. Figure 20.34 shows the distribution of the major systemic arteries in the lower limb. Table 20.10 summarizes the major systemic arteries discussed in the text.

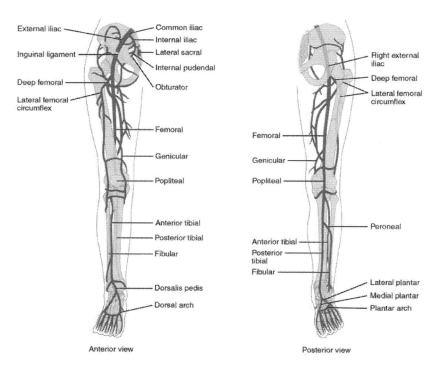

Figure 20.33 Major Arteries Serving the Lower Limb Major arteries serving the lower limb are shown in anterior and posterior views.

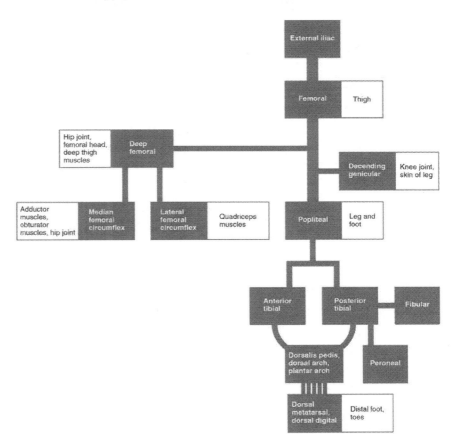

Figure 20.34 Systemic Arteries of the Lower Limb The flow chart summarizes the distribution of the systemic arteries from the external iliac artery into the lower limb.

Arteries Serving the Lower Limbs

Vessel	Description
Femoral artery	Continuation of the external iliac artery after it passes through the body cavity; divides into several smaller branches, the lateral deep femoral artery, and the genicular artery; becomes the popliteal artery as it passes posterior to the knee
Deep femoral artery	Branch of the femoral artery; gives rise to the lateral circumflex arteries
Lateral circumflex artery	Branch of the deep femoral artery; supplies blood to the deep muscles of the thigh and the ventral and lateral regions of the integument
Genicular artery	Branch of the femoral artery; supplies blood to the region of the knee

Table 20.10

Arteries Serving the Lower Limbs

Vessel	Description
Popliteal artery	Continuation of the femoral artery posterior to the knee; branches into the anterior and posterior tibial arteries
Anterior tibial artery	Branches from the popliteal artery; supplies blood to the anterior tibial region; becomes the dorsalis pedis artery
Dorsalis pedis artery	Forms from the anterior tibial artery; branches repeatedly to supply blood to the tarsal and dorsal regions of the foot
Posterior tibial artery	Branches from the popliteal artery and gives rise to the fibular or peroneal artery; supplies blood to the posterior tibial region
Medial plantar artery	Arises from the bifurcation of the posterior tibial arteries; supplies blood to the medial plantar surfaces of the foot
Lateral plantar artery	Arises from the bifurcation of the posterior tibial arteries; supplies blood to the lateral plantar surfaces of the foot
Dorsal or arcuate arch	Formed from the anastomosis of the dorsalis pedis artery and the medial and plantar arteries; branches supply the distal portions of the foot and digits
Plantar arch	Formed from the anastomosis of the dorsalis pedis artery and the medial and plantar arteries; branches supply the distal portions of the foot and digits

Table 20.10

Overview of Systemic Veins

Systemic veins return blood to the right atrium. Since the blood has already passed through the systemic capillaries, it will be relatively low in oxygen concentration. In many cases, there will be veins draining organs and regions of the body with the same name as the arteries that supplied these regions and the two often parallel one another. This is often described as a "complementary" pattern. However, there is a great deal more variability in the venous circulation than normally occurs in the arteries. For the sake of brevity and clarity, this text will discuss only the most commonly encountered patterns. However, keep this variation in mind when you move from the classroom to clinical practice.

In both the neck and limb regions, there are often both superficial and deeper levels of veins. The deeper veins generally correspond to the complementary arteries. The superficial veins do not normally have direct arterial counterparts, but in addition to returning blood, they also make contributions to the maintenance of body temperature. When the ambient temperature is warm, more blood is diverted to the superficial veins where heat can be more easily dissipated to the environment. In colder weather, there is more constriction of the superficial veins and blood is diverted deeper where the body can retain more of the heat.

The "Voyage of Discovery" analogy and stick drawings mentioned earlier remain valid techniques for the study of systemic veins, but veins present a more difficult challenge because there are numerous anastomoses and multiple branches. It is like following a river with many tributaries and channels, several of which interconnect. Tracing blood flow through arteries follows the current in the direction of blood flow, so that we move from the heart through the large arteries and into the smaller arteries to the capillaries. From the capillaries, we move into the smallest veins and follow the direction of blood flow into larger veins and back to the heart. Figure 20.35 outlines the path of the major systemic veins.

Visit this site (http://openstaxcollege.org/l/veinsum) for a brief online summary of the veins.

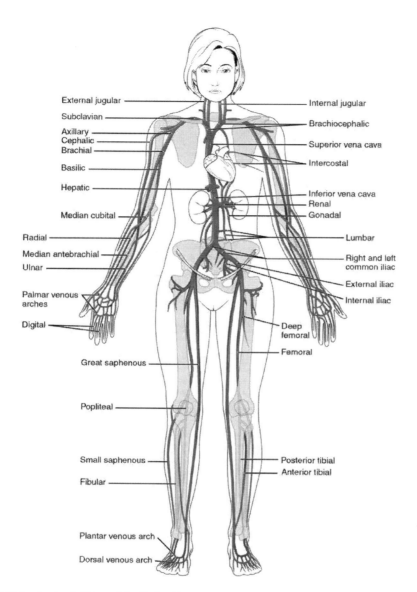

Figure 20.35 Major Systemic Veins of the Body The major systemic veins of the body are shown here in an anterior view.

The right atrium receives all of the systemic venous return. Most of the blood flows into either the superior vena cava or inferior vena cava. If you draw an imaginary line at the level of the diaphragm, systemic venous circulation from above that line will generally flow into the superior vena cava; this includes blood from the head, neck, chest, shoulders, and upper limbs. The exception to this is that most venous blood flow from the coronary veins flows directly into the coronary sinus and from there directly into the right atrium. Beneath the diaphragm, systemic venous flow enters the inferior vena cava, that is, blood from the abdominal and pelvic regions and the lower limbs.

The Superior Vena Cava

The **superior vena cava** drains most of the body superior to the diaphragm (Figure 20.36). On both the left and right sides, the **subclavian vein** forms when the axillary vein passes through the body wall from the axillary region. It fuses with the external and internal jugular veins from the head and neck to form the **brachiocephalic vein**. Each **vertebral vein** also flows into the brachiocephalic vein close to this fusion. These veins arise from the base of the brain and the cervical region of the spinal cord, and flow largely through the intervertebral foramina in the cervical vertebrae. They are the counterparts of the vertebral arteries. Each **internal thoracic vein**, also known as an internal mammary vein, drains the anterior surface of the chest wall and flows into the brachiocephalic vein.

The remainder of the blood supply from the thorax drains into the azygos vein. Each **intercostal vein** drains muscles of the thoracic wall, each **esophageal vein** delivers blood from the inferior portions of the esophagus, each **bronchial vein** drains the systemic circulation from the lungs, and several smaller veins drain the mediastinal region. Bronchial veins carry approximately 13 percent of the blood that flows into the bronchial arteries; the remainder intermingles with the pulmonary circulation and returns to the heart via the pulmonary veins. These veins flow into the **azygos vein**, and with the smaller **hemiazygos vein** (hemi- = "half") on the left of the vertebral column, drain blood from the thoracic region. The hemiazygos vein does not drain directly into the superior vena cava but enters the brachiocephalic vein via the superior intercostal vein.

The azygos vein passes through the diaphragm from the thoracic cavity on the right side of the vertebral column and begins in the lumbar region of the thoracic cavity. It flows into the superior vena cava at approximately the level of T2, making a significant contribution to the flow of blood. It combines with the two large left and right brachiocephalic veins to form the superior vena cava.

Table 20.11 summarizes the veins of the thoracic region that flow into the superior vena cava.

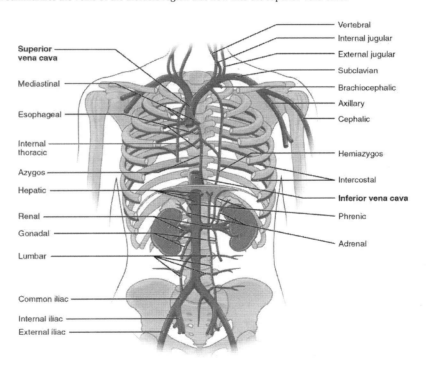

Figure 20.36 Veins of the Thoracic and Abdominal Regions Veins of the thoracic and abdominal regions drain blood from the area above the diaphragm, returning it to the right atrium via the superior vena cava.

Veins of the Thoracic Region

Vessel	Description
Superior vena cava	Large systemic vein; drains blood from most areas superior to the diaphragm; empties into the right atrium
Subclavian vein	Located deep in the thoracic cavity; formed by the axillary vein as it enters the thoracic cavity from the axillary region; drains the axillary and smaller local veins near the scapular region and leads to the brachiocephalic vein
Brachiocephalic veins	Pair of veins that form from a fusion of the external and internal jugular veins and the subclavian vein; subclavian, external and internal jugulars, vertebral, and internal thoracic veins flow into it; drain the upper thoracic region and lead to the superior vena cava
Vertebral vein	Arises from the base of the brain and the cervical region of the spinal cord; passes through the intervertebral foramina in the cervical vertebrae; drains smaller veins from the cranium, spinal cord, and vertebrae, and leads to the brachiocephalic vein; counterpart of the vertebral artery
Internal thoracic veins	Also called internal mammary veins; drain the anterior surface of the chest wall and lead to the brachiocephalic vein
Intercostal vein	Drains the muscles of the thoracic wall and leads to the azygos vein
Esophageal vein	Drains the inferior portions of the esophagus and leads to the azygos vein
Bronchial vein	Drains the systemic circulation from the lungs and leads to the azygos vein
Azygos vein	Originates in the lumbar region and passes through the diaphragm into the thoracic cavity on the right side of the vertebral column; drains blood from the intercostal veins, esophageal veins, bronchial veins, and other veins draining the mediastinal region, and leads to the superior vena cava
Hemiazygos vein	Smaller vein complementary to the azygos vein; drains the esophageal veins from the esophagus and the left intercostal veins, and leads to the brachiocephalic vein via the superior intercostal vein

Table 20.11

Veins of the Head and Neck

Blood from the brain and the superficial facial vein flow into each **internal jugular vein** (Figure 20.37). Blood from the more superficial portions of the head, scalp, and cranial regions, including the **temporal vein** and **maxillary vein**, flow into each **external jugular vein**. Although the external and internal jugular veins are separate vessels, there are anastomoses between them close to the thoracic region. Blood from the external jugular vein empties into the subclavian vein. Table 20.12 summarizes the major veins of the head and neck.

Major Veins of the Head and Neck

Vessel	Description
Internal jugular vein	Parallel to the common carotid artery, which is more or less its counterpart, and passes through the jugular foramen and canal; primarily drains blood from the brain, receives the superficial facial vein, and empties into the subclavian vein
Temporal vein	Drains blood from the temporal region and flows into the external jugular vein
Maxillary vein	Drains blood from the maxillary region and flows into the external jugular vein

Table 20.12

Major Veins of the Head and Neck

Vessel	Description
External jugular vein	Drains blood from the more superficial portions of the head, scalp, and cranial regions, and leads to the subclavian vein

Table 20.12

Venous Drainage of the Brain

Circulation to the brain is both critical and complex (see Figure 20.37). Many smaller veins of the brain stem and the superficial veins of the cerebrum lead to larger vessels referred to as intracranial sinuses. These include the superior and inferior sagittal sinuses, straight sinus, cavernous sinuses, left and right sinuses, the petrosal sinuses, and the occipital sinuses. Ultimately, sinuses will lead back to either the inferior jugular vein or vertebral vein.

Most of the veins on the superior surface of the cerebrum flow into the largest of the sinuses, the **superior sagittal sinus**. It is located midsagittally between the meningeal and periosteal layers of the dura mater within the falx cerebri and, at first glance in images or models, can be mistaken for the subarachnoid space. Most reabsorption of cerebrospinal fluid occurs via the chorionic villi (arachnoid granulations) into the superior sagittal sinus. Blood from most of the smaller vessels originating from the inferior cerebral veins flows into the **great cerebral vein** and into the **straight sinus**. Other cerebral veins and those from the eye socket flow into the **cavernous sinus**, which flows into the **petrosal sinus** and then into the internal jugular vein. The **occipital sinus**, sagittal sinus, and straight sinuses all flow into the left and right transverse sinuses near the lambdoid suture. The **transverse sinuses** in turn flow into the **sigmoid sinuses** that pass through the jugular foramen and into the internal jugular vein. The internal jugular vein flows parallel to the common carotid artery and is more or less its counterpart. It empties into the brachiocephalic vein. The veins draining the cervical vertebrae and the posterior surface of the skull, including some blood from the occipital sinus, flow into the vertebral veins. These parallel the vertebral arteries and travel through the transverse foramina of the cervical vertebrae. The vertebral veins also flow into the brachiocephalic veins. Table 20.13 summarizes the major veins of the brain.

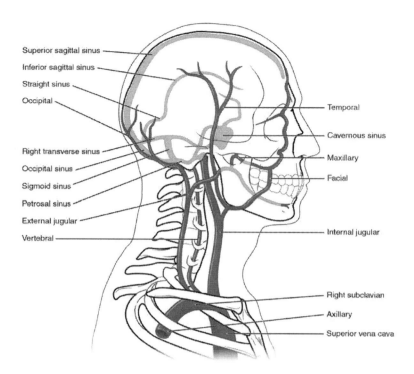

Figure 20.37 Veins of the Head and Neck This left lateral view shows the veins of the head and neck, including the intercranial sinuses.

Major Veins of the Brain

Vessel	Description
Superior sagittal sinus	Enlarged vein located midsagittally between the meningeal and periosteal layers of the dura mater within the falx cerebri; receives most of the blood drained from the superior surface of the cerebrum and leads to the inferior jugular vein and the vertebral vein
Great cerebral vein	Receives most of the smaller vessels from the inferior cerebral veins and leads to the straight sinus
Straight sinus	Enlarged vein that drains blood from the brain; receives most of the blood from the great cerebral vein and leads to the left or right transverse sinus
Cavernous sinus	Enlarged vein that receives blood from most of the other cerebral veins and the eye socket, and leads to the petrosal sinus
Petrosal sinus	Enlarged vein that receives blood from the cavernous sinus and leads into the internal jugular veins
Occipital sinus	Enlarged vein that drains the occipital region near the falx cerebelli and leads to the left and right transverse sinuses, and also the vertebral veins
Transverse sinuses	Pair of enlarged veins near the lambdoid suture that drains the occipital, sagittal, and straight sinuses, and leads to the sigmoid sinuses

Table 20.13

Major Veins of the Brain

Vessel	Description
Sigmoid sinuses	Enlarged vein that receives blood from the transverse sinuses and leads through the jugular foramen to the internal jugular vein

Table 20.13

Veins Draining the Upper Limbs

The **digital veins** in the fingers come together in the hand to form the **palmar venous arches** (Figure 20.38). From here, the veins come together to form the radial vein, the ulnar vein, and the median antebrachial vein. The **radial vein** and the **ulnar vein** parallel the bones of the forearm and join together at the antebrachium to form the **brachial vein**, a deep vein that flows into the axillary vein in the brachium.

The **median antebrachial vein** parallels the ulnar vein, is more medial in location, and joins the **basilic vein** in the forearm. As the basilic vein reaches the antecubital region, it gives off a branch called the **median cubital vein** that crosses at an angle to join the cephalic vein. The median cubital vein is the most common site for drawing venous blood in humans. The basilic vein continues through the arm medially and superficially to the axillary vein.

The **cephalic vein** begins in the antebrachium and drains blood from the superficial surface of the arm into the axillary vein. It is extremely superficial and easily seen along the surface of the biceps brachii muscle in individuals with good muscle tone and in those without excessive subcutaneous adipose tissue in the arms.

The **subscapular vein** drains blood from the subscapular region and joins the cephalic vein to form the **axillary vein**. As it passes through the body wall and enters the thorax, the axillary vein becomes the subclavian vein.

Many of the larger veins of the thoracic and abdominal region and upper limb are further represented in the flow chart in Figure 20.39. Table 20.14 summarizes the veins of the upper limbs.

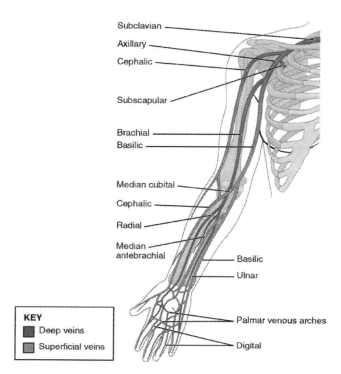

Figure 20.38 Veins of the Upper Limb This anterior view shows the veins that drain the upper limb.

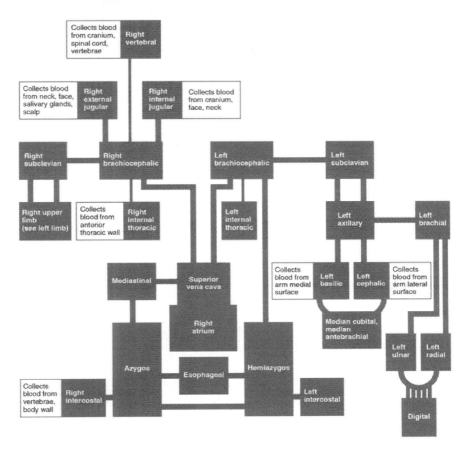

Figure 20.39 Veins Flowing into the Superior Vena Cava The flow chart summarizes the distribution of the veins flowing into the superior vena cava.

Veins of the Upper Limbs

Vessel	Description
Digital veins	Drain the digits and lead to the palmar arches of the hand and dorsal venous arch of the foot
Palmar venous arches	Drain the hand and digits, and lead to the radial vein, ulnar veins, and the median antebrachial vein
Radial vein	Vein that parallels the radius and radial artery; arises from the palmar venous arches and leads to the brachial vein
Ulnar vein	Vein that parallels the ulna and ulnar artery; arises from the palmar venous arches and leads to the brachial vein
Brachial vein	Deeper vein of the arm that forms from the radial and ulnar veins in the lower arm; leads to the axillary vein

Table 20.14

Veins of the Upper Limbs

Vessel	Description
Median antebrachial vein	Vein that parallels the ulnar vein but is more medial in location; intertwines with the palmar venous arches; leads to the basilic vein
Basilic vein	Superficial vein of the arm that arises from the median antebrachial vein, intersects with the median cubital vein, parallels the ulnar vein, and continues into the upper arm; along with the brachial vein, it leads to the axillary vein
Median cubital vein	Superficial vessel located in the antecubital region that links the cephalic vein to the basilic vein in the form of a v; a frequent site from which to draw blood
Cephalic vein	Superficial vessel in the upper arm; leads to the axillary vein
Subscapular vein	Drains blood from the subscapular region and leads to the axillary vein
Axillary vein	The major vein in the axillary region; drains the upper limb and becomes the subclavian vein

Table 20.14

The Inferior Vena Cava

Other than the small amount of blood drained by the azygos and hemiazygos veins, most of the blood inferior to the diaphragm drains into the inferior vena cava before it is returned to the heart (see Figure 20.36). Lying just beneath the parietal peritoneum in the abdominal cavity, the **inferior vena cava** parallels the abdominal aorta, where it can receive blood from abdominal veins. The lumbar portions of the abdominal wall and spinal cord are drained by a series of **lumbar veins**, usually four on each side. The ascending lumbar veins drain into either the azygos vein on the right or the hemiazygos vein on the left, and return to the superior vena cava. The remaining lumbar veins drain directly into the inferior vena cava.

Blood supply from the kidneys flows into each **renal vein**, normally the largest veins entering the inferior vena cava. A number of other, smaller veins empty into the left renal vein. Each **adrenal vein** drains the adrenal or suprarenal glands located immediately superior to the kidneys. The right adrenal vein enters the inferior vena cava directly, whereas the left adrenal vein enters the left renal vein.

From the male reproductive organs, each **testicular vein** flows from the scrotum, forming a portion of the spermatic cord. Each **ovarian vein** drains an ovary in females. Each of these veins is generically called a **gonadal vein**. The right gonadal vein empties directly into the inferior vena cava, and the left gonadal vein empties into the left renal vein.

Each side of the diaphragm drains into a **phrenic vein**; the right phrenic vein empties directly into the inferior vena cava, whereas the left phrenic vein empties into the left renal vein. Blood supply from the liver drains into each **hepatic vein** and directly into the inferior vena cava. Since the inferior vena cava lies primarily to the right of the vertebral column and aorta, the left renal vein is longer, as are the left phrenic, adrenal, and gonadal veins. The longer length of the left renal vein makes the left kidney the primary target of surgeons removing this organ for donation. Figure 20.40 provides a flow chart of the veins flowing into the inferior vena cava. Table 20.15 summarizes the major veins of the abdominal region.

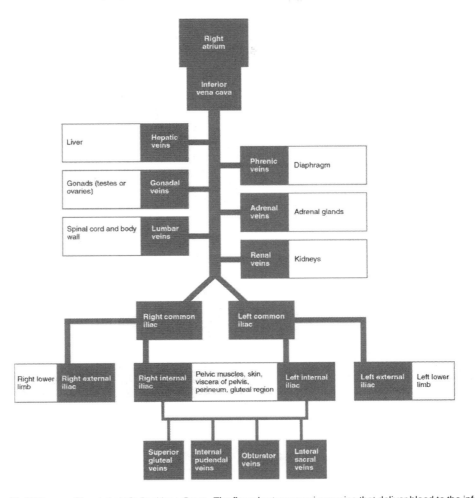

Figure 20.40 Venous Flow into Inferior Vena Cava The flow chart summarizes veins that deliver blood to the inferior vena cava.

Major Veins of the Abdominal Region

Vessel	Description
Inferior vena cava	Large systemic vein that drains blood from areas largely inferior to the diaphragm; empties into the right atrium
Lumbar veins	Series of veins that drain the lumbar portion of the abdominal wall and spinal cord; the ascending lumbar veins drain into the azygos vein on the right or the hemiazygos vein on the left; the remaining lumbar veins drain directly into the inferior vena cava
Renal vein	Largest vein entering the inferior vena cava; drains the kidneys and flows into the inferior vena cava

Table 20.15

Major Veins of the Abdominal Region

Vessel	Description
Adrenal vein	Drains the adrenal or suprarenal; the right adrenal vein enters the inferior vena cava directly and the left adrenal vein enters the left renal vein
Testicular vein	Drains the testes and forms part of the spermatic cord; the right testicular vein empties directly into the inferior vena cava and the left testicular vein empties into the left renal vein
Ovarian vein	Drains the ovary; the right ovarian vein empties directly into the inferior vena cava and the left ovarian vein empties into the left renal vein
Gonadal vein	Generic term for a vein draining a reproductive organ; may be either an ovarian vein or a testicular vein, depending on the sex of the individual
Phrenic vein	Drains the diaphragm; the right phrenic vein flows into the inferior vena cava and the left phrenic vein empties into the left renal vein
Hepatic vein	Drains systemic blood from the liver and flows into the inferior vena cava

Table 20.15

Veins Draining the Lower Limbs

The superior surface of the foot drains into the digital veins, and the inferior surface drains into the **plantar veins**, which flow into a complex series of anastomoses in the feet and ankles, including the **dorsal venous arch** and the **plantar venous arch** (Figure 20.41). From the dorsal venous arch, blood supply drains into the anterior and posterior tibial veins. The **anterior tibial vein** drains the area near the tibialis anterior muscle and combines with the posterior tibial vein and the fibular vein to form the popliteal vein. The **posterior tibial vein** drains the posterior surface of the tibia and joins the popliteal vein. The **fibular vein** drains the muscles and integument in proximity to the fibula and also joins the popliteal vein. The **small saphenous vein** located on the lateral surface of the leg drains blood from the superficial regions of the lower leg and foot, and flows into to the **popliteal vein**. As the popliteal vein passes behind the knee in the popliteal region, it becomes the femoral vein. It is palpable in patients without excessive adipose tissue.

Close to the body wall, the great saphenous vein, the deep femoral vein, and the femoral circumflex vein drain into the femoral vein. The **great saphenous vein** is a prominent surface vessel located on the medial surface of the leg and thigh that collects blood from the superficial portions of these areas. The **deep femoral vein**, as the name suggests, drains blood from the deeper portions of the thigh. The **femoral circumflex vein** forms a loop around the femur just inferior to the trochanters and drains blood from the areas in proximity to the head and neck of the femur.

As the **femoral vein** penetrates the body wall from the femoral portion of the upper limb, it becomes the **external iliac vein**, a large vein that drains blood from the leg to the common iliac vein. The pelvic organs and integument drain into the **internal iliac vein**, which forms from several smaller veins in the region, including the umbilical veins that run on either side of the bladder. The external and internal iliac veins combine near the inferior portion of the sacroiliac joint to form the common iliac vein. In addition to blood supply from the external and internal iliac veins, the **middle sacral vein** drains the sacral region into the **common iliac vein**. Similar to the common iliac arteries, the common iliac veins come together at the level of L5 to form the inferior vena cava.

Figure 20.42 is a flow chart of veins flowing into the lower limb. Table 20.16 summarizes the major veins of the lower limbs.

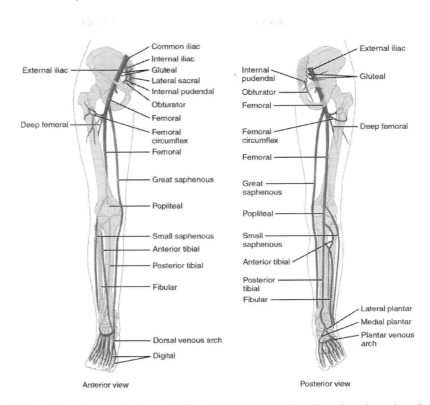

Figure 20.41 Major Veins Serving the Lower Limbs Anterior and posterior views show the major veins that drain the lower limb into the inferior vena cava.

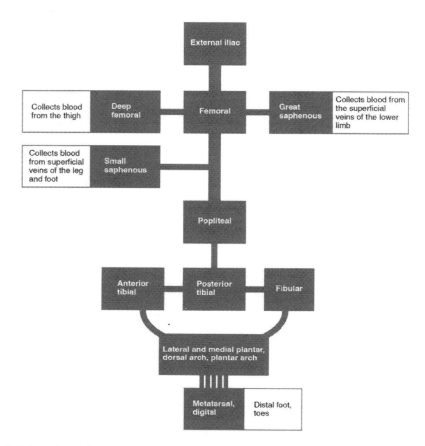

Figure 20.42 Major Veins of the Lower Limb The flow chart summarizes venous flow from the lower limb.

Veins of the Lower Limbs

Vessel	Description
Plantar veins	Drain the foot and flow into the plantar venous arch
Dorsal venous arch	Drains blood from digital veins and vessels on the superior surface of the foot
Plantar venous arch	Formed from the plantar veins; flows into the anterior and posterior tibial veins through anastomoses
Anterior tibial vein	Formed from the dorsal venous arch; drains the area near the tibialis anterior muscle and flows into the popliteal vein
Posterior tibial vein	Formed from the dorsal venous arch; drains the area near the posterior surface of the tibia and flows into the popliteal vein
Fibular vein	Drains the muscles and integument near the fibula and flows into the popliteal vein

Table 20.16

Veins of the Lower Limbs

Vessel	Description
Small saphenous vein	Located on the lateral surface of the leg; drains blood from the superficial regions of the lower leg and foot, and flows into the popliteal vein
Popliteal vein	Drains the region behind the knee and forms from the fusion of the fibular, anterior, and posterior tibial veins; flows into the femoral vein
Great saphenous vein	Prominent surface vessel located on the medial surface of the leg and thigh; drains the superficial portions of these areas and flows into the femoral vein
Deep femoral vein	Drains blood from the deeper portions of the thigh and flows into the femoral vein
Femoral circumflex vein	Forms a loop around the femur just inferior to the trochanters; drains blood from the areas around the head and neck of the femur; flows into the femoral vein
Femoral vein	Drains the upper leg; receives blood from the great saphenous vein, the deep femoral vein, and the femoral circumflex vein; becomes the external iliac vein when it crosses the body wall
External iliac vein	Formed when the femoral vein passes into the body cavity; drains the legs and flows into the common iliac vein
Internal iliac vein	Drains the pelvic organs and integument; formed from several smaller veins in the region; flows into the common iliac vein
Middle sacral vein	Drains the sacral region and flows into the left common iliac vein
Common iliac vein	Flows into the inferior vena cava at the level of L5; the left common iliac vein drains the sacral region; formed from the union of the external and internal iliac veins near the inferior portion of the sacroiliac joint

Table 20.16

Hepatic Portal System

The liver is a complex biochemical processing plant. It packages nutrients absorbed by the digestive system; produces plasma proteins, clotting factors, and bile; and disposes of worn-out cell components and waste products. Instead of entering the circulation directly, absorbed nutrients and certain wastes (for example, materials produced by the spleen) travel to the liver for processing. They do so via the **hepatic portal system** (Figure 20.43). Portal systems begin and end in capillaries. In this case, the initial capillaries from the stomach, small intestine, large intestine, and spleen lead to the hepatic portal vein and end in specialized capillaries within the liver, the hepatic sinusoids. You saw the only other portal system with the hypothalamic-hypophyseal portal vessel in the endocrine chapter.

The hepatic portal system consists of the hepatic portal vein and the veins that drain into it. The hepatic portal vein itself is relatively short, beginning at the level of L2 with the confluence of the superior mesenteric and splenic veins. It also receives branches from the inferior mesenteric vein, plus the splenic veins and all their tributaries. The superior mesenteric vein receives blood from the small intestine, two-thirds of the large intestine, and the stomach. The inferior mesenteric vein drains the distal third of the large intestine, including the descending colon, the sigmoid colon, and the rectum. The splenic vein is formed from branches from the spleen, pancreas, and portions of the stomach, and the inferior mesenteric vein. After its formation, the hepatic portal vein also receives branches from the gastric veins of the stomach and cystic veins from the gall bladder. The hepatic portal vein delivers materials from these digestive and circulatory organs directly to the liver for processing.

Because of the hepatic portal system, the liver receives its blood supply from two different sources: from normal systemic circulation via the hepatic artery and from the hepatic portal vein. The liver processes the blood from the portal system to remove certain wastes and excess nutrients, which are stored for later use. This processed blood, as well as the systemic blood that came from the hepatic artery, exits the liver via the right, left, and middle hepatic veins, and flows into the inferior vena cava. Overall systemic blood composition remains relatively stable, since the liver is able to metabolize the absorbed digestive components.

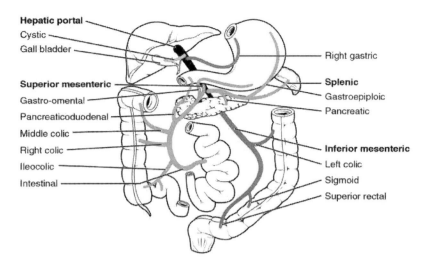

Figure 20.43 Hepatic Portal System The liver receives blood from the normal systemic circulation via the hepatic artery. It also receives and processes blood from other organs, delivered via the veins of the hepatic portal system. All blood exits the liver via the hepatic vein, which delivers the blood to the inferior vena cava. (Different colors are used to help distinguish among the different vessels in the system.)

20.6 | Development of Blood Vessels and Fetal Circulation

By the end of this section, you will be able to:
- Describe the development of blood vessels
- Describe the fetal circulation

In a developing embryo, the heart has developed enough by day 21 post-fertilization to begin beating. Circulation patterns are clearly established by the fourth week of embryonic life. It is critical to the survival of the developing human that the circulatory system forms early to supply the growing tissue with nutrients and gases, and to remove waste products. Blood cells and vessel production in structures outside the embryo proper called the yolk sac, chorion, and connecting stalk begin about 15 to 16 days following fertilization. Development of these circulatory elements within the embryo itself begins approximately 2 days later. You will learn more about the formation and function of these early structures when you study the chapter on development. During those first few weeks, blood vessels begin to form from the embryonic mesoderm. The precursor cells are known as **hemangioblasts**. These in turn differentiate into **angioblasts**, which give rise to the blood vessels and pluripotent stem cells, which differentiate into the formed elements of blood. (Seek additional content for more detail on fetal development and circulation.) Together, these cells form masses known as **blood islands** scattered throughout the embryonic disc. Spaces appear on the blood islands that develop into vessel lumens. The endothelial lining of the vessels arise from the angioblasts within these islands. Surrounding mesenchymal cells give rise to the smooth muscle and connective tissue layers of the vessels. While the vessels are developing, the pluripotent stem cells begin to form the blood.

Vascular tubes also develop on the blood islands, and they eventually connect to one another as well as to the developing, tubular heart. Thus, the developmental pattern, rather than beginning from the formation of one central vessel and spreading outward, occurs in many regions simultaneously with vessels later joining together. This **angiogenesis**—the creation of new blood vessels from existing ones—continues as needed throughout life as we grow and develop.

Blood vessel development often follows the same pattern as nerve development and travels to the same target tissues and organs. This occurs because the many factors directing growth of nerves also stimulate blood vessels to follow a similar pattern. Whether a given vessel develops into an artery or a vein is dependent upon local concentrations of signaling proteins.

As the embryo grows within the mother's uterus, its requirements for nutrients and gas exchange also grow. The placenta—a circulatory organ unique to pregnancy—develops jointly from the embryo and uterine wall structures to fill this need. Emerging from the placenta is the **umbilical vein**, which carries oxygen-rich blood from the mother to the fetal inferior vena cava via the ductus venosus to the heart that pumps it into fetal circulation. Two **umbilical arteries** carry oxygen-depleted fetal blood, including wastes and carbon dioxide, to the placenta. Remnants of the umbilical arteries remain in the adult. (Seek additional content for more information on the role of the placenta in fetal circulation.)

There are three major shunts—alternate paths for blood flow—found in the circulatory system of the fetus. Two of these shunts divert blood from the pulmonary to the systemic circuit, whereas the third connects the umbilical vein to the inferior vena cava. The first two shunts are critical during fetal life, when the lungs are compressed, filled with amniotic fluid, and nonfunctional, and gas exchange is provided by the placenta. These shunts close shortly after birth, however, when the newborn begins to breathe. The third shunt persists a bit longer but becomes nonfunctional once the umbilical cord is severed. The three shunts are as follows (Figure 20.44):

- The **foramen ovale** is an opening in the interatrial septum that allows blood to flow from the right atrium to the left atrium. A valve associated with this opening prevents backflow of blood during the fetal period. As the newborn begins to breathe and blood pressure in the atria increases, this shunt closes. The fossa ovalis remains in the interatrial septum after birth, marking the location of the former foramen ovale.

- The **ductus arteriosus** is a short, muscular vessel that connects the pulmonary trunk to the aorta. Most of the blood pumped from the right ventricle into the pulmonary trunk is thereby diverted into the aorta. Only enough blood reaches the fetal lungs to maintain the developing lung tissue. When the newborn takes the first breath, pressure within the lungs drops dramatically, and both the lungs and the pulmonary vessels expand. As the amount of oxygen increases, the smooth muscles in the wall of the ductus arteriosus constrict, sealing off the passage. Eventually, the muscular and endothelial components of the ductus arteriosus degenerate, leaving only the connective tissue component of the ligamentum arteriosum.

- The **ductus venosus** is a temporary blood vessel that branches from the umbilical vein, allowing much of the freshly oxygenated blood from the placenta—the organ of gas exchange between the mother and fetus—to bypass the fetal liver and go directly to the fetal heart. The ductus venosus closes slowly during the first weeks of infancy and degenerates to become the ligamentum venosum.

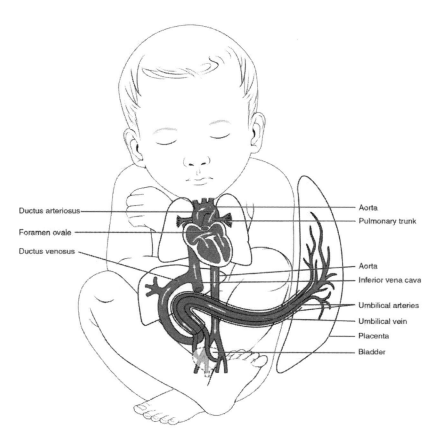

Figure 20.44 Fetal Shunts The foramen ovale in the interatrial septum allows blood to flow from the right atrium to the left atrium. The ductus arteriosus is a temporary vessel, connecting the aorta to the pulmonary trunk. The ductus venosus links the umbilical vein to the inferior vena cava largely through the liver.

KEY TERMS

abdominal aorta portion of the aorta inferior to the aortic hiatus and superior to the common iliac arteries

adrenal artery branch of the abdominal aorta; supplies blood to the adrenal (suprarenal) glands

adrenal vein drains the adrenal or suprarenal glands that are immediately superior to the kidneys; the right adrenal vein enters the inferior vena cava directly and the left adrenal vein enters the left renal vein

anaphylactic shock type of shock that follows a severe allergic reaction and results from massive vasodilation

angioblasts stem cells that give rise to blood vessels

angiogenesis development of new blood vessels from existing vessels

anterior cerebral artery arises from the internal carotid artery; supplies the frontal lobe of the cerebrum

anterior communicating artery anastomosis of the right and left internal carotid arteries; supplies blood to the brain

anterior tibial artery branches from the popliteal artery; supplies blood to the anterior tibial region; becomes the dorsalis pedis artery

anterior tibial vein forms from the dorsal venous arch; drains the area near the tibialis anterior muscle and leads to the popliteal vein

aorta largest artery in the body, originating from the left ventricle and descending to the abdominal region where it bifurcates into the common iliac arteries at the level of the fourth lumbar vertebra; arteries originating from the aorta distribute blood to virtually all tissues of the body

aortic arch arc that connects the ascending aorta to the descending aorta; ends at the intervertebral disk between the fourth and fifth thoracic vertebrae

aortic hiatus opening in the diaphragm that allows passage of the thoracic aorta into the abdominal region where it becomes the abdominal aorta

aortic sinuses small pockets in the ascending aorta near the aortic valve that are the locations of the baroreceptors (stretch receptors) and chemoreceptors that trigger a reflex that aids in the regulation of vascular homeostasis

arterial circle (also, circle of Willis) anastomosis located at the base of the brain that ensures continual blood supply; formed from branches of the internal carotid and vertebral arteries; supplies blood to the brain

arteriole (also, resistance vessel) very small artery that leads to a capillary

arteriovenous anastomosis short vessel connecting an arteriole directly to a venule and bypassing the capillary beds

artery blood vessel that conducts blood away from the heart; may be a conducting or distributing vessel

ascending aorta initial portion of the aorta, rising from the left ventricle for a distance of approximately 5 cm

atrial reflex mechanism for maintaining vascular homeostasis involving atrial baroreceptors: if blood is returning to the right atrium more rapidly than it is being ejected from the left ventricle, the atrial receptors will stimulate the cardiovascular centers to increase sympathetic firing and increase cardiac output until the situation is reversed; the opposite is also true

axillary artery continuation of the subclavian artery as it penetrates the body wall and enters the axillary region; supplies blood to the region near the head of the humerus (humeral circumflex arteries); the majority of the vessel continues into the brachium and becomes the brachial artery

axillary vein major vein in the axillary region; drains the upper limb and becomes the subclavian vein

azygos vein originates in the lumbar region and passes through the diaphragm into the thoracic cavity on the right side of the vertebral column; drains blood from the intercostal veins, esophageal veins, bronchial veins, and other veins draining the mediastinal region; leads to the superior vena cava

basilar artery formed from the fusion of the two vertebral arteries; sends branches to the cerebellum, brain stem, and the posterior cerebral arteries; the main blood supply to the brain stem

basilic vein superficial vein of the arm that arises from the palmar venous arches, intersects with the median cubital vein, parallels the ulnar vein, and continues into the upper arm; along with the brachial vein, it leads to the axillary vein

blood colloidal osmotic pressure (BCOP) pressure exerted by colloids suspended in blood within a vessel; a primary determinant is the presence of plasma proteins

blood flow movement of blood through a vessel, tissue, or organ that is usually expressed in terms of volume per unit of time

blood hydrostatic pressure force blood exerts against the walls of a blood vessel or heart chamber

blood islands masses of developing blood vessels and formed elements from mesodermal cells scattered throughout the embryonic disc

blood pressure force exerted by the blood against the wall of a vessel or heart chamber; can be described with the more generic term hydrostatic pressure

brachial artery continuation of the axillary artery in the brachium; supplies blood to much of the brachial region; gives off several smaller branches that provide blood to the posterior surface of the arm in the region of the elbow; bifurcates into the radial and ulnar arteries at the coronoid fossa

brachial vein deeper vein of the arm that forms from the radial and ulnar veins in the lower arm; leads to the axillary vein

brachiocephalic artery single vessel located on the right side of the body; the first vessel branching from the aortic arch; gives rise to the right subclavian artery and the right common carotid artery; supplies blood to the head, neck, upper limb, and wall of the thoracic region

brachiocephalic vein one of a pair of veins that form from a fusion of the external and internal jugular veins and the subclavian vein; subclavian, external and internal jugulars, vertebral, and internal thoracic veins lead to it; drains the upper thoracic region and flows into the superior vena cava

bronchial artery systemic branch from the aorta that provides oxygenated blood to the lungs in addition to the pulmonary circuit

bronchial vein drains the systemic circulation from the lungs and leads to the azygos vein

capacitance ability of a vein to distend and store blood

capacitance vessels veins

capillary smallest of blood vessels where physical exchange occurs between the blood and tissue cells surrounded by interstitial fluid

capillary bed network of 10–100 capillaries connecting arterioles to venules

capillary hydrostatic pressure (CHP) force blood exerts against a capillary

cardiogenic shock type of shock that results from the inability of the heart to maintain cardiac output

carotid sinuses small pockets near the base of the internal carotid arteries that are the locations of the baroreceptors and chemoreceptors that trigger a reflex that aids in the regulation of vascular homeostasis

cavernous sinus enlarged vein that receives blood from most of the other cerebral veins and the eye socket, and leads to the petrosal sinus

celiac trunk (also, celiac artery) major branch of the abdominal aorta; gives rise to the left gastric artery, the splenic artery, and the common hepatic artery that forms the hepatic artery to the liver, the right gastric artery to the stomach, and the cystic artery to the gall bladder

cephalic vein superficial vessel in the upper arm; leads to the axillary vein

cerebrovascular accident (CVA) blockage of blood flow to the brain; also called a stroke

circle of Willis (also, arterial circle) anastomosis located at the base of the brain that ensures continual blood supply; formed from branches of the internal carotid and vertebral arteries; supplies blood to the brain

circulatory shock also simply called shock; a life-threatening medical condition in which the circulatory system is unable to supply enough blood flow to provide adequate oxygen and other nutrients to the tissues to maintain cellular metabolism

common carotid artery right common carotid artery arises from the brachiocephalic artery, and the left common carotid arises from the aortic arch; gives rise to the external and internal carotid arteries; supplies the respective sides of the head and neck

common hepatic artery branch of the celiac trunk that forms the hepatic artery, the right gastric artery, and the cystic artery

common iliac artery branch of the aorta that leads to the internal and external iliac arteries

common iliac vein one of a pair of veins that flows into the inferior vena cava at the level of L5; the left common iliac vein drains the sacral region; divides into external and internal iliac veins near the inferior portion of the sacroiliac joint

compliance degree to which a blood vessel can stretch as opposed to being rigid

continuous capillary most common type of capillary, found in virtually all tissues except epithelia and cartilage; contains very small gaps in the endothelial lining that permit exchange

cystic artery branch of the common hepatic artery; supplies blood to the gall bladder

deep femoral artery branch of the femoral artery; gives rise to the lateral circumflex arteries

deep femoral vein drains blood from the deeper portions of the thigh and leads to the femoral vein

descending aorta portion of the aorta that continues downward past the end of the aortic arch; subdivided into the thoracic aorta and the abdominal aorta

diastolic pressure lower number recorded when measuring arterial blood pressure; represents the minimal value corresponding to the pressure that remains during ventricular relaxation

digital arteries formed from the superficial and deep palmar arches; supply blood to the digits

digital veins drain the digits and feed into the palmar arches of the hand and dorsal venous arch of the foot

dorsal arch (also, arcuate arch) formed from the anastomosis of the dorsalis pedis artery and medial and plantar arteries; branches supply the distal portions of the foot and digits

dorsal venous arch drains blood from digital veins and vessels on the superior surface of the foot

dorsalis pedis artery forms from the anterior tibial artery; branches repeatedly to supply blood to the tarsal and dorsal regions of the foot

ductus arteriosus shunt in the fetal pulmonary trunk that diverts oxygenated blood back to the aorta

ductus venosus shunt that causes oxygenated blood to bypass the fetal liver on its way to the inferior vena cava

elastic artery (also, conducting artery) artery with abundant elastic fibers located closer to the heart, which maintains the pressure gradient and conducts blood to smaller branches

esophageal artery branch of the thoracic aorta; supplies blood to the esophagus

esophageal vein drains the inferior portions of the esophagus and leads to the azygos vein

external carotid artery arises from the common carotid artery; supplies blood to numerous structures within the face, lower jaw, neck, esophagus, and larynx

external elastic membrane membrane composed of elastic fibers that separates the tunica media from the tunica externa; seen in larger arteries

external iliac artery branch of the common iliac artery that leaves the body cavity and becomes a femoral artery; supplies blood to the lower limbs

external iliac vein formed when the femoral vein passes into the body cavity; drains the legs and leads to the common iliac vein

external jugular vein one of a pair of major veins located in the superficial neck region that drains blood from the more superficial portions of the head, scalp, and cranial regions, and leads to the subclavian vein

femoral artery continuation of the external iliac artery after it passes through the body cavity; divides into several smaller branches, the lateral deep femoral artery, and the genicular artery; becomes the popliteal artery as it passes posterior to the knee

femoral circumflex vein forms a loop around the femur just inferior to the trochanters; drains blood from the areas around the head and neck of the femur; leads to the femoral vein

femoral vein drains the upper leg; receives blood from the great saphenous vein, the deep femoral vein, and the femoral circumflex vein; becomes the external iliac vein when it crosses the body wall

fenestrated capillary type of capillary with pores or fenestrations in the endothelium that allow for rapid passage of certain small materials

fibular vein drains the muscles and integument near the fibula and leads to the popliteal vein

filtration in the cardiovascular system, the movement of material from a capillary into the interstitial fluid, moving from an area of higher pressure to lower pressure

foramen ovale shunt that directly connects the right and left atria and helps to divert oxygenated blood from the fetal pulmonary circuit

genicular artery branch of the femoral artery; supplies blood to the region of the knee

gonadal artery branch of the abdominal aorta; supplies blood to the gonads or reproductive organs; also described as ovarian arteries or testicular arteries, depending upon the sex of the individual

gonadal vein generic term for a vein draining a reproductive organ; may be either an ovarian vein or a testicular vein, depending on the sex of the individual

great cerebral vein receives most of the smaller vessels from the inferior cerebral veins and leads to the straight sinus

great saphenous vein prominent surface vessel located on the medial surface of the leg and thigh; drains the superficial portions of these areas and leads to the femoral vein

hemangioblasts embryonic stem cells that appear in the mesoderm and give rise to both angioblasts and pluripotent stem cells

hemiazygos vein smaller vein complementary to the azygos vein; drains the esophageal veins from the esophagus and the left intercostal veins, and leads to the brachiocephalic vein via the superior intercostal vein

hepatic artery proper branch of the common hepatic artery; supplies systemic blood to the liver

hepatic portal system specialized circulatory pathway that carries blood from digestive organs to the liver for processing before being sent to the systemic circulation

hepatic vein drains systemic blood from the liver and flows into the inferior vena cava

hypertension chronic and persistent blood pressure measurements of 140/90 mm Hg or above

hypervolemia abnormally high levels of fluid and blood within the body

hypovolemia abnormally low levels of fluid and blood within the body

hypovolemic shock type of circulatory shock caused by excessive loss of blood volume due to hemorrhage or possibly dehydration

hypoxia lack of oxygen supply to the tissues

inferior mesenteric artery branch of the abdominal aorta; supplies blood to the distal segment of the large intestine and rectum

inferior phrenic artery branch of the abdominal aorta; supplies blood to the inferior surface of the diaphragm

inferior vena cava large systemic vein that drains blood from areas largely inferior to the diaphragm; empties into the right atrium

intercostal artery branch of the thoracic aorta; supplies blood to the muscles of the thoracic cavity and vertebral column

intercostal vein drains the muscles of the thoracic wall and leads to the azygos vein

internal carotid artery arises from the common carotid artery and begins with the carotid sinus; goes through the carotid canal of the temporal bone to the base of the brain; combines with branches of the vertebral artery forming the arterial circle; supplies blood to the brain

internal elastic membrane membrane composed of elastic fibers that separates the tunica intima from the tunica media; seen in larger arteries

internal iliac artery branch from the common iliac arteries; supplies blood to the urinary bladder, walls of the pelvis, external genitalia, and the medial portion of the femoral region; in females, also provide blood to the uterus and vagina

internal iliac vein drains the pelvic organs and integument; formed from several smaller veins in the region; leads to the common iliac vein

internal jugular vein one of a pair of major veins located in the neck region that passes through the jugular foramen and canal, flows parallel to the common carotid artery that is more or less its counterpart; primarily drains blood from the brain, receives the superficial facial vein, and empties into the subclavian vein

internal thoracic artery (also, mammary artery) arises from the subclavian artery; supplies blood to the thymus, pericardium of the heart, and the anterior chest wall

internal thoracic vein (also, internal mammary vein) drains the anterior surface of the chest wall and leads to the brachiocephalic vein

interstitial fluid colloidal osmotic pressure (IFCOP) pressure exerted by the colloids within the interstitial fluid

interstitial fluid hydrostatic pressure (IFHP) force exerted by the fluid in the tissue spaces

ischemia insufficient blood flow to the tissues

Korotkoff sounds noises created by turbulent blood flow through the vessels

lateral circumflex artery branch of the deep femoral artery; supplies blood to the deep muscles of the thigh and the ventral and lateral regions of the integument

lateral plantar artery arises from the bifurcation of the posterior tibial arteries; supplies blood to the lateral plantar surfaces of the foot

left gastric artery branch of the celiac trunk; supplies blood to the stomach

lumbar arteries branches of the abdominal aorta; supply blood to the lumbar region, the abdominal wall, and spinal cord

lumbar veins drain the lumbar portion of the abdominal wall and spinal cord; the superior lumbar veins drain into the azygos vein on the right or the hemiazygos vein on the left; blood from these vessels is returned to the superior vena cava rather than the inferior vena cava

lumen interior of a tubular structure such as a blood vessel or a portion of the alimentary canal through which blood, chyme, or other substances travel

maxillary vein drains blood from the maxillary region and leads to the external jugular vein

mean arterial pressure (MAP) average driving force of blood to the tissues; approximated by taking diastolic pressure and adding 1/3 of pulse pressure

medial plantar artery arises from the bifurcation of the posterior tibial arteries; supplies blood to the medial plantar surfaces of the foot

median antebrachial vein vein that parallels the ulnar vein but is more medial in location; intertwines with the palmar venous arches

median cubital vein superficial vessel located in the antecubital region that links the cephalic vein to the basilic vein in the form of a v; a frequent site for a blood draw

median sacral artery continuation of the aorta into the sacrum

mediastinal artery branch of the thoracic aorta; supplies blood to the mediastinum

metarteriole short vessel arising from a terminal arteriole that branches to supply a capillary bed

microcirculation blood flow through the capillaries

middle cerebral artery another branch of the internal carotid artery; supplies blood to the temporal and parietal lobes of the cerebrum

middle sacral vein drains the sacral region and leads to the left common iliac vein

muscular artery (also, distributing artery) artery with abundant smooth muscle in the tunica media that branches to distribute blood to the arteriole network

myogenic response constriction or dilation in the walls of arterioles in response to pressures related to blood flow; reduces high blood flow or increases low blood flow to help maintain consistent flow to the capillary network

nervi vasorum small nerve fibers found in arteries and veins that trigger contraction of the smooth muscle in their walls

net filtration pressure (NFP) force driving fluid out of the capillary and into the tissue spaces; equal to the difference of the capillary hydrostatic pressure and the blood colloidal osmotic pressure

neurogenic shock type of shock that occurs with cranial or high spinal injuries that damage the cardiovascular centers in the medulla oblongata or the nervous fibers originating from this region

obstructive shock type of shock that occurs when a significant portion of the vascular system is blocked

occipital sinus enlarged vein that drains the occipital region near the falx cerebelli and flows into the left and right transverse sinuses, and also into the vertebral veins

ophthalmic artery branch of the internal carotid artery; supplies blood to the eyes

ovarian artery branch of the abdominal aorta; supplies blood to the ovary, uterine (Fallopian) tube, and uterus

ovarian vein drains the ovary; the right ovarian vein leads to the inferior vena cava and the left ovarian vein leads to the left renal vein

palmar arches superficial and deep arches formed from anastomoses of the radial and ulnar arteries; supply blood to the hand and digital arteries

palmar venous arches drain the hand and digits, and feed into the radial and ulnar veins

parietal branches (also, somatic branches) group of arterial branches of the thoracic aorta; includes those that supply blood to the thoracic cavity, vertebral column, and the superior surface of the diaphragm

perfusion distribution of blood into the capillaries so the tissues can be supplied

pericardial artery branch of the thoracic aorta; supplies blood to the pericardium

petrosal sinus enlarged vein that receives blood from the cavernous sinus and flows into the internal jugular vein

phrenic vein drains the diaphragm; the right phrenic vein flows into the inferior vena cava and the left phrenic vein leads to the left renal vein

plantar arch formed from the anastomosis of the dorsalis pedis artery and medial and plantar arteries; branches supply the distal portions of the foot and digits

plantar veins drain the foot and lead to the plantar venous arch

plantar venous arch formed from the plantar veins; leads to the anterior and posterior tibial veins through anastomoses

popliteal artery continuation of the femoral artery posterior to the knee; branches into the anterior and posterior tibial arteries

popliteal vein continuation of the femoral vein behind the knee; drains the region behind the knee and forms from the fusion of the fibular and anterior and posterior tibial veins

posterior cerebral artery branch of the basilar artery that forms a portion of the posterior segment of the arterial circle; supplies blood to the posterior portion of the cerebrum and brain stem

posterior communicating artery branch of the posterior cerebral artery that forms part of the posterior portion of the arterial circle; supplies blood to the brain

posterior tibial artery branch from the popliteal artery that gives rise to the fibular or peroneal artery; supplies blood to the posterior tibial region

posterior tibial vein forms from the dorsal venous arch; drains the area near the posterior surface of the tibia and leads to the popliteal vein

precapillary sphincters circular rings of smooth muscle that surround the entrance to a capillary and regulate blood flow into that capillary

pulmonary artery one of two branches, left and right, that divides off from the pulmonary trunk and leads to smaller arterioles and eventually to the pulmonary capillaries

pulmonary circuit system of blood vessels that provide gas exchange via a network of arteries, veins, and capillaries that run from the heart, through the body, and back to the lungs

pulmonary trunk single large vessel exiting the right ventricle that divides to form the right and left pulmonary arteries

pulmonary veins two sets of paired vessels, one pair on each side, that are formed from the small venules leading away from the pulmonary capillaries that flow into the left atrium

pulse alternating expansion and recoil of an artery as blood moves through the vessel; an indicator of heart rate

pulse pressure difference between the systolic and diastolic pressures

radial artery formed at the bifurcation of the brachial artery; parallels the radius; gives off smaller branches until it reaches the carpal region where it fuses with the ulnar artery to form the superficial and deep palmar arches; supplies blood to the lower arm and carpal region

radial vein parallels the radius and radial artery; arises from the palmar venous arches and leads to the brachial vein

reabsorption in the cardiovascular system, the movement of material from the interstitial fluid into the capillaries

renal artery branch of the abdominal aorta; supplies each kidney

renal vein largest vein entering the inferior vena cava; drains the kidneys and leads to the inferior vena cava

resistance any condition or parameter that slows or counteracts the flow of blood

respiratory pump increase in the volume of the thorax during inhalation that decreases air pressure, enabling venous blood to flow into the thoracic region, then exhalation increases pressure, moving blood into the atria

right gastric artery branch of the common hepatic artery; supplies blood to the stomach

sepsis (also, septicemia) organismal-level inflammatory response to a massive infection

septic shock (also, blood poisoning) type of shock that follows a massive infection resulting in organism-wide inflammation

sigmoid sinuses enlarged veins that receive blood from the transverse sinuses; flow through the jugular foramen and into the internal jugular vein

sinusoid capillary rarest type of capillary, which has extremely large intercellular gaps in the basement membrane in addition to clefts and fenestrations; found in areas such as the bone marrow and liver where passage of large molecules occurs

skeletal muscle pump effect on increasing blood pressure within veins by compression of the vessel caused by the contraction of nearby skeletal muscle

small saphenous vein located on the lateral surface of the leg; drains blood from the superficial regions of the lower leg and foot, and leads to the popliteal vein

sphygmomanometer blood pressure cuff attached to a device that measures blood pressure

splenic artery branch of the celiac trunk; supplies blood to the spleen

straight sinus enlarged vein that drains blood from the brain; receives most of the blood from the great cerebral vein and flows into the left or right transverse sinus

subclavian artery right subclavian arises from the brachiocephalic artery, whereas the left subclavian artery arises from the aortic arch; gives rise to the internal thoracic, vertebral, and thyrocervical arteries; supplies blood to the arms, chest, shoulders, back, and central nervous system

subclavian vein located deep in the thoracic cavity; becomes the axillary vein as it enters the axillary region; drains the axillary and smaller local veins near the scapular region; leads to the brachiocephalic vein

subscapular vein drains blood from the subscapular region and leads to the axillary vein

superior mesenteric artery branch of the abdominal aorta; supplies blood to the small intestine (duodenum, jejunum, and ileum), the pancreas, and a majority of the large intestine

superior phrenic artery branch of the thoracic aorta; supplies blood to the superior surface of the diaphragm

superior sagittal sinus enlarged vein located midsagittally between the meningeal and periosteal layers of the dura mater within the falx cerebri; receives most of the blood drained from the superior surface of the cerebrum and leads to the inferior jugular vein and the vertebral vein

superior vena cava large systemic vein; drains blood from most areas superior to the diaphragm; empties into the right atrium

systolic pressure larger number recorded when measuring arterial blood pressure; represents the maximum value following ventricular contraction

temporal vein drains blood from the temporal region and leads to the external jugular vein

testicular artery branch of the abdominal aorta; will ultimately travel outside the body cavity to the testes and form one component of the spermatic cord

testicular vein drains the testes and forms part of the spermatic cord; the right testicular vein empties directly into the inferior vena cava and the left testicular vein empties into the left renal vein

thoracic aorta portion of the descending aorta superior to the aortic hiatus

thoroughfare channel continuation of the metarteriole that enables blood to bypass a capillary bed and flow directly into a venule, creating a vascular shunt

thyrocervical artery arises from the subclavian artery; supplies blood to the thyroid, the cervical region, the upper back, and shoulder

transient ischemic attack (TIA) temporary loss of neurological function caused by a brief interruption in blood flow; also known as a mini-stroke

transverse sinuses pair of enlarged veins near the lambdoid suture that drain the occipital, sagittal, and straight sinuses, and leads to the sigmoid sinuses

trunk large vessel that gives rise to smaller vessels

tunica externa (also, tunica adventitia) outermost layer or tunic of a vessel (except capillaries)

tunica intima (also, tunica interna) innermost lining or tunic of a vessel

tunica media middle layer or tunic of a vessel (except capillaries)

ulnar artery formed at the bifurcation of the brachial artery; parallels the ulna; gives off smaller branches until it reaches the carpal region where it fuses with the radial artery to form the superficial and deep palmar arches; supplies blood to the lower arm and carpal region

ulnar vein parallels the ulna and ulnar artery; arises from the palmar venous arches and leads to the brachial vein

umbilical arteries pair of vessels that runs within the umbilical cord and carries fetal blood low in oxygen and high in waste to the placenta for exchange with maternal blood

umbilical vein single vessel that originates in the placenta and runs within the umbilical cord, carrying oxygen- and nutrient-rich blood to the fetal heart

vasa vasorum small blood vessels located within the walls or tunics of larger vessels that supply nourishment to and remove wastes from the cells of the vessels

vascular shock type of shock that occurs when arterioles lose their normal muscular tone and dilate dramatically

vascular shunt continuation of the metarteriole and thoroughfare channel that allows blood to bypass the capillary beds to flow directly from the arterial to the venous circulation

vascular tone contractile state of smooth muscle in a blood vessel

vascular tubes rudimentary blood vessels in a developing fetus

vasoconstriction constriction of the smooth muscle of a blood vessel, resulting in a decreased vascular diameter

vasodilation relaxation of the smooth muscle in the wall of a blood vessel, resulting in an increased vascular diameter

vasomotion irregular, pulsating flow of blood through capillaries and related structures

vein blood vessel that conducts blood toward the heart

venous reserve volume of blood contained within systemic veins in the integument, bone marrow, and liver that can be returned to the heart for circulation, if needed

venule small vessel leading from the capillaries to veins

vertebral artery arises from the subclavian artery and passes through the vertebral foramen through the foramen magnum to the brain; joins with the internal carotid artery to form the arterial circle; supplies blood to the brain and spinal cord

vertebral vein arises from the base of the brain and the cervical region of the spinal cord; passes through the intervertebral foramina in the cervical vertebrae; drains smaller veins from the cranium, spinal cord, and vertebrae, and leads to the brachiocephalic vein; counterpart of the vertebral artery

visceral branches branches of the descending aorta that supply blood to the viscera

CHAPTER REVIEW

20.1 Structure and Function of Blood Vessels

Blood pumped by the heart flows through a series of vessels known as arteries, arterioles, capillaries, venules, and veins before returning to the heart. Arteries transport blood away from the heart and branch into smaller vessels, forming arterioles. Arterioles distribute blood to capillary beds, the sites of exchange with the body tissues. Capillaries lead back to small vessels known as venules that flow into the larger veins and eventually back to the heart.

The arterial system is a relatively high-pressure system, so arteries have thick walls that appear round in cross section. The venous system is a lower-pressure system, containing veins that have larger lumens and thinner walls. They often appear flattened. Arteries, arterioles, venules, and veins are composed of three tunics known as the tunica intima, tunica media, and tunica externa. Capillaries have only a tunica intima layer. The tunica intima is a thin layer composed of a simple squamous epithelium known as endothelium and a small amount of connective tissue. The tunica media is a thicker area composed of variable amounts of smooth muscle and connective tissue. It is the thickest layer in all but the largest arteries. The tunica externa is primarily a layer of connective tissue, although in veins, it also contains some smooth muscle. Blood flow through vessels can be dramatically influenced by vasoconstriction and vasodilation in their walls.

20.2 Blood Flow, Blood Pressure, and Resistance

Blood flow is the movement of blood through a vessel, tissue, or organ. The slowing or blocking of blood flow is called resistance. Blood pressure is the force that blood exerts upon the walls of the blood vessels or chambers of the heart. The components of blood pressure include systolic pressure, which results from ventricular contraction, and diastolic pressure, which results from ventricular relaxation. Pulse pressure is the difference between systolic and diastolic measures, and mean arterial pressure is the "average" pressure of blood in the arterial system, driving blood into the tissues. Pulse, the expansion and recoiling of an artery, reflects the heartbeat. The variables affecting blood flow and blood pressure in the systemic circulation are cardiac output, compliance, blood volume, blood viscosity, and the length and diameter of the blood vessels. In the arterial system, vasodilation and vasoconstriction of the arterioles is a significant factor in systemic blood pressure: Slight vasodilation greatly decreases resistance and increases flow, whereas slight vasoconstriction greatly increases resistance and decreases flow. In the arterial system, as resistance increases, blood pressure increases and flow decreases. In the venous system, constriction increases blood pressure as it does in arteries; the increasing pressure helps to return blood to the heart. In addition, constriction causes the vessel lumen to become more rounded, decreasing resistance and increasing blood flow. Venoconstriction, while less important than arterial vasoconstriction, works with the skeletal muscle pump, the respiratory pump, and their valves to promote venous return to the heart.

20.3 Capillary Exchange

Small molecules can cross into and out of capillaries via simple or facilitated diffusion. Some large molecules can cross in vesicles or through clefts, fenestrations, or gaps between cells in capillary walls. However, the bulk flow of capillary and tissue fluid occurs via filtration and reabsorption. Filtration, the movement of fluid out of the capillaries, is driven by the CHP. Reabsorption, the influx of tissue fluid into the capillaries, is driven by the BCOP. Filtration predominates in the arterial end of the capillary; in the middle section, the opposing pressures are virtually identical so there is no net exchange, whereas reabsorption predominates at the venule end of the capillary. The hydrostatic and colloid osmotic pressures in the interstitial fluid are negligible in healthy circumstances.

20.4 Homeostatic Regulation of the Vascular System

Neural, endocrine, and autoregulatory mechanisms affect blood flow, blood pressure, and eventually perfusion of blood to body tissues. Neural mechanisms include the cardiovascular centers in the medulla oblongata, baroreceptors in the aorta and carotid arteries and right atrium, and associated chemoreceptors that monitor blood levels of oxygen, carbon dioxide, and hydrogen ions. Endocrine controls include epinephrine and norepinephrine, as well as ADH, the renin-angiotensin-aldosterone mechanism, ANH, and EPO. Autoregulation is the local control of vasodilation and constriction by chemical signals and the myogenic response. Exercise greatly improves cardiovascular function and reduces the risk of cardiovascular diseases, including hypertension, a leading cause of heart attacks and strokes. Significant hemorrhage can lead to a form of circulatory shock known as hypovolemic shock. Sepsis, obstruction, and widespread inflammation can also cause circulatory shock.

20.5 Circulatory Pathways

The right ventricle pumps oxygen-depleted blood into the pulmonary trunk and right and left pulmonary arteries, which carry it to the right and left lungs for gas exchange. Oxygen-rich blood is transported by pulmonary veins to the left atrium. The left ventricle pumps this blood into the aorta. The main regions of the aorta are the ascending aorta, aortic arch, and descending aorta, which is further divided into the thoracic and abdominal aorta. The coronary arteries branch from the ascending aorta. After oxygenating tissues in the capillaries, systemic blood is returned to the right atrium from the venous system via the superior vena cava, which drains most of the veins superior to the diaphragm, the inferior vena cava, which drains most of the veins inferior to the diaphragm, and the coronary veins via the coronary sinus. The hepatic portal system carries blood to the liver for processing before it enters circulation. Review the figures provided in this section for circulation of blood through the blood vessels.

20.6 Development of Blood Vessels and Fetal Circulation

Blood vessels begin to form from the embryonic mesoderm. The precursor hemangioblasts differentiate into angioblasts, which give rise to the blood vessels and pluripotent stem cells that differentiate into the formed elements of the blood. Together, these cells form blood islands scattered throughout the embryo. Extensions known as vascular tubes eventually connect the vascular network. As the embryo grows within the mother's womb, the placenta develops to supply blood rich in oxygen and nutrients via the umbilical vein and to remove wastes in oxygen-depleted blood via the umbilical arteries. Three major shunts found in the fetus are the foramen ovale and ductus arteriosus, which divert blood from the pulmonary to the systemic circuit, and the ductus venosus, which carries freshly oxygenated blood high in nutrients to the fetal heart.

INTERACTIVE LINK QUESTIONS

1. Watch this video (http://openstaxcollege.org/l/capillaryfunct) to explore capillaries and how they function in the body. Capillaries are never more than 100 micrometers away. What is the main component of interstitial fluid?

2. Listen to this CDC podcast (http://openstaxcollege.org/l/CDCpodcast) to learn about hypertension, often described as a "silent killer." What steps can you take to reduce your risk of a heart attack or stroke?

REVIEW QUESTIONS

3. The endothelium is found in the _____.
 a. tunica intima
 b. tunica media
 c. tunica externa
 d. lumen

4. Nervi vasorum control _____.
 a. vasoconstriction
 b. vasodilation
 c. capillary permeability
 d. both vasoconstriction and vasodilation

5. Closer to the heart, arteries would be expected to have a higher percentage of _____.
 a. endothelium
 b. smooth muscle fibers
 c. elastic fibers
 d. collagenous fibers

6. Which of the following best describes veins?
 a. thick walled, small lumens, low pressure, lack valves
 b. thin walled, large lumens, low pressure, have valves
 c. thin walled, small lumens, high pressure, have valves

d. thick walled, large lumens, high pressure, lack valves

7. An especially leaky type of capillary found in the liver and certain other tissues is called a _____.
   a. capillary bed
   b. fenestrated capillary
   c. sinusoid capillary
   d. metarteriole

8. In a blood pressure measurement of 110/70, the number 70 is the _____.
   a. systolic pressure
   b. diastolic pressure
   c. pulse pressure
   d. mean arterial pressure

9. A healthy elastic artery _____.
   a. is compliant
   b. reduces blood flow
   c. is a resistance artery
   d. has a thin wall and irregular lumen

10. Which of the following statements is *true*?
   a. The longer the vessel, the lower the resistance and the greater the flow.
   b. As blood volume decreases, blood pressure and blood flow also decrease.
   c. Increased viscosity increases blood flow.
   d. All of the above are true.

11. Slight vasodilation in an arteriole prompts a _____.
   a. slight increase in resistance
   b. huge increase in resistance
   c. slight decrease in resistance
   d. huge decrease in resistance

12. Venoconstriction increases which of the following?
   a. blood pressure within the vein
   b. blood flow within the vein
   c. return of blood to the heart
   d. all of the above

13. Hydrostatic pressure is _____.
   a. greater than colloid osmotic pressure at the venous end of the capillary bed
   b. the pressure exerted by fluid in an enclosed space
   c. about zero at the midpoint of a capillary bed
   d. all of the above

14. Net filtration pressure is calculated by _____.
   a. adding the capillary hydrostatic pressure to the interstitial fluid hydrostatic pressure
   b. subtracting the fluid drained by the lymphatic vessels from the total fluid in the interstitial fluid
   c. adding the blood colloid osmotic pressure to the capillary hydrostatic pressure
   d. subtracting the blood colloid osmotic pressure from the capillary hydrostatic pressure

15. Which of the following statements is true?
   a. In one day, more fluid exits the capillary through filtration than enters through reabsorption.
   b. In one day, approximately 35 mm of blood are filtered and 7 mm are reabsorbed.
   c. In one day, the capillaries of the lymphatic system absorb about 20.4 liters of fluid.
   d. None of the above are true.

16. Clusters of neurons in the medulla oblongata that regulate blood pressure are known collectively as _____.
   a. baroreceptors
   b. angioreceptors
   c. the cardiomotor mechanism
   d. the cardiovascular center

17. In the renin-angiotensin-aldosterone mechanism, _____.
   a. decreased blood pressure prompts the release of renin from the liver
   b. aldosterone prompts increased urine output
   c. aldosterone prompts the kidneys to reabsorb sodium
   d. all of the above

18. In the myogenic response, _____.
   a. muscle contraction promotes venous return to the heart
   b. ventricular contraction strength is decreased
   c. vascular smooth muscle responds to stretch
   d. endothelins dilate muscular arteries

19. A form of circulatory shock common in young children with severe diarrhea or vomiting is _____.
   a. hypovolemic shock
   b. anaphylactic shock
   c. obstructive shock
   d. hemorrhagic shock

20. The coronary arteries branch off of the _____.
   a. aortic valve
   b. ascending aorta
   c. aortic arch
   d. thoracic aorta

21. Which of the following statements is true?
   a. The left and right common carotid arteries both branch off of the brachiocephalic trunk.
   b. The brachial artery is the distal branch of the axillary artery.
   c. The radial and ulnar arteries join to form the palmar arch.
   d. All of the above are true.

22. Arteries serving the stomach, pancreas, and liver all branch from the _____.
   a. superior mesenteric artery
   b. inferior mesenteric artery
   c. celiac trunk
   d. splenic artery

23. The right and left brachiocephalic veins _____.
    a. drain blood from the right and left internal jugular veins
    b. drain blood from the right and left subclavian veins
    c. drain into the superior vena cava
    d. all of the above are true

24. The hepatic portal system delivers blood from the digestive organs to the _____.
    a. liver
    b. hypothalamus
    c. spleen
    d. left atrium

25. Blood islands are _____.
    a. clusters of blood-filtering cells in the placenta
    b. masses of pluripotent stem cells scattered throughout the fetal bone marrow
    c. vascular tubes that give rise to the embryonic tubular heart
    d. masses of developing blood vessels and formed elements scattered throughout the embryonic disc

26. Which of the following statements is true?
    a. Two umbilical veins carry oxygen-depleted blood from the fetal circulation to the placenta.
    b. One umbilical vein carries oxygen-rich blood from the placenta to the fetal heart.
    c. Two umbilical arteries carry oxygen-depleted blood to the fetal lungs.
    d. None of the above are true.

27. The ductus venosus is a shunt that allows _____.
    a. fetal blood to flow from the right atrium to the left atrium
    b. fetal blood to flow from the right ventricle to the left ventricle
    c. most freshly oxygenated blood to flow into the fetal heart
    d. most oxygen-depleted fetal blood to flow directly into the fetal pulmonary trunk

CRITICAL THINKING QUESTIONS

28. Arterioles are often referred to as resistance vessels. Why?

29. Cocaine use causes vasoconstriction. Is this likely to increase or decrease blood pressure, and why?

30. A blood vessel with a few smooth muscle fibers and connective tissue, and only a very thin tunica externa conducts blood toward the heart. What type of vessel is this?

31. You measure a patient's blood pressure at 130/85. Calculate the patient's pulse pressure and mean arterial pressure. Determine whether each pressure is low, normal, or high.

32. An obese patient comes to the clinic complaining of swollen feet and ankles, fatigue, shortness of breath, and often feeling "spaced out." She is a cashier in a grocery store, a job that requires her to stand all day. Outside of work, she engages in no physical activity. She confesses that, because of her weight, she finds even walking uncomfortable. Explain how the skeletal muscle pump might play a role in this patient's signs and symptoms.

33. A patient arrives at the emergency department with dangerously low blood pressure. The patient's blood colloid osmotic pressure is normal. How would you expect this situation to affect the patient's net filtration pressure?

34. True or false? The plasma proteins suspended in blood cross the capillary cell membrane and enter the tissue fluid via facilitated diffusion. Explain your thinking.

35. A patient arrives in the emergency department with a blood pressure of 70/45 confused and complaining of thirst. Why?

36. Nitric oxide is broken down very quickly after its release. Why?

37. Identify the ventricle of the heart that pumps oxygen-depleted blood and the arteries of the body that carry oxygen-depleted blood.

38. What organs do the gonadal veins drain?

39. What arteries play the leading roles in supplying blood to the brain?

40. All tissues, including malignant tumors, need a blood supply. Explain why drugs called angiogenesis inhibitors would be used in cancer treatment.

41. Explain the location and importance of the ductus arteriosus in fetal circulation.

21 | THE LYMPHATIC AND IMMUNE SYSTEM

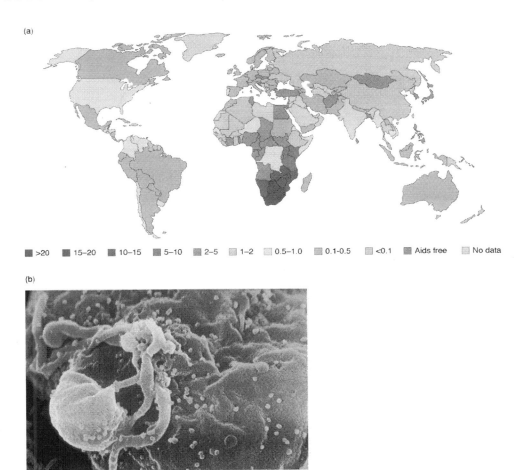

Figure 21.1 The Worldwide AIDS Epidemic (a) As of 2008, more than 15 percent of adults were infected with HIV in certain African countries. This grim picture had changed little by 2012. (b) In this scanning electron micrograph, HIV virions (green particles) are budding off the surface of a macrophage (pink structure). (credit b: C. Goldsmith)

Introduction

Chapter Objectives

After studying this chapter, you will be able to:

- Identify the components and anatomy of the lymphatic system
- Discuss the role of the innate immune response against pathogens
- Describe the power of the adaptive immune response to cure disease
- Explain immunological deficiencies and over-reactions of the immune system
- Discuss the role of the immune response in transplantation and cancer
- Describe the interaction of the immune and lymphatic systems with other body systems

In June 1981, the Centers for Disease Control and Prevention (CDC), in Atlanta, Georgia, published a report of an unusual cluster of five patients in Los Angeles, California. All five were diagnosed with a rare pneumonia caused by a fungus called *Pneumocystis jirovecii* (formerly known as *Pneumocystis carinii*).

Why was this unusual? Although commonly found in the lungs of healthy individuals, this fungus is an opportunistic pathogen that causes disease in individuals with suppressed or underdeveloped immune systems. The very young, whose immune systems have yet to mature, and the elderly, whose immune systems have declined with age, are particularly susceptible. The five patients from LA, though, were between 29 and 36 years of age and should have been in the prime of their lives, immunologically speaking. What could be going on?

A few days later, a cluster of eight cases was reported in New York City, also involving young patients, this time exhibiting a rare form of skin cancer known as Kaposi's sarcoma. This cancer of the cells that line the blood and lymphatic vessels was previously observed as a relatively innocuous disease of the elderly. The disease that doctors saw in 1981 was frighteningly more severe, with multiple, fast-growing lesions that spread to all parts of the body, including the trunk and face. Could the immune systems of these young patients have been compromised in some way? Indeed, when they were tested, they exhibited extremely low numbers of a specific type of white blood cell in their bloodstreams, indicating that they had somehow lost a major part of the immune system.

Acquired immune deficiency syndrome, or AIDS, turned out to be a new disease caused by the previously unknown human immunodeficiency virus (HIV). Although nearly 100 percent fatal in those with active HIV infections in the early years, the development of anti-HIV drugs has transformed HIV infection into a chronic, manageable disease and not the certain death sentence it once was. One positive outcome resulting from the emergence of HIV disease was that the public's attention became focused as never before on the importance of having a functional and healthy immune system.

21.1 | Anatomy of the Lymphatic and Immune Systems

By the end of this section, you will be able to:

- Describe the structure and function of the lymphatic tissue (lymph fluid, vessels, ducts, and organs)
- Describe the structure and function of the primary and secondary lymphatic organs
- Discuss the cells of the immune system, how they function, and their relationship with the lymphatic system

The **immune system** is the complex collection of cells and organs that destroys or neutralizes pathogens that would otherwise cause disease or death. The lymphatic system, for most people, is associated with the immune system to such a degree that the two systems are virtually indistinguishable. The **lymphatic system** is the system of vessels, cells, and organs that carries excess fluids to the bloodstream and filters pathogens from the blood. The swelling of lymph nodes during an infection and the transport of lymphocytes via the lymphatic vessels are but two examples of the many connections between these critical organ systems.

Functions of the Lymphatic System

A major function of the lymphatic system is to drain body fluids and return them to the bloodstream. Blood pressure causes leakage of fluid from the capillaries, resulting in the accumulation of fluid in the interstitial space—that is, spaces between individual cells in the tissues. In humans, 20 liters of plasma is released into the interstitial space of the tissues each day due to capillary filtration. Once this filtrate is out of the bloodstream and in the tissue spaces, it is referred to as interstitial fluid. Of this, 17 liters is reabsorbed directly by the blood vessels. But what happens to the remaining three liters? This is where the lymphatic system comes into play. It drains the excess fluid and empties it back into the bloodstream via a series of vessels, trunks, and ducts. **Lymph** is the term used to describe interstitial fluid once it has entered the lymphatic system. When the lymphatic system is damaged in some way, such as by being blocked by cancer cells or destroyed by injury, protein-rich interstitial fluid accumulates (sometimes "backs up" from the lymph vessels) in the tissue spaces. This inappropriate accumulation of fluid referred to as lymphedema may lead to serious medical consequences.

As the vertebrate immune system evolved, the network of lymphatic vessels became convenient avenues for transporting the cells of the immune system. Additionally, the transport of dietary lipids and fat-soluble vitamins absorbed in the gut uses this system.

Cells of the immune system not only use lymphatic vessels to make their way from interstitial spaces back into the circulation, but they also use lymph nodes as major staging areas for the development of critical immune responses. A **lymph node** is one of the small, bean-shaped organs located throughout the lymphatic system.

Visit this website (http://openstaxcollege.org/l/lymphsystem) for an overview of the lymphatic system. What are the three main components of the lymphatic system?

Structure of the Lymphatic System

The lymphatic vessels begin as open-ended capillaries, which feed into larger and larger lymphatic vessels, and eventually empty into the bloodstream by a series of ducts. Along the way, the lymph travels through the lymph nodes, which are commonly found near the groin, armpits, neck, chest, and abdomen. Humans have about 500–600 lymph nodes throughout the body (Figure 21.2).

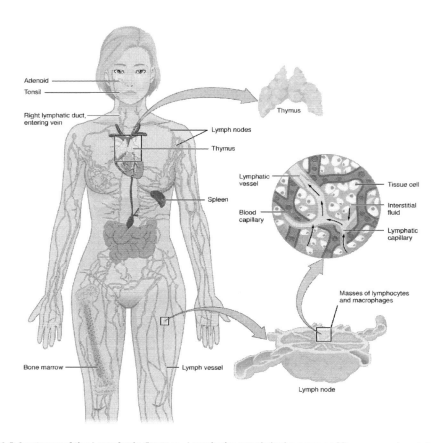

Figure 21.2 Anatomy of the Lymphatic System   Lymphatic vessels in the arms and legs convey lymph to the larger lymphatic vessels in the torso.

A major distinction between the lymphatic and cardiovascular systems in humans is that lymph is not actively pumped by the heart, but is forced through the vessels by the movements of the body, the contraction of skeletal muscles during body movements, and breathing. One-way valves (semi-lunar valves) in lymphatic vessels keep the lymph moving toward the heart. Lymph flows from the lymphatic capillaries, through lymphatic vessels, and then is dumped into the circulatory system via the lymphatic ducts located at the junction of the jugular and subclavian veins in the neck.

Lymphatic Capillaries

Lymphatic capillaries, also called the terminal lymphatics, are vessels where interstitial fluid enters the lymphatic system to become lymph fluid. Located in almost every tissue in the body, these vessels are interlaced among the arterioles and venules of the circulatory system in the soft connective tissues of the body (Figure 21.3). Exceptions are the central nervous system, bone marrow, bones, teeth, and the cornea of the eye, which do not contain lymph vessels.

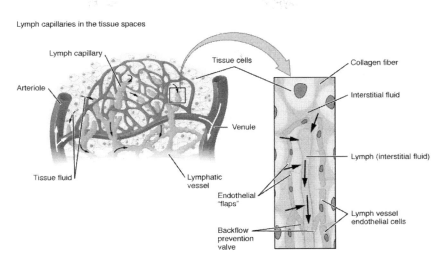

Figure 21.3 Lymphatic Capillaries Lymphatic capillaries are interlaced with the arterioles and venules of the cardiovascular system. Collagen fibers anchor a lymphatic capillary in the tissue (inset). Interstitial fluid slips through spaces between the overlapping endothelial cells that compose the lymphatic capillary.

Lymphatic capillaries are formed by a one cell-thick layer of endothelial cells and represent the open end of the system, allowing interstitial fluid to flow into them via overlapping cells (see Figure 21.3). When interstitial pressure is low, the endothelial flaps close to prevent "backflow." As interstitial pressure increases, the spaces between the cells open up, allowing the fluid to enter. Entry of fluid into lymphatic capillaries is also enabled by the collagen filaments that anchor the capillaries to surrounding structures. As interstitial pressure increases, the filaments pull on the endothelial cell flaps, opening up them even further to allow easy entry of fluid.

In the small intestine, lymphatic capillaries called lacteals are critical for the transport of dietary lipids and lipid-soluble vitamins to the bloodstream. In the small intestine, dietary triglycerides combine with other lipids and proteins, and enter the lacteals to form a milky fluid called **chyle**. The chyle then travels through the lymphatic system, eventually entering the liver and then the bloodstream.

Larger Lymphatic Vessels, Trunks, and Ducts

The lymphatic capillaries empty into larger lymphatic vessels, which are similar to veins in terms of their three-tunic structure and the presence of valves. These one-way valves are located fairly close to one another, and each one causes a bulge in the lymphatic vessel, giving the vessels a beaded appearance (see Figure 21.3).

The superficial and deep lymphatics eventually merge to form larger lymphatic vessels known as **lymphatic trunks**. On the right side of the body, the right sides of the head, thorax, and right upper limb drain lymph fluid into the right subclavian vein via the right lymphatic duct (Figure 21.4). On the left side of the body, the remaining portions of the body drain into the larger thoracic duct, which drains into the left subclavian vein. The thoracic duct itself begins just beneath the diaphragm in the **cisterna chyli**, a sac-like chamber that receives lymph from the lower abdomen, pelvis, and lower limbs by way of the left and right lumbar trunks and the intestinal trunk.

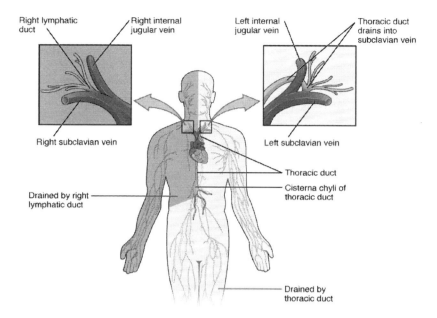

Figure 21.4 Major Trunks and Ducts of the Lymphatic System The thoracic duct drains a much larger portion of the body than does the right lymphatic duct.

The overall drainage system of the body is asymmetrical (see Figure 21.4). The **right lymphatic duct** receives lymph from only the upper right side of the body. The lymph from the rest of the body enters the bloodstream through the **thoracic duct** via all the remaining lymphatic trunks. In general, lymphatic vessels of the subcutaneous tissues of the skin, that is, the superficial lymphatics, follow the same routes as veins, whereas the deep lymphatic vessels of the viscera generally follow the paths of arteries.

The Organization of Immune Function

The immune system is a collection of barriers, cells, and soluble proteins that interact and communicate with each other in extraordinarily complex ways. The modern model of immune function is organized into three phases based on the timing of their effects. The three temporal phases consist of the following:

- **Barrier defenses** such as the skin and mucous membranes, which act instantaneously to prevent pathogenic invasion into the body tissues
- The rapid but nonspecific **innate immune response**, which consists of a variety of specialized cells and soluble factors
- The slower but more specific and effective **adaptive immune response**, which involves many cell types and soluble factors, but is primarily controlled by white blood cells (leukocytes) known as **lymphocytes**, which help control immune responses

The cells of the blood, including all those involved in the immune response, arise in the bone marrow via various differentiation pathways from hematopoietic stem cells (Figure 21.5). In contrast with embryonic stem cells, hematopoietic stem cells are present throughout adulthood and allow for the continuous differentiation of blood cells to replace those lost to age or function. These cells can be divided into three classes based on function:

- Phagocytic cells, which ingest pathogens to destroy them
- Lymphocytes, which specifically coordinate the activities of adaptive immunity
- Cells containing cytoplasmic granules, which help mediate immune responses against parasites and intracellular pathogens such as viruses

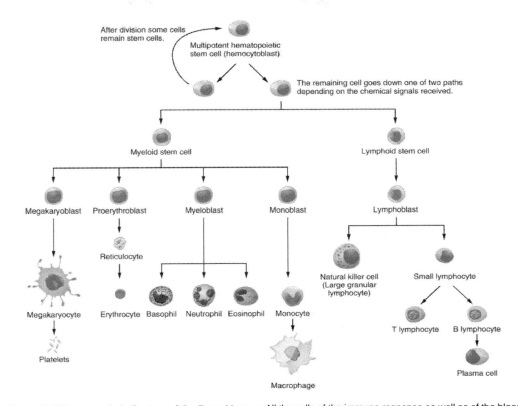

Figure 21.5 Hematopoietic System of the Bone Marrow All the cells of the immune response as well as of the blood arise by differentiation from hematopoietic stem cells. Platelets are cell fragments involved in the clotting of blood.

Lymphocytes: B Cells, T Cells, Plasma Cells, and Natural Killer Cells

As stated above, lymphocytes are the primary cells of adaptive immune responses (Table 21.1). The two basic types of lymphocytes, B cells and T cells, are identical morphologically with a large central nucleus surrounded by a thin layer of cytoplasm. They are distinguished from each other by their surface protein markers as well as by the molecules they secrete. While B cells mature in red bone marrow and T cells mature in the thymus, they both initially develop from bone marrow. T cells migrate from bone marrow to the thymus gland where they further mature. B cells and T cells are found in many parts of the body, circulating in the bloodstream and lymph, and residing in secondary lymphoid organs, including the spleen and lymph nodes, which will be described later in this section. The human body contains approximately 10^{12} lymphocytes.

B Cells

B cells are immune cells that function primarily by producing antibodies. An **antibody** is any of the group of proteins that binds specifically to pathogen-associated molecules known as antigens. An **antigen** is a chemical structure on the surface of a pathogen that binds to T or B lymphocyte antigen receptors. Once activated by binding to antigen, B cells differentiate into cells that secrete a soluble form of their surface antibodies. These activated B cells are known as plasma cells.

T Cells

The **T cell**, on the other hand, does not secrete antibody but performs a variety of functions in the adaptive immune response. Different T cell types have the ability to either secrete soluble factors that communicate with other cells of the adaptive immune response or destroy cells infected with intracellular pathogens. The roles of T and B lymphocytes in the adaptive immune response will be discussed further in this chapter.

Plasma Cells

Another type of lymphocyte of importance is the plasma cell. A **plasma cell** is a B cell that has differentiated in response to antigen binding, and has thereby gained the ability to secrete soluble antibodies. These cells differ in morphology from standard B and T cells in that they contain a large amount of cytoplasm packed with the protein-synthesizing machinery known as rough endoplasmic reticulum.

Natural Killer Cells

A fourth important lymphocyte is the natural killer cell, a participant in the innate immune response. A **natural killer cell (NK)** is a circulating blood cell that contains cytotoxic (cell-killing) granules in its extensive cytoplasm. It shares this mechanism with the cytotoxic T cells of the adaptive immune response. NK cells are among the body's first lines of defense against viruses and certain types of cancer.

Lymphocytes

Type of lymphocyte	Primary function
B lymphocyte	Generates diverse antibodies
T lymphocyte	Secretes chemical messengers
Plasma cell	Secretes antibodies
NK cell	Destroys virally infected cells

Table 21.1

Visit this website (http://openstaxcollege.org/l/immunecells) to learn about the many different cell types in the immune system and their very specialized jobs. What is the role of the dendritic cell in an HIV infection?

Primary Lymphoid Organs and Lymphocyte Development

Understanding the differentiation and development of B and T cells is critical to the understanding of the adaptive immune response. It is through this process that the body (ideally) learns to destroy only pathogens and leaves the body's own cells relatively intact. The **primary lymphoid organs** are the bone marrow and thymus gland. The lymphoid organs are where lymphocytes mature, proliferate, and are selected, which enables them to attack pathogens without harming the cells of the body.

Bone Marrow

In the embryo, blood cells are made in the yolk sac. As development proceeds, this function is taken over by the spleen, lymph nodes, and liver. Later, the bone marrow takes over most hematopoietic functions, although the final stages of the differentiation of some cells may take place in other organs. The red **bone marrow** is a loose collection of cells where hematopoiesis occurs, and the yellow bone marrow is a site of energy storage, which consists largely of fat cells (Figure 21.6). The B cell undergoes nearly all of its development in the red bone marrow, whereas the immature T cell, called a **thymocyte**, leaves the bone marrow and matures largely in the thymus gland.

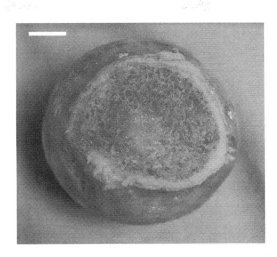

Figure 21.6 Bone Marrow Red bone marrow fills the head of the femur, and a spot of yellow bone marrow is visible in the center. The white reference bar is 1 cm.

Thymus

The **thymus** gland is a bilobed organ found in the space between the sternum and the aorta of the heart (Figure 21.7). Connective tissue holds the lobes closely together but also separates them and forms a capsule.

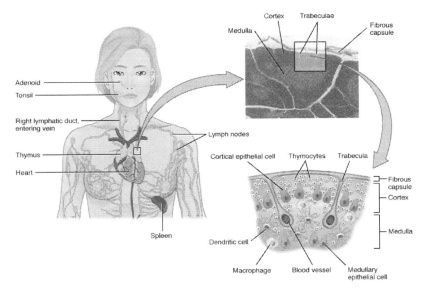

Figure 21.7 Location, Structure, and Histology of the Thymus The thymus lies above the heart. The trabeculae and lobules, including the darkly staining cortex and the lighter staining medulla of each lobule, are clearly visible in the light micrograph of the thymus of a newborn. LM × 100. (Micrograph provided by the Regents of the University of Michigan Medical School © 2012)

Interactive Link

View the University of Michigan WebScope at http://141.214.65.171/Histology/Lymphatic%20System/140_HISTO_40X.svs/view.apml (http://openstaxcollege.org/l/thymusMG) to explore the tissue sample in greater detail.

The connective tissue capsule further divides the thymus into lobules via extensions called trabeculae. The outer region of the organ is known as the cortex and contains large numbers of thymocytes with some epithelial cells, macrophages, and dendritic cells (two types of phagocytic cells that are derived from monocytes). The cortex is densely packed so it stains more intensely than the rest of the thymus (see Figure 21.7). The medulla, where thymocytes migrate before leaving the thymus, contains a less dense collection of thymocytes, epithelial cells, and dendritic cells.

Aging AND THE...

Immune System

By the year 2050, 25 percent of the population of the United States will be 60 years of age or older. The CDC estimates that 80 percent of those 60 years and older have one or more chronic disease associated with deficiencies of the immune systems. This loss of immune function with age is called immunosenescence. To treat this growing population, medical professionals must better understand the aging process. One major cause of age-related immune deficiencies is thymic involution, the shrinking of the thymus gland that begins at birth, at a rate of about three percent tissue loss per year, and continues until 35–45 years of age, when the rate declines to about one percent loss per year for the rest of one's life. At that pace, the total loss of thymic epithelial tissue and thymocytes would occur at about 120 years of age. Thus, this age is a theoretical limit to a healthy human lifespan.

Thymic involution has been observed in all vertebrate species that have a thymus gland. Animal studies have shown that transplanted thymic grafts between inbred strains of mice involuted according to the age of the donor and not of the recipient, implying the process is genetically programmed. There is evidence that the thymic microenvironment, so vital to the development of naïve T cells, loses thymic epithelial cells according to the decreasing expression of the FOXN1 gene with age.

It is also known that thymic involution can be altered by hormone levels. Sex hormones such as estrogen and testosterone enhance involution, and the hormonal changes in pregnant women cause a temporary thymic involution that reverses itself, when the size of the thymus and its hormone levels return to normal, usually after lactation ceases. What does all this tell us? Can we reverse immunosenescence, or at least slow it down? The potential is there for using thymic transplants from younger donors to keep thymic output of naïve T cells high. Gene therapies that target gene expression are also seen as future possibilities. The more we learn through immunosenescence research, the more opportunities there will be to develop therapies, even though these therapies will likely take decades to develop. The ultimate goal is for everyone to live and be healthy longer, but there may be limits to immortality imposed by our genes and hormones.

Secondary Lymphoid Organs and their Roles in Active Immune Responses

Lymphocytes develop and mature in the primary lymphoid organs, but they mount immune responses from the **secondary lymphoid organs**. A **naïve lymphocyte** is one that has left the primary organ and entered a secondary lymphoid organ.

Naïve lymphocytes are fully functional immunologically, but have yet to encounter an antigen to respond to. In addition to circulating in the blood and lymph, lymphocytes concentrate in secondary lymphoid organs, which include the lymph nodes, spleen, and lymphoid nodules. All of these tissues have many features in common, including the following:

- The presence of lymphoid follicles, the sites of the formation of lymphocytes, with specific B cell-rich and T cell-rich areas
- An internal structure of reticular fibers with associated fixed macrophages
- **Germinal centers**, which are the sites of rapidly dividing B lymphocytes and plasma cells, with the exception of the spleen
- Specialized post-capillary vessels known as **high endothelial venules**; the cells lining these venules are thicker and more columnar than normal endothelial cells, which allow cells from the blood to directly enter these tissues

Lymph Nodes

Lymph nodes function to remove debris and pathogens from the lymph, and are thus sometimes referred to as the "filters of the lymph" (Figure 21.8). Any bacteria that infect the interstitial fluid are taken up by the lymphatic capillaries and transported to a regional lymph node. Dendritic cells and macrophages within this organ internalize and kill many of the pathogens that pass through, thereby removing them from the body. The lymph node is also the site of adaptive immune responses mediated by T cells, B cells, and accessory cells of the adaptive immune system. Like the thymus, the bean-shaped lymph nodes are surrounded by a tough capsule of connective tissue and are separated into compartments by trabeculae, the extensions of the capsule. In addition to the structure provided by the capsule and trabeculae, the structural support of the lymph node is provided by a series of reticular fibers laid down by fibroblasts.

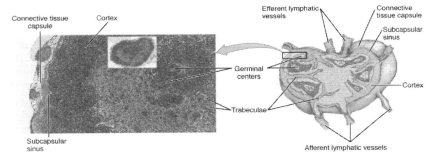

Figure 21.8 Structure and Histology of a Lymph Node Lymph nodes are masses of lymphatic tissue located along the larger lymph vessels. The micrograph of the lymph nodes shows a germinal center, which consists of rapidly dividing B cells surrounded by a layer of T cells and other accessory cells. LM × 128. (Micrograph provided by the Regents of the University of Michigan Medical School © 2012)

View the University of Michigan WebScope at http://141.214.65.171/Histology/Lymphatic%20System/142_HISTO_40X.svs/view.apml (http://openstaxcollege.org/l/lymphnodeMG) to explore the tissue sample in greater detail.

The major routes into the lymph node are via **afferent lymphatic vessels** (see Figure 21.8). Cells and lymph fluid that leave the lymph node may do so by another set of vessels known as the **efferent lymphatic vessels**. Lymph enters the lymph node via the subcapsular sinus, which is occupied by dendritic cells, macrophages, and reticular fibers. Within the cortex of the lymph node are lymphoid follicles, which consist of germinal centers of rapidly dividing B cells surrounded by a layer of T cells and other accessory cells. As the lymph continues to flow through the node, it enters the medulla, which consists of medullary cords of B cells and plasma cells, and the medullary sinuses where the lymph collects before leaving the node via the efferent lymphatic vessels.

Spleen

In addition to the lymph nodes, the **spleen** is a major secondary lymphoid organ (Figure 21.9). It is about 12 cm (5 in) long and is attached to the lateral border of the stomach via the gastrosplenic ligament. The spleen is a fragile organ without a strong capsule, and is dark red due to its extensive vascularization. The spleen is sometimes called the "filter of the blood" because of its extensive vascularization and the presence of macrophages and dendritic cells that remove microbes and other materials from the blood, including dying red blood cells. The spleen also functions as the location of immune responses to blood-borne pathogens.

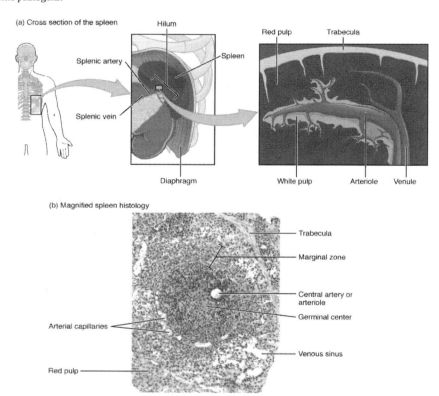

Figure 21.9 Spleen (a) The spleen is attached to the stomach. (b) A micrograph of spleen tissue shows the germinal center. The marginal zone is the region between the red pulp and white pulp, which sequesters particulate antigens from the circulation and presents these antigens to lymphocytes in the white pulp. EM × 660. (Micrograph provided by the Regents of the University of Michigan Medical School © 2012)

The spleen is also divided by trabeculae of connective tissue, and within each splenic nodule is an area of red pulp, consisting of mostly red blood cells, and white pulp, which resembles the lymphoid follicles of the lymph nodes. Upon entering the spleen, the splenic artery splits into several arterioles (surrounded by white pulp) and eventually into sinusoids. Blood from the capillaries subsequently collects in the venous sinuses and leaves via the splenic vein. The red pulp consists of reticular fibers with fixed macrophages attached, free macrophages, and all of the other cells typical of the blood, including some lymphocytes. The white pulp surrounds a central arteriole and consists of germinal centers of dividing B cells surrounded by T cells and accessory cells, including macrophages and dendritic cells. Thus, the red pulp primarily functions as a filtration system of the blood, using cells of the relatively nonspecific immune response, and white pulp is where adaptive T and B cell responses are mounted.

Lymphoid Nodules

The other lymphoid tissues, the **lymphoid nodules**, have a simpler architecture than the spleen and lymph nodes in that they consist of a dense cluster of lymphocytes without a surrounding fibrous capsule. These nodules are located in the respiratory and digestive tracts, areas routinely exposed to environmental pathogens.

Tonsils are lymphoid nodules located along the inner surface of the pharynx and are important in developing immunity to oral pathogens (Figure 21.10). The tonsil located at the back of the throat, the pharyngeal tonsil, is sometimes referred to as the adenoid when swollen. Such swelling is an indication of an active immune response to infection. Histologically, tonsils do not contain a complete capsule, and the epithelial layer invaginates deeply into the interior of the tonsil to form tonsillar crypts. These structures, which accumulate all sorts of materials taken into the body through eating and breathing, actually "encourage" pathogens to penetrate deep into the tonsillar tissues where they are acted upon by numerous lymphoid follicles and eliminated. This seems to be the major function of tonsils—to help children's bodies recognize, destroy, and develop immunity to common environmental pathogens so that they will be protected in their later lives. Tonsils are often removed in those children who have recurring throat infections, especially those involving the palatine tonsils on either side of the throat, whose swelling may interfere with their breathing and/or swallowing.

344 Chapter 21 | The Lymphatic and Immune System

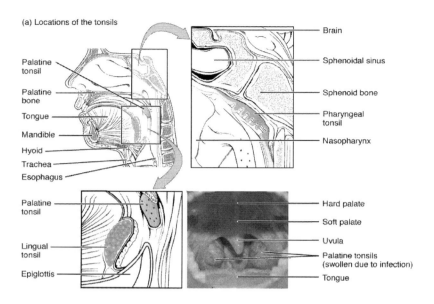

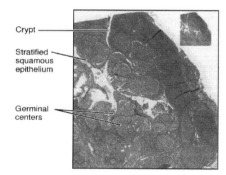

Figure 21.10 Locations and Histology of the Tonsils (a) The pharyngeal tonsil is located on the roof of the posterior superior wall of the nasopharynx. The palatine tonsils lay on each side of the pharynx. (b) A micrograph shows the palatine tonsil tissue. LM × 40. (Micrograph provided by the Regents of the University of Michigan Medical School © 2012)

View the University of Michigan WebScope at http://141.214.65.171/Histology/Lymphatic%20System/138_HISTO_20X.svs/view.apml (http://openstaxcollege.org/l/tonsilMG) to explore the tissue sample in greater detail.

Mucosa-associated lymphoid tissue (MALT) consists of an aggregate of lymphoid follicles directly associated with the mucous membrane epithelia. MALT makes up dome-shaped structures found underlying the mucosa of the gastrointestinal tract, breast tissue, lungs, and eyes. Peyer's patches, a type of MALT in the small intestine, are especially important for immune responses against ingested substances (Figure 21.11). Peyer's patches contain specialized endothelial cells called M (or microfold) cells that sample material from the intestinal lumen and transport it to nearby follicles so that adaptive immune responses to potential pathogens can be mounted.

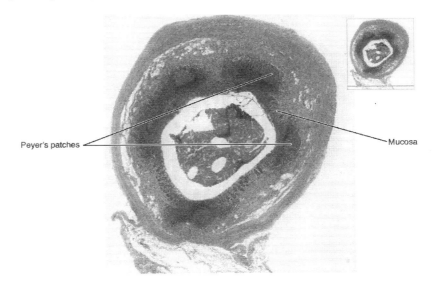

Figure 21.11 Mucosa-associated Lymphoid Tissue (MALT) Nodule LM × 40. (Micrograph provided by the Regents of the University of Michigan Medical School © 2012)

Bronchus-associated lymphoid tissue (BALT) consists of lymphoid follicular structures with an overlying epithelial layer found along the bifurcations of the bronchi, and between bronchi and arteries. They also have the typically less-organized structure of other lymphoid nodules. These tissues, in addition to the tonsils, are effective against inhaled pathogens.

21.2 | Barrier Defenses and the Innate Immune Response

By the end of this section, you will be able to:

- Describe the barrier defenses of the body
- Show how the innate immune response is important and how it helps guide and prepare the body for adaptive immune responses
- Describe various soluble factors that are part of the innate immune response
- Explain the steps of inflammation and how they lead to destruction of a pathogen
- Discuss early induced immune responses and their level of effectiveness

The immune system can be divided into two overlapping mechanisms to destroy pathogens: the innate immune response, which is relatively rapid but nonspecific and thus not always effective, and the adaptive immune response, which is slower in its development during an initial infection with a pathogen, but is highly specific and effective at attacking a wide variety of pathogens (Figure 21.12).

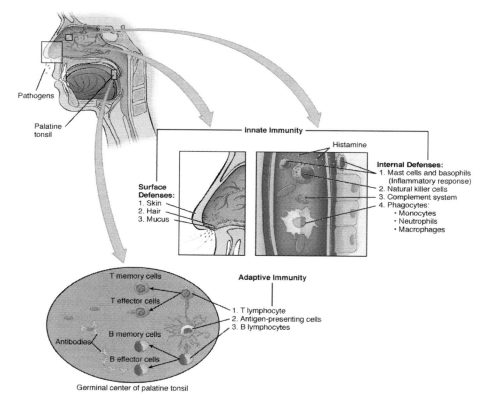

Figure 21.12 Cooperation between Innate and Adaptive Immune Responses The innate immune system enhances adaptive immune responses so they can be more effective.

Any discussion of the innate immune response usually begins with the physical barriers that prevent pathogens from entering the body, destroy them after they enter, or flush them out before they can establish themselves in the hospitable environment of the body's soft tissues. Barrier defenses are part of the body's most basic defense mechanisms. The barrier defenses are not a response to infections, but they are continuously working to protect against a broad range of pathogens.

The different modes of barrier defenses are associated with the external surfaces of the body, where pathogens may try to enter (Table 21.2). The primary barrier to the entrance of microorganisms into the body is the skin. Not only is the skin covered with a layer of dead, keratinized epithelium that is too dry for bacteria in which to grow, but as these cells are continuously sloughed off from the skin, they carry bacteria and other pathogens with them. Additionally, sweat and other skin secretions may lower pH, contain toxic lipids, and physically wash microbes away.

Barrier Defenses

Site	Specific defense	Protective aspect
Skin	Epidermal surface	Keratinized cells of surface, Langerhans cells
Skin (sweat/secretions)	Sweat glands, sebaceous glands	Low pH, washing action
Oral cavity	Salivary glands	Lysozyme
Stomach	Gastrointestinal tract	Low pH
Mucosal surfaces	Mucosal epithelium	Nonkeratinized epithelial cells
Normal flora (nonpathogenic bacteria)	Mucosal tissues	Prevent pathogens from growing on mucosal surfaces

Table 21.2

Another barrier is the saliva in the mouth, which is rich in lysozyme—an enzyme that destroys bacteria by digesting their cell walls. The acidic environment of the stomach, which is fatal to many pathogens, is also a barrier. Additionally, the mucus layer of the gastrointestinal tract, respiratory tract, reproductive tract, eyes, ears, and nose traps both microbes and debris, and facilitates their removal. In the case of the upper respiratory tract, ciliated epithelial cells move potentially contaminated mucus upwards to the mouth, where it is then swallowed into the digestive tract, ending up in the harsh acidic environment of the stomach. Considering how often you breathe compared to how often you eat or perform other activities that expose you to pathogens, it is not surprising that multiple barrier mechanisms have evolved to work in concert to protect this vital area.

Cells of the Innate Immune Response

A phagocyte is a cell that is able to surround and engulf a particle or cell, a process called **phagocytosis**. The phagocytes of the immune system engulf other particles or cells, either to clean an area of debris, old cells, or to kill pathogenic organisms such as bacteria. The phagocytes are the body's fast acting, first line of immunological defense against organisms that have breached barrier defenses and have entered the vulnerable tissues of the body.

Phagocytes: Macrophages and Neutrophils

Many of the cells of the immune system have a phagocytic ability, at least at some point during their life cycles. Phagocytosis is an important and effective mechanism of destroying pathogens during innate immune responses. The phagocyte takes the organism inside itself as a phagosome, which subsequently fuses with a lysosome and its digestive enzymes, effectively killing many pathogens. On the other hand, some bacteria including *Mycobacteria tuberculosis*, the cause of tuberculosis, may be resistant to these enzymes and are therefore much more difficult to clear from the body. Macrophages, neutrophils, and dendritic cells are the major phagocytes of the immune system.

A **macrophage** is an irregularly shaped phagocyte that is amoeboid in nature and is the most versatile of the phagocytes in the body. Macrophages move through tissues and squeeze through capillary walls using pseudopodia. They not only participate in innate immune responses but have also evolved to cooperate with lymphocytes as part of the adaptive immune response. Macrophages exist in many tissues of the body, either freely roaming through connective tissues or fixed to reticular fibers within specific tissues such as lymph nodes. When pathogens breach the body's barrier defenses, macrophages are the first line of defense (Table 21.3). They are called different names, depending on the tissue: Kupffer cells in the liver, histiocytes in connective tissue, and alveolar macrophages in the lungs.

A **neutrophil** is a phagocytic cell that is attracted via chemotaxis from the bloodstream to infected tissues. These spherical cells are granulocytes. A granulocyte contains cytoplasmic granules, which in turn contain a variety of vasoactive mediators such as histamine. In contrast, macrophages are agranulocytes. An agranulocyte has few or no cytoplasmic granules. Whereas macrophages act like sentries, always on guard against infection, neutrophils can be thought of as military reinforcements that are called into a battle to hasten the destruction of the enemy. Although, usually thought of as the primary pathogen-killing cell of the inflammatory process of the innate immune response, new research has suggested that neutrophils play a role in the adaptive immune response as well, just as macrophages do.

A **monocyte** is a circulating precursor cell that differentiates into either a macrophage or dendritic cell, which can be rapidly attracted to areas of infection by signal molecules of inflammation.

Phagocytic Cells of the Innate Immune System

Cell	Cell type	Primary location	Function in the innate immune response
Macrophage	Agranulocyte	Body cavities/organs	Phagocytosis
Neutrophil	Granulocyte	Blood	Phagocytosis
Monocyte	Agranulocyte	Blood	Precursor of macrophage/dendritic cell

Table 21.3

Natural Killer Cells

NK cells are a type of lymphocyte that have the ability to induce apoptosis, that is, programmed cell death, in cells infected with intracellular pathogens such as obligate intracellular bacteria and viruses. NK cells recognize these cells by mechanisms that are still not well understood, but presumably involve their surface receptors. NK cells can induce apoptosis, in which a cascade of events inside the cell causes its own death by either of two mechanisms:

1) NK cells are able to respond to chemical signals and express the fas ligand. The **fas ligand** is a surface molecule that binds to the fas molecule on the surface of the infected cell, sending it apoptotic signals, thus killing the cell and the pathogen within it; or

2) The granules of the NK cells release perforins and granzymes. A **perforin** is a protein that forms pores in the membranes of infected cells. A **granzyme** is a protein-digesting enzyme that enters the cell via the perforin pores and triggers apoptosis intracellularly.

Both mechanisms are especially effective against virally infected cells. If apoptosis is induced before the virus has the ability to synthesize and assemble all its components, no infectious virus will be released from the cell, thus preventing further infection.

Recognition of Pathogens

Cells of the innate immune response, the phagocytic cells, and the cytotoxic NK cells recognize patterns of pathogen-specific molecules, such as bacterial cell wall components or bacterial flagellar proteins, using pattern recognition receptors. A **pattern recognition receptor (PRR)** is a membrane-bound receptor that recognizes characteristic features of a pathogen and molecules released by stressed or damaged cells.

These receptors, which are thought to have evolved prior to the adaptive immune response, are present on the cell surface whether they are needed or not. Their variety, however, is limited by two factors. First, the fact that each receptor type must be encoded by a specific gene requires the cell to allocate most or all of its DNA to make receptors able to recognize all pathogens. Secondly, the variety of receptors is limited by the finite surface area of the cell membrane. Thus, the innate immune system must "get by" using only a limited number of receptors that are active against as wide a variety of pathogens as possible. This strategy is in stark contrast to the approach used by the adaptive immune system, which uses large numbers of different receptors, each highly specific to a particular pathogen.

Should the cells of the innate immune system come into contact with a species of pathogen they recognize, the cell will bind to the pathogen and initiate phagocytosis (or cellular apoptosis in the case of an intracellular pathogen) in an effort to destroy the offending microbe. Receptors vary somewhat according to cell type, but they usually include receptors for bacterial components and for complement, discussed below.

Soluble Mediators of the Innate Immune Response

The previous discussions have alluded to chemical signals that can induce cells to change various physiological characteristics, such as the expression of a particular receptor. These soluble factors are secreted during innate or early induced responses, and later during adaptive immune responses.

Cytokines and Chemokines

A **cytokine** is signaling molecule that allows cells to communicate with each other over short distances. Cytokines are secreted into the intercellular space, and the action of the cytokine induces the receiving cell to change its physiology. A **chemokine** is a soluble chemical mediator similar to cytokines except that its function is to attract cells (chemotaxis) from longer distances.

Visit this website (http://openstaxcollege.org/l/chemotaxis) to learn about phagocyte chemotaxis. Phagocyte chemotaxis is the movement of phagocytes according to the secretion of chemical messengers in the form of interleukins and other chemokines. By what means does a phagocyte destroy a bacterium that it has ingested?

Early induced Proteins

Early induced proteins are those that are not constitutively present in the body, but are made as they are needed early during the innate immune response. **Interferons** are an example of early induced proteins. Cells infected with viruses secrete interferons that travel to adjacent cells and induce them to make antiviral proteins. Thus, even though the initial cell is sacrificed, the surrounding cells are protected. Other early induced proteins specific for bacterial cell wall components are mannose-binding protein and C-reactive protein, made in the liver, which bind specifically to polysaccharide components of the bacterial cell wall. Phagocytes such as macrophages have receptors for these proteins, and they are thus able to recognize them as they are bound to the bacteria. This brings the phagocyte and bacterium into close proximity and enhances the phagocytosis of the bacterium by the process known as opsonization. **Opsonization** is the tagging of a pathogen for phagocytosis by the binding of an antibody or an antimicrobial protein.

Complement System

The **complement** system is a series of proteins constitutively found in the blood plasma. As such, these proteins are not considered part of the **early induced immune response**, even though they share features with some of the antibacterial proteins of this class. Made in the liver, they have a variety of functions in the innate immune response, using what is known as the "alternate pathway" of complement activation. Additionally, complement functions in the adaptive immune response as well, in what is called the classical pathway. The complement system consists of several proteins that enzymatically alter and fragment later proteins in a series, which is why it is termed cascade. Once activated, the series of reactions is irreversible, and releases fragments that have the following actions:

- Bind to the cell membrane of the pathogen that activates it, labeling it for phagocytosis (opsonization)
- Diffuse away from the pathogen and act as chemotactic agents to attract phagocytic cells to the site of inflammation
- Form damaging pores in the plasma membrane of the pathogen

Figure 21.13 shows the classical pathway, which requires antibodies of the adaptive immune response. The alternate pathway does not require an antibody to become activated.

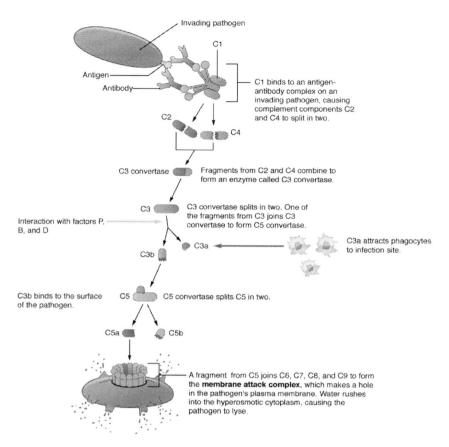

Figure 21.13 Complement Cascade and Function The classical pathway, used during adaptive immune responses, occurs when C1 reacts with antibodies that have bound an antigen.

The splitting of the C3 protein is the common step to both pathways. In the alternate pathway, C3 is activated spontaneously and, after reacting with the molecules factor P, factor B, and factor D, splits apart. The larger fragment, C3b, binds to the surface of the pathogen and C3a, the smaller fragment, diffuses outward from the site of activation and attracts phagocytes to the site of infection. Surface-bound C3b then activates the rest of the cascade, with the last five proteins, C5–C9, forming the membrane-attack complex (MAC). The MAC can kill certain pathogens by disrupting their osmotic balance. The MAC is especially effective against a broad range of bacteria. The classical pathway is similar, except the early stages of activation require the presence of antibody bound to antigen, and thus is dependent on the adaptive immune response. The earlier fragments of the cascade also have important functions. Phagocytic cells such as macrophages and neutrophils are attracted to an infection site by chemotactic attraction to smaller complement fragments. Additionally, once they arrive, their receptors for surface-bound C3b opsonize the pathogen for phagocytosis and destruction.

Inflammatory Response

The hallmark of the innate immune response is **inflammation**. Inflammation is something everyone has experienced. Stub a toe, cut a finger, or do any activity that causes tissue damage and inflammation will result, with its four characteristics: heat, redness, pain, and swelling ("loss of function" is sometimes mentioned as a fifth characteristic). It is important to note that inflammation does not have to be initiated by an infection, but can also be caused by tissue injuries. The release of damaged cellular contents into the site of injury is enough to stimulate the response, even in the absence of breaks in physical barriers that would allow pathogens to enter (by hitting your thumb with a hammer, for example). The inflammatory reaction brings in phagocytic cells to the damaged area to clear cellular debris and to set the stage for wound repair (Figure 21.14).

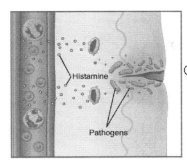

1. Mast cells detect injury to nearby cells and release histamine, initiating inflammatory response.

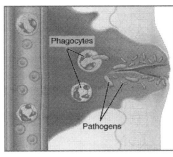

2. Histamine increases blood flow to the wound sites, bringing in phagocytes and other immune cells that neutralize pathogens. The blood influx causes the wound to swell, redden, and become warm and painful.

Figure 21.14

This reaction also brings in the cells of the innate immune system, allowing them to get rid of the sources of a possible infection. Inflammation is part of a very basic form of immune response. The process not only brings fluid and cells into the site to destroy the pathogen and remove it and debris from the site, but also helps to isolate the site, limiting the spread of the pathogen. **Acute inflammation** is a short-term inflammatory response to an insult to the body. If the cause of the inflammation is not resolved, however, it can lead to chronic inflammation, which is associated with major tissue destruction and fibrosis. **Chronic inflammation** is ongoing inflammation. It can be caused by foreign bodies, persistent pathogens, and autoimmune diseases such as rheumatoid arthritis.

There are four important parts to the inflammatory response:

- *Tissue Injury.* The released contents of injured cells stimulate the release of **mast cell** granules and their potent inflammatory mediators such as histamine, leukotrienes, and prostaglandins. **Histamine** increases the diameter of local blood vessels (vasodilation), causing an increase in blood flow. Histamine also increases the permeability of local capillaries, causing plasma to leak out and form interstitial fluid. This causes the swelling associated with inflammation.
  Additionally, injured cells, phagocytes, and basophils are sources of inflammatory mediators, including prostaglandins and leukotrienes. Leukotrienes attract neutrophils from the blood by chemotaxis and increase vascular permeability. Prostaglandins cause vasodilation by relaxing vascular smooth muscle and are a major cause of the pain associated with inflammation. Nonsteroidal anti-inflammatory drugs such as aspirin and ibuprofen relieve pain by inhibiting prostaglandin production.

- *Vasodilation.* Many inflammatory mediators such as histamine are vasodilators that increase the diameters of local capillaries. This causes increased blood flow and is responsible for the heat and redness of inflamed tissue. It allows greater access of the blood to the site of inflammation.

- *Increased Vascular Permeability.* At the same time, inflammatory mediators increase the permeability of the local vasculature, causing leakage of fluid into the interstitial space, resulting in the swelling, or edema, associated with inflammation.

- *Recruitment of Phagocytes.* Leukotrienes are particularly good at attracting neutrophils from the blood to the site of infection by chemotaxis. Following an early neutrophil infiltrate stimulated by macrophage cytokines, more macrophages are recruited to clean up the debris left over at the site. When local infections are severe, neutrophils are attracted to the sites of infections in large numbers, and as they phagocytose the pathogens and subsequently die, their accumulated cellular remains are visible as pus at the infection site.

Overall, inflammation is valuable for many reasons. Not only are the pathogens killed and debris removed, but the increase in vascular permeability encourages the entry of clotting factors, the first step towards wound repair. Inflammation also facilitates the transport of antigen to lymph nodes by dendritic cells for the development of the adaptive immune response.

21.3 | The Adaptive Immune Response: T lymphocytes and Their Functional Types

By the end of this section, you will be able to:
- Explain the advantages of the adaptive immune response over the innate immune response
- List the various characteristics of an antigen
- Describe the types of T cell antigen receptors
- Outline the steps of T cell development
- Describe the major T cell types and their functions

Innate immune responses (and early induced responses) are in many cases ineffective at completely controlling pathogen growth. However, they slow pathogen growth and allow time for the adaptive immune response to strengthen and either control or eliminate the pathogen. The innate immune system also sends signals to the cells of the adaptive immune system, guiding them in how to attack the pathogen. Thus, these are the two important arms of the immune response.

The Benefits of the Adaptive Immune Response

The specificity of the adaptive immune response—its ability to specifically recognize and make a response against a wide variety of pathogens—is its great strength. Antigens, the small chemical groups often associated with pathogens, are recognized by receptors on the surface of B and T lymphocytes. The adaptive immune response to these antigens is so versatile that it can respond to nearly any pathogen. This increase in specificity comes because the adaptive immune response has a unique way to develop as many as 10^{11}, or 100 trillion, different receptors to recognize nearly every conceivable pathogen. How could so many different types of antibodies be encoded? And what about the many specificities of T cells? There is not nearly enough DNA in a cell to have a separate gene for each specificity. The mechanism was finally worked out in the 1970s and 1980s using the new tools of molecular genetics

Primary Disease and Immunological Memory

The immune system's first exposure to a pathogen is called a **primary adaptive response**. Symptoms of a first infection, called primary disease, are always relatively severe because it takes time for an initial adaptive immune response to a pathogen to become effective.

Upon re-exposure to the same pathogen, a secondary adaptive immune response is generated, which is stronger and faster that the primary response. The **secondary adaptive response** often eliminates a pathogen before it can cause significant tissue damage or any symptoms. Without symptoms, there is no disease, and the individual is not even aware of the infection. This secondary response is the basis of **immunological memory**, which protects us from getting diseases repeatedly from the same pathogen. By this mechanism, an individual's exposure to pathogens early in life spares the person from these diseases later in life.

Self Recognition

A third important feature of the adaptive immune response is its ability to distinguish between self-antigens, those that are normally present in the body, and foreign antigens, those that might be on a potential pathogen. As T and B cells mature, there are mechanisms in place that prevent them from recognizing self-antigen, preventing a damaging immune response against the body. These mechanisms are not 100 percent effective, however, and their breakdown leads to autoimmune diseases, which will be discussed later in this chapter.

T Cell-Mediated Immune Responses

The primary cells that control the adaptive immune response are the lymphocytes, the T and B cells. T cells are particularly important, as they not only control a multitude of immune responses directly, but also control B cell immune responses in many cases as well. Thus, many of the decisions about how to attack a pathogen are made at the T cell level, and knowledge of their functional types is crucial to understanding the functioning and regulation of adaptive immune responses as a whole.

T lymphocytes recognize antigens based on a two-chain protein receptor. The most common and important of these are the alpha-beta T cell receptors (Figure 21.15).

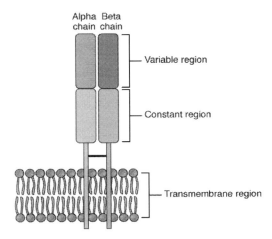

Figure 21.15 Alpha-beta T Cell Receptor Notice the constant and variable regions of each chain, anchored by the transmembrane region.

There are two chains in the T cell receptor, and each chain consists of two domains. The **variable region domain** is furthest away from the T cell membrane and is so named because its amino acid sequence varies between receptors. In contrast, the **constant region domain** has less variation. The differences in the amino acid sequences of the variable domains are the molecular basis of the diversity of antigens the receptor can recognize. Thus, the antigen-binding site of the receptor consists of the terminal ends of both receptor chains, and the amino acid sequences of those two areas combine to determine its antigenic specificity. Each T cell produces only one type of receptor and thus is specific for a single particular antigen.

Antigens

Antigens on pathogens are usually large and complex, and consist of many antigenic determinants. An **antigenic determinant** (epitope) is one of the small regions within an antigen to which a receptor can bind, and antigenic determinants are limited by the size of the receptor itself. They usually consist of six or fewer amino acid residues in a protein, or one or two sugar moieties in a carbohydrate antigen. Antigenic determinants on a carbohydrate antigen are usually less diverse than on a protein antigen. Carbohydrate antigens are found on bacterial cell walls and on red blood cells (the ABO blood group antigens). Protein antigens are complex because of the variety of three-dimensional shapes that proteins can assume, and are especially important for the immune responses to viruses and worm parasites. It is the interaction of the shape of the antigen and the complementary shape of the amino acids of the antigen-binding site that accounts for the chemical basis of specificity (Figure 21.16).

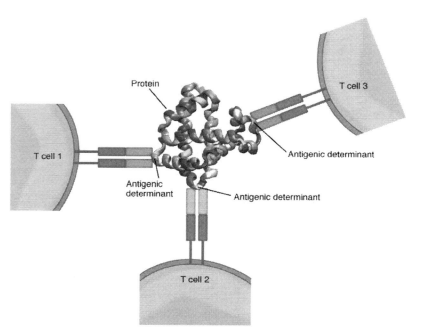

Figure 21.16 Antigenic Determinants A typical protein antigen has multiple antigenic determinants, shown by the ability of T cells with three different specificities to bind to different parts of the same antigen.

Antigen Processing and Presentation

Although Figure 21.16 shows T cell receptors interacting with antigenic determinants directly, the mechanism that T cells use to recognize antigens is, in reality, much more complex. T cells do not recognize free-floating or cell-bound antigens as they appear on the surface of the pathogen. They only recognize antigen on the surface of specialized cells called antigen-presenting cells. Antigens are internalized by these cells. **Antigen processing** is a mechanism that enzymatically cleaves the antigen into smaller pieces. The antigen fragments are then brought to the cell's surface and associated with a specialized type of antigen-presenting protein known as a **major histocompatibility complex (MHC)** molecule. The MHC is the cluster of genes that encode these antigen-presenting molecules. The association of the antigen fragments with an MHC molecule on the surface of a cell is known as **antigen presentation** and results in the recognition of antigen by a T cell. This association of antigen and MHC occurs inside the cell, and it is the complex of the two that is brought to the surface. The peptide-binding cleft is a small indentation at the end of the MHC molecule that is furthest away from the cell membrane; it is here that the processed fragment of antigen sits. MHC molecules are capable of presenting a variety of antigens, depending on the amino acid sequence, in their peptide-binding clefts. It is the combination of the MHC molecule and the fragment of the original peptide or carbohydrate that is actually physically recognized by the T cell receptor (Figure 21.17).

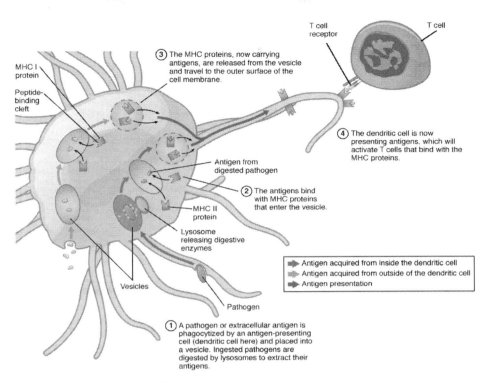

Figure 21.17 Antigen Processing and Presentation

Two distinct types of MHC molecules, **MHC class I** and **MHC class II**, play roles in antigen presentation. Although produced from different genes, they both have similar functions. They bring processed antigen to the surface of the cell via a transport vesicle and present the antigen to the T cell and its receptor. Antigens from different classes of pathogens, however, use different MHC classes and take different routes through the cell to get to the surface for presentation. The basic mechanism, though, is the same. Antigens are processed by digestion, are brought into the endomembrane system of the cell, and then are expressed on the surface of the antigen-presenting cell for antigen recognition by a T cell. Intracellular antigens are typical of viruses, which replicate inside the cell, and certain other intracellular parasites and bacteria. These antigens are processed in the cytosol by an enzyme complex known as the proteasome and are then brought into the endoplasmic reticulum by the transporter associated with antigen processing (TAP) system, where they interact with class I MHC molecules and are eventually transported to the cell surface by a transport vesicle.

Extracellular antigens, characteristic of many bacteria, parasites, and fungi that do not replicate inside the cell's cytoplasm, are brought into the endomembrane system of the cell by receptor-mediated endocytosis. The resulting vesicle fuses with vesicles from the Golgi complex, which contain pre-formed MHC class II molecules. After fusion of these two vesicles and the association of antigen and MHC, the new vesicle makes its way to the cell surface.

Professional Antigen-presenting Cells

Many cell types express class I molecules for the presentation of intracellular antigens. These MHC molecules may then stimulate a cytotoxic T cell immune response, eventually destroying the cell and the pathogen within. This is especially important when it comes to the most common class of intracellular pathogens, the virus. Viruses infect nearly every tissue of the body, so all these tissues must necessarily be able to express class I MHC or no T cell response can be made.

On the other hand, class II MHC molecules are expressed only on the cells of the immune system, specifically cells that affect other arms of the immune response. Thus, these cells are called "professional" antigen-presenting cells to distinguish them from those that bear class I MHC. The three types of professional antigen presenters are macrophages, dendritic cells, and B cells (Table 21.4).

Macrophages stimulate T cells to release cytokines that enhance phagocytosis. Dendritic cells also kill pathogens by phagocytosis (see Figure 21.17), but their major function is to bring antigens to regional draining lymph nodes. The lymph nodes are the locations in which most T cell responses against pathogens of the interstitial tissues are mounted. Macrophages are found in the skin and in the lining of mucosal surfaces, such as the nasopharynx, stomach, lungs, and intestines. B cells may also present antigens to T cells, which are necessary for certain types of antibody responses, to be covered later in this chapter.

Classes of Antigen-presenting Cells

MHC	Cell type	Phagocytic?	Function
Class I	Many	No	Stimulates cytotoxic T cell immune response
Class II	Macrophage	Yes	Stimulates phagocytosis and presentation at primary infection site
Class II	Dendritic	Yes, in tissues	Brings antigens to regional lymph nodes
Class II	B cell	Yes, internalizes surface Ig and antigen	Stimulates antibody secretion by B cells

Table 21.4

T Cell Development and Differentiation

The process of eliminating T cells that might attack the cells of one's own body is referred to as **T cell tolerance**. While thymocytes are in the cortex of the thymus, they are referred to as "double negatives," meaning that they do not bear the CD4 or CD8 molecules that you can use to follow their pathways of differentiation (Figure 21.18). In the cortex of the thymus, they are exposed to cortical epithelial cells. In a process known as **positive selection**, double-negative thymocytes bind to the MHC molecules they observe on the thymic epithelia, and the MHC molecules of "self" are selected. This mechanism kills many thymocytes during T cell differentiation. In fact, only two percent of the thymocytes that enter the thymus leave it as mature, functional T cells.

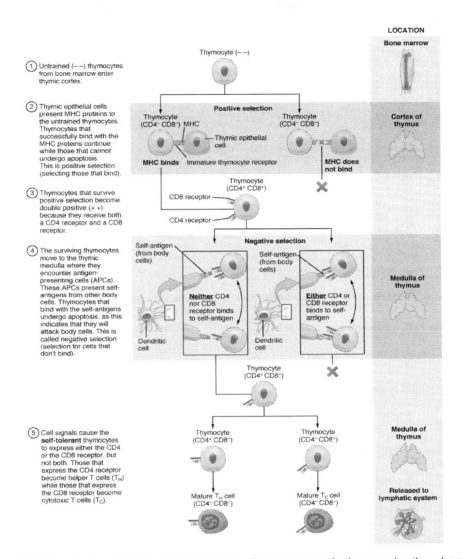

Figure 21.18 Differentiation of T Cells within the Thymus   Thymocytes enter the thymus and go through a series of developmental stages that ensures both function and tolerance before they leave and become functional components of the adaptive immune response.

Later, the cells become double positives that express both CD4 and CD8 markers and move from the cortex to the junction between the cortex and medulla. It is here that negative selection takes place. In **negative selection**, self-antigens are brought into the thymus from other parts of the body by professional antigen-presenting cells. The T cells that bind to these self-antigens are selected for negatively and are killed by apoptosis. In summary, the only T cells left are those that can bind to MHC molecules of the body with foreign antigens presented on their binding clefts, preventing an attack on one's own body tissues, at least under normal circumstances. Tolerance can be broken, however, by the development of an autoimmune response, to be discussed later in this chapter.

The cells that leave the thymus become single positives, expressing either CD4 or CD8, but not both (see Figure 21.18). The $CD4^+$ T cells will bind to class II MHC and the $CD8^+$ cells will bind to class I MHC. The discussion that follows explains the functions of these molecules and how they can be used to differentiate between the different T cell functional types.

Mechanisms of T Cell-mediated Immune Responses

Mature T cells become activated by recognizing processed foreign antigen in association with a self-MHC molecule and begin dividing rapidly by mitosis. This proliferation of T cells is called **clonal expansion** and is necessary to make the immune response strong enough to effectively control a pathogen. How does the body select only those T cells that are needed against a specific pathogen? Again, the specificity of a T cell is based on the amino acid sequence and the three-dimensional shape of the antigen-binding site formed by the variable regions of the two chains of the T cell receptor (Figure 21.19). **Clonal selection** is the process of antigen binding only to those T cells that have receptors specific to that antigen. Each T cell that is activated has a specific receptor "hard-wired" into its DNA, and all of its progeny will have identical DNA and T cell receptors, forming clones of the original T cell.

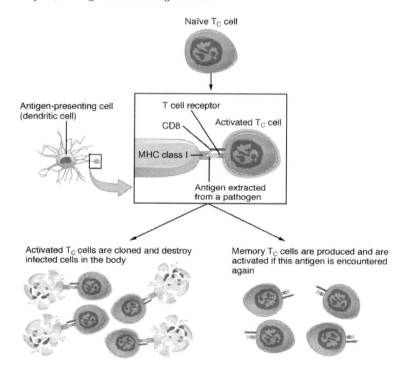

Figure 21.19 Clonal Selection and Expansion of T Lymphocytes Stem cells differentiate into T cells with specific receptors, called clones. The clones with receptors specific for antigens on the pathogen are selected for and expanded.

Clonal Selection and Expansion

The clonal selection theory was proposed by Frank Burnet in the 1950s. However, the term clonal selection is not a complete description of the theory, as clonal expansion goes hand in glove with the selection process. The main tenet of the theory is that a typical individual has a multitude (10^{11}) of different types of T cell clones based on their receptors. In this use, a **clone** is a group of lymphocytes that share the same **antigen receptor**. Each clone is necessarily present in the body in low numbers. Otherwise, the body would not have room for lymphocytes with so many specificities.

Only those clones of lymphocytes whose receptors are activated by the antigen are stimulated to proliferate. Keep in mind that most antigens have multiple antigenic determinants, so a T cell response to a typical antigen involves a polyclonal response. A **polyclonal response** is the stimulation of multiple T cell clones. Once activated, the selected clones increase in number and make many copies of each cell type, each clone with its unique receptor. By the time this process is complete, the body will have large numbers of specific lymphocytes available to fight the infection (see Figure 21.19).

The Cellular Basis of Immunological Memory

As already discussed, one of the major features of an adaptive immune response is the development of immunological memory.

During a primary adaptive immune response, both **memory T cells** and **effector T cells** are generated. Memory T cells are long-lived and can even persist for a lifetime. Memory cells are primed to act rapidly. Thus, any subsequent exposure to the pathogen will elicit a very rapid T cell response. This rapid, secondary adaptive response generates large numbers of effector T cells so fast that the pathogen is often overwhelmed before it can cause any symptoms of disease. This is what is meant by immunity to a disease. The same pattern of primary and secondary immune responses occurs in B cells and the antibody response, as will be discussed later in the chapter.

T Cell Types and their Functions

In the discussion of T cell development, you saw that mature T cells express either the CD4 marker or the CD8 marker, but not both. These markers are cell adhesion molecules that keep the T cell in close contact with the antigen-presenting cell by directly binding to the MHC molecule (to a different part of the molecule than does the antigen). Thus, T cells and antigen-presenting cells are held together in two ways: by CD4 or CD8 attaching to MHC and by the T cell receptor binding to antigen (Figure 21.20).

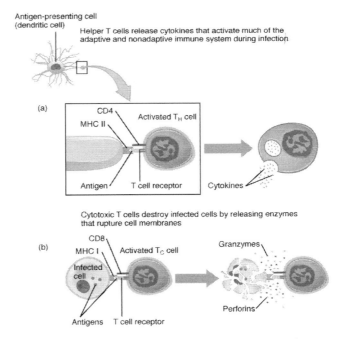

Figure 21.20 Pathogen Presentation (a) CD4 is associated with helper and regulatory T cells. An extracellular pathogen is processed and presented in the binding cleft of a class II MHC molecule, and this interaction is strengthened by the CD4 molecule. (b) CD8 is associated with cytotoxic T cells. An intracellular pathogen is presented by a class I MHC molecule, and CD8 interacts with it.

Although the correlation is not 100 percent, CD4-bearing T cells are associated with helper functions and CD8-bearing T cells are associated with cytotoxicity. These functional distinctions based on CD4 and CD8 markers are useful in defining the function of each type.

Helper T Cells and their Cytokines

Helper T cells (Th), bearing the CD4 molecule, function by secreting cytokines that act to enhance other immune responses. There are two classes of Th cells, and they act on different components of the immune response. These cells are not distinguished by their surface molecules but by the characteristic set of cytokines they secrete (Table 21.5).

Th1 cells are a type of helper T cell that secretes cytokines that regulate the immunological activity and development of a variety of cells, including macrophages and other types of T cells.

Th2 cells, on the other hand, are cytokine-secreting cells that act on B cells to drive their differentiation into plasma cells that make antibody. In fact, T cell help is required for antibody responses to most protein antigens, and these are called T cell-dependent antigens.

Cytotoxic T cells

Cytotoxic T cells (Tc) are T cells that kill target cells by inducing apoptosis using the same mechanism as NK cells. They either express Fas ligand, which binds to the fas molecule on the target cell, or act by using perforins and granzymes contained in their cytoplasmic granules. As was discussed earlier with NK cells, killing a virally infected cell before the virus can complete its replication cycle results in the production of no infectious particles. As more Tc cells are developed during an immune response, they overwhelm the ability of the virus to cause disease. In addition, each Tc cell can kill more than one target cell, making them especially effective. Tc cells are so important in the antiviral immune response that some speculate that this was the main reason the adaptive immune response evolved in the first place.

Regulatory T Cells

Regulatory T cells (Treg), or suppressor T cells, are the most recently discovered of the types listed here, so less is understood about them. In addition to CD4, they bear the molecules CD25 and FOXP3. Exactly how they function is still under investigation, but it is known that they suppress other T cell immune responses. This is an important feature of the immune response, because if clonal expansion during immune responses were allowed to continue uncontrolled, these responses could lead to autoimmune diseases and other medical issues.

Not only do T cells directly destroy pathogens, but they regulate nearly all other types of the adaptive immune response as well, as evidenced by the functions of the T cell types, their surface markers, the cells they work on, and the types of pathogens they work against (see Table 21.5).

Functions of T Cell Types and Their Cytokines

T cell	Main target	Function	Pathogen	Surface marker	MHC	Cytokines or mediators
Tc	Infected cells	Cytotoxicity	Intracellular	CD8	Class I	Perforins, granzymes, and fas ligand
Th1	Macrophage	Helper inducer	Extracellular	CD4	Class II	Interferon-γ and TGF-β
Th2	B cell	Helper inducer	Extracellular	CD4	Class II	IL-4, IL-6, IL-10, and others
Treg	Th cell	Suppressor	None	CD4, CD25	?	TGF-β and IL-10

Table 21.5

21.4 | The Adaptive Immune Response: B-lymphocytes and Antibodies

By the end of this section, you will be able to:
- Explain how B cells mature and how B cell tolerance develops
- Discuss how B cells are activated and differentiate into plasma cells
- Describe the structure of the antibody classes and their functions

Antibodies were the first component of the adaptive immune response to be characterized by scientists working on the immune system. It was already known that individuals who survived a bacterial infection were immune to re-infection with the same pathogen. Early microbiologists took serum from an immune patient and mixed it with a fresh culture of the same type of bacteria, then observed the bacteria under a microscope. The bacteria became clumped in a process called agglutination. When a different bacterial species was used, the agglutination did not happen. Thus, there was something in the serum of immune individuals that could specifically bind to and agglutinate bacteria.

Scientists now know the cause of the agglutination is an antibody molecule, also called an **immunoglobulin**. What is an antibody? An antibody protein is essentially a secreted form of a B cell receptor. (In fact, surface immunoglobulin is another name for the B cell receptor.) Not surprisingly, the same genes encode both the secreted antibodies and the surface immunoglobulins. One minor difference in the way these proteins are synthesized distinguishes a naïve B cell with antibody on its surface from an antibody-secreting plasma cell with no antibodies on its surface. The antibodies of the plasma cell have the exact same antigen-binding site and specificity as their B cell precursors.

There are five different classes of antibody found in humans: IgM, IgD, IgG, IgA, and IgE. Each of these has specific functions in the immune response, so by learning about them, researchers can learn about the great variety of antibody functions critical to many adaptive immune responses.

B cells do not recognize antigen in the complex fashion of T cells. B cells can recognize native, unprocessed antigen and do not require the participation of MHC molecules and antigen-presenting cells.

B Cell Differentiation and Activation

B cells differentiate in the bone marrow. During the process of maturation, up to 100 trillion different clones of B cells are generated, which is similar to the diversity of antigen receptors seen in T cells.

B cell differentiation and the development of tolerance are not quite as well understood as it is in T cells. **Central tolerance** is the destruction or inactivation of B cells that recognize self-antigens in the bone marrow, and its role is critical and well established. In the process of **clonal deletion**, immature B cells that bind strongly to self-antigens expressed on tissues are signaled to commit suicide by apoptosis, removing them from the population. In the process of **clonal anergy**, however, B cells exposed to soluble antigen in the bone marrow are not physically deleted, but become unable to function.

Another mechanism called peripheral tolerance is a direct result of T cell tolerance. In **peripheral tolerance**, functional, mature B cells leave the bone marrow but have yet to be exposed to self-antigen. Most protein antigens require signals from helper T cells (Th2) to proceed to make antibody. When a B cell binds to a self-antigen but receives no signals from a nearby Th2 cell to produce antibody, the cell is signaled to undergo apoptosis and is destroyed. This is yet another example of the control that T cells have over the adaptive immune response.

After B cells are activated by their binding to antigen, they differentiate into plasma cells. Plasma cells often leave the secondary lymphoid organs, where the response is generated, and migrate back to the bone marrow, where the whole differentiation process started. After secreting antibodies for a specific period, they die, as most of their energy is devoted to making antibodies and not to maintaining themselves. Thus, plasma cells are said to be terminally differentiated.

The final B cell of interest is the memory B cell, which results from the clonal expansion of an activated B cell. Memory B cells function in a way similar to memory T cells. They lead to a stronger and faster secondary response when compared to the primary response, as illustrated below.

Antibody Structure

Antibodies are glycoproteins consisting of two types of polypeptide chains with attached carbohydrates. The **heavy chain** and the **light chain** are the two polypeptides that form the antibody. The main differences between the classes of antibodies are in the differences between their heavy chains, but as you shall see, the light chains have an important role, forming part of the antigen-binding site on the antibody molecules.

Four-chain Models of Antibody Structures

All antibody molecules have two identical heavy chains and two identical light chains. (Some antibodies contain multiple units of this four-chain structure.) The **Fc region** of the antibody is formed by the two heavy chains coming together, usually linked by disulfide bonds (Figure 21.21). The Fc portion of the antibody is important in that many effector cells of the immune system have Fc receptors. Cells having these receptors can then bind to antibody-coated pathogens, greatly increasing the specificity of the effector cells. At the other end of the molecule are two identical antigen-binding sites.

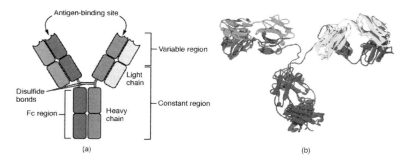

Figure 21.21 Antibody and IgG2 Structures The typical four chain structure of a generic antibody (a) and the corresponding three-dimensional structure of the antibody IgG2 (b). (credit b: modification of work by Tim Vickers)

Five Classes of Antibodies and their Functions

In general, antibodies have two basic functions. They can act as the B cell antigen receptor or they can be secreted, circulate, and bind to a pathogen, often labeling it for identification by other forms of the immune response. Of the five antibody classes, notice that only two can function as the antigen receptor for naïve B cells: IgM and **IgD** (Figure 21.22). Mature B cells that leave the bone marrow express both IgM and IgD, but both antibodies have the same antigen specificity. Only IgM is secreted, however, and no other nonreceptor function for IgD has been discovered.

	The Five Immunoglobulin (Ig) Classes				
	IgM pentamer	IgG monomer	Secretory IgA dimer	IgE monomer	IgD monomer
Heavy chains	μ	γ	α	ε	δ
Number of antigen binding sites	10	2	4	2	2
Molecular weight (Daltons)	900,000	150,000	385,000	200,000	180,000
Percentage of total antibody in serum	6%	80%	13%	0.002%	1%
Crosses placenta	no	yes	no	no	no
Fixes complement	yes	yes	no	no	no
Fc binds to		phagocytes		mast cells and basophils	
Function	Main antibody of primary responses, best at fixing complement; the monomer form of IgM serves as the B cell receptor	Main blood antibody of secondary responses, neutralizes toxins, opsonization	Secreted into mucus, tears, saliva, colostrum	Antibody of allergy and antiparasitic activity	B cell receptor

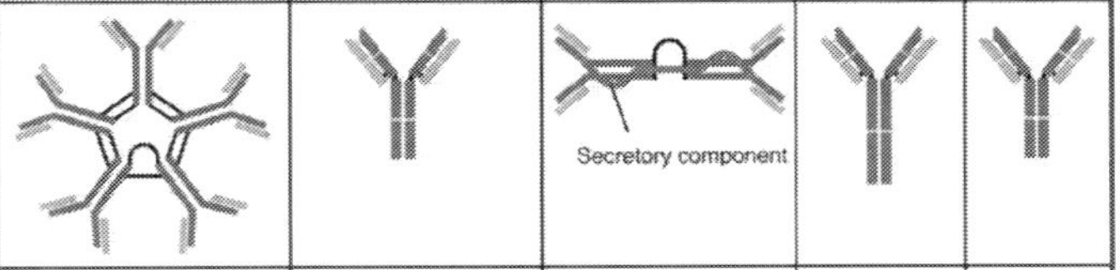

Figure 21.22 Five Classes of Antibodies

IgM consists of five four-chain structures (20 total chains with 10 identical antigen-binding sites) and is thus the largest of the antibody molecules. IgM is usually the first antibody made during a primary response. Its 10 antigen-binding sites and large shape allow it to bind well to many bacterial surfaces. It is excellent at binding complement proteins and activating the complement cascade, consistent with its role in promoting chemotaxis, opsonization, and cell lysis. Thus, it is a very effective antibody against bacteria at early stages of a primary antibody response. As the primary response proceeds, the antibody produced in a B cell can change to IgG, IgA, or IgE by the process known as class switching. **Class switching** is the change of one antibody class to another. While the class of antibody changes, the specificity and the antigen-binding sites do not. Thus, the antibodies made are still specific to the pathogen that stimulated the initial IgM response.

IgG is a major antibody of late primary responses and the main antibody of secondary responses in the blood. This is because class switching occurs during primary responses. IgG is a monomeric antibody that clears pathogens from the blood and can activate complement proteins (although not as well as IgM), taking advantage of its antibacterial activities. Furthermore, this class of antibody is the one that crosses the placenta to protect the developing fetus from disease exits the blood to the interstitial fluid to fight extracellular pathogens.

IgA exists in two forms, a four-chain monomer in the blood and an eight-chain structure, or dimer, in exocrine gland secretions of the mucous membranes, including mucus, saliva, and tears. Thus, dimeric IgA is the only antibody to leave the interior of the body to protect body surfaces. IgA is also of importance to newborns, because this antibody is present in mother's breast milk (colostrum), which serves to protect the infant from disease.

IgE is usually associated with allergies and anaphylaxis. It is present in the lowest concentration in the blood, because its Fc region binds strongly to an IgE-specific Fc receptor on the surfaces of mast cells. IgE makes mast cell degranulation very specific, such that if a person is allergic to peanuts, there will be peanut-specific IgE bound to his or her mast cells. In this person, eating peanuts will cause the mast cells to degranulate, sometimes causing severe allergic reactions, including anaphylaxis, a severe, systemic allergic response that can cause death.

Clonal Selection of B Cells

Clonal selection and expansion work much the same way in B cells as in T cells. Only B cells with appropriate antigen specificity are selected for and expanded (Figure 21.23). Eventually, the plasma cells secrete antibodies with antigenic specificity identical to those that were on the surfaces of the selected B cells. Notice in the figure that both plasma cells and memory B cells are generated simultaneously.

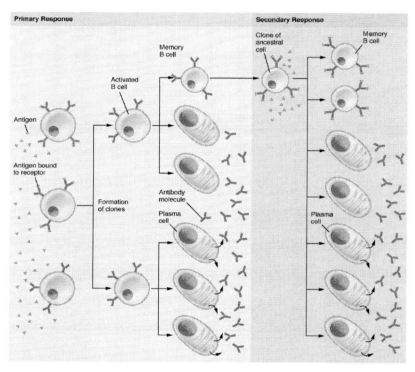

Figure 21.23 Clonal Selection of B Cells During a primary B cell immune response, both antibody-secreting plasma cells and memory B cells are produced. These memory cells lead to the differentiation of more plasma cells and memory B cells during secondary responses.

Primary versus Secondary B Cell Responses

Primary and secondary responses as they relate to T cells were discussed earlier. This section will look at these responses with B cells and antibody production. Because antibodies are easily obtained from blood samples, they are easy to follow and graph (Figure 21.24). As you will see from the figure, the primary response to an antigen (representing a pathogen) is delayed by several days. This is the time it takes for the B cell clones to expand and differentiate into plasma cells. The level of antibody produced is low, but it is sufficient for immune protection. The second time a person encounters the same antigen, there is no time delay, and the amount of antibody made is much higher. Thus, the secondary antibody response overwhelms the pathogens quickly and, in most situations, no symptoms are felt. When a different antigen is used, another primary response is made with its low antibody levels and time delay.

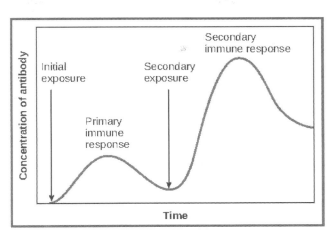

Figure 21.24 Primary and Secondary Antibody Responses Antigen A is given once to generate a primary response and later to generate a secondary response. When a different antigen is given for the first time, a new primary response is made.

Active versus Passive Immunity

Immunity to pathogens, and the ability to control pathogen growth so that damage to the tissues of the body is limited, can be acquired by (1) the active development of an immune response in the infected individual or (2) the passive transfer of immune components from an immune individual to a nonimmune one. Both active and passive immunity have examples in the natural world and as part of medicine.

Active immunity is the resistance to pathogens acquired during an adaptive immune response within an individual (Table 21.6). Naturally acquired active immunity, the response to a pathogen, is the focus of this chapter. Artificially acquired active immunity involves the use of vaccines. A vaccine is a killed or weakened pathogen or its components that, when administered to a healthy individual, leads to the development of immunological memory (a weakened primary immune response) without causing much in the way of symptoms. Thus, with the use of vaccines, one can avoid the damage from disease that results from the first exposure to the pathogen, yet reap the benefits of protection from immunological memory. The advent of vaccines was one of the major medical advances of the twentieth century and led to the eradication of smallpox and the control of many infectious diseases, including polio, measles, and whooping cough.

Active versus Passive Immunity

	Natural	**Artificial**
Active	Adaptive immune response	Vaccine response
Passive	Trans-placental antibodies/breastfeeding	Immune globulin injections

Table 21.6

Passive immunity arises from the transfer of antibodies to an individual without requiring them to mount their own active immune response. Naturally acquired passive immunity is seen during fetal development. IgG is transferred from the maternal circulation to the fetus via the placenta, protecting the fetus from infection and protecting the newborn for the first few months of its life. As already stated, a newborn benefits from the IgA antibodies it obtains from milk during breastfeeding. The fetus and newborn thus benefit from the immunological memory of the mother to the pathogens to which she has been exposed. In medicine, artificially acquired passive immunity usually involves injections of immunoglobulins, taken from animals previously exposed to a specific pathogen. This treatment is a fast-acting method of temporarily protecting an individual who was possibly exposed to a pathogen. The downside to both types of passive immunity is the lack of the development of immunological memory. Once the antibodies are transferred, they are effective for only a limited time before they degrade.

Immunity can be acquired in an active or passive way, and it can be natural or artificial. Watch this video (http://openstaxcollege.org/l/immunity) to see an animated discussion of passive and active immunity. What is an example of natural immunity acquired passively?

T cell-dependent versus T cell-independent Antigens

As discussed previously, Th2 cells secrete cytokines that drive the production of antibodies in a B cell, responding to complex antigens such as those made by proteins. On the other hand, some antigens are T cell independent. A **T cell-independent antigen** usually is in the form of repeated carbohydrate moieties found on the cell walls of bacteria. Each antibody on the B cell surface has two binding sites, and the repeated nature of T cell-independent antigen leads to crosslinking of the surface antibodies on the B cell. The crosslinking is enough to activate it in the absence of T cell cytokines.

A **T cell-dependent antigen**, on the other hand, usually is not repeated to the same degree on the pathogen and thus does not crosslink surface antibody with the same efficiency. To elicit a response to such antigens, the B and T cells must come close together (Figure 21.25). The B cell must receive two signals to become activated. Its surface immunoglobulin must recognize native antigen. Some of this antigen is internalized, processed, and presented to the Th2 cells on a class II MHC molecule. The T cell then binds using its antigen receptor and is activated to secrete cytokines that diffuse to the B cell, finally activating it completely. Thus, the B cell receives signals from both its surface antibody and the T cell via its cytokines, and acts as a professional antigen-presenting cell in the process.

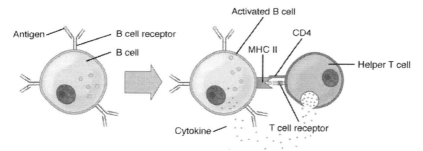

Figure 21.25 **T and B Cell Binding** To elicit a response to a T cell-dependent antigen, the B and T cells must come close together. To become fully activated, the B cell must receive two signals from the native antigen and the T cell's cytokines.

21.5 | The Immune Response against Pathogens

By the end of this section, you will be able to:
- Explain the development of immunological competence
- Describe the mucosal immune response
- Discuss immune responses against bacterial, viral, fungal, and animal pathogens
- Describe different ways pathogens evade immune responses

Now that you understand the development of mature, naïve B cells and T cells, and some of their major functions, how do all of these various cells, proteins, and cytokines come together to actually resolve an infection? Ideally, the immune response will rid the body of a pathogen entirely. The adaptive immune response, with its rapid clonal expansion, is well suited to this purpose. Think of a primary infection as a race between the pathogen and the immune system. The pathogen bypasses barrier defenses and starts multiplying in the host's body. During the first 4 to 5 days, the innate immune response will partially control, but not stop, pathogen growth. As the adaptive immune response gears up, however, it will begin to clear the pathogen from the body, while at the same time becoming stronger and stronger. When following antibody responses in patients with a particular disease such as a virus, this clearance is referred to as seroconversion (sero- = "serum"). **Seroconversion** is the reciprocal relationship between virus levels in the blood and antibody levels. As the antibody levels rise, the virus levels decline, and this is a sign that the immune response is being at least partially effective (partially, because in many diseases, seroconversion does not necessarily mean a patient is getting well).

An excellent example of this is seroconversion during HIV disease (Figure 21.26). Notice that antibodies are made early in this disease, and the increase in anti-HIV antibodies correlates with a decrease in detectable virus in the blood. Although these antibodies are an important marker for diagnosing the disease, they are not sufficient to completely clear the virus. Several years later, the vast majority of these individuals, if untreated, will lose their entire adaptive immune response, including the ability to make antibodies, during the final stages of AIDS.

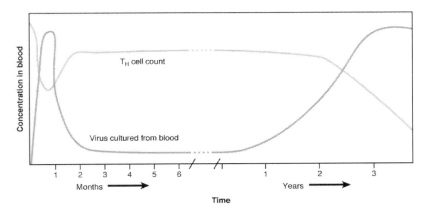

Figure 21.26 HIV Disease Progression Seroconversion, the rise of anti-HIV antibody levels and the concomitant decline in measurable virus levels, happens during the first several months of HIV disease. Unfortunately, this antibody response is ineffective at controlling the disease, as seen by the progression of the disease towards AIDS, in which all adaptive immune responses are compromised.

Everyday CONNECTION

Disinfectants: Fighting the Good Fight?

"Wash your hands!" Parents have been telling their children this for generations. Dirty hands can spread disease. But is it possible to get rid of enough pathogens that children will never get sick? Are children who avoid exposure to pathogens better off? The answers to both these questions appears to be no.

Antibacterial wipes, soaps, gels, and even toys with antibacterial substances embedded in their plastic are ubiquitous in our society. Still, these products do not rid the skin and gastrointestinal tract of bacteria, and it would be harmful to our health if they did. We need these nonpathogenic bacteria on and within our bodies to keep the pathogenic ones from growing. The urge to keep children perfectly clean is thus probably misguided. Children will get sick anyway, and the later benefits of immunological memory far outweigh the minor discomforts of most childhood diseases. In fact, getting diseases such as chickenpox or measles later in life is much harder on the adult and are associated with symptoms significantly worse than those seen in the childhood illnesses. Of course, vaccinations help children avoid some illnesses, but there are so many pathogens, we will never be immune to them all.

Could over-cleanliness be the reason that allergies are increasing in more developed countries? Some scientists think so. Allergies are based on an IgE antibody response. Many scientists think the system evolved to help the body rid itself of worm parasites. The hygiene theory is the idea that the immune system is geared to respond to antigens, and if pathogens are not present, it will respond instead to inappropriate antigens such as allergens and self-antigens. This is one explanation for the rising incidence of allergies in developed countries, where the response to nonpathogens like pollen, shrimp, and cat dander cause allergic responses while not serving any protective function.

The Mucosal Immune Response

Mucosal tissues are major barriers to the entry of pathogens into the body. The IgA (and sometimes IgM) antibodies in mucus and other secretions can bind to the pathogen, and in the cases of many viruses and bacteria, neutralize them. **Neutralization** is the process of coating a pathogen with antibodies, making it physically impossible for the pathogen to bind to receptors. Neutralization, which occurs in the blood, lymph, and other body fluids and secretions, protects the body constantly. Neutralizing antibodies are the basis for the disease protection offered by vaccines. Vaccinations for diseases that commonly enter the body via mucous membranes, such as influenza, are usually formulated to enhance IgA production.

Immune responses in some mucosal tissues such as the Peyer's patches (see Figure 21.11) in the small intestine take up particulate antigens by specialized cells known as microfold or M cells (Figure 21.27). These cells allow the body to sample potential pathogens from the intestinal lumen. Dendritic cells then take the antigen to the regional lymph nodes, where an immune response is mounted.

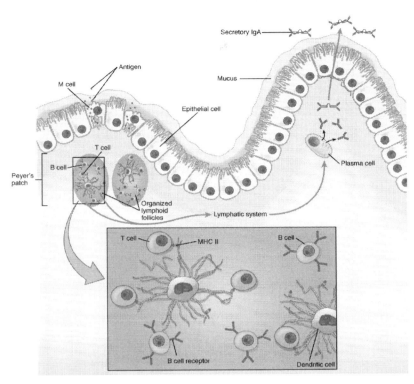

Figure 21.27 IgA Immunity The nasal-associated lymphoid tissue and Peyer's patches of the small intestine generate IgA immunity. Both use M cells to transport antigen inside the body so that immune responses can be mounted.

Defenses against Bacteria and Fungi

The body fights bacterial pathogens with a wide variety of immunological mechanisms, essentially trying to find one that is effective. Bacteria such as *Mycobacterium leprae*, the cause of leprosy, are resistant to lysosomal enzymes and can persist in macrophage organelles or escape into the cytosol. In such situations, infected macrophages receiving cytokine signals from Th1 cells turn on special metabolic pathways. **Macrophage oxidative metabolism** is hostile to intracellular bacteria, often relying on the production of nitric oxide to kill the bacteria inside the macrophage.

Fungal infections, such as those from *Aspergillus*, *Candida*, and *Pneumocystis*, are largely opportunistic infections that take advantage of suppressed immune responses. Most of the same immune mechanisms effective against bacteria have similar effects on fungi, both of which have characteristic cell wall structures that protect their cells.

Defenses against Parasites

Worm parasites such as helminths are seen as the primary reason why the mucosal immune response, IgE-mediated allergy and asthma, and eosinophils evolved. These parasites were at one time very common in human society. When infecting a human, often via contaminated food, some worms take up residence in the gastrointestinal tract. Eosinophils are attracted to the site by T cell cytokines, which release their granule contents upon their arrival. Mast cell degranulation also occurs, and the fluid leakage caused by the increase in local vascular permeability is thought to have a flushing action on the parasite, expelling its larvae from the body. Furthermore, if IgE labels the parasite, the eosinophils can bind to it by its Fc receptor.

Defenses against Viruses

The primary mechanisms against viruses are NK cells, interferons, and cytotoxic T cells. Antibodies are effective against viruses mostly during protection, where an immune individual can neutralize them based on a previous exposure.

Antibodies have no effect on viruses or other intracellular pathogens once they enter the cell, since antibodies are not able to penetrate the plasma membrane of the cell. Many cells respond to viral infections by downregulating their expression of MHC class I molecules. This is to the advantage of the virus, because without class I expression, cytotoxic T cells have no activity. NK cells, however, can recognize virally infected class I-negative cells and destroy them. Thus, NK and cytotoxic T cells have complementary activities against virally infected cells.

Interferons have activity in slowing viral replication and are used in the treatment of certain viral diseases, such as hepatitis B and C, but their ability to eliminate the virus completely is limited. The cytotoxic T cell response, though, is key, as it eventually overwhelms the virus and kills infected cells before the virus can complete its replicative cycle. Clonal expansion and the ability of cytotoxic T cells to kill more than one target cell make these cells especially effective against viruses. In fact, without cytotoxic T cells, it is likely that humans would all die at some point from a viral infection (if no vaccine were available).

Evasion of the Immune System by Pathogens

It is important to keep in mind that although the immune system has evolved to be able to control many pathogens, pathogens themselves have evolved ways to evade the immune response. An example already mentioned is in *Mycobactrium tuberculosis*, which has evolved a complex cell wall that is resistant to the digestive enzymes of the macrophages that ingest them, and thus persists in the host, causing the chronic disease tuberculosis. This section briefly summarizes other ways in which pathogens can "outwit" immune responses. But keep in mind, although it seems as if pathogens have a will of their own, they do not. All of these evasive "strategies" arose strictly by evolution, driven by selection.

Bacteria sometimes evade immune responses because they exist in multiple strains, such as different groups of *Staphylococcus aureus*. *S. aureus* is commonly found in minor skin infections, such as boils, and some healthy people harbor it in their nose. One small group of strains of this bacterium, however, called methicillin-resistant *Staphylococcus aureus*, has become resistant to multiple antibiotics and is essentially untreatable. Different bacterial strains differ in the antigens on their surfaces. The immune response against one strain (antigen) does not affect the other; thus, the species survives.

Another method of immune evasion is mutation. Because viruses' surface molecules mutate continuously, viruses like influenza change enough each year that the flu vaccine for one year may not protect against the flu common to the next. New vaccine formulations must be derived for each flu season.

Genetic recombination—the combining of gene segments from two different pathogens—is an efficient form of immune evasion. For example, the influenza virus contains gene segments that can recombine when two different viruses infect the same cell. Recombination between human and pig influenza viruses led to the 2010 H1N1 swine flu outbreak.

Pathogens can produce immunosuppressive molecules that impair immune function, and there are several different types. Viruses are especially good at evading the immune response in this way, and many types of viruses have been shown to suppress the host immune response in ways much more subtle than the wholesale destruction caused by HIV.

21.6 | Diseases Associated with Depressed or Overactive Immune Responses

By the end of this section, you will be able to:
- Discuss inherited and acquired immunodeficiencies
- Explain the four types of hypersensitivity and how they differ
- Give an example of how autoimmune disease breaks tolerance

This section is about how the immune system goes wrong. When it goes haywire, and becomes too weak or too strong, it leads to a state of disease. The factors that maintain immunological homeostasis are complex and incompletely understood.

Immunodeficiencies

As you have seen, the immune system is quite complex. It has many pathways using many cell types and signals. Because it is so complex, there are many ways for it to go wrong. Inherited immunodeficiencies arise from gene mutations that affect specific components of the immune response. There are also acquired immunodeficiencies with potentially devastating effects on the immune system, such as HIV.

Inherited Immunodeficiencies

A list of all inherited immunodeficiencies is well beyond the scope of this book. The list is almost as long as the list of cells, proteins, and signaling molecules of the immune system itself. Some deficiencies, such as those for complement, cause only a higher susceptibility to some Gram-negative bacteria. Others are more severe in their consequences. Certainly, the most serious of the inherited immunodeficiencies is **severe combined immunodeficiency disease (SCID)**. This disease is complex because it is caused by many different genetic defects. What groups them together is the fact that both the B cell and T cell arms of the adaptive immune response are affected.

Children with this disease usually die of opportunistic infections within their first year of life unless they receive a bone marrow transplant. Such a procedure had not yet been perfected for David Vetter, the "boy in the bubble," who was treated for SCID by having to live almost his entire life in a sterile plastic cocoon for the 12 years before his death from infection in 1984. One of the features that make bone marrow transplants work as well as they do is the proliferative capability of hematopoietic stem cells of the bone marrow. Only a small amount of bone marrow from a healthy donor is given intravenously to the recipient. It finds its own way to the bone where it populates it, eventually reconstituting the patient's immune system, which is usually destroyed beforehand by treatment with radiation or chemotherapeutic drugs.

New treatments for SCID using gene therapy, inserting nondefective genes into cells taken from the patient and giving them back, have the advantage of not needing the tissue match required for standard transplants. Although not a standard treatment, this approach holds promise, especially for those in whom standard bone marrow transplantation has failed.

Human Immunodeficiency Virus/AIDS

Although many viruses cause suppression of the immune system, only one wipes it out completely, and that is the previously mentioned HIV. It is worth discussing the biology of this virus, which can lead to the well-known AIDS, so that its full effects on the immune system can be understood. The virus is transmitted through semen, vaginal fluids, and blood, and can be caught by risky sexual behaviors and the sharing of needles by intravenous drug users. There are sometimes, but not always, flu-like symptoms in the first 1 to 2 weeks after infection. This is later followed by seroconversion. The anti-HIV antibodies formed during seroconversion are the basis for most initial HIV screening done in the United States. Because seroconversion takes different lengths of time in different individuals, multiple AIDS tests are given months apart to confirm or eliminate the possibility of infection.

After seroconversion, the amount of virus circulating in the blood drops and stays at a low level for several years. During this time, the levels of $CD4^+$ cells, especially helper T cells, decline steadily, until at some point, the immune response is so weak that opportunistic disease and eventually death result. CD4 is the receptor that HIV uses to get inside T cells and reproduce. Given that $CD4^+$ helper T cells play an important role in other in T cell immune responses and antibody responses, it should be no surprise that both types of immune responses are eventually seriously compromised.

Treatment for the disease consists of drugs that target virally encoded proteins that are necessary for viral replication but are absent from normal human cells. By targeting the virus itself and sparing the cells, this approach has been successful in significantly prolonging the lives of HIV-positive individuals. On the other hand, an HIV vaccine has been 30 years in development and is still years away. Because the virus mutates rapidly to evade the immune system, scientists have been looking for parts of the virus that do not change and thus would be good targets for a vaccine candidate.

Hypersensitivities

The word "hypersensitivity" simply means sensitive beyond normal levels of activation. Allergies and inflammatory responses to nonpathogenic environmental substances have been observed since the dawn of history. Hypersensitivity is a medical term describing symptoms that are now known to be caused by unrelated mechanisms of immunity. Still, it is useful for this discussion to use the four types of hypersensitivities as a guide to understand these mechanisms (Figure 21.28).

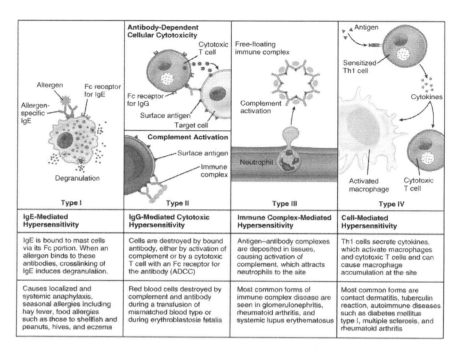

Figure 21.28 Immune Hypersensitivity Components of the immune system cause four types of hypersensitivity. Notice that types I–III are B cell mediated, whereas type IV hypersensitivity is exclusively a T cell phenomenon.

Immediate (Type I) Hypersensitivity

Antigens that cause allergic responses are often referred to as allergens. The specificity of the **immediate hypersensitivity** response is predicated on the binding of allergen-specific IgE to the mast cell surface. The process of producing allergen-specific IgE is called sensitization, and is a necessary prerequisite for the symptoms of immediate hypersensitivity to occur. Allergies and allergic asthma are mediated by mast cell degranulation that is caused by the crosslinking of the antigen-specific IgE molecules on the mast cell surface. The mediators released have various vasoactive effects already discussed, but the major symptoms of inhaled allergens are the nasal edema and runny nose caused by the increased vascular permeability and increased blood flow of nasal blood vessels. As these mediators are released with mast cell degranulation, **type I hypersensitivity** reactions are usually rapid and occur within just a few minutes, hence the term immediate hypersensitivity.

Most allergens are in themselves nonpathogenic and therefore innocuous. Some individuals develop mild allergies, which are usually treated with antihistamines. Others develop severe allergies that may cause anaphylactic shock, which can potentially be fatal within 20 to 30 minutes if untreated. This drop in blood pressure (shock) with accompanying contractions of bronchial smooth muscle is caused by systemic mast cell degranulation when an allergen is eaten (for example, shellfish and peanuts), injected (by a bee sting or being administered penicillin), or inhaled (asthma). Because epinephrine raises blood pressure and relaxes bronchial smooth muscle, it is routinely used to counteract the effects of anaphylaxis and can be lifesaving. Patients with known severe allergies are encouraged to keep automatic epinephrine injectors with them at all times, especially when away from easy access to hospitals.

Allergists use skin testing to identify allergens in type I hypersensitivity. In skin testing, allergen extracts are injected into the epidermis, and a positive result of a soft, pale swelling at the site surrounded by a red zone (called the wheal and flare response), caused by the release of histamine and the granule mediators, usually occurs within 30 minutes. The soft center is due to fluid leaking from the blood vessels and the redness is caused by the increased blood flow to the area that results from the dilation of local blood vessels at the site.

Type II and Type III Hypersensitivities

Type II hypersensitivity, which involves IgG-mediated lysis of cells by complement proteins, occurs during mismatched blood transfusions and blood compatibility diseases such as erythroblastosis fetalis (see section on transplantation). **Type III hypersensitivity** occurs with diseases such as systemic lupus erythematosus, where soluble antigens, mostly DNA and other material from the nucleus, and antibodies accumulate in the blood to the point that the antigen and antibody precipitate along blood vessel linings. These immune complexes often lodge in the kidneys, joints, and other organs where they can activate complement proteins and cause inflammation.

Delayed (Type IV) Hypersensitivity

Delayed hypersensitivity, or type IV hypersensitivity, is basically a standard cellular immune response. In delayed hypersensitivity, the first exposure to an antigen is called **sensitization**, such that on re-exposure, a secondary cellular response results, secreting cytokines that recruit macrophages and other phagocytes to the site. These sensitized T cells, of the Th1 class, will also activate cytotoxic T cells. The time it takes for this reaction to occur accounts for the 24- to 72-hour delay in development.

The classical test for delayed hypersensitivity is the tuberculin test for tuberculosis, where bacterial proteins from *M. tuberculosis* are injected into the skin. A couple of days later, a positive test is indicated by a raised red area that is hard to the touch, called an induration, which is a consequence of the cellular infiltrate, an accumulation of activated macrophages. A positive tuberculin test means that the patient has been exposed to the bacteria and exhibits a cellular immune response to it.

Another type of delayed hypersensitivity is contact sensitivity, where substances such as the metal nickel cause a red and swollen area upon contact with the skin. The individual must have been previously sensitized to the metal. A much more severe case of contact sensitivity is poison ivy, but many of the harshest symptoms of the reaction are associated with the toxicity of its oils and are not T cell mediated.

Autoimmune Responses

The worst cases of the immune system over-reacting are autoimmune diseases. Somehow, tolerance breaks down and the immune systems in individuals with these diseases begin to attack their own bodies, causing significant damage. The trigger for these diseases is, more often than not, unknown, and the treatments are usually based on resolving the symptoms using immunosuppressive and anti-inflammatory drugs such as steroids. These diseases can be localized and crippling, as in rheumatoid arthritis, or diffuse in the body with multiple symptoms that differ in different individuals, as is the case with systemic lupus erythematosus (Figure 21.29).

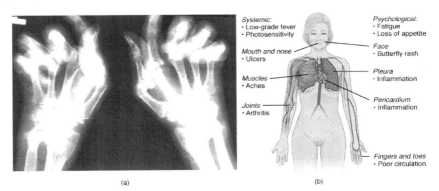

Figure 21.29 Autoimmune Disorders: Rheumatoid Arthritis and Lupus (a) Extensive damage to the right hand of a rheumatoid arthritis sufferer is shown in the x-ray. (b) The diagram shows a variety of possible symptoms of systemic lupus erythematosus.

Environmental triggers seem to play large roles in autoimmune responses. One explanation for the breakdown of tolerance is that, after certain bacterial infections, an immune response to a component of the bacterium cross-reacts with a self-antigen. This mechanism is seen in rheumatic fever, a result of infection with *Streptococcus* bacteria, which causes strep throat. The antibodies to this pathogen's M protein cross-react with an antigenic component of heart myosin, a major contractile protein of the heart that is critical to its normal function. The antibody binds to these molecules and activates complement proteins, causing damage to the heart, especially to the heart valves. On the other hand, some theories propose that having multiple common infectious diseases actually prevents autoimmune responses. The fact that autoimmune diseases are rare in countries that have a high incidence of infectious diseases supports this idea, another example of the hygiene hypothesis discussed earlier in this chapter.

There are genetic factors in autoimmune diseases as well. Some diseases are associated with the MHC genes that an individual expresses. The reason for this association is likely because if one's MHC molecules are not able to present a certain self-antigen, then that particular autoimmune disease cannot occur. Overall, there are more than 80 different autoimmune diseases, which are a significant health problem in the elderly. Table 21.7 lists several of the most common autoimmune diseases, the antigens that are targeted, and the segment of the adaptive immune response that causes the damage.

Autoimmune Diseases

Disease	Autoantigen	Symptoms
Celiac disease	Tissue transglutaminase	Damage to small intestine
Diabetes mellitus type I	Beta cells of pancreas	Low insulin production; inability to regulate serum glucose
Graves' disease	Thyroid-stimulating hormone receptor (antibody blocks receptor)	Hyperthyroidism
Hashimoto's thyroiditis	Thyroid-stimulating hormone receptor (antibody mimics hormone and stimulates receptor)	Hypothyroidism
Lupus erythematosus	Nuclear DNA and proteins	Damage of many body systems
Myasthenia gravis	Acetylcholine receptor in neuromuscular junctions	Debilitating muscle weakness
Rheumatoid arthritis	Joint capsule antigens	Chronic inflammation of joints

Table 21.7

21.7 | Transplantation and Cancer Immunology

By the end of this section, you will be able to:

- Explain why blood typing is important and what happens when mismatched blood is used in a transfusion
- Describe how tissue typing is done during organ transplantation and the role of transplant anti-rejection drugs
- Show how the immune response is able to control some cancers and how this immune response might be enhanced by cancer vaccines

The immune responses to transplanted organs and to cancer cells are both important medical issues. With the use of tissue typing and anti-rejection drugs, transplantation of organs and the control of the anti-transplant immune response have made huge strides in the past 50 years. Today, these procedures are commonplace. **Tissue typing** is the determination of MHC molecules in the tissue to be transplanted to better match the donor to the recipient. The immune response to cancer, on the other hand, has been more difficult to understand and control. Although it is clear that the immune system can recognize some cancers and control them, others seem to be resistant to immune mechanisms.

The Rh Factor

Red blood cells can be typed based on their surface antigens. ABO blood type, in which individuals are type A, B, AB, or O according to their genetics, is one example. A separate antigen system seen on red blood cells is the Rh antigen. When someone is "A positive" for example, the positive refers to the presence of the Rh antigen, whereas someone who is "A negative" would lack this molecule.

An interesting consequence of Rh factor expression is seen in **erythroblastosis fetalis**, a hemolytic disease of the newborn (Figure 21.30). This disease occurs when mothers negative for Rh antigen have multiple Rh-positive children. During the birth of a first Rh-positive child, the mother makes a primary anti-Rh antibody response to the fetal blood cells that enter the maternal bloodstream. If the mother has a second Rh-positive child, IgG antibodies against Rh-positive blood mounted during this secondary response cross the placenta and attack the fetal blood, causing anemia. This is a consequence of the fact that the fetus is not genetically identical to the mother, and thus the mother is capable of mounting an immune response against it. This disease is treated with antibodies specific for Rh factor. These are given to the mother during the subsequent births, destroying any fetal blood that might enter her system and preventing the immune response.

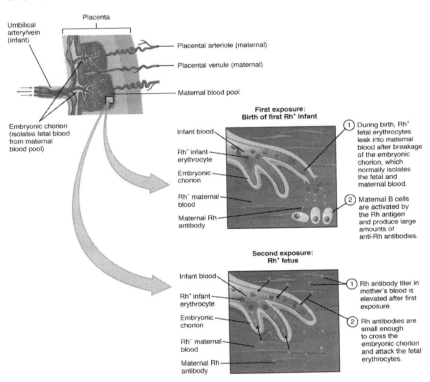

Figure 21.30 Erythroblastosis Fetalis Erythroblastosis fetalis (hemolytic disease of the newborn) is the result of an immune response in an Rh-negative mother who has multiple children with an Rh-positive father. During the first birth, fetal blood enters the mother's circulatory system, and anti-Rh antibodies are made. During the gestation of the second child, these antibodies cross the placenta and attack the blood of the fetus. The treatment for this disease is to give the mother anti-Rh antibodies (RhoGAM) during the first pregnancy to destroy Rh-positive fetal red blood cells from entering her system and causing the anti-Rh antibody response in the first place.

Tissue Transplantation

Tissue transplantation is more complicated than blood transfusions because of two characteristics of MHC molecules. These molecules are the major cause of transplant rejection (hence the name "histocompatibility"). **MHC polygeny** refers to the multiple MHC proteins on cells, and **MHC polymorphism** refers to the multiple alleles for each individual MHC locus. Thus, there are many alleles in the human population that can be expressed (Table 21.8 and Table 21.9). When a donor organ expresses MHC molecules that are different from the recipient, the latter will often mount a cytotoxic T cell response to the organ and reject it. Histologically, if a biopsy of a transplanted organ exhibits massive infiltration of T lymphocytes within the first weeks after transplant, it is a sign that the transplant is likely to fail. The response is a classical, and very specific, primary T cell immune response. As far as medicine is concerned, the immune response in this scenario does the patient no good at all and causes significant harm.

Partial Table of Alleles of the Human MHC (Class I)

Gene	# of alleles	# of possible MHC I protein components
A	2132	1527
B	2798	2110
C	1672	1200
E	11	3
F	22	4
G	50	16

Table 21.8

Partial Table of Alleles of the Human MHC (Class II)

Gene	# of alleles	# of possible MHC II protein components
DRA	7	2
DRB	1297	958
DQA1	49	31
DQB1	179	128
DPA1	36	18
DPB1	158	136
DMA	7	4
DMB	13	7
DOA	12	3
DOB	13	5

Table 21.9

Immunosuppressive drugs such as cyclosporine A have made transplants more successful, but matching the MHC molecules is still key. In humans, there are six MHC molecules that show the most polymorphisms, three class I molecules (A, B, and C) and three class II molecules called DP, DQ, and DR. A successful transplant usually requires a match between at least 3–4 of these molecules, with more matches associated with greater success. Family members, since they share a similar genetic background, are much more likely to share MHC molecules than unrelated individuals do. In fact, due to the extensive polymorphisms in these MHC molecules, unrelated donors are found only through a worldwide database. The system is not foolproof however, as there are not enough individuals in the system to provide the organs necessary to treat all patients needing them.

One disease of transplantation occurs with bone marrow transplants, which are used to treat various diseases, including SCID and leukemia. Because the bone marrow cells being transplanted contain lymphocytes capable of mounting an immune response, and because the recipient's immune response has been destroyed before receiving the transplant, the donor cells may attack the recipient tissues, causing **graft-versus-host disease**. Symptoms of this disease, which usually include a rash and damage to the liver and mucosa, are variable, and attempts have been made to moderate the disease by first removing mature T cells from the donor bone marrow before transplanting it.

Immune Responses Against Cancer

It is clear that with some cancers, for example Kaposi's sarcoma, a healthy immune system does a good job at controlling them (Figure 21.31). This disease, which is caused by the human herpesvirus, is almost never observed in individuals with strong immune systems, such as the young and immunocompetent. Other examples of cancers caused by viruses include liver cancer caused by the hepatitis B virus and cervical cancer caused by the human papilloma virus. As these last two viruses have vaccines available for them, getting vaccinated can help prevent these two types of cancer by stimulating the immune response.

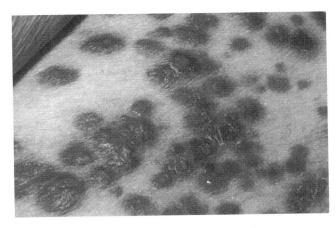

Figure 21.31 Karposi's Sarcoma Lesions (credit: National Cancer Institute)

On the other hand, as cancer cells are often able to divide and mutate rapidly, they may escape the immune response, just as certain pathogens such as HIV do. There are three stages in the immune response to many cancers: elimination, equilibrium, and escape. Elimination occurs when the immune response first develops toward tumor-specific antigens specific to the cancer and actively kills most cancer cells, followed by a period of controlled equilibrium during which the remaining cancer cells are held in check. Unfortunately, many cancers mutate, so they no longer express any specific antigens for the immune system to respond to, and a subpopulation of cancer cells escapes the immune response, continuing the disease process.

This fact has led to extensive research in trying to develop ways to enhance the early immune response to completely eliminate the early cancer and thus prevent a later escape. One method that has shown some success is the use of cancer vaccines, which differ from viral and bacterial vaccines in that they are directed against the cells of one's own body. Treated cancer cells are injected into cancer patients to enhance their anti-cancer immune response and thereby prolong survival. The immune system has the capability to detect these cancer cells and proliferate faster than the cancer cells do, overwhelming the cancer in a similar way as they do for viruses. Cancer vaccines have been developed for malignant melanoma, a highly fatal skin cancer, and renal (kidney) cell carcinoma. These vaccines are still in the development stages, but some positive and encouraging results have been obtained clinically.

It is tempting to focus on the complexity of the immune system and the problems it causes as a negative. The upside to immunity, however, is so much greater: The benefit of staying alive far outweighs the negatives caused when the system does sometimes go awry. Working on "autopilot," the immune system helps to maintain your health and kill pathogens. The only time you really miss the immune response is when it is not being effective and illness results, or, as in the extreme case of HIV disease, the immune system is gone completely.

Everyday CONNECTION

How Stress Affects the Immune Response: The Connections between the Immune, Nervous, and Endocrine Systems of the Body

The immune system cannot exist in isolation. After all, it has to protect the entire body from infection. Therefore, the immune system is required to interact with other organ systems, sometimes in complex ways. Thirty years of research focusing on the connections between the immune system, the central nervous system, and the endocrine system have led to a new science with the unwieldy name of called **psychoneuroimmunology**. The physical connections between these systems have been known for centuries: All primary and secondary organs are connected to sympathetic nerves. What is more complex, though, is the interaction of neurotransmitters, hormones, cytokines, and other soluble signaling molecules, and the mechanism of "crosstalk" between the systems. For example, white blood cells, including lymphocytes and phagocytes, have receptors for various neurotransmitters released by associated neurons. Additionally, hormones such as cortisol (naturally produced by the adrenal cortex) and prednisone (synthetic) are well known for their abilities to suppress T cell immune mechanisms, hence, their prominent use in medicine as long-term, anti-inflammatory drugs.

One well-established interaction of the immune, nervous, and endocrine systems is the effect of stress on immune health. In the human vertebrate evolutionary past, stress was associated with the fight-or-flight response, largely mediated by the central nervous system and the adrenal medulla. This stress was necessary for survival. The physical action of fighting or running, whichever the animal decides, usually resolves the problem in one way or another. On the other hand, there are no physical actions to resolve most modern day stresses, including short-term stressors like taking examinations and long-term stressors such as being unemployed or losing a spouse. The effect of stress can be felt by nearly every organ system, and the immune system is no exception (Table 21.10).

Effects of Stress on Body Systems

System	Stress-related illness
Integumentary system	Acne, skin rashes, irritation
Nervous system	Headaches, depression, anxiety, irritability, loss of appetite, lack of motivation, reduced mental performance
Muscular and skeletal systems	Muscle and joint pain, neck and shoulder pain
Circulatory system	Increased heart rate, hypertension, increased probability of heart attacks
Digestive system	Indigestion, heartburn, stomach pain, nausea, diarrhea, constipation, weight gain or loss
Immune system	Depressed ability to fight infections
Male reproductive system	Lowered sperm production, impotence, reduced sexual desire
Female reproductive system	Irregular menstrual cycle, reduced sexual desire

Table 21.10

At one time, it was assumed that all types of stress reduced all aspects of the immune response, but the last few decades of research have painted a different picture. First, most short-term stress does not impair the immune system in healthy individuals enough to lead to a greater incidence of diseases. However, older individuals and those with suppressed immune responses due to disease or immunosuppressive drugs may respond even to short-term stressors by getting sicker more often. It has been found that short-term stress diverts the body's resources towards enhancing innate immune responses, which have the ability to act fast and would seem to help the body prepare better for possible infections associated with the trauma that may result from a fight-or-flight exchange. The diverting of resources away from the adaptive immune response, however, causes its own share of problems in fighting disease.

Chronic stress, unlike short-term stress, may inhibit immune responses even in otherwise healthy adults. The suppression of both innate and adaptive immune responses is clearly associated with increases in some diseases, as seen when individuals lose a spouse or have other long-term stresses, such as taking care of a spouse with a fatal disease or dementia. The new science of psychoneuroimmunology, while still in its relative infancy, has great potential to make exciting advances in our understanding of how the nervous, endocrine, and immune systems have evolved together and communicate with each other.

KEY TERMS

active immunity immunity developed from an individual's own immune system

acute inflammation inflammation occurring for a limited time period; rapidly developing

adaptive immune response relatively slow but very specific and effective immune response controlled by lymphocytes

afferent lymphatic vessels lead into a lymph node

antibody antigen-specific protein secreted by plasma cells; immunoglobulin

antigen molecule recognized by the receptors of B and T lymphocytes

antigen presentation binding of processed antigen to the protein-binding cleft of a major histocompatibility complex molecule

antigen processing internalization and digestion of antigen in an antigen-presenting cell

antigen receptor two-chain receptor by which lymphocytes recognize antigen

antigenic determinant (also, epitope) one of the chemical groups recognized by a single type of lymphocyte antigen receptor

B cells lymphocytes that act by differentiating into an antibody-secreting plasma cell

barrier defenses antipathogen defenses deriving from a barrier that physically prevents pathogens from entering the body to establish an infection

bone marrow tissue found inside bones; the site of all blood cell differentiation and maturation of B lymphocytes

bronchus-associated lymphoid tissue (BALT) lymphoid nodule associated with the respiratory tract

central tolerance B cell tolerance induced in immature B cells of the bone marrow

chemokine soluble, long-range, cell-to-cell communication molecule

chronic inflammation inflammation occurring for long periods of time

chyle lipid-rich lymph inside the lymphatic capillaries of the small intestine

cisterna chyli bag-like vessel that forms the beginning of the thoracic duct

class switching ability of B cells to change the class of antibody they produce without altering the specificity for antigen

clonal anergy process whereby B cells that react to soluble antigens in bone marrow are made nonfunctional

clonal deletion removal of self-reactive B cells by inducing apoptosis

clonal expansion growth of a clone of selected lymphocytes

clonal selection stimulating growth of lymphocytes that have specific receptors

clone group of lymphocytes sharing the same antigen receptor

complement enzymatic cascade of constitutive blood proteins that have antipathogen effects, including the direct killing of bacteria

constant region domain part of a lymphocyte antigen receptor that does not vary much between different receptor types

cytokine soluble, short-range, cell-to-cell communication molecule

cytotoxic T cells (Tc) T lymphocytes with the ability to induce apoptosis in target cells

delayed hypersensitivity (type IV) T cell-mediated immune response against pathogens infiltrating interstitial tissues, causing cellular infiltrate

early induced immune response includes antimicrobial proteins stimulated during the first several days of an infection

effector T cells immune cells with a direct, adverse effect on a pathogen

efferent lymphatic vessels lead out of a lymph node

erythroblastosis fetalis disease of Rh factor-positive newborns in Rh-negative mothers with multiple Rh-positive children; resulting from the action of maternal antibodies against fetal blood

fas ligand molecule expressed on cytotoxic T cells and NK cells that binds to the fas molecule on a target cell and induces it do undergo apoptosis

Fc region in an antibody molecule, the site where the two termini of the heavy chains come together; many cells have receptors for this portion of the antibody, adding functionality to these molecules

germinal centers clusters of rapidly proliferating B cells found in secondary lymphoid tissues

graft-versus-host disease in bone marrow transplants; occurs when the transplanted cells mount an immune response against the recipient

granzyme apoptosis-inducing substance contained in granules of NK cells and cytotoxic T cells

heavy chain larger protein chain of an antibody

helper T cells (Th) T cells that secrete cytokines to enhance other immune responses, involved in activation of both B and T cell lymphocytes

high endothelial venules vessels containing unique endothelial cells specialized to allow migration of lymphocytes from the blood to the lymph node

histamine vasoactive mediator in granules of mast cells and is the primary cause of allergies and anaphylactic shock

IgA antibody whose dimer is secreted by exocrine glands, is especially effective against digestive and respiratory pathogens, and can pass immunity to an infant through breastfeeding

IgD class of antibody whose only known function is as a receptor on naive B cells; important in B cell activation

IgE antibody that binds to mast cells and causes antigen-specific degranulation during an allergic response

IgG main blood antibody of late primary and early secondary responses; passed from mother to unborn child via placenta

IgM antibody whose monomer is a surface receptor of naive B cells; the pentamer is the first antibody made blood plasma during primary responses

immediate hypersensitivity (type I) IgE-mediated mast cell degranulation caused by crosslinking of surface IgE by antigen

immune system series of barriers, cells, and soluble mediators that combine to response to infections of the body with pathogenic organisms

immunoglobulin protein antibody; occurs as one of five main classes

immunological memory ability of the adaptive immune response to mount a stronger and faster immune response upon re-exposure to a pathogen

inflammation basic innate immune response characterized by heat, redness, pain, and swelling

innate immune response rapid but relatively nonspecific immune response

interferons early induced proteins made in virally infected cells that cause nearby cells to make antiviral proteins

light chain small protein chain of an antibody

lymph fluid contained within the lymphatic system

lymph node one of the bean-shaped organs found associated with the lymphatic vessels

lymphatic capillaries smallest of the lymphatic vessels and the origin of lymph flow

lymphatic system network of lymphatic vessels, lymph nodes, and ducts that carries lymph from the tissues and back to the bloodstream.

lymphatic trunks large lymphatics that collect lymph from smaller lymphatic vessels and empties into the blood via lymphatic ducts

lymphocytes white blood cells characterized by a large nucleus and small rim of cytoplasm

lymphoid nodules unencapsulated patches of lymphoid tissue found throughout the body

macrophage ameboid phagocyte found in several tissues throughout the body

macrophage oxidative metabolism metabolism turned on in macrophages by T cell signals that help destroy intracellular bacteria

major histocompatibility complex (MHC) gene cluster whose proteins present antigens to T cells

mast cell cell found in the skin and the lining of body cells that contains cytoplasmic granules with vasoactive mediators such as histamine

memory T cells long-lived immune cell reserved for future exposure to an pathogen

MHC class I found on most cells of the body, it binds to the CD8 molecule on T cells

MHC class II found on macrophages, dendritic cells, and B cells, it binds to CD4 molecules on T cells

MHC polygeny multiple MHC genes and their proteins found in body cells

MHC polymorphism multiple alleles for each individual MHC locus

monocyte precursor to macrophages and dendritic cells seen in the blood

mucosa-associated lymphoid tissue (MALT) lymphoid nodule associated with the mucosa

natural killer cell (NK) cytotoxic lymphocyte of innate immune response

naïve lymphocyte mature B or T cell that has not yet encountered antigen for the first time

negative selection selection against thymocytes in the thymus that react with self-antigen

neutralization inactivation of a virus by the binding of specific antibody

neutrophil phagocytic white blood cell recruited from the bloodstream to the site of infection via the bloodstream

opsonization enhancement of phagocytosis by the binding of antibody or antimicrobial protein

passive immunity transfer of immunity to a pathogen to an individual that lacks immunity to this pathogen usually by the injection of antibodies

pattern recognition receptor (PRR) leukocyte receptor that binds to specific cell wall components of different bacterial species

perforin molecule in NK cell and cytotoxic T cell granules that form pores in the membrane of a target cell

peripheral tolerance mature B cell made tolerant by lack of T cell help

phagocytosis movement of material from the outside to the inside of the cells via vesicles made from invaginations of the plasma membrane

plasma cell differentiated B cell that is actively secreting antibody

polyclonal response response by multiple clones to a complex antigen with many determinants

positive selection selection of thymocytes within the thymus that interact with self, but not non-self, MHC molecules

primary adaptive response immune system's response to the first exposure to a pathogen

primary lymphoid organ site where lymphocytes mature and proliferate; red bone marrow and thymus gland

psychoneuroimmunology study of the connections between the immune, nervous, and endocrine systems

regulatory T cells (Treg) (also, suppressor T cells) class of CD4 T cells that regulates other T cell responses

right lymphatic duct drains lymph fluid from the upper right side of body into the right subclavian vein

secondary adaptive response immune response observed upon re-exposure to a pathogen, which is stronger and faster than a primary response

secondary lymphoid organs sites where lymphocytes mount adaptive immune responses; examples include lymph nodes and spleen

sensitization first exposure to an antigen

seroconversion clearance of pathogen in the serum and the simultaneous rise of serum antibody

severe combined immunodeficiency disease (SCID) genetic mutation that affects both T cell and B cell arms of the immune response

spleen secondary lymphoid organ that filters pathogens from the blood (white pulp) and removes degenerating or damaged blood cells (red pulp)

T cell lymphocyte that acts by secreting molecules that regulate the immune system or by causing the destruction of foreign cells, viruses, and cancer cells

T cell tolerance process during T cell differentiation where most T cells that recognize antigens from one's own body are destroyed

T cell-dependent antigen antigen that binds to B cells, which requires signals from T cells to make antibody

T cell-independent antigen binds to B cells, which do not require signals from T cells to make antibody

Th1 cells cells that secrete cytokines that enhance the activity of macrophages and other cells

Th2 cells cells that secrete cytokines that induce B cells to differentiate into antibody-secreting plasma cells

thoracic duct large duct that drains lymph from the lower limbs, left thorax, left upper limb, and the left side of the head

thymocyte immature T cell found in the thymus

thymus primary lymphoid organ; where T lymphocytes proliferate and mature

tissue typing typing of MHC molecules between a recipient and donor for use in a potential transplantation procedure

tonsils lymphoid nodules associated with the nasopharynx

type I hypersensitivity immediate response mediated by mast cell degranulation caused by the crosslinking of the antigen-specific IgE molecules on the mast cell surface

type II hypersensitivity cell damage caused by the binding of antibody and the activation of complement, usually against red blood cells

type III hypersensitivity damage to tissues caused by the deposition of antibody-antigen (immune) complexes followed by the activation of complement

variable region domain part of a lymphocyte antigen receptor that varies considerably between different receptor types

CHAPTER REVIEW

21.1 Anatomy of the Lymphatic and Immune Systems

The lymphatic system is a series of vessels, ducts, and trunks that remove interstitial fluid from the tissues and return it the blood. The lymphatics are also used to transport dietary lipids and cells of the immune system. Cells of the immune system all come from the hematopoietic system of the bone marrow. Primary lymphoid organs, the bone marrow and thymus gland, are the locations where lymphocytes of the adaptive immune system proliferate and mature. Secondary lymphoid organs are site in which mature lymphocytes congregate to mount immune responses. Many immune system cells use the lymphatic and circulatory systems for transport throughout the body to search for and then protect against pathogens.

21.2 Barrier Defenses and the Innate Immune Response

Innate immune responses are critical to the early control of infections. Whereas barrier defenses are the body's first line of physical defense against pathogens, innate immune responses are the first line of physiological defense. Innate responses occur rapidly, but with less specificity and effectiveness than the adaptive immune response. Innate responses can be caused by a variety of cells, mediators, and antibacterial proteins such as complement. Within the first few days of an infection, another series of antibacterial proteins are induced, each with activities against certain bacteria, including opsonization of certain species. Additionally, interferons are induced that protect cells from viruses in their vicinity. Finally, the innate immune response does not stop when the adaptive immune response is developed. In fact, both can cooperate and one can influence the other in their responses against pathogens.

21.3 The Adaptive Immune Response: T lymphocytes and Their Functional Types

T cells recognize antigens with their antigen receptor, a complex of two protein chains on their surface. They do not recognize self-antigens, however, but only processed antigen presented on their surfaces in a binding groove of a major histocompatibility complex molecule. T cells develop in the thymus, where they learn to use self-MHC molecules to recognize only foreign antigens, thus making them tolerant to self-antigens. There are several functional types of T lymphocytes, the major ones being helper, regulatory, and cytotoxic T cells.

21.4 The Adaptive Immune Response: B-lymphocytes and Antibodies

B cells, which develop within the bone marrow, are responsible for making five different classes of antibodies, each with its own functions. B cells have their own mechanisms for tolerance, but in peripheral tolerance, the B cells that leave the bone marrow remain inactive due to T cell tolerance. Some B cells do not need T cell cytokines to make antibody, and they bypass this need by the crosslinking of their surface immunoglobulin by repeated carbohydrate residues found in the cell walls of many bacterial species. Others require T cells to become activated.

21.5 The Immune Response against Pathogens

Early childhood is a time when the body develops much of its immunological memory that protects it from diseases in adulthood. The components of the immune response that have the maximum effectiveness against a pathogen are often associated with the class of pathogen involved. Bacteria and fungi are especially susceptible to damage by complement proteins, whereas viruses are taken care of by interferons and cytotoxic T cells. Worms are attacked by eosinophils. Pathogens have shown the ability, however, to evade the body's immune responses, some leading to chronic infections or

21.6 Diseases Associated with Depressed or Overactive Immune Responses

The immune response can be under-reactive or over-reactive. Suppressed immunity can result from inherited genetic defects or by acquiring viruses. Over-reactive immune responses include the hypersensitivities: B cell- and T cell-mediated immune responses designed to control pathogens, but that lead to symptoms or medical complications. The worst cases of over-reactive immune responses are autoimmune diseases, where an individual's immune system attacks his or her own body because of the breakdown of immunological tolerance. These diseases are more common in the aged, so treating them will be a challenge in the future as the aged population in the world increases.

21.7 Transplantation and Cancer Immunology

Blood transfusion and organ transplantation both require an understanding of the immune response to prevent medical complications. Blood needs to be typed so that natural antibodies against mismatched blood will not destroy it, causing more harm than good to the recipient. Transplanted organs must be matched by their MHC molecules and, with the use of immunosuppressive drugs, can be successful even if an exact tissue match cannot be made. Another aspect to the immune response is its ability to control and eradicate cancer. Although this has been shown to occur with some rare cancers and those caused by known viruses, the normal immune response to most cancers is not sufficient to control cancer growth. Thus, cancer vaccines designed to enhance these immune responses show promise for certain types of cancer.

INTERACTIVE LINK QUESTIONS

1. Visit this website (http://openstaxcollege.org/l/lymphsystem) for an overview of the lymphatic system. What are the three main components of the lymphatic system?

2. Visit this website (http://openstaxcollege.org/l/immunecells) to learn about the many different cell types in the immune system and their very specialized jobs. What is the role of the dendritic cell in infection by HIV?

3. Visit this website (http://openstaxcollege.org/l/chemotaxis) to learn about phagocyte chemotaxis. Phagocyte chemotaxis is the movement of phagocytes according to the secretion of chemical messengers in the form of interleukins and other chemokines. By what means does a phagocyte destroy a bacterium that it has ingested?

4. Immunity can be acquired in an active or passive way, and it can be natural or artificial. Watch this video (http://openstaxcollege.org/l/immunity) to see an animated discussion of passive and active immunity. What is an example of natural immunity acquired passively?

REVIEW QUESTIONS

5. Which of the following cells is phagocytic?
    a. plasma cell
    b. macrophage
    c. B cell
    d. NK cell

6. Which structure allows lymph from the lower right limb to enter the bloodstream?
    a. thoracic duct
    b. right lymphatic duct
    c. right lymphatic trunk
    d. left lymphatic trunk

7. Which of the following cells is important in the innate immune response?
    a. B cells
    b. T cells
    c. macrophages
    d. plasma cells

8. Which of the following cells would be most active in early, antiviral immune responses the first time one is exposed to pathogen?
    a. macrophage
    b. T cell
    c. neutrophil
    d. natural killer cell

9. Which of the lymphoid nodules is most likely to see food antigens first?
    a. tonsils
    b. Peyer's patches
    c. bronchus-associated lymphoid tissue
    d. mucosa-associated lymphoid tissue

10. Which of the following signs is *not* characteristic of inflammation?
    a. redness
    b. pain
    c. cold
    d. swelling

11. Which of the following is *not* important in the antiviral innate immune response?
    a. interferons
    b. natural killer cells

c. complement
d. microphages

12. Enhanced phagocytosis of a cell by the binding of a specific protein is called _____.
a. endocytosis
b. opsonization
c. anaphylaxis
d. complement activation

13. Which of the following leads to the redness of inflammation?
a. increased vascular permeability
b. anaphylactic shock
c. increased blood flow
d. complement activation

14. T cells that secrete cytokines that help antibody responses are called _____.
a. Th1
b. Th2
c. regulatory T cells
d. thymocytes

15. The taking in of antigen and digesting it for later presentation is called _____.
a. antigen presentation
b. antigen processing
c. endocytosis
d. exocytosis

16. Why is clonal expansion so important?
a. to select for specific cells
b. to secrete cytokines
c. to kill target cells
d. to increase the numbers of specific cells

17. The elimination of self-reactive thymocytes is called _____.
a. positive selection.
b. negative selection.
c. tolerance.
d. clonal selection.

18. Which type of T cell is most effective against viruses?
a. Th1
b. Th2
c. cytotoxic T cells
d. regulatory T cells

19. Removing functionality from a B cell without killing it is called _____.
a. clonal selection
b. clonal expansion
c. clonal deletion
d. clonal anergy

20. Which class of antibody crosses the placenta in pregnant women?
a. IgM
b. IgA
c. IgE
d. IgG

21. Which class of antibody has no known function other than as an antigen receptor?
a. IgM
b. IgA
c. IgE
d. IgD

22. When does class switching occur?
a. primary response
b. secondary response
c. tolerance
d. memory response

23. Which class of antibody is found in mucus?
a. IgM
b. IgA
c. IgE
d. IgD

24. Which enzymes in macrophages are important for clearing intracellular bacteria?
a. metabolic
b. mitochondrial
c. nuclear
d. lysosomal

25. What type of chronic lung disease is caused by a *Mycobacterium*?
a. asthma
b. emphysema
c. tuberculosis
d. leprosy

26. Which type of immune response is most *directly* effective against bacteria?
a. natural killer cells
b. complement
c. cytotoxic T cells
d. helper T cells

27. What is the reason that you have to be immunized with a new influenza vaccine each year?
a. the vaccine is only protective for a year
b. mutation
c. macrophage oxidative metabolism
d. memory response

28. Which type of immune response works in concert with cytotoxic T cells against virally infected cells?
a. natural killer cells
b. complement
c. antibodies
d. memory

29. Which type of hypersensitivity involves soluble antigen-antibody complexes?
a. type I
b. type II
c. type III
d. type IV

30. What causes the delay in delayed hypersensitivity?

a. inflammation

b. cytokine release
c. recruitment of immune cells
d. histamine release

31. Which of the following is a critical feature of immediate hypersensitivity?
a. inflammation
b. cytotoxic T cells
c. recruitment of immune cells
d. histamine release

32. Which of the following is an autoimmune disease of the heart?
a. rheumatoid arthritis
b. lupus
c. rheumatic fever
d. Hashimoto's thyroiditis

33. What drug is used to counteract the effects of anaphylactic shock?
a. epinephrine
b. antihistamines
c. antibiotics
d. aspirin

34. Which of the following terms means "many genes"?

a. polymorphism
b. polygeny

c. polypeptide
d. multiple alleles

35. Why do we have natural antibodies?
a. We don't know why.
b. immunity to environmental bacteria
c. immunity to transplants
d. from clonal selection

36. Which type of cancer is associated with HIV disease?
a. Kaposi's sarcoma
b. melanoma
c. lymphoma
d. renal cell carcinoma

37. How does cyclosporine A work?
a. suppresses antibodies
b. suppresses T cells
c. suppresses macrophages
d. suppresses neutrophils

38. What disease is associated with bone marrow transplants?
a. diabetes mellitus type I
b. melanoma
c. headache
d. graft-versus-host disease

CRITICAL THINKING QUESTIONS

39. Describe the flow of lymph from its origins in interstitial fluid to its emptying into the venous bloodstream.

40. Describe the process of inflammation in an area that has been traumatized, but not infected.

41. Describe two early induced responses and what pathogens they affect.

42. Describe the processing and presentation of an intracellular antigen.

43. Describe clonal selection and expansion.

44. Describe how secondary B cell responses are developed.

45. Describe the role of IgM in immunity.

46. Describe how seroconversion works in HIV disease.

47. Describe tuberculosis and the innocent bystander effect.

48. Describe anaphylactic shock in someone sensitive to peanuts?

49. Describe rheumatic fever and how tolerance is broken.

50. Describe how stress affects immune responses.

22 | THE RESPIRATORY SYSTEM

Figure 22.1 Mountain Climbers The thin air at high elevations can strain the human respiratory system. (credit: "bortescristian"/flickr.com)

Introduction

Chapter Objectives

After studying this chapter, you will be able to:

- List the structures of the respiratory system
- List the major functions of the respiratory system
- Outline the forces that allow for air movement into and out of the lungs
- Outline the process of gas exchange
- Summarize the process of oxygen and carbon dioxide transport within the respiratory system
- Create a flow chart illustrating how respiration is controlled
- Discuss how the respiratory system responds to exercise
- Describe the development of the respiratory system in the embryo

Hold your breath. Really! See how long you can hold your breath as you continue reading…How long can you do it? Chances are you are feeling uncomfortable already. A typical human cannot survive without breathing for more than 3 minutes, and even if you wanted to hold your breath longer, your autonomic nervous system would take control. This is because every cell in the body needs to run the oxidative stages of cellular respiration, the process by which energy is produced in the form of adenosine triphosphate (ATP). For oxidative phosphorylation to occur, oxygen is used as a reactant and carbon dioxide is released as a waste product. You may be surprised to learn that although oxygen is a critical need for cells, it is actually the accumulation of carbon dioxide that primarily drives your need to breathe. Carbon dioxide is exhaled and oxygen is inhaled through the respiratory system, which includes muscles to move air into and out of the lungs, passageways through which air moves, and microscopic gas exchange surfaces covered by capillaries. The circulatory system transports gases from the lungs to tissues throughout the body and vice versa. A variety of diseases can affect the respiratory system, such as asthma, emphysema, chronic obstruction pulmonary disorder (COPD), and lung cancer. All of these conditions affect the gas exchange process and result in labored breathing and other difficulties.

22.1 | Organs and Structures of the Respiratory System

By the end of this section, you will be able to:
- List the structures that make up the respiratory system
- Describe how the respiratory system processes oxygen and CO_2
- Compare and contrast the functions of upper respiratory tract with the lower respiratory tract

The major organs of the respiratory system function primarily to provide oxygen to body tissues for cellular respiration, remove the waste product carbon dioxide, and help to maintain acid-base balance. Portions of the respiratory system are also used for non-vital functions, such as sensing odors, speech production, and for straining, such as during childbirth or coughing (Figure 22.2).

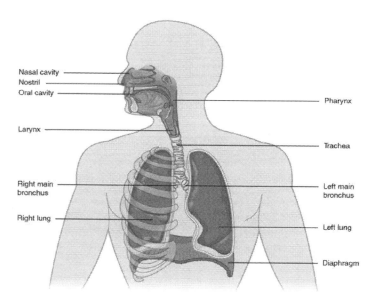

Figure 22.2 Major Respiratory Structures The major respiratory structures span the nasal cavity to the diaphragm.

Functionally, the respiratory system can be divided into a conducting zone and a respiratory zone. The **conducting zone** of the respiratory system includes the organs and structures not directly involved in gas exchange. The gas exchange occurs in the **respiratory zone**.

Conducting Zone

The major functions of the conducting zone are to provide a route for incoming and outgoing air, remove debris and pathogens from the incoming air, and warm and humidify the incoming air. Several structures within the conducting zone perform other functions as well. The epithelium of the nasal passages, for example, is essential to sensing odors, and the bronchial epithelium that lines the lungs can metabolize some airborne carcinogens.

The Nose and its Adjacent Structures

The major entrance and exit for the respiratory system is through the nose. When discussing the nose, it is helpful to divide it into two major sections: the external nose, and the nasal cavity or internal nose.

The **external nose** consists of the surface and skeletal structures that result in the outward appearance of the nose and contribute to its numerous functions (Figure 22.3). The **root** is the region of the nose located between the eyebrows. The **bridge** is the part of the nose that connects the root to the rest of the nose. The **dorsum nasi** is the length of the nose. The **apex** is the tip of the nose. On either side of the apex, the nostrils are formed by the alae (singular = ala). An **ala** is a cartilaginous structure that forms the lateral side of each **naris** (plural = nares), or nostril opening. The **philtrum** is the concave surface that connects the apex of the nose to the upper lip.

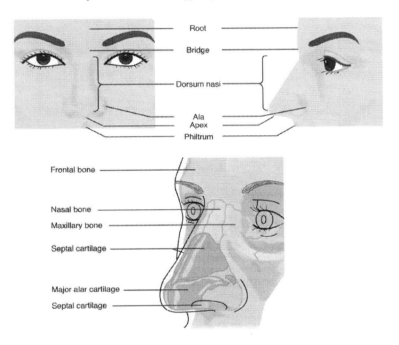

Figure 22.3 Nose This illustration shows features of the external nose (top) and skeletal features of the nose (bottom).

Underneath the thin skin of the nose are its skeletal features (see Figure 22.3, lower illustration). While the root and bridge of the nose consist of bone, the protruding portion of the nose is composed of cartilage. As a result, when looking at a skull, the nose is missing. The **nasal bone** is one of a pair of bones that lies under the root and bridge of the nose. The nasal bone articulates superiorly with the frontal bone and laterally with the maxillary bones. Septal cartilage is flexible hyaline cartilage connected to the nasal bone, forming the dorsum nasi. The **alar cartilage** consists of the apex of the nose; it surrounds the naris.

The nares open into the nasal cavity, which is separated into left and right sections by the nasal septum (Figure 22.4). The **nasal septum** is formed anteriorly by a portion of the septal cartilage (the flexible portion you can touch with your fingers) and posteriorly by the perpendicular plate of the ethmoid bone (a cranial bone located just posterior to the nasal bones) and the thin vomer bones (whose name refers to its plough shape). Each lateral wall of the nasal cavity has three bony projections, called the superior, middle, and inferior nasal conchae. The inferior conchae are separate bones, whereas the superior and middle conchae are portions of the ethmoid bone. Conchae serve to increase the surface area of the nasal cavity and to disrupt the flow of air as it enters the nose, causing air to bounce along the epithelium, where it is cleaned and warmed. The conchae and **meatuses** also conserve water and prevent dehydration of the nasal epithelium by trapping water during exhalation. The floor of the nasal cavity is composed of the palate. The hard palate at the anterior region of the nasal cavity is composed of bone. The soft palate at the posterior portion of the nasal cavity consists of muscle tissue. Air exits the nasal cavities via the internal nares and moves into the pharynx.

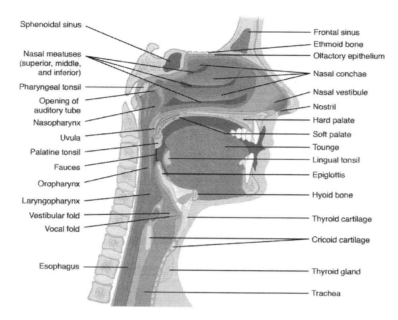

Figure 22.4 Upper Airway

Several bones that help form the walls of the nasal cavity have air-containing spaces called the paranasal sinuses, which serve to warm and humidify incoming air. Sinuses are lined with a mucosa. Each **paranasal sinus** is named for its associated bone: frontal sinus, maxillary sinus, sphenoidal sinus, and ethmoidal sinus. The sinuses produce mucus and lighten the weight of the skull.

The nares and anterior portion of the nasal cavities are lined with mucous membranes, containing sebaceous glands and hair follicles that serve to prevent the passage of large debris, such as dirt, through the nasal cavity. An olfactory epithelium used to detect odors is found deeper in the nasal cavity.

The conchae, meatuses, and paranasal sinuses are lined by **respiratory epithelium** composed of pseudostratified ciliated columnar epithelium (Figure 22.5). The epithelium contains goblet cells, one of the specialized, columnar epithelial cells that produce mucus to trap debris. The cilia of the respiratory epithelium help remove the mucus and debris from the nasal cavity with a constant beating motion, sweeping materials towards the throat to be swallowed. Interestingly, cold air slows the movement of the cilia, resulting in accumulation of mucus that may in turn lead to a runny nose during cold weather. This moist epithelium functions to warm and humidify incoming air. Capillaries located just beneath the nasal epithelium warm the air by convection. Serous and mucus-producing cells also secrete the lysozyme enzyme and proteins called defensins, which have antibacterial properties. Immune cells that patrol the connective tissue deep to the respiratory epithelium provide additional protection.

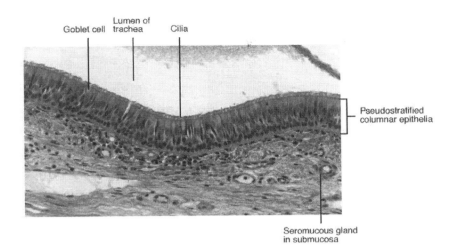

Figure 22.5 Pseudostratified Ciliated Columnar Epithelium Respiratory epithelium is pseudostratified ciliated columnar epithelium. Seromucous glands provide lubricating mucus. LM × 680. (Micrograph provided by the Regents of University of Michigan Medical School © 2012)

View the University of Michigan WebScope at http://141.214.65.171/Histology/Basic%20Tissues/Epithelium%20and%20CT/040_HISTO_40X.svs/view.apml? (http://openstaxcollege.org/l/pseudoMG) to explore the tissue sample in greater detail.

Pharynx

The **pharynx** is a tube formed by skeletal muscle and lined by mucous membrane that is continuous with that of the nasal cavities (see Figure 22.4). The pharynx is divided into three major regions: the nasopharynx, the oropharynx, and the laryngopharynx (Figure 22.6).

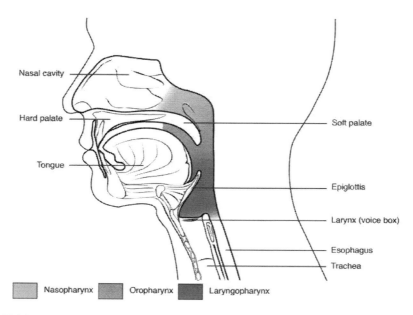

Figure 22.6 Divisions of the Pharynx The pharynx is divided into three regions: the nasopharynx, the oropharynx, and the laryngopharynx.

The **nasopharynx** is flanked by the conchae of the nasal cavity, and it serves only as an airway. At the top of the nasopharynx are the pharyngeal tonsils. A **pharyngeal tonsil**, also called an adenoid, is an aggregate of lymphoid reticular tissue similar to a lymph node that lies at the superior portion of the nasopharynx. The function of the pharyngeal tonsil is not well understood, but it contains a rich supply of lymphocytes and is covered with ciliated epithelium that traps and destroys invading pathogens that enter during inhalation. The pharyngeal tonsils are large in children, but interestingly, tend to regress with age and may even disappear. The uvula is a small bulbous, teardrop-shaped structure located at the apex of the soft palate. Both the uvula and soft palate move like a pendulum during swallowing, swinging upward to close off the nasopharynx to prevent ingested materials from entering the nasal cavity. In addition, auditory (Eustachian) tubes that connect to each middle ear cavity open into the nasopharynx. This connection is why colds often lead to ear infections.

The **oropharynx** is a passageway for both air and food. The oropharynx is bordered superiorly by the nasopharynx and anteriorly by the oral cavity. The **fauces** is the opening at the connection between the oral cavity and the oropharynx. As the nasopharynx becomes the oropharynx, the epithelium changes from pseudostratified ciliated columnar epithelium to stratified squamous epithelium. The oropharynx contains two distinct sets of tonsils, the palatine and lingual tonsils. A **palatine tonsil** is one of a pair of structures located laterally in the oropharynx in the area of the fauces. The **lingual tonsil** is located at the base of the tongue. Similar to the pharyngeal tonsil, the palatine and lingual tonsils are composed of lymphoid tissue, and trap and destroy pathogens entering the body through the oral or nasal cavities.

The **laryngopharynx** is inferior to the oropharynx and posterior to the larynx. It continues the route for ingested material and air until its inferior end, where the digestive and respiratory systems diverge. The stratified squamous epithelium of the oropharynx is continuous with the laryngopharynx. Anteriorly, the laryngopharynx opens into the larynx, whereas posteriorly, it enters the esophagus.

Larynx

The **larynx** is a cartilaginous structure inferior to the laryngopharynx that connects the pharynx to the trachea and helps regulate the volume of air that enters and leaves the lungs (Figure 22.7). The structure of the larynx is formed by several pieces of cartilage. Three large cartilage pieces—the thyroid cartilage (anterior), epiglottis (superior), and cricoid cartilage (inferior)—form the major structure of the larynx. The **thyroid cartilage** is the largest piece of cartilage that makes up the larynx. The thyroid cartilage consists of the **laryngeal prominence**, or "Adam's apple," which tends to be more prominent in males. The thick **cricoid cartilage** forms a ring, with a wide posterior region and a thinner anterior region. Three smaller, paired cartilages—the arytenoids, corniculates, and cuneiforms—attach to the epiglottis and the vocal cords and muscle that help move the vocal cords to produce speech.

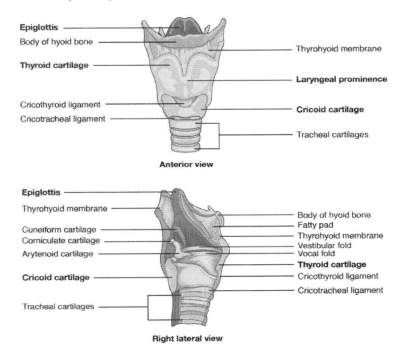

Figure 22.7 Larynx The larynx extends from the laryngopharynx and the hyoid bone to the trachea.

The **epiglottis**, attached to the thyroid cartilage, is a very flexible piece of elastic cartilage that covers the opening of the trachea (see Figure 22.4). When in the "closed" position, the unattached end of the epiglottis rests on the glottis. The **glottis** is composed of the vestibular folds, the true vocal cords, and the space between these folds (Figure 22.8). A **vestibular fold**, or false vocal cord, is one of a pair of folded sections of mucous membrane. A **true vocal cord** is one of the white, membranous folds attached by muscle to the thyroid and arytenoid cartilages of the larynx on their outer edges. The inner edges of the true vocal cords are free, allowing oscillation to produce sound. The size of the membranous folds of the true vocal cords differs between individuals, producing voices with different pitch ranges. Folds in males tend to be larger than those in females, which create a deeper voice. The act of swallowing causes the pharynx and larynx to lift upward, allowing the pharynx to expand and the epiglottis of the larynx to swing downward, closing the opening to the trachea. These movements produce a larger area for food to pass through, while preventing food and beverages from entering the trachea.

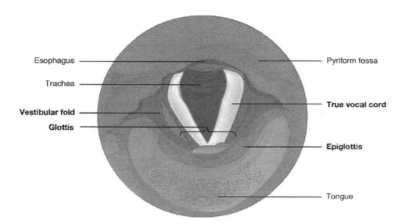

Figure 22.8 Vocal Cords The true vocal cords and vestibular folds of the larynx are viewed inferiorly from the laryngopharynx.

Continuous with the laryngopharynx, the superior portion of the larynx is lined with stratified squamous epithelium, transitioning into pseudostratified ciliated columnar epithelium that contains goblet cells. Similar to the nasal cavity and nasopharynx, this specialized epithelium produces mucus to trap debris and pathogens as they enter the trachea. The cilia beat the mucus upward towards the laryngopharynx, where it can be swallowed down the esophagus.

Trachea

The trachea (windpipe) extends from the larynx toward the lungs (Figure 22.9a). The **trachea** is formed by 16 to 20 stacked, C-shaped pieces of hyaline cartilage that are connected by dense connective tissue. The **trachealis muscle** and elastic connective tissue together form the **fibroelastic membrane**, a flexible membrane that closes the posterior surface of the trachea, connecting the C-shaped cartilages. The fibroelastic membrane allows the trachea to stretch and expand slightly during inhalation and exhalation, whereas the rings of cartilage provide structural support and prevent the trachea from collapsing. In addition, the trachealis muscle can be contracted to force air through the trachea during exhalation. The trachea is lined with pseudostratified ciliated columnar epithelium, which is continuous with the larynx. The esophagus borders the trachea posteriorly.

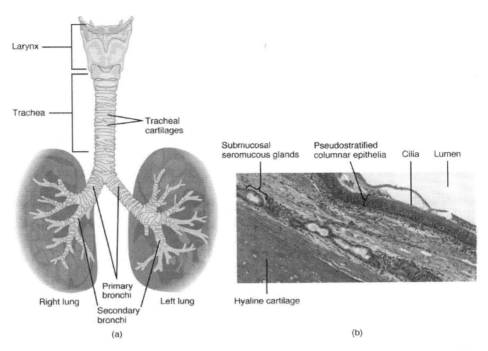

Figure 22.9 Trachea (a) The tracheal tube is formed by stacked, C-shaped pieces of hyaline cartilage. (b) The layer visible in this cross-section of tracheal wall tissue between the hyaline cartilage and the lumen of the trachea is the mucosa, which is composed of pseudostratified ciliated columnar epithelium that contains goblet cells. LM × 1220. (Micrograph provided by the Regents of University of Michigan Medical School © 2012)

Bronchial Tree

The trachea branches into the right and left primary **bronchi** at the carina. These bronchi are also lined by pseudostratified ciliated columnar epithelium containing mucus-producing goblet cells (Figure 22.9**b**). The carina is a raised structure that contains specialized nervous tissue that induces violent coughing if a foreign body, such as food, is present. Rings of cartilage, similar to those of the trachea, support the structure of the bronchi and prevent their collapse. The primary bronchi enter the lungs at the hilum, a concave region where blood vessels, lymphatic vessels, and nerves also enter the lungs. The bronchi continue to branch into bronchial a tree. A **bronchial tree** (or respiratory tree) is the collective term used for these multiple-branched bronchi. The main function of the bronchi, like other conducting zone structures, is to provide a passageway for air to move into and out of each lung. In addition, the mucous membrane traps debris and pathogens.

A **bronchiole** branches from the tertiary bronchi. Bronchioles, which are about 1 mm in diameter, further branch until they become the tiny terminal bronchioles, which lead to the structures of gas exchange. There are more than 1000 terminal bronchioles in each lung. The muscular walls of the bronchioles do not contain cartilage like those of the bronchi. This muscular wall can change the size of the tubing to increase or decrease airflow through the tube.

Respiratory Zone

In contrast to the conducting zone, the respiratory zone includes structures that are directly involved in gas exchange. The respiratory zone begins where the terminal bronchioles join a **respiratory bronchiole**, the smallest type of bronchiole (Figure 22.10), which then leads to an alveolar duct, opening into a cluster of alveoli.

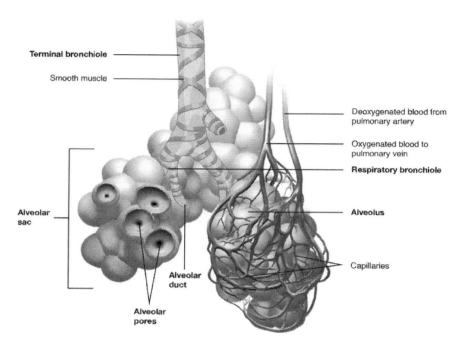

Figure 22.10 Respiratory Zone Bronchioles lead to alveolar sacs in the respiratory zone, where gas exchange occurs.

Alveoli

An **alveolar duct** is a tube composed of smooth muscle and connective tissue, which opens into a cluster of alveoli. An **alveolus** is one of the many small, grape-like sacs that are attached to the alveolar ducts.

An **alveolar sac** is a cluster of many individual alveoli that are responsible for gas exchange. An alveolus is approximately 200 μm in diameter with elastic walls that allow the alveolus to stretch during air intake, which greatly increases the surface area available for gas exchange. Alveoli are connected to their neighbors by **alveolar pores**, which help maintain equal air pressure throughout the alveoli and lung (Figure 22.11).

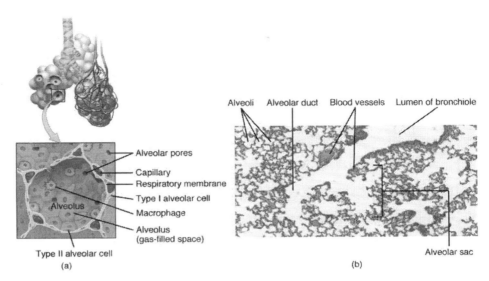

Figure 22.11 Structures of the Respiratory Zone (a) The alveolus is responsible for gas exchange. (b) A micrograph shows the alveolar structures within lung tissue. LM × 178. (Micrograph provided by the Regents of University of Michigan Medical School © 2012)

The alveolar wall consists of three major cell types: type I alveolar cells, type II alveolar cells, and alveolar macrophages. A **type I alveolar cell** is a squamous epithelial cell of the alveoli, which constitute up to 97 percent of the alveolar surface area. These cells are about 25 nm thick and are highly permeable to gases. A **type II alveolar cell** is interspersed among the type I cells and secretes **pulmonary surfactant**, a substance composed of phospholipids and proteins that reduces the surface tension of the alveoli. Roaming around the alveolar wall is the **alveolar macrophage**, a phagocytic cell of the immune system that removes debris and pathogens that have reached the alveoli.

The simple squamous epithelium formed by type I alveolar cells is attached to a thin, elastic basement membrane. This epithelium is extremely thin and borders the endothelial membrane of capillaries. Taken together, the alveoli and capillary membranes form a **respiratory membrane** that is approximately 0.5 mm thick. The respiratory membrane allows gases to cross by simple diffusion, allowing oxygen to be picked up by the blood for transport and CO_2 to be released into the air of the alveoli.

Respiratory System: Asthma

Asthma is common condition that affects the lungs in both adults and children. Approximately 8.2 percent of adults (18.7 million) and 9.4 percent of children (7 million) in the United States suffer from asthma. In addition, asthma is the most frequent cause of hospitalization in children.

Asthma is a chronic disease characterized by inflammation and edema of the airway, and bronchospasms (that is, constriction of the bronchioles), which can inhibit air from entering the lungs. In addition, excessive mucus secretion can occur, which further contributes to airway occlusion (Figure 22.12). Cells of the immune system, such as eosinophils and mononuclear cells, may also be involved in infiltrating the walls of the bronchi and bronchioles.

Bronchospasms occur periodically and lead to an "asthma attack." An attack may be triggered by environmental factors such as dust, pollen, pet hair, or dander, changes in the weather, mold, tobacco smoke, and respiratory infections, or by exercise and stress.

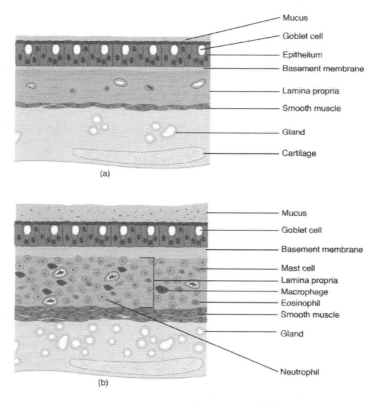

Figure 22.12 Normal and Bronchial Asthma Tissues (a) Normal lung tissue does not have the characteristics of lung tissue during (b) an asthma attack, which include thickened mucosa, increased mucus-producing goblet cells, and eosinophil infiltrates.

Symptoms of an asthma attack involve coughing, shortness of breath, wheezing, and tightness of the chest. Symptoms of a severe asthma attack that requires immediate medical attention would include difficulty breathing that results in blue (cyanotic) lips or face, confusion, drowsiness, a rapid pulse, sweating, and severe anxiety. The severity of the condition, frequency of attacks, and identified triggers influence the type of medication that an individual may require. Longer-term treatments are used for those with more severe asthma. Short-term, fast-acting drugs that are used to treat an asthma attack are typically administered via an inhaler. For young children or individuals who have difficulty using an inhaler, asthma medications can be administered via a nebulizer.

In many cases, the underlying cause of the condition is unknown. However, recent research has demonstrated that certain viruses, such as human rhinovirus C (HRVC), and the bacteria *Mycoplasma pneumoniae* and *Chlamydia pneumoniae* that are contracted in infancy or early childhood, may contribute to the development of many cases of asthma.

Visit this site (http://openstaxcollege.org/l/asthma) to learn more about what happens during an asthma attack. What are the three changes that occur inside the airways during an asthma attack?

22.2 | The Lungs

By the end of this section, you will be able to:
- Describe the overall function of the lung
- Summarize the blood flow pattern associated with the lungs
- Outline the anatomy of the blood supply to the lungs
- Describe the pleura of the lungs and their function

A major organ of the respiratory system, each **lung** houses structures of both the conducting and respiratory zones. The main function of the lungs is to perform the exchange of oxygen and carbon dioxide with air from the atmosphere. To this end, the lungs exchange respiratory gases across a very large epithelial surface area—about 70 square meters—that is highly permeable to gases.

Gross Anatomy of the Lungs

The lungs are pyramid-shaped, paired organs that are connected to the trachea by the right and left bronchi; on the inferior surface, the lungs are bordered by the diaphragm. The diaphragm is the flat, dome-shaped muscle located at the base of the lungs and thoracic cavity. The lungs are enclosed by the pleurae, which are attached to the mediastinum. The right lung is shorter and wider than the left lung, and the left lung occupies a smaller volume than the right. The **cardiac notch** is an indentation on the surface of the left lung, and it allows space for the heart (Figure 22.13). The apex of the lung is the superior region, whereas the base is the opposite region near the diaphragm. The costal surface of the lung borders the ribs. The mediastinal surface faces the midline.

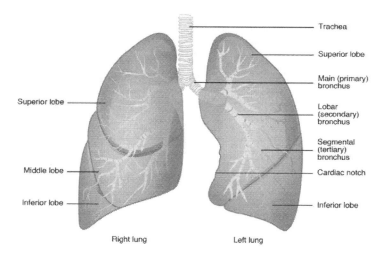

Figure 22.13 Gross Anatomy of the Lungs

Each lung is composed of smaller units called lobes. Fissures separate these lobes from each other. The right lung consists of three lobes: the superior, middle, and inferior lobes. The left lung consists of two lobes: the superior and inferior lobes. A bronchopulmonary segment is a division of a lobe, and each lobe houses multiple bronchopulmonary segments. Each segment receives air from its own tertiary bronchus and is supplied with blood by its own artery. Some diseases of the lungs typically affect one or more bronchopulmonary segments, and in some cases, the diseased segments can be surgically removed with little influence on neighboring segments. A pulmonary lobule is a subdivision formed as the bronchi branch into bronchioles. Each lobule receives its own large bronchiole that has multiple branches. An interlobular septum is a wall, composed of connective tissue, which separates lobules from one another.

Blood Supply and Nervous Innervation of the Lungs

The blood supply of the lungs plays an important role in gas exchange and serves as a transport system for gases throughout the body. In addition, innervation by the both the parasympathetic and sympathetic nervous systems provides an important level of control through dilation and constriction of the airway.

Blood Supply

The major function of the lungs is to perform gas exchange, which requires blood from the pulmonary circulation. This blood supply contains deoxygenated blood and travels to the lungs where erythrocytes, also known as red blood cells, pick up oxygen to be transported to tissues throughout the body. The **pulmonary artery** is an artery that arises from the pulmonary trunk and carries deoxygenated, arterial blood to the alveoli. The pulmonary artery branches multiple times as it follows the bronchi, and each branch becomes progressively smaller in diameter. One arteriole and an accompanying venule supply and drain one pulmonary lobule. As they near the alveoli, the pulmonary arteries become the pulmonary capillary network. The pulmonary capillary network consists of tiny vessels with very thin walls that lack smooth muscle fibers. The capillaries branch and follow the bronchioles and structure of the alveoli. It is at this point that the capillary wall meets the alveolar wall, creating the respiratory membrane. Once the blood is oxygenated, it drains from the alveoli by way of multiple pulmonary veins, which exit the lungs through the **hilum**.

Nervous Innervation

Dilation and constriction of the airway are achieved through nervous control by the parasympathetic and sympathetic nervous systems. The parasympathetic system causes **bronchoconstriction**, whereas the sympathetic nervous system stimulates **bronchodilation**. Reflexes such as coughing, and the ability of the lungs to regulate oxygen and carbon dioxide levels, also result from this autonomic nervous system control. Sensory nerve fibers arise from the vagus nerve, and from the second to fifth thoracic ganglia. The **pulmonary plexus** is a region on the lung root formed by the entrance of the nerves at the hilum. The nerves then follow the bronchi in the lungs and branch to innervate muscle fibers, glands, and blood vessels.

Pleura of the Lungs

Each lung is enclosed within a cavity that is surrounded by the pleura. The pleura (plural = pleurae) is a serous membrane that surrounds the lung. The right and left pleurae, which enclose the right and left lungs, respectively, are separated by the mediastinum. The pleurae consist of two layers. The **visceral pleura** is the layer that is superficial to the lungs, and extends into and lines the lung fissures (Figure 22.14). In contrast, the **parietal pleura** is the outer layer that connects to the thoracic wall, the mediastinum, and the diaphragm. The visceral and parietal pleurae connect to each other at the hilum. The **pleural cavity** is the space between the visceral and parietal layers.

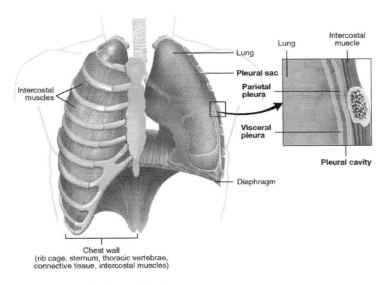

Figure 22.14 Parietal and Visceral Pleurae of the Lungs

The pleurae perform two major functions: They produce pleural fluid and create cavities that separate the major organs. **Pleural fluid** is secreted by mesothelial cells from both pleural layers and acts to lubricate their surfaces. This lubrication reduces friction between the two layers to prevent trauma during breathing, and creates surface tension that helps maintain the position of the lungs against the thoracic wall. This adhesive characteristic of the pleural fluid causes the lungs to enlarge when the thoracic wall expands during ventilation, allowing the lungs to fill with air. The pleurae also create a division between major organs that prevents interference due to the movement of the organs, while preventing the spread of infection.

Everyday CONNECTION

The Effects of Second-Hand Tobacco Smoke

The burning of a tobacco cigarette creates multiple chemical compounds that are released through mainstream smoke, which is inhaled by the smoker, and through sidestream smoke, which is the smoke that is given off by the burning cigarette. Second-hand smoke, which is a combination of sidestream smoke and the mainstream smoke that is exhaled by the smoker, has been demonstrated by numerous scientific studies to cause disease. At least 40 chemicals in sidestream smoke have been identified that negatively impact human health, leading to the development of cancer or other conditions, such as immune system dysfunction, liver toxicity, cardiac arrhythmias, pulmonary edema, and neurological dysfunction. Furthermore, second-hand smoke has been found to harbor at least 250 compounds that are known to be toxic, carcinogenic, or both. Some major classes of carcinogens in second-hand smoke are polyaromatic hydrocarbons (PAHs), N-nitrosamines, aromatic amines, formaldehyde, and acetaldehyde.

Tobacco and second-hand smoke are considered to be carcinogenic. Exposure to second-hand smoke can cause lung cancer in individuals who are not tobacco users themselves. It is estimated that the risk of developing lung cancer is increased by up to 30 percent in nonsmokers who live with an individual who smokes in the house, as compared to nonsmokers who are not regularly exposed to second-hand smoke. Children are especially affected by second-hand smoke. Children who live with an individual who smokes inside the home have a larger number of lower respiratory infections, which are associated with hospitalizations, and higher risk of sudden infant death syndrome (SIDS). Second-hand smoke in the home has also been linked to a greater number of ear infections in children, as well as worsening symptoms of asthma.

22.3 | The Process of Breathing

By the end of this section, you will be able to:
- Describe the mechanisms that drive breathing
- Discuss how pressure, volume, and resistance are related
- List the steps involved in pulmonary ventilation
- Discuss the physical factors related to breathing
- Discuss the meaning of respiratory volume and capacities
- Define respiratory rate
- Outline the mechanisms behind the control of breathing
- Describe the respiratory centers of the medulla oblongata
- Describe the respiratory centers of the pons
- Discuss factors that can influence the respiratory rate

Pulmonary ventilation is the act of breathing, which can be described as the movement of air into and out of the lungs. The major mechanisms that drive pulmonary ventilation are atmospheric pressure (P_{atm}); the air pressure within the alveoli, called alveolar pressure (P_{alv}); and the pressure within the pleural cavity, called intrapleural pressure (P_{ip}).

Mechanisms of Breathing

The alveolar and intrapleural pressures are dependent on certain physical features of the lung. However, the ability to breathe—to have air enter the lungs during inspiration and air leave the lungs during expiration—is dependent on the air pressure of the atmosphere and the air pressure within the lungs.

Pressure Relationships

Inspiration (or inhalation) and expiration (or exhalation) are dependent on the differences in pressure between the atmosphere and the lungs. In a gas, pressure is a force created by the movement of gas molecules that are confined. For example, a certain number of gas molecules in a two-liter container has more room than the same number of gas molecules in a one-liter container (Figure 22.15). In this case, the force exerted by the movement of the gas molecules against the walls of the two-liter container is lower than the force exerted by the gas molecules in the one-liter container. Therefore, the pressure is lower in the two-liter container and higher in the one-liter container. At a constant temperature, changing the volume occupied by the gas changes the pressure, as does changing the number of gas molecules. **Boyle's law** describes the relationship between volume and pressure in a gas at a constant temperature. Boyle discovered that the pressure of a gas is inversely proportional to its volume: If volume increases, pressure decreases. Likewise, if volume decreases, pressure increases. Pressure and volume are inversely related ($P = k/V$). Therefore, the pressure in the one-liter container (one-half the volume of the two-liter container) would be twice the pressure in the two-liter container. Boyle's law is expressed by the following formula:

$$P_1 V_1 = P_2 V_2$$

In this formula, P_1 represents the initial pressure and V_1 represents the initial volume, whereas the final pressure and volume are represented by P_2 and V_2, respectively. If the two- and one-liter containers were connected by a tube and the volume of one of the containers were changed, then the gases would move from higher pressure (lower volume) to lower pressure (higher volume).

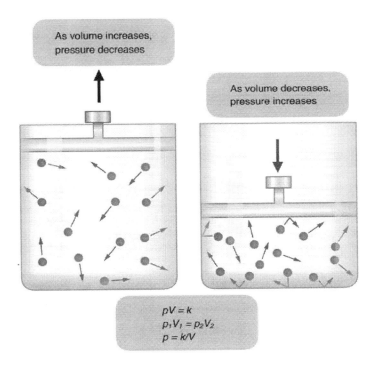

Figure 22.15 Boyle's Law   In a gas, pressure increases as volume decreases.

Pulmonary ventilation is dependent on three types of pressure: atmospheric, intra-alveolar, and interpleural. **Atmospheric pressure** is the amount of force that is exerted by gases in the air surrounding any given surface, such as the body. Atmospheric pressure can be expressed in terms of the unit atmosphere, abbreviated atm, or in millimeters of mercury (mm Hg). One atm is equal to 760 mm Hg, which is the atmospheric pressure at sea level. Typically, for respiration, other pressure values are discussed in relation to atmospheric pressure. Therefore, negative pressure is pressure lower than the atmospheric pressure, whereas positive pressure is pressure that it is greater than the atmospheric pressure. A pressure that is equal to the atmospheric pressure is expressed as zero.

Intra-alveolar pressure is the pressure of the air within the alveoli, which changes during the different phases of breathing (Figure 22.16). Because the alveoli are connected to the atmosphere via the tubing of the airways (similar to the two- and one-liter containers in the example above), the interpulmonary pressure of the alveoli always equalizes with the atmospheric pressure.

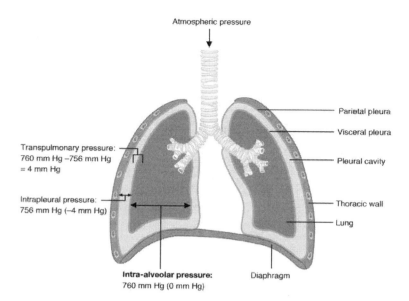

Figure 22.16 Intrapulmonary and Intrapleural Pressure Relationships Alveolar pressure changes during the different phases of the cycle. It equalizes at 760 mm Hg but does not remain at 760 mm Hg.

Intrapleural pressure is the pressure of the air within the pleural cavity, between the visceral and parietal pleurae. Similar to intra-alveolar pressure, intrapleural pressure also changes during the different phases of breathing. However, due to certain characteristics of the lungs, the intrapleural pressure is always lower than, or negative to, the intra-alveolar pressure (and therefore also to atmospheric pressure). Although it fluctuates during inspiration and expiration, intrapleural pressure remains approximately –4 mm Hg throughout the breathing cycle.

Competing forces within the thorax cause the formation of the negative intrapleural pressure. One of these forces relates to the elasticity of the lungs themselves—elastic tissue pulls the lungs inward, away from the thoracic wall. Surface tension of alveolar fluid, which is mostly water, also creates an inward pull of the lung tissue. This inward tension from the lungs is countered by opposing forces from the pleural fluid and thoracic wall. Surface tension within the pleural cavity pulls the lungs outward. Too much or too little pleural fluid would hinder the creation of the negative intrapleural pressure; therefore, the level must be closely monitored by the mesothelial cells and drained by the lymphatic system. Since the parietal pleura is attached to the thoracic wall, the natural elasticity of the chest wall opposes the inward pull of the lungs. Ultimately, the outward pull is slightly greater than the inward pull, creating the –4 mm Hg intrapleural pressure relative to the intra-alveolar pressure. **Transpulmonary pressure** is the difference between the intrapleural and intra-alveolar pressures, and it determines the size of the lungs. A higher transpulmonary pressure corresponds to a larger lung.

Physical Factors Affecting Ventilation

In addition to the differences in pressures, breathing is also dependent upon the contraction and relaxation of muscle fibers of both the diaphragm and thorax. The lungs themselves are passive during breathing, meaning they are not involved in creating the movement that helps inspiration and expiration. This is because of the adhesive nature of the pleural fluid, which allows the lungs to be pulled outward when the thoracic wall moves during inspiration. The recoil of the thoracic wall during expiration causes compression of the lungs. Contraction and relaxation of the diaphragm and intercostals muscles (found between the ribs) cause most of the pressure changes that result in inspiration and expiration. These muscle movements and subsequent pressure changes cause air to either rush in or be forced out of the lungs.

Other characteristics of the lungs influence the effort that must be expended to ventilate. Resistance is a force that slows motion, in this case, the flow of gases. The size of the airway is the primary factor affecting resistance. A small tubular diameter forces air through a smaller space, causing more collisions of air molecules with the walls of the airways. The following formula helps to describe the relationship between airway resistance and pressure changes:

$$F = \Delta P / R$$

As noted earlier, there is surface tension within the alveoli caused by water present in the lining of the alveoli. This surface tension tends to inhibit expansion of the alveoli. However, pulmonary surfactant secreted by type II alveolar cells mixes with that water and helps reduce this surface tension. Without pulmonary surfactant, the alveoli would collapse during expiration.

Thoracic wall compliance is the ability of the thoracic wall to stretch while under pressure. This can also affect the effort expended in the process of breathing. In order for inspiration to occur, the thoracic cavity must expand. The expansion of the thoracic cavity directly influences the capacity of the lungs to expand. If the tissues of the thoracic wall are not very compliant, it will be difficult to expand the thorax to increase the size of the lungs.

Pulmonary Ventilation

The difference in pressures drives pulmonary ventilation because air flows down a pressure gradient, that is, air flows from an area of higher pressure to an area of lower pressure. Air flows into the lungs largely due to a difference in pressure; atmospheric pressure is greater than intra-alveolar pressure, and intra-alveolar pressure is greater than intrapleural pressure. Air flows out of the lungs during expiration based on the same principle; pressure within the lungs becomes greater than the atmospheric pressure.

Pulmonary ventilation comprises two major steps: inspiration and expiration. **Inspiration** is the process that causes air to enter the lungs, and **expiration** is the process that causes air to leave the lungs (Figure 22.17). A **respiratory cycle** is one sequence of inspiration and expiration. In general, two muscle groups are used during normal inspiration: the diaphragm and the external intercostal muscles. Additional muscles can be used if a bigger breath is required. When the diaphragm contracts, it moves inferiorly toward the abdominal cavity, creating a larger thoracic cavity and more space for the lungs. Contraction of the external intercostal muscles moves the ribs upward and outward, causing the rib cage to expand, which increases the volume of the thoracic cavity. Due to the adhesive force of the pleural fluid, the expansion of the thoracic cavity forces the lungs to stretch and expand as well. This increase in volume leads to a decrease in intra-alveolar pressure, creating a pressure lower than atmospheric pressure. As a result, a pressure gradient is created that drives air into the lungs.

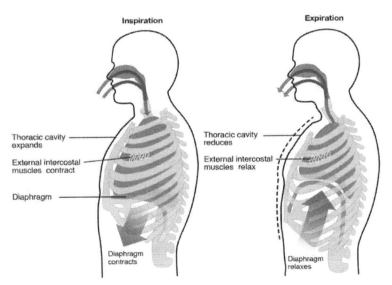

Figure 22.17 Inspiration and Expiration Inspiration and expiration occur due to the expansion and contraction of the thoracic cavity, respectively.

The process of normal expiration is passive, meaning that energy is not required to push air out of the lungs. Instead, the elasticity of the lung tissue causes the lung to recoil, as the diaphragm and intercostal muscles relax following inspiration. In turn, the thoracic cavity and lungs decrease in volume, causing an increase in interpulmonary pressure. The interpulmonary pressure rises above atmospheric pressure, creating a pressure gradient that causes air to leave the lungs.

There are different types, or modes, of breathing that require a slightly different process to allow inspiration and expiration. **Quiet breathing**, also known as eupnea, is a mode of breathing that occurs at rest and does not require the cognitive thought of the individual. During quiet breathing, the diaphragm and external intercostals must contract.

A deep breath, called diaphragmatic breathing, requires the diaphragm to contract. As the diaphragm relaxes, air passively leaves the lungs. A shallow breath, called costal breathing, requires contraction of the intercostal muscles. As the intercostal muscles relax, air passively leaves the lungs.

In contrast, **forced breathing**, also known as hyperpnea, is a mode of breathing that can occur during exercise or actions that require the active manipulation of breathing, such as singing. During forced breathing, inspiration and expiration both occur due to muscle contractions. In addition to the contraction of the diaphragm and intercostal muscles, other accessory muscles must also contract. During forced inspiration, muscles of the neck, including the scalenes, contract and lift the thoracic wall, increasing lung volume. During forced expiration, accessory muscles of the abdomen, including the obliques, contract, forcing abdominal organs upward against the diaphragm. This helps to push the diaphragm further into the thorax, pushing more air out. In addition, accessory muscles (primarily the internal intercostals) help to compress the rib cage, which also reduces the volume of the thoracic cavity.

Respiratory Volumes and Capacities

Respiratory volume is the term used for various volumes of air moved by or associated with the lungs at a given point in the respiratory cycle. There are four major types of respiratory volumes: tidal, residual, inspiratory reserve, and expiratory reserve (Figure 22.18). **Tidal volume (TV)** is the amount of air that normally enters the lungs during quiet breathing, which is about 500 milliliters. **Expiratory reserve volume (ERV)** is the amount of air you can forcefully exhale past a normal tidal expiration, up to 1200 milliliters for men. **Inspiratory reserve volume (IRV)** is produced by a deep inhalation, past a tidal inspiration. This is the extra volume that can be brought into the lungs during a forced inspiration. **Residual volume (RV)** is the air left in the lungs if you exhale as much air as possible. The residual volume makes breathing easier by preventing the alveoli from collapsing. Respiratory volume is dependent on a variety of factors, and measuring the different types of respiratory volumes can provide important clues about a person's respiratory health (Figure 22.19).

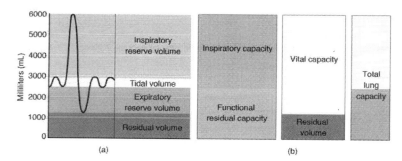

Figure 22.18 Respiratory Volumes and Capacities These two graphs show (a) respiratory volumes and (b) the combination of volumes that results in respiratory capacity.

Pulmonary function test	Instrument	Measures	Function
Spirometry	Spirometer	Forced vital capacity (FVC)	Volume of air that is exhaled after maximum inhalation
		Forced expiratory volume (FEV)	Volume of air exhaled in one breath
		Forced expiratory flow, 25–75 percent	Air flow in the middle of exhalation
		Peak expiratory flow (PEF)	Rate of exhalation
		Maximum voluntary ventilation (MVV)	Volume of air that can be inspired and expired in 1 minute
		Slow vital capacity (SVC)	Volume of air that can be slowly exhaled after inhaling past the tidal volume
		Total lung capacity (TLC)	Volume of air in the lungs after maximum inhalation
		Functional residual capacity (FRC)	Volume of air left in the lungs after normal expiration
		Residual volume (RV)	Volume of air in the lungs after maximum exhalation
		Total lung capacity (TLC)	Maximum volume of air that the lungs can hold
		Expiratory reserve volume (ERV)	The volume of air that can be exhaled beyond normal exhalation
Gas diffusion	Blood gas analyzer	Arterial blood gases	Concentration of oxygen and carbon dioxide in the blood

Figure 22.19 Pulmonary Function Testing

Respiratory capacity is the combination of two or more selected volumes, which further describes the amount of air in the lungs during a given time. For example, **total lung capacity (TLC)** is the sum of all of the lung volumes (TV, ERV, IRV, and RV), which represents the total amount of air a person can hold in the lungs after a forceful inhalation. TLC is about 6000 mL air for men, and about 4200 mL for women. **Vital capacity (VC)** is the amount of air a person can move into or out of his or her lungs, and is the sum of all of the volumes except residual volume (TV, ERV, and IRV), which is between 4000 and 5000 milliliters. **Inspiratory capacity (IC)** is the maximum amount of air that can be inhaled past a normal tidal expiration, is the sum of the tidal volume and inspiratory reserve volume. On the other hand, the **functional residual capacity (FRC)** is the amount of air that remains in the lung after a normal tidal expiration; it is the sum of expiratory reserve volume and residual volume (see Figure 22.18).

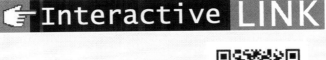

Watch this video (http://openstaxcollege.org/l/spirometers) to learn more about lung volumes and spirometers. Explain how spirometry test results can be used to diagnose respiratory diseases or determine the effectiveness of disease treatment.

In addition to the air that creates respiratory volumes, the respiratory system also contains **anatomical dead space**, which is air that is present in the airway that never reaches the alveoli and therefore never participates in gas exchange. **Alveolar dead space** involves air found within alveoli that are unable to function, such as those affected by disease or abnormal blood flow. **Total dead space** is the anatomical dead space and alveolar dead space together, and represents all of the air in the respiratory system that is not being used in the gas exchange process.

Respiratory Rate and Control of Ventilation

Breathing usually occurs without thought, although at times you can consciously control it, such as when you swim under water, sing a song, or blow bubbles. The **respiratory rate** is the total number of breaths, or respiratory cycles, that occur each minute. Respiratory rate can be an important indicator of disease, as the rate may increase or decrease during an illness or in a disease condition. The respiratory rate is controlled by the respiratory center located within the medulla oblongata in the brain, which responds primarily to changes in carbon dioxide, oxygen, and pH levels in the blood.

The normal respiratory rate of a child decreases from birth to adolescence. A child under 1 year of age has a normal respiratory rate between 30 and 60 breaths per minute, but by the time a child is about 10 years old, the normal rate is closer to 18 to 30. By adolescence, the normal respiratory rate is similar to that of adults, 12 to 18 breaths per minute.

Ventilation Control Centers

The control of ventilation is a complex interplay of multiple regions in the brain that signal the muscles used in pulmonary ventilation to contract (Table 22.1). The result is typically a rhythmic, consistent ventilation rate that provides the body with sufficient amounts of oxygen, while adequately removing carbon dioxide.

Summary of Ventilation Regulation

System component	Function
Medullary respiratory renter	Sets the basic rhythm of breathing
Ventral respiratory group (VRG)	Generates the breathing rhythm and integrates data coming into the medulla
Dorsal respiratory group (DRG)	Integrates input from the stretch receptors and the chemoreceptors in the periphery
Pontine respiratory group (PRG)	Influences and modifies the medulla oblongata's functions
Aortic body	Monitors blood PCO_2, PO_2, and pH
Carotid body	Monitors blood PCO_2, PO_2, and pH
Hypothalamus	Monitors emotional state and body temperature
Cortical areas of the brain	Control voluntary breathing
Proprioceptors	Send impulses regarding joint and muscle movements
Pulmonary irritant reflexes	Protect the respiratory zones of the system from foreign material
Inflation reflex	Protects the lungs from over-inflating

Table 22.1

Neurons that innervate the muscles of the respiratory system are responsible for controlling and regulating pulmonary ventilation. The major brain centers involved in pulmonary ventilation are the medulla oblongata and the pontine respiratory group (Figure 22.20).

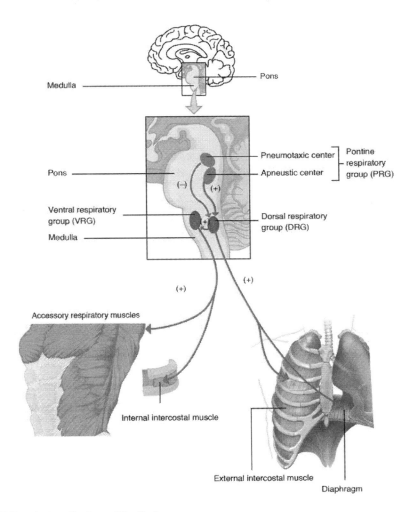

Figure 22.20 Respiratory Centers of the Brain

The medulla oblongata contains the **dorsal respiratory group (DRG)** and the **ventral respiratory group (VRG)**. The DRG is involved in maintaining a constant breathing rhythm by stimulating the diaphragm and intercostal muscles to contract, resulting in inspiration. When activity in the DRG ceases, it no longer stimulates the diaphragm and intercostals to contract, allowing them to relax, resulting in expiration. The VRG is involved in forced breathing, as the neurons in the VRG stimulate the accessory muscles involved in forced breathing to contract, resulting in forced inspiration. The VRG also stimulates the accessory muscles involved in forced expiration to contract.

The second respiratory center of the brain is located within the pons, called the pontine respiratory group, and consists of the apneustic and pneumotaxic centers. The **apneustic center** is a double cluster of neuronal cell bodies that stimulate neurons in the DRG, controlling the depth of inspiration, particularly for deep breathing. The **pneumotaxic center** is a network of neurons that inhibits the activity of neurons in the DRG, allowing relaxation after inspiration, and thus controlling the overall rate.

Factors That Affect the Rate and Depth of Respiration

The respiratory rate and the depth of inspiration are regulated by the medulla oblongata and pons; however, these regions of the brain do so in response to systemic stimuli. It is a dose-response, positive-feedback relationship in which the greater the stimulus, the greater the response. Thus, increasing stimuli results in forced breathing. Multiple systemic factors are involved in stimulating the brain to produce pulmonary ventilation.

The major factor that stimulates the medulla oblongata and pons to produce respiration is surprisingly not oxygen concentration, but rather the concentration of carbon dioxide in the blood. As you recall, carbon dioxide is a waste product of cellular respiration and can be toxic. Concentrations of chemicals are sensed by chemoreceptors. A **central chemoreceptor** is one of the specialized receptors that are located in the brain and brainstem, whereas a **peripheral chemoreceptor** is one of the specialized receptors located in the carotid arteries and aortic arch. Concentration changes in certain substances, such as carbon dioxide or hydrogen ions, stimulate these receptors, which in turn signal the respiration centers of the brain. In the case of carbon dioxide, as the concentration of CO_2 in the blood increases, it readily diffuses across the blood-brain barrier, where it collects in the extracellular fluid. As will be explained in more detail later, increased carbon dioxide levels lead to increased levels of hydrogen ions, decreasing pH. The increase in hydrogen ions in the brain triggers the central chemoreceptors to stimulate the respiratory centers to initiate contraction of the diaphragm and intercostal muscles. As a result, the rate and depth of respiration increase, allowing more carbon dioxide to be expelled, which brings more air into and out of the lungs promoting a reduction in the blood levels of carbon dioxide, and therefore hydrogen ions, in the blood. In contrast, low levels of carbon dioxide in the blood cause low levels of hydrogen ions in the brain, leading to a decrease in the rate and depth of pulmonary ventilation, producing shallow, slow breathing.

Another factor involved in influencing the respiratory activity of the brain is systemic arterial concentrations of hydrogen ions. Increasing carbon dioxide levels can lead to increased H^+ levels, as mentioned above, as well as other metabolic activities, such as lactic acid accumulation after strenuous exercise. Peripheral chemoreceptors of the aortic arch and carotid arteries sense arterial levels of hydrogen ions. When peripheral chemoreceptors sense decreasing, or more acidic, pH levels, they stimulate an increase in ventilation to remove carbon dioxide from the blood at a quicker rate. Removal of carbon dioxide from the blood helps to reduce hydrogen ions, thus increasing systemic pH.

Blood levels of oxygen are also important in influencing respiratory rate. The peripheral chemoreceptors are responsible for sensing large changes in blood oxygen levels. If blood oxygen levels become quite low—about 60 mm Hg or less—then peripheral chemoreceptors stimulate an increase in respiratory activity. The chemoreceptors are only able to sense dissolved oxygen molecules, not the oxygen that is bound to hemoglobin. As you recall, the majority of oxygen is bound by hemoglobin; when dissolved levels of oxygen drop, hemoglobin releases oxygen. Therefore, a large drop in oxygen levels is required to stimulate the chemoreceptors of the aortic arch and carotid arteries.

The hypothalamus and other brain regions associated with the limbic system also play roles in influencing the regulation of breathing by interacting with the respiratory centers. The hypothalamus and other regions associated with the limbic system are involved in regulating respiration in response to emotions, pain, and temperature. For example, an increase in body temperature causes an increase in respiratory rate. Feeling excited or the fight-or-flight response will also result in an increase in respiratory rate.

Respiratory System: Sleep Apnea

Sleep apnea is a chronic disorder that can occur in children or adults, and is characterized by the cessation of breathing during sleep. These episodes may last for several seconds or several minutes, and may differ in the frequency with which they are experienced. Sleep apnea leads to poor sleep, which is reflected in the symptoms of fatigue, evening napping, irritability, memory problems, and morning headaches. In addition, many individuals with sleep apnea experience a dry throat in the morning after waking from sleep, which may be due to excessive snoring.

There are two types of sleep apnea: obstructive sleep apnea and central sleep apnea. Obstructive sleep apnea is caused by an obstruction of the airway during sleep, which can occur at different points in the airway, depending on the underlying cause of the obstruction. For example, the tongue and throat muscles of some individuals with obstructive sleep apnea may relax excessively, causing the muscles to push into the airway. Another example is obesity, which is a known risk factor for sleep apnea, as excess adipose tissue in the neck region can push the soft tissues towards the lumen of the airway, causing the trachea to narrow.

In central sleep apnea, the respiratory centers of the brain do not respond properly to rising carbon dioxide levels and therefore do not stimulate the contraction of the diaphragm and intercostal muscles regularly. As a result, inspiration does not occur and breathing stops for a short period. In some cases, the cause of central sleep apnea is unknown. However, some medical conditions, such as stroke and congestive heart failure, may cause damage to the pons or medulla oblongata. In addition, some pharmacologic agents, such as morphine, can affect the respiratory centers, causing a decrease in the respiratory rate. The symptoms of central sleep apnea are similar to those of obstructive sleep apnea.

A diagnosis of sleep apnea is usually done during a sleep study, where the patient is monitored in a sleep laboratory for several nights. The patient's blood oxygen levels, heart rate, respiratory rate, and blood pressure are monitored, as are brain activity and the volume of air that is inhaled and exhaled. Treatment of sleep apnea commonly includes the use of a device called a continuous positive airway pressure (CPAP) machine during sleep. The CPAP machine has a mask that covers the nose, or the nose and mouth, and forces air into the airway at regular intervals. This pressurized air can help to gently force the airway to remain open, allowing more normal ventilation to occur. Other treatments include lifestyle changes to decrease weight, eliminate alcohol and other sleep apnea–promoting drugs, and changes in sleep position. In addition to these treatments, patients with central sleep apnea may need supplemental oxygen during sleep.

22.4 | Gas Exchange

By the end of this section, you will be able to:
- Compare the composition of atmospheric air and alveolar air
- Describe the mechanisms that drive gas exchange
- Discuss the importance of sufficient ventilation and perfusion, and how the body adapts when they are insufficient
- Discuss the process of external respiration
- Describe the process of internal respiration

The purpose of the respiratory system is to perform gas exchange. Pulmonary ventilation provides air to the alveoli for this gas exchange process. At the respiratory membrane, where the alveolar and capillary walls meet, gases move across the membranes, with oxygen entering the bloodstream and carbon dioxide exiting. It is through this mechanism that blood is oxygenated and carbon dioxide, the waste product of cellular respiration, is removed from the body.

Gas Exchange

In order to understand the mechanisms of gas exchange in the lung, it is important to understand the underlying princ[.] of gases and their behavior. In addition to Boyle's law, several other gas laws help to describe the behavior of gases.

Gas Laws and Air Composition

Gas molecules exert force on the surfaces with which they are in contact; this force is called pressure. In natural systems, gases are normally present as a mixture of different types of molecules. For example, the atmosphere consists of oxygen, nitrogen, carbon dioxide, and other gaseous molecules, and this gaseous mixture exerts a certain pressure referred to as atmospheric pressure (Table 22.2). **Partial pressure** (P_X) is the pressure of a single type of gas in a mixture of gases. For example, in the atmosphere, oxygen exerts a partial pressure, and nitrogen exerts another partial pressure, independent of the partial pressure of oxygen (Figure 22.21). **Total pressure** is the sum of all the partial pressures of a gaseous mixture. **Dalton's law** describes the behavior of nonreactive gases in a gaseous mixture and states that a specific gas type in a mixture exerts its own pressure; thus, the total pressure exerted by a mixture of gases is the sum of the partial pressures of the gases in the mixture.

Partial Pressures of Atmospheric Gases

Gas	Percent of total composition	Partial pressure (mm Hg)
Nitrogen (N_2)	78.6	597.4
Oxygen (O_2)	20.9	158.8
Water (H_2O)	0.04	3.0
Carbon dioxide (CO_2)	0.004	0.3
Others	0.0006	0.5
Total composition/total atmospheric pressure	100%	760.0

Table 22.2

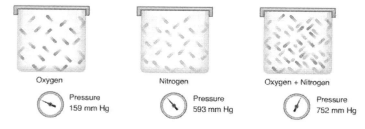

Figure 22.21 Partial and Total Pressures of a Gas Partial pressure is the force exerted by a gas. The sum of the partial pressures of all the gases in a mixture equals the total pressure.

Partial pressure is extremely important in predicting the movement of gases. Recall that gases tend to equalize their pressure in two regions that are connected. A gas will move from an area where its partial pressure is higher to an area where its partial pressure is lower. In addition, the greater the partial pressure difference between the two areas, the more rapid is the movement of gases.

Solubility of Gases in Liquids

Henry's law describes the behavior of gases when they come into contact with a liquid, such as blood. Henry's law states that the concentration of gas in a liquid is directly proportional to the solubility and partial pressure of that gas. The greater the partial pressure of the gas, the greater the number of gas molecules that will dissolve in the liquid. The concentration of the gas in a liquid is also dependent on the solubility of the gas in the liquid. For example, although nitrogen is present in the atmosphere, very little nitrogen dissolves into the blood, because the solubility of nitrogen in blood is very low. The exception to this occurs in scuba divers; the composition of the compressed air that divers breathe causes nitrogen to have a higher pressure than normal, causing it to dissolve in the blood in greater amounts than normal. Too much nitrogen in the blood results in a serious condition that can be fatal if not corrected. Gas molecules establish an equilibrium between those dissolved in liquid and those in air.

The composition of air in the atmosphere and in the alveoli differs. In both cases, the relative concentration of gases is nitrogen > oxygen > water vapor > carbon dioxide. The amount of water vapor present in alveolar air is greater than that in atmospheric air (Table 22.3). Recall that the respiratory system works to humidify incoming air, thereby causing the air present in the alveoli to have a greater amount of water vapor than atmospheric air. In addition, alveolar air contains a greater amount of carbon dioxide and less oxygen than atmospheric air. This is no surprise, as gas exchange removes oxygen from and adds carbon dioxide to alveolar air. Both deep and forced breathing cause the alveolar air composition to be changed more rapidly than during quiet breathing. As a result, the partial pressures of oxygen and carbon dioxide change, affecting the diffusion process that moves these materials across the membrane. This will cause oxygen to enter and carbon dioxide to leave the blood more quickly.

Composition and Partial Pressures of Alveolar Air

Gas	Percent of total composition	Partial pressure (mm Hg)
Nitrogen (N_2)	74.9	569
Oxygen (O_2)	13.7	104
Water (H_2O)	6.2	40
Carbon dioxide (CO_2)	5.2	47
Total composition/total alveolar pressure	100%	760.0

Table 22.3

Ventilation and Perfusion

Two important aspects of gas exchange in the lung are ventilation and perfusion. **Ventilation** is the movement of air into and out of the lungs, and perfusion is the flow of blood in the pulmonary capillaries. For gas exchange to be efficient, the volumes involved in ventilation and perfusion should be compatible. However, factors such as regional gravity effects on blood, blocked alveolar ducts, or disease can cause ventilation and perfusion to be imbalanced.

The partial pressure of oxygen in alveolar air is about 104 mm Hg, whereas the partial pressure of the oxygenated pulmonary venous blood is about 100 mm Hg. When ventilation is sufficient, oxygen enters the alveoli at a high rate, and the partial pressure of oxygen in the alveoli remains high. In contrast, when ventilation is insufficient, the partial pressure of oxygen in the alveoli drops. Without the large difference in partial pressure between the alveoli and the blood, oxygen does not diffuse efficiently across the respiratory membrane. The body has mechanisms that counteract this problem. In cases when ventilation is not sufficient for an alveolus, the body redirects blood flow to alveoli that are receiving sufficient ventilation. This is achieved by constricting the pulmonary arterioles that serves the dysfunctional alveolus, which redirects blood to other alveoli that have sufficient ventilation. At the same time, the pulmonary arterioles that serve alveoli receiving sufficient ventilation vasodilate, which brings in greater blood flow. Factors such as carbon dioxide, oxygen, and pH levels can all serve as stimuli for adjusting blood flow in the capillary networks associated with the alveoli.

Ventilation is regulated by the diameter of the airways, whereas perfusion is regulated by the diameter of the blood vessels. The diameter of the bronchioles is sensitive to the partial pressure of carbon dioxide in the alveoli. A greater partial pressure of carbon dioxide in the alveoli causes the bronchioles to increase their diameter as will a decreased level of oxygen in the blood supply, allowing carbon dioxide to be exhaled from the body at a greater rate. As mentioned above, a greater partial pressure of oxygen in the alveoli causes the pulmonary arterioles to dilate, increasing blood flow.

Gas Exchange

Gas exchange occurs at two sites in the body: in the lungs, where oxygen is picked up and carbon dioxide is released at the respiratory membrane, and at the tissues, where oxygen is released and carbon dioxide is picked up. External respiration is the exchange of gases with the external environment, and occurs in the alveoli of the lungs. Internal respiration is the exchange of gases with the internal environment, and occurs in the tissues. The actual exchange of gases occurs due to simple diffusion. Energy is not required to move oxygen or carbon dioxide across membranes. Instead, these gases foll pressure gradients that allow them to diffuse. The anatomy of the lung maximizes the diffusion of gases: The respira membrane is highly permeable to gases; the respiratory and blood capillary membranes are very thin; and there is a surface area throughout the lungs.

External Respiration

The pulmonary artery carries deoxygenated blood into the lungs from the heart, where it branches and eventually becomes the capillary network composed of pulmonary capillaries. These pulmonary capillaries create the respiratory membrane with the alveoli (Figure 22.22). As the blood is pumped through this capillary network, gas exchange occurs. Although a small amount of the oxygen is able to dissolve directly into plasma from the alveoli, most of the oxygen is picked up by erythrocytes (red blood cells) and binds to a protein called hemoglobin, a process described later in this chapter. Oxygenated hemoglobin is red, causing the overall appearance of bright red oxygenated blood, which returns to the heart through the pulmonary veins. Carbon dioxide is released in the opposite direction of oxygen, from the blood to the alveoli. Some of the carbon dioxide is returned on hemoglobin, but can also be dissolved in plasma or is present as a converted form, also explained in greater detail later in this chapter.

External respiration occurs as a function of partial pressure differences in oxygen and carbon dioxide between the alveoli and the blood in the pulmonary capillaries.

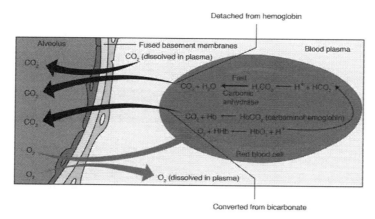

Figure 22.22 External Respiration In external respiration, oxygen diffuses across the respiratory membrane from the alveolus to the capillary, whereas carbon dioxide diffuses out of the capillary into the alveolus.

Although the solubility of oxygen in blood is not high, there is a drastic difference in the partial pressure of oxygen in the alveoli versus in the blood of the pulmonary capillaries. This difference is about 64 mm Hg: The partial pressure of oxygen in the alveoli is about 104 mm Hg, whereas its partial pressure in the blood of the capillary is about 40 mm Hg. This large difference in partial pressure creates a very strong pressure gradient that causes oxygen to rapidly cross the respiratory membrane from the alveoli into the blood.

The partial pressure of carbon dioxide is also different between the alveolar air and the blood of the capillary. However, the partial pressure difference is less than that of oxygen, about 5 mm Hg. The partial pressure of carbon dioxide in the blood of the capillary is about 45 mm Hg, whereas its partial pressure in the alveoli is about 40 mm Hg. However, the solubility of carbon dioxide is much greater than that of oxygen—by a factor of about 20—in both blood and alveolar fluids. As a result, the relative concentrations of oxygen and carbon dioxide that diffuse across the respiratory membrane are similar.

Internal Respiration

Internal respiration is gas exchange that occurs at the level of body tissues (Figure 22.23). Similar to external respiration, internal respiration also occurs as simple diffusion due to a partial pressure gradient. However, the partial pressure gradients are opposite of those present at the respiratory membrane. The partial pressure of oxygen in tissues is low, about 40 mm Hg, because oxygen is continuously used for cellular respiration. In contrast, the partial pressure of oxygen in the blood is about 100 mm Hg. This creates a pressure gradient that causes oxygen to dissociate from hemoglobin, diffuse out of the blood, cross the interstitial space, and enter the tissue. Hemoglobin that has little oxygen bound to it loses much of its brightness, so that blood returning to the heart is more burgundy in color.

Considering that cellular respiration continuously produces carbon dioxide, the partial pressure of carbon dioxide is lower in the blood than in the tissue, causing carbon dioxide to diffuse out of the tissue, cross the interstitial fluid, and enter the blood. It is then carried back to the lungs either bound to hemoglobin, dissolved in plasma, or in a converted form. By the time blood returns to the lungs, the partial pressure of oxygen has returned to about 40 mm Hg, and the partial pressure of carbon dioxide has returned to about 45 mm Hg. The blood is then pumped back to the lungs to be oxygenated once again during external respiration.

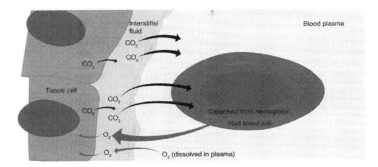

Figure 22.23 Internal Respiration Oxygen diffuses out of the capillary and into cells, whereas carbon dioxide diffuses out of cells and into the capillary.

Everyday CONNECTION

Hyperbaric Chamber Treatment

A type of device used in some areas of medicine that exploits the behavior of gases is hyperbaric chamber treatment. A hyperbaric chamber is a unit that can be sealed and expose a patient to either 100 percent oxygen with increased pressure or a mixture of gases that includes a higher concentration of oxygen than normal atmospheric air, also at a higher partial pressure than the atmosphere. There are two major types of chambers: monoplace and multiplace. Monoplace chambers are typically for one patient, and the staff tending to the patient observes the patient from outside of the chamber (Figure 22.24). Some facilities have special monoplace hyperbaric chambers that allow multiple patients to be treated at once, usually in a sitting or reclining position, to help ease feelings of isolation or claustrophobia. Multiplace chambers are large enough for multiple patients to be treated at one time, and the staff attending these patients is present inside the chamber. In a multiplace chamber, patients are often treated with air via a mask or hood, and the chamber is pressurized.

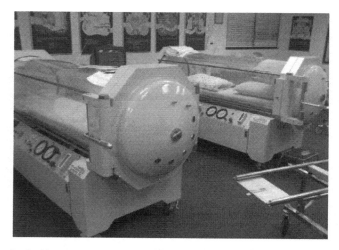

Figure 22.24 Hyperbaric Chamber (credit: "komunews"/flickr.com)

Hyperbaric chamber treatment is based on the behavior of gases. As you recall, gases move from a region of higher partial pressure to a region of lower partial pressure. In a hyperbaric chamber, the atmospheric pressure is increased, causing a greater amount of oxygen than normal to diffuse into the bloodstream of the patient. Hyperbaric chamber therapy is used to treat a variety of medical problems, such as wound and graft healing, anaerobic bacterial infections, and carbon monoxide poisoning. Exposure to and poisoning by carbon monoxide is difficult to reverse, because hemoglobin's affinity for carbon monoxide is much stronger than its affinity for oxygen, causing carbon monoxide to replace oxygen in the blood. Hyperbaric chamber therapy can treat carbon monoxide poisoning, because the increased atmospheric pressure causes more oxygen to diffuse into the bloodstream. At this increased pressure and increased concentration of oxygen, carbon monoxide is displaced from hemoglobin. Another example is the treatment of anaerobic bacterial infections, which are created by bacteria that cannot or prefer not to live in the presence of oxygen. An increase in blood and tissue levels of oxygen helps to kill the anaerobic bacteria that are responsible for the infection, as oxygen is toxic to anaerobic bacteria. For wounds and grafts, the chamber stimulates the healing process by increasing energy production needed for repair. Increasing oxygen transport allows cells to ramp up cellular respiration and thus ATP production, the energy needed to build new structures.

22.5 | Transport of Gases

By the end of this section, you will be able to:
- Describe the principles of oxygen transport
- Describe the structure of hemoglobin
- Compare and contrast fetal and adult hemoglobin
- Describe the principles of carbon dioxide transport

The other major activity in the lungs is the process of respiration, the process of gas exchange. The function of respiration is to provide oxygen for use by body cells during cellular respiration and to eliminate carbon dioxide, a waste product of cellular respiration, from the body. In order for the exchange of oxygen and carbon dioxide to occur, both gases must be transported between the external and internal respiration sites. Although carbon dioxide is more soluble than oxygen in blood, both gases require a specialized transport system for the majority of the gas molecules to be moved between the lungs and other tissues.

Oxygen Transport in the Blood

Even though oxygen is transported via the blood, you may recall that oxygen is not very soluble in liquids. A small amount of oxygen does dissolve in the blood and is transported in the bloodstream, but it is only about 1.5% of the total amount. The majority of oxygen molecules are carried from the lungs to the body's tissues by a specialized transport system, which relies on the erythrocyte—the red blood cell. Erythrocytes contain a metalloprotein, hemoglobin, which serves to bind oxygen molecules to the erythrocyte (Figure 22.25). Heme is the portion of hemoglobin that contains iron, and it is heme that binds oxygen. One hemoglobin molecule contains iron-containing Heme molecules, and because of this, each hemoglobin molecule is capable of carrying up to four molecules of oxygen. As oxygen diffuses across the respiratory membrane from the alveolus to the capillary, it also diffuses into the red blood cell and is bound by hemoglobin. The following reversible chemical reaction describes the production of the final product, **oxyhemoglobin** (Hb–O_2), which is formed when oxygen binds to hemoglobin. Oxyhemoglobin is a bright red-colored molecule that contributes to the bright red color of oxygenated blood.

$$Hb + O_2 \leftrightarrow Hb - O_2$$

In this formula, Hb represents reduced hemoglobin, that is, hemoglobin that does not have oxygen bound to it. There are multiple factors involved in how readily heme binds to and dissociates from oxygen, which will be discussed in the subsequent sections.

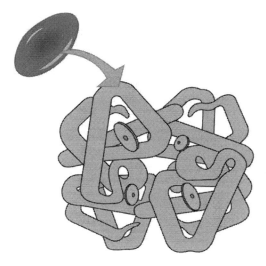

Figure 22.25 **Erythrocyte and Hemoglobin** Hemoglobin consists of four subunits, each of which contains one molecule of iron.

Function of Hemoglobin

Hemoglobin is composed of subunits, a protein structure that is referred to as a quaternary structure. Each of the four subunits that make up hemoglobin is arranged in a ring-like fashion, with an iron atom covalently bound to the heme in the center of each subunit. Binding of the first oxygen molecule causes a conformational change in hemoglobin that allows the second molecule of oxygen to bind more readily. As each molecule of oxygen is bound, it further facilitates the binding of the next molecule, until all four heme sites are occupied by oxygen. The opposite occurs as well: After the first oxygen molecule dissociates and is "dropped off" at the tissues, the next oxygen molecule dissociates more readily. When all four heme sites are occupied, the hemoglobin is said to be saturated. When one to three heme sites are occupied, the hemoglobin is said to be partially saturated. Therefore, when considering the blood as a whole, the percent of the available heme units that are bound to oxygen at a given time is called hemoglobin saturation. Hemoglobin saturation of 100 percent means that every heme unit in all of the erythrocytes of the body is bound to oxygen. In a healthy individual with normal hemoglobin levels, hemoglobin saturation generally ranges from 95 percent to 99 percent.

Oxygen Dissociation from Hemoglobin

Partial pressure is an important aspect of the binding of oxygen to and disassociation from heme. An **oxygen–hemoglobin dissociation curve** is a graph that describes the relationship of partial pressure to the binding of oxygen to heme and its subsequent dissociation from heme (Figure 22.26). Remember that gases travel from an area of higher partial pressure to an area of lower partial pressure. In addition, the affinity of an oxygen molecule for heme increases as more oxygen molecules are bound. Therefore, in the oxygen–hemoglobin saturation curve, as the partial pressure of oxygen increases, a proportionately greater number of oxygen molecules are bound by heme. Not surprisingly, the oxygen–hemoglobin saturation/dissociation curve also shows that the lower the partial pressure of oxygen, the fewer oxygen molecules are bound to heme. As a result, the partial pressure of oxygen plays a major role in determining the degree of binding of oxygen to heme at the site of the respiratory membrane, as well as the degree of dissociation of oxygen from heme at the site of body tissues.

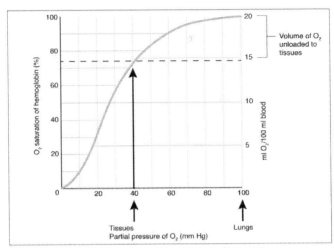

(a) Partial pressure of oxygen and hemoglobin saturation

(a)

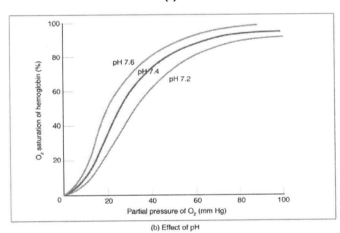

(b) Effect of pH

(b)

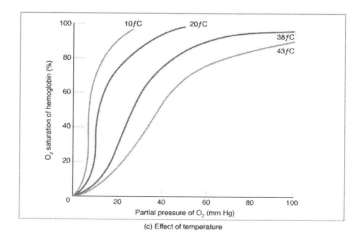

(c)

Figure 22.26 Oxygen-Hemoglobin Dissociation and Effects of pH and Temperature These three graphs show (a) the relationship between the partial pressure of oxygen and hemoglobin saturation, (b) the effect of pH on the oxygen–hemoglobin dissociation curve, and (c) the effect of temperature on the oxygen–hemoglobin dissociation curve.

The mechanisms behind the oxygen–hemoglobin saturation/dissociation curve also serve as automatic control mechanisms that regulate how much oxygen is delivered to different tissues throughout the body. This is important because some tissues have a higher metabolic rate than others. Highly active tissues, such as muscle, rapidly use oxygen to produce ATP, lowering the partial pressure of oxygen in the tissue to about 20 mm Hg. The partial pressure of oxygen inside capillaries is about 100 mm Hg, so the difference between the two becomes quite high, about 80 mm Hg. As a result, a greater number of oxygen molecules dissociate from hemoglobin and enter the tissues. The reverse is true of tissues, such as adipose (body fat), which have lower metabolic rates. Because less oxygen is used by these cells, the partial pressure of oxygen within such tissues remains relatively high, resulting in fewer oxygen molecules dissociating from hemoglobin and entering the tissue interstitial fluid. Although venous blood is said to be deoxygenated, some oxygen is still bound to hemoglobin in its red blood cells. This provides an oxygen reserve that can be used when tissues suddenly demand more oxygen.

Factors other than partial pressure also affect the oxygen–hemoglobin saturation/dissociation curve. For example, a higher temperature promotes hemoglobin and oxygen to dissociate faster, whereas a lower temperature inhibits dissociation (see Figure 22.26, **middle**). However, the human body tightly regulates temperature, so this factor may not affect gas exchange throughout the body. The exception to this is in highly active tissues, which may release a larger amount of energy than is given off as heat. As a result, oxygen readily dissociates from hemoglobin, which is a mechanism that helps to provide active tissues with more oxygen.

Certain hormones, such as androgens, epinephrine, thyroid hormones, and growth hormone, can affect the oxygen–hemoglobin saturation/disassociation curve by stimulating the production of a compound called 2,3-bisphosphoglycerate (BPG) by erythrocytes. BPG is a byproduct of glycolysis. Because erythrocytes do not contain mitochondria, glycolysis is the sole method by which these cells produce ATP. BPG promotes the disassociation of oxygen from hemoglobin. Therefore, the greater the concentration of BPG, the more readily oxygen dissociates from hemoglobin, despite its partial pressure.

The pH of the blood is another factor that influences the oxygen–hemoglobin saturation/dissociation curve (see Figure 22.26). The **Bohr effect** is a phenomenon that arises from the relationship between pH and oxygen's affinity for hemoglobin: A lower, more acidic pH promotes oxygen dissociation from hemoglobin. In contrast, a higher, or more basic, pH inhibits oxygen dissociation from hemoglobin. The greater the amount of carbon dioxide in the blood, the more molecules that must be converted, which in turn generates hydrogen ions and thus lowers blood pH. Furthermore, blood pH may become more acidic when certain byproducts of cell metabolism, such as lactic acid, carbonic acid, and carbon dioxide, are released into the bloodstream.

Hemoglobin of the Fetus

The fetus has its own circulation with its own erythrocytes; however, it is dependent on the mother for oxygen. Blood is supplied to the fetus by way of the umbilical cord, which is connected to the placenta and separated from maternal blood by the chorion. The mechanism of gas exchange at the chorion is similar to gas exchange at the respiratory membrane. However, the partial pressure of oxygen is lower in the maternal blood in the placenta, at about 35 to 50 mm Hg, than it is in maternal arterial blood. The difference in partial pressures between maternal and fetal blood is not large, as the partial pressure of oxygen in fetal blood at the placenta is about 20 mm Hg. Therefore, there is not as much diffusion of oxygen into the fetal blood supply. The fetus' hemoglobin overcomes this problem by having a greater affinity for oxygen than maternal hemoglobin (Figure 22.27). Both fetal and adult hemoglobin have four subunits, but two of the subunits of fetal hemoglobin have a different structure that causes fetal hemoglobin to have a greater affinity for oxygen than does adult hemoglobin.

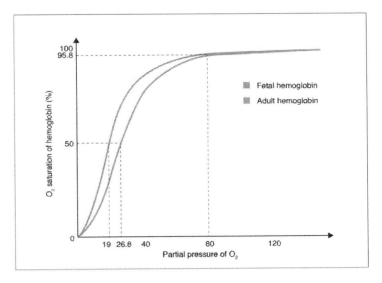

Figure 22.27 Oxygen-Hemoglobin Dissociation Curves in Fetus and Adult Fetal hemoglobin has a greater affinity for oxygen than does adult hemoglobin.

Carbon Dioxide Transport in the Blood

Carbon dioxide is transported by three major mechanisms. The first mechanism of carbon dioxide transport is by blood plasma, as some carbon dioxide molecules dissolve in the blood. The second mechanism is transport in the form of bicarbonate (HCO_3^-), which also dissolves in plasma. The third mechanism of carbon dioxide transport is similar to the transport of oxygen by erythrocytes (Figure 22.28).

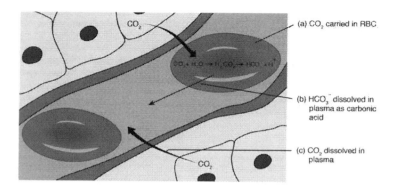

Figure 22.28 Carbon Dioxide Transport Carbon dioxide is transported by three different methods: (a) in erythrocytes; (b) after forming carbonic acid (H_2CO_3), which is dissolved in plasma; (c) and in plasma.

Dissolved Carbon Dioxide

Although carbon dioxide is not considered to be highly soluble in blood, a small fraction—about 7 to 10 percent—of the carbon dioxide that diffuses into the blood from the tissues dissolves in plasma. The dissolved carbon dioxide then travels in the bloodstream and when the blood reaches the pulmonary capillaries, the dissolved carbon dioxide diffuses across the respiratory membrane into the alveoli, where it is then exhaled during pulmonary ventilation.

Bicarbonate Buffer

A large fraction—about 70 percent—of the carbon dioxide molecules that diffuse into the blood is transported to the lungs as bicarbonate. Most bicarbonate is produced in erythrocytes after carbon dioxide diffuses into the capillaries, and subsequently into red blood cells. **Carbonic anhydrase (CA)** causes carbon dioxide and water to form carbonic acid (H_2CO_3), which dissociates into two ions: bicarbonate (HCO_3^-) and hydrogen (H^+). The following formula depicts this reaction:

$$CO_2 + H_2O \overset{CA}{\leftrightarrow} H_2CO_3 \leftrightarrow H^+ + HCO_3^-$$

Bicarbonate tends to build up in the erythrocytes, so that there is a greater concentration of bicarbonate in the erythrocytes than in the surrounding blood plasma. As a result, some of the bicarbonate will leave the erythrocytes and move down its concentration gradient into the plasma in exchange for chloride (Cl^-) ions. This phenomenon is referred to as the **chloride shift** and occurs because by exchanging one negative ion for another negative ion, neither the electrical charge of the erythrocytes nor that of the blood is altered.

At the pulmonary capillaries, the chemical reaction that produced bicarbonate (shown above) is reversed, and carbon dioxide and water are the products. Much of the bicarbonate in the plasma re-enters the erythrocytes in exchange for chloride ions. Hydrogen ions and bicarbonate ions join to form carbonic acid, which is converted into carbon dioxide and water by carbonic anhydrase. Carbon dioxide diffuses out of the erythrocytes and into the plasma, where it can further diffuse across the respiratory membrane into the alveoli to be exhaled during pulmonary ventilation.

Carbaminohemoglobin

About 20 percent of carbon dioxide is bound by hemoglobin and is transported to the lungs. Carbon dioxide does not bind to iron as oxygen does; instead, carbon dioxide binds amino acid moieties on the globin portions of hemoglobin to form **carbaminohemoglobin**, which forms when hemoglobin and carbon dioxide bind. When hemoglobin is not transporting oxygen, it tends to have a bluish-purple tone to it, creating the darker maroon color typical of deoxygenated blood. The following formula depicts this reversible reaction:

$$CO_2 + Hb \leftrightarrow HbCO_2$$

Similar to the transport of oxygen by heme, the binding and dissociation of carbon dioxide to and from hemoglobin is dependent on the partial pressure of carbon dioxide. Because carbon dioxide is released from the lungs, blood that leaves the lungs and reaches body tissues has a lower partial pressure of carbon dioxide than is found in the tissues. As a result, carbon dioxide leaves the tissues because of its higher partial pressure, enters the blood, and then moves into red blood cells, binding to hemoglobin. In contrast, in the pulmonary capillaries, the partial pressure of carbon dioxide is high compared to within the alveoli. As a result, carbon dioxide dissociates readily from hemoglobin and diffuses across the respiratory membrane into the air.

In addition to the partial pressure of carbon dioxide, the oxygen saturation of hemoglobin and the partial pressure of oxygen in the blood also influence the affinity of hemoglobin for carbon dioxide. The **Haldane effect** is a phenomenon that arises from the relationship between the partial pressure of oxygen and the affinity of hemoglobin for carbon dioxide. Hemoglobin that is saturated with oxygen does not readily bind carbon dioxide. However, when oxygen is not bound to heme and the partial pressure of oxygen is low, hemoglobin readily binds to carbon dioxide.

Watch this video (http://openstaxcollege.org/l/oxyblood) to see the transport of oxygen from the lungs to the tissues. Why is oxygenated blood bright red, whereas deoxygenated blood tends to be more of a purple color?

22.6 | Modifications in Respiratory Functions

By the end of this section, you will be able to:
- Define the terms hyperpnea and hyperventilation
- Describe the effect of exercise on the respiratory system
- Describe the effect of high altitude on the respiratory system
- Discuss the process of acclimatization

At rest, the respiratory system performs its functions at a constant, rhythmic pace, as regulated by the respiratory centers of the brain. At this pace, ventilation provides sufficient oxygen to all the tissues of the body. However, there are times that the respiratory system must alter the pace of its functions in order to accommodate the oxygen demands of the body.

Hyperpnea

Hyperpnea is an increased depth and rate of ventilation to meet an increase in oxygen demand as might be seen in exercise or disease, particularly diseases that target the respiratory or digestive tracts. This does not significantly alter blood oxygen or carbon dioxide levels, but merely increases the depth and rate of ventilation to meet the demand of the cells. In contrast, **hyperventilation** is an increased ventilation rate that is independent of the cellular oxygen needs and leads to abnormally low blood carbon dioxide levels and high (alkaline) blood pH.

Interestingly, exercise does not cause hyperpnea as one might think. Muscles that perform work during exercise do increase their demand for oxygen, stimulating an increase in ventilation. However, hyperpnea during exercise appears to occur before a drop in oxygen levels within the muscles can occur. Therefore, hyperpnea must be driven by other mechanisms, either instead of or in addition to a drop in oxygen levels. The exact mechanisms behind exercise hyperpnea are not well understood, and some hypotheses are somewhat controversial. However, in addition to low oxygen, high carbon dioxide, and low pH levels, there appears to be a complex interplay of factors related to the nervous system and the respiratory centers of the brain.

First, a conscious decision to partake in exercise, or another form of physical exertion, results in a psychological stimulus that may trigger the respiratory centers of the brain to increase ventilation. In addition, the respiratory centers of the brain may be stimulated through the activation of motor neurons that innervate muscle groups that are involved in the physical activity. Finally, physical exertion stimulates proprioceptors, which are receptors located within the muscles, joints, and tendons, which sense movement and stretching; proprioceptors thus create a stimulus that may also trigger the respiratory centers of the brain. These neural factors are consistent with the sudden increase in ventilation that is observed immediately as exercise begins. Because the respiratory centers are stimulated by psychological, motor neuron, and proprioceptor inputs throughout exercise, the fact that there is also a sudden decrease in ventilation immediately after the exercise ends when these neural stimuli cease, further supports the idea that they are involved in triggering the changes of ventilation.

High Altitude Effects

An increase in altitude results in a decrease in atmospheric pressure. Although the proportion of oxygen relative to gases in the atmosphere remains at 21 percent, its partial pressure decreases (Table 22.4). As a result, it is more difficult for a body to achieve the same level of oxygen saturation at high altitude than at low altitude, due to lower atmospheric pressure. In fact, hemoglobin saturation is lower at high altitudes compared to hemoglobin saturation at sea level. For example, hemoglobin saturation is about 67 percent at 19,000 feet above sea level, whereas it reaches about 98 percent at sea level.

Partial Pressure of Oxygen at Different Altitudes

Example location	Altitude (feet above sea level)	Atmospheric pressure (mm Hg)	Partial pressure of oxygen (mm Hg)
New York City, New York	0	760	159
Boulder, Colorado	5000	632	133
Aspen, Colorado	8000	565	118
Pike's Peak, Colorado	14,000	447	94
Denali (Mt. McKinley), Alaska	20,000	350	73
Mt. Everest, Tibet	29,000	260	54

Table 22.4

As you recall, partial pressure is extremely important in determining how much gas can cross the respiratory membrane and enter the blood of the pulmonary capillaries. A lower partial pressure of oxygen means that there is a smaller difference in partial pressures between the alveoli and the blood, so less oxygen crosses the respiratory membrane. As a result, fewer oxygen molecules are bound by hemoglobin. Despite this, the tissues of the body still receive a sufficient amount of oxygen during rest at high altitudes. This is due to two major mechanisms. First, the number of oxygen molecules that enter the tissue from the blood is nearly equal between sea level and high altitudes. At sea level, hemoglobin saturation is higher, but only a quarter of the oxygen molecules are actually released into the tissue. At high altitudes, a greater proportion of molecules of oxygen are released into the tissues. Secondly, at high altitudes, a greater amount of BPG is produced by erythrocytes, which enhances the dissociation of oxygen from hemoglobin. Physical exertion, such as skiing or hiking, can lead to altitude sickness due to the low amount of oxygen reserves in the blood at high altitudes. At sea level, there is a large amount of oxygen reserve in venous blood (even though venous blood is thought of as "deoxygenated") from which the muscles can draw during physical exertion. Because the oxygen saturation is much lower at higher altitudes, this venous reserve is small, resulting in pathological symptoms of low blood oxygen levels. You may have heard that it is important to drink more water when traveling at higher altitudes than you are accustomed to. This is because your body will increase micturition (urination) at high altitudes to counteract the effects of lower oxygen levels. By removing fluids, blood plasma levels drop but not the total number of erythrocytes. In this way, the overall concentration of erythrocytes in the blood increases, which helps tissues obtain the oxygen they need.

Acute mountain sickness (AMS), or altitude sickness, is a condition that results from acute exposure to high altitudes due to a low partial pressure of oxygen at high altitudes. AMS typically can occur at 2400 meters (8000 feet) above sea level. AMS is a result of low blood oxygen levels, as the body has acute difficulty adjusting to the low partial pressure of oxygen. In serious cases, AMS can cause pulmonary or cerebral edema. Symptoms of AMS include nausea, vomiting, fatigue, lightheadedness, drowsiness, feeling disoriented, increased pulse, and nosebleeds. The only treatment for AMS is descending to a lower altitude; however, pharmacologic treatments and supplemental oxygen can improve symptoms. AMS can be prevented by slowly ascending to the desired altitude, allowing the body to acclimate, as well as maintaining proper hydration.

Acclimatization

Especially in situations where the ascent occurs too quickly, traveling to areas of high altitude can cause AMS. **Acclimatization** is the process of adjustment that the respiratory system makes due to chronic exposure to a high altitude. Over a period of time, the body adjusts to accommodate the lower partial pressure of oxygen. The low partial pressure of oxygen at high altitudes results in a lower oxygen saturation level of hemoglobin in the blood. In turn, the tissue levels of oxygen are also lower. As a result, the kidneys are stimulated to produce the hormone erythropoietin (EPO), which stimulates the production of erythrocytes, resulting in a greater number of circulating erythrocytes in an individual at a high altitude over a long period. With more red blood cells, there is more hemoglobin to help transport the available oxygen. Even though there is low saturation of each hemoglobin molecule, there will be more hemoglobin present, and therefore more oxygen in the blood. Over time, this allows the person to partake in physical exertion without developing AMS.

22.7 | Embryonic Development of the Respiratory System

By the end of this section, you will be able to:
- Create a timeline of the phases of respiratory development in the fetus
- Propose reasons for fetal breathing movements
- Explain how the lungs become inflated after birth

Development of the respiratory system begins early in the fetus. It is a complex process that includes many structures, most of which arise from the endoderm. Towards the end of development, the fetus can be observed making breathing movements. Until birth, however, the mother provides all of the oxygen to the fetus as well as removes all of the fetal carbon dioxide via the placenta.

Time Line

The development of the respiratory system begins at about week 4 of gestation. By week 28, enough alveoli have matured that a baby born prematurely at this time can usually breathe on its own. The respiratory system, however, is not fully developed until early childhood, when a full complement of mature alveoli is present.

Weeks 4–7

Respiratory development in the embryo begins around week 4. Ectodermal tissue from the anterior head region invaginates posteriorly to form olfactory pits, which fuse with endodermal tissue of the developing pharynx. An **olfactory pit** is one of a pair of structures that will enlarge to become the nasal cavity. At about this same time, the lung bud forms. The **lung bud** is a dome-shaped structure composed of tissue that bulges from the foregut. The **foregut** is endoderm just inferior to the pharyngeal pouches. The **laryngotracheal bud** is a structure that forms from the longitudinal extension of the lung bud as development progresses. The portion of this structure nearest the pharynx becomes the trachea, whereas the distal end becomes more bulbous, forming bronchial buds. A **bronchial bud** is one of a pair of structures that will eventually become the bronchi and all other lower respiratory structures (Figure 22.29).

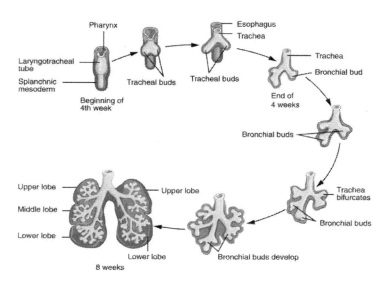

Figure 22.29 Development of the Lower Respiratory System

Weeks 7–16

Bronchial buds continue to branch as development progresses until all of the segmental bronchi have been formed. Beginning around week 13, the lumens of the bronchi begin to expand in diameter. By week 16, respiratory bronchioles form. The fetus now has all major lung structures involved in the airway.

Weeks 16–24

Once the respiratory bronchioles form, further development includes extensive vascularization, or the development of the blood vessels, as well as the formation of alveolar ducts and alveolar precursors. At about week 19, the respiratory bronchioles have formed. In addition, cells lining the respiratory structures begin to differentiate to form type I and type II pneumocytes. Once type II cells have differentiated, they begin to secrete small amounts of pulmonary surfactant. Around week 20, fetal breathing movements may begin.

Weeks 24–Term

Major growth and maturation of the respiratory system occurs from week 24 until term. More alveolar precursors develop, and larger amounts of pulmonary surfactant are produced. Surfactant levels are not generally adequate to create effective lung compliance until about the eighth month of pregnancy. The respiratory system continues to expand, and the surfaces that will form the respiratory membrane develop further. At this point, pulmonary capillaries have formed and continue to expand, creating a large surface area for gas exchange. The major milestone of respiratory development occurs at around week 28, when sufficient alveolar precursors have matured so that a baby born prematurely at this time can usually breathe on its own. However, alveoli continue to develop and mature into childhood. A full complement of functional alveoli does not appear until around 8 years of age.

Fetal "Breathing"

Although the function of fetal breathing movements is not entirely clear, they can be observed starting at 20–21 weeks of development. Fetal breathing movements involve muscle contractions that cause the inhalation of amniotic fluid and exhalation of the same fluid, with pulmonary surfactant and mucus. Fetal breathing movements are not continuous and may include periods of frequent movements and periods of no movements. Maternal factors can influence the frequency of breathing movements. For example, high blood glucose levels, called hyperglycemia, can boost the number of breathing movements. Conversely, low blood glucose levels, called hypoglycemia, can reduce the number of fetal breathing movements. Tobacco use is also known to lower fetal breathing rates. Fetal breathing may help tone the muscles in preparation for breathing movements once the fetus is born. It may also help the alveoli to form and mature. Fetal breathing movements are considered a sign of robust health.

Birth

Prior to birth, the lungs are filled with amniotic fluid, mucus, and surfactant. As the fetus is squeezed through the birth canal, the fetal thoracic cavity is compressed, expelling much of this fluid. Some fluid remains, however, but is rapidly absorbed by the body shortly after birth. The first inhalation occurs within 10 seconds after birth and not only serves as the first inspiration, but also acts to inflate the lungs. Pulmonary surfactant is critical for inflation to occur, as it reduces the surface tension of the alveoli. Preterm birth around 26 weeks frequently results in severe respiratory distress, although with current medical advancements, some babies may survive. Prior to 26 weeks, sufficient pulmonary surfactant is not produced, and the surfaces for gas exchange have not formed adequately; therefore, survival is low.

Respiratory System: Respiratory Distress Syndrome

Respiratory distress syndrome (RDS) primarily occurs in infants born prematurely. Up to 50 percent of infants born between 26 and 28 weeks and fewer than 30 percent of infants born between 30 and 31 weeks develop RDS. RDS results from insufficient production of pulmonary surfactant, thereby preventing the lungs from properly inflating at birth. A small amount of pulmonary surfactant is produced beginning at around 20 weeks; however, this is not sufficient for inflation of the lungs. As a result, dyspnea occurs and gas exchange cannot be performed properly. Blood oxygen levels are low, whereas blood carbon dioxide levels and pH are high.

The primary cause of RDS is premature birth, which may be due to a variety of known or unknown causes. Other risk factors include gestational diabetes, cesarean delivery, second-born twins, and family history of RDS. The presence of RDS can lead to other serious disorders, such as septicemia (infection of the blood) or pulmonary hemorrhage. Therefore, it is important that RDS is immediately recognized and treated to prevent death and reduce the risk of developing other disorders.

Medical advances have resulted in an improved ability to treat RDS and support the infant until proper lung development can occur. At the time of delivery, treatment may include resuscitation and intubation if the infant does not breathe on his or her own. These infants would need to be placed on a ventilator to mechanically assist with the breathing process. If spontaneous breathing occurs, application of nasal continuous positive airway pressure (CPAP) may be required. In addition, pulmonary surfactant is typically administered. Death due to RDS has been reduced by 50 percent due to the introduction of pulmonary surfactant therapy. Other therapies may include corticosteroids, supplemental oxygen, and assisted ventilation. Supportive therapies, such as temperature regulation, nutritional support, and antibiotics, may be administered to the premature infant as well.

KEY TERMS

acclimatization process of adjustment that the respiratory system makes due to chronic exposure to high altitudes

acute mountain sickness (AMS) condition that occurs a result of acute exposure to high altitude due to a low partial pressure of oxygen

ala (plural = alae) small, flaring structure of a nostril that forms the lateral side of the nares

alar cartilage cartilage that supports the apex of the nose and helps shape the nares; it is connected to the septal cartilage and connective tissue of the alae

alveolar dead space air space within alveoli that are unable to participate in gas exchange

alveolar duct small tube that leads from the terminal bronchiole to the respiratory bronchiole and is the point of attachment for alveoli

alveolar macrophage immune system cell of the alveolus that removes debris and pathogens

alveolar pore opening that allows airflow between neighboring alveoli

alveolar sac cluster of alveoli

alveolus small, grape-like sac that performs gas exchange in the lungs

anatomical dead space air space present in the airway that never reaches the alveoli and therefore never participates in gas exchange

apex tip of the external nose

apneustic center network of neurons within the pons that stimulate the neurons in the dorsal respiratory group; controls the depth of inspiration

atmospheric pressure amount of force that is exerted by gases in the air surrounding any given surface

Bohr effect relationship between blood pH and oxygen dissociation from hemoglobin

Boyle's law relationship between volume and pressure as described by the formula: $P_1V_1 = P_2V_2$

bridge portion of the external nose that lies in the area of the nasal bones

bronchial bud structure in the developing embryo that forms when the laryngotracheal bud extends and branches to form two bulbous structures

bronchial tree collective name for the multiple branches of the bronchi and bronchioles of the respiratory system

bronchiole branch of bronchi that are 1 mm or less in diameter and terminate at alveolar sacs

bronchoconstriction decrease in the size of the bronchiole due to contraction of the muscular wall

bronchodilation increase in the size of the bronchiole due to contraction of the muscular wall

bronchus tube connected to the trachea that branches into many subsidiaries and provides a passageway for air to enter and leave the lungs

carbaminohemoglobin bound form of hemoglobin and carbon dioxide

carbonic anhydrase (CA) enzyme that catalyzes the reaction that causes carbon dioxide and water to form carbonic acid

cardiac notch indentation on the surface of the left lung that allows space for the heart

central chemoreceptor one of the specialized receptors that are located in the brain that sense changes in hydrogen ion, oxygen, or carbon dioxide concentrations in the brain

chloride shift facilitated diffusion that exchanges bicarbonate (HCO_3^-) with chloride (Cl^-) ions

conducting zone region of the respiratory system that includes the organs and structures that provide passageways for air and are not directly involved in gas exchange

cricoid cartilage portion of the larynx composed of a ring of cartilage with a wide posterior region and a thinner anterior region; attached to the esophagus

Dalton's law statement of the principle that a specific gas type in a mixture exerts its own pressure, as if that specific gas type was not part of a mixture of gases

dorsal respiratory group (DRG) region of the medulla oblongata that stimulates the contraction of the diaphragm and intercostal muscles to induce inspiration

dorsum nasi intermediate portion of the external nose that connects the bridge to the apex and is supported by the nasal bone

epiglottis leaf-shaped piece of elastic cartilage that is a portion of the larynx that swings to close the trachea during swallowing

expiration (also, exhalation) process that causes the air to leave the lungs

expiratory reserve volume (ERV) amount of air that can be forcefully exhaled after a normal tidal exhalation

external nose region of the nose that is easily visible to others

external respiration gas exchange that occurs in the alveoli

fauces portion of the posterior oral cavity that connects the oral cavity to the oropharynx

fibroelastic membrane specialized membrane that connects the ends of the C-shape cartilage in the trachea; contains smooth muscle fibers

forced breathing (also, hyperpnea) mode of breathing that occurs during exercise or by active thought that requires muscle contraction for both inspiration and expiration

foregut endoderm of the embryo towards the head region

functional residual capacity (FRC) sum of ERV and RV, which is the amount of air that remains in the lungs after a tidal expiration

glottis opening between the vocal folds through which air passes when producing speech

Haldane effect relationship between the partial pressure of oxygen and the affinity of hemoglobin for carbon dioxide

Henry's law statement of the principle that the concentration of gas in a liquid is directly proportional to the solubility and partial pressure of that gas

hilum concave structure on the mediastinal surface of the lungs where blood vessels, lymphatic vessels, nerves, and a bronchus enter the lung

hyperpnea increased rate and depth of ventilation due to an increase in oxygen demand that does not significantly alter blood oxygen or carbon dioxide levels

hyperventilation increased ventilation rate that leads to abnormally low blood carbon dioxide levels and high (alkaline) blood pH

inspiration (also, inhalation) process that causes air to enter the lungs

inspiratory capacity (IC) sum of the TV and IRV, which is the amount of air that can maximally be inhaled past a tidal expiration

inspiratory reserve volume (IRV) amount of air that enters the lungs due to deep inhalation past the tidal volume

internal respiration gas exchange that occurs at the level of body tissues

intra-alveolar pressure (intrapulmonary pressure) pressure of the air within the alveoli

intrapleural pressure pressure of the air within the pleural cavity

laryngeal prominence region where the two lamina of the thyroid cartilage join, forming a protrusion known as "Adam's apple"

laryngopharynx portion of the pharynx bordered by the oropharynx superiorly and esophagus and trachea inferiorly; serves as a route for both air and food

laryngotracheal bud forms from the lung bud, has a tracheal end and bulbous bronchial buds at the distal end

larynx cartilaginous structure that produces the voice, prevents food and beverages from entering the trachea, and regulates the volume of air that enters and leaves the lungs

lingual tonsil lymphoid tissue located at the base of the tongue

lung organ of the respiratory system that performs gas exchange

lung bud median dome that forms from the endoderm of the foregut

meatus one of three recesses (superior, middle, and inferior) in the nasal cavity attached to the conchae that increase the surface area of the nasal cavity

naris (plural = nares) opening of the nostrils

nasal bone bone of the skull that lies under the root and bridge of the nose and is connected to the frontal and maxillary bones

nasal septum wall composed of bone and cartilage that separates the left and right nasal cavities

nasopharynx portion of the pharynx flanked by the conchae and oropharynx that serves as an airway

olfactory pit invaginated ectodermal tissue in the anterior portion of the head region of an embryo that will form the nasal cavity

oropharynx portion of the pharynx flanked by the nasopharynx, oral cavity, and laryngopharynx that is a passageway for both air and food

oxygen–hemoglobin dissociation curve graph that describes the relationship of partial pressure to the binding and disassociation of oxygen to and from heme

oxyhemoglobin ($Hb-O_2$) bound form of hemoglobin and oxygen

palatine tonsil one of the paired structures composed of lymphoid tissue located anterior to the uvula at the roof of isthmus of the fauces

paranasal sinus one of the cavities within the skull that is connected to the conchae that serve to warm and humidify incoming air, produce mucus, and lighten the weight of the skull; consists of frontal, maxillary, sphenoidal, and ethmoidal sinuses

parietal pleura outermost layer of the pleura that connects to the thoracic wall, mediastinum, and diaphragm

partial pressure force exerted by each gas in a mixture of gases

peripheral chemoreceptor one of the specialized receptors located in the aortic arch and carotid arteries that sense changes in pH, carbon dioxide, or oxygen blood levels

pharyngeal tonsil structure composed of lymphoid tissue located in the nasopharynx

pharynx region of the conducting zone that forms a tube of skeletal muscle lined with respiratory epithelium; located between the nasal conchae and the esophagus and trachea

philtrum concave surface of the face that connects the apex of the nose to the top lip

pleural cavity space between the visceral and parietal pleurae

pleural fluid substance that acts as a lubricant for the visceral and parietal layers of the pleura during the movement of breathing

pneumotaxic center network of neurons within the pons that inhibit the activity of the neurons in the dorsal respiratory group; controls rate of breathing

pulmonary artery artery that arises from the pulmonary trunk and carries deoxygenated, arterial blood to the alveoli

pulmonary plexus network of autonomic nervous system fibers found near the hilum of the lung

pulmonary surfactant substance composed of phospholipids and proteins that reduces the surface tension of the alveoli; made by type II alveolar cells

pulmonary ventilation exchange of gases between the lungs and the atmosphere; breathing

quiet breathing (also, eupnea) mode of breathing that occurs at rest and does not require the cognitive thought of the individual

residual volume (RV) amount of air that remains in the lungs after maximum exhalation

respiratory bronchiole specific type of bronchiole that leads to alveolar sacs

respiratory cycle one sequence of inspiration and expiration

respiratory epithelium ciliated lining of much of the conducting zone that is specialized to remove debris and pathogens, and produce mucus

respiratory membrane alveolar and capillary wall together, which form an air-blood barrier that facilitates the simple diffusion of gases

respiratory rate total number of breaths taken each minute

respiratory volume varying amounts of air within the lung at a given time

respiratory zone includes structures of the respiratory system that are directly involved in gas exchange

root region of the external nose between the eyebrows

thoracic wall compliance ability of the thoracic wall to stretch while under pressure

thyroid cartilage largest piece of cartilage that makes up the larynx and consists of two lamina

tidal volume (TV) amount of air that normally enters the lungs during quiet breathing

total dead space sum of the anatomical dead space and alveolar dead space

total lung capacity (TLC) total amount of air that can be held in the lungs; sum of TV, ERV, IRV, and RV

total pressure sum of all the partial pressures of a gaseous mixture

trachea tube composed of cartilaginous rings and supporting tissue that connects the lung bronchi and the larynx; provides a route for air to enter and exit the lung

trachealis muscle smooth muscle located in the fibroelastic membrane of the trachea

transpulmonary pressure pressure difference between the intrapleural and intra-alveolar pressures

true vocal cord one of the pair of folded, white membranes that have a free inner edge that oscillates as air passes through to produce sound

type I alveolar cell squamous epithelial cells that are the major cell type in the alveolar wall; highly permeable to gases

type II alveolar cell cuboidal epithelial cells that are the minor cell type in the alveolar wall; secrete pulmonary surfactant

ventilation movement of air into and out of the lungs; consists of inspiration and expiration

ventral respiratory group (VRG) region of the medulla oblongata that stimulates the contraction of the accessory muscles involved in respiration to induce forced inspiration and expiration

vestibular fold part of the folded region of the glottis composed of mucous membrane; supports the epiglottis during swallowing

visceral pleura innermost layer of the pleura that is superficial to the lungs and extends into the lung fissures

vital capacity (VC) sum of TV, ERV, and IRV, which is all the volumes that participate in gas exchange

CHAPTER REVIEW

22.1 Organs and Structures of the Respiratory System

The respiratory system is responsible for obtaining oxygen and getting rid of carbon dioxide, and aiding in speech production and in sensing odors. From a functional perspective, the respiratory system can be divided into two major areas: the conducting zone and the respiratory zone. The conducting zone consists of all of the structures that provide passageways for air to travel into and out of the lungs: the nasal cavity, pharynx, trachea, bronchi, and most bronchioles. The nasal passages contain the conchae and meatuses that expand the surface area of the cavity, which helps to warm and humidify incoming air, while removing debris and pathogens. The pharynx is composed of three major sections: the nasopharynx, which is continuous with the nasal cavity; the oropharynx, which borders the nasopharynx and the oral cavity; and the laryngopharynx, which borders the oropharynx, trachea, and esophagus. The respiratory zone includes the structures of the lung that are directly involved in gas exchange: the terminal bronchioles and alveoli.

The lining of the conducting zone is composed mostly of pseudostratified ciliated columnar epithelium with goblet cells. The mucus traps pathogens and debris, whereas beating cilia move the mucus superiorly toward the throat, where it is swallowed. As the bronchioles become smaller and smaller, and nearer the alveoli, the epithelium thins and is simple squamous epithelium in the alveoli. The endothelium of the surrounding capillaries, together with the alveolar epithelium, forms the respiratory membrane. This is a blood-air barrier through which gas exchange occurs by simple diffusion.

22.2 The Lungs

The lungs are the major organs of the respiratory system and are responsible for performing gas exchange. The lungs are paired and separated into lobes; The left lung consists of two lobes, whereas the right lung consists of three lobes. Blood circulation is very important, as blood is required to transport oxygen from the lungs to other tissues throughout the body. The function of the pulmonary circulation is to aid in gas exchange. The pulmonary artery provides deoxygenated blood to the capillaries that form respiratory membranes with the alveoli, and the pulmonary veins return newly oxygenated blood to the heart for further transport throughout the body. The lungs are innervated by the parasympathetic and sympathetic nervous systems, which coordinate the bronchodilation and bronchoconstriction of the airways. The lungs are enclosed by the pleura, a membrane that is composed of visceral and parietal pleural layers. The space between these two layers is called the pleural cavity. The mesothelial cells of the pleural membrane create pleural fluid, which serves as both a lubricant (to reduce friction during breathing) and as an adhesive to adhere the lungs to the thoracic wall (to facilitate movement of the lungs during ventilation).

22.3 The Process of Breathing

Pulmonary ventilation is the process of breathing, which is driven by pressure differences between the lungs and the atmosphere. Atmospheric pressure is the force exerted by gases present in the atmosphere. The force exerted by gases within the alveoli is called intra-alveolar (intrapulmonary) pressure, whereas the force exerted by gases in the pleural cavity is called intrapleural pressure. Typically, intrapleural pressure is lower, or negative to, intra-alveolar pressure. The difference in pressure between intrapleural and intra-alveolar pressures is called transpulmonary pressure. In addition, intra-alveolar pressure will equalize with the atmospheric pressure. Pressure is determined by the volume of the space occupied by a gas and is influenced by resistance. Air flows when a pressure gradient is created, from a space of higher pressure to a space of lower pressure. Boyle's law describes the relationship between volume and pressure. A gas is at lower pressure in a larger volume because the gas molecules have more space to in which to move. The same quantity of gas in a smaller volume results in gas molecules crowding together, producing increased pressure.

Resistance is created by inelastic surfaces, as well as the diameter of the airways. Resistance reduces the flow of gases. The surface tension of the alveoli also influences pressure, as it opposes the expansion of the alveoli. However, pulmonary surfactant helps to reduce the surface tension so that the alveoli do not collapse during expiration. The ability of the lungs to stretch, called lung compliance, also plays a role in gas flow. The more the lungs can stretch, the greater the potential volume of the lungs. The greater the volume of the lungs, the lower the air pressure within the lungs.

Pulmonary ventilation consists of the process of inspiration (or inhalation), where air enters the lungs, and expiration (or exhalation), where air leaves the lungs. During inspiration, the diaphragm and external intercostal muscles contract, causing the rib cage to expand and move outward, and expanding the thoracic cavity and lung volume. This creates a lower pressure within the lung than that of the atmosphere, causing air to be drawn into the lungs. During expiration, the diaphragm and intercostals relax, causing the thorax and lungs to recoil. The air pressure within the lungs increases to above the pressure of the atmosphere, causing air to be forced out of the lungs. However, during forced exhalation, the internal intercostals and abdominal muscles may be involved in forcing air out of the lungs.

Respiratory volume describes the amount of air in a given space within the lungs, or which can be moved by the lung, and is dependent on a variety of factors. Tidal volume refers to the amount of air that enters the lungs during quiet breathing, whereas inspiratory reserve volume is the amount of air that enters the lungs when a person inhales past the tidal volume. Expiratory reserve volume is the extra amount of air that can leave with forceful expiration, following tidal expiration. Residual volume is the amount of air that is left in the lungs after expelling the expiratory reserve volume. Respiratory capacity is the combination of two or more volumes. Anatomical dead space refers to the air within the respiratory structures that never participates in gas exchange, because it does not reach functional alveoli. Respiratory rate is the number of breaths taken per minute, which may change during certain diseases or conditions.

Both respiratory rate and depth are controlled by the respiratory centers of the brain, which are stimulated by factors such as chemical and pH changes in the blood. These changes are sensed by central chemoreceptors, which are located in the brain, and peripheral chemoreceptors, which are located in the aortic arch and carotid arteries. A rise in carbon dioxide or a decline in oxygen levels in the blood stimulates an increase in respiratory rate and depth.

22.4 Gas Exchange

The behavior of gases can be explained by the principles of Dalton's law and Henry's law, both of which describe aspects of gas exchange. Dalton's law states that each specific gas in a mixture of gases exerts force (its partial pressure) independently of the other gases in the mixture. Henry's law states that the amount of a specific gas that dissolves in a liquid is a function of its partial pressure. The greater the partial pressure of a gas, the more of that gas will dissolve in a liquid, as the gas moves toward equilibrium. Gas molecules move down a pressure gradient; in other words, gas moves from a region of high pressure to a region of low pressure. The partial pressure of oxygen is high in the alveoli and low in the blood of the pulmonary capillaries. As a result, oxygen diffuses across the respiratory membrane from the alveoli into the blood. In contrast, the partial pressure of carbon dioxide is high in the pulmonary capillaries and low in the alveoli. Therefore, carbon dioxide diffuses across the respiratory membrane from the blood into the alveoli. The amount of oxygen and carbon dioxide that diffuses across the respiratory membrane is similar.

Ventilation is the process that moves air into and out of the alveoli, and perfusion affects the flow of blood in the capillaries. Both are important in gas exchange, as ventilation must be sufficient to create a high partial pressure of oxygen in the alveoli. If ventilation is insufficient and the partial pressure of oxygen drops in the alveolar air, the capillary is constricted and blood flow is redirected to alveoli with sufficient ventilation. External respiration refers to gas exchange that occurs in the alveoli, whereas internal respiration refers to gas exchange that occurs in the tissue. Both are driven by partial pressure differences.

22.5 Transport of Gases

Oxygen is primarily transported through the blood by erythrocytes. These cells contain a metalloprotein called hemoglobin, which is composed of four subunits with a ring-like structure. Each subunit contains one atom of iron bound to a molecule of heme. Heme binds oxygen so that each hemoglobin molecule can bind up to four oxygen molecules. When all of the heme units in the blood are bound to oxygen, hemoglobin is considered to be saturated. Hemoglobin is partially saturated when only some heme units are bound to oxygen. An oxygen–hemoglobin saturation/dissociation curve is a common way to depict the relationship of how easily oxygen binds to or dissociates from hemoglobin as a function of the partial pressure of oxygen. As the partial pressure of oxygen increases, the more readily hemoglobin binds to oxygen. At the same time, once one molecule of oxygen is bound by hemoglobin, additional oxygen molecules more readily bind to hemoglobin. Other factors such as temperature, pH, the partial pressure of carbon dioxide, and the concentration of 2,3-bisphosphoglycerate can enhance or inhibit the binding of hemoglobin and oxygen as well. Fetal hemoglobin has a different structure than adult hemoglobin, which results in fetal hemoglobin having a greater affinity for oxygen than adult hemoglobin.

Carbon dioxide is transported in blood by three different mechanisms: as dissolved carbon dioxide, as bicarbonate, or as carbaminohemoglobin. A small portion of carbon dioxide remains. The largest amount of transported carbon dioxide is as bicarbonate, formed in erythrocytes. For this conversion, carbon dioxide is combined with water with the aid of an enzyme called carbonic anhydrase. This combination forms carbonic acid, which spontaneously dissociates into bicarbonate and hydrogen ions. As bicarbonate builds up in erythrocytes, it is moved across the membrane into the plasma in exchange for chloride ions by a mechanism called the chloride shift. At the pulmonary capillaries, bicarbonate re-enters erythrocytes in exchange for chloride ions, and the reaction with carbonic anhydrase is reversed, recreating carbon dioxide and water. Carbon dioxide then diffuses out of the erythrocyte and across the respiratory membrane into the air. An intermediate amount of carbon dioxide binds directly to hemoglobin to form carbaminohemoglobin. The partial pressures of carbon dioxide and oxygen, as well as the oxygen saturation of hemoglobin, influence how readily hemoglobin binds carbon dioxide. The less saturated hemoglobin is and the lower the partial pressure of oxygen in the blood is, the more readily hemoglobin binds to carbon dioxide. This is an example of the Haldane effect.

22.6 Modifications in Respiratory Functions

Normally, the respiratory centers of the brain maintain a consistent, rhythmic breathing cycle. However, in certain cases, the respiratory system must adjust to situational changes in order to supply the body with sufficient oxygen. For example, exercise results in increased ventilation, and chronic exposure to a high altitude results in a greater number of circulating erythrocytes. Hyperpnea, an increase in the rate and depth of ventilation, appears to be a function of three neural mechanisms that include a psychological stimulus, motor neuron activation of skeletal muscles, and the activation of proprioceptors in the muscles, joints, and tendons. As a result, hyperpnea related to exercise is initiated when exercise begins, as opposed to when tissue oxygen demand actually increases.

In contrast, acute exposure to a high altitude, particularly during times of physical exertion, does result in low blood and tissue levels of oxygen. This change is caused by a low partial pressure of oxygen in the air, because the atmospheric pressure at high altitudes is lower than the atmospheric pressure at sea level. This can lead to a condition called acute mountain sickness (AMS) with symptoms that include headaches, disorientation, fatigue, nausea, and lightheadedness. Over a long period of time, a person's body will adjust to the high altitude, a process called acclimatization. During acclimatization, the low tissue levels of oxygen will cause the kidneys to produce greater amounts of the hormone erythropoietin, which stimulates the production of erythrocytes. Increased levels of circulating erythrocytes provide an increased amount of hemoglobin that helps supply an individual with more oxygen, preventing the symptoms of AMS.

22.7 Embryonic Development of the Respiratory System

The development of the respiratory system in the fetus begins at about 4 weeks and continues into childhood. Ectodermal tissue in the anterior portion of the head region invaginates posteriorly, forming olfactory pits, which ultimately fuse with endodermal tissue of the early pharynx. At about this same time, an protrusion of endodermal tissue extends anteriorly from the foregut, producing a lung bud, which continues to elongate until it forms the laryngotracheal bud. The proximal portion of this structure will mature into the trachea, whereas the bulbous end will branch to form two bronchial buds. These buds then branch repeatedly, so that at about week 16, all major airway structures are present. Development progresses after week 16 as respiratory bronchioles and alveolar ducts form, and extensive vascularization occurs. Alveolar type I cells also begin to take shape. Type II pulmonary cells develop and begin to produce small amounts of surfactant. As the fetus grows, the respiratory system continues to expand as more alveoli develop and more surfactant is produced. Beginning at about week 36 and lasting into childhood, alveolar precursors mature to become fully functional alveoli. At birth, compression of the thoracic cavity forces much of the fluid in the lungs to be expelled. The first inhalation inflates the lungs. Fetal breathing movements begin around week 20 or 21, and occur when contractions of the respiratory muscles cause the fetus to inhale and exhale amniotic fluid. These movements continue until birth and may help to tone the muscles in preparation for breathing after birth and are a sign of good health.

INTERACTIVE LINK QUESTIONS

1. Visit this site (http://openstaxcollege.org/l/asthma) to learn more about what happens during an asthma attack. What are the three changes that occur inside the airways during an asthma attack?

2. Watch this video (http://openstaxcollege.org/l/spirometers) to learn more about lung volumes and spirometers. Explain how spirometry test results can be used to diagnose respiratory diseases or determine the effectiveness of disease treatment.

3. Watch this video (http://openstaxcollege.org/l/oxyblood) to see the transport of oxygen from the lungs to the tissues. Why is oxygenated blood bright red, whereas deoxygenated blood tends to be more of a purple color?

REVIEW QUESTIONS

4. Which of the following anatomical structures is *not* part of the conducting zone?
   a. pharynx
   b. nasal cavity
   c. alveoli
   d. bronchi

5. What is the function of the conchae in the nasal cavity?
   a. increase surface area
   b. exchange gases
   c. maintain surface tension
   d. maintain air pressure

6. The fauces connects which of the following structures to the oropharynx?
   a. nasopharynx
   b. laryngopharynx
   c. nasal cavity
   d. oral cavity

7. Which of the following are structural features of the trachea?
   a. C-shaped cartilage
   b. smooth muscle fibers
   c. cilia
   d. all of the above

8. Which of the following structures is *not* part of the bronchial tree?
   a. alveoli
   b. bronchi
   c. terminal bronchioles
   d. respiratory bronchioles

9. What is the role of alveolar macrophages?
   a. to secrete pulmonary surfactant
   b. to secrete antimicrobial proteins
   c. to remove pathogens and debris
   d. to facilitate gas exchange

10. Which of the following structures separates the lung into lobes?
   a. mediastinum
   b. fissure
   c. root
   d. pleura

11. A section of the lung that receives its own tertiary bronchus is called the _____.
   a. bronchopulmonary segment
   b. pulmonary lobule
   c. interpulmonary segment
   d. respiratory segment

12. The _____ circulation picks up oxygen for cellular use and drops off carbon dioxide for removal from the body.
   a. pulmonary
   b. interlobular
   c. respiratory
   d. bronchial

13. The pleura that surrounds the lungs consists of two layers, the _____.
   a. visceral and parietal pleurae.
   b. mediastinum and parietal pleurae.
   c. visceral and mediastinum pleurae.
   d. none of the above

14. Which of the following processes does atmospheric pressure play a role in?
   a. pulmonary ventilation
   b. production of pulmonary surfactant
   c. resistance
   d. surface tension

15. A decrease in volume leads to a(n) _____ pressure.
   a. decrease in
   b. equalization of
   c. increase in
   d. zero

16. The pressure difference between the intra-alveolar and intrapleural pressures is called _____.
   a. atmospheric pressure
   b. pulmonary pressure
   c. negative pressure
   d. transpulmonary pressure

17. Gas flow decreases as _____ increases.
   a. resistance
   b. pressure
   c. airway diameter

d. friction

18. Contraction of the external intercostal muscles causes which of the following to occur?
a. The diaphragm moves downward.
b. The rib cage is compressed.
c. The thoracic cavity volume decreases.
d. The ribs and sternum move upward.

19. Which of the following prevents the alveoli from collapsing?
a. residual volume
b. tidal volume
c. expiratory reserve volume
d. inspiratory reserve volume

20. Gas moves from an area of _____ partial pressure to an area of _____ partial pressure.
a. low; high
b. low; low
c. high; high
d. high; low

21. When ventilation is not sufficient, which of the following occurs?
a. The capillary constricts.
b. The capillary dilates.
c. The partial pressure of oxygen in the affected alveolus increases.
d. The bronchioles dilate.

22. Gas exchange that occurs at the level of the tissues is called _____.
a. external respiration
b. interpulmonary respiration
c. internal respiration
d. pulmonary ventilation

23. The partial pressure of carbon dioxide is 45 mm Hg in the blood and 40 mm Hg in the alveoli. What happens to the carbon dioxide?
a. It diffuses into the blood.
b. It diffuses into the alveoli.
c. The gradient is too small for carbon dioxide to diffuse.
d. It decomposes into carbon and oxygen.

24. Oxyhemoglobin forms by a chemical reaction between which of the following?
a. hemoglobin and carbon dioxide
b. carbonic anhydrase and carbon dioxide
c. hemoglobin and oxygen
d. carbonic anhydrase and oxygen

25. Which of the following factors play a role in the oxygen–hemoglobin saturation/dissociation curve?
a. temperature
b. pH
c. BPG
d. all of the above

26. Which of the following occurs during the chloride shift?
a. Chloride is removed from the erythrocyte.
b. Chloride is exchanged for bicarbonate.
c. Bicarbonate is removed from the erythrocyte.
d. Bicarbonate is removed from the blood.

27. A low partial pressure of oxygen promotes hemoglobin binding to carbon dioxide. This is an example of the _____.
a. Haldane effect
b. Bohr effect
c. Dalton's law
d. Henry's law

28. Increased ventilation that results in an increase in blood pH is called _____.
a. hyperventilation
b. hyperpnea
c. acclimatization
d. apnea

29. Exercise can trigger symptoms of AMS due to which of the following?
a. low partial pressure of oxygen
b. low atmospheric pressure
c. abnormal neural signals
d. small venous reserve of oxygen

30. Which of the following stimulates the production of erythrocytes?
a. AMS
b. high blood levels of carbon dioxide
c. low atmospheric pressure
d. erythropoietin

31. The olfactory pits form from which of the following?
a. mesoderm
b. cartilage
c. ectoderm
d. endoderm

32. A full complement of mature alveoli are present by _____.
a. early childhood, around 8 years of age
b. birth
c. 37 weeks
d. 16 weeks

33. If a baby is born prematurely before type II cells produce sufficient pulmonary surfactant, which of the following might you expect?
a. difficulty expressing fluid
b. difficulty inflating the lungs
c. difficulty with pulmonary capillary flow
d. no difficulty as type I cells can provide enough surfactant for normal breathing

34. When do fetal breathing movements begin?
a. around week 20
b. around week 37
c. around week 16
d. after birth

35. What happens to the fluid that remains in the lungs after birth?

a. It reduces the surface tension of the alveoli.
b. It is expelled shortly after birth.
c. It is absorbed shortly after birth.
d. It lubricates the pleurae.

CRITICAL THINKING QUESTIONS

36. Describe the three regions of the pharynx and their functions.

37. If a person sustains an injury to the epiglottis, what would be the physiological result?

38. Compare and contrast the conducting and respiratory zones.

39. Compare and contrast the right and left lungs.

40. Why are the pleurae not damaged during normal breathing?

41. Describe what is meant by the term "lung compliance."

42. Outline the steps involved in quiet breathing.

43. What is respiratory rate and how is it controlled?

44. Compare and contrast Dalton's law and Henry's law.

45. A smoker develops damage to several alveoli that then can no longer function. How does this affect gas exchange?

46. Compare and contrast adult hemoglobin and fetal hemoglobin.

47. Describe the relationship between the partial pressure of oxygen and the binding of oxygen to hemoglobin.

48. Describe three ways in which carbon dioxide can be transported.

49. Describe the neural factors involved in increasing ventilation during exercise.

50. What is the major mechanism that results in acclimatization?

51. During what timeframe does a fetus have enough mature structures to breathe on its own if born prematurely? Describe the other structures that develop during this phase.

52. Describe fetal breathing movements and their purpose.

23 | THE DIGESTIVE SYSTEM

Figure 23.1 Eating Apples Eating may be one of the simple pleasures in life, but digesting even one apple requires the coordinated work of many organs. (credit: "Aimanness Photography"/Flickr)

Introduction

Chapter Objectives

After studying this chapter, you will be able to:

- List and describe the functional anatomy of the organs and accessory organs of the digestive system
- Discuss the processes and control of ingestion, propulsion, mechanical digestion, chemical digestion, absorption, and defecation
- Discuss the roles of the liver, pancreas, and gallbladder in digestion
- Compare and contrast the digestion of the three macronutrients

The digestive system is continually at work, yet people seldom appreciate the complex tasks it performs in a choreographed biologic symphony. Consider what happens when you eat an apple. Of course, you enjoy the apple's taste as you chew it, but in the hours that follow, unless something goes amiss and you get a stomachache, you don't notice that your digestive system is working. You may be taking a walk or studying or sleeping, having forgotten all about the apple, but your stomach and intestines are busy digesting it and absorbing its vitamins and other nutrients. By the time any waste material is excreted, the body has appropriated all it can use from the apple. In short, whether you pay attention or not, the organs of the digestive system perform their specific functions, allowing you to use the food you eat to keep you going. This chapter examines the structure and functions of these organs, and explores the mechanics and chemistry of the digestive processes.

23.1 | Overview of the Digestive System

By the end of this section, you will be able to:

- Identify the organs of the alimentary canal from proximal to distal, and briefly state their function
- Identify the accessory digestive organs and briefly state their function
- Describe the four fundamental tissue layers of the alimentary canal
- Contrast the contributions of the enteric and autonomic nervous systems to digestive system functioning
- Explain how the peritoneum anchors the digestive organs

The function of the digestive system is to break down the foods you eat, release their nutrients, and absorb those nutrients into the body. Although the small intestine is the workhorse of the system, where the majority of digestion occurs, and where most of the released nutrients are absorbed into the blood or lymph, each of the digestive system organs makes a vital contribution to this process (Figure 23.2).

Chapter 23 | The Digestive System

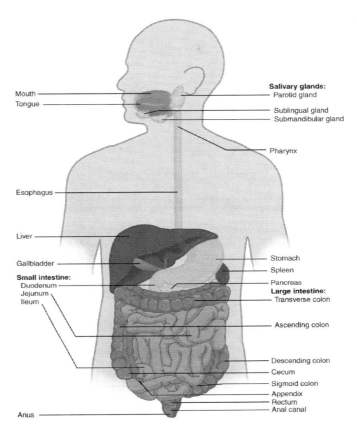

Figure 23.2 Components of the Digestive System   All digestive organs play integral roles in the life-sustaining process of digestion.

As is the case with all body systems, the digestive system does not work in isolation; it functions cooperatively with the other systems of the body. Consider for example, the interrelationship between the digestive and cardiovascular systems. Arteries supply the digestive organs with oxygen and processed nutrients, and veins drain the digestive tract. These intestinal veins, constituting the hepatic portal system, are unique; they do not return blood directly to the heart. Rather, this blood is diverted to the liver where its nutrients are off-loaded for processing before blood completes its circuit back to the heart. At the same time, the digestive system provides nutrients to the heart muscle and vascular tissue to support their functioning. The interrelationship of the digestive and endocrine systems is also critical. Hormones secreted by several endocrine glands, as well as endocrine cells of the pancreas, the stomach, and the small intestine, contribute to the control of digestion and nutrient metabolism. In turn, the digestive system provides the nutrients to fuel endocrine function. Table 23.1 gives a quick glimpse at how these other systems contribute to the functioning of the digestive system.

Contribution of Other Body Systems to the Digestive System

Body system	Benefits received by the digestive system
Cardiovascular	Blood supplies digestive organs with oxygen and processed nutrients
Endocrine	Endocrine hormones help regulate secretion in digestive glands and accessory organs

Table 23.1

Contribution of Other Body Systems to the Digestive System

Body system	Benefits received by the digestive system
Integumentary	Skin helps protect digestive organs and synthesizes vitamin D for calcium absorption
Lymphatic	Mucosa-associated lymphoid tissue and other lymphatic tissue defend against entry of pathogens; lacteals absorb lipids; and lymphatic vessels transport lipids to bloodstream
Muscular	Skeletal muscles support and protect abdominal organs
Nervous	Sensory and motor neurons help regulate secretions and muscle contractions in the digestive tract
Respiratory	Respiratory organs provide oxygen and remove carbon dioxide
Skeletal	Bones help protect and support digestive organs
Urinary	Kidneys convert vitamin D into its active form, allowing calcium absorption in the small intestine

Table 23.1

Digestive System Organs

The easiest way to understand the digestive system is to divide its organs into two main categories. The first group is the organs that make up the alimentary canal. Accessory digestive organs comprise the second group and are critical for orchestrating the breakdown of food and the assimilation of its nutrients into the body. Accessory digestive organs, despite their name, are critical to the function of the digestive system.

Alimentary Canal Organs

Also called the gastrointestinal (GI) tract or gut, the **alimentary canal** (aliment- = "to nourish") is a one-way tube about 7.62 meters (25 feet) in length during life and closer to 10.67 meters (35 feet) in length when measured after death, once smooth muscle tone is lost. The main function of the organs of the alimentary canal is to nourish the body. This tube begins at the mouth and terminates at the anus. Between those two points, the canal is modified as the pharynx, esophagus, stomach, and small and large intestines to fit the functional needs of the body. Both the mouth and anus are open to the external environment; thus, food and wastes within the alimentary canal are technically considered to be outside the body. Only through the process of absorption do the nutrients in food enter into and nourish the body's "inner space."

Accessory Structures

Each **accessory digestive organ** aids in the breakdown of food (Figure 23.3). Within the mouth, the teeth and tongue begin mechanical digestion, whereas the salivary glands begin chemical digestion. Once food products enter the small intestine, the gallbladder, liver, and pancreas release secretions—such as bile and enzymes—essential for digestion to continue. Together, these are called accessory organs because they sprout from the lining cells of the developing gut (mucosa) and augment its function; indeed, you could not live without their vital contributions, and many significant diseases result from their malfunction. Even after development is complete, they maintain a connection to the gut by way of ducts.

Histology of the Alimentary Canal

Throughout its length, the alimentary tract is composed of the same four tissue layers; the details of their structural arrangements vary to fit their specific functions. Starting from the lumen and moving outwards, these layers are the mucosa, submucosa, muscularis, and serosa, which is continuous with the mesentery (see Figure 23.3).

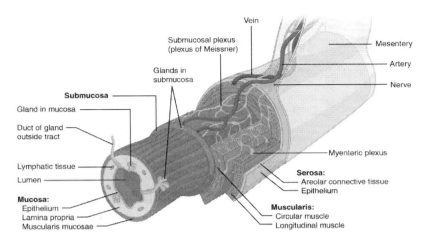

Figure 23.3 Layers of the Alimentary Canal   The wall of the alimentary canal has four basic tissue layers: the mucosa, submucosa, muscularis, and serosa.

The **mucosa** is referred to as a mucous membrane, because mucus production is a characteristic feature of gut epithelium. The membrane consists of epithelium, which is in direct contact with ingested food, and the lamina propria, a layer of connective tissue analogous to the dermis. In addition, the mucosa has a thin, smooth muscle layer, called the muscularis mucosa (not to be confused with the muscularis layer, described below).

Epithelium—In the mouth, pharynx, esophagus, and anal canal, the epithelium is primarily a non-keratinized, stratified squamous epithelium. In the stomach and intestines, it is a simple columnar epithelium. Notice that the epithelium is in direct contact with the lumen, the space inside the alimentary canal. Interspersed among its epithelial cells are goblet cells, which secrete mucus and fluid into the lumen, and enteroendocrine cells, which secrete hormones into the interstitial spaces between cells. Epithelial cells have a very brief lifespan, averaging from only a couple of days (in the mouth) to about a week (in the gut). This process of rapid renewal helps preserve the health of the alimentary canal, despite the wear and tear resulting from continued contact with foodstuffs.

Lamina propria—In addition to loose connective tissue, the lamina propria contains numerous blood and lymphatic vessels that transport nutrients absorbed through the alimentary canal to other parts of the body. The lamina propria also serves an immune function by housing clusters of lymphocytes, making up the mucosa-associated lymphoid tissue (MALT). These lymphocyte clusters are particularly substantial in the distal ileum where they are known as Peyer's patches. When you consider that the alimentary canal is exposed to foodborne bacteria and other foreign matter, it is not hard to appreciate why the immune system has evolved a means of defending against the pathogens encountered within it.

Muscularis mucosa—This thin layer of smooth muscle is in a constant state of tension, pulling the mucosa of the stomach and small intestine into undulating folds. These folds dramatically increase the surface area available for digestion and absorption.

As its name implies, the **submucosa** lies immediately beneath the mucosa. A broad layer of dense connective tissue, it connects the overlying mucosa to the underlying muscularis. It includes blood and lymphatic vessels (which transport absorbed nutrients), and a scattering of submucosal glands that release digestive secretions. Additionally, it serves as a conduit for a dense branching network of nerves, the submucosal plexus, which functions as described below.

The third layer of the alimentary canal is the **muscalaris** (also called the muscularis externa). The muscularis in the small intestine is made up of a double layer of smooth muscle: an inner circular layer and an outer longitudinal layer. The contractions of these layers promote mechanical digestion, expose more of the food to digestive chemicals, and move the food along the canal. In the most proximal and distal regions of the alimentary canal, including the mouth, pharynx, anterior part of the esophagus, and external anal sphincter, the muscularis is made up of skeletal muscle, which gives you voluntary control over swallowing and defecation. The basic two-layer structure found in the small intestine is modified in the organs proximal and distal to it. The stomach is equipped for its churning function by the addition of a third layer, the oblique muscle. While the colon has two layers like the small intestine, its longitudinal layer is segregated into three narrow parallel bands, the tenia coli, which make it look like a series of pouches rather than a simple tube.

The **serosa** is the portion of the alimentary canal superficial to the muscularis. Present only in the region of the alimentary canal within the abdominal cavity, it consists of a layer of visceral peritoneum overlying a layer of loose connective tissue. Instead of serosa, the mouth, pharynx, and esophagus have a dense sheath of collagen fibers called the adventitia. These tissues serve to hold the alimentary canal in place near the ventral surface of the vertebral column.

Nerve Supply

As soon as food enters the mouth, it is detected by receptors that send impulses along the sensory neurons of cranial nerves. Without these nerves, not only would your food be without taste, but you would also be unable to feel either the food or the structures of your mouth, and you would be unable to avoid biting yourself as you chew, an action enabled by the motor branches of cranial nerves.

Intrinsic innervation of much of the alimentary canal is provided by the enteric nervous system, which runs from the esophagus to the anus, and contains approximately 100 million motor, sensory, and interneurons (unique to this system compared to all other parts of the peripheral nervous system). These enteric neurons are grouped into two plexuses. The **myenteric plexus** (plexus of Auerbach) lies in the muscularis layer of the alimentary canal and is responsible for **motility**, especially the rhythm and force of the contractions of the muscularis. The **submucosal plexus** (plexus of Meissner) lies in the submucosal layer and is responsible for regulating digestive secretions and reacting to the presence of food (see Figure 23.3).

Extrinsic innervations of the alimentary canal are provided by the autonomic nervous system, which includes both sympathetic and parasympathetic nerves. In general, sympathetic activation (the fight-or-flight response) restricts the activity of enteric neurons, thereby decreasing GI secretion and motility. In contrast, parasympathetic activation (the rest-and-digest response) increases GI secretion and motility by stimulating neurons of the enteric nervous system.

Blood Supply

The blood vessels serving the digestive system have two functions. They transport the protein and carbohydrate nutrients absorbed by mucosal cells after food is digested in the lumen. Lipids are absorbed via lacteals, tiny structures of the lymphatic system. The blood vessels' second function is to supply the organs of the alimentary canal with the nutrients and oxygen needed to drive their cellular processes.

Specifically, the more anterior parts of the alimentary canal are supplied with blood by arteries branching off the aortic arch and thoracic aorta. Below this point, the alimentary canal is supplied with blood by arteries branching from the abdominal aorta. The celiac trunk services the liver, stomach, and duodenum, whereas the superior and inferior mesenteric arteries supply blood to the remaining small and large intestines.

The veins that collect nutrient-rich blood from the small intestine (where most absorption occurs) empty into the hepatic portal system. This venous network takes the blood into the liver where the nutrients are either processed or stored for later use. Only then does the blood drained from the alimentary canal viscera circulate back to the heart. To appreciate just how demanding the digestive process is on the cardiovascular system, consider that while you are "resting and digesting," about one-fourth of the blood pumped with each heartbeat enters arteries serving the intestines.

The Peritoneum

The digestive organs within the abdominal cavity are held in place by the peritoneum, a broad serous membranous sac made up of squamous epithelial tissue surrounded by connective tissue. It is composed of two different regions: the parietal peritoneum, which lines the abdominal wall, and the visceral peritoneum, which envelopes the abdominal organs (Figure 23.4). The peritoneal cavity is the space bounded by the visceral and parietal peritoneal surfaces. A few milliliters of watery fluid act as a lubricant to minimize friction between the serosal surfaces of the peritoneum.

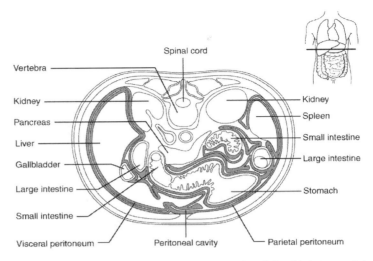

Figure 23.4 The Peritoneum A cross-section of the abdomen shows the relationship between abdominal organs and the peritoneum (darker lines).

Digestive System: Peritonitis

Inflammation of the peritoneum is called peritonitis. Chemical peritonitis can develop any time the wall of the alimentary canal is breached, allowing the contents of the lumen entry into the peritoneal cavity. For example, when an ulcer perforates the stomach wall, gastric juices spill into the peritoneal cavity. Hemorrhagic peritonitis occurs after a ruptured tubal pregnancy or traumatic injury to the liver or spleen fills the peritoneal cavity with blood. Even more severe peritonitis is associated with bacterial infections seen with appendicitis, colonic diverticulitis, and pelvic inflammatory disease (infection of uterine tubes, usually by sexually transmitted bacteria). Peritonitis is life threatening and often results in emergency surgery to correct the underlying problem and intensive antibiotic therapy. When your great grandparents and even your parents were young, the mortality from peritonitis was high. Aggressive surgery, improvements in anesthesia safety, the advance of critical care expertise, and antibiotics have greatly improved the mortality rate from this condition. Even so, the mortality rate still ranges from 30 to 40 percent.

The visceral peritoneum includes multiple large folds that envelope various abdominal organs, holding them to the dorsal surface of the body wall. Within these folds are blood vessels, lymphatic vessels, and nerves that innervate the organs with which they are in contact, supplying their adjacent organs. The five major peritoneal folds are described in Table 23.2. Note that during fetal development, certain digestive structures, including the first portion of the small intestine (called the duodenum), the pancreas, and portions of the large intestine (the ascending and descending colon, and the rectum) remain completely or partially posterior to the peritoneum. Thus, the location of these organs is described as **retroperitoneal**.

The Five Major Peritoneal Folds

Fold	Description
Greater omentum	Apron-like structure that lies superficial to the small intestine and transverse colon; a site of fat deposition in people who are overweight

Table 23.2

The Five Major Peritoneal Folds

Fold	Description
Falciform ligament	Anchors the liver to the anterior abdominal wall and inferior border of the diaphragm
Lesser omentum	Suspends the stomach from the inferior border of the liver; provides a pathway for structures connecting to the liver
Mesentery	Vertical band of tissue anterior to the lumbar vertebrae and anchoring all of the small intestine except the initial portion (the duodenum)
Mesocolon	Attaches two portions of the large intestine (the transverse and sigmoid colon) to the posterior abdominal wall

Table 23.2

By clicking on this link (http://openstaxcollege.org/l/fooddigestion) you can watch a short video of what happens to the food you eat, as it passes from your mouth to your intestine. Along the way, note how the food changes consistency and form. How does this change in consistency facilitate your gaining nutrients from food?

23.2 | Digestive System Processes and Regulation

By the end of this section, you will be able to:
- Discuss six fundamental activities of the digestive system, giving an example of each
- Compare and contrast the neural and hormonal controls involved in digestion

The digestive system uses mechanical and chemical activities to break food down into absorbable substances during its journey through the digestive system. Table 23.3 provides an overview of the basic functions of the digestive organs.

Visit this site (http://openstaxcollege.org/l/fooddigestion2) for an overview of digestion of food in different regions of the digestive tract. Note the route of non-fat nutrients from the small intestine to their release as nutrients to the body.

Functions of the Digestive Organs

Organ	Major functions	Other functions
Mouth	Ingests food Chews and mixes food Begins chemical breakdown of carbohydrates Moves food into the pharynx Begins breakdown of lipids via lingual lipase	Moistens and dissolves food, allowing you to taste it Cleans and lubricates the teeth and oral cavity Has some antimicrobial activity
Pharynx	Propels food from the oral cavity to the esophagus	Lubricates food and passageways
Esophagus	Propels food to the stomach	Lubricates food and passageways
Stomach	Mixes and churns food with gastric juices to form chyme Begins chemical breakdown of proteins Releases food into the duodenum as chyme Absorbs some fat-soluble substances (for example, alcohol, aspirin) Possesses antimicrobial functions	Stimulates protein-digesting enzymes Secretes intrinsic factor required for vitamin B_{12} absorption in small intestine
Small intestine	Mixes chyme with digestive juices Propels food at a rate slow enough for digestion and absorption Absorbs breakdown products of carbohydrates, proteins, lipids, and nucleic acids, along with vitamins, minerals, and water Performs physical digestion via segmentation	Provides optimal medium for enzymatic activity

Table 23.3

Functions of the Digestive Organs

Organ	Major functions	Other functions
Accessory organs	Liver: produces bile salts, which emulsify lipids, aiding their digestion and absorption Gallbladder: stores, concentrates, and releases bile Pancreas: produces digestive enzymes and bicarbonate	Bicarbonate-rich pancreatic juices help neutralize acidic chyme and provide optimal environment for enzymatic activity
Large intestine	Further breaks down food residues Absorbs most residual water, electrolytes, and vitamins produced by enteric bacteria Propels feces toward rectum Eliminates feces	Food residue is concentrated and temporarily stored prior to defecation Mucus eases passage of feces through colon

Table 23.3

Digestive Processes

The processes of digestion include six activities: ingestion, propulsion, mechanical or physical digestion, chemical digestion, absorption, and defecation.

The first of these processes, **ingestion**, refers to the entry of food into the alimentary canal through the mouth. There, the food is chewed and mixed with saliva, which contains enzymes that begin breaking down the carbohydrates in the food plus some lipid digestion via lingual lipase. Chewing increases the surface area of the food and allows an appropriately sized bolus to be produced.

Food leaves the mouth when the tongue and pharyngeal muscles propel it into the esophagus. This act of swallowing, the last voluntary act until defecation, is an example of **propulsion**, which refers to the movement of food through the digestive tract. It includes both the voluntary process of swallowing and the involuntary process of peristalsis. **Peristalsis** consists of sequential, alternating waves of contraction and relaxation of alimentary wall smooth muscles, which act to propel food along (Figure 23.5). These waves also play a role in mixing food with digestive juices. Peristalsis is so powerful that foods and liquids you swallow enter your stomach even if you are standing on your head.

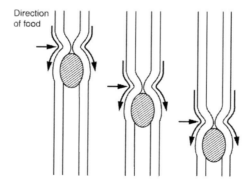

Figure 23.5 Peristalsis   Peristalsis moves food through the digestive tract with alternating waves of muscle contraction and relaxation.

Digestion includes both mechanical and chemical processes. **Mechanical digestion** is a purely physical process that does not change the chemical nature of the food. Instead, it makes the food smaller to increase both surface area and mobility. It includes **mastication**, or chewing, as well as tongue movements that help break food into smaller bits and mix food with saliva. Although there may be a tendency to think that mechanical digestion is limited to the first steps of the digestive process, it occurs after the food leaves the mouth, as well. The mechanical churning of food in the stomach serves to further break it apart and expose more of its surface area to digestive juices, creating an acidic "soup" called **chyme**. **Segmentation**, which occurs mainly in the small intestine, consists of localized contractions of circular muscle of the muscularis layer of the alimentary canal. These contractions isolate small sections of the intestine, moving their contents back and forth while continuously subdividing, breaking up, and mixing the contents. By moving food back and forth in the intestinal lumen, segmentation mixes food with digestive juices and facilitates absorption.

In **chemical digestion**, starting in the mouth, digestive secretions break down complex food molecules into their chemical building blocks (for example, proteins into separate amino acids). These secretions vary in composition, but typically contain water, various enzymes, acids, and salts. The process is completed in the small intestine.

Food that has been broken down is of no value to the body unless it enters the bloodstream and its nutrients are put to work. This occurs through the process of **absorption**, which takes place primarily within the small intestine. There, most nutrients are absorbed from the lumen of the alimentary canal into the bloodstream through the epithelial cells that make up the mucosa. Lipids are absorbed into lacteals and are transported via the lymphatic vessels to the bloodstream (the subclavian veins near the heart). The details of these processes will be discussed later.

In **defecation**, the final step in digestion, undigested materials are removed from the body as feces.

Digestive System: From Appetite Suppression to Constipation

Age-related changes in the digestive system begin in the mouth and can affect virtually every aspect of the digestive system. Taste buds become less sensitive, so food isn't as appetizing as it once was. A slice of pizza is a challenge, not a treat, when you have lost teeth, your gums are diseased, and your salivary glands aren't producing enough saliva. Swallowing can be difficult, and ingested food moves slowly through the alimentary canal because of reduced strength and tone of muscular tissue. Neurosensory feedback is also dampened, slowing the transmission of messages that stimulate the release of enzymes and hormones.

Pathologies that affect the digestive organs—such as hiatal hernia, gastritis, and peptic ulcer disease—can occur at greater frequencies as you age. Problems in the small intestine may include duodenal ulcers, maldigestion, and malabsorption. Problems in the large intestine include hemorrhoids, diverticular disease, and constipation. Conditions that affect the function of accessory organs—and their abilities to deliver pancreatic enzymes and bile to the small intestine—include jaundice, acute pancreatitis, cirrhosis, and gallstones.

In some cases, a single organ is in charge of a digestive process. For example, ingestion occurs only in the mouth and defecation only in the anus. However, most digestive processes involve the interaction of several organs and occur gradually as food moves through the alimentary canal (Figure 23.6).

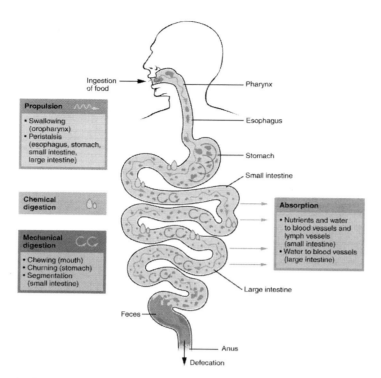

Figure 23.6 Digestive Processes The digestive processes are ingestion, propulsion, mechanical digestion, chemical digestion, absorption, and defecation.

Some chemical digestion occurs in the mouth. Some absorption can occur in the mouth and stomach, for example, alcohol and aspirin.

Regulatory Mechanisms

Neural and endocrine regulatory mechanisms work to maintain the optimal conditions in the lumen needed for digestion and absorption. These regulatory mechanisms, which stimulate digestive activity through mechanical and chemical activity, are controlled both extrinsically and intrinsically.

Neural Controls

The walls of the alimentary canal contain a variety of sensors that help regulate digestive functions. These include mechanoreceptors, chemoreceptors, and osmoreceptors, which are capable of detecting mechanical, chemical, and osmotic stimuli, respectively. For example, these receptors can sense when the presence of food has caused the stomach to expand, whether food particles have been sufficiently broken down, how much liquid is present, and the type of nutrients in the food (lipids, carbohydrates, and/or proteins). Stimulation of these receptors provokes an appropriate reflex that furthers the process of digestion. This may entail sending a message that activates the glands that secrete digestive juices into the lumen, or it may mean the stimulation of muscles within the alimentary canal, thereby activating peristalsis and segmentation that move food along the intestinal tract.

The walls of the entire alimentary canal are embedded with nerve plexuses that interact with the central nervous system and other nerve plexuses—either within the same digestive organ or in different ones. These interactions prompt several types of reflexes. Extrinsic nerve plexuses orchestrate long reflexes, which involve the central and autonomic nervous systems and work in response to stimuli from outside the digestive system. Short reflexes, on the other hand, are orchestrated by intrinsic nerve plexuses within the alimentary canal wall. These two plexuses and their connections were introduced earlier as the enteric nervous system. Short reflexes regulate activities in one area of the digestive tract and may coordinate local peristaltic movements and stimulate digestive secretions. For example, the sight, smell, and taste of food initiate long reflexes that begin with a sensory neuron delivering a signal to the medulla oblongata. The response to the signal is to stimulate cells in the stomach to begin secreting digestive juices in preparation for incoming food. In contrast, food that distends the stomach initiates short reflexes that cause cells in the stomach wall to increase their secretion of digestive juices.

Hormonal Controls

A variety of hormones are involved in the digestive process. The main digestive hormone of the stomach is gastrin, which is secreted in response to the presence of food. Gastrin stimulates the secretion of gastric acid by the parietal cells of the stomach mucosa. Other GI hormones are produced and act upon the gut and its accessory organs. Hormones produced by the duodenum include secretin, which stimulates a watery secretion of bicarbonate by the pancreas; cholecystokinin (CCK), which stimulates the secretion of pancreatic enzymes and bile from the liver and release of bile from the gallbladder; and gastric inhibitory peptide, which inhibits gastric secretion and slows gastric emptying and motility. These GI hormones are secreted by specialized epithelial cells, called endocrinocytes, located in the mucosal epithelium of the stomach and small intestine. These hormones then enter the bloodstream, through which they can reach their target organs.

23.3 | The Mouth, Pharynx, and Esophagus

By the end of this section, you will be able to:
- Describe the structures of the mouth, including its three accessory digestive organs
- Group the 32 adult teeth according to name, location, and function
- Describe the process of swallowing, including the roles of the tongue, upper esophageal sphincter, and epiglottis
- Trace the pathway food follows from ingestion into the mouth through release into the stomach

In this section, you will examine the anatomy and functions of the three main organs of the upper alimentary canal—the mouth, pharynx, and esophagus—as well as three associated accessory organs—the tongue, salivary glands, and teeth.

The Mouth

The cheeks, tongue, and palate frame the mouth, which is also called the **oral cavity** (or buccal cavity). The structures of the mouth are illustrated in Figure 23.7.

At the entrance to the mouth are the lips, or **labia** (singular = labium). Their outer covering is skin, which transitions to a mucous membrane in the mouth proper. Lips are very vascular with a thin layer of keratin; hence, the reason they are "red." They have a huge representation on the cerebral cortex, which probably explains the human fascination with kissing! The lips cover the orbicularis oris muscle, which regulates what comes in and goes out of the mouth. The **labial frenulum** is a midline fold of mucous membrane that attaches the inner surface of each lip to the gum. The cheeks make up the oral cavity's sidewalls. While their outer covering is skin, their inner covering is mucous membrane. This membrane is made up of non-keratinized, stratified squamous epithelium. Between the skin and mucous membranes are connective tissue and buccinator muscles. The next time you eat some food, notice how the buccinator muscles in your cheeks and the orbicularis oris muscle in your lips contract, helping you keep the food from falling out of your mouth. Additionally, notice how these muscles work when you are speaking.

The pocket-like part of the mouth that is framed on the inside by the gums and teeth, and on the outside by the cheeks and lips is called the **oral vestibule**. Moving farther into the mouth, the opening between the oral cavity and throat (oropharynx) is called the **fauces** (like the kitchen "faucet"). The main open area of the mouth, or oral cavity proper, runs from the gums and teeth to the fauces.

When you are chewing, you do not find it difficult to breathe simultaneously. The next time you have food in your mouth, notice how the arched shape of the roof of your mouth allows you to handle both digestion and respiration at the same time. This arch is called the palate. The anterior region of the palate serves as a wall (or septum) between the oral and nasal cavities as well as a rigid shelf against which the tongue can push food. It is created by the maxillary and palatine bones of the skull and, given its bony structure, is known as the hard palate. If you run your tongue along the roof of your mouth, you'll notice that the hard palate ends in the posterior oral cavity, and the tissue becomes fleshier. This part of the palate, known as the **soft palate**, is composed mainly of skeletal muscle. You can therefore manipulate, subconsciously, the soft palate—for instance, to yawn, swallow, or sing (see Figure 23.7).

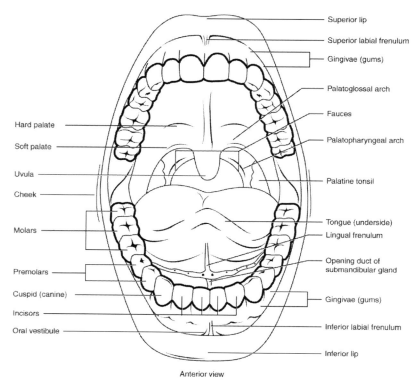

Figure 23.7 Mouth The mouth includes the lips, tongue, palate, gums, and teeth.

A fleshy bead of tissue called the uvula drops down from the center of the posterior edge of the soft palate. Although some have suggested that the uvula is a vestigial organ, it serves an important purpose. When you swallow, the soft palate and uvula move upward, helping to keep foods and liquid from entering the nasal cavity. Unfortunately, it can also contribute to the sound produced by snoring. Two muscular folds extend downward from the soft palate, on either side of the uvula. Toward the front, the **palatoglossal arch** lies next to the base of the tongue; behind it, the **palatopharyngeal arch** forms the superior and lateral margins of the fauces. Between these two arches are the palatine tonsils, clusters of lymphoid tissue that protect the pharynx. The lingual tonsils are located at the base of the tongue.

The Tongue

Perhaps you have heard it said that the **tongue** is the strongest muscle in the body. Those who stake this claim cite its strength proportionate to its size. Although it is difficult to quantify the relative strength of different muscles, it remains indisputable that the tongue is a workhorse, facilitating ingestion, mechanical digestion, chemical digestion (lingual lipase), sensation (of taste, texture, and temperature of food), swallowing, and vocalization.

The tongue is attached to the mandible, the styloid processes of the temporal bones, and the hyoid bone. The hyoid is unique in that it only distantly/indirectly articulates with other bones. The tongue is positioned over the floor of the oral cavity. A medial septum extends the entire length of the tongue, dividing it into symmetrical halves.

Beneath its mucous membrane covering, each half of the tongue is composed of the same number and type of intrinsic and extrinsic skeletal muscles. The intrinsic muscles (those within the tongue) are the longitudinalis inferior, longitudinalis superior, transversus linguae, and verticalis linguae muscles. These allow you to change the size and shape of your tongue, as well as to stick it out, if you wish. Having such a flexible tongue facilitates both swallowing and speech.

As you learned in your study of the muscular system, the extrinsic muscles of the tongue are the mylohyoid, hyoglossus, styloglossus, and genioglossus muscles. These muscles originate outside the tongue and insert into connective tissues within the tongue. The mylohyoid is responsible for raising the tongue, the hyoglossus pulls it down and back, the styloglossus pulls it up and back, and the genioglossus pulls it forward. Working in concert, these muscles perform three important digestive functions in the mouth: (1) position food for optimal chewing, (2) gather food into a **bolus** (rounded mass), and (3) position food so it can be swallowed.

The top and sides of the tongue are studded with papillae, extensions of lamina propria of the mucosa, which are covered in stratified squamous epithelium (Figure 23.8). Fungiform papillae, which are mushroom shaped, cover a large area of the tongue; they tend to be larger toward the rear of the tongue and smaller on the tip and sides. In contrast, filiform papillae are long and thin. Fungiform papillae contain taste buds, and filiform papillae have touch receptors that help the tongue move food around in the mouth. The filiform papillae create an abrasive surface that performs mechanically, much like a cat's rough tongue that is used for grooming. Lingual glands in the lamina propria of the tongue secrete mucus and a watery serous fluid that contains the enzyme **lingual lipase**, which plays a minor role in breaking down triglycerides but does not begin working until it is activated in the stomach. A fold of mucous membrane on the underside of the tongue, the **lingual frenulum**, tethers the tongue to the floor of the mouth. People with the congenital anomaly ankyloglossia, also known by the non-medical term "tongue tie," have a lingual frenulum that is too short or otherwise malformed. Severe ankyloglossia can impair speech and must be corrected with surgery.

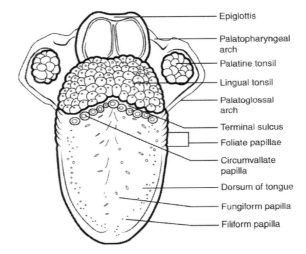

Figure 23.8 Tongue   This superior view of the tongue shows the locations and types of lingual papillae.

The Salivary Glands

Many small **salivary glands** are housed within the mucous membranes of the mouth and tongue. These minor exocrine glands are constantly secreting saliva, either directly into the oral cavity or indirectly through ducts, even while you sleep. In fact, an average of 1 to 1.5 liters of saliva is secreted each day. Usually just enough saliva is present to moisten the mouth and teeth. Secretion increases when you eat, because saliva is essential to moisten food and initiate the chemical breakdown of carbohydrates. Small amounts of saliva are also secreted by the labial glands in the lips. In addition, the buccal glands in the cheeks, palatal glands in the palate, and lingual glands in the tongue help ensure that all areas of the mouth are supplied with adequate saliva.

The Major Salivary Glands

Outside the oral mucosa are three pairs of major salivary glands, which secrete the majority of saliva into ducts that open into the mouth:

- The **submandibular glands**, which are in the floor of the mouth, secrete saliva into the mouth through the submandibular ducts.
- The **sublingual glands**, which lie below the tongue, use the lesser sublingual ducts to secrete saliva into the oral cavity.
- The **parotid glands** lie between the skin and the masseter muscle, near the ears. They secrete saliva into the mouth through the parotid duct, which is located near the second upper molar tooth (Figure 23.9).

Saliva

Saliva is essentially (95.5 percent) water. The remaining 4.5 percent is a complex mixture of ions, glycoproteins, enzymes, growth factors, and waste products. Perhaps the most important ingredient in salvia from the perspective of digestion is the enzyme **salivary amylase**, which initiates the breakdown of carbohydrates. Food does not spend enough time in the mouth to allow all the carbohydrates to break down, but salivary amylase continues acting until it is inactivated by stomach acids. Bicarbonate and phosphate ions function as chemical buffers, maintaining saliva at a pH between 6.35 and 6.85. Salivary mucus helps lubricate food, facilitating movement in the mouth, bolus formation, and swallowing. Saliva contains immunoglobulin A, which prevents microbes from penetrating the epithelium, and lysozyme, which makes saliva antimicrobial. Saliva also contains epidermal growth factor, which might have given rise to the adage "a mother's kiss can heal a wound."

Each of the major salivary glands secretes a unique formulation of saliva according to its cellular makeup. For example, the parotid glands secrete a watery solution that contains salivary amylase. The submandibular glands have cells similar to those of the parotid glands, as well as mucus-secreting cells. Therefore, saliva secreted by the submandibular glands also contains amylase but in a liquid thickened with mucus. The sublingual glands contain mostly mucous cells, and they secrete the thickest saliva with the least amount of salivary amylase.

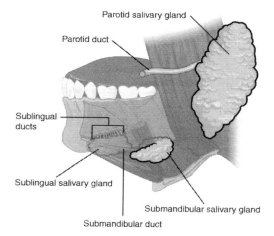

Figure 23.9 Salivary glands The major salivary glands are located outside the oral mucosa and deliver saliva into the mouth through ducts.

The Parotid Glands: Mumps

Infections of the nasal passages and pharynx can attack any salivary gland. The parotid glands are the usual site of infection with the virus that causes mumps (paramyxovirus). Mumps manifests by enlargement and inflammation of the parotid glands, causing a characteristic swelling between the ears and the jaw. Symptoms include fever and throat pain, which can be severe when swallowing acidic substances such as orange juice.

In about one-third of men who are past puberty, mumps also causes testicular inflammation, typically affecting only one testis and rarely resulting in sterility. With the increasing use and effectiveness of mumps vaccines, the incidence of mumps has decreased dramatically. According to the U.S. Centers for Disease Control and Prevention (CDC), the number of mumps cases dropped from more than 150,000 in 1968 to fewer than 1700 in 1993 to only 11 reported cases in 2011.

Regulation of Salivation

The autonomic nervous system regulates **salivation** (the secretion of saliva). In the absence of food, parasympathetic stimulation keeps saliva flowing at just the right level for comfort as you speak, swallow, sleep, and generally go about life. Over-salivation can occur, for example, if you are stimulated by the smell of food, but that food is not available for you to eat. Drooling is an extreme instance of the overproduction of saliva. During times of stress, such as before speaking in public, sympathetic stimulation takes over, reducing salivation and producing the symptom of dry mouth often associated with anxiety. When you are dehydrated, salivation is reduced, causing the mouth to feel dry and prompting you to take action to quench your thirst.

Salivation can be stimulated by the sight, smell, and taste of food. It can even be stimulated by thinking about food. You might notice whether reading about food and salivation right now has had any effect on your production of saliva.

How does the salivation process work while you are eating? Food contains chemicals that stimulate taste receptors on the tongue, which send impulses to the superior and inferior salivatory nuclei in the brain stem. These two nuclei then send back parasympathetic impulses through fibers in the glossopharyngeal and facial nerves, which stimulate salivation. Even after you swallow food, salivation is increased to cleanse the mouth and to water down and neutralize any irritating chemical remnants, such as that hot sauce in your burrito. Most saliva is swallowed along with food and is reabsorbed, so that fluid is not lost.

The Teeth

The teeth, or **dentes** (singular = dens), are organs similar to bones that you use to tear, grind, and otherwise mechanically break down food.

Types of Teeth

During the course of your lifetime, you have two sets of teeth (one set of teeth is a **dentition**). Your 20 **deciduous teeth**, or baby teeth, first begin to appear at about 6 months of age. Between approximately age 6 and 12, these teeth are replaced by 32 **permanent teeth**. Moving from the center of the mouth toward the side, these are as follows (Figure 23.10):

- The eight **incisors**, four top and four bottom, are the sharp front teeth you use for biting into food.
- The four **cuspids** (or canines) flank the incisors and have a pointed edge (cusp) to tear up food. These fang-like teeth are superb for piercing tough or fleshy foods.
- Posterior to the cuspids are the eight **premolars** (or bicuspids), which have an overall flatter shape with two rounded cusps useful for mashing foods.
- The most posterior and largest are the 12 **molars**, which have several pointed cusps used to crush food so it is ready for swallowing. The third members of each set of three molars, top and bottom, are commonly referred to as the wisdom teeth, because their eruption is commonly delayed until early adulthood. It is not uncommon for wisdom teeth to fail to erupt; that is, they remain impacted. In these cases, the teeth are typically removed by orthodontic surgery.

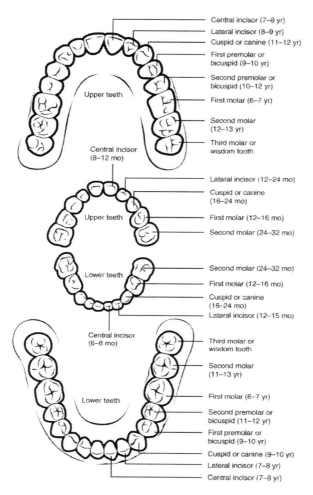

Figure 23.10 Permanent and Deciduous Teeth This figure of two human dentitions shows the arrangement of teeth in the maxilla and mandible, and the relationship between the deciduous and permanent teeth.

Anatomy of a Tooth

The teeth are secured in the alveolar processes (sockets) of the maxilla and the mandible. **Gingivae** (commonly called the gums) are soft tissues that line the alveolar processes and surround the necks of the teeth. Teeth are also held in their sockets by a connective tissue called the periodontal ligament.

The two main parts of a tooth are the **crown**, which is the portion projecting above the gum line, and the **root**, which is embedded within the maxilla and mandible. Both parts contain an inner **pulp cavity**, containing loose connective tissue through which run nerves and blood vessels. The region of the pulp cavity that runs through the root of the tooth is called the root canal. Surrounding the pulp cavity is **dentin**, a bone-like tissue. In the root of each tooth, the dentin is covered by an even harder bone-like layer called **cementum**. In the crown of each tooth, the dentin is covered by an outer layer of **enamel**, the hardest substance in the body (Figure 23.11).

Although enamel protects the underlying dentin and pulp cavity, it is still nonetheless susceptible to mechanical and chemical erosion, or what is known as tooth decay. The most common form, dental caries (cavities) develops when colonies of bacteria feeding on sugars in the mouth release acids that cause soft tissue inflammation and degradation of the calcium crystals of the enamel. The digestive functions of the mouth are summarized in Table 23.4.

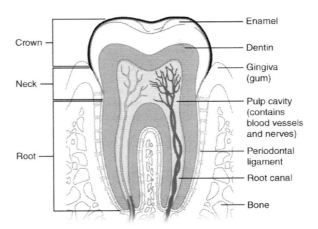

Figure 23.11 **The Structure of the Tooth** This longitudinal section through a molar in its alveolar socket shows the relationships between enamel, dentin, and pulp.

Digestive Functions of the Mouth

Structure	Action	Outcome
Lips and cheeks	Confine food between teeth	Food is chewed evenly during mastication
Salivary glands	Secrete saliva	Moisten and lubricate the lining of the mouth and pharynx Moisten, soften, and dissolve food Clean the mouth and teeth Salivary amylase breaks down starch
Tongue's extrinsic muscles	Move tongue sideways, and in and out	Manipulate food for chewing Shape food into a bolus Manipulate food for swallowing
Tongue's intrinsic muscles	Change tongue shape	Manipulate food for swallowing
Taste buds	Sense food in mouth and sense taste	Nerve impulses from taste buds are conducted to salivary nuclei in the brain stem and then to salivary glands, stimulating saliva secretion
Lingual glands	Secrete lingual lipase	Activated in the stomach Break down triglycerides into fatty acids and diglycerides
Teeth	Shred and crush food	Break down solid food into smaller particles for deglutition

Table 23.4

The Pharynx

The **pharynx** (throat) is involved in both digestion and respiration. It receives food and air from the mouth, and air from the nasal cavities. When food enters the pharynx, involuntary muscle contractions close off the air passageways.

A short tube of skeletal muscle lined with a mucous membrane, the pharynx runs from the posterior oral and nasal cavities to the opening of the esophagus and larynx. It has three subdivisions. The most superior, the nasopharynx, is involved only in breathing and speech. The other two subdivisions, the **oropharynx** and the **laryngopharynx**, are used for both breathing and digestion. The oropharynx begins inferior to the nasopharynx and is continuous below with the laryngopharynx (Figure 23.12). The inferior border of the laryngopharynx connects to the esophagus, whereas the anterior portion connects to the larynx, allowing air to flow into the bronchial tree.

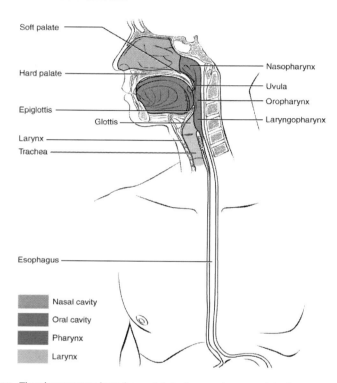

Figure 23.12 Pharynx   The pharynx runs from the nostrils to the esophagus and the larynx.

Histologically, the wall of the oropharynx is similar to that of the oral cavity. The mucosa includes a stratified squamous epithelium that is endowed with mucus-producing glands. During swallowing, the elevator skeletal muscles of the pharynx contract, raising and expanding the pharynx to receive the bolus of food. Once received, these muscles relax and the constrictor muscles of the pharynx contract, forcing the bolus into the esophagus and initiating peristalsis.

Usually during swallowing, the soft palate and uvula rise reflexively to close off the entrance to the nasopharynx. At the same time, the larynx is pulled superiorly and the cartilaginous epiglottis, its most superior structure, folds inferiorly, covering the glottis (the opening to the larynx); this process effectively blocks access to the trachea and bronchi. When the food "goes down the wrong way," it goes into the trachea. When food enters the trachea, the reaction is to cough, which usually forces the food up and out of the trachea, and back into the pharynx.

The Esophagus

The **esophagus** is a muscular tube that connects the pharynx to the stomach. It is approximately 25.4 cm (10 in) in length, located posterior to the trachea, and remains in a collapsed form when not engaged in swallowing. As you can see in

Figure 23.13, the esophagus runs a mainly straight route through the mediastinum of the thorax. To enter the abdomen, the esophagus penetrates the diaphragm through an opening called the esophageal hiatus.

Passage of Food through the Esophagus

The **upper esophageal sphincter**, which is continuous with the inferior pharyngeal constrictor, controls the movement of food from the pharynx into the esophagus. The upper two-thirds of the esophagus consists of both smooth and skeletal muscle fibers, with the latter fading out in the bottom third of the esophagus. Rhythmic waves of peristalsis, which begin in the upper esophagus, propel the bolus of food toward the stomach. Meanwhile, secretions from the esophageal mucosa lubricate the esophagus and food. Food passes from the esophagus into the stomach at the **lower esophageal sphincter** (also called the gastroesophageal or cardiac sphincter). Recall that sphincters are muscles that surround tubes and serve as valves, closing the tube when the sphincters contract and opening it when they relax. The lower esophageal sphincter relaxes to let food pass into the stomach, and then contracts to prevent stomach acids from backing up into the esophagus. Surrounding this sphincter is the muscular diaphragm, which helps close off the sphincter when no food is being swallowed. When the lower esophageal sphincter does not completely close, the stomach's contents can reflux (that is, back up into the esophagus), causing heartburn or gastroesophageal reflux disease (GERD).

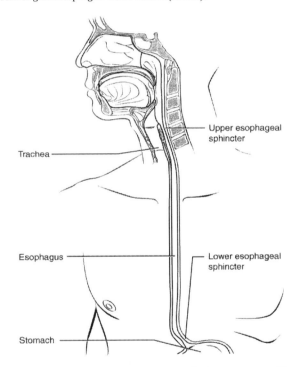

Figure 23.13 Esophagus The upper esophageal sphincter controls the movement of food from the pharynx to the esophagus. The lower esophageal sphincter controls the movement of food from the esophagus to the stomach.

Histology of the Esophagus

The mucosa of the esophagus is made up of an epithelial lining that contains non-keratinized, stratified squamous epithelium, with a layer of basal and parabasal cells. This epithelium protects against erosion from food particles. The mucosa's lamina propria contains mucus-secreting glands. The muscularis layer changes according to location: In the upper third of the esophagus, the muscularis is skeletal muscle. In the middle third, it is both skeletal and smooth muscle. In the lower third, it is smooth muscle. As mentioned previously, the most superficial layer of the esophagus is called the adventitia, not the serosa. In contrast to the stomach and intestines, the loose connective tissue of the adventitia is not covered by a fold of visceral peritoneum. The digestive functions of the esophagus are identified in Table 23.5.

Digestive Functions of the Esophagus

Action	Outcome
Upper esophageal sphincter relaxation	Allows the bolus to move from the laryngopharynx to the esophagus
Peristalsis	Propels the bolus through the esophagus
Lower esophageal sphincter relaxation	Allows the bolus to move from the esophagus into the stomach and prevents chime from entering the esophagus
Mucus secretion	Lubricates the esophagus, allowing easy passage of the bolus

Table 23.5

Deglutition

Deglutition is another word for swallowing—the movement of food from the mouth to the stomach. The entire process takes about 4 to 8 seconds for solid or semisolid food, and about 1 second for very soft food and liquids. Although this sounds quick and effortless, deglutition is, in fact, a complex process that involves both the skeletal muscle of the tongue and the muscles of the pharynx and esophagus. It is aided by the presence of mucus and saliva. There are three stages in deglutition: the voluntary phase, the pharyngeal phase, and the esophageal phase (Figure 23.14). The autonomic nervous system controls the latter two phases.

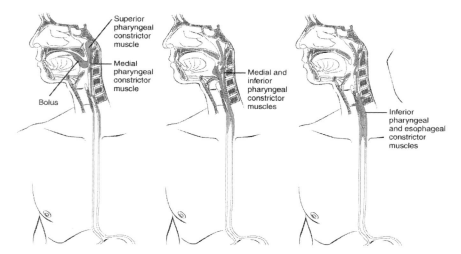

Figure 23.14 Deglutition Deglutition includes the voluntary phase and two involuntary phases: the pharyngeal phase and the esophageal phase.

The Voluntary Phase

The **voluntary phase** of deglutition (also known as the oral or buccal phase) is so called because you can control when you swallow food. In this phase, chewing has been completed and swallowing is set in motion. The tongue moves upward and backward against the palate, pushing the bolus to the back of the oral cavity and into the oropharynx. Other muscles keep the mouth closed and prevent food from falling out. At this point, the two involuntary phases of swallowing begin.

The Pharyngeal Phase

In the pharyngeal phase, stimulation of receptors in the oropharynx sends impulses to the deglutition center (a collection of neurons that controls swallowing) in the medulla oblongata. Impulses are then sent back to the uvula and soft palate, causing them to move upward and close off the nasopharynx. The laryngeal muscles also constrict to prevent aspiration of food into the trachea. At this point, deglutition apnea takes place, which means that breathing ceases for a very brief time.

Contractions of the pharyngeal constrictor muscles move the bolus through the oropharynx and laryngopharynx. Relaxation of the upper esophageal sphincter then allows food to enter the esophagus.

The Esophageal Phase

The entry of food into the esophagus marks the beginning of the esophageal phase of deglutition and the initiation of peristalsis. As in the previous phase, the complex neuromuscular actions are controlled by the medulla oblongata. Peristalsis propels the bolus through the esophagus and toward the stomach. The circular muscle layer of the muscularis contracts, pinching the esophageal wall and forcing the bolus forward. At the same time, the longitudinal muscle layer of the muscularis also contracts, shortening this area and pushing out its walls to receive the bolus. In this way, a series of contractions keeps moving food toward the stomach. When the bolus nears the stomach, distention of the esophagus initiates a short reflex relaxation of the lower esophageal sphincter that allows the bolus to pass into the stomach. During the esophageal phase, esophageal glands secrete mucus that lubricates the bolus and minimizes friction.

Watch this animation (http://openstaxcollege.org/l/swallowing) to see how swallowing is a complex process that involves the nervous system to coordinate the actions of upper respiratory and digestive activities. During which stage of swallowing is there a risk of food entering respiratory pathways and how is this risk blocked?

23.4 | The Stomach

By the end of this section, you will be able to:
- Label on a diagram the four main regions of the stomach, its curvatures, and its sphincter
- Identify the four main types of secreting cells in gastric glands, and their important products
- Explain why the stomach does not digest itself
- Describe the mechanical and chemical digestion of food entering the stomach

Although a minimal amount of carbohydrate digestion occurs in the mouth, chemical digestion really gets underway in the stomach. An expansion of the alimentary canal that lies immediately inferior to the esophagus, the stomach links the esophagus to the first part of the small intestine (the duodenum) and is relatively fixed in place at its esophageal and duodenal ends. In between, however, it can be a highly active structure, contracting and continually changing position and size. These contractions provide mechanical assistance to digestion. The empty stomach is only about the size of your fist, but can stretch to hold as much as 4 liters of food and fluid, or more than 75 times its empty volume, and then return to its resting size when empty. Although you might think that the size of a person's stomach is related to how much food that individual consumes, body weight does not correlate with stomach size. Rather, when you eat greater quantities of food—such as at holiday dinner—you stretch the stomach more than when you eat less.

Popular culture tends to refer to the stomach as the location where all digestion takes place. Of course, this is not true. An important function of the stomach is to serve as a temporary holding chamber. You can ingest a meal far more quickly than it can be digested and absorbed by the small intestine. Thus, the stomach holds food and parses only small amounts into the small intestine at a time. Foods are not processed in the order they are eaten; rather, they are mixed together with digestive juices in the stomach until they are converted into chyme, which is released into the small intestine.

As you will see in the sections that follow, the stomach plays several important roles in chemical digestion, including the continued digestion of carbohydrates and the initial digestion of proteins and triglycerides. Little if any nutrient absorption occurs in the stomach, with the exception of the negligible amount of nutrients in alcohol.

Structure

There are four main regions in the **stomach**: the cardia, fundus, body, and pylorus (Figure 23.15). The **cardia** (or cardiac region) is the point where the esophagus connects to the stomach and through which food passes into the stomach. Located inferior to the diaphragm, above and to the left of the cardia, is the dome-shaped **fundus**. Below the fundus is the **body**, the main part of the stomach. The funnel-shaped **pylorus** connects the stomach to the duodenum. The wider end of the funnel, the **pyloric antrum**, connects to the body of the stomach. The narrower end is called the **pyloric canal**, which connects to the duodenum. The smooth muscle **pyloric sphincter** is located at this latter point of connection and controls stomach emptying. In the absence of food, the stomach deflates inward, and its mucosa and submucosa fall into a large fold called a **ruga**.

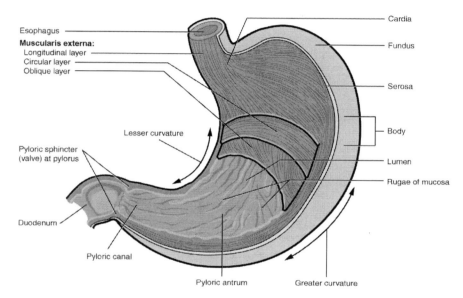

Figure 23.15 Stomach The stomach has four major regions: the cardia, fundus, body, and pylorus. The addition of an inner oblique smooth muscle layer gives the muscularis the ability to vigorously churn and mix food.

The convex lateral surface of the stomach is called the greater curvature; the concave medial border is the lesser curvature. The stomach is held in place by the lesser omentum, which extends from the liver to the lesser curvature, and the greater omentum, which runs from the greater curvature to the posterior abdominal wall.

Histology

The wall of the stomach is made of the same four layers as most of the rest of the alimentary canal, but with adaptations to the mucosa and muscularis for the unique functions of this organ. In addition to the typical circular and longitudinal smooth muscle layers, the muscularis has an inner oblique smooth muscle layer (Figure 23.16). As a result, in addition to moving food through the canal, the stomach can vigorously churn food, mechanically breaking it down into smaller particles.

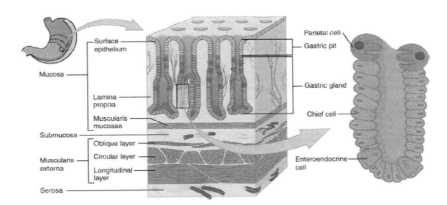

Figure 23.16 Histology of the Stomach The stomach wall is adapted for the functions of the stomach. In the epithelium, gastric pits lead to gastric glands that secrete gastric juice. The gastric glands (one gland is shown enlarged on the right) contain different types of cells that secrete a variety of enzymes, including hydrochloride acid, which activates the protein-digesting enzyme pepsin.

The stomach mucosa's epithelial lining consists only of surface mucus cells, which secrete a protective coat of alkaline mucus. A vast number of **gastric pits** dot the surface of the epithelium, giving it the appearance of a well-used pincushion, and mark the entry to each **gastric gland**, which secretes a complex digestive fluid referred to as gastric juice.

Although the walls of the gastric pits are made up primarily of mucus cells, the gastric glands are made up of different types of cells. The glands of the cardia and pylorus are composed primarily of mucus-secreting cells. Cells that make up the pyloric antrum secrete mucus and a number of hormones, including the majority of the stimulatory hormone, **gastrin**. The much larger glands of the fundus and body of the stomach, the site of most chemical digestion, produce most of the gastric secretions. These glands are made up of a variety of secretory cells. These include parietal cells, chief cells, mucous neck cells, and enteroendocrine cells.

Parietal cells—Located primarily in the middle region of the gastric glands are **parietal cells**, which are among the most highly differentiated of the body's epithelial cells. These relatively large cells produce both **hydrochloric acid (HCl)** and **intrinsic factor**. HCl is responsible for the high acidity (pH 1.5 to 3.5) of the stomach contents and is needed to activate the protein-digesting enzyme, pepsin. The acidity also kills much of the bacteria you ingest with food and helps to denature proteins, making them more available for enzymatic digestion. Intrinsic factor is a glycoprotein necessary for the absorption of vitamin B_{12} in the small intestine.

Chief cells—Located primarily in the basal regions of gastric glands are **chief cells**, which secrete **pepsinogen**, the inactive proenzyme form of pepsin. HCl is necessary for the conversion of pepsinogen to pepsin.

Mucous neck cells—Gastric glands in the upper part of the stomach contain **mucous neck cells** that secrete thin, acidic mucus that is much different from the mucus secreted by the goblet cells of the surface epithelium. The role of this mucus is not currently known.

Enteroendocrine cells—Finally, **enteroendocrine cells** found in the gastric glands secrete various hormones into the interstitial fluid of the lamina propria. These include gastrin, which is released mainly by enteroendocrine **G cells**.

Table 23.6 describes the digestive functions of important hormones secreted by the stomach.

Interactive LINK

Watch this animation (http://openstaxcollege.org/l/stomach1) that depicts the structure of the stomach and how this structure functions in the initiation of protein digestion. This view of the stomach shows the characteristic rugae. What is the function of these rugae?

Hormones Secreted by the Stomach

Hormone	Production site	Production stimulus	Target organ	Action
Gastrin	Stomach mucosa, mainly G cells of the pyloric antrum	Presence of peptides and amino acids in stomach	Stomach	Increases secretion by gastric glands; promotes gastric emptying
Gastrin	Stomach mucosa, mainly G cells of the pyloric antrum	Presence of peptides and amino acids in stomach	Small intestine	Promotes intestinal muscle contraction
Gastrin	Stomach mucosa, mainly G cells of the pyloric antrum	Presence of peptides and amino acids in stomach	Ileocecal valve	Relaxes valve
Gastrin	Stomach mucosa, mainly G cells of the pyloric antrum	Presence of peptides and amino acids in stomach	Large intestine	Triggers mass movements
Ghrelin	Stomach mucosa, mainly fundus	Fasting state (levels increase just prior to meals)	Hypothalamus	Regulates food intake, primarily by stimulating hunger and satiety
Histamine	Stomach mucosa	Presence of food in the stomach	Stomach	Stimulates parietal cells to release HCl
Serotonin	Stomach mucosa	Presence of food in the stomach	Stomach	Contracts stomach muscle
Somatostatin	Mucosa of stomach, especially pyloric antrum; also duodenum	Presence of food in the stomach; sympathetic axon stimulation	Stomach	Restricts all gastric secretions, gastric motility, and emptying
Somatostatin	Mucosa of stomach, especially pyloric antrum; also duodenum	Presence of food in the stomach; sympathetic axon stimulation	Pancreas	Restricts pancreatic secretions
Somatostatin	Mucosa of stomach, especially pyloric antrum; also duodenum	Presence of food in the stomach; sympathetic axon stimulation	Small intestine	Reduces intestinal absorption by reducing blood flow

Table 23.6

Gastric Secretion

The secretion of gastric juice is controlled by both nerves and hormones. Stimuli in the brain, stomach, and small intestine activate or inhibit gastric juice production. This is why the three phases of gastric secretion are called the cephalic, gastric, and intestinal phases (Figure 23.17). However, once gastric secretion begins, all three phases can occur simultaneously.

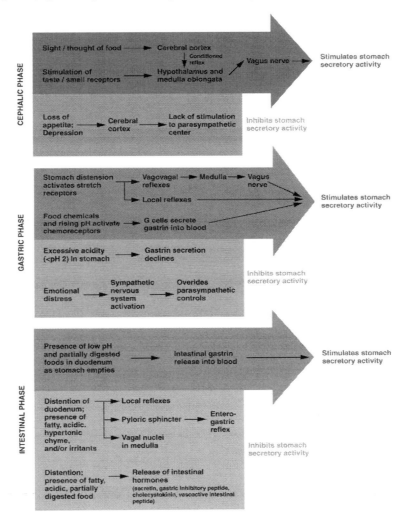

Figure 23.17 The Three Phases of Gastric Secretion Gastric secretion occurs in three phases: cephalic, gastric, and intestinal. During each phase, the secretion of gastric juice can be stimulated or inhibited.

The **cephalic phase** (reflex phase) of gastric secretion, which is relatively brief, takes place before food enters the stomach. The smell, taste, sight, or thought of food triggers this phase. For example, when you bring a piece of sushi to your lips, impulses from receptors in your taste buds or the nose are relayed to your brain, which returns signals that increase gastric secretion to prepare your stomach for digestion. This enhanced secretion is a conditioned reflex, meaning it occurs only if you like or want a particular food. Depression and loss of appetite can suppress the cephalic reflex.

The **gastric phase** of secretion lasts 3 to 4 hours, and is set in motion by local neural and hormonal mechanisms triggered by the entry of food into the stomach. For example, when your sushi reaches the stomach, it creates distention that activates the stretch receptors. This stimulates parasympathetic neurons to release acetylcholine, which then provokes increased secretion of gastric juice. Partially digested proteins, caffeine, and rising pH stimulate the release of gastrin from enteroendocrine G cells, which in turn induces parietal cells to increase their production of HCl, which is needed to create an acidic environment for the conversion of pepsinogen to pepsin, and protein digestion. Additionally, the release of gastrin activates vigorous smooth muscle contractions. However, it should be noted that the stomach does have a natural means of avoiding excessive acid secretion and potential heartburn. Whenever pH levels drop too low, cells in the stomach react by suspending HCl secretion and increasing mucous secretions.

The **intestinal phase** of gastric secretion has both excitatory and inhibitory elements. The duodenum has a major role in regulating the stomach and its emptying. When partially digested food fills the duodenum, intestinal mucosal cells release a hormone called intestinal (enteric) gastrin, which further excites gastric juice secretion. This stimulatory activity is brief, however, because when the intestine distends with chyme, the enterogastric reflex inhibits secretion. One of the effects of this reflex is to close the pyloric sphincter, which blocks additional chyme from entering the duodenum.

The Mucosal Barrier

The mucosa of the stomach is exposed to the highly corrosive acidity of gastric juice. Gastric enzymes that can digest protein can also digest the stomach itself. The stomach is protected from self-digestion by the **mucosal barrier**. This barrier has several components. First, the stomach wall is covered by a thick coating of bicarbonate-rich mucus. This mucus forms a physical barrier, and its bicarbonate ions neutralize acid. Second, the epithelial cells of the stomach's mucosa meet at tight junctions, which block gastric juice from penetrating the underlying tissue layers. Finally, stem cells located where gastric glands join the gastric pits quickly replace damaged epithelial mucosal cells, when the epithelial cells are shed. In fact, the surface epithelium of the stomach is completely replaced every 3 to 6 days.

Ulcers: When the Mucosal Barrier Breaks Down

As effective as the mucosal barrier is, it is not a "fail-safe" mechanism. Sometimes, gastric juice eats away at the superficial lining of the stomach mucosa, creating erosions, which mostly heal on their own. Deeper and larger erosions are called ulcers.

Why does the mucosal barrier break down? A number of factors can interfere with its ability to protect the stomach lining. The majority of all ulcers are caused by either excessive intake of non-steroidal anti-inflammatory drugs (NSAIDs), including aspirin, or *Helicobacter pylori* infection.

Antacids help relieve symptoms of ulcers such as "burning" pain and indigestion. When ulcers are caused by NSAID use, switching to other classes of pain relievers allows healing. When caused by *H. pylori* infection, antibiotics are effective.

A potential complication of ulcers is perforation: Perforated ulcers create a hole in the stomach wall, resulting in peritonitis (inflammation of the peritoneum). These ulcers must be repaired surgically.

Digestive Functions of the Stomach

The stomach participates in virtually all the digestive activities with the exception of ingestion and defecation. Although almost all absorption takes place in the small intestine, the stomach does absorb some nonpolar substances, such as alcohol and aspirin.

Mechanical Digestion

Within a few moments after food after enters your stomach, mixing waves begin to occur at intervals of approximately 20 seconds. A **mixing wave** is a unique type of peristalsis that mixes and softens the food with gastric juices to create chyme. The initial mixing waves are relatively gentle, but these are followed by more intense waves, starting at the body of the stomach and increasing in force as they reach the pylorus. It is fair to say that long before your sushi exits through the pyloric sphincter, it bears little resemblance to the sushi you ate.

The pylorus, which holds around 30 mL (1 fluid ounce) of chyme, acts as a filter, permitting only liquids and small food particles to pass through the mostly, but not fully, closed pyloric sphincter. In a process called **gastric emptying**, rhythmic mixing waves force about 3 mL of chyme at a time through the pyloric sphincter and into the duodenum. Release of a greater amount of chyme at one time would overwhelm the capacity of the small intestine to handle it. The rest of the chyme is pushed back into the body of the stomach, where it continues mixing. This process is repeated when the next mixing waves force more chyme into the duodenum.

Gastric emptying is regulated by both the stomach and the duodenum. The presence of chyme in the duodenum activates receptors that inhibit gastric secretion. This prevents additional chyme from being released by the stomach before the duodenum is ready to process it.

Chemical Digestion

The fundus plays an important role, because it stores both undigested food and gases that are released during the process of chemical digestion. Food may sit in the fundus of the stomach for a while before being mixed with the chyme. While the food is in the fundus, the digestive activities of salivary amylase continue until the food begins mixing with the acidic chyme. Ultimately, mixing waves incorporate this food with the chyme, the acidity of which inactivates salivary amylase and activates lingual lipase. Lingual lipase then begins breaking down triglycerides into free fatty acids, and mono- and diglycerides.

The breakdown of protein begins in the stomach through the actions of HCl and the enzyme pepsin. During infancy, gastric glands also produce rennin, an enzyme that helps digest milk protein.

Its numerous digestive functions notwithstanding, there is only one stomach function necessary to life: the production of intrinsic factor. The intestinal absorption of vitamin B_{12}, which is necessary for both the production of mature red blood cells and normal neurological functioning, cannot occur without intrinsic factor. People who undergo total gastrectomy (stomach removal)—for life-threatening stomach cancer, for example—can survive with minimal digestive dysfunction if they receive vitamin B_{12} injections.

The contents of the stomach are completely emptied into the duodenum within 2 to 4 hours after you eat a meal. Different types of food take different amounts of time to process. Foods heavy in carbohydrates empty fastest, followed by high-protein foods. Meals with a high triglyceride content remain in the stomach the longest. Since enzymes in the small intestine digest fats slowly, food can stay in the stomach for 6 hours or longer when the duodenum is processing fatty chyme. However, note that this is still a fraction of the 24 to 72 hours that full digestion typically takes from start to finish.

23.5 | The Small and Large Intestines

By the end of this section, you will be able to:
- Compare and contrast the location and gross anatomy of the small and large intestines
- Identify three main adaptations of the small intestine wall that increase its absorptive capacity
- Describe the mechanical and chemical digestion of chyme upon its release into the small intestine
- List three features unique to the wall of the large intestine and identify their contributions to its function
- Identify the beneficial roles of the bacterial flora in digestive system functioning
- Trace the pathway of food waste from its point of entry into the large intestine through its exit from the body as feces

The word intestine is derived from a Latin root meaning "internal," and indeed, the two organs together nearly fill the interior of the abdominal cavity. In addition, called the small and large bowel, or colloquially the "guts," they constitute the greatest mass and length of the alimentary canal and, with the exception of ingestion, perform all digestive system functions.

The Small Intestine

Chyme released from the stomach enters the **small intestine**, which is the primary digestive organ in the body. Not only is this where most digestion occurs, it is also where practically all absorption occurs. The longest part of the alimentary canal, the small intestine is about 3.05 meters (10 feet) long in a living person (but about twice as long in a cadaver due to the loss of muscle tone). Since this makes it about five times longer than the large intestine, you might wonder why it is called "small." In fact, its name derives from its relatively smaller diameter of only about 2.54 cm (1 in), compared with 7.62 cm (3 in) for the large intestine. As we'll see shortly, in addition to its length, the folds and projections of the lining of the small intestine work to give it an enormous surface area, which is approximately 200 m^2, more than 100 times the surface area of your skin. This large surface area is necessary for complex processes of digestion and absorption that occur within it.

Structure

The coiled tube of the small intestine is subdivided into three regions. From proximal (at the stomach) to distal, these are the duodenum, jejunum, and ileum (Figure 23.18).

The shortest region is the 25.4-cm (10-in) **duodenum**, which begins at the pyloric sphincter. Just past the pyloric sphincter, it bends posteriorly behind the peritoneum, becoming retroperitoneal, and then makes a C-shaped curve around the head of the pancreas before ascending anteriorly again to return to the peritoneal cavity and join the jejunum. The duodenum can therefore be subdivided into four segments: the superior, descending, horizontal, and ascending duodenum.

Of particular interest is the **hepatopancreatic ampulla** (ampulla of Vater). Located in the duodenal wall, the ampulla marks the transition from the anterior portion of the alimentary canal to the mid-region, and is where the bile duct (through which bile passes from the liver) and the **main pancreatic duct** (through which pancreatic juice passes from the pancreas) join. This ampulla opens into the duodenum at a tiny volcano-shaped structure called the **major duodenal papilla**. The **hepatopancreatic sphincter** (sphincter of Oddi) regulates the flow of both bile and pancreatic juice from the ampulla into the duodenum.

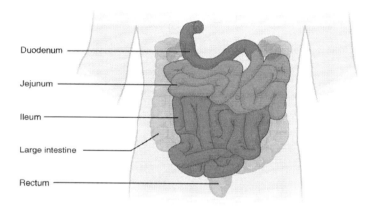

Figure 23.18 Small Intestine The three regions of the small intestine are the duodenum, jejunum, and ileum.

The **jejunum** is about 0.9 meters (3 feet) long (in life) and runs from the duodenum to the ileum. Jejunum means "empty" in Latin and supposedly was so named by the ancient Greeks who noticed it was always empty at death. No clear demarcation exists between the jejunum and the final segment of the small intestine, the ileum.

The **ileum** is the longest part of the small intestine, measuring about 1.8 meters (6 feet) in length. It is thicker, more vascular, and has more developed mucosal folds than the jejunum. The ileum joins the cecum, the first portion of the large intestine, at the **ileocecal sphincter** (or valve). The jejunum and ileum are tethered to the posterior abdominal wall by the mesentery. The large intestine frames these three parts of the small intestine.

Parasympathetic nerve fibers from the vagus nerve and sympathetic nerve fibers from the thoracic splanchnic nerve provide extrinsic innervation to the small intestine. The superior mesenteric artery is its main arterial supply. Veins run parallel to the arteries and drain into the superior mesenteric vein. Nutrient-rich blood from the small intestine is then carried to the liver via the hepatic portal vein.

Histology

The wall of the small intestine is composed of the same four layers typically present in the alimentary system. However, three features of the mucosa and submucosa are unique. These features, which increase the absorptive surface area of the small intestine more than 600-fold, include circular folds, villi, and microvilli (Figure 23.19). These adaptations are most abundant in the proximal two-thirds of the small intestine, where the majority of absorption occurs.

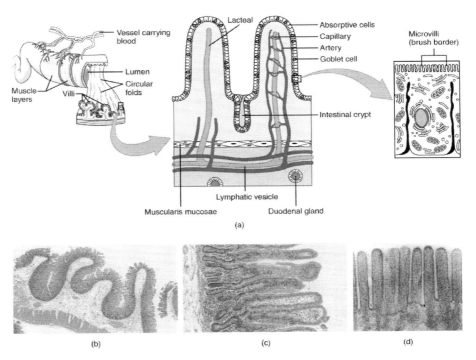

Figure 23.19 Histology of the Small Intestine (a) The absorptive surface of the small intestine is vastly enlarged by the presence of circular folds, villi, and microvilli. (b) Micrograph of the circular folds. (c) Micrograph of the villi. (d) Electron micrograph of the microvilli. From left to right, LM × 56, LM × 508, EM × 196,000. (credit b-d: Micrograph provided by the Regents of University of Michigan Medical School © 2012)

Circular folds

Also called a plica circulare, a **circular fold** is a deep ridge in the mucosa and submucosa. Beginning near the proximal part of the duodenum and ending near the middle of the ileum, these folds facilitate absorption. Their shape causes the chyme to spiral, rather than move in a straight line, through the small intestine. Spiraling slows the movement of chyme and provides the time needed for nutrients to be fully absorbed.

Villi

Within the circular folds are small (0.5–1 mm long) hairlike vascularized projections called **villi** (singular = villus) that give the mucosa a furry texture. There are about 20 to 40 villi per square millimeter, increasing the surface area of the epithelium tremendously. The mucosal epithelium, primarily composed of absorptive cells, covers the villi. In addition to muscle and connective tissue to support its structure, each villus contains a capillary bed composed of one arteriole and one venule, as well as a lymphatic capillary called a **lacteal**. The breakdown products of carbohydrates and proteins (sugars and amino acids) can enter the bloodstream directly, but lipid breakdown products are absorbed by the lacteals and transported to the bloodstream via the lymphatic system.

Microvilli

As their name suggests, **microvilli** (singular = microvillus) are much smaller (1 μm) than villi. They are cylindrical apical surface extensions of the plasma membrane of the mucosa's epithelial cells, and are supported by microfilaments within those cells. Although their small size makes it difficult to see each microvillus, their combined microscopic appearance suggests a mass of bristles, which is termed the **brush border**. Fixed to the surface of the microvilli membranes are enzymes that finish digesting carbohydrates and proteins. There are an estimated 200 million microvilli per square millimeter of small intestine, greatly expanding the surface area of the plasma membrane and thus greatly enhancing absorption.

Intestinal Glands

In addition to the three specialized absorptive features just discussed, the mucosa between the villi is dotted with deep crevices that each lead into a tubular **intestinal gland** (crypt of Lieberkühn), which is formed by cells that line the crevices (see Figure 23.19). These produce **intestinal juice**, a slightly alkaline (pH 7.4 to 7.8) mixture of water and mucus. Each day, about 0.95 to 1.9 liters (1 to 2 quarts) are secreted in response to the distention of the small intestine or the irritating effects of chyme on the intestinal mucosa.

The submucosa of the duodenum is the only site of the complex mucus-secreting **duodenal glands** (Brunner's glands), which produce a bicarbonate-rich alkaline mucus that buffers the acidic chyme as it enters from the stomach.

The roles of the cells in the small intestinal mucosa are detailed in Table 23.7.

Cells of the Small Intestinal Mucosa

Cell type	Location in the mucosa	Function
Absorptive	Epithelium/intestinal glands	Digestion and absorption of nutrients in chyme
Goblet	Epithelium/intestinal glands	Secretion of mucus
Paneth	Intestinal glands	Secretion of the bactericidal enzyme lysozyme; phagocytosis
G cells	Intestinal glands of duodenum	Secretion of the hormone intestinal gastrin
I cells	Intestinal glands of duodenum	Secretion of the hormone cholecystokinin, which stimulates release of pancreatic juices and bile
K cells	Intestinal glands	Secretion of the hormone glucose-dependent insulinotropic peptide, which stimulates the release of insulin
M cells	Intestinal glands of duodenum and jejunum	Secretion of the hormone motilin, which accelerates gastric emptying, stimulates intestinal peristalsis, and stimulates the production of pepsin
S cells	Intestinal glands	Secretion of the hormone secretin

Table 23.7

Intestinal MALT

The lamina propria of the small intestine mucosa is studded with quite a bit of MALT. In addition to solitary lymphatic nodules, aggregations of intestinal MALT, which are typically referred to as Peyer's patches, are concentrated in the distal ileum, and serve to keep bacteria from entering the bloodstream. Peyer's patches are most prominent in young people and become less distinct as you age, which coincides with the general activity of our immune system.

Interactive LINK

Watch this animation (http://openstaxcollege.org/l/sintestine) that depicts the structure of the small intestine, and, in particular, the villi. Epithelial cells continue the digestion and absorption of nutrients and transport these nutrients to the lymphatic and circulatory systems. In the small intestine, the products of food digestion are absorbed by different structures in the villi. Which structure absorbs and transports fats?

Mechanical Digestion in the Small Intestine

The movement of intestinal smooth muscles includes both segmentation and a form of peristalsis called migrating motility complexes. The kind of peristaltic mixing waves seen in the stomach are not observed here.

If you could see into the small intestine when it was going through segmentation, it would look as if the contents were being shoved incrementally back and forth, as the rings of smooth muscle repeatedly contract and then relax. Segmentation in the small intestine does not force chyme through the tract. Instead, it combines the chyme with digestive juices and pushes food particles against the mucosa to be absorbed. The duodenum is where the most rapid segmentation occurs, at a rate of about 12 times per minute. In the ileum, segmentations are only about eight times per minute (Figure 23.20).

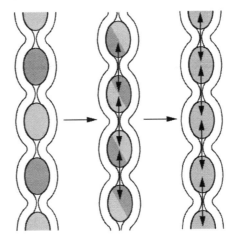

Figure 23.20 Segmentation Segmentation separates chyme and then pushes it back together, mixing it and providing time for digestion and absorption.

When most of the chyme has been absorbed, the small intestinal wall becomes less distended. At this point, the localized segmentation process is replaced by transport movements. The duodenal mucosa secretes the hormone **motilin**, which initiates peristalsis in the form of a **migrating motility complex**. These complexes, which begin in the duodenum, force chyme through a short section of the small intestine and then stop. The next contraction begins a little bit farther down than the first, forces chyme a bit farther through the small intestine, then stops. These complexes move slowly down the small intestine, forcing chyme on the way, taking around 90 to 120 minutes to finally reach the end of the ileum. At this point, the process is repeated, starting in the duodenum.

The ileocecal valve, a sphincter, is usually in a constricted state, but when motility in the ileum increases, this sphincter relaxes, allowing food residue to enter the first portion of the large intestine, the cecum. Relaxation of the ileocecal sphincter is controlled by both nerves and hormones. First, digestive activity in the stomach provokes the **gastroileal reflex**, which increases the force of ileal segmentation. Second, the stomach releases the hormone gastrin, which enhances ileal motility, thus relaxing the ileocecal sphincter. After chyme passes through, backward pressure helps close the sphincter, preventing backflow into the ileum. Because of this reflex, your lunch is completely emptied from your stomach and small intestine by the time you eat your dinner. It takes about 3 to 5 hours for all chyme to leave the small intestine.

Chemical Digestion in the Small Intestine

The digestion of proteins and carbohydrates, which partially occurs in the stomach, is completed in the small intestine with the aid of intestinal and pancreatic juices. Lipids arrive in the intestine largely undigested, so much of the focus here is on lipid digestion, which is facilitated by bile and the enzyme pancreatic lipase.

Moreover, intestinal juice combines with pancreatic juice to provide a liquid medium that facilitates absorption. The intestine is also where most water is absorbed, via osmosis. The small intestine's absorptive cells also synthesize digestive enzymes and then place them in the plasma membranes of the microvilli. This distinguishes the small intestine from the stomach; that is, enzymatic digestion occurs not only in the lumen, but also on the luminal surfaces of the mucosal cells.

For optimal chemical digestion, chyme must be delivered from the stomach slowly and in small amounts. This is because chyme from the stomach is typically hypertonic, and if large quantities were forced all at once into the small intestine, the resulting osmotic water loss from the blood into the intestinal lumen would result in potentially life-threatening low blood volume. In addition, continued digestion requires an upward adjustment of the low pH of stomach chyme, along with rigorous mixing of the chyme with bile and pancreatic juices. Both processes take time, so the pumping action of the pylorus must be carefully controlled to prevent the duodenum from being overwhelmed with chyme.

Small Intestine: Lactose Intolerance

Lactose intolerance is a condition characterized by indigestion caused by dairy products. It occurs when the absorptive cells of the small intestine do not produce enough lactase, the enzyme that digests the milk sugar lactose. In most mammals, lactose intolerance increases with age. In contrast, some human populations, most notably Caucasians, are able to maintain the ability to produce lactase as adults.

In people with lactose intolerance, the lactose in chyme is not digested. Bacteria in the large intestine ferment the undigested lactose, a process that produces gas. In addition to gas, symptoms include abdominal cramps, bloating, and diarrhea. Symptom severity ranges from mild discomfort to severe pain; however, symptoms resolve once the lactose is eliminated in feces.

The hydrogen breath test is used to help diagnose lactose intolerance. Lactose-tolerant people have very little hydrogen in their breath. Those with lactose intolerance exhale hydrogen, which is one of the gases produced by the bacterial fermentation of lactose in the colon. After the hydrogen is absorbed from the intestine, it is transported through blood vessels into the lungs. There are a number of lactose-free dairy products available in grocery stores. In addition, dietary supplements are available. Taken with food, they provide lactase to help digest lactose.

The Large Intestine

The **large intestine** is the terminal part of the alimentary canal. The primary function of this organ is to finish absorption of nutrients and water, synthesize certain vitamins, form feces, and eliminate feces from the body.

Structure

The large intestine runs from the appendix to the anus. It frames the small intestine on three sides. Despite its being about one-half as long as the small intestine, it is called large because it is more than twice the diameter of the small intestine, about 3 inches.

Subdivisions

The large intestine is subdivided into four main regions: the cecum, the colon, the rectum, and the anus. The ileocecal valve, located at the opening between the ileum and the large intestine, controls the flow of chyme from the small intestine to the large intestine.

Cecum

The first part of the large intestine is the **cecum**, a sac-like structure that is suspended inferior to the ileocecal valve. It is about 6 cm (2.4 in) long, receives the contents of the ileum, and continues the absorption of water and salts. The **appendix** (or vermiform appendix) is a winding tube that attaches to the cecum. Although the 7.6-cm (3-in) long appendix contains lymphoid tissue, suggesting an immunologic function, this organ is generally considered vestigial. However, at least one recent report postulates a survival advantage conferred by the appendix: In diarrheal illness, the appendix may serve as a bacterial reservoir to repopulate the enteric bacteria for those surviving the initial phases of the illness. Moreover, its twisted anatomy provides a haven for the accumulation and multiplication of enteric bacteria. The **mesoappendix**, the mesentery of the appendix, tethers it to the mesentery of the ileum.

Colon

The cecum blends seamlessly with the **colon**. Upon entering the colon, the food residue first travels up the **ascending colon** on the right side of the abdomen. At the inferior surface of the liver, the colon bends to form the **right colic flexure** (hepatic flexure) and becomes the **transverse colon**. The region defined as hindgut begins with the last third of the transverse colon and continues on. Food residue passing through the transverse colon travels across to the left side of the abdomen, where the colon angles sharply immediately inferior to the spleen, at the **left colic flexure** (splenic flexure). From there, food residue passes through the **descending colon**, which runs down the left side of the posterior abdominal wall. After entering the pelvis inferiorly, it becomes the s-shaped **sigmoid colon**, which extends medially to the midline (Figure 23.21). The ascending and descending colon, and the rectum (discussed next) are located in the retroperitoneum. The transverse and sigmoid colon are tethered to the posterior abdominal wall by the mesocolon.

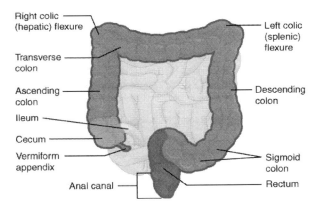

Figure 23.21 Large Intestine The large intestine includes the cecum, colon, and rectum.

Colorectal Cancer

Each year, approximately 140,000 Americans are diagnosed with colorectal cancer, and another 49,000 die from it, making it one of the most deadly malignancies. People with a family history of colorectal cancer are at increased risk. Smoking, excessive alcohol consumption, and a diet high in animal fat and protein also increase the risk. Despite popular opinion to the contrary, studies support the conclusion that dietary fiber and calcium do not reduce the risk of colorectal cancer.

Colorectal cancer may be signaled by constipation or diarrhea, cramping, abdominal pain, and rectal bleeding. Bleeding from the rectum may be either obvious or occult (hidden in feces). Since most colon cancers arise from benign mucosal growths called polyps, cancer prevention is focused on identifying these polyps. The colonoscopy is both diagnostic and therapeutic. Colonoscopy not only allows identification of precancerous polyps, the procedure also enables them to be removed before they become malignant. Screening for fecal occult blood tests and colonoscopy is recommended for those over 50 years of age.

Rectum

Food residue leaving the sigmoid colon enters the **rectum** in the pelvis, near the third sacral vertebra. The final 20.3 cm (8 in) of the alimentary canal, the rectum extends anterior to the sacrum and coccyx. Even though rectum is Latin for "straight," this structure follows the curved contour of the sacrum and has three lateral bends that create a trio of internal transverse folds called the **rectal valves**. These valves help separate the feces from gas to prevent the simultaneous passage of feces and gas.

Anal Canal

Finally, food residue reaches the last part of the large intestine, the **anal canal**, which is located in the perineum, completely outside of the abdominopelvic cavity. This 3.8–5 cm (1.5–2 in) long structure opens to the exterior of the body at the anus. The anal canal includes two sphincters. The **internal anal sphincter** is made of smooth muscle, and its contractions are involuntary. The **external anal sphincter** is made of skeletal muscle, which is under voluntary control. Except when defecating, both usually remain closed.

Histology

There are several notable differences between the walls of the large and small intestines (Figure 23.22). For example, few enzyme-secreting cells are found in the wall of the large intestine, and there are no circular folds or villi. Other than in the anal canal, the mucosa of the colon is simple columnar epithelium made mostly of enterocytes (absorptive cells) and goblet cells. In addition, the wall of the large intestine has far more intestinal glands, which contain a vast population of enterocytes and goblet cells. These goblet cells secrete mucus that eases the movement of feces and protects the intestine from the effects of the acids and gases produced by enteric bacteria. The enterocytes absorb water and salts as well as vitamins produced by your intestinal bacteria.

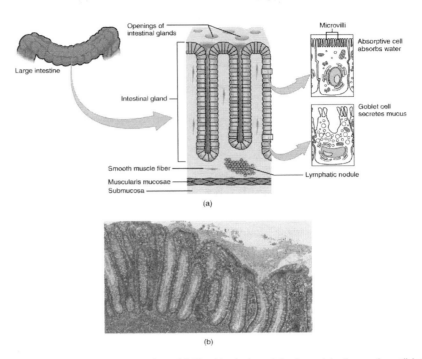

Figure 23.22 Histology of the large Intestine (a) The histologies of the large intestine and small intestine (not shown) are adapted for the digestive functions of each organ. (b) This micrograph shows the colon's simple columnar epithelium and goblet cells. LM × 464. (credit b: Micrograph provided by the Regents of University of Michigan Medical School © 2012)

Anatomy

Three features are unique to the large intestine: teniae coli, haustra, and epiploic appendages (Figure 23.23). The **teniae coli** are three bands of smooth muscle that make up the longitudinal muscle layer of the muscularis of the large intestine, except at its terminal end. Tonic contractions of the teniae coli bunch up the colon into a succession of pouches called **haustra** (singular = hostrum), which are responsible for the wrinkled appearance of the colon. Attached to the teniae coli are small, fat-filled sacs of visceral peritoneum called **epiploic appendages**. The purpose of these is unknown. Although the rectum and anal canal have neither teniae coli nor haustra, they do have well-developed layers of muscularis that create the strong contractions needed for defecation.

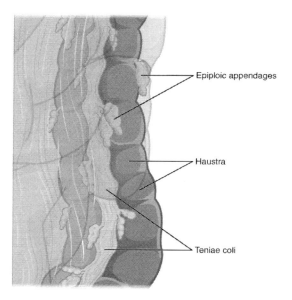

Figure 23.23 Teniae Coli, Haustra, and Epiploic Appendages

The stratified squamous epithelial mucosa of the anal canal connects to the skin on the outside of the anus. This mucosa varies considerably from that of the rest of the colon to accommodate the high level of abrasion as feces pass through. The anal canal's mucous membrane is organized into longitudinal folds, each called an **anal column**, which house a grid of arteries and veins. Two superficial venous plexuses are found in the anal canal: one within the anal columns and one at the anus.

Depressions between the anal columns, each called an **anal sinus**, secrete mucus that facilitates defecation. The **pectinate line** (or dentate line) is a horizontal, jagged band that runs circumferentially just below the level of the anal sinuses, and represents the junction between the hindgut and external skin. The mucosa above this line is fairly insensitive, whereas the area below is very sensitive. The resulting difference in pain threshold is due to the fact that the upper region is innervated by visceral sensory fibers, and the lower region is innervated by somatic sensory fibers.

Bacterial Flora

Most bacteria that enter the alimentary canal are killed by lysozyme, defensins, HCl, or protein-digesting enzymes. However, trillions of bacteria live within the large intestine and are referred to as the **bacterial flora**. Most of the more than 700 species of these bacteria are nonpathogenic commensal organisms that cause no harm as long as they stay in the gut lumen. In fact, many facilitate chemical digestion and absorption, and some synthesize certain vitamins, mainly biotin, pantothenic acid, and vitamin K. Some are linked to increased immune response. A refined system prevents these bacteria from crossing the mucosal barrier. First, peptidoglycan, a component of bacterial cell walls, activates the release of chemicals by the mucosa's epithelial cells, which draft immune cells, especially dendritic cells, into the mucosa. Dendritic cells open the tight junctions between epithelial cells and extend probes into the lumen to evaluate the microbial antigens. The dendritic cells with antigens then travel to neighboring lymphoid follicles in the mucosa where T cells inspect for antigens. This process triggers an IgA-mediated response, if warranted, in the lumen that blocks the commensal organisms from infiltrating the mucosa and setting off a far greater, widespread systematic reaction.

Digestive Functions of the Large Intestine

The residue of chyme that enters the large intestine contains few nutrients except water, which is reabsorbed as the residue lingers in the large intestine, typically for 12 to 24 hours. Thus, it may not surprise you that the large intestine can be completely removed without significantly affecting digestive functioning. For example, in severe cases of inflammatory bowel disease, the large intestine can be removed by a procedure known as a colectomy. Often, a new fecal pouch can be crafted from the small intestine and sutured to the anus, but if not, an ileostomy can be created by bringing the distal ileum through the abdominal wall, allowing the watery chyme to be collected in a bag-like adhesive appliance.

Mechanical Digestion

In the large intestine, mechanical digestion begins when chyme moves from the ileum into the cecum, an activity regulated by the ileocecal sphincter. Right after you eat, peristalsis in the ileum forces chyme into the cecum. When the cecum is distended with chyme, contractions of the ileocecal sphincter strengthen. Once chyme enters the cecum, colon movements begin.

Mechanical digestion in the large intestine includes a combination of three types of movements. The presence of food residues in the colon stimulates a slow-moving **haustral contraction**. This type of movement involves sluggish segmentation, primarily in the transverse and descending colons. When a haustrum is distended with chyme, its muscle contracts, pushing the residue into the next haustrum. These contractions occur about every 30 minutes, and each last about 1 minute. These movements also mix the food residue, which helps the large intestine absorb water. The second type of movement is peristalsis, which, in the large intestine, is slower than in the more proximal portions of the alimentary canal. The third type is a **mass movement**. These strong waves start midway through the transverse colon and quickly force the contents toward the rectum. Mass movements usually occur three or four times per day, either while you eat or immediately afterward. Distension in the stomach and the breakdown products of digestion in the small intestine provoke the **gastrocolic reflex**, which increases motility, including mass movements, in the colon. Fiber in the diet both softens the stool and increases the power of colonic contractions, optimizing the activities of the colon.

Chemical Digestion

Although the glands of the large intestine secrete mucus, they do not secrete digestive enzymes. Therefore, chemical digestion in the large intestine occurs exclusively because of bacteria in the lumen of the colon. Through the process of **saccharolytic fermentation**, bacteria break down some of the remaining carbohydrates. This results in the discharge of hydrogen, carbon dioxide, and methane gases that create **flatus** (gas) in the colon; flatulence is excessive flatus. Each day, up to 1500 mL of flatus is produced in the colon. More is produced when you eat foods such as beans, which are rich in otherwise indigestible sugars and complex carbohydrates like soluble dietary fiber.

Absorption, Feces Formation, and Defecation

The small intestine absorbs about 90 percent of the water you ingest (either as liquid or within solid food). The large intestine absorbs most of the remaining water, a process that converts the liquid chyme residue into semisolid **feces** ("stool"). Feces is composed of undigested food residues, unabsorbed digested substances, millions of bacteria, old epithelial cells from the GI mucosa, inorganic salts, and enough water to let it pass smoothly out of the body. Of every 500 mL (17 ounces) of food residue that enters the cecum each day, about 150 mL (5 ounces) become feces.

Feces are eliminated through contractions of the rectal muscles. You help this process by a voluntary procedure called **Valsalva's maneuver**, in which you increase intra-abdominal pressure by contracting your diaphragm and abdominal wall muscles, and closing your glottis.

The process of defecation begins when mass movements force feces from the colon into the rectum, stretching the rectal wall and provoking the defecation reflex, which eliminates feces from the rectum. This parasympathetic reflex is mediated by the spinal cord. It contracts the sigmoid colon and rectum, relaxes the internal anal sphincter, and initially contracts the external anal sphincter. The presence of feces in the anal canal sends a signal to the brain, which gives you the choice of voluntarily opening the external anal sphincter (defecating) or keeping it temporarily closed. If you decide to delay defecation, it takes a few seconds for the reflex contractions to stop and the rectal walls to relax. The next mass movement will trigger additional defecation reflexes until you defecate.

If defecation is delayed for an extended time, additional water is absorbed, making the feces firmer and potentially leading to constipation. On the other hand, if the waste matter moves too quickly through the intestines, not enough water is absorbed, and diarrhea can result. This can be caused by the ingestion of foodborne pathogens. In general, diet, health, and stress determine the frequency of bowel movements. The number of bowel movements varies greatly between individuals, ranging from two or three per day to three or four per week.

Interactive Link

By watching this animation (http://openstaxcollege.org/l/foodgroups) you will see that for the various food groups—proteins, fats, and carbohydrates—digestion begins in different parts of the digestion system, though all end in the same place. Of the three major food classes (carbohydrates, fats, and proteins), which is digested in the mouth, the stomach, and the small intestine?

23.6 | Accessory Organs in Digestion: The Liver, Pancreas, and Gallbladder

By the end of this section, you will be able to:
- State the main digestive roles of the liver, pancreas, and gallbladder
- Identify three main features of liver histology that are critical to its function
- Discuss the composition and function of bile
- Identify the major types of enzymes and buffers present in pancreatic juice

Chemical digestion in the small intestine relies on the activities of three accessory digestive organs: the liver, pancreas, and gallbladder (Figure 23.24). The digestive role of the liver is to produce bile and export it to the duodenum. The gallbladder primarily stores, concentrates, and releases bile. The pancreas produces pancreatic juice, which contains digestive enzymes and bicarbonate ions, and delivers it to the duodenum.

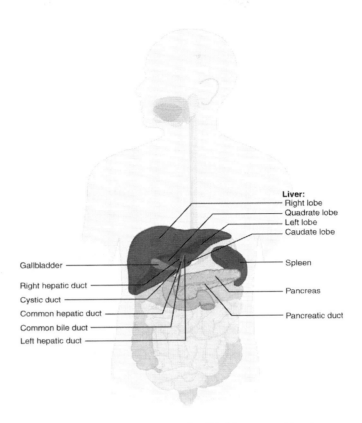

Figure 23.24 Accessory Organs   The liver, pancreas, and gallbladder are considered accessory digestive organs, but their roles in the digestive system are vital.

The Liver

The **liver** is the largest gland in the body, weighing about three pounds in an adult. It is also one of the most important organs. In addition to being an accessory digestive organ, it plays a number of roles in metabolism and regulation. The liver lies inferior to the diaphragm in the right upper quadrant of the abdominal cavity and receives protection from the surrounding ribs.

The liver is divided into two primary lobes: a large right lobe and a much smaller left lobe. In the right lobe, some anatomists also identify an inferior quadrate lobe and a posterior caudate lobe, which are defined by internal features. The liver is connected to the abdominal wall and diaphragm by five peritoneal folds referred to as ligaments. These are the falciform ligament, the coronary ligament, two lateral ligaments, and the ligamentum teres hepatis. The falciform ligament and ligamentum teres hepatis are actually remnants of the umbilical vein, and separate the right and left lobes anteriorly. The lesser omentum tethers the liver to the lesser curvature of the stomach.

The **porta hepatis** ("gate to the liver") is where the **hepatic artery** and **hepatic portal vein** enter the liver. These two vessels, along with the common hepatic duct, run behind the lateral border of the lesser omentum on the way to their destinations. As shown in Figure 23.25, the hepatic artery delivers oxygenated blood from the heart to the liver. The hepatic portal vein delivers partially deoxygenated blood containing nutrients absorbed from the small intestine and actually supplies more oxygen to the liver than do the much smaller hepatic arteries. In addition to nutrients, drugs and toxins are also absorbed. After processing the bloodborne nutrients and toxins, the liver releases nutrients needed by other cells back into the blood, which drains into the central vein and then through the hepatic vein to the inferior vena cava. With this hepatic portal circulation, all blood from the alimentary canal passes through the liver. This largely explains why the liver is the most common site for the metastasis of cancers that originate in the alimentary canal.

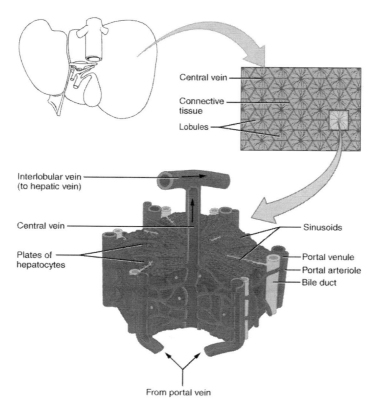

Figure 23.25 Microscopic Anatomy of the Liver The liver receives oxygenated blood from the hepatic artery and nutrient-rich deoxygenated blood from the hepatic portal vein.

Histology

The liver has three main components: hepatocytes, bile canaliculi, and hepatic sinusoids. A **hepatocyte** is the liver's main cell type, accounting for around 80 percent of the liver's volume. These cells play a role in a wide variety of secretory, metabolic, and endocrine functions. Plates of hepatocytes called hepatic laminae radiate outward from the portal vein in each **hepatic lobule**.

Between adjacent hepatocytes, grooves in the cell membranes provide room for each **bile canaliculus** (plural = canaliculi). These small ducts accumulate the bile produced by hepatocytes. From here, bile flows first into bile ductules and then into bile ducts. The bile ducts unite to form the larger right and left hepatic ducts, which themselves merge and exit the liver as the **common hepatic duct**. This duct then joins with the cystic duct from the gallbladder, forming the **common bile duct** through which bile flows into the small intestine.

A **hepatic sinusoid** is an open, porous blood space formed by fenestrated capillaries from nutrient-rich hepatic portal veins and oxygen-rich hepatic arteries. Hepatocytes are tightly packed around the fenestrated endothelium of these spaces, giving them easy access to the blood. From their central position, hepatocytes process the nutrients, toxins, and waste materials carried by the blood. Materials such as bilirubin are processed and excreted into the bile canaliculi. Other materials including proteins, lipids, and carbohydrates are processed and secreted into the sinusoids or just stored in the cells until called upon. The hepatic sinusoids combine and send blood to a **central vein**. Blood then flows through a **hepatic vein** into the inferior vena cava. This means that blood and bile flow in opposite directions. The hepatic sinusoids also contain star-shaped **reticuloendothelial cells** (Kupffer cells), phagocytes that remove dead red and white blood cells, bacteria, and other foreign material that enter the sinusoids. The **portal triad** is a distinctive arrangement around the perimeter of hepatic lobules, consisting of three basic structures: a bile duct, a hepatic artery branch, and a hepatic portal vein branch.

Bile

Recall that lipids are hydrophobic, that is, they do not dissolve in water. Thus, before they can be digested in the watery environment of the small intestine, large lipid globules must be broken down into smaller lipid globules, a process called emulsification. **Bile** is a mixture secreted by the liver to accomplish the emulsification of lipids in the small intestine.

Hepatocytes secrete about one liter of bile each day. A yellow-brown or yellow-green alkaline solution (pH 7.6 to 8.6), bile is a mixture of water, bile salts, bile pigments, phospholipids (such as lecithin), electrolytes, cholesterol, and triglycerides. The components most critical to emulsification are bile salts and phospholipids, which have a nonpolar (hydrophobic) region as well as a polar (hydrophilic) region. The hydrophobic region interacts with the large lipid molecules, whereas the hydrophilic region interacts with the watery chyme in the intestine. This results in the large lipid globules being pulled apart into many tiny lipid fragments of about 1 μm in diameter. This change dramatically increases the surface area available for lipid-digesting enzyme activity. This is the same way dish soap works on fats mixed with water.

Bile salts act as emulsifying agents, so they are also important for the absorption of digested lipids. While most constituents of bile are eliminated in feces, bile salts are reclaimed by the **enterohepatic circulation**. Once bile salts reach the ileum, they are absorbed and returned to the liver in the hepatic portal blood. The hepatocytes then excrete the bile salts into newly formed bile. Thus, this precious resource is recycled.

Bilirubin, the main bile pigment, is a waste product produced when the spleen removes old or damaged red blood cells from the circulation. These breakdown products, including proteins, iron, and toxic bilirubin, are transported to the liver via the splenic vein of the hepatic portal system. In the liver, proteins and iron are recycled, whereas bilirubin is excreted in the bile. It accounts for the green color of bile. Bilirubin is eventually transformed by intestinal bacteria into stercobilin, a brown pigment that gives your stool its characteristic color! In some disease states, bile does not enter the intestine, resulting in white ('acholic') stool with a high fat content, since virtually no fats are broken down or absorbed.

Hepatocytes work non-stop, but bile production increases when fatty chyme enters the duodenum and stimulates the secretion of the gut hormone secretin. Between meals, bile is produced but conserved. The valve-like hepatopancreatic ampulla closes, allowing bile to divert to the gallbladder, where it is concentrated and stored until the next meal.

Watch this video (http://openstaxcollege.org/l/liver) to see the structure of the liver and how this structure supports the functions of the liver, including the processing of nutrients, toxins, and wastes. At rest, about 1500 mL of blood per minute flow through the liver. What percentage of this blood flow comes from the hepatic portal system?

The Pancreas

The soft, oblong, glandular **pancreas** lies transversely in the retroperitoneum behind the stomach. Its head is nestled into the "c-shaped" curvature of the duodenum with the body extending to the left about 15.2 cm (6 in) and ending as a tapering tail in the hilum of the spleen. It is a curious mix of exocrine (secreting digestive enzymes) and endocrine (releasing hormones into the blood) functions (Figure 23.26).

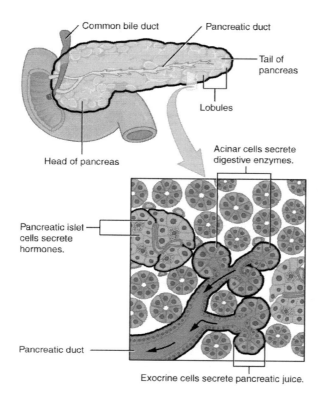

Figure 23.26 Exocrine and Endocrine Pancreas The pancreas has a head, a body, and a tail. It delivers pancreatic juice to the duodenum through the pancreatic duct.

The exocrine part of the pancreas arises as little grape-like cell clusters, each called an **acinus** (plural = acini), located at the terminal ends of pancreatic ducts. These acinar cells secrete enzyme-rich **pancreatic juice** into tiny merging ducts that form two dominant ducts. The larger duct fuses with the common bile duct (carrying bile from the liver and gallbladder) just before entering the duodenum via a common opening (the hepatopancreatic ampulla). The smooth muscle sphincter of the hepatopancreatic ampulla controls the release of pancreatic juice and bile into the small intestine. The second and smaller pancreatic duct, the **accessory duct** (duct of Santorini), runs from the pancreas directly into the duodenum, approximately 1 inch above the hepatopancreatic ampulla. When present, it is a persistent remnant of pancreatic development.

Scattered through the sea of exocrine acini are small islands of endocrine cells, the islets of Langerhans. These vital cells produce the hormones pancreatic polypeptide, insulin, glucagon, and somatostatin.

Pancreatic Juice

The pancreas produces over a liter of pancreatic juice each day. Unlike bile, it is clear and composed mostly of water along with some salts, sodium bicarbonate, and several digestive enzymes. Sodium bicarbonate is responsible for the slight alkalinity of pancreatic juice (pH 7.1 to 8.2), which serves to buffer the acidic gastric juice in chyme, inactivate pepsin from the stomach, and create an optimal environment for the activity of pH-sensitive digestive enzymes in the small intestine. Pancreatic enzymes are active in the digestion of sugars, proteins, and fats.

The pancreas produces protein-digesting enzymes in their inactive forms. These enzymes are activated in the duodenum. If produced in an active form, they would digest the pancreas (which is exactly what occurs in the disease, pancreatitis). The intestinal brush border enzyme **enteropeptidase** stimulates the activation of trypsin from trypsinogen of the pancreas, which in turn changes the pancreatic enzymes procarboxypeptidase and chymotrypsinogen into their active forms, carboxypeptidase and chymotrypsin.

The enzymes that digest starch (amylase), fat (lipase), and nucleic acids (nuclease) are secreted in their active forms, since they do not attack the pancreas as do the protein-digesting enzymes.

Pancreatic Secretion

Regulation of pancreatic secretion is the job of hormones and the parasympathetic nervous system. The entry of acidic chyme into the duodenum stimulates the release of secretin, which in turn causes the duct cells to release bicarbonate-rich pancreatic juice. The presence of proteins and fats in the duodenum stimulates the secretion of CCK, which then stimulates the acini to secrete enzyme-rich pancreatic juice and enhances the activity of secretin. Parasympathetic regulation occurs mainly during the cephalic and gastric phases of gastric secretion, when vagal stimulation prompts the secretion of pancreatic juice.

Usually, the pancreas secretes just enough bicarbonate to counterbalance the amount of HCl produced in the stomach. Hydrogen ions enter the blood when bicarbonate is secreted by the pancreas. Thus, the acidic blood draining from the pancreas neutralizes the alkaline blood draining from the stomach, maintaining the pH of the venous blood that flows to the liver.

The Gallbladder

The **gallbladder** is 8–10 cm (~3–4 in) long and is nested in a shallow area on the posterior aspect of the right lobe of the liver. This muscular sac stores, concentrates, and, when stimulated, propels the bile into the duodenum via the common bile duct. It is divided into three regions. The fundus is the widest portion and tapers medially into the body, which in turn narrows to become the neck. The neck angles slightly superiorly as it approaches the hepatic duct. The cystic duct is 1–2 cm (less than 1 in) long and turns inferiorly as it bridges the neck and hepatic duct.

The simple columnar epithelium of the gallbladder mucosa is organized in rugae, similar to those of the stomach. There is no submucosa in the gallbladder wall. The wall's middle, muscular coat is made of smooth muscle fibers. When these fibers contract, the gallbladder's contents are ejected through the **cystic duct** and into the bile duct (Figure 23.27). Visceral peritoneum reflected from the liver capsule holds the gallbladder against the liver and forms the outer coat of the gallbladder. The gallbladder's mucosa absorbs water and ions from bile, concentrating it by up to 10-fold.

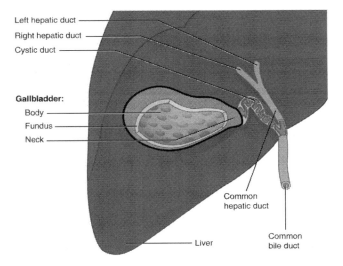

Figure 23.27 Gallbladder The gallbladder stores and concentrates bile, and releases it into the two-way cystic duct when it is needed by the small intestine.

23.7 | Chemical Digestion and Absorption: A Closer Look

By the end of this section, you will be able to:
- Identify the locations and primary secretions involved in the chemical digestion of carbohydrates, proteins, lipids, and nucleic acids
- Compare and contrast absorption of the hydrophilic and hydrophobic nutrients

As you have learned, the process of mechanical digestion is relatively simple. It involves the physical breakdown of food but does not alter its chemical makeup. Chemical digestion, on the other hand, is a complex process that reduces food into its chemical building blocks, which are then absorbed to nourish the cells of the body (Figure 23.28). In this section, you will look more closely at the processes of chemical digestion and absorption.

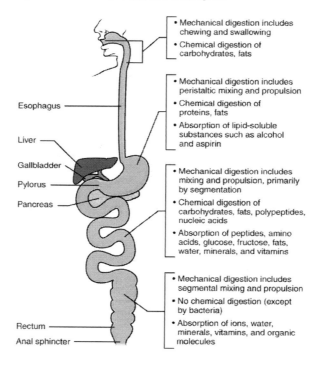

Figure 23.28 Digestion and Absorption Digestion begins in the mouth and continues as food travels through the small intestine. Most absorption occurs in the small intestine.

Chemical Digestion

Large food molecules (for example, proteins, lipids, nucleic acids, and starches) must be broken down into subunits that are small enough to be absorbed by the lining of the alimentary canal. This is accomplished by enzymes through hydrolysis. The many enzymes involved in chemical digestion are summarized in Table 23.8.

The Digestive Enzymes

Enzyme Category	Enzyme Name	Source	Substrate	Product
Salivary Enzymes	Lingual lipase	Lingual glands	Triglycerides	Free fatty acids, and mono- and diglycerides
Salivary Enzymes	Salivary amylase	Salivary glands	Polysaccharides	Disaccharides and trisaccharides
Gastric enzymes	Gastric lipase	Chief cells	Triglycerides	Fatty acids and monoacylglycerides
Gastric enzymes	Pepsin*	Chief cells	Proteins	Peptides
Brush border enzymes	α-Dextrinase	Small intestine	α-Dextrins	Glucose
Brush border enzymes	Enteropeptidase	Small intestine	Trypsinogen	Trypsin
Brush border enzymes	Lactase	Small intestine	Lactose	Glucose and galactose
Brush border enzymes	Maltase	Small intestine	Maltose	Glucose
Brush border enzymes	Nucleosidases and phosphatases	Small intestine	Nucleotides	Phosphates, nitrogenous bases, and pentoses
Brush border enzymes	Peptidases	Small intestine	Aminopeptidase: amino acids at the amino end of peptides Dipeptidase: dipeptides	Aminopeptidase: amino acids and peptides Dipeptidase: amino acids
Brush border enzymes	Sucrase	Small intestine	Sucrose	Glucose and fructose
Pancreatic enzymes	Carboxypeptidase*	Pancreatic acinar cells	Amino acids at the carboxyl end of peptides	Amino acids and peptides
Pancreatic enzymes	Chymotrypsin*	Pancreatic acinar cells	Proteins	Peptides
Pancreatic enzymes	Elastase*	Pancreatic acinar cells	Proteins	Peptides
Pancreatic enzymes	Nucleases	Pancreatic acinar cells	Ribonuclease: ribonucleic acids Deoxyribonuclease: deoxyribonucleic acids	Nucleotides
Pancreatic enzymes	Pancreatic amylase	Pancreatic acinar cells	Polysaccharides (starches)	α-Dextrins, disaccharides (maltose), trisaccharides (maltotriose)
Pancreatic enzymes	Pancreatic lipase	Pancreatic acinar cells	Triglycerides that have been emulsified by bile salts	Fatty acids and monoacylglycerides
Pancreatic enzymes	Trypsin*	Pancreatic acinar cells	Proteins	Peptides

Table 23.8 *These enzymes have been activated by other substances.

Carbohydrate Digestion

The average American diet is about 50 percent carbohydrates, which may be classified according to the number of monomers they contain of simple sugars (monosaccharides and disaccharides) and/or complex sugars (polysaccharides). Glucose, galactose, and fructose are the three monosaccharides that are commonly consumed and are readily absorbed. Your digestive system is also able to break down the disaccharide sucrose (regular table sugar: glucose + fructose), lactose (milk sugar: glucose + galactose), and maltose (grain sugar: glucose + glucose), and the polysaccharides glycogen and starch (chains of monosaccharides). Your bodies do not produce enzymes that can break down most fibrous polysaccharides, such as cellulose. While indigestible polysaccharides do not provide any nutritional value, they do provide dietary fiber, which helps propel food through the alimentary canal.

The chemical digestion of starches begins in the mouth and has been reviewed above.

In the small intestine, **pancreatic amylase** does the 'heavy lifting' for starch and carbohydrate digestion (Figure 23.29). After amylases break down starch into smaller fragments, the brush border enzyme **α-dextrinase** starts working on **α-dextrin**, breaking off one glucose unit at a time. Three brush border enzymes hydrolyze sucrose, lactose, and maltose into monosaccharides. **Sucrase** splits sucrose into one molecule of fructose and one molecule of glucose; **maltase** breaks down maltose and maltotriose into two and three glucose molecules, respectively; and **lactase** breaks down lactose into one molecule of glucose and one molecule of galactose. Insufficient lactase can lead to lactose intolerance.

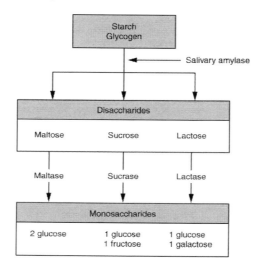

Figure 23.29 Carbohydrate Digestion Flow Chart Carbohydrates are broken down into their monomers in a series of steps.

Protein Digestion

Proteins are polymers composed of amino acids linked by peptide bonds to form long chains. Digestion reduces them to their constituent amino acids. You usually consume about 15 to 20 percent of your total calorie intake as protein.

The digestion of protein starts in the stomach, where HCl and pepsin break proteins into smaller polypeptides, which then travel to the small intestine (Figure 23.30). Chemical digestion in the small intestine is continued by pancreatic enzymes, including chymotrypsin and trypsin, each of which act on specific bonds in amino acid sequences. At the same time, the cells of the brush border secrete enzymes such as **aminopeptidase** and **dipeptidase**, which further break down peptide chains. This results in molecules small enough to enter the bloodstream (Figure 23.31).

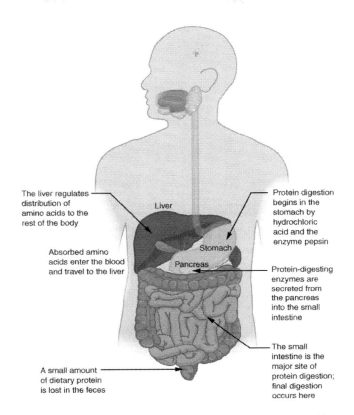

Figure 23.30 Digestion of Protein The digestion of protein begins in the stomach and is completed in the small intestine.

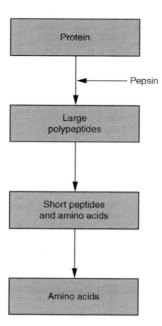

Figure 23.31 Digestion of Protein Flow Chart Proteins are successively broken down into their amino acid components.

Lipid Digestion

A healthy diet limits lipid intake to 35 percent of total calorie intake. The most common dietary lipids are triglycerides, which are made up of a glycerol molecule bound to three fatty acid chains. Small amounts of dietary cholesterol and phospholipids are also consumed.

The three lipases responsible for lipid digestion are lingual lipase, gastric lipase, and **pancreatic lipase**. However, because the pancreas is the only consequential source of lipase, virtually all lipid digestion occurs in the small intestine. Pancreatic lipase breaks down each triglyceride into two free fatty acids and a monoglyceride. The fatty acids include both short-chain (less than 10 to 12 carbons) and long-chain fatty acids.

Nucleic Acid Digestion

The nucleic acids DNA and RNA are found in most of the foods you eat. Two types of **pancreatic nuclease** are responsible for their digestion: **deoxyribonuclease**, which digests DNA, and **ribonuclease**, which digests RNA. The nucleotides produced by this digestion are further broken down by two intestinal brush border enzymes (**nucleosidase** and **phosphatase**) into pentoses, phosphates, and nitrogenous bases, which can be absorbed through the alimentary canal wall. The large food molecules that must be broken down into subunits are summarized Table 23.9

Absorbable Food Substances

Source	Substance
Carbohydrates	Monosaccharides: glucose, galactose, and fructose
Proteins	Single amino acids, dipeptides, and tripeptides
Triglycerides	Monoacylglycerides, glycerol, and free fatty acids
Nucleic acids	Pentose sugars, phosphates, and nitrogenous bases

Table 23.9

Absorption

The mechanical and digestive processes have one goal: to convert food into molecules small enough to be absorbed by the epithelial cells of the intestinal villi. The absorptive capacity of the alimentary canal is almost endless. Each day, the alimentary canal processes up to 10 liters of food, liquids, and GI secretions, yet less than one liter enters the large intestine. Almost all ingested food, 80 percent of electrolytes, and 90 percent of water are absorbed in the small intestine. Although the entire small intestine is involved in the absorption of water and lipids, most absorption of carbohydrates and proteins occurs in the jejunum. Notably, bile salts and vitamin B_{12} are absorbed in the terminal ileum. By the time chyme passes from the ileum into the large intestine, it is essentially indigestible food residue (mainly plant fibers like cellulose), some water, and millions of bacteria (Figure 23.32).

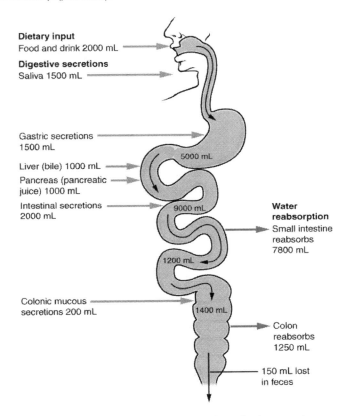

Figure 23.32 Digestive Secretions and Absorption of Water Absorption is a complex process, in which nutrients from digested food are harvested.

Absorption can occur through five mechanisms: (1) active transport, (2) passive diffusion, (3) facilitated diffusion, (4) co-transport (or secondary active transport), and (5) endocytosis. As you will recall from Chapter 3, active transport refers to the movement of a substance across a cell membrane going from an area of lower concentration to an area of higher concentration (up the concentration gradient). In this type of transport, proteins within the cell membrane act as "pumps," using cellular energy (ATP) to move the substance. Passive diffusion refers to the movement of substances from an area of higher concentration to an area of lower concentration, while facilitated diffusion refers to the movement of substances from an area of higher to an area of lower concentration using a carrier protein in the cell membrane. Co-transport uses the movement of one molecule through the membrane from higher to lower concentration to power the movement of another from lower to higher. Finally, endocytosis is a transportation process in which the cell membrane engulfs material. It requires energy, generally in the form of ATP.

Because the cell's plasma membrane is made up of hydrophobic phospholipids, water-soluble nutrients must use transport molecules embedded in the membrane to enter cells. Moreover, substances cannot pass between the epithelial cells of the intestinal mucosa because these cells are bound together by tight junctions. Thus, substances can only enter blood capillaries by passing through the apical surfaces of epithelial cells and into the interstitial fluid. Water-soluble nutrients enter the capillary blood in the villi and travel to the liver via the hepatic portal vein.

In contrast to the water-soluble nutrients, lipid-soluble nutrients can diffuse through the plasma membrane. Once inside the cell, they are packaged for transport via the base of the cell and then enter the lacteals of the villi to be transported by lymphatic vessels to the systemic circulation via the thoracic duct. The absorption of most nutrients through the mucosa of the intestinal villi requires active transport fueled by ATP. The routes of absorption for each food category are summarized in Table 23.10.

Absorption in the Alimentary Canal

Food	Breakdown products	Absorption mechanism	Entry to bloodstream	Destination
Carbohydrates	Glucose	Co-transport with sodium ions	Capillary blood in villi	Liver via hepatic portal vein
Carbohydrates	Galactose	Co-transport with sodium ions	Capillary blood in villi	Liver via hepatic portal vein
Carbohydrates	Fructose	Facilitated diffusion	Capillary blood in villi	Liver via hepatic portal vein
Protein	Amino acids	Co-transport with sodium ions	Capillary blood in villi	Liver via hepatic portal vein
Lipids	Long-chain fatty acids	Diffusion into intestinal cells, where they are combined with proteins to create chylomicrons	Lacteals of villi	Systemic circulation via lymph entering thoracic duct
Lipids	Monoacylglycerides	Diffusion into intestinal cells, where they are combined with proteins to create chylomicrons	Lacteals of villi	Systemic circulation via lymph entering thoracic duct
Lipids	Short-chain fatty acids	Simple diffusion	Capillary blood in villi	Liver via hepatic portal vein
Lipids	Glycerol	Simple diffusion	Capillary blood in villi	Liver via hepatic portal vein
Lipids	Nucleic acid digestion products	Active transport via membrane carriers	Capillary blood in villi	Liver via hepatic portal vein

Table 23.10

Carbohydrate Absorption

All carbohydrates are absorbed in the form of monosaccharides. The small intestine is highly efficient at this, absorbing monosaccharides at an estimated rate of 120 grams per hour. All normally digested dietary carbohydrates are absorbed; indigestible fibers are eliminated in the feces. The monosaccharides glucose and galactose are transported into the epithelial cells by common protein carriers via secondary active transport (that is, co-transport with sodium ions). The monosaccharides leave these cells via facilitated diffusion and enter the capillaries through intercellular clefts. The monosaccharide fructose (which is in fruit) is absorbed and transported by facilitated diffusion alone. The monosaccharides combine with the transport proteins immediately after the disaccharides are broken down.

Protein Absorption

Active transport mechanisms, primarily in the duodenum and jejunum, absorb most proteins as their breakdown products, amino acids. Almost all (95 to 98 percent) protein is digested and absorbed in the small intestine. The type of carrier that transports an amino acid varies. Most carriers are linked to the active transport of sodium. Short chains of two amino acids (dipeptides) or three amino acids (tripeptides) are also transported actively. However, after they enter the absorptive epithelial cells, they are broken down into their amino acids before leaving the cell and entering the capillary blood via diffusion.

Lipid Absorption

About 95 percent of lipids are absorbed in the small intestine. Bile salts not only speed up lipid digestion, they are also essential to the absorption of the end products of lipid digestion. Short-chain fatty acids are relatively water soluble and can enter the absorptive cells (enterocytes) directly. Despite being hydrophobic, the small size of short-chain fatty acids enables them to be absorbed by enterocytes via simple diffusion, and then take the same path as monosaccharides and amino acids into the blood capillary of a villus.

The large and hydrophobic long-chain fatty acids and monoacylglycerides are not so easily suspended in the watery intestinal chyme. However, bile salts and lecithin resolve this issue by enclosing them in a **micelle**, which is a tiny sphere with polar (hydrophilic) ends facing the watery environment and hydrophobic tails turned to the interior, creating a receptive environment for the long-chain fatty acids. The core also includes cholesterol and fat-soluble vitamins. Without micelles, lipids would sit on the surface of chyme and never come in contact with the absorptive surfaces of the epithelial cells. Micelles can easily squeeze between microvilli and get very near the luminal cell surface. At this point, lipid substances exit the micelle and are absorbed via simple diffusion.

The free fatty acids and monoacylglycerides that enter the epithelial cells are reincorporated into triglycerides. The triglycerides are mixed with phospholipids and cholesterol, and surrounded with a protein coat. This new complex, called a **chylomicron**, is a water-soluble lipoprotein. After being processed by the Golgi apparatus, chylomicrons are released from the cell (Figure 23.33). Too big to pass through the basement membranes of blood capillaries, chylomicrons instead enter the large pores of lacteals. The lacteals come together to form the lymphatic vessels. The chylomicrons are transported in the lymphatic vessels and empty through the thoracic duct into the subclavian vein of the circulatory system. Once in the bloodstream, the enzyme **lipoprotein lipase** breaks down the triglycerides of the chylomicrons into free fatty acids and glycerol. These breakdown products then pass through capillary walls to be used for energy by cells or stored in adipose tissue as fat. Liver cells combine the remaining chylomicron remnants with proteins, forming lipoproteins that transport cholesterol in the blood.

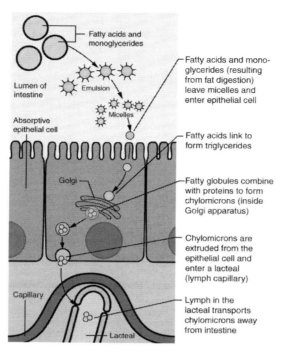

Figure 23.33 Lipid Absorption Unlike amino acids and simple sugars, lipids are transformed as they are absorbed through epithelial cells.

Nucleic Acid Absorption

The products of nucleic acid digestion—pentose sugars, nitrogenous bases, and phosphate ions—are transported by carriers across the villus epithelium via active transport. These products then enter the bloodstream.

Mineral Absorption

The electrolytes absorbed by the small intestine are from both GI secretions and ingested foods. Since electrolytes dissociate into ions in water, most are absorbed via active transport throughout the entire small intestine. During absorption, co-transport mechanisms result in the accumulation of sodium ions inside the cells, whereas anti-port mechanisms reduce the potassium ion concentration inside the cells. To restore the sodium-potassium gradient across the cell membrane, a sodium-potassium pump requiring ATP pumps sodium out and potassium in.

In general, all minerals that enter the intestine are absorbed, whether you need them or not. Iron and calcium are exceptions; they are absorbed in the duodenum in amounts that meet the body's current requirements, as follows:

Iron—The ionic iron needed for the production of hemoglobin is absorbed into mucosal cells via active transport. Once inside mucosal cells, ionic iron binds to the protein ferritin, creating iron-ferritin complexes that store iron until needed. When the body has enough iron, most of the stored iron is lost when worn-out epithelial cells slough off. When the body needs iron because, for example, it is lost during acute or chronic bleeding, there is increased uptake of iron from the intestine and accelerated release of iron into the bloodstream. Since women experience significant iron loss during menstruation, they have around four times as many iron transport proteins in their intestinal epithelial cells as do men.

Calcium—Blood levels of ionic calcium determine the absorption of dietary calcium. When blood levels of ionic calcium drop, parathyroid hormone (PTH) secreted by the parathyroid glands stimulates the release of calcium ions from bone matrices and increases the reabsorption of calcium by the kidneys. PTH also upregulates the activation of vitamin D in the kidney, which then facilitates intestinal calcium ion absorption.

Vitamin Absorption

The small intestine absorbs the vitamins that occur naturally in food and supplements. Fat-soluble vitamins (A, D, E, and K) are absorbed along with dietary lipids in micelles via simple diffusion. This is why you are advised to eat some fatty foods when you take fat-soluble vitamin supplements. Most water-soluble vitamins (including most B vitamins and vitamin C) also are absorbed by simple diffusion. An exception is vitamin B_{12}, which is a very large molecule. Intrinsic factor secreted in the stomach binds to vitamin B_{12}, preventing its digestion and creating a complex that binds to mucosal receptors in the terminal ileum, where it is taken up by endocytosis.

Water Absorption

Each day, about nine liters of fluid enter the small intestine. About 2.3 liters are ingested in foods and beverages, and the rest is from GI secretions. About 90 percent of this water is absorbed in the small intestine. Water absorption is driven by the concentration gradient of the water: The concentration of water is higher in chyme than it is in epithelial cells. Thus, water moves down its concentration gradient from the chyme into cells. As noted earlier, much of the remaining water is then absorbed in the colon.

KEY TERMS

absorption passage of digested products from the intestinal lumen through mucosal cells and into the bloodstream or lacteals

accessory digestive organ includes teeth, tongue, salivary glands, gallbladder, liver, and pancreas

accessory duct (also, duct of Santorini) duct that runs from the pancreas into the duodenum

acinus cluster of glandular epithelial cells in the pancreas that secretes pancreatic juice in the pancreas

alimentary canal continuous muscular digestive tube that extends from the mouth to the anus

aminopeptidase brush border enzyme that acts on proteins

anal canal final segment of the large intestine

anal column long fold of mucosa in the anal canal

anal sinus recess between anal columns

appendix (vermiform appendix) coiled tube attached to the cecum

ascending colon first region of the colon

bacterial flora bacteria in the large intestine

bile alkaline solution produced by the liver and important for the emulsification of lipids

bile canaliculus small duct between hepatocytes that collects bile

bilirubin main bile pigment, which is responsible for the brown color of feces

body mid-portion of the stomach

bolus mass of chewed food

brush border fuzzy appearance of the small intestinal mucosa created by microvilli

cardia (also, cardiac region) part of the stomach surrounding the cardiac orifice (esophageal hiatus)

cecum pouch forming the beginning of the large intestine

cementum bone-like tissue covering the root of a tooth

central vein vein that receives blood from hepatic sinusoids

cephalic phase (also, reflex phase) initial phase of gastric secretion that occurs before food enters the stomach

chemical digestion enzymatic breakdown of food

chief cell gastric gland cell that secretes pepsinogen

chylomicron large lipid-transport compound made up of triglycerides, phospholipids, cholesterol, and proteins

chyme soupy liquid created when food is mixed with digestive juices

circular fold (also, plica circulare) deep fold in the mucosa and submucosa of the small intestine

colon part of the large intestine between the cecum and the rectum

common bile duct structure formed by the union of the common hepatic duct and the gallbladder's cystic duct

common hepatic duct duct formed by the merger of the two hepatic ducts

crown portion of tooth visible superior to the gum line

cuspid (also, canine) pointed tooth used for tearing and shredding food

cystic duct duct through which bile drains and enters the gallbladder

deciduous tooth one of 20 "baby teeth"

defecation elimination of undigested substances from the body in the form of feces

deglutition three-stage process of swallowing

dens tooth

dentin bone-like tissue immediately deep to the enamel of the crown or cementum of the root of a tooth

dentition set of teeth

deoxyribonuclease pancreatic enzyme that digests DNA

descending colon part of the colon between the transverse colon and the sigmoid colon

dipeptidase brush border enzyme that acts on proteins

duodenal gland (also, Brunner's gland) mucous-secreting gland in the duodenal submucosa

duodenum first part of the small intestine, which starts at the pyloric sphincter and ends at the jejunum

enamel covering of the dentin of the crown of a tooth

enteroendocrine cell gastric gland cell that releases hormones

enterohepatic circulation recycling mechanism that conserves bile salts

enteropeptidase intestinal brush-border enzyme that activates trypsinogen to trypsin

epiploic appendage small sac of fat-filled visceral peritoneum attached to teniae coli

esophagus muscular tube that runs from the pharynx to the stomach

external anal sphincter voluntary skeletal muscle sphincter in the anal canal

fauces opening between the oral cavity and the oropharynx

feces semisolid waste product of digestion

flatus gas in the intestine

fundus dome-shaped region of the stomach above and to the left of the cardia

G cell gastrin-secreting enteroendocrine cell

gallbladder accessory digestive organ that stores and concentrates bile

gastric emptying process by which mixing waves gradually cause the release of chyme into the duodenum

gastric gland gland in the stomach mucosal epithelium that produces gastric juice

gastric phase phase of gastric secretion that begins when food enters the stomach

gastric pit narrow channel formed by the epithelial lining of the stomach mucosa

gastrin peptide hormone that stimulates secretion of hydrochloric acid and gut motility

gastrocolic reflex propulsive movement in the colon activated by the presence of food in the stomach

gastroileal reflex long reflex that increases the strength of segmentation in the ileum

gingiva gum

haustral contraction slow segmentation in the large intestine

haustrum small pouch in the colon created by tonic contractions of teniae coli

hepatic artery artery that supplies oxygenated blood to the liver

hepatic lobule hexagonal-shaped structure composed of hepatocytes that radiate outward from a central vein

hepatic portal vein vein that supplies deoxygenated nutrient-rich blood to the liver

hepatic sinusoid blood capillaries between rows of hepatocytes that receive blood from the hepatic portal vein and the branches of the hepatic artery

hepatic vein vein that drains into the inferior vena cava

hepatocytes major functional cells of the liver

hepatopancreatic ampulla (also, ampulla of Vater) bulb-like point in the wall of the duodenum where the bile duct and main pancreatic duct unite

hepatopancreatic sphincter (also, sphincter of Oddi) sphincter regulating the flow of bile and pancreatic juice into the duodenum

hydrochloric acid (HCl) digestive acid secreted by parietal cells in the stomach

ileocecal sphincter sphincter located where the small intestine joins with the large intestine

ileum end of the small intestine between the jejunum and the large intestine

incisor midline, chisel-shaped tooth used for cutting into food

ingestion taking food into the GI tract through the mouth

internal anal sphincter involuntary smooth muscle sphincter in the anal canal

intestinal gland (also, crypt of Lieberkühn) gland in the small intestinal mucosa that secretes intestinal juice

intestinal juice mixture of water and mucus that helps absorb nutrients from chyme

intestinal phase phase of gastric secretion that begins when chyme enters the intestine

intrinsic factor glycoprotein required for vitamin B_{12} absorption in the small intestine

jejunum middle part of the small intestine between the duodenum and the ileum

labial frenulum midline mucous membrane fold that attaches the inner surface of the lips to the gums

labium lip

lactase brush border enzyme that breaks down lactose into glucose and galactose

lacteal lymphatic capillary in the villi

large intestine terminal portion of the alimentary canal

laryngopharynx part of the pharynx that functions in respiration and digestion

left colic flexure (also, splenic flexure) point where the transverse colon curves below the inferior end of the spleen

lingual frenulum mucous membrane fold that attaches the bottom of the tongue to the floor of the mouth

lingual lipase digestive enzyme from glands in the tongue that acts on triglycerides

lipoprotein lipase enzyme that breaks down triglycerides in chylomicrons into fatty acids and monoglycerides

liver largest gland in the body whose main digestive function is the production of bile

lower esophageal sphincter smooth muscle sphincter that regulates food movement from the esophagus to the stomach

main pancreatic duct (also, duct of Wirsung) duct through which pancreatic juice drains from the pancreas

major duodenal papilla point at which the hepatopancreatic ampulla opens into the duodenum

maltase brush border enzyme that breaks down maltose and maltotriose into two and three molecules of glucose, respectively

mass movement long, slow, peristaltic wave in the large intestine

mastication chewing

mechanical digestion chewing, mixing, and segmentation that prepares food for chemical digestion

mesoappendix mesentery of the appendix

micelle tiny lipid-transport compound composed of bile salts and phospholipids with a fatty acid and monoacylglyceride core

microvillus small projection of the plasma membrane of the absorptive cells of the small intestinal mucosa

migrating motility complex form of peristalsis in the small intestine

mixing wave unique type of peristalsis that occurs in the stomach

molar tooth used for crushing and grinding food

motilin hormone that initiates migrating motility complexes

motility movement of food through the GI tract

mucosa innermost lining of the alimentary canal

mucosal barrier protective barrier that prevents gastric juice from destroying the stomach itself

mucous neck cell gastric gland cell that secretes a uniquely acidic mucus

muscularis muscle (skeletal or smooth) layer of the alimentary canal wall

myenteric plexus (plexus of Auerbach) major nerve supply to alimentary canal wall; controls motility

nucleosidase brush border enzyme that digests nucleotides

oral cavity (also, buccal cavity) mouth

oral vestibule part of the mouth bounded externally by the cheeks and lips, and internally by the gums and teeth

oropharynx part of the pharynx continuous with the oral cavity that functions in respiration and digestion

palatoglossal arch muscular fold that extends from the lateral side of the soft palate to the base of the tongue

palatopharyngeal arch muscular fold that extends from the lateral side of the soft palate to the side of the pharynx

pancreas accessory digestive organ that secretes pancreatic juice

pancreatic amylase enzyme secreted by the pancreas that completes the chemical digestion of carbohydrates in the small intestine

pancreatic juice secretion of the pancreas containing digestive enzymes and bicarbonate

pancreatic lipase enzyme secreted by the pancreas that participates in lipid digestion

pancreatic nuclease enzyme secreted by the pancreas that participates in nucleic acid digestion

parietal cell gastric gland cell that secretes hydrochloric acid and intrinsic factor

parotid gland one of a pair of major salivary glands located inferior and anterior to the ears

pectinate line horizontal line that runs like a ring, perpendicular to the inferior margins of the anal sinuses

pepsinogen inactive form of pepsin

peristalsis muscular contractions and relaxations that propel food through the GI tract

permanent tooth one of 32 adult teeth

pharynx throat

phosphatase brush border enzyme that digests nucleotides

porta hepatis "gateway to the liver" where the hepatic artery and hepatic portal vein enter the liver

portal triad bile duct, hepatic artery branch, and hepatic portal vein branch

premolar (also, bicuspid) transitional tooth used for mastication, crushing, and grinding food

propulsion voluntary process of swallowing and the involuntary process of peristalsis that moves food through the digestive tract

pulp cavity deepest portion of a tooth, containing nerve endings and blood vessels

pyloric antrum wider, more superior part of the pylorus

pyloric canal narrow, more inferior part of the pylorus

pyloric sphincter sphincter that controls stomach emptying

pylorus lower, funnel-shaped part of the stomach that is continuous with the duodenum

rectal valve one of three transverse folds in the rectum where feces is separated from flatus

rectum part of the large intestine between the sigmoid colon and anal canal

reticuloendothelial cell (also, Kupffer cell) phagocyte in hepatic sinusoids that filters out material from venous blood from the alimentary canal

retroperitoneal located posterior to the peritoneum

ribonuclease pancreatic enzyme that digests RNA

right colic flexure (also, hepatic flexure) point, at the inferior surface of the liver, where the ascending colon turns abruptly to the left

root portion of a tooth embedded in the alveolar processes beneath the gum line

ruga fold of alimentary canal mucosa and submucosa in the empty stomach and other organs

saccharolytic fermentation anaerobic decomposition of carbohydrates

saliva aqueous solution of proteins and ions secreted into the mouth by the salivary glands

salivary amylase digestive enzyme in saliva that acts on starch

salivary gland an exocrine gland that secretes a digestive fluid called saliva

salivation secretion of saliva

segmentation alternating contractions and relaxations of non-adjacent segments of the intestine that move food forward and backward, breaking it apart and mixing it with digestive juices

serosa outermost layer of the alimentary canal wall present in regions within the abdominal cavity

sigmoid colon end portion of the colon, which terminates at the rectum

small intestine section of the alimentary canal where most digestion and absorption occurs

soft palate posterior region of the bottom portion of the nasal cavity that consists of skeletal muscle

stomach alimentary canal organ that contributes to chemical and mechanical digestion of food from the esophagus before releasing it, as chyme, to the small intestine

sublingual gland one of a pair of major salivary glands located beneath the tongue

submandibular gland one of a pair of major salivary glands located in the floor of the mouth

submucosa layer of dense connective tissue in the alimentary canal wall that binds the overlying mucosa to the underlying muscularis

submucosal plexus (plexus of Meissner) nerve supply that regulates activity of glands and smooth muscle

sucrase brush border enzyme that breaks down sucrose into glucose and fructose

tenia coli one of three smooth muscle bands that make up the longitudinal muscle layer of the muscularis in all of the large intestine except the terminal end

tongue accessory digestive organ of the mouth, the bulk of which is composed of skeletal muscle

transverse colon part of the colon between the ascending colon and the descending colon

upper esophageal sphincter skeletal muscle sphincter that regulates food movement from the pharynx to the esophagus

Valsalva's maneuver voluntary contraction of the diaphragm and abdominal wall muscles and closing of the glottis, which increases intra-abdominal pressure and facilitates defecation

villus projection of the mucosa of the small intestine

voluntary phase initial phase of deglutition, in which the bolus moves from the mouth to the oropharynx

α-dextrin breakdown product of starch

α-dextrinase brush border enzyme that acts on α-dextrins

CHAPTER REVIEW

23.1 Overview of the Digestive System

The digestive system includes the organs of the alimentary canal and accessory structures. The alimentary canal forms a continuous tube that is open to the outside environment at both ends. The organs of the alimentary canal are the mouth, pharynx, esophagus, stomach, small intestine, and large intestine. The accessory digestive structures include the teeth, tongue, salivary glands, liver, pancreas, and gallbladder. The wall of the alimentary canal is composed of four basic tissue layers: mucosa, submucosa, muscularis, and serosa. The enteric nervous system provides intrinsic innervation, and the autonomic nervous system provides extrinsic innervation.

23.2 Digestive System Processes and Regulation

The digestive system ingests and digests food, absorbs released nutrients, and excretes food components that are indigestible. The six activities involved in this process are ingestion, motility, mechanical digestion, chemical digestion, absorption, and defecation. These processes are regulated by neural and hormonal mechanisms.

23.3 The Mouth, Pharynx, and Esophagus

In the mouth, the tongue and the teeth begin mechanical digestion, and saliva begins chemical digestion. The pharynx, which plays roles in breathing and vocalization as well as digestion, runs from the nasal and oral cavities superiorly to the esophagus inferiorly (for digestion) and to the larynx anteriorly (for respiration). During deglutition (swallowing), the soft palate rises to close off the nasopharynx, the larynx elevates, and the epiglottis folds over the glottis. The esophagus includes an upper esophageal sphincter made of skeletal muscle, which regulates the movement of food from the pharynx to the esophagus. It also has a lower esophageal sphincter, made of smooth muscle, which controls the passage of food from the esophagus to the stomach. Cells in the esophageal wall secrete mucus that eases the passage of the food bolus.

23.4 The Stomach

The stomach participates in all digestive activities except ingestion and defecation. It vigorously churns food. It secretes gastric juices that break down food and absorbs certain drugs, including aspirin and some alcohol. The stomach begins the digestion of protein and continues the digestion of carbohydrates and fats. It stores food as an acidic liquid called chyme, and releases it gradually into the small intestine through the pyloric sphincter.

23.5 The Small and Large Intestines

The three main regions of the small intestine are the duodenum, the jejunum, and the ileum. The small intestine is where digestion is completed and virtually all absorption occurs. These two activities are facilitated by structural adaptations that increase the mucosal surface area by 600-fold, including circular folds, villi, and microvilli. There are around 200 million microvilli per square millimeter of small intestine, which contain brush border enzymes that complete the digestion of carbohydrates and proteins. Combined with pancreatic juice, intestinal juice provides the liquid medium needed to further digest and absorb substances from chyme. The small intestine is also the site of unique mechanical digestive movements. Segmentation moves the chyme back and forth, increasing mixing and opportunities for absorption. Migrating motility complexes propel the residual chyme toward the large intestine.

The main regions of the large intestine are the cecum, the colon, and the rectum. The large intestine absorbs water and forms feces, and is responsible for defecation. Bacterial flora break down additional carbohydrate residue, and synthesize certain vitamins. The mucosa of the large intestinal wall is generously endowed with goblet cells, which secrete mucus that eases the passage of feces. The entry of feces into the rectum activates the defecation reflex.

23.6 Accessory Organs in Digestion: The Liver, Pancreas, and Gallbladder

Chemical digestion in the small intestine cannot occur without the help of the liver and pancreas. The liver produces bile and delivers it to the common hepatic duct. Bile contains bile salts and phospholipids, which emulsify large lipid globules into tiny lipid droplets, a necessary step in lipid digestion and absorption. The gallbladder stores and concentrates bile, releasing it when it is needed by the small intestine.

The pancreas produces the enzyme- and bicarbonate-rich pancreatic juice and delivers it to the small intestine through ducts. Pancreatic juice buffers the acidic gastric juice in chyme, inactivates pepsin from the stomach, and enables the optimal functioning of digestive enzymes in the small intestine.

23.7 Chemical Digestion and Absorption: A Closer Look

The small intestine is the site of most chemical digestion and almost all absorption. Chemical digestion breaks large food molecules down into their chemical building blocks, which can then be absorbed through the intestinal wall and into the general circulation. Intestinal brush border enzymes and pancreatic enzymes are responsible for the majority of chemical digestion. The breakdown of fat also requires bile.

Most nutrients are absorbed by transport mechanisms at the apical surface of enterocytes. Exceptions include lipids, fat-soluble vitamins, and most water-soluble vitamins. With the help of bile salts and lecithin, the dietary fats are emulsified to form micelles, which can carry the fat particles to the surface of the enterocytes. There, the micelles release their fats to diffuse across the cell membrane. The fats are then reassembled into triglycerides and mixed with other lipids and proteins into chylomicrons that can pass into lacteals. Other absorbed monomers travel from blood capillaries in the villus to the hepatic portal vein and then to the liver.

INTERACTIVE LINK QUESTIONS

1. By clicking on this link (http://openstaxcollege.org/l/fooddigestion) , you can watch a short video of what happens to the food you eat as it passes from your mouth to your intestine. Along the way, note how the food changes consistency and form. How does this change in consistency facilitate your gaining nutrients from food?

2. Visit this site (http://openstaxcollege.org/l/fooddigestion2) for an overview of digestion of food in different regions of the digestive tract. Note the route of non-fat nutrients from the small intestine to their release as nutrients to the body.

3. Watch this animation (http://openstaxcollege.org/l/swallowing) to see how swallowing is a complex process that involves the nervous system to coordinate the actions of upper respiratory and digestive activities. During which stage of swallowing is there a risk of food entering respiratory pathways and how is this risk blocked?

4. Watch this animation (http://openstaxcollege.org/l/stomach1) that depicts the structure of the stomach and how this structure functions in the initiation of protein digestion. This view of the stomach shows the characteristic rugae. What is the function of these rugae?

5. Watch this animation (http://openstaxcollege.org/l/sintestine) that depicts the structure of the small intestine, and, in particular, the villi. Epithelial cells continue the digestion and absorption of nutrients and transport these nutrients to the lymphatic and circulatory systems. In the small intestine, the products of food digestion are absorbed by different structures in the villi. Which structure absorbs and transports fats?

6. By watching this animation (http://openstaxcollege.org/l/foodgroups) , you will see that for the various food groups—proteins, fats, and carbohydrates—digestion begins in different parts of the digestion system, though all end in the same place. Of the three major food classes (carbohydrates, fats, and proteins), which is digested in the mouth, the stomach, and the small intestine?

7. Watch this video (http://openstaxcollege.org/l/liver) to see the structure of the liver and how this structure supports the functions of the liver, including the processing of nutrients, toxins, and wastes. At rest, about 1500 mL of blood per minute flow through the liver. What percentage of this blood flow comes from the hepatic portal system?

REVIEW QUESTIONS

8. Which of these organs is not considered an accessory digestive structure?
   a. mouth
   b. salivary glands
   c. pancreas
   d. liver

9. Which of the following organs is supported by a layer of adventitia rather than serosa?
   a. esophagus
   b. stomach
   c. small intestine
   d. large intestine

10. Which of the following membranes covers the stomach?
   a. falciform ligament
   b. mesocolon
   c. parietal peritoneum
   d. visceral peritoneum

11. Which of these processes occurs in the mouth?
   a. ingestion
   b. mechanical digestion
   c. chemical digestion
   d. all of the above

12. Which of these processes occurs throughout most of the alimentary canal?
   a. ingestion
   b. propulsion
   c. segmentation
   d. absorption

13. Which of the following stimuli activates sensors in the walls of digestive organs?
   a. breakdown products of digestion
   b. distension
   c. pH of chyme
   d. all of the above

14. Which of these statements about reflexes in the GI tract is false?
   a. Short reflexes are provoked by nerves near the GI tract.
   b. Short reflexes are mediated by the enteric nervous system.
   c. Food that distends the stomach initiates long reflexes.
   d. Long reflexes can be provoked by stimuli originating outside the GI tract.

15. Which of these ingredients in saliva is responsible for activating salivary amylase?

a. mucus
b. phosphate ions
c. chloride ions
d. urea

16. Which of these statements about the pharynx is true?

a. It extends from the nasal and oral cavities superiorly to the esophagus anteriorly.
b. The oropharynx is continuous superiorly with the nasopharynx.
c. The nasopharynx is involved in digestion.
d. The laryngopharynx is composed partially of cartilage.

17. Which structure is located where the esophagus penetrates the diaphragm?
a. esophageal hiatus
b. cardiac orifice
c. upper esophageal sphincter
d. lower esophageal sphincter

18. Which phase of deglutition involves contraction of the longitudinal muscle layer of the muscularis?
a. voluntary phase
b. buccal phase
c. pharyngeal phase
d. esophageal phase

19. Which of these cells secrete hormones?
a. parietal cells
b. mucous neck cells
c. enteroendocrine cells
d. chief cells

20. Where does the majority of chemical digestion in the stomach occur?
a. fundus and body
b. cardia and fundus
c. body and pylorus
d. body

21. During gastric emptying, chyme is released into the duodenum through the _____.
a. esophageal hiatus
b. pyloric antrum
c. pyloric canal
d. pyloric sphincter

22. Parietal cells secrete _____.
a. gastrin
b. hydrochloric acid
c. pepsin
d. pepsinogen

23. In which part of the alimentary canal does most digestion occur?
a. stomach
b. proximal small intestine
c. distal small intestine
d. ascending colon

24. Which of these is most associated with villi?
a. haustra
b. lacteals
c. bacterial flora
d. intestinal glands

25. What is the role of the small intestine's MALT?
a. secreting mucus
b. buffering acidic chyme
c. activating pepsin
d. preventing bacteria from entering the bloodstream

26. Which part of the large intestine attaches to the appendix?
a. cecum
b. ascending colon
c. transverse colon
d. descending colon

27. Which of these statements about bile is true?
a. About 500 mL is secreted daily.
b. Its main function is the denaturation of proteins.
c. It is synthesized in the gallbladder.
d. Bile salts are recycled.

28. Pancreatic juice _____.
a. deactivates bile.
b. is secreted by pancreatic islet cells.
c. buffers chyme.
d. is released into the cystic duct.

29. Where does the chemical digestion of starch begin?
a. mouth
b. esophagus
c. stomach
d. small intestine

30. Which of these is involved in the chemical digestion of protein?
a. pancreatic amylase
b. trypsin
c. sucrase
d. pancreatic nuclease

31. Where are most fat-digesting enzymes produced?
a. small intestine
b. gallbladder
c. liver
d. pancreas

32. Which of these nutrients is absorbed mainly in the duodenum?
a. glucose
b. iron
c. sodium
d. water

CRITICAL THINKING QUESTIONS

33. Explain how the enteric nervous system supports the digestive system. What might occur that could result in the autonomic nervous system having a negative impact on digestion?

34. What layer of the alimentary canal tissue is capable of helping to protect the body against disease, and through what mechanism?

35. Offer a theory to explain why segmentation occurs and peristalsis slows in the small intestine.

36. It has been several hours since you last ate. Walking past a bakery, you catch a whiff of freshly baked bread. What type of reflex is triggered, and what is the result?

37. The composition of saliva varies from gland to gland. Discuss how saliva produced by the parotid gland differs in action from saliva produced by the sublingual gland.

38. During a hockey game, the puck hits a player in the mouth, knocking out all eight of his most anterior teeth. Which teeth did the player lose and how does this loss affect food ingestion?

39. What prevents swallowed food from entering the airways?

40. Explain the mechanism responsible for gastroesophageal reflux.

41. Describe the three processes involved in the esophageal phase of deglutition.

42. Explain how the stomach is protected from self-digestion and why this is necessary.

43. Describe unique anatomical features that enable the stomach to perform digestive functions.

44. Explain how nutrients absorbed in the small intestine pass into the general circulation.

45. Why is it important that chyme from the stomach is delivered to the small intestine slowly and in small amounts?

46. Describe three of the differences between the walls of the large and small intestines.

47. Why does the pancreas secrete some enzymes in their inactive forms, and where are these enzymes activated?

48. Describe the location of hepatocytes in the liver and how this arrangement enhances their function.

49. Explain the role of bile salts and lecithin in the emulsification of lipids (fats).

50. How is vitamin B_{12} absorbed?

24 | METABOLISM AND NUTRITION

Figure 24.1 Metabolism Metabolism is the sum of all energy-requiring and energy-consuming processes of the body. Many factors contribute to overall metabolism, including lean muscle mass, the amount and quality of food consumed, and the physical demands placed on the human body. (credit: "tableatny"/flickr.com)

Introduction

Chapter Objectives

After studying this chapter, you will be able to:

- Describe the processes involved in anabolic and catabolic reactions
- List and describe the steps necessary for carbohydrate, lipid, and protein metabolism
- Explain the processes that regulate glucose levels during the absorptive and postabsorptive states
- Explain how metabolism is essential to maintaining body temperature (thermoregulation)
- Summarize the importance of vitamins and minerals in the diet

Eating is essential to life. Many of us look to eating as not only a necessity, but also a pleasure. You may have been told since childhood to start the day with a good breakfast to give you the energy to get through most of the day. You most likely have heard about the importance of a balanced diet, with plenty of fruits and vegetables. But what does this all mean to your body and the physiological processes it carries out each day? You need to absorb a range of nutrients so that your cells have the building blocks for metabolic processes that release the energy for the cells to carry out their daily jobs, to manufacture new proteins, cells, and body parts, and to recycle materials in the cell.

This chapter will take you through some of the chemical reactions essential to life, the sum of which is referred to as metabolism. The focus of these discussions will be anabolic reactions and catabolic reactions. You will examine the various chemical reactions that are important to sustain life, including why you must have oxygen, how mitochondria transfer energy, and the importance of certain "metabolic" hormones and vitamins.

Metabolism varies, depending on age, gender, activity level, fuel consumption, and lean body mass. Your own metabolic rate fluctuates throughout life. By modifying your diet and exercise regimen, you can increase both lean body mass and metabolic rate. Factors affecting metabolism also play important roles in controlling muscle mass. Aging is known to decrease the metabolic rate by as much as 5 percent per year. Additionally, because men tend to have more lean muscle mass then women, their basal metabolic rate (metabolic rate at rest) is higher; therefore, men tend to burn more calories than women do. Lastly, an individual's inherent metabolic rate is a function of the proteins and enzymes derived from their genetic background. Thus, your genes play a big role in your metabolism. Nonetheless, each person's body engages in the same overall metabolic processes.

24.1 | Overview of Metabolic Reactions

By the end of this section, you will be able to:
- Describe the process by which polymers are broken down into monomers
- Describe the process by which monomers are combined into polymers
- Discuss the role of ATP in metabolism
- Explain oxidation-reduction reactions
- Describe the hormones that regulate anabolic and catabolic reactions

Metabolic processes are constantly taking place in the body. **Metabolism** is the sum of all of the chemical reactions that are involved in catabolism and anabolism. The reactions governing the breakdown of food to obtain energy are called catabolic reactions. Conversely, anabolic reactions use the energy produced by catabolic reactions to synthesize larger molecules from smaller ones, such as when the body forms proteins by stringing together amino acids. Both sets of reactions are critical to maintaining life.

Because catabolic reactions produce energy and anabolic reactions use energy, ideally, energy usage would balance the energy produced. If the net energy change is positive (catabolic reactions release more energy than the anabolic reactions use), then the body stores the excess energy by building fat molecules for long-term storage. On the other hand, if the net energy change is negative (catabolic reactions release less energy than anabolic reactions use), the body uses stored energy to compensate for the deficiency of energy released by catabolism.

Catabolic Reactions

Catabolic reactions break down large organic molecules into smaller molecules, releasing the energy contained in the chemical bonds. These energy releases (conversions) are not 100 percent efficient. The amount of energy released is less than the total amount contained in the molecule. Approximately 40 percent of energy yielded from catabolic reactions is directly transferred to the high-energy molecule adenosine triphosphate (ATP). ATP, the energy currency of cells, can be used immediately to power molecular machines that support cell, tissue, and organ function. This includes building new tissue and repairing damaged tissue. ATP can also be stored to fulfill future energy demands. The remaining 60 percent of the energy released from catabolic reactions is given off as heat, which tissues and body fluids absorb.

Structurally, ATP molecules consist of an adenine, a ribose, and three phosphate groups (Figure 24.2). The chemical bond between the second and third phosphate groups, termed a high-energy bond, represents the greatest source of energy in a cell. It is the first bond that catabolic enzymes break when cells require energy to do work. The products of this reaction are a molecule of adenosine diphosphate (ADP) and a lone phosphate group (P_i). ATP, ADP, and P_i are constantly being cycled through reactions that build ATP and store energy, and reactions that break down ATP and release energy.

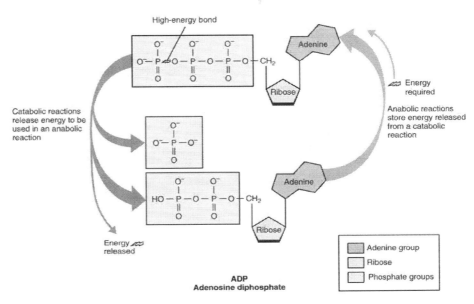

Figure 24.2 Structure of ATP Molecule Adenosine triphosphate (ATP) is the energy molecule of the cell. During catabolic reactions, ATP is created and energy is stored until needed during anabolic reactions.

The energy from ATP drives all bodily functions, such as contracting muscles, maintaining the electrical potential of nerve cells, and absorbing food in the gastrointestinal tract. The metabolic reactions that produce ATP come from various sources (Figure 24.3).

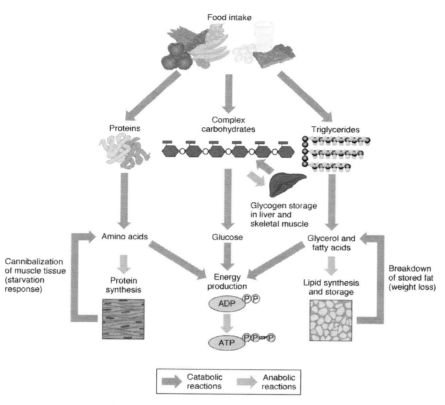

Figure 24.3 Sources of ATP During catabolic reactions, proteins are broken down into amino acids, lipids are broken down into fatty acids, and polysaccharides are broken down into monosaccharides. These building blocks are then used for the synthesis of molecules in anabolic reactions.

Of the four major macromolecular groups (carbohydrates, lipids, proteins, and nucleic acids) that are processed by digestion, carbohydrates are considered the most common source of energy to fuel the body. They take the form of either complex carbohydrates, polysaccharides like starch and glycogen, or simple sugars (monosaccharides) like glucose and fructose. Sugar catabolism breaks polysaccharides down into their individual monosaccharides. Among the monosaccharides, glucose is the most common fuel for ATP production in cells, and as such, there are a number of endocrine control mechanisms to regulate glucose concentration in the bloodstream. Excess glucose is either stored as an energy reserve in the liver and skeletal muscles as the complex polymer glycogen, or it is converted into fat (triglyceride) in adipose cells (adipocytes).

Among the lipids (fats), triglycerides are most often used for energy via a metabolic process called β-oxidation. About one-half of excess fat is stored in adipocytes that accumulate in the subcutaneous tissue under the skin, whereas the rest is stored in adipocytes in other tissues and organs.

Proteins, which are polymers, can be broken down into their monomers, individual amino acids. Amino acids can be used as building blocks of new proteins or broken down further for the production of ATP. When one is chronically starving, this use of amino acids for energy production can lead to a wasting away of the body, as more and more proteins are broken down.

Nucleic acids are present in most of the foods you eat. During digestion, nucleic acids including DNA and various RNAs are broken down into their constituent nucleotides. These nucleotides are readily absorbed and transported throughout the body to be used by individual cells during nucleic acid metabolism.

Anabolic Reactions

In contrast to catabolic reactions, **anabolic reactions** involve the joining of smaller molecules into larger ones. Anabolic reactions combine monosaccharides to form polysaccharides, fatty acids to form triglycerides, amino acids to form proteins, and nucleotides to form nucleic acids. These processes require energy in the form of ATP molecules generated by catabolic reactions. Anabolic reactions, also called **biosynthesis reactions**, create new molecules that form new cells and tissues, and revitalize organs.

Hormonal Regulation of Metabolism

Catabolic and anabolic hormones in the body help regulate metabolic processes. **Catabolic hormones** stimulate the breakdown of molecules and the production of energy. These include cortisol, glucagon, adrenaline/epinephrine, and cytokines. All of these hormones are mobilized at specific times to meet the needs of the body. **Anabolic hormones** are required for the synthesis of molecules and include growth hormone, insulin-like growth factor, insulin, testosterone, and estrogen. Table 24.1 summarizes the function of each of the catabolic hormones and Table 24.2 summarizes the functions of the anabolic hormones.

Catabolic Hormones

Hormone	Function
Cortisol	Released from the adrenal gland in response to stress; its main role is to increase blood glucose levels by gluconeogenesis (breaking down fats and proteins)
Glucagon	Released from alpha cells in the pancreas either when starving or when the body needs to generate additional energy; it stimulates the breakdown of glycogen in the liver to increase blood glucose levels; its effect is the opposite of insulin; glucagon and insulin are a part of a negative-feedback system that stabilizes blood glucose levels
Adrenaline/ epinephrine	Released in response to the activation of the sympathetic nervous system; increases heart rate and heart contractility, constricts blood vessels, is a bronchodilator that opens (dilates) the bronchi of the lungs to increase air volume in the lungs, and stimulates gluconeogenesis

Table 24.1

Anabolic Hormones

Hormone	Function
Growth hormone (GH)	Synthesized and released from the pituitary gland; stimulates the growth of cells, tissues, and bones
Insulin-like growth factor (IGF)	Stimulates the growth of muscle and bone while also inhibiting cell death (apoptosis)
Insulin	Produced by the beta cells of the pancreas; plays an essential role in carbohydrate and fat metabolism, controls blood glucose levels, and promotes the uptake of glucose into body cells; causes cells in muscle, adipose tissue, and liver to take up glucose from the blood and store it in the liver and muscle as glucagon; its effect is the opposite of glucagon; glucagon and insulin are a part of a negative-feedback system that stabilizes blood glucose levels
Testosterone	Produced by the testes in males and the ovaries in females; stimulates an increase in muscle mass and strength as well as the growth and strengthening of bone
Estrogen	Produced primarily by the ovaries, it is also produced by the liver and adrenal glands; its anabolic functions include increasing metabolism and fat deposition

Table 24.2

Metabolic Processes: Cushing Syndrome and Addison's Disease

As might be expected for a fundamental physiological process like metabolism, errors or malfunctions in metabolic processing lead to a pathophysiology or—if uncorrected—a disease state. Metabolic diseases are most commonly the result of malfunctioning proteins or enzymes that are critical to one or more metabolic pathways. Protein or enzyme malfunction can be the consequence of a genetic alteration or mutation. However, normally functioning proteins and enzymes can also have deleterious effects if their availability is not appropriately matched with metabolic need. For example, excessive production of the hormone cortisol (see Table 24.1) gives rise to Cushing syndrome. Clinically, Cushing syndrome is characterized by rapid weight gain, especially in the trunk and face region, depression, and anxiety. It is worth mentioning that tumors of the pituitary that produce adrenocorticotropic hormone (ACTH), which subsequently stimulates the adrenal cortex to release excessive cortisol, produce similar effects. This indirect mechanism of cortisol overproduction is referred to as Cushing disease.

Patients with Cushing syndrome can exhibit high blood glucose levels and are at an increased risk of becoming obese. They also show slow growth, accumulation of fat between the shoulders, weak muscles, bone pain (because cortisol causes proteins to be broken down to make glucose via gluconeogenesis), and fatigue. Other symptoms include excessive sweating (hyperhidrosis), capillary dilation, and thinning of the skin, which can lead to easy bruising. The treatments for Cushing syndrome are all focused on reducing excessive cortisol levels. Depending on the cause of the excess, treatment may be as simple as discontinuing the use of cortisol ointments. In cases of tumors, surgery is often used to remove the offending tumor. Where surgery is inappropriate, radiation therapy can be used to reduce the size of a tumor or ablate portions of the adrenal cortex. Finally, medications are available that can help to regulate the amounts of cortisol.

Insufficient cortisol production is equally problematic. Adrenal insufficiency, or Addison's disease, is characterized by the reduced production of cortisol from the adrenal gland. It can result from malfunction of the adrenal glands—they do not produce enough cortisol—or it can be a consequence of decreased ACTH availability from the pituitary. Patients with Addison's disease may have low blood pressure, paleness, extreme weakness, fatigue, slow or sluggish movements, lightheadedness, and salt cravings due to the loss of sodium and high blood potassium levels (hyperkalemia). Victims also may suffer from loss of appetite, chronic diarrhea, vomiting, mouth lesions, and patchy skin color. Diagnosis typically involves blood tests and imaging tests of the adrenal and pituitary glands. Treatment involves cortisol replacement therapy, which usually must be continued for life.

Oxidation-Reduction Reactions

The chemical reactions underlying metabolism involve the transfer of electrons from one compound to another by processes catalyzed by enzymes. The electrons in these reactions commonly come from hydrogen atoms, which consist of an electron and a proton. A molecule gives up a hydrogen atom, in the form of a hydrogen ion (H^+) and an electron, breaking the molecule into smaller parts. The loss of an electron, or **oxidation**, releases a small amount of energy; both the electron and the energy are then passed to another molecule in the process of **reduction**, or the gaining of an electron. These two reactions always happen together in an **oxidation-reduction reaction** (also called a redox reaction)—when an electron is passed between molecules, the donor is oxidized and the recipient is reduced. Oxidation-reduction reactions often happen in a series, so that a molecule that is reduced is subsequently oxidized, passing on not only the electron it just received but also the energy it received. As the series of reactions progresses, energy accumulates that is used to combine P_i and ADP to form ATP, the high-energy molecule that the body uses for fuel.

Oxidation-reduction reactions are catalyzed by enzymes that trigger the removal of hydrogen atoms. Coenzymes work with enzymes and accept hydrogen atoms. The two most common coenzymes of oxidation-reduction reactions are **nicotinamide adenine dinucleotide (NAD)** and **flavin adenine dinucleotide (FAD)**. Their respective reduced coenzymes are **NADH** and **FADH$_2$**, which are energy-containing molecules used to transfer energy during the creation of ATP.

24.2 | Carbohydrate Metabolism

By the end of this section, you will be able to:
- Explain the processes of glycolysis
- Describe the pathway of a pyruvate molecule through the Krebs cycle
- Explain the transport of electrons through the electron transport chain
- Describe the process of ATP production through oxidative phosphorylation
- Summarize the process of gluconeogenesis

Carbohydrates are organic molecules composed of carbon, hydrogen, and oxygen atoms. The family of carbohydrates includes both simple and complex sugars. Glucose and fructose are examples of simple sugars, and starch, glycogen, and cellulose are all examples of complex sugars. The complex sugars are also called **polysaccharides** and are made of multiple **monosaccharide** molecules. Polysaccharides serve as energy storage (e.g., starch and glycogen) and as structural components (e.g., chitin in insects and cellulose in plants).

During digestion, carbohydrates are broken down into simple, soluble sugars that can be transported across the intestinal wall into the circulatory system to be transported throughout the body. Carbohydrate digestion begins in the mouth with the action of **salivary amylase** on starches and ends with monosaccharides being absorbed across the epithelium of the small intestine. Once the absorbed monosaccharides are transported to the tissues, the process of **cellular respiration** begins (Figure 24.4). This section will focus first on glycolysis, a process where the monosaccharide glucose is oxidized, releasing the energy stored in its bonds to produce ATP.

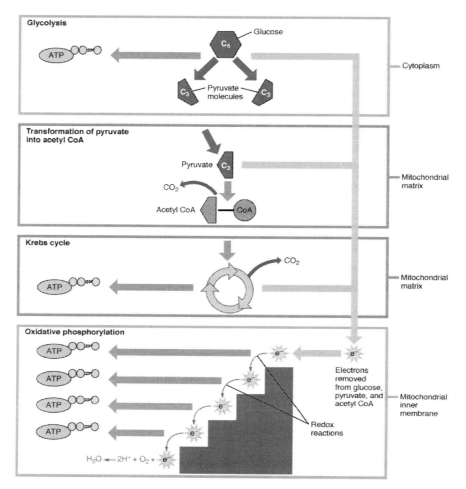

Figure 24.4 Cellular Respiration Cellular respiration oxidizes glucose molecules through glycolysis, the Krebs cycle, and oxidative phosphorylation to produce ATP.

Glycolysis

Glucose is the body's most readily available source of energy. After digestive processes break polysaccharides down into monosaccharides, including glucose, the monosaccharides are transported across the wall of the small intestine and into the circulatory system, which transports them to the liver. In the liver, hepatocytes either pass the glucose on through the circulatory system or store excess glucose as glycogen. Cells in the body take up the circulating glucose in response to insulin and, through a series of reactions called **glycolysis**, transfer some of the energy in glucose to ADP to form ATP (Figure 24.5). The last step in glycolysis produces the product **pyruvate**.

Glycolysis begins with the phosphorylation of glucose by hexokinase to form glucose-6-phosphate. This step uses one ATP, which is the donor of the phosphate group. Under the action of phosphofructokinase, glucose-6-phosphate is converted into fructose-6-phosphate. At this point, a second ATP donates its phosphate group, forming fructose-1,6-bisphosphate. This six-carbon sugar is split to form two phosphorylated three-carbon molecules, glyceraldehyde-3-phosphate and dihydroxyacetone phosphate, which are both converted into glyceraldehyde-3-phosphate. The glyceraldehyde-3-phosphate is further phosphorylated with groups donated by dihydrogen phosphate present in the cell to form the three-carbon molecule 1,3-bisphosphoglycerate. The energy of this reaction comes from the oxidation of (removal of electrons from) glyceraldehyde-3-phosphate. In a series of reactions leading to pyruvate, the two phosphate groups are then transferred to two ADPs to form two ATPs. Thus, glycolysis uses two ATPs but generates four ATPs, yielding a net gain of two ATPs and two molecules of pyruvate. In the presence of oxygen, pyruvate continues on to the Krebs cycle (also called the **citric acid cycle** or **tricarboxylic acid cycle (TCA)**, where additional energy is extracted and passed on.

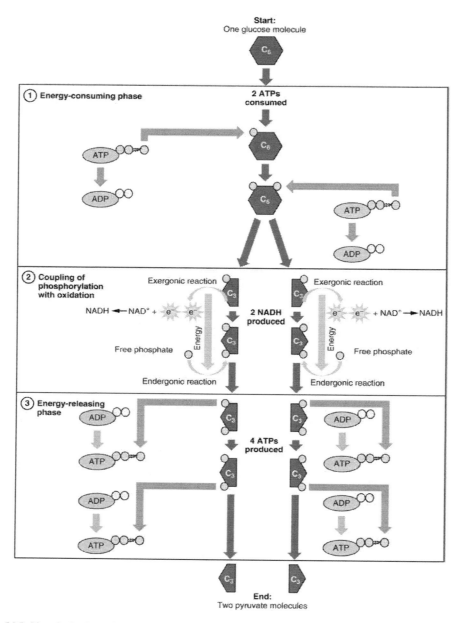

Figure 24.5 Glycolysis Overview During the energy-consuming phase of glycolysis, two ATPs are consumed, transferring two phosphates to the glucose molecule. The glucose molecule then splits into two three-carbon compounds, each containing a phosphate. During the second phase, an additional phosphate is added to each of the three-carbon compounds. The energy for this endergonic reaction is provided by the removal (oxidation) of two electrons from each three-carbon compound. During the energy-releasing phase, the phosphates are removed from both three-carbon compounds and used to produce four ATP molecules.

Interactive Link

Watch this video (http://openstaxcollege.org/l/glycolysis1) to learn about glycolysis.

Glycolysis can be divided into two phases: energy consuming (also called chemical priming) and energy yielding. The first phase is the **energy-consuming phase**, so it requires two ATP molecules to start the reaction for each molecule of glucose. However, the end of the reaction produces four ATPs, resulting in a net gain of two ATP energy molecules.

Glycolysis can be expressed as the following equation:

$$\text{Glucose} + 2\text{ATP} + 2\text{NAD}^+ + 4\text{ADP} + 2P_i \rightarrow 2 \text{ Pyruvate} + 4\text{ATP} + 2\text{NADH} + 2\text{H}^+$$

This equation states that glucose, in combination with ATP (the energy source), NAD^+ (a coenzyme that serves as an electron acceptor), and inorganic phosphate, breaks down into two pyruvate molecules, generating four ATP molecules—for a net yield of two ATP—and two energy-containing NADH coenzymes. The NADH that is produced in this process will be used later to produce ATP in the mitochondria. Importantly, by the end of this process, one glucose molecule generates two pyruvate molecules, two high-energy ATP molecules, and two electron-carrying NADH molecules.

The following discussions of glycolysis include the enzymes responsible for the reactions. When glucose enters a cell, the enzyme hexokinase (or glucokinase, in the liver) rapidly adds a phosphate to convert it into **glucose-6-phosphate**. A kinase is a type of enzyme that adds a phosphate molecule to a substrate (in this case, glucose, but it can be true of other molecules also). This conversion step requires one ATP and essentially traps the glucose in the cell, preventing it from passing back through the plasma membrane, thus allowing glycolysis to proceed. It also functions to maintain a concentration gradient with higher glucose levels in the blood than in the tissues. By establishing this concentration gradient, the glucose in the blood will be able to flow from an area of high concentration (the blood) into an area of low concentration (the tissues) to be either used or stored. **Hexokinase** is found in nearly every tissue in the body. **Glucokinase**, on the other hand, is expressed in tissues that are active when blood glucose levels are high, such as the liver. Hexokinase has a higher affinity for glucose than glucokinase and therefore is able to convert glucose at a faster rate than glucokinase. This is important when levels of glucose are very low in the body, as it allows glucose to travel preferentially to those tissues that require it more.

In the next step of the first phase of glycolysis, the enzyme glucose-6-phosphate isomerase converts glucose-6-phosphate into fructose-6-phosphate. Like glucose, fructose is also a six carbon-containing sugar. The enzyme phosphofructokinase-1 then adds one more phosphate to convert fructose-6-phosphate into fructose-1-6-bisphosphate, another six-carbon sugar, using another ATP molecule. Aldolase then breaks down this fructose-1-6-bisphosphate into two three-carbon molecules, glyceraldehyde-3-phosphate and dihydroxyacetone phosphate. The triosephosphate isomerase enzyme then converts dihydroxyacetone phosphate into a second glyceraldehyde-3-phosphate molecule. Therefore, by the end of this chemical-priming or energy-consuming phase, one glucose molecule is broken down into two glyceraldehyde-3-phosphate molecules.

The second phase of glycolysis, the **energy-yielding phase**, creates the energy that is the product of glycolysis. Glyceraldehyde-3-phosphate dehydrogenase converts each three-carbon glyceraldehyde-3-phosphate produced during the energy-consuming phase into 1,3-bisphosphoglycerate. This reaction releases an electron that is then picked up by NAD^+ to create an NADH molecule. NADH is a high-energy molecule, like ATP, but unlike ATP, it is not used as energy currency by the cell. Because there are two glyceraldehyde-3-phosphate molecules, two NADH molecules are synthesized during this step. Each 1,3-bisphosphoglycerate is subsequently dephosphorylated (i.e., a phosphate is removed) by phosphoglycerate kinase into 3-phosphoglycerate. Each phosphate released in this reaction can convert one molecule of ADP into one high-energy ATP molecule, resulting in a gain of two ATP molecules.

The enzyme phosphoglycerate mutase then converts the 3-phosphoglycerate molecules into 2-phosphoglycerate. The enolase enzyme then acts upon the 2-phosphoglycerate molecules to convert them into phosphoenolpyruvate molecules.

The last step of glycolysis involves the dephosphorylation of the two phosphoenolpyruvate molecules by pyruvate kinase to create two pyruvate molecules and two ATP molecules.

In summary, one glucose molecule breaks down into two pyruvate molecules, and creates two net ATP molecules and two NADH molecules by glycolysis. Therefore, glycolysis generates energy for the cell and creates pyruvate molecules that can be processed further through the aerobic Krebs cycle (also called the citric acid cycle or tricarboxylic acid cycle); converted into lactic acid or alcohol (in yeast) by fermentation; or used later for the synthesis of glucose through gluconeogenesis.

Anaerobic Respiration

When oxygen is limited or absent, pyruvate enters an anaerobic pathway. In these reactions, pyruvate can be converted into lactic acid. In addition to generating an additional ATP, this pathway serves to keep the pyruvate concentration low so glycolysis continues, and it oxidizes NADH into the NAD^+ needed by glycolysis. In this reaction, lactic acid replaces oxygen as the final electron acceptor. Anaerobic respiration occurs in most cells of the body when oxygen is limited or mitochondria are absent or nonfunctional. For example, because erythrocytes (red blood cells) lack mitochondria, they must produce their ATP from anaerobic respiration. This is an effective pathway of ATP production for short periods of time, ranging from seconds to a few minutes. The lactic acid produced diffuses into the plasma and is carried to the liver, where it is converted back into pyruvate or glucose via the Cori cycle. Similarly, when a person exercises, muscles use ATP faster than oxygen can be delivered to them. They depend on glycolysis and lactic acid production for rapid ATP production.

Aerobic Respiration

In the presence of oxygen, pyruvate can enter the Krebs cycle where additional energy is extracted as electrons are transferred from the pyruvate to the receptors NAD^+, GDP, and FAD, with carbon dioxide being a "waste product" (Figure 24.6). The NADH and $FADH_2$ pass electrons on to the electron transport chain, which uses the transferred energy to produce ATP. As the terminal step in the electron transport chain, oxygen is the **terminal electron acceptor** and creates water inside the mitochondria.

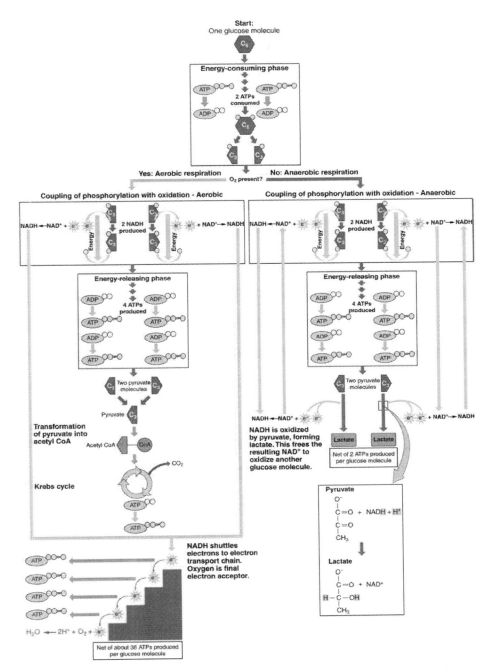

Figure 24.6 Aerobic versus Anaerobic Respiration The process of anaerobic respiration converts glucose into two lactate molecules in the absence of oxygen or within erythrocytes that lack mitochondria. During aerobic respiration, glucose is oxidized into two pyruvate molecules.

Krebs Cycle/Citric Acid Cycle/Tricarboxylic Acid Cycle

The pyruvate molecules generated during glycolysis are transported across the mitochondrial membrane into the inner mitochondrial matrix, where they are metabolized by enzymes in a pathway called the **Krebs cycle** (Figure 24.7). The Krebs cycle is also commonly called the citric acid cycle or the tricarboxylic acid (TCA) cycle. During the Krebs cycle, high-energy molecules, including ATP, NADH, and FADH$_2$, are created. NADH and FADH$_2$ then pass electrons through the electron transport chain in the mitochondria to generate more ATP molecules.

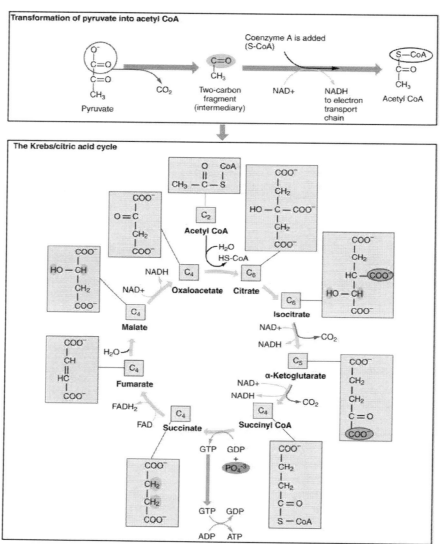

Figure 24.7 Krebs Cycle During the Krebs cycle, each pyruvate that is generated by glycolysis is converted into a two-carbon acetyl CoA molecule. The acetyl CoA is systematically processed through the cycle and produces high-energy NADH, FADH$_2$, and ATP molecules.

Watch this animation (http://openstaxcollege.org/l/krebscycle) to observe the Krebs cycle.

The three-carbon pyruvate molecule generated during glycolysis moves from the cytoplasm into the mitochondrial matrix, where it is converted by the enzyme pyruvate dehydrogenase into a two-carbon **acetyl coenzyme A (acetyl CoA)** molecule. This reaction is an oxidative decarboxylation reaction. It converts the three-carbon pyruvate into a two-carbon acetyl CoA molecule, releasing carbon dioxide and transferring two electrons that combine with NAD^+ to form NADH. Acetyl CoA enters the Krebs cycle by combining with a four-carbon molecule, oxaloacetate, to form the six-carbon molecule citrate, or citric acid, at the same time releasing the coenzyme A molecule.

The six-carbon citrate molecule is systematically converted to a five-carbon molecule and then a four-carbon molecule, ending with oxaloacetate, the beginning of the cycle. Along the way, each citrate molecule will produce one ATP, one $FADH_2$, and three NADH. The $FADH_2$ and NADH will enter the oxidative phosphorylation system located in the inner mitochondrial membrane. In addition, the Krebs cycle supplies the starting materials to process and break down proteins and fats.

To start the Krebs cycle, citrate synthase combines acetyl CoA and oxaloacetate to form a six-carbon citrate molecule; CoA is subsequently released and can combine with another pyruvate molecule to begin the cycle again. The aconitase enzyme converts citrate into isocitrate. In two successive steps of oxidative decarboxylation, two molecules of CO_2 and two NADH molecules are produced when isocitrate dehydrogenase converts isocitrate into the five-carbon α-ketoglutarate, which is then catalyzed and converted into the four-carbon succinyl CoA by α-ketoglutarate dehydrogenase. The enzyme succinyl CoA dehydrogenase then converts succinyl CoA into succinate and forms the high-energy molecule GTP, which transfers its energy to ADP to produce ATP. Succinate dehydrogenase then converts succinate into fumarate, forming a molecule of $FADH_2$. Fumarase then converts fumarate into malate, which malate dehydrogenase then converts back into oxaloacetate while reducing NAD^+ to NADH. Oxaloacetate is then ready to combine with the next acetyl CoA to start the Krebs cycle again (see Figure 24.7). For each turn of the cycle, three NADH, one ATP (through GTP), and one $FADH_2$ are created. Each carbon of pyruvate is converted into CO_2, which is released as a byproduct of oxidative (aerobic) respiration.

Oxidative Phosphorylation and the Electron Transport Chain

The **electron transport chain (ETC)** uses the NADH and $FADH_2$ produced by the Krebs cycle to generate ATP. Electrons from NADH and $FADH_2$ are transferred through protein complexes embedded in the inner mitochondrial membrane by a series of enzymatic reactions. The electron transport chain consists of a series of four enzyme complexes (Complex I – Complex IV) and two coenzymes (ubiquinone and Cytochrome c), which act as electron carriers and proton pumps used to transfer H^+ ions into the space between the inner and outer mitochondrial membranes (Figure 24.8). The ETC couples the transfer of electrons between a donor (like NADH) and an electron acceptor (like O_2) with the transfer of protons (H^+ ions) across the inner mitochondrial membrane, enabling the process of **oxidative phosphorylation**. In the presence of oxygen, energy is passed, stepwise, through the electron carriers to collect gradually the energy needed to attach a phosphate to ADP and produce ATP. The role of molecular oxygen, O_2, is as the terminal electron acceptor for the ETC. This means that once the electrons have passed through the entire ETC, they must be passed to another, separate molecule. These electrons, O_2, and H^+ ions from the matrix combine to form new water molecules. This is the basis for your need to breathe in oxygen. Without oxygen, electron flow through the ETC ceases.

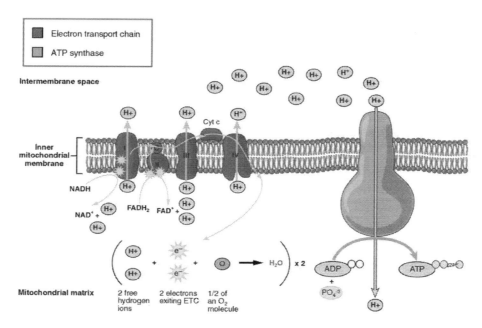

Figure 24.8 Electron Transport Chain The electron transport chain is a series of electron carriers and ion pumps that are used to pump H⁺ ions out of the inner mitochondrial matrix.

Watch this video (http://openstaxcollege.org/l/ETchain) to learn about the electron transport chain.

The electrons released from NADH and FADH$_2$ are passed along the chain by each of the carriers, which are reduced when they receive the electron and oxidized when passing it on to the next carrier. Each of these reactions releases a small amount of energy, which is used to pump H⁺ ions across the inner membrane. The accumulation of these protons in the space between the membranes creates a proton gradient with respect to the mitochondrial matrix.

Also embedded in the inner mitochondrial membrane is an amazing protein pore complex called **ATP synthase**. Effectively, it is a turbine that is powered by the flow of H⁺ ions across the inner membrane down a gradient and into the mitochondrial matrix. As the H⁺ ions traverse the complex, the shaft of the complex rotates. This rotation enables other portions of ATP synthase to encourage ADP and P$_i$ to create ATP. In accounting for the total number of ATP produced per glucose molecule through aerobic respiration, it is important to remember the following points:

- A net of two ATP are produced through glycolysis (four produced and two consumed during the energy-consuming stage). However, these two ATP are used for transporting the NADH produced during glycolysis from the cytoplasm into the mitochondria. Therefore, the net production of ATP during glycolysis is zero.

- In all phases after glycolysis, the number of ATP, NADH, and FADH$_2$ produced must be multiplied by two to reflect how each glucose molecule produces two pyruvate molecules.
- In the ETC, about three ATP are produced for every oxidized NADH. However, only about two ATP are produced for every oxidized FADH$_2$. The electrons from FADH$_2$ produce less ATP, because they start at a lower point in the ETC (Complex II) compared to the electrons from NADH (Complex I) (see Figure 24.8).

Therefore, for every glucose molecule that enters aerobic respiration, a net total of 36 ATPs are produced (Figure 24.9).

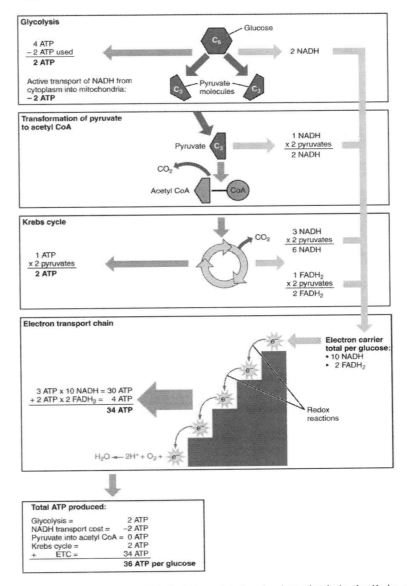

Figure 24.9 Carbohydrate Metabolism Carbohydrate metabolism involves glycolysis, the Krebs cycle, and the electron transport chain.

Gluconeogenesis

Gluconeogenesis is the synthesis of new glucose molecules from pyruvate, lactate, glycerol, or the amino acids alanine or glutamine. This process takes place primarily in the liver during periods of low glucose, that is, under conditions of fasting, starvation, and low carbohydrate diets. So, the question can be raised as to why the body would create something it has just spent a fair amount of effort to break down? Certain key organs, including the brain, can use only glucose as an energy source; therefore, it is essential that the body maintain a minimum blood glucose concentration. When the blood glucose concentration falls below that certain point, new glucose is synthesized by the liver to raise the blood concentration to normal.

Gluconeogenesis is not simply the reverse of glycolysis. There are some important differences (Figure 24.10). Pyruvate is a common starting material for gluconeogenesis. First, the pyruvate is converted into oxaloacetate. Oxaloacetate then serves as a substrate for the enzyme phosphoenolpyruvate carboxykinase (PEPCK), which transforms oxaloacetate into phosphoenolpyruvate (PEP). From this step, gluconeogenesis is nearly the reverse of glycolysis. PEP is converted back into 2-phosphoglycerate, which is converted into 3-phosphoglycerate. Then, 3-phosphoglycerate is converted into 1,3 bisphosphoglycerate and then into glyceraldehyde-3-phosphate. Two molecules of glyceraldehyde-3-phosphate then combine to form fructose-1-6-bisphosphate, which is converted into fructose 6-phosphate and then into glucose-6-phosphate. Finally, a series of reactions generates glucose itself. In gluconeogenesis (as compared to glycolysis), the enzyme hexokinase is replaced by glucose-6-phosphatase, and the enzyme phosphofructokinase-1 is replaced by fructose-1,6-bisphosphatase. This helps the cell to regulate glycolysis and gluconeogenesis independently of each other.

As will be discussed as part of lipolysis, fats can be broken down into glycerol, which can be phosphorylated to form dihydroxyacetone phosphate or DHAP. DHAP can either enter the glycolytic pathway or be used by the liver as a substrate for gluconeogenesis.

Figure 24.10 Gluconeogenesis   Gluconeogenesis is the synthesis of glucose from pyruvate, lactate, glycerol, alanine, or glutamate.

Body's Metabolic Rate

The human body's metabolic rate decreases nearly 2 percent per decade after age 30. Changes in body composition, including reduced lean muscle mass, are mostly responsible for this decrease. The most dramatic loss of muscle mass, and consequential decline in metabolic rate, occurs between 50 and 70 years of age. Loss of muscle mass is the equivalent of reduced strength, which tends to inhibit seniors from engaging in sufficient physical activity. This results in a positive-feedback system where the reduced physical activity leads to even more muscle loss, further reducing metabolism.

There are several things that can be done to help prevent general declines in metabolism and to fight back against the cyclic nature of these declines. These include eating breakfast, eating small meals frequently, consuming plenty of lean protein, drinking water to remain hydrated, exercising (including strength training), and getting enough sleep. These measures can help keep energy levels from dropping and curb the urge for increased calorie consumption from excessive snacking. While these strategies are not guaranteed to maintain metabolism, they do help prevent muscle loss and may increase energy levels. Some experts also suggest avoiding sugar, which can lead to excess fat storage. Spicy foods and green tea might also be beneficial. Because stress activates cortisol release, and cortisol slows metabolism, avoiding stress, or at least practicing relaxation techniques, can also help.

24.3 | Lipid Metabolism

By the end of this section, you will be able to:
- Explain how energy can be derived from fat
- Explain the purpose and process of ketogenesis
- Describe the process of ketone body oxidation
- Explain the purpose and the process of lipogenesis

Fats (or triglycerides) within the body are ingested as food or synthesized by adipocytes or hepatocytes from carbohydrate precursors (Figure 24.11). Lipid metabolism entails the oxidation of fatty acids to either generate energy or synthesize new lipids from smaller constituent molecules. Lipid metabolism is associated with carbohydrate metabolism, as products of glucose (such as acetyl CoA) can be converted into lipids.

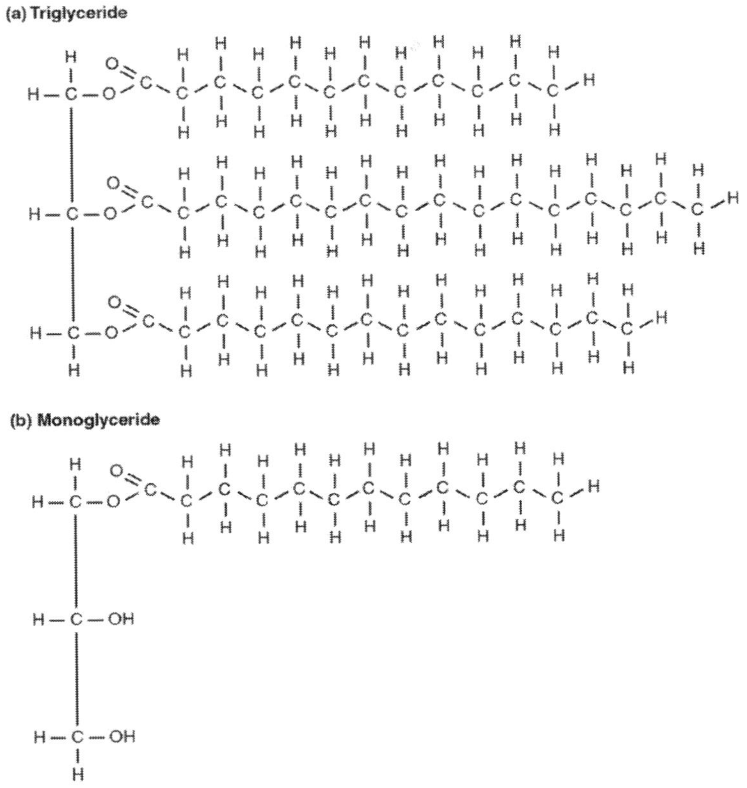

(a) Triglyceride

(b) Monoglyceride

Figure 24.11 Triglyceride Broken Down into a Monoglyceride A triglyceride molecule (a) breaks down into a monoglyceride (b).

Lipid metabolism begins in the intestine where ingested **triglycerides** are broken down into smaller chain fatty acids and subsequently into **monoglyceride molecules** (see Figure 24.11b) by **pancreatic lipases**, enzymes that break down fats after they are emulsified by **bile salts**. When food reaches the small intestine in the form of chyme, a digestive hormone called **cholecystokinin (CCK)** is released by intestinal cells in the intestinal mucosa. CCK stimulates the release of pancreatic lipase from the pancreas and stimulates the contraction of the gallbladder to release stored bile salts into the intestine. CCK also travels to the brain, where it can act as a hunger suppressant.

Together, the pancreatic lipases and bile salts break down triglycerides into free fatty acids. These fatty acids can be transported across the intestinal membrane. However, once they cross the membrane, they are recombined to again form triglyceride molecules. Within the intestinal cells, these triglycerides are packaged along with cholesterol molecules in phospholipid vesicles called **chylomicrons** (Figure 24.12). The chylomicrons enable fats and cholesterol to move within the aqueous environment of your lymphatic and circulatory systems. Chylomicrons leave the enterocytes by exocytosis and enter the lymphatic system via lacteals in the villi of the intestine. From the lymphatic system, the chylomicrons are transported to the circulatory system. Once in the circulation, they can either go to the liver or be stored in fat cells (adipocytes) that comprise adipose (fat) tissue found throughout the body.

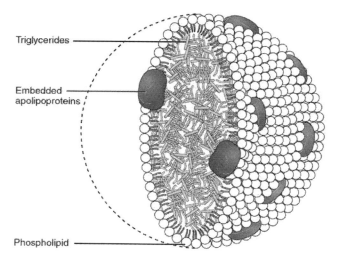

Figure 24.12 Chylomicrons Chylomicrons contain triglycerides, cholesterol molecules, and other apolipoproteins (protein molecules). They function to carry these water-insoluble molecules from the intestine, through the lymphatic system, and into the bloodstream, which carries the lipids to adipose tissue for storage.

Lipolysis

To obtain energy from fat, triglycerides must first be broken down by hydrolysis into their two principal components, fatty acids and glycerol. This process, called **lipolysis**, takes place in the cytoplasm. The resulting fatty acids are oxidized by β-oxidation into acetyl CoA, which is used by the Krebs cycle. The glycerol that is released from triglycerides after lipolysis directly enters the glycolysis pathway as DHAP. Because one triglyceride molecule yields three fatty acid molecules with as much as 16 or more carbons in each one, fat molecules yield more energy than carbohydrates and are an important source of energy for the human body. Triglycerides yield more than twice the energy per unit mass when compared to carbohydrates and proteins. Therefore, when glucose levels are low, triglycerides can be converted into acetyl CoA molecules and used to generate ATP through aerobic respiration.

The breakdown of fatty acids, called **fatty acid oxidation** or **beta (β)-oxidation**, begins in the cytoplasm, where fatty acids are converted into fatty acyl CoA molecules. This fatty acyl CoA combines with carnitine to create a fatty acyl carnitine molecule, which helps to transport the fatty acid across the mitochondrial membrane. Once inside the mitochondrial matrix, the fatty acyl carnitine molecule is converted back into fatty acyl CoA and then into acetyl CoA (Figure 24.13). The newly formed acetyl CoA enters the Krebs cycle and is used to produce ATP in the same way as acetyl CoA derived from pyruvate.

Figure 24.13 Breakdown of Fatty Acids During fatty acid oxidation, triglycerides can be broken down into acetyl CoA molecules and used for energy when glucose levels are low.

Ketogenesis

If excessive acetyl CoA is created from the oxidation of fatty acids and the Krebs cycle is overloaded and cannot handle it, the acetyl CoA is diverted to create **ketone bodies**. These ketone bodies can serve as a fuel source if glucose levels are too low in the body. Ketones serve as fuel in times of prolonged starvation or when patients suffer from uncontrolled diabetes and cannot utilize most of the circulating glucose. In both cases, fat stores are liberated to generate energy through the Krebs cycle and will generate ketone bodies when too much acetyl CoA accumulates.

In this ketone synthesis reaction, excess acetyl CoA is converted into **hydroxymethylglutaryl CoA (HMG CoA)**. HMG CoA is a precursor of cholesterol and is an intermediate that is subsequently converted into β-hydroxybutyrate, the primary ketone body in the blood (Figure 24.14).

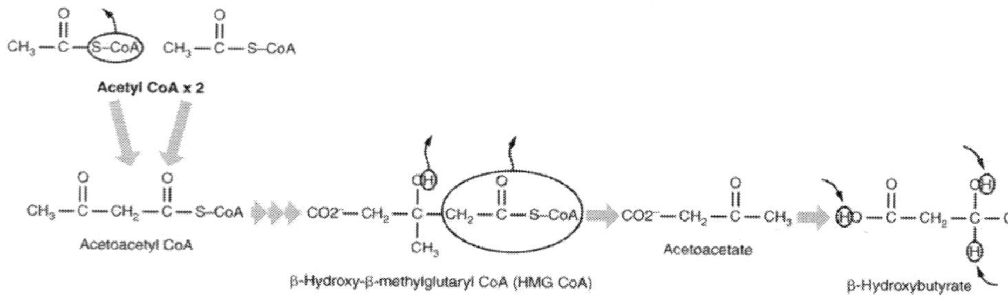

Figure 24.14 Ketogenesis Excess acetyl CoA is diverted from the Krebs cycle to the ketogenesis pathway. This reaction occurs in the mitochondria of liver cells. The result is the production of β-hydroxybutyrate, the primary ketone body found in the blood.

Ketone Body Oxidation

Organs that have classically been thought to be dependent solely on glucose, such as the brain, can actually use ketones as an alternative energy source. This keeps the brain functioning when glucose is limited. When ketones are produced faster than they can be used, they can be broken down into CO_2 and acetone. The acetone is removed by exhalation. One symptom of ketogenesis is that the patient's breath smells sweet like alcohol. This effect provides one way of telling if a diabetic is properly controlling the disease. The carbon dioxide produced can acidify the blood, leading to diabetic ketoacidosis, a dangerous condition in diabetics.

Ketones oxidize to produce energy for the brain. **beta (β)-hydroxybutyrate** is oxidized to acetoacetate and NADH is released. An HS-CoA molecule is added to acetoacetate, forming acetoacetyl CoA. The carbon within the acetoacetyl CoA that is not bonded to the CoA then detaches, splitting the molecule in two. This carbon then attaches to another free HS-CoA, resulting in two acetyl CoA molecules. These two acetyl CoA molecules are then processed through the Krebs cycle to generate energy (Figure 24.15).

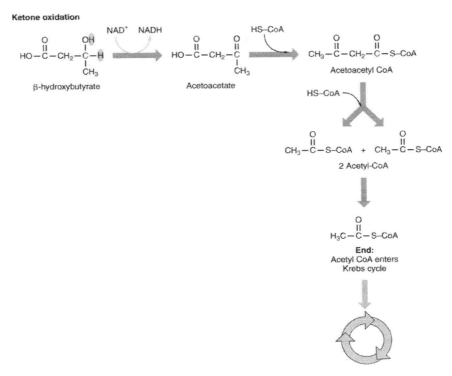

Figure 24.15 Ketone Oxidation When glucose is limited, ketone bodies can be oxidized to produce acetyl CoA to be used in the Krebs cycle to generate energy.

Lipogenesis

When glucose levels are plentiful, the excess acetyl CoA generated by glycolysis can be converted into fatty acids, triglycerides, cholesterol, steroids, and bile salts. This process, called **lipogenesis**, creates lipids (fat) from the acetyl CoA and takes place in the cytoplasm of adipocytes (fat cells) and hepatocytes (liver cells). When you eat more glucose or carbohydrates than your body needs, your system uses acetyl CoA to turn the excess into fat. Although there are several metabolic sources of acetyl CoA, it is most commonly derived from glycolysis. Acetyl CoA availability is significant, because it initiates lipogenesis. Lipogenesis begins with acetyl CoA and advances by the subsequent addition of two carbon atoms from another acetyl CoA; this process is repeated until fatty acids are the appropriate length. Because this is a bond-creating anabolic process, ATP is consumed. However, the creation of triglycerides and lipids is an efficient way of storing the energy available in carbohydrates. Triglycerides and lipids, high-energy molecules, are stored in adipose tissue until they are needed.

Although lipogenesis occurs in the cytoplasm, the necessary acetyl CoA is created in the mitochondria and cannot be transported across the mitochondrial membrane. To solve this problem, pyruvate is converted into both oxaloacetate and acetyl CoA. Two different enzymes are required for these conversions. Oxaloacetate forms via the action of pyruvate carboxylase, whereas the action of pyruvate dehydrogenase creates acetyl CoA. Oxaloacetate and acetyl CoA combine to form citrate, which can cross the mitochondrial membrane and enter the cytoplasm. In the cytoplasm, citrate is converted back into oxaloacetate and acetyl CoA. Oxaloacetate is converted into malate and then into pyruvate. Pyruvate crosses back across the mitochondrial membrane to wait for the next cycle of lipogenesis. The acetyl CoA is converted into malonyl CoA that is used to synthesize fatty acids. Figure 24.16 summarizes the pathways of lipid metabolism.

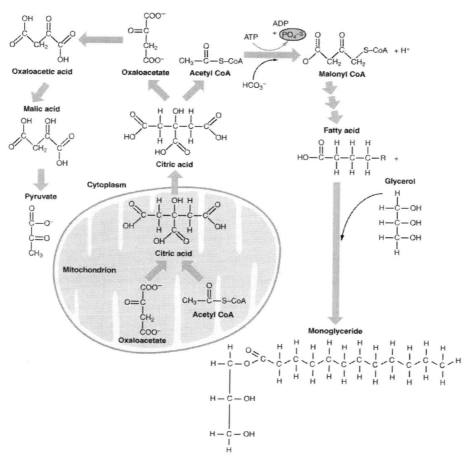

Figure 24.16 Lipid Metabolism Lipids may follow one of several pathways during metabolism. Glycerol and fatty acids follow different pathways.

24.4 | Protein Metabolism

By the end of this section, you will be able to:
- Describe how the body digests proteins
- Explain how the urea cycle prevents toxic concentrations of nitrogen
- Differentiate between glucogenic and ketogenic amino acids
- Explain how protein can be used for energy

Much of the body is made of protein, and these proteins take on a myriad of forms. They represent cell signaling receptors, signaling molecules, structural members, enzymes, intracellular trafficking components, extracellular matrix scaffolds, ion pumps, ion channels, oxygen and CO_2 transporters (hemoglobin). That is not even the complete list! There is protein in bones (collagen), muscles, and tendons; the hemoglobin that transports oxygen; and enzymes that catalyze all biochemical reactions. Protein is also used for growth and repair. Amid all these necessary functions, proteins also hold the potential to serve as a metabolic fuel source. Proteins are not stored for later use, so excess proteins must be converted into glucose or triglycerides, and used to supply energy or build energy reserves. Although the body can synthesize proteins from amino acids, food is an important source of those amino acids, especially because humans cannot synthesize all of the 20 amino acids used to build proteins.

The digestion of proteins begins in the stomach. When protein-rich foods enter the stomach, they are greeted by a mixture of the enzyme **pepsin** and hydrochloric acid (HCl; 0.5 percent). The latter produces an environmental pH of 1.5–3.5 that denatures proteins within food. Pepsin cuts proteins into smaller polypeptides and their constituent amino acids. When the food-gastric juice mixture (chyme) enters the small intestine, the pancreas releases **sodium bicarbonate** to neutralize the HCl. This helps to protect the lining of the intestine. The small intestine also releases digestive hormones, including **secretin** and CCK, which stimulate digestive processes to break down the proteins further. Secretin also stimulates the pancreas to release sodium bicarbonate. The pancreas releases most of the digestive enzymes, including the proteases trypsin, chymotrypsin, and **elastase**, which aid protein digestion. Together, all of these enzymes break complex proteins into smaller individual amino acids (Figure 24.17), which are then transported across the intestinal mucosa to be used to create new proteins, or to be converted into fats or acetyl CoA and used in the Krebs cycle.

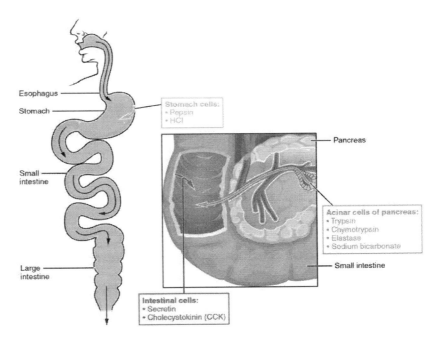

Figure 24.17 Digestive Enzymes and Hormones   Enzymes in the stomach and small intestine break down proteins into amino acids. HCl in the stomach aids in proteolysis, and hormones secreted by intestinal cells direct the digestive processes.

In order to avoid breaking down the proteins that make up the pancreas and small intestine, pancreatic enzymes are released as **inactive proenzymes** that are only activated in the small intestine. In the pancreas, vesicles store **trypsin** and **chymotrypsin** as **trypsinogen** and **chymotrypsinogen**. Once released into the small intestine, an enzyme found in the wall of the small intestine, called **enterokinase**, binds to trypsinogen and converts it into its active form, trypsin. Trypsin then binds to chymotrypsinogen to convert it into the active chymotrypsin. Trypsin and chymotrypsin break down large proteins into smaller peptides, a process called **proteolysis**. These smaller peptides are catabolized into their constituent amino acids, which are transported across the apical surface of the intestinal mucosa in a process that is mediated by sodium-amino acid transporters. These transporters bind sodium and then bind the amino acid to transport it across the membrane. At the basal surface of the mucosal cells, the sodium and amino acid are released. The sodium can be reused in the transporter, whereas the amino acids are transferred into the bloodstream to be transported to the liver and cells throughout the body for protein synthesis.

Freely available amino acids are used to create proteins. If amino acids exist in excess, the body has no capacity or mechanism for their storage; thus, they are converted into glucose or ketones, or they are decomposed. Amino acid decomposition results in hydrocarbons and nitrogenous waste. However, high concentrations of nitrogen are toxic. The urea cycle processes nitrogen and facilitates its excretion from the body.

Urea Cycle

The **urea cycle** is a set of biochemical reactions that produces urea from ammonium ions in order to prevent a toxic level of ammonium in the body. It occurs primarily in the liver and, to a lesser extent, in the kidney. Prior to the urea cycle, ammonium ions are produced from the breakdown of amino acids. In these reactions, an amine group, or ammonium ion, from the amino acid is exchanged with a keto group on another molecule. This **transamination** event creates a molecule that is necessary for the Krebs cycle and an ammonium ion that enters into the urea cycle to be eliminated.

In the urea cycle, ammonium is combined with CO_2, resulting in urea and water. The urea is eliminated through the kidneys in the urine (Figure 24.18).

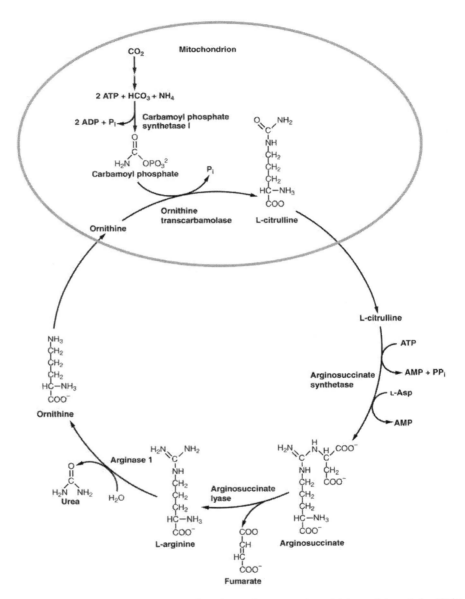

Figure 24.18 Urea Cycle Nitrogen is transaminated, creating ammonia and intermediates of the Krebs cycle. Ammonia is processed in the urea cycle to produce urea that is eliminated through the kidneys.

Amino acids can also be used as a source of energy, especially in times of starvation. Because the processing of amino acids results in the creation of metabolic intermediates, including pyruvate, acetyl CoA, acetoacyl CoA, oxaloacetate, and α-ketoglutarate, amino acids can serve as a source of energy production through the Krebs cycle (Figure 24.19). Figure 24.20 summarizes the pathways of catabolism and anabolism for carbohydrates, lipids, and proteins.

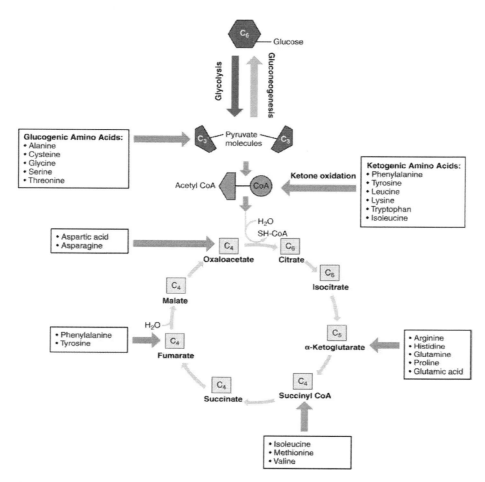

Figure 24.19 Energy from Amino Acids Amino acids can be broken down into precursors for glycolysis or the Krebs cycle. Amino acids (in bold) can enter the cycle through more than one pathway.

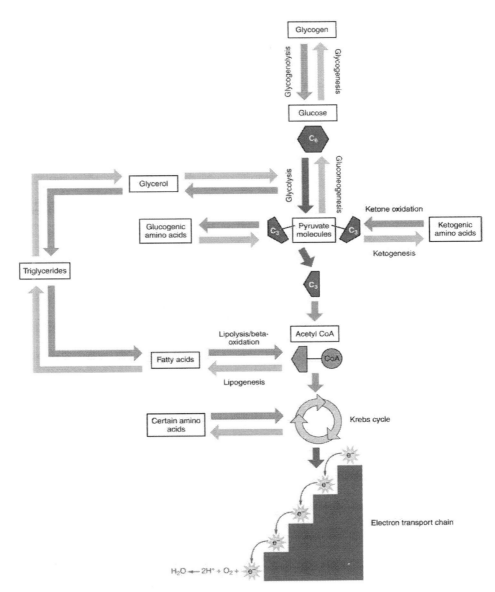

Figure 24.20 Catabolic and Anabolic Pathways Nutrients follow a complex pathway from ingestion through anabolism and catabolism to energy production.

Metabolism: Pyruvate Dehydrogenase Complex Deficiency and Phenylketonuria

Pyruvate dehydrogenase complex deficiency (PDCD) and phenylketonuria (PKU) are genetic disorders. Pyruvate dehydrogenase is the enzyme that converts pyruvate into acetyl CoA, the molecule necessary to begin the Krebs cycle to produce ATP. With low levels of the pyruvate dehydrogenase complex (PDC), the rate of cycling through the Krebs cycle is dramatically reduced. This results in a decrease in the total amount of energy that is produced by the cells of the body. PDC deficiency results in a neurodegenerative disease that ranges in severity, depending on the levels of the PDC enzyme. It may cause developmental defects, muscle spasms, and death. Treatments can include diet modification, vitamin supplementation, and gene therapy; however, damage to the central nervous system usually cannot be reversed.

PKU affects about 1 in every 15,000 births in the United States. People afflicted with PKU lack sufficient activity of the enzyme phenylalanine hydroxylase and are therefore unable to break down phenylalanine into tyrosine adequately. Because of this, levels of phenylalanine rise to toxic levels in the body, which results in damage to the central nervous system and brain. Symptoms include delayed neurological development, hyperactivity, mental retardation, seizures, skin rash, tremors, and uncontrolled movements of the arms and legs. Pregnant women with PKU are at a high risk for exposing the fetus to too much phenylalanine, which can cross the placenta and affect fetal development. Babies exposed to excess phenylalanine in utero may present with heart defects, physical and/or mental retardation, and microcephaly. Every infant in the United States and Canada is tested at birth to determine whether PKU is present. The earlier a modified diet is begun, the less severe the symptoms will be. The person must closely follow a strict diet that is low in phenylalanine to avoid symptoms and damage. Phenylalanine is found in high concentrations in artificial sweeteners, including aspartame. Therefore, these sweeteners must be avoided. Some animal products and certain starches are also high in phenylalanine, and intake of these foods should be carefully monitored.

24.5 | Metabolic States of the Body

By the end of this section, you will be able to:
- Describe what defines each of the three metabolic states
- Describe the processes that occur during the absorptive state of metabolism
- Describe the processes that occur during the postabsorptive state of metabolism
- Explain how the body processes glucose when the body is starved of fuel

You eat periodically throughout the day; however, your organs, especially the brain, need a continuous supply of glucose. How does the body meet this constant demand for energy? Your body processes the food you eat both to use immediately and, importantly, to store as energy for later demands. If there were no method in place to store excess energy, you would need to eat constantly in order to meet energy demands. Distinct mechanisms are in place to facilitate energy storage, and to make stored energy available during times of fasting and starvation.

The Absorptive State

The **absorptive state**, or the fed state, occurs after a meal when your body is digesting the food and absorbing the nutrients (anabolism exceeds catabolism). Digestion begins the moment you put food into your mouth, as the food is broken down into its constituent parts to be absorbed through the intestine. The digestion of carbohydrates begins in the mouth, whereas the digestion of proteins and fats begins in the stomach and small intestine. The constituent parts of these carbohydrates, fats, and proteins are transported across the intestinal wall and enter the bloodstream (sugars and amino acids) or the lymphatic system (fats). From the intestines, these systems transport them to the liver, adipose tissue, or muscle cells that will process and use, or store, the energy.

Depending on the amounts and types of nutrients ingested, the absorptive state can linger for up to 4 hours. The ingestion of food and the rise of glucose concentrations in the bloodstream stimulate pancreatic beta cells to release **insulin** into the bloodstream, where it initiates the absorption of blood glucose by liver hepatocytes, and by adipose and muscle cells. Once inside these cells, glucose is immediately converted into glucose-6-phosphate. By doing this, a concentration gradient is established where glucose levels are higher in the blood than in the cells. This allows for glucose to continue moving from the blood to the cells where it is needed. Insulin also stimulates the storage of glucose as glycogen in the liver and muscle cells where it can be used for later energy needs of the body. Insulin also promotes the synthesis of protein in muscle. As you will see, muscle protein can be catabolized and used as fuel in times of starvation.

If energy is exerted shortly after eating, the dietary fats and sugars that were just ingested will be processed and used immediately for energy. If not, the excess glucose is stored as glycogen in the liver and muscle cells, or as fat in adipose tissue; excess dietary fat is also stored as triglycerides in adipose tissues.

Figure 24.21 summarizes the metabolic processes occurring in the body during the absorptive state.

540 Chapter 24 | Metabolism and Nutrition

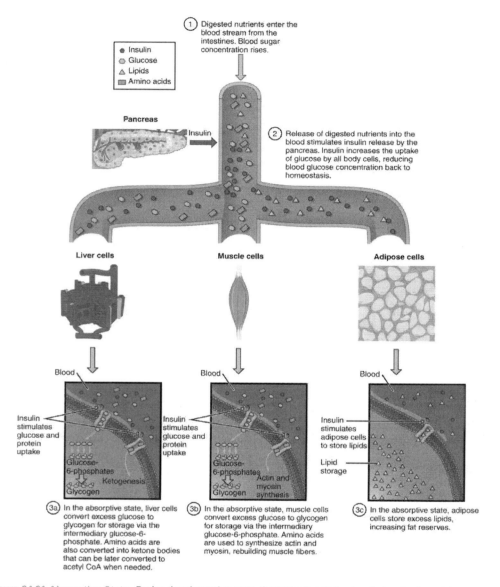

Figure 24.21 Absorptive State During the absorptive state, the body digests food and absorbs the nutrients.

The Postabsorptive State

The **postabsorptive state**, or the fasting state, occurs when the food has been digested, absorbed, and stored. You commonly fast overnight, but skipping meals during the day puts your body in the postabsorptive state as well. During this state, the body must rely initially on stored **glycogen**. Glucose levels in the blood begin to drop as it is absorbed and used by the cells. In response to the decrease in glucose, insulin levels also drop. Glycogen and triglyceride storage slows. However, due to the demands of the tissues and organs, blood glucose levels must be maintained in the normal range of 80–120 mg/dL. In response to a drop in blood glucose concentration, the hormone glucagon is released from the alpha cells of the pancreas. Glucagon acts upon the liver cells, where it inhibits the synthesis of glycogen and stimulates the breakdown of stored glycogen back into glucose. This glucose is released from the liver to be used by the peripheral tissues and the brain. As a result, blood glucose levels begin to rise. Gluconeogenesis will also begin in the liver to replace the glucose that has been used by the peripheral tissues.

After ingestion of food, fats and proteins are processed as described previously; however, the glucose processing changes a bit. The peripheral tissues preferentially absorb glucose. The liver, which normally absorbs and processes glucose, will not do so after a prolonged fast. The gluconeogenesis that has been ongoing in the liver will continue after fasting to replace the glycogen stores that were depleted in the liver. After these stores have been replenished, excess glucose that is absorbed by the liver will be converted into triglycerides and fatty acids for long-term storage. Figure 24.22 summarizes the metabolic processes occurring in the body during the postabsorptive state.

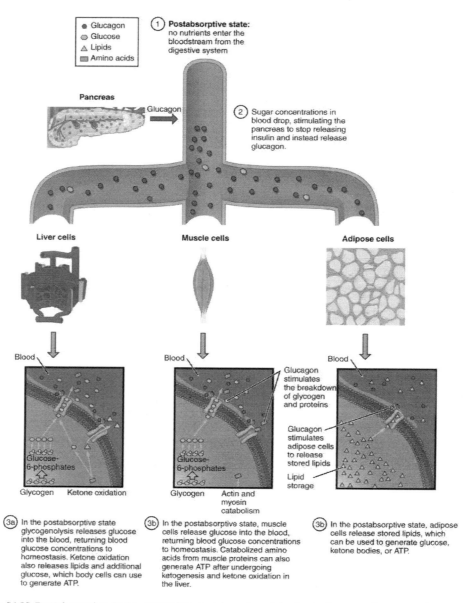

Figure 24.22 Postabsorptive State During the postabsorptive state, the body must rely on stored glycogen for energy.

Starvation

When the body is deprived of nourishment for an extended period of time, it goes into "survival mode." The first priority for survival is to provide enough glucose or fuel for the brain. The second priority is the conservation of amino acids for proteins. Therefore, the body uses ketones to satisfy the energy needs of the brain and other glucose-dependent organs, and to maintain proteins in the cells (see Figure 24.2). Because glucose levels are very low during starvation, glycolysis will shut off in cells that can use alternative fuels. For example, muscles will switch from using glucose to fatty acids as fuel.

As previously explained, fatty acids can be converted into acetyl CoA and processed through the Krebs cycle to make ATP. Pyruvate, lactate, and alanine from muscle cells are not converted into acetyl CoA and used in the Krebs cycle, but are exported to the liver to be used in the synthesis of glucose. As starvation continues, and more glucose is needed, glycerol from fatty acids can be liberated and used as a source for gluconeogenesis.

After several days of starvation, ketone bodies become the major source of fuel for the heart and other organs. As starvation continues, fatty acids and triglyceride stores are used to create ketones for the body. This prevents the continued breakdown of proteins that serve as carbon sources for gluconeogenesis. Once these stores are fully depleted, proteins from muscles are released and broken down for glucose synthesis. Overall survival is dependent on the amount of fat and protein stored in the body.

24.6 | Energy and Heat Balance

By the end of this section, you will be able to:
- Describe how the body regulates temperature
- Explain the significance of the metabolic rate

The body tightly regulates the body temperature through a process called **thermoregulation**, in which the body can maintain its temperature within certain boundaries, even when the surrounding temperature is very different. The core temperature of the body remains steady at around 36.5–37.5 °C (or 97.7–99.5 °F). In the process of ATP production by cells throughout the body, approximately 60 percent of the energy produced is in the form of heat used to maintain body temperature. Thermoregulation is an example of negative feedback.

The hypothalamus in the brain is the master switch that works as a thermostat to regulate the body's core temperature (Figure 24.23). If the temperature is too high, the hypothalamus can initiate several processes to lower it. These include increasing the circulation of the blood to the surface of the body to allow for the dissipation of heat through the skin and initiation of sweating to allow evaporation of water on the skin to cool its surface. Conversely, if the temperature falls below the set core temperature, the hypothalamus can initiate shivering to generate heat. The body uses more energy and generates more heat. In addition, thyroid hormone will stimulate more energy use and heat production by cells throughout the body. An environment is said to be **thermoneutral** when the body does not expend or release energy to maintain its core temperature. For a naked human, this is an ambient air temperature of around 84 °F. If the temperature is higher, for example, when wearing clothes, the body compensates with cooling mechanisms. The body loses heat through the mechanisms of heat exchange.

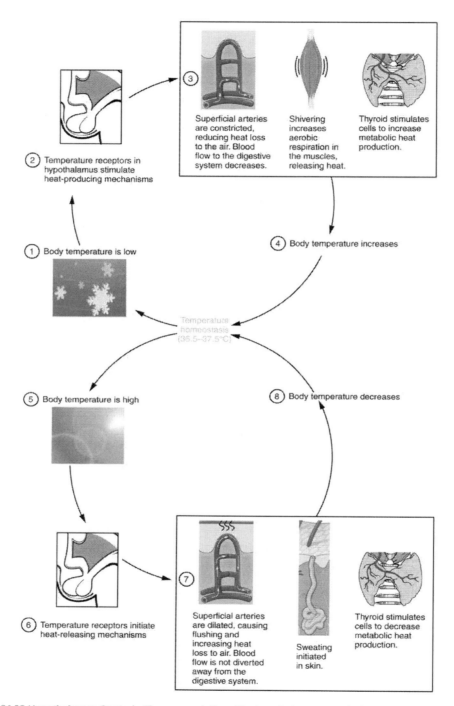

Figure 24.23 Hypothalamus Controls Thermoregulation The hypothalamus controls thermoregulation.

Mechanisms of Heat Exchange

When the environment is not thermoneutral, the body uses four mechanisms of heat exchange to maintain homeostasis: conduction, convection, radiation, and evaporation. Each of these mechanisms relies on the property of heat to flow from a higher concentration to a lower concentration; therefore, each of the mechanisms of heat exchange varies in rate according to the temperature and conditions of the environment.

Conduction is the transfer of heat by two objects that are in direct contact with one another. It occurs when the skin comes in contact with a cold or warm object. For example, when holding a glass of ice water, the heat from your skin will warm the glass and in turn melt the ice. Alternatively, on a cold day, you might warm up by wrapping your cold hands around a hot mug of coffee. Only about 3 percent of the body's heat is lost through conduction.

Convection is the transfer of heat to the air surrounding the skin. The warmed air rises away from the body and is replaced by cooler air that is subsequently heated. Convection can also occur in water. When the water temperature is lower than the body's temperature, the body loses heat by warming the water closest to the skin, which moves away to be replaced by cooler water. The convection currents created by the temperature changes continue to draw heat away from the body more quickly than the body can replace it, resulting in hyperthermia. About 15 percent of the body's heat is lost through convection.

Radiation is the transfer of heat via infrared waves. This occurs between any two objects when their temperatures differ. A radiator can warm a room via radiant heat. On a sunny day, the radiation from the sun warms the skin. The same principle works from the body to the environment. About 60 percent of the heat lost by the body is lost through radiation.

Evaporation is the transfer of heat by the evaporation of water. Because it takes a great deal of energy for a water molecule to change from a liquid to a gas, evaporating water (in the form of sweat) takes with it a great deal of energy from the skin. However, the rate at which evaporation occurs depends on relative humidity—more sweat evaporates in lower humidity environments. Sweating is the primary means of cooling the body during exercise, whereas at rest, about 20 percent of the heat lost by the body occurs through evaporation.

Metabolic Rate

The **metabolic rate** is the amount of energy consumed minus the amount of energy expended by the body. The **basal metabolic rate (BMR)** describes the amount of daily energy expended by humans at rest, in a neutrally temperate environment, while in the postabsorptive state. It measures how much energy the body needs for normal, basic, daily activity. About 70 percent of all daily energy expenditure comes from the basic functions of the organs in the body. Another 20 percent comes from physical activity, and the remaining 10 percent is necessary for body thermoregulation or temperature control. This rate will be higher if a person is more active or has more lean body mass. As you age, the BMR generally decreases as the percentage of less lean muscle mass decreases.

24.7 | Nutrition and Diet

By the end of this section, you will be able to:
- Explain how different foods can affect metabolism
- Describe a healthy diet, as recommended by the U.S. Department of Agriculture (USDA)
- List reasons why vitamins and minerals are critical to a healthy diet

The carbohydrates, lipids, and proteins in the foods you eat are used for energy to power molecular, cellular, and organ system activities. Importantly, the energy is stored primarily as fats. The quantity and quality of food that is ingested, digested, and absorbed affects the amount of fat that is stored as excess calories. Diet—both what you eat and how much you eat—has a dramatic impact on your health. Eating too much or too little food can lead to serious medical issues, including cardiovascular disease, cancer, anorexia, and diabetes, among others. Combine an unhealthy diet with unhealthy environmental conditions, such as smoking, and the potential medical complications increase significantly.

Food and Metabolism

The amount of energy that is needed or ingested per day is measured in calories. The nutritional **Calorie** (C) is the amount of heat it takes to raise 1 kg (1000 g) of water by 1 °C. This is different from the calorie (c) used in the physical sciences, which is the amount of heat it takes to raise 1 g of water by 1 °C. When we refer to "calorie," we are referring to the nutritional Calorie.

On average, a person needs 1500 to 2000 calories per day to sustain (or carry out) daily activities. The total number of calories needed by one person is dependent on their body mass, age, height, gender, activity level, and the amount of exercise per day. If exercise is regular part of one's day, more calories are required. As a rule, people underestimate the number of calories ingested and overestimate the amount they burn through exercise. This can lead to ingestion of too many calories per day. The accumulation of an extra 3500 calories adds one pound of weight. If an excess of 200 calories per day is ingested, one extra pound of body weight will be gained every 18 days. At that rate, an extra 20 pounds can be gained over the course of a year. Of course, this increase in calories could be offset by increased exercise. Running or jogging one mile burns almost 100 calories.

The type of food ingested also affects the body's metabolic rate. Processing of carbohydrates requires less energy than processing of proteins. In fact, the breakdown of carbohydrates requires the least amount of energy, whereas the processing of proteins demands the most energy. In general, the amount of calories ingested and the amount of calories burned determines the overall weight. To lose weight, the number of calories burned per day must exceed the number ingested. Calories are in almost everything you ingest, so when considering calorie intake, beverages must also be considered.

To help provide guidelines regarding the types and quantities of food that should be eaten every day, the USDA has updated their food guidelines from MyPyramid to MyPlate. They have put the recommended elements of a healthy meal into the context of a place setting of food. MyPlate categorizes food into the standard six food groups: fruits, vegetables, grains, protein foods, dairy, and oils. The accompanying website gives clear recommendations regarding quantity and type of each food that you should consume each day, as well as identifying which foods belong in each category. The accompanying graphic (Figure 24.24) gives a clear visual with general recommendations for a healthy and balanced meal. The guidelines recommend to "Make half your plate fruits and vegetables." The other half is grains and protein, with a slightly higher quantity of grains than protein. Dairy products are represented by a drink, but the quantity can be applied to other dairy products as well.

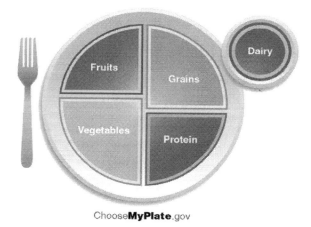

Figure 24.24 MyPlate The U.S. Department of Agriculture developed food guidelines called MyPlate to help demonstrate how to maintain a healthy lifestyle.

ChooseMyPlate.gov provides extensive online resources for planning a healthy diet and lifestyle, including offering weight management tips and recommendations for physical activity. It also includes the SuperTracker, a web-based application to help you analyze your own diet and physical activity.

Everyday CONNECTION

Metabolism and Obesity

Obesity in the United States is epidemic. The rate of obesity has been steadily rising since the 1980s. In the 1990s, most states reported that less than 10 percent of their populations was obese, and the state with the highest rate reported that only 15 percent of their population was considered obese. By 2010, the U.S. Centers for Disease Control and Prevention reported that nearly 36 percent of adults over 20 years old were obese and an additional 33 percent were overweight, leaving only about 30 percent of the population at a healthy weight. These studies find the highest levels of obesity are concentrated in the southern states. They also find the level of childhood obesity is rising.

Obesity is defined by the **body mass index (BMI)**, which is a measure of an individual's weight-to-height ratio. The normal, or healthy, BMI range is between 18 and 24.9 kg/m^2. Overweight is defined as a BMI of 25 to 29.9 kg/m^2, and obesity is considered to be a BMI greater than 30 kg/m^2. Obesity can arise from a number of factors, including overeating, poor diet, sedentary lifestyle, limited sleep, genetic factors, and even diseases or drugs. Severe obesity (morbid obesity) or long-term obesity can result in serious medical conditions, including coronary heart disease; type 2 diabetes; endometrial, breast, or colon cancer; hypertension (high blood pressure); dyslipidemia (high cholesterol or elevated triglycerides); stroke; liver disease; gall bladder disease; sleep apnea or respiratory diseases; osteoarthritis; and infertility. Research has shown that losing weight can help reduce or reverse the complications associated with these conditions.

Vitamins

Vitamins are organic compounds found in foods and are a necessary part of the biochemical reactions in the body. They are involved in a number of processes, including mineral and bone metabolism, and cell and tissue growth, and they act as cofactors for energy metabolism. The B vitamins play the largest role of any vitamins in metabolism (Table 24.3 and Table 24.4).

You get most of your vitamins through your diet, although some can be formed from the precursors absorbed during digestion. For example, the body synthesizes vitamin A from the β-carotene in orange vegetables like carrots and sweet potatoes. Vitamins are either fat-soluble or water-soluble. Fat-soluble vitamins A, D, E, and K, are absorbed through the intestinal tract with lipids in chylomicrons. Vitamin D is also synthesized in the skin through exposure to sunlight. Because they are carried in lipids, fat-soluble vitamins can accumulate in the lipids stored in the body. If excess vitamins are retained in the lipid stores in the body, hypervitaminosis can result.

Water-soluble vitamins, including the eight B vitamins and vitamin C, are absorbed with water in the gastrointestinal tract. These vitamins move easily through bodily fluids, which are water based, so they are not stored in the body. Excess water-soluble vitamins are excreted in the urine. Therefore, hypervitaminosis of water-soluble vitamins rarely occurs, except with an excess of vitamin supplements.

Fat-soluble Vitamins

Vitamin and alternative name	Sources	Recommended daily allowance	Function	Problems associated with deficiency
A retinal or β-carotene	Yellow and orange fruits and vegetables, dark green leafy vegetables, eggs, milk, liver	700–900 µg	Eye and bone development, immune function	Night blindness, epithelial changes, immune system deficiency

Table 24.3

Fat-soluble Vitamins

Vitamin and alternative name	Sources	Recommended daily allowance	Function	Problems associated with deficiency
D cholecalciferol	Dairy products, egg yolks; also synthesized in the skin from exposure to sunlight	5–15 μg	Aids in calcium absorption, promoting bone growth	Rickets, bone pain, muscle weakness, increased risk of death from cardiovascular disease, cognitive impairment, asthma in children, cancer
E tocopherols	Seeds, nuts, vegetable oils, avocados, wheat germ	15 mg	Antioxidant	Anemia
K phylloquinone	Dark green leafy vegetables, broccoli, Brussels sprouts, cabbage	90–120 μg	Blood clotting, bone health	Hemorrhagic disease of newborn in infants; uncommon in adults

Table 24.3

Water-soluble Vitamins

Vitamin and alternative name	Sources	Recommended daily allowance	Function	Problems associated with deficiency
B_1 thiamine	Whole grains, enriched bread and cereals, milk, meat	1.1–1.2 mg	Carbohydrate metabolism	Beriberi, Wernicke-Korsikoff syndrome
B_2 riboflavin	Brewer's yeast, almonds, milk, organ meats, legumes, enriched breads and cereals, broccoli, asparagus	1.1–1.3 mg	Synthesis of FAD for metabolism, production of red blood cells	Fatigue, slowed growth, digestive problems, light sensitivity, epithelial problems like cracks in the corners of the mouth
B_3 niacin	Meat, fish, poultry, enriched breads and cereals, peanuts	14–16 mg	Synthesis of NAD, nerve function, cholesterol production	Cracked, scaly skin; dementia; diarrhea; also known as pellagra
B_5 pantothenic acid	Meat, poultry, potatoes, oats, enriched breads and cereals, tomatoes	5 mg	Synthesis of coenzyme A in fatty acid metabolism	Rare: symptoms may include fatigue, insomnia, depression, irritability
B_6 pyridoxine	Potatoes, bananas, beans, seeds, nuts, meat, poultry, fish, eggs, dark green leafy vegetables, soy, organ meats	1.3–1.5 mg	Sodium and potassium balance, red blood cell synthesis, protein metabolism	Confusion, irritability, depression, mouth and tongue sores

Table 24.4

Water-soluble Vitamins

Vitamin and alternative name	Sources	Recommended daily allowance	Function	Problems associated with deficiency
B_7 biotin	Liver, fruits, meats	30 μg	Cell growth, metabolism of fatty acids, production of blood cells	Rare in developed countries; symptoms include dermatitis, hair loss, loss of muscular coordination
B_9 folic acid	Liver, legumes, dark green leafy vegetables, enriched breads and cereals, citrus fruits	400 μg	DNA/protein synthesis	Poor growth, gingivitis, appetite loss, shortness of breath, gastrointestinal problems, mental deficits
B_{12} cyanocobalamin	Fish, meat, poultry, dairy products, eggs	2.4 μg	Fatty acid oxidation, nerve cell function, red blood cell production	Pernicious anemia, leading to nerve cell damage
C ascorbic acid	Citrus fruits, red berries, peppers, tomatoes, broccoli, dark green leafy vegetables	75–90 mg	Necessary to produce collagen for formation of connective tissue and teeth, and for wound healing	Dry hair, gingivitis, bleeding gums, dry and scaly skin, slow wound healing, easy bruising, compromised immunity; can lead to scurvy

Table 24.4

Minerals

Minerals in food are inorganic compounds that work with other nutrients to ensure the body functions properly. Minerals cannot be made in the body; they come from the diet. The amount of minerals in the body is small—only 4 percent of the total body mass—and most of that consists of the minerals that the body requires in moderate quantities: potassium, sodium, calcium, phosphorus, magnesium, and chloride.

The most common minerals in the body are calcium and phosphorous, both of which are stored in the skeleton and necessary for the hardening of bones. Most minerals are ionized, and their ionic forms are used in physiological processes throughout the body. Sodium and chloride ions are electrolytes in the blood and extracellular tissues, and iron ions are critical to the formation of hemoglobin. There are additional trace minerals that are still important to the body's functions, but their required quantities are much lower.

Like vitamins, minerals can be consumed in toxic quantities (although it is rare). A healthy diet includes most of the minerals your body requires, so supplements and processed foods can add potentially toxic levels of minerals. Table 24.5 and Table 24.6 provide a summary of minerals and their function in the body.

Major Minerals

Mineral	Sources	Recommended daily allowance	Function	Problems associated with deficiency
Potassium	Meats, some fish, fruits, vegetables, legumes, dairy products	4700 mg	Nerve and muscle function; acts as an electrolyte	Hypokalemia: weakness, fatigue, muscle cramping, gastrointestinal problems, cardiac problems
Sodium	Table salt, milk, beets, celery, processed foods	2300 mg	Blood pressure, blood volume, muscle and nerve function	Rare
Calcium	Dairy products, dark green leafy vegetables, blackstrap molasses, nuts, brewer's yeast, some fish	1000 mg	Bone structure and health; nerve and muscle functions, especially cardiac function	Slow growth, weak and brittle bones
Phosphorous	Meat, milk	700 mg	Bone formation, metabolism, ATP production	Rare
Magnesium	Whole grains, nuts, leafy green vegetables	310–420 mg	Enzyme activation, production of energy, regulation of other nutrients	Agitation, anxiety, sleep problems, nausea and vomiting, abnormal heart rhythms, low blood pressure, muscular problems
Chloride	Most foods, salt, vegetables, especially seaweed, tomatoes, lettuce, celery, olives	2300 mg	Balance of body fluids, digestion	Loss of appetite, muscle cramps

Table 24.5

Trace Minerals

Mineral	Sources	Recommended daily allowance	Function	Problems associated with deficiency
Iron	Meat, poultry, fish, shellfish, legumes, nuts, seeds, whole grains, dark leafy green vegetables	8–18 mg	Transport of oxygen in blood, production of ATP	Anemia, weakness, fatigue
Zinc	Meat, fish, poultry, cheese, shellfish	8–11 mg	Immunity, reproduction, growth, blood clotting, insulin and thyroid function	Loss of appetite, poor growth, weight loss, skin problems, hair loss, vision problems, lack of taste or smell

Table 24.6

Trace Minerals

Mineral	Sources	Recommended daily allowance	Function	Problems associated with deficiency
Copper	Seafood, organ meats, nuts, legumes, chocolate, enriched breads and cereals, some fruits and vegetables	900 µg	Red blood cell production, nerve and immune system function, collagen formation, acts as an antioxidant	Anemia, low body temperature, bone fractures, low white blood cell concentration, irregular heartbeat, thyroid problems
Iodine	Fish, shellfish, garlic, lima beans, sesame seeds, soybeans, dark leafy green vegetables	150 µg	Thyroid function	Hypothyroidism: fatigue, weight gain, dry skin, temperature sensitivity
Sulfur	Eggs, meat, poultry, fish, legumes	None	Component of amino acids	Protein deficiency
Fluoride	Fluoridated water	3–4 mg	Maintenance of bone and tooth structure	Increased cavities, weak bones and teeth
Manganese	Nuts, seeds, whole grains, legumes	1.8–2.3 mg	Formation of connective tissue and bones, blood clotting, sex hormone development, metabolism, brain and nerve function	Infertility, bone malformation, weakness, seizures
Cobalt	Fish, nuts, leafy green vegetables, whole grains	None	Component of B_{12}	None
Selenium	Brewer's yeast, wheat germ, liver, butter, fish, shellfish, whole grains	55 µg	Antioxidant, thyroid function, immune system function	Muscle pain
Chromium	Whole grains, lean meats, cheese, black pepper, thyme, brewer's yeast	25–35 µg	Insulin function	High blood sugar, triglyceride, and cholesterol levels
Molybdenum	Legumes, whole grains, nuts	45 µg	Cofactor for enzymes	Rare

Table 24.6

KEY TERMS

absorptive state also called the fed state; the metabolic state occurring during the first few hours after ingesting food in which the body is digesting food and absorbing the nutrients

acetyl coenzyme A (acetyl CoA) starting molecule of the Krebs cycle

anabolic hormones hormones that stimulate the synthesis of new, larger molecules

anabolic reactions reactions that build smaller molecules into larger molecules

ATP synthase protein pore complex that creates ATP

basal metabolic rate (BMR) amount of energy expended by the body at rest

beta (β)-hydroxybutyrate primary ketone body produced in the body

beta (β)-oxidation fatty acid oxidation

bile salts salts that are released from the liver in response to lipid ingestion and surround the insoluble triglycerides to aid in their conversion to monoglycerides and free fatty acids

biosynthesis reactions reactions that create new molecules, also called anabolic reactions

body mass index (BMI) relative amount of body weight compared to the overall height; a BMI ranging from 18–24.9 is considered normal weight, 25–29.9 is considered overweight, and greater than 30 is considered obese

calorie amount of heat it takes to raise 1 kg (1000 g) of water by 1 °C

catabolic hormones hormones that stimulate the breakdown of larger molecules

catabolic reactions reactions that break down larger molecules into their constituent parts

cellular respiration production of ATP from glucose oxidation via glycolysis, the Krebs cycle, and oxidative phosphorylation

cholecystokinin (CCK) hormone that stimulates the release of pancreatic lipase and the contraction of the gallbladder to release bile salts

chylomicrons vesicles containing cholesterol and triglycerides that transport lipids out of the intestinal cells and into the lymphatic and circulatory systems

chymotrypsin pancreatic enzyme that digests protein

chymotrypsinogen proenzyme that is activated by trypsin into chymotrypsin

citric acid cycle also called the Krebs cycle or the tricarboxylic acid cycle; converts pyruvate into CO_2 and high-energy $FADH_2$, NADH, and ATP molecules

conduction transfer of heat through physical contact

convection transfer of heat between the skin and air or water

elastase pancreatic enzyme that digests protein

electron transport chain (ETC) ATP production pathway in which electrons are passed through a series of oxidation-reduction reactions that forms water and produces a proton gradient

energy-consuming phase first phase of glycolysis, in which two molecules of ATP are necessary to start the reaction

energy-yielding phase second phase of glycolysis, during which energy is produced

enterokinase enzyme located in the wall of the small intestine that activates trypsin

evaporation transfer of heat that occurs when water changes from a liquid to a gas

FADH$_2$ high-energy molecule needed for glycolysis

fatty acid oxidation breakdown of fatty acids into smaller chain fatty acids and acetyl CoA

flavin adenine dinucleotide (FAD) coenzyme used to produce FADH$_2$

glucokinase cellular enzyme, found in the liver, which converts glucose into glucose-6-phosphate upon uptake into the cell

gluconeogenesis process of glucose synthesis from pyruvate or other molecules

glucose-6-phosphate phosphorylated glucose produced in the first step of glycolysis

glycogen form that glucose assumes when it is stored

glycolysis series of metabolic reactions that breaks down glucose into pyruvate and produces ATP

hexokinase cellular enzyme, found in most tissues, that converts glucose into glucose-6-phosphate upon uptake into the cell

hydroxymethylglutaryl CoA (HMG CoA) molecule created in the first step of the creation of ketone bodies from acetyl CoA

inactive proenzymes forms in which proteases are stored and released to prevent the inappropriate digestion of the native proteins of the stomach, pancreas, and small intestine

insulin hormone secreted by the pancreas that stimulates the uptake of glucose into the cells

ketone bodies alternative source of energy when glucose is limited, created when too much acetyl CoA is created during fatty acid oxidation

Krebs cycle also called the citric acid cycle or the tricarboxylic acid cycle, converts pyruvate into CO$_2$ and high-energy FADH$_2$, NADH, and ATP molecules

lipogenesis synthesis of lipids that occurs in the liver or adipose tissues

lipolysis breakdown of triglycerides into glycerol and fatty acids

metabolic rate amount of energy consumed minus the amount of energy expended by the body

metabolism sum of all catabolic and anabolic reactions that take place in the body

minerals inorganic compounds required by the body to ensure proper function of the body

monoglyceride molecules lipid consisting of a single fatty acid chain attached to a glycerol backbone

monosaccharide smallest, monomeric sugar molecule

NADH high-energy molecule needed for glycolysis

nicotinamide adenine dinucleotide (NAD) coenzyme used to produce NADH

oxidation loss of an electron

oxidation-reduction reaction (also, redox reaction) pair of reactions in which an electron is passed from one molecule to another, oxidizing one and reducing the other

oxidative phosphorylation process that converts high-energy NADH and FADH$_2$ into ATP

pancreatic lipases enzymes released from the pancreas that digest lipids in the diet

pepsin enzyme that begins to break down proteins in the stomach

polysaccharides complex carbohydrates made up of many monosaccharides

postabsorptive state also called the fasting state; the metabolic state occurring after digestion when food is no longer the body's source of energy and it must rely on stored glycogen

proteolysis process of breaking proteins into smaller peptides

pyruvate three-carbon end product of glycolysis and starting material that is converted into acetyl CoA that enters the Krebs cycle

radiation transfer of heat via infrared waves

reduction gaining of an electron

salivary amylase digestive enzyme that is found in the saliva and begins the digestion of carbohydrates in the mouth

secretin hormone released in the small intestine to aid in digestion

sodium bicarbonate anion released into the small intestine to neutralize the pH of the food from the stomach

terminal electron acceptor oxygen, the recipient of the free hydrogen at the end of the electron transport chain

thermoneutral external temperature at which the body does not expend any energy for thermoregulation, about 84 °F

thermoregulation process of regulating the temperature of the body

transamination transfer of an amine group from one molecule to another as a way to turn nitrogen waste into ammonia so that it can enter the urea cycle

tricarboxylic acid cycle (TCA) also called the Krebs cycle or the citric acid cycle; converts pyruvate into CO_2 and high-energy $FADH_2$, NADH, and ATP molecules

triglycerides lipids, or fats, consisting of three fatty acid chains attached to a glycerol backbone

trypsin pancreatic enzyme that activates chymotrypsin and digests protein

trypsinogen proenzyme form of trypsin

urea cycle process that converts potentially toxic nitrogen waste into urea that can be eliminated through the kidneys

vitamins organic compounds required by the body to perform biochemical reactions like metabolism and bone, cell, and tissue growth

CHAPTER REVIEW

24.1 Overview of Metabolic Reactions

Metabolism is the sum of all catabolic (break down) and anabolic (synthesis) reactions in the body. The metabolic rate measures the amount of energy used to maintain life. An organism must ingest a sufficient amount of food to maintain its metabolic rate if the organism is to stay alive for very long.

Catabolic reactions break down larger molecules, such as carbohydrates, lipids, and proteins from ingested food, into their constituent smaller parts. They also include the breakdown of ATP, which releases the energy needed for metabolic processes in all cells throughout the body.

Anabolic reactions, or biosynthetic reactions, synthesize larger molecules from smaller constituent parts, using ATP as the energy source for these reactions. Anabolic reactions build bone, muscle mass, and new proteins, fats, and nucleic acids. Oxidation-reduction reactions transfer electrons across molecules by oxidizing one molecule and reducing another, and collecting the released energy to convert P_i and ADP into ATP. Errors in metabolism alter the processing of carbohydrates, lipids, proteins, and nucleic acids, and can result in a number of disease states.

24.2 Carbohydrate Metabolism

Metabolic enzymes catalyze catabolic reactions that break down carbohydrates contained in food. The energy released is used to power the cells and systems that make up your body. Excess or unutilized energy is stored as fat or glycogen for later use. Carbohydrate metabolism begins in the mouth, where the enzyme salivary amylase begins to break down complex sugars into monosaccharides. These can then be transported across the intestinal membrane into the bloodstream and then to body tissues. In the cells, glucose, a six-carbon sugar, is processed through a sequence of reactions into smaller sugars, and the energy stored inside the molecule is released. The first step of carbohydrate catabolism is glycolysis, which produces pyruvate, NADH, and ATP. Under anaerobic conditions, the pyruvate can be converted into lactate to keep glycolysis working. Under aerobic conditions, pyruvate enters the Krebs cycle, also called the citric acid cycle or tricarboxylic acid cycle. In addition to ATP, the Krebs cycle produces high-energy $FADH_2$ and NADH molecules, which provide electrons to the oxidative phosphorylation process that generates more high-energy ATP molecules. For each molecule of glucose that is processed in glycolysis, a net of 36 ATPs can be created by aerobic respiration.

Under anaerobic conditions, ATP production is limited to those generated by glycolysis. While a total of four ATPs are produced by glycolysis, two are needed to begin glycolysis, so there is a net yield of two ATP molecules.

In conditions of low glucose, such as fasting, starvation, or low carbohydrate diets, glucose can be synthesized from lactate, pyruvate, glycerol, alanine, or glutamate. This process, called gluconeogenesis, is almost the reverse of glycolysis and serves to create glucose molecules for glucose-dependent organs, such as the brain, when glucose levels fall below normal.

24.3 Lipid Metabolism

Lipids are available to the body from three sources. They can be ingested in the diet, stored in the adipose tissue of the body, or synthesized in the liver. Fats ingested in the diet are digested in the small intestine. The triglycerides are broken down into monoglycerides and free fatty acids, then imported across the intestinal mucosa. Once across, the triglycerides are resynthesized and transported to the liver or adipose tissue. Fatty acids are oxidized through fatty acid or β-oxidation into two-carbon acetyl CoA molecules, which can then enter the Krebs cycle to generate ATP. If excess acetyl CoA is created and overloads the capacity of the Krebs cycle, the acetyl CoA can be used to synthesize ketone bodies. When glucose is limited, ketone bodies can be oxidized and used for fuel. Excess acetyl CoA generated from excess glucose or carbohydrate ingestion can be used for fatty acid synthesis or lipogenesis. Acetyl CoA is used to create lipids, triglycerides, steroid hormones, cholesterol, and bile salts. Lipolysis is the breakdown of triglycerides into glycerol and fatty acids, making them easier for the body to process.

24.4 Protein Metabolism

Digestion of proteins begins in the stomach, where HCl and pepsin begin the process of breaking down proteins into their constituent amino acids. As the chyme enters the small intestine, it mixes with bicarbonate and digestive enzymes. The bicarbonate neutralizes the acidic HCl, and the digestive enzymes break down the proteins into smaller peptides and amino acids. Digestive hormones secretin and CCK are released from the small intestine to aid in digestive processes, and digestive proenzymes are released from the pancreas (trypsinogen and chymotrypsinogen). Enterokinase, an enzyme located in the wall of the small intestine, activates trypsin, which in turn activates chymotrypsin. These enzymes liberate the individual amino acids that are then transported via sodium-amino acid transporters across the intestinal wall into the cell. The amino acids are then transported into the bloodstream for dispersal to the liver and cells throughout the body to be used to create new proteins. When in excess, the amino acids are processed and stored as glucose or ketones. The nitrogen waste that is liberated in this process is converted to urea in the urea acid cycle and eliminated in the urine. In times of starvation, amino acids can be used as an energy source and processed through the Krebs cycle.

24.5 Metabolic States of the Body

There are three main metabolic states of the body: absorptive (fed), postabsorptive (fasting), and starvation. During any given day, your metabolism switches between absorptive and postabsorptive states. Starvation states happen very rarely in generally well-nourished individuals. When the body is fed, glucose, fats, and proteins are absorbed across the intestinal membrane and enter the bloodstream and lymphatic system to be used immediately for fuel. Any excess is stored for later fasting stages. As blood glucose levels rise, the pancreas releases insulin to stimulate the uptake of glucose by hepatocytes in the liver, muscle cells/fibers, and adipocytes (fat cells), and to promote its conversion to glycogen. As the postabsorptive state begins, glucose levels drop, and there is a corresponding drop in insulin levels. Falling glucose levels trigger the pancreas to release glucagon to turn off glycogen synthesis in the liver and stimulate its breakdown into glucose. The glucose is released into the bloodstream to serve as a fuel source for cells throughout the body. If glycogen stores are depleted during fasting, alternative sources, including fatty acids and proteins, can be metabolized and used as fuel. When the body once again enters the absorptive state after fasting, fats and proteins are digested and used to replenish fat and protein stores, whereas glucose is processed and used first to replenish the glycogen stores in the peripheral tissues, then in the liver. If the fast is not broken and starvation begins to set in, during the initial days, glucose produced from gluconeogenesis is still used by the brain and organs. After a few days, however, ketone bodies are created from fats and serve as the preferential fuel source for the heart and other organs, so that the brain can still use glucose. Once these stores are depleted, proteins will be catabolized first from the organs with fast turnover, such as the intestinal lining. Muscle will be spared to prevent the wasting of muscle tissue; however, these proteins will be used if alternative stores are not available.

24.6 Energy and Heat Balance

Some of the energy from the food that is ingested is used to maintain the core temperature of the body. Most of the energy derived from the food is released as heat. The core temperature is kept around 36.5–37.5 °C (97.7–99.5 °F). This is tightly regulated by the hypothalamus in the brain, which senses changes in the core temperature and operates like a thermostat to increase sweating or shivering, or inducing other mechanisms to return the temperature to its normal range. The body can also gain or lose heat through mechanisms of heat exchange. Conduction transfers heat from one object to another through physical contact. Convection transfers heat to air or water. Radiation transfers heat via infrared radiation. Evaporation transfers heat as water changes state from a liquid to a gas.

24.7 Nutrition and Diet

Nutrition and diet affect your metabolism. More energy is required to break down fats and proteins than carbohydrates; however, all excess calories that are ingested will be stored as fat in the body. On average, a person requires 1500 to 2000 calories for normal daily activity, although routine exercise will increase that amount. If you ingest more than that, the remainder is stored for later use. Conversely, if you ingest less than that, the energy stores in your body will be depleted. Both the quantity and quality of the food you eat affect your metabolism and can affect your overall health. Eating too much or too little can result in serious medical conditions, including cardiovascular disease, cancer, and diabetes.

Vitamins and minerals are essential parts of the diet. They are needed for the proper function of metabolic pathways in the body. Vitamins are not stored in the body, so they must be obtained from the diet or synthesized from precursors available in the diet. Minerals are also obtained from the diet, but they are also stored, primarily in skeletal tissues.

REVIEW QUESTIONS

1. A monosaccharide is formed from a polysaccharide in what kind of reaction?
   a. oxidation–reduction reaction
   b. anabolic reaction
   c. catabolic reaction
   d. biosynthetic reaction

2. If anabolic reactions exceed catabolic reactions, the result will be _____.
   a. weight loss
   b. weight gain
   c. metabolic rate change
   d. development of disease

3. When NAD becomes NADH, the coenzyme has been _____.
   a. reduced
   b. oxidized
   c. metabolized
   d. hydrolyzed

4. Anabolic reactions use energy by _____.
   a. turning ADP into ATP
   b. removing a phosphate group from ATP
   c. producing heat
   d. breaking down molecules into smaller parts

5. Glycolysis results in the production of two _____ molecules from a single molecule of glucose. In the absence of _____, the end product of glycolysis is _____.
   a. acetyl CoA, pyruvate, lactate
   b. ATP, carbon, pyruvate
   c. pyruvate, oxygen, lactate
   d. pyruvate, carbon, acetyl CoA

6. The Krebs cycle converts _____ through a cycle of reactions. In the process, ATP, _____, and _____ are produced.
   a. acetyl CoA; FAD, NAD
   b. acetyl CoA; FADH$_2$; NADH
   c. pyruvate; NAD; FADH$_2$
   d. pyruvate; oxygen; oxaloacetate

7. Which pathway produces the most ATP molecules?
   a. lactic acid fermentation
   b. the Krebs cycle
   c. the electron transport chain
   d. glycolysis

8. Aerobic cellular respiration results in the production of these two products.
   a. NADH and FADH$_2$
   b. ATP and pyruvate
   c. ATP and glucose
   d. ATP and H$_2$O

9. When NAD^+ becomes NADH, the coenzyme has been _____.
   a. reduced
   b. oxidized
   c. metabolized
   d. hydrolyzed

10. Lipids in the diet can be _____.
   a. broken down into energy for the body
   b. stored as triglycerides for later use
   c. converted into acetyl CoA
   d. all of the above

11. The gallbladder provides _____ that aid(s) in transport of lipids across the intestinal membrane.
   a. lipases
   b. cholesterol
   c. proteins
   d. bile salts

12. Triglycerides are transported by chylomicrons because _____.
   a. they cannot move easily in the blood stream because they are fat based, while the blood is water based
   b. they are too small to move by themselves
   c. the chylomicrons contain enzymes they need for anabolism
   d. they cannot fit across the intestinal membrane

13. Which molecule produces the most ATP?
   a. carbohydrates
   b. $FADH_2$
   c. triglycerides
   d. NADH

14. Which molecules can enter the Krebs cycle?
   a. chylomicrons
   b. acetyl CoA
   c. monoglycerides
   d. ketone bodies

15. Acetyl CoA can be converted to all of the following except _____.
   a. ketone bodies
   b. fatty acids
   c. polysaccharides
   d. triglycerides

16. Digestion of proteins begins in the _____ where _____ and _____ mix with food to break down protein into _____.
   a. stomach; amylase; HCl; amino acids
   b. mouth; pepsin; HCl; fatty acids
   c. stomach; lipase; HCl; amino acids
   d. stomach; pepsin; HCl; amino acids

17. Amino acids are needed to _____.
   a. build new proteins
   b. serve as fat stores
   c. supply energy for the cell
   d. create red blood cells

18. If an amino acid is not used to create new proteins, it can be _____.
   a. converted to acetyl CoA
   b. converted to glucose or ketones
   c. converted to nitrogen
   d. stored to be used later

19. During the absorptive state, glucose levels are _____, insulin levels are _____, and glucagon levels _____.
   a. high; low; stay the same
   b. low; low; stay the same
   c. high; high; are high
   d. high; high; are low

20. Starvation sets in after 3 to 4 days without food. Which hormones change in response to low glucose levels?
   a. glucagon and insulin
   b. ketones and glucagon
   c. insulin, glucose, and glucagon
   d. insulin and ketones

21. The postabsorptive state relies on stores of _____ in the _____.
   a. insulin; pancreas
   b. glucagon; pancreas
   c. glycogen; liver
   d. glucose; liver

22. The body's temperature is controlled by the _____. This temperature is always kept between _____.
   a. pituitary; 36.5–37.5 °C
   b. hypothalamus; 97.7–99.5 °F
   c. hypothalamus; 36.5–37.5 °F
   d. pituitary; 97.7–99.5 °F

23. Fever increases the body temperature and can induce chills to help cool the temperature back down. What other mechanisms are in place to regulate the body temperature?
   a. shivering
   b. sweating
   c. erection of the hairs on the arms and legs
   d. all of the above

24. The heat you feel on your chair when you stand up was transferred from your skin via _____.
   a. conduction
   b. convection
   c. radiation
   d. evaporation

25. A crowded room warms up through the mechanism of _____.
   a. conduction
   b. convection
   c. radiation
   d. evaporation

26. A deficiency in vitamin A can result in _____.

a. improper bone development
b. scurvy
c. improper eye development or sight
d. all of the above

27. Rickets results in improper bone development in children that arises from the malabsorption of calcium and a deficiency in _____.
a. vitamin D
b. vitamin C
c. vitamin B_{12}
d. niacin

28. Consuming which type of food will help the most with weight loss?
a. fats
b. vegetables
c. lean meats
d. fruits

29. Which of the following is stored in the body?
a. thiamine
b. phosphorous
c. folic acid
d. vitamin C

CRITICAL THINKING QUESTIONS

30. Describe how metabolism can be altered.

31. Describe how Addison's disease can be treated.

32. Explain how glucose is metabolized to yield ATP.

33. Insulin is released when food is ingested and stimulates the uptake of glucose into the cell. Discuss the mechanism cells employ to create a concentration gradient to ensure continual uptake of glucose from the bloodstream.

34. Discuss how carbohydrates can be stored as fat.

35. If a diabetic's breath smells like alcohol, what could this mean?

36. Amino acids are not stored in the body. Describe how excess amino acids are processed in the cell.

37. Release of trypsin and chymotrypsin in their active form can result in the digestion of the pancreas or small intestine itself. What mechanism does the body employ to prevent its self-destruction?

38. In type II diabetes, insulin is produced but is nonfunctional. These patients are described as "starving in a sea of plenty," because their blood glucose levels are high, but none of the glucose is transported into the cells. Describe how this leads to malnutrition.

39. Ketone bodies are used as an alternative source of fuel during starvation. Describe how ketones are synthesized.

40. How does vasoconstriction help increase the core temperature of the body?

41. How can the ingestion of food increase the body temperature?

42. Weight loss and weight gain are complex processes. What are some of the main factors that influence weight gain in people?

43. Some low-fat or non-fat foods contain a large amount of sugar to replace the fat content of the food. Discuss how this leads to increased fat in the body (and weight gain) even though the item is non-fat.

25 | THE URINARY SYSTEM

Figure 25.1 Sewage Treatment Plant (credit: "eutrophication&hypoxia"/flickr.com)

Introduction

Chapter Objectives

After studying this chapter, you will be able to:

- Describe the composition of urine
- Label structures of the urinary system
- Characterize the roles of each of the parts of the urinary system
- Illustrate the macroscopic and microscopic structures of the kidney
- Trace the flow of blood through the kidney
- Outline how blood is filtered in the kidney nephron
- Provide symptoms of kidney failure
- List some of the solutes filtered, secreted, and reabsorbed in different parts of the nephron
- Describe the role of a portal system in the kidney
- Explain how urine osmolarity is hormonally regulated
- Describe the regulation of major ions by the kidney
- Summarize the role of the kidneys in maintaining acid–base balance

The urinary system has roles you may be well aware of: cleansing the blood and ridding the body of wastes probably come to mind. However, there are additional, equally important functions played by the system. Take for example, regulation of pH, a function shared with the lungs and the buffers in the blood. Additionally, the regulation of blood pressure is a role shared with the heart and blood vessels. What about regulating the concentration of solutes in the blood? Did you know that the kidney is important in determining the concentration of red blood cells? Eighty-five percent of the erythropoietin (EPO) produced to stimulate red blood cell production is produced in the kidneys. The kidneys also perform the final synthesis step of vitamin D production, converting calcidiol to calcitriol, the active form of vitamin D.

If the kidneys fail, these functions are compromised or lost altogether, with devastating effects on homeostasis. The affected individual might experience weakness, lethargy, shortness of breath, anemia, widespread edema (swelling), metabolic acidosis, rising potassium levels, heart arrhythmias, and more. Each of these functions is vital to your well-being and survival. The urinary system, controlled by the nervous system, also stores urine until a convenient time for disposal and then provides the anatomical structures to transport this waste liquid to the outside of the body. Failure of nervous control or the anatomical structures leading to a loss of control of urination results in a condition called incontinence.

This chapter will help you to understand the anatomy of the urinary system and how it enables the physiologic functions critical to homeostasis. It is best to think of the kidney as a regulator of plasma makeup rather than simply a urine producer. As you read each section, ask yourself this question: "What happens if this does not work?" This question will help you to understand how the urinary system maintains homeostasis and affects all the other systems of the body and the quality of one's life.

Watch this video (http://openstaxcollege.org/l/urineintro) from the Howard Hughes Medical Institute for an introduction to the urinary system.

25.1 | Physical Characteristics of Urine

By the end of this section, you will be able to:
- Compare and contrast blood plasma, glomerular filtrate, and urine characteristics
- Describe the characteristics of a normal urine sample, including normal range of pH, osmolarity, and volume

The urinary system's ability to filter the blood resides in about 2 to 3 million tufts of specialized capillaries—the glomeruli—distributed more or less equally between the two kidneys. Because the glomeruli filter the blood based mostly on particle size, large elements like blood cells, platelets, antibodies, and albumen are excluded. The glomerulus is the first part of the nephron, which then continues as a highly specialized tubular structure responsible for creating the final urine composition. All other solutes, such as ions, amino acids, vitamins, and wastes, are filtered to create a filtrate composition very similar to plasma. The glomeruli create about 200 liters (189 quarts) of this filtrate every day, yet you excrete less than two liters of waste you call urine.

Characteristics of the urine change, depending on influences such as water intake, exercise, environmental temperature, nutrient intake, and other factors (Table 25.1). Some of the characteristics such as color and odor are rough descriptors of your state of hydration. For example, if you exercise or work outside, and sweat a great deal, your urine will turn darker and produce a slight odor, even if you drink plenty of water. Athletes are often advised to consume water until their urine is clear. This is good advice; however, it takes time for the kidneys to process body fluids and store it in the bladder. Another way of looking at this is that the quality of the urine produced is an average over the time it takes to make that urine. Producing clear urine may take only a few minutes if you are drinking a lot of water or several hours if you are working outside and not drinking much.

Normal Urine Characteristics

Characteristic	Normal values
Color	Pale yellow to deep amber
Odor	Odorless
Volume	750–2000 mL/24 hour
pH	4.5–8.0
Specific gravity	1.003–1.032
Osmolarity	40–1350 mOsmol/kg
Urobilinogen	0.2–1.0 mg/100 mL
White blood cells	0–2 HPF (per high-power field of microscope)
Leukocyte esterase	None
Protein	None or trace
Bilirubin	<0.3 mg/100 mL
Ketones	None
Nitrites	None
Blood	None
Glucose	None

Table 25.1

Urinalysis (urine analysis) often provides clues to renal disease. Normally, only traces of protein are found in urine, and when higher amounts are found, damage to the glomeruli is the likely basis. Unusually large quantities of urine may point to diseases like diabetes mellitus or hypothalamic tumors that cause diabetes insipidus. The color of urine is determined mostly by the breakdown products of red blood cell destruction (Figure 25.2). The "heme" of hemoglobin is converted by the liver into water-soluble forms that can be excreted into the bile and indirectly into the urine. This yellow pigment is **urochrome**. Urine color may also be affected by certain foods like beets, berries, and fava beans. A kidney stone or a cancer of the urinary system may produce sufficient bleeding to manifest as pink or even bright red urine. Diseases of the liver or obstructions of bile drainage from the liver impart a dark "tea" or "cola" hue to the urine. Dehydration produces darker, concentrated urine that may also possess the slight odor of ammonia. Most of the ammonia produced from protein breakdown is converted into urea by the liver, so ammonia is rarely detected in fresh urine. The strong ammonia odor you may detect in bathrooms or alleys is due to the breakdown of urea into ammonia by bacteria in the environment. About one in five people detect a distinctive odor in their urine after consuming asparagus; other foods such as onions, garlic, and fish can impart their own aromas! These food-caused odors are harmless.

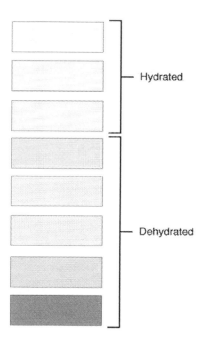

Figure 25.2 Urine Color

Urine volume varies considerably. The normal range is one to two liters per day (Table 25.2). The kidneys must produce a minimum urine volume of about 500 mL/day to rid the body of wastes. Output below this level may be caused by severe dehydration or renal disease and is termed **oliguria**. The virtual absence of urine production is termed **anuria**. Excessive urine production is **polyuria**, which may be due to diabetes mellitus or diabetes insipidus. In diabetes mellitus, blood glucose levels exceed the number of available sodium-glucose transporters in the kidney, and glucose appears in the urine. The osmotic nature of glucose attracts water, leading to its loss in the urine. In the case of diabetes insipidus, insufficient pituitary antidiuretic hormone (ADH) release or insufficient numbers of ADH receptors in the collecting ducts means that too few water channels are inserted into the cell membranes that line the collecting ducts of the kidney. Insufficient numbers of water channels (aquaporins) reduce water absorption, resulting in high volumes of very dilute urine.

Urine Volumes

Volume condition	Volume	Causes
Normal	1–2 L/day	
Polyuria	>2.5 L/day	Diabetes mellitus; diabetes insipidus; excess caffeine or alcohol; kidney disease; certain drugs, such as diuretics; sickle cell anemia; excessive water intake
Oliguria	300–500 mL/day	Dehydration; blood loss; diarrhea; cardiogenic shock; kidney disease; enlarged prostate
Anuria	<50 mL/day	Kidney failure; obstruction, such as kidney stone or tumor; enlarged prostate

Table 25.2

The pH (hydrogen ion concentration) of the urine can vary more than 1000-fold, from a normal low of 4.5 to a maximum of 8.0. Diet can influence pH; meats lower the pH, whereas citrus fruits, vegetables, and dairy products raise the pH. Chronically high or low pH can lead to disorders, such as the development of kidney stones or osteomalacia.

Specific gravity is a measure of the quantity of solutes per unit volume of a solution and is traditionally easier to measure than osmolarity. Urine will always have a specific gravity greater than pure water (water = 1.0) due to the presence of solutes. Laboratories can now measure urine osmolarity directly, which is a more accurate indicator of urinary solutes than **specific gravity**. Remember that osmolarity is the number of osmoles or milliosmoles per liter of fluid (mOsmol/L). Urine osmolarity ranges from a low of 50–100 mOsmol/L to as high as 1200 mOsmol/L H_2O.

Cells are not normally found in the urine. The presence of leukocytes may indicate a urinary tract infection. **Leukocyte esterase** is released by leukocytes; if detected in the urine, it can be taken as indirect evidence of a urinary tract infection (UTI).

Protein does not normally leave the glomerular capillaries, so only trace amounts of protein should be found in the urine, approximately 10 mg/100 mL in a random sample. If excessive protein is detected in the urine, it usually means that the glomerulus is damaged and is allowing protein to "leak" into the filtrate.

Ketones are byproducts of fat metabolism. Finding ketones in the urine suggests that the body is using fat as an energy source in preference to glucose. In diabetes mellitus when there is not enough insulin (type I diabetes mellitus) or because of insulin resistance (type II diabetes mellitus), there is plenty of glucose, but without the action of insulin, the cells cannot take it up, so it remains in the bloodstream. Instead, the cells are forced to use fat as their energy source, and fat consumed at such a level produces excessive ketones as byproducts. These excess ketones will appear in the urine. Ketones may also appear if there is a severe deficiency of proteins or carbohydrates in the diet.

Nitrates (NO_3^-) occur normally in the urine. Gram-negative bacteria metabolize nitrate into nitrite (NO_2^-), and its presence in the urine is indirect evidence of infection.

There should be no blood found in the urine. It may sometimes appear in urine samples as a result of menstrual contamination, but this is not an abnormal condition. Now that you understand what the normal characteristics of urine are, the next section will introduce you to how you store and dispose of this waste product and how you make it.

25.2 | Gross Anatomy of Urine Transport

By the end of this section, you will be able to:
- Identify the ureters, urinary bladder, and urethra, as well as their location, structure, histology, and function
- Compare and contrast male and female urethras
- Describe the micturition reflex
- Describe voluntary and involuntary neural control of micturition

Rather than start with urine formation, this section will start with urine excretion. Urine is a fluid of variable composition that requires specialized structures to remove it from the body safely and efficiently. Blood is filtered, and the filtrate is transformed into urine at a relatively constant rate throughout the day. This processed liquid is stored until a convenient time for excretion. All structures involved in the transport and storage of the urine are large enough to be visible to the naked eye. This transport and storage system not only stores the waste, but it protects the tissues from damage due to the wide range of pH and osmolarity of the urine, prevents infection by foreign organisms, and for the male, provides reproductive functions.

Urethra

The **urethra** transports urine from the bladder to the outside of the body for disposal. The urethra is the only urologic organ that shows any significant anatomic difference between males and females; all other urine transport structures are identical (Figure 25.3).

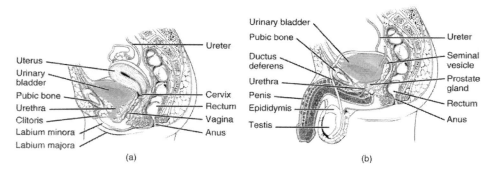

Figure 25.3 Female and Male Urethras The urethra transports urine from the bladder to the outside of the body. This image shows (a) a female urethra and (b) a male urethra.

The urethra in both males and females begins inferior and central to the two ureteral openings forming the three points of a triangular-shaped area at the base of the bladder called the **trigone** (Greek tri- = "triangle" and the root of the word "trigonometry"). The urethra tracks posterior and inferior to the pubic symphysis (see Figure 25.3a). In both males and females, the proximal urethra is lined by transitional epithelium, whereas the terminal portion is a nonkeratinized, stratified squamous epithelium. In the male, pseudostratified columnar epithelium lines the urethra between these two cell types. Voiding is regulated by an involuntary autonomic nervous system-controlled **internal urinary sphincter**, consisting of smooth muscle and voluntary skeletal muscle that forms the **external urinary sphincter** below it.

Female Urethra

The external urethral orifice is embedded in the anterior vaginal wall inferior to the clitoris, superior to the vaginal opening (introitus), and medial to the labia minora. Its short length, about 4 cm, is less of a barrier to fecal bacteria than the longer male urethra and the best explanation for the greater incidence of UTI in women. Voluntary control of the external urethral sphincter is a function of the pudendal nerve. It arises in the sacral region of the spinal cord, traveling via the S2–S4 nerves of the sacral plexus.

Male Urethra

The male urethra passes through the prostate gland immediately inferior to the bladder before passing below the pubic symphysis (see Figure 25.3b). The length of the male urethra varies between men but averages 20 cm in length. It is divided into four regions: the preprostatic urethra, the prostatic urethra, the membranous urethra, and the spongy or penile urethra. The preprostatic urethra is very short and incorporated into the bladder wall. The prostatic urethra passes through the prostate gland. During sexual intercourse, it receives sperm via the ejaculatory ducts and secretions from the seminal vesicles. Paired Cowper's glands (bulbourethral glands) produce and secrete mucus into the urethra to buffer urethral pH during sexual stimulation. The mucus neutralizes the usually acidic environment and lubricates the urethra, decreasing the resistance to ejaculation. The membranous urethra passes through the deep muscles of the perineum, where it is invested by the overlying urethral sphincters. The spongy urethra exits at the tip (external urethral orifice) of the penis after passing through the corpus spongiosum. Mucous glands are found along much of the length of the urethra and protect the urethra from extremes of urine pH. Innervation is the same in both males and females.

Bladder

The urinary bladder collects urine from both ureters (Figure 25.4). The bladder lies anterior to the uterus in females, posterior to the pubic bone and anterior to the rectum. During late pregnancy, its capacity is reduced due to compression by the enlarging uterus, resulting in increased frequency of urination. In males, the anatomy is similar, minus the uterus, and with the addition of the prostate inferior to the bladder. The bladder is partially **retroperitoneal** (outside the peritoneal cavity) with its peritoneal-covered "dome" projecting into the abdomen when the bladder is distended with urine.

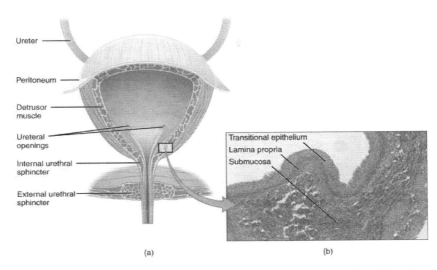

Figure 25.4 Bladder (a) Anterior cross section of the bladder. (b) The detrusor muscle of the bladder (source: monkey tissue) LM × 448. (Micrograph provided by the Regents of the University of Michigan Medical School © 2012)

View the University of Michigan WebScope at http://141.214.65.171/Histology/Urinary%20System/212N_HISTO_40X.svs/view.apml (http://openstaxcollege.org/l/bladderMG) to explore the tissue sample in greater detail.

The bladder is a highly distensible organ comprised of irregular crisscrossing bands of smooth muscle collectively called the **detrusor muscle**. The interior surface is made of transitional cellular epithelium that is structurally suited for the large volume fluctuations of the bladder. When empty, it resembles columnar epithelia, but when stretched, it "transitions" (hence the name) to a squamous appearance (see Figure 25.4). Volumes in adults can range from nearly zero to 500–600 mL.

The detrusor muscle contracts with significant force in the young. The bladder's strength diminishes with age, but voluntary contractions of abdominal skeletal muscles can increase intra-abdominal pressure to promote more forceful bladder emptying. Such voluntary contraction is also used in forceful defecation and childbirth.

Micturition Reflex

Micturition is a less-often used, but proper term for urination or voiding. It results from an interplay of involuntary and voluntary actions by the internal and external urethral sphincters. When bladder volume reaches about 150 mL, an urge to void is sensed but is easily overridden. Voluntary control of urination relies on consciously preventing relaxation of the external urethral sphincter to maintain urinary continence. As the bladder fills, subsequent urges become harder to ignore. Ultimately, voluntary constraint fails with resulting **incontinence**, which will occur as bladder volume approaches 300 to 400 mL.

Normal micturition is a result of stretch receptors in the bladder wall that transmit nerve impulses to the sacral region of the spinal cord to generate a spinal reflex. The resulting parasympathetic neural outflow causes contraction of the detrusor muscle and relaxation of the involuntary internal urethral sphincter. At the same time, the spinal cord inhibits somatic motor neurons, resulting in the relaxation of the skeletal muscle of the external urethral sphincter. The micturition reflex is active in infants but with maturity, children learn to override the reflex by asserting external sphincter control, thereby delaying voiding (potty training). This reflex may be preserved even in the face of spinal cord injury that results in paraplegia or quadriplegia. However, relaxation of the external sphincter may not be possible in all cases, and therefore, periodic catheterization may be necessary for bladder emptying.

Nerves involved in the control of urination include the hypogastric, pelvic, and pudendal (Figure 25.5). Voluntary micturition requires an intact spinal cord and functional pudendal nerve arising from the **sacral micturition center**. Since the external urinary sphincter is voluntary skeletal muscle, actions by cholinergic neurons maintain contraction (and thereby continence) during filling of the bladder. At the same time, sympathetic nervous activity via the hypogastric nerves suppresses contraction of the detrusor muscle. With further bladder stretch, afferent signals traveling over sacral pelvic nerves activate parasympathetic neurons. This activates efferent neurons to release acetylcholine at the neuromuscular junctions, producing detrusor contraction and bladder emptying.

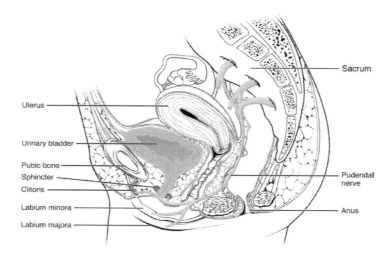

Figure 25.5 Nerves Innervating the Urinary System

Ureters

The kidneys and ureters are completely retroperitoneal, and the bladder has a peritoneal covering only over the dome. As urine is formed, it drains into the calyces of the kidney, which merge to form the funnel-shaped renal pelvis in the hilum of each kidney. The hilum narrows to become the ureter of each kidney. As urine passes through the ureter, it does not passively drain into the bladder but rather is propelled by waves of peristalsis. As the ureters enter the pelvis, they sweep laterally, hugging the pelvic walls. As they approach the bladder, they turn medially and pierce the bladder wall obliquely. This is important because it creates an one-way valve (a **physiological sphincter** rather than an **anatomical sphincter**) that allows urine into the bladder but prevents reflux of urine from the bladder back into the ureter. Children born lacking this oblique course of the ureter through the bladder wall are susceptible to "vesicoureteral reflux," which dramatically increases their risk of serious UTI. Pregnancy also increases the likelihood of reflux and UTI.

The ureters are approximately 30 cm long. The inner mucosa is lined with transitional epithelium (Figure 25.6) and scattered goblet cells that secrete protective mucus. The muscular layer of the ureter consists of longitudinal and circular smooth muscles that create the peristaltic contractions to move the urine into the bladder without the aid of gravity. Finally, a loose adventitial layer composed of collagen and fat anchors the ureters between the parietal peritoneum and the posterior abdominal wall.

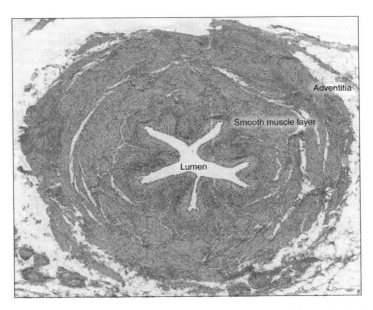

Figure 25.6 Ureter Peristaltic contractions help to move urine through the lumen with contributions from fluid pressure and gravity. LM × 128. (Micrograph provided by the Regents of the University of Michigan Medical School © 2012)

25.3 | Gross Anatomy of the Kidney

By the end of this section, you will be able to:
- Describe the external structure of the kidney, including its location, support structures, and covering
- Identify the major internal divisions and structures of the kidney
- Identify the major blood vessels associated with the kidney and trace the path of blood through the kidney
- Compare and contrast the cortical and juxtamedullary nephrons
- Name structures found in the cortex and medulla
- Describe the physiological characteristics of the cortex and medulla

The kidneys lie on either side of the spine in the retroperitoneal space between the parietal peritoneum and the posterior abdominal wall, well protected by muscle, fat, and ribs. They are roughly the size of your fist, and the male kidney is typically a bit larger than the female kidney. The kidneys are well vascularized, receiving about 25 percent of the cardiac output at rest.

Interactive Link

There have never been sufficient kidney donations to provide a kidney to each person needing one. Watch this video (http://openstaxcollege.org/l/TED) to learn about the TED (Technology, Entertainment, Design) Conference held in March 2011. In this video, Dr. Anthony Atala discusses a cutting-edge technique in which a new kidney is "printed." The successful utilization of this technology is still several years in the future, but imagine a time when you can print a replacement organ or tissue on demand.

External Anatomy

The left kidney is located at about the T12 to L3 vertebrae, whereas the right is lower due to slight displacement by the liver. Upper portions of the kidneys are somewhat protected by the eleventh and twelfth ribs (Figure 25.7). Each kidney weighs about 125–175 g in males and 115–155 g in females. They are about 11–14 cm in length, 6 cm wide, and 4 cm thick, and are directly covered by a fibrous capsule composed of dense, irregular connective tissue that helps to hold their shape and protect them. This capsule is covered by a shock-absorbing layer of adipose tissue called the **renal fat pad**, which in turn is encompassed by a tough renal fascia. The fascia and, to a lesser extent, the overlying peritoneum serve to firmly anchor the kidneys to the posterior abdominal wall in a retroperitoneal position.

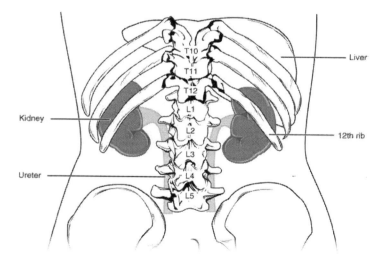

Figure 25.7 Kidneys The kidneys are slightly protected by the ribs and are surrounded by fat for protection (not shown).

On the superior aspect of each kidney is the adrenal gland. The adrenal cortex directly influences renal function through the production of the hormone aldosterone to stimulate sodium reabsorption.

Internal Anatomy

A frontal section through the kidney reveals an outer region called the **renal cortex** and an inner region called the **medulla** (Figure 25.8). The **renal columns** are connective tissue extensions that radiate downward from the cortex through the medulla to separate the most characteristic features of the medulla, the **renal pyramids** and **renal papillae**. The papillae are bundles of collecting ducts that transport urine made by nephrons to the **calyces** of the kidney for excretion. The renal columns also serve to divide the kidney into 6–8 lobes and provide a supportive framework for vessels that enter and exit the cortex. The pyramids and renal columns taken together constitute the kidney lobes.

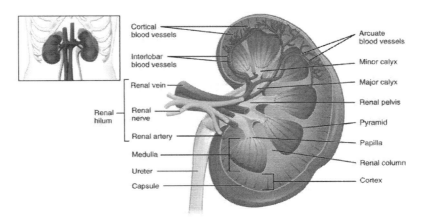

Figure 25.8 Left Kidney

Renal Hilum

The **renal hilum** is the entry and exit site for structures servicing the kidneys: vessels, nerves, lymphatics, and ureters. The medial-facing hila are tucked into the sweeping convex outline of the cortex. Emerging from the hilum is the renal pelvis, which is formed from the major and minor calyxes in the kidney. The smooth muscle in the renal pelvis funnels urine via peristalsis into the ureter. The renal arteries form directly from the descending aorta, whereas the renal veins return cleansed blood directly to the inferior vena cava. The artery, vein, and renal pelvis are arranged in an anterior-to-posterior order.

Nephrons and Vessels

The renal artery first divides into segmental arteries, followed by further branching to form interlobar arteries that pass through the renal columns to reach the cortex (Figure 25.9). The interlobar arteries, in turn, branch into arcuate arteries, cortical radiate arteries, and then into afferent arterioles. The afferent arterioles service about 1.3 million nephrons in each kidney.

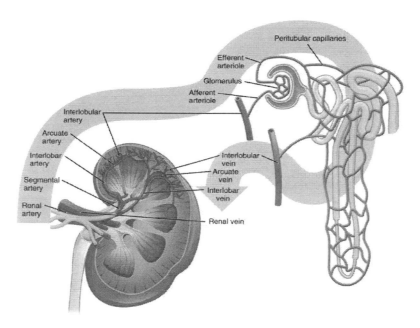

Figure 25.9 Blood Flow in the Kidney

Nephrons are the "functional units" of the kidney; they cleanse the blood and balance the constituents of the circulation. The afferent arterioles form a tuft of high-pressure capillaries about 200 μm in diameter, the **glomerulus**. The rest of the nephron consists of a continuous sophisticated tubule whose proximal end surrounds the glomerulus in an intimate embrace—this is **Bowman's capsule**. The glomerulus and Bowman's capsule together form the **renal corpuscle**. As mentioned earlier, these glomerular capillaries filter the blood based on particle size. After passing through the renal corpuscle, the capillaries form a second arteriole, the **efferent arteriole** (Figure 25.10). These will next form a capillary network around the more distal portions of the nephron tubule, the **peritubular capillaries** and **vasa recta**, before returning to the venous system. As the glomerular filtrate progresses through the nephron, these capillary networks recover most of the solutes and water, and return them to the circulation. Since a capillary bed (the glomerulus) drains into a vessel that in turn forms a second capillary bed, the definition of a portal system is met. This is the only portal system in which an arteriole is found between the first and second capillary beds. (Portal systems also link the hypothalamus to the anterior pituitary, and the blood vessels of the digestive viscera to the liver.)

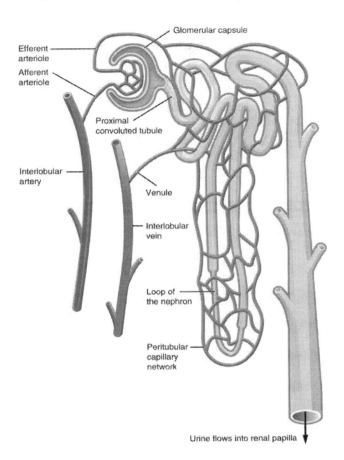

Figure 25.10 **Blood Flow in the Nephron** The two capillary beds are clearly shown in this figure. The efferent arteriole is the connecting vessel between the glomerulus and the peritubular capillaries and vasa recta.

Visit this link (http://openstaxcollege.org/l/bloodflow5) to view an interactive tutorial of the flow of blood through the kidney.

Cortex

In a dissected kidney, it is easy to identify the cortex; it appears lighter in color compared to the rest of the kidney. All of the renal corpuscles as well as both the **proximal convoluted tubules (PCTs)** and **distal convoluted tubules** are found here. Some nephrons have a short **loop of Henle** that does not dip beyond the cortex. These nephrons are called **cortical nephrons**. About 15 percent of nephrons have long loops of Henle that extend deep into the medulla and are called **juxtamedullary nephrons**.

25.4 | Microscopic Anatomy of the Kidney

By the end of this section, you will be able to:

- Distinguish the histological differences between the renal cortex and medulla
- Describe the structure of the filtration membrane
- Identify the major structures and subdivisions of the renal corpuscles, renal tubules, and renal capillaries
- Discuss the function of the peritubular capillaries and vasa recta
- Identify the location of the juxtaglomerular apparatus and describe the cells that line it
- Describe the histology of the proximal convoluted tubule, loop of Henle, distal convoluted tubule, and collecting ducts

The renal structures that conduct the essential work of the kidney cannot be seen by the naked eye. Only a light or electron microscope can reveal these structures. Even then, serial sections and computer reconstruction are necessary to give us a comprehensive view of the functional anatomy of the nephron and its associated blood vessels.

Nephrons: The Functional Unit

Nephrons take a simple filtrate of the blood and modify it into urine. Many changes take place in the different parts of the nephron before urine is created for disposal. The term **forming urine** will be used hereafter to describe the filtrate as it is modified into true urine. The principle task of the nephron population is to balance the plasma to homeostatic set points and excrete potential toxins in the urine. They do this by accomplishing three principle functions—filtration, reabsorption, and secretion. They also have additional secondary functions that exert control in three areas: blood pressure (via production of **renin**), red blood cell production (via the hormone EPO), and calcium absorption (via conversion of calcidiol into calcitriol, the active form of vitamin D).

Renal Corpuscle

As discussed earlier, the renal corpuscle consists of a tuft of capillaries called the glomerulus that is largely surrounded by Bowman's (glomerular) capsule. The glomerulus is a high-pressure capillary bed between afferent and efferent arterioles. Bowman's capsule surrounds the glomerulus to form a lumen, and captures and directs this filtrate to the PCT. The outermost part of Bowman's capsule, the parietal layer, is a simple squamous epithelium. It transitions onto the glomerular capillaries in an intimate embrace to form the visceral layer of the capsule. Here, the cells are not squamous, but uniquely shaped cells (**podocytes**) extending finger-like arms (**pedicels**) to cover the glomerular capillaries (Figure 25.11). These projections interdigitate to form **filtration slits**, leaving small gaps between the digits to form a sieve. As blood passes through the glomerulus, 10 to 20 percent of the plasma filters between these sieve-like fingers to be captured by Bowman's capsule and funneled to the PCT. Where the fenestrae (windows) in the glomerular capillaries match the spaces between the podocyte "fingers," the only thing separating the capillary lumen and the lumen of Bowman's capsule is their shared basement membrane (Figure 25.12). These three features comprise what is known as the filtration membrane. This membrane permits very rapid movement of filtrate from capillary to capsule though pores that are only 70 nm in diameter.

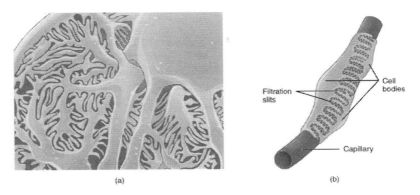

Figure 25.11 Podocytes Podocytes interdigitate with structures called pedicels and filter substances in a way similar to fenestrations. In (a), the large cell body can be seen at the top right corner, with branches extending from the cell body. The smallest finger-like extensions are the pedicels. Pedicels on one podocyte always interdigitate with the pedicels of another podocyte. (b) This capillary has three podocytes wrapped around it.

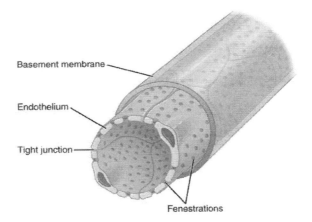

Figure 25.12 Fenestrated Capillary Fenestrations allow many substances to diffuse from the blood based primarily on size.

The **fenestrations** prevent filtration of blood cells or large proteins, but allow most other constituents through. These substances cross readily if they are less than 4 nm in size and most pass freely up to 8 nm in size. An additional factor affecting the ability of substances to cross this barrier is their electric charge. The proteins associated with these pores are negatively charged, so they tend to repel negatively charged substances and allow positively charged substances to pass more readily. The basement membrane prevents filtration of medium-to-large proteins such as globulins. There are also **mesangial** cells in the filtration membrane that can contract to help regulate the rate of filtration of the glomerulus. Overall, filtration is regulated by fenestrations in capillary endothelial cells, podocytes with filtration slits, membrane charge, and the basement membrane between capillary cells. The result is the creation of a filtrate that does not contain cells or large proteins, and has a slight predominance of positively charged substances.

Lying just outside Bowman's capsule and the glomerulus is the **juxtaglomerular apparatus (JGA)** (Figure 25.13). At the juncture where the afferent and efferent arterioles enter and leave Bowman's capsule, the initial part of the distal convoluted tubule (DCT) comes into direct contact with the arterioles. The wall of the DCT at that point forms a part of the JGA known as the **macula densa**. This cluster of cuboidal epithelial cells monitors the fluid composition of fluid flowing through the DCT. In response to the concentration of Na^+ in the fluid flowing past them, these cells release paracrine signals. They also have a single, nonmotile cilium that responds to the rate of fluid movement in the tubule. The paracrine signals released in response to changes in flow rate and Na$^+$ concentration are adenosine triphosphate (ATP) and adenosine.

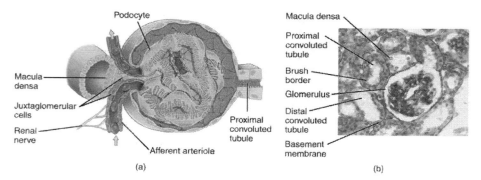

Figure 25.13 Juxtaglomerular Apparatus and Glomerulus (a) The JGA allows specialized cells to monitor the composition of the fluid in the DCT and adjust the glomerular filtration rate. (b) This micrograph shows the glomerulus and surrounding structures. LM × 1540. (Micrograph provided by the Regents of University of Michigan Medical School © 2012)

A second cell type in this apparatus is the **juxtaglomerular cell**. This is a modified, smooth muscle cell lining the afferent arteriole that can contract or relax in response to ATP or adenosine released by the macula densa. Such contraction and relaxation regulate blood flow to the glomerulus. If the osmolarity of the filtrate is too high (hyperosmotic), the juxtaglomerular cells will contract, decreasing the glomerular filtration rate (GFR) so less plasma is filtered, leading to less urine formation and greater retention of fluid. This will ultimately decrease blood osmolarity toward the physiologic norm. If the osmolarity of the filtrate is too low, the juxtaglomerular cells will relax, increasing the GFR and enhancing the loss of water to the urine, causing blood osmolarity to rise. In other words, when osmolarity goes up, filtration and urine formation decrease and water is retained. When osmolarity goes down, filtration and urine formation increase and water is lost by way of the urine. The net result of these opposing actions is to keep the rate of filtration relatively constant. A second function of the macula densa cells is to regulate renin release from the juxtaglomerular cells of the afferent arteriole (Figure 25.14). Active renin is a protein comprised of 304 amino acids that cleaves several amino acids from **angiotensinogen** to produce **angiotensin I**. Angiotensin I is not biologically active until converted to angiotensin II by **angiotensin-converting enzyme (ACE)** from the lungs. **Angiotensin II** is a systemic vasoconstrictor that helps to regulate blood pressure by increasing it. Angiotensin II also stimulates the release of the steroid hormone aldosterone from the adrenal cortex. Aldosterone stimulates Na$^+$ reabsorption by the kidney, which also results in water retention and increased blood pressure.

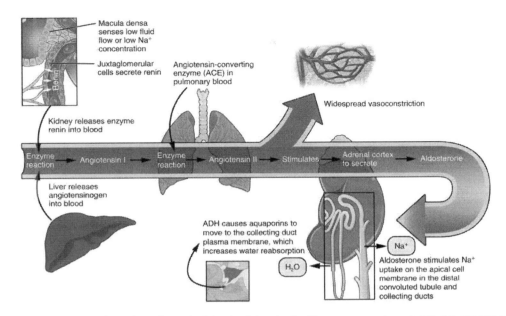

Figure 25.14 Conversion of Angiotensin I to Angiotensin II The enzyme renin converts the pro-enzyme angiotensin I; the lung-derived enzyme ACE converts angiotensin I into active angiotensin II.

Proximal Convoluted Tubule (PCT)

Filtered fluid collected by Bowman's capsule enters into the PCT. It is called convoluted due to its tortuous path. Simple cuboidal cells form this tubule with prominent microvilli on the luminal surface, forming a **brush border**. These microvilli create a large surface area to maximize the absorption and secretion of solutes (Na^+, Cl^-, glucose, etc.), the most essential function of this portion of the nephron. These cells actively transport ions across their membranes, so they possess a high concentration of mitochondria in order to produce sufficient ATP.

Loop of Henle

The descending and ascending portions of the loop of Henle (sometimes referred to as the nephron loop) are, of course, just continuations of the same tubule. They run adjacent and parallel to each other after having made a hairpin turn at the deepest point of their descent. The descending loop of Henle consists of an initial short, thick portion and long, thin portion, whereas the ascending loop consists of an initial short, thin portion followed by a long, thick portion. The descending thick portion consists of simple cuboidal epithelium similar to that of the PCT. The descending and ascending thin portions consists of simple squamous epithelium. As you will see later, these are important differences, since different portions of the loop have different permeabilities for solutes and water. The ascending thick portion consists of simple cuboidal epithelium similar to the DCT.

Distal Convoluted Tubule (DCT)

The DCT, like the PCT, is very tortuous and formed by simple cuboidal epithelium, but it is shorter than the PCT. These cells are not as active as those in the PCT; thus, there are fewer microvilli on the apical surface. However, these cells must also pump ions against their concentration gradient, so you will find of large numbers of mitochondria, although fewer than in the PCT.

Collecting Ducts

The collecting ducts are continuous with the nephron but not technically part of it. In fact, each duct collects filtrate from several nephrons for final modification. Collecting ducts merge as they descend deeper in the medulla to form about 30 terminal ducts, which empty at a papilla. They are lined with simple squamous epithelium with receptors for ADH. When stimulated by ADH, these cells will insert **aquaporin** channel proteins into their membranes, which as their name suggests, allow water to pass from the duct lumen through the cells and into the interstitial spaces to be recovered by the vasa recta. This process allows for the recovery of large amounts of water from the filtrate back into the blood. In the absence of ADH, these channels are not inserted, resulting in the excretion of water in the form of dilute urine. Most, if not all, cells of the body contain aquaporin molecules, whose channels are so small that only water can pass. At least 10 types of aquaporins are known in humans, and six of those are found in the kidney. The function of all aquaporins is to allow the movement of water across the lipid-rich, hydrophobic cell membrane (Figure 25.15).

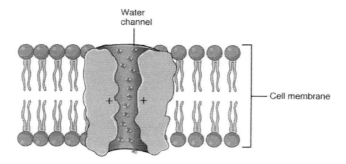

Figure 25.15 Aquaporin Water Channel Positive charges inside the channel prevent the leakage of electrolytes across the cell membrane, while allowing water to move due to osmosis.

25.5 | Physiology of Urine Formation

By the end of this section, you will be able to:
- Describe the hydrostatic and colloid osmotic forces that favor and oppose filtration
- Describe glomerular filtration rate (GFR), state the average value of GFR, and explain how clearance rate can be used to measure GFR
- Predict specific factors that will increase or decrease GFR
- State the percent of the filtrate that is normally reabsorbed and explain why the process of reabsorption is so important
- Calculate daily urine production
- List common symptoms of kidney failure

Having reviewed the anatomy and microanatomy of the urinary system, now is the time to focus on the physiology. You will discover that different parts of the nephron utilize specific processes to produce urine: filtration, reabsorption, and secretion. You will learn how each of these processes works and where they occur along the nephron and collecting ducts. The physiologic goal is to modify the composition of the plasma and, in doing so, produce the waste product urine.

Failure of the renal anatomy and/or physiology can lead suddenly or gradually to renal failure. In this event, a number of symptoms, signs, or laboratory findings point to the diagnosis (Table 25.3).

Symptoms of Kidney Failure
Weakness
Lethargy
Shortness of breath
Widespread edema
Anemia

Table 25.3

Symptoms of Kidney Failure

Metabolic acidosis
Metabolic alkalosis
Heart arrhythmias
Uremia (high urea level in the blood)
Loss of appetite
Fatigue
Excessive urination
Oliguria (too little urine output)

Table 25.3

Glomerular Filtration Rate (GFR)

The volume of filtrate formed by both kidneys per minute is termed the **glomerular filtration rate (GFR)**. The heart pumps about 5 L blood per min under resting conditions. Approximately 20 percent or one liter enters the kidneys to be filtered. On average, this liter results in the production of about 125 mL/min filtrate produced in men (range of 90 to 140 mL/min) and 105 mL/min filtrate produced in women (range of 80 to 125 mL/min). This amount equates to a volume of about 180 L/day in men and 150 L/day in women. Ninety-nine percent of this filtrate is returned to the circulation by reabsorption so that only about 1–2 liters of urine are produced per day (Table 25.4).

Calculating Urine Formation per Day

	Flow per minute (mL)	Calculation
Renal blood flow	1050	Cardiac output is about 5000 mL/minute, of which 21 percent flows through the kidney. 5000*0.21 = 1050 mL blood/min
Renal plasma flow	578	Renal plasma flow equals the blood flow per minute times the hematocrit. If a person has a hematocrit of 45, then the renal plasma flow is 55 percent. 1050*0.55 = 578 mL plasma/min
Glomerular filtration rate	110	The GFR is the amount of plasma entering Bowman's capsule per minute. It is the renal plasma flow times the fraction that enters the renal capsule (19 percent). 578*0.19 = 110 mL filtrate/min
Urine	1296 ml/day	The filtrate not recovered by the kidney is the urine that will be eliminated. It is the GFR times the fraction of the filtrate that is not reabsorbed (0.8 percent). 110*.008 = 0.9 mL urine /min Multiply urine/min times 60 minutes times 24 hours to get daily urine production. 0.9*60*24 = 1296 mL/day urine

Table 25.4

GFR is influenced by the hydrostatic pressure and colloid osmotic pressure on either side of the capillary membrane of the glomerulus. Recall that filtration occurs as pressure forces fluid and solutes through a semipermeable barrier with the solute movement constrained by particle size. Hydrostatic pressure is the pressure produced by a fluid against a surface. If you have a fluid on both sides of a barrier, both fluids exert a pressure in opposing directions. Net fluid movement will be in the direction of the lower pressure. Osmosis is the movement of solvent (water) across a membrane that is impermeable to a solute in the solution. This creates a pressure, osmotic pressure, which will exist until the solute concentration is the same on both sides of a semipermeable membrane. As long as the concentration differs, water will move. Glomerular filtration occurs when glomerular hydrostatic pressure exceeds the luminal hydrostatic pressure of Bowman's capsule. There is also an opposing force, the osmotic pressure, which is typically higher in the glomerular capillary.

To understand why this is so, look more closely at the microenvironment on either side of the filtration membrane. You will find osmotic pressure exerted by the solutes inside the lumen of the capillary as well as inside of Bowman's capsule. Since the filtration membrane limits the size of particles crossing the membrane, the osmotic pressure inside the glomerular capillary is higher than the osmotic pressure in Bowman's capsule. Recall that cells and the medium-to-large proteins cannot pass between the podocyte processes or through the fenestrations of the capillary endothelial cells. This means that red and white blood cells, platelets, albumins, and other proteins too large to pass through the filter remain in the capillary, creating an average colloid osmotic pressure of 30 mm Hg within the capillary. The absence of proteins in Bowman's space (the lumen within Bowman's capsule) results in an osmotic pressure near zero. Thus, the only pressure moving fluid across the capillary wall into the lumen of Bowman's space is hydrostatic pressure. Hydrostatic (fluid) pressure is sufficient to push water through the membrane despite the osmotic pressure working against it. The sum of all of the influences, both osmotic and hydrostatic, results in a **net filtration pressure (NFP)** of about 10 mm Hg (Figure 25.16).

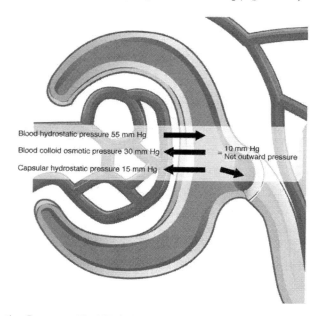

Figure 25.16 Net Filtration Pressure   The NFP is the sum of osmotic and hydrostatic pressures.

A proper concentration of solutes in the blood is important in maintaining osmotic pressure both in the glomerulus and systemically. There are disorders in which too much protein passes through the filtration slits into the kidney filtrate. This excess protein in the filtrate leads to a deficiency of circulating plasma proteins. In turn, the presence of protein in the urine increases its osmolarity; this holds more water in the filtrate and results in an increase in urine volume. Because there is less circulating protein, principally albumin, the osmotic pressure of the blood falls. Less osmotic pressure pulling water into the capillaries tips the balance towards hydrostatic pressure, which tends to push it out of the capillaries. The net effect is that water is lost from the circulation to interstitial tissues and cells. This "plumps up" the tissues and cells, a condition termed **systemic edema**.

Net Filtration Pressure (NFP)

NFP determines filtration rates through the kidney. It is determined as follows:

NFP = Glomerular blood hydrostatic pressure (GBHP) – [capsular hydrostatic pressure (CHP) + blood colloid osmotic pressure (BCOP)] = 10 mm Hg

That is:

NFP = GBHP – [CHP + BCOP] = 10 mm Hg

Or:

NFP = 55 – [15 + 30] = 10 mm Hg

As you can see, there is a low net pressure across the filtration membrane. Intuitively, you should realize that minor changes in osmolarity of the blood or changes in capillary blood pressure result in major changes in the amount of filtrate formed at any given point in time. The kidney is able to cope with a wide range of blood pressures. In large part, this is due to the autoregulatory nature of smooth muscle. When you stretch it, it contracts. Thus, when blood pressure goes up, smooth muscle in the afferent capillaries contracts to limit any increase in blood flow and filtration rate. When blood pressure drops, the same capillaries relax to maintain blood flow and filtration rate. The net result is a relatively steady flow of blood into the glomerulus and a relatively steady filtration rate in spite of significant systemic blood pressure changes. Mean arterial blood pressure is calculated by adding 1/3 of the difference between the systolic and diastolic pressures to the diastolic pressure. Therefore, if the blood pressure is 110/80, the difference between systolic and diastolic pressure is 30. One third of this is 10, and when you add this to the diastolic pressure of 80, you arrive at a calculated mean arterial pressure of 90 mm Hg. Therefore, if you use mean arterial pressure for the GBHP in the formula for calculating NFP, you can determine that as long as mean arterial pressure is above approximately 60 mm Hg, the pressure will be adequate to maintain glomerular filtration. Blood pressures below this level will impair renal function and cause systemic disorders that are severe enough to threaten survival. This condition is called shock.

Determination of the GFR is one of the tools used to assess the kidney's excretory function. This is more than just an academic exercise. Since many drugs are excreted in the urine, a decline in renal function can lead to toxic accumulations. Additionally, administration of appropriate drug dosages for those drugs primarily excreted by the kidney requires an accurate assessment of GFR. GFR can be estimated closely by intravenous administration of **inulin**. Inulin is a plant polysaccharide that is neither reabsorbed nor secreted by the kidney. Its appearance in the urine is directly proportional to the rate at which it is filtered by the renal corpuscle. However, since measuring inulin clearance is cumbersome in the clinical setting, most often, the GFR is estimated by measuring naturally occurring creatinine, a protein-derived molecule produced by muscle metabolism that is not reabsorbed and only slightly secreted by the nephron.

25.6 | Tubular Reabsorption

By the end of this section, you will be able to:
- List specific transport mechanisms occurring in different parts of the nephron, including active transport, osmosis, facilitated diffusion, and passive electrochemical gradients
- List the different membrane proteins of the nephron, including channels, transporters, and ATPase pumps
- Compare and contrast passive and active tubular reabsorption
- Explain why the differential permeability or impermeability of specific sections of the nephron tubules is necessary for urine formation
- Describe how and where water, organic compounds, and ions are reabsorbed in the nephron
- Explain the role of the loop of Henle, the vasa recta, and the countercurrent multiplication mechanisms in the concentration of urine
- List the locations in the nephron where tubular secretion occurs

With up to 180 liters per day passing through the nephrons of the kidney, it is quite obvious that most of that fluid and its contents must be reabsorbed. That recovery occurs in the PCT, loop of Henle, DCT, and the collecting ducts (Table 25.5 and Figure 25.17). Various portions of the nephron differ in their capacity to reabsorb water and specific solutes. While much of the reabsorption and secretion occur passively based on concentration gradients, the amount of water that is reabsorbed or lost is tightly regulated. This control is exerted directly by ADH and aldosterone, and indirectly by renin. Most water is recovered in the PCT, loop of Henle, and DCT. About 10 percent (about 18 L) reaches the collecting ducts. The collecting ducts, under the influence of ADH, can recover almost all of the water passing through them, in cases of dehydration, or almost none of the water, in cases of over-hydration.

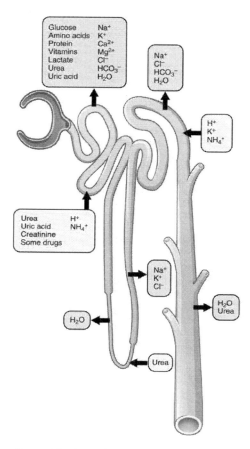

Figure 25.17 Locations of Secretion and Reabsorption in the Nephron

Substances Secreted or Reabsorbed in the Nephron and Their Locations

Substance	PCT	Loop of Henle	DCT	Collecting ducts
Glucose	Almost 100 percent reabsorbed; secondary active transport with Na^+			
Oligopeptides, proteins, amino acids	Almost 100 percent reabsorbed; symport with Na^+			
Vitamins	Reabsorbed			

Table 25.5

Substances Secreted or Reabsorbed in the Nephron and Their Locations

Substance	PCT	Loop of Henle	DCT	Collecting ducts
Lactate	Reabsorbed			
Creatinine	Secreted			
Urea	50 percent reabsorbed by diffusion; also secreted	Secretion, diffusion in descending limb		Reabsorption in medullary collecting ducts; diffusion
Sodium	65 percent actively reabsorbed	25 percent reabsorbed in thick ascending limb; active transport	5 percent reabsorbed; active	5 percent reabsorbed, stimulated by aldosterone; active
Chloride	Reabsorbed, symport with Na^+, diffusion	Reabsorbed in thin and thick ascending limb; diffusion in ascending limb	Reabsorbed; diffusion	Reabsorbed; symport
Water	67 percent reabsorbed osmotically with solutes	15 percent reabsorbed in descending limb; osmosis	8 percent reabsorbed if ADH; osmosis	Variable amounts reabsorbed, controlled by ADH, osmosis
Bicarbonate	80–90 percent symport reabsorption with Na^+	Reabsorbed, symport with Na^+ and antiport with Cl^-; in ascending limb		Reabsorbed antiport with Cl^-
H^+	Secreted; diffusion		Secreted; active	Secreted; active
NH_4^+	Secreted; diffusion		Secreted; diffusion	Secreted; diffusion
HCO_3^-	Reabsorbed; diffusion	Reabsorbed; diffusion in ascending limb	Reabsorbed; diffusion	Reabsorbed; antiport with Na^+
Some drugs	Secreted		Secreted; active	Secreted; active
Potassium	65 percent reabsorbed; diffusion	20 percent reabsorbed in thick ascending limb; symport	Secreted; active	Secretion controlled by aldosterone; active
Calcium	Reabsorbed; diffusion	Reabsorbed in thick ascending limb; diffusion		Reabsorbed if parathyroid hormone present; active
Magnesium	Reabsorbed; diffusion	Reabsorbed in thick ascending limb; diffusion	Reabsorbed	
Phosphate	85 percent reabsorbed, inhibited by parathyroid hormone, diffusion		Reabsorbed; diffusion	

Table 25.5

Mechanisms of Recovery

Mechanisms by which substances move across membranes for reabsorption or secretion include active transport, diffusion, facilitated diffusion, secondary active transport, and osmosis. These were discussed in an earlier chapter, and you may wish to review them.

Active transport utilizes energy, usually the energy found in a phosphate bond of ATP, to move a substance across a membrane from a low to a high concentration. It is very specific and must have an appropriately shaped receptor for the substance to be transported. An example would be the active transport of Na^+ out of a cell and K^+ into a cell by the Na^+/K^+ pump. Both ions are moved in opposite directions from a lower to a higher concentration.

Simple diffusion moves a substance from a higher to a lower concentration down its concentration gradient. It requires no energy and only needs to be soluble.

Facilitated diffusion is similar to diffusion in that it moves a substance down its concentration gradient. The difference is that it requires specific membrane receptors or channel proteins for movement. The movement of glucose and, in certain situations, Na^+ ions, is an example of facilitated diffusion. In some cases of facilitated diffusion, two different substances share the same channel protein port; these mechanisms are described by the terms symport and antiport.

Symport mechanisms move two or more substances in the same direction at the same time, whereas antiport mechanisms move two or more substances in opposite directions across the cell membrane. Both mechanisms may utilize concentration gradients maintained by ATP pumps. This is a mechanism described by the term "secondary active transport." For example, a Na^+ ATPase pump on the basilar membrane of a cell may constantly pump Na^+ out of a cell, maintaining a strong electrochemical gradient. On the opposite (apical) surface, a Na^+/glucose symport protein channel assists both Na^+ and glucose into the cell as Na^+ moves down the concentration gradient created by the basilar Na^+ ATPase pumps. The glucose molecule then diffuses across the basal membrane by facilitated diffusion into the interstitial space and from there into peritubular capillaries.

Most of the Ca^{++}, Na^+, glucose, and amino acids must be reabsorbed by the nephron to maintain homeostatic plasma concentrations. Other substances, such as urea, K^+, ammonia (NH_3), creatinine, and some drugs are secreted into the filtrate as waste products. Acid–base balance is maintained through actions of the lungs and kidneys: The lungs rid the body of H^+, whereas the kidneys secrete or reabsorb H^+ and HCO_3^- (Table 25.6). In the case of urea, about 50 percent is passively reabsorbed by the PCT. More is recovered by in the collecting ducts as needed. ADH induces the insertion of urea transporters and aquaporin channel proteins.

Substances Filtered and Reabsorbed by the Kidney per 24 Hours

Substance	Amount filtered (grams)	Amount reabsorbed (grams)	Amount in urine (grams)
Water	180 L	179 L	1 L
Proteins	10–20	10–20	0
Chlorine	630	625	5
Sodium	540	537	3
Bicarbonate	300	299.7	0.3
Glucose	180	180	0
Urea	53	28	25
Potassium	28	24	4
Uric acid	8.5	7.7	0.8
Creatinine	1.4	0	1.4

Table 25.6

Reabsorption and Secretion in the PCT

The renal corpuscle filters the blood to create a filtrate that differs from blood mainly in the absence of cells and large proteins. From this point to the ends of the collecting ducts, the filtrate or forming urine is undergoing modification through secretion and reabsorption before true urine is produced. The first point at which the forming urine is modified is in the PCT. Here, some substances are reabsorbed, whereas others are secreted. Note the use of the term "reabsorbed." All of these substances were "absorbed" in the digestive tract—99 percent of the water and most of the solutes filtered by the nephron must be reabsorbed. Water and substances that are reabsorbed are returned to the circulation by the peritubular and vasa recta capillaries. It is important to understand the difference between the glomerulus and the peritubular and vasa recta capillaries. The glomerulus has a relatively high pressure inside its capillaries and can sustain this by dilating the afferent arteriole while constricting the efferent arteriole. This assures adequate filtration pressure even as the systemic blood pressure varies. Movement of water into the peritubular capillaries and vasa recta will be influenced primarily by osmolarity and concentration gradients. Sodium is actively pumped out of the PCT into the interstitial spaces between cells and diffuses down its concentration gradient into the peritubular capillary. As it does so, water will follow passively to maintain an isotonic fluid environment inside the capillary. This is called obligatory water reabsorption, because water is "obliged" to follow the Na$^+$ (Figure 25.18).

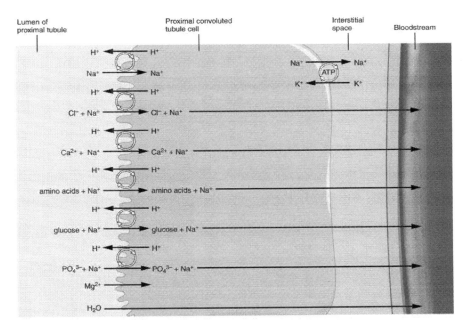

Figure 25.18 Substances Reabsorbed and Secreted by the PCT

More substances move across the membranes of the PCT than any other portion of the nephron. Many of these substances (amino acids and glucose) use symport mechanisms for transport along with Na$^+$. Antiport, active transport, diffusion, and facilitated diffusion are additional mechanisms by which substances are moved from one side of a membrane to the other. Recall that cells have two surfaces: apical and basal. The apical surface is the one facing the lumen or open space of a cavity or tube, in this case, the inside of the PCT. The basal surface of the cell faces the connective tissue base to which the cell attaches (basement membrane) or the cell membrane closer to the basement membrane if there is a stratified layer of cells. In the PCT, there is a single layer of simple cuboidal endothelial cells against the basement membrane. The numbers and particular types of pumps and channels vary between the apical and basilar surfaces (Table 25.7). A few of the substances that are transported with Na$^+$ (symport mechanism) on the apical membrane include Cl$^-$, Ca^{++}, amino acids, glucose, and PO$_4^{3-}$. Sodium is actively exchanged for K$^+$ using ATP on the basal membrane. Most of the substances transported by a symport mechanism on the apical membrane are transported by facilitated diffusion on the basal membrane. At least three ions, K$^+$, Ca^{++}, and Mg^{++}, diffuse laterally between adjacent cell membranes (transcellular).

Reabsorption of Major Solutes by the PCT

Basal membrane	Apical membrane
Active transport	Symport with Na^+
Na^+ (exchange for K^+)	K^+
Facilitated diffusion	Cl^-
K^+	Ca^{++}
Cl^-	Mg^{++}
Ca^{++}	HCO_3^-
HCO_3^-	PO_4^{3-}
PO_4^{3-}	Amino acids
Amino acids	Glucose
Glucose	Fructose
Fructose	Galactose
Galactose	Lactate
Lactate	Succinate
Succinate	Citrate
Citrate	Diffusion between nephron cells
	K^+
	Ca^{++}
	Mg^{++}

Table 25.7

About 67 percent of the water, Na^+, and K^+ entering the nephron is reabsorbed in the PCT and returned to the circulation. Almost 100 percent of glucose, amino acids, and other organic substances such as vitamins are normally recovered here. Some glucose may appear in the urine if circulating glucose levels are high enough that all the glucose transporters in the PCT are saturated, so that their capacity to move glucose is exceeded (transport maximum, or T_m). In men, the maximum amount of glucose that can be recovered is about 375 mg/min, whereas in women, it is about 300 mg/min. This recovery rate translates to an arterial concentration of about 200 mg/dL. Though an exceptionally high sugar intake might cause sugar to appear briefly in the urine, the appearance of **glycosuria** usually points to type I or II diabetes mellitus. The transport of glucose from the lumen of the PCT to the interstitial space is similar to the way it is absorbed by the small intestine. Both glucose and Na^+ bind simultaneously to the same symport proteins on the apical surface of the cell to be transported in the same direction, toward the interstitial space. Sodium moves down its electrochemical and concentration gradient into the cell and takes glucose with it. Na^+ is then actively pumped out of the cell at the basal surface of the cell into the interstitial space. Glucose leaves the cell to enter the interstitial space by facilitated diffusion. The energy to move glucose comes from the Na^+/K^+ ATPase that pumps Na^+ out of the cell on the basal surface. Fifty percent of Cl^- and variable quantities of Ca^{++}, Mg^{++}, and HPO_4^{2-} are also recovered in the PCT.

Recovery of bicarbonate (HCO_3^-) is vital to the maintenance of acid–base balance, since it is a very powerful and fast-acting buffer. An important enzyme is used to catalyze this mechanism: carbonic anhydrase (CA). This same enzyme and reaction is used in red blood cells in the transportation of CO_2, in the stomach to produce hydrochloric acid, and in the pancreas to produce HCO_3^- to buffer acidic chyme from the stomach. In the kidney, most of the CA is located within the cell, but a small amount is bound to the brush border of the membrane on the apical surface of the cell. In the lumen of the PCT,

Chapter 25 | The Urinary System

HCO_3^- combines with hydrogen ions to form carbonic acid (H_2CO_3). This is enzymatically catalyzed into CO_2 and water, which diffuse across the apical membrane into the cell. Water can move osmotically across the lipid bilayer membrane due to the presence of aquaporin water channels. Inside the cell, the reverse reaction occurs to produce bicarbonate ions (HCO_3^-). These bicarbonate ions are cotransported with Na^+ across the basal membrane to the interstitial space around the PCT (Figure 25.19). At the same time this is occurring, a Na^+/H^+ antiporter excretes H^+ into the lumen, while it recovers Na^+. Note how the hydrogen ion is recycled so that bicarbonate can be recovered. Also, note that a Na^+ gradient is created by the Na^+/K^+ pump.

$$HCO_3^- + H^+ \leftrightarrow H_2CO_3 \leftrightarrow CO_2 + H_2O$$

The significant recovery of solutes from the PCT lumen to the interstitial space creates an osmotic gradient that promotes water recovery. As noted before, water moves through channels created by the aquaporin proteins. These proteins are found in all cells in varying amounts and help regulate water movement across membranes and through cells by creating a passageway across the hydrophobic lipid bilayer membrane. Changing the number of aquaporin proteins in membranes of the collecting ducts also helps to regulate the osmolarity of the blood. The movement of many positively charged ions also creates an electrochemical gradient. This charge promotes the movement of negative ions toward the interstitial spaces and the movement of positive ions toward the lumen.

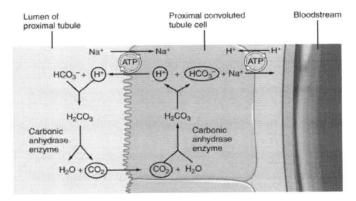

Figure 25.19 Reabsorption of Bicarbonate from the PCT

Reabsorption and Secretion in the Loop of Henle

The loop of Henle consists of two sections: thick and thin descending and thin and thick ascending sections. The loops of cortical nephrons do not extend into the renal medulla very far, if at all. Juxtamedullary nephrons have loops that extend variable distances, some very deep into the medulla. The descending and ascending portions of the loop are highly specialized to enable recovery of much of the Na^+ and water that were filtered by the glomerulus. As the forming urine moves through the loop, the osmolarity will change from isosmotic with blood (about 278–300 mOsmol/kg) to both a very hypertonic solution of about 1200 mOsmol/kg and a very hypotonic solution of about 100 mOsmol/kg. These changes are accomplished by osmosis in the descending limb and active transport in the ascending limb. Solutes and water recovered from these loops are returned to the circulation by way of the vasa recta.

Descending Loop

The majority of the descending loop is comprised of simple squamous epithelial cells; to simplify the function of the loop, this discussion focuses on these cells. These membranes have permanent aquaporin channel proteins that allow unrestricted movement of water from the descending loop into the surrounding interstitium as osmolarity increases from about 300 mOsmol/kg to about 1200 mOsmol/kg. This increase results in reabsorption of up to 15 percent of the water entering the nephron. Modest amounts of urea, Na^+, and other ions are also recovered here.

Most of the solutes that were filtered in the glomerulus have now been recovered along with a majority of water, about 82 percent. As the forming urine enters the ascending loop, major adjustments will be made to the concentration of solutes to create what you perceive as urine.

Ascending Loop

The ascending loop is made of very short thin and longer thick portions. Once again, to simplify the function, this section only considers the thick portion. The thick portion is lined with simple cuboidal epithelium without a brush border. It is completely impermeable to water due to the absence of aquaporin proteins, but ions, mainly Na^+, are actively pumped out of the loop by large quantities of the Na^+/K^+ ATPase pump. This has two significant effects: Removal of Na^+ while retaining water leads to a hypotonic filtrate by the time it reaches the DCT; pumping Na^+ into the interstitial space contributes to the hyperosmotic environment in the kidney medulla.

The Na^+/K^+ ATPase pumps in the basal membrane create an electrochemical gradient, allowing reabsorption of Cl^- by Na^+/Cl^- symporters in the apical membrane. At the same time that Na^+ is actively pumped from the basal side of the cell into the interstitial fluid, Cl^- follows the Na^+ from the lumen into the interstitial fluid by a paracellular route between cells through **leaky tight junctions**. These are found between cells of the ascending loop, where they allow certain solutes to move according to their concentration gradient. Most of the K^+ that enters the cell via symporters returns to the lumen (down its concentration gradient) through leaky channels in the apical membrane. Note the environment now created in the interstitial space: With the "back door exiting" K^+, there is one Na^+ and two Cl^- ions left in the interstitium surrounding the ascending loop. Therefore, in comparison to the lumen of the loop, the interstitial space is now a negatively charged environment. This negative charge attracts cations (Na^+, K^+, Ca^{++}, and Mg^{++}) from the lumen via a paracellular route to the interstitial space and vasa recta.

Countercurrent Multiplier System

The structure of the loop of Henle and associated vasa recta create a **countercurrent multiplier system** (Figure 25.20). The countercurrent term comes from the fact that the descending and ascending loops are next to each other and their fluid flows in opposite directions (countercurrent). The multiplier term is due to the action of solute pumps that increase (multiply) the concentrations of urea and Na^+ deep in the medulla.

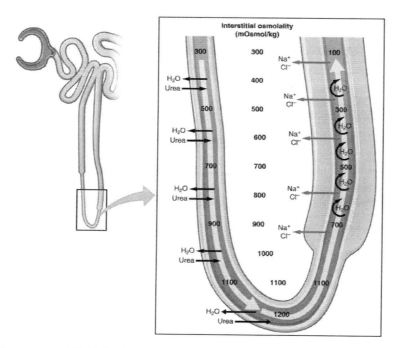

Figure 25.20 Countercurrent Multiplier System

As discussed above, the ascending loop has many Na^+ pumps that actively pump Na^+ out of the forming urine into the interstitial spaces. In addition, collecting ducts have urea pumps that actively pump urea into the interstitial spaces. This results in the recovery of Na^+ to the circulation via the vasa recta and creates a high osmolar environment in the depths of the medulla.

Ammonia (NH_3) is a toxic byproduct of protein metabolism. It is formed as amino acids are deaminated by liver hepatocytes. That means that the amine group, NH_2, is removed from amino acids as they are broken down. Most of the resulting ammonia is converted into urea by liver hepatocytes. Urea is not only less toxic but is utilized to aid in the recovery of water by the loop of Henle and collecting ducts. At the same time that water is freely diffusing out of the descending loop through aquaporin channels into the interstitial spaces of the medulla, urea freely diffuses into the lumen of the descending loop as it descends deeper into the medulla, much of it to be reabsorbed from the forming urine when it reaches the collecting duct. Thus, the movement of Na^+ and urea into the interstitial spaces by these mechanisms creates the hyperosmotic environment of the medulla. The net result of this countercurrent multiplier system is to recover both water and Na^+ in the circulation.

The amino acid glutamine can be deaminated by the kidney. As NH_2 from the amino acid is converted into NH_3 and pumped into the lumen of the PCT, Na^+ and HCO_3^- are excreted into the interstitial fluid of the renal pyramid via a symport mechanism. When this process occurs in the cells of the PCT, the added benefit is a net loss of a hydrogen ion (complexed to ammonia to form the weak acid NH_4^+) in the urine and a gain of a bicarbonate ion (HCO_3^-) in the blood. Ammonia and bicarbonate are exchanged in a one-to-one ratio. This exchange is yet another means by which the body can buffer and excrete acid. The presence of aquaporin channels in the descending loop allows prodigious quantities of water to leave the loop and enter the hyperosmolar interstitium of the pyramid, where it is returned to the circulation by the vasa recta. As the loop turns to become the ascending loop, there is an absence of aquaporin channels, so water cannot leave the loop. However, in the basal membrane of cells of the thick ascending loop, ATPase pumps actively remove Na^+ from the cell. A $Na^+/K^+/2Cl^-$ symporter in the apical membrane passively allows these ions to enter the cell cytoplasm from the lumen of the loop down a concentration gradient created by the pump. This mechanism works to dilute the fluid of the ascending loop ultimately to approximately 50–100 mOsmol/L.

At the transition from the DCT to the collecting duct, about 20 percent of the original water is still present and about 10 percent of the sodium. If no other mechanism for water reabsorption existed, about 20–25 liters of urine would be produced. Now consider what is happening in the adjacent capillaries, the vasa recta. They are recovering both solutes and water at a rate that preserves the countercurrent multiplier system. In general, blood flows slowly in capillaries to allow time for exchange of nutrients and wastes. In the vasa recta particularly, this rate of flow is important for two additional reasons. The flow must be slow to allow blood cells to lose and regain water without either crenating or bursting. Second, a rapid flow would remove too much Na^+ and urea, destroying the osmolar gradient that is necessary for the recovery of solutes and water. Thus, by flowing slowly to preserve the countercurrent mechanism, as the vasa recta descend, Na^+ and urea are freely able to enter the capillary, while water freely leaves; as they ascend, Na^+ and urea are secreted into the surrounding medulla, while water reenters and is removed.

Watch this video (http://openstaxcollege.org/l/multiplier) to learn about the countercurrent multiplier system.

Reabsorption and Secretion in the Distal Convoluted Tubule

Approximately 80 percent of filtered water has been recovered by the time the dilute forming urine enters the DCT. The DCT will recover another 10–15 percent before the forming urine enters the collecting ducts. Aldosterone increases the amount of Na^+/K^+ ATPase in the basal membrane of the DCT and collecting duct. The movement of Na^+ out of the lumen of the collecting duct creates a negative charge that promotes the movement of Cl^- out of the lumen into the interstitial space by a paracellular route across tight junctions. Peritubular capillaries receive the solutes and water, returning them to the circulation.

Cells of the DCT also recover Ca^{++} from the filtrate. Receptors for parathyroid hormone (PTH) are found in DCT cells and when bound to PTH, induce the insertion of calcium channels on their luminal surface. The channels enhance Ca^{++} recovery from the forming urine. In addition, as Na^+ is pumped out of the cell, the resulting electrochemical gradient attracts Ca^{++} into the cell. Finally, calcitriol (1,25 dihydroxyvitamin D, the active form of vitamin D) is very important for calcium recovery. It induces the production of calcium-binding proteins that transport Ca^{++} into the cell. These binding proteins are also important for the movement of calcium inside the cell and aid in exocytosis of calcium across the basolateral membrane. Any Ca^{++} not reabsorbed at this point is lost in the urine.

Collecting Ducts and Recovery of Water

Solutes move across the membranes of the collecting ducts, which contain two distinct cell types, principal cells and intercalated cells. A **principal cell** possesses channels for the recovery or loss of sodium and potassium. An **intercalated cell** secretes or absorbs acid or bicarbonate. As in other portions of the nephron, there is an array of micromachines (pumps and channels) on display in the membranes of these cells.

Regulation of urine volume and osmolarity are major functions of the collecting ducts. By varying the amount of water that is recovered, the collecting ducts play a major role in maintaining the body's normal osmolarity. If the blood becomes hyperosmotic, the collecting ducts recover more water to dilute the blood; if the blood becomes hyposmotic, the collecting ducts recover less of the water, leading to concentration of the blood. Another way of saying this is: If plasma osmolarity rises, more water is recovered and urine volume decreases; if plasma osmolarity decreases, less water is recovered and urine volume increases. This function is regulated by the posterior pituitary hormone ADH (vasopressin). With mild dehydration, plasma osmolarity rises slightly. This increase is detected by osmoreceptors in the hypothalamus, which stimulates the release of ADH from the posterior pituitary. If plasma osmolarity decreases slightly, the opposite occurs.

When stimulated by ADH, aquaporin channels are inserted into the apical membrane of principal cells, which line the collecting ducts. As the ducts descend through the medulla, the osmolarity surrounding them increases (due to the countercurrent mechanisms described above). If aquaporin water channels are present, water will be osmotically pulled from the collecting duct into the surrounding interstitial space and into the peritubular capillaries. Therefore, the final urine will be more concentrated. If less ADH is secreted, fewer aquaporin channels are inserted and less water is recovered, resulting in dilute urine. By altering the number of aquaporin channels, the volume of water recovered or lost is altered. This, in turn, regulates the blood osmolarity, blood pressure, and osmolarity of the urine.

As Na^+ is pumped from the forming urine, water is passively recaptured for the circulation; this preservation of vascular volume is critically important for the maintenance of a normal blood pressure. Aldosterone is secreted by the adrenal cortex in response to angiotensin II stimulation. As an extremely potent vasoconstrictor, angiotensin II functions immediately to increase blood pressure. By also stimulating aldosterone production, it provides a longer-lasting mechanism to support blood pressure by maintaining vascular volume (water recovery).

In addition to receptors for ADH, principal cells have receptors for the steroid hormone aldosterone. While ADH is primarily involved in the regulation of water recovery, aldosterone regulates Na^+ recovery. Aldosterone stimulates principal cells to manufacture luminal Na^+ and K^+ channels as well as Na^+/K^+ ATPase pumps on the basal membrane of the cells. When aldosterone output increases, more Na^+ is recovered from the forming urine and water follows the Na^+ passively. As the pump recovers Na^+ for the body, it is also pumping K^+ into the forming urine, since the pump moves K^+ in the opposite direction. When aldosterone decreases, more Na^+ remains in the forming urine and more K^+ is recovered in the circulation. Symport channels move Na^+ and Cl^- together. Still other channels in the principal cells secrete K^+ into the collecting duct in direct proportion to the recovery of Na^+.

Intercalated cells play significant roles in regulating blood pH. Intercalated cells reabsorb K^+ and HCO_3^- while secreting H^+. This function lowers the acidity of the plasma while increasing the acidity of the urine.

25.7 | Regulation of Renal Blood Flow

By the end of this section, you will be able to:
- Describe the myogenic and tubuloglomerular feedback mechanisms and explain how they affect urine volume and composition
- Describe the function of the juxtaglomerular apparatus

It is vital that the flow of blood through the kidney be at a suitable rate to allow for filtration. This rate determines how much solute is retained or discarded, how much water is retained or discarded, and ultimately, the osmolarity of blood and the blood pressure of the body.

Sympathetic Nerves

The kidneys are innervated by the sympathetic neurons of the autonomic nervous system via the celiac plexus and splanchnic nerves. Reduction of sympathetic stimulation results in vasodilation and increased blood flow through the kidneys during resting conditions. When the frequency of action potentials increases, the arteriolar smooth muscle constricts (vasoconstriction), resulting in diminished glomerular flow, so less filtration occurs. Under conditions of stress, sympathetic nervous activity increases, resulting in the direct vasoconstriction of afferent arterioles (norepinephrine effect) as well as stimulation of the adrenal medulla. The adrenal medulla, in turn, produces a generalized vasoconstriction through the release of epinephrine. This includes vasoconstriction of the afferent arterioles, further reducing the volume of blood flowing through the kidneys. This process redirects blood to other organs with more immediate needs. If blood pressure falls, the sympathetic nerves will also stimulate the release of renin. Additional renin increases production of the powerful vasoconstrictor angiotensin II. Angiotensin II, as discussed above, will also stimulate aldosterone production to augment blood volume through retention of more Na^+ and water. Only a 10 mm Hg pressure differential across the glomerulus is required for normal GFR, so very small changes in afferent arterial pressure significantly increase or decrease GFR.

Autoregulation

The kidneys are very effective at regulating the rate of blood flow over a wide range of blood pressures. Your blood pressure will decrease when you are relaxed or sleeping. It will increase when exercising. Yet, despite these changes, the filtration rate through the kidney will change very little. This is due to two internal autoregulatory mechanisms that operate without outside influence: the myogenic mechanism and the tubuloglomerular feedback mechanism.

Arteriole Myogenic Mechanism

The **myogenic mechanism** regulating blood flow within the kidney depends upon a characteristic shared by most smooth muscle cells of the body. When you stretch a smooth muscle cell, it contracts; when you stop, it relaxes, restoring its resting length. This mechanism works in the afferent arteriole that supplies the glomerulus. When blood pressure increases, smooth muscle cells in the wall of the arteriole are stretched and respond by contracting to resist the pressure, resulting in little change in flow. When blood pressure drops, the same smooth muscle cells relax to lower resistance, allowing a continued even flow of blood.

Tubuloglomerular Feedback

The **tubuloglomerular feedback** mechanism involves the JGA and a paracrine signaling mechanism utilizing ATP, adenosine, and nitric oxide (NO). This mechanism stimulates either contraction or relaxation of afferent arteriolar smooth muscle cells (Table 25.8). Recall that the DCT is in intimate contact with the afferent and efferent arterioles of the glomerulus. Specialized macula densa cells in this segment of the tubule respond to changes in the fluid flow rate and Na^+ concentration. As GFR increases, there is less time for NaCl to be reabsorbed in the PCT, resulting in higher osmolarity in the filtrate. The increased fluid movement more strongly deflects single nonmotile cilia on macula densa cells. This increased osmolarity of the forming urine, and the greater flow rate within the DCT, activates macula densa cells to respond by releasing ATP and adenosine (a metabolite of ATP). ATP and adenosine act locally as paracrine factors to stimulate the myogenic juxtaglomerular cells of the afferent arteriole to constrict, slowing blood flow and reducing GFR. Conversely, when GFR decreases, less Na^+ is in the forming urine, and most will be reabsorbed before reaching the macula densa, which will result in decreased ATP and adenosine, allowing the afferent arteriole to dilate and increase GFR. NO has the opposite effect, relaxing the afferent arteriole at the same time ATP and adenosine are stimulating it to contract. Thus, NO fine-tunes the effects of adenosine and ATP on GFR.

Paracrine Mechanisms Controlling Glomerular Filtration Rate

Change in GFR	NaCl Absorption	Role of ATP and adenosine/Role of NO	Effect on GFR
Increased GFR	Tubular NaCl increases	ATP and adenosine increase, causing vasoconstriction	Vasoconstriction slows GFR
Decreased GFR	Tubular NaCl decreases	ATP and adenosine decrease, causing vasodilation	Vasodilation increases GFR
Increased GFR	Tubular NaCl increases	NO increases, causing vasodilation	Vasodilation increases GFR
Decreased GFR	Tubular NaCl decreases	NO decreases, causing vasoconstricton	Vasoconstriction decreases GFR

Table 25.8

25.8 | Endocrine Regulation of Kidney Function

By the end of this section, you will be able to:
- Describe how each of the following functions in the extrinsic control of GFR: renin–angiotensin mechanism, natriuretic peptides, and sympathetic adrenergic activity
- Describe how each of the following works to regulate reabsorption and secretion, so as to affect urine volume and composition: renin–angiotensin system, aldosterone, antidiuretic hormone, and natriuretic peptides
- Name and define the roles of other hormones that regulate kidney control

Several hormones have specific, important roles in regulating kidney function. They act to stimulate or inhibit blood flow. Some of these are endocrine, acting from a distance, whereas others are paracrine, acting locally.

Renin–Angiotensin–Aldosterone

Renin is an enzyme that is produced by the granular cells of the afferent arteriole at the JGA. It enzymatically converts angiotensinogen (made by the liver, freely circulating) into angiotensin I. Its release is stimulated by prostaglandins and NO from the JGA in response to decreased extracellular fluid volume.

ACE is not a hormone but it is functionally important in regulating systemic blood pressure and kidney function. It is produced in the lungs but binds to the surfaces of endothelial cells in the afferent arterioles and glomerulus. It enzymatically converts inactive angiotensin I into active angiotensin II. ACE is important in raising blood pressure. People with high blood pressure are sometimes prescribed ACE inhibitors to lower their blood pressure.

Angiotensin II is a potent vasoconstrictor that plays an immediate role in the regulation of blood pressure. It acts systemically to cause vasoconstriction as well as constriction of both the afferent and efferent arterioles of the glomerulus. In instances of blood loss or dehydration, it reduces both GFR and renal blood flow, thereby limiting fluid loss and preserving blood volume. Its release is usually stimulated by decreases in blood pressure, and so the preservation of adequate blood pressure is its primary role.

Aldosterone, often called the "salt-retaining hormone," is released from the adrenal cortex in response to angiotensin II or directly in response to increased plasma K^+. It promotes Na^+ reabsorption by the nephron, promoting the retention of water. It is also important in regulating K^+, promoting its excretion. (This dual effect on two minerals and its origin in the adrenal cortex explains its designation as a mineralocorticoid.) As a result, renin has an immediate effect on blood pressure due to angiotensin II–stimulated vasoconstriction and a prolonged effect through Na^+ recovery due to aldosterone. At the same time that aldosterone causes increased recovery of Na^+, it also causes greater loss of K^+. Progesterone is a steroid that is structurally similar to aldosterone. It binds to the aldosterone receptor and weakly stimulates Na^+ reabsorption and increased water recovery. This process is unimportant in men due to low levels of circulating progesterone. It may cause increased retention of water during some periods of the menstrual cycle in women when progesterone levels increase.

Antidiuretic Hormone (ADH)

Diuretics are drugs that can increase water loss by interfering with the recapture of solutes and water from the forming urine. They are often prescribed to lower blood pressure. Coffee, tea, and alcoholic beverages are familiar diuretics. ADH, a 9-amino acid peptide released by the posterior pituitary, works to do the exact opposite. It promotes the recovery of water, decreases urine volume, and maintains plasma osmolarity and blood pressure. It does so by stimulating the movement of aquaporin proteins into the apical cell membrane of principal cells of the collecting ducts to form water channels, allowing the transcellular movement of water from the lumen of the collecting duct into the interstitial space in the medulla of the kidney by osmosis. From there, it enters the vasa recta capillaries to return to the circulation. Water is attracted by the high osmotic environment of the deep kidney medulla.

Endothelin

Endothelins, 21-amino acid peptides, are extremely powerful vasoconstrictors. They are produced by endothelial cells of the renal blood vessels, mesangial cells, and cells of the DCT. Hormones stimulating endothelin release include angiotensin II, bradykinin, and epinephrine. They do not typically influence blood pressure in healthy people. On the other hand, in people with diabetic kidney disease, endothelin is chronically elevated, resulting in sodium retention. They also diminish GFR by damaging the podocytes and by potently vasoconstricting both the afferent and efferent arterioles.

Natriuretic Hormones

Natriuretic hormones are peptides that stimulate the kidneys to excrete sodium—an effect opposite that of aldosterone. Natriuretic hormones act by inhibiting aldosterone release and therefore inhibiting Na^+ recovery in the collecting ducts. If Na^+ remains in the forming urine, its osmotic force will cause a concurrent loss of water. Natriuretic hormones also inhibit ADH release, which of course will result in less water recovery. Therefore, natriuretic peptides inhibit both Na^+ and water recovery. One example from this family of hormones is atrial natriuretic hormone (ANH), a 28-amino acid peptide produced by heart atria in response to over-stretching of the atrial wall. The over-stretching occurs in persons with elevated blood pressure or heart failure. It increases GFR through concurrent vasodilation of the afferent arteriole and vasoconstriction of the efferent arteriole. These events lead to an increased loss of water and sodium in the forming urine. It also decreases sodium reabsorption in the DCT. There is also B-type natriuretic peptide (BNP) of 32 amino acids produced in the ventricles of the heart. It has a 10-fold lower affinity for its receptor, so its effects are less than those of ANH. Its role may be to provide "fine tuning" for the regulation of blood pressure. BNP's longer biologic half-life makes it a good diagnostic marker of congestive heart failure (Figure 25.21).

Parathyroid Hormone

Parathyroid hormone (PTH) is an 84-amino acid peptide produced by the parathyroid glands in response to decreased circulating Ca^{++} levels. Among its targets is the PCT, where it stimulates the hydroxylation of calcidiol to calcitriol (1,25-hydroxycholecalciferol, the active form of vitamin D). It also blocks reabsorption of phosphate (PO_3^-), causing its loss in the urine. The retention of phosphate would result in the formation of calcium phosphate in the plasma, reducing circulating Ca^{++} levels. By ridding the blood of phosphate, higher circulating Ca^{++} levels are permitted.

	Stimulus	Effect on GFR	Effect on RBF
VASOCONSTRICTORS			
Sympathetic nerves (epinephrine and norepinephrine)	↓ECFV	↓	↓
Angiotensin II	↓ECFV	↓	↓
Endothelin	↑Stretch, bradykinin, angiotensin II, epinephrine ↓ECFV	↓	↓
VASODILATORS			
Prostaglandins (PGE1, PGE2, and PGI2)	↓ECFV ↑shear stress, angiotensin II	No change/↑	↑
Nitric oxide (NO)	↑shear stress, acetylcholine, histamine, bradykinin, ATP, adenosine	↑	↑
Bradykinin	Prostaglandins, ↓ACE	↑	↑
Natriuretic peptides (ANP, B-type)	↑ECFV	↑	No change

ACE = angiotensin-converting enzyme; ECFV = extracellular fluid volume; GFR = glomerular filtration rate; RBF = renal blood flow; ANP = atrial natriuretic peptide; B-type = ventricular natriuretic peptide

Figure 25.21 Major Hormones That Influence GFR and RFB

25.9 | Regulation of Fluid Volume and Composition

By the end of this section, you will be able to:
- Explain the mechanism of action of diuretics
- Explain why the differential permeability or impermeability of specific sections of the nephron tubules is necessary for urine formation

The major hormones influencing total body water are ADH, aldosterone, and ANH. Circumstances that lead to fluid depletion in the body include blood loss and dehydration. Homeostasis requires that volume and osmolarity be preserved. Blood volume is important in maintaining sufficient blood pressure, and there are nonrenal mechanisms involved in its preservation, including vasoconstriction, which can act within seconds of a drop in pressure. Thirst mechanisms are also activated to promote the consumption of water lost through respiration, evaporation, or urination. Hormonal mechanisms are activated to recover volume while maintaining a normal osmotic environment. These mechanisms act principally on the kidney.

Volume-sensing Mechanisms

The body cannot directly measure blood volume, but blood pressure can be measured. Blood pressure often reflects blood volume and is measured by baroreceptors in the aorta and carotid sinuses. When blood pressure increases, baroreceptors send more frequent action potentials to the central nervous system, leading to widespread vasodilation. Included in this vasodilation are the afferent arterioles supplying the glomerulus, resulting in increased GFR, and water loss by the kidneys. If pressure decreases, fewer action potentials travel to the central nervous system, resulting in more sympathetic stimulation-producing vasoconstriction, which will result in decreased filtration and GFR, and water loss.

Decreased blood pressure is also sensed by the granular cells in the afferent arteriole of the JGA. In response, the enzyme renin is released. You saw earlier in the chapter that renin activity leads to an almost immediate rise in blood pressure as activated angiotensin II produces vasoconstriction. The rise in pressure is sustained by the aldosterone effects initiated by angiotensin II; this includes an increase in Na^+ retention and water volume. As an aside, late in the menstrual cycle, progesterone has a modest influence on water retention. Due to its structural similarity to aldosterone, progesterone binds to the aldosterone receptor in the collecting duct of the kidney, causing the same, albeit weaker, effect on Na^+ and water retention.

Cardiomyocytes of the atria also respond to greater stretch (as blood pressure rises) by secreting ANH. ANH opposes the action of aldosterone by inhibiting the recovery of Na^+ by the DCT and collecting ducts. More Na^+ is lost, and as water follows, total blood volume and pressure decline. In low-pressure states, ANH does not seem to have much effect.

ADH is also called vasopressin. Early researchers found that in cases of unusually high secretion of ADH, the hormone caused vasoconstriction (vasopressor activity, hence the name). Only later were its antidiuretic properties identified. Synthetic ADH is still used occasionally to stem life-threatening esophagus bleeding in alcoholics.

When blood volume drops 5–10 percent, causing a decrease in blood pressure, there is a rapid and significant increase in ADH release from the posterior pituitary. Immediate vasoconstriction to increase blood pressure is the result. ADH also causes activation of aquaporin channels in the collecting ducts to affect the recovery of water to help restore vascular volume.

Diuretics and Fluid Volume

A **diuretic** is a compound that increases urine volume. Three familiar drinks contain diuretic compounds: coffee, tea, and alcohol. The caffeine in coffee and tea works by promoting vasodilation in the nephron, which increases GFR. Alcohol increases GFR by inhibiting ADH release from the posterior pituitary, resulting in less water recovery by the collecting duct. In cases of high blood pressure, diuretics may be prescribed to reduce blood volume and, thereby, reduce blood pressure. The most frequently prescribed anti-hypertensive diuretic is hydrochlorothiazide. It inhibits the Na^+/Cl^- symporter in the DCT and collecting duct. The result is a loss of Na^+ with water following passively by osmosis.

Osmotic diuretics promote water loss by osmosis. An example is the indigestible sugar mannitol, which is most often administered to reduce brain swelling after head injury. However, it is not the only sugar that can produce a diuretic effect. In cases of poorly controlled diabetes mellitus, glucose levels exceed the capacity of the tubular glucose symporters, resulting in glucose in the urine. The unrecovered glucose becomes a powerful osmotic diuretic. Classically, in the days before glucose could be detected in the blood and urine, clinicians identified diabetes mellitus by the three Ps: polyuria (diuresis), polydipsia (increased thirst), and polyphagia (increased hunger).

Regulation of Extracellular Na^+

Sodium has a very strong osmotic effect and attracts water. It plays a larger role in the osmolarity of the plasma than any other circulating component of the blood. If there is too much Na^+ present, either due to poor control or excess dietary consumption, a series of metabolic problems ensue. There is an increase in total volume of water, which leads to hypertension (high blood pressure). Over a long period, this increases the risk of serious complications such as heart attacks, strokes, and aneurysms. It can also contribute to system-wide edema (swelling).

Mechanisms for regulating Na^+ concentration include the renin–angiotensin–aldosterone system and ADH (see Figure 25.14). Aldosterone stimulates the uptake of Na^+ on the apical cell membrane of cells in the DCT and collecting ducts, whereas ADH helps to regulate Na^+ concentration indirectly by regulating the reabsorption of water.

Regulation of Extracellular K^+

Potassium is present in a 30-fold greater concentration inside the cell than outside the cell. A generalization can be made that K^+ and Na^+ concentrations will move in opposite directions. When more Na^+ is reabsorbed, more K^+ is secreted; when less Na^+ is reabsorbed (leading to excretion by the kidney), more K^+ is retained. When aldosterone causes a recovery of Na^+ in the nephron, a negative electrical gradient is created that promotes the secretion of K^+ and Cl^- into the lumen.

Regulation of Cl^-

Chloride is important in acid–base balance in the extracellular space and has other functions, such as in the stomach, where it combines with hydrogen ions in the stomach lumen to form hydrochloric acid, aiding digestion. Its close association with Na^+ in the extracellular environment makes it the dominant anion of this compartment, and its regulation closely mirrors that of Na^+.

Regulation of Ca^{++} and Phosphate

The parathyroid glands monitor and respond to circulating levels of Ca^{++} in the blood. When levels drop too low, PTH is released to stimulate the DCT to reabsorb Ca^{++} from the forming urine. When levels are adequate or high, less PTH is released and more Ca^{++} remains in the forming urine to be lost. Phosphate levels move in the opposite direction. When Ca^{++} levels are low, PTH inhibits reabsorption of HPO_4^{2-} so that its blood level drops, allowing Ca^{++} levels to rise. PTH also stimulates the renal conversion of calcidiol into calcitriol, the active form of vitamin D. Calcitriol then stimulates the intestines to absorb more Ca^{++} from the diet.

Regulation of H$^+$, Bicarbonate, and pH

The acid–base homeostasis of the body is a function of chemical buffers and physiologic buffering provided by the lungs and kidneys. Buffers, especially proteins, HCO_3^{2-}, and ammonia have a very large capacity to absorb or release H$^+$ as needed to resist a change in pH. They can act within fractions of a second. The lungs can rid the body of excess acid very rapidly (seconds to minutes) through the conversion of HCO_3^- into CO_2, which is then exhaled. It is rapid but has limited capacity in the face of a significant acid challenge. The kidneys can rid the body of both acid and base. The renal capacity is large but slow (minutes to hours). The cells of the PCT actively secrete H$^+$ into the forming urine as Na$^+$ is reabsorbed. The body rids itself of excess H$^+$ and raises blood pH. In the collecting ducts, the apical surfaces of intercalated cells have proton pumps that actively secrete H$^+$ into the luminal, forming urine to remove it from the body.

As hydrogen ions are pumped into the forming urine, it is buffered by bicarbonate (HCO_3^-), $H_2PO_4^-$ (dihydrogen phosphate ion), or ammonia (forming NH_4^+, ammonium ion). Urine pH typically varies in a normal range from 4.5 to 8.0.

Regulation of Nitrogen Wastes

Nitrogen wastes are produced by the breakdown of proteins during normal metabolism. Proteins are broken down into amino acids, which in turn are deaminated by having their nitrogen groups removed. Deamination converts the amino (NH_2) groups into ammonia (NH_3), ammonium ion (NH_4^+), urea, or uric acid (Figure 25.22). Ammonia is extremely toxic, so most of it is very rapidly converted into urea in the liver. Human urinary wastes typically contain primarily urea with small amounts of ammonium and very little uric acid.

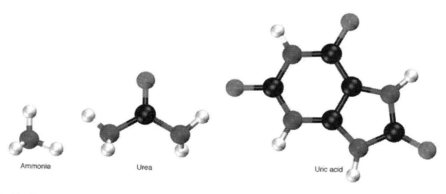

Figure 25.22 Nitrogen Wastes

Elimination of Drugs and Hormones

Water-soluble drugs may be excreted in the urine and are influenced by one or all of the following processes: glomerular filtration, tubular secretion, or tubular reabsorption. Drugs that are structurally small can be filtered by the glomerulus with the filtrate. Large drug molecules such as heparin or those that are bound to plasma proteins cannot be filtered and are not readily eliminated. Some drugs can be eliminated by carrier proteins that enable secretion of the drug into the tubule lumen. There are specific carriers that eliminate basic (such as dopamine or histamine) or acidic drugs (such as penicillin or indomethacin). As is the case with other substances, drugs may be both filtered and reabsorbed passively along a concentration gradient.

25.10 | The Urinary System and Homeostasis

By the end of this section, you will be able to:
- Describe the role of the kidneys in vitamin D activation
- Describe the role of the kidneys in regulating erythropoiesis
- Provide specific examples to demonstrate how the urinary system responds to maintain homeostasis in the body
- Explain how the urinary system relates to other body systems in maintaining homeostasis
- Predict factors or situations affecting the urinary system that could disrupt homeostasis
- Predict the types of problems that would occur in the body if the urinary system could not maintain homeostasis

All systems of the body are interrelated. A change in one system may affect all other systems in the body, with mild to devastating effects. A failure of urinary continence can be embarrassing and inconvenient, but is not life threatening. The loss of other urinary functions may prove fatal. A failure to synthesize vitamin D is one such example.

Vitamin D Synthesis

In order for vitamin D to become active, it must undergo a hydroxylation reaction in the kidney, that is, an –OH group must be added to calcidiol to make calcitriol (1,25-dihydroxycholecalciferol). Activated vitamin D is important for absorption of Ca^{++} in the digestive tract, its reabsorption in the kidney, and the maintenance of normal serum concentrations of Ca^{++} and phosphate. Calcium is vitally important in bone health, muscle contraction, hormone secretion, and neurotransmitter release. Inadequate Ca^{++} leads to disorders like osteoporosis and **osteomalacia** in adults and rickets in children. Deficits may also result in problems with cell proliferation, neuromuscular function, blood clotting, and the inflammatory response. Recent research has confirmed that vitamin D receptors are present in most, if not all, cells of the body, reflecting the systemic importance of vitamin D. Many scientists have suggested it be referred to as a hormone rather than a vitamin.

Erythropoiesis

EPO is a 193-amino acid protein that stimulates the formation of red blood cells in the bone marrow. The kidney produces 85 percent of circulating EPO; the liver, the remainder. If you move to a higher altitude, the partial pressure of oxygen is lower, meaning there is less pressure to push oxygen across the alveolar membrane and into the red blood cell. One way the body compensates is to manufacture more red blood cells by increasing EPO production. If you start an aerobic exercise program, your tissues will need more oxygen to cope, and the kidney will respond with more EPO. If erythrocytes are lost due to severe or prolonged bleeding, or under produced due to disease or severe malnutrition, the kidneys come to the rescue by producing more EPO. Renal failure (loss of EPO production) is associated with anemia, which makes it difficult for the body to cope with increased oxygen demands or to supply oxygen adequately even under normal conditions. Anemia diminishes performance and can be life threatening.

Blood Pressure Regulation

Due to osmosis, water follows where Na^+ leads. Much of the water the kidneys recover from the forming urine follows the reabsorption of Na^+. ADH stimulation of aquaporin channels allows for regulation of water recovery in the collecting ducts. Normally, all of the glucose is recovered, but loss of glucose control (diabetes mellitus) may result in an osmotic dieresis severe enough to produce severe dehydration and death. A loss of renal function means a loss of effective vascular volume control, leading to hypotension (low blood pressure) or hypertension (high blood pressure), which can lead to stroke, heart attack, and aneurysm formation.

The kidneys cooperate with the lungs, liver, and adrenal cortex through the renin–angiotensin–aldosterone system (see Figure 25.14). The liver synthesizes and secretes the inactive precursor angiotensinogen. When the blood pressure is low, the kidney synthesizes and releases renin. Renin converts angiotensinogen into angiotensin I, and ACE produced in the lung converts angiotensin I into biologically active angiotensin II (Figure 25.23). The immediate and short-term effect of angiotensin II is to raise blood pressure by causing widespread vasoconstriction. angiotensin II also stimulates the adrenal cortex to release the steroid hormone aldosterone, which results in renal reabsorption of Na^+ and its associated osmotic recovery of water. The reabsorption of Na^+ helps to raise and maintain blood pressure over a longer term.

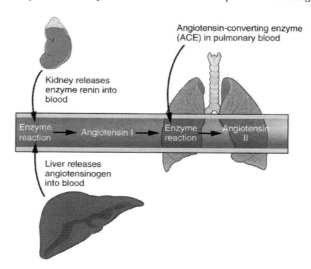

Figure 25.23 **The Enzyme Renin Converts the Pro-enzyme Angiotensin**

Regulation of Osmolarity

Blood pressure and osmolarity are regulated in a similar fashion. Severe hypo-osmolarity can cause problems like lysis (rupture) of blood cells or widespread edema, which is due to a solute imbalance. Inadequate solute concentration (such as protein) in the plasma results in water moving toward an area of greater solute concentration, in this case, the interstitial space and cell cytoplasm. If the kidney glomeruli are damaged by an autoimmune illness, large quantities of protein may be lost in the urine. The resultant drop in serum osmolarity leads to widespread edema that, if severe, may lead to damaging or fatal brain swelling. Severe hypertonic conditions may arise with severe dehydration from lack of water intake, severe vomiting, or uncontrolled diarrhea. When the kidney is unable to recover sufficient water from the forming urine, the consequences may be severe (lethargy, confusion, muscle cramps, and finally, death).

Recovery of Electrolytes

Sodium, calcium, and potassium must be closely regulated. The role of Na^+ and Ca^{++} homeostasis has been discussed at length. Failure of K^+ regulation can have serious consequences on nerve conduction, skeletal muscle function, and most significantly, on cardiac muscle contraction and rhythm.

pH Regulation

Recall that enzymes lose their three-dimensional conformation and, therefore, their function if the pH is too acidic or basic. This loss of conformation may be a consequence of the breaking of hydrogen bonds. Move the pH away from the optimum for a specific enzyme and you may severely hamper its function throughout the body, including hormone binding, central nervous system signaling, or myocardial contraction. Proper kidney function is essential for pH homeostasis.

Everyday CONNECTION

Stem Cells and Repair of Kidney Damage

Stem cells are unspecialized cells that can reproduce themselves via cell division, sometimes after years of inactivity. Under certain conditions, they may differentiate into tissue-specific or organ-specific cells with special functions. In some cases, stem cells may continually divide to produce a mature cell and to replace themselves. Stem cell therapy has an enormous potential to improve the quality of life or save the lives of people suffering from debilitating or life-threatening diseases. There have been several studies in animals, but since stem cell therapy is still in its infancy, there have been limited experiments in humans.

Acute kidney injury can be caused by a number of factors, including transplants and other surgeries. It affects 7–10 percent of all hospitalized patients, resulting in the deaths of 35–40 percent of inpatients. In limited studies using mesenchymal stem cells, there have been fewer instances of kidney damage after surgery, the length of hospital stays has been reduced, and there have been fewer readmissions after release.

How do these stem cells work to protect or repair the kidney? Scientists are unsure at this point, but some evidence has shown that these stem cells release several growth factors in endocrine and paracrine ways. As further studies are conducted to assess the safety and effectiveness of stem cell therapy, we will move closer to a day when kidney injury is rare, and curative treatments are routine.

KEY TERMS

anatomical sphincter smooth or skeletal muscle surrounding the lumen of a vessel or hollow organ that can restrict flow when contracted

angiotensin I protein produced by the enzymatic action of renin on angiotensinogen; inactive precursor of angiotensin II

angiotensin II protein produced by the enzymatic action of ACE on inactive angiotensin I; actively causes vasoconstriction and stimulates aldosterone release by the adrenal cortex

angiotensin-converting enzyme (ACE) enzyme produced by the lungs that catalyzes the reaction of inactive angiotensin I into active angiotensin II

angiotensinogen inactive protein in the circulation produced by the liver; precursor of angiotensin I; must be modified by the enzymes renin and ACE to be activated

anuria absence of urine produced; production of 50 mL or less per day

aquaporin protein-forming water channels through the lipid bilayer of the cell; allows water to cross; activation in the collecting ducts is under the control of ADH

Bowman's capsule cup-shaped sack lined by a simple squamous epithelium (parietal surface) and specialized cells called podocytes (visceral surface) that participate in the filtration process; receives the filtrate which then passes on to the PCTs

brush border formed by microvilli on the surface of certain cuboidal cells; in the kidney it is found in the PCT; increases surface area for absorption in the kidney

calyces cup-like structures receiving urine from the collecting ducts where it passes on to the renal pelvis and ureter

cortical nephrons nephrons with loops of Henle that do not extend into the renal medulla

countercurrent multiplier system involves the descending and ascending loops of Henle directing forming urine in opposing directions to create a concentration gradient when combined with variable permeability and sodium pumping

detrusor muscle smooth muscle in the bladder wall; fibers run in all directions to reduce the size of the organ when emptying it of urine

distal convoluted tubules portions of the nephron distal to the loop of Henle that receive hyposmotic filtrate from the loop of Henle and empty into collecting ducts

diuretic compound that increases urine output, leading to decreased water conservation

efferent arteriole arteriole carrying blood from the glomerulus to the capillary beds around the convoluted tubules and loop of Henle; portion of the portal system

endothelins group of vasoconstrictive, 21-amino acid peptides; produced by endothelial cells of the renal blood vessels, mesangial cells, and cells of the DCT

external urinary sphincter skeletal muscle; must be relaxed consciously to void urine

fenestrations small windows through a cell, allowing rapid filtration based on size; formed in such a way as to allow substances to cross through a cell without mixing with cell contents

filtration slits formed by pedicels of podocytes; substances filter between the pedicels based on size

forming urine filtrate undergoing modifications through secretion and reabsorption before true urine is produced

glomerular filtration rate (GFR) rate of renal filtration

glomerulus tuft of capillaries surrounded by Bowman's capsule; filters the blood based on size

glycosuria presence of glucose in the urine; caused by high blood glucose levels that exceed the ability of the kidneys to reabsorb the glucose; usually the result of untreated or poorly controlled diabetes mellitus

incontinence loss of ability to control micturition

intercalated cell specialized cell of the collecting ducts that secrete or absorb acid or bicarbonate; important in acid–base balance

internal urinary sphincter smooth muscle at the juncture of the bladder and urethra; relaxes as the bladder fills to allow urine into the urethra

inulin plant polysaccharide injected to determine GFR; is neither secreted nor absorbed by the kidney, so its appearance in the urine is directly proportional to its filtration rate

juxtaglomerular apparatus (JGA) located at the juncture of the DCT and the afferent and efferent arterioles of the glomerulus; plays a role in the regulation of renal blood flow and GFR

juxtaglomerular cell modified smooth muscle cells of the afferent arteriole; secretes renin in response to a drop in blood pressure

juxtamedullary nephrons nephrons adjacent to the border of the cortex and medulla with loops of Henle that extend into the renal medulla

leaky tight junctions tight junctions in which the sealing strands of proteins between the membranes of adjacent cells are fewer in number and incomplete; allows limited intercellular movement of solvent and solutes

leukocyte esterase enzyme produced by leukocytes that can be detected in the urine and that serves as an indirect indicator of urinary tract infection

loop of Henle descending and ascending portions between the proximal and distal convoluted tubules; those of cortical nephrons do not extend into the medulla, whereas those of juxtamedullary nephrons do extend into the medulla

macula densa cells found in the part of the DCT forming the JGA; sense Na^+ concentration in the forming urine

medulla inner region of kidney containing the renal pyramids

mesangial contractile cells found in the glomerulus; can contract or relax to regulate filtration rate

micturition also called urination or voiding

myogenic mechanism mechanism by which smooth muscle responds to stretch by contracting; an increase in blood pressure causes vasoconstriction and a decrease in blood pressure causes vasodilation so that blood flow downstream remains steady

nephrons functional units of the kidney that carry out all filtration and modification to produce urine; consist of renal corpuscles, proximal and distal convoluted tubules, and descending and ascending loops of Henle; drain into collecting ducts

net filtration pressure (NFP) pressure of fluid across the glomerulus; calculated by taking the hydrostatic pressure of the capillary and subtracting the colloid osmotic pressure of the blood and the hydrostatic pressure of Bowman's capsule

oliguria below normal urine production of 400–500 mL/day

osteomalacia softening of bones due to a lack of mineralization with calcium and phosphate; most often due to lack of vitamin D; in children, osteomalacia is termed rickets; not to be confused with osteoporosis

pedicels finger-like projections of podocytes surrounding glomerular capillaries; interdigitate to form a filtration membrane

peritubular capillaries second capillary bed of the renal portal system; surround the proximal and distal convoluted tubules; associated with the vasa recta

physiological sphincter sphincter consisting of circular smooth muscle indistinguishable from adjacent muscle but possessing differential innervations, permitting its function as a sphincter; structurally weak

podocytes cells forming finger-like processes; form the visceral layer of Bowman's capsule; pedicels of the podocytes interdigitate to form a filtration membrane

polyuria urine production in excess of 2.5 L/day; may be caused by diabetes insipidus, diabetes mellitus, or excessive use of diuretics

principal cell found in collecting ducts and possess channels for the recovery or loss of sodium and potassium; under the control of aldosterone; also have aquaporin channels under ADH control to regulate recovery of water

proximal convoluted tubules (PCTs) tortuous tubules receiving filtrate from Bowman's capsule; most active part of the nephron in reabsorption and secretion

renal columns extensions of the renal cortex into the renal medulla; separates the renal pyramids; contains blood vessels and connective tissues

renal corpuscle consists of the glomerulus and Bowman's capsule

renal cortex outer part of kidney containing all of the nephrons; some nephrons have loops of Henle extending into the medulla

renal fat pad adipose tissue between the renal fascia and the renal capsule that provides protective cushioning to the kidney

renal hilum recessed medial area of the kidney through which the renal artery, renal vein, ureters, lymphatics, and nerves pass

renal papillae medullary area of the renal pyramids where collecting ducts empty urine into the minor calyces

renal pyramids six to eight cone-shaped tissues in the medulla of the kidney containing collecting ducts and the loops of Henle of juxtamedullary nephrons

renin enzyme produced by juxtaglomerular cells in response to decreased blood pressure or sympathetic nervous activity; catalyzes the conversion of angiotensinogen into angiotensin I

retroperitoneal outside the peritoneal cavity; in the case of the kidney and ureters, between the parietal peritoneum and the abdominal wall

sacral micturition center group of neurons in the sacral region of the spinal cord that controls urination; acts reflexively unless its action is modified by higher brain centers to allow voluntary urination

specific gravity weight of a liquid compared to pure water, which has a specific gravity of 1.0; any solute added to water will increase its specific gravity

systemic edema increased fluid retention in the interstitial spaces and cells of the body; can be seen as swelling over large areas of the body, particularly the lower extremities

trigone area at the base of the bladder marked by the two ureters in the posterior–lateral aspect and the urethral orifice in the anterior aspect oriented like points on a triangle

tubuloglomerular feedback feedback mechanism involving the JGA; macula densa cells monitor Na^+ concentration in the terminal portion of the ascending loop of Henle and act to cause vasoconstriction or vasodilation of afferent and efferent arterioles to alter GFR

urethra transports urine from the bladder to the outside environment

urinalysis analysis of urine to diagnose disease

urochrome heme-derived pigment that imparts the typical yellow color of urine

vasa recta branches of the efferent arterioles that parallel the course of the loops of Henle and are continuous with the peritubular capillaries; with the glomerulus, form a portal system

CHAPTER REVIEW

25.1 Physical Characteristics of Urine

The kidney glomerulus filters blood mainly based on particle size to produce a filtrate lacking cells or large proteins. Most of the ions and molecules in the filtrate are needed by the body and must be reabsorbed farther down the nephron tubules, resulting in the formation of urine. Urine characteristics change depending on water intake, exercise, environmental temperature, and nutrient intake. Urinalysis analyzes characteristics of the urine and is used to diagnose diseases. A minimum of 400 to 500 mL urine must be produced daily to rid the body of wastes. Excessive quantities of urine may indicate diabetes insipidus or diabetes mellitus. The pH range of urine is 4.5 to 8.0, and is affected by diet. Osmolarity ranges from 50 to 1200 milliosmoles, and is a reflection of the amount of water being recovered or lost by renal nephrons.

25.2 Gross Anatomy of Urine Transport

The urethra is the only urinary structure that differs significantly between males and females. This is due to the dual role of the male urethra in transporting both urine and semen. The urethra arises from the trigone area at the base of the bladder. Urination is controlled by an involuntary internal sphincter of smooth muscle and a voluntary external sphincter of skeletal muscle. The shorter female urethra contributes to the higher incidence of bladder infections in females. The male urethra receives secretions from the prostate gland, Cowper's gland, and seminal vesicles as well as sperm. The bladder is largely retroperitoneal and can hold up to 500–600 mL urine. Micturition is the process of voiding the urine and involves both involuntary and voluntary actions. Voluntary control of micturition requires a mature and intact sacral micturition center. It also requires an intact spinal cord. Loss of control of micturition is called incontinence and results in voiding when the bladder contains about 250 mL urine. The ureters are retroperitoneal and lead from the renal pelvis of the kidney to the trigone area at the base of the bladder. A thick muscular wall consisting of longitudinal and circular smooth muscle helps move urine toward the bladder by way of peristaltic contractions.

25.3 Gross Anatomy of the Kidney

As noted previously, the structure of the kidney is divided into two principle regions—the peripheral rim of cortex and the central medulla. The two kidneys receive about 25 percent of cardiac output. They are protected in the retroperitoneal space by the renal fat pad and overlying ribs and muscle. Ureters, blood vessels, lymph vessels, and nerves enter and leave at the renal hilum. The renal arteries arise directly from the aorta, and the renal veins drain directly into the inferior vena cava. Kidney function is derived from the actions of about 1.3 million nephrons per kidney; these are the "functional units." A capillary bed, the glomerulus, filters blood and the filtrate is captured by Bowman's capsule. A portal system is formed when the blood flows through a second capillary bed surrounding the proximal and distal convoluted tubules and the loop of Henle. Most water and solutes are recovered by this second capillary bed. This filtrate is processed and finally gathered by collecting ducts that drain into the minor calyces, which merge to form major calyces; the filtrate then proceeds to the renal pelvis and finally the ureters.

25.4 Microscopic Anatomy of the Kidney

The functional unit of the kidney, the nephron, consists of the renal corpuscle, PCT, loop of Henle, and DCT. Cortical nephrons have short loops of Henle, whereas juxtamedullary nephrons have long loops of Henle extending into the medulla. About 15 percent of nephrons are juxtamedullary. The glomerulus is a capillary bed that filters blood principally based on particle size. The filtrate is captured by Bowman's capsule and directed to the PCT. A filtration membrane is formed by the fused basement membranes of the podocytes and the capillary endothelial cells that they embrace. Contractile mesangial cells further perform a role in regulating the rate at which the blood is filtered. Specialized cells in the JGA produce paracrine signals to regulate blood flow and filtration rates of the glomerulus. Other JGA cells produce the enzyme renin, which plays a central role in blood pressure regulation. The filtrate enters the PCT where absorption and secretion of several substances occur. The descending and ascending limbs of the loop of Henle consist of thick and thin segments. Absorption and secretion continue in the DCT but to a lesser extent than in the PCT. Each collecting duct collects forming urine from several nephrons and responds to the posterior pituitary hormone ADH by inserting aquaporin water channels into the cell membrane to fine tune water recovery.

25.5 Physiology of Urine Formation

The entire volume of the blood is filtered through the kidneys about 300 times per day, and 99 percent of the water filtered is recovered. The GFR is influenced by hydrostatic pressure and colloid osmotic pressure. Under normal circumstances, hydrostatic pressure is significantly greater and filtration occurs. The hydrostatic pressure of the glomerulus depends on systemic blood pressure, autoregulatory mechanisms, sympathetic nervous activity, and paracrine hormones. The kidney can function normally under a wide range of blood pressures due to the autoregulatory nature of smooth muscle.

25.6 Tubular Reabsorption

The kidney regulates water recovery and blood pressure by producing the enzyme renin. It is renin that starts a series of reactions, leading to the production of the vasoconstrictor angiotensin II and the salt-retaining steroid aldosterone. Water recovery is also powerfully and directly influenced by the hormone ADH. Even so, it only influences the last 10 percent of water available for recovery after filtration at the glomerulus, because 90 percent of water is recovered before reaching the collecting ducts. Depending on the body's fluid status at any given time, the collecting ducts can recover none or almost all of the water reaching them.

Mechanisms of solute recovery include active transport, simple diffusion, and facilitated diffusion. Most filtered substances are reabsorbed. Urea, NH_3, creatinine, and some drugs are filtered or secreted as wastes. H^+ and HCO_3^- are secreted or reabsorbed as needed to maintain acid–base balance. Movement of water from the glomerulus is primarily due to pressure, whereas that of peritubular capillaries and vasa recta is due to osmolarity and concentration gradients. The PCT is the most metabolically active part of the nephron and uses a wide array of protein micromachines to maintain homeostasis—symporters, antiporters, and ATPase active transporters—in conjunction with diffusion, both simple and facilitated. Almost 100 percent of glucose, amino acids, and vitamins are recovered in the PCT. Bicarbonate (HCO_3^-) is recovered using the same enzyme, carbonic anhydrase (CA), found in erythrocytes. The recovery of solutes creates an osmotic gradient to promote the recovery of water. The descending loop of the juxtaglomerular nephrons reaches an osmolarity of up to 1200 mOsmol/kg, promoting the recovery of water. The ascending loop is impervious to water but actively recovers Na^+, reducing filtrate osmolarity to 50–100 mOsmol/kg. The descending and ascending loop and vasa recta form a countercurrent multiplier system to increase Na^+ concentration in the kidney medulla. The collecting ducts actively pump urea into the medulla, further contributing to the high osmotic environment. The vasa recta recover the solute and water in the medulla, returning them to the circulation. Nearly 90 percent of water is recovered before the forming urine reaches the DCT, which will recover another 10 percent. Calcium recovery in the DCT is influenced by PTH and active vitamin D. In the collecting ducts, ADH stimulates aquaporin channel insertion to increase water recovery and thereby regulate osmolarity of the blood. Aldosterone stimulates Na^+ recovery by the collecting duct.

25.7 Regulation of Renal Blood Flow

The kidneys are innervated by sympathetic nerves of the autonomic nervous system. Sympathetic nervous activity decreases blood flow to the kidney, making more blood available to other areas of the body during times of stress. The arteriolar myogenic mechanism maintains a steady blood flow by causing arteriolar smooth muscle to contract when blood pressure increases and causing it to relax when blood pressure decreases. Tubuloglomerular feedback involves paracrine signaling at the JGA to cause vasoconstriction or vasodilation to maintain a steady rate of blood flow.

25.8 Endocrine Regulation of Kidney Function

Endocrine hormones act from a distance and paracrine hormones act locally. The renal enzyme renin converts angiotensinogen into angiotensin I. The lung enzyme, ACE, converts angiotensin I into active angiotensin II. Angiotensin II is an active vasoconstrictor that increases blood pressure. Angiotensin II also stimulates aldosterone release from the adrenal cortex, causing the collecting duct to retain Na^+, which promotes water retention and a longer-term rise in blood pressure. ADH promotes water recovery by the collecting ducts by stimulating the insertion of aquaporin water channels into cell membranes. Endothelins are elevated in cases of diabetic kidney disease, increasing Na^+ retention and decreasing GFR. Natriuretic hormones, released primarily from the atria of the heart in response to stretching of the atrial walls, stimulate Na^+ excretion and thereby decrease blood pressure. PTH stimulates the final step in the formation of active vitamin D3 and reduces phosphate reabsorption, resulting in higher circulating Ca^{++} levels.

25.9 Regulation of Fluid Volume and Composition

The major hormones regulating body fluids are ADH, aldosterone and ANH. Progesterone is similar in structure to aldosterone and can bind to and weakly stimulate aldosterone receptors, providing a similar but diminished response. Blood pressure is a reflection of blood volume and is monitored by baroreceptors in the aortic arch and carotid sinuses. When blood pressure increases, more action potentials are sent to the central nervous system, resulting in greater vasodilation, greater GFR, and more water lost in the urine. ANH is released by the cardiomyocytes when blood pressure increases, causing Na^+ and water loss. ADH at high levels causes vasoconstriction in addition to its action on the collecting ducts to recover more water. Diuretics increase urine volume. Mechanisms for controlling Na^+ concentration in the blood include the renin–angiotensin–aldosterone system and ADH. When Na^+ is retained, K^+ is excreted; when Na^+ is lost, K^+ is retained. When circulating Ca^{++} decreases, PTH stimulates the reabsorption of Ca^{++} and inhibits reabsorption of HPO_4^{2-}. pH is regulated through buffers, expiration of CO_2, and excretion of acid or base by the kidneys. The breakdown of amino acids produces ammonia. Most ammonia is converted into less-toxic urea in the liver and excreted in the urine. Regulation of drugs is by glomerular filtration, tubular secretion, and tubular reabsorption.

25.10 The Urinary System and Homeostasis

The effects of failure of parts of the urinary system may range from inconvenient (incontinence) to fatal (loss of filtration and many others). The kidneys catalyze the final reaction in the synthesis of active vitamin D that in turn helps regulate Ca^{++}. The kidney hormone EPO stimulates erythrocyte development and promotes adequate O_2 transport. The kidneys help regulate blood pressure through Na^+ and water retention and loss. The kidneys work with the adrenal cortex, lungs, and liver in the renin–angiotensin–aldosterone system to regulate blood pressure. They regulate osmolarity of the blood by regulating both solutes and water. Three electrolytes are more closely regulated than others: Na^+, Ca^{++}, and K^+. The kidneys share pH regulation with the lungs and plasma buffers, so that proteins can preserve their three-dimensional conformation and thus their function.

REVIEW QUESTIONS

1. Diabetes insipidus or diabetes mellitus would most likely be indicated by _____.
   a. anuria
   b. polyuria
   c. oliguria
   d. none of the above

2. The color of urine is determined mainly by _____.

   a. diet
   b. filtration rate
   c. byproducts of red blood cell breakdown
   d. filtration efficiency

3. Production of less than 50 mL/day of urine is called _____.
   a. normal
   b. polyuria
   c. oliguria
   d. anuria

4. Peristaltic contractions occur in the _____.

   a. urethra
   b. bladder
   c. ureters
   d. urethra, bladder, and ureters

5. Somatic motor neurons must be _____ to relax the external urethral sphincter to allow urination.
   a. stimulated
   b. inhibited

6. Which part of the urinary system is *not* completely retroperitoneal?
   a. kidneys
   b. ureters
   c. bladder
   d. nephrons

7. The renal pyramids are separated from each other by extensions of the renal cortex called _____.
   a. renal medulla
   b. minor calyces
   c. medullary cortices
   d. renal columns

8. The primary structure found within the medulla is the _____.
   a. loop of Henle
   b. minor calyces
   c. portal system
   d. ureter

9. The right kidney is slightly lower because _____.

   a. it is displaced by the liver
   b. it is displace by the heart
   c. it is slightly smaller
   d. it needs protection of the lower ribs

10. Blood filtrate is captured in the lumen of the _____.

a. glomerulus
b. Bowman's capsule
c. calyces
d. renal papillae

11. What are the names of the capillaries following the efferent arteriole?
a. arcuate and medullary
b. interlobar and interlobular
c. peritubular and vasa recta
d. peritubular and medullary

12. The functional unit of the kidney is called _____.

a. the renal hilus
b. the renal corpuscle
c. the nephron
d. Bowman's capsule

13. _____ pressure must be greater on the capillary side of the filtration membrane to achieve filtration.
a. Osmotic
b. Hydrostatic

14. Production of urine to modify plasma makeup is the result of _____.
a. filtration
b. absorption
c. secretion
d. filtration, absorption, and secretion

15. Systemic blood pressure must stay above 60 so that the proper amount of filtration occurs.
a. true
b. false

16. Aquaporin channels are only found in the collecting duct.
a. true
b. false

17. Most absorption and secretion occurs in this part of the nephron.
a. proximal convoluted tubule
b. descending loop of Henle
c. ascending loop of Henle
d. distal convoluted tubule
e. collecting ducts

18. The fine tuning of water recovery or disposal occurs in _____.
a. the proximal convoluted tubule
b. the collecting ducts
c. the ascending loop of Henle
d. the distal convoluted tubule

19. Vasodilation of blood vessels to the kidneys is due to _____.
a. more frequent action potentials
b. less frequent action potentials

20. When blood pressure increases, blood vessels supplying the kidney will _____ to mount a steady rate of filtration.

a. contract
b. relax

21. Which of these three paracrine chemicals cause vasodilation?
a. ATP
b. adenosine
c. nitric oxide

22. What hormone directly opposes the actions of natriuretic hormones?
a. renin
b. nitric oxide
c. dopamine
d. aldosterone

23. Which of these is a vasoconstrictor?
a. nitric oxide
b. natriuretic hormone
c. bradykinin
d. angiotensin II

24. What signal causes the heart to secrete atrial natriuretic hormone?
a. increased blood pressure
b. decreased blood pressure
c. increased Na^+ levels
d. decreased Na^+ levels

25. Which of these beverages does *not* have a diuretic effect?
a. tea
b. coffee
c. alcohol
d. milk

26. Progesterone can bind to receptors for which hormone that, when released, activates water retention?
a. aldosterone
b. ADH
c. PTH
d. ANH

27. Renin is released in response to _____.
a. increased blood pressure
b. decreased blood pressure
c. ACE
d. diuretics

28. Which step in vitamin D production does the kidney perform?
a. converts cholecalciferol into calcidiol
b. converts calcidiol into calcitriol
c. stores vitamin D
d. none of these

29. Which hormone does the kidney produce that stimulates red blood cell production?
a. thrombopoeitin
b. vitamin D
c. EPO
d. renin

30. If there were no aquaporin channels in the collecting duct, _____.
    a. you would develop systemic edema
    b. you would retain excess Na^+
    c. you would lose vitamins and electrolytes
    d. you would suffer severe dehydration

CRITICAL THINKING QUESTIONS

31. What is suggested by the presence of white blood cells found in the urine?

32. Both diabetes mellitus and diabetes insipidus produce large urine volumes, but how would other characteristics of the urine differ between the two diseases?

33. Why are females more likely to contract bladder infections than males?

34. Describe how forceful urination is accomplished.

35. What anatomical structures provide protection to the kidney?

36. How does the renal portal system differ from the hypothalamo–hypophyseal and digestive portal systems?

37. Name the structures found in the renal hilum.

38. Which structures make up the renal corpuscle?

39. What are the major structures comprising the filtration membrane?

40. Give the formula for net filtration pressure.

41. Name at least five symptoms of kidney failure.

42. Which vessels and what part of the nephron are involved in countercurrent multiplication?

43. Give the approximate osmolarity of fluid in the proximal convoluted tubule, deepest part of the loop of Henle, distal convoluted tubule, and the collecting ducts.

44. Explain what happens to Na^+ concentration in the nephron when GFR increases.

45. If you want the kidney to excrete more Na^+ in the urine, what do you want the blood flow to do?

46. What organs produce which hormones or enzymes in the renin–angiotensin system?

47. PTH affects absorption and reabsorption of what?

48. Why is ADH also called vasopressin?

49. How can glucose be a diuretic?

50. How does lack of protein in the blood cause edema?

51. Which three electrolytes are most closely regulated by the kidney?

26 | FLUID, ELECTROLYTE, AND ACID-BASE BALANCE

Figure 26.1 Venus Williams Perspiring on the Tennis Court The body has critically important mechanisms for balancing the intake and output of bodily fluids. An athlete must continuously replace the water and electrolytes lost in sweat. (credit: "Edwin Martinez1"/Wikimedia Commons)

Introduction

Chapter Objectives

After studying this chapter, you will be able to:

- Identify the body's main fluid compartments
- Define plasma osmolality and identify two ways in which plasma osmolality is maintained
- Identify the six ions most important to the function of the body
- Define buffer and discuss the role of buffers in the body
- Explain why bicarbonate must be conserved rather than reabsorbed in the kidney
- Identify the normal range of blood pH and name the conditions where one has a blood pH that is either too high or too low

Homeostasis, or the maintenance of constant conditions in the body, is a fundamental property of all living things. In the human body, the substances that participate in chemical reactions must remain within narrows ranges of concentration. Too much or too little of a single substance can disrupt your bodily functions. Because metabolism relies on reactions that are all interconnected, any disruption might affect multiple organs or even organ systems. Water is the most ubiquitous substance in the chemical reactions of life. The interactions of various aqueous solutions—solutions in which water is the solvent—are continuously monitored and adjusted by a large suite of interconnected feedback systems in your body. Understanding the ways in which the body maintains these critical balances is key to understanding good health.

26.1 | Body Fluids and Fluid Compartments

By the end of this section, you will be able to:
- Explain the importance of water in the body
- Contrast the composition of the intracellular fluid with that of the extracellular fluid
- Explain the importance of protein channels in the movement of solutes
- Identify the causes and symptoms of edema

The chemical reactions of life take place in aqueous solutions. The dissolved substances in a solution are called solutes. In the human body, solutes vary in different parts of the body, but may include proteins—including those that transport lipids, carbohydrates, and, very importantly, electrolytes. Often in medicine, a mineral dissociated from a salt that carries an electrical charge (an ion) is called and electrolyte. For instance, sodium ions (Na^+) and chloride ions (Cl^-) are often referred to as electrolytes.

In the body, water moves through semi-permeable membranes of cells and from one compartment of the body to another by a process called osmosis. Osmosis is basically the diffusion of water from regions of higher concentration to regions of lower concentration, along an osmotic gradient across a semi-permeable membrane. As a result, water will move into and out of cells and tissues, depending on the relative concentrations of the water and solutes found there. An appropriate balance of solutes inside and outside of cells must be maintained to ensure normal function.

Body Water Content

Human beings are mostly water, ranging from about 75 percent of body mass in infants to about 50–60 percent in adult men and women, to as low as 45 percent in old age. The percent of body water changes with development, because the proportions of the body given over to each organ and to muscles, fat, bone, and other tissues change from infancy to adulthood (Figure 26.2). Your brain and kidneys have the highest proportions of water, which composes 80–85 percent of their masses. In contrast, teeth have the lowest proportion of water, at 8–10 percent.

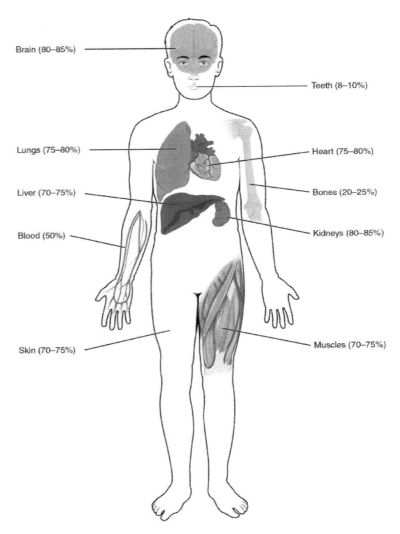

Figure 26.2 Water Content of the Body's Organs and Tissues Water content varies in different body organs and tissues, from as little as 8 percent in the teeth to as much as 85 percent in the brain.

Fluid Compartments

Body fluids can be discussed in terms of their specific **fluid compartment**, a location that is largely separate from another compartment by some form of a physical barrier. The **intracellular fluid (ICF)** compartment is the system that includes all fluid enclosed in cells by their plasma membranes. **Extracellular fluid (ECF)** surrounds all cells in the body. Extracellular fluid has two primary constituents: the fluid component of the blood (called plasma) and the **interstitial fluid (IF)** that surrounds all cells not in the blood (Figure 26.3).

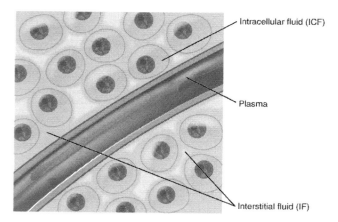

Figure 26.3 Fluid Compartments in the Human Body The intracellular fluid (ICF) is the fluid within cells. The interstitial fluid (IF) is part of the extracellular fluid (ECF) between the cells. Blood plasma is the second part of the ECF. Materials travel between cells and the plasma in capillaries through the IF.

Intracellular Fluid

The ICF lies within cells and is the principal component of the cytosol/cytoplasm. The ICF makes up about 60 percent of the total water in the human body, and in an average-size adult male, the ICF accounts for about 25 liters (seven gallons) of fluid (Figure 26.4). This fluid volume tends to be very stable, because the amount of water in living cells is closely regulated. If the amount of water inside a cell falls to a value that is too low, the cytosol becomes too concentrated with solutes to carry on normal cellular activities; if too much water enters a cell, the cell may burst and be destroyed.

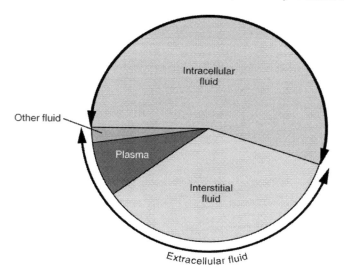

Figure 26.4 A Pie Graph Showing the Proportion of Total Body Fluid in Each of the Body's Fluid Compartments Most of the water in the body is intracellular fluid. The second largest volume is the interstitial fluid, which surrounds cells that are not blood cells.

Extracellular Fluid

The ECF accounts for the other one-third of the body's water content. Approximately 20 percent of the ECF is found in plasma. Plasma travels through the body in blood vessels and transports a range of materials, including blood cells, proteins (including clotting factors and antibodies), electrolytes, nutrients, gases, and wastes. Gases, nutrients, and waste materials travel between capillaries and cells through the IF. Cells are separated from the IF by a selectively permeable cell membrane that helps regulate the passage of materials between the IF and the interior of the cell.

The body has other water-based ECF. These include the cerebrospinal fluid that bathes the brain and spinal cord, lymph, the synovial fluid in joints, the pleural fluid in the pleural cavities, the pericardial fluid in the cardiac sac, the peritoneal fluid in the peritoneal cavity, and the aqueous humor of the eye. Because these fluids are outside of cells, these fluids are also considered components of the ECF compartment.

Composition of Body Fluids

The compositions of the two components of the ECF—plasma and IF—are more similar to each other than either is to the ICF (Figure 26.5). Blood plasma has high concentrations of sodium, chloride, bicarbonate, and protein. The IF has high concentrations of sodium, chloride, and bicarbonate, but a relatively lower concentration of protein. In contrast, the ICF has elevated amounts of potassium, phosphate, magnesium, and protein. Overall, the ICF contains high concentrations of potassium and phosphate (HPO_4^{2-}), whereas both plasma and the ECF contain high concentrations of sodium and chloride.

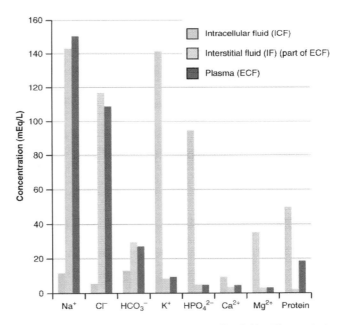

Figure 26.5 **The Concentrations of Different Elements in Key Bodily Fluids** The graph shows the composition of the ICF, IF, and plasma. The compositions of plasma and IF are similar to one another but are quite different from the composition of the ICF.

Interactive LINK

Watch this video (http://openstaxcollege.org/l/bodyfluids) to learn more about body fluids, fluid compartments, and electrolytes. When blood volume decreases due to sweating, from what source is water taken in by the blood?

Most body fluids are neutral in charge. Thus, cations, or positively charged ions, and anions, or negatively charged ions, are balanced in fluids. As seen in the previous graph, sodium (Na^+) ions and chloride (Cl^-) ions are concentrated in the ECF of the body, whereas potassium (K^+) ions are concentrated inside cells. Although sodium and potassium can "leak" through "pores" into and out of cells, respectively, the high levels of potassium and low levels of sodium in the ICF are maintained by sodium-potassium pumps in the cell membranes. These pumps use the energy supplied by ATP to pump sodium out of the cell and potassium into the cell (Figure 26.6).

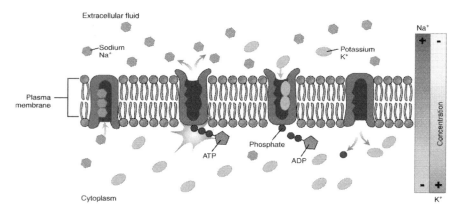

Figure 26.6 The Sodium-Potassium Pump The sodium-potassium pump is powered by ATP to transfer sodium out of the cytoplasm and into the ECF. The pump also transfers potassium out of the ECF and into the cytoplasm. (credit: modification of work by Mariana Ruiz Villarreal)

Fluid Movement between Compartments

Hydrostatic pressure, the force exerted by a fluid against a wall, causes movement of fluid between compartments. The hydrostatic pressure of blood is the pressure exerted by blood against the walls of the blood vessels by the pumping action of the heart. In capillaries, hydrostatic pressure (also known as capillary blood pressure) is higher than the opposing "colloid osmotic pressure" in blood—a "constant" pressure primarily produced by circulating albumin—at the arteriolar end of the capillary (Figure 26.7). This pressure forces plasma and nutrients out of the capillaries and into surrounding tissues. Fluid and the cellular wastes in the tissues enter the capillaries at the venule end, where the hydrostatic pressure is less than the osmotic pressure in the vessel. Filtration pressure squeezes fluid from the plasma in the blood to the IF surrounding the tissue cells. The surplus fluid in the interstitial space that is not returned directly back to the capillaries is drained from tissues by the lymphatic system, and then re-enters the vascular system at the subclavian veins.

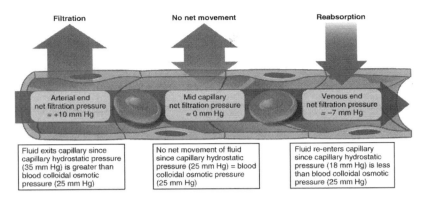

Figure 26.7 Capillary Exchange Net filtration occurs near the arterial end of the capillary since capillary hydrostatic pressure (CHP) is greater than blood colloidal osmotic pressure (BCOP). There is no net movement of fluid near the midpoint of the capillary since CHP = BCOP. Net reabsorption occurs near the venous end of the capillary since BCOP is greater than CHP.

Watch this video (http://openstaxcollege.org/l/dynamicfluid) to see an explanation of the dynamics of fluid in the body's compartments. What happens in the tissue when capillary blood pressure is less than osmotic pressure?

Hydrostatic pressure is especially important in governing the movement of water in the nephrons of the kidneys to ensure proper filtering of the blood to form urine. As hydrostatic pressure in the kidneys increases, the amount of water leaving the capillaries also increases, and more urine filtrate is formed. If hydrostatic pressure in the kidneys drops too low, as can happen in dehydration, the functions of the kidneys will be impaired, and less nitrogenous wastes will be removed from the bloodstream. Extreme dehydration can result in kidney failure.

Fluid also moves between compartments along an osmotic gradient. Recall that an osmotic gradient is produced by the difference in concentration of all solutes on either side of a semi-permeable membrane. The magnitude of the osmotic gradient is proportional to the difference in the concentration of solutes on one side of the cell membrane to that on the other side. Water will move by osmosis from the side where its concentration is high (and the concentration of solute is low) to the side of the membrane where its concentration is low (and the concentration of solute is high). In the body, water moves by osmosis from plasma to the IF (and the reverse) and from the IF to the ICF (and the reverse). In the body, water moves constantly into and out of fluid compartments as conditions change in different parts of the body.

For example, if you are sweating, you will lose water through your skin. Sweating depletes your tissues of water and increases the solute concentration in those tissues. As this happens, water diffuses from your blood into sweat glands and surrounding skin tissues that have become dehydrated because of the osmotic gradient. Additionally, as water leaves the blood, it is replaced by the water in other tissues throughout your body that are not dehydrated. If this continues, dehydration spreads throughout the body. When a dehydrated person drinks water and rehydrates, the water is redistributed by the same gradient, but in the opposite direction, replenishing water in all of the tissues.

Solute Movement between Compartments

The movement of some solutes between compartments is active, which consumes energy and is an active transport process, whereas the movement of other solutes is passive, which does not require energy. Active transport allows cells to move a specific substance against its concentration gradient through a membrane protein, requiring energy in the form of ATP. For example, the sodium-potassium pump employs active transport to pump sodium out of cells and potassium into cells, with both substances moving against their concentration gradients.

Passive transport of a molecule or ion depends on its ability to pass through the membrane, as well as the existence of a concentration gradient that allows the molecules to diffuse from an area of higher concentration to an area of lower concentration. Some molecules, like gases, lipids, and water itself (which also utilizes water channels in the membrane called aquaporins), slip fairly easily through the cell membrane; others, including polar molecules like glucose, amino acids, and ions do not. Some of these molecules enter and leave cells using facilitated transport, whereby the molecules move down a concentration gradient through specific protein channels in the membrane. This process does not require energy. For example, glucose is transferred into cells by glucose transporters that use facilitated transport (Figure 26.8).

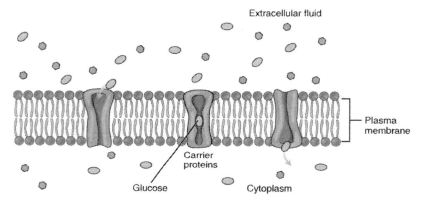

Figure 26.8 Facilitated Diffusion   Glucose molecules use facilitated diffusion to move down a concentration gradient through the carrier protein channels in the membrane. (credit: modification of work by Mariana Ruiz Villarreal)

Disorders OF THE...

Fluid Balance: Edema

Edema is the accumulation of excess water in the tissues. It is most common in the soft tissues of the extremities. The physiological causes of edema include water leakage from blood capillaries. Edema is almost always caused by an underlying medical condition, by the use of certain therapeutic drugs, by pregnancy, by localized injury, or by an allergic reaction. In the limbs, the symptoms of edema include swelling of the subcutaneous tissues, an increase in the normal size of the limb, and stretched, tight skin. One quick way to check for subcutaneous edema localized in a limb is to press a finger into the suspected area. Edema is likely if the depression persists for several seconds after the finger is removed (which is called "pitting").

Pulmonary edema is excess fluid in the air sacs of the lungs, a common symptom of heart and/or kidney failure. People with pulmonary edema likely will experience difficulty breathing, and they may experience chest pain. Pulmonary edema can be life threatening, because it compromises gas exchange in the lungs, and anyone having symptoms should immediately seek medical care.

In pulmonary edema resulting from heart failure, excessive leakage of water occurs because fluids get "backed up" in the pulmonary capillaries of the lungs, when the left ventricle of the heart is unable to pump sufficient blood into the systemic circulation. Because the left side of the heart is unable to pump out its normal volume of blood, the blood in the pulmonary circulation gets "backed up," starting with the left atrium, then into the pulmonary veins, and then into pulmonary capillaries. The resulting increased hydrostatic pressure within pulmonary capillaries, as blood is still coming in from the pulmonary arteries, causes fluid to be pushed out of them and into lung tissues.

Other causes of edema include damage to blood vessels and/or lymphatic vessels, or a decrease in osmotic pressure in chronic and severe liver disease, where the liver is unable to manufacture plasma proteins (Figure 26.9). A decrease in the normal levels of plasma proteins results in a decrease of colloid osmotic pressure (which counterbalances the hydrostatic pressure) in the capillaries. This process causes loss of water from the blood to the surrounding tissues, resulting in edema.

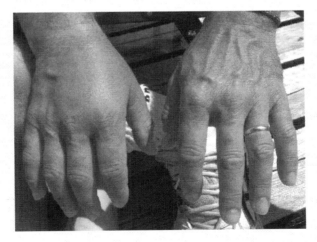

Figure 26.9 Edema An allergic reaction can cause capillaries in the hand to leak excess fluid that accumulates in the tissues. (credit: Jane Whitney)

Mild, transient edema of the feet and legs may be caused by sitting or standing in the same position for long periods of time, as in the work of a toll collector or a supermarket cashier. This is because deep veins in the lower limbs rely on skeletal muscle contractions to push on the veins and thus "pump" blood back to the heart. Otherwise, the venous blood pools in the lower limbs and can leak into surrounding tissues.

Medications that can result in edema include vasodilators, calcium channel blockers used to treat hypertension, non-steroidal anti-inflammatory drugs, estrogen therapies, and some diabetes medications. Underlying medical conditions that can contribute to edema include congestive heart failure, kidney damage and kidney disease, disorders that affect the veins of the legs, and cirrhosis and other liver disorders.

Therapy for edema usually focuses on elimination of the cause. Activities that can reduce the effects of the condition include appropriate exercises to keep the blood and lymph flowing through the affected areas. Other therapies include elevation of the affected part to assist drainage, massage and compression of the areas to move the fluid out of the tissues, and decreased salt intake to decrease sodium and water retention.

26.2 | Water Balance

By the end of this section, you will be able to:
- Explain how water levels in the body influence the thirst cycle
- Identify the main route by which water leaves the body
- Describe the role of ADH and its effect on body water levels
- Define dehydration and identify common causes of dehydration

On a typical day, the average adult will take in about 2500 mL (almost 3 quarts) of aqueous fluids. Although most of the intake comes through the digestive tract, about 230 mL (8 ounces) per day is generated metabolically, in the last steps of aerobic respiration. Additionally, each day about the same volume (2500 mL) of water leaves the body by different routes; most of this lost water is removed as urine. The kidneys also can adjust blood volume though mechanisms that draw water out of the filtrate and urine. The kidneys can regulate water levels in the body; they conserve water if you are dehydrated, and they can make urine more dilute to expel excess water if necessary. Water is lost through the skin through evaporation from the skin surface without overt sweating and from air expelled from the lungs. This type of water loss is called insensible water loss because a person is usually unaware of it.

Regulation of Water Intake

Osmolality is the ratio of solutes in a solution to a volume of solvent in a solution. **Plasma osmolality** is thus the ratio of solutes to water in blood plasma. A person's plasma osmolality value reflects his or her state of hydration. A healthy body maintains plasma osmolality within a narrow range, by employing several mechanisms that regulate both water intake and output.

Drinking water is considered voluntary. So how is water intake regulated by the body? Consider someone who is experiencing **dehydration**, a net loss of water that results in insufficient water in blood and other tissues. The water that leaves the body, as exhaled air, sweat, or urine, is ultimately extracted from blood plasma. As the blood becomes more concentrated, the thirst response—a sequence of physiological processes—is triggered (Figure 26.10). Osmoreceptors are sensory receptors in the thirst center in the hypothalamus that monitor the concentration of solutes (osmolality) of the blood. If blood osmolality increases above its ideal value, the hypothalamus transmits signals that result in a conscious awareness of thirst. The person should (and normally does) respond by drinking water. The hypothalamus of a dehydrated person also releases antidiuretic hormone (ADH) through the posterior pituitary gland. ADH signals the kidneys to recover water from urine, effectively diluting the blood plasma. To conserve water, the hypothalamus of a dehydrated person also sends signals via the sympathetic nervous system to the salivary glands in the mouth. The signals result in a decrease in watery, serous output (and an increase in stickier, thicker mucus output). These changes in secretions result in a "dry mouth" and the sensation of thirst.

Chapter 26 | Fluid, Electrolyte, and Acid-Base Balance

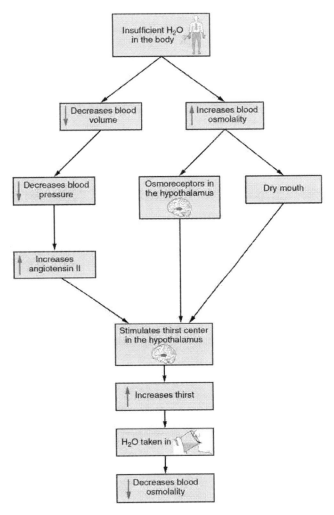

Figure 26.10 A Flowchart Showing the Thirst Response The thirst response begins when osmoreceptors detect a decrease in water levels in the blood.

Decreased blood volume resulting from water loss has two additional effects. First, baroreceptors, blood-pressure receptors in the arch of the aorta and the carotid arteries in the neck, detect a decrease in blood pressure that results from decreased blood volume. The heart is ultimately signaled to increase its rate and/or strength of contractions to compensate for the lowered blood pressure.

Second, the kidneys have a renin-angiotensin hormonal system that increases the production of the active form of the hormone angiotensin II, which helps stimulate thirst, but also stimulates the release of the hormone aldosterone from the adrenal glands. Aldosterone increases the reabsorption of sodium in the distal tubules of the nephrons in the kidneys, and water follows this reabsorbed sodium back into the blood.

If adequate fluids are not consumed, dehydration results and a person's body contains too little water to function correctly. A person who repeatedly vomits or who has diarrhea may become dehydrated, and infants, because their body mass is so low, can become dangerously dehydrated very quickly. Endurance athletes such as distance runners often become dehydrated during long races. Dehydration can be a medical emergency, and a dehydrated person may lose consciousness, become comatose, or die, if his or her body is not rehydrated quickly.

Regulation of Water Output

Water loss from the body occurs predominantly through the renal system. A person produces an average of 1.5 liters (1.6 quarts) of urine per day. Although the volume of urine varies in response to hydration levels, there is a minimum volume of urine production required for proper bodily functions. The kidney excretes 100 to 1200 milliosmoles of solutes per day to rid the body of a variety of excess salts and other water-soluble chemical wastes, most notably creatinine, urea, and uric acid. Failure to produce the minimum volume of urine means that metabolic wastes cannot be effectively removed from the body, a situation that can impair organ function. The minimum level of urine production necessary to maintain normal function is about 0.47 liters (0.5 quarts) per day.

The kidneys also must make adjustments in the event of ingestion of too much fluid. **Diuresis**, which is the production of urine in excess of normal levels, begins about 30 minutes after drinking a large quantity of fluid. Diuresis reaches a peak after about 1 hour, and normal urine production is reestablished after about 3 hours.

Role of ADH

Antidiuretic hormone (ADH), also known as vasopressin, controls the amount of water reabsorbed from the collecting ducts and tubules in the kidney. This hormone is produced in the hypothalamus and is delivered to the posterior pituitary for storage and release (Figure 26.11). When the osmoreceptors in the hypothalamus detect an increase in the concentration of blood plasma, the hypothalamus signals the release of ADH from the posterior pituitary into the blood.

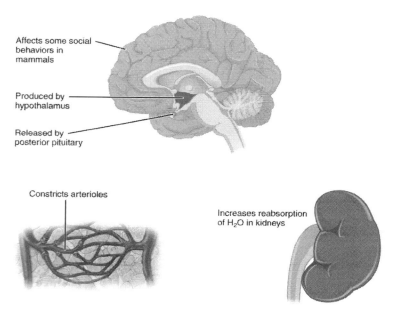

Figure 26.11 Antidiuretic Hormone (ADH) ADH is produced in the hypothalamus and released by the posterior pituitary gland. It causes the kidneys to retain water, constricts arterioles in the peripheral circulation, and affects some social behaviors in mammals.

ADH has two major effects. It constricts the arterioles in the peripheral circulation, which reduces the flow of blood to the extremities and thereby increases the blood supply to the core of the body. ADH also causes the epithelial cells that line the renal collecting tubules to move water channel proteins, called aquaporins, from the interior of the cells to the apical surface, where these proteins are inserted into the cell membrane (Figure 26.12). The result is an increase in the water permeability of these cells and, thus, a large increase in water passage from the urine through the walls of the collecting tubules, leading to more reabsorption of water into the bloodstream. When the blood plasma becomes less concentrated and the level of ADH decreases, aquaporins are removed from collecting tubule cell membranes, and the passage of water out of urine and into the blood decreases.

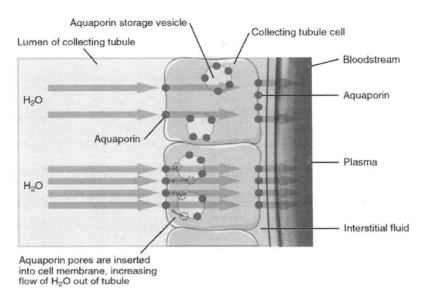

Figure 26.12 Aquaporins The binding of ADH to receptors on the cells of the collecting tubule results in aquaporins being inserted into the plasma membrane, shown in the lower cell. This dramatically increases the flow of water out of the tubule and into the bloodstream.

A diuretic is a compound that increases urine output and therefore decreases water conservation by the body. Diuretics are used to treat hypertension, congestive heart failure, and fluid retention associated with menstruation. Alcohol acts as a diuretic by inhibiting the release of ADH. Additionally, caffeine, when consumed in high concentrations, acts as a diuretic.

26.3 | Electrolyte Balance

By the end of this section, you will be able to:
- List the role of the six most important electrolytes in the body
- Name the disorders associated with abnormally high and low levels of the six electrolytes
- Identify the predominant extracellular anion
- Describe the role of aldosterone on the level of water in the body

The body contains a large variety of ions, or electrolytes, which perform a variety of functions. Some ions assist in the transmission of electrical impulses along cell membranes in neurons and muscles. Other ions help to stabilize protein structures in enzymes. Still others aid in releasing hormones from endocrine glands. All of the ions in plasma contribute to the osmotic balance that controls the movement of water between cells and their environment.

Electrolytes in living systems include sodium, potassium, chloride, bicarbonate, calcium, phosphate, magnesium, copper, zinc, iron, manganese, molybdenum, copper, and chromium. In terms of body functioning, six electrolytes are most important: sodium, potassium, chloride, bicarbonate, calcium, and phosphate.

Roles of Electrolytes

These six ions aid in nerve excitability, endocrine secretion, membrane permeability, buffering body fluids, and controlling the movement of fluids between compartments. These ions enter the body through the digestive tract. More than 90 percent of the calcium and phosphate that enters the body is incorporated into bones and teeth, with bone serving as a mineral reserve for these ions. In the event that calcium and phosphate are needed for other functions, bone tissue can be broken down to supply the blood and other tissues with these minerals. Phosphate is a normal constituent of nucleic acids; hence, blood levels of phosphate will increase whenever nucleic acids are broken down.

Excretion of ions occurs mainly through the kidneys, with lesser amounts lost in sweat and in feces. Excessive sweating may cause a significant loss, especially of sodium and chloride. Severe vomiting or diarrhea will cause a loss of chloride and bicarbonate ions. Adjustments in respiratory and renal functions allow the body to regulate the levels of these ions in the ECF.

Table 26.1 lists the reference values for blood plasma, cerebrospinal fluid (CSF), and urine for the six ions addressed in this section. In a clinical setting, sodium, potassium, and chloride are typically analyzed in a routine urine sample. In contrast, calcium and phosphate analysis requires a collection of urine across a 24-hour period, because the output of these ions can vary considerably over the course of a day. Urine values reflect the rates of excretion of these ions. Bicarbonate is the one ion that is not normally excreted in urine; instead, it is conserved by the kidneys for use in the body's buffering systems.

Electrolyte and Ion Reference Values

Name	Chemical symbol	Plasma	CSF	Urine
Sodium	Na^+	136.00–146.00 (mM)	138.00–150.00 (mM)	40.00–220.00 (mM)
Potassium	K^+	3.50–5.00 (mM)	0.35–3.5 (mM)	25.00–125.00 (mM)
Chloride	Cl^-	98.00–107.00 (mM)	118.00–132.00 (mM)	110.00–250.00 (mM)
Bicarbonate	HCO_3^-	22.00–29.00 (mM)	------	------
Calcium	Ca^{++}	2.15–2.55 (mmol/day)	------	Up to 7.49 (mmol/day)
Phosphate	HPO_4^{2-}	0.81–1.45 (mmol/day)	------	12.90–42.00 (mmol/day)

Table 26.1

Sodium

Sodium is the major cation of the extracellular fluid. It is responsible for one-half of the osmotic pressure gradient that exists between the interior of cells and their surrounding environment. People eating a typical Western diet, which is very high in NaCl, routinely take in 130 to 160 mmol/day of sodium, but humans require only 1 to 2 mmol/day. This excess sodium appears to be a major factor in hypertension (high blood pressure) in some people. Excretion of sodium is accomplished primarily by the kidneys. Sodium is freely filtered through the glomerular capillaries of the kidneys, and although much of the filtered sodium is reabsorbed in the proximal convoluted tubule, some remains in the filtrate and urine, and is normally excreted.

Hyponatremia is a lower-than-normal concentration of sodium, usually associated with excess water accumulation in the body, which dilutes the sodium. An absolute loss of sodium may be due to a decreased intake of the ion coupled with its continual excretion in the urine. An abnormal loss of sodium from the body can result from several conditions, including excessive sweating, vomiting, or diarrhea; the use of diuretics; excessive production of urine, which can occur in diabetes; and acidosis, either metabolic acidosis or diabetic ketoacidosis.

A relative decrease in blood sodium can occur because of an imbalance of sodium in one of the body's other fluid compartments, like IF, or from a dilution of sodium due to water retention related to edema or congestive heart failure. At the cellular level, hyponatremia results in increased entry of water into cells by osmosis, because the concentration of solutes within the cell exceeds the concentration of solutes in the now-diluted ECF. The excess water causes swelling of the cells; the swelling of red blood cells—decreasing their oxygen-carrying efficiency and making them potentially too large to fit through capillaries—along with the swelling of neurons in the brain can result in brain damage or even death.

Hypernatremia is an abnormal increase of blood sodium. It can result from water loss from the blood, resulting in the hemoconcentration of all blood constituents. Hormonal imbalances involving ADH and aldosterone may also result in higher-than-normal sodium values.

Potassium

Potassium is the major intracellular cation. It helps establish the resting membrane potential in neurons and muscle fibers after membrane depolarization and action potentials. In contrast to sodium, potassium has very little effect on osmotic pressure. The low levels of potassium in blood and CSF are due to the sodium-potassium pumps in cell membranes, which maintain the normal potassium concentration gradients between the ICF and ECF. The recommendation for daily intake/consumption of potassium is 4700 mg. Potassium is excreted, both actively and passively, through the renal tubules, especially the distal convoluted tubule and collecting ducts. Potassium participates in the exchange with sodium in the renal tubules under the influence of aldosterone, which also relies on basolateral sodium-potassium pumps.

Hypokalemia is an abnormally low potassium blood level. Similar to the situation with hyponatremia, hypokalemia can occur because of either an absolute reduction of potassium in the body or a relative reduction of potassium in the blood due to the redistribution of potassium. An absolute loss of potassium can arise from decreased intake, frequently related to starvation. It can also come about from vomiting, diarrhea, or alkalosis.

Some insulin-dependent diabetic patients experience a relative reduction of potassium in the blood from the redistribution of potassium. When insulin is administered and glucose is taken up by cells, potassium passes through the cell membrane along with glucose, decreasing the amount of potassium in the blood and IF, which can cause hyperpolarization of the cell membranes of neurons, reducing their responses to stimuli.

Hyperkalemia, an elevated potassium blood level, also can impair the function of skeletal muscles, the nervous system, and the heart. Hyperkalemia can result from increased dietary intake of potassium. In such a situation, potassium from the blood ends up in the ECF in abnormally high concentrations. This can result in a partial depolarization (excitation) of the plasma membrane of skeletal muscle fibers, neurons, and cardiac cells of the heart, and can also lead to an inability of cells to repolarize. For the heart, this means that it won't relax after a contraction, and will effectively "seize" and stop pumping blood, which is fatal within minutes. Because of such effects on the nervous system, a person with hyperkalemia may also exhibit mental confusion, numbness, and weakened respiratory muscles.

Chloride

Chloride is the predominant extracellular anion. Chloride is a major contributor to the osmotic pressure gradient between the ICF and ECF, and plays an important role in maintaining proper hydration. Chloride functions to balance cations in the ECF, maintaining the electrical neutrality of this fluid. The paths of secretion and reabsorption of chloride ions in the renal system follow the paths of sodium ions.

Hypochloremia, or lower-than-normal blood chloride levels, can occur because of defective renal tubular absorption. Vomiting, diarrhea, and metabolic acidosis can also lead to hypochloremia. **Hyperchloremia**, or higher-than-normal blood chloride levels, can occur due to dehydration, excessive intake of dietary salt (NaCl) or swallowing of sea water, aspirin intoxication, congestive heart failure, and the hereditary, chronic lung disease, cystic fibrosis. In people who have cystic fibrosis, chloride levels in sweat are two to five times those of normal levels, and analysis of sweat is often used in the diagnosis of the disease.

Watch this video (http://openstaxcollege.org/l/saltwater) to see an explanation of the effect of seawater on humans. What effect does drinking seawater have on the body?

Bicarbonate

Bicarbonate is the second most abundant anion in the blood. Its principal function is to maintain your body's acid-base balance by being part of buffer systems. This role will be discussed in a different section.

Bicarbonate ions result from a chemical reaction that starts with carbon dioxide (CO_2) and water, two molecules that are produced at the end of aerobic metabolism. Only a small amount of CO_2 can be dissolved in body fluids. Thus, over 90 percent of the CO_2 is converted into bicarbonate ions, HCO_3^-, through the following reactions:

$$CO_2 + H_2O \leftrightarrow H_2CO_3 \leftrightarrow H_2CO_3^- + H^+$$

The bidirectional arrows indicate that the reactions can go in either direction, depending on the concentrations of the reactants and products. Carbon dioxide is produced in large amounts in tissues that have a high metabolic rate. Carbon dioxide is converted into bicarbonate in the cytoplasm of red blood cells through the action of an enzyme called carbonic anhydrase. Bicarbonate is transported in the blood. Once in the lungs, the reactions reverse direction, and CO_2 is regenerated from bicarbonate to be exhaled as metabolic waste.

Calcium

About two pounds of calcium in your body are bound up in bone, which provides hardness to the bone and serves as a mineral reserve for calcium and its salts for the rest of the tissues. Teeth also have a high concentration of calcium within them. A little more than one-half of blood calcium is bound to proteins, leaving the rest in its ionized form. Calcium ions, Ca^{2+}, are necessary for muscle contraction, enzyme activity, and blood coagulation. In addition, calcium helps to stabilize cell membranes and is essential for the release of neurotransmitters from neurons and of hormones from endocrine glands.

Calcium is absorbed through the intestines under the influence of activated vitamin D. A deficiency of vitamin D leads to a decrease in absorbed calcium and, eventually, a depletion of calcium stores from the skeletal system, potentially leading to rickets in children and osteomalacia in adults, contributing to osteoporosis.

Hypocalcemia, or abnormally low calcium blood levels, is seen in hypoparathyroidism, which may follow the removal of the thyroid gland, because the four nodules of the parathyroid gland are embedded in it. **Hypercalcemia**, or abnormally high calcium blood levels, is seen in primary hyperparathyroidism. Some malignancies may also result in hypercalcemia.

Phosphate

Phosphate is present in the body in three ionic forms: $H_2PO_4^-$, HPO_4^{2-}, and PO_4^{3-}. The most common form is HPO_4^{2-}. Bone and teeth bind up 85 percent of the body's phosphate as part of calcium-phosphate salts. Phosphate is found in phospholipids, such as those that make up the cell membrane, and in ATP, nucleotides, and buffers.

Hypophosphatemia, or abnormally low phosphate blood levels, occurs with heavy use of antacids, during alcohol withdrawal, and during malnourishment. In the face of phosphate depletion, the kidneys usually conserve phosphate, but during starvation, this conservation is impaired greatly. **Hyperphosphatemia**, or abnormally increased levels of phosphates in the blood, occurs if there is decreased renal function or in cases of acute lymphocytic leukemia. Additionally, because phosphate is a major constituent of the ICF, any significant destruction of cells can result in dumping of phosphate into the ECF.

Regulation of Sodium and Potassium

Sodium is reabsorbed from the renal filtrate, and potassium is excreted into the filtrate in the renal collecting tubule. The control of this exchange is governed principally by two hormones—aldosterone and angiotensin II.

Aldosterone

Recall that aldosterone increases the excretion of potassium and the reabsorption of sodium in the distal tubule. Aldosterone is released if blood levels of potassium increase, if blood levels of sodium severely decrease, or if blood pressure decreases. Its net effect is to conserve and increase water levels in the plasma by reducing the excretion of sodium, and thus water, from the kidneys. In a negative feedback loop, increased osmolality of the ECF (which follows aldosterone-stimulated sodium absorption) inhibits the release of the hormone (Figure 26.13).

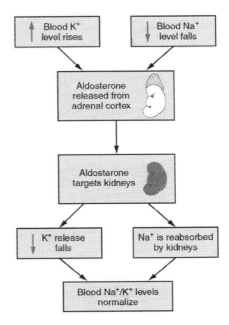

Figure 26.13 The Aldosterone Feedback Loop Aldosterone, which is released by the adrenal gland, facilitates reabsorption of Na^+ and thus the reabsorption of water.

Angiotensin II

Angiotensin II causes vasoconstriction and an increase in systemic blood pressure. This action increases the glomerular filtration rate, resulting in more material filtered out of the glomerular capillaries and into Bowman's capsule. Angiotensin II also signals an increase in the release of aldosterone from the adrenal cortex.

In the distal convoluted tubules and collecting ducts of the kidneys, aldosterone stimulates the synthesis and activation of the sodium-potassium pump (Figure 26.14). Sodium passes from the filtrate, into and through the cells of the tubules and ducts, into the ECF and then into capillaries. Water follows the sodium due to osmosis. Thus, aldosterone causes an increase in blood sodium levels and blood volume. Aldosterone's effect on potassium is the reverse of that of sodium; under its influence, excess potassium is pumped into the renal filtrate for excretion from the body.

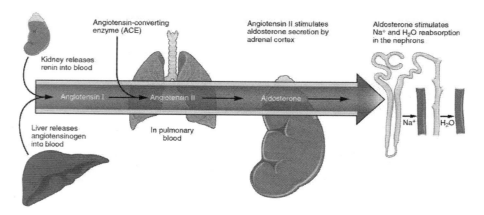

Figure 26.14 The Renin-Angiotensin System Angiotensin II stimulates the release of aldosterone from the adrenal cortex.

Regulation of Calcium and Phosphate

Calcium and phosphate are both regulated through the actions of three hormones: parathyroid hormone (PTH), dihydroxyvitamin D (calcitriol), and calcitonin. All three are released or synthesized in response to the blood levels of calcium.

PTH is released from the parathyroid gland in response to a decrease in the concentration of blood calcium. The hormone activates osteoclasts to break down bone matrix and release inorganic calcium-phosphate salts. PTH also increases the gastrointestinal absorption of dietary calcium by converting vitamin D into **dihydroxyvitamin D** (calcitriol), an active form of vitamin D that intestinal epithelial cells require to absorb calcium.

PTH raises blood calcium levels by inhibiting the loss of calcium through the kidneys. PTH also increases the loss of phosphate through the kidneys.

Calcitonin is released from the thyroid gland in response to elevated blood levels of calcium. The hormone increases the activity of osteoblasts, which remove calcium from the blood and incorporate calcium into the bony matrix.

26.4 | Acid-Base Balance

By the end of this section, you will be able to:
- Identify the most powerful buffer system in the body
- Explain the way in which the respiratory system affects blood pH

Proper physiological functioning depends on a very tight balance between the concentrations of acids and bases in the blood. Acid-balance balance is measured using the pH scale, as shown in Figure 26.15. A variety of buffering systems permits blood and other bodily fluids to maintain a narrow pH range, even in the face of perturbations. A buffer is a chemical system that prevents a radical change in fluid pH by dampening the change in hydrogen ion concentrations in the case of excess acid or base. Most commonly, the substance that absorbs the ions is either a weak acid, which takes up hydroxyl ions, or a weak base, which takes up hydrogen ions.

pH	Examples of solutions
0	Battery acid, strong hydrofluoric acid
1	Hydrochloric acid secreted by stomach lining
2	Lemon juice, gastric acid, vinegar
3	Grapefruit juice, orange juice, soda
4	Tomato juice, acid rain
5	Soft drinking water, black coffee
6	Urine, saliva
7	"Pure" water
8	Sea water
9	Baking soda
10	Great Salt Lake, milk of magnesia
11	Ammonia solution
12	Soapy water
13	Bleach, oven cleaner
14	Liquid drain cleaner

Figure 26.15 The pH Scale This chart shows where many common substances fall on the pH scale.

Buffer Systems in the Body

The buffer systems in the human body are extremely efficient, and different systems work at different rates. It takes only seconds for the chemical buffers in the blood to make adjustments to pH. The respiratory tract can adjust the blood pH upward in minutes by exhaling CO_2 from the body. The renal system can also adjust blood pH through the excretion of hydrogen ions (H^+) and the conservation of bicarbonate, but this process takes hours to days to have an effect.

The buffer systems functioning in blood plasma include plasma proteins, phosphate, and bicarbonate and carbonic acid buffers. The kidneys help control acid-base balance by excreting hydrogen ions and generating bicarbonate that helps maintain blood plasma pH within a normal range. Protein buffer systems work predominantly inside cells.

Protein Buffers in Blood Plasma and Cells

Nearly all proteins can function as buffers. Proteins are made up of amino acids, which contain positively charged amino groups and negatively charged carboxyl groups. The charged regions of these molecules can bind hydrogen and hydroxyl ions, and thus function as buffers. Buffering by proteins accounts for two-thirds of the buffering power of the blood and most of the buffering within cells.

Hemoglobin as a Buffer

Hemoglobin is the principal protein inside of red blood cells and accounts for one-third of the mass of the cell. During the conversion of CO_2 into bicarbonate, hydrogen ions liberated in the reaction are buffered by hemoglobin, which is reduced by the dissociation of oxygen. This buffering helps maintain normal pH. The process is reversed in the pulmonary capillaries to re-form CO_2, which then can diffuse into the air sacs to be exhaled into the atmosphere. This process is discussed in detail in the chapter on the respiratory system.

Phosphate Buffer

Phosphates are found in the blood in two forms: sodium dihydrogen phosphate ($Na_2H_2PO_4^-$), which is a weak acid, and sodium monohydrogen phosphate ($Na_2HPO_4^{2-}$), which is a weak base. When $Na_2HPO_4^{2-}$ comes into contact with a strong acid, such as HCl, the base picks up a second hydrogen ion to form the weak acid $Na_2H_2PO_4^-$ and sodium chloride, NaCl. When $Na_2HPO_4^{2-}$ (the weak acid) comes into contact with a strong base, such as sodium hydroxide (NaOH), the weak acid reverts back to the weak base and produces water. Acids and bases are still present, but they hold onto the ions.

$$HCl + Na_2HPO_4 \rightarrow NaH_2PO_4 + NaCl$$
(strong acid) + (weak base) → (weak acid) + (salt)

$$NaOH + NaH_2PO_4 \rightarrow Na_2HPO_4 + H_2O$$
(strong base) + (weak acid) → (weak base) + (water)

Bicarbonate-Carbonic Acid Buffer

The bicarbonate-carbonic acid buffer works in a fashion similar to phosphate buffers. The bicarbonate is regulated in the blood by sodium, as are the phosphate ions. When sodium bicarbonate ($NaHCO_3$), comes into contact with a strong acid, such as HCl, carbonic acid (H_2CO_3), which is a weak acid, and NaCl are formed. When carbonic acid comes into contact with a strong base, such as NaOH, bicarbonate and water are formed.

$$NaHCO_3 + HCl \rightarrow H_2CO_3 + NaCl$$
(sodium bicarbonate) + (strong acid) → (weak acid) + (salt)

$$H_2CO_3 + NaOH \rightarrow HCO_3^- + H_2O$$
(weak acid) + (strong base) → (bicarbonate) + (water)

As with the phosphate buffer, a weak acid or weak base captures the free ions, and a significant change in pH is prevented. Bicarbonate ions and carbonic acid are present in the blood in a 20:1 ratio if the blood pH is within the normal range. With 20 times more bicarbonate than carbonic acid, this capture system is most efficient at buffering changes that would make the blood more acidic. This is useful because most of the body's metabolic wastes, such as lactic acid and ketones, are acids. Carbonic acid levels in the blood are controlled by the expiration of CO_2 through the lungs. In red blood cells, carbonic anhydrase forces the dissociation of the acid, rendering the blood less acidic. Because of this acid dissociation, CO_2 is exhaled (see equations above). The level of bicarbonate in the blood is controlled through the renal system, where bicarbonate ions in the renal filtrate are conserved and passed back into the blood. However, the bicarbonate buffer is the primary buffering system of the IF surrounding the cells in tissues throughout the body.

Respiratory Regulation of Acid-Base Balance

The respiratory system contributes to the balance of acids and bases in the body by regulating the blood levels of carbonic acid (Figure 26.16). CO_2 in the blood readily reacts with water to form carbonic acid, and the levels of CO_2 and carbonic acid in the blood are in equilibrium. When the CO_2 level in the blood rises (as it does when you hold your breath), the excess CO_2 reacts with water to form additional carbonic acid, lowering blood pH. Increasing the rate and/or depth of respiration (which you might feel the "urge" to do after holding your breath) allows you to exhale more CO_2. The loss of CO_2 from the body reduces blood levels of carbonic acid and thereby adjusts the pH upward, toward normal levels. As you might have surmised, this process also works in the opposite direction. Excessive deep and rapid breathing (as in hyperventilation) rids the blood of CO_2 and reduces the level of carbonic acid, making the blood too alkaline. This brief alkalosis can be remedied by rebreathing air that has been exhaled into a paper bag. Rebreathing exhaled air will rapidly bring blood pH down toward normal.

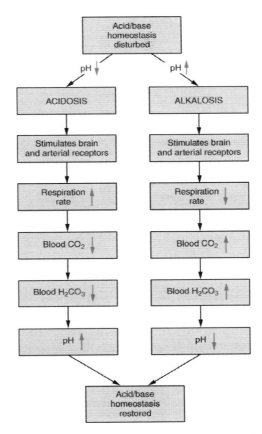

Figure 26.16 Respiratory Regulation of Blood pH The respiratory system can reduce blood pH by removing CO_2 from the blood.

The chemical reactions that regulate the levels of CO_2 and carbonic acid occur in the lungs when blood travels through the lung's pulmonary capillaries. Minor adjustments in breathing are usually sufficient to adjust the pH of the blood by changing how much CO_2 is exhaled. In fact, doubling the respiratory rate for less than 1 minute, removing "extra" CO_2, would increase the blood pH by 0.2. This situation is common if you are exercising strenuously over a period of time. To keep up the necessary energy production, you would produce excess CO_2 (and lactic acid if exercising beyond your aerobic threshold). In order to balance the increased acid production, the respiration rate goes up to remove the CO_2. This helps to keep you from developing acidosis.

The body regulates the respiratory rate by the use of chemoreceptors, which primarily use CO_2 as a signal. Peripheral blood sensors are found in the walls of the aorta and carotid arteries. These sensors signal the brain to provide immediate adjustments to the respiratory rate if CO_2 levels rise or fall. Yet other sensors are found in the brain itself. Changes in the pH of CSF affect the respiratory center in the medulla oblongata, which can directly modulate breathing rate to bring the pH back into the normal range.

Hypercapnia, or abnormally elevated blood levels of CO_2, occurs in any situation that impairs respiratory functions, including pneumonia and congestive heart failure. Reduced breathing (hypoventilation) due to drugs such as morphine, barbiturates, or ethanol (or even just holding one's breath) can also result in hypercapnia. **Hypocapnia**, or abnormally low blood levels of CO_2, occurs with any cause of hyperventilation that drives off the CO_2, such as salicylate toxicity, elevated room temperatures, fever, or hysteria.

Renal Regulation of Acid-Base Balance

The renal regulation of the body's acid-base balance addresses the metabolic component of the buffering system. Whereas the respiratory system (together with breathing centers in the brain) controls the blood levels of carbonic acid by controlling the exhalation of CO_2, the renal system controls the blood levels of bicarbonate. A decrease of blood bicarbonate can result from the inhibition of carbonic anhydrase by certain diuretics or from excessive bicarbonate loss due to diarrhea. Blood bicarbonate levels are also typically lower in people who have Addison's disease (chronic adrenal insufficiency), in which aldosterone levels are reduced, and in people who have renal damage, such as chronic nephritis. Finally, low bicarbonate blood levels can result from elevated levels of ketones (common in unmanaged diabetes mellitus), which bind bicarbonate in the filtrate and prevent its conservation.

Bicarbonate ions, HCO_3^-, found in the filtrate, are essential to the bicarbonate buffer system, yet the cells of the tubule are not permeable to bicarbonate ions. The steps involved in supplying bicarbonate ions to the system are seen in Figure 26.17 and are summarized below:

- Step 1: Sodium ions are reabsorbed from the filtrate in exchange for H^+ by an antiport mechanism in the apical membranes of cells lining the renal tubule.
- Step 2: The cells produce bicarbonate ions that can be shunted to peritubular capillaries.
- Step 3: When CO_2 is available, the reaction is driven to the formation of carbonic acid, which dissociates to form a bicarbonate ion and a hydrogen ion.
- Step 4: The bicarbonate ion passes into the peritubular capillaries and returns to the blood. The hydrogen ion is secreted into the filtrate, where it can become part of new water molecules and be reabsorbed as such, or removed in the urine.

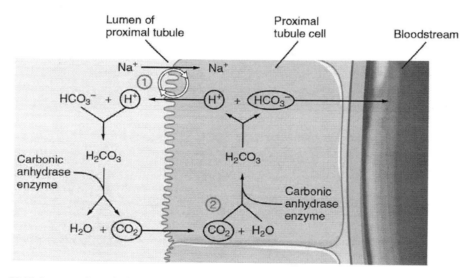

Figure 26.17 **Conservation of Bicarbonate in the Kidney** Tubular cells are not permeable to bicarbonate; thus, bicarbonate is conserved rather than reabsorbed. Steps 1 and 2 of bicarbonate conservation are indicated.

It is also possible that salts in the filtrate, such as sulfates, phosphates, or ammonia, will capture hydrogen ions. If this occurs, the hydrogen ions will not be available to combine with bicarbonate ions and produce CO_2. In such cases, bicarbonate ions are not conserved from the filtrate to the blood, which will also contribute to a pH imbalance and acidosis.

The hydrogen ions also compete with potassium to exchange with sodium in the renal tubules. If more potassium is present than normal, potassium, rather than the hydrogen ions, will be exchanged, and increased potassium enters the filtrate. When this occurs, fewer hydrogen ions in the filtrate participate in the conversion of bicarbonate into CO_2 and less bicarbonate is conserved. If there is less potassium, more hydrogen ions enter the filtrate to be exchanged with sodium and more bicarbonate is conserved.

Chloride ions are important in neutralizing positive ion charges in the body. If chloride is lost, the body uses bicarbonate ions in place of the lost chloride ions. Thus, lost chloride results in an increased reabsorption of bicarbonate by the renal system.

Acid-Base Balance: Ketoacidosis

Diabetic acidosis, or ketoacidosis, occurs most frequently in people with poorly controlled diabetes mellitus. When certain tissues in the body cannot get adequate amounts of glucose, they depend on the breakdown of fatty acids for energy. When acetyl groups break off the fatty acid chains, the acetyl groups then non-enzymatically combine to form ketone bodies, acetoacetic acid, beta-hydroxybutyric acid, and acetone, all of which increase the acidity of the blood. In this condition, the brain isn't supplied with enough of its fuel—glucose—to produce all of the ATP it requires to function.

Ketoacidosis can be severe and, if not detected and treated properly, can lead to diabetic coma, which can be fatal. A common early symptom of ketoacidosis is deep, rapid breathing as the body attempts to drive off CO_2 and compensate for the acidosis. Another common symptom is fruity-smelling breath, due to the exhalation of acetone. Other symptoms include dry skin and mouth, a flushed face, nausea, vomiting, and stomach pain. Treatment for diabetic coma is ingestion or injection of sugar; its prevention is the proper daily administration of insulin.

A person who is diabetic and uses insulin can initiate ketoacidosis if a dose of insulin is missed. Among people with type 2 diabetes, those of Hispanic and African-American descent are more likely to go into ketoacidosis than those of other ethnic backgrounds, although the reason for this is unknown.

26.5 | Disorders of Acid-Base Balance

By the end of this section, you will be able to:
- Identify the three blood variables considered when making a diagnosis of acidosis or alkalosis
- Identify the source of compensation for blood pH problems of a respiratory origin
- Identify the source of compensation for blood pH problems of a metabolic/renal origin

Normal arterial blood pH is restricted to a very narrow range of 7.35 to 7.45. A person who has a blood pH below 7.35 is considered to be in acidosis (actually, "physiological acidosis," because blood is not truly acidic until its pH drops below 7), and a continuous blood pH below 7.0 can be fatal. Acidosis has several symptoms, including headache and confusion, and the individual can become lethargic and easily fatigued (Figure 26.18). A person who has a blood pH above 7.45 is considered to be in alkalosis, and a pH above 7.8 is fatal. Some symptoms of alkalosis include cognitive impairment (which can progress to unconsciousness), tingling or numbness in the extremities, muscle twitching and spasm, and nausea and vomiting. Both acidosis and alkalosis can be caused by either metabolic or respiratory disorders.

As discussed earlier in this chapter, the concentration of carbonic acid in the blood is dependent on the level of CO_2 in the body and the amount of CO_2 gas exhaled through the lungs. Thus, the respiratory contribution to acid-base balance is usually discussed in terms of CO_2 (rather than of carbonic acid). Remember that a molecule of carbonic acid is lost for every molecule of CO_2 exhaled, and a molecule of carbonic acid is formed for every molecule of CO_2 retained.

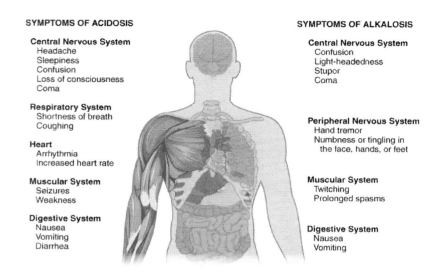

Figure 26.18 Symptoms of Acidosis and Alkalosis Symptoms of acidosis affect several organ systems. Both acidosis and alkalosis can be diagnosed using a blood test.

Metabolic Acidosis: Primary Bicarbonate Deficiency

Metabolic acidosis occurs when the blood is too acidic (pH below 7.35) due to too little bicarbonate, a condition called primary bicarbonate deficiency. At the normal pH of 7.40, the ratio of bicarbonate to carbonic acid buffer is 20:1. If a person's blood pH drops below 7.35, then he or she is in metabolic acidosis. The most common cause of metabolic acidosis is the presence of organic acids or excessive ketones in the blood. Table 26.2 lists some other causes of metabolic acidosis.

Common Causes of Metabolic Acidosis and Blood Metabolites

Cause	Metabolite
Diarrhea	Bicarbonate
Uremia	Phosphoric, sulfuric, and lactic acids
Diabetic ketoacidosis	Increased ketones
Strenuous exercise	Lactic acid
Methanol	Formic acid*
Paraldehyde	β-Hydroxybutyric acid*
Isopropanol	Propionic acid*
Ethylene glycol	Glycolic acid, and some oxalic and formic acids*
Salicylate/aspirin	Sulfasalicylic acid (SSA)*

Table 26.2 *Acid metabolites from ingested chemical.

The first three of the eight causes of metabolic acidosis listed are medical (or unusual physiological) conditions. Strenuous exercise can cause temporary metabolic acidosis due to the production of lactic acid. The last five causes result from the ingestion of specific substances. The active form of aspirin is its metabolite, sulfasalicylic acid. An overdose of aspirin causes acidosis due to the acidity of this metabolite. Metabolic acidosis can also result from uremia, which is the retention of urea and uric acid. Metabolic acidosis can also arise from diabetic ketoacidosis, wherein an excess of ketones is present in the blood. Other causes of metabolic acidosis are a decrease in the excretion of hydrogen ions, which inhibits the conservation of bicarbonate ions, and excessive loss of bicarbonate ions through the gastrointestinal tract due to diarrhea.

Metabolic Alkalosis: Primary Bicarbonate Excess

Metabolic alkalosis is the opposite of metabolic acidosis. It occurs when the blood is too alkaline (pH above 7.45) due to too much bicarbonate (called primary bicarbonate excess).

A transient excess of bicarbonate in the blood can follow ingestion of excessive amounts of bicarbonate, citrate, or antacids for conditions such as stomach acid reflux—known as heartburn. Cushing's disease, which is the chronic hypersecretion of adrenocorticotrophic hormone (ACTH) by the anterior pituitary gland, can cause chronic metabolic alkalosis. The oversecretion of ACTH results in elevated aldosterone levels and an increased loss of potassium by urinary excretion. Other causes of metabolic alkalosis include the loss of hydrochloric acid from the stomach through vomiting, potassium depletion due to the use of diuretics for hypertension, and the excessive use of laxatives.

Respiratory Acidosis: Primary Carbonic Acid/CO_2 Excess

Respiratory acidosis occurs when the blood is overly acidic due to an excess of carbonic acid, resulting from too much CO_2 in the blood. Respiratory acidosis can result from anything that interferes with respiration, such as pneumonia, emphysema, or congestive heart failure.

Respiratory Alkalosis: Primary Carbonic Acid/CO_2 Deficiency

Respiratory alkalosis occurs when the blood is overly alkaline due to a deficiency in carbonic acid and CO_2 levels in the blood. This condition usually occurs when too much CO_2 is exhaled from the lungs, as occurs in hyperventilation, which is breathing that is deeper or more frequent than normal. An elevated respiratory rate leading to hyperventilation can be due to extreme emotional upset or fear, fever, infections, hypoxia, or abnormally high levels of catecholamines, such as epinephrine and norepinephrine. Surprisingly, aspirin overdose—salicylate toxicity—can result in respiratory alkalosis as the body tries to compensate for initial acidosis.

Watch this video (http://openstaxcollege.org/l/altitude) to see a demonstration of the effect altitude has on blood pH. What effect does high altitude have on blood pH, and why?

Compensation Mechanisms

Various compensatory mechanisms exist to maintain blood pH within a narrow range, including buffers, respiration, and renal mechanisms. Although compensatory mechanisms usually work very well, when one of these mechanisms is not working properly (like kidney failure or respiratory disease), they have their limits. If the pH and bicarbonate to carbonic acid ratio are changed too drastically, the body may not be able to compensate. Moreover, extreme changes in pH can denature proteins. Extensive damage to proteins in this way can result in disruption of normal metabolic processes, serious tissue damage, and ultimately death.

Respiratory Compensation

Respiratory compensation for metabolic acidosis increases the respiratory rate to drive off CO_2 and readjust the bicarbonate to carbonic acid ratio to the 20:1 level. This adjustment can occur within minutes. Respiratory compensation for metabolic alkalosis is not as adept as its compensation for acidosis. The normal response of the respiratory system to elevated pH is to increase the amount of CO_2 in the blood by decreasing the respiratory rate to conserve CO_2. There is a limit to the decrease in respiration, however, that the body can tolerate. Hence, the respiratory route is less efficient at compensating for metabolic alkalosis than for acidosis.

Metabolic Compensation

Metabolic and renal compensation for respiratory diseases that can create acidosis revolves around the conservation of bicarbonate ions. In cases of respiratory acidosis, the kidney increases the conservation of bicarbonate and secretion of H^+ through the exchange mechanism discussed earlier. These processes increase the concentration of bicarbonate in the blood, reestablishing the proper relative concentrations of bicarbonate and carbonic acid. In cases of respiratory alkalosis, the kidneys decrease the production of bicarbonate and reabsorb H^+ from the tubular fluid. These processes can be limited by the exchange of potassium by the renal cells, which use a K^+-H^+ exchange mechanism (antiporter).

Diagnosing Acidosis and Alkalosis

Lab tests for pH, CO_2 partial pressure (pCO_2), and HCO_3^- can identify acidosis and alkalosis, indicating whether the imbalance is respiratory or metabolic, and the extent to which compensatory mechanisms are working. The blood pH value, as shown in Table 26.3, indicates whether the blood is in acidosis, the normal range, or alkalosis. The pCO_2 and total HCO_3^- values aid in determining whether the condition is metabolic or respiratory, and whether the patient has been able to compensate for the problem. Table 26.3 lists the conditions and laboratory results that can be used to classify these conditions. Metabolic acid-base imbalances typically result from kidney disease, and the respiratory system usually responds to compensate.

Types of Acidosis and Alkalosis

	pH	pCO$_2$	Total HCO$_3^-$
Metabolic acidosis	↓	N, then ↓	↓
Respiratory acidosis	↓	↑	N, then ↑
Metabolic alkalosis	↑	N, then ↑	↑
Respiratory alkalosis	↑	↓	N, then ↓

Table 26.3 Reference values (arterial): pH: 7.35–7.45; pCO$_2$: male: 35–48 mm Hg, female: 32–45 mm Hg; total venous bicarbonate: 22–29 mM. N denotes normal; ↑ denotes a rising or increased value; and ↓ denotes a falling or decreased value.

Metabolic acidosis is problematic, as lower-than-normal amounts of bicarbonate are present in the blood. The pCO_2 would be normal at first, but if compensation has occurred, it would decrease as the body reestablishes the proper ratio of bicarbonate and carbonic acid/CO_2.

Respiratory acidosis is problematic, as excess CO_2 is present in the blood. Bicarbonate levels would be normal at first, but if compensation has occurred, they would increase in an attempt to reestablish the proper ratio of bicarbonate and carbonic acid/CO_2.

Alkalosis is characterized by a higher-than-normal pH. Metabolic alkalosis is problematic, as elevated pH and excess bicarbonate are present. The pCO_2 would again be normal at first, but if compensation has occurred, it would increase as the body attempts to reestablish the proper ratios of bicarbonate and carbonic acid/CO_2.

Respiratory alkalosis is problematic, as CO_2 deficiency is present in the bloodstream. The bicarbonate concentration would be normal at first. When renal compensation occurs, however, the bicarbonate concentration in blood decreases as the kidneys attempt to reestablish the proper ratios of bicarbonate and carbonic acid/CO_2 by eliminating more bicarbonate to bring the pH into the physiological range.

KEY TERMS

antidiuretic hormone (ADH) also known as vasopressin, a hormone that increases the volume of water reabsorbed from the collecting tubules of the kidney

dehydration state of containing insufficient water in blood and other tissues

dihydroxyvitamin D active form of vitamin D required by the intestinal epithelial cells for the absorption of calcium

diuresis excess production of urine

extracellular fluid (ECF) fluid exterior to cells; includes the interstitial fluid, blood plasma, and fluids found in other reservoirs in the body

fluid compartment fluid inside all cells of the body constitutes a compartment system that is largely segregated from other systems

hydrostatic pressure pressure exerted by a fluid against a wall, caused by its own weight or pumping force

hypercalcemia abnormally increased blood levels of calcium

hypercapnia abnormally elevated blood levels of CO_2

hyperchloremia higher-than-normal blood chloride levels

hyperkalemia higher-than-normal blood potassium levels

hypernatremia abnormal increase in blood sodium levels

hyperphosphatemia abnormally increased blood phosphate levels

hypocalcemia abnormally low blood levels of calcium

hypocapnia abnormally low blood levels of CO_2

hypochloremia lower-than-normal blood chloride levels

hypokalemia abnormally decreased blood levels of potassium

hyponatremia lower-than-normal levels of sodium in the blood

hypophosphatemia abnormally low blood phosphate levels

interstitial fluid (IF) fluid in the small spaces between cells not contained within blood vessels

intracellular fluid (ICF) fluid in the cytosol of cells

metabolic acidosis condition wherein a deficiency of bicarbonate causes the blood to be overly acidic

metabolic alkalosis condition wherein an excess of bicarbonate causes the blood to be overly alkaline

plasma osmolality ratio of solutes to a volume of solvent in the plasma; plasma osmolality reflects a person's state of hydration

respiratory acidosis condition wherein an excess of carbonic acid or CO_2 causes the blood to be overly acidic

respiratory alkalosis condition wherein a deficiency of carbonic acid/CO_2 levels causes the blood to be overly alkaline

CHAPTER REVIEW

26.1 Body Fluids and Fluid Compartments

Your body is mostly water. Body fluids are aqueous solutions with differing concentrations of materials, called solutes. An appropriate balance of water and solute concentrations must be maintained to ensure cellular functions. If the cytosol becomes too concentrated due to water loss, cell functions deteriorate. If the cytosol becomes too dilute due to water intake by cells, cell membranes can be damaged, and the cell can burst. Hydrostatic pressure is the force exerted by a fluid against a wall and causes movement of fluid between compartments. Fluid can also move between compartments along an osmotic gradient. Active transport processes require ATP to move some solutes against their concentration gradients between compartments. Passive transport of a molecule or ion depends on its ability to pass easily through the membrane, as well as the existence of a high to low concentration gradient.

26.2 Water Balance

Homeostasis requires that water intake and output be balanced. Most water intake comes through the digestive tract via liquids and food, but roughly 10 percent of water available to the body is generated at the end of aerobic respiration during cellular metabolism. Urine produced by the kidneys accounts for the largest amount of water leaving the body. The kidneys can adjust the concentration of the urine to reflect the body's water needs, conserving water if the body is dehydrated or making urine more dilute to expel excess water when necessary. ADH is a hormone that helps the body to retain water by increasing water reabsorption by the kidneys.

26.3 Electrolyte Balance

Electrolytes serve various purposes, such as helping to conduct electrical impulses along cell membranes in neurons and muscles, stabilizing enzyme structures, and releasing hormones from endocrine glands. The ions in plasma also contribute to the osmotic balance that controls the movement of water between cells and their environment. Imbalances of these ions can result in various problems in the body, and their concentrations are tightly regulated. Aldosterone and angiotensin II control the exchange of sodium and potassium between the renal filtrate and the renal collecting tubule. Calcium and phosphate are regulated by PTH, calcitrol, and calcitonin.

26.4 Acid-Base Balance

A variety of buffering systems exist in the body that helps maintain the pH of the blood and other fluids within a narrow range—between pH 7.35 and 7.45. A buffer is a substance that prevents a radical change in fluid pH by absorbing excess hydrogen or hydroxyl ions. Most commonly, the substance that absorbs the ion is either a weak acid, which takes up a hydroxyl ion (OH^-), or a weak base, which takes up a hydrogen ion (H^+). Several substances serve as buffers in the body, including cell and plasma proteins, hemoglobin, phosphates, bicarbonate ions, and carbonic acid. The bicarbonate buffer is the primary buffering system of the IF surrounding the cells in tissues throughout the body. The respiratory and renal systems also play major roles in acid-base homeostasis by removing CO_2 and hydrogen ions, respectively, from the body.

26.5 Disorders of Acid-Base Balance

Acidosis and alkalosis describe conditions in which a person's blood is, respectively, too acidic (pH below 7.35) and too alkaline (pH above 7.45). Each of these conditions can be caused either by metabolic problems related to bicarbonate levels or by respiratory problems related to carbonic acid and CO_2 levels. Several compensatory mechanisms allow the body to maintain a normal pH.

INTERACTIVE LINK QUESTIONS

1. Watch this video (http://openstaxcollege.org/l/bodyfluids) to learn more about body fluids, fluid compartments, and electrolytes. When blood volume decreases due to sweating, from what source is water taken in by the blood?

2. Watch this video (http://openstaxcollege.org/l/dynamicfluid) to see an explanation of the dynamics of fluid in the body's compartments. What happens in tissues when capillary blood pressure is less than osmotic pressure?

3. Watch this video (http://openstaxcollege.org/l/saltwater) to see an explanation of the effect of seawater on humans. What effect does drinking seawater have on the body?

4. Watch this video (http://openstaxcollege.org/l/altitude) to see a demonstration of the effect altitude has on blood pH. What effect does high altitude have on blood pH, and why?

REVIEW QUESTIONS

5. Solute contributes to the movement of water between cells and the surrounding medium by _____.
   a. osmotic pressure
   b. hydrostatic pressure
   c. Brownian movement
   d. random motion

6. A cation has a(n) _____ charge.
   a. neutral
   b. positive
   c. alternating
   d. negative

7. Interstitial fluid (IF) is _____.
   a. the fluid in the cytosol of the cells
   b. the fluid component of blood
   c. the fluid that bathes all of the body's cells except for blood cells
   d. the intracellular fluids found between membranes

8. The largest amount of water comes into the body via _____.
   a. metabolism
   b. foods
   c. liquids
   d. humidified air

9. The largest amount of water leaves the body via _____.
   a. the GI tract
   b. the skin as sweat
   c. expiration
   d. urine

10. Insensible water loss is water lost via _____.
   a. skin evaporation and in air from the lungs
   b. urine
   c. excessive sweating
   d. vomiting or diarrhea

11. How soon after drinking a large glass of water will a person start increasing their urine output?
   a. 5 minutes
   b. 30 minutes
   c. 1 hour
   d. 3 hours

12. Bone serves as a mineral reserve for which two ions?
   a. sodium and potassium
   b. calcium and phosphate
   c. chloride and bicarbonate
   d. calcium and bicarbonate

13. Electrolytes are lost mostly through _____.
   a. renal function
   b. sweating
   c. feces
   d. respiration

14. The major cation in extracellular fluid is _____.
   a. sodium
   b. potassium
   c. chloride
   d. bicarbonate

15. The major cation in intracellular fluid is _____.
   a. sodium
   b. potassium
   c. chloride
   d. bicarbonate

16. The major anion in extracellular fluid is _____.
   a. sodium
   b. potassium
   c. chloride
   d. bicarbonate

17. Most of the body's calcium is found in _____.
   a. teeth
   b. bone
   c. plasma
   d. extracellular fluids

18. Abnormally increased blood levels of sodium are termed _____.
   a. hyperkalemia
   b. hyperchloremia
   c. hypernatremia
   d. hypercalcemia

19. The ion with the lowest blood level is _____.
   a. sodium
   b. potassium
   c. chloride
   d. bicarbonate

20. Which two ions are most affected by aldosterone?
   a. sodium and potassium
   b. chloride and bicarbonate
   c. calcium and phosphate
   d. sodium and phosphate

21. Which of the following is the most important buffer inside red blood cells?
   a. plasma proteins
   b. hemoglobin
   c. phosphate buffers
   d. bicarbonate: carbonic acid buffer

22. Which explanation best describes why plasma proteins can function as buffers?
   a. Plasma proteins combine with bicarbonate to make a stronger buffer.

b. Plasma proteins are immune to damage from acids.
c. Proteins have both positive and negative charges on their surface.
d. Proteins are alkaline.

23. The buffer that is adjusted to control acid-base balance is _____.
a. plasma protein
b. hemoglobin
c. phosphate buffer
d. bicarbonate: carbonic acid buffer

24. Carbonic acid levels are controlled through the _____.
a. respiratory system
b. renal system
c. digestive system
d. metabolic rate of cells

25. Bicarbonate ion concentrations in the blood are controlled through the _____.
a. respiratory system
b. renal system
c. digestive system
d. metabolic rate of cells

26. Which reaction is catalyzed by carbonic anhydrase?
a. $HPO_4^{2-} + H^+ \leftrightarrow H_2PO_4^-$
b. $CO_2 + H_2O \leftrightarrow H_2CO_3$
c. $H_2PO_4^- + OH^- \leftrightarrow HPO_4^{2-} + H_2O$
d. $H_2CO_3 \leftrightarrow HCO_3^- + H^+$

27. Which of the following is a cause of metabolic acidosis?
a. excessive HCl loss
b. increased aldosterone
c. diarrhea
d. prolonged use of diuretics

28. Which of the following is a cause of respiratory acidosis?
a. emphysema
b. low blood K^+
c. increased aldosterone
d. increased blood ketones

29. At a pH of 7.40, the carbonic acid ratio is _____.
a. 35:1
b. 4:1
c. 20:1
d. 3:1

30. Which of the following is characterized as metabolic alkalosis?
a. increased pH, decreased pCO_2, decreased HCO_3^-
b. increased pH, increased pCO_2, increased HCO_3^-
c. decreased pH, decreased pCO_2, decreased HCO_3^-
d. decreased pH, increased pCO_2, increased HCO_3^-

CRITICAL THINKING QUESTIONS

31. Plasma contains more sodium than chloride. How can this be if individual ions of sodium and chloride exactly balance each other out, and plasma is electrically neutral?

32. How is fluid moved from compartment to compartment?

33. Describe the effect of ADH on renal collecting tubules.

34. Why is it important for the amount of water intake to equal the amount of water output?

35. Explain how the CO_2 generated by cells and exhaled in the lungs is carried as bicarbonate in the blood.

36. How can one have an imbalance in a substance, but not actually have elevated or deficient levels of that substance in the body?

37. Describe the conservation of bicarbonate ions in the renal system.

38. Describe the control of blood carbonic acid levels through the respiratory system.

39. Case Study: Bob is a 64-year-old male admitted to the emergency room for asthma. His laboratory results are as follows: pH 7.31, pCO_2 higher than normal, and total HCO_3^- also higher than normal. Classify his acid-base balance as acidosis or alkalosis, and as metabolic or respiratory. Is there evidence of compensation? Propose the mechanism by which asthma contributed to the lab results seen.

40. Case Study: Kim is a 38-year-old women admitted to the hospital for bulimia. Her laboratory results are as follows: pH 7.48, pCO_2 in the normal range, and total HCO_3^- higher than normal. Classify her acid-base balance as acidosis or alkalosis, and as metabolic or respiratory. Is there evidence of compensation? Propose the mechanism by which bulimia contributed to the lab results seen.

27 | THE REPRODUCTIVE SYSTEM

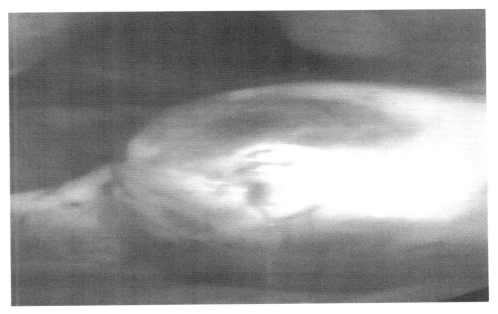

Figure 27.1 Ovulation Following a surge of luteinizing hormone (LH), an oocyte (immature egg cell) will be released into the uterine tube, where it will then be available to be fertilized by a male's sperm. Ovulation marks the end of the follicular phase of the ovarian cycle and the start of the luteal phase.

Introduction

Chapter Objectives

After studying this chapter, you will be able to:

- Describe the anatomy of the male and female reproductive systems, including their accessory structures
- Explain the role of hypothalamic and pituitary hormones in male and female reproductive function
- Trace the path of a sperm cell from its initial production through fertilization of an oocyte
- Explain the events in the ovary prior to ovulation
- Describe the development and maturation of the sex organs and the emergence of secondary sex characteristics during puberty

Small, uncoordinated, and slick with amniotic fluid, a newborn encounters the world outside of her mother's womb. We do not often consider that a child's birth is proof of the healthy functioning of both her mother's and father's reproductive systems. Moreover, her parents' endocrine systems had to secrete the appropriate regulating hormones to induce the production and release of unique male and female gametes, reproductive cells containing the parents' genetic material (one set of 23 chromosomes). Her parent's reproductive behavior had to facilitate the transfer of male gametes—the sperm—to the female reproductive tract at just the right time to encounter the female gamete, an oocyte (egg). Finally, combination of the gametes (fertilization) had to occur, followed by implantation and development. In this chapter, you will explore the male and female reproductive systems, whose healthy functioning can culminate in the powerful sound of a newborn's first cry.

27.1 | Anatomy and Physiology of the Male Reproductive System

By the end of this section, you will be able to:
- Describe the structure and function of the organs of the male reproductive system
- Describe the structure and function of the sperm cell
- Explain the events during spermatogenesis that produce haploid sperm from diploid cells
- Identify the importance of testosterone in male reproductive function

Unique for its role in human reproduction, a **gamete** is a specialized sex cell carrying 23 chromosomes—one half the number in body cells. At fertilization, the chromosomes in one male gamete, called a **sperm** (or spermatozoon), combine with the chromosomes in one female gamete, called an oocyte. The function of the male reproductive system (Figure 27.2) is to produce sperm and transfer them to the female reproductive tract. The paired testes are a crucial component in this process, as they produce both sperm and androgens, the hormones that support male reproductive physiology. In humans, the most important male androgen is testosterone. Several accessory organs and ducts aid the process of sperm maturation and transport the sperm and other seminal components to the penis, which delivers sperm to the female reproductive tract. In this section, we examine each of these different structures, and discuss the process of sperm production and transport.

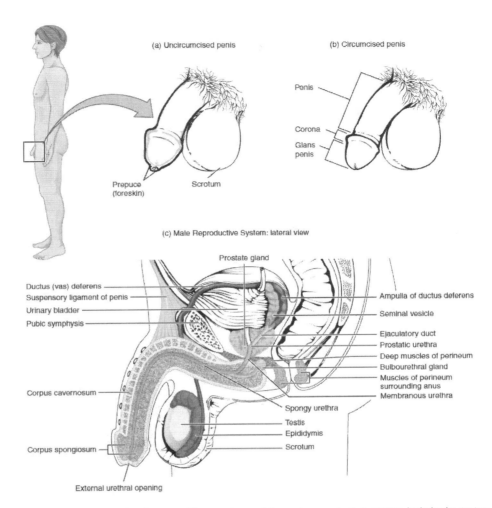

Figure 27.2 Male Reproductive System The structures of the male reproductive system include the testes, the epididymides, the penis, and the ducts and glands that produce and carry semen. Sperm exit the scrotum through the ductus deferens, which is bundled in the spermatic cord. The seminal vesicles and prostate gland add fluids to the sperm to create semen.

Scrotum

The testes are located in a skin-covered, highly pigmented, muscular sack called the **scrotum** that extends from the body behind the penis (see Figure 27.2). This location is important in sperm production, which occurs within the testes, and proceeds more efficiently when the testes are kept 2 to 4°C below core body temperature.

The dartos muscle makes up the subcutaneous muscle layer of the scrotum (Figure 27.3). It continues internally to make up the scrotal septum, a wall that divides the scrotum into two compartments, each housing one testis. Descending from the internal oblique muscle of the abdominal wall are the two cremaster muscles, which cover each testis like a muscular net. By contracting simultaneously, the dartos and cremaster muscles can elevate the testes in cold weather (or water), moving the testes closer to the body and decreasing the surface area of the scrotum to retain heat. Alternatively, as the environmental temperature increases, the scrotum relaxes, moving the testes farther from the body core and increasing scrotal surface area, which promotes heat loss. Externally, the scrotum has a raised medial thickening on the surface called the raphae.

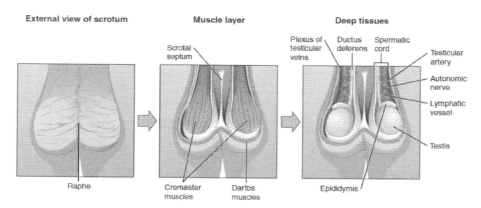

Figure 27.3 The Scrotum and Testes This anterior view shows the structures of the scrotum and testes.

Testes

The **testes** (singular = testis) are the male **gonads**—that is, the male reproductive organs. They produce both sperm and androgens, such as testosterone, and are active throughout the reproductive lifespan of the male.

Paired ovals, the testes are each approximately 4 to 5 cm in length and are housed within the scrotum (see Figure 27.3). They are surrounded by two distinct layers of protective connective tissue (Figure 27.4). The outer tunica vaginalis is a serous membrane that has both a parietal and a thin visceral layer. Beneath the tunica vaginalis is the tunica albuginea, a tough, white, dense connective tissue layer covering the testis itself. Not only does the tunica albuginea cover the outside of the testis, it also invaginates to form septa that divide the testis into 300 to 400 structures called lobules. Within the lobules, sperm develop in structures called seminiferous tubules. During the seventh month of the developmental period of a male fetus, each testis moves through the abdominal musculature to descend into the scrotal cavity. This is called the "descent of the testis." Cryptorchidism is the clinical term used when one or both of the testes fail to descend into the scrotum prior to birth.

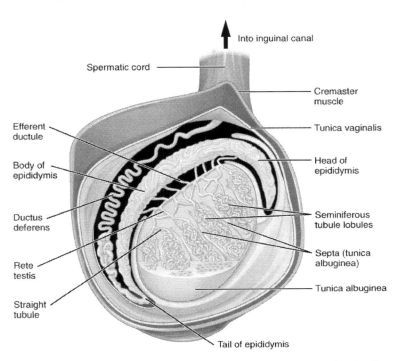

Figure 27.4 Anatomy of the Testis This sagittal view shows the seminiferous tubules, the site of sperm production. Formed sperm are transferred to the epididymis, where they mature. They leave the epididymis during an ejaculation via the ductus deferens.

The tightly coiled **seminiferous tubules** form the bulk of each testis. They are composed of developing sperm cells surrounding a lumen, the hollow center of the tubule, where formed sperm are released into the duct system of the testis. Specifically, from the lumens of the seminiferous tubules, sperm move into the straight tubules (or tubuli recti), and from there into a fine meshwork of tubules called the rete testes. Sperm leave the rete testes, and the testis itself, through the 15 to 20 efferent ductules that cross the tunica albuginea.

Inside the seminiferous tubules are six different cell types. These include supporting cells called sustentacular cells, as well as five types of developing sperm cells called germ cells. Germ cell development progresses from the basement membrane—at the perimeter of the tubule—toward the lumen. Let's look more closely at these cell types.

Sertoli Cells

Surrounding all stages of the developing sperm cells are elongate, branching **Sertoli cells**. Sertoli cells are a type of supporting cell called a sustentacular cell, or sustenocyte, that are typically found in epithelial tissue. Sertoli cells secrete signaling molecules that promote sperm production and can control whether germ cells live or die. They extend physically around the germ cells from the peripheral basement membrane of the seminiferous tubules to the lumen. Tight junctions between these sustentacular cells create the **blood–testis barrier**, which keeps bloodborne substances from reaching the germ cells and, at the same time, keeps surface antigens on developing germ cells from escaping into the bloodstream and prompting an autoimmune response.

Germ Cells

The least mature cells, the **spermatogonia** (singular = spermatogonium), line the basement membrane inside the tubule. Spermatogonia are the stem cells of the testis, which means that they are still able to differentiate into a variety of different cell types throughout adulthood. Spermatogonia divide to produce primary and secondary spermatocytes, then spermatids, which finally produce formed sperm. The process that begins with spermatogonia and concludes with the production of sperm is called **spermatogenesis**.

Spermatogenesis

As just noted, spermatogenesis occurs in the seminiferous tubules that form the bulk of each testis (see Figure 27.4). The process begins at puberty, after which time sperm are produced constantly throughout a man's life. One production cycle, from spermatogonia through formed sperm, takes approximately 64 days. A new cycle starts approximately every 16 days, although this timing is not synchronous across the seminiferous tubules. Sperm counts—the total number of sperm a man produces—slowly decline after age 35, and some studies suggest that smoking can lower sperm counts irrespective of age.

The process of spermatogenesis begins with mitosis of the diploid spermatogonia (Figure 27.5). Because these cells are diploid (2n), they each have a complete copy of the father's genetic material, or 46 chromosomes. However, mature gametes are haploid (1n), containing 23 chromosomes—meaning that daughter cells of spermatogonia must undergo a second cellular division through the process of meiosis.

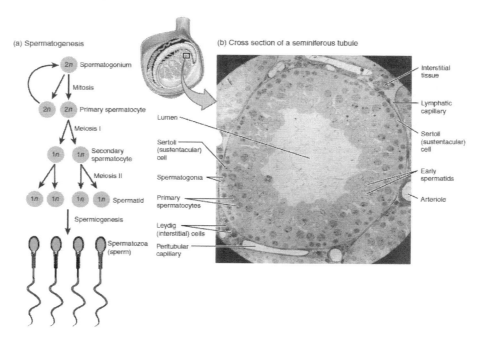

Figure 27.5 Spermatogenesis (a) Mitosis of a spermatogonial stem cell involves a single cell division that results in two identical, diploid daughter cells (spermatogonia to primary spermatocyte). Meiosis has two rounds of cell division: primary spermatocyte to secondary spermatocyte, and then secondary spermatocyte to spermatid. This produces four haploid daughter cells (spermatids). (b) In this electron micrograph of a cross-section of a seminiferous tubule from a rat, the lumen is the light-shaded area in the center of the image. The location of the primary spermatocytes is near the basement membrane, and the early spermatids are approaching the lumen (tissue source: rat). EM × 900. (Micrograph provided by the Regents of University of Michigan Medical School © 2012)

Two identical diploid cells result from spermatogonia mitosis. One of these cells remains a spermatogonium, and the other becomes a primary **spermatocyte**, the next stage in the process of spermatogenesis. As in mitosis, DNA is replicated in a primary spermatocyte, and the cell undergoes cell division to produce two cells with identical chromosomes. Each of these is a secondary spermatocyte. Now a second round of cell division occurs in both of the secondary spermatocytes, separating the chromosome pairs. This second meiotic division results in a total of four cells with only half of the number of chromosomes. Each of these new cells is a **spermatid**. Although haploid, early spermatids look very similar to cells in the earlier stages of spermatogenesis, with a round shape, central nucleus, and large amount of cytoplasm. A process called **spermiogenesis** transforms these early spermatids, reducing the cytoplasm, and beginning the formation of the parts of a true sperm. The fifth stage of germ cell formation—spermatozoa, or formed sperm—is the end result of this process, which occurs in the portion of the tubule nearest the lumen. Eventually, the sperm are released into the lumen and are moved along a series of ducts in the testis toward a structure called the epididymis for the next step of sperm maturation.

Structure of Formed Sperm

Sperm are smaller than most cells in the body; in fact, the volume of a sperm cell is 85,000 times less than that of the female gamete. Approximately 100 to 300 million sperm are produced each day, whereas women typically ovulate only one oocyte per month as is true for most cells in the body, the structure of sperm cells speaks to their function. Sperm have a distinctive head, mid-piece, and tail region (Figure 27.6). The head of the sperm contains the extremely compact haploid nucleus with very little cytoplasm. These qualities contribute to the overall small size of the sperm (the head is only 5 μm long). A structure called the acrosome covers most of the head of the sperm cell as a "cap" that is filled with lysosomal enzymes important for preparing sperm to participate in fertilization. Tightly packed mitochondria fill the mid-piece of the sperm. ATP produced by these mitochondria will power the flagellum, which extends from the neck and the mid-piece through the tail of the sperm, enabling it to move the entire sperm cell. The central strand of the flagellum, the axial filament, is formed from one centriole inside the maturing sperm cell during the final stages of spermatogenesis.

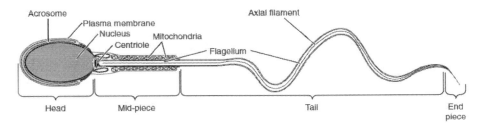

Figure 27.6 Structure of Sperm Sperm cells are divided into a head, containing DNA; a mid-piece, containing mitochondria; and a tail, providing motility. The acrosome is oval and somewhat flattened.

Sperm Transport

To fertilize an egg, sperm must be moved from the seminiferous tubules in the testes, through the epididymis, and—later during ejaculation—along the length of the penis and out into the female reproductive tract.

Role of the Epididymis

From the lumen of the seminiferous tubules, the immotile sperm are surrounded by testicular fluid and moved to the **epididymis** (plural = epididymides), a coiled tube attached to the testis where newly formed sperm continue to mature (see Figure 27.4). Though the epididymis does not take up much room in its tightly coiled state, it would be approximately 6 m (20 feet) long if straightened. It takes an average of 12 days for sperm to move through the coils of the epididymis, with the shortest recorded transit time in humans being one day. Sperm enter the head of the epididymis and are moved along predominantly by the contraction of smooth muscles lining the epididymal tubes. As they are moved along the length of the epididymis, the sperm further mature and acquire the ability to move under their own power. Once inside the female reproductive tract, they will use this ability to move independently toward the unfertilized egg. The more mature sperm are then stored in the tail of the epididymis (the final section) until ejaculation occurs.

Duct System

During ejaculation, sperm exit the tail of the epididymis and are pushed by smooth muscle contraction to the **ductus deferens** (also called the vas deferens). The ductus deferens is a thick, muscular tube that is bundled together inside the scrotum with connective tissue, blood vessels, and nerves into a structure called the **spermatic cord** (see Figure 27.2 and Figure 27.3). Because the ductus deferens is physically accessible within the scrotum, surgical sterilization to interrupt sperm delivery can be performed by cutting and sealing a small section of the ductus (vas) deferens. This procedure is called a vasectomy, and it is an effective form of male birth control. Although it may be possible to reverse a vasectomy, clinicians consider the procedure permanent, and advise men to undergo it only if they are certain they no longer wish to father children.

Interactive LINK

Watch this video (http://openstaxcollege.org/l/vasectomy) to learn about a vasectomy. As described in this video, a vasectomy is a procedure in which a small section of the ductus (vas) deferens is removed from the scrotum. This interrupts the path taken by sperm through the ductus deferens. If sperm do not exit through the vas, either because the man has had a vasectomy or has not ejaculated, in what region of the testis do they remain?

From each epididymis, each ductus deferens extends superiorly into the abdominal cavity through the **inguinal canal** in the abdominal wall. From here, the ductus deferens continues posteriorly to the pelvic cavity, ending posterior to the bladder where it dilates in a region called the ampulla (meaning "flask").

Sperm make up only 5 percent of the final volume of **semen**, the thick, milky fluid that the male ejaculates. The bulk of semen is produced by three critical accessory glands of the male reproductive system: the seminal vesicles, the prostate, and the bulbourethral glands.

Seminal Vesicles

As sperm pass through the ampulla of the ductus deferens at ejaculation, they mix with fluid from the associated **seminal vesicle** (see Figure 27.2). The paired seminal vesicles are glands that contribute approximately 60 percent of the semen volume. Seminal vesicle fluid contains large amounts of fructose, which is used by the sperm mitochondria to generate ATP to allow movement through the female reproductive tract.

The fluid, now containing both sperm and seminal vesicle secretions, next moves into the associated **ejaculatory duct**, a short structure formed from the ampulla of the ductus deferens and the duct of the seminal vesicle. The paired ejaculatory ducts transport the seminal fluid into the next structure, the prostate gland.

Prostate Gland

As shown in Figure 27.2, the centrally located **prostate gland** sits anterior to the rectum at the base of the bladder surrounding the prostatic urethra (the portion of the urethra that runs within the prostate). About the size of a walnut, the prostate is formed of both muscular and glandular tissues. It excretes an alkaline, milky fluid to the passing seminal fluid—now called semen—that is critical to first coagulate and then decoagulate the semen following ejaculation. The temporary thickening of semen helps retain it within the female reproductive tract, providing time for sperm to utilize the fructose provided by seminal vesicle secretions. When the semen regains its fluid state, sperm can then pass farther into the female reproductive tract.

The prostate normally doubles in size during puberty. At approximately age 25, it gradually begins to enlarge again. This enlargement does not usually cause problems; however, abnormal growth of the prostate, or benign prostatic hyperplasia (BPH), can cause constriction of the urethra as it passes through the middle of the prostate gland, leading to a number of lower urinary tract symptoms, such as a frequent and intense urge to urinate, a weak stream, and a sensation that the bladder has not emptied completely. By age 60, approximately 40 percent of men have some degree of BPH. By age 80, the number of affected individuals has jumped to as many as 80 percent. Treatments for BPH attempt to relieve the pressure on the urethra so that urine can flow more normally. Mild to moderate symptoms are treated with medication, whereas severe enlargement of the prostate is treated by surgery in which a portion of the prostate tissue is removed.

Another common disorder involving the prostate is prostate cancer. According to the Centers for Disease Control and Prevention (CDC), prostate cancer is the second most common cancer in men. However, some forms of prostate cancer grow very slowly and thus may not ever require treatment. Aggressive forms of prostate cancer, in contrast, involve metastasis to vulnerable organs like the lungs and brain. There is no link between BPH and prostate cancer, but the symptoms are similar. Prostate cancer is detected by a medical history, a blood test, and a rectal exam that allows physicians to palpate the prostate and check for unusual masses. If a mass is detected, the cancer diagnosis is confirmed by biopsy of the cells.

Bulbourethral Glands

The final addition to semen is made by two **bulbourethral glands** (or Cowper's glands) that release a thick, salty fluid that lubricates the end of the urethra and the vagina, and helps to clean urine residues from the penile urethra. The fluid from these accessory glands is released after the male becomes sexually aroused, and shortly before the release of the semen. It is therefore sometimes called pre-ejaculate. It is important to note that, in addition to the lubricating proteins, it is possible for bulbourethral fluid to pick up sperm already present in the urethra, and therefore it may be able to cause pregnancy.

Watch this video (http://openstaxcollege.org/l/spermpath) to explore the structures of the male reproductive system and the path of sperm, which starts in the testes and ends as the sperm leave the penis through the urethra. Where are sperm deposited after they leave the ejaculatory duct?

The Penis

The **penis** is the male organ of copulation (sexual intercourse). It is flaccid for non-sexual actions, such as urination, and turgid and rod-like with sexual arousal. When erect, the stiffness of the organ allows it to penetrate into the vagina and deposit semen into the female reproductive tract.

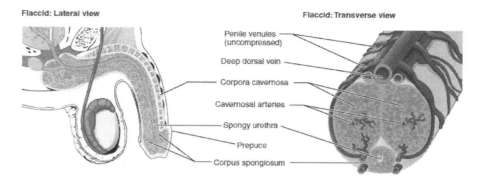

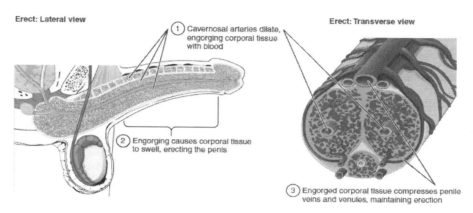

Figure 27.7 Cross-Sectional Anatomy of the Penis Three columns of erectile tissue make up most of the volume of the penis.

The shaft of the penis surrounds the urethra (Figure 27.7). The shaft is composed of three column-like chambers of erectile tissue that span the length of the shaft. Each of the two larger lateral chambers is called a **corpus cavernosum** (plural = corpora cavernosa). Together, these make up the bulk of the penis. The **corpus spongiosum**, which can be felt as a raised ridge on the erect penis, is a smaller chamber that surrounds the spongy, or penile, urethra. The end of the penis, called the **glans penis**, has a high concentration of nerve endings, resulting in very sensitive skin that influences the likelihood of ejaculation (see Figure 27.2). The skin from the shaft extends down over the glans and forms a collar called the **prepuce** (or foreskin). The foreskin also contains a dense concentration of nerve endings, and both lubricate and protect the sensitive skin of the glans penis. A surgical procedure called circumcision, often performed for religious or social reasons, removes the prepuce, typically within days of birth.

Both sexual arousal and REM sleep (during which dreaming occurs) can induce an erection. Penile erections are the result of vasocongestion, or engorgement of the tissues because of more arterial blood flowing into the penis than is leaving in the veins. During sexual arousal, nitric oxide (NO) is released from nerve endings near blood vessels within the corpora cavernosa and spongiosum. Release of NO activates a signaling pathway that results in relaxation of the smooth muscles that surround the penile arteries, causing them to dilate. This dilation increases the amount of blood that can enter the penis and induces the endothelial cells in the penile arterial walls to also secrete NO and perpetuate the vasodilation. The rapid increase in blood volume fills the erectile chambers, and the increased pressure of the filled chambers compresses the thin-walled penile venules, preventing venous drainage of the penis. The result of this increased blood flow to the penis and reduced blood return from the penis is erection. Depending on the flaccid dimensions of a penis, it can increase in size slightly or greatly during erection, with the average length of an erect penis measuring approximately 15 cm.

Male Reproductive System

Erectile dysfunction (ED) is a condition in which a man has difficulty either initiating or maintaining an erection. The combined prevalence of minimal, moderate, and complete ED is approximately 40 percent in men at age 40, and reaches nearly 70 percent by 70 years of age. In addition to aging, ED is associated with diabetes, vascular disease, psychiatric disorders, prostate disorders, the use of some drugs such as certain antidepressants, and problems with the testes resulting in low testosterone concentrations. These physical and emotional conditions can lead to interruptions in the vasodilation pathway and result in an inability to achieve an erection.

Recall that the release of NO induces relaxation of the smooth muscles that surround the penile arteries, leading to the vasodilation necessary to achieve an erection. To reverse the process of vasodilation, an enzyme called phosphodiesterase (PDE) degrades a key component of the NO signaling pathway called cGMP. There are several different forms of this enzyme, and PDE type 5 is the type of PDE found in the tissues of the penis. Scientists discovered that inhibiting PDE5 increases blood flow, and allows vasodilation of the penis to occur.

PDEs and the vasodilation signaling pathway are found in the vasculature in other parts of the body. In the 1990s, clinical trials of a PDE5 inhibitor called sildenafil were initiated to treat hypertension and angina pectoris (chest pain caused by poor blood flow through the heart). The trial showed that the drug was not effective at treating heart conditions, but many men experienced erection and priapism (erection lasting longer than 4 hours). Because of this, a clinical trial was started to investigate the ability of sildenafil to promote erections in men suffering from ED. In 1998, the FDA approved the drug, marketed as Viagra®. Since approval of the drug, sildenafil and similar PDE inhibitors now generate over a billion dollars a year in sales, and are reported to be effective in treating approximately 70 to 85 percent of cases of ED. Importantly, men with health problems—especially those with cardiac disease taking nitrates—should avoid Viagra or talk to their physician to find out if they are a candidate for the use of this drug, as deaths have been reported for at-risk users.

Testosterone

Testosterone, an androgen, is a steroid hormone produced by **Leydig cells**. The alternate term for Leydig cells, interstitial cells, reflects their location between the seminiferous tubules in the testes. In male embryos, testosterone is secreted by Leydig cells by the seventh week of development, with peak concentrations reached in the second trimester. This early release of testosterone results in the anatomical differentiation of the male sexual organs. In childhood, testosterone concentrations are low. They increase during puberty, activating characteristic physical changes and initiating spermatogenesis.

Functions of Testosterone

The continued presence of testosterone is necessary to keep the male reproductive system working properly, and Leydig cells produce approximately 6 to 7 mg of testosterone per day. Testicular steroidogenesis (the manufacture of androgens, including testosterone) results in testosterone concentrations that are 100 times higher in the testes than in the circulation. Maintaining these normal concentrations of testosterone promotes spermatogenesis, whereas low levels of testosterone can lead to infertility. In addition to intratesticular secretion, testosterone is also released into the systemic circulation and plays an important role in muscle development, bone growth, the development of secondary sex characteristics, and maintaining libido (sex drive) in both males and females. In females, the ovaries secrete small amounts of testosterone, although most is converted to estradiol. A small amount of testosterone is also secreted by the adrenal glands in both sexes.

Control of Testosterone

The regulation of testosterone concentrations throughout the body is critical for male reproductive function. The intricate interplay between the endocrine system and the reproductive system is shown in Figure 27.8.

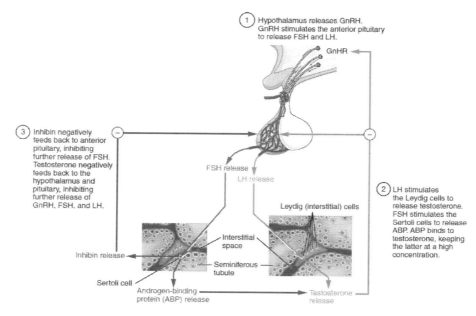

Figure 27.8 Regulation of Testosterone Production The hypothalamus and pituitary gland regulate the production of testosterone and the cells that assist in spermatogenesis. GnRH activates the anterior pituitary to produce LH and FSH, which in turn stimulate Leydig cells and Sertoli cells, respectively. The system is a negative feedback loop because the end products of the pathway, testosterone and inhibin, interact with the activity of GnRH to inhibit their own production.

The regulation of Leydig cell production of testosterone begins outside of the testes. The hypothalamus and the pituitary gland in the brain integrate external and internal signals to control testosterone synthesis and secretion. The regulation begins in the hypothalamus. Pulsatile release of a hormone called **gonadotropin-releasing hormone (GnRH)** from the hypothalamus stimulates the endocrine release of hormones from the pituitary gland. Binding of GnRH to its receptors on the anterior pituitary gland stimulates release of the two gonadotropins: luteinizing hormone (LH) and follicle-stimulating hormone (FSH). These two hormones are critical for reproductive function in both men and women. In men, FSH binds predominantly to the Sertoli cells within the seminiferous tubules to promote spermatogenesis. FSH also stimulates the Sertoli cells to produce hormones called inhibins, which function to inhibit FSH release from the pituitary, thus reducing testosterone secretion. These polypeptide hormones correlate directly with Sertoli cell function and sperm number; inhibin B can be used as a marker of spermatogenic activity. In men, LH binds to receptors on Leydig cells in the testes and upregulates the production of testosterone.

A negative feedback loop predominantly controls the synthesis and secretion of both FSH and LH. Low blood concentrations of testosterone stimulate the hypothalamic release of GnRH. GnRH then stimulates the anterior pituitary to secrete LH into the bloodstream. In the testis, LH binds to LH receptors on Leydig cells and stimulates the release of testosterone. When concentrations of testosterone in the blood reach a critical threshold, testosterone itself will bind to androgen receptors on both the hypothalamus and the anterior pituitary, inhibiting the synthesis and secretion of GnRH and LH, respectively. When the blood concentrations of testosterone once again decline, testosterone no longer interacts with the receptors to the same degree and GnRH and LH are once again secreted, stimulating more testosterone production. This same process occurs with FSH and inhibin to control spermatogenesis.

Male Reproductive System

Declines in Leydig cell activity can occur in men beginning at 40 to 50 years of age. The resulting reduction in circulating testosterone concentrations can lead to symptoms of andropause, also known as male menopause. While the reduction in sex steroids in men is akin to female menopause, there is no clear sign—such as a lack of a menstrual period—to denote the initiation of andropause. Instead, men report feelings of fatigue, reduced muscle mass, depression, anxiety, irritability, loss of libido, and insomnia. A reduction in spermatogenesis resulting in lowered fertility is also reported, and sexual dysfunction can also be associated with andropausal symptoms.

Whereas some researchers believe that certain aspects of andropause are difficult to tease apart from aging in general, testosterone replacement is sometimes prescribed to alleviate some symptoms. Recent studies have shown a benefit from androgen replacement therapy on the new onset of depression in elderly men; however, other studies caution against testosterone replacement for long-term treatment of andropause symptoms, showing that high doses can sharply increase the risk of both heart disease and prostate cancer.

27.2 | Anatomy and Physiology of the Female Reproductive System

By the end of this section, you will be able to:
- Describe the structure and function of the organs of the female reproductive system
- List the steps of oogenesis
- Describe the hormonal changes that occur during the ovarian and menstrual cycles
- Trace the path of an oocyte from ovary to fertilization

The female reproductive system functions to produce gametes and reproductive hormones, just like the male reproductive system; however, it also has the additional task of supporting the developing fetus and delivering it to the outside world. Unlike its male counterpart, the female reproductive system is located primarily inside the pelvic cavity (Figure 27.9). Recall that the ovaries are the female gonads. The gamete they produce is called an **oocyte**. We'll discuss the production of oocytes in detail shortly. First, let's look at some of the structures of the female reproductive system.

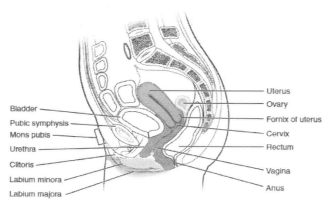

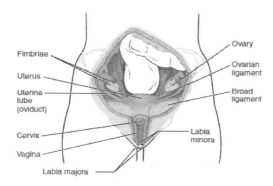

Figure 27.9 Female Reproductive System The major organs of the female reproductive system are located inside the pelvic cavity.

External Female Genitals

The external female reproductive structures are referred to collectively as the **vulva** (Figure 27.10). The **mons pubis** is a pad of fat that is located at the anterior, over the pubic bone. After puberty, it becomes covered in pubic hair. The **labia majora** (labia = "lips"; majora = "larger") are folds of hair-covered skin that begin just posterior to the mons pubis. The thinner and more pigmented **labia minora** (labia = "lips"; minora = "smaller") extend medial to the labia majora. Although they naturally vary in shape and size from woman to woman, the labia minora serve to protect the female urethra and the entrance to the female reproductive tract.

The superior, anterior portions of the labia minora come together to encircle the **clitoris** (or glans clitoris), an organ that originates from the same cells as the glans penis and has abundant nerves that make it important in sexual sensation and orgasm. The **hymen** is a thin membrane that sometimes partially covers the entrance to the vagina. An intact hymen cannot be used as an indication of "virginity"; even at birth, this is only a partial membrane, as menstrual fluid and other secretions must be able to exit the body, regardless of penile–vaginal intercourse. The vaginal opening is located between the opening of the urethra and the anus. It is flanked by outlets to the **Bartholin's glands** (or greater vestibular glands).

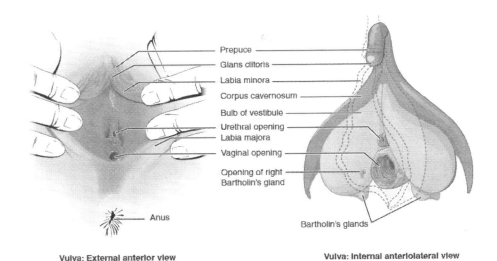

Figure 27.10 The Vulva The external female genitalia are referred to collectively as the vulva.

Vagina

The **vagina**, shown at the bottom of Figure 27.9 and Figure 27.9, is a muscular canal (approximately 10 cm long) that serves as the entrance to the reproductive tract. It also serves as the exit from the uterus during menses and childbirth. The outer walls of the anterior and posterior vagina are formed into longitudinal columns, or ridges, and the superior portion of the vagina—called the fornix—meets the protruding uterine cervix. The walls of the vagina are lined with an outer, fibrous adventitia; a middle layer of smooth muscle; and an inner mucous membrane with transverse folds called **rugae**. Together, the middle and inner layers allow the expansion of the vagina to accommodate intercourse and childbirth. The thin, perforated hymen can partially surround the opening to the vaginal orifice. The hymen can be ruptured with strenuous physical exercise, penile–vaginal intercourse, and childbirth. The Bartholin's glands and the lesser vestibular glands (located near the clitoris) secrete mucus, which keeps the vestibular area moist.

The vagina is home to a normal population of microorganisms that help to protect against infection by pathogenic bacteria, yeast, or other organisms that can enter the vagina. In a healthy woman, the most predominant type of vaginal bacteria is from the genus *Lactobacillus*. This family of beneficial bacterial flora secretes lactic acid, and thus protects the vagina by maintaining an acidic pH (below 4.5). Potential pathogens are less likely to survive in these acidic conditions. Lactic acid, in combination with other vaginal secretions, makes the vagina a self-cleansing organ. However, douching—or washing out the vagina with fluid—can disrupt the normal balance of healthy microorganisms, and actually increase a woman's risk for infections and irritation. Indeed, the American College of Obstetricians and Gynecologists recommend that women do not douche, and that they allow the vagina to maintain its normal healthy population of protective microbial flora.

Ovaries

The **ovaries** are the female gonads (see Figure 27.9). Paired ovals, they are each about 2 to 3 cm in length, about the size of an almond. The ovaries are located within the pelvic cavity, and are supported by the mesovarium, an extension of the peritoneum that connects the ovaries to the **broad ligament**. Extending from the mesovarium itself is the suspensory ligament that contains the ovarian blood and lymph vessels. Finally, the ovary itself is attached to the uterus via the ovarian ligament.

The ovary comprises an outer covering of cuboidal epithelium called the ovarian surface epithelium that is superficial to a dense connective tissue covering called the tunica albuginea. Beneath the tunica albuginea is the cortex, or outer portion, of the organ. The cortex is composed of a tissue framework called the ovarian stroma that forms the bulk of the adult ovary. Oocytes develop within the outer layer of this stroma, each surrounded by supporting cells. This grouping of an oocyte and its supporting cells is called a **follicle**. The growth and development of ovarian follicles will be described shortly. Beneath the cortex lies the inner ovarian medulla, the site of blood vessels, lymph vessels, and the nerves of the ovary. You will learn more about the overall anatomy of the female reproductive system at the end of this section.

The Ovarian Cycle

The **ovarian cycle** is a set of predictable changes in a female's oocytes and ovarian follicles. During a woman's reproductive years, it is a roughly 28-day cycle that can be correlated with, but is not the same as, the menstrual cycle (discussed shortly). The cycle includes two interrelated processes: oogenesis (the production of female gametes) and folliculogenesis (the growth and development of ovarian follicles).

Oogenesis

Gametogenesis in females is called **oogenesis**. The process begins with the ovarian stem cells, or **oogonia** (Figure 27.11). Oogonia are formed during fetal development, and divide via mitosis, much like spermatogonia in the testis. Unlike spermatogonia, however, oogonia form primary oocytes in the fetal ovary prior to birth. These primary oocytes are then arrested in this stage of meiosis I, only to resume it years later, beginning at puberty and continuing until the woman is near menopause (the cessation of a woman's reproductive functions). The number of primary oocytes present in the ovaries declines from one to two million in an infant, to approximately 400,000 at puberty, to zero by the end of menopause.

The initiation of **ovulation**—the release of an oocyte from the ovary—marks the transition from puberty into reproductive maturity for women. From then on, throughout a woman's reproductive years, ovulation occurs approximately once every 28 days. Just prior to ovulation, a surge of luteinizing hormone triggers the resumption of meiosis in a primary oocyte. This initiates the transition from primary to secondary oocyte. However, as you can see in Figure 27.11, this cell division does not result in two identical cells. Instead, the cytoplasm is divided unequally, and one daughter cell is much larger than the other. This larger cell, the secondary oocyte, eventually leaves the ovary during ovulation. The smaller cell, called the first **polar body**, may or may not complete meiosis and produce second polar bodies; in either case, it eventually disintegrates. Therefore, even though oogenesis produces up to four cells, only one survives.

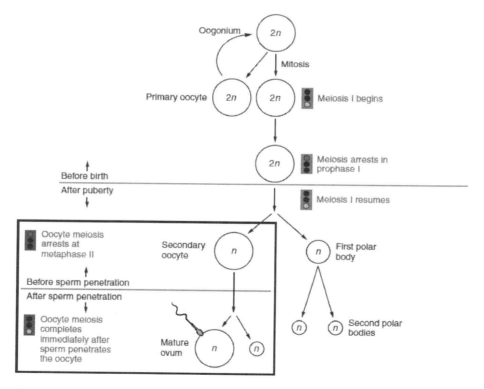

Figure 27.11 Oogenesis The unequal cell division of oogenesis produces one to three polar bodies that later degrade, as well as a single haploid ovum, which is produced only if there is penetration of the secondary oocyte by a sperm cell.

How does the diploid secondary oocyte become an **ovum**—the haploid female gamete? Meiosis of a secondary oocyte is completed only if a sperm succeeds in penetrating its barriers. Meiosis II then resumes, producing one haploid ovum that, at the instant of fertilization by a (haploid) sperm, becomes the first diploid cell of the new offspring (a zygote). Thus, the ovum can be thought of as a brief, transitional, haploid stage between the diploid oocyte and diploid zygote.

The larger amount of cytoplasm contained in the female gamete is used to supply the developing zygote with nutrients during the period between fertilization and implantation into the uterus. Interestingly, sperm contribute only DNA at fertilization —not cytoplasm. Therefore, the cytoplasm and all of the cytoplasmic organelles in the developing embryo are of maternal origin. This includes mitochondria, which contain their own DNA. Scientific research in the 1980s determined that mitochondrial DNA was maternally inherited, meaning that you can trace your mitochondrial DNA directly to your mother, her mother, and so on back through your female ancestors.

Everyday CONNECTION

Mapping Human History with Mitochondrial DNA

When we talk about human DNA, we're usually referring to nuclear DNA; that is, the DNA coiled into chromosomal bundles in the nucleus of our cells. We inherit half of our nuclear DNA from our father, and half from our mother. However, mitochondrial DNA (mtDNA) comes only from the mitochondria in the cytoplasm of the fat ovum we inherit from our mother. She received her mtDNA from her mother, who got it from her mother, and so on. Each of our cells contains approximately 1700 mitochondria, with each mitochondrion packed with mtDNA containing approximately 37 genes.

Mutations (changes) in mtDNA occur spontaneously in a somewhat organized pattern at regular intervals in human history. By analyzing these mutational relationships, researchers have been able to determine that we can all trace our ancestry back to one woman who lived in Africa about 200,000 years ago. Scientists have given this woman the biblical name Eve, although she is not, of course, the first *Homo sapiens* female. More precisely, she is our most recent common ancestor through matrilineal descent.

This doesn't mean that everyone's mtDNA today looks exactly like that of our ancestral Eve. Because of the spontaneous mutations in mtDNA that have occurred over the centuries, researchers can map different "branches" off of the "main trunk" of our mtDNA family tree. Your mtDNA might have a pattern of mutations that aligns more closely with one branch, and your neighbor's may align with another branch. Still, all branches eventually lead back to Eve.

But what happened to the mtDNA of all of the other *Homo sapiens* females who were living at the time of Eve? Researchers explain that, over the centuries, their female descendants died childless or with only male children, and thus, their maternal line—and its mtDNA—ended.

Folliculogenesis

Again, ovarian follicles are oocytes and their supporting cells. They grow and develop in a process called **folliculogenesis**, which typically leads to ovulation of one follicle approximately every 28 days, along with death to multiple other follicles. The death of ovarian follicles is called atresia, and can occur at any point during follicular development. Recall that, a female infant at birth will have one to two million oocytes within her ovarian follicles, and that this number declines throughout life until menopause, when no follicles remain. As you'll see next, follicles progress from primordial, to primary, to secondary and tertiary stages prior to ovulation—with the oocyte inside the follicle remaining as a primary oocyte until right before ovulation.

Folliculogenesis begins with follicles in a resting state. These small **primordial follicles** are present in newborn females and are the prevailing follicle type in the adult ovary (Figure 27.12). Primordial follicles have only a single flat layer of support cells, called **granulosa cells**, that surround the oocyte, and they can stay in this resting state for years—some until right before menopause.

After puberty, a few primordial follicles will respond to a recruitment signal each day, and will join a pool of immature growing follicles called **primary follicles**. Primary follicles start with a single layer of granulosa cells, but the granulosa cells then become active and transition from a flat or squamous shape to a rounded, cuboidal shape as they increase in size and proliferate. As the granulosa cells divide, the follicles—now called **secondary follicles** (see Figure 27.12)—increase in diameter, adding a new outer layer of connective tissue, blood vessels, and **theca cells**—cells that work with the granulosa cells to produce estrogens.

Within the growing secondary follicle, the primary oocyte now secretes a thin acellular membrane called the zona pellucida that will play a critical role in fertilization. A thick fluid, called follicular fluid, that has formed between the granulosa cells also begins to collect into one large pool, or **antrum**. Follicles in which the antrum has become large and fully formed are considered **tertiary follicles** (or antral follicles). Several follicles reach the tertiary stage at the same time, and most of these will undergo atresia. The one that does not die will continue to grow and develop until ovulation, when it will expel its secondary oocyte surrounded by several layers of granulosa cells from the ovary. Keep in mind that most follicles don't make it to this point. In fact, roughly 99 percent of the follicles in the ovary will undergo atresia, which can occur at any stage of folliculogenesis.

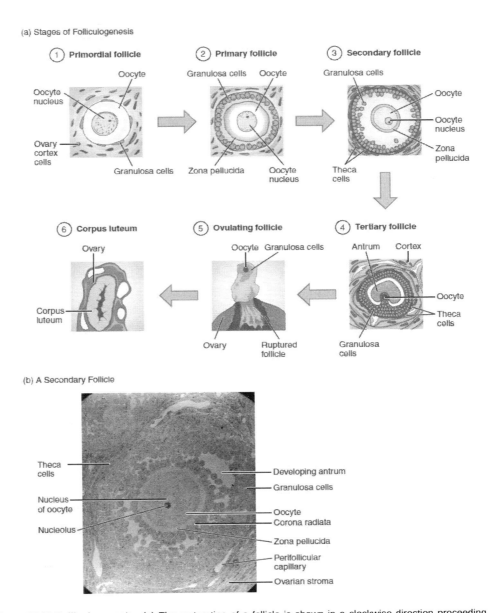

Figure 27.12 Folliculogenesis (a) The maturation of a follicle is shown in a clockwise direction proceeding from the primordial follicles. FSH stimulates the growth of a tertiary follicle, and LH stimulates the production of estrogen by granulosa and theca cells. Once the follicle is mature, it ruptures and releases the oocyte. Cells remaining in the follicle then develop into the corpus luteum. (b) In this electron micrograph of a secondary follicle, the oocyte, theca cells (thecae folliculi), and developing antrum are clearly visible. EM × 1100. (Micrograph provided by the Regents of University of Michigan Medical School © 2012)

Hormonal Control of the Ovarian Cycle

The process of development that we have just described, from primordial follicle to early tertiary follicle, takes approximately two months in humans. The final stages of development of a small cohort of tertiary follicles, ending with ovulation of a secondary oocyte, occur over a course of approximately 28 days. These changes are regulated by many of the same hormones that regulate the male reproductive system, including GnRH, LH, and FSH.

As in men, the hypothalamus produces GnRH, a hormone that signals the anterior pituitary gland to produce the gonadotropins FSH and LH (Figure 27.13). These gonadotropins leave the pituitary and travel through the bloodstream to the ovaries, where they bind to receptors on the granulosa and theca cells of the follicles. FSH stimulates the follicles to grow (hence its name of follicle-stimulating hormone), and the five or six tertiary follicles expand in diameter. The release of LH also stimulates the granulosa and theca cells of the follicles to produce the sex steroid hormone estradiol, a type of estrogen. This phase of the ovarian cycle, when the tertiary follicles are growing and secreting estrogen, is known as the follicular phase.

The more granulosa and theca cells a follicle has (that is, the larger and more developed it is), the more estrogen it will produce in response to LH stimulation. As a result of these large follicles producing large amounts of estrogen, systemic plasma estrogen concentrations increase. Following a classic negative feedback loop, the high concentrations of estrogen will stimulate the hypothalamus and pituitary to reduce the production of GnRH, LH, and FSH. Because the large tertiary follicles require FSH to grow and survive at this point, this decline in FSH caused by negative feedback leads most of them to die (atresia). Typically only one follicle, now called the dominant follicle, will survive this reduction in FSH, and this follicle will be the one that releases an oocyte. Scientists have studied many factors that lead to a particular follicle becoming dominant: size, the number of granulosa cells, and the number of FSH receptors on those granulosa cells all contribute to a follicle becoming the one surviving dominant follicle.

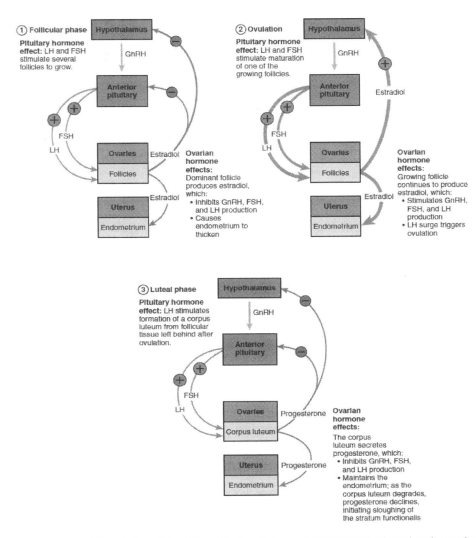

Figure 27.13 Hormonal Regulation of Ovulation The hypothalamus and pituitary gland regulate the ovarian cycle and ovulation. GnRH activates the anterior pituitary to produce LH and FSH, which stimulate the production of estrogen and progesterone by the ovaries.

When only the one dominant follicle remains in the ovary, it again begins to secrete estrogen. It produces more estrogen than all of the developing follicles did together before the negative feedback occurred. It produces so much estrogen that the normal negative feedback doesn't occur. Instead, these extremely high concentrations of systemic plasma estrogen trigger a regulatory switch in the anterior pituitary that responds by secreting large amounts of LH and FSH into the bloodstream (see Figure 27.13). The positive feedback loop by which more estrogen triggers release of more LH and FSH only occurs at this point in the cycle.

It is this large burst of LH (called the LH surge) that leads to ovulation of the dominant follicle. The LH surge induces many changes in the dominant follicle, including stimulating the resumption of meiosis of the primary oocyte to a secondary oocyte. As noted earlier, the polar body that results from unequal cell division simply degrades. The LH surge also triggers proteases (enzymes that cleave proteins) to break down structural proteins in the ovary wall on the surface of the bulging dominant follicle. This degradation of the wall, combined with pressure from the large, fluid-filled antrum, results in the expulsion of the oocyte surrounded by granulosa cells into the peritoneal cavity. This release is ovulation.

In the next section, you will follow the ovulated oocyte as it travels toward the uterus, but there is one more important event that occurs in the ovarian cycle. The surge of LH also stimulates a change in the granulosa and theca cells that remain in the follicle after the oocyte has been ovulated. This change is called luteinization (recall that the full name of LH is luteinizing hormone), and it transforms the collapsed follicle into a new endocrine structure called the **corpus luteum**, a term meaning "yellowish body" (see Figure 27.12). Instead of estrogen, the luteinized granulosa and theca cells of the corpus luteum begin to produce large amounts of the sex steroid hormone progesterone, a hormone that is critical for the establishment and maintenance of pregnancy. Progesterone triggers negative feedback at the hypothalamus and pituitary, which keeps GnRH, LH, and FSH secretions low, so no new dominant follicles develop at this time.

The post-ovulatory phase of progesterone secretion is known as the luteal phase of the ovarian cycle. If pregnancy does not occur within 10 to 12 days, the corpus luteum will stop secreting progesterone and degrade into the **corpus albicans**, a nonfunctional "whitish body" that will disintegrate in the ovary over a period of several months. During this time of reduced progesterone secretion, FSH and LH are once again stimulated, and the follicular phase begins again with a new cohort of early tertiary follicles beginning to grow and secrete estrogen.

The Uterine Tubes

The **uterine tubes** (also called fallopian tubes or oviducts) serve as the conduit of the oocyte from the ovary to the uterus (Figure 27.14). Each of the two uterine tubes is close to, but not directly connected to, the ovary and divided into sections. The **isthmus** is the narrow medial end of each uterine tube that is connected to the uterus. The wide distal **infundibulum** flares out with slender, finger-like projections called **fimbriae**. The middle region of the tube, called the **ampulla**, is where fertilization often occurs. The uterine tubes also have three layers: an outer serosa, a middle smooth muscle layer, and an inner mucosal layer. In addition to its mucus-secreting cells, the inner mucosa contains ciliated cells that beat in the direction of the uterus, producing a current that will be critical to move the oocyte.

Following ovulation, the secondary oocyte surrounded by a few granulosa cells is released into the peritoneal cavity. The nearby uterine tube, either left or right, receives the oocyte. Unlike sperm, oocytes lack flagella, and therefore cannot move on their own. So how do they travel into the uterine tube and toward the uterus? High concentrations of estrogen that occur around the time of ovulation induce contractions of the smooth muscle along the length of the uterine tube. These contractions occur every 4 to 8 seconds, and the result is a coordinated movement that sweeps the surface of the ovary and the pelvic cavity. Current flowing toward the uterus is generated by coordinated beating of the cilia that line the outside and lumen of the length of the uterine tube. These cilia beat more strongly in response to the high estrogen concentrations that occur around the time of ovulation. As a result of these mechanisms, the oocyte–granulosa cell complex is pulled into the interior of the tube. Once inside, the muscular contractions and beating cilia move the oocyte slowly toward the uterus. When fertilization does occur, sperm typically meet the egg while it is still moving through the ampulla.

Watch this video (http://openstaxcollege.org/l/ovulation) to observe ovulation and its initiation in response to the release of FSH and LH from the pituitary gland. What specialized structures help guide the oocyte from the ovary into the uterine tube?

If the oocyte is successfully fertilized, the resulting zygote will begin to divide into two cells, then four, and so on, as it makes its way through the uterine tube and into the uterus. There, it will implant and continue to grow. If the egg is not fertilized, it will simply degrade—either in the uterine tube or in the uterus, where it may be shed with the next menstrual period.

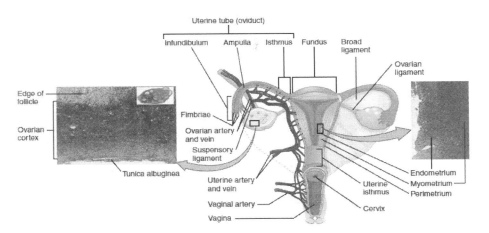

Figure 27.14 Ovaries, Uterine Tubes, and Uterus This anterior view shows the relationship of the ovaries, uterine tubes (oviducts), and uterus. Sperm enter through the vagina, and fertilization of an ovulated oocyte usually occurs in the distal uterine tube. From left to right, LM × 400, LM × 20. (Micrographs provided by the Regents of University of Michigan Medical School © 2012)

The open-ended structure of the uterine tubes can have significant health consequences if bacteria or other contagions enter through the vagina and move through the uterus, into the tubes, and then into the pelvic cavity. If this is left unchecked, a bacterial infection (sepsis) could quickly become life-threatening. The spread of an infection in this manner is of special concern when unskilled practitioners perform abortions in non-sterile conditions. Sepsis is also associated with sexually transmitted bacterial infections, especially gonorrhea and chlamydia. These increase a woman's risk for pelvic inflammatory disease (PID), infection of the uterine tubes or other reproductive organs. Even when resolved, PID can leave scar tissue in the tubes, leading to infertility.

Watch this series of videos (http://openstaxcollege.org/l/oocyte) to look at the movement of the oocyte through the ovary. The cilia in the uterine tube promote movement of the oocyte. What would likely occur if the cilia were paralyzed at the time of ovulation?

The Uterus and Cervix

The **uterus** is the muscular organ that nourishes and supports the growing embryo (see Figure 27.14). Its average size is approximately 5 cm wide by 7 cm long (approximately 2 in by 3 in) when a female is not pregnant. It has three sections. The portion of the uterus superior to the opening of the uterine tubes is called the **fundus**. The middle section of the uterus is called the **body of uterus** (or corpus). The **cervix** is the narrow inferior portion of the uterus that projects into the vagina. The cervix produces mucus secretions that become thin and stringy under the influence of high systemic plasma estrogen concentrations, and these secretions can facilitate sperm movement through the reproductive tract.

Several ligaments maintain the position of the uterus within the abdominopelvic cavity. The broad ligament is a fold of peritoneum that serves as a primary support for the uterus, extending laterally from both sides of the uterus and attaching it to the pelvic wall. The round ligament attaches to the uterus near the uterine tubes, and extends to the labia majora. Finally, the uterosacral ligament stabilizes the uterus posteriorly by its connection from the cervix to the pelvic wall.

The wall of the uterus is made up of three layers. The most superficial layer is the serous membrane, or **perimetrium**, which consists of epithelial tissue that covers the exterior portion of the uterus. The middle layer, or **myometrium**, is a thick layer of smooth muscle responsible for uterine contractions. Most of the uterus is myometrial tissue, and the muscle fibers run horizontally, vertically, and diagonally, allowing the powerful contractions that occur during labor and the less powerful contractions (or cramps) that help to expel menstrual blood during a woman's period. Anteriorly directed myometrial contractions also occur near the time of ovulation, and are thought to possibly facilitate the transport of sperm through the female reproductive tract.

The innermost layer of the uterus is called the **endometrium**. The endometrium contains a connective tissue lining, the lamina propria, which is covered by epithelial tissue that lines the lumen. Structurally, the endometrium consists of two layers: the stratum basalis and the stratum functionalis (the basal and functional layers). The stratum basalis layer is part of the lamina propria and is adjacent to the myometrium; this layer does not shed during menses. In contrast, the thicker stratum functionalis layer contains the glandular portion of the lamina propria and the endothelial tissue that lines the uterine lumen. It is the stratum functionalis that grows and thickens in response to increased levels of estrogen and progesterone. In the luteal phase of the menstrual cycle, special branches off of the uterine artery called spiral arteries supply the thickened stratum functionalis. This inner functional layer provides the proper site of implantation for the fertilized egg, and—should fertilization not occur—it is only the stratum functionalis layer of the endometrium that sheds during menstruation.

Recall that during the follicular phase of the ovarian cycle, the tertiary follicles are growing and secreting estrogen. At the same time, the stratum functionalis of the endometrium is thickening to prepare for a potential implantation. The post-ovulatory increase in progesterone, which characterizes the luteal phase, is key for maintaining a thick stratum functionalis. As long as a functional corpus luteum is present in the ovary, the endometrial lining is prepared for implantation. Indeed, if an embryo implants, signals are sent to the corpus luteum to continue secreting progesterone to maintain the endometrium, and thus maintain the pregnancy. If an embryo does not implant, no signal is sent to the corpus luteum and it degrades, ceasing progesterone production and ending the luteal phase. Without progesterone, the endometrium thins and, under the influence of prostaglandins, the spiral arteries of the endometrium constrict and rupture, preventing oxygenated blood from reaching the endometrial tissue. As a result, endometrial tissue dies and blood, pieces of the endometrial tissue, and white blood cells are shed through the vagina during menstruation, or the **menses**. The first menses after puberty, called **menarche**, can occur either before or after the first ovulation.

The Menstrual Cycle

Now that we have discussed the maturation of the cohort of tertiary follicles in the ovary, the build-up and then shedding of the endometrial lining in the uterus, and the function of the uterine tubes and vagina, we can put everything together to talk about the three phases of the **menstrual cycle**—the series of changes in which the uterine lining is shed, rebuilds, and prepares for implantation.

The timing of the menstrual cycle starts with the first day of menses, referred to as day one of a woman's period. Cycle length is determined by counting the days between the onset of bleeding in two subsequent cycles. Because the average length of a woman's menstrual cycle is 28 days, this is the time period used to identify the timing of events in the cycle. However, the length of the menstrual cycle varies among women, and even in the same woman from one cycle to the next, typically from 21 to 32 days.

Just as the hormones produced by the granulosa and theca cells of the ovary "drive" the follicular and luteal phases of the ovarian cycle, they also control the three distinct phases of the menstrual cycle. These are the menses phase, the proliferative phase, and the secretory phase.

Menses Phase

The **menses phase** of the menstrual cycle is the phase during which the lining is shed; that is, the days that the woman menstruates. Although it averages approximately five days, the menses phase can last from 2 to 7 days, or longer. As shown in Figure 27.15, the menses phase occurs during the early days of the follicular phase of the ovarian cycle, when progesterone, FSH, and LH levels are low. Recall that progesterone concentrations decline as a result of the degradation of the corpus luteum, marking the end of the luteal phase. This decline in progesterone triggers the shedding of the stratum functionalis of the endometrium.

Chapter 27 | The Reproductive System

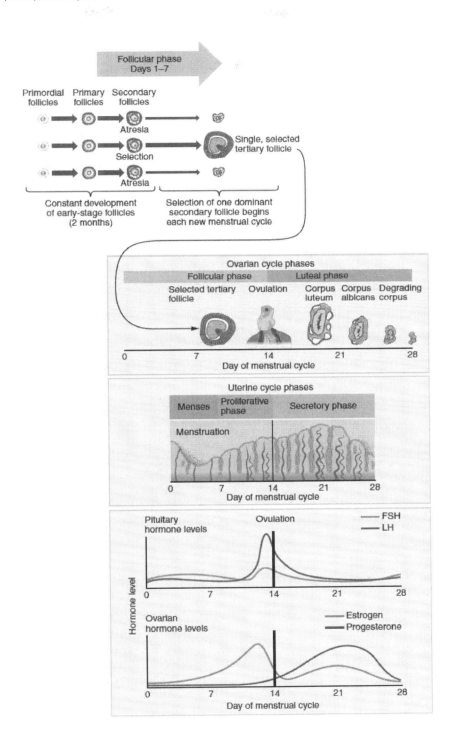

Figure 27.15 Hormone Levels in Ovarian and Menstrual Cycles The correlation of the hormone levels and their effects on the female reproductive system is shown in this timeline of the ovarian and menstrual cycles. The menstrual cycle begins at day one with the start of menses. Ovulation occurs around day 14 of a 28-day cycle, triggered by the LH surge.

Proliferative Phase

Once menstrual flow ceases, the endometrium begins to proliferate again, marking the beginning of the **proliferative phase** of the menstrual cycle (see Figure 27.15). It occurs when the granulosa and theca cells of the tertiary follicles begin to produce increased amounts of estrogen. These rising estrogen concentrations stimulate the endometrial lining to rebuild.

Recall that the high estrogen concentrations will eventually lead to a decrease in FSH as a result of negative feedback, resulting in atresia of all but one of the developing tertiary follicles. The switch to positive feedback—which occurs with the elevated estrogen production from the dominant follicle—then stimulates the LH surge that will trigger ovulation. In a typical 28-day menstrual cycle, ovulation occurs on day 14. Ovulation marks the end of the proliferative phase as well as the end of the follicular phase.

Secretory Phase

In addition to prompting the LH surge, high estrogen levels increase the uterine tube contractions that facilitate the pick-up and transfer of the ovulated oocyte. High estrogen levels also slightly decrease the acidity of the vagina, making it more hospitable to sperm. In the ovary, the luteinization of the granulosa cells of the collapsed follicle forms the progesterone-producing corpus luteum, marking the beginning of the luteal phase of the ovarian cycle. In the uterus, progesterone from the corpus luteum begins the **secretory phase** of the menstrual cycle, in which the endometrial lining prepares for implantation (see Figure 27.15). Over the next 10 to 12 days, the endometrial glands secrete a fluid rich in glycogen. If fertilization has occurred, this fluid will nourish the ball of cells now developing from the zygote. At the same time, the spiral arteries develop to provide blood to the thickened stratum functionalis.

If no pregnancy occurs within approximately 10 to 12 days, the corpus luteum will degrade into the corpus albicans. Levels of both estrogen and progesterone will fall, and the endometrium will grow thinner. Prostaglandins will be secreted that cause constriction of the spiral arteries, reducing oxygen supply. The endometrial tissue will die, resulting in menses—or the first day of the next cycle.

Female Reproductive System

Research over many years has confirmed that cervical cancer is most often caused by a sexually transmitted infection with human papillomavirus (HPV). There are over 100 related viruses in the HPV family, and the characteristics of each strain determine the outcome of the infection. In all cases, the virus enters body cells and uses its own genetic material to take over the host cell's metabolic machinery and produce more virus particles.

HPV infections are common in both men and women. Indeed, a recent study determined that 42.5 percent of females had HPV at the time of testing. These women ranged in age from 14 to 59 years and differed in race, ethnicity, and number of sexual partners. Of note, the prevalence of HPV infection was 53.8 percent among women aged 20 to 24 years, the age group with the highest infection rate.

HPV strains are classified as high or low risk according to their potential to cause cancer. Though most HPV infections do not cause disease, the disruption of normal cellular functions in the low-risk forms of HPV can cause the male or female human host to develop genital warts. Often, the body is able to clear an HPV infection by normal immune responses within 2 years. However, the more serious, high-risk infection by certain types of HPV can result in cancer of the cervix (Figure 27.16). Infection with either of the cancer-causing variants HPV 16 or HPV 18 has been linked to more than 70 percent of all cervical cancer diagnoses. Although even these high-risk HPV strains can be cleared from the body over time, infections persist in some individuals. If this happens, the HPV infection can influence the cells of the cervix to develop precancerous changes.

Risk factors for cervical cancer include having unprotected sex; having multiple sexual partners; a first sexual experience at a younger age, when the cells of the cervix are not fully mature; failure to receive the HPV vaccine; a compromised immune system; and smoking. The risk of developing cervical cancer is doubled with cigarette smoking.

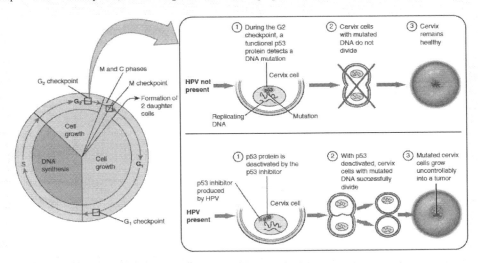

Figure 27.16 Development of Cervical Cancer In most cases, cells infected with the HPV virus heal on their own. In some cases, however, the virus continues to spread and becomes an invasive cancer.

When the high-risk types of HPV enter a cell, two viral proteins are used to neutralize proteins that the host cells use as checkpoints in the cell cycle. The best studied of these proteins is p53. In a normal cell, p53 detects DNA damage in the cell's genome and either halts the progression of the cell cycle—allowing time for DNA repair to occur—or initiates apoptosis. Both of these processes prevent the accumulation of mutations in a cell's genome. High-risk HPV can neutralize p53, keeping the cell in a state in which fast growth is possible and impairing apoptosis, allowing mutations to accumulate in the cellular DNA.

The prevalence of cervical cancer in the United States is very low because of regular screening exams called pap smears. Pap smears sample cells of the cervix, allowing the detection of abnormal cells. If pre-cancerous cells are detected, there are several highly effective techniques that are currently in use to remove them before they pose a danger. However, women in developing countries often do not have access to regular pap smears. As a result, these women account for as many as 80 percent of the cases of cervical cancer worldwide.

In 2006, the first vaccine against the high-risk types of HPV was approved. There are now two HPV vaccines available: Gardasil® and Cervarix®. Whereas these vaccines were initially only targeted for women, because HPV is sexually transmitted, both men and women require vaccination for this approach to achieve its maximum efficacy. A recent study suggests that the HPV vaccine has cut the rates of HPV infection by the four targeted strains at least in half. Unfortunately, the high cost of manufacturing the vaccine is currently limiting access to many women worldwide.

The Breasts

Whereas the breasts are located far from the other female reproductive organs, they are considered accessory organs of the female reproductive system. The function of the breasts is to supply milk to an infant in a process called lactation. The external features of the breast include a nipple surrounded by a pigmented **areola** (Figure 27.17), whose coloration may deepen during pregnancy. The areola is typically circular and can vary in size from 25 to 100 mm in diameter. The areolar region is characterized by small, raised areolar glands that secrete lubricating fluid during lactation to protect the nipple from chafing. When a baby nurses, or draws milk from the breast, the entire areolar region is taken into the mouth.

Breast milk is produced by the **mammary glands**, which are modified sweat glands. The milk itself exits the breast through the nipple via 15 to 20 **lactiferous ducts** that open on the surface of the nipple. These lactiferous ducts each extend to a **lactiferous sinus** that connects to a glandular lobe within the breast itself that contains groups of milk-secreting cells in clusters called **alveoli** (see Figure 27.17). The clusters can change in size depending on the amount of milk in the alveolar lumen. Once milk is made in the alveoli, stimulated myoepithelial cells that surround the alveoli contract to push the milk to the lactiferous sinuses. From here, the baby can draw milk through the lactiferous ducts by suckling. The lobes themselves are surrounded by fat tissue, which determines the size of the breast; breast size differs between individuals and does not affect the amount of milk produced. Supporting the breasts are multiple bands of connective tissue called **suspensory ligaments** that connect the breast tissue to the dermis of the overlying skin.

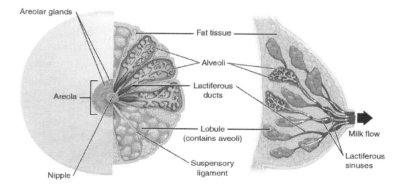

Figure 27.17 Anatomy of the Breast During lactation, milk moves from the alveoli through the lactiferous ducts to the nipple.

During the normal hormonal fluctuations in the menstrual cycle, breast tissue responds to changing levels of estrogen and progesterone, which can lead to swelling and breast tenderness in some individuals, especially during the secretory phase. If pregnancy occurs, the increase in hormones leads to further development of the mammary tissue and enlargement of the breasts.

Hormonal Birth Control

Birth control pills take advantage of the negative feedback system that regulates the ovarian and menstrual cycles to stop ovulation and prevent pregnancy. Typically they work by providing a constant level of both estrogen and progesterone, which negatively feeds back onto the hypothalamus and pituitary, thus preventing the release of FSH and LH. Without FSH, the follicles do not mature, and without the LH surge, ovulation does not occur. Although the estrogen in birth control pills does stimulate some thickening of the endometrial wall, it is reduced compared with a normal cycle and is less likely to support implantation.

Some birth control pills contain 21 active pills containing hormones, and 7 inactive pills (placebos). The decline in hormones during the week that the woman takes the placebo pills triggers menses, although it is typically lighter than a normal menstrual flow because of the reduced endometrial thickening. Newer types of birth control pills have been developed that deliver low-dose estrogens and progesterone for the entire cycle (these are meant to be taken 365 days a year), and menses never occurs. While some women prefer to have the proof of a lack of pregnancy that a monthly period provides, menstruation every 28 days is not required for health reasons, and there are no reported adverse effects of not having a menstrual period in an otherwise healthy individual.

Because birth control pills function by providing constant estrogen and progesterone levels and disrupting negative feedback, skipping even just one or two pills at certain points of the cycle (or even being several hours late taking the pill) can lead to an increase in FSH and LH and result in ovulation. It is important, therefore, that the woman follow the directions on the birth control pill package to successfully prevent pregnancy.

Female Reproductive System

Female fertility (the ability to conceive) peaks when women are in their twenties, and is slowly reduced until a women reaches 35 years of age. After that time, fertility declines more rapidly, until it ends completely at the end of menopause. Menopause is the cessation of the menstrual cycle that occurs as a result of the loss of ovarian follicles and the hormones that they produce. A woman is considered to have completed menopause if she has not menstruated in a full year. After that point, she is considered postmenopausal. The average age for this change is consistent worldwide at between 50 and 52 years of age, but it can normally occur in a woman's forties, or later in her fifties. Poor health, including smoking, can lead to earlier loss of fertility and earlier menopause.

As a woman reaches the age of menopause, depletion of the number of viable follicles in the ovaries due to atresia affects the hormonal regulation of the menstrual cycle. During the years leading up to menopause, there is a decrease in the levels of the hormone inhibin, which normally participates in a negative feedback loop to the pituitary to control the production of FSH. The menopausal decrease in inhibin leads to an increase in FSH. The presence of FSH stimulates more follicles to grow and secrete estrogen. Because small, secondary follicles also respond to increases in FSH levels, larger numbers of follicles are stimulated to grow; however, most undergo atresia and die. Eventually, this process leads to the depletion of all follicles in the ovaries, and the production of estrogen falls off dramatically. It is primarily the lack of estrogens that leads to the symptoms of menopause.

The earliest changes occur during the menopausal transition, often referred to as peri-menopause, when a women's cycle becomes irregular but does not stop entirely. Although the levels of estrogen are still nearly the same as before the transition, the level of progesterone produced by the corpus luteum is reduced. This decline in progesterone can lead to abnormal growth, or hyperplasia, of the endometrium. This condition is a concern because it increases the risk of developing endometrial cancer. Two harmless conditions that can develop during the transition are uterine fibroids, which are benign masses of cells, and irregular bleeding. As estrogen levels change, other symptoms that occur are hot flashes and night sweats, trouble sleeping, vaginal dryness, mood swings, difficulty focusing, and thinning of hair on the head along with the growth of more hair on the face. Depending on the individual, these symptoms can be entirely absent, moderate, or severe.

After menopause, lower amounts of estrogens can lead to other changes. Cardiovascular disease becomes as prevalent in women as in men, possibly because estrogens reduce the amount of cholesterol in the blood vessels. When estrogen is lacking, many women find that they suddenly have problems with high cholesterol and the cardiovascular issues that accompany it. Osteoporosis is another problem because bone density decreases rapidly in the first years after menopause. The reduction in bone density leads to a higher incidence of fractures.

Hormone therapy (HT), which employs medication (synthetic estrogens and progestins) to increase estrogen and progestin levels, can alleviate some of the symptoms of menopause. In 2002, the Women's Health Initiative began a study to observe women for the long-term outcomes of hormone replacement therapy over 8.5 years. However, the study was prematurely terminated after 5.2 years because of evidence of a higher than normal risk of breast cancer in patients taking estrogen-only HT. The potential positive effects on cardiovascular disease were also not realized in the estrogen-only patients. The results of other hormone replacement studies over the last 50 years, including a 2012 study that followed over 1,000 menopausal women for 10 years, have shown cardiovascular benefits from estrogen and no increased risk for cancer. Some researchers believe that the age group tested in the 2002 trial may have been too old to benefit from the therapy, thus skewing the results. In the meantime, intense debate and study of the benefits and risks of replacement therapy is ongoing. Current guidelines approve HT for the reduction of hot flashes or flushes, but this treatment is generally only considered when women first start showing signs of menopausal changes, is used in the lowest dose possible for the shortest time possible (5 years or less), and it is suggested that women on HT have regular pelvic and breast exams.

27.3 | Development of the Male and Female Reproductive Systems

By the end of this section, you will be able to:
- Explain how bipotential tissues are directed to develop into male or female sex organs
- Name the rudimentary duct systems in the embryo that are precursors to male or female internal sex organs
- Describe the hormonal changes that bring about puberty, and the secondary sex characteristics of men and women

The development of the reproductive systems begins soon after fertilization of the egg, with primordial gonads beginning to develop approximately one month after conception. Reproductive development continues in utero, but there is little change in the reproductive system between infancy and puberty.

Development of the Sexual Organs in the Embryo and Fetus

Females are considered the "fundamental" sex—that is, without much chemical prompting, all fertilized eggs would develop into females. To become a male, an individual must be exposed to the cascade of factors initiated by a single gene on the male Y chromosome. This is called the SRY (Sex-determining Region of the Y chromosome). Because females do not have a Y chromosome, they do not have the *SRY* gene. Without a functional *SRY* gene, an individual will be female.

In both male and female embryos, the same group of cells has the potential to develop into either the male or female gonads; this tissue is considered bipotential. The *SRY* gene actively recruits other genes that begin to develop the testes, and suppresses genes that are important in female development. As part of this *SRY*-prompted cascade, germ cells in the bipotential gonads differentiate into spermatogonia. Without *SRY*, different genes are expressed, oogonia form, and primordial follicles develop in the primitive ovary.

Soon after the formation of the testis, the Leydig cells begin to secrete testosterone. Testosterone can influence tissues that are bipotential to become male reproductive structures. For example, with exposure to testosterone, cells that could become either the glans penis or the glans clitoris form the glans penis. Without testosterone, these same cells differentiate into the clitoris.

Not all tissues in the reproductive tract are bipotential. The internal reproductive structures (for example the uterus, uterine tubes, and part of the vagina in females; and the epididymis, ductus deferens, and seminal vesicles in males) form from one of two rudimentary duct systems in the embryo. For proper reproductive function in the adult, one set of these ducts must develop properly, and the other must degrade. In males, secretions from sustentacular cells trigger a degradation of the female duct, called the **Müllerian duct**. At the same time, testosterone secretion stimulates growth of the male tract, the **Wolffian duct**. Without such sustentacular cell secretion, the Müllerian duct will develop; without testosterone, the Wolffian duct will degrade. Thus, the developing offspring will be female. For more information and a figure of differentiation of the gonads, seek additional content on fetal development.

A baby's gender is determined at conception, and the different genitalia of male and female fetuses develop from the same tissues in the embryo. View this animation (http://openstaxcollege.org/l/fetus) to see a comparison of the development of structures of the female and male reproductive systems in a growing fetus. Where are the testes located for most of gestational time?

Further Sexual Development Occurs at Puberty

Puberty is the stage of development at which individuals become sexually mature. Though the outcomes of puberty for boys and girls are very different, the hormonal control of the process is very similar. In addition, though the timing of these events varies between individuals, the sequence of changes that occur is predictable for male and female adolescents. As shown in Figure 27.18, a concerted release of hormones from the hypothalamus (GnRH), the anterior pituitary (LH and FSH), and the gonads (either testosterone or estrogen) is responsible for the maturation of the reproductive systems and the development of **secondary sex characteristics**, which are physical changes that serve auxiliary roles in reproduction.

The first changes begin around the age of eight or nine when the production of LH becomes detectable. The release of LH occurs primarily at night during sleep and precedes the physical changes of puberty by several years. In pre-pubertal children, the sensitivity of the negative feedback system in the hypothalamus and pituitary is very high. This means that very low concentrations of androgens or estrogens will negatively feed back onto the hypothalamus and pituitary, keeping the production of GnRH, LH, and FSH low.

As an individual approaches puberty, two changes in sensitivity occur. The first is a decrease of sensitivity in the hypothalamus and pituitary to negative feedback, meaning that it takes increasingly larger concentrations of sex steroid hormones to stop the production of LH and FSH. The second change in sensitivity is an increase in sensitivity of the gonads to the FSH and LH signals, meaning the gonads of adults are more responsive to gonadotropins than are the gonads of children. As a result of these two changes, the levels of LH and FSH slowly increase and lead to the enlargement and maturation of the gonads, which in turn leads to secretion of higher levels of sex hormones and the initiation of spermatogenesis and folliculogenesis.

In addition to age, multiple factors can affect the age of onset of puberty, including genetics, environment, and psychological stress. One of the more important influences may be nutrition; historical data demonstrate the effect of better and more consistent nutrition on the age of menarche in girls in the United States, which decreased from an average age of approximately 17 years of age in 1860 to the current age of approximately 12.75 years in 1960, as it remains today. Some studies indicate a link between puberty onset and the amount of stored fat in an individual. This effect is more pronounced in girls, but has been documented in both sexes. Body fat, corresponding with secretion of the hormone leptin by adipose cells, appears to have a strong role in determining menarche. This may reflect to some extent the high metabolic costs of gestation and lactation. In girls who are lean and highly active, such as gymnasts, there is often a delay in the onset of puberty.

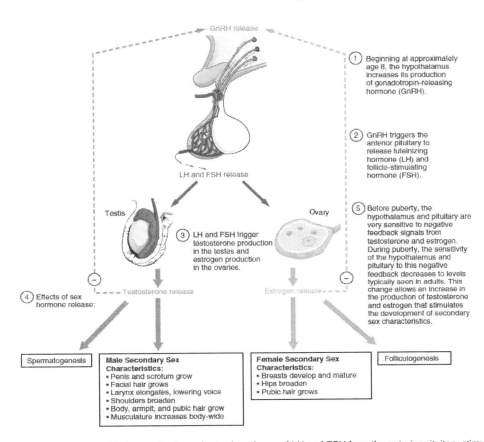

Figure 27.18 Hormones of Puberty During puberty, the release of LH and FSH from the anterior pituitary stimulates the gonads to produce sex hormones in both male and female adolescents.

Signs of Puberty

Different sex steroid hormone concentrations between the sexes also contribute to the development and function of secondary sexual characteristics. Examples of secondary sexual characteristics are listed in Table 27.1.

Development of the Secondary Sexual Characteristics

Male	Female
Increased larynx size and deepening of the voice	Deposition of fat, predominantly in breasts and hips
Increased muscular development	Breast development
Growth of facial, axillary, and pubic hair, and increased growth of body hair	Broadening of the pelvis and growth of axillary and pubic hair

Table 27.1

As a girl reaches puberty, typically the first change that is visible is the development of the breast tissue. This is followed by the growth of axillary and pubic hair. A growth spurt normally starts at approximately age 9 to 11, and may last two years or more. During this time, a girl's height can increase 3 inches a year. The next step in puberty is menarche, the start of menstruation.

In boys, the growth of the testes is typically the first physical sign of the beginning of puberty, which is followed by growth and pigmentation of the scrotum and growth of the penis. The next step is the growth of hair, including armpit, pubic, chest, and facial hair. Testosterone stimulates the growth of the larynx and thickening and lengthening of the vocal folds, which causes the voice to drop in pitch. The first fertile ejaculations typically appear at approximately 15 years of age, but this age can vary widely across individual boys. Unlike the early growth spurt observed in females, the male growth spurt occurs toward the end of puberty, at approximately age 11 to 13, and a boy's height can increase as much as 4 inches a year. In some males, pubertal development can continue through the early 20s.

KEY TERMS

alveoli (of the breast) milk-secreting cells in the mammary gland

ampulla (of the uterine tube) middle portion of the uterine tube in which fertilization often occurs

antrum fluid-filled chamber that characterizes a mature tertiary (antral) follicle

areola highly pigmented, circular area surrounding the raised nipple and containing areolar glands that secrete fluid important for lubrication during suckling

Bartholin's glands (also, greater vestibular glands) glands that produce a thick mucus that maintains moisture in the vulva area; also referred to as the greater vestibular glands

blood–testis barrier tight junctions between Sertoli cells that prevent bloodborne pathogens from gaining access to later stages of spermatogenesis and prevent the potential for an autoimmune reaction to haploid sperm

body of uterus middle section of the uterus

broad ligament wide ligament that supports the uterus by attaching laterally to both sides of the uterus and pelvic wall

bulbourethral glands (also, Cowper's glands) glands that secrete a lubricating mucus that cleans and lubricates the urethra prior to and during ejaculation

cervix elongate inferior end of the uterus where it connects to the vagina

clitoris (also, glans clitoris) nerve-rich area of the vulva that contributes to sexual sensation during intercourse

corpus albicans nonfunctional structure remaining in the ovarian stroma following structural and functional regression of the corpus luteum

corpus cavernosum either of two columns of erectile tissue in the penis that fill with blood during an erection

corpus luteum transformed follicle after ovulation that secretes progesterone

corpus spongiosum (plural = corpora cavernosa) column of erectile tissue in the penis that fills with blood during an erection and surrounds the penile urethra on the ventral portion of the penis

ductus deferens (also, vas deferens) duct that transports sperm from the epididymis through the spermatic cord and into the ejaculatory duct; also referred as the vas deferens

ejaculatory duct duct that connects the ampulla of the ductus deferens with the duct of the seminal vesicle at the prostatic urethra

endometrium inner lining of the uterus, part of which builds up during the secretory phase of the menstrual cycle and then sheds with menses

epididymis (plural = epididymides) coiled tubular structure in which sperm start to mature and are stored until ejaculation

fimbriae fingerlike projections on the distal uterine tubes

follicle ovarian structure of one oocyte and surrounding granulosa (and later theca) cells

folliculogenesis development of ovarian follicles from primordial to tertiary under the stimulation of gonadotropins

fundus (of the uterus) domed portion of the uterus that is superior to the uterine tubes

gamete haploid reproductive cell that contributes genetic material to form an offspring

glans penis bulbous end of the penis that contains a large number of nerve endings

gonadotropin-releasing hormone (GnRH) hormone released by the hypothalamus that regulates the production of follicle-stimulating hormone and luteinizing hormone from the pituitary gland

gonads reproductive organs (testes in men and ovaries in women) that produce gametes and reproductive hormones

granulosa cells supportive cells in the ovarian follicle that produce estrogen

hymen membrane that covers part of the opening of the vagina

infundibulum (of the uterine tube) wide, distal portion of the uterine tube terminating in fimbriae

inguinal canal opening in abdominal wall that connects the testes to the abdominal cavity

isthmus narrow, medial portion of the uterine tube that joins the uterus

labia majora hair-covered folds of skin located behind the mons pubis

labia minora thin, pigmented, hairless flaps of skin located medial and deep to the labia majora

lactiferous ducts ducts that connect the mammary glands to the nipple and allow for the transport of milk

lactiferous sinus area of milk collection between alveoli and lactiferous duct

Leydig cells cells between the seminiferous tubules of the testes that produce testosterone; a type of interstitial cell

mammary glands glands inside the breast that secrete milk

menarche first menstruation in a pubertal female

menses shedding of the inner portion of the endometrium out though the vagina; also referred to as menstruation

menses phase phase of the menstrual cycle in which the endometrial lining is shed

menstrual cycle approximately 28-day cycle of changes in the uterus consisting of a menses phase, a proliferative phase, and a secretory phase

mons pubis mound of fatty tissue located at the front of the vulva

myometrium smooth muscle layer of uterus that allows for uterine contractions during labor and expulsion of menstrual blood

Müllerian duct duct system present in the embryo that will eventually form the internal female reproductive structures

oocyte cell that results from the division of the oogonium and undergoes meiosis I at the LH surge and meiosis II at fertilization to become a haploid ovum

oogenesis process by which oogonia divide by mitosis to primary oocytes, which undergo meiosis to produce the secondary oocyte and, upon fertilization, the ovum

oogonia ovarian stem cells that undergo mitosis during female fetal development to form primary oocytes

ovarian cycle approximately 28-day cycle of changes in the ovary consisting of a follicular phase and a luteal phase

ovaries female gonads that produce oocytes and sex steroid hormones (notably estrogen and progesterone)

ovulation release of a secondary oocyte and associated granulosa cells from an ovary

ovum haploid female gamete resulting from completion of meiosis II at fertilization

penis male organ of copulation

perimetrium outer epithelial layer of uterine wall

polar body smaller cell produced during the process of meiosis in oogenesis

prepuce (also, foreskin) flap of skin that forms a collar around, and thus protects and lubricates, the glans penis; also referred as the foreskin

primary follicles ovarian follicles with a primary oocyte and one layer of cuboidal granulosa cells

primordial follicles least developed ovarian follicles that consist of a single oocyte and a single layer of flat (squamous) granulosa cells

proliferative phase phase of the menstrual cycle in which the endometrium proliferates

prostate gland doughnut-shaped gland at the base of the bladder surrounding the urethra and contributing fluid to semen during ejaculation

puberty life stage during which a male or female adolescent becomes anatomically and physiologically capable of reproduction

rugae (of the vagina) folds of skin in the vagina that allow it to stretch during intercourse and childbirth

scrotum external pouch of skin and muscle that houses the testes

secondary follicles ovarian follicles with a primary oocyte and multiple layers of granulosa cells

secondary sex characteristics physical characteristics that are influenced by sex steroid hormones and have supporting roles in reproductive function

secretory phase phase of the menstrual cycle in which the endometrium secretes a nutrient-rich fluid in preparation for implantation of an embryo

semen ejaculatory fluid composed of sperm and secretions from the seminal vesicles, prostate, and bulbourethral glands

seminal vesicle gland that produces seminal fluid, which contributes to semen

seminiferous tubules tube structures within the testes where spermatogenesis occurs

Sertoli cells cells that support germ cells through the process of spermatogenesis; a type of sustentacular cell

sperm (also, spermatozoon) male gamete

spermatic cord bundle of nerves and blood vessels that supplies the testes; contains ductus deferens

spermatid immature sperm cells produced by meiosis II of secondary spermatocytes

spermatocyte cell that results from the division of spermatogonium and undergoes meiosis I and meiosis II to form spermatids

spermatogenesis formation of new sperm, occurs in the seminiferous tubules of the testes

spermatogonia (singular = spermatogonium) diploid precursor cells that become sperm

spermiogenesis transformation of spermatids to spermatozoa during spermatogenesis

suspensory ligaments bands of connective tissue that suspend the breast onto the chest wall by attachment to the overlying dermis

tertiary follicles (also, antral follicles) ovarian follicles with a primary or secondary oocyte, multiple layers of granulosa cells, and a fully formed antrum

testes (singular = testis) male gonads

theca cells estrogen-producing cells in a maturing ovarian follicle

uterine tubes (also, fallopian tubes or oviducts) ducts that facilitate transport of an ovulated oocyte to the uterus

uterus muscular hollow organ in which a fertilized egg develops into a fetus

vagina tunnel-like organ that provides access to the uterus for the insertion of semen and from the uterus for the birth of a baby

vulva external female genitalia

Wolffian duct duct system present in the embryo that will eventually form the internal male reproductive structures

CHAPTER REVIEW

27.1 Anatomy and Physiology of the Male Reproductive System

Gametes are the reproductive cells that combine to form offspring. Organs called gonads produce the gametes, along with the hormones that regulate human reproduction. The male gametes are called sperm. Spermatogenesis, the production of sperm, occurs within the seminiferous tubules that make up most of the testis. The scrotum is the muscular sac that holds the testes outside of the body cavity.

Spermatogenesis begins with mitotic division of spermatogonia (stem cells) to produce primary spermatocytes that undergo the two divisions of meiosis to become secondary spermatocytes, then the haploid spermatids. During spermiogenesis, spermatids are transformed into spermatozoa (formed sperm). Upon release from the seminiferous tubules, sperm are moved to the epididymis where they continue to mature. During ejaculation, sperm exit the epididymis through the ductus deferens, a duct in the spermatic cord that leaves the scrotum. The ampulla of the ductus deferens meets the seminal vesicle, a gland that contributes fructose and proteins, at the ejaculatory duct. The fluid continues through the prostatic urethra, where secretions from the prostate are added to form semen. These secretions help the sperm to travel through the urethra and into the female reproductive tract. Secretions from the bulbourethral glands protect sperm and cleanse and lubricate the penile (spongy) urethra.

The penis is the male organ of copulation. Columns of erectile tissue called the corpora cavernosa and corpus spongiosum fill with blood when sexual arousal activates vasodilatation in the blood vessels of the penis. Testosterone regulates and maintains the sex organs and sex drive, and induces the physical changes of puberty. Interplay between the testes and the endocrine system precisely control the production of testosterone with a negative feedback loop.

27.2 Anatomy and Physiology of the Female Reproductive System

The external female genitalia are collectively called the vulva. The vagina is the pathway into and out of the uterus. The man's penis is inserted into the vagina to deliver sperm, and the baby exits the uterus through the vagina during childbirth.

The ovaries produce oocytes, the female gametes, in a process called oogenesis. As with spermatogenesis, meiosis produces the haploid gamete (in this case, an ovum); however, it is completed only in an oocyte that has been penetrated by a sperm. In the ovary, an oocyte surrounded by supporting cells is called a follicle. In folliculogenesis, primordial follicles develop into primary, secondary, and tertiary follicles. Early tertiary follicles with their fluid-filled antrum will be stimulated by an increase in FSH, a gonadotropin produced by the anterior pituitary, to grow in the 28-day ovarian cycle. Supporting granulosa and theca cells in the growing follicles produce estrogens, until the level of estrogen in the bloodstream is high enough that it triggers negative feedback at the hypothalamus and pituitary. This results in a reduction of FSH and LH, and most tertiary follicles in the ovary undergo atresia (they die). One follicle, usually the one with the most FSH receptors, survives this period and is now called the dominant follicle. The dominant follicle produces more estrogen, triggering positive feedback and the LH surge that will induce ovulation. Following ovulation, the granulosa cells of the empty follicle luteinize and transform into the progesterone-producing corpus luteum. The ovulated oocyte with its surrounding granulosa cells is picked up by the infundibulum of the uterine tube, and beating cilia help to transport it through the tube toward the uterus. Fertilization occurs within the uterine tube, and the final stage of meiosis is completed.

The uterus has three regions: the fundus, the body, and the cervix. It has three layers: the outer perimetrium, the muscular myometrium, and the inner endometrium. The endometrium responds to estrogen released by the follicles during the menstrual cycle and grows thicker with an increase in blood vessels in preparation for pregnancy. If the egg is not fertilized, no signal is sent to extend the life of the corpus luteum, and it degrades, stopping progesterone production. This decline in progesterone results in the sloughing of the inner portion of the endometrium in a process called menses, or menstruation.

The breasts are accessory sexual organs that are utilized after the birth of a child to produce milk in a process called lactation. Birth control pills provide constant levels of estrogen and progesterone to negatively feed back on the hypothalamus and pituitary, and suppress the release of FSH and LH, which inhibits ovulation and prevents pregnancy.

27.3 Development of the Male and Female Reproductive Systems

The reproductive systems of males and females begin to develop soon after conception. A gene on the male's Y chromosome called *SRY* is critical in stimulating a cascade of events that simultaneously stimulate testis development and repress the development of female structures. Testosterone produced by Leydig cells in the embryonic testis stimulates the development of male sexual organs. If testosterone is not present, female sexual organs will develop.

Whereas the gonads and some other reproductive tissues are considered bipotential, the tissue that forms the internal reproductive structures stems from ducts that will develop into only male (Wolffian) or female (Müllerian) structures. To be able to reproduce as an adult, one of these systems must develop properly and the other must degrade.

Further development of the reproductive systems occurs at puberty. The initiation of the changes that occur in puberty is the result of a decrease in sensitivity to negative feedback in the hypothalamus and pituitary gland, and an increase in sensitivity of the gonads to FSH and LH stimulation. These changes lead to increases in either estrogen or testosterone, in female and male adolescents, respectively. The increase in sex steroid hormones leads to maturation of the gonads and other reproductive organs. The initiation of spermatogenesis begins in boys, and girls begin ovulating and menstruating. Increases in sex steroid hormones also lead to the development of secondary sex characteristics such as breast development in girls and facial hair and larynx growth in boys.

INTERACTIVE LINK QUESTIONS

1. Watch this video (http://openstaxcollege.org/l/vasectomy) to learn about vasectomy. As described in this video, a vasectomy is a procedure in which a small section of the ductus (vas) deferens is removed from the scrotum. This interrupts the path taken by sperm through the ductus deferens. If sperm do not exit through the vas, either because the man has had a vasectomy or has not ejaculated, in what region of the testis do they remain?

2. Watch this video (http://openstaxcollege.org/l/spermpath) to explore the structures of the male reproductive system and the path of sperm that starts in the testes and ends as the sperm leave the penis through the urethra. Where are sperm deposited after they leave the ejaculatory duct?

3. Watch this video (http://openstaxcollege.org/l/ovulation) to observe ovulation and its initiation in response to the release of FSH and LH from the pituitary gland. What specialized structures help guide the oocyte from the ovary into the uterine tube?

4. Watch this series of videos (http://openstaxcollege.org/l/oocyte) to look at the movement of the oocyte through the ovary. The cilia in the uterine tube promote movement of the oocyte. What would likely occur if the cilia were paralyzed at the time of ovulation?

5. A baby's gender is determined at conception, and the different genitalia of male and female fetuses develop from the same tissues in the embryo. View this animation (http://openstaxcollege.org/l/fetus) that compares the development of structures of the female and male reproductive systems in a growing fetus. Where are the testes located for most of gestational time?

REVIEW QUESTIONS

6. What are male gametes called?
   a. ova
   b. sperm
   c. testes
   d. testosterone

7. Leydig cells _____.
   a. secrete testosterone
   b. activate the sperm flagellum
   c. support spermatogenesis
   d. secrete seminal fluid

8. Which hypothalamic hormone contributes to the regulation of the male reproductive system?
   a. luteinizing hormone
   b. gonadotropin-releasing hormone
   c. follicle-stimulating hormone
   d. androgens

9. What is the function of the epididymis?
   a. sperm maturation and storage
   b. produces the bulk of seminal fluid
   c. provides nitric oxide needed for erections
   d. spermatogenesis

10. Spermatogenesis takes place in the _____.
   a. prostate gland
   b. glans penis
   c. seminiferous tubules
   d. ejaculatory duct

11. What are the female gonads called?
   a. oocytes
   b. ova
   c. oviducts
   d. ovaries

12. When do the oogonia undergo mitosis?
   a. before birth
   b. at puberty
   c. at the beginning of each menstrual cycle

d. during fertilization

13. From what structure does the corpus luteum originate?

a. uterine corpus
b. dominant follicle
c. fallopian tube
d. corpus albicans

14. Where does fertilization of the egg by the sperm typically occur?

a. vagina
b. uterus
c. uterine tube
d. ovary

15. Why do estrogen levels fall after menopause?

a. The ovaries degrade.
b. There are no follicles left to produce estrogen.
c. The pituitary secretes a menopause-specific hormone.
d. The cells of the endometrium degenerate.

16. The vulva includes the _____.

a. lactiferous duct, rugae, and hymen
b. lactiferous duct, endometrium, and bulbourethral glands
c. mons pubis, endometrium, and hymen
d. mons pubis, labia majora, and Bartholin's glands

17. What controls whether an embryo will develop testes or ovaries?

a. pituitary gland
b. hypothalamus
c. Y chromosome
d. presence or absence of estrogen

18. Without *SRY* expression, an embryo will develop _____.

a. male reproductive structures
b. female reproductive structures
c. no reproductive structures
d. male reproductive structures 50 percent of the time and female reproductive structures 50 percent of the time

19. The timing of puberty can be influenced by which of the following?

a. genes
b. stress
c. amount of body fat
d. all of the above

CRITICAL THINKING QUESTIONS

20. Briefly explain why mature gametes carry only one set of chromosomes.

21. What special features are evident in sperm cells but not in somatic cells, and how do these specializations function?

22. What do each of the three male accessory glands contribute to the semen?

23. Describe how penile erection occurs.

24. While anabolic steroids (synthetic testosterone) bulk up muscles, they can also affect testosterone production in the testis. Using what you know about negative feedback, describe what would happen to testosterone production in the testis if a male takes large amounts of synthetic testosterone.

25. Follow the path of ejaculated sperm from the vagina to the oocyte. Include all structures of the female reproductive tract that the sperm must swim through to reach the egg.

26. Identify some differences between meiosis in men and women.

27. Explain the hormonal regulation of the phases of the menstrual cycle.

28. Endometriosis is a disorder in which endometrial cells implant and proliferate outside of the uterus—in the uterine tubes, on the ovaries, or even in the pelvic cavity. Offer a theory as to why endometriosis increases a woman's risk of infertility.

29. Identify the changes in sensitivity that occur in the hypothalamus, pituitary, and gonads as a boy or girl approaches puberty. Explain how these changes lead to the increases of sex steroid hormone secretions that drive many pubertal changes.

30. Explain how the internal female and male reproductive structures develop from two different duct systems.

31. Explain what would occur during fetal development to an XY individual with a mutation causing a nonfunctional *SRY* gene.

28 | DEVELOPMENT AND INHERITANCE

Figure 28.1 Newborn   A single fertilized egg develops over the span of nine months into an infant consisting of trillions of cells and capable of surviving outside the womb. (credit: "Seattleye"/flickr.com)

Introduction

Chapter Objectives

After studying this chapter, you will be able to:

- List and explain the steps involved in fertilization
- Describe the major events in embryonic development
- Describe the major events in fetal development
- Discuss the adaptations of a woman's body to pregnancy
- Describe the physiologic adjustments that the newborn must make in the first hours of extrauterine life
- Summarize the physiology of lactation
- Classify and describe the different patterns of inheritance

In approximately nine months, a single cell—a fertilized egg—develops into a fully formed infant consisting of trillions of cells with myriad specialized functions. The dramatic changes of fertilization, embryonic development, and fetal development are followed by remarkable adaptations of the newborn to life outside the womb. An offspring's normal development depends upon the appropriate synthesis of structural and functional proteins. This, in turn, is governed by the genetic material inherited from the parental egg and sperm, as well as environmental factors.

28.1 | Fertilization

By the end of this section, you will be able to:

- Describe the obstacles that sperm must overcome to reach an oocyte
- Explain capacitation and its importance in fertilization
- Summarize the events that occur as a sperm fertilizes an oocyte

Fertilization occurs when a sperm and an oocyte (egg) combine and their nuclei fuse. Because each of these reproductive cells is a haploid cell containing half of the genetic material needed to form a human being, their combination forms a diploid cell. This new single cell, called a **zygote**, contains all of the genetic material needed to form a human—half from the mother and half from the father.

Transit of Sperm

Fertilization is a numbers game. During ejaculation, hundreds of millions of sperm (spermatozoa) are released into the vagina. Almost immediately, millions of these sperm are overcome by the acidity of the vagina (approximately pH 3.8), and millions more may be blocked from entering the uterus by thick cervical mucus. Of those that do enter, thousands are destroyed by phagocytic uterine leukocytes. Thus, the race into the uterine tubes, which is the most typical site for sperm to encounter the oocyte, is reduced to a few thousand contenders. Their journey—thought to be facilitated by uterine contractions—usually takes from 30 minutes to 2 hours. If the sperm do not encounter an oocyte immediately, they can survive in the uterine tubes for another 3–5 days. Thus, fertilization can still occur if intercourse takes place a few days before ovulation. In comparison, an oocyte can survive independently for only approximately 24 hours following ovulation. Intercourse more than a day after ovulation will therefore usually not result in fertilization.

During the journey, fluids in the female reproductive tract prepare the sperm for fertilization through a process called **capacitation**, or priming. The fluids improve the motility of the spermatozoa. They also deplete cholesterol molecules embedded in the membrane of the head of the sperm, thinning the membrane in such a way that will help facilitate the release of the lysosomal (digestive) enzymes needed for the sperm to penetrate the oocyte's exterior once contact is made. Sperm must undergo the process of capacitation in order to have the "capacity" to fertilize an oocyte. If they reach the oocyte before capacitation is complete, they will be unable to penetrate the oocyte's thick outer layer of cells.

Contact Between Sperm and Oocyte

Upon ovulation, the oocyte released by the ovary is swept into—and along—the uterine tube. Fertilization must occur in the distal uterine tube because an unfertilized oocyte cannot survive the 72-hour journey to the uterus. As you will recall from your study of the oogenesis, this oocyte (specifically a secondary oocyte) is surrounded by two protective layers. The **corona radiata** is an outer layer of follicular (granulosa) cells that form around a developing oocyte in the ovary and remain with it upon ovulation. The underlying **zona pellucida** (pellucid = "transparent") is a transparent, but thick, glycoprotein membrane that surrounds the cell's plasma membrane.

As it is swept along the distal uterine tube, the oocyte encounters the surviving capacitated sperm, which stream toward it in response to chemical attractants released by the cells of the corona radiata. To reach the oocyte itself, the sperm must penetrate the two protective layers. The sperm first burrow through the cells of the corona radiata. Then, upon contact with the zona pellucida, the sperm bind to receptors in the zona pellucida. This initiates a process called the **acrosomal reaction** in which the enzyme-filled "cap" of the sperm, called the **acrosome**, releases its stored digestive enzymes. These enzymes clear a path through the zona pellucida that allows sperm to reach the oocyte. Finally, a single sperm makes contact with sperm-binding receptors on the oocyte's plasma membrane (Figure 28.2). The plasma membrane of that sperm then fuses with the oocyte's plasma membrane, and the head and mid-piece of the "winning" sperm enter the oocyte interior.

How do sperm penetrate the corona radiata? Some sperm undergo a spontaneous acrosomal reaction, which is an acrosomal reaction not triggered by contact with the zona pellucida. The digestive enzymes released by this reaction digest the extracellular matrix of the corona radiata. As you can see, the first sperm to reach the oocyte is never the one to fertilize it. Rather, hundreds of sperm cells must undergo the acrosomal reaction, each helping to degrade the corona radiata and zona pellucida until a path is created to allow one sperm to contact and fuse with the plasma membrane of the oocyte. If you consider the loss of millions of sperm between entry into the vagina and degradation of the zona pellucida, you can understand why a low sperm count can cause male infertility.

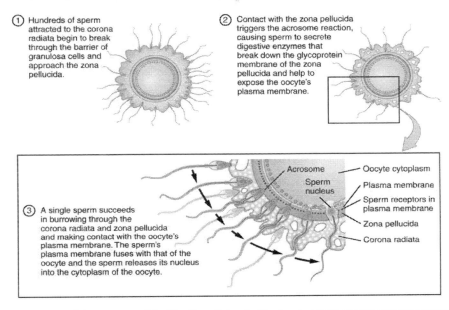

Figure 28.2 Sperm and the Process of Fertilization Before fertilization, hundreds of capacitated sperm must break through the surrounding corona radiata and zona pellucida so that one can contact and fuse with the oocyte plasma membrane.

When the first sperm fuses with the oocyte, the oocyte deploys two mechanisms to prevent **polyspermy**, which is penetration by more than one sperm. This is critical because if more than one sperm were to fertilize the oocyte, the resulting zygote would be a triploid organism with three sets of chromosomes. This is incompatible with life.

The first mechanism is the fast block, which involves a near instantaneous change in sodium ion permeability upon binding of the first sperm, depolarizing the oocyte plasma membrane and preventing the fusion of additional sperm cells. The fast block sets in almost immediately and lasts for about a minute, during which time an influx of calcium ions following sperm penetration triggers the second mechanism, the slow block. In this process, referred to as the **cortical reaction**, cortical granules sitting immediately below the oocyte plasma membrane fuse with the membrane and release zonal inhibiting proteins and mucopolysaccharides into the space between the plasma membrane and the zona pellucida. Zonal inhibiting proteins cause the release of any other attached sperm and destroy the oocyte's sperm receptors, thus preventing any more sperm from binding. The mucopolysaccharides then coat the nascent zygote in an impenetrable barrier that, together with hardened zona pellucida, is called a **fertilization membrane**.

The Zygote

Recall that at the point of fertilization, the oocyte has not yet completed meiosis; all secondary oocytes remain arrested in metaphase of meiosis II until fertilization. Only upon fertilization does the oocyte complete meiosis. The unneeded complement of genetic material that results is stored in a second polar body that is eventually ejected. At this moment, the oocyte has become an ovum, the female haploid gamete. The two haploid nuclei derived from the sperm and oocyte and contained within the egg are referred to as pronuclei. They decondense, expand, and replicate their DNA in preparation for mitosis. The pronuclei then migrate toward each other, their nuclear envelopes disintegrate, and the male- and female-derived genetic material intermingles. This step completes the process of fertilization and results in a single-celled diploid zygote with all the genetic instructions it needs to develop into a human.

Most of the time, a woman releases a single egg during an ovulation cycle. However, in approximately 1 percent of ovulation cycles, two eggs are released and both are fertilized. Two zygotes form, implant, and develop, resulting in the birth of dizygotic (or fraternal) twins. Because dizygotic twins develop from two eggs fertilized by two sperm, they are no more identical than siblings born at different times.

Much less commonly, a zygote can divide into two separate offspring during early development. This results in the birth of monozygotic (or identical) twins. Although the zygote can split as early as the two-cell stage, splitting occurs most commonly during the early blastocyst stage, with roughly 70–100 cells present. These two scenarios are distinct from each other, in that the twin embryos that separated at the two-cell stage will have individual placentas, whereas twin embryos that form from separation at the blastocyst stage will share a placenta and a chorionic cavity.

Everyday CONNECTION

In Vitro Fertilization

IVF, which stands for in vitro fertilization, is an assisted reproductive technology. In vitro, which in Latin translates to "in glass," refers to a procedure that takes place outside of the body. There are many different indications for IVF. For example, a woman may produce normal eggs, but the eggs cannot reach the uterus because the uterine tubes are blocked or otherwise compromised. A man may have a low sperm count, low sperm motility, sperm with an unusually high percentage of morphological abnormalities, or sperm that are incapable of penetrating the zona pellucida of an egg.

A typical IVF procedure begins with egg collection. A normal ovulation cycle produces only one oocyte, but the number can be boosted significantly (to 10–20 oocytes) by administering a short course of gonadotropins. The course begins with follicle-stimulating hormone (FSH) analogs, which support the development of multiple follicles, and ends with a luteinizing hormone (LH) analog that triggers ovulation. Right before the ova would be released from the ovary, they are harvested using ultrasound-guided oocyte retrieval. In this procedure, ultrasound allows a physician to visualize mature follicles. The ova are aspirated (sucked out) using a syringe.

In parallel, sperm are obtained from the male partner or from a sperm bank. The sperm are prepared by washing to remove seminal fluid because seminal fluid contains a peptide, FPP (or, fertilization promoting peptide), that—in high concentrations—prevents capacitation of the sperm. The sperm sample is also concentrated, to increase the sperm count per milliliter.

Next, the eggs and sperm are mixed in a petri dish. The ideal ratio is 75,000 sperm to one egg. If there are severe problems with the sperm—for example, the count is exceedingly low, or the sperm are completely nonmotile, or incapable of binding to or penetrating the zona pellucida—a sperm can be injected into an egg. This is called intracytoplasmic sperm injection (ICSI).

The embryos are then incubated until they either reach the eight-cell stage or the blastocyst stage. In the United States, fertilized eggs are typically cultured to the blastocyst stage because this results in a higher pregnancy rate. Finally, the embryos are transferred to a woman's uterus using a plastic catheter (tube). Figure 28.3 illustrates the steps involved in IVF.

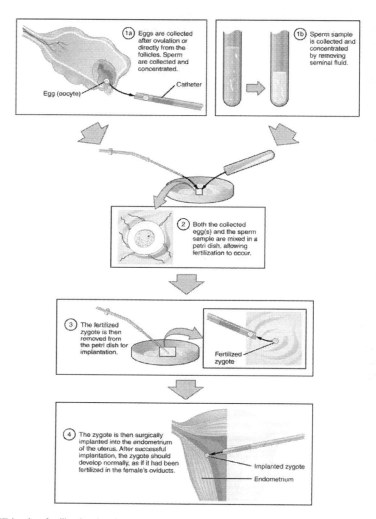

Figure 28.3 IVF In vitro fertilization involves egg collection from the ovaries, fertilization in a petri dish, and the transfer of embryos into the uterus.

IVF is a relatively new and still evolving technology, and until recently it was necessary to transfer multiple embryos to achieve a good chance of a pregnancy. Today, however, transferred embryos are much more likely to implant successfully, so countries that regulate the IVF industry cap the number of embryos that can be transferred per cycle at two. This reduces the risk of multiple-birth pregnancies.

The rate of success for IVF is correlated with a woman's age. More than 40 percent of women under 35 succeed in giving birth following IVF, but the rate drops to a little over 10 percent in women over 40.

Go to this site (http://openstaxcollege.org/l/fertilization) to view resources covering various aspects of fertilization, including movies and animations showing sperm structure and motility, ovulation, and fertilization.

28.2 | Embryonic Development

By the end of this section, you will be able to:
- Distinguish the stages of embryonic development that occur before implantation
- Describe the process of implantation
- List and describe four embryonic membranes
- Explain gastrulation
- Describe how the placenta is formed and identify its functions
- Explain how an embryo transforms from a flat disc of cells into a three-dimensional shape resembling a human
- Summarize the process of organogenesis

Throughout this chapter, we will express embryonic and fetal ages in terms of weeks from fertilization, commonly called conception. The period of time required for full development of a fetus in utero is referred to as **gestation** (gestare = "to carry" or "to bear"). It can be subdivided into distinct gestational periods. The first 2 weeks of prenatal development are referred to as the pre-embryonic stage. A developing human is referred to as an **embryo** during weeks 3–8, and a **fetus** from the ninth week of gestation until birth. In this section, we'll cover the pre-embryonic and embryonic stages of development, which are characterized by cell division, migration, and differentiation. By the end of the embryonic period, all of the organ systems are structured in rudimentary form, although the organs themselves are either nonfunctional or only semi-functional.

Pre-implantation Embryonic Development

Following fertilization, the zygote and its associated membranes, together referred to as the **conceptus**, continue to be projected toward the uterus by peristalsis and beating cilia. During its journey to the uterus, the zygote undergoes five or six rapid mitotic cell divisions. Although each **cleavage** results in more cells, it does not increase the total volume of the conceptus (Figure 28.4). Each daughter cell produced by cleavage is called a **blastomere** (blastos = "germ," in the sense of a seed or sprout).

Approximately 3 days after fertilization, a 16-cell conceptus reaches the uterus. The cells that had been loosely grouped are now compacted and look more like a solid mass. The name given to this structure is the **morula** (morula = "little mulberry"). Once inside the uterus, the conceptus floats freely for several more days. It continues to divide, creating a ball of approximately 100 cells, and consuming nutritive endometrial secretions called uterine milk while the uterine lining thickens. The ball of now tightly bound cells starts to secrete fluid and organize themselves around a fluid-filled cavity, the **blastocoel**. At this developmental stage, the conceptus is referred to as a **blastocyst**. Within this structure, a group of cells forms into an **inner cell mass**, which is fated to become the embryo. The cells that form the outer shell are called **trophoblasts** (trophe = "to feed" or "to nourish"). These cells will develop into the chorionic sac and the fetal portion of the **placenta** (the organ of nutrient, waste, and gas exchange between mother and the developing offspring).

The inner mass of embryonic cells is totipotent during this stage, meaning that each cell has the potential to differentiate into any cell type in the human body. Totipotency lasts for only a few days before the cells' fates are set as being the precursors to a specific lineage of cells.

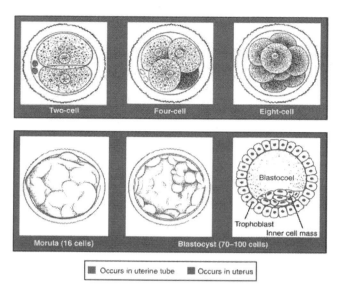

Figure 28.4 Pre-Embryonic Cleavages Pre-embryonic cleavages make use of the abundant cytoplasm of the conceptus as the cells rapidly divide without changing the total volume.

As the blastocyst forms, the trophoblast excretes enzymes that begin to degrade the zona pellucida. In a process called "hatching," the conceptus breaks free of the zona pellucida in preparation for implantation.

View this time-lapse movie (http://openstaxcollege.org/l/conceptus) of a conceptus starting at day 3. What is the first structure you see? At what point in the movie does the blastocoel first appear? What event occurs at the end of the movie?

Implantation

At the end of the first week, the blastocyst comes in contact with the uterine wall and adheres to it, embedding itself in the uterine lining via the trophoblast cells. Thus begins the process of **implantation**, which signals the end of the pre-embryonic stage of development (Figure 28.5). Implantation can be accompanied by minor bleeding. The blastocyst typically implants in the fundus of the uterus or on the posterior wall. However, if the endometrium is not fully developed and ready to receive the blastocyst, the blastocyst will detach and find a better spot. A significant percentage (50–75 percent) of blastocysts fail to implant; when this occurs, the blastocyst is shed with the endometrium during menses. The high rate of implantation failure is one reason why pregnancy typically requires several ovulation cycles to achieve.

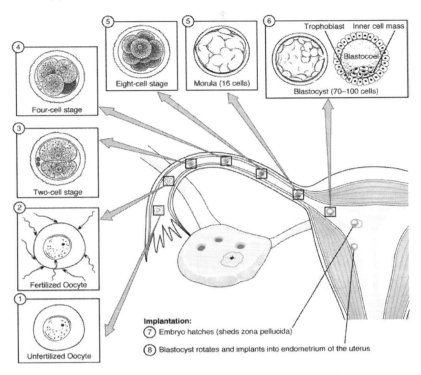

Figure 28.5 Pre-Embryonic Development Ovulation, fertilization, pre-embryonic development, and implantation occur at specific locations within the female reproductive system in a time span of approximately 1 week.

When implantation succeeds and the blastocyst adheres to the endometrium, the superficial cells of the trophoblast fuse with each other, forming the **syncytiotrophoblast**, a multinucleated body that digests endometrial cells to firmly secure the blastocyst to the uterine wall. In response, the uterine mucosa rebuilds itself and envelops the blastocyst (Figure 28.6). The trophoblast secretes **human chorionic gonadotropin (hCG)**, a hormone that directs the corpus luteum to survive, enlarge, and continue producing progesterone and estrogen to suppress menses. These functions of hCG are necessary for creating an environment suitable for the developing embryo. As a result of this increased production, hCG accumulates in the maternal bloodstream and is excreted in the urine. Implantation is complete by the middle of the second week. Just a few days after implantation, the trophoblast has secreted enough hCG for an at-home urine pregnancy test to give a positive result.

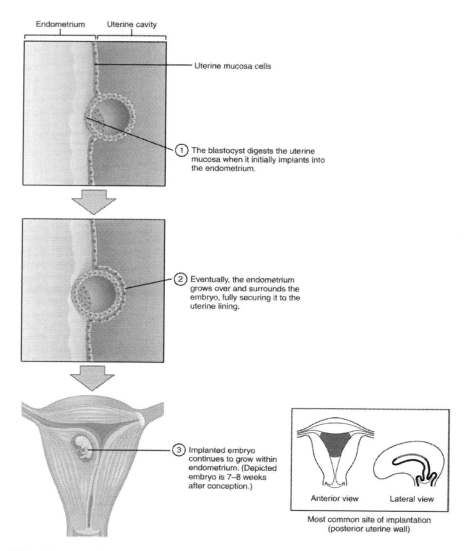

Figure 28.6 Implantation During implantation, the trophoblast cells of the blastocyst adhere to the endometrium and digest endometrial cells until it is attached securely.

Most of the time an embryo implants within the body of the uterus in a location that can support growth and development. However, in one to two percent of cases, the embryo implants either outside the uterus (an **ectopic pregnancy**) or in a region of uterus that can create complications for the pregnancy. If the embryo implants in the inferior portion of the uterus, the placenta can potentially grow over the opening of the cervix, a condition call **placenta previa**.

Development of the Embryo

In the vast majority of ectopic pregnancies, the embryo does not complete its journey to the uterus and implants in the uterine tube, referred to as a tubal pregnancy. However, there are also ovarian ectopic pregnancies (in which the egg never left the ovary) and abdominal ectopic pregnancies (in which an egg was "lost" to the abdominal cavity during the transfer from ovary to uterine tube, or in which an embryo from a tubal pregnancy re-implanted in the abdomen). Once in the abdominal cavity, an embryo can implant into any well-vascularized structure—the rectouterine cavity (Douglas' pouch), the mesentery of the intestines, and the greater omentum are some common sites.

Tubal pregnancies can be caused by scar tissue within the tube following a sexually transmitted bacterial infection. The scar tissue impedes the progress of the embryo into the uterus—in some cases "snagging" the embryo and, in other cases, blocking the tube completely. Approximately one half of tubal pregnancies resolve spontaneously. Implantation in a uterine tube causes bleeding, which appears to stimulate smooth muscle contractions and expulsion of the embryo. In the remaining cases, medical or surgical intervention is necessary. If an ectopic pregnancy is detected early, the embryo's development can be arrested by the administration of the cytotoxic drug methotrexate, which inhibits the metabolism of folic acid. If diagnosis is late and the uterine tube is already ruptured, surgical repair is essential.

Even if the embryo has successfully found its way to the uterus, it does not always implant in an optimal location (the fundus or the posterior wall of the uterus). Placenta previa can result if an embryo implants close to the internal os of the uterus (the internal opening of the cervix). As the fetus grows, the placenta can partially or completely cover the opening of the cervix (Figure 28.7). Although it occurs in only 0.5 percent of pregnancies, placenta previa is the leading cause of antepartum hemorrhage (profuse vaginal bleeding after week 24 of pregnancy but prior to childbirth).

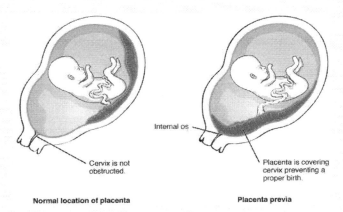

Figure 28.7 Placenta Previa An embryo that implants too close to the opening of the cervix can lead to placenta previa, a condition in which the placenta partially or completely covers the cervix.

Embryonic Membranes

During the second week of development, with the embryo implanted in the uterus, cells within the blastocyst start to organize into layers. Some grow to form the extra-embryonic membranes needed to support and protect the growing embryo: the amnion, the yolk sac, the allantois, and the chorion.

At the beginning of the second week, the cells of the inner cell mass form into a two-layered disc of embryonic cells, and a space—the **amniotic cavity**—opens up between it and the trophoblast (Figure 28.8). Cells from the upper layer of the disc (the **epiblast**) extend around the amniotic cavity, creating a membranous sac that forms into the **amnion** by the end of the second week. The amnion fills with amniotic fluid and eventually grows to surround the embryo. Early in development, amniotic fluid consists almost entirely of a filtrate of maternal plasma, but as the kidneys of the fetus begin to function at approximately the eighth week, they add urine to the volume of amniotic fluid. Floating within the amniotic fluid, the embryo—and later, the fetus—is protected from trauma and rapid temperature changes. It can move freely within the fluid and can prepare for swallowing and breathing out of the uterus.

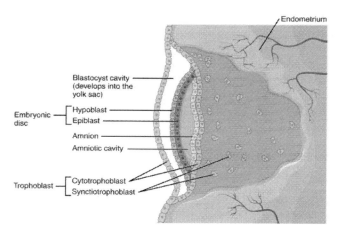

Figure 28.8 Development of the Embryonic Disc Formation of the embryonic disc leaves spaces on either side that develop into the amniotic cavity and the yolk sac.

On the ventral side of the embryonic disc, opposite the amnion, cells in the lower layer of the embryonic disk (the **hypoblast**) extend into the blastocyst cavity and form a **yolk sac**. The yolk sac supplies some nutrients absorbed from the trophoblast and also provides primitive blood circulation to the developing embryo for the second and third week of development. When the placenta takes over nourishing the embryo at approximately week 4, the yolk sac has been greatly reduced in size and its main function is to serve as the source of blood cells and germ cells (cells that will give rise to gametes). During week 3, a finger-like outpocketing of the yolk sac develops into the **allantois**, a primitive excretory duct of the embryo that will become part of the urinary bladder. Together, the stalks of the yolk sac and allantois establish the outer structure of the umbilical cord.

The last of the extra-embryonic membranes is the **chorion**, which is the one membrane that surrounds all others. The development of the chorion will be discussed in more detail shortly, as it relates to the growth and development of the placenta.

Embryogenesis

As the third week of development begins, the two-layered disc of cells becomes a three-layered disc through the process of **gastrulation**, during which the cells transition from totipotency to multipotency. The embryo, which takes the shape of an oval-shaped disc, forms an indentation called the **primitive streak** along the dorsal surface of the epiblast. A node at the caudal or "tail" end of the primitive streak emits growth factors that direct cells to multiply and migrate. Cells migrate toward and through the primitive streak and then move laterally to create two new layers of cells. The first layer is the **endoderm**, a sheet of cells that displaces the hypoblast and lies adjacent to the yolk sac. The second layer of cells fills in as the middle layer, or **mesoderm**. The cells of the epiblast that remain (not having migrated through the primitive streak) become the **ectoderm** (Figure 28.9).

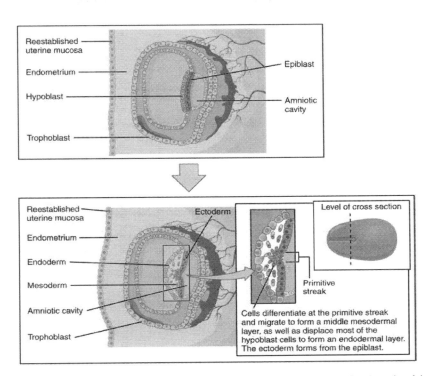

Figure 28.9 Germ Layers Formation of the three primary germ layers occurs during the first 2 weeks of development. The embryo at this stage is only a few millimeters in length.

Each of these germ layers will develop into specific structures in the embryo. Whereas the ectoderm and endoderm form tightly connected epithelial sheets, the mesodermal cells are less organized and exist as a loosely connected cell community. The ectoderm gives rise to cell lineages that differentiate to become the central and peripheral nervous systems, sensory organs, epidermis, hair, and nails. Mesodermal cells ultimately become the skeleton, muscles, connective tissue, heart, blood vessels, and kidneys. The endoderm goes on to form the epithelial lining of the gastrointestinal tract, liver, and pancreas, as well as the lungs (Figure 28.10).

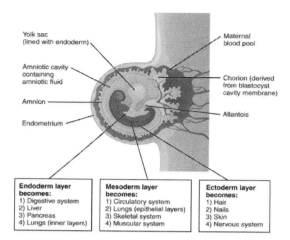

Figure 28.10 Fates of Germ Layers in Embryo Following gastrulation of the embryo in the third week, embryonic cells of the ectoderm, mesoderm, and endoderm begin to migrate and differentiate into the cell lineages that will give rise to mature organs and organ systems in the infant.

Development of the Placenta

During the first several weeks of development, the cells of the endometrium—referred to as decidual cells—nourish the nascent embryo. During prenatal weeks 4–12, the developing placenta gradually takes over the role of feeding the embryo, and the decidual cells are no longer needed. The mature placenta is composed of tissues derived from the embryo, as well as maternal tissues of the endometrium. The placenta connects to the conceptus via the **umbilical cord**, which carries deoxygenated blood and wastes from the fetus through two umbilical arteries; nutrients and oxygen are carried from the mother to the fetus through the single umbilical vein. The umbilical cord is surrounded by the amnion, and the spaces within the cord around the blood vessels are filled with Wharton's jelly, a mucous connective tissue.

The maternal portion of the placenta develops from the deepest layer of the endometrium, the decidua basalis. To form the embryonic portion of the placenta, the syncytiotrophoblast and the underlying cells of the trophoblast (cytotrophoblast cells) begin to proliferate along with a layer of extraembryonic mesoderm cells. These form the **chorionic membrane**, which envelops the entire conceptus as the chorion. The chorionic membrane forms finger-like structures called **chorionic villi** that burrow into the endometrium like tree roots, making up the fetal portion of the placenta. The cytotrophoblast cells perforate the chorionic villi, burrow farther into the endometrium, and remodel maternal blood vessels to augment maternal blood flow surrounding the villi. Meanwhile, fetal mesenchymal cells derived from the mesoderm fill the villi and differentiate into blood vessels, including the three umbilical blood vessels that connect the embryo to the developing placenta (Figure 28.11).

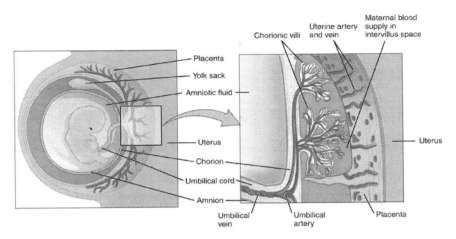

Figure 28.11 Cross-Section of the Placenta In the placenta, maternal and fetal blood components are conducted through the surface of the chorionic villi, but maternal and fetal bloodstreams never mix directly.

The placenta develops throughout the embryonic period and during the first several weeks of the fetal period; **placentation** is complete by weeks 14–16. As a fully developed organ, the placenta provides nutrition and excretion, respiration, and endocrine function (Table 28.1 and Figure 28.12). It receives blood from the fetus through the umbilical arteries. Capillaries in the chorionic villi filter fetal wastes out of the blood and return clean, oxygenated blood to the fetus through the umbilical vein. Nutrients and oxygen are transferred from maternal blood surrounding the villi through the capillaries and into the fetal bloodstream. Some substances move across the placenta by simple diffusion. Oxygen, carbon dioxide, and any other lipid-soluble substances take this route. Other substances move across by facilitated diffusion. This includes water-soluble glucose. The fetus has a high demand for amino acids and iron, and those substances are moved across the placenta by active transport.

Maternal and fetal blood does not commingle because blood cells cannot move across the placenta. This separation prevents the mother's cytotoxic T cells from reaching and subsequently destroying the fetus, which bears "non-self" antigens. Further, it ensures the fetal red blood cells do not enter the mother's circulation and trigger antibody development (if they carry "non-self" antigens)—at least until the final stages of pregnancy or birth. This is the reason that, even in the absence of preventive treatment, an Rh^- mother doesn't develop antibodies that could cause hemolytic disease in her first Rh^+ fetus.

Although blood cells are not exchanged, the chorionic villi provide ample surface area for the two-way exchange of substances between maternal and fetal blood. The rate of exchange increases throughout gestation as the villi become thinner and increasingly branched. The placenta is permeable to lipid-soluble fetotoxic substances: alcohol, nicotine, barbiturates, antibiotics, certain pathogens, and many other substances that can be dangerous or fatal to the developing embryo or fetus. For these reasons, pregnant women should avoid fetotoxic substances. Alcohol consumption by pregnant women, for example, can result in a range of abnormalities referred to as fetal alcohol spectrum disorders (FASD). These include organ and facial malformations, as well as cognitive and behavioral disorders.

Functions of the Placenta

Nutrition and digestion	Respiration	Endocrine function
Mediates diffusion of maternal glucose, amino acids, fatty acids, vitamins, and minerals	Mediates maternal-to-fetal oxygen transport and fetal-to-maternal carbon dioxide transport	Secretes several hormones, including hCG, estrogens, and progesterone, to maintain the pregnancy and stimulate maternal and fetal development
Stores nutrients during early pregnancy to accommodate increased fetal demand later in pregnancy		
Excretes and filters fetal nitrogenous wastes into maternal blood		Mediates the transmission of maternal hormones into fetal blood and vice versa

Table 28.1

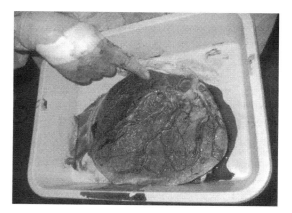

Figure 28.12 Placenta   This post-expulsion placenta and umbilical cord (white) are viewed from the fetal side.

Organogenesis

Following gastrulation, rudiments of the central nervous system develop from the ectoderm in the process of **neurulation** (Figure 28.13). Specialized neuroectodermal tissues along the length of the embryo thicken into the **neural plate**. During the fourth week, tissues on either side of the plate fold upward into a **neural fold**. The two folds converge to form the **neural tube**. The tube lies atop a rod-shaped, mesoderm-derived **notochord**, which eventually becomes the nucleus pulposus of intervertebral discs. Block-like structures called **somites** form on either side of the tube, eventually differentiating into the axial skeleton, skeletal muscle, and dermis. During the fourth and fifth weeks, the anterior neural tube dilates and subdivides to form vesicles that will become the brain structures.

Folate, one of the B vitamins, is important to the healthy development of the neural tube. A deficiency of maternal folate in the first weeks of pregnancy can result in neural tube defects, including spina bifida—a birth defect in which spinal tissue protrudes through the newborn's vertebral column, which has failed to completely close. A more severe neural tube defect is anencephaly, a partial or complete absence of brain tissue.

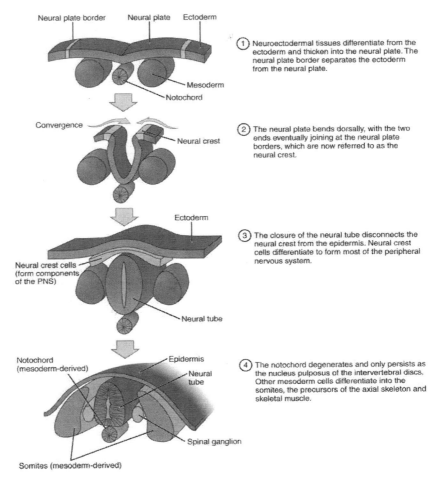

Figure 28.13 Neurulation The embryonic process of neurulation establishes the rudiments of the future central nervous system and skeleton.

The embryo, which begins as a flat sheet of cells, begins to acquire a cylindrical shape through the process of **embryonic folding** (Figure 28.14). The embryo folds laterally and again at either end, forming a C-shape with distinct head and tail ends. The embryo envelops a portion of the yolk sac, which protrudes with the umbilical cord from what will become the abdomen. The folding essentially creates a tube, called the primitive gut, that is lined by the endoderm. The amniotic sac, which was sitting on top of the flat embryo, envelops the embryo as it folds.

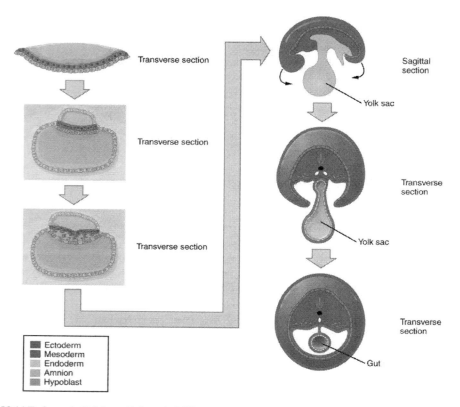

Figure 28.14 Embryonic Folding Embryonic folding converts a flat sheet of cells into a hollow, tube-like structure.

Within the first 8 weeks of gestation, a developing embryo establishes the rudimentary structures of all of its organs and tissues from the ectoderm, mesoderm, and endoderm. This process is called **organogenesis**.

Like the central nervous system, the heart also begins its development in the embryo as a tube-like structure, connected via capillaries to the chorionic villi. Cells of the primitive tube-shaped heart are capable of electrical conduction and contraction. The heart begins beating in the beginning of the fourth week, although it does not actually pump embryonic blood until a week later, when the oversized liver has begun producing red blood cells. (This is a temporary responsibility of the embryonic liver that the bone marrow will assume during fetal development.) During weeks 4–5, the eye pits form, limb buds become apparent, and the rudiments of the pulmonary system are formed.

During the sixth week, uncontrolled fetal limb movements begin to occur. The gastrointestinal system develops too rapidly for the embryonic abdomen to accommodate it, and the intestines temporarily loop into the umbilical cord. Paddle-shaped hands and feet develop fingers and toes by the process of apoptosis (programmed cell death), which causes the tissues between the fingers to disintegrate. By week 7, the facial structure is more complex and includes nostrils, outer ears, and lenses (Figure 28.15). By the eighth week, the head is nearly as large as the rest of the embryo's body, and all major brain structures are in place. The external genitalia are apparent, but at this point, male and female embryos are indistinguishable. Bone begins to replace cartilage in the embryonic skeleton through the process of ossification. By the end of the embryonic period, the embryo is approximately 3 cm (1.2 in) from crown to rump and weighs approximately 8 g (0.25 oz).

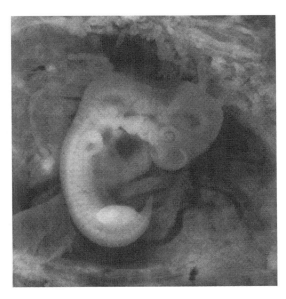

Figure 28.15 Embryo at 7 Weeks An embryo at the end of 7 weeks of development is only 10 mm in length, but its developing eyes, limb buds, and tail are already visible. (This embryo was derived from an ectopic pregnancy.) (credit: Ed Uthman)

Use this interactive tool (http://openstaxcollege.org/l/embryogenesis) to view the process of embryogenesis from the perspective of the conceptus (left panel), as well as fetal development viewed from a maternal cross-section (right panel). Can you identify when neurulation occurs in the embryo?

28.3 | Fetal Development

By the end of this section, you will be able to:
- Differentiate between the embryonic period and the fetal period
- Briefly describe the process of sexual differentiation
- Describe the fetal circulatory system and explain the role of the shunts
- Trace the development of a fetus from the end of the embryonic period to birth

As you will recall, a developing human is called a fetus from the ninth week of gestation until birth. This 30-week period of development is marked by continued cell growth and differentiation, which fully develop the structures and functions of the immature organ systems formed during the embryonic period. The completion of fetal development results in a newborn who, although still immature in many ways, is capable of survival outside the womb.

Sexual Differentiation

Sexual differentiation does not begin until the fetal period, during weeks 9–12. Embryonic males and females, though genetically distinguishable, are morphologically identical (Figure 28.16). Bipotential gonads, or gonads that can develop into male or female sexual organs, are connected to a central cavity called the cloaca via Müllerian ducts and Wolffian ducts. (The cloaca is an extension of the primitive gut.) Several events lead to sexual differentiation during this period.

During male fetal development, the bipotential gonads become the testes and associated epididymis. The Müllerian ducts degenerate. The Wolffian ducts become the vas deferens, and the cloaca becomes the urethra and rectum.

During female fetal development, the bipotential gonads develop into ovaries. The Wolffian ducts degenerate. The Müllerian ducts become the uterine tubes and uterus, and the cloaca divides and develops into a vagina, a urethra, and a rectum.

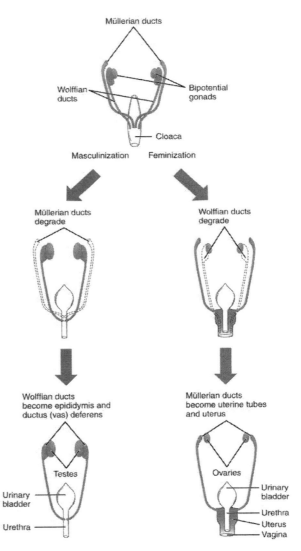

Figure 28.16 Sexual Differentiation Differentiation of the male and female reproductive systems does not occur until the fetal period of development.

The Fetal Circulatory System

During prenatal development, the fetal circulatory system is integrated with the placenta via the umbilical cord so that the fetus receives both oxygen and nutrients from the placenta. However, after childbirth, the umbilical cord is severed, and the newborn's circulatory system must be reconfigured. When the heart first forms in the embryo, it exists as two parallel tubes derived from mesoderm and lined with endothelium, which then fuse together. As the embryo develops into a fetus, the tube-shaped heart folds and further differentiates into the four chambers present in a mature heart. Unlike a mature cardiovascular system, however, the fetal cardiovascular system also includes circulatory shortcuts, or shunts. A **shunt** is an anatomical (or sometimes surgical) diversion that allows blood flow to bypass immature organs such as the lungs and liver until childbirth.

The placenta provides the fetus with necessary oxygen and nutrients via the umbilical vein. (Remember that veins carry blood toward the heart. In this case, the blood flowing to the fetal heart is oxygenated because it comes from the placenta. The respiratory system is immature and cannot yet oxygenate blood on its own.) From the umbilical vein, the oxygenated blood flows toward the inferior vena cava, all but bypassing the immature liver, via the **ductus venosus** shunt (Figure 28.17). The liver receives just a trickle of blood, which is all that it needs in its immature, semifunctional state. Blood flows from the inferior vena cava to the right atrium, mixing with fetal venous blood along the way.

Although the fetal liver is semifunctional, the fetal lungs are nonfunctional. The fetal circulation therefore bypasses the lungs by shifting some of the blood through the **foramen ovale**, a shunt that directly connects the right and left atria and avoids the pulmonary trunk altogether. Most of the rest of the blood is pumped to the right ventricle, and from there, into the pulmonary trunk, which splits into pulmonary arteries. However, a shunt within the pulmonary artery, the **ductus arteriosus**, diverts a portion of this blood into the aorta. This ensures that only a small volume of oxygenated blood passes through the immature pulmonary circuit, which has only minor metabolic requirements. Blood vessels of uninflated lungs have high resistance to flow, a condition that encourages blood to flow to the aorta, which presents much lower resistance. The oxygenated blood moves through the foramen ovale into the left atrium, where it mixes with the now deoxygenated blood returning from the pulmonary circuit. This blood then moves into the left ventricle, where it is pumped into the aorta. Some of this blood moves through the coronary arteries into the myocardium, and some moves through the carotid arteries to the brain.

The descending aorta carries partially oxygenated and partially deoxygenated blood into the lower regions of the body. It eventually passes into the umbilical arteries through branches of the internal iliac arteries. The deoxygenated blood collects waste as it circulates through the fetal body and returns to the umbilical cord. Thus, the two umbilical arteries carry blood low in oxygen and high in carbon dioxide and fetal wastes. This blood is filtered through the placenta, where wastes diffuse into the maternal circulation. Oxygen and nutrients from the mother diffuse into the placenta and from there into the fetal blood, and the process repeats.

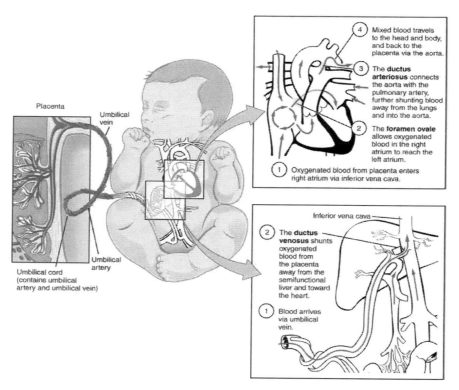

Figure 28.17 Fetal Circulatory System The fetal circulatory system includes three shunts to divert blood from undeveloped and partially functioning organs, as well as blood supply to and from the placenta.

Other Organ Systems

During weeks 9–12 of fetal development, the brain continues to expand, the body elongates, and ossification continues. Fetal movements are frequent during this period, but are jerky and not well-controlled. The bone marrow begins to take over the process of erythrocyte production—a task that the liver performed during the embryonic period. The liver now secretes bile. The fetus circulates amniotic fluid by swallowing it and producing urine. The eyes are well-developed by this stage, but the eyelids are fused shut. The fingers and toes begin to develop nails. By the end of week 12, the fetus measures approximately 9 cm (3.5 in) from crown to rump.

Weeks 13–16 are marked by sensory organ development. The eyes move closer together; blinking motions begin, although the eyes remain sealed shut. The lips exhibit sucking motions. The ears move upward and lie flatter against the head. The scalp begins to grow hair. The excretory system is also developing: the kidneys are well-formed, and **meconium**, or fetal feces, begins to accumulate in the intestines. Meconium consists of ingested amniotic fluid, cellular debris, mucus, and bile.

During approximately weeks 16–20, as the fetus grows and limb movements become more powerful, the mother may begin to feel **quickening**, or fetal movements. However, space restrictions limit these movements and typically force the growing fetus into the "fetal position," with the arms crossed and the legs bent at the knees. Sebaceous glands coat the skin with a waxy, protective substance called **vernix caseosa** that protects and moisturizes the skin and may provide lubrication during childbirth. A silky hair called **lanugo** also covers the skin during weeks 17–20, but it is shed as the fetus continues to grow. Extremely premature infants sometimes exhibit residual lanugo.

Developmental weeks 21–30 are characterized by rapid weight gain, which is important for maintaining a stable body temperature after birth. The bone marrow completely takes over erythrocyte synthesis, and the axons of the spinal cord begin to be myelinated, or coated in the electrically insulating glial cell sheaths that are necessary for efficient nervous system functioning. (The process of myelination is not completed until adolescence.) During this period, the fetus grows eyelashes. The eyelids are no longer fused and can be opened and closed. The lungs begin producing surfactant, a substance that reduces surface tension in the lungs and assists proper lung expansion after birth. Inadequate surfactant production in premature newborns may result in respiratory distress syndrome, and as a result, the newborn may require surfactant replacement therapy, supplemental oxygen, or maintenance in a continuous positive airway pressure (CPAP) chamber during their first days or weeks of life. In male fetuses, the testes descend into the scrotum near the end of this period. The fetus at 30 weeks measures 28 cm (11 in) from crown to rump and exhibits the approximate body proportions of a full-term newborn, but still is much leaner.

Visit this site (http://openstaxcollege.org/l/pregstages) for a summary of the stages of pregnancy, as experienced by the mother, and view the stages of development of the fetus throughout gestation. At what point in fetal development can a regular heartbeat be detected?

The fetus continues to lay down subcutaneous fat from week 31 until birth. The added fat fills out the hypodermis, and the skin transitions from red and wrinkled to soft and pink. Lanugo is shed, and the nails grow to the tips of the fingers and toes. Immediately before birth, the average crown-to-rump length is 35.5–40.5 cm (14–16 in), and the fetus weighs approximately 2.5–4 kg (5.5–8.8 lbs). Once born, the newborn is no longer confined to the fetal position, so subsequent measurements are made from head-to-toe instead of from crown-to-rump. At birth, the average length is approximately 51 cm (20 in).

Developing Fetus

Throughout the second half of gestation, the fetal intestines accumulate a tarry, greenish black meconium. The newborn's first stools consist almost entirely of meconium; they later transition to seedy yellow stools or slightly formed tan stools as meconium is cleared and replaced with digested breast milk or formula, respectively. Unlike these later stools, meconium is sterile; it is devoid of bacteria because the fetus is in a sterile environment and has not consumed any breast milk or formula. Typically, an infant does not pass meconium until after birth. However, in 5–20 percent of births, the fetus has a bowel movement in utero, which can cause major complications in the newborn.

The passage of meconium in the uterus signals fetal distress, particularly fetal hypoxia (i.e., oxygen deprivation). This may be caused by maternal drug abuse (especially tobacco or cocaine), maternal hypertension, depletion of amniotic fluid, long labor or difficult birth, or a defect in the placenta that prevents it from delivering adequate oxygen to the fetus. Meconium passage is typically a complication of full-term or post-term newborns because it is rarely passed before 34 weeks of gestation, when the gastrointestinal system has matured and is appropriately controlled by nervous system stimuli. Fetal distress can stimulate the vagus nerve to trigger gastrointestinal peristalsis and relaxation of the anal sphincter. Notably, fetal hypoxic stress also induces a gasping reflex, increasing the likelihood that meconium will be inhaled into the fetal lungs.

Although meconium is a sterile substance, it interferes with the antibiotic properties of the amniotic fluid and makes the newborn and mother more vulnerable to bacterial infections at birth and during the perinatal period. Specifically, inflammation of the fetal membranes, inflammation of the uterine lining, or neonatal sepsis (infection in the newborn) may occur. Meconium also irritates delicate fetal skin and can cause a rash.

The first sign that a fetus has passed meconium usually does not come until childbirth, when the amniotic sac ruptures. Normal amniotic fluid is clear and watery, but amniotic fluid in which meconium has been passed is stained greenish or yellowish. Antibiotics given to the mother may reduce the incidence of maternal bacterial infections, but it is critical that meconium is aspirated from the newborn before the first breath. Under these conditions, an obstetrician will extensively aspirate the infant's airways as soon as the head is delivered, while the rest of the infant's body is still inside the birth canal.

Aspiration of meconium with the first breath can result in labored breathing, a barrel-shaped chest, or a low Apgar score. An obstetrician can identify meconium aspiration by listening to the lungs with a stethoscope for a coarse rattling sound. Blood gas tests and chest X-rays of the infant can confirm meconium aspiration. Inhaled meconium after birth could obstruct a newborn's airways leading to alveolar collapse, interfere with surfactant function by stripping it from the lungs, or cause pulmonary inflammation or hypertension. Any of these complications will make the newborn much more vulnerable to pulmonary infection, including pneumonia.

28.4 | Maternal Changes During Pregnancy, Labor, and Birth

By the end of this section, you will be able to:

- Explain how estrogen, progesterone, and hCG are involved in maintaining pregnancy
- List the contributors to weight gain during pregnancy
- Describe the major changes to the maternal digestive, circulatory, and integumentary systems during pregnancy
- Summarize the events leading to labor
- Identify and describe each of the three stages of childbirth

A full-term pregnancy lasts approximately 270 days (approximately 38.5 weeks) from conception to birth. Because it is easier to remember the first day of the last menstrual period (LMP) than to estimate the date of conception, obstetricians set the due date as 284 days (approximately 40.5 weeks) from the LMP. This assumes that conception occurred on day 14 of the woman's cycle, which is usually a good approximation. The 40 weeks of an average pregnancy are usually discussed in terms of three **trimesters**, each approximately 13 weeks. During the second and third trimesters, the pre-pregnancy uterus—about the size of a fist—grows dramatically to contain the fetus, causing a number of anatomical changes in the mother (Figure 28.18).

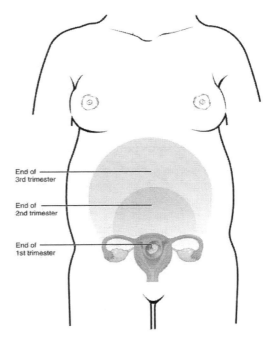

Figure 28.18 Size of Uterus throughout Pregnancy The uterus grows throughout pregnancy to accommodate the fetus.

Effects of Hormones

Virtually all of the effects of pregnancy can be attributed in some way to the influence of hormones—particularly estrogens, progesterone, and hCG. During weeks 7–12 from the LMP, the pregnancy hormones are primarily generated by the corpus luteum. Progesterone secreted by the corpus luteum stimulates the production of decidual cells of the endometrium that nourish the blastocyst before placentation. As the placenta develops and the corpus luteum degenerates during weeks 12–17, the placenta gradually takes over as the endocrine organ of pregnancy.

The placenta converts weak androgens secreted by the maternal and fetal adrenal glands to estrogens, which are necessary for pregnancy to progress. Estrogen levels climb throughout the pregnancy, increasing 30-fold by childbirth. Estrogens have the following actions:

- They suppress FSH and LH production, effectively preventing ovulation. (This function is the biological basis of hormonal birth control pills.)
- They induce the growth of fetal tissues and are necessary for the maturation of the fetal lungs and liver.
- They promote fetal viability by regulating progesterone production and triggering fetal synthesis of cortisol, which helps with the maturation of the lungs, liver, and endocrine organs such as the thyroid gland and adrenal gland.
- They stimulate maternal tissue growth, leading to uterine enlargement and mammary duct expansion and branching.

Relaxin, another hormone secreted by the corpus luteum and then by the placenta, helps prepare the mother's body for childbirth. It increases the elasticity of the symphysis pubis joint and pelvic ligaments, making room for the growing fetus and allowing expansion of the pelvic outlet for childbirth. Relaxin also helps dilate the cervix during labor.

The placenta takes over the synthesis and secretion of progesterone throughout pregnancy as the corpus luteum degenerates. Like estrogen, progesterone suppresses FSH and LH. It also inhibits uterine contractions, protecting the fetus from preterm birth. This hormone decreases in late gestation, allowing uterine contractions to intensify and eventually progress to true labor. The placenta also produces hCG. In addition to promoting survival of the corpus luteum, hCG stimulates the male fetal gonads to secrete testosterone, which is essential for the development of the male reproductive system.

The anterior pituitary enlarges and ramps up its hormone production during pregnancy, raising the levels of thyrotropin, prolactin, and adrenocorticotropic hormone (ACTH). Thyrotropin, in conjunction with placental hormones, increases the production of thyroid hormone, which raises the maternal metabolic rate. This can markedly augment a pregnant woman's appetite and cause hot flashes. Prolactin stimulates enlargement of the mammary glands in preparation for milk production. ACTH stimulates maternal cortisol secretion, which contributes to fetal protein synthesis. In addition to the pituitary hormones, increased parathyroid levels mobilize calcium from maternal bones for fetal use.

Weight Gain

The second and third trimesters of pregnancy are associated with dramatic changes in maternal anatomy and physiology. The most obvious anatomical sign of pregnancy is the dramatic enlargement of the abdominal region, coupled with maternal weight gain. This weight results from the growing fetus as well as the enlarged uterus, amniotic fluid, and placenta. Additional breast tissue and dramatically increased blood volume also contribute to weight gain (Table 28.2). Surprisingly, fat storage accounts for only approximately 2.3 kg (5 lbs) in a normal pregnancy and serves as a reserve for the increased metabolic demand of breastfeeding.

During the first trimester, the mother does not need to consume additional calories to maintain a healthy pregnancy. However, a weight gain of approximately 0.45 kg (1 lb) per month is common. During the second and third trimesters, the mother's appetite increases, but it is only necessary for her to consume an additional 300 calories per day to support the growing fetus. Most women gain approximately 0.45 kg (1 lb) per week.

Contributors to Weight Gain During Pregnancy

Component	Weight (kg)	Weight (lb)
Fetus	3.2–3.6	7–8
Placenta and fetal membranes	0.9–1.8	2–4
Amniotic fluid	0.9–1.4	2–3
Breast tissue	0.9–1.4	2–3
Blood	1.4	4
Fat	0.9–4.1	3–9
Uterus	0.9–2.3	2–5
Total	10–16.3	22–36

Table 28.2

Changes in Organ Systems During Pregnancy

As the woman's body adapts to pregnancy, characteristic physiologic changes occur. These changes can sometimes prompt symptoms often referred to collectively as the common discomforts of pregnancy.

Digestive and Urinary System Changes

Nausea and vomiting, sometimes triggered by an increased sensitivity to odors, are common during the first few weeks to months of pregnancy. This phenomenon is often referred to as "morning sickness," although the nausea may persist all day. The source of pregnancy nausea is thought to be the increased circulation of pregnancy-related hormones, specifically circulating estrogen, progesterone, and hCG. Decreased intestinal peristalsis may also contribute to nausea. By about week 12 of pregnancy, nausea typically subsides.

A common gastrointestinal complaint during the later stages of pregnancy is gastric reflux, or heartburn, which results from the upward, constrictive pressure of the growing uterus on the stomach. The same decreased peristalsis that may contribute to nausea in early pregnancy is also thought to be responsible for pregnancy-related constipation as pregnancy progresses.

The downward pressure of the uterus also compresses the urinary bladder, leading to frequent urination. The problem is exacerbated by increased urine production. In addition, the maternal urinary system processes both maternal and fetal wastes, further increasing the total volume of urine.

Circulatory System Changes

Blood volume increases substantially during pregnancy, so that by childbirth, it exceeds its preconception volume by 30 percent, or approximately 1–2 liters. The greater blood volume helps to manage the demands of fetal nourishment and fetal waste removal. In conjunction with increased blood volume, the pulse and blood pressure also rise moderately during pregnancy. As the fetus grows, the uterus compresses underlying pelvic blood vessels, hampering venous return from the legs and pelvic region. As a result, many pregnant women develop varicose veins or hemorrhoids.

Respiratory System Changes

During the second half of pregnancy, the respiratory minute volume (volume of gas inhaled or exhaled by the lungs per minute) increases by 50 percent to compensate for the oxygen demands of the fetus and the increased maternal metabolic rate. The growing uterus exerts upward pressure on the diaphragm, decreasing the volume of each inspiration and potentially causing shortness of breath, or dyspnea. During the last several weeks of pregnancy, the pelvis becomes more elastic, and the fetus descends lower in a process called **lightening**. This typically ameliorates dyspnea.

The respiratory mucosa swell in response to increased blood flow during pregnancy, leading to nasal congestion and nose bleeds, particularly when the weather is cold and dry. Humidifier use and increased fluid intake are often recommended to counteract congestion.

Integumentary System Changes

The dermis stretches extensively to accommodate the growing uterus, breast tissue, and fat deposits on the thighs and hips. Torn connective tissue beneath the dermis can cause striae (stretch marks) on the abdomen, which appear as red or purple marks during pregnancy that fade to a silvery white color in the months after childbirth.

An increase in melanocyte-stimulating hormone, in conjunction with estrogens, darkens the areolae and creates a line of pigment from the umbilicus to the pubis called the linea nigra (Figure 28.19). Melanin production during pregnancy may also darken or discolor skin on the face to create a chloasma, or "mask of pregnancy."

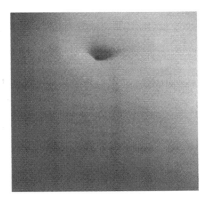

Figure 28.19 Linea Nigra The linea nigra, a dark medial line running from the umbilicus to the pubis, forms during pregnancy and persists for a few weeks following childbirth. The linea nigra shown here corresponds to a pregnancy that is 22 weeks along.

Physiology of Labor

Childbirth, or **parturition**, typically occurs within a week of a woman's due date, unless the woman is pregnant with more than one fetus, which usually causes her to go into labor early. As a pregnancy progresses into its final weeks, several physiological changes occur in response to hormones that trigger labor.

First, recall that progesterone inhibits uterine contractions throughout the first several months of pregnancy. As the pregnancy enters its seventh month, progesterone levels plateau and then drop. Estrogen levels, however, continue to rise in the maternal circulation (Figure 28.20). The increasing ratio of estrogen to progesterone makes the myometrium (the uterine smooth muscle) more sensitive to stimuli that promote contractions (because progesterone no longer inhibits them).

Moreover, in the eighth month of pregnancy, fetal cortisol rises, which boosts estrogen secretion by the placenta and further overpowers the uterine-calming effects of progesterone. Some women may feel the result of the decreasing levels of progesterone in late pregnancy as weak and irregular peristaltic **Braxton Hicks contractions**, also called false labor. These contractions can often be relieved with rest or hydration.

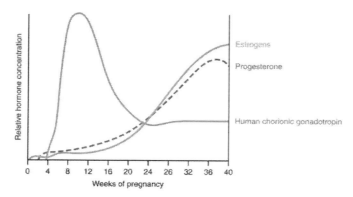

Figure 28.20 Hormones Initiating Labor   A positive feedback loop of hormones works to initiate labor.

A common sign that labor will be short is the so-called "bloody show." During pregnancy, a plug of mucus accumulates in the cervical canal, blocking the entrance to the uterus. Approximately 1–2 days prior to the onset of true labor, this plug loosens and is expelled, along with a small amount of blood.

Meanwhile, the posterior pituitary has been boosting its secretion of oxytocin, a hormone that stimulates the contractions of labor. At the same time, the myometrium increases its sensitivity to oxytocin by expressing more receptors for this hormone. As labor nears, oxytocin begins to stimulate stronger, more painful uterine contractions, which—in a positive feedback loop—stimulate the secretion of prostaglandins from fetal membranes. Like oxytocin, prostaglandins also enhance uterine contractile strength. The fetal pituitary also secretes oxytocin, which increases prostaglandins even further. Given the importance of oxytocin and prostaglandins to the initiation and maintenance of labor, it is not surprising that, when a pregnancy is not progressing to labor and needs to be induced, a pharmaceutical version of these compounds (called pitocin) is administered by intravenous drip.

Finally, stretching of the myometrium and cervix by a full-term fetus in the vertex (head-down) position is regarded as a stimulant to uterine contractions. The sum of these changes initiates the regular contractions known as **true labor**, which become more powerful and more frequent with time. The pain of labor is attributed to myometrial hypoxia during uterine contractions.

Stages of Childbirth

The process of childbirth can be divided into three stages: cervical dilation, expulsion of the newborn, and afterbirth (Figure 28.21).

Cervical Dilation

For vaginal birth to occur, the cervix must dilate fully to 10 cm in diameter—wide enough to deliver the newborn's head. The **dilation** stage is the longest stage of labor and typically takes 6–12 hours. However, it varies widely and may take minutes, hours, or days, depending in part on whether the mother has given birth before; in each subsequent labor, this stage tends to be shorter.

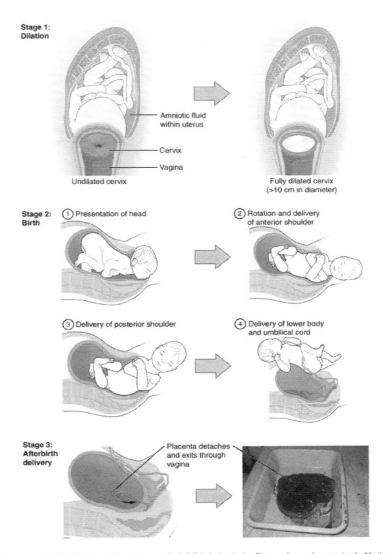

Figure 28.21 Stages of Childbirth   The stages of childbirth include Stage 1, early cervical dilation; Stage 2, full dilation and expulsion of the newborn; and Stage 3, delivery of the placenta and associated fetal membranes. (The position of the newborn's shoulder is described relative to the mother.)

True labor progresses in a positive feedback loop in which uterine contractions stretch the cervix, causing it to dilate and efface, or become thinner. Cervical stretching induces reflexive uterine contractions that dilate and efface the cervix further. In addition, cervical dilation boosts oxytocin secretion from the pituitary, which in turn triggers more powerful uterine contractions. When labor begins, uterine contractions may occur only every 3–30 minutes and last only 20–40 seconds; however, by the end of this stage, contractions may occur as frequently as every 1.5–2 minutes and last for a full minute.

Each contraction sharply reduces oxygenated blood flow to the fetus. For this reason, it is critical that a period of relaxation occur after each contraction. Fetal distress, measured as a sustained decrease or increase in the fetal heart rate, can result from severe contractions that are too powerful or lengthy for oxygenated blood to be restored to the fetus. Such a situation can be cause for an emergency birth with vacuum, forceps, or surgically by Caesarian section.

The amniotic membranes rupture before the onset of labor in about 12 percent of women; they typically rupture at the end of the dilation stage in response to excessive pressure from the fetal head entering the birth canal.

Expulsion Stage

The **expulsion** stage begins when the fetal head enters the birth canal and ends with birth of the newborn. It typically takes up to 2 hours, but it can last longer or be completed in minutes, depending in part on the orientation of the fetus. The vertex presentation known as the occiput anterior vertex is the most common presentation and is associated with the greatest ease of vaginal birth. The fetus faces the maternal spinal cord and the smallest part of the head (the posterior aspect called the occiput) exits the birth canal first.

In fewer than 5 percent of births, the infant is oriented in the breech presentation, or buttocks down. In a complete breech, both legs are crossed and oriented downward. In a frank breech presentation, the legs are oriented upward. Before the 1960s, it was common for breech presentations to be delivered vaginally. Today, most breech births are accomplished by Caesarian section.

Vaginal birth is associated with significant stretching of the vaginal canal, the cervix, and the perineum. Until recent decades, it was routine procedure for an obstetrician to numb the perineum and perform an **episiotomy**, an incision in the posterior vaginal wall and perineum. The perineum is now more commonly allowed to tear on its own during birth. Both an episiotomy and a perineal tear need to be sutured shortly after birth to ensure optimal healing. Although suturing the jagged edges of a perineal tear may be more difficult than suturing an episiotomy, tears heal more quickly, are less painful, and are associated with less damage to the muscles around the vagina and rectum.

Upon birth of the newborn's head, an obstetrician will aspirate mucus from the mouth and nose before the newborn's first breath. Once the head is birthed, the rest of the body usually follows quickly. The umbilical cord is then double-clamped, and a cut is made between the clamps. This completes the second stage of childbirth.

Afterbirth

The delivery of the placenta and associated membranes, commonly referred to as the **afterbirth**, marks the final stage of childbirth. After expulsion of the newborn, the myometrium continues to contract. This movement shears the placenta from the back of the uterine wall. It is then easily delivered through the vagina. Continued uterine contractions then reduce blood loss from the site of the placenta. Delivery of the placenta marks the beginning of the postpartum period—the period of approximately 6 weeks immediately following childbirth during which the mother's body gradually returns to a non-pregnant state. If the placenta does not birth spontaneously within approximately 30 minutes, it is considered retained, and the obstetrician may attempt manual removal. If this is not successful, surgery may be required.

It is important that the obstetrician examines the expelled placenta and fetal membranes to ensure that they are intact. If fragments of the placenta remain in the uterus, they can cause postpartum hemorrhage. Uterine contractions continue for several hours after birth to return the uterus to its pre-pregnancy size in a process called **involution**, which also allows the mother's abdominal organs to return to their pre-pregnancy locations. Breastfeeding facilitates this process.

Although postpartum uterine contractions limit blood loss from the detachment of the placenta, the mother does experience a postpartum vaginal discharge called **lochia**. This is made up of uterine lining cells, erythrocytes, leukocytes, and other debris. Thick, dark, lochia rubra (red lochia) typically continues for 2–3 days, and is replaced by lochia serosa, a thinner, pinkish form that continues until about the tenth postpartum day. After this period, a scant, creamy, or watery discharge called lochia alba (white lochia) may continue for another 1–2 weeks.

28.5 | Adjustments of the Infant at Birth and Postnatal Stages

By the end of this section, you will be able to:
- Discuss the importance of an infant's first breath
- Explain the closing of the cardiac shunts
- Describe thermoregulation in the newborn
- Summarize the importance of intestinal flora in the newborn

From a fetal perspective, the process of birth is a crisis. In the womb, the fetus was snuggled in a soft, warm, dark, and quiet world. The placenta provided nutrition and oxygen continuously. Suddenly, the contractions of labor and vaginal childbirth forcibly squeeze the fetus through the birth canal, limiting oxygenated blood flow during contractions and shifting the skull bones to accommodate the small space. After birth, the newborn's system must make drastic adjustments to a world that is colder, brighter, and louder, and where he or she will experience hunger and thirst. The neonatal period (neo- = "new"; -natal = "birth") spans the first to the thirtieth day of life outside of the uterus.

Respiratory Adjustments

Although the fetus "practices" breathing by inhaling amniotic fluid in utero, there is no air in the uterus and thus no true opportunity to breathe. (There is also no need to breathe because the placenta supplies the fetus with all the oxygenated blood it needs.) During gestation, the partially collapsed lungs are filled with amniotic fluid and exhibit very little metabolic activity. Several factors stimulate newborns to take their first breath at birth. First, labor contractions temporarily constrict umbilical blood vessels, reducing oxygenated blood flow to the fetus and elevating carbon dioxide levels in the blood. High carbon dioxide levels cause acidosis and stimulate the respiratory center in the brain, triggering the newborn to take a breath.

The first breath typically is taken within 10 seconds of birth, after mucus is aspirated from the infant's mouth and nose. The first breaths inflate the lungs to nearly full capacity and dramatically decrease lung pressure and resistance to blood flow, causing a major circulatory reconfiguration. Pulmonary alveoli open, and alveolar capillaries fill with blood. Amniotic fluid in the lungs drains or is absorbed, and the lungs immediately take over the task of the placenta, exchanging carbon dioxide for oxygen by the process of respiration.

Circulatory Adjustments

The process of clamping and cutting the umbilical cord collapses the umbilical blood vessels. In the absence of medical assistance, this occlusion would occur naturally within 20 minutes of birth because the Wharton's jelly within the umbilical cord would swell in response to the lower temperature outside of the mother's body, and the blood vessels would constrict. Natural occlusion has occurred when the umbilical cord is no longer pulsating. For the most part, the collapsed vessels atrophy and become fibrotic remnants, existing in the mature circulatory system as ligaments of the abdominal wall and liver. The ductus venosus degenerates to become the ligamentum venosum beneath the liver. Only the proximal sections of the two umbilical arteries remain functional, taking on the role of supplying blood to the upper part of the bladder (Figure 28.22).

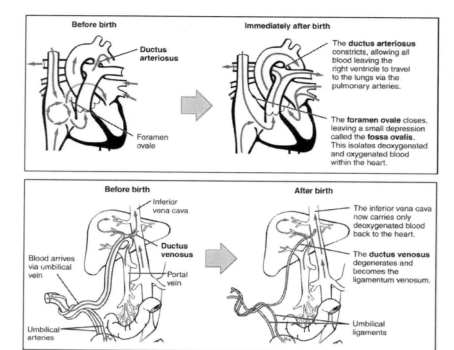

Figure 28.22 Neonatal Circulatory System A newborn's circulatory system reconfigures immediately after birth. The three fetal shunts have been closed permanently, facilitating blood flow to the liver and lungs.

The newborn's first breath is vital to initiate the transition from the fetal to the neonatal circulatory pattern. Inflation of the lungs decreases blood pressure throughout the pulmonary system, as well as in the right atrium and ventricle. In response to this pressure change, the flow of blood temporarily reverses direction through the foramen ovale, moving from the left to the right atrium, and blocking the shunt with two flaps of tissue. Within 1 year, the tissue flaps usually fuse over the shunt, turning the foramen ovale into the fossa ovalis. The ductus arteriosus constricts as a result of increased oxygen concentration, and becomes the ligamentum arteriosum. Closing of the ductus arteriosus ensures that all blood pumped to the pulmonary circuit will be oxygenated by the newly functional neonatal lungs.

Thermoregulatory Adjustments

The fetus floats in warm amniotic fluid that is maintained at a temperature of approximately 98.6°F with very little fluctuation. Birth exposes newborns to a cooler environment in which they have to regulate their own body temperature. Newborns have a higher ratio of surface area to volume than adults. This means that their body has less volume throughout which to produce heat, and more surface area from which to lose heat. As a result, newborns produce heat more slowly and lose it more quickly. Newborns also have immature musculature that limits their ability to generate heat by shivering. Moreover, their nervous systems are underdeveloped, so they cannot quickly constrict superficial blood vessels in response to cold. They also have little subcutaneous fat for insulation. All these factors make it harder for newborns to maintain their body temperature.

Newborns, however, do have a special method for generating heat: **nonshivering thermogenesis**, which involves the breakdown of **brown adipose tissue**, or brown fat, which is distributed over the back, chest, and shoulders. Brown fat differs from the more familiar white fat in two ways:

- It is highly vascularized. This allows for faster delivery of oxygen, which leads to faster cellular respiration.
- It is packed with a special type of mitochondria that are able to engage in cellular respiration reactions that produce less ATP and more heat than standard cellular respiration reactions.

The breakdown of brown fat occurs automatically upon exposure to cold, so it is an important heat regulator in newborns. During fetal development, the placenta secretes inhibitors that prevent metabolism of brown adipose fat and promote its accumulation in preparation for birth.

Gastrointestinal and Urinary Adjustments

In adults, the gastrointestinal tract harbors bacterial flora—trillions of bacteria that aid in digestion, produce vitamins, and protect from the invasion or replication of pathogens. In stark contrast, the fetal intestine is sterile. The first consumption of breast milk or formula floods the neonatal gastrointestinal tract with beneficial bacteria that begin to establish the bacterial flora.

The fetal kidneys filter blood and produce urine, but the neonatal kidneys are still immature and inefficient at concentrating urine. Therefore, newborns produce very dilute urine, making it particularly important for infants to obtain sufficient fluids from breast milk or formula.

Homeostasis in the Newborn: Apgar Score

In the minutes following birth, a newborn must undergo dramatic systemic changes to be able to survive outside the womb. An obstetrician, midwife, or nurse can estimate how well a newborn is doing by obtaining an Apgar score. The Apgar score was introduced in 1952 by the anesthesiologist Dr. Virginia Apgar as a method to assess the effects on the newborn of anesthesia given to the laboring mother. Healthcare providers now use it to assess the general wellbeing of the newborn, whether or not analgesics or anesthetics were used.

Five criteria—skin color, heart rate, reflex, muscle tone, and respiration—are assessed, and each criterion is assigned a score of 0, 1, or 2. Scores are taken at 1 minute after birth and again at 5 minutes after birth. Each time that scores are taken, the five scores are added together. High scores (out of a possible 10) indicate the baby has made the transition from the womb well, whereas lower scores indicate that the baby may be in distress.

The technique for determining an Apgar score is quick and easy, painless for the newborn, and does not require any instruments except for a stethoscope. A convenient way to remember the five scoring criteria is to apply the mnemonic APGAR, for "appearance" (skin color), "pulse" (heart rate), "grimace" (reflex), "activity" (muscle tone), and "respiration."

Of the five Apgar criteria, heart rate and respiration are the most critical. Poor scores for either of these measurements may indicate the need for immediate medical attention to resuscitate or stabilize the newborn. In general, any score lower than 7 at the 5-minute mark indicates that medical assistance may be needed. A total score below 5 indicates an emergency situation. Normally, a newborn will get an intermediate score of 1 for some of the Apgar criteria and will progress to a 2 by the 5-minute assessment. Scores of 8 or above are normal.

28.6 | Lactation

By the end of this section, you will be able to:
- Describe the structure of the lactating breast
- Summarize the process of lactation
- Explain how the composition of breast milk changes during the first days of lactation and in the course of a single feeding

Lactation is the process by which milk is synthesized and secreted from the mammary glands of the postpartum female breast in response to an infant sucking at the nipple. Breast milk provides ideal nutrition and passive immunity for the infant, encourages mild uterine contractions to return the uterus to its pre-pregnancy size (i.e., involution), and induces a substantial metabolic increase in the mother, consuming the fat reserves stored during pregnancy.

Structure of the Lactating Breast

Mammary glands are modified sweat glands. The non-pregnant and non-lactating female breast is composed primarily of adipose and collagenous tissue, with mammary glands making up a very minor proportion of breast volume. The mammary gland is composed of milk-transporting lactiferous ducts, which expand and branch extensively during pregnancy in response to estrogen, growth hormone, cortisol, and prolactin. Moreover, in response to progesterone, clusters of breast alveoli bud from the ducts and expand outward toward the chest wall. Breast alveoli are balloon-like structures lined with milk-secreting cuboidal cells, or lactocytes, that are surrounded by a net of contractile myoepithelial cells. Milk is secreted from the lactocytes, fills the alveoli, and is squeezed into the ducts. Clusters of alveoli that drain to a common duct are called lobules; the lactating female has 12–20 lobules organized radially around the nipple. Milk drains from lactiferous ducts into lactiferous sinuses that meet at 4 to 18 perforations in the nipple, called nipple pores. The small bumps of the areola (the darkened skin around the nipple) are called Montgomery glands. They secrete oil to cleanse the nipple opening and prevent chapping and cracking of the nipple during breastfeeding.

The Process of Lactation

The pituitary hormone **prolactin** is instrumental in the establishment and maintenance of breast milk supply. It also is important for the mobilization of maternal micronutrients for breast milk.

Near the fifth week of pregnancy, the level of circulating prolactin begins to increase, eventually rising to approximately 10–20 times the pre-pregnancy concentration. We noted earlier that, during pregnancy, prolactin and other hormones prepare the breasts anatomically for the secretion of milk. The level of prolactin plateaus in late pregnancy, at a level high enough to initiate milk production. However, estrogen, progesterone, and other placental hormones inhibit prolactin-mediated milk synthesis during pregnancy. It is not until the placenta is expelled that this inhibition is lifted and milk production commences.

After childbirth, the baseline prolactin level drops sharply, but it is restored for a 1-hour spike during each feeding to stimulate the production of milk for the next feeding. With each prolactin spike, estrogen and progesterone also increase slightly.

When the infant suckles, sensory nerve fibers in the areola trigger a neuroendocrine reflex that results in milk secretion from lactocytes into the alveoli. The posterior pituitary releases oxytocin, which stimulates myoepithelial cells to squeeze milk from the alveoli so it can drain into the lactiferous ducts, collect in the lactiferous sinuses, and discharge through the nipple pores. It takes less than 1 minute from the time when an infant begins suckling (the latent period) until milk is secreted (the let-down). Figure 28.23 summarizes the positive feedback loop of the **let-down reflex**.

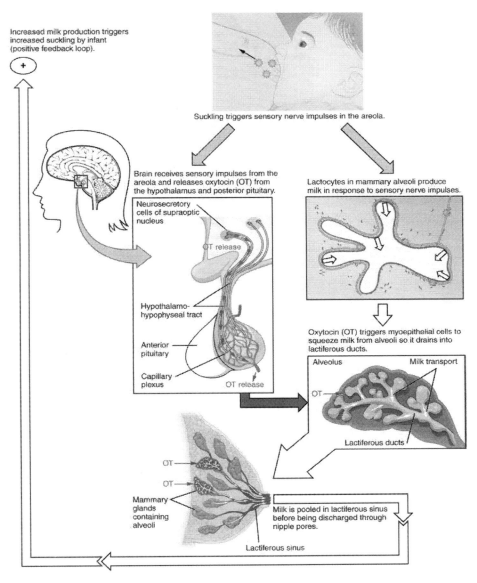

Figure 28.23 Let-Down Reflex A positive feedback loop ensures continued milk production as long as the infant continues to breastfeed.

The prolactin-mediated synthesis of milk changes with time. Frequent milk removal by breastfeeding (or pumping) will maintain high circulating prolactin levels for several months. However, even with continued breastfeeding, baseline prolactin will decrease over time to its pre-pregnancy level. In addition to prolactin and oxytocin, growth hormone, cortisol, parathyroid hormone, and insulin contribute to lactation, in part by facilitating the transport of maternal amino acids, fatty acids, glucose, and calcium to breast milk.

Changes in the Composition of Breast Milk

In the final weeks of pregnancy, the alveoli swell with **colostrum**, a thick, yellowish substance that is high in protein but contains less fat and glucose than mature breast milk (Table 28.3). Before childbirth, some women experience leakage of colostrum from the nipples. In contrast, mature breast milk does not leak during pregnancy and is not secreted until several days after childbirth.

Compositions of Human Colostrum, Mature Breast Milk, and Cow's Milk (g/L)

	Human colostrum	Human breast milk	Cow's milk*
Total protein	23	11	31
Immunoglobulins	19	0.1	1
Fat	30	45	38
Lactose	57	71	47
Calcium	0.5	0.3	1.4
Phosphorus	0.16	0.14	0.90
Sodium	0.50	0.15	0.41

Table 28.3 *Cow's milk should never be given to an infant. Its composition is not suitable and its proteins are difficult for the infant to digest.

Colostrum is secreted during the first 48–72 hours postpartum. Only a small volume of colostrum is produced—approximately 3 ounces in a 24-hour period—but it is sufficient for the newborn in the first few days of life. Colostrum is rich with immunoglobulins, which confer gastrointestinal, and also likely systemic, immunity as the newborn adjusts to a nonsterile environment.

After about the third postpartum day, the mother secretes transitional milk that represents an intermediate between mature milk and colostrum. This is followed by mature milk from approximately postpartum day 10 (see Table 28.3). As you can see in the accompanying table, cow's milk is not a substitute for breast milk. It contains less lactose, less fat, and more protein and minerals. Moreover, the proteins in cow's milk are difficult for an infant's immature digestive system to metabolize and absorb.

The first few weeks of breastfeeding may involve leakage, soreness, and periods of milk engorgement as the relationship between milk supply and infant demand becomes established. Once this period is complete, the mother will produce approximately 1.5 liters of milk per day for a single infant, and more if she has twins or triplets. As the infant goes through growth spurts, the milk supply constantly adjusts to accommodate changes in demand. A woman can continue to lactate for years, but once breastfeeding is stopped for approximately 1 week, any remaining milk will be reabsorbed; in most cases, no more will be produced, even if suckling or pumping is resumed.

Mature milk changes from the beginning to the end of a feeding. The early milk, called **foremilk**, is watery, translucent, and rich in lactose and protein. Its purpose is to quench the infant's thirst. **Hindmilk** is delivered toward the end of a feeding. It is opaque, creamy, and rich in fat, and serves to satisfy the infant's appetite.

During the first days of a newborn's life, it is important for meconium to be cleared from the intestines and for bilirubin to be kept low in the circulation. Recall that bilirubin, a product of erythrocyte breakdown, is processed by the liver and secreted in bile. It enters the gastrointestinal tract and exits the body in the stool. Breast milk has laxative properties that help expel meconium from the intestines and clear bilirubin through the excretion of bile. A high concentration of bilirubin in the blood causes jaundice. Some degree of jaundice is normal in newborns, but a high level of bilirubin—which is neurotoxic—can cause brain damage. Newborns, who do not yet have a fully functional blood–brain barrier, are highly vulnerable to the bilirubin circulating in the blood. Indeed, hyperbilirubinemia, a high level of circulating bilirubin, is the most common condition requiring medical attention in newborns. Newborns with hyperbilirubinemia are treated with phototherapy because UV light helps to break down the bilirubin quickly.

28.7 | Patterns of Inheritance

By the end of this section, you will be able to:
- Differentiate between genotype and phenotype
- Describe how alleles determine a person's traits
- Summarize Mendel's experiments and relate them to human genetics
- Explain the inheritance of autosomal dominant and recessive and sex-linked genetic disorders

We have discussed the events that lead to the development of a newborn. But what makes each newborn unique? The answer lies, of course, in the DNA in the sperm and oocyte that combined to produce that first diploid cell, the human zygote.

From Genotype to Phenotype

Each human body cell has a full complement of DNA stored in 23 pairs of chromosomes. Figure 28.24 shows the pairs in a systematic arrangement called a **karyotype**. Among these is one pair of chromosomes, called the **sex chromosomes**, that determines the sex of the individual (XX in females, XY in males). The remaining 22 chromosome pairs are called **autosomal chromosomes**. Each of these chromosomes carries hundreds or even thousands of genes, each of which codes for the assembly of a particular protein—that is, genes are "expressed" as proteins. An individual's complete genetic makeup is referred to as his or her **genotype**. The characteristics that the genes express, whether they are physical, behavioral, or biochemical, are a person's **phenotype**.

You inherit one chromosome in each pair—a full complement of 23—from each parent. This occurs when the sperm and oocyte combine at the moment of your conception. Homologous chromosomes—those that make up a complementary pair—have genes for the same characteristics in the same location on the chromosome. Because one copy of a gene, an **allele**, is inherited from each parent, the alleles in these complementary pairs may vary. Take for example an allele that encodes for dimples. A child may inherit the allele encoding for dimples on the chromosome from the father and the allele that encodes for smooth skin (no dimples) on the chromosome from the mother.

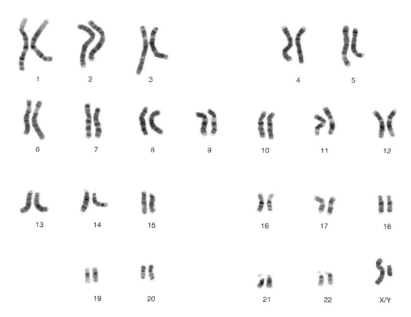

Figure 28.24 **Chromosomal Complement of a Male** Each pair of chromosomes contains hundreds to thousands of genes. The banding patterns are nearly identical for the two chromosomes within each pair, indicating the same organization of genes. As is visible in this karyotype, the only exception to this is the XY sex chromosome pair in males. (credit: National Human Genome Research Institute)

Although a person can have two identical alleles for a single gene (a **homozygous** state), it is also possible for a person to have two different alleles (a **heterozygous** state). The two alleles can interact in several different ways. The expression of an allele can be dominant, for which the activity of this gene will mask the expression of a nondominant, or recessive, allele. Sometimes dominance is complete; at other times, it is incomplete. In some cases, both alleles are expressed at the same time in a form of expression known as codominance.

In the simplest scenario, a single pair of genes will determine a single heritable characteristic. However, it is quite common for multiple genes to interact to confer a feature. For instance, eight or more genes—each with their own alleles—determine eye color in humans. Moreover, although any one person can only have two alleles corresponding to a given gene, more than two alleles commonly exist in a population. This phenomenon is called multiple alleles. For example, there are three different alleles that encode ABO blood type; these are designated I^A, I^B, and i.

Over 100 years of theoretical and experimental genetics studies, and the more recent sequencing and annotation of the human genome, have helped scientists to develop a better understanding of how an individual's genotype is expressed as their phenotype. This body of knowledge can help scientists and medical professionals to predict, or at least estimate, some of the features that an offspring will inherit by examining the genotypes or phenotypes of the parents. One important application of this knowledge is to identify an individual's risk for certain heritable genetic disorders. However, most diseases have a multigenic pattern of inheritance and can also be affected by the environment, so examining the genotypes or phenotypes of a person's parents will provide only limited information about the risk of inheriting a disease. Only for a handful of single-gene disorders can genetic testing allow clinicians to calculate the probability with which a child born to the two parents tested may inherit a specific disease.

Mendel's Theory of Inheritance

Our contemporary understanding of genetics rests on the work of a nineteenth-century monk. Working in the mid-1800s, long before anyone knew about genes or chromosomes, Gregor Mendel discovered that garden peas transmit their physical characteristics to subsequent generations in a discrete and predictable fashion. When he mated, or crossed, two pure-breeding pea plants that differed by a certain characteristic, the first-generation offspring all looked like one of the parents. For instance, when he crossed tall and dwarf pure-breeding pea plants, all of the offspring were tall. Mendel called tallness **dominant** because it was expressed in offspring when it was present in a purebred parent. He called dwarfism **recessive** because it was masked in the offspring if one of the purebred parents possessed the dominant characteristic. Note that tallness and dwarfism are variations on the characteristic of height. Mendel called such a variation a **trait**. We now know that these traits are the expression of different alleles of the gene encoding height.

Mendel performed thousands of crosses in pea plants with differing traits for a variety of characteristics. And he repeatedly came up with the same results—among the traits he studied, one was always dominant, and the other was always recessive. (Remember, however, that this dominant–recessive relationship between alleles is not always the case; some alleles are codominant, and sometimes dominance is incomplete.)

Using his understanding of dominant and recessive traits, Mendel tested whether a recessive trait could be lost altogether in a pea lineage or whether it would resurface in a later generation. By crossing the second-generation offspring of purebred parents with each other, he showed that the latter was true: recessive traits reappeared in third-generation plants in a ratio of 3:1 (three offspring having the dominant trait and one having the recessive trait). Mendel then proposed that characteristics such as height were determined by heritable "factors" that were transmitted, one from each parent, and inherited in pairs by offspring.

In the language of genetics, Mendel's theory applied to humans says that if an individual receives two dominant alleles, one from each parent, the individual's phenotype will express the dominant trait. If an individual receives two recessive alleles, then the recessive trait will be expressed in the phenotype. Individuals who have two identical alleles for a given gene, whether dominant or recessive, are said to be homozygous for that gene (homo- = "same"). Conversely, an individual who has one dominant allele and one recessive allele is said to be heterozygous for that gene (hetero- = "different" or "other"). In this case, the dominant trait will be expressed, and the individual will be phenotypically identical to an individual who possesses two dominant alleles for the trait.

It is common practice in genetics to use capital and lowercase letters to represent dominant and recessive alleles. Using Mendel's pea plants as an example, if a tall pea plant is homozygous, it will possess two tall alleles (*TT*). A dwarf pea plant must be homozygous because its dwarfism can only be expressed when two recessive alleles are present (*tt*). A heterozygous pea plant (*Tt*) would be tall and phenotypically indistinguishable from a tall homozygous pea plant because of the dominant tall allele. Mendel deduced that a 3:1 ratio of dominant to recessive would be produced by the random segregation of heritable factors (genes) when crossing two heterozygous pea plants. In other words, for any given gene, parents are equally likely to pass down either one of their alleles to their offspring in a haploid gamete, and the result will be expressed in a dominant–recessive pattern if both parents are heterozygous for the trait.

Because of the random segregation of gametes, the laws of chance and probability come into play when predicting the likelihood of a given phenotype. Consider a cross between an individual with two dominant alleles for a trait (*AA*) and an individual with two recessive alleles for the same trait (*aa*). All of the parental gametes from the dominant individual would be *A*, and all of the parental gametes from the recessive individual would be *a* (Figure 28.25). All of the offspring of that second generation, inheriting one allele from each parent, would have the genotype *Aa*, and the probability of expressing the phenotype of the dominant allele would be 4 out of 4, or 100 percent.

This seems simple enough, but the inheritance pattern gets interesting when the second-generation *Aa* individuals are crossed. In this generation, 50 percent of each parent's gametes are *A* and the other 50 percent are *a*. By Mendel's principle of random segregation, the possible combinations of gametes that the offspring can receive are *AA*, *Aa*, *aA* (which is the same as *Aa*), and *aa*. Because segregation and fertilization are random, each offspring has a 25 percent chance of receiving any of these combinations. Therefore, if an *Aa* × *Aa* cross were performed 1000 times, approximately 250 (25 percent) of the offspring would be *AA*; 500 (50 percent) would be *Aa* (that is, *Aa* plus *aA*); and 250 (25 percent) would be *aa*. The genotypic ratio for this inheritance pattern is 1:2:1. However, we have already established that *AA* and *Aa* (and *aA*) individuals all express the dominant trait (i.e., share the same phenotype), and can therefore be combined into one group. The result is Mendel's third-generation phenotype ratio of 3:1.

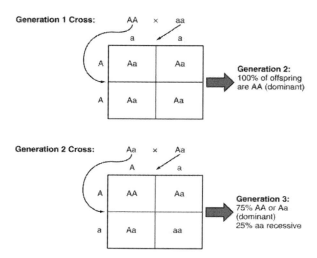

Figure 28.25 Random Segregation In the formation of gametes, it is equally likely that either one of a pair alleles from one parent will be passed on to the offspring. This figure follows the possible combinations of alleles through two generations following a first-generation cross of homozygous dominant and homozygous recessive parents. The recessive phenotype, which is masked in the second generation, has a 1 in 4, or 25 percent, chance of reappearing in the third generation.

Mendel's observation of pea plants also included many crosses that involved multiple traits, which prompted him to formulate the principle of independent assortment. The law states that the members of one pair of genes (alleles) from a parent will sort independently from other pairs of genes during the formation of gametes. Applied to pea plants, that means that the alleles associated with the different traits of the plant, such as color, height, or seed type, will sort independently of one another. This holds true except when two alleles happen to be located close to one other on the same chromosome. Independent assortment provides for a great degree of diversity in offspring.

Mendelian genetics represent the fundamentals of inheritance, but there are two important qualifiers to consider when applying Mendel's findings to inheritance studies in humans. First, as we've already noted, not all genes are inherited in a dominant–recessive pattern. Although all diploid individuals have two alleles for every gene, allele pairs may interact to create several types of inheritance patterns, including incomplete dominance and codominance.

Secondly, Mendel performed his studies using thousands of pea plants. He was able to identify a 3:1 phenotypic ratio in second-generation offspring because his large sample size overcame the influence of variability resulting from chance. In contrast, no human couple has ever had thousands of children. If we know that a man and woman are both heterozygous for a recessive genetic disorder, we would predict that one in every four of their children would be affected by the disease. In real life, however, the influence of chance could change that ratio significantly. For example, if a man and a woman are both heterozygous for cystic fibrosis, a recessive genetic disorder that is expressed only when the individual has two defective alleles, we would expect one in four of their children to have cystic fibrosis. However, it is entirely possible for them to have seven children, none of whom is affected, or for them to have two children, both of whom are affected. For each individual child, the presence or absence of a single gene disorder depends on which alleles that child inherits from his or her parents.

Autosomal Dominant Inheritance

In the case of cystic fibrosis, the disorder is recessive to the normal phenotype. However, a genetic abnormality may be dominant to the normal phenotype. When the dominant allele is located on one of the 22 pairs of autosomes (non-sex chromosomes), we refer to its inheritance pattern as **autosomal dominant**. An example of an autosomal dominant disorder is neurofibromatosis type I, a disease that induces tumor formation within the nervous system that leads to skin and skeletal deformities. Consider a couple in which one parent is heterozygous for this disorder (and who therefore has neurofibromatosis), *Nn*, and one parent is homozygous for the normal gene, *nn*. The heterozygous parent would have a 50 percent chance of passing the dominant allele for this disorder to his or her offspring, and the homozygous parent would always pass the normal allele. Therefore, four possible offspring genotypes are equally likely to occur: *Nn, Nn, nn*, and *nn*. That is, every child of this couple would have a 50 percent chance of inheriting neurofibromatosis. This inheritance pattern is shown in Figure 28.26, in a form called a **Punnett square**, named after its creator, the British geneticist Reginald Punnett.

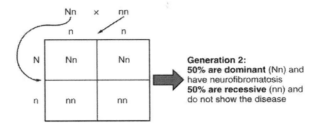

Figure 28.25 Autosomal Dominant Inheritance Inheritance pattern of an autosomal dominant disorder, such as neurofibromatosis, is shown in a Punnett square.

Other genetic diseases that are inherited in this pattern are achondroplastic dwarfism, Marfan syndrome, and Huntington's disease. Because autosomal dominant disorders are expressed by the presence of just one gene, an individual with the disorder will know that he or she has at least one faulty gene. The expression of the disease may manifest later in life, after the childbearing years, which is the case in Huntington's disease (discussed in more detail later in this section).

Autosomal Recessive Inheritance

When a genetic disorder is inherited in an **autosomal recessive** pattern, the disorder corresponds to the recessive phenotype. Heterozygous individuals will not display symptoms of this disorder, because their unaffected gene will compensate. Such an individual is called a **carrier**. Carriers for an autosomal recessive disorder may never know their genotype unless they have a child with the disorder.

An example of an autosomal recessive disorder is cystic fibrosis (CF), which we introduced earlier. CF is characterized by the chronic accumulation of a thick, tenacious mucus in the lungs and digestive tract. Decades ago, children with CF rarely lived to adulthood. With advances in medical technology, the average lifespan in developed countries has increased into middle adulthood. CF is a relatively common disorder that occurs in approximately 1 in 2000 Caucasians. A child born to two CF carriers would have a 25 percent chance of inheriting the disease. This is the same 3:1 dominant:recessive ratio that Mendel observed in his pea plants would apply here. The pattern is shown in Figure 28.27, using a diagram that tracks the likely incidence of an autosomal recessive disorder on the basis of parental genotypes.

On the other hand, a child born to a CF carrier and someone with two unaffected alleles would have a 0 percent probability of inheriting CF, but would have a 50 percent chance of being a carrier. Other examples of autosome recessive genetic illnesses include the blood disorder sickle-cell anemia, the fatal neurological disorder Tay–Sachs disease, and the metabolic disorder phenylketonuria.

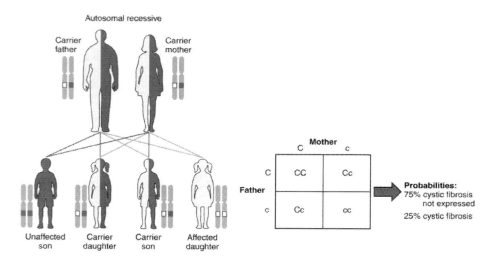

Figure 28.27 Autosomal Recessive Inheritance The inheritance pattern of an autosomal recessive disorder with two carrier parents reflects a 3:1 probability of expression among offspring. (credit: U.S. National Library of Medicine)

X-linked Dominant or Recessive Inheritance

An **X-linked** transmission pattern involves genes located on the X chromosome of the 23rd pair (Figure 28.28). Recall that a male has one X and one Y chromosome. When a father transmits a Y chromosome, the child is male, and when he transmits an X chromosome, the child is female. A mother can transmit only an X chromosome, as both her sex chromosomes are X chromosomes.

When an abnormal allele for a gene that occurs on the X chromosome is dominant over the normal allele, the pattern is described as **X-linked dominant**. This is the case with vitamin D–resistant rickets: an affected father would pass the disease gene to all of his daughters, but none of his sons, because he donates only the Y chromosome to his sons (see Figure 28.28a). If it is the mother who is affected, all of her children—male or female—would have a 50 percent chance of inheriting the disorder because she can only pass an X chromosome on to her children (see Figure 28.28b). For an affected female, the inheritance pattern would be identical to that of an autosomal dominant inheritance pattern in which one parent is heterozygous and the other is homozygous for the normal gene.

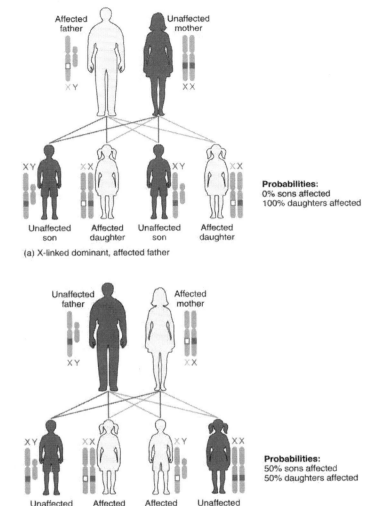

Figure 28.28 X-Linked Patterns of Inheritance   A chart of X-linked dominant inheritance patterns differs depending on whether (a) the father or (b) the mother is affected with the disease. (credit: U.S. National Library of Medicine)

X-linked recessive inheritance is much more common because females can be carriers of the disease yet still have a normal phenotype. Diseases transmitted by X-linked recessive inheritance include color blindness, the blood-clotting disorder hemophilia, and some forms of muscular dystrophy. For an example of X-linked recessive inheritance, consider parents in which the mother is an unaffected carrier and the father is normal. None of the daughters would have the disease because they receive a normal gene from their father. However, they have a 50 percent chance of receiving the disease gene from their mother and becoming a carrier. In contrast, 50 percent of the sons would be affected (Figure 28.29).

With X-linked recessive diseases, males either have the disease or are genotypically normal—they cannot be carriers. Females, however, can be genotypically normal, a carrier who is phenotypically normal, or affected with the disease. A daughter can inherit the gene for an X-linked recessive illness when her mother is a carrier or affected, or her father is affected. The daughter will be affected by the disease only if she inherits an X-linked recessive gene from both parents. As you can imagine, X-linked recessive disorders affect many more males than females. For example, color blindness affects at least 1 in 20 males, but only about 1 in 400 females.

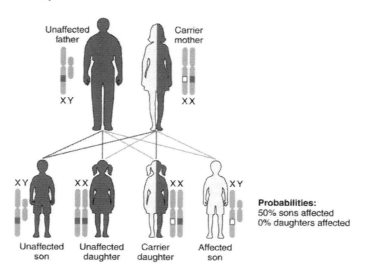

Figure 28.29 X-Linked Recessive Inheritance Given two parents in which the father is normal and the mother is a carrier of an X-linked recessive disorder, a son would have a 50 percent probability of being affected with the disorder, whereas daughters would either be carriers or entirely unaffected. (credit: U.S. National Library of Medicine)

Other Inheritance Patterns: Incomplete Dominance, Codominance, and Lethal Alleles

Not all genetic disorders are inherited in a dominant–recessive pattern. In **incomplete dominance**, the offspring express a heterozygous phenotype that is intermediate between one parent's homozygous dominant trait and the other parent's homozygous recessive trait. An example of this can be seen in snapdragons when red-flowered plants and white-flowered plants are crossed to produce pink-flowered plants. In humans, incomplete dominance occurs with one of the genes for hair texture. When one parent passes a curly hair allele (the incompletely dominant allele) and the other parent passes a straight-hair allele, the effect on the offspring will be intermediate, resulting in hair that is wavy.

Codominance is characterized by the equal, distinct, and simultaneous expression of both parents' different alleles. This pattern differs from the intermediate, blended features seen in incomplete dominance. A classic example of codominance in humans is ABO blood type. People are blood type A if they have an allele for an enzyme that facilitates the production of surface antigen A on their erythrocytes. This allele is designated I^A. In the same manner, people are blood type B if they express an enzyme for the production of surface antigen B. People who have alleles for both enzymes (I^A and I^B) produce both surface antigens A and B. As a result, they are blood type AB. Because the effect of both alleles (or enzymes) is observed, we say that the I^A and I^B alleles are codominant. There is also a third allele that determines blood type. This allele (i) produces a nonfunctional enzyme. People who have two i alleles do not produce either A or B surface antigens: they have type O blood. If a person has I^A and i alleles, the person will have blood type A. Notice that it does not make any difference whether a person has two I^A alleles or one I^A and one i allele. In both cases, the person is blood type A. Because I^A masks i, we say that I^A is dominant to i. Table 28.4 summarizes the expression of blood type.

Expression of Blood Types

Blood type	Genotype	Pattern of inheritance
A	I^AI^A or I^Ai	I^A is dominant to i
B	I^BI^B or I^Bi	I^B is dominant to i
AB	I^AI^B	I^A is co-dominant to I^B
O	ii	Two recessive alleles

Table 28.4

Certain combinations of alleles can be lethal, meaning they prevent the individual from developing in utero, or cause a shortened life span. In **recessive lethal** inheritance patterns, a child who is born to two heterozygous (carrier) parents and who inherited the faulty allele from both would not survive. An example of this is Tay–Sachs, a fatal disorder of the nervous system. In this disorder, parents with one copy of the allele for the disorder are carriers. If they both transmit their abnormal allele, their offspring will develop the disease and will die in childhood, usually before age 5.

Dominant lethal inheritance patterns are much more rare because neither heterozygotes nor homozygotes survive. Of course, dominant lethal alleles that arise naturally through mutation and cause miscarriages or stillbirths are never transmitted to subsequent generations. However, some dominant lethal alleles, such as the allele for Huntington's disease, cause a shortened life span but may not be identified until after the person reaches reproductive age and has children. Huntington's disease causes irreversible nerve cell degeneration and death in 100 percent of affected individuals, but it may not be expressed until the individual reaches middle age. In this way, dominant lethal alleles can be maintained in the human population. Individuals with a family history of Huntington's disease are typically offered genetic counseling, which can help them decide whether or not they wish to be tested for the faulty gene.

Mutations

A **mutation** is a change in the sequence of DNA nucleotides that may or may not affect a person's phenotype. Mutations can arise spontaneously from errors during DNA replication, or they can result from environmental insults such as radiation, certain viruses, or exposure to tobacco smoke or other toxic chemicals. Because genes encode for the assembly of proteins, a mutation in the nucleotide sequence of a gene can change amino acid sequence and, consequently, a protein's structure and function. Spontaneous mutations occurring during meiosis are thought to account for many spontaneous abortions (miscarriages).

Chromosomal Disorders

Sometimes a genetic disease is not caused by a mutation in a gene, but by the presence of an incorrect number of chromosomes. For example, Down syndrome is caused by having three copies of chromosome 21. This is known as trisomy 21. The most common cause of trisomy 21 is chromosomal nondisjunction during meiosis. The frequency of nondisjunction events appears to increase with age, so the frequency of bearing a child with Down syndrome increases in women over 36. The age of the father matters less because nondisjunction is much less likely to occur in a sperm than in an egg.

Whereas Down syndrome is caused by having three copies of a chromosome, Turner syndrome is caused by having just one copy of the X chromosome. This is known as monosomy. The affected child is always female. Women with Turner syndrome are sterile because their sexual organs do not mature.

Genetic Counselor

Given the intricate orchestration of gene expression, cell migration, and cell differentiation during prenatal development, it is amazing that the vast majority of newborns are healthy and free of major birth defects. When a woman over 35 is pregnant or intends to become pregnant, or her partner is over 55, or if there is a family history of a genetic disorder, she and her partner may want to speak to a genetic counselor to discuss the likelihood that their child may be affected by a genetic or chromosomal disorder. A genetic counselor can interpret a couple's family history and estimate the risks to their future offspring.

For many genetic diseases, a DNA test can determine whether a person is a carrier. For instance, carrier status for Fragile X, an X-linked disorder associated with mental retardation, or for cystic fibrosis can be determined with a simple blood draw to obtain DNA for testing. A genetic counselor can educate a couple about the implications of such a test and help them decide whether to undergo testing. For chromosomal disorders, the available testing options include a blood test, amniocentesis (in which amniotic fluid is tested), and chorionic villus sampling (in which tissue from the placenta is tested). Each of these has advantages and drawbacks. A genetic counselor can also help a couple cope with the news that either one or both partners is a carrier of a genetic illness, or that their unborn child has been diagnosed with a chromosomal disorder or other birth defect.

To become a genetic counselor, one needs to complete a 4-year undergraduate program and then obtain a Master of Science in Genetic Counseling from an accredited university. Board certification is attained after passing examinations by the American Board of Genetic Counseling. Genetic counselors are essential professionals in many branches of medicine, but there is a particular demand for preconception and prenatal genetic counselors.

Visit the National Society of Genetic Counselors website (http://openstaxcollege.org/l/gencounselor1) for more information about genetic counselors.

Visit the American Board of Genetic Counselors, Inc., website (http://openstaxcollege.org/l/gencounselor2) for more information about genetic counselors.

KEY TERMS

acrosomal reaction release of digestive enzymes by sperm that enables them to burrow through the corona radiata and penetrate the zona pellucida of an oocyte prior to fertilization

acrosome cap-like vesicle located at the anterior-most region of a sperm that is rich with lysosomal enzymes capable of digesting the protective layers surrounding the oocyte

afterbirth third stage of childbirth in which the placenta and associated fetal membranes are expelled

allantois finger-like outpocketing of yolk sac forms the primitive excretory duct of the embryo; precursor to the urinary bladder

allele alternative forms of a gene that occupy a specific locus on a specific gene

amnion transparent membranous sac that encloses the developing fetus and fills with amniotic fluid

amniotic cavity cavity that opens up between the inner cell mass and the trophoblast; develops into amnion

autosomal chromosome in humans, the 22 pairs of chromosomes that are not the sex chromosomes (XX or XY)

autosomal dominant pattern of dominant inheritance that corresponds to a gene on one of the 22 autosomal chromosomes

autosomal recessive pattern of recessive inheritance that corresponds to a gene on one of the 22 autosomal chromosomes

blastocoel fluid-filled cavity of the blastocyst

blastocyst term for the conceptus at the developmental stage that consists of about 100 cells shaped into an inner cell mass that is fated to become the embryo and an outer trophoblast that is fated to become the associated fetal membranes and placenta

blastomere daughter cell of a cleavage

Braxton Hicks contractions weak and irregular peristaltic contractions that can occur in the second and third trimesters; they do not indicate that childbirth is imminent

brown adipose tissue highly vascularized fat tissue that is packed with mitochondria; these properties confer the ability to oxidize fatty acids to generate heat

capacitation process that occurs in the female reproductive tract in which sperm are prepared for fertilization; leads to increased motility and changes in their outer membrane that improve their ability to release enzymes capable of digesting an oocyte's outer layers

carrier heterozygous individual who does not display symptoms of a recessive genetic disorder but can transmit the disorder to his or her offspring

chorion membrane that develops from the syncytiotrophoblast, cytotrophoblast, and mesoderm; surrounds the embryo and forms the fetal portion of the placenta through the chorionic villi

chorionic membrane precursor to the chorion; forms from extra-embryonic mesoderm cells

chorionic villi projections of the chorionic membrane that burrow into the endometrium and develop into the placenta

cleavage form of mitotic cell division in which the cell divides but the total volume remains unchanged; this process serves to produce smaller and smaller cells

codominance pattern of inheritance that corresponds to the equal, distinct, and simultaneous expression of two different alleles

colostrum thick, yellowish substance secreted from a mother's breasts in the first postpartum days; rich in immunoglobulins

conceptus pre-implantation stage of a fertilized egg and its associated membranes

corona radiata in an oocyte, a layer of granulosa cells that surrounds the oocyte and that must be penetrated by sperm before fertilization can occur

cortical reaction following fertilization, the release of cortical granules from the oocyte's plasma membrane into the zona pellucida creating a fertilization membrane that prevents any further attachment or penetration of sperm; part of the slow block to polyspermy

dilation first stage of childbirth, involving an increase in cervical diameter

dominant describes a trait that is expressed both in homozygous and heterozygous form

dominant lethal inheritance pattern in which individuals with one or two copies of a lethal allele do not survive in utero or have a shortened life span

ductus arteriosus shunt in the pulmonary trunk that diverts oxygenated blood back to the aorta

ductus venosus shunt that causes oxygenated blood to bypass the fetal liver on its way to the inferior vena cava

ectoderm primary germ layer that develops into the central and peripheral nervous systems, sensory organs, epidermis, hair, and nails

ectopic pregnancy implantation of an embryo outside of the uterus

embryo developing human during weeks 3–8

embryonic folding process by which an embryo develops from a flat disc of cells to a three-dimensional shape resembling a cylinder

endoderm primary germ layer that goes on to form the gastrointestinal tract, liver, pancreas, and lungs

epiblast upper layer of cells of the embryonic disc that forms from the inner cell mass; gives rise to all three germ layers

episiotomy incision made in the posterior vaginal wall and perineum that facilitates vaginal birth

expulsion second stage of childbirth, during which the mother bears down with contractions; this stage ends in birth

fertilization unification of genetic material from male and female haploid gametes

fertilization membrane impenetrable barrier that coats a nascent zygote; part of the slow block to polyspermy

fetus developing human during the time from the end of the embryonic period (week 9) to birth

foramen ovale shunt that directly connects the right and left atria and helps divert oxygenated blood from the fetal pulmonary circuit

foremilk watery, translucent breast milk that is secreted first during a feeding and is rich in lactose and protein; quenches the infant's thirst

gastrulation process of cell migration and differentiation into three primary germ layers following cleavage and implantation

genotype complete genetic makeup of an individual

gestation in human development, the period required for embryonic and fetal development in utero; pregnancy

heterozygous having two different alleles for a given gene

hindmilk opaque, creamy breast milk delivered toward the end of a feeding; rich in fat; satisfies the infant's appetite

homozygous having two identical alleles for a given gene

human chorionic gonadotropin (hCG) hormone that directs the corpus luteum to survive, enlarge, and continue producing progesterone and estrogen to suppress menses and secure an environment suitable for the developing embryo

hypoblast lower layer of cells of the embryonic disc that extend into the blastocoel to form the yolk sac

implantation process by which a blastocyst embeds itself in the uterine endometrium

incomplete dominance pattern of inheritance in which a heterozygous genotype expresses a phenotype intermediate between dominant and recessive phenotypes

inner cell mass cluster of cells within the blastocyst that is fated to become the embryo

involution postpartum shrinkage of the uterus back to its pre-pregnancy volume

karyotype systematic arrangement of images of chromosomes into homologous pairs

lactation process by which milk is synthesized and secreted from the mammary glands of the postpartum female breast in response to sucking at the nipple

lanugo silk-like hairs that coat the fetus; shed later in fetal development

let-down reflex release of milk from the alveoli triggered by infant suckling

lightening descent of the fetus lower into the pelvis in late pregnancy; also called "dropping"

lochia postpartum vaginal discharge that begins as blood and ends as a whitish discharge; the end of lochia signals that the site of placental attachment has healed

meconium fetal wastes consisting of ingested amniotic fluid, cellular debris, mucus, and bile

mesoderm primary germ layer that becomes the skeleton, muscles, connective tissue, heart, blood vessels, and kidneys

morula tightly packed sphere of blastomeres that has reached the uterus but has not yet implanted itself

mutation change in the nucleotide sequence of DNA

neural fold elevated edge of the neural groove

neural plate thickened layer of neuroepithelium that runs longitudinally along the dorsal surface of an embryo and gives rise to nervous system tissue

neural tube precursor to structures of the central nervous system, formed by the invagination and separation of neuroepithelium

neurulation embryonic process that establishes the central nervous system

nonshivering thermogenesis process of breaking down brown adipose tissue to produce heat in the absence of a shivering response

notochord rod-shaped, mesoderm-derived structure that provides support for growing fetus

organogenesis development of the rudimentary structures of all of an embryo's organs from the germ layers

parturition childbirth

phenotype physical or biochemical manifestation of the genotype; expression of the alleles

placenta organ that forms during pregnancy to nourish the developing fetus; also regulates waste and gas exchange between mother and fetus

placenta previa low placement of fetus within uterus causes placenta to partially or completely cover the opening of the cervix as it grows

placentation formation of the placenta; complete by weeks 14–16 of pregnancy

polyspermy penetration of an oocyte by more than one sperm

primitive streak indentation along the dorsal surface of the epiblast through which cells migrate to form the endoderm and mesoderm during gastrulation

prolactin pituitary hormone that establishes and maintains the supply of breast milk; also important for the mobilization of maternal micronutrients for breast milk

Punnett square grid used to display all possible combinations of alleles transmitted by parents to offspring and predict the mathematical probability of offspring inheriting a given genotype

quickening fetal movements that are strong enough to be felt by the mother

recessive describes a trait that is only expressed in homozygous form and is masked in heterozygous form

recessive lethal inheritance pattern in which individuals with two copies of a lethal allele do not survive in utero or have a shortened life span

sex chromosomes pair of chromosomes involved in sex determination; in males, the XY chromosomes; in females, the XX chromosomes

shunt circulatory shortcut that diverts the flow of blood from one region to another

somite one of the paired, repeating blocks of tissue located on either side of the notochord in the early embryo

syncytiotrophoblast superficial cells of the trophoblast that fuse to form a multinucleated body that digests endometrial cells to firmly secure the blastocyst to the uterine wall

trait variation of an expressed characteristic

trimester division of the duration of a pregnancy into three 3-month terms

trophoblast fluid-filled shell of squamous cells destined to become the chorionic villi, placenta, and associated fetal membranes

true labor regular contractions that immediately precede childbirth; they do not abate with hydration or rest, and they become more frequent and powerful with time

umbilical cord connection between the developing conceptus and the placenta; carries deoxygenated blood and wastes from the fetus and returns nutrients and oxygen from the mother

vernix caseosa waxy, cheese-like substance that protects the delicate fetal skin until birth

X-linked pattern of inheritance in which an allele is carried on the X chromosome of the 23rd pair

X-linked dominant pattern of dominant inheritance that corresponds to a gene on the X chromosome of the 23rd pair

X-linked recessive pattern of recessive inheritance that corresponds to a gene on the X chromosome of the 23rd pair

yolk sac membrane associated with primitive circulation to the developing embryo; source of the first blood cells and germ cells and contributes to the umbilical cord structure

zona pellucida thick, gel-like glycoprotein membrane that coats the oocyte and must be penetrated by sperm before fertilization can occur

zygote fertilized egg; a diploid cell resulting from the fertilization of haploid gametes from the male and female lines

CHAPTER REVIEW

28.1 Fertilization

Hundreds of millions of sperm deposited in the vagina travel toward the oocyte, but only a few hundred actually reach it. The number of sperm that reach the oocyte is greatly reduced because of conditions within the female reproductive tract. Many sperm are overcome by the acidity of the vagina, others are blocked by mucus in the cervix, whereas others are attacked by phagocytic leukocytes in the uterus. Those sperm that do survive undergo a change in response to those conditions. They go through the process of capacitation, which improves their motility and alters the membrane surrounding the acrosome, the cap-like structure in the head of a sperm that contains the digestive enzymes needed for it to attach to and penetrate the oocyte.

The oocyte that is released by ovulation is protected by a thick outer layer of granulosa cells known as the corona radiata and by the zona pellucida, a thick glycoprotein membrane that lies just outside the oocyte's plasma membrane. When capacitated sperm make contact with the oocyte, they release the digestive enzymes in the acrosome (the acrosomal reaction) and are thus able to attach to and burrow through to the oocyte's zona pellucida. One of the sperm will then break through to the oocyte's plasma membrane and release its haploid nucleus into the oocyte. The oocyte's membrane structure changes in response (cortical reaction), preventing any further penetration by another sperm and forming a fertilization membrane. Fertilization is complete upon unification of the haploid nuclei of the two gametes, producing a diploid zygote.

28.2 Embryonic Development

As the zygote travels toward the uterus, it undergoes numerous cleavages in which the number of cells doubles (blastomeres). Upon reaching the uterus, the conceptus has become a tightly packed sphere of cells called the morula, which then forms into a blastocyst consisting of an inner cell mass within a fluid-filled cavity surrounded by trophoblasts. The blastocyst implants in the uterine wall, the trophoblasts fuse to form a syncytiotrophoblast, and the conceptus is enveloped by the endometrium. Four embryonic membranes form to support the growing embryo: the amnion, the yolk sac, the allantois, and the chorion. The chorionic villi of the chorion extend into the endometrium to form the fetal portion of the placenta. The placenta supplies the growing embryo with oxygen and nutrients; it also removes carbon dioxide and other metabolic wastes.

Following implantation, embryonic cells undergo gastrulation, in which they differentiate and separate into an embryonic disc and establish three primary germ layers (the endoderm, mesoderm, and ectoderm). Through the process of embryonic folding, the fetus begins to take shape. Neurulation starts the process of the development of structures of the central nervous system and organogenesis establishes the basic plan for all organ systems.

28.3 Fetal Development

The fetal period lasts from the ninth week of development until birth. During this period, male and female gonads differentiate. The fetal circulatory system becomes much more specialized and efficient than its embryonic counterpart. It includes three shunts—the ductus venosus, the foramen ovale, and the ductus arteriosus—that enable it to bypass the semifunctional liver and pulmonary circuit until after childbirth. The brain continues to grow and its structures differentiate. Facial features develop, the body elongates, and the skeleton ossifies. In the womb, the developing fetus moves, blinks, practices sucking, and circulates amniotic fluid. The fetus grows from an embryo measuring approximately 3.3 cm (1.3 in) and weighing 7 g (0.25 oz) to an infant measuring approximately 51 cm (20 in) and weighing an average of approximately 3.4 kg (7.5 lbs). Embryonic organ structures that were primitive and nonfunctional develop to the point that the newborn can survive in the outside world.

28.4 Maternal Changes During Pregnancy, Labor, and Birth

Hormones (especially estrogens, progesterone, and hCG) secreted by the corpus luteum and later by the placenta are responsible for most of the changes experienced during pregnancy. Estrogen maintains the pregnancy, promotes fetal viability, and stimulates tissue growth in the mother and developing fetus. Progesterone prevents new ovarian follicles from developing and suppresses uterine contractility.

Pregnancy weight gain primarily occurs in the breasts and abdominal region. Nausea, heartburn, and frequent urination are common during pregnancy. Maternal blood volume increases by 30 percent during pregnancy and respiratory minute volume increases by 50 percent. The skin may develop stretch marks and melanin production may increase.

Toward the late stages of pregnancy, a drop in progesterone and stretching forces from the fetus lead to increasing uterine irritability and prompt labor. Contractions serve to dilate the cervix and expel the newborn. Delivery of the placenta and associated fetal membranes follows.

28.5 Adjustments of the Infant at Birth and Postnatal Stages

The first breath a newborn takes at birth inflates the lungs and dramatically alters the circulatory system, closing the three shunts that directed oxygenated blood away from the lungs and liver during fetal life. Clamping and cutting the umbilical cord collapses the three umbilical blood vessels. The proximal umbilical arteries remain a part of the circulatory system, whereas the distal umbilical arteries and the umbilical vein become fibrotic. The newborn keeps warm by breaking down brown adipose tissue in the process of nonshivering thermogenesis. The first consumption of breast milk or formula floods the newborn's sterile gastrointestinal tract with beneficial bacteria that eventually establish themselves as the bacterial flora, which aid in digestion.

28.6 Lactation

The lactating mother supplies all the hydration and nutrients that a growing infant needs for the first 4–6 months of life. During pregnancy, the body prepares for lactation by stimulating the growth and development of branching lactiferous ducts and alveoli lined with milk-secreting lactocytes, and by creating colostrum. These functions are attributable to the actions of several hormones, including prolactin. Following childbirth, suckling triggers oxytocin release, which stimulates myoepithelial cells to squeeze milk from alveoli. Breast milk then drains toward the nipple pores to be consumed by the infant. Colostrum, the milk produced in the first postpartum days, provides immunoglobulins that increase the newborn's immune defenses. Colostrum, transitional milk, and mature breast milk are ideally suited to each stage of the newborn's development, and breastfeeding helps the newborn's digestive system expel meconium and clear bilirubin. Mature milk changes from the beginning to the end of a feeding. Foremilk quenches the infant's thirst, whereas hindmilk satisfies the infant's appetite.

28.7 Patterns of Inheritance

There are two aspects to a person's genetic makeup. Their genotype refers to the genetic makeup of the chromosomes found in all their cells and the alleles that are passed down from their parents. Their phenotype is the expression of that genotype, based on the interaction of the paired alleles, as well as how environmental conditions affect that expression.

Working with pea plants, Mendel discovered that the factors that account for different traits in parents are discretely transmitted to offspring in pairs, one from each parent. He articulated the principles of random segregation and independent assortment to account for the inheritance patterns he observed. Mendel's factors are genes, with differing variants being referred to as alleles and those alleles being dominant or recessive in expression. Each parent passes one allele for every gene on to offspring, and offspring are equally likely to inherit any combination of allele pairs. When Mendel crossed heterozygous individuals, he repeatedly found a 3:1 dominant–recessive ratio. He correctly postulated that the expression of the recessive trait was masked in heterozygotes but would resurface in their offspring in a predictable manner.

Human genetics focuses on identifying different alleles and understanding how they express themselves. Medical researchers are especially interested in the identification of inheritance patterns for genetic disorders, which provides the means to estimate the risk that a given couple's offspring will inherit a genetic disease or disorder. Patterns of inheritance in humans include autosomal dominance and recessiveness, X-linked dominance and recessiveness, incomplete dominance, codominance, and lethality. A change in the nucleotide sequence of DNA, which may or may not manifest in a phenotype, is called a mutation.

INTERACTIVE LINK QUESTIONS

1. View this time-lapse movie (http://openstaxcollege.org/l/conceptus) of a conceptus starting at day 3. What is the first structure you see? At what point in the movie does the blastocoel first appear? What event occurs at the end of the movie?

2. Use this interactive tool (http://openstaxcollege.org/l/embryogenesis) to view the process of embryogenesis from the perspective of the conceptus (left panel), as well as fetal development viewed from a maternal cross-section (right panel). Can you identify when neurulation occurs in the embryo?

3. Visit this site (http://openstaxcollege.org/l/pregstages) for a summary of the stages of pregnancy, as experienced by the mother, and view the stages of development of the fetus throughout gestation. At what point in fetal development can a regular heartbeat be detected?

REVIEW QUESTIONS

4. Sperm and ova are similar in terms of _____.
   a. size
   b. quantity produced per year
   c. chromosome number
   d. flagellar motility

5. Although the male ejaculate contains hundreds of millions of sperm, _____.
   a. most do not reach the oocyte
   b. most are destroyed by the alkaline environment of the uterus
   c. it takes millions to penetrate the outer layers of the oocyte
   d. most are destroyed by capacitation

6. As sperm first reach the oocyte, they will contact the _____.
   a. acrosome
   b. corona radiata
   c. sperm-binding receptors
   d. zona pellucida

7. Fusion of pronuclei occurs during _____.
   a. spermatogenesis
   b. ovulation
   c. fertilization
   d. capacitation

8. Sperm must first complete _____ to enable the fertilization of an oocyte.
   a. capacitation
   b. the acrosomal reaction
   c. the cortical reaction
   d. the fast block

9. Cleavage produces daughter cells called _____.
   a. trophoblasts
   b. blastocysts
   c. morulae
   d. blastomeres

10. The conceptus, upon reaching the uterus, first _____.
   a. implants
   b. divides
   c. disintegrates
   d. hatches

11. The inner cell mass of the blastocyst is destined to become the _____.
   a. embryo
   b. trophoblast
   c. chorionic villi
   d. placenta

12. Which primary germ layer gave rise to the cells that eventually became the central nervous system?
   a. endoderm
   b. ectoderm
   c. acrosome
   d. mesoderm

13. What would happen if the trophoblast did not secrete hCG upon implantation of the blastocyst?
   a. The cells would not continue to divide.
   b. The corpus luteum would continue to produce progesterone and estrogen.
   c. Menses would flush the blastocyst out of the uterus.
   d. The uterine mucosa would not envelop the blastocyst.

14. During what process does the amnion envelop the embryo?
   a. embryonic folding
   b. gastrulation
   c. implantation
   d. organogenesis

15. The placenta is formed from _____.
   a. the embryo's mesenchymal cells
   b. the mother's endometrium only
   c. the mother's endometrium and the embryo's chorionic membrane
   d. the mother's endometrium and the embryo's umbilical cord

16. The foramen ovale causes the fetal circulatory system to bypass the _____.
   a. liver
   b. lungs
   c. kidneys
   d. gonads

17. What happens to the urine excreted by the fetus when the kidneys begin to function?
   a. The umbilical cord carries it to the placenta for removal.
   b. The endometrium absorbs it.
   c. It adds to the amniotic fluid.
   d. It is turned into meconium.

18. During weeks 9–12 of fetal development, _____.
   a. bone marrow begins to assume erythrocyte production
   b. meconium begins to accumulate in the intestines
   c. surfactant production begins in the fetal lungs
   d. the spinal cord begins to be myelinated

19. Progesterone secreted by the placenta suppresses _____ to prevent maturation of ovarian follicles.
   a. LH and estrogen
   b. hCG and FSH
   c. FSH and LH
   d. estrogen and hCG

20. Which of the following is a possible culprit of "morning sickness"?
   a. increased minute respiration
   b. decreased intestinal peristalsis
   c. decreased aldosterone secretion
   d. increased blood volume

21. How does the decrease in progesterone at the last weeks of pregnancy help to bring on labor?
   a. stimulating FSH production
   b. decreasing the levels of estrogens
   c. dilating the cervix
   d. decreasing the inhibition of uterine contractility

22. Which of these fetal presentations is the easiest for vaginal birth?
   a. complete breech
   b. vertex occiput anterior
   c. frank breech
   d. vertex occiput posterior

23. Which of these shunts exists between the right and left atria?
   a. foramen ovale
   b. ductus venosus
   c. ductus arteriosis
   d. foramen venosus

24. Why is brown fat important?
   a. It is the newborn's primary source of insulation.
   b. It can be broken down to generate heat for thermoregulation.
   c. It can be broken down for energy between feedings.
   d. It can be converted to white fat.

25. Constriction of umbilical blood vessels during vaginal birth _____.
   a. causes respiratory alkalosis
   b. inhibits the respiratory center in the brain
   c. elevates carbon dioxide levels in the blood
   d. both a and b

26. Alveoli are connected to the lactiferous sinuses by _____.
   a. lactocytes
   b. lactiferous ducts
   c. nipple pores
   d. lobules

27. How is colostrum most important to a newborn?
   a. It helps boost the newborn's immune system.
   b. It provides much needed fat.
   c. It satisfies the newborn's thirst.
   d. It satisfies the infant's appetite.

28. Mature breast milk _____.
   a. has more sodium than cow's milk
   b. has more calcium than cow's milk
   c. has more protein than cow's milk
   d. has more fat than cow's milk

29. Marfan syndrome is inherited in an autosomal dominant pattern. Which of the following is true?
   a. Female offspring are more likely to be carriers of the disease.
   b. Male offspring are more likely to inherit the disease.
   c. Male and female offspring have the same likelihood of inheriting the disease.
   d. Female offspring are more likely to inherit the disease.

30. In addition to codominance, the ABO blood group antigens are also an example of _____.
   a. incomplete dominance
   b. X-linked recessive inheritance
   c. multiple alleles
   d. recessive lethal inheritance

31. Zoe has cystic fibrosis. Which of the following is the most likely explanation?
   a. Zoe probably inherited one faulty allele from her father, who is a carrier, and one normal allele from her mother.
   b. Zoe probably inherited one faulty allele from her mother, who must also have cystic fibrosis, and one normal allele from her father.
   c. Zoe must have inherited faulty alleles from both parents, both of whom must also have cystic fibrosis.
   d. Zoe must have inherited faulty alleles from both parents, both of whom are carriers.

CRITICAL THINKING QUESTIONS

32. Darcy and Raul are having difficulty conceiving a child. Darcy ovulates every 28 days, and Raul's sperm count is normal. If we could observe Raul's sperm about an hour after ejaculation, however, we'd see that they appear to be moving only sluggishly. When Raul's sperm eventually encounter Darcy's oocyte, they appear to be incapable of generating an adequate acrosomal reaction. Which process has probably gone wrong?

33. Sherrise is a sexually active college student. On Saturday night, she has unprotected sex with her boyfriend. On Tuesday morning, she experiences the twinge of mid-cycle pain that she typically feels when she is ovulating. This makes Sherrise extremely anxious that she might soon learn she is pregnant. Is Sherrise's concern valid? Why or why not?

34. Approximately 3 weeks after her last menstrual period, a sexually active woman experiences a brief episode of abdominopelvic cramping and minor bleeding. What might be the explanation?

35. The Food and Nutrition Board of the Institute of Medicine recommends that all women who might become pregnant consume at least 400 μg/day of folate from supplements or fortified foods. Why?

36. What is the physiological benefit of incorporating shunts into the fetal circulatory system?

37. Why would a premature infant require supplemental oxygen?

38. Devin is 35 weeks pregnant with her first child when she arrives at the birthing unit reporting that she believes she is in labor. She states that she has been experiencing diffuse, mild contractions for the past few hours. Examination reveals, however, that the plug of mucus blocking her cervix is intact and her cervix has not yet begun to dilate. She is advised to return home. Why?

39. Janine is 41 weeks pregnant with her first child when she arrives at the birthing unit reporting that she believes she has been in labor "for days" but that "it's just not going anywhere." During the clinical exam, she experiences a few mild contractions, each lasting about 15–20 seconds; however, her cervix is found to be only 2 cm dilated, and the amniotic sac is intact. Janine is admitted to the birthing unit and an IV infusion of pitocin is started. Why?

40. Describe how the newborn's first breath alters the circulatory pattern.

41. Newborns are at much higher risk for dehydration than adults. Why?

42. Describe the transit of breast milk from lactocytes to nipple pores.

43. A woman who stopped breastfeeding suddenly is experiencing breast engorgement and leakage, just like she did in the first few weeks of breastfeeding. Why?

44. Explain why it was essential that Mendel perform his crosses using a large sample size?

45. How can a female carrier of an X-linked recessive disorder have a daughter who is affected?

ANSWER KEY

Chapter 15

1 The heart rate increases to send more blood to the muscles, and the liver releases stored glucose to fuel the muscles. **3** The effect of gravity on circulation means that it is harder to get blood up from the legs as the body takes on a vertical orientation. **5** The release of urine in extreme fear. The sympathetic system normally constricts sphincters such as that of the urethra. **7** D **9** C **11** A **13** D **15** A **17** A **19** B **21** B **23** C **25** D **27** Whereas energy is needed for running away from the threat, blood needs to be sent to the skeletal muscles for oxygen supply. The additional fuel, in the form of carbohydrates, probably wouldn't improve the ability to escape the threat as much as the diversion of oxygen-rich blood would hinder it. **29** The nerves that carry sensory information from the diaphragm enter the spinal cord in the cervical region where somatic sensory fibers from the shoulder and neck would enter. The brain superimposes this experience onto the sensory homunculus where the somatic nerves are connected. **31** Pupillary dilation and sweating, two functions lost in Horner's syndrome, are caused by the sympathetic system. A tumor in the thoracic cavity may interrupt the output of the thoracic ganglia that project to the head and face. **33** Blood vessels, and therefore blood pressure, are primarily influenced by only the sympathetic system. There is no parasympathetic influence on blood pressure, so nicotine activation of autonomic ganglia will preferentially increase blood pressure. Also, cardiac muscle tissue is only modulated by autonomic inputs, so the conflicting information from both sympathetic and parasympathetic postganglionic fibers will cause arrhythmias. Both hypertension and arrhythmias are cardiac risk factors.

Chapter 16

1 Coordination and gait were tested first, followed by mental status, motor, sensory, and reflexes. There were no specific tests of the cranial nerves. **3** The patient was unable to form episodic memories during the events described in the case, so the medial temporal lobe structures might have been affected by the antibodies. **5** She has just demonstrated voluntary control by closing her eyes, but when he provides the resistance that she needs to hold tight against, she has already relaxed the muscles enough for him to pull them open. She needs to squeeze them tighter to demonstrate the strength she has in the orbicular oculi. **7** The region lateral to the umbilicus is innervated by T9–T11, approximately. A lack of contraction following that stimulation would therefore suggest damage at those levels. **9** D **11** C **13** D **15** D **17** A **19** A **21** D **23** C **25** D **27** C **29** C **31** B **33** D **34** If an ischemic event has occurred, nervous tissue may be compromised, but quick intervention—possibly within a few hours—may be the critical aspect of recovery. **36** The patient has suffered a stroke to the prefrontal cortex where working memory is localized. **38** If the person already has problems focusing on far objects, and wears corrective lenses to see farther objects, then as accommodation changes, focusing on a reading surface might still be in their naturally near-sighted range. **40** Where spinal nerves innervate the skin is represented by "slices" of the body surface referred to as dermatomes. The fibers originating in each region are contained within the same spinal nerve, which relates to the perception of that localization. **42** The spinocerebellum is related to controlling the axial muscles and keeps the body balanced on the bike. The cerebrocerebellum is related to controlling the appendicular muscles and keeps the legs moving to pedal the bike. The vestibulocerebellum receives input about equilibrium to help keep everything balanced as the bike is moving forward.

Chapter 17

1 cAMP **3** Cortisol. **5** Insulin is overproduced. **6** C **8** B **10** C **12** C **14** B **16** B **18** C **20** B **22** A **24** D **26** B **28** D **30** D **32** B **34** C **36** A **38** The endocrine system uses chemical signals called hormones to convey information from one part of the body to a distant part of the body. Hormones are released from the endocrine cell into the extracellular environment, but then travel in the bloodstream to target tissues. This communication and response can take seconds to days. In contrast, neurons transmit electrical signals along their axons. At the axon terminal, the electrical signal prompts the release of a chemical signal called a neurotransmitter that carries the message across the synaptic cleft to elicit a response in the neighboring cell. This method of communication is nearly instantaneous, of very brief duration, and is highly specific. **40** True. Neurotransmitters can be classified as paracrines because, upon their release from a neuron's axon terminals, they travel across a microscopically small cleft to exert their effect on a nearby neuron or muscle cell. **42** An intracellular hormone receptor is located within the cell. A hydrophobic hormone diffuses through the cell membrane and binds to the intracellular hormone receptor, which may be in the cytosol or in the cell nucleus. This hormone–receptor complex binds to a segment of DNA. This initiates the transcription of a target gene, the end result of which is protein assembly and the hormonal response. **44** The mammary glands are the target tissues for prolactin. **46** Hyperthyroidism is an abnormally elevated blood level of thyroid hormones due to an overproduction of T_3 and T_4. An individual with hyperthyroidism is likely to lose weight because one of the primary roles of thyroid hormones is to increase the body's basal metabolic rate, increasing the breakdown of nutrients and the production of ATP. **48** A parathyroid gland tumor can prompt hypersecretion of PTH. This can raise blood calcium levels so excessively that calcium deposits begin to accumulate throughout the body, including in the kidney tubules, where they are referred to as kidney stones. **50** Damage to the innervation of the adrenal medulla would prevent the adrenal glands from responding to the hypothalamus during the fight-or-flight response. Therefore, the response would be reduced. **52** SAD is thought to occur in part because low levels and duration of sunlight allow excessive and prolonged secretion of melatonin. Light therapy—daytime exposure to very bright lighting—is one common therapy. **54** Both estrogens and progesterone are steroid hormones produced by the ovaries that help regulate the menstrual cycle. Estrogens play an important role in the development of the female reproductive tract and secondary sex characteristics. They also help maintain pregnancy. Progesterone prepares the body for pregnancy and helps maintain pregnancy. **56** The beta cells produce the hormone insulin, which is important in the regulation of blood glucose levels. All insulin-dependent cells of the body require insulin in order to take up glucose from the bloodstream. Destruction of the beta cells would result in an inability to produce and secrete insulin, leading to abnormally high blood glucose levels and the disease called type 1 diabetes mellitus. **58** The presence of food in the GI tract stimulates the release of hormones that aid in digestion. For example, gastrin is secreted in response to stomach distention and causes the release of hydrochloric acid in the stomach. Secretin is secreted when acidic chyme enters the small intestine, and stimulates the release of pancreatic bicarbonate. In the presence of fat and protein in the duodenum, CCK stimulates the release of pancreatic digestive enzymes and bile from the gallbladder. Other GI tract hormones aid in glucose metabolism and other functions. **60** Menopause occurs as the result of a progressive decline in the function of the ovaries, resulting in low estrogen and progesterone levels. Ovulation ceases, and postmenopausal woman can no longer conceive a child. In contrast, andropause is a much more gradual and subtle decline in testosterone levels and functioning. A man typically maintains fertility until very old age, although the quantity, quality, and motility of the sperm he produces may be reduced.

Chapter 18

1 There are values given for percent saturation, tension, and blood gas, and there are listings for different types of hemoglobin. **3** Figure 18.13 This should appear to be a normal blood smear. **5** C **7** D **9** A **11** A **13** D **15** D **17** B **19** A **21** A **23** B **25** B **27** The patient's blood is approximately 58 percent plasma (since the buffy coat is less than 1 percent). **29** False. The buffy coat is the portion of blood that is made up of its leukocytes and platelets. **31** The adjective myelogenous suggests a condition originating from (generated by) myeloid cells. Acute myelogenous leukemia impairs the production of erythrocytes and other mature formed elements of the myeloid stem cell lineage. Lymphocytes arise from the lymphoid stem cell line. **33** Bilirubin is a breakdown product of the non-iron component of heme, which is cleaved from globin when erythrocytes are degraded. Excessive erythrocyte destruction would deposit excessive bilirubin in the blood. Bilirubin is a yellowish pigment, and high blood levels can manifest as yellowed skin. **35** Any severe stress can increase the leukocyte count, resulting in leukocytosis. A burn is especially likely to increase the proliferation of leukocytes in order to ward off infection, a significant risk when the barrier function of the skin is destroyed. **37** In a thrombotic stroke, a blood vessel to the brain has been blocked by a thrombus, an aggregation of platelets and erythrocytes within a blood vessel. A thrombolytic agent is a medication that promotes the breakup of thrombi. **39** The lab technician has not made an error. Blood type AB has both A and B surface antigens, and neither anti-A nor anti-B antibodies circulating in the plasma. When anti-A antibodies (added to the first well) contact A antigens on AB erythrocytes, they will cause agglutination. Similarly, when anti-B antibodies contact B antigens on AB erythrocytes, they will cause agglutination.

Chapter 19

1 The pressure gradient between the atria and the ventricles is much greater than that between the ventricles and the pulmonary trunk and aorta. Without the presence of the chordae tendineae and papillary muscles, the valves would be blown back (prolapsed) into the atria and blood would regurgitate. **2** D **4** A **6** B **8** C **10** D **12** D **14** B **16** B **18** A **20** A **22** D **24** D **26** D **27** When the ventricles contract and pressure begins to rise in the ventricles, there is an initial tendency for blood to flow back (regurgitate) to the atria. However, the papillary muscles also contract, placing tension on the chordae tendineae and holding the atrioventricular valves (tricuspid and mitral) in place to prevent the valves from prolapsing and being forced back into the atria. The semilunar valves (pulmonary and aortic) lack chordae tendineae and papillary muscles, but do not face the same pressure gradients as do the atrioventricular valves. As the ventricles relax and pressure drops within the ventricles, there is a tendency for the blood to flow backward. However, the valves, consisting of reinforced endothelium and connective tissue, fill with blood and seal off the opening preventing the return of blood. **29** It prevents additional impulses from spreading through the heart prematurely, thereby allowing the muscle sufficient time to contract and pump blood effectively. **31** Gap junctions within the intercalated disks allow impulses to spread from one cardiac muscle cell to another, allowing sodium, potassium, and calcium ions to flow between adjacent cells, propagating the action potential, and ensuring coordinated contractions. **33** The cardiac cycle comprises a complete relaxation and contraction of both the atria and ventricles, and lasts approximately 0.8 seconds. Beginning with all chambers in diastole, blood flows passively from the veins into the atria and past the atrioventricular valves into the ventricles. The atria begin to contract following depolarization of the atria and pump blood into the ventricles. The ventricles begin to contract, raising pressure within the ventricles. When ventricular pressure rises above the pressure in the two major arteries, blood pushes open the two semilunar valves and moves into the pulmonary trunk and aorta in the ventricular ejection phase.

Answer Key 735

Following ventricular repolarization, the ventricles begin to relax, and pressure within the ventricles drops. When the pressure falls below that of the atria, blood moves from the atria into the ventricles, opening the atrioventricular valves and marking one complete heart cycle. **35** Afterload represents the resistance within the arteries to the flow of blood ejected from the ventricles. If uncompensated, if afterload increases, flow will decrease. In order for the heart to maintain adequate flow to overcome increasing afterload, it must pump more forcefully. This is one of the negative consequences of high blood pressure or hypertension. **37** After fusion of the two endocardial tubes into the single primitive heart, five regions quickly become visible. From the head, these are the truncus arteriosus, bulbus cordis, primitive ventricle, primitive atrium, and sinus venosus. Contractions propel the blood from the sinus venosus to the truncus arteriosus. About day 23, the heart begins to form an S-shaped structure within the pericardium. The bulbus cordis develops into the right ventricle, whereas the primitive ventricle becomes the left ventricle. The interventricular septum separating these begins to form about day 28. The atrioventricular valves form between weeks five to eight. At this point, the heart ventricles resemble the adult structure.

Chapter 20

1 Water. **3** A **5** C **7** C **9** A **11** D **13** B **15** A **17** C **19** A **21** C **23** D **25** D **27** C **28** Arterioles receive blood from arteries, which are vessels with a much larger lumen. As their own lumen averages just 30 micrometers or less, arterioles are critical in slowing down—or resisting—blood flow. The arterioles can also constrict or dilate, which varies their resistance, to help distribute blood flow to the tissues. **30** This is a venule. **32** People who stand upright all day and are inactive overall have very little skeletal muscle activity in the legs. Pooling of blood in the legs and feet is common. Venous return to the heart is reduced, a condition that in turn reduces cardiac output and therefore oxygenation of tissues throughout the body. This could at least partially account for the patient's fatigue and shortness of breath, as well as her "spaced out" feeling, which commonly reflects reduced oxygen to the brain. **34** False. The plasma proteins suspended in blood cannot cross the semipermeable capillary cell membrane, and so they remain in the plasma within the vessel, where they account for the blood colloid osmotic pressure. **36** Nitric oxide is a very powerful local vasodilator that is important in the autoregulation of tissue perfusion. If it were not broken down very quickly after its release, blood flow to the region could exceed metabolic needs. **38** The gonadal veins drain the testes in males and the ovaries in females. **40** Angiogenesis inhibitors are drugs that inhibit the growth of new blood vessels. They can impede the growth of tumors by limiting their blood supply and therefore their access to gas and nutrient exchange.

Chapter 21

1 The three main components are the lymph vessels, the lymph nodes, and the lymph. **3** The bacterium is digested by the phagocyte's digestive enzymes (contained in its lysosomes). **5** B **7** C **9** A **11** D **13** C **15** B **17** D **19** D **21** D **23** B **25** C **27** B **29** C **31** D **33** A **35** B **37** B **39** The lymph enters through lymphatic capillaries, and then into larger lymphatic vessels. The lymph can only go in one direction due to valves in the vessels. The larger lymphatics merge to form trunks that enter into the blood via lymphatic ducts. **41** Interferons are produced in virally infected cells and cause them to secrete signals for surrounding cells to make antiviral proteins. C-reactive protein is induced to be made by the liver and will opsonize certain species of bacteria. **43** Antigen-specific clones are stimulated as their antigen receptor binds to antigen. They are then activated and proliferate, expanding their numbers. The result is a large number of antigen-specific lymphocytes. **45** IgM is an antigen receptor on naïve B cells. Upon activation, naïve B cells make IgM first. IgM is good at binding complement and thus has good antibacterial effects. IgM is replaced with other classes of antibodies later on in the primary response due to class switching. **47** Tuberculosis is caused by bacteria resistant to lysosomal enzymes in alveolar macrophages, resulting in chronic infection. The immune response to these bacteria actually causes most of the lung damage that is characteristic of this life-threatening disease. **49** Antibody response to the cell walls of β-*Streptococcus* cross-reacts with the heart muscle. Complement is then activated and the heart is damaged, leading to abnormal function. Tolerance is broken because heart myosin antigens are similar to antigens on the β- *Streptococcus* bacteria.

Chapter 22

1 Inflammation and the production of a thick mucus; constriction of the airway muscles, or bronchospasm; and an increased sensitivity to allergens. **3** When oxygen binds to the hemoglobin molecule, oxyhemoglobin is created, which has a red color to it. Hemoglobin that is not bound to oxygen tends to be more of a blue–purple color. Oxygenated blood traveling through the systemic arteries has large amounts of oxyhemoglobin. As blood passes through the tissues, much of the oxygen is released into systemic capillaries. The deoxygenated blood returning through the systemic veins, therefore, contains much smaller amounts of oxyhemoglobin. The more oxyhemoglobin that is present in the blood, the redder the fluid will be. As a result, oxygenated blood will be much redder in color than deoxygenated blood. **4** C **6** D **8** C **10** B **12** C **14** A **16** D **18** D **20** D **22** C **24** C **26** B **28** A **30** D **32** A **34** A **36** The pharynx has three major regions. The first region is the nasopharynx, which is connected to the posterior nasal cavity and functions as an airway. The second region is the oropharynx, which is continuous with the nasopharynx and is connected to the oral cavity at the fauces. The laryngopharynx is connected to the oropharynx and the esophagus and trachea. Both the oropharynx and laryngopharynx are passageways for air and food and drink. **38** The conducting zone of the respiratory system includes the organs and structures that are not directly involved in gas exchange, but perform other duties such as providing a passageway for air, trapping and removing debris and pathogens, and warming and humidifying incoming air. Such structures include the nasal cavity, pharynx, larynx, trachea, and most of the bronchial tree. The respiratory zone includes all the organs and structures that are directly involved in gas exchange, including the respiratory bronchioles, alveolar ducts, and alveoli. **40** There is a cavity, called the pleural cavity, between the parietal and visceral layers of the pleura. Mesothelial cells produce and secrete pleural fluid into the pleural cavity that acts as a lubricant. Therefore, as you breathe, the pleural fluid prevents the two layers of the pleura from rubbing against each other and causing damage due to friction. **42** Quiet breathing occurs at rest and without active thought. During quiet breathing, the diaphragm and external intercostal muscles work at different extents, depending on the situation. For inspiration, the diaphragm contracts, causing the diaphragm to flatten and drop towards the abdominal cavity, helping to expand the thoracic cavity. The external intercostal muscles contract as well, causing the rib cage to expand, and the rib cage and sternum to move outward, also expanding the thoracic cavity. Expansion of the thoracic cavity also causes the lungs to expand, due to the adhesiveness of the pleural fluid. As a result, the pressure within the lungs drops below that of the atmosphere, causing air to rush into the lungs. In contrast, expiration is a passive process. As the diaphragm and intercostal muscles relax, the lungs and thoracic tissues recoil, and the volume of the lungs decreases. This causes the pressure within the lungs to increase above that of the atmosphere, causing air to leave the lungs. **44** Both Dalton's and Henry's laws describe the behavior of gases. Dalton's law states that any gas in a mixture of gases exerts force as if it were not in a mixture. Henry's law states that gas molecules dissolve in a liquid proportional to their partial pressure. **46** Both adult and fetal hemoglobin transport oxygen via iron molecules. However, fetal hemoglobin has about a 20-fold greater affinity for oxygen than does adult hemoglobin. This is due to a difference in structure; fetal hemoglobin has two subunits that have a slightly different structure than the subunits of adult hemoglobin. **48** Carbon dioxide can be transported by three mechanisms: dissolved in plasma, as bicarbonate, or as carbaminohemoglobin. Dissolved in plasma, carbon dioxide molecules simply diffuse into the blood from the tissues. Bicarbonate is created by a chemical reaction that occurs mostly in erythrocytes, joining carbon dioxide and water by carbonic anhydrase, producing carbonic acid, which breaks down into bicarbonate and hydrogen ions. Carbaminohemoglobin is the bound form of hemoglobin and carbon dioxide. **50** A major mechanism involved in acclimatization is the increased production of erythrocytes. A drop in tissue levels of oxygen stimulates the kidneys to produce the hormone erythropoietin, which signals the bone marrow to produce erythrocytes. As a result, individuals exposed to a high altitude for long periods of time have a greater number of circulating erythrocytes than do individuals at lower altitudes. **52** Fetal breathing movements occur due to the contraction of respiratory muscles, causing the fetus to inhale and exhale amniotic fluid. It is thought that these movements are a way to "practice" breathing, which results in toning the muscles in preparation for breathing after birth. In addition, fetal breathing movements may help alveoli to form and mature.

Chapter 23

1 Answers may vary. **3** Answers may vary. **5** Answers may vary. **7** Answers may vary. **8** A **10** D **12** B **14** A **16** B **18** D **20** A **22** B **24** B **26** A **28** C **30** B **32** B **33** The enteric nervous system helps regulate alimentary canal motility and the secretion of digestive juices, thus facilitating digestion. If a person becomes overly anxious, sympathetic innervation of the alimentary canal is stimulated, which can result in a slowing of digestive activity. **35** The majority of digestion and absorption occurs in the small intestine. By slowing the transit of chyme, segmentation and a reduced rate of peristalsis allow time for these processes to occur. **37** Parotid gland saliva is watery with little mucus but a lot of amylase, which allows it to mix freely with food during mastication and begin the digestion of carbohydrates. In contrast, sublingual gland saliva has a lot of mucus with the least amount of amylase of all the salivary glands. The high mucus content serves to lubricate the food for swallowing. **39** Usually when food is swallowed, involuntary muscle contractions cause the soft palate to rise and close off the nasopharynx. The larynx also is pulled up, and the epiglottis folds over the glottis. These actions block off the air passages. **41** Peristalsis moves the bolus down the esophagus and toward the stomach. Esophageal glands secrete mucus that lubricates the bolus and reduces friction. When the bolus nears the stomach, the lower esophageal sphincter relaxes, allowing the bolus to pass into the stomach. **43** The stomach has an additional inner oblique smooth muscle layer that helps the muscularis churn and mix food. The epithelium includes gastric glands that secrete gastric fluid. The gastric fluid consists mainly of mucous, HCl, and the enzyme pepsin released as pepsinogen. **45** If large quantities of chyme were forced into the small intestine, it would result in osmotic water loss from the blood into the intestinal lumen that could cause potentially life-threatening low blood volume and erosion of the duodenum. **47** The pancreas secretes protein-digesting enzymes in their inactive forms. If secreted in their active forms, they would self-digest the pancreas. These enzymes are activated in the duodenum. **49** Bile salts and lecithin can emulsify large lipid globules because they are amphipathic; they have a nonpolar (hydrophobic) region that attaches to the large fat molecules as well as a polar (hydrophilic) region that interacts with the watery chime in the intestine.

Chapter 24

1 C **3** A **5** C **7** C **9** A **11** D **13** C **15** C **17** A **19** D **21** C **23** D **25** C **27** A **29** B **30** An increase or decrease in lean muscle mass will result in an increase or decrease in metabolism. **32** Glucose is oxidized during glycolysis, creating pyruvate, which is processed through the Krebs cycle to produce NADH, FADH$_2$, ATP, and CO$_2$. The FADH$_2$ and NADH yield ATP. **34** Carbohydrates are converted into pyruvate during glycolysis. This pyruvate is converted into acetyl CoA and proceeds through the Krebs cycle. When excess acetyl CoA is produced that cannot be processed through the Krebs cycle, the acetyl CoA is converted into triglycerides and fatty acids to be stored in the liver and adipose tissue. **36** Amino acids are not stored in the body. The individual amino acids are broken down into pyruvate, acetyl CoA, or intermediates of the Krebs cycle, and used for energy or for lipogenesis reactions to be stored as fats. **38** Insulin stimulates the uptake of glucose into the cells. In diabetes, the insulin does not function properly; therefore, the blood glucose is unable to be transported across the cell membrane for processing. These patients

Answer Key

are unable to process the glucose in their blood and therefore must rely on other sources of fuel. If the disease is not controlled properly, this inability to process the glucose can lead to starvation states even though the patient is eating. **40** When blood flows to the outer layers of the skin or to the extremities, heat is lost to the environment by the mechanisms of conduction, convection, or radiation. This will cool the blood and the body. Vasoconstriction helps increase the core body temperature by preventing the flow of blood to the outer layer of the skin and outer parts of the extremities. **42** Factors that influence weight gain are food intake (both quantity and quality), environmental factors, height, exercise level, some drugs or disease states, and genes.

Chapter 25

1 B **3** D **5** B **7** D **9** A **11** C **13** B **15** B **17** A **19** B **21** C **23** D **25** D **27** B **29** C **31** The presence of white blood cells found in the urine suggests urinary tract infection. **33** The longer urethra of males means bacteria must travel farther to the bladder to cause an infection. **35** Retroperitoneal anchoring, renal fat pads, and ribs provide protection to the kidney. **37** The structures found in the renal hilum are arteries, veins, ureters, lymphatics, and nerves. **39** The major structures comprising the filtration membrane are fenestrations and podocyte fenestra, fused basement membrane, and filtration slits. **41** Symptoms of kidney failure are weakness, lethargy, shortness of breath, widespread edema, anemia, metabolic acidosis or alkalosis, heart arrhythmias, uremia, loss of appetite, fatigue, excessive urination, and oliguria. **43** The approximate osmolarities are: CT = 300; deepest loop = 1200; DCT = 100; and collecting ducts = 100–1200. **45** To excrete more Na^+ in the urine, increase the flow rate. **47** PTH affects absorption and reabsorption of calcium. **49** In cases of diabetes mellitus, there is more glucose present than the kidney can recover and the excess glucose is lost in the urine. It possesses osmotic character so that it attracts water to the forming urine. **51** The three electrolytes are most closely regulated by the kidney are calcium, sodium, and potassium.

Chapter 26

1 The interstitial fluid (IF). **3** Drinking seawater dehydrates the body as the body must pass sodium through the kidneys, and water follows. **5** A **7** C **9** D **11** B **13** A **15** B **17** B **19** B **21** B **23** D **25** B **27** C **29** C **31** There are additional negatively charged molecules in plasma besides chloride. The additional sodium balances the total negative charges. **33** ADH constricts the arterioles in the peripheral circulation, limiting blood to the extremities and increasing the blood supply to the core of the body. ADH also causes the epithelial cells lining the renal collecting tubules to move water channel proteins called aquaporins from the sides of the cells to the apical surface. This greatly increases the passage of water from the renal filtrate through the wall of the collecting tubule as well as the reabsorption of water into the bloodstream. **35** Very little of the carbon dioxide in the blood is carried dissolved in the plasma. It is transformed into carbonic acid and then into bicarbonate in order to mix in plasma for transportation to the lungs, where it reverts back to its gaseous form. **37** Bicarbonate ions are freely filtered through the glomerulus. They cannot pass freely into the renal tubular cells and must be converted into CO_2 in the filtrate, which can pass through the cell membrane. Sodium ions are reabsorbed at the membrane, and hydrogen ions are expelled into the filtrate. The hydrogen ions combine with bicarbonate, forming carbonic acid, which dissociates into CO_2 gas and water. The gas diffuses into the renal cells where carbonic anhydrase catalyzes its conversion back into a bicarbonate ion, which enters the blood. **39** Respiratory acidosis is present as evidenced by the decreased pH and increased pCO_2, with some compensation as shown by the increased total HCO_3^-. His asthma has compromised his respiratory functions, and excess CO_2 is being retained in his blood.

Chapter 27

1 Sperm remain in the epididymis until they degenerate. **3** The fimbriae sweep the oocyte into the uterine tube. **5** The testes are located in the abdomen. **6** b **8** b **10** c **12** a **14** c **16** d **18** b **20** A single gamete must combine with a gamete from an individual of the opposite sex to produce a fertilized egg, which has a complete set of chromosomes and is the first cell of a new individual. **22** The three accessory glands make the following contributions to semen: the seminal vesicle contributes about 60 percent of the semen volume, with fluid that contains large amounts of fructose to power the movement of sperm; the prostate gland contributes substances critical to sperm maturation; and the bulbourethral glands contribute a thick fluid that lubricates the ends of the urethra and the vagina and helps to clean urine residues from the urethra. **24** Testosterone production by the body would be reduced if a male were taking anabolic steroids. This is because the hypothalamus responds to rising testosterone levels by reducing its secretion of GnRH, which would in turn reduce the anterior pituitary's release of LH, finally reducing the manufacture of testosterone in the testes. **26** Meiosis in the man results in four viable haploid sperm, whereas meiosis in the woman results in a secondary oocyte and, upon completion following fertilization by a sperm, one viable haploid ovum with abundant cytoplasm and up to three polar bodies with little cytoplasm that are destined to die. **28** Endometrial tissue proliferating outside of the endometrium—for example, in the uterine tubes, on the ovaries, or within the pelvic cavity—could block the passage of sperm, ovulated oocytes, or a zygote, thus reducing fertility. **30** The internal reproductive structures form from one of two rudimentary duct systems in the embryo. Testosterone secretion stimulates growth of the male tract, the Wolffian duct. Secretions of sustentacular cells trigger a degradation of the female tract, the Müllerian duct. Without these stimuli, the Müllerian duct will develop and the Wolffian duct will degrade, resulting in a female embryo.

Chapter 28

1 The first structure shown is the morula. The blastocoel appears at approximately 20 seconds. The movie ends with the hatching of the conceptus. **3** A regular heartbeat can be detected at approximately 8 weeks. **4** C **6** B **8** A **10** B **12** B **14** A **16** B **18** A **20** B **22** B **24** B **26** B **28** D **30** C **32** The process of capacitation appears to be incomplete. Capacitation increases sperm motility and makes the sperm membrane more fragile. This enables it to release its digestive enzymes during the acrosomal reaction. When capacitation is inadequate, sperm cannot reach the oocyte membrane. **34** The timing of this discomfort and bleeding suggests that it is probably caused by implantation of the blastocyst into the uterine wall. **36** Circulatory shunts bypass the fetal lungs and liver, bestowing them with just enough oxygenated blood to fulfill their metabolic requirements. Because these organs are only semifunctional in the fetus, it is more efficient to bypass them and divert oxygen and nutrients to the organs that need it more. **38** Devin is very likely experiencing Braxton Hicks contractions, also known as false labor. These are mild contractions that do not promote cervical dilation and are not associated with impending birth. They will probably dissipate with rest. **40** The first breath inflates the lungs, which drops blood pressure throughout the pulmonary system, as well as in the right atrium and ventricle. In response to this pressure change, the flow of blood temporarily reverses direction through the foramen ovale, moving from the left to the right atrium, and blocking the shunt with two flaps of tissue. The increased oxygen concentration also constricts the ductus arteriosus, ensuring that these shunts no longer prevent blood from reaching the lungs to be oxygenated. **42** Milk is secreted by lactocytes into alveoli. Suckling stimulates the contraction of myoepithelial cells that squeeze milk into lactiferous ducts. It then collects in lactiferous sinuses and is secreted through the nipple pores. **44** By using large sample sizes, Mendel minimized the effect of random variability resulting from chance. This allowed him to identify true ratios corresponding to dominant–recessive inheritance.

REFERENCES

18.6 Blood Typing

American Red Cross (US). Blood types [Internet]. c2013 [cited 2013 Apr 3]. Available from: http://www.redcrossblood.org/learn-about-blood/blood-types (http://www.redcrossblood.org/learn-about-blood/blood-types) 2013

20.4 Homeostatic Regulation of the Vascular System

Centers for Disease Control and Prevention (US). Getting blood pressure under control: high blood pressure is out of control for too many Americans [Internet]. Atlanta (GA); [cited 2013 Apr 26]. Available from: http://www.cdc.gov/features/vitalsigns/hypertension/ (http://www.cdc.gov/features/vitalsigns/hypertension/)

21.7 Transplantation and Cancer Immunology

Robinson J, Mistry K, McWilliam H, Lopez R, Parham P, Marsh SG. Nucleic acid research. IMGT/HLA Database [Internet]. 2011 [cited 2013 Apr 1]; 39:D1171–1176. Available from: http://europepmc.org/abstract/MED/21071412 (http://europepmc.org/abstract/MED/21071412)

Robinson J, Malik A, Parham P, Bodmer JG, Marsh SG. Tissue antigens. IMGT/HLA Database [Internet]. 2000 [cited 2013 Apr 1]; 55(3):280–287. Available from: http://europepmc.org/abstract/MED/10777106/reload=0;jsessionid=otkdw3M0TIVSa2zhvimg.6 (http://europepmc.org/abstract/MED/10777106/reload=0;jsessionid=otkdw3M0TIVSa2zhvimg.6)

22.1 Organs and Structures of the Respiratory System

Bizzintino J, Lee WM, Laing IA, Vang F, Pappas T, Zhang G, Martin AC, Khoo SK, Cox DW, Geelhoed GC, et al. Association between human rhinovirus C and severity of acute asthma in children. Eur Respir J [Internet]. 2010 [cited 2013 Mar 22]; 37(5):1037–1042. Available from: http://erj.ersjournals.com/gca?submit=Go&gca=erj%3B37%2F5%2F1037&allch= (http://erj.ersjournals.com/gca?submit=Go&gca=erj%3B37%2F5%2F1037&allch=)

Kumar V, Ramzi S, Robbins SL. Robbins Basic Pathology. 7th ed. Philadelphia (PA): Elsevier Ltd; 2005.

Martin RJ, Kraft M, Chu HW, Berns, EA, Cassell GH. A link between chronic asthma and chronic infection. J Allergy Clin Immunol [Internet]. 2001 [cited 2013 Mar 22]; 107(4):595-601. Available from: http://erj.ersjournals.com/gca?submit=Go&gca=erj%3B37%2F5%2F1037&allch= (http://www.jacionline.org/article/S0091-6749(01)31561-0/fulltext)

23.3 The Mouth, Pharynx, and Esophagus

van Loon FPL, Holmes SJ, Sirotkin B, Williams W, Cochi S, Hadler S, Lindegren ML. Morbidity and Mortality Weekly Report: Mumps surveillance -- United States, 1988–1993 [Internet]. Atlanta, GA: Center for Disease Control; [cited 2013 Apr 3]. Available from: http://www.cdc.gov/mmwr/preview/mmwrhtml/00038546.htm (http://www.cdc.gov/mmwr/preview/mmwrhtml/00038546.htm).

23.5 The Small and Large Intestines

American Cancer Society (US). Cancer facts and figures: colorectal cancer: 2011–2013 [Internet]. c2013 [cited 2013 Apr 3]. Available from: http://www.cancer.org/Research/CancerFactsFigures/ColorectalCancerFactsFigures/colorectal-cancer-facts-figures-2011-2013-page (http://www.cancer.org/Research/CancerFactsFigures/ColorectalCancerFactsFigures/colorectal-cancer-facts-figures-2011-2013-page).

The Nutrition Source. Fiber and colon cancer: following the scientific trail [Internet]. Boston (MA): Harvard School of Public Health; c2012 [cited 2013 Apr 3]. Available from: http://www.hsph.harvard.edu/nutritionsource/nutrition-news/fiber-and-colon-cancer/index.html (http://www.hsph.harvard.edu/nutritionsource/nutrition-news/fiber-and-colon-cancer/index.html).

Centers for Disease Control and Prevention (US). Morbidity and mortality weekly report: notifiable diseases and mortality tables [Internet]. Atlanta (GA); [cited 2013 Apr 3]. Available from: http://www.cdc.gov/mmwr/preview/mmwrhtml/mm6101md.htm?s_cid=mm6101md_w (http://www.cdc.gov/mmwr/preview/mmwrhtml/mm6101md.htm?s_cid=mm6101md_w).

25.10 The Urinary System and Homeostasis

Bagul A, Frost JH, Drage M. Stem cells and their role in renal ischaemia reperfusion injury. Am J Nephrol [Internet]. 2013 [cited 2013 Apr 15]; 37(1):16–29. Available from: http://www.karger.com/Article/FullText/345731 (http://www.karger.com/Article/FullText/345731)

INDEX

Symbols

α-dextrin, 488, 501
α-dextrinase, 488, 501

A

abdominal aorta, 283, 317
ABO blood group, 165, 170
absorption, 451, 496
absorptive state, 538, 552
accessory digestive organ, 444, 496
accessory duct, 484, 496
Acclimatization, 427
acclimatization, 430
accommodation, 61, 76
accommodation-convergence reflex, 61, 76
acetyl coenzyme A (acetyl CoA), 521, 552
acetylcholine (ACh), 17, 38
acinus, 484, 496
acromegaly, 102, 128
acrosomal reaction, 678, 723
acrosome, 678, 723
Active immunity, 365
active immunity, 380
Acute inflammation, 351
acute inflammation, 380
Acute mountain sickness (AMS), 426
acute mountain sickness (AMS), 430
adaptive immune response, 336, 380
adenylyl cyclase, 93, 128
adrenal artery, 289, 317
adrenal cortex, 114, 128
adrenal glands, 113, 128
adrenal medulla, 15, 38, 114, 128
adrenal vein, 308, 317
adrenergic, 17, 38
adrenocorticotropic hormone (ACTH), 103, 128
afferent branch, 19, 38
afferent lymphatic vessels, 342, 380
afterbirth, 706, 723
Afterload, 230
afterload, 234
agglutination, 165, 170
agonist, 33, 38
agranular leukocytes, 156, 170
ala, 391, 430
alar cartilage, 391, 430
alarm reaction, 114, 128
Albumin, 140
albumin, 170
Aldosterone, 115
aldosterone, 128
alimentary canal, 444, 496

allantois, 688, 723
allele, 713, 723
alpha (α)-adrenergic receptor, 17, 38
alpha cell, 119, 128
Alveolar dead space, 409
alveolar dead space, 430
alveolar duct, 398, 430
alveolar macrophage, 399, 430
alveolar pore, 430
alveolar pores, 398
alveolar sac, 398, 430
alveoli, 664, 671
alveolus, 398, 430
aminopeptidase, 488, 496
amnion, 687, 723
amniotic cavity, 687, 723
ampulla, 658, 671
Anabolic hormones, 511
anabolic hormones, 552
anabolic reactions, 511, 552
anal canal, 476, 496
anal column, 478, 496
anal sinus, 478, 496
Anaphylactic shock, 278
anaphylactic shock, 317
anastomosis, 198, 234
anatomical dead space, 409, 430
anatomical sphincter, 566, 598
anemia, 151, 170
angioblasts, 314, 317
angiogenesis, 314, 317
angiotensin I, 574, 598
Angiotensin II, 574
angiotensin II, 598
angiotensin-converting enzyme, 115, 128
angiotensin-converting enzyme (ACE), 574, 598
angiotensinogen, 574, 598
antagonist, 34, 38
anterior cardiac veins, 200, 234
anterior cerebral artery, 284, 317
anterior communicating artery, 284, 317
anterior interventricular artery, 198, 234
anterior interventricular sulcus, 186, 234
anterior tibial artery, 295, 317
anterior tibial vein, 310, 317
anterograde amnesia, 53, 76
antibodies, 140, 170
antibody, 337, 380
anticholinergic drugs, 35, 38
anticoagulant, 163, 170
antidiuretic hormone (ADH), 100, 128, 633
Antidiuretic hormone (ADH), 618
antigen, 337, 380
antigen presentation, 354, 380
Antigen processing, 354
antigen processing, 380

antigen receptor, 358, 380
antigenic determinant, 353, 380
Antithrombin, 163
antithrombin, 170
antrum, 654, 671
anuria, 562, 598
aorta, 282, 317
aortic arch, 282, 317
aortic hiatus, 283, 317
aortic sinuses, 271, 317
aortic valve, 193, 234
apex, 391, 430
aphasia, 54, 76
apneustic center, 411, 430
appendix, 475, 496
aquaporin, 575, 598
areola, 664, 671
arterial circle, 284, 317
arteriole, 249, 317
arteriovenous anastomosis, 250, 317
artery, 248, 317
artificial pacemaker, 216, 234
ascending aorta, 282, 317
ascending colon, 475, 496
ataxia, 74, 76
Atmospheric pressure, 405
atmospheric pressure, 430
ATP synthase, 522, 552
atrial natriuretic peptide (ANP), 124, 128
atrial reflex, 226, 234, 272, 317
atrioventricular (AV) node, 205, 234
atrioventricular bundle, 206, 234
atrioventricular bundle branches, 206, 234
atrioventricular septum, 188, 234
atrioventricular valves, 188, 234
atrium, 183, 234
auricle, 186, 234
autocrine, 88, 128
autonomic tone, 26, 38, 223, 234
autorhythmicity, 202, 234
autosomal chromosome, 723
autosomal chromosomes, 713
autosomal dominant, 716, 723
autosomal recessive, 717, 723
axillary artery, 292, 317
axillary vein, 305, 317
azygos vein, 301, 318

B

B cells, 337, 380
B lymphocytes, 157, 170
Babinski sign, 70, 76
Bachmann's bundle, 205, 234
bacterial flora, 478, 496
Bainbridge reflex, 226, 234
baroreceptor, 20, 38
baroreceptor reflex, 226, 234

Barrier defenses, 336
barrier defenses, 380
Bartholin's glands, 650, 671
basal metabolic rate (BMR), 545, 552
basilar artery, 284, 318
basilic vein, 305, 318
Basophils, 156
basophils, 170
beta (β)-adrenergic receptor, 17, 38
beta (β)-hydroxybutyrate, 530, 552
beta (β)-oxidation, 528, 552
beta cell, 119, 128
bicuspid valve, 193, 235
Bile, 483
bile, 496
bile canaliculus, 482, 496
bile salts, 527, 552
bilirubin, 149, 170, 496
Bilirubin, 483
biliverdin, 149, 170
biosynthesis reactions, 511, 552
blastocoel, 683, 723
blastocyst, 683, 723
blastomere, 683, 723
blood, 138, 170
blood colloidal osmotic pressure (BCOP), 267, 318
Blood flow, 256
blood flow, 318
Blood hydrostatic pressure, 266
blood hydrostatic pressure, 318
blood islands, 314, 318
blood pressure, 256, 318
blood-testis barrier, 641, 671
body, 464, 496
body mass index (BMI), 547, 552
body of uterus, 659, 671
Bohr effect, 422, 430
bolus, 455, 496
bone marrow, 338, 380
bone marrow biopsy, 145, 170
bone marrow transplant, 145, 170
Bowman's capsule, 570, 598
Boyle's law, 405, 430
brachial artery, 292, 318
brachial vein, 305, 318
brachiocephalic artery, 318
brachiocephalic vein, 301, 318
Braxton Hicks contractions, 704, 723
bridge, 391, 430
broad ligament, 651, 671
bronchi, 397
bronchial artery, 287, 318
bronchial bud, 427, 430
bronchial tree, 397, 430
bronchial vein, 301, 318
bronchiole, 397, 430
bronchoconstriction, 402, 430

bronchodilation, 402, 430
bronchus, 430
Bronchus-associated lymphoid tissue (BALT), 345
bronchus-associated lymphoid tissue (BALT), 380
brown adipose tissue, 708, 723
brush border, 471, 496, 575, 598
buffy coat, 139, 170
bulbourethral glands, 645, 671
bulbus cordis, 233, 235
bundle of His, 206, 235

C

calcitonin, 110, 128
Calorie, 545
calorie, 552
calyces, 569, 598
capacitance, 254, 318
capacitance vessels, 254, 318
capacitation, 678, 723
capillary, 249, 318
capillary bed, 250, 318
capillary hydrostatic pressure (CHP), 266, 318
carbaminohemoglobin, 148, 170, 424, 430
Carbonic anhydrase (CA), 424
carbonic anhydrase (CA), 430
cardia, 464, 496
cardiac accelerator nerves, 30, 38
cardiac cycle, 216, 235
cardiac notch, 180, 235, 401, 430
Cardiac output (CO), 221
cardiac output (CO), 235
cardiac plexus, 224, 235
cardiac reflexes, 225, 235
cardiac reserve, 222, 235
cardiac skeleton, 188, 235
cardiogenic area, 232, 235
cardiogenic cords, 232, 235
Cardiogenic shock, 277
cardiogenic shock, 318
cardiomyocyte, 198, 235
cardiovascular center, 30, 38
carotid sinuses, 271, 318
carrier, 717, 723
Catabolic hormones, 511
catabolic hormones, 552
Catabolic reactions, 508
catabolic reactions, 552
cavernous sinus, 303, 319
cecum, 475, 496
celiac ganglion, 13, 38
celiac trunk, 289, 319
cellular respiration, 513, 552
cementum, 458, 496
central chemoreceptor, 412, 431

central neuron, 11, 38
Central tolerance, 361
central tolerance, 380
central vein, 482, 496
cephalic phase, 467, 496
cephalic vein, 305, 319
cerebrocerebellum, 72, 76
cerebrovascular accident (CVA), 284, 319
cervix, 659, 671
check reflex, 73, 76
chemical digestion, 451, 496
chemokine, 349, 380
chief cell, 496
chief cells, 465
chloride shift, 424, 431
cholecystokinin (CCK), 527, 552
cholinergic, 17, 38
chordae tendineae, 191, 235
chorion, 688, 723
chorionic membrane, 690, 723
chorionic villi, 690, 723
chromaffin, 115, 128
chromaffin cells, 15, 38
Chronic inflammation, 351
chronic inflammation, 380
chyle, 335, 380
chylomicron, 493, 496
chylomicrons, 527, 552
chyme, 451, 496
chymotrypsin, 533, 552
chymotrypsinogen, 533, 552
ciliary ganglion, 15, 38
circle of Willis, 284, 319
circular fold, 471, 496
circulatory shock, 277, 319
circumflex artery, 198, 235
cisterna chyli, 335, 380
citric acid cycle, 515, 552
clasp-knife response, 70, 76
Class switching, 363
class switching, 380
cleavage, 683, 723
clitoris, 650, 671
clonal anergy, 361, 380
clonal deletion, 361, 380
clonal expansion, 358, 380
Clonal selection, 358
clonal selection, 380
clone, 358, 380
clotting factors, 161, 170
coagulation, 160, 170
Codominance, 720
codominance, 723
Collateral ganglia, 13
collateral ganglia, 38
colloid, 105, 128
colon, 475, 496
Colony-stimulating factors (CSFs), 144

Download for free at http://cnx.org/content/col11496/latest/

colony-stimulating factors (CSFs), 170
colostrum, 712, 724
common bile duct, 482, 496
common carotid artery, 284, 319
common hepatic artery, 289, 319
common hepatic duct, 482, 496
common iliac artery, 289, 319
common iliac vein, 310, 319
common pathway, 163, 170
complement, 349, 380
Compliance, 260
compliance, 319
conceptus, 683, 724
conducting zone, 390, 431
Conduction, 545
conduction, 552
Conduction aphasia, 54
conduction aphasia, 76
conductive hearing, 59, 76
conjugate gaze, 60, 76
constant region domain, 353, 380
continuous capillary, 249, 319
Convection, 545
convection, 552
convergence, 61, 76
coordination exam, 46, 76
corona radiata, 678, 724
Coronary arteries, 198
coronary arteries, 235
coronary sinus, 191, 235
coronary sulcus, 186, 235
Coronary veins, 200
coronary veins, 235
corpus albicans, 658, 671
corpus cavernosum, 646, 671
corpus luteum, 658, 671
corpus spongiosum, 646, 671
cortical nephrons, 572, 598
cortical reaction, 679, 724
cortico-ponto-cerebellar pathway, 72, 76
cortisol, 115, 128
countercurrent multiplier system, 586, 598
cranial nerve exam, 46, 76
craniosacral system, 15, 38
cricoid cartilage, 394, 431
cross matching, 170
crown, 458, 497
cuspid, 497
cuspids, 457
cyclic adenosine monophosphate (cAMP), 93, 128
cystic artery, 289, 319
cystic duct, 485, 497
cytoarchitecture, 51, 76
cytokine, 349, 381
Cytokines, 144
cytokines, 170

Cytotoxic T cells (Tc), 360
cytotoxic T cells (Tc), 381

D

Dalton's law, 414, 431
deciduous teeth, 457
deciduous tooth, 497
deep femoral artery, 295, 319
deep femoral vein, 310, 319
deep tendon reflex, 69, 76
defecation, 451, 497
defensins, 156, 171
deglutition, 497
Deglutition, 462
dehydration, 616, 633
Delayed hypersensitivity, 373
delayed hypersensitivity, 381
delta cell, 119, 128
dens, 497
dentes, 457
dentin, 458, 497
dentition, 457, 497
deoxyhemoglobin, 148, 171
deoxyribonuclease, 490, 497
descending aorta, 283, 319
descending colon, 475, 497
detrusor muscle, 565, 598
diabetes mellitus, 123, 128
diacylglycerol (DAG), 94, 128
diapedesis, 154, 171
diastole, 216, 235
diastolic pressure, 256, 319
digital arteries, 292, 319
digital veins, 305, 319
dihydroxyvitamin D, 624, 633
dilation, 704, 724
dipeptidase, 488, 497
diplopia, 61, 76
distal convoluted tubules, 572, 598
Diuresis, 618
diuresis, 633
diuretic, 593, 598
dominant, 714, 724
Dominant lethal, 721
dominant lethal, 724
dorsal arch, 295, 319
dorsal longitudinal fasciculus, 28, 38
dorsal nucleus of the vagus nerve, 15, 38
dorsal respiratory group (DRG), 411, 431
dorsal venous arch, 310, 319
dorsalis pedis artery, 295, 319
dorsum nasi, 391, 431
downregulation, 95, 129
ductus arteriosus, 315, 319, 698, 724
ductus deferens, 643, 671
ductus venosus, 315, 319, 698, 724
duodenal gland, 497

duodenal glands, 472
duodenum, 470, 497

E

early induced immune response, 349, 381
ectoderm, 688, 724
ectopic pregnancy, 686, 724
Eddinger-Westphal nucleus, 38
edema, 48, 76
Edinger-Westphal nucleus, 15
effector T cells, 359, 381
efferent arteriole, 570, 598
efferent branch, 19, 39
efferent lymphatic vessels, 342, 381
ejaculatory duct, 644, 671
ejection fraction, 222, 235
elastase, 533, 552
elastic artery, 248, 320
electrocardiogram (ECG), 209, 235
electron transport chain (ETC), 521, 552
embolus, 48, 76, 164, 171
embryo, 683, 724
embryonic folding, 693, 724
emigration, 154, 171
enamel, 458, 497
end diastolic volume (EDV), 218, 235
end systolic volume (ESV), 218, 235
endocardial tubes, 232, 235
endocardium, 188, 236
endocrine gland, 87, 129
endocrine system, 86, 129
endoderm, 688, 724
endogenous, 17, 39
endogenous chemical, 32, 39
endometrium, 660, 671
Endothelins, 591
endothelins, 598
endothelium, 188, 236
energy-consuming phase, 517, 552
energy-yielding phase, 517, 552
enteroendocrine cell, 497
enteroendocrine cells, 465
enterohepatic circulation, 483, 497
enterokinase, 533, 552
enteropeptidase, 484, 497
Eosinophils, 156
eosinophils, 171
epiblast, 687, 724
epicardial coronary arteries, 198, 236
epicardium, 184, 236
epididymis, 643, 671
epiglottis, 395, 431
epinephrine, 17, 39, 115, 129
epiploic appendage, 497
epiploic appendages, 477
episiotomy, 706, 724
episodic memory, 53, 76

erythroblastosis fetalis, 375, 381
erythrocyte, 145, 171
erythropoietin (EPO), 124, 129, 171
Erythropoietin (EPO), 144
esophageal artery, 287, 320
esophageal vein, 301, 320
esophagus, 460, 497
estrogens, 117, 129
Evaporation, 545
evaporation, 553
exocrine system, 88, 129
exogenous, 17, 39
exogenous chemical, 32, 39
expiration, 407, 431
Expiratory reserve volume (ERV), 408
expiratory reserve volume (ERV), 431
expressive aphasia, 54, 76
expulsion, 706, 724
external anal sphincter, 476, 497
external carotid artery, 284, 320
external elastic membrane, 248, 320
external iliac artery, 289, 320
external iliac vein, 310, 320
external jugular vein, 302, 320
external nose, 391, 431
External respiration, 416
external respiration, 431
external urinary sphincter, 564, 598
Extracellular fluid (ECF), 609
extracellular fluid (ECF), 633
extrinsic muscles of the tongue, 63, 77
extrinsic pathway, 162, 171

F

FADH$_2$, 512, 553
fas ligand, 348, 381
fasciculation, 70, 77
fatty acid oxidation, 528, 553
fauces, 62, 77, 394, 431, 453, 497
Fc region, 362, 381
feces, 479, 497
femoral artery, 295, 320
femoral circumflex vein, 310, 320
femoral vein, 310, 320
fenestrated capillary, 250, 320
fenestrations, 573, 598
ferritin, 149, 171
Fertilization, 678
fertilization, 724
fertilization membrane, 679, 724
fetus, 683, 724
fibrillation, 70, 77
fibrin, 160, 171
fibrinogen, 140, 171
Fibrinolysis, 163
fibrinolysis, 171
fibroelastic membrane, 396, 431

fibular vein, 310, 320
fight-or-flight response, 10, 39
filling time, 229, 236
filtration, 266, 320
filtration slits, 572, 598
fimbriae, 658, 671
first messenger, 93, 129
flaccid paralysis, 70, 77
flaccidity, 69, 77
flatus, 479, 497
flavin adenine dinucleotide (FAD), 512, 553
flocculonodular lobe, 72, 77
fluid compartment, 609, 633
follicle, 651, 671
follicle-stimulating hormone (FSH), 103, 129
folliculogenesis, 653, 671
foramen ovale, 188, 236, 315, 320, 698, 724
forced breathing, 408, 431
foregut, 427, 431
foremilk, 712, 724
formed elements, 138, 171
forming urine, 572, 598
fossa ovalis, 188, 236
Frank-Starling mechanism, 229, 236
functional residual capacity (FRC), 409, 431
fundus, 464, 497, 659, 671

G

G cell, 497
G cells, 465
G protein, 93, 129
G protein-coupled receptor, 17, 39
gait, 72, 77
gait exam, 46, 77
gallbladder, 485, 497
gamete, 638, 671
ganglionic neuron, 13, 39
gastric emptying, 468, 497
gastric gland, 465, 497
gastric phase, 467, 497
gastric pit, 497
gastric pits, 465
gastrin, 465, 497
gastrocolic reflex, 479, 498
gastroileal reflex, 474, 498
gastrulation, 688, 724
general adaptation syndrome (GAS), 114, 129
genicular artery, 295, 320
genotype, 713, 724
Germinal centers, 341
germinal centers, 381
gestation, 683, 724

gigantism, 102, 129
gingiva, 498
Gingivae, 458
glans penis, 646, 671
globin, 148, 171
globulins, 140, 171
glomerular filtration rate (GFR), 577, 598
glomerulus, 570, 599
glottis, 395, 431
glucagon, 120, 129
glucocorticoids, 115, 129
Glucokinase, 517
glucokinase, 553
Gluconeogenesis, 524
gluconeogenesis, 553
glucose-6-phosphate, 517, 553
glycogen, 540, 553
glycolysis, 514, 553
glycosuria, 584, 599
gnosis, 55, 77
goiter, 109, 129
gonadal artery, 289, 320
gonadal vein, 308, 320
gonadotropin-releasing hormone (GnRH), 648, 672
gonadotropins, 103, 129
gonads, 640, 672
graft-versus-host disease, 376, 381
Granular leukocytes, 156
granular leukocytes, 171
granulosa cells, 653, 672
granzyme, 348, 381
graphesthesia, 55, 77
gray rami communicantes, 13, 39
great cardiac vein, 200, 236
great cerebral vein, 303, 320
great saphenous vein, 310, 320
greater splanchnic nerve, 13, 39
growth hormone (GH), 101, 129

H

Haldane effect, 425, 431
haustra, 477
haustral contraction, 479, 498
haustrum, 498
heart block, 215, 236
heart bulge, 232, 236
heart rate (HR), 221, 236
heart sounds, 219, 236
heavy chain, 361, 381
Helper T cells (Th), 360
helper T cells (Th), 381
hemangioblasts, 314, 320
hematocrit, 139, 171
heme, 148, 171
hemiazygos vein, 301, 320
hemisection, 68, 77

hemocytoblast, 143, 171
Hemoglobin, 148
hemoglobin, 171
hemolysis, 165, 171
hemolytic disease of the newborn (HDN), 166, 171
hemophilia, 164, 171
hemopoiesis, 142, 171
hemopoietic growth factors, 143, 171
hemopoietic stem cell, 143, 172
hemorrhage, 159, 172
hemorrhagic stroke, 48, 77
hemosiderin, 149, 172
hemostasis, 159, 172
Henry's law, 414, 431
heparin, 163, 172
hepatic artery, 481, 498
hepatic artery proper, 289, 320
hepatic lobule, 482, 498
hepatic portal system, 313, 321
hepatic portal vein, 481, 498
hepatic sinusoid, 482, 498
hepatic vein, 308, 321, 482, 498
hepatocyte, 482
hepatocytes, 498
hepatopancreatic ampulla, 470, 498
hepatopancreatic sphincter, 470, 498
heterozygous, 714, 724
Hexokinase, 517
hexokinase, 553
high endothelial venules, 341, 381
hilum, 402, 431
Hindmilk, 712
hindmilk, 725
histamine, 381
Histamine, 351
homozygous, 714, 725
hormone, 86, 129
hormone receptor, 92, 129
human chorionic gonadotropin (hCG), 685, 725
hydrochloric acid (HCl), 465, 498
Hydrostatic pressure, 612
hydrostatic pressure, 633
hydroxymethylglutaryl CoA (HMG CoA), 530, 553
hymen, 650, 672
hypercalcemia, 633
Hypercalcemia, 622
Hypercapnia, 627
hypercapnia, 633
Hyperchloremia, 621
hyperchloremia, 633
hyperflexia, 70, 77
hyperglycemia, 123, 129
Hyperkalemia, 621
hyperkalemia, 633
Hypernatremia, 620

hypernatremia, 633
hyperparathyroidism, 112, 129
Hyperphosphatemia, 622
hyperphosphatemia, 633
Hyperpnea, 425
hyperpnea, 431
hypertension, 276, 321
hyperthyroidism, 109, 129
hypertrophic cardiomyopathy, 183, 236
hyperventilation, 425, 431
Hypervolemia, 261
hypervolemia, 321
hypoblast, 688, 725
Hypocalcemia, 622
hypocalcemia, 633
Hypocapnia, 627
hypocapnia, 633
Hypochloremia, 621
hypochloremia, 633
Hypokalemia, 621
hypokalemia, 633
Hyponatremia, 620
hyponatremia, 633
hypoparathyroidism, 112, 129
Hypophosphatemia, 622
hypophosphatemia, 633
hypophyseal portal system, 100, 129
hypothalamus, 97, 130
hypothyroidism, 109, 130
hypotonicity, 69, 77
hypovolemia, 48, 77, 261, 321
Hypovolemic shock, 277
hypovolemic shock, 321
hypoxemia, 148, 172
hypoxia, 257, 321

I

IgA, 363, 381
IgD, 362, 381
IgE, 363, 381
IgG, 363, 381
IgM, 363, 381
ileocecal sphincter, 470, 498
ileum, 470, 498
immediate hypersensitivity, 372, 381
immune system, 332, 381
immunoglobulin, 361, 381
immunoglobulins, 140, 172
immunological memory, 352, 381
implantation, 684, 725
inactive proenzymes, 533, 553
incisor, 498
incisors, 457
incomplete dominance, 720, 725
incontinence, 565, 599
inferior cerebellar peduncle (ICP), 72, 77
inferior mesenteric artery, 289, 321

inferior mesenteric ganglion, 13, 39
inferior olive, 72, 77
inferior phrenic artery, 289, 321
inferior vena cava, 183, 236, 308, 321
inflammation, 350, 382
infundibulum, 98, 130, 658, 672
ingestion, 450, 498
inguinal canal, 644, 672
inhibin, 117, 130
innate immune response, 336, 382
inner cell mass, 683, 725
inositol triphosphate (IP3), 94, 130
Inspiration, 407
inspiration, 431
Inspiratory capacity (IC), 409
inspiratory capacity (IC), 432
Inspiratory reserve volume (IRV), 408
inspiratory reserve volume (IRV), 432
insulin, 122, 130, 538, 553
insulin-like growth factors (IGF), 130
insulin-like growth factors (IGFs), 102
interatrial band, 205, 236
interatrial septum, 188, 236
intercalated cell, 588, 599
intercalated disc, 202, 236
intercostal artery, 287, 321
intercostal vein, 301, 321
Interferons, 349
interferons, 382
Interleukins, 144
interleukins, 172
internal anal sphincter, 476, 498
internal carotid artery, 284, 321
internal elastic membrane, 247, 321
internal iliac artery, 289, 321
internal iliac vein, 310, 321
internal jugular vein, 302, 321
Internal respiration, 416
internal respiration, 432
internal thoracic artery, 284, 321
internal thoracic vein, 301, 321
internal urinary sphincter, 564, 599
internodal pathways, 205, 236
internuclear ophthalmoplegia, 61, 77
interstitial fluid (IF), 609, 633
interstitial fluid colloidal osmotic pressure (IFCOP), 267, 321
interstitial fluid hydrostatic pressure (IFHP), 266, 321
interventricular septum, 188, 236
intestinal gland, 472, 498
intestinal juice, 472, 498
intestinal phase, 468, 498
intorsion, 60, 77
Intra-alveolar pressure, 405
intra-alveolar pressure, 432
intracellular fluid (ICF), 609, 633
intramural ganglia, 15, 39

Intrapleural pressure, 406
intrapleural pressure, 432
intrinsic factor, 465, 498
intrinsic muscles of the tongue, 63, 77
intrinsic pathway, 163, 172
inulin, 579, 599
involution, 706, 725
ischemia, 257, 321
ischemic stroke, 48, 77
isovolumic contraction, 218, 236
isovolumic ventricular relaxation phase, 218, 236
isthmus, 658, 672

J

jaw-jerk reflex, 60, 77
jejunum, 470, 498
juxtaglomerular apparatus (JGA), 573, 599
juxtaglomerular cell, 574, 599
juxtamedullary nephrons, 572, 599

K

karyotype, 713, 725
ketone bodies, 530, 553
Korotkoff sounds, 259, 321
Krebs cycle, 520, 553

L

labia, 453
labia majora, 650, 672
labia minora, 650, 672
labial frenulum, 453, 498
labium, 498
lactase, 488, 498
Lactation, 709
lactation, 725
lacteal, 471, 498
lactiferous ducts, 664, 672
lactiferous sinus, 664, 672
lanugo, 699, 725
large intestine, 474, 498
laryngeal prominence, 394, 432
laryngopharynx, 394, 432, 460, 498
laryngotracheal, 432
laryngotracheal bud, 427
larynx, 394, 432
lateral circumflex artery, 295, 321
lateral plantar artery, 295, 322
leaky tight junctions, 586, 599
left atrioventricular valve, 193, 236
left colic flexure, 475, 498
left gastric artery, 289, 322
leptin, 125, 130
lesser splanchnic nerve, 13, 39

let-down reflex, 710, 725
Leukemia, 157
leukemia, 172
leukocyte, 153, 172
Leukocyte esterase, 563
leukocyte esterase, 599
leukocytosis, 157, 172
Leukopenia, 157
leukopenia, 172
Leydig cells, 647, 672
ligand-gated cation channel, 17, 39
light chain, 361, 382
lightening, 703, 725
limbic lobe, 29, 39
lingual frenulum, 455, 499
lingual lipase, 455, 499
lingual tonsil, 394, 432
lipogenesis, 531, 553
lipolysis, 528, 553
lipoprotein lipase, 493, 499
liver, 481, 499
Localization of function, 47
localization of function, 77
lochia, 706, 725
long reflex, 22, 39
loop of Henle, 572, 599
lower esophageal sphincter, 461, 499
lumbar arteries, 289, 322
lumbar veins, 308, 322
lumen, 245, 322
lung, 401, 432
lung bud, 427, 432
Luteinizing hormone (LH), 103
luteinizing hormone (LH), 130
Lymph, 333
lymph, 382
lymph node, 333, 382
Lymphatic capillaries, 334
lymphatic capillaries, 382
lymphatic system, 332, 382
lymphatic trunks, 335, 382
Lymphocytes, 157
lymphocytes, 172, 336, 382
lymphoid nodules, 343, 382
Lymphoid stem cells, 143
lymphoid stem cells, 172
Lymphoma, 158
lymphoma, 172
lysozyme, 156, 172

M

macrophage, 149, 172, 347, 382
Macrophage oxidative metabolism, 369
macrophage oxidative metabolism, 382
macula densa, 573, 599
main pancreatic duct, 470, 499
major duodenal papilla, 470, 499

major histocompatibility complex (MHC), 354, 382
maltase, 488, 499
mammary glands, 664, 672
marginal arteries, 199, 236
mass movement, 479, 499
mast cell, 351, 382
mastication, 450, 499
maxillary vein, 302, 322
Mean arterial pressure (MAP), 257
mean arterial pressure (MAP), 322
meatus, 432
meatuses, 391
Mechanical digestion, 450
mechanical digestion, 499
meconium, 699, 725
medial forebrain bundle, 28, 39
medial longitudinal fasciculus (MLF), 60, 77
medial plantar artery, 295, 322
median antebrachial vein, 305, 322
median cubital vein, 305, 322
median sacral artery, 289, 322
mediastinal artery, 287, 322
medulla, 569, 599
megakaryocyte, 158, 172
melatonin, 116, 130
memory cell, 157, 172
memory T cells, 359, 382
menarche, 660, 672
menses, 660, 672
menses phase, 660, 672
menstrual cycle, 660, 672
mental status exam, 46, 77
mesangial, 573, 599
mesenteric plexus, 15, 39
mesoappendix, 475, 499
mesoderm, 232, 236, 688, 725
mesothelium, 185, 237
Metabolic acidosis, 630
metabolic acidosis, 633
Metabolic alkalosis, 631
metabolic alkalosis, 633
metabolic rate, 545, 553
Metabolism, 508
metabolism, 553
metarteriole, 250, 322
MHC class I, 355, 382
MHC class II, 355, 382
MHC polygeny, 375, 382
MHC polymorphism, 375, 382
micelle, 493, 499
microcirculation, 249, 322
microvilli, 471
microvillus, 499
Micturition, 565
micturition, 599
middle cardiac vein, 200, 237

middle cerebellar peduncle (MCP), 72, 78
middle cerebral artery, 284, 322
middle sacral vein, 310, 322
migrating motility complex, 473, 499
mineralocorticoids, 115, 130
Minerals, 549
minerals, 553
mitral valve, 193, 237
mixing wave, 468, 499
moderator band , 192, 237
molar, 499
molars, 457
monocyte, 348, 382
Monocytes, 157
monocytes, 172
monoglyceride molecules, 527, 553
monosaccharide, 513, 553
mons pubis, 650, 672
morula, 683, 725
motilin, 473, 499
motility, 446, 499
motor exam, 46, 78
mucosa, 445, 499
Mucosa-associated lymphoid tissue (MALT), 345
mucosa-associated lymphoid tissue (MALT), 382
mucosal barrier, 468, 499
mucous neck cell, 499
mucous neck cells, 465
Müllerian duct, 667, 672
murmur, 220, 237
muscalaris, 445
muscarinic receptor, 17, 39
muscular artery, 249, 322
muscularis, 499
mutation, 721, 725
mydriasis, 34, 39
Myeloid stem cells, 143
myeloid stem cells, 172
myenteric plexus, 446, 499
myocardial conducting cells, 202, 237
myocardial contractile cells, 202, 237
myocardium, 186, 237
myogenic mechanism, 589, 599
myogenic response, 274, 322
myometrium, 660, 672

N

NADH, 512, 553
naïve lymphocyte, 340, 382
naris, 391, 432
nasal bone, 391, 432
nasal septum, 391, 432
nasopharynx, 394, 432
Natural killer (NK) cells, 157
natural killer (NK) cells, 172

natural killer cell (NK), 338, 382
negative inotropic factors, 229, 237
negative selection, 357, 382
Neonatal hypothyroidism, 109
neonatal hypothyroidism, 130
Nephrons, 570
nephrons, 599
nervi vasorum, 248, 322
net filtration pressure (NFP), 267, 322, 578, 599
neural fold, 692, 725
neural plate, 692, 725
neural tube, 692, 725
Neurogenic shock, 278
neurogenic shock, 322
neurological exam, 46, 78
neurulation, 692, 725
Neutralization, 368
neutralization, 382
neutrophil, 347, 382
neutrophils, 156, 172
nicotinamide adenine dinucleotide (NAD), 512, 553
nicotinic receptor, 17, 39
nonshivering thermogenesis, 708, 725
norepinephrine, 17, 39, 115, 130
notochord, 692, 725
nucleosidase, 490, 499
nucleus ambiguus, 15, 40

O

Obstructive shock, 278
obstructive shock, 322
occipital sinus, 303, 322
olfactory pit, 427, 432
oliguria, 562, 599
oocyte, 649, 672
oogenesis, 652, 672
oogonia, 652, 672
ophthalmic artery, 284, 322
Opsonization, 349
opsonization, 382
oral cavity, 453, 499
oral vestibule, 453, 499
organogenesis, 694, 725
oropharynx, 394, 432, 460, 499
osmoreceptor, 130
osmoreceptors, 100
osteomalacia, 595, 599
ovarian artery, 289, 323
ovarian cycle, 652, 672
ovarian vein, 308, 323
ovaries, 651, 672
ovulation, 652, 672
ovum, 653, 672
oxidation, 512, 553
oxidation-reduction reaction, 512, 553

oxidative phosphorylation, 521, 553
oxygen-hemoglobin dissociation curve, 420, 432
oxyhemoglobin, 148, 172, 419, 432
oxytocin, 99, 130

P

P wave, 210, 237
pacemaker, 205, 237
packed cell volume (PCV), 139, 172
palatine tonsil, 394, 432
palatoglossal arch, 454, 499
palatopharyngeal arch, 454, 499
palmar arches, 292, 323
palmar venous arches, 305, 323
pancreas, 118, 130, 483, 499
pancreatic amylase, 488, 500
pancreatic islets, 118, 130
pancreatic juice, 484, 500
pancreatic lipase, 490, 500
pancreatic lipases, 527, 553
pancreatic nuclease, 490, 500
papillary muscle, 191, 237
paracrine, 88, 130
paramedian pontine reticular formation (PPRF), 60, 78
paranasal sinus, 392, 432
parasympathetic division, 10, 40
parasympathomimetic drugs, 35, 40
parathyroid glands, 110, 130
parathyroid hormone (PTH), 110, 130
paravertebral ganglia, 13, 40
paresis, 70, 78
parietal branches, 287, 323
parietal cell, 500
parietal cells, 465
parietal pleura, 403, 432
parotid gland, 500
parotid glands, 455
Partial pressure, 414
partial pressure, 432
parturition, 703, 725
Passive immunity, 365
passive immunity, 382
pattern recognition receptor (PRR), 348, 383
pectinate line, 478, 500
pectinate muscles, 191, 237
pedicels, 572, 599
penis, 645, 672
pepsin, 533, 554
pepsinogen, 465, 500
perforin, 348, 383
perfusion, 249, 323
pericardial artery, 287, 323
pericardial cavity, 180, 237
pericardial sac, 184, 237

pericardium, 184, 237
perimetrium, 660, 672
peripheral chemoreceptor, 412, 433
peripheral tolerance, 361, 383
Peristalsis, 450
peristalsis, 500
peritubular capillaries, 570, 600
permanent teeth, 457
permanent tooth, 500
petrosal sinus, 303, 323
phagocytosis, 347, 383
pharyngeal tonsil, 394, 433
pharynx, 393, 433, 460, 500
phenotype, 713, 725
philtrum, 391, 433
phosphatase, 490, 500
phosphodiesterase (PDE), 94, 130
phosphorylation cascade, 93, 130
phrenic vein, 308, 323
physiological sphincter, 566, 600
pineal gland, 116, 130
pinealocyte, 116, 130
pituitary dwarfism, 102, 130
pituitary gland, 98, 131
placenta, 683, 726
placenta previa, 686, 726
placentation, 691, 726
plantar arch, 295, 323
plantar reflex, 70, 78
plantar veins, 310, 323
plantar venous arch, 310, 323
plasma, 138, 173
plasma cell, 338, 383
Plasma osmolality, 616
plasma osmolality, 633
plasmin, 163, 173
platelet plug, 160, 173
platelets, 138, 173
pleural cavity, 403, 433
Pleural fluid, 403
pleural fluid, 433
pluripotent stem cell, 143, 173
pneumotaxic center, 411, 433
podocytes, 572, 600
polar body, 652, 672
polyclonal response, 358, 383
polycythemia, 153, 173
polymorphonuclear, 156, 173
polysaccharides, 513, 554
polyspermy, 679, 726
polyuria, 562, 600
popliteal artery, 295, 323
popliteal vein, 310, 323
porta hepatis, 481, 500
portal triad, 482, 500
positive chemotaxis, 154, 173
positive inotropic factors, 229, 237
positive selection, 356, 383

postabsorptive state, 540, 554
posterior cardiac vein, 200, 237
posterior cerebral artery, 284, 323
posterior communicating artery, 284, 323
posterior interventricular artery, 199, 237
posterior interventricular sulcus, 186, 237
posterior tibial artery, 295, 323
posterior tibial vein, 310, 323
postganglionic fiber, 14, 40
PP cell, 119, 131
praxis, 54, 78
precapillary sphincters, 250, 323
preganglionic fiber, 14, 40
preload, 218, 237
premolar, 500
premolars, 457
prepotential depolarization, 206, 237
prepuce, 646, 673
prevertebral ganglia, 13, 40
primary adaptive response, 352, 383
primary follicles, 653, 673
primary lymphoid organ, 383
primary lymphoid organs, 338
primitive atrium, 233, 238
primitive heart tube, 232, 238
primitive streak, 688, 726
primitive ventricle, 233, 238
primordial follicles, 653, 673
principal cell, 588, 600
procedural memory, 53, 78
progesterone, 117, 131
prolactin, 710, 726
prolactin (PRL), 103, 131
proliferative phase, 662, 673
pronator drift, 69, 78
propulsion, 450, 500
prostate gland, 644, 673
protein kinase, 93, 131
proteolysis, 533, 554
proximal convoluted tubules (PCTs), 572, 600
psychoneuroimmunology, 378, 383
Puberty, 668
puberty, 673
pulmonary arteries, 183, 238
pulmonary artery, 280, 323, 402, 433
pulmonary capillaries, 183, 238
pulmonary circuit, 183, 238, 280, 323
pulmonary plexus, 402, 433
pulmonary surfactant, 399, 433
pulmonary trunk, 183, 238, 280, 323
pulmonary valve, 193, 238
pulmonary veins, 183, 238, 280, 323
Pulmonary ventilation, 404
pulmonary ventilation, 433
pulp cavity, 458, 500
pulse, 258, 323
pulse pressure, 257, 324

Punnett square, 717, 726
Purkinje fibers, 206, 238
pyloric antrum, 464, 500
pyloric canal, 464, 500
pyloric sphincter, 464, 500
pylorus, 464, 500
pyruvate, 514, 554

Q

QRS complex, 210, 238
quickening, 699, 726
Quiet breathing, 408
quiet breathing, 433

R

radial artery, 292, 324
radial vein, 305, 324
Radiation, 545
radiation, 554
reabsorption, 266, 324
receptive aphasia, 54, 78
recessive, 714, 726
recessive lethal, 721, 726
rectal valve, 500
rectal valves, 476
rectum, 476, 500
red blood cells (RBCs), 138, 173
red nucleus, 72, 78
reduction, 512, 554
referred pain, 21, 40
reflex arc, 19, 40
Regulatory T cells (Treg), 360
regulatory T cells (Treg), 383
renal artery, 289, 324
renal columns, 569, 600
renal corpuscle, 570, 600
renal cortex, 569, 600
renal fat pad, 568, 600
renal hilum, 569, 600
renal papillae, 569, 600
renal pyramids, 569, 600
renal vein, 308, 324
renin, 572, 600
Residual volume (RV), 408
residual volume (RV), 433
resistance, 256, 324
Respiratory acidosis, 631
respiratory acidosis, 633
Respiratory alkalosis, 631
respiratory alkalosis, 633
respiratory bronchiole, 397, 433
respiratory cycle, 407, 433
respiratory epithelium, 392, 433
respiratory membrane, 399, 433
respiratory pump, 265, 324
respiratory rate, 410, 433

Respiratory volume, 408
respiratory volume, 433
respiratory zone, 390, 433
rest and digest, 10, 40
reticulocyte, 147, 173
reticuloendothelial cell, 500
reticuloendothelial cells, 482
retrograde amnesia, 53, 78
retroperitoneal, 447, 500, 564, 600
Rh blood group, 166, 173
ribonuclease, 490, 500
right atrioventricular valve, 193, 238
right colic flexure, 475, 500
right gastric artery, 289, 324
right lymphatic duct, 336, 383
Rinne test, 59, 78
Romberg test, 68, 78
root, 391, 433, 458, 500
rubrospinal tract, 72, 78
ruga, 464, 500
rugae, 651, 673

S

saccade, 60, 78
saccharolytic fermentation, 479, 500
sacral micturition center, 566, 600
Saliva, 456
saliva, 501
salivary amylase, 456, 501, 513, 554
salivary gland, 501
salivary glands, 455
salivation, 457, 501
scrotum, 639, 673
second messenger, 93, 131
secondary adaptive response, 352, 383
secondary follicles, 653, 673
secondary lymphoid organs, 340, 383
secondary sex characteristics, 668, 673
secretin, 533, 554
secretory phase, 662, 673
Segmentation, 451
segmentation, 501
semen, 644, 673
semilunar valves, 188, 238
seminal vesicle, 644, 673
seminiferous tubules, 641, 673
sensitization, 373, 383
sensorineural hearing, 59, 78
sensory exam, 46, 78
sepsis, 278, 324
septic shock, 278, 324
septum, 188, 238
septum primum, 188, 238
Seroconversion, 367
seroconversion, 383
serosa, 446, 501
Sertoli cells, 641, 673

serum, 163, 173
severe combined immunodeficiency disease (SCID), 371, 383
sex chromosomes, 713, 726
short reflex, 22, 40
short-term memory, 53, 78
shunt, 697, 726
sickle cell disease, 152, 173
sigmoid colon, 475, 501
sigmoid sinuses, 303, 324
sinoatrial (SA) node, 204, 238
sinus rhythm, 205, 238
sinus venosus, 233, 238
sinusoid capillary, 250, 324
skeletal muscle pump, 264, 324
small cardiac vein, 200, 238
small intestine, 469, 501
small saphenous vein, 310, 324
Snellen chart, 58, 78
sodium bicarbonate, 533, 554
soft palate, 453, 501
somatic reflex, 19, 40
somite, 726
somites, 692
spasticity, 70, 78
specific gravity, 563, 600
sperm, 638, 673
spermatic cord, 643, 673
spermatid, 642, 673
spermatocyte, 642, 673
spermatogenesis, 641, 673
spermatogonia, 641, 673
spermiogenesis, 642, 673
sphygmomanometer, 259, 324
spinocerebellar tract, 68, 78
spinocerebellum, 72, 78
spleen, 342, 383
splenic artery, 289, 324
spontaneous depolarization, 206, 238
stage of exhaustion, 114, 131
stage of resistance, 114, 131
stereognosis, 55, 78
stomach, 464, 501
straight sinus, 303, 324
stroke, 48, 79
stroke volume (SV), 221, 238
subclavian artery, 284, 324
subclavian vein, 301, 324
sublingual gland, 501
sublingual glands, 455
submandibular gland, 501
submandibular glands, 455
submucosa, 445, 501
submucosal plexus, 446, 501
subscapular vein, 305, 324
Sucrase, 488
sucrase, 501
sulcus, 186, 238

superficial reflex, 69, 79
superior cerebellar peduncle (SCP), 72, 79
superior cervical ganglion, 13, 40
superior mesenteric artery, 289, 324
superior mesenteric ganglion, 13, 40
superior phrenic artery, 287, 324
superior sagittal sinus, 303, 324
superior vena cava, 183, 238, 301, 325
suspensory ligaments, 664, 673
sympathetic chain ganglia, 11, 40
sympathetic division, 10, 40
sympatholytic drug, 33, 40
sympathomimetic drug, 33, 40
syncytiotrophoblast, 685, 726
systemic circuit, 183, 238
systemic edema, 578, 600
systole, 216, 239
systolic pressure, 256, 325

T

T cell, 337, 383
T cell tolerance, 356, 383
T cell-dependent antigen, 366, 383
T cell-independent antigen, 366, 383
T lymphocytes, 157, 173
T wave, 210, 239
target effector, 13, 40
target heart rate, 223, 239
temporal vein, 302, 325
tenia coli, 501
teniae coli, 477
terminal electron acceptor, 518, 554
terminal ganglia, 15, 40
tertiary follicles, 654, 673
testes, 640, 673
testicular artery, 289, 325
testicular vein, 308, 325
testosterone, 117, 131
Th1 cells, 360, 383
Th2 cells, 360, 383
Thalassemia, 153
thalassemia, 173
theca cells, 653, 673
thermoneutral, 543, 554
thermoregulation, 543, 554
thoracic aorta, 283, 325
thoracic duct, 336, 383
Thoracic wall compliance, 407
thoracic wall compliance, 433
thoracolumbar system, 11, 40
thoroughfare channel, 250, 325
thrombin, 163, 173
thrombocytes, 158, 173
thrombocytopenia, 158, 173
Thrombocytosis, 158
thrombocytosis, 173

Thrombopoietin, 144
thrombopoietin, 173
thrombosis, 164, 173
thrombus, 164, 173
thymocyte, 338, 383
thymosins, 125, 131
thymus, 125, 131, 339, 383
thyrocervical artery, 284, 325
thyroid cartilage, 394, 433
thyroid gland, 105, 131
thyroid-stimulating hormone (TSH), 102, 131
thyroxine, 107, 131
Tidal volume (TV), 408
tidal volume (TV), 433
tissue factor, 162, 173
Tissue typing, 374
tissue typing, 384
tongue, 454, 501
Tonsils, 343
tonsils, 384
Total dead space, 410
total dead space, 433
total lung capacity (TLC), 409, 433
Total pressure, 414
total pressure, 433
totipotent stem cell, 143, 173
trabeculae carneae, 192, 239
trachea, 396, 434
trachealis muscle, 396, 434
trait, 715, 726
transamination, 534, 554
transferrin, 149, 173
transient ischemic attack (TIA), 48, 79, 284, 325
Transpulmonary pressure, 406
transpulmonary pressure, 434
transverse colon, 475, 501
transverse sinuses, 303, 325
tricarboxylic acid cycle (TCA), 515, 554
tricuspid valve, 193, 239
triglycerides, 527, 554
trigone, 564, 600
triiodothyronine, 107, 131
trimester, 726
trimesters, 701
trophoblast, 726
trophoblasts, 683
true labor, 704, 726
true vocal cord, 395, 434
truncus arteriosus, 233, 239
trunk, 280, 325
trypsin, 533, 554
trypsinogen, 533, 554
tubuloglomerular feedback, 589, 600
tunica externa, 248, 325
tunica intima, 247, 325
tunica media, 248, 325

type I alveolar cell, 399, 434
type I hypersensitivity, 372, 384
type II alveolar cell, 399, 434
Type II hypersensitivity, 373
type II hypersensitivity, 384
Type III hypersensitivity, 373
type III hypersensitivity, 384

U

ulnar artery, 292, 325
ulnar vein, 305, 325
umbilical arteries, 315, 325
umbilical cord, 690, 726
umbilical vein, 315, 325
universal donor, 168, 173
universal recipient, 168, 173
upper esophageal sphincter, 461, 501
upregulation, 95, 131
urea cycle, 534, 554
urethra, 563, 600
Urinalysis, 561
urinalysis, 600
urochrome, 561, 601
uterine tubes, 658, 673
uterus, 659, 674

V

vagina, 651, 674
Valsalva's maneuver, 479, 501
valve, 188, 239
variable region domain, 353, 384
varicosity, 18, 40
vasa recta, 570, 601
vasa vasorum, 246, 325
Vascular shock, 278
vascular shock, 325
vascular shunt, 250, 325
vascular spasm, 159, 174
vascular tone, 261, 325
Vascular tubes, 314
vascular tubes, 325
vasoconstriction, 248, 325
vasodilation, 248, 325
vasomotion, 250, 326
vasomotor nerves, 30, 40
vein, 251, 326
venous reserve, 254, 326
Ventilation, 415
ventilation, 434
ventral respiratory group (VRG), 411, 434
ventricle, 183, 239
ventricular ejection phase, 218, 239
venule, 251, 326
vermis, 72, 79
vernix caseosa, 699, 726
vertebral artery, 284, 326

vertebral vein, 301, 326
vestibular fold, 395, 434
vestibulo-ocular reflex (VOR), 61, 79
vestibulocerebellum, 72, 79
villi, 471
villus, 501
visceral branches, 287, 326
visceral pleura, 403, 434
visceral reflex, 19, 40
Vital capacity (VC), 409
vital capacity (VC), 434
Vitamins, 547
vitamins, 554
voluntary phase, 462, 501
vulva, 650, 674

W

Weber test, 59, 79
Wernicke's area, 54, 79
white blood cells (WBCs), 138, 174
white rami communicantes, 13, 40
Wolffian duct, 667, 674

X

X-linked, 718, 726
X-linked dominant, 718, 726
X-linked recessive, 719, 726

Y

yolk sac, 688, 726

Z

zona fasciculata, 114, 131
zona glomerulosa, 114, 131
zona pellucida, 678, 726
zona reticularis, 114, 131
zygote, 678, 727

Download for free at http://cnx.org/content/col11496/latest/

Made in the USA
Middletown, DE
15 June 2017